SOUTH CAROLINA

Abbeville
Abbeville County Historical Society & Archives • Historical Museum, 211 N Main St, P.O. Box 12 • Abbeville, SC 29620 • (864) 459-8193

Abbeville County Library • 201 S Main St • Abbeville, SC 29620 • (864) 459-4009

Abbeville County Museum Association • P.O. Box 607 • Abbeville, SC 29620 • (864) 459-2696

Abbeville Historic Preservation Commission • 313 Greenville, P.O. Box 164 • Abbeville, SC 29620 • (864) 459-4297

Adams Run
Clan MacLennan Association USA • Willtown Bluff • Adams Run, SC 29426 • (843) 889-2979 • *Clan MacLennan Newsletter*

Aiken
Aiken County Historical Commission & Archives • Historical Museum, 433 Newberry St SW • Aiken, SC 29801 • (803) 642-2015 • *Journal of the Aiken County Historical Commission*

Aiken County Historical Museum Archives • 433 Newberry St NW • Aiken, SC 29801 • (803) 642-2015 • *Aiken County Historical Museum Newsletter*

Aiken County Historical Society & Library • P.O. Box 1775 • Aiken, SC 29803 • (803) 649-6050 • *Journal of the Aiken County Historical Society*

Aiken-Bamberg-Barnell-Edgefield Regional Library System • 314 Chesterfield St • Aiken, SC 29801-7171 • (803) 642-7575

Aiken-Barnwell Genealogical Society Chapter, SCGS & Library • P.O. Box 415 • Aiken, SC 29802 • (803) 648-3898 • http://www.abgs.org • *Newsletter of the Aiken-Barnwell Genealogical Society Chapter, SCGS*; *Journal of the Aiken-Barnwell Genealogical Society Chapter, SCGS*

Gregg-Graniteville Library • University of South Carolina-Aiken, 471 University Pkwy • Aiken, SC 29801 • (803) 648-6851 • http://ibrary.usca.sc.edu

Historic Aiken Foundation • P.O. Box 959 • Aiken, SC 29802 • (803) 648-0242

Twamley Surname Research • 827 Legare Rd • Aiken, SC 29803 • (803) 649-2680

Aledo
Pickens County Chapter, SCGS • P.O. Box 338 • Aledo, SC 29803

Allendale
Allendale County Historical Society • P.O. Box 545 • Allendale, SC 29810 • (803) 584-0899

Allendale-Hampton-Jasper Regional Library • War Memorial Bldg, 158 McNair St, P.O. Drawer 280 • Allendale, SC 29810-0280 • (803) 584-3513 • http://www.ahjlibrary.org

Salkehatchie Regional Campus Library • University of South Carolina, P.O. Box 617 • Allendale, SC 29810-0617 • (803) 584-3446 • http://www.rcce.sc.edu/salkehatchie/

Anderson
Anderson County Genealogical Society • P.O. Box 5743 • Anderson, SC 29623 • http://www.rootsweb.com/~scanders/andgensoc.html

Anderson County Historical Society • 1208 Northampton Rd, P.O. Drawer 785 • Anderson, SC 29622 • (864) 646-3782 • *Anderson County Historical Society News*; *New Highland Sentinel*

Anderson County Library • 300 N McDuffie St, P.O. Box 4047 • Anderson, SC 29622-4047 • (864) 260-4500 • http://www.andersonlibrary.org

Anderson County Museum Archives • 202 E Greenville St, P.O. Box 8002 • Anderson, SC 29622 • (864) 260-4737 • http://www.andersoncountysc.org/museum.htm • *Musings*; *Muse News*

Anderson Heritage • P.O. Box 58 • Anderson, SC 29622 • (864) 375-1739

Bamberg
Historical Society of Bamberg • 1611 Heritage Hwy • Bamberg, SC 29003 • (803) 245-2261

Barnwell
Aiken-Bamberg-[illegible] well County • 617 Hagood Av[illegible]

Barnwell County [illegible] arnwell, SC 29812 • (803) 2[illegible]

Barnwell County Museums Archives • Hagood & Marlboro Aves, P.O. Box 422 • Barnwell, SC 29812 • (803) 259-1916 • http://www.barnwellsc.com

Beaufort
Beaufort County Historical Society • 807 Craven, P.O. Box 55 • Beaufort, SC 29901-0055 • (843) 525-4064

Beaufort County Library • 311 Scott St • Beaufort, SC 29902-5591 • (843) 525-4000 • http://www.co.beaufort.sc.us/bftlib/desault

Beaufort Museum Archives • 713 Craven St, P.O. Drawer 1167 • Beaufort, SC 29901 • (843) 525-7077 • http://www.besufortcity.sc.com • *Museum Muse*

Carroll Family Organization • P.O. Box 660 • Beaufort, SC 29901 • (843) 524-5860

Historic Beaufort Foundation & Library • Verdier House Museum, 801 Bay St, P.O. Box 11 • Beaufort, SC 29901 • (843) 379-3331 • http://www.historic-beaufort.org • *Historic Beaufort Foundation Newsletter*

University of South Carolina at Beaufort Library • 801 Carteret St • Beaufort, SC 29902 • (843) 521-4121 • http://www.sc.edu/beaufort/library

US Marine Corps Air Station Library • P.O. Box 55018 • Beaufort, SC 29904-5018 • (843) 228-7682

Beech Island
Beech Island Historical Society • 144 Old Jackson Highway • Beech Island, SC 29842 • (803) 867-3600 • http://www.beech-islandhistory.org

Bennetsville
Marlborough Historical Society & Archives • Historical Museum, 123 S Marlboro St • Bennetsville, SC 29512-4031 • (803) 479-5624 • *Marlborough Historical Society Newsletter*

Marlboro County Library • 200 John Corry Rd • Bennettsville, SC 29512 • (843) 479-5630

Marlborough County Historical Preservation Commission & Library • Jennings-Brown House Museum, 123 S Marlboro St, P.O. Box 178 • Bennettsville, SC 29512 • (803) 479-5624

Marlborough Historical Society & Archives • Historical Museum, 123 S Marlboro St, P.O. Box 178 • Bennettsville, SC 29512-4031 • (843) 479-5624 • *Marlborough Historical Society Newsletter*

Bishopville
Lee County Historical Society • 208 N Dennis Ave • Bishopville, SC 29010 • (803) 484-6146

Lee County Historical Society • 208 N Dennis Ave, P.O. Box 684 • Bishopville, SC 29010 • (803) 484-6146

South Carolina Cotton Museum Archives • 121 W Cedar Lane • Bishopville, SC 29010 • (803) 484-4497 • http://www.sccotton.org • *South Carolina Cotton Museum Newsletter*

Blacksburg
Kings Mountain National Military Park Library • 2625 Park Rd • Blacksburg, SC 29702 • (864) 936-7921 • http://www.nps.gov/kimo

Blackville
Blackville Area Historical Society • 95 Pascallas St • Blackville, SC 29817 • (843) 284-3267

Bluffton
Bluffton Historical Preservation Society & Archives • Heywood House, P.O. Box 742 • Bluffton, SC 29910 • (843) 757-6293 • http://www.heywardhouse.org • *Newsletter of the Bluffton Historical Preservation Society*

South Carolina

Branchville
Branchville Railroad Shrine and Museum Archives • 7505 Freedom Rd, P.O. Box 85 • Branchville, SC 29432 • (803) 274-8820

Camden
Ansley Family Association • 1800 Forest Dr • Camden, SC 29020 • (803) 432-8075 • *Ansley Reunion Newsletter*

Camden Museum Archives and DAR Collection • 1314 Broad St • Camden, SC 29020 • (803) 425-6050 • http://www.mindspring.com/~camdenarchives/

Catawba-Wateree Genealogical Society & Library • 1314 Broad St • Camden, SC 29020 • http://hometown.aol.com/catawbawatereegs/ • *Catawba-Wateree Messenger*

Historic Camden and Revolutionary War Site & Library • Historical Museum, 222 Broad St, P.O. Box 710 • Camden, SC 29020-0710 • (803) 432-9841 • http://www.historic-camden.net • *Historic Camden Newsletter*

Kershaw County Historical Society & Archives • Bonds Conway House Museum, 811 S Fair St, P.O. Box 501 • Camden, SC 29020 • (803) 425-1123 • http://www.mindspring.com/~kchistory • *Update: Newsletter of the Kershaw County Historical Society*

Kershaw County Library • 1304 Broad St • Camden, SC 29020-3595 • (803) 425-1508 • http://www.kershaw.lib.sc.us

Phelps Family Association • 1002 Queen St • Camden, SC 29020-3113 • (803) 432-8432 • *Phelps Family Association Newsletter*

Reich Family Association • 514 Kirkwood Ln • Camden, SC 29020-2410

Cayce
Cayce Historical Museum Archives • P.O. Box 2004 • Cayce, SC 29171 • (803) 739-5385

Central
Central Heritage Society • 416 Church St, P.O. Box 1162 • Central, SC 29630 • (864) 639-2156 • http://www.centralheritage.org

Claude R Rickman Library • Southern Wesleyan Univ, 916 Wesleyan Dr, P.O. Box 1020 • Central, SC 29630-1020 • (864) 644-5060 • http://www.swu.edu/library

Chapin
Dutch Fork Chapter, SCGS • P.O. Box 481 • Chapin, SC 29036-0481 • (803) 279-0322 • *Dutch Fork Digest*

Charleston
American Military Museum Archives • 360 Concord St, P.o. Box 31351 • Charleston, SC 29401 • (843) 723-9620 • http://www.americanmilitarymuseum.org

Avery Institute of Afro-American History and Culture & Library • College of Charleston, 125 Bull St • Charleston, SC 29424 • (843) 953-7609 • http://www.cofc.edu/~avery.rsc • *Bulletin of the Avery Institute of Afro-American History and Culture; Avery Review*

Best Friend of Charleston Museum Archives • 44 John St • Charleston, SC 29464 • http://www.bestfriendofcharleston.org • *Best Friend*

Charles Towne Landing 1620 & Archives • Historical Museum, 1500 Old Towne Rd • Charleston, SC 29407-6099 • (843) 852-4200 • http://www.southcarolinaparks.com • *Instruc'ns*

Charleston County Genealogical Society & Library • 1300 N Edgewater, P.O. Box 20266 • Charleston, SC 29413-0266 • (843) 766-1667 • http://www.scgen.org/charlestonmain.htm • *Low Country Courier*; *Preston Scoop*; *Kilgore Clan*; *Bethany Cemetery Inscriptions*

Charleston County Public Library • 68 Calhoun St • Charleston, SC 29401 • (843) 805-6801 • http://www.ccpl.org

Charleston Library Society • Historical Museum, 164 King St • Charleston, SC 29401 • (843) 723-9912 • http://www.sciway.net/lib/cls_home.html

Charleston Museum Archives • 360 Meeting St • Charleston, SC 29403 • (843) 723-2926 • http://www.charlestonmuseum.org • *Charleston Museum Newsletter*

Church Street Historic Foundation • 59 Church St • Charleston, SC 29401 • (843) 723-5424

Citadel • Dept of English • Charleston, SC 29409-0001 • (843) 792-5140 • *Nineteenth-Century Studies*

Citadel Archives and Museum • 171 Moultrie St • Charleston, SC 29409 • (843) 953-6846 • http://www.citadel.edu/archivesandmuseum

Clan Hamilton Society • P.O. Box 71881 • Charleston, SC 29415-1881 • (843) 873-2430 • http://www.sysconn.com/hamilton/welcome.htm • *An Darach*

Daniel Library • The Citadel, 171 Moultrie St • Charleston, SC 29409-6140 • (843) 953-2569 • http://www.citadel.edu/library/

Drayton Hall Museum Archives • 3380 Ashley River Rd • Charleston, SC 29414-7105 • (843) 766-0188 • http://www.draytonhall.org

Federation of Museums • P.O. Box 100107 • Charleston, SC 29202 • (803) 898-4982

German Friendly Society • 29 Chalmers St • Charleston, SC 29401 • (843) 723-3040

Historic Charleston Foundation & Archives • Historical Museum, 40 E Bay St, P.O. Box 1120 • Charleston, SC 29402 • (843) 723-1623 • http://www.historiccharleston.org

Huguenot Society of South Carolina & Library • 138 Logan St • Charleston, SC 29401 • (843) 723-3235 • http://www.huguenotsociety.org • *Transactions of Huguenot Society of South Carolina*

Jewish Historical Society of South Carolina • 66 George St • Charleston, SC 29424-0001 • (843) 953-3918

John Rivers Communications Museum Archives • 58 George St • Charleston, SC 29424 • (843) 953-5810 • http://www.cofc.edu/~jrmuseum

Joyner-Williams Reunion • 3277 Dublin Rd N • Charleston, SC 29420 • (843) 552-2758

Macaulay Museum of Dental History Archives • Medical Univ of SC, 175 Ashley Ave • Charleston, SC 29425 • (843) 792-2288 • http://waring.library.musc.edu

Magnolia Plantation Museum Archives • 3550 Ashley River Rd • Charleston, SC 29414 • (843) 571-1266 • http://www.magnoliaplantation.com

Middleton Place Foundation • 4600 Ashley River Rd • Charleston, SC 29414 • (843) 556-6020 • http://www.middletonplace.org • *Middleton Place Notebook*

National Society of the Colonial Dames of America in the State of South Carolina & Library • 79 Cumberland St, P.O. Box 22127 • Charleston, SC 29401 • (843) 722-3767

National Trust for Historic Preservation, South Region • 456 King St • Charleston, SC 29403 • (843) 722-8552 • http://www.nthp.org

Old Exchange and Provost Dungeon Archives • 122 E Bay St • Charleston, SC 29401 • (843) 727-2165 • http://www.oldexchange.com

Orangeburg German-Swiss Genealogical Society • P.O. Box 20266 • Charleston, SC 29413

Powder Magazine Museum Archives • 79 Cumberland St, P.O. Box 22127 • Charleston, SC 29413 • (843) 722-9350

Preservation Society of Charleston • 147 King St, P.O. Box 521 • Charleston, SC 29402 • (843) 722-4630 • http://www.preservationsociety.org • *Preservation Progress*

Robert Scott Small Library • College of Charleston, 175 Calhoun St • Charleston, SC 29401-3519 • (843) 953-8000 • http://www.cofc.edu/~library

Society of First Families of South Carolina 1670-1700 & Library • P.O. Box 21328 • Charleston, SC 29413-2564 • (843) 577-4324

South Carolina Historical Society & Archives • Historical Museum, 100 Meeting St • Charleston, SC 29401-2215 • (843) 723-3225 • http://www.schistory.org • *Carologue: A Bulletin of South Carolina History*; *South Carolina Historical Magazine*

Waring Historical Medical Museum Archives • 175 Ashley Ave, P.O. Box 250403 • Charleston, SC 29425 • (843) 792-288 • http://waring.library.musc.edu

Charleston AFB

Charleston Air Force Base Library FL4418 • 437 SVS/SVMG, 106 W McCaw St, Bldg 215 • Charleston AFB, SC 29404-4700 • (843) 963-3320

Cheraw

Cheraw Lyceum Museum Archives • 200 Market St, P.O. Box 111 • Cheraw, SC 29520 • (843) 537-8407 • http://www.cheraw.com

Chesterfield County Historic Preservation Commission • 230 3rd St • Cheraw, SC 29520 • (843) 537-3387

Historic Cheraw • 230 3rd St • Cheraw, SC 29520

Northeastern Technical College Library • 1201 Chesterfield Hwy, P.O. Box 1007 • Cheraw, SC 29520-1007 • (843) 921-6953 • http://www.northeasterntech.org

Chesnee

Cowpens National Battlefield Archives • 4001 Chesnee Hwy, P.O. Box 308 • Chesnee, SC 29323 • (864) 461-2828 • http://www.nps.gov/cowp/

Chester

Amzi Neely Grant and Descendants • 1225 Peden Bridge Rd • Chester, SC 29706-8596

Chester County Historical Society & Archives • Historical Museum, 107 McAlily St, P.O. Box 811 • Chester, SC 29706 • (803) 385-2330 • *Chester County Historical Society Quarterly Newsletter*

Chester County Library • 100 Center St • Chester, SC 29706 • (803) 377-8145

Chesterfield

Chesterfield County Library • 119 W Main St • Chesterfield, SC 29709-1512 • (843) 623-7489

Chesterfield District Chapter, SCGS & Library • Main St, P.O. Box 167 • Chesterfield, SC 29709 • (843) 634-5136 • http://www.chesterfielddistrictchapter.org/chesterfieldsc/ • *Chesterfield District Chronicle*

Genealogical Society of Chesterfield County • 115 Green St • Chesterfield, SC 29709 • (843) 623-2244

Historical Society of Chesterfield County • P.O. Box 291 • Chesterfield, SC 29709 • (843) 523-2984

Clemson

Fort Hill Museum Archives • John C Calhoun House, Fort Hill St, P.O. Box 345615 • Clemson, SC 29634 • (804) 656-2475 • http://www.clemson.edu/welcome/history/forthill.htm

Hanover House Museum Archives • Perimeter Rd, P.O. Box 345615 • Clemson, SC 29634 • (864) 656-2241 • http://www.clemson.edu/welcome/history.hanover.htm • *Hanover House Newsletter*

Strom Thurmond Institute Archives • Clemson Univ, Pearman Blvd • Clemson, SC 29634 • (864) 656-4700 • http://www.strom.clemson.edu

Clinton

James H Thomason Library • Presbyterian College, 211 E Maple St • Clinton, SC 29325 • (864) 833-7080 • http://www.presby.edu/library/

Old Newberry District Chapter, SCGS • 406 E Florida St • Clinton, SC 29325

Reid Family Data • 801 Musgove St, Cottage 101 • Clinton, SC 29325-1752 • (864) 938-0410

Clover

Clover Historical Society • 114 Faulkner St • Clover, SC 29710 • (803) 684-1189

Columbia

African-American Heritage Commission • 8301 Parklane Rd • Columbia, SC 29223-4905 • (803) 896-6100 • http://www.state.sc.us/scdah/hpafricanamerher.htm

Afro-American Historical and Genealogical Society, Columbia Chapter • P.O. Box 25615 • Columbia, SC 29224

Chicora Foundation • 861 Arbutus Dr, P.O. Box 8664 • Columbia, SC 29202-8664 • (803) 787-6910 • http://www.chicora.org • *Chicora Foundation Research*

Columbia Chapter, SCGS & Library • P.O. Box 11353 • Columbia, SC 29211 • (803) 787-4918 • http://www.rootsweb.com/~scccscgs/ • *Columbia Chronicle*

Columbia Fire Department Museum Archives • 1800 Laurel St • Columbia, SC 29201 • (803) 733-8350 • http://www.columbiasc.net/fire2.htm • *Columbia Fire Department Museum Newsletter*

Confederation of South Carolina Local Historical Societies • 8301 Parklane Rd • Columbia, SC 29223-4905 • (803) 359-8369

Eastern Cherokee Southern Iroquois and United Tribes • P.O. Box 7062 • Columbia, SC 29202 • (803) 699-0446 • http://www.cherokeesofsouthcarolina.com

Flynt-Flint Research • 7 Northlake Rd • Columbia, SC 2923-5909 • *Flynt-Flint Newsletter*

Governor's Mansion Museum Archives • 800 Richland St • Columbia, SC 29201 • (803) 737-3000 • http://www.scgovernorsmansion.org

High Family Association • P.O. Box 5841 • Columbia, SC 29250 • (803) 782-9595 • http://www.highfamily.org • *High Family Association Newsletter*

Historic Columbia Foundation & Archives • Hampton-Preston Mansion, 1601 Richland St • Columbia, SC 29201-2633 • (803) 252-1770 • http://www.historiccolumbia.org

Jewish Historical Society of South Carolina • 5827 N Trenholm Rd • Columbia, SC 29208 • (803) 953-5682 • http://www.scsn.net/users/efolley/jhssc/jhssc_home.html

Johnson-Johnston Research • 5821 Satchelford Rd • Columbia, SC 29206-1508 • Johnsons and Johnstons of Alabama

Lake Murray Historical Society • 1634 Emerald Valley Rd • Columbia, SC 29210-6706 • (803) 772-9486

Palmetto Trust for Historic Preservation • 8301 Parklane Rd • Columbia, SC 29204-2413 • (803) 771-6132

Parker-Lumpkin Reunion • 531 Lockshire Rd • Columbia, SC 29210 • (803) 772-4788

Richland County Public Library • 1431 Assembly St • Columbia, SC 29201 • (803) 799-9084 • http://www.richland.lib.sc.us

South Carolina Archives Department • 1430 Senate St • Columbia, SC 29201 • (803) 734-8577 • http://www.scdah.sc.edu/homepage.htm

South Carolina Confederate Relic Room and Museum Library • 301 Gervais St • Columbia, SC 29201 • (803) 898-8095 • http://www.crr.sc.gov

South Carolina Department of Archives and History • 8301 Parkland Rd • Columbia, SC 29223-4905 • (803) 896-6100 • http://www.state.sc.us/scdah

South Carolina Genealogical Society • 2910 Duncan St, P.O. Box 492 • Columbia, SC 29202 • (843) 766-1476 • http://www.scgen.org • *Carolina Herald*

South Carolina Law Enforcement Officers Hall of Fame • 5490 Broad River Rd • Columbia, SC 29212 • (873) 896-8199 • http://www.sodps.org/cja/halloffame

South Carolina Magazine • P.O. Box 21766 • Columbia, SC 29221 • (803) 772-6919 • http://www.scmar.com • *South Carolina Magazine of Ancestral Research*

South Carolina Military Museum Archives • 1 National Guard Rd • Columbia, SC 29201 • (803) 806-4440

South Carolina State Library • 301 Gervais St, P.O. Box 100107 • Columbia, SC 29211 • (803) 734-8666 • http://www.museum.state.sc.us

South Carolina State Museum Archives • 301 Gervais St • Columbia, SC 29201-3027 • (803) 737-8095 • http://www.museum.state.sc.us

South Caroliniana Library • Univ of South Carolina • Columbia, SC 29208-0103 • (803) 777-3131 • http://www.sc.edu/library/socar/

South Caroliniana Society • South Caroliniana Library, Univ of South Carolina • Columbia, SC 29208 • (803)777-3131

Thomas Cooper Library • Univ of South Carolina • Columbia, SC 29208-0103 • (803) 777-3142 • http://www.sc.edu/library • Ex Libris; Reflections

Walter Stewart Family Association • 6336 Briarwood Rd • Columbia, SC 29206 • (803) 782-1464 • *Stewart Family Newsletter*

Conway
Horry County Historical Society • 606 Main St, P.O. Box 2025 • Conway, SC 29528-4340 • (843) 488-1966 • http://www.hchsonline.org • *Independent Republic Quarterly*

Horry County Memorial Library • 1008 5th Ave • Conway, SC 29526-5196 • (843) 248-1543 • http://www.horry.lib.sc.us

Horry County Museum Archives • 428 Main St • Conway, SC 29526 • (803) 248-1542 • http://www.horrycountymuseum.org

Cowpens
Micah Martin Family Organization • Route 1, Box 803A • Cowpens, SC 29330 • (864) 463-4576

Darlington
Darlington County Historical Commission & Library • 204 Hewitt St • Darlington, SC 29532 • (843) 398-4710

Darlington County Historical Society • P. O. Box 546 • Darlington, SC 29532

Darlington County Library • 204 N Main St • Darlington, SC 29532 • (843) 398-4940 • http://www.darlington-lib.org

Denmark
Wright Potts Library • Voorhees College, Voorhees Rd, P.O. Box 678 • Denmark, SC 29042-0678 • (803) 793-3351

Dillon
Dillon County Historical Society • P.O. Box 1806 • Dillon, SC 29536 • (843) 774-6122 • http://www.dillonmuseum.com

Dillon County Library • 600 E Main St • Dillon, SC 29536 • (843) 774-0330 • http://www.dillon.lib.sc.us

J W Dillion House Museum Archives • 1302 W Main St • Dillon, SC 29536 • (843) 774-9051 • http://www.dillonmuseum.com

Donalds
Boonesborough Historical Society • 134 Drake Rd • Donalds, SC 29638 • (864) 379-8245 • http://web.infoave.net/~kfleming/bhs.html

Due West
McCain Library • Erskine College & Theological Seminary, 1 Depot St • Due West, SC 29639 • (864) 379-8898 • http://www.erskine.edu/library

Easley
Ocenee County Genealogical Society • 247 Cross Hill Rd • Easley, SC 29640-8857 • (864) 859-2392

Old Pendleton District Chapter, SCGS • 247 Cross Hill Rd • Easley, SC 29640-8857 • (864) 859-2392 • http://www.oldpendleton.homestead.com • *Old Pendleton District Chapter Newsletter*

Pickens County Library • 110 W 1st Ave • Easley, SC 29640-2998 • (864) 850-7077

Eastover
Kensington Mansion Museum Archives • McCords Ferry Rd, P.O. Box 237 • Eastover, SC 29044 • (803) 353-0456 • http://kensington.sumtercountymuseum.org • *Kensington Times*

Edgefield
Edgefield County Genealogical Society • P.O. Box 486 • Edgefield, SC 29824 • http://www.oedegs.com • *Quill*

Edgefield County Historical Society & Library • 108-1/2 Court House Sq, P.O. Box 174 • Edgefield, SC 29824 • (803) 637-2233

Oakley Park Museum Archives • 300 Columbia Rd, P.O. Box 26 • Edgefield, SC 29824 • (803) 637-4027

Old Edgefield District Archives • P.O. Box 468 • Edgefield, SC 29824

Old Edgefield District Chapter, SCGS & Library • 104 Courthouse Sq, P.O. Box 546 • Edgefield, SC 29824-0546 • (803) 637-5652 • *Annals of Edgefield District*; *Quill*

Tompkins Memorial Library • 104 Courthouse Sq • Edgefield, SC 29824 • (803) 637-4010

Edisto Island
Edisto Island Historic Preservation Society & Archives • Historical Museum, 8123 Chisholm Plantation Rd, P.O. Box 393 • Edisto Island, SC 29438 • (843) 869-1954 • http://www.edistomuseum.com • *Edisto Echoes*

Florence
Florence County Historical Society • P.O. Drawer 150 • Florence, SC 29503

Florence County Library • 319 S Irby St • Florence, SC 29501-4795 • (843) 662-8424

Florence Heritage Foundation • 1159 Brunwood, P.O. Box 1909 • Florence, SC 29503-1909 • (843) 662-3258

Florence Museum of History Archives • 558 Spruce St • Florence, SC 29501 • (843) 662-3351 • *Florence Museum Newsletter*

James A Rogers Library • Francis Marion University, Hwy 301 N, P.O. Box 100547 • Florence, SC 29501-0547 • (843) 661-1310 • http://library.fmarion.edu • *Axis*

Locke Family Association • 325 Park Ave • Florence, SC 29501-4738 • *Locke Family Association Newsletter*

Mars Bluff Society • 6701 E Palmetto St • Florence, SC 29500 • (843) 669-2183

Fort Jackson
Fort Jackson Main Post Library • Thomas Lee Hall, Bldg 4679 • Fort Jackson, SC 29207 • (803) 751-4816

Fort Jackson Museum Library • 4442 Jackson Blvd • Fort Jackson, SC 29207 • (803) 751-7419 • http://www.jackson.army.mil/museum/

US Army Chaplain Museum Archives • 10100 Lee Rd • Fort Jackson, SC 29207 • (803) 751-8827 • http://www.usaches.army.mil • *US Army Chaplain Museum Newsletter*

US Army Finance Corps Museum Archives • 10000 Hampton Pkwy • Fort Jackson, SC 29207 • (803) 751-8566 • http://www.jackson.army.mil

Gaffney
A J Eastwood Library • Limestone College, 1115 College Dr • Gaffney, SC 29340 • (864) 488-4611 • http://lib.limestone.edu

Cherokee County Public Library • 300 E Rutledge Ave • Gaffney, SC 29340-2227 • (864) 487-2711 • http://www.cherokeecountylibrary.org • *Genealogically Speaking*; *Friendly Notes*

Cherokee Historic and Preservation Society • 301 S Johnson St • Gaffney, SC 29340 • (864) 489-3988

Winnie Davis Museum of History Archives • Limestone College, 1115 College Dr • Gaffney, SC 29340 • (864) 489-7151 • http://www.limestone.edu

Gaston
King Family Reunion • Route 1, Box 83-B1 • Gaston, SC 29053

Georgetown
Georgetown County Historical Commission • 633 Front St • Georgetown, SC 29440 • (843) 546-7423 • http://ricemuseum.com

Georgetown County Historical Society • P.O. Box 861 • Georgetown, SC 29442 • (843) 546-0462

Georgetown County Library System • 405 Cleland St • Georgetown, SC 29440-3200 • (843) 546-2521 • http://www.gcpl.lib.sc.us • *Friends*

Hopsewee Plantation Museum Archives • 494 Hopsewee Rd • Georgetown, SC 29440 • (843) 546-7891 • http://www.hopsewee.com

Kaminski House Museum Archives • 1003 Front St, P.O. Box 939 • Georgetown, SC 29442 • (843) 546-7706 • http://www.cityofgeorgetownsc.com

Rice Museum Archives • Front & Screven Sts, P.O. Box 902 • Georgetown, SC 29440 • (843) 546-7423 • http://www.ricemuseum.com

Goose Creek
Berkeley County Historical Society • 108 The Oaks Ave • Goose Creek, SC 29445 • http://www.rootsweb.com/~scbchs/

Gray Court
Gray Court-Owing Historical Society • 944 Hwy 92 • Gray Court, SC 29645 • (843) 876-2667

Greenville
Cathey Reunion Association • 620 Halton Rd #3102 • Greenville, SC 29607-3456 • (910) 454-4121 • *Cathey Kith and Kin*

Greenville County Genealogical Society & Library • P.O. Box 16236 • Greenville, SC 29606-7236 • (803) 246-4519 • *Carolina Herald*; *Greenville County Genealogical Society Newsletter*, *Greenville Chapter Journal*

Greenville County Historic Preservation Commission • 301 University Ridge, Ste 100 • Greenville, SC 29601 • (864) 467-7105 • http://www.greenvillehistoricpreservation.org

Greenville County Historical Society & Library • 211 E Washington St, P.O. Box 10472 • Greenville, SC 29603 • (864) 233-4103 • http://greenvillehistory.org • *New Greenville Mountaineer*, *Greenville County Historical Society Proceedings and Papers*

Greenville County Library • 300 College St • Greenville, SC 29601 • (864) 242-5000 x269

Greenville County Library System-Hughes Main Library • 25 Heritage Green Pl • Greenville, SC 29601-2034 • (864) 242-5000 • http://www.greenvillelibrary.org

Historic Greenville Foundation • 540 Buncombe St • Greenville, SC 29601 • (864) 467-3100 • http://www.upcountryhistory.org

International Clan Macfie • 620 Halton Rd #3102 • Greenville, SC 29607-3456 • (910) 454-4121

James B Duke Library • Furman Univ, 3300 Poinsett Hwy • Greenville, SC 29613-0600 • (864) 294-2195 • http://library.furman.edu

Southern Historical Press • 275 W Broad St, P.O. Box 1267 • Greenville, SC 29601-2634 • (864) 233-2346 • *Georgia Genealogical Magazine*

Greenwood
Glasgow Family Association • 117 Sunnywide Dr • Greenwood, SC 29646 • (864) 223-3047

Greenwood County Genealogical Society • P.O. Box 3468 • Greenwood, SC 29648

Greenwood County Historical Society & Archives • c/o Abbeville-Greenwood Regional Library, 106 N Main St, P.O. Box 782 • Greenwood, SC 29646 • (864) 223-0398

Greenwood County Library • 106 N Main St • Greenwood, SC 29646 • (864) 941-4650 • http://www.greenwoodcountylibrary.org

Greenwood Museum Archives • 106 Main St, P.O. Box 3131 • Greenwood, SC 29648 • (864) 229-7093 • http://www.themuseum-greenwood.org • *Greenwood Museum Newsletter*

Old Ninety Six District, SCGS & Library • P.O. Box 3468 • Greenwood, SC 29648-3468 • (864) 223-7374 • http://www.scgen.org/OldNinetySix.htm • *Genealogical Roots and Branches*

Skelton Reunion • 223 Puckett's Pointe Rd • Greenwood, SC 29649 • (864) 223-6090

Greer
Henderson, Peck Family Reunion • 119 Pinewood Dr • Greer, SC 29651 • (864) 877-2424

Hampton
Hampton County Historical Society & Archives • Historical Museum, 601 S Hampton • Hampton, SC 29924 • (803) 943-2784

Hardeeville
Purysburg Preservation Foundation • P.O. Box 1732 • Hardeeville, SC 29927

Hartsville
Darlington County Genealogical Society • Genealogical Research Library, 114 S 4th St, P.O. Box 175 • Hartsville, SC 29551 • (843) 857-0300 • http://www.geocities.com/heartland/estates/7212

Hartsville Genealogical Research Library • 114 S 4th St • Hartsville, SC 29551 • (843) 857-0300

Hartsville Museum Archives • 222 N 5th St, P.O. Box 431 • Hartsville, SC 29551 • (843) 383-3005 • http://www.hartsvillemuseum.org

Kelley Jacob House Museum Archives • 2585 Kelleytown Rd • Hartsville, SC 29550 • (843) 339-9093

Old Darlington District Chapter, SCGS • 307 Kings Place, P.O. Box 175 • Hartsville, SC 29551-1075 • (843) 332-1071 • http://www.geocities.com/Heartland/Estates/7212 • *Old Darlington Flag Quarterly*, *Darlington Flag*

Robinson Visitors Center Museum Archives • 3581 W Entrance Rd • Hartsville, SC 29550 • (843) 857-5291

Hemingway
Browntown Museum Archives • Hwy 341, P.O. Box 811 • Hemingway, SC 29544 • (803) 558-2355

Three Rivers Historical Society & Library • 414 Main St, P.O. Box 811 • Hemingway, SC 29554 • (843) 558-2355 • http://www.threeriversshistsoc.org • *Three Rivers Chronicle*

Hickory Grove
Broad River Basin Historical Society • P.O. Box 215 • Hickory Grove, SC 29717

Broad River Genealogical Society • P.O. Box 215 • Hickory Grove, SC 29717 • *Broad River Genealogical Society Quarterly*

Hilton Head Island
Beaufort County Genealogical Society • P.O. Box 5492 • Hilton Head Island, SC 29928

Coastal Discovery Museum Archives • 10 William Hilton Pkwy • Hilton Head Island, SC 29926 • (843) 689-6767 • http://www.coastaldiscovery.org • Coastal Discovery Museum Newsletter

Heritage Library • 32 Office Park Rd, Suite 300 • Hilton Head Island, SC 29928-4640 • (843) 686-6560

Hilton Head Island Genealogical Society • c/o Heritage Library, 32 Office Park Rd, Ste 300, P.O. Box 5492 • Hilton Head Island, SC 29928-5492 • (843) 686-6560 • http://ourtown.islandpacket.com/32/ • *Hilton Head Island Genealogical Society Newsletter*

Hilton Head Island Historical Society • 8 Moon Shell Rd • Hilton Head Island, SC 29928-5444 • (843) 785-3967

Parris Island Historical Society • Heritage Library, Courtyard Building • Hilton Head Island, SC 29928 • (843)686-6560 • http://www.parrisisland.com/historic.htm

Hodges
Cokesbury Historical and Recreational Commission • P.O. Box 206 • Hodges, SC 29653 • (864) 374-3237

Iva
REVIVA • P.O. Box 402 • Iva, SC 29655 • (864) 348-6544

South Carolina

Johnston
Ridge Heritage Association • P.O. Box 117 • Johnston, SC 29832 • (803) 275-3775

Kershaw
McNaughton-Hearon Family Association • 4560 Bethune Rd • Kershaw, SC 29067 • (803) 475-5600

Kingstree
Williamsburg County Historical Society & Archives • Historical Museum, 135 Hampton Ave, P.O. Box 24 • Kingstree, SC 29556 • (843) 355-3306

Williamsburg County Library • 215 N Jackson • Kingstree, SC 29556-3319 • (843) 354-9486 • http://www.wlbg.lib.sc.us

Lake City
Browntown Museum Archives • Hwy 341 • Lake City, SC 29560 • (843) 558-2355 • http://www.threeriversh istsoc.org • *Three Rivers Chronicle*

Lancaster
Lancaster County Historical Commission & Library • P.O. Box 67 • Lancaster, SC 29744 • (803) 285-6465

Lancaster County Library • 313 S White St • Lancaster, SC 29720 • (803) 285-1502 • http://www.lanclib.org

Lancaster County Society for Historic Preservation • P.O. Box 1075 • Lancaster, SC 29721 • (803) 285-9455 • *Lancaster County Society for Historic Preservation Newsletter*

Medford Library • University of South Carolina, P.O. Box 889 • Lancaster, SC 29721-0889 • (803) 313-7060 • http://www.usc.lancaster.sc.edu/library

University of South Carolina Historical Association • USC-Lancaster, P.O. Box 889 • Lancaster, SC 29721 • http://www.state.sc.us/scdah/scha/scha.htm

Latta
Pee Dee Chapter, SCGS • P.O. Box 236 • Latta, SC 29565 • *Pee Dee Queue*

Laurens
Laurens County Historical Commission • P.O. Box 49 • Laurens, SC 29360

Laurens County Historical Society • P.O. Box 292 • Laurens, SC 29360 • (864) 984-0596

Laurens County Landmarks Foundation & Archives • James Dunklin House Museum, 544 W Main St • Laurens, SC 29360 • (864) 984-4735

Laurens County Library • 101 W Main St • Laurens, SC 29360 • (864) 984-0596 • http://www.lcpl.org

Laurens District Genealogical Society • P.O. Box 1217 • Laurens, SC 29360-1217 • *Tree Climber*

Lexington
Chavis Surname Organization • 164 Bluefield Rd • Lexington, SC 29072 • (803) 957-6736

House of Baillie USA • 114 Meadow Wood Dr • Lexington, SC 29073 • (803) 356-1409 • http://www.tartans.com/clans/Baillie/baillie.html

Lexington County Genealogical Association • P.O. Box 1442 • Lexington, SC 29072 • *Lexington Genealogical Exchange*

Lexington County Historical Society • 231 Fox St • Lexington, SC 29071 • (803) 359-8369

Lexington County Museum Archives • 231 Fox St, P.O. Box 637 • Lexington, SC 29071 • (803) 359-8369

Lexington County Public Library • 5440 Augusta Rd • Lexington, SC 29072 • (803) 808-2600 • http://www.lex.lib.sc.us

Manning
Clarendon County Archives • P.O. Box 486 • Manning, SC 29102 • (803) 435-0328

Clarendon County Historical Society • 211 N Brooks St • Manning, SC 29102 • (803) 435-0328

Harvin Clarendon County Library • 215 N Brooks St • Manning, SC 29102-3209 • (803) 435-8633 • http://www.hccl.lib.sc.us

Marion
Horry County Genealogical Society • P.O. Box 1428 • Marion, SC 29571

Marion County Historical Society • P.O. Box 7 • Marion, SC 29571 • (843) 423-8299 • *Marion County Historical Society Newsletter*

Marion County Library • 101 E Court St • Marion, SC 29571-3699 • (843) 423-8300 • http://www.marioncountylibrary.org

Marion County Museum Archives • 101 Willcox Ave, P.O. Box 220 • Marion, SC 29571 • (843) 423-8299

Pee Dee Chapter, SCGS & Library • 400 N Main St, P.O. Box 1428 • Marion, SC 29571-1428 • http://scgen.org/peedee.htm • *Pee Dee Queue*

McClellanville
Hampton Plantation Museum Archives • 1950 Rutledge Rd • McClellanville, SC 29458 • (843) 546-9361 • http://www.southcarolinaparks.com

McConnells
Historic Brattonsville & Archives • Historical Museum, 1444 Brattonsville Rd • McConnells, SC 29726 • (803) 684-2327 • http://www.chmuseums.org

McCormick
Dorn Historical Restoration Association • 1000 Cedar Hill Rd • McCormick, SC 29835 • (864) 465-2347

McCormick County Historical Commission • P.O. Box 578 • McCormick, SC 29835 • (864) 465-2347

McCormick County Historical Society • P.O. Box 1498 • McCormick, SC 29835 • (864) 465-2144

Moncks Corner
Berkeley County Historical Society & Archives • Historical Museum, 950 Stoney Landing Rd, P.O. Box 504 • Moncks Corner, SC 29461 • (843) 899-5101

Berkeley County Library • 100 Library St • Moncks Corner, SC 29461-2326 • (843) 719-4223 • http://www.berkeley.lib.sc.us

Old Santee Canal Park Archives • 900 Stony Landing Rd • Moncks Corner, SC 29461 • (843) 899-5200 • http://www.oldsanteecanalpark.org

Mount Carmel
Old Abbeville District Historical Commission • P.O. Drawer 257 • Mount Carmel, SC 29840 • (864) 391-2121

Mount Pleasant
Charles Pinckney National Historic Site Archives • 1254 Long Point Rd • Mount Pleasant, SC 29464 • (843) 881-5516 • http://www.nps.gov/chps

Christ Church Parish Preservation Society • P.O. Box 165 • Mount Pleasant, SC 29465 • (843) 884-4265

Patriots Point Naval and Maritime Museum Archives • 40 Patriots Point Rd • Mount Pleasant, SC 29464 • (843) 884-2727 • http://www.state.sc.us/pdp • *To the Point*

Society of Mayflower Descendants • 843 O'Sullivan Dr • Mount Pleasant, SC 29464

Myrtle Beach
Chapin Memorial Library • 400 14th Ave N • Myrtle Beach, SC 29557-3612 • (843) 918-1275 • http://www.chapinlibrary.org

Neeses
Neese's Farm Museum Archives • 6149 Savannah Hwy • Neeses, SC 29107 • (803) 247-5818

Newberry
Newberry County Historical Society • 1905 Benedict, P.O. Box 186 • Newberry, SC 29108-0364 • (803) 276-1597 • *Newberry County Historical Society Bulletin*

Newberry County Library • 1300 Friend St • Newberry, SC 29108-3400 • (803) 276-0854 • http://www.newberrylibrary.org

Wessels Library • Newberry College, 2100 College St • Newberry, SC 29108-2197 • (803) 321-5229 • http://www.newberry.edu/wessels/

Ninety-Six
Ninety-Six National Historic Site Archives • 1103 Hwy 248, P.O. Box 295 • Ninety-Six, SC 29666 • (864) 543-4068 • http://www.nps.gov/nisi

North Augusta
Hammond Family Association • P.O. Box 6545 • North Augusta, SC 29841 • (803) 279-7632 • *Hammond Family Association Newsletter*

Olde Towne Preservation Association of North Augusta • P.O. Box 7915 • North Augusta, SC 29841 • (803) 279-7560 • http://www.colonialtimes.us

North Myrtle Beach
Atlantic Beach Historical Society • 1100 David St • North Myrtle Beach, SC 29582 • (843) 272-8900

Orangeburg
H V Manning Library • Claflin University, 400 Magnolia St • Orangeburg, SC 29115 • (803) 535-5307

Louthan-Louthen Families • 1571 Green Valley NW • Orangeburg, SC 29115 • (803) 534-4589

Orangeburg County Historical Society • 1421 Middleton St, P.O. Box 1891 • Orangeburg, SC 29116-1891 • (803) 535-0022 • *Orangeburg County Historical Society Newsletter*

Orangeburg County Library • 510 Louis St NE, P.O. Box 1367 • Orangeburg, SC 29116-1367 • (803) 531-4636

Orangeburg Historical and Genealogical Society • 467 Palmetto Pkwy NE, P.O. Box 959 • Orangeburg, SC 29116 • (803) 531-1002 • *Orangeburg Historical and Genealogical Record*

Orangeburgh German-Swiss Genealogical Society & Library • P.O. Box 974 • Orangeburg, SC 29116-0974 • (843) 723-2235 • http://netside.com/~genealogy/orangeburgh.htm • *Orangeburgh German-Swiss Newsletter*

Parris Island
Parris Island Historical Society • P.O. Box 5202 • Parris Island, SC 29905

Parris Island Museum Archives • Attn MUS, MCRD ERR, Box 19001 • Parris Island, SC 29905-9001 • (843) 525-3765 • http://mcmsmo3.usmc.mil/museum/ • *Parris Island Museum Quarterly*

Pendleton
Pendleton District Agricultural Museum Archives • Highway 76, P.O. Box 565 • Pendleton, SC 29670 • (800) 862-1795 • http://www.pendleton-district.org

Pendleton District Historical, Recreational and Tourism Commission & Library • 125 E Queen St, P.O. Box 565 • Pendleton, SC 29670-0565 • (864) 646-3782 • http://www.pendleton-district.org • *Friends of the Pendleton District Commission Newsletter*

Pendleton Foundation for Black History and Culture • P.O. Box 806 • Pendleton, SC 29670 • (864) 656-1587

Pendleton Historic Foundation • Ashtabula Plantation, Hwy 88, P.O. Box 444 • Pendleton, SC 29670 • (864) 646-7249 • http://www.home.earthlink.net/~historicfnd • Pendleton Historic Foundation Newsletter

Woodburn Historic House Archives • 130 History Ln • Pendleton, SC 29670 • (864) 646-7249 • http://www.home.earthlink.net/!histfnd • *Woodburn Historic House Newsletter*

Pickens
Pickens County Historical Society • 104 N Lewis St, P.O. Box 755 • Pickens, SC 29671 • (864) 878-9459 • *Pickens County Historical Museum Newsletter*

Pickens County Museum Archives • 307 Johnson St • Pickens, SC 29671 • (864) 898-5963 • http://www.co.pickens.sc.us/culturalcommission • *Old Gaol Gazette*

Pinewood
Daughters of the American Revolution • P.O. Box 68 • Pinewood, SC 29125 • (803) 452-5341

Reidville
Reidville Historical Society • P.O. Box 375 • Reidville, SC 29375 • (864) 486-0547

Richburg
Chester District Genealogical Society & Library • P.O. Box 336 • Richburg, SC 29729-0336 • http://hometown.aol.com/catawbawatereegs/ • *Chester District Genealogical Society Bulletin*

Ridgeland
Jasper County Historical Society • P.O. Box 2111 • Ridgeland, SC 29936 • (843) 726-8136

Rock Hill
Biggerstaff Genealogical Society and Family Association • 1671 Huntmoor Dr • Rock Hill, SC 29732 • (803) 325-7859 • http://www.uftree.com UFT/WebPages/RichardBiggerstaff/BIGGERST/ • *Biggerstaff Family Association Quarterly*

Historic Rock Hill • P.O. Box 651 • Rock Hill, SC 29731 • (803) 980-1603

Ida Jane Dacus Library • Winthrop Univ, 810 Oakland Ave • Rock Hill, SC 29733 • (803) 323-2131 • http://www.winthrop.edu/dacus

Museum of York County Archives • 4621 Mount Gallant Rd • Rock Hill, SC 29732-9905 • (803) 329-2121 • http://www.yorkcounty.org • *Museum of York County Newsletter*

York County Culture and Heritage Commission • 4621 Mount Gallant Rd • Rock Hill, SC 29732-8666 • (803) 329-2121 • http://www.yorkcounty.org

York County Genealogical and Historical Society • P.O. Box 3061, Cherry Rd Sta • Rock Hill, SC 29731 • (803) 327-4667 • http://www.rootsweb.com/~scycghs/ • *York County, South Carolina Quarterly*

York County Library • 138 E Black St, P.O. Box 10032 • Rock Hill, SC 29731 • (803) 324-3055

York County Library-Rock Hill Public • 138 E Black St, P.O. Box 10032 • Rock Hill, SC 29731 • (803) 981-5825 • http://www.yclibrary.org

Roebuck
Historic Price House Museum Archives • 1200 Oak View Farms Rd • Roebuck, SC 29376 • (864) 576-6546 • http://www.spartanarts.org/history/ • *Drover's Post*

Spartanburg Historical Association & Archives • Walnut Grove Plantation Museum, 1200 Otts' Shoals Rd • Roebuck, SC 29376 • (864) 576-6546 • http://www.spartanarts.org/history

Saint George
Dorchester County Library • 506 N Parler Ave • Saint George, SC 29477-2297 • (803) 563-9189 • http://www.dcl.lib.sc.us

Saint Helena Island
Beaufort Genealogical Society • P.O. Box 1070 • Saint Helena Island, SC 29920

York W Bailey Museum Archives • Cope Industrial Bldg., P.O. Box 126 • Saint Helena Island, SC 29920 • (843) 838-2432 • http://www.penncenter.com

Saint Matthews
Calhoun County Museum Archives • 313 Butler St • Saint Matthews, SC 29135 • (843) 874-3964

Saluda
Saluda County Historical Society • 109 Law Range St, P.O. Box 22 • Saluda, SC 29138 • (864) 445-8550 • http://www.saludaschistorical.org • *Saluda County Historical Society Newsletter*

Saluda County Library • 101 S Main St • Saluda, SC 29138 • (864) 445-2267 • http://www.saluda.lib.sc.us

Sardinia
MacFaddien Family Society • Route 1, Box 28 • Sardinia, SC 29143 • (803) 473-2643 • *MacFaddien News*

Seneca

Addington Research • 100 Honeybee Ln • Seneca, SC 29678 • http://www.association.addington.com • *Addington Newsletter: Keeping Descendants of Henry and Sarah Addington Informed*

Oconee County Museum Association & Archives • Lunney Museum, 211 WS 1st St • Seneca, SC 29678 • (864) 882-4811

Sharon

Broad River Basin Historical Society • P.O. Box 86 • Sharon, SC 29742 • (803) 927-7558

Simpsonville

Simpsonville Historical Society • 216 Jones Ave • Simpsonville, SC 29681 • (864) 963-4374

Spartanburg

Descendants of John B and Eli S Clark • 1009 Oak Creek Dr • Spartanburg, SC 29302-2981 • (864) 591-1438 • http://www3.teleplex.net/gclark/homepage/clarkstart.html

Piedmont Historical Society • P.O. Box 8096 • Spartanburg, SC 29305-8096 • (864) 574-3056 • http://www.piedmont-historical-society.org • *Upper South Carolina Genealogy and History*

Pinckney District Chapter, SCGS • 385 S Spring St, P.O. Box 5281 • Spartanburg, SC 29304 • *Pinckney District Chapter Quarterly*; *SCGS Bulletin*

Preservation Trust of Spartanburg • P.O. Box 2223 • Spartanburg, SC 29304

Sandor Teszler Library • Wofford College, 429 N Church St • Spartanburg, SC 29303-3663 • (864) 497-4300 • http://www.wofford.edu/library

Sons of the American Revolution, South Carolina Society • P.O. Box 2413 • Spartanburg, SC 29303

Spartanburg County Historical Association & Library • Seay House Museum, 106 Darby Rd, P.O. Box 887 • Spartanburg, SC 29304-0887 • (864) 596-3501 • http://www.spartanarts.org/history/ • *Drover's Post*

Spartanburg County Public Library • 151 S Church St • Spartanburg, SC 29306-3241 • (864) 596-3507 • http://www.infodepot.org

Spartanburg County Regional Museum Archives • 100 E Main St #1, P.O. Box 887 • Spartanburg, SC 29304 • (864) 596-3501 • http://www.spartanarts.org/history

Spartanburg Historical Association • 501 Otis Blvd • Spartanburg, SC 29306

Sullivan's Island

Charles Pinckney National Historic Site Archives • 1214 Middle St • Sullivan's Island, SC 29482 • (843) 881-5516 • http://www.nps.gov/chpi

Fort Moultrie Museum Archives • 1214 Middle St • Sullivan's Island, SC 29482 • (843) 883-3123

Fort Sumter National Monument Library • 1214 Middle St • Sullivan's Island, SC 29482 • (843) 883-3123 • http://www.nps.gov/fosu

Saint James Santee Parish Historical Society • 2513 I'on Ave • Sullivan's Island, SC 29482 • (843) 883-3741

Summerville

Kilgore-Preston Research • 106 Mikel Ct • Summerville, SC 29485 • (843) 873-7897 • *Kilgore Clan*; *Preston Scoop*

Old Dorchester State Historic Site Archives • 300 State Park Rd • Summerville, SC 29485 • (843) 873-1740 • http://www.southcarolinaparks.com

Summerville Preservation Society • 201 W Caroline Ave, P.O. Box 511 • Summerville, SC 29484 • (843) 871-4276

Timrod Library • 217 Central Ave • Summerville, SC 29483 • (843) 871-4600

Sumter

Kay Family Association • 26 Paisley Park • Sumter, SC 29150 • Kay Quarterly

South Carolina National Guard Museum Archives • 395 N Pike Rd • Sumter, SC 29150 • (803) 806-1107

Stockbridge Reunion • 9 Fair Ct • Sumter, SC 29150-3244 • (803) 773-5005

Sumter County Genealogical Society & Archives • Old Carnegie Library, Liberty St, P.O. Box 2543 • Sumter, SC 29151-2543 • (803) 773-9144 • http://www.rootsweb.com/~scscgs/ • *Sumpter Black River Watchman*

Sumter County Historical Commission & Library • 406 N Magnolia St P.O. Box 306 • Sumter, SC 29150-0306 • (803) 775-7503

Sumter County Historical Society & Archives • Historical Museum, P.O. Box 1456 • Sumter, SC 29150 • (803) 775-0908 • http://www.sumtercountymuseum.com

Sumter County Library • 111 N Harvin St • Sumter, SC 29150 • (803) 773-7273 • http://www.midnet.sc.edu/sumtercls • *Bookings*

Sumter County Museum Archives • 122 N Washington St, P.O. Box 1456 • Sumter, SC 29150 • (803) 775-0908 • http://www.sumtercountymuseum.com • Sumter County Museum Newsletter

Surfside Beach

Halbert-Holbert History Association • 154 Cooper River Rd • Surfside Beach, SC 29575-7446 • (843) 215-9496

Taylors

Sons of the American Revolution, South Carolina Society • 2805 Hwy 414 • Taylors, SC 29687

Travlers Rest

Old Pendleton District Chapter, SCGS • 228 McElhaney Dr #25 • Travlers Rest, SC 29609 • http://www.oldpendleton.homestead.com

Union

Rose Hill Plantation Museum Archives • 2677 Sardis Rd • Union, SC 29379 • (864) 427-5966 • http://www.southcarolinaparks.com

Union County Carnegie Library • 300 E South St • Union, SC 29379-2392 • (864) 427-7140 • http://www.unionlibrary.org

Union County Historical Foundation & Archives • Historical Museum, E Main & Church Sts, P.O. Box 220 • Union, SC 29379 • (803) 427-2029 • *Union County Historical Foundation Newsletter*

Wadmalaw Island

Charleston Tea Garden Archives • 6617 Maybank Hwy • Wadmalaw Island, SC 29487 • (843) 559-0383

First Families of SC 1670-1700 • P.O. Box 23 • Wadmalaw Island, SC 29487

Walhalla

Oconee County Library • 501 W South Broad St • Walhalla, SC 29691 • (864) 638-4133 • http://ocplibrary.org

Oconee Heritage Center • 123 Brown Square Dr, P.O. Box 395 • Walhalla, SC 29691

Oconee Station Historic Site Archives • 500 Oconee Station Rd • Walhalla, SC 29691 • (864) 638-0079

Walterboro

Colleton County Genealogical Society • 125 Wade Hampton Ave • Walterboro, SC 29488

Colleton County Historical and Preservation Society • 205 Church St • Walterboro, SC 29488 • (843) 549-9633

Colleton County Memorial Library • 600 Hampton St • Walterboro, SC 29488-4098 • (803) 549-5621

Colleton Museum Archives • 239 N Jeffries Blvd • Walterboro, SC 29488 • (803) 549-2303 • http://www.walterboro.org • *Notes from the Old Jail*

Old Saint Bartholomew Chapter, SCGS • 104 Wade Hampton Ave • Walterboro, SC 29488-9261 • (843) 549-5757 • http://www.rootsweb.com/~scosbc/ • *Rice Planter*

West Union

Clan Macaulay • P.O. Box 343 • West Union, SC 29696 • (803) 638-6945

Williamston

Williamston Area Historic Commission • P.O. Box 577 • Williamston, SC 29697

Winnsboro

Fairfield County Genealogical Society • P.O. Box 696 • Winnsboro, SC 29180 • http://www.rootsweb.com/~scfairfi/gensoc.html • *Fairfield County Genealogical Society Newsletter*

Fairfield County Historical Society • P.O. Box 632 • Winnsboro, SC 29180 • (803) 635-9811 • http://fairfieldchamber.org

Fairfield County Library • 300 Washington St • Winnsboro, SC 29180 • (803) 635-4971 • http://www.fairfield.lib.sc.us

Fairfield County Museum and Genealogy Room • 231 S Congress St, P.O. Box 6 • Winnsboro, SC 29180 • (803) 635-9811 • http://www.fairfieldchamber.org

South Carolina Railroad Museum Archives • 110 Industrial Park Rd, P.O. Box 643 • Winnsboro, SC 29180 • (803) 635-4242 • http://www.scrm.org

York

York County Historical Commission • 212 E Jefferson St • York, SC 29745 • (803) 684-2327

Yorkville Historical Society • 37 Pinckney St, P.O. Box 1122 • York, SC 29745 • (843) 684-7722 • http://www.yorkvillehs.org

South Carolina

SOUTH DAKOTA

Aberdeen
Aberdeen Area Genealogical Society & Library • c/o Alexander Mitchell Public Library, 519 S Kline St, P.O. Box 493 • Aberdeen, SD 57402-0493 • *Tree Climber*

Alexander Mitchell Public Library • 519 S Kline St • Aberdeen, SD 57401-4495 • (605) 626-7097 • http://ampl.sdln.net • *AMPL News*

Beulah Williams Library • Northern State University, 1200 S Jay St • Aberdeen, SD 57401-7198 • (605) 626-2645 • http://lib.northern.edu/library

Dacotah Prairie Museum Library • 21 S Main St, P.O. Box 395 • Aberdeen, SD 57401-0395 • (605) 622-7117 • http://www.dacotahprairiemuseum.com • *Dacotah Prairie Times*

Hamilton Family: Fifer's Clan • 5219 8th Ave NE • Aberdeen, SD 57401-8181 • (605) 226-2358

Allen
Bennett County Genealogical Society • P.O. Box 483 • Allen, SD 57714

Armour
Douglas County Historical Society & Archives • Historical Museum, 710 Braddock, P.O. Box 638 • Armour, SD 57313 • (605) 724-2115 • *Little Giant*

Belle Fourche
Belle Fourche Public Library • 905 5th Ave • Belle Fourche, SD 57717-1795 • (605) 892-4407

CTC Families Association • P.O. Box 641 • Belle Fourche, SD 57717-0641 • (605) 892-2891 • *Cousin-to-Cousin-Coast-to-Coast CTC Courier*

Tri-State Genealogical Society • c/o Belle Fourche Public Library, 905 5th Ave • Belle Fourche, SD 57717-1702 • (605) 892-4407 • *WyMonDak Messenger*

Beresford
Beresford Public Library • 115 S 3rd St • Beresford, SD 57004-1798 • (605) 763-2782 • http://www.bmtc.net/~libone

Bowdle
Descendants of Michael and Mary Sheppard • HCR, Box 78 • Bowdle, SD 57428

Brookings
Brookings Area Genealogical Society & Library • 524 4th St • Brookings, SD 57006 • *Dakota Frontier Days*; *Brookings Area Genealogical Society Newsletter*

Brookings Public Library • 515 3rd St • Brookings, SD 57006 • (605) 692-9407 • http://www.brookings.com/library/ • *News & Events at Brookings Public Library*

State Agricultural Heritage Museum Archives • South Dakota State Univ, 925 11th St • Brookings, SD 57007 • (605) 688-6226 • http://www.agmuseum.com

Buffalo
Buffalo Historical Museum Archives • One-Room Schoolhouse, Hwy 85, P.O. Box 63 • Buffalo, SD 57720 • (605) 375-3800

Centerville
Centerville Community Library • 421 Florida, P.O. Box 100 • Centerville, SD 57014-0100 • (605) 563-2540

Chamberlain
Akta Lakota Museum Archives • St Joseph's Indian School, Box 89 • Chamberlain, SD 57325 • (605) 734-3452 • http://www.stjo.org

Chamberlain Area Historical Preservation Association • 115 W Lawler • Chamberlain, SD 57325 • (605) 734-6542

Cozard Memorial Library • 110 E Lawler • Chamberlain, SD 57325

Lyman-Brule Genealogical Society • c/o Cozard Memorial Library, 110 E Lawler, P.O. Box 555 • Chamberlain, SD 57325 • (605) 734-5862

South Dakota Hall of Fame Archives • 1480 S Main, P.O. Box 180 • Chamberlain, SD 57325 • (605) 734-4216 • http://www.sdhalloffame.com • *South Dakota Hall of Fame Magazine*

Clark
Clark County Historical Society & Archives • Beauvais Heritage Center, Hwy 212 • Clark, SD 57236 • (605) 532-3722 • *Clark County Historical Society Newsletter*

Crazy Horse
Indian Museum of North America Library • Crazy Horse Memorial Ave of the Chiefs • Crazy Horse, SD 57730-9506 • (605) 673-4681 • http://www.crazyhorse.org

Custer
Custer County Historical Society & Archives • 1881 Courthouse Museum, 411 Mt Rushmore Rd, P.O. Box 826 • Custer, SD 57730 • (605) 673-2443

Custer County Library • 447 Crook St, Suite 4 • Custer, SD 57730-1509 • (605) 673-8178 • http://custerlibrary.com

Custer State Park Museum Archives • Hwy 16A • Custer, SD 57730 • (605) 255-4460 • http://www.custerstatepark.info

De Smet
De Smet Depot Museum Archives • 104 Calumet Ave NE, P.O. Drawer 70 • De Smet, SD 57231 • (605) 854-3991

Kingsbury Genealogical Society • P.O. Box 330 • De Smet, SD 57231-0330

Laura Ingalls Wilder Memorial Society • Historical Museum, P.O. Box 426 • De Smet, SD 57231 • (605) 854-3383 • http://www.liwms.com • *Laura Ingalls Wilder Lore*

Standing Rock Sioux Tribal Offices • general delivery • De Smet, SD 57231 • (605) 854-2120

Deadwood
Adams Museum and House Archives • 54 Sherman, P.O. Box 252 • Deadwood, SD 57732 • (605) 578-1714 • http://www.adamsmuseumandhouse.org • *Adams Banner*

Deadwood Public Library • 435 Williams St • Deadwood, SD 57732-1113 • (605) 578-2821 • http://dwdlib.sdln.net

House of Roses Library • Senator Wilson Home, 15 Forest Ave • Deadwood, SD 57732 • (605) 578-1879

TDG Communication • 93 Sherman St • Deadwood, SD 57732 • (605) 722-7111 • *Deadwood Magazine*

Dell Rapids
Carnegie Public Library • 513 N Orleans Ave • Dell Rapids, SD 57022-1637 • (605) 428-3280

Edgemont
Edgemont Public Library • 412 2nd Ave, P.O. Box 449 • Edgemont, SD 57735-0449 • (605) 602-7712

Elk Point
Union County Historical Society • P.O. Box 552 • Elk Point, SD 57025

Ellsworth AFB
Holbrook Library, Ellsworth Air Force Base FL4690 • 28 SVS/SVMG, 2650 Doolittle Dr • Ellsworth AFB, SD 57706-4820 • (605) 385-1688 • http://www.ellsworth.af.mil/~library/home.shtml

Eureka
Eureka Pioneer Museum Archives • 1610 J Ave, P.O. Box 902 • Eureka, SD 57437 • (605) 284-2987 • http://www.glpta.org/eurekamuseum.htm

Faith
Faith Public Library • 204 W 5th St, P.O. Box 172 • Faith, SD 57626-0172 • (605) 967-2262

Faulkton
Faulk County Historical Society • Pickler Mansion Museum, 900 8th Ave, P.O. Box 584 • Faulkton, SD 57438 • (605) 598-4285

Flandreau
Moody County Genealogical Society • 501 W 1st Ave • Flandreau, SD 57028-1003 • (605) 997-2786

South Dakota

Moody County Historical Society & Archives • Historical Museum, 706 E Pipestone Ave, P.O. Box 25 • Flandreau, SD 57028 • (605) 997-3191 • http://www.rootsweb.com/~sdmoody/ • *Moody County Historical Society Newsletter*

Moody County Library • 700 W Community Dr • Flandreau, SD 57028-1061 • (605) 997-3326

Fort Meade
Old Fort Meade Museum Archives • Bldg 55, P.O. Box 164 • Fort Meade, SD 57741 • (605) 347-9822 • http://www.fortmeademuseum.org

Fort Pierre
Wakpa Sica Historical Society • 28 E Main Ave • Fort Pierre, SD 57532 • (605) 223-9099

Frankfort
Fisher Grove Country School Museum Archives • 17290 Fishers Ln • Frankfort, SD 57440 • (605) 472-1212

Freeman
Freeman Academy Library • Heritage Hall Museum, 748 S Main St, P.O. Box 1000 • Freeman, SD 57209 • (605) 925-4237 • http://www.freemanmuseum.org

Freeman Public Library • 185 E 3rd St, P.O. Box 1 • Freeman, SD 57029-0080 • (605) 925-7003

Geddes
Geddes Historic District Village Archives • P.O. Box 97 • Geddes, SD 57342 • (605) 337-2501 • http://www.geddes.og

Gettysburg
Dakota Sunset Museum Archives • 205 W Commercial Ave, Ste 104 • Gettysburg, SD 57442 • (605) 765-9480 • *Dakota Sunset Newsletter*

Gregory
Gregory Public Library • 112 E 5th • Gregory, SD 57533-1463 • (605) 835-8531

Hermosa
Schaub Reunion • 777 Ranch, HC 83, Box 11 • Hermosa, SD 57744

Highmore
Hyde County Historical and Genealogical Society • 400 1st St SW, P.O. Box 392 • Highmore, SD 57345 • (605) 852-3148

Hyde Historical and Genealogical Society • 400 1st St SW • Highmore, SD 57345 • (605) 852-3148

Hot Springs
Fall River County Historical Society & Archives • Historical Museum, P.O. Box 361 • Hot Springs, SD 57747 • (605) 745-5147

Hot Springs Public Library • 1543 Baltimore Ave • Hot Springs, SD 57747-1631 • (605) 745-3151

Pioneer Historical Museum of South Dakota • 300 S Chicago St • Hot Springs, SD 57747 • (605) 745-5147 • http://www.pioneer-museum.com

Huron
Dakotaland Museum Archives • State Fairgrounds, P.O. Box 1254 • Huron, SD 57350 • (605) 352-4626

Huron Public Library • 521 Dakota Ave S • Huron, SD 57350 • (605) 353-8530

Pyle House Museum Archives • 376 Idaho Ave SE • Huron, SD 57350 • (605) 352-2528

Ipswich
J W Parmely Historical Museum Archives • 35324 133rd St, P.O. Box 104 • Ipswich, SD 57451 • (605) 426-6949

Kadoka
Jackson-Washabough County Historical Society & Archives • Historical Museum, S Main St, P.O. Box 58 • Kadoka, SD 57543 • (605) 837-2229

Keystone
Big Thunder Gold Mine Museum Archives • 604 Blair, P.O. Box 459 • Keystone, SD 57751 • (605) 666-4847 • http://www.bigthundergoldmine.net

Keystone Area Historical Society & Archives • Historical Museum, 410 3rd St, P.O. Box 177 • Keystone, SD 57751 • (605) 666-4824 • http://www.keystonehistory.com • Holy Terror Tattler

Mount Rushmore National Memorial Archives • Hwy 244 • Keystone, SD 57751 • (605) 574-2523 • http://www.nps.gov/moru/

Kimball
South Dakota Tractor Museum Archives • 501 S West St, P.O. Box 418 • Kimball, SD 57355 • (605) 733-6513 • http://sdtractormuseum.home.comcast.net/news.htm

Kyle
Oglala Lakota College Library • P.O. Box 310 • Kyle, SD 57752-0310 • (605) 455-6069

Lake City
Fort Sisseton State Historic Park Archives • 11907 434th Ave • Lake City, SD 57427 • (605) 448-5701

Lead
Black Hills Mining Museum Archives • 323 W Main, P.O. Box 694 • Lead, SD 57754 • (605) 584-1605 • http://www.mning-museum.blackhills.com • *Black Hills Mining Museum Newsletter*

Phoebe Apperson Hearst Library • 315 W Main • Lead, SD 57754-1604 • (605) 584-2013

Lemmon
Grand River Museum Archives • 114 10th St W • Lemmon, SD 57638 • (605) 374-3911 • http://www.grandrivermuseum.org • *Grand River Museum Newsletter*

Letcher
Letcher Public Library • P.O. Box 176 • Letcher, SD 57359 • (605) 248-2689

Madison
Karl E Mundt Library and Museum • Dakota State Univ, 820 N Washington Ave, P.O. Box 483 • Madison, SD 57042 • (605) 256-5203 • http://www.departments.dsu.edu/library

Lake County Genealogical Society • c/o Karl Mundt Library, Dakota State Univ • Madison, SD 57042 • (605) 256-5203

Madison Public Library • 209 E Center St • Madison, SD 57042-2998 • (605) 256-7525

Prairie Village Archives • W Hwy 34, P.O. Box 256 • Madison, SD 57402 • (605) 256-3644 • http://www.prairievillage.org

Smith-Zimmerman State Museum Archives • Dakota State College, 221 NE 8th St • Madison, SD 57042 • (605) 256-5308 • http://www.smith-zimmerman.dsu.edu • *Smith-Zimmerman State Museum Newsletter*

Marvin
Blue Cloud Abbey Library • 46561 147th St, P.O. Box 98 • Marvin, SD 57251-0098 • (605) 398-9200 • http://www.bluecloud.org

Midland
Pioneer Club of Western South Dakota & Archives • Historical Museum, Main St • Midland, SD 57552 • (605) 843-2150 • http://www.gwic.net/~kry

Milbank
Grant County Public Library • 207 E Park Ave • Milbank, SD 57252-2497 • (605) 432-6543 • http://grantcountylibrary.com

Miller
Arbogast Reunion • 622 E 2nd St • Miller, SD 57362

Hand County Library • 402 N Broadway • Miller, SD 57362 • (605) 853-3693

Mina
North Central South Dakota Genealogical Society • 178 Southshore Dr • Mina, SD 57462-3000

Missions Hills
Yankton Genealogical Society • P.O. Box 71 • Missions Hills, SD 57406

Mitchell
Carl G Dittmann Family Organization • 620 N Edmunds • Mitchell, SD 57301 • (605) 996-5448

Dakota Discovery Museum Archives • 1300 E University St, P.O. Box 1071 • Mitchell, SD 57301 • (605) 996-2122 • http://www.dakotadicovery.com • *Dakota Discovery Museum Newsletter*

Davison County Genealogical Society • 41004 259th St • Mitchell, SD 57301

Enchanted World Doll Museum Archives • 615 N Main • Mitchell, SD 57301 • (605) 996-9896

Middle Border Museum Archives • 1311 S Duff St, P.O. Box 1071 • Mitchell, SD 57301 • (605) 996-2122

Mitchell Area Genealogical Society & Library • 620 N Edmunds • Mitchell, SD 57301 • (605) 996-6693

Mitchell Public Library • 221 N Duff St • Mitchell, SD 57301-2596 • (605) 995-8480 • http://mitlib.sdln.net

Mobridge
A H Brown Public Library • 521 N Main St • Mobridge, SD 57601-2130 • (605) 845-2808

Klein Museum Archives • 1820 W Grand Crossing • Mobridge, SD 57601 • (605) 845-7243

Murdo
1880 Town Museum Archives • I-90, P.O. Box 507 • Murdo, SD 57559 • (605) 344-2259

Murdo Genealogical Society • P.O. Box 441 • Murdo, SD 57559-0441

Pioneer Auto Museum Archives • I-90 & US 16, P.O. Box 76 • Murdo, SD 57559 • (605) 669-2691 • http://www.pioneersautoshow.com

Newell
Newell Museum Archives • 108 3rd St, P.O. Box 433 • Newell, SD 57760 • (605) 456-1310 • http://www.cityofnewell.com

Parker
Parker Public Library • 115 N Main Ave, P.O. Box 576 • Parker, SD 57053-0576 • (605) 297-5552

Philip
Prairie Homestead Museum Archives • 21141 Hwy 240 • Philip, SD 57567 • (605) 433-5400 • http://www.prairiehomestead.com

West River Museum Society & Archives • Historical Museum, Center Ave, P.O. Box 221 • Philip, SD 57567

Pierre
Pierre-Fort Pierre Genealogical Society & Library • P.O. Box 925 • Pierre, SD 57501 • (605) 223-9773 • *Pierre-Fort Pierre Genealogical Society Newsletter*

Rawlins Municipal Library • 1000 E Church St • Pierre, SD 57501 • (605) 773-7421 • http://www.sdln.net/libs/rawlins/rawlins.html

South Dakota Genealogical Society • P.O. Box 1101 • Pierre, SD 57501-1101 • *South Dakota Genealogical Society Quarterly*; *South Dakota Genealogical Society Newsletter*

South Dakota National Guard Museum Archives • 301 E Dakota Ave • Pierre, SD 57501 • (605) 224-9991 • http://www.state.sd.us/military/museum.htm

South Dakota State Archives • Memorial Bldg Branch, 900 Governors Dr • Pierre, SD 57501-2217 • (605) 773-3804 • http://www.sdhistory.org

South Dakota State Historical Society & Library • Cultural Heritage Center, 900 Governors Dr • Pierre, SD 57501-2217 • (605) 773-3458 • http://www.sdhistory.org/archives.htm • *South Dakota History*; *History Notes*

South Dakota State Library • Memorial Bldg Branch, 800 Governors Dr • Pierre, SD 57501-2294 • (605) 773-3131 • http://www.sdstatelibrary.com

Pine Ridge
Heritage Center Archives • Red Cloud Indian School, 100 Mission Dr, P.O. Box 100 • Pine Ridge, SD 57770 • (605) 867-5491 • http://www.redcloudindianschool.org

Platte
Platte Heritage Club • Route 2, Box 128 • Platte, SD 57369-0128

Rapid City
Keystone Area Historical Society • 410 3rd St • Rapid City, SD 57701 • (605) 666-4494

Rapid City
Minnilusa Historical Association & Archives • Pioneer Journey Museum, 222 New York St • Rapid City, SD 57701 • (605) 394-6923 • http://www.journeymuseum.org • *Minnilusa Historical Association Newsletter*

Motion Unlimited Museum Archives • 6180 S Hwy 79 • Rapid City, SD 57702 • (605) 348-7373 • http://www.motionunlimitedmuseum.com

Rapid City Public Library • 610 Quincy St • Rapid City, SD 57701-3655 • (605) 394-4171 • http://www.rapidcitylibrary.org

Rapid City Society for Genealogical Research & Library • P.O. Box 1495 • Rapid City, SD 57709 • Black Hills Nuggets

Samuel Sellers Family Organization • 255 Texas St #E459 • Rapid City, SD 57701-7325

Redfield
Spink County Historical Society • Historical Society, 225 E 8th Ave • Redfield, SD 57469 • (605) 472-0758

Revillo
Billings County Historical Society • general delivery • Revillo, SD 57259 • (605) 623-4829

Saint Francis
Buechel Memorial Lakota Museum Archives • 350 S Oak St, P.O. Box 499 • Saint Francis, SD 57572 • (605) 747-2745 • http://www.sfmission.org

Salem
McCook County Historical Society & Archives • Historical Museum, 44476 251st St • Salem, SD 57058 • (605) 425-2340

Scotland
Scotland Heritage Chapel and Museum Archives • 811 6th St, P.O. Box 112 • Scotland, SD 57059 • (605) 583-2344

Sioux Falls
Battleship South Dakota Museum Archives • 12th & Kiwanis • Sioux Falls, SD 57104 • (605) 367-7141

Center for Western Studies • Augustana College, 2201 S Summit • Sioux Falls, SD 57197 • (605) 274-4007 • http://www.augic.edu/cws/

Disbrow Research • 435 N Franklin Ave • Sioux Falls, SD 57103 • (605) 336-8012 • *Disbrow Family Newsletter*

Little Cornwall on the Prarie • 2805 S 4th Ave • Sioux Falls, SD 57105

Mears Library • University of Sioux Falls, 1101 W 22nd St • Sioux Falls, SD 57105-1699 • (605) 331-6660 • http://www.usioux.edu/is/library

Nordland Heritage Foundation • c/o Augustana College Library, 29th & Summit St, P.O. Box 727 • Sioux Falls, SD 57197 • (605) 336-4007 • http://www.augie.edu/cws

North American Baptist Heritage Commission & Library • Kaiser-Ramaker Library, 1525 S Grange Ave • Sioux Falls, SD 57105-1526 • (605) 335-9080 • http://www.nabs.edu • *Heritage Horizons*

North American Baptists Archives • 1605 S Euclid Ave • Sioux Falls, SD 57105 • (605) 336-6588

Pettigrew Home Museum Archives • 8th & Duluth • Sioux Falls, SD 57104 • (605) 367-7097

Sioux Empire Medical Museum Archives • 1305 W 18th St • Sioux Falls, SD 57117 • (605) 333-6397

South Dakota

Sioux Valley Genealogical Society & Archives • Old Courthouse Museum, 200 W 6th St • Sioux Falls, SD 57104-6001 • (605) 367-4210 • http://www.rootsweb.com/~sdsvgs • *Pioneer Pathfinder*

Siouxland Heritage Museums Library • Old Courthouse, 200 W 6th St • Sioux Falls, SD 57104 • (605) 367-4210 • http://www.siouxlandmuseums.com • *Museums Report*

Siouxland Libraries • 201 N Main Ave • Sioux Falls, SD 57104-6002 • (605) 367-8701 • http://www.siouxland.lib.sd.us • *GroupLetter*

Sisseton
Roberts County Historical Society & Archives • c/o Sisseton Memorial Library, 305 E Maple St, P.O. Box 289 • Sisseton, SD 57262-0289 • (605) 698-7391

Sisseton Memorial Library • 305 E Maple St, P.O. Box 289 • Sisseton, SD 57262-0289 • (605) 698-7391

Sisseton Wahpeton Community College Library • Agency Village, P.O. Box 689 • Sisseton, SD 57262-0698 • (605) 698-3966 • http://www.swcc.cc.sd.us/vlibrary

Spearfish
D C Booth Historic Fish Hatchery Museum Archives • 423 Hatchery Cr • Spearfish, SD 57783 • (605) 642-7730 • http://www.debooth.fws.gov • *D C Booth Historic Fish Hatchery Museum Newsletter*

E Y Berry Library • Black Hills State Univ, 1200 University Ave • Spearfish, SD 57799-9676 • (605) 642-6833 • http://www.bhsu.edu/resources/library

Grace Balloch Memorial Library • 625 N 5th St • Spearfish, SD 57783-2311 • (605) 642-1330 • http://www.spflib.sdln.net

High Plains Heritage Society & Archives • Historical Museum, 825 Heritage Dr, P.O. Box 542 • Spearfish, SD 57783 • (605) 642-9378 • http://www.westernheritagecenter.com • *High Plains News*

Stratford
Tilton Ishmael Family Organization • 588 N 3rd St • Stratford, SD 57474 • (605) 395-6411

Sturgis
Sturgis Public Library • 1040 2nd St • Sturgis, SD 57785 • (605) 347-2624

Tabor
Czech Heritage Preservation Society • P.O. Box 3 • Tabor, SD 57063 • (605) 589-3494 • *Czech Heritage Preservation Society Annual Newsletter*

Timber Lake
Dewey County Library • 212 S Main, P.O. Box 68 • Timber Lake, SD 57656-0068 • (605) 865-3541

Turton
Lagesse Family Association • P.O. Box 45 • Turton, SD 57477 • (605) 897-6528

Norbert Barrie Family Organization • P.O. Box 45 • Turton, SD 57477 • (605) 897-6528

Vermillion
I D Weeks Library • University of South Dakota, 414 E Clark St • Vermillion, SD 57069 • (605) 677-5371 • http://www.usd.edu/library

Samuel Chaney Family Organization • 403 E Main St #A • Vermillion, SD 57069-3225 • (605) 539-9087

Vermillion Public Library • 18 Church St • Vermillion, SD 57069-3093 • (605) 677-7060

W H Over State Museum Archives • 1110 Ratingen St • Vermillion, SD 57069 • (605) 677-5228 • http://www.usd.edu/whover/ • *W H Over State Museum Newsletter*

Volga
Brookings County Historical Society & Archives • Historical Museum, 101 Lincoln Ln, P.O. Box 608 • Volga, SD 57071 • (605) 627-9149 • Window

Wall
Wounded Knee Museum Archives • I-90 • Wall, SD 57790 • (605) 279-2573 • http://www.woundedkneemuseum.org

Watertown
Codington County Historical Society & Archives • Heritage Museum, 27 1st Ave SE • Watertown, SD 57201 • (605) 886-7335 • http://www.cchsmuseum.org • Codington County Historical Society Newsletter

Mellette House Museum Archives • 421 5th Ave NW • Watertown, SD 57201 • (605) 886-4730

Watertown Genealogical Society & Library • 611 NE B Avenue • Watertown, SD 57201 • (605) 882-6220

Watertown Regional Library • 611 B Avenue NE, P.O. Box 250 • Watertown, SD 57201-0250 • (605) 882-6220 • http://watweb.sdln.net

Webster
Webster Public Library • 800 Main St • Webster, SD 57274-1494 • (605) 345-3263

Wessington
Wessington Public Library • 240 Wessington St, P.O. Box 108 • Wessington, SD 57381-0108 • (605) 458-2596

Wessington Springs
Wessington Springs Carnegie Library • 109 W Main St, P.O. Box 336 • Wessington Springs, SD 57382-0336 • (605) 539-1803

White River
Edwin Elliot Brooking Descendants • P.O. Box 282 • White River, SD 57579 • (605) 259-3479

Winner
Family Tree Genealogical Society • P.O. Box 202 • Winner, SD 57580-0202

Tripp County Historical Society • 100 E 4th St • Winner, SD 57580 • (605) 842-0704

Tripp County Library • 442 W Monroe St • Winner, SD 57580 • (605) 842-0330

Wolsey
East River Genealogical Forum • RR 2, Box 148 • Wolsey, SD 57384

East River Genealogical Society • 20084 387th Ave • Wolsey, SD 57384 • (605) 883-4117

Yankton
Cramer-Kenyon Heritage Home Museum Archives • 509 Pine St • Yankton, SD 57078 • (605) 665-7470

Lewis and Clark Museum Archives • NE Hwy 121, P.O. Box 710 • Yankton, SD 57078 • (402) 667-7873

Yankton Community Library • 515 Walnut St • Yankton, SD 57078-4042 • (605) 668-5275 • http://ycllib.sdln.net

Yankton County Historical Society & Archives • Dakota Territorial Museum, 610 Summit St, P.O. Box 1033 • Yankton, SD 57078 • (605) 665-2919 • *Museum Chronicle*

Yankton Genealogical Society • 1803 Douglas Ave • Yankton, SD 57078

TENNESSEE

Adams
Port Royal State Historic Area Archives • 3300 Old Clarksville-Springfield Rd • Adams, TN 37010 • (931) 358-9696

Alamo
Crockett Memorial Library • 258 E Church St • Alamo, TN 38001-1108 • (731) 696-4220

Alcoa
Doane Family Association • P.O. Box 43 • Alcoa, TN 37701-0043 • *Doane Doin's and Diggin's*

Ashland City
Cheatham County Historical and Genealogical Society • 199 Court St • Ashland City, TN 37015-1297 • (615) 792-3623 • http://www.rootsweb.com/~tncheath/

Cheatham County Public Library • 188 County Services Dr, Suite 200 • Ashland City, TN 37015-1726 • (615) 792-4828 • http://www.members.tripod.com/cheatham_library/

Athens
Fort Loudoun Regional Library Center • 718 George St NW • Athens, TN 37303-2214 • (423) 745-5194 • http://www.state.tn.us/sos/statelib/p&d/fortloudoun/

McMinn County Living Heritage Museum Archives • 522 W Madison Ave, P.O. Box 889 • Athens, TN 37303 • (423) 745-0329 • http://www.livingheritagemuseum.com

McMinn Historical Society • 6 E Madison Ave • Athens, TN 37303 • (423) 744-3911

Merner-Pfeiffer Library • Tennessee Wesleyan College, Coach Farmer Dr, P.O. Box 40 • Athens, TN 37371 • (423) 746-5250 • http://www.library.twcnet.edu

Bartlett
Bartlett Historical Society & Archives • Bartlett Museum, 2969 Court St • Bartlett, TN 38134 • (901) 373-8433

Tennessee Genealogical Society • 9140 Davies Plantation Rd • Bartlett, TN 38134 • (901) 381-1447

Wood-Woods Research • 6025 Stage Rd #42287 • Bartlett, TN 38134-8374 • *Wood-Woods Family Magazine*

Benton
Lillard Family Association • 1669 Mountain View Rd • Benton, TN 37307 • (423) 338-5777 • *Lillard Lines*

Polk County Historical and Genealogical Society • P.O. Box 636 • Benton, TN 37307 • (423) 338-1005 • http://www.tngenweb.usit.com/polk • *Polk County Historical and Genealogical Society Quarterly*

Blountville
Harr Family Organization • 141 Oak St • Blountville, TN 37617 • (423) 323-5590

Spurlock Family Association • P.O. Box 567 • Blountville, TN 37617-0567 • http://www.geocities.com/Heartland/Hills/4411/ • *Spurlock Family Quarterly*

Sullivan County Genealogy Club • c/o Sullivan County Public Library, 1655 State Route 37, P.O. Box 568 • Blountville, TN 37617 • (423) 279-2714 • http://www.usit.net/tngenweb/sullivan/sullclub.htm

Sullivan County Public Library • 1655 Blountville Blvd, P.O. Box 510 • Blountville, TN 37617-0510 • (423) 279-2714 • http://www.wrlibrary.org/sullivan

Bluff City
Family of Bruce Society in America • 1172 Weaver Branch Rd • Bluff City, TN 37618-2546

Bolivar
Bolivar-Hardeman County Public Library • 213 N Washington St • Bolivar, TN 38008-2020 • (731) 658-3436

Brentwood
Brentwood Library • 8109 Concord Rd • Brentwood, TN 37027 • (615) 371-0090 • http://www.brentwood-tn.org/library

Bristol
E W King Library • King College, 1350 King College Rd • Bristol, TN 37620 • (423) 652-4791 • http://www.king.edu/library

Holston Territory Genealogical Society • P.O. Box 433 • Bristol, TN 37621

Sullivan County Genealogical Society • P.O. Box 433 • Bristol, TN 37621

Brownsville
Elma Ross Public Library • 1011 E Main St • Brownsville, TN 38012-2652 • (731) 772-9534

Brunswick
Tennessee Genealogical Society • 9114 Davies Plantation Rd, P.O. Box 247 • Brunswick, TN 38014-0247 • (901) 381-1447 • *Tennessee Genealogical Magazine: Ansearchin' News*

Burns
Cumberland Presbyterian Church Birthplace Archives • Montgomery Bell State Park • Burns, TN 37029 • (901) 276-8602 • http://www.cumberland.org/hfcpc

Butler
William Bunton Descendants • Route 1, Box 210 • Butler, TN 37640

Camden
Benton County Genealogical Society • P. O. Box 775 • Camden, TN 38320

Benton County Public Library • 121 S Forrest Ave • Camden, TN 38320-2055 • (731) 584-4772

Carthage
Futral Genealogy Trails • 6 Wonderland Ln • Carthage, TN 37030-9546 • (615) 735-0093 • *Ancestors-Descendants of Futral-Cliffords, Watkins-Wood*

Smith County Historical and Genealogical Society • P.O. Box 112 • Carthage, TN 37030

Smith County Public Library • 215 Main St N • Carthage, TN 37030 • (615) 735-1326 • http://www.webman.addr.com/library/

Castalian Springs
Bledsoe's Lick Historical Association • P.O. Box 210 • Castalian Springs, TN 37031

Historic Cragfont Archives • 200 Cragfront Rd • Castalian Springs, TN 37031 • (615) 452-7070 • http://www.srlab.net/cragfont/

Wynnewood State Historical Site Archives • Castilian Springs • Castalian Springs, TN 37031 • (615) 452-5463

Centerville
Hickman County Historical Society • 13 Courthouse • Centerville, TN 37033 • (931) 729-3279

Hickman County Public Library • 120 W Swan St • Centerville, TN 37033 • (931) 729-5130 • http://www.hickmancountylibrary.homestead.com

Chattanooga
Chattanooga African-American Heritage Museum Archives • 200 E Martin L King Blvd, P.O. Box 11493 • Chattanooga, TN 37416 • (423) 266-8658 • http://www.caamhistory.com • *Heritage*

Chattanooga Regional History Museum Archives • 400 Chestnut St • Chattanooga, TN 37402 • (423) 265-3247 • http://www.chattanoogahistory.com • Chattanooga Regional History Museum Newsletter

Chattanooga-Hamilton County Bicentennial Library • 1001 Broad St • Chattanooga, TN 37402 • (423) 757-5310 • http://www.lib.chattanooga.gov/

National Medal of Honor Museum of Military History Archives • Northgate Mall, Hwy 153, P.O. Box 11467 • Chattanooga, TN 37401-2467 • (423) 267-1737 • http://www.mohm.org • *National Medal of Honor Museum of Military History Newsletter*

Overall Research • 133 Kingwood Dr • Chattanooga, TN 37412 • *Overalls All Over*

T Cartter & Margaret Rawlings Lupton Library • University of Tennessee at Chattanooga, Vine St • Chattanooga, TN 37403-2598 • (423) 425-4510 • http://www.lib.utc.edu • *T Cartter & Margaret Rawlings Lupton Library Newsletter*

Tennessee Civil War Museum Archives • 3914 St Elmo Ave • Chattanooga, TN 37409 • (423) 821-4954

Tennessee Valley Railroad Museum Archives • 4119 Cromwell • Chattanooga, TN 37421 • (423) 894-8028 • http://www.tvrail.com • *Smoke and Cinders*

Church Hill
Netherland Family Society • 107 S Holston Dr • Church Hill, TN 37642 • (423) 245-6844

Clarksville
Clarksville-Montgomery County Historical Museum Archives • 200 S 2nd St, P.O. Box 383 • Clarksville, TN 37040 • (931) 648-5780 • http://www.customshousemuseum.org • *Art-N-Facts*

Clarksville-Montgomery County Public Library • 350 Pageant Lane, Suite 501 • Clarksville, TN 37040 • (615) 648-8826 • http://www.clarksville.org • *Friends of the Library Newsletter*

Hastings Family Organization • P.O. Box 585 • Clarksville, TN 37040

Montgomery County Historical Society • 189 S 10th St • Clarksville, TN 37040 • (931) 553-2486

Montgomery County Historical Society & Archives • c/o Clarksville-Montgomery County Library, 350 Pageant Ln #501, P.O. Box 262 • Clarksville, TN 37041 • (615) 648-8824 • *Montgomery County Historical Journal*

Smith-Trahern Mansion Archives • 101 McClure St • Clarksville, TN 37040 • (931) 648-9998

Cleveland
Bradley County Genealogical Society • P.O. Box 1384 • Cleveland, TN 37364

Bradley County Historical Society & Library • Lee College, 833 N Ocoee St, P.O. Box 4845 • Cleveland, TN 37320 • (423) 479-8367

Cleveland Public Library • 795 Church St NE • Cleveland, TN 37311-5295 • (423) 472-2163 • http://www.clevelandlibrary.org • *Friends of the Library Newsletter*

Cleveland State Community College Library • 3535 Adkisson Dr, P.O. Box 3570 • Cleveland, TN 37320-3570 • (423) 478-6209 • http://www.clscc.cc.tn.us/library/

Red Clay State Historic Park Archives • 1140 Red Clay Park Rd SW • Cleveland, TN 37311 • (423) 478-0339

Clinton
Clinton Public Library • 118 S Hicks St • Clinton, TN 37716 • (865) 457-0519

Museum of Appalachia Archives • 2819 Andersonville Hwy • Clinton, TN 37716 • (865) 494-7680 • http://www.museumofappalachia.com

Pellissippi Genealogical and Historical Society • c/o Clinton Public Library, 118 S Hicks St • Clinton, TN 37716 • (865) 457-5400 x379 • http://pghs.home.att.net • *Pellissippian*

Collegedale
McKee Library • Southern Adventist University, P.O. Box 629 • Collegedale, TN 37315-0629 • (423) 238-2794 • http://www.library.southern.edu • *LNN News*

Collierville
Biblical Resource Center Museum Archives • 140 E Mulberry • Collierville, TN 38017 • (901) 854-8578 • http://www.biblical-museum.org

Columbia
Athenaeum Archives • 808 Athenaeum St • Columbia, TN 38401 • (931) 381-4822

James K Polk Ancestral Home Archives • 301 W 7th St, P.O. Box 741 • Columbia, TN 38402 • (931) 388-2354 • http://www.jameskpolk.com

Maury County Historical Society & Library • P.O. Box 147 • Columbia, TN 38401 • (931) 381-1673 • *Historic Maury*; *Maury County Historical Society Newsletter*

Maury County Public Library • 211 W 8th St • Columbia, TN 38401 • (931) 388-6332 • http://www.maurycountylibrary.org

Polk Family Reunion • James K Polk Ancestral Home, 303 W 7th St, P.O. Box 741 • Columbia, TN 38401 • (931) 388-2354 • http://www.jameskpolk.com

Sons of Confederate Veterans & Library • P.O. Box 592 • Columbia, TN 38401 • (931) 380-1844 • http://www.scv.org • *Confederate Veteran*

Cookeville
Cookeville Depot Museum Archives • 116 N Cedar Ave • Cookeville, TN 38501 • (931) 628-8559 • http://www.cookeville-tn.org • *Highballer*

Putnam County Library • 50 E Broad St • Cookeville, TN 38501 • (931) 526-2416 • http://www.pclibrary.org

University Library • Tennessee Technical Univ, P.O. Box 5066 • Cookeville, TN 38505 • (931) 372-3326

Upper Cumberland Genealogical Association • c/o Putnam County Library, 50 E Broad St, P.O. Box 575 • Cookeville, TN 38503-0575 • (931) 526-2416 • http://www.jagunet.com/~mbar/ucga.htm • *Quarterly of the Upper Cumberland Genealogical Association*; *Upper Cumberland Genealogical Association Bulletin*; *Upper Cumberland Researcher*

Volpe Library • Tennessee Technological University, 1100 N Peachtree, Box 5066 • Cookeville, TN 38505 • (931) 372-3408 • http://www.tntech.edu/library

Covington
Tipton County Historical Society • 120 W Pleasant Ave • Covington, TN 38019 • (901) 475-6608

Tipton County Museum Veterans Memorial Archives • 451 Bert Robinson Ave • Covington, TN 38019 • (901) 476-0242

Tipton County Public Library • 300 W Church St • Covington, TN 38019-2729 • (901) 476-8289

Cowan
Franklin County Old Jail Museum Archives • 7895 Sewanee Hwy • Cowan, TN 37318 • (931) 967-0524

Crossville
Art Circle Public Library • 154 E 1st St • Crossville, TN 38555-4696 • (931) 484-6790 • http://www.artcircle.crossville.com

Brough Family Association • 223 Kings Row • Crossville, TN 38555

Cumberland County Historical and Genealical Society • 20 S Main St • Crossville, TN 38555 • (931) 456-5520

Cypress Inn
Wayne and Lawrence, TN Brewer Reunion • Route 1, Box 99 • Cypress Inn, TN 38452 • (731) 724-9029

Dandridge
Dandridge Memorial Library • 1235 Circle Dr, P.O. Box 339 • Dandridge, TN 37725-0339 • (865) 397-9758

Goddard Historical and Genealogical Society • P.O. Box 688 • Dandridge, TN 37725 • *Goddard Newsletter*

Jefferson County Historical Society • P.O. Box 325 • Dandridge, TN 37725

Dayton
Rhea County Historical and Genealogical Society • P.O. Box 31 • Dayton, TN 37321

Decaturville
Decatur County Historical Society • P.O. Box 700 • Decaturville, TN 38329

Deer Lodge
Deer Lodge Abner Ross Memorial Center Library • Harker St, P.O. Box 127 • Deer Lodge, TN 37726-0127 • (423) 965-3472

Deer Lodge Historical Society • 302 Old Deer Lodge Pike • Deer Lodge, TN 37726 • (423) 965-2525

Dickson
Dickson County Public Library • 206 Henslee Dr • Dickson, TN 37055-2020 • (615) 446-8293 • http://www.dicksonpubliclibrary.org

Dover
Fort Donelson National Battlefield Archives • 120 Fort Donelson Rd, P.O. Boc 434 • Dover, TN 37058 • (931) 232-5706 • http://www.nps.gov

Stewart County Historical Society • 174 Church St • Dover, TN 37058 • (931) 232-9773

Dyersburg
McIver's Grant Public Library • 204 N Mill • Dyersburg, TN 38024-4631 • (731) 285-5032

Elizabethton
Carter County and Its People 1796-1993 • P.O. Box 176 • Elizabethton, TN 37643

Elizabethton Public Library • 201 N Sycamore St • Elizabethton, TN 37643 • (423) 547-6360 • http://www.eccpl.org

Erin
Houston County Historical Society • P.O. Box 401 • Erin, TN 37061

Erwin
Unicoi County Public Library • 201 Nolichucky Ave • Erwin, TN 37650-1237 • (423) 743-6533 • http://www.wrlibrary.org/Library/uupage.html

Farragut
Farragut Folklife Museum Archives • 11408 Municipal Center • Farragut, TN 37922 • (865) 966-8057 • *Farragut Folklife Museum Newsletter*

Fayetteville
Fayetteville-Lincoln County Public Library • 400 Rocky Knob Ln • Fayetteville, TN 37334-2558 • (931) 433-3286

William Ables Family Organization • 5 Shadetree Ln • Fayetteville, TN 37334-6669 • (931) 433-6812 • *William Ables Family Organization Newsletter*

Franklin
Arbogast Database • 121 Yorktown Rd • Franklin, TN 37064-3277 • (615) 591-7032

Carnton Plantation Association & Archives • Historical Museum, 1345 Carnton Ln • Franklin, TN 37064 • (615) 794-0903 • http://www.carnton.org

Carter House Association & Archives • Historical Museum, 1140 Columbia Ave, P.O. Box 555 • Franklin, TN 37065 • (615) 791-1861 • http://www.carterhouse.org

Spencer Family Historical and Genealogical Society • 376 Sims Ln • Franklin, TN 37069-1893 • (615) 591-7373 • http://www.spectrumdata.com/shgs • *Le Despencer*

Williamson County Historical Society • P.O. Box 71 • Franklin, TN 37065 • *Williamson County Historical Society Journal*

Williamson County Public Library • 611 W Main St • Franklin, TN 37064-2723 • (615) 595-1243 • http://lib.williamson-tn.org

Gainesboro
Charles Ralph Holland Memorial Library • 205 Hull St, P.O. Box 647 • Gainesboro, TN 38562 • (615) 268-9190

Gallatin
Rose Mont Archives • 810 S Water Ave • Gallatin, TN 37066 • (615) 451-2331

Sumner County Archives • 155 E Main St • Gallatin, TN 37066 • (615) 452-0037

Sumner County Historical Society • P.O. Box 1871 • Gallatin, TN 37066 • (615) 452-2701

Sumner County Public Library • 658 Hartsville Pk • Gallatin, TN 37066-2509 • (615) 452-1722

Trousdale Place Archives • 183 W Main • Gallatin, TN 37066 • (615) 452-5648

Gatlinburg
Anna Porter Public Library • 207 Cherokee Orchard Rd • Gatlinburg, TN 37738-3417 • (865) 436-5588 • http://www.annaporterpl.org

Great Smoky Mountains National Park Library • 107 Park Headquarters Rd • Gatlinburg, TN 37738 • (865) 436-1296

Germantown
Buffum Family Association • 2386 Oak Trail Cove • Germantown, TN 38139-6410 • *Buffum Family Bulletin*

Capoot Surname Organization • 1862 Brooksedge • Germantown, TN 38138 • (901) 756-6510

Clan Donnachaidh Society, Mid-South States • 1507 Miller Farms Rd • Germantown, TN 38138 • (901) 754-8468

P T Boat Museum Archives • 1986 Cordova Rd • Germantown, TN 38498 • (901) 956-8640 • http://www.ptboat.org

Goodlettsville
Kerr Family Association of North America • 7980 Ridgewood Rd • Goodlettsville, TN 37072

Ridgetop Historical Society • 110 O'Bryan St • Goodlettsville, TN 37072-7146 • (615) 851-9468

Granville
Granville Museum Archives • Clover St, P.O. Box 26 • Granville, TN 38560 • (901) 453-4511 • http://www.granvillemuseum.com

Greeneville
Andrew Johnson National Historic Site Library • 101 N College St, P.O. Box 1088 • Greeneville, TN 37744-1088 • (423) 638-3551 • http://www.nps.gov

Doak House Museum Archives • Tusculum College, P.O. Box 5028 • Greeneville, TN 37743 • (423) 626-6554 • http://www.tusculum.edu

Greene County Genealogical Society • c/o Greeneville Public Library, P.O. Box 1903 • Greeneville, TN 37744 • *Greene County Pioneer*

Greene County Public Library • 210 N Main St • Greeneville, TN 37745-3816 • (423) 638-5034 • http://www.ggcpl.org

President Andrew Johnson Museum and Library • Tusculum College, P.O. Box 5026 • Greeneville, TN 37743 • (423) 636-7438 • http://www.tusculum.edu/museum/johnson.html

Halls
Forked Deer Regional Library Center • 220 N Front St, P.O. Box 68 • Halls, TN 38040-0068 • (731) 836-5812

Harriman
Harriman Public Library • 601 Walden St • Harriman, TN 37748-2506 • (865) 882-3195

Tidwell, Ledford Database • 2913 Roane State Hwy • Harriman, TN 37748 • (865) 882-7944

Harrogate
Abraham Lincoln Museum Archives • Hwy 25E, Cumberland Gap Pkwy • Harrogate, TN 37752 • (423) 869-6235 • http://www.lmvnet.edu/musfront1.htm • *Lincoln Herald*; *Lincoln Letters*

Carnegie Vincent Library • Lincoln Memorial University, Cumberland Gap Pkwy • Harrogate, TN 37752 • (423) 869-6436 • http://www.lmunet.edu

Henderson
Peddy Family Organization • 615 Allen Peddy Loop • Henderson, TN 38340

Hendersonville
Rock Castle Archives • 139 Rock Castle Ln • Hendersonville, TN 37075 • (615) 824-0502

Hermitage
Hermitage: Home of President Andrew Jackson Archives • 4580 Rachels Ln • Hermitage, TN 37076-1344 • (615) 889-2941 • http://www.thehermitage.com

Tulip Grove Mansion Archives • 4580 Rachel's Ln • Hermitage, TN 37076 • (615) 889-2941

Tennessee

Hixson
Venable Research • P.O. Box 211 • Hixson, TN 37343-0211 • *Venable Letter*

Hohenwald
Meriwether Lewis National Monument Archives • 189 Meriwether Lewis Park • Hohenwald, TN 38462 • (800) 308-7417 • http://www.nps.gov

Huntingdon
Carroll County Library • 159 E Main St • Huntingdon, TN 38344-3903 • (731) 986-1919

Huntsville
Scott County Historical Society & Library • 198 Woodland Pl, P.O. Box 7 • Huntsville, TN 37756 • (423) 663-3887 • *Scott County Historical Society Newsletter*

Jackson
Casey Jones Home and Railroad Museum Archives • Casey Jones Village, P.O. Box 11597 • Jackson, TN 38305 • (731) 668-1222 • http://www.caseyjonesvillage.com

Emma Waters Summar Library • Union University, 1050 Union University Dr • Jackson, TN 38305 • (731) 661-5070 • http://www.uu.edu/library/ • *Compass*

Jackson-Madison County Library • 433 E Lafayette St • Jackson, TN 38301-6386 • (731) 425-8600 • http://www.jmcl.tn.org

Luther L Gobbel Library • Lambuth Univ, 705 Lambuth Blvd • Jackson, TN 38301 • (731) 425-3290 • http://www.lambuth.edu/academics/library/library.html

Mid-West Tennessee Genealogical Society • P.O. Box 3343 • Jackson, TN 38303-0343 • (731) 784-2236 • http://erc.jscc.cc.tn.us/jfn/libjmc/Genealogical.html • *Family Findings*

Shiloh Regional Library • 573 Old Hickford Blvd • Jackson, TN 38305-2901 • (731) 668-0710

Utley Reunion • 590 Wallace Rd • Jackson, TN 38305-2839 • (731) 668-5409 • *Utley Reunion Update*

Jamestown
Fentress County Genealogical Society • P.O. Box 178 • Jamestown, TN 38556

Fentress County Historical Society & Library • P.O. Box 178 • Jamestown, TN 38556 • (931) 879-7512 • http://www.dsenter.com/~overton/fent.htm • *Fentress County Historical Society Newsletter*

Jefferson
Clan Gillean Association, USA • 742 Lakewood Dr • Jefferson, TN 37760 • (865) 475-2015 • *Pipings of MacLean*

Jefferson City
Jefferson County Genealogical Society • P.O. Box 267 • Jefferson City, TN 37760-0267 • (931) 397-9050 • *Jefferson County Genealogical Society Journal*

Joelton
Gower History • 2076 Valley View Rd • Joelton, TN 37080 • (615) 876-3473

Johnson City
Carroll Reece Museum Archives • East Tennesse State Univ, P.O. Box 70660 • Johnson City, TN 37614-0660 • (423) 929-4392 • http://cass.etsu.edu/museum

Garland Family Research Association • 3154 Antioch Rd • Johnson City, TN 37604 • (423) 926-5010

Johnson City Historical Society • general delivery • Johnson City, TN 37601

Johnson City Public Library • 100 W Millard St • Johnson City, TN 37604 • (423) 434-4469 • http://www.jcpl.net

Joseph Francis Kiener Family Organization • 2403 Camelot Cr • Johnson City, TN 37604 • (423) 282-0906

Museum at Mountain Home • East Tennessee State Univ, P.O. Box 70693 • Johnson City, TN 37604 • (423) 439-8049

Pelham Humphries Heirs Association • P.O. Box 1023 • Johnson City, TN 37605 • (423) 926-3012

Sherrod Library • East Tennessee State Univ, Seehorn Dr & Lake St, P.O. Box 70665 • Johnson City, TN 37614 • (423) 439-4307 • http://sherrod.etsu.edu

Tipton-Haynes Historic Site Archives • 2620 S Roan St • Johnson City, TN 37804 • (423) 926-5623 • http://www.tipton-haynes.org

Watauga Regional Library Center • 2700 S Roan St, Suite 435 • Johnson City, TN 37601 • (423) 926-2951 • http://www.wrlibrary.org

Jonesborough
Jonesborough-Washington County History Museum Archives • 117 Boone St • Jonesborough, TN 37659 • (423) 753-1015 • http://www.jwcheritagealliance.org

Washington County-Jonesboro Public Library • 200 Sabin Dr • Jonesborough, TN 37659-1306 • (423) 753-1800 • http://www.wrlibrary.org

Kingsport
Chesnutt-Griffin Family • 1000 Hanover Ct • Kingsport, TN 37660

Clan Maxwell Society of the USA • 246 DeLee Dr • Kingsport, TN 37663 • (615) 239-8426

Kingsport Public Library • 400 Broad St • Kingsport, TN 37660-4292 • (423) 224-2539 • http://www.kingsportlibrary.org • *Footnotes*

Netherland Inn House Museum Archives • 2144 Netherland Inn Rd • Kingsport, TN 37664 • (423) 247-3211 • *Netherland Inn House Museum Newsletter*

Simon Granser Marshall Association • 1514 Ardmore Pl • Kingsport, TN 37664 • (615) 378-4172 • *Marshall Newsletter*

Kingston
Anubis Society • 1816 Oak Hill Dr • Kingston, TN 37763

Kingston City Library • 10004 Bradford Wy • Kingston, TN 37763 • (865) 376-9905 • http://kpltn.org

Roane County Genealogical Society & Archives • c/o Kingston Public Library, 10004 Bradford Wy, P.O. Box 297 • Kingston, TN 37763-0297 • (865) 376-9905 • http://www.roanetn.com/rcgs.htm • *Roane Ramblings*

Roane County Heritage Commission • 119 Court St, P.O. Box 738 • Kingston, TN 37763 • (615) 376-9211 • http://www.roanetnheritage.com • *Heritage Newsletter*

Roane County Museum of History Archives • 119 Court St • Kingston, TN 37763 • (865) 376-9211

Knoxville
Acuff Archives • P.O. Box 6764 • Knoxville, TN 37919 • http://www.acuff.org

Barnhill Family Association • P.O. Box 22621 • Knoxville, TN 37933

Beck Cultural Exchange Center Archives • 1927 Dandridge Ave • Knoxville, TN 37915 • (865) 524-8461 • http://www.korrnet.org/beckcec

Blount Mansion Archives • 200 W Hill Ave, P.O. Box 1703 • Knoxville, TN 37901 • (865-525-2375 • http://www.blountmnsion.org

Clan Skene Association • 485 Hiawassee Ave • Knoxville, TN 37917-3641 • http://www.parsonage.net/ClanSkene/ • *Clan Skene Association Newsletter*

Clan Stewart Society in America • P.O. Box 9538 • Knoxville, TN 37940 • *Fesse Chequy*

Confederate Memorial Hall Archives • Bleak House, 3148 Kingston Pike • Knoxville, TN 37919 • (865) 522-2371 • http://www.knoxville.cmh.org

Crawford County Historical Society & Archives • County Courthouse • Knoxville, TN 37950

Crescent Bend Museum Archives • Armstrong-Lockett House, 2728 Kingston Pk • Knoxville, TN 37919 • (865) 637-3163 • http://www.kornet.org/cresbend

East Tennessee Historical Center • 500 W Church Ave • Knoxville, TN 37902-2505 • (865) 215-8700 • http://www.knoxlib.org

East Tennessee Historical Society & Archives • Historical Museum, 600 Market St, P.O. Box 1629 • Knoxville, TN 37901-1629 • (865) 544-5732 • http://www.east-tennessee-history.org • *Journal of East Tennessee History*; *East Tennessee Historical Society's Publications*; *Newsline*; *Tennessee Ancestors*

Folk Family • P.O. Box 52048 • Knoxville, TN 37950-2048 • *McMahan Families; Winston Families; Ragsdale Register; Garland Gazette; Michie Families; Allen Families; Dabney Families; Quarles Queries; Carr-Kerr Chronicle; Capps Families; Campbell Clans; Bird Branches; Owenby-Ownby Families; Overton Observer; McFatridge Family Newsletter; Yates of Yore; Stockton Links; Rook Roots; Marney Monitor Newsletter; Maupin Families; Blake Banner; Cabbage Campbell Capps; Lindsay Letters; Priddy Press; Daniel-Daniels Newsletter; Tiner Times; Adams Families; Stockton Links; Keener Kinfolk; Rook Roots; McFatridge Family Newsletter; Fontaine Families; Stinnett Family Newsletter; Kilgore Kith and Kin Newsletter; Isbell Inquirer; Waller Wanderings; Rust Family Newsletter; Whaley Family Newsletter*

Frank H McClung Museum Archives • Univ of Tennessee, 1327 Circle Park Dr • Knoxville, TN 37996-3200 • (865) 974-2144 • http://mcclungmuseum.utk.edu

Frost Reunion • 730 Cherokee Blvd • Knoxville, TN 37919 • (865) 524-7887

Georgia-Pennsylvania-Revolutionary War-South Carolina-Virginia Research • 407 Ascot Ct • Knoxville, TN 37923-5807 • (865) 690-7831 • *Georgia Genealogical Research*; *Pennsylvania Genealogical Research*; *Revolutionary War Genealogy*; *South Carolina Genealogical Research*; *Virginia Genealogical Research*

Goff-Gough Family Association • 8624 Wimbledon Dr • Knoxville, TN 37923 • (865) 690-2432 • *Goffs-Goughs: Their Ancestors and Descendants*

Goodenow Family Association • 1212 Nighthawk Ln • Knoxville, TN 37923-2040 • (865) 693-3797 • http://users.ilnk.com/ejcornell.goodenow.htm • *Goodenows' Ghosts*

James Family Reunion • 2029 Harris Rd • Knoxville, TN 37924

Jewett Family of America • 209 Marchmont Rd • Knoxville, TN 37923

John C Hodges Library • Univ of Tennessee, Knoxville, 1015 Volunteer Blvd • Knoxville, TN 37996-1000 • (865) 974-4240 • http://www.lib.utk.edu

John Willis Hooker Family Organization • 5520 Timbercrest Tr • Knoxville, TN 37909 • (865) 584-3106

Knox County Public Library System • 500 W Church Ave • Knoxville, TN 37902 • (865) 544-5750

Mabry-Hazen House Archives • 1711 Dandridge Ave • Knoxville, TN 37915 • (865) 522-8661 • http://www.kornet.org/mabry

Marble Springs, Gov John Sevier Farm Home Archives • 1220 W Gov John Sevier Hwy • Knoxville, TN 37920 • (865) 573-5508 • http://www.marblesprings.org

Meates Family Association • P.O. Box 53071 • Knoxville, TN 37950

Pendleton Database • 5348 Amherst Woods Rd • Knoxville, TN 37921

Phillip-Chandler Reunion • 1025 Ohio Ave • Knoxville, TN 37921-1827 • (865) 546-1934

Ramsey House Museum Plantation Archives • 2614 Thorngrove Pk • Knoxville, TN 37914 • (865) 546-0745 • http://www.ramseyhouse.org • *Ramsey House Museum Plantation Newsletter*

Tennessee Valley Authority Archives • 400 W Summit Hill Dr • Knoxville, TN 37902 • (423) 532-3464 • http://www.tva.gov

White James Fort Association Archives • 205 E Hill Ave • Knoxville, TN 37915 • (865) 525-6514

Wooldridge Family Reunion • 730 Cherokee Blvd • Knoxville, TN 37919 • (865) 524-7887

La Follette

Campbell County Historical Society • 101 S 6th St • La Follette, TN 37766 • (423) 566-2127 • *Campbell Countian*

Campbell County Historical Society & Archives • Historical Museum, 235 E Central Ave • La Follette, TN 37766 • (423) 566-3581

Lafayette

Macon County Historical Society & Archives • c/o Macon County Public Library, 311 Church St, P.O Box 231 • Lafayette, TN 37083-0231 • (615) 666-4340 • http://members.aol.com/tngenweb/mhistsoc.htm • *History Happenings*; *Macon County Historical Society Quarterly*; *Macon County Tennessee Historical Society Newsletter*

Macon County Public Library • 311 Church St • Lafayette, TN 37083-1607 • (615) 666-4340

Lawrenceburg

Lawrence County Genealogical Society • 218 N Military Ave, Ste B-1 • Lawrenceburg, TN 38464 • (931) 766-1576 • http://web.infoave.net/~lcarchives/lcgenso.htm

Lawrence County Historical Society • 233 Waterloo St, P.O. Box 431 • Lawrenceburg, TN 38464 • (931) 766-3646 • *Yesterday and Today in Lawrence County*

Lawrence County Public Library • 519 E Gaines St • Lawrenceburg, TN 38464-3599 • (931) 762-4627 • http://www.co.lawrence.tn.us/departments/library/county_library.htm

Lebanon

Bond Family Reunion • 710 Bond Rd • Lebanon, TN 37090

Doris & Harry Vise Library • Cumberland Univ, 1 Cumberland Sq • Lebanon, TN 37087 • (615) 444-2562 • http://library.cumberland.edu

Roy Bailey African American History Center Archives • 115 E Main St • Lebanon, TN 37087 • (615) 449-2911

Lewisburg

Marshall County Historical Society • 224 3rd Ave N • Lewisburg, TN 37091 • (931) 359-2383 • *Marshall County Historical Quarterly*

Marshall County Memorial Library • 310 Old Farmington Rd • Lewisburg, TN 37091 • (931) 359-3335

Linden

Perry County Public Library • Route 10, Box 3A • Linden, TN 37096-9802 • (931) 589-5011

Perry County Historical Society • c/o Linden Public Library, Route 10, Box 3A • Linden, TN 37096 • (931) 593-3373 • http://www.tngenweb.usit.com/perry • *Perry County Historical Society Quarterly*

Livingston

Overton County Public Library • 225 E Main St • Livingston, TN 38570-1959 • (931) 823-1888 • http://www.overtoncolibrary.com

Lookout Mountain

Battles for Chattanooga Museum Archives • 1110 E Brow Rd • Lookout Mountain, TN 37350-1016 • (423) 821-2812

Cravens House Museum Archives • Point Park Visitor Center • Lookout Mountain, TN 37756 • (423) 821-7786

Madisonville

Madisonville Public Library • 305 College St • Madisonville, TN 37354-1128 • (423) 442-6617 • http://www.madisonvillelibrary.org

Manchester

Coffee County Historical Society & Library • 101 W Fort St, Ste 2, P.O. Box 524 • Manchester, TN 37355-7502 • (931) 728-0145 • http://www.cafes.net/jlewis/pubs.htm • Coffee County Historical Quarterly

Martin

C E Weldon Public Library • 100 Main St • Martin, TN 38237-2445 • (731) 587-3148 • http://www.ceweldonlibrary.org • *C E Weldon Public Library Newsletter*

Paul Meek Library • University of Tennessee at Martin, 1 Wayne Fisher Dr • Martin, TN 38238 • (731) 587-7065 • http://www.utm.edu/departments/acadpro/library/

University Museum Archives • Univ of Tennessee at Martin • Martin, TN 38236 • (731) 881-7094

Weakley County Genealogical Society & Library • P.O. Box 92 • Martin, TN 38237 • *Forget Me Not*

Maryville

Alexander-Smith Library • New Providence Presbyterian Church, 703 W Broadway • Maryville, TN 37801 • (865) 983-0182 • http://www.newprovidencepres.org

Blount County Genealogical and Historical Society • 301 McGhee St, P.O. Box 653 • Maryville, TN 37802-0653 • (865) 982-0981 • *Blount Journal*

Blount County Public Library • 508 N Cusick St • Maryville, TN 37804-5714 • (865) 982-0981 • http://www.kornet.org/bcpl

Sam Houston Historical Schoolhouse Archives • 3650 Old Sam Houston School Rd • Maryville, TN 37804 • (805) 985-1556 • http://www.geocities.com/samhoustonschoolhouse

Maynardville

Maynardville Public Library • 296 Main St • Maynardville, TN 37807-3400 • (865) 992-7106 • http://www.maynardville.com

Union County Historical Society • 3824 Maynardville Hwy, P.O. Box 95 • Maynardville, TN 37807 • (865) 992-2136 • *Pathways: History and Genealogical Journal*

McKenzie

Burroughs Library • Bethel College, 325 Cherry Ave • McKenzie, TN 38201 • (731) 352-4081 • http://www.bethel-college.edu/library/

Carroll County Historical Society & Archives • Gordon Browning Museum and Genealogical Library, 640 Main St • McKenzie, TN 38201 • (731) 352-3510

McKenzie Memorial Library • 15 N Broadway • McKenzie, TN 38201-2101 • (731) 352-5741

McMinnville

Lance Research • 419 W Main • McMinnville, TN 37110 • *Charger: The Lance Family Newsletter*

Magness Memorial Library • 118 W Main St • McMinnville, TN 37110 • (931) 473-2428 • http://www.magnesslibrary.org

Warren County Genealogical Association & Archives • c/o Magness Memorial Library, 118 W Main St, P.O. Box 411 • McMinnville, TN 37110-0411 • (423) 473-2428 • Warren County Genealogical Association Bulletin

Memphis

Auxier Family Association • 890 Winchester Rd • Memphis, TN 38116 • (901) 396-4979 • *Auxier Family Newsletter*

Center for Southern Folklore Archives • 119 S Main St, P.O. Box 226 • Memphis, TN 38101-0226 • (901) 525-3655 • http://www.southernfolklore.com

Cossitt-Goodwyn Library • 33 S Front St • Memphis, TN 38103 • (901) 526-1712

Fire Museum of Memphis Archives • 118 Adams Ave • Memphis, TN 38103 • (901) 320-5650 • http://www.firemuseum.com • *Fire Museum of Memphis Quarterly*

Hendren Surname Organization • 626 McConwell • Memphis, TN 38112-1822 • (901) 458-3554

Mageveny House Museum Archives • 198 Adams • Memphis, TN 38103 • (901) 526-4464 • http://www.memphismuseums.org

Mallory-Neely House Museum Archives • 652 Adams Ave • Memphis, TN 38105 • (901) 523-1484 • http://www.memphismuseums.org

McWherter Library • University of Memphis • Memphis, TN 38152-3250 • (901) 678-2208 • http://exlibris.memphis.edu

Memphis Belle B17 Flying Fortress Museum Archives • Mud Island, P.O. Box 1942 • Memphis, TN 38111 • (901) 521-1265 • http://www.memphisbelle.com

Memphis Pink Palace Museum Library • 3050 Central Ave • Memphis, TN 38111-3399 • (901) 320-6322 • http://www.memphisguide.com

Memphis Theological Seminary Library • 168 E Parkway S • Memphis, TN 38104 • (901) 458-8232 • http://www.mtscampus.edu/library

Memphis-Shelby County Public Library Center • 3030 Poplar Ave • Memphis, TN 38111-3527 • (901) 415-2700 • http://www.memphislibrary.org

Miller Research • 126 Perkins Extended • Memphis, TN 38117-3125 • *Miller Newsletter*

Mississippi River Museum at Mud Island Archives • 125 N front St • Memphis, TN 38103 • (901) 576-7230 • http://www.mudisland.com

National Civil Rights Museum Archives • 450 Mulberry St • Memphis, TN 38103 • (901) 521-9699 • http://www.civilrightsmuseum.org • *Movement Newsletter*

P.T. Boats Museum & Library • 1384 Cordova Cove, Suite 2, P.O. Box 38070 • Memphis, TN 38183-0070 • (901) 755-8440 • http://www.ptboats.org

Plough Library • Christian Brothers University, 650 E Pkwy South • Memphis, TN 38104 • (901) 321-3432 • http://www.cbu.edu/library

Ricks Family and Friends • 3747 Graves Rd • Memphis, TN 38116

Sigler Family Reunion • 1972 Whitney Ave • Memphis, TN 38127 • (901) 357-6097

Smith-Myers Reunion • 2035 Big Bend • Memphis, TN 38116 • (901) 396-2815

Southern Bean Association • 6133 Mary Elizabeth Cove • Memphis, TN 38134 • (901) 388-6736 • *Bean Stalk*

Tennessee Genealogical Society • 9114 Davies Plantation Rd, P.O. Box 111249 • Memphis, TN 38111-1249 • (901) 381-1447 • http://www.rootsweb.com/~tngs/ • *Tennessee Genealogical Magazine: the Ansearchin' News*

Washingtons of Pontotoc County, Mississippi • 2702 Chatworth St • Memphis, TN 38127 • (901) 358-0595

West Tennessee Historical Society & Library • P.O. Box 111046 • Memphis, TN 38111 • (901) 567-4518 • http://www.wths.tn.org • *West Tennessee Historical Society Papers*

Wheeler Research • 4060 Mary Lee • Memphis, TN 38116 • (901) 332-2109 • *Wheeler Cousins*

Morristown

Association for the Preservation of Tennessee Antiquities, Hamblen County Chapter & Archives • Crockett Tavern Museum, 2002 E Morningside Dr, P.O. Box 524 • Morristown, TN 37815 • (615) 587-9900 • http://www.discoveret.org.crockett • *Hamblen County Chapter APTA Newsletter*

Hamblen County Genealogical and Historical Society & Archives • c/o Morristown-Hamblen Library, 417 W Main St, P.O. Box 1213 • Morristown, TN 37816-1213 • (423) 586-6410 • *Hamblen Heritage*

Jones Family Association • 6132 Silver Fox Tr • Morristown, TN 37814 • (423) 581-7066

Morristown-Hamblen Public Library • 417 W Main St • Morristown, TN 37814-4686 • (423) 586-6410

Mount Juliet

Macfie Clan Society of North America • 7501 Hickory Ridge Rd • Mount Juliet, TN 37122

Mount Juliet Public Library • 2765 N Mt Juliet Rd, P.O. Box 319 • Mount Juliet, TN 37122-0319 • (615) 758-7051

Mount Juliet-West Wilson County Historical Society & Library • 144 Mount Juliet Rd, P.O. Box 319 • Mount Juliet, TN 37212 • (615) 754-2418 • *Mount Juliet-West Wilson Historical Society Chronicle*

West Wilson County Historical Society • P.O. Box 337 • Mount Juliet, TN 37122

Mount Pleasant

Maury County Public Library-Mount Pleasant Branch • 200 Hay Long Ave, P.O. Box 71 • Mount Pleasant, TN 38474-0071 • (931) 379-3752

Mountain City

Johnson County Historical Society • P.O. Box 1 • Mountain City, TN 37683 • http://www.mainmenu.com/jcwc/history.htm

Mountain Home

Museum at Mountain Home Archives • P.O. Box 1186 • Mountain Home, TN 37684 • (423) 439-7083 • http://qcom_etso.edu/medlib

Murfreesboro

Center for Historic Preservation, Todd Library • Middle Tennessee State Univ, P.O. Box 80 • Murfreesboro, TN 37132 • (615) 898-2947 • http://frank.mtsu.edu/kmiddlet/history/women.html

Highland Rim Regional Library Center • 2118 E Main St • Murfreesboro, TN 37130 • (615) 893-3380

James E Walker Library • Middle Tennessee State University, MTSU, P.O. Box 13 • Murfreesboro, TN 37132 • (615) 898-2817 • http://www.mtsu.edu/~library • *Library Update*

Linebaugh Public Library System of Rutherford County • 105 W Vine St • Murfreesboro, TN 37130-3673 • (615) 893-4131 • http://www.linebaugh.org

Oaklands Historic House Museum Archives • 900 N Maney Ave, P.O. Box 432 • Murfreesboro, TN 37133-0432 • (615) 893-0022 • http://www.oaklandsmuseum.org

Rutherford County Historical Society • P.O. Box 906 • Murfreesboro, TN 37133-0906 • *Rutherford County Historical Society Newsletter*; *Rutherford County Historical Society Publications*

Stones River National Battlefield Archives • 3501 Old Nashville Hwy • Murfreesboro, TN 37129-3094 • (615) 893-9501 • http://www.mps.gov/stri

Vaught Association of the US • 313 Chamberlain, P.O. Box 2044 • Murfreesboro, TN 37133 • (615) 896-0182 • *Vaught Connections*

Nashville

American Association for State and Local History • 1717 Church St • Nashville, TN 37203 • (615) 255-2971 • http://www.aaslh.org • *Dispatch*; *History News Magazine*

Association for the Preservation of Tennessee Antiquities & Library • *Belle Meade Mansion*, 110 Leake Ave • Nashville, TN 37205 • (615) 352-8247 • http://www.bellemeadeplantation.com • *Intercom*

Bragg Family Association • 707 Ringgold Dr • Nashville, TN 37207

Brown-Daniel Library • Tennessee State University, 3500 John A Merritt Blvd • Nashville, TN 37209-1561 • (615) 963-5201 • http://www.tnstate.edu/library/

Carney Research • 839 Battery Ln • Nashville, TN 37220 • *Carney Chronicles Newsletter*

Central of Georgia Railway Historical Society • 4403 Sunnybrook Dr • Nashville, TN 37205 • (615) 665-0556 • http://www.cofg.org

Corew Reunion • 522 American Rd • Nashville, TN 37209

Cumberland Science Museum Archives • 800 Fort Negley Blvd • Nashville, TN 37203 • (615) 862-5160

Disciples of Christ Historical Society & Library • 1101 19th Ave S • Nashville, TN 37212-2196 • (615) 327-1444 • http://www.dishistsoc.org • *Discipliana*

Fort Nashborough Museum Archives • 170 1st Ave N • Nashville, TN 37201 • (615) 862-8400 • http://www.nashville.gov/parks

Gospel Advocate Archives and Library • 1006 Elm Hill Pk • Nashville, TN 37210 • (615) 254-8781

Historic Nashville & Archives • Historical Museum, 154 5th Ave N, P.O. Box 190516 • Nashville, TN 37219 • (615) 244-7835 • http://www.historicnashville.org • *Historic Register*, *Historic Ink*

Historical Commission of the Southern Baptist Convention & Library • 901 Commerce St • Nashville, TN 37203-3620 • (615) 242-0344 • *Baptist Heritage Update*; Baptist History and Heritage

Jewish Federation of Nashville and Middle Tennessee & Library • 801 Percy Warner Blvd • Nashville, TN 37205 • (615) 356-3242

Measures Family Association • P.O. Box 90054 • Nashville, TN 37209 • (615) 356-7192 • *Measure's Advisor*

Middle Tennessee Genealogical Society • P.O. Box 330948 • Nashville, TN 37203-7507 • (615) 297-3085 • http://www.mtgs.org • *Middle Tennessee Journal of Genealogy and History*

Nashville Public Library • 615 Church St • Nashville, TN 37219-2314 • (615) 862-5800 • http://www.library.nashville.org

Nashville Zoo and Historic Farm Archives • 3777 Nolensville Road • Nashville, TN 37211 • (615) 833-1534 • http://www.nashvillezoo.org

National Society, Daughters of the American Revolution • 3322 West End Ave, Ste 700 • Nashville, TN 37203 • (866) 327-6242 • *American Spirit Magazine*

Southern Baptist Historical Library and Archives • 901 Commerce St, Suite 400 • Nashville, TN 37203 • (615) 244-0344 • http://www.sbhla.org

Sumner Family Association • 7540 Rolling River Pkwy • Nashville, TN 37221-3322 • (585) 334-2989 • http://homepages.rootsweb.com/~lcompton/sumner/SFA • *Sumner Search*

Tennessee Central Railway Museum Archives • 220 Willow St • Nashville, TN 37210 • (615) 244-9001 • http://www.tcry.org • *Order Board*

Tennessee Historical Commission & Archives • Historical Museum, 2941 Lebanon Rd • Nashville, TN 37243-0440 • (615) 532-1550 • http://www.state.tn.us/environment/hist • *Courier*, *Tennessee Conservationist*

Tennessee Historical Society & Archives • War Memorial Bldg Museum, 300 Capitol Blvd • Nashville, TN 37243-0084 • (615) 741-8934 • http://www.tennesseehistory.org • *Tennessee Historical Quarterly*, *Tennessee Genealogist & Family Historian*; *News in Tennessee History*

Tennessee State Library and Archives • 403 7th Ave N • Nashville, TN 37243-0312 • (615) 741-2764 • http://www.state.tn.us/sos/statelib

Tennessee State Museum Archives • Polk Cultural Center, 505 Deaderick St • Nashville, TN 37243-1120 • (615) 741-2692 • http://www.tnmuseum.org • *Tennessee State Museum Newsletter*

Tennessee Western History Library • P.O. Box 111864 • Nashville, TN 37222 • (615) 834-5069

Travellers Rest Plantation Museum Archives • 636 Farrell Pkwy • Nashville, TN 37220 • (615) 832-8197 • http://www.travellersrestplantation.org

United Methodist Publishing House Library • 201 8th Ave S • Nashville, TN 37203 • (615) 749-6335

Upper Room Chapel Museum Archives • 1908 Grand Ave, P.O. Box 340004 • Nashville, TN 37203 • (615) 340-7206 • http://www.upperroom.org

Voter Family History Association • 1402-B Sweetbriar Ave • Nashville, TN 37212-5523

Welch Library • Free Will Baptist Bible College, 3630 W End Ave • Nashville, TN 37205 • (615) 844-5274

Newport

Johannes Michael Schneider Descendants • 1001 Sierra Rd • Newport, TN 37821-6006 • (423) 625-9325

Stokely Memorial Library • 383 E Broadway • Newport, TN 37821-3105 • (423) 623-3832

Norris

Museum of Appalachia Archives • Hwy 61, Box 1189 • Norris, TN 37828 • (865) 494-7680

Tennessee Valley Authority Archives • Ridgeway Rd, Natural Resources Bldg • Norris, TN 37828 • (865) 632-1578 • http://www.tva.gov

Oak Ridge

East Tennessee Heritage Foundation • 1345 Oak Ridge Tpke, #318 • Oak Ridge, TN 37830 • (865) 691-4031 • *East Tennessee Roots*

Highland Rim Keene and Kin Reunion • 105 E Newcomb Rd • Oak Ridge, TN 37830-5358 • (865) 483-7549 • http://hometown.aol.com/cathelk/sumner/keen.htm • *Highland Rim Kim & Keene Newsletter*, *Keen(e) Reunion Newsletter*

Kylander-Kilander Gatherings • 838 W Outer Dr • Oak Ridge, TN 37830 • (865) 483-3805 • *Kylander, Kilander, Callendar Families of America Newsletter*

Oak Ridge Public Library • Civic Center, 1401 Turnpike • Oak Ridge, TN 37830 • (865) 482-8455

Old Hickory
Wissel-Wessel Research • 40 Jones Cr • Old Hickory, TN 37138-3431 • (615) 847-2269 • *Wissel-Wessel Family Newsletter*

Oliver Springs
Oliver Springs Historical Society • 727 Main St • Oliver Springs, TN 37840 • http://www.roanetn.com/oshs/

Oliver Springs Public Library • 610 Walker Ave • Oliver Springs, TN 37840 • (865) 435-2509

Palmer
Grundy County Swiss Historical Society • 329 Swiss Colony Cemetery Rd • Palmer, TN 37365 • (931) 779-3730

Paris
Paris Area Genealogical Society • P.O. Box 636 • Paris, TN 38242 • http://pw2.netcom.com/~dmartin2/henry-co-tn.html

Paris-Henry County Heritage Center Archives • 615 N Prospect, P.O. Box 822 • Paris, TN 38242 • (731) 642-1030 • http://www.phchc.com • *Inkwell*

Paschill Genealogy Committee • 203 Maple St • Paris, TN 38242 • *Paschill Genealogy Bulletin*

W G Rhea Library • 400 W Washington St • Paris, TN 38242-3903 • (731) 642-1702

Pikeville
Bledsoe County Public Library • 102 E Cumberland Ave, P.O. Box 465 • Pikeville, TN 37367-0465 • (423) 447-2817

Piney Flats
Rocky Mount Historical Association & Archives • Rocky Mount Museum, 200 Hyder Hill Rd, P.O. Box 160 • Piney Flats, TN 37686-0160 • (423) 538-7396 • http://www.rockymountmuseum.com • *Rocky Mount Gazette*

Portland
Portland Public Library • 301 Portland Blvd • Portland, TN 37148-1229 • (931) 325-2279 • http://www.portlandtn.com/library.htm

Pulaski
Giles County Historical Society & Library • 122 S 2nd St, P.O. Box 693 • Pulaski, TN 38478 • (931) 363-2720 • http://www.rootsweb.com/~tngiles/hist/histsoc.htm • *Giles County Historical Society Bulletin*

Giles County Public Library • 122 S 2nd St • Pulaski, TN 38478-3285 • (931) 363-2720 • http://gilescountylibrary.org • *Giles County Public Library Bulletin*

Warden Memorial Library • Martin Methodist College, 433 W Madison St • Pulaski, TN 38478-2799 • (931) 363-9844 • http://martinlib.igiles.net

Ripley
Lauderdale County Library • 120 Lafayette St • Ripley, TN 38063-1321 • (731) 635-1872

Rockwood
McCuistion-Turk Reunion • 433 W Rockwood St • Rockwood, TN 37854

Rockwood Public Library • 117 N Front St • Rockwood, TN 37854-2320 • (865) 354-1281 • http://www.rockwoodlibrary.org

Rogersville
H B Stamps Memorial Library • 407 E Main St • Rogersville, TN 37857 • (423) 272-8710

Hawkins County Genealogical and Historical Society • P.O. Box 429 • Rogersville, TN 37587-0429 • http://www.rootsweb.com/~tnhcghs • *Distant Crossroads*

Rosemark
Moffatt Clan Society of North America • P.O. Box 18 • Rosemark, TN 38053

Rugby
Historic Rugby & Archives • Historic Museum, 5517 Rugby Hwy, P.O. Box 8 • Rugby, TN 37733 • (423) 628-2441 • http://www.historicrugby.org • *Rugbeian*

Thomas Hughes Free Public Library • Hwy 52, P.O. Box 8 • Rugby, TN 37733 • (423) 628-2441

Rutherford
David Crockett Cabin Museum Archives • 219 N Trenton St • Rutherford, TN 38369 • (731) 665-7258 • http://www.davycrockettcabin.org

Rutledge
Fennell Surname Organization • Langley Mansion, Route 2, Box 135 • Rutledge, TN 37861 • (865) 828-5621

Sale Creek
Kerr Family Association of North America • 14623 Back Valley Rd • Sale Creek, TN 37373

Savannah
Hardin County Historical Society & Library • 601 Main St, P.O. Box 1012 • Savannah, TN 38372 • (731) 925-3106 • *Hardin County Historical Quarterly*

Hardin County Library • 1365 Pickwick St • Savannah, TN 38372 • (731) 925-4314 • *Hardin County Library Newsletter*

Selmer
Jack McConnico Memorial Library • 225 Oak Grove Rd • Selmer, TN 38375 • (731) 645-5571

Sevierville
Sevier County Public Library • 321 Court Ave • Sevierville, TN 37862 • (865) 453-3532 • http://www.sevierlibrary.org

Smoky Mountain Historical Society • 167 E Bruce St, P.O. Box 5078 • Sevierville, TN 37864-5078 • http://www.smokykin.com/smhs • *Smoky Mountain Historical Society Newsletter*

Sons Of The Revolution, Gen John Sevier Chapter • 624 George Davis Ave • Sevierville, TN 37862

Tennessee Museum of Aviation Archives • 135 Air Museum Wy, P.O. Box 5587 • Sevierville, TN 37862 • (865) 908-0171 • http://www.tnairmuseum.com

Sewanee
Jessie Ball duPont Library • Univ of the South, 735 University Ave • Sewanee, TN 37383-1000 • (931) 598-1368 • http://library.sewanee.edu • *Friends of the Library*

Shelbyville
Argie Cooper Public Library • 100 S Main St • Shelbyville, TN 37160-3984 • (931) 684-7323

Shiloh
Shiloh National Military Park Library • 1055 Pittsburg Landing Rd • Shiloh, TN 38376 • (731) 689-5275 • http://www.nps.gov/shil

Signal Mountain
Mountain Press • 4503 Anderson Pike, P.O. Box 400 • Signal Mountain, TN 37377-0400 • (423) 886-6369 • http://www.mountainpress.com • *McGill Family News*; *Locke Family News*; *Moore Family News*; *Morgan Family News*; *Tennessee Genealogy and History*; *Bennett Family News*; *Mercer Family*; *Jones Newsletter*

Town of Signal Mountain Library • 1114 James Blvd • Signal Mountain, TN 37377-2509 • (423) 886-7323 • http://www.signalmtnlibrary.org • *Bookmark*

Smyrna
Sam Davis Home Memorial Association • 1399 Sam Davis Rd • Smyrna, TN 37167 • (615) 459-2341

Somerville
Somerville-Fayette County Library • 216 W Market St • Somerville, TN 38068-1592 • (901) 465-5248

Sparta
White County Genealogical and Historical Society • P.O. Box 721 • Sparta, TN 38583-0721 • http://www.midtenn.net/~rocketman/wcghs.htm

White County Public Library • 144 S Main St • Sparta, TN 38583-2299 • (931) 836-3613 • http://www.wtclibrary.org

Spencer
Van Buren County Historical Society & Library • P.O. Box 126 • Spencer, TN 38585 • (931) 946-7607 • *Van Buren County Historical Journal*; *Van Buren County Historical Society Newsletter*

Spring Hill
Spring Hill Genealogy and Historical Society • 5317 Main St, P.O. Box 311 • Spring Hill, TN 37716 • (931) 486-2933 • *Spring Hill Genealogy and Historical Society Newsletter*

Springfield
Gorham-MacBane Public Library • 405 White St • Springfield, TN 37172-2340 • (615) 384-5123

Sunbright
Sunbright Public Library • 142 Melton Dr • Sunbright, TN 37872 • (423) 628-2439 • http://www.korrnet.org/sunlibry

Surgoinsville
Small Family • 784 Caney Valley Loop • Surgoinsville, TN 37873 • (423) 357-3442 • http://homepages.rootsweb.com/~smalljd/

Sweetwater
Sweetwater Public Library • 210 Mayes Ave • Sweetwater, TN 37874 • (423) 337-5274

Tazewell
Claiborne County Historical Society • P.O. Box 32 • Tazewell, TN 37879 • (423) 626-7261 • Reflections

Townsend
Cades Cove Open-Air Museum Archives • Great Smoky Mountains National Park, 16042 Campgrounds Dr • Townsend, TN 37882 • http://www.nps.gov/grsm

Trenton
Gibson County Memorial Library • 303 S High St • Trenton, TN 38382-2027 • (731) 855-1991

Tullahoma
Coffee County Lannom Memorial Public Library • 312 N Collins St • Tullahoma, TN 37388-3229 • (931) 455-2460 • http://www.lannom.org

Unicoi
Callaway Family Association • 138 Buffalo Ridge Dr • Unicoi, TN 37692 • (423) 743-6613 • *Callaway Journal*; *Callaway Communique*; *Callaway Bulletin*

Union City
Dixie Gun Works' Old Car Museum Archives • 1412 W Reelfoot Ave • Union City, TN 38261 • (731) 885-0561 • http://www.dixiegunworks.com

Obion County Genealogical Society & Library • 1004 Edwards St, P.O. Box 241 • Union City, TN 38261 • http://www.tngenweb.usit.com/obion/obiohsoc.htm • *Obion Origins*

Wartburg
Morgan County Genealogical and Historical Society • Rt 2, Box 992 • Wartburg, TN 37887 • (423) 346-3137 • *Morgan County Messenger*

Washburn
Cabbage-Cabage Surname Organization • Route 2, Box 97A • Washburn, TN 37888 • (865) 497-2287 • *Cabbage-Cabage Surname Organization Annual*

Waverly
Humphreys County Historical Society • 105 Carroll Ave • Waverly, TN 37185 • (615) 296-3445 • Humphreys County Historical Society Publication

Waynesboro
Wayne County Historical Society • Public Square, P.O. Box 866 • Waynesboro, TN 38485-0866 • http://www.netease.net/wayne/wchs.htm • *Wayne County Historian*

Westmoreland
Northeast Sumner Historical Society • P.O. Box 417 • Westmoreland, TN 37186-0417

White House
White House Historical Society • 412 Hwy 76 • White House, TN 37188

White Pine
McClanahan Family Reunion • 938 Hwy 25-32 • White Pine, TN 37890

White Pine Public Library • 1708 Main St • White Pine, TN 37890 • (865) 674-6313

Whitwell
Marion County Genealogical and Historical Group • 6611 Old Dunlap Rd • Whitwell, TN 37397

Winchester
Franklin County Historical Society & Archives • c/o Franklin County Library, 105 S Porter, P.O. Box 130 • Winchester, TN 37398-0130 • (931) 962-1476 • *Franklin County Historical Review*, *Historical Tidings*

Franklin County Library • 105 S Porter St • Winchester, TN 37298-1546 • (931) 967-3706

Franklin County Old Jail Museum Archives • 400 Dinah Shore Blvd • Winchester, TN 37398 • (931) 967-0524

TEXAS

Abernathy
Kemp Research • 210 Ave M • Abernathy, TX 79311 • (806) 298-4048 • *Kemps with Roots in the South*

Abilene
Abilene Preservation League • 1174 N 1st St • Abilene, TX 79601 • (325) 676-3775

Abilene Public Library • 202 Cedar St • Abilene, TX 79601-5793 • (325) 676-6021 • http://www.abilenetx.com/apl • *Big Country News*

Abilene
Forster-Foster and their Royal Descendants • 2625 N 6th St • Abilene, TX 79603-7259 • (915) 673-3918

Gilleland Endowment • 940 Bacacita Farms Rd • Abilene, TX 79602 • (915) 698-0824 • *Gilleland Endowment Newsletter*

Grace Museum Archives • 102 Cypress St • Abilene, TX 79601 • (325) 673-4587 • http://www.thegracemuseum.org

Jay-Rollins Library • McMurray College, Sayles Blvd & S 14th, McMurry Sta, Box 218 • Abilene, TX 79697-0218 • (325) 793-4692 • http://www.mcm.edu

Margaret and Herman Brown Library • Abilene Christian Univ, ACU Box 29208 • Abilene, TX 79699-9208 • (915) 674-2344 • http://www.acu.edu/academics/library/ • *Library Friends News*

Richardson Library • Hardin-Simmons Univ, 2341 Hickory St, P.O. Box 16195 • Abilene, TX 79698-6195 • (325) 670-1236 • http://www.hsutx.edu/library/

Swanton-Nyberg Reunion • 1261 Beechwood Ln • Abilene, TX 79603-4635

West Texas Genealogical Society & Library • P.O. Box 2307 • Abilene, TX 79606 • *West Texas Genealogical Society Bulletin*

West Texas Historical Association & Archives • c/o Richardson Library, Hardin Simmons Univ, P.O. Box 16172 • Abilene, TX 79698 • (915) 677-8351 • *West Texas Historical Association Year Book*

Alamo
Clifton James Biggar-Conklin-George Henry Mills-Albertson Family Organization • 938 S Alamo Rd Lot 42 • Alamo, TX 78516 • (716) 257-9488

Albany
McFarland Family Association • P.O. Box 37 • Albany, TX 76430

Aledo
East Parker County Library • 201 FM 1187 N, P.O. Box 275 • Aledo, TX 76008-0275 • (817) 441-6545

Living Word National Bible Museum Archives • 3909 Snow Creek Dr • Aledo, TX 76008 • (817) 244-4504 • http://webpages.charter.net/johnellstern/

Pickens County Genealogical Society • P.O. Box 338 • Aledo, TX 76008

Alice
Alice Public Library • 401 E 3rd St • Alice, TX 78332 • (361) 664-9506

South Texas Museum Archives • 66 S Wright St, P.O. Box 3232 • Alice, TX 78333 • (361) 668-8891 • *STM Newsletter*

Alpine
Alpine Public Library • 203 N 7th St • Alpine, TX 79830 • (915) 837-2621

Big Bend Genealogical Society • 300 John Rd W • Alpine, TX 79830-2032

Bryan Wildenthal Memorial Library • Sul Ross State University, P.O. Box C-109 • Alpine, TX 79832-0001 • (432) 837-8123 • http://www.libit.sulross.edu

Museum and Archives of the Big Bend Archives • Sul Ross State Univ, P.O. Box C-210 • Alpine, TX 79832 • (915) 837-8143 • http://www.sulross.edu/~museum

Alto
Stella Hill Memorial Lbirary • 200 W San Antonio St, Route 1, Box 724 • Alto, TX 75925-0724 • (936) 858-4343 • http://www.netdot.com/altolib/

Alvin
Clan Gillean Association USA • P.O. Box 4061 • Alvin, TX 77511 • (713) 581-2845 • *Pipings*

Amarillo
Amarillo Genealogical Society & Archives • c/o Amarillo Public Library, 300 E 4th St, P.O. Box 2171 • Amarillo, TX 79189 • (806) 378-3054 • *Reflector, Amarillo Genealogical Society Newsletter*

Amarillo Public Library • 413 E 4th St, P.O. Box 2171 • Amarillo, TX 79105-2171 • (806) 378-3054 • http://www.amarillolibrary.org

American Quarter Horse Heritage Center Museum Archives • 2601 I-40 E • Amarillo, TX 79104 • (806) 376-5181 • http://www.aqha.org

Catholic Historical Society of the Diocese of Amarillo & Library • 1800 N Spring, P.O. Box 5644 • Amarillo, TX 79117-5644 • (806) 383-2243 • http://www.amarillodiocese.org

Lawrence Joseph Keily Family Organization • 1 Snead Ln • Amarillo, TX 79124-1717 • (806) 374-3362

Morris-Earnest-Mills-Cunningham-Gatlin-Beatty-Stiger-Murray-Hodapp-Holte Surname Organization • 5341 Whitney Ln • Amarillo, TX 79110 • (806) 359-1012

Perez Family Association • 5222 Floyd • Amarillo, TX 79106 • (806) 353-7532

Skaggs-Miller Family Association • 3308 Linda Dr • Amarillo, TX 79109 • (806) 352-0818 • http://members.amaonline.com/freecards/skaggsfamily.htm

Texas Pharmacy Museum Archives • Texas Tech, School of Pharmacy, 1300 Coulter • Amarillo, TX 79106 • (806) 356-4000 • http://www.texas.pharmacy.museum

Anahuac
Chambers County Library • 202 Cummings St, P.O. Box 520 • Anahuac, TX 77514-0520 • (409) 267-8263 • http://www.chambers.lib.tx.us

Andrews
Andrews County Library • 109 NW 1st St • Andrews, TX 79714 • (915) 523-9819 • http://www.andrews.lib.tx.us

Angleton
Brazoria County Historical Museum Library • 100 E Cedar St • Angleton, TX 77515 • (979) 849-5711 • http://www.bchm.org • *Brazoria County Historical Museum Newsletter*

Brazoria County Library System • 131 E Live Oak • Angleton, TX 77515-4641 • (979) 864-1505 • http://bcls.lib.tx.us • *Library News*

Liberty P Hardwick Family Organization • 1126 E Cedar St • Angleton, TX 77515-5802 • (979) 849-6227 • *Roots, Branches, Leaves, Hardwick Edition*

Anton
Harrell Family Association • P.O. Box 360 • Anton, TX 79313 • (806) 997-2951 • *Harrell Family News*

Aransas Pass
Ed and Hazel Richmond Public Library • 110 N Lamont St • Aransas Pass, TX 78336-3698 • (512) 758-2350

Archer City
Archer County Historical Society • P.O. Box 815 • Archer City, TX 76351

Archer County Museum Archives • 201 N Sycamore, P.O. Box 102 • Archer City, TX 76351 • (940) 423-6426

Arlington
Arlington Genealogical Society & Archives • c/o Arlington Public Library, 101 E Abram St • Arlington, TX 76010-1183 • (817) 459-6900 • *Newsletter of the Arlington Genealogical Society*

Arlington Historical Society • 1616 W Abram St • Arlington, TX 76013-1709 • (817) 460-4001

Arlington Public Library • 101 E Abram St • Arlington, TX 76010-1183 • (817) 459-6900 • http://www.pub-lib.ci.arlington.tx.us

Clan Armstrong • 2008 Oak Bluff Dr • Arlington, TX 76006 • http://www.tartans.com/clans/Armstrong/armstrong.html

Clan MacLachlan Association of North America • 509 S Fielder Rd • Arlington, TX 76013-1743 • (703) 635-5497 • http://www.maclachlans.org • *Roebuck*

Gochenour Family Genealogical Society • 4901 Arborgate Dr • Arlington, TX 76017-1049 • (817) 478-1970 • http://thetrailseekers.com • *Trail Seekers: Gochenour Family Genealogical Society Newsletter*

Landis-Keyes-Bogart-Ball Surname Organization • 9 Twin Lakes Ct • Arlington, TX 76016 • (817) 467-0158

North Texas Cornish Society • 1300 Canterbury Ct • Arlington, TX 76013-1002

University of Texas at Arlington Library • 702 College St, P.O. Box 19497 • Arlington, TX 76019-0497 • (817) 272-3394 • http://www.uta.edu/library/ • *Compass Rose*

Woodard Family Association • 2106 Creekside Ct • Arlington, TX 76013 • (817) 496-1606

Atascocita

Clan Morrison Society (US and Canada) • 20111 Sunny Shores Dr • Atascocita, TX 77346 • (281) 852-1381

Athens

Athens Genealogical Organization & Archives • c/o Henderson Public Library, 121 S Prairieville St • Athens, TX 75751 • (903) 675-2694 • *Texas Athens Genealogical Organization Newsletter*

Henderson County Historical Commission • Old Henderson Jail, 201 E Larkin St, P.O. Box 1412 • Athens, TX 75751 • (903) 677-7269

Henderson County Historical Society • 217 N Prairieville St, P.O. Box 1412 • Athens, TX 75751 • (903) 677-3611

Henderson County Library • 121 S Prairieville St • Athens, TX 75751 • (903) 677-7295

Ira Dabney Lewis Family Organization • Route 1, Box 1570 • Athens, TX 75751 • (903) 675-2448

Atlanta

Atlanta Public Library • 101 W Hiram St • Atlanta, TX 75551 • (903) 796-2112

Cass County Conservancy • 101 N East St • Atlanta, TX 75551 • (903) 796-8811

Cass County Genealogical Society • P.O. Box 880 • Atlanta, TX 75551-0880 • (903) 796-2107 • http://www.rootsweb.com/~txcass/ • *Cass County Genealogical Society Quarterly*; *Cass County Connections*

Austin

Austin Genealogical Society & Library • P.O. Box 1507 • Austin, TX 78767-1507 • (512) 345-4409 • *Austin Genealogical Society Quarterly*

Austin History Center • 810 Guadalupe St • Austin, TX 78701 • (512) 499-7480 • http://www.cityofaustin.org/library/ahc • *Austin Archives*

Austin Public Library • 800 Guadalupe, P.O. Box 2287 • Austin, TX 78768-2287 • (512) 974-7400 • http://www.ci.austin.tx.us/library/

Austin Public Library-Carver • 1607 Pennsylvania Ave • Austin, TX 78702 • (512) 472-8954

Bob Bullock Texas State History Museum Archives • 1800 N Congress Ave • Austin, TX 78701 • (512) 936-8946 • http://www.TheStoryofTexas.com

Booher Library • Episcopal Theological Seminary of the Southwest, 606 Rathervue Pl, P.O. Box 2247 • Austin, TX 78768-2247 • (512) 478-5212 • http://www.etss.edu

Catholic Diocese of Austin • 1600 N Congress Ave, P.O. Box 13124, Capitol Sta • Austin, TX 78711-3124 • (512) 476-6296 • http://www.onr.com/user/cat

Center for American History • University of Texas Library, SRH 2.101 • Austin, TX 78712 • (512) 495-4532 • http://www.cah.utexas.edu • *Center for American History Newsletter*

Clan Scott Society of the Americas • P.O. Box 13021 • Austin, TX 78711 • (512) 932-7700 • http://www.clanscottsociety.org • *Stag and Thistle*

Cree Family History Society • 11009 Country Knoll • Austin, TX 78750 • http://www.leicester.co.uk/cree/ • *Cree News*

Daughters of the Republic of Texas & Archives • French Legation Museum, 802 San Marcos • Austin, TX 78702 • (512) 472-8180 • http://www.french-legation.mus.tx.us

Eggert Surname Organization • 2413B Burleson Ct • Austin, TX 78741-5603 • (512) 462-3951

Elisabet Ney Museum Library • 304 E 44th St • Austin, TX 78751 • (512) 458-2255 • http://www.ci.austin.tx.us/elisabetney

Episcopal Church Historical Society & Library • 606 Ratherview Pl, P.O. Box 2247 • Austin, TX 78768-2247 • (512) 282-3234 • *Anglican and Episcopal History*

Federation of Genealogical Societies • 12705 Twisted Briar Ln, P.O. Box 200940 • Austin, TX 78720-0940 • (512) 336-2731 • http://www.fgs.org • *FGS Forum*; *FGS Membership Directory*

Foster Pioneer Families of Adams County, Ohio • 8006 El Dorado Dr • Austin, TX 78737-1343 • (512) 288-0254

French Legation Museum Archives • 802 San Marcos St • Austin, TX 78702 • (512) 472-8180 • http://www.french-legation.mus.tx.us

Gafford Family Association • 10607 Spicewood Pkwy • Austin, TX 78750 • (512) 258-5840 • *Gafford Newsletter*

George Washington Carver Museum Library • 1165 Angelina St • Austin, TX 78702 • (512) 472-4809

German-Texan Heritage Society & Library • 507 E 10th St, P.O. Box 684171 • Austin, TX 78768 • (512) 482-0927 • *Journal of the German-Texan Heritage Society*; *German-Texan Heritage Society Newsletter*

Hargrave-Hardgrave Family Association • 10603 Parkfield • Austin, TX 78758 • *Hargrave Family Newsletter*

Heritage Society of Austin • 101 W 6th St, P.O. Box 2113 • Austin, TX 78701 • (512) 474-5198

Jewish Genealogical Society of Austin • 11713 Jollyville Rd • Austin, TX 78759

Journal of Texas Catholic History and Culture • 3001 S Congress Ave • Austin, TX 78704-6425 • (512) 447-4032 • *Journal of Texas Catholic History and Culture*

Lloyd Exchange • 4826 Twin Valley Dr • Austin, TX 78731

Lyndon Baines Johnson Library and Museum • 2313 Red River St • Austin, TX 78705-5702 • (512) 721-0212 • http://www.lbjlib.utexas.edu

Mirabeau B Lamar Library • Univ of Texas • Austin, TX 78712 • (512) 495-4350

Neill-Cochran House Museum Archives • 2310 San Gabriel St • Austin, TX 78705 • (512) 478-3258 • http://www.neill-cochranmuseum.com

O Henry Museum Archives • 409 E 5th St • Austin, TX 78701 • (512) 472-1903 • http://www.ci.austin.tx.us/parks/ohenry.htm • *Pun-Intended*

Pierre Baudouin Family Association • 903 Chatsworth Cr • Austin, TX 78704-5230 • (512) 442-7932

Preservation Texas • 1204 San Antonio St • Austin, TX 78701 • (512) 472-0102

Roots Family Organization • P.O. Box 160185 • Austin, TX 78716 • (512) 263-5226 • *Roots Roots*

Sheldon Family Association • 3402 Mt Bonnell Dr • Austin, TX 78731-5729 • (512) 453-1184 • http://www.sheldonfamily.org • *Sheldon Family Association Quarterly*

State Preservation Board • Capitol Visitors Center, 112 E 11th St, P.O. Box 13286 • Austin, TX 78711 • (512) 305-8400 • http://www.texascapitolvisitorscenter.com

Texas Association of Museums & Library • 3939 Bee Caves, Bldg A, Ste 1B • Austin, TX 78746 • (512) 328-6812 • http://www.texasmuseums.org • *Museline*

Texas Catholic Historical Society • Saint Edward's Univ, 1625 Rutherford Ln, P.O. Box 704 • Austin, TX 78704 • (512) 447-4032 • http://www.history.swt.edu/Catholic_Southwest.htm • *Texas Catholic Historical Society Newsletter*; *Catholic Southwest: A Journal of History and Culture*; *Texas Catholic Historian*

Texas General Land Office-Archives & Records Division Library • Stephen F Austin Bldg, 1700 N Congress St • Austin, TX 78701 • (512) 364-5277 • http://www.glo.state.tx.us

Texas Governor's Museum Archives • 1010 Colorado • Austin, TX 78701 • (512) 463-5518 • http://www.txfgm.org

Texas Historical Commission & Library • 1511 N Colorado, P.O. Box 12276, Capitol Sta • Austin, TX 78711-2276 • (512) 475-3122 • http://www.thc.state.tx.us • *Medallion*

Texas Historical Foundation & Library • 221 E 9th St, P.O. Box 50314 • Austin, TX 78763 • (512) 453-2154 • http://www.texashf.org • *Heritage*

Texas Military Forces Museum Archives • 2200 W 35th St, P.O. Box 5218 • Austin, TX 78763 • (512) 782-5659 • http://www.kwanah.com/txmilmus • *Texas Military Forces Museum Newsletter*

Texas Research Library • 400 W 15th St, Suite 400 • Austin, TX 78701 • (512) 472-3127 • http://www.ttara.org

Texas State Historical Association • Univ of Texas at Austin, 1 University Sta, D0901 • Austin, TX 78712-0332 • (512) 232-1516 • *Riding Line*; *Southwest Historical Quarterly*; *Texas Historian*

Texas State Library • 1201 Brazos St, P.O. Box 12927, Capitol Sta • Austin, TX 78711-2927 • (512) 463-5455 • http://www.tsl.state.tx.us

Texas Supreme Court Historical Society • 205 W 14th St • Austin, TX 78701 • (512) 481-1840

Texian Heritage Society • 15742 Fitzhugh Rd • Austin, TX 78736

Timothy Joseph Kelty and Idona Irene Davis Descendants • 2212 Tallow Ct • Austin, TX 78744

University of Texas Press • P.O. Box 7819 • Austin, TX 78713 • (512) 471-1525 • *Southwestern Historical Quarterly*

W H Passon Historical Society • 1501 E 12th St • Austin, TX 78702 • (512) 220-1157

Azle

Azle Public Library • 609 Southeast Pkwy • Azle, TX 76020 • (817) 444-7114 • http://www.ci.azle.tx.us

Peacock Family Association of the South • 8045 Person Ln • Azle, TX 76020-5457 • (817) 279-1414 • http://www.peacockfamily.org • Peacock Paths

Baird

Callahan County Pioneer Museum Archives • 100 W 4th, B1 • Baird, TX 79504 • (325) 954-1718

Bandera

Bandera County Library • 515 Main St, P.O. Box 1568 • Bandera, TX 78003-1568 • (830) 796-4213 • http://www.banderalibrary.org

Frontier Times Museum Archives • 506 13th St, P.O. Box 1918 • Bandera, TX 78003-1918 • (830) 796-3864 • http://www.frontiertimesmuseum.com • Frontier Times Museum Newsletter

Barksdale

Hanson, Henson, Hinson, Hynson Research Association • P.O. Box 249 • Barksdale, TX 78828-0249 • *Hanson, Henson, Hinson, Hynson Research Associates Newsletter*

Bartlett

Teinert Memorial Public Library • Hwy 95 & Professor Paul Blvd, P.O. Box 12 • Bartlett, TX 76511-0012 • (254) 527-3208

Bastrop

Bastrop County Historical Society & Archives • Historical Museum, 702 Main St, P.O. Box 279 • Bastrop, TX 78602 • (512) 303-0057

Bastrop Public Library • 1100 Church St, P.O. Drawer 670 • Bastrop, TX 78602-0670 • (512) 321-5441 • http://www.bastroplibrary.org

Bay City

Bay City Public Library • 1100 7th St • Bay City, TX 77414 • (979) 245-6931

Matagorda County Genealogical Society & Library • c/o Bay City Public Library, 1100 7th St, P.O. Box 264 • Bay City, TX 77414-0264 • (979) 245-6931 • *Oak Leaves*

Matagorda County Museum Archives • 2100 Avenue F • Bay City, TX 77414 • (979) 245-7502 • http://www.matagordacountymuseum.org • *Matagorda County Musings*

Baytown

Bay Area Heritage Society • 220 W Defee • Baytown, TX 77520-4010

Baytown Genealogical Society & Archives • c/o Sterling Municipal Library, Mary E Wilbanks Ave, P.O. Box 2486 • Baytown, TX 77522 • (281) 427-7331 • *Baytown Genealogical Society Newsletter*

Baytown Historical Museum Archives • 200 W Defee Ave • Baytown, TX 77520-4010 • (281) 427-8768

Lee College Library • 150 Lee Dr, P.O. Box 818 • Baytown, TX 77522-0818 • (281) 425-6379 • http://www.lee.edu/library

Sterling Municipal Library • Mary E Wilbanks Ave • Baytown, TX 77520 • (281) 427-7331 • http://www.sml.lib.tx.us

Beaumont

Beaumont Heritage Society & Archives • John Jay French House, 3025 French Rd • Beaumont, TX 77706 • (409) 898-0348 • http://www.beaumontheritage.org • *Trading Post Times*; *We're Making History*

Beaumont Public Library • 801 Pearl St, P.O. Box 3827 • Beaumont, TX 77704 • (409) 838-6606

Edison Museum Archives • 350 Pine St, P.O. Box 2951 • Beaumont, TX 77704 • (409) 839-3089 • http://www.edisonmuseum.org

Fire Museum of Texas Archives • 400 Walnut, P.O. Box 3827 • Beaumont, TX 77704 • (409) 880-3927 • http://www.firemuseumoftexas.org • *Fire Museum of Texas Newsletter*

Knott Ancestors • 3490 Brentwood • Beaumont, TX 77706

Mary and John Gray Library • Lamar Univ, 1 Redbird Lane, P.O. Box 10021 • Beaumont, TX 77710-0021 • (409) 880-1898 • http://library.lamar.edu • *Library News*

McFaddin-Ward House Archives • 1906 McFaddin Ave • Beaumont, TX 77701 • (409) 832-1906 • http://www.mcfaddin-ward.org • *McFaddin-Ward House Newsletter*

Southeast Texas Genealogical and Historical Society • Tyrrell Historical Library, 695 Pearl St, P.O. Box 3827 • Beaumont, TX 77704-3827 • (409) 833-2759 • http://www.rootsweb.com/~txsetghs • *Yellowed Pages*; *Tyrrell Historical Library Association Newsletter*; *SoutheastTexas Genealogical and Historical Society Newsletter*

Spindletop-Gladys City Boomtown Museum Archives • Lamar Univ, Hwy 69 & Univ Dr, P.O. Box 10070 • Beaumont, TX 77710 • (409) 880-8896

Texas Energy Museum Archives • 600 Main St • Beaumont, TX 77701 • (409) 833-5100 • http://www.texasenergymuseum.org

Bedford

Baldwin, Lucas, Bridwell, Wallace Reunion • P.O. Box 211993 • Bedford, TX 76095 • (817) 358-0604

Bedford Public Library • 1805 L Don Dodgson Dr • Bedford, TX 76021-1897 • (817) 952-2342 • http://www.bedfordlibrary.org

Mid-Cities Genealogical Society • P.O. Box 407 • Bedford, TX 76021-0407 • (817) 285-9945 • *A Tale of Mid-Cities*; *Mid-Cities Genealogical Society Newsletter*

Pitman-Pittman Reunion • 2116 Shady Brook Dr • Bedford, TX 76021 • (817) 267-1645 • *Pitman-Pittman Reunion Newsletter*

Beeville

Bee County Public Library • 110 W Corpus Christi St • Beeville, TX 78102-5604 • (361) 362-4901 • http://www.bclib.org

Family Bookshelf • P.O. Box 339 • Beeville, TX 78104-0339 • (361) 362-0422 • http://www.eggertweb.com/grigsby/ • *Sinkler, Sinclair, St Clair Quarterly*

Grady C Hogue Library • 3800 Charco Rd • Beeville, TX 78102-2110 • (361) 354-2740 • http://www.coastalbend.edu • *BookSampler, Recent Titles*

South Texas Genealogical Society • c/o Bee County Public Library, 210 E Corpus Christi, P.O. Box 754 • Beeville, TX 78104-0754 • (512) 358-5541 • *South Texas Genealogical Society Quarterly*

Bellaire
Andrew Tennant and His 33 Grandchildren • 5112 Huisache • Bellaire, TX 77401 • (713) 667-4190

Bellaire City Library • 5111 Jessamine St • Bellaire, TX 77401-4498 • (713) 662-8160 • http://www.ci.bellaire.tx.us

Bellville
Bellville Historical Society • 15 N Masonic St, P.O. Box 67 • Bellville, TX 77418 • (979) 865-9116

Belton
Baylor Townsend Memorial Library • University of Mary Hardin, 900 College St, UMHB Sta, Box 8016 • Belton, TX 76513-2599 • (254) 295-4641 • http://umhblib.umhb.edu

Bell County Museum Archives • 201 N Main St, P.O. Box 1381 • Belton, TX 76513 • (254) 933-5243 • http://www.bellcountytx.com/museum • *Bell County Museum Newsletter*

Lena Armstrong Public Library-Belton City Branch • 301 E 1st Ave, P.O. Box 120 • Belton, TX 76513-0120 • (254) 933-5830 • http://www.cityofbelton.org

Petty Reunion • 709 Maple • Belton, TX 76513 • (254) 780-2249

Benbrook
Ryker Family Association • 448 Meadowhill Dr • Benbrook, TX 76126-4017 • (817) 249-2877

Benjamin
Knox County Historical Commission & Archives • Courthouse Museum, P.O. Box 124 • Benjamin, TX 79505 • (940) 454-2241 • http://www.knoxcountytexas.com

Big Spring
Columbus B Gray-Martha Hurd-Benjamin Jackson Jenkins Family Organization • 2702 Cindy Ln • Big Spring, TX 79720 • (915) 263-0391

Genealogical Society of the Big Spring • c/o Howard County Library, 500 Main St • Big Spring, TX 79720 • (915) 264-2260 • *Signal Peak*

Heritage Museum Archives • Potton House, 510 Scurry St • Big Spring, TX 79720 • (915) 267-8255 • http://www.bigspringmuseum.com • *Heritage Museum Newsletter*

Howard County Library • 500 Main St • Big Spring, TX 79720-2532 • (915) 264-2260 • http://www.howard-county.lib.tx.us

Boerne
Agricultural Heritage Museum Archives • Hwy 46 E, P.O. Box 4092 • Boerne, TX 78006 • (830) 249-6007 • http://www.agmuseum.org • *Agricultural Heritage Museum Newsletter*

Boerne Area Historical Society & Library • 402 E Blanco Rd, P.O. Box 178 • Boerne, TX 78006 • (830) 249-2030

Boerne Public Library • 210 N Main St • Boerne, TX 78006 • (830) 249-3053 • http://www.boerne.lib.tx.us

Kendall County Genealogical Society & Library • 201 N Main, P.O. Box 623 • Boerne, TX 78006 • (830) 249-3053 • *Keys to the Past*

Kuhlmann King Historical House and Museum Archives • 402 E Blanco, P.O. Box 178 • Boerne, TX 78006 • (830) 249-2030 • http://www.rootsweb.com/~txkendal

Bonham
Bonham Public Library • 305 E 5th St • Bonham, TX 75418 • (903) 583-3128

Fannin County Genealogical and Historical Society • 605 Agnew St • Bonham, TX 75418 • (972) 583-5215 • *Fannin County Genealogical and Historical Society Quarterly*

Fannin County Historical Society & Archives • Historical Museum, 1 N Main St • Bonham, TX 75418-4345 • (903) 583-8042

Fort Inglish Museum Archives • Hwy 56 & Chinner St, P.O. Box 395 • Bonham, TX 75418 • (903) 583-3943 • *Fort Inglish Courier*

Sam Rayburn Library & Museum Archives • 800 W Sam Rayburn Dr, P.O. Box 308 • Bonham, TX 75418-0309 • (903) 583-2455 • http://www.thc.state.tx.us/samrayhouse/srhoefault.html • *Sam Rayburn Library Newsletter*

Borger
Hutchinson County Genealogical Society • c/o Hutchinson County Library, 625 Weatherly St • Borger, TX 79007 • (806) 273-0126

Hutchinson County Historical Museum Archives • 618 N Main • Borger, TX 79007 • (806) 273-0130 • http://www.hutchinsoncountymuseum.org • *Hutchinson County Historical Museum Newsletter*

Hutchinson County Library • 625 N Weatherly St • Borger, TX 79007-3621 • (806) 273-0126

Bowie
Bowie Public Library • 301 Walnut St • Bowie, TX 76230 • (940) 872-2681

Montague County Genealogical Society • P.O. Box 795 • Bowie, TX 76230

Brackettville
Fort Clark Historical Society & Archives • Old Guardhouse Museum, P.O. Box 1061 • Brackettville, TX 78832-1061 • (830) 563-9150 • http://www.hilconet.com/~fchstex/museum

Kinney County Public Library • 510 S Ellen, P.O. Box 975 • Brackettville, TX 78832 • (830) 563-2884

Brazoria
Brazoria County Library System-Brazoria Branch Genealogical Library • 620 S Brooks, P.O. Drawer 1550 • Brazoria, TX 77422-1550 • (979) 798-2372

Breckenridge
Breckenridge Public Library • 209 N Breckenridge Ave • Breckenridge, TX 76424 • (254) 559-5505

Stephens County Genealogical Society & Archives • Swenson Memorial Museum, 116 W Walker, P.O. Box 350 • Breckenridge, TX 76424 • (254) 559-8471

Swenson Memorial Museum of Stephens County Archives • 116 W Walker, P.O. Box 350 • Breckenridge, TX 76024 • (254) 559-8471

Brenham
Nancy Carol Roberts Memorial Library • 100 W Academy St • Brenham, TX 77833-3107 • (979) 337-7201

Polk Family • 550 Farmers Rd • Brenham, TX 77833-9131 • (979) 830-9199

Texas Baptist Historical Center Archives • 10405 FM 50 • Brenham, TX 77833 • (979) 836-5117

W L Moody Jr Library • Blinn College, 902 College Ave • Brenham, TX 77833 • (979) 830-4250 • http://www.blinn.edu/library/

Ward Family Association • Route 6, Box 6442 • Brenham, TX 77833-4127

Washington County Heritage Society • 2203 Century Cr, P.O. Box 1123 • Brenham, TX 77833 • (979) 836-1690

Bronte
Scott Family Reunion • P.O. Box 33 • Bronte, TX 76933 • (915) 473-5331

Brooks AFB
Edward H White II Memorial Museum Archives • 311 AG/MU, 8008 Inner Circle Dr • Brooks AFB, TX 78235 • (210) 536-2203 • http://www.brooks.af.mil/ABG/mh/general.html

Brookshire
Waller County Historical Society • P.O. Box 1548 • Brookshire, TX 77423

Brownfield
Kendrick Memorial Library • 301 W Tate St • Brownfield, TX 79316-4387 • (806) 637-3848

Brownsville
Arnulfo Oliviera Memorial Library • University of Texas at Brownsville, 80 Fort Brown • Brownsville, TX 78521 • (956) 983-7206 • http://www.utb.edu/lib • *Arnulfo Oliviera Memorial Library Newsletter*

Brownsville Historical Association & Library • 1335 E Washington St, P.O. Box 846 • Brownsville, TX 78520 • (956) 546-3745 • *Brownsville Historical Association Newsletter*

Brownsville Public Library • 2600 Central Blvd • Brownsville, TX 78250-8824 • (956) 548-1055 • http://www.brownsville.lib.tx.us

Fort Brown Genealogical Society • 608 E Adams • Brownsville, TX 78520-6087 • (956) 542-4824

Brownwood
Brownwood Public Library • 600 Carnegie Blvd • Brownwood, TX 76801 • (915) 646-0155

Pecan Valley Genealogical Society • 2018 Elizabeth St • Brownwood, TX 76801-4811

Walker Memorial Library • Howard Payne University, 1000 Fisk Ave • Brownwood, TX 76801 • (325) 649-8602 • http://www.hputx.edu/library

Bruceville
Higginbotham Descendants • P.O. Box 1153 • Bruceville, TX 76630-1153 • (254) 859-5337

Bryan
Brazos Genealogical Association • P.O. Box 5493 • Bryan, TX 77805-5493 • *Brazos Genealogical Advertiser*

Bryan & College Station Public Library • 201 E 26th St • Bryan, TX 77803-5356 • (979) 209-5600 • http://www.bcslibrary.org

McCulley Depository • 205 Staiger Rd • Bryan, TX 77801 • (979) 846-6311

Mogingo, Monzingo, Montzingo Depository • 205 Hensel Dr • Bryan, TX 77801 • (979) 846-6311

Texas Research Ramblers • 740 Garden Acres • Bryan, TX 77802-4005 • (979) 846-8278 • *Texas Research Ramblers Newsletter*

Buchanan Dam
Schulz and Marks Reunion • P.O. Box 367 • Buchanan Dam, TX 78609 • (512) 793-2623

Buffalo Gap
Buffalo Gap Historic Village Archives • State Hwy 89, P.O. Box 818 • Buffalo Gap, TX 79508 • (325) 572-3365

Bullard
Bullard Community Library • 211 W Main, P.O. Box 368 • Bullard, TX 75757-0368 • (903) 894-6125 • http://www.bullardlibrary.org

Dewberry Plantation Archives • 14007 FM 346 W • Bullard, TX 75757 • (903) 825-9000

Buna
Michael Rhoads Family Organization • Route 1, Box 68 • Buna, TX 77612 • (409) 994-2776

Burkburnett
Burkburnett Genealogical Society • c/o Burkburnett Library, 215 E 4th St • Burkburnett, TX 76354 • (940) 569-2991

Burkburnett Library • 215 E 4th St • Burkburnett, TX 76354-3446 • (940) 569-2991

Trails and Tales of Boom Town USA • 104 W 3rd St • Burkburnett, TX 76354 • (940) 569-0460

Burkeville
Curry-Berry-Rogers-Lawrence-Killgore-John R Jones-McInvale Surname Organization • Hwy 87 N, P.O. Box 340 • Burkeville, TX 75932 • (409) 565-4751

Burleson
Bewley Reunion • 32 Oakridge Rd • Burleson, TX 76028

Burnet
Burnet County Genealogical Society & Archives • c/o Herman Brown Free Library, 100 E Washington St • Burnet, TX 78611 • (512) 756-2328 • http://www.rootsweb.com/~txburnet/ • *Newsletter of the Burnet County Genealogical Society; Shin Oaks Folks*

Burnet County Heritage Society & Archives • Fort Croghan Museum, 703 Buchanan Dr, P.O. Box 74 • Burnet, TX 78611 • (512) 756-8281 • http://www.fortcoghan.org

Ellett Family • P.O. Box 45 • Burnet, TX 78611 • (512) 756-4452

Herman Brown Free Library • 100 E Washington St • Burnet, TX 78611 • (512) 756-2328

Caldwell
Burleson County Historical Museum Archives • Burleson County Courthouse, P.O. Box 127 • Caldwell, TX 77836 • (979) 567-7196

Weeks Research • 401 Molly #206 • Caldwell, TX 77836 • *Weeks Newsletter: Weeks Family and Its Many Branches*

Cameron
Boney-Stutts Family Organization • P.O. Box 702 • Cameron, TX 76520 • (254) 697-2321

Cameron Public Library • 304 E 3rd St • Cameron, TX 76520 • (254) 697-2401

Magnolia House Archives • 502 N Travis Ave • Cameron, TX 76520 • (254) 697-4395

Milam County Historical Museum Archives • Main & Fannin, P.O. Box 966 • Cameron, TX 76520 • (254) 697-4770 • http://www.cameron-tx.com

Canadian
Hemphill County Historical and Genealogical Society • Route 2 • Canadian, TX 79014

Hemphill County Library • 500 Main St • Canadian, TX 79014 • (806) 323-5282

Canton
Genealogical Society of Van Zandt County & Library • Van Zandr County Courthouse Annex Bldg, Hwy 19 & Terrell St, P.O. Box 716 • Canton, TX 75103-0716 • (903) 567-5012 • http://www.rootsweb.com/txvanzan/vzcpage.html • *Our Heritage*

Van Zandt County Library • 317 First Monday Ln • Canton, TX 75103 • (903) 567-4276

Canyon
Cornette Library • West Texas A&M University, 2nd Ave & 26th St, WTAMU Box 60748 • Canyon, TX 79016-0001 • (806) 651-2215 • http://www.wtamu.edu/library • *Cornette Library Newsletter*

High Plains Genealogical Society • West Texas State University • Canyon, TX 79015

Panhandle Plains Historical Society & Archives • Historical Museum, 2503 4th Ave, P.O. Box 60967 • Canyon, TX 79016 • (806) 656-2244 • http://www.panhandleplains.org • *Panhandle Plains Historical Review*; *Corral Dust*; *PPHM News*

Canyon Lake
Tye Preston Memorial Library • 1321 FM 2673 • Canyon Lake, TX 78133-5301 • (830) 964-3744 • http://www.tyeprestonlib.org

Carrollton
Carrollton Public Library • 4220 N Josey Ln • Carrollton, TX 75010-4600 • (972) 466-4800

Dafft-Daft Research • 1605 Cottonwood Rd • Carrollton, TX 75006-3856 • (214) 466-0336 • *Dafft-Daft Family Newsletter*

Peters Colony Historical Society of Dallas County • P.O. Box 110846 • Carrollton, TX 75011-0846 • (214) 382-3643 • *Elm Fork Echoes*

Carthage
M P Baker Library • Panola College, 1109 W Panola St • Carthage, TX 75633 • (903) 693-1181 • http://www.panola.edu/library.htm • *Library News*

Panola County Historical and Genealogical Association • 113 S Shelby St • Carthage, TX 75633 • (903) 693-3388 • http://www.panola.cc.tx.us/Carthage-PanolaCounty/1891jail.htm • *Old Red Review*

Castroville
Castro Colonies Heritage Association • P.O. Box 636 • Castroville, TX 78009

Castroville Public Library • 802 London St • Castroville, TX 78009-0532 • (830) 931-4095 • http://www.castroville.lib.tx.us

Cedar Hill
Zula-Bryant-Wylie Library • 225 Cedar St • Cedar Hill, TX 75104-2655 • (972) 291-7323 • http://www.zulabwylielib.org

Cedar Park
Cedar Park Public Library • 550 Discovery Blvd • Cedar Park, TX 78613 • (512) 259-5353 • http://www.ci.cedar-park.tx.us/library

Garner Research • 701 Lobo St • Cedar Park, TX 79613 • *Raking for Garner Newsletter*

McNew-Carroll-Hockett History Association • 465 Sunset Terr • Cedar Park, TX 78513 • (512) 259-4796

Center
Shelby County Historical Commission • 600 Pine St • Center, TX 75935 • (936) 598-3863 • http://obewan.ktsnet.com/schc/

Shelby County Historical Society & Archives • Weaver-Oates House, 230 Pecan St, P.O. Box 1542 • Center, TX 75935 • (936) 598-3613 • http://www.panola.cc.tx.us/~schs/

Shelby County Museum Archives • 230 Pecan St, P.O. Box 1542 • Center, TX 75935 • (936) 593-3613

Centerville
Leon County Genealogical Society & Archives • Old Courthouse, P.O. Box 400 • Centerville, TX 75833 • *Leon Hunters Dispatch*

Chappell Hill
Chappell Hill Historical Society & Archives • Historical Museum, 9220 Poplar St, P.O. Box 211 • Chappell Hill, TX 77426 • (979) 836-6033 • http://www.chappellhillmuseum.org • *Chappell Hill Historical Review*

Childress
Byers-Byars Research • 2108 Denfield Ln • Childress, TX 79201 • *Byers-Byars Family Report*

Childress Genealogical Society • c/o Childress Public Library, 117 Avenue B NE • Childress, TX 79201 • (940) 937-8421

Childress Heritage Museum Archives • 210 3rd St NW • Childress, TX 79201 • (940) 937-2261

Childress Public Library • 117 Avenue B NE • Childress, TX 79201-4509 • (940) 937-8421

Cisco
Maner Memorial Library • Cisco Junior College, 101 College Heights • Cisco, TX 76437 • (254) 442-2567 • http://www.cisco.cc.tx.us/library.html • *Maner Messenger*

Clarendon
Clarendon College Library • 1122 College Dr, P.O. Box 968 • Clarendon, TX 79226-0968 • (806) 874-3571 • http://www.clarendoncollege.edu

Donley County Genealogical Society • P.O. Box 116 • Clarendon, TX 79226

Clarksville
Red River County Genealogical Society & Archives • c/o Red River County Public Library, 307 N Walnut St, P.O. Box 516 • Clarksville, TX 75426 • (903) 427-3991 • *Red River County Texas Genealogical Society Newsletter*

Cleburne
Cleburne Public Library • 302 W Henderson St, P.O. Box 657 • Cleburne, TX 76033-0657 • (817) 645-0934 • http://www.ci.cleburne.tx.us/library/

Johnson County Genealogical Society & Library • P.O. Box 10246 • Cleburne, TX 76033-1256 • (817) 558-8241 • http://www.htcomp.net/jcgs/soc/soc.htm • *Finders Keepers*

Layland Museum Library • 201 N Caddo St • Cleburne, TX 76031 • (817) 645-0940

Printus Clifford Evans Family Organization • 1510 N Robinson • Cleburne, TX 76031 • (817) 641-0196

Cleveland
Austin Memorial Library • 220 S Bonham Ave • Cleveland, TX 77327-4591 • (281) 593-3920 • http://www.austinmemlib.org

Cleveland Area Genealogical Society • c/o Austin Memorial Library, 220 S Bonham • Cleveland, TX 77327 • (281) 593-3920 • *Cleveland Area Pioneer*

Clifton
Moseley Database • Route 2, Box 47A • Clifton, TX 76634-9608

Clute
Brazasport Facts Library • 720 S Main St, P.O. Box 549 • Clute, TX 77531-0549 • (979) 265-7411

Clyde
Clyde Public Library • 125 Oak St, P.O. Box 1779 • Clyde, TX 79510-1779 • (915) 893-5315

Coldspring
San Jacinto County Heritage Society and Historical Commission • P.O. Box 505 • Coldspring, TX 77331 • (409) 653-2009

Coleman
Coleman Public Library • 402 Commercial Ave • Coleman, TX 76834-9737 • (915) 625-3043

College Station
Cushing Library • Texas A&M University • College Station, TX 77843-5000 • (979) 845-1951

George Bush Presidential Library • 1000 George Bush Dr W • College Station, TX 77845 • (979) 260-9552 • http://bushlibrary.tamu.edu

Seventeenth-Century News • Dept. of English, 4227 Texas A & M University • College Station, TX 77843-4227 • (979) 845-8340 • http://www.english.tamu.edu/pubs/scn • *Seventeenth-Century News*

Sterling C Evans Library • Texas A&M University • College Station, TX 77843-5000 • (979) 845-8111 • http://library.tamu.edu

Colorado City
Heart of West Texas Museum Archives • 340 E 3rd St • Colorado City, TX 79512 • (915) 728-8285 • http://www.coloradocity.net/MuseumHartOfWestTexas

Mitchell County Public Library • 340 Oak St • Colorado City, TX 79512 • (325) 728-3968

Columbus
Nesbitt Memorial Library • 529 Washington St • Columbus, TX 78934-2326 • (979) 732-3392 • http://www.columbustexus.net/library

Comanche
Comanche Genealogical Society • P.O. Box 411 • Comanche, TX 76442

Comanche Public Library • 311 N Austin St, P.O. Box 777 • Comanche, TX 76442-0777 • (915) 356-2122

Comfort
Comfort Heritage Foundation & Archives • c/o Comfort Public Library, 701 High St, P.O. Box 443 • Comfort, TX 78013 • (830) 995-2398

Comfort Public Library • 701 High St, P.O. Box 536 • Comfort, TX 78013-0036 • (830) 995-2398 • http://www.comfort-library.txed.net

Commerce
Commerce Public Library • 1210 Park St, P.O. Box 308 • Commerce, TX 75428-0308 • (903) 886-6858 • http://www.geocities.com/commercepubliclibrary

James Gilliam Gee Library • East Texas State University, P.O. Box 3011 • Commerce, TX 75429-3011 • (903) 885-5720 • http://www7.tamu-commerce.edu/library

Comstock
Seminold Canyon State Park and Historic Site Archives • US Hwy 30 W, P.O. Box 820 • Comstock, TX 78837 • (432) 292-4464 • http://www.tpwd.state.tx.us

Conroe
Montgomery County Genealogical and Historical Society • P.O. Box 867 • Conroe, TX 77305-0867 • (936) 788-8363 • http://mcia.com/gsociety.htm • *Herald*

Montgomery County Library • 104 I-45 N • Conroe, TX 77301-2720 • (936) 788-8361 • http://www.countylibrary.org

Copperas Cove
Ballentine, Huxford and Connected Families • 2714 Phyllis Dr • Copperas Cove, TX 76522-4311 • (254) 542-7259 • http://www.dashlink.com/~georgeball/ • *Ballentine Branches*

Copperas Cove Public Library • 501 S Main St • Copperas Cove, TX 76522 • (254) 547-3826 • http://www.ci.copperas-cove.tx.us

Corpus Christi
Coastal Bend Genealogical Society & Library • 2801 Lawnview St, P.O. Box 2711 • Corpus Christi, TX 78403 • (361) 776-7376 • http://www.rootsweb.com/~txebgs/ • *Reflections*

Corpus Christi Museum of Science and History Archives • 1900 N Chaparral • Corpus Christi, TX 78401 • (361) 883-2862 • http://www.ccmuseum.com

Corpus Christi Public Library • 805 Comanche • Corpus Christi, TX 78401 • (361) 880-7000 • http://www.library.ci.corpus-christi.tx.us

Geyer Society of America • P.O. Box 270396 • Corpus Christi, TX 78427-0396 • (361) 850-9268 • *Geyer Newsletter*

Hanson, Henson, Hinson, Hynson Research Association • 6922 Roseland Dr • Corpus Christi, TX 78414-2714 • *Hanson, Henson, Hinson, Hynson Research Associates Newsletter*

Haymore Research • 4518 Clearwater Dr • Corpus Christi, TX 78413 • *Haymore Family of North America Newsletter*

Mary and Jeff Bell Library • Texas A&M-Corpus Christi, 6300 Ocean Dr • Corpus Christi, TX 78412-5501 • (361) 994-2643 • http://rattler.tamucc.edu

McBurney Research • P.O. Box 6577 • Corpus Christi, TX 78411 • *McBurney Family News*

McLouth-Pratt Family of America Association • P.O. Box 3202 • Corpus Christi, TX 78463 • (361) 992-1826

Naval Air Station Library • Bldg 5 • Corpus Christi, TX 78419 • (361) 961-3574

Spanish American Genealogical Association • 4601 Cosner, P.O. Box 794 • Corpus Christi, TX 78403 • (361) 855-1183 • http://members.aol.com/sagacorpus/saga.htm

USS Lexington Museum Archives • 2914 N Shoreline Blvd, P.O. Box 23076 • Corpus Christi, TX 78403-3076 • (800) ladylex • http://www.usslexington.com • USS Lexington Museum Newsletter

Youngblood (Jungblut) Society of America • P.O. Box 270396 • Corpus Christi, TX 78427-0396 • (361) 850-9268 • *Youngblood News Letter*

Corrigan
Mickey Reily Public Library • 604 S Mathews St • Corrigan, TX 75939 • (936) 398-4156

Corsicana
Corsicana Public Library • 100 N 12th St • Corsicana, TX 75110 • (903) 654-4810 • http://www.ci.corsicana.tx.us

Gaston T Gooch Library • Navarro College, 3200 W 7th Ave • Corsicana, TX 75110-4899 • (903) 875-7442 • http://www.navarrocollege.edu

Navarro County Genealogical Society & Archives • c/o Corsicana Public Library, 100 N 12th St, P.O. Box 2278 • Corsicana, TX 75151-2278 • (903) 872-3071 • *Navarro Leaves and Branches*

Navarro County Historical Society & Archives • Pioneer Village Museum, 912 W Park Ave • Corsicana, TX 75110 • (903) 654-4846

Pearce Collections Museum Archives • 3100 W Collins St • Corsicana, TX 75110 • (903) 875-7438 • http://www.pearcecollections.us

Cortulla
Brush Country Museum Archives • 201 S Stewart, P.O. Box 369 • Cortulla, TX 78014 • (830) 879-2429 • http://www.historicdistrict.com/museum

Covington
Pennington Research Association • P.O. Box 456 • Covington, TX 76636 • (254) 654-2502 • http://penningtonresearch.org • *Penninton Pedigrees*

Cresson
Pate Museum of Transportation Archives • Hwy 37 • Cresson, TX 76104 • (817) 396-4305

Crockett
Houston County Historical Commission & Library • Houston County Courthouse Annex, 401 E Goliad • Crockett, TX 75835-4035 • (936) 544-3255 • *Discovery*

Houston County Museum Archives • 303 S 1st St, P.O. Box 449 • Crockett, TX 75835 • (936) 544-9520

John H Wootters-Crocket Public Library • 708 E Goliad Ave, P.O. Box 1226 • Crockett, TX 75835-1226 • (936) 544-3089

Crosbyton
Crosby County Historical Society • 101 Main St • Crosbyton, TX 79322

Crosby County Pioneer Memorial Museum Archives • 101 W Main St • Crosbyton, TX 79322 • (806) 675-2331 • http://www.crosbycountymuseum.com

Crowley
Eller Research • 500 E Mission St • Crowley, TX 76036 • *Eller Chronicles*

Crystal City
Crystal City Memorial Library • 101 E Dimmit St • Crystal City, TX 78839 • (830) 374-3477

Cuero
Cuero Public Library • 207 E Main St • Cuero, TX 77954 • (361) 275-2864 • http://www.cuero.tx-lib.com

DeWitt County Historical Museum Archives • 312 E Broadway, P.O. Box 745 • Cuero, TX 77954 • (361) 275-6322 • http://www.cuero.org

Dalhart
Dallam-Hartley Counties Historical Association & Archives • Dallam-Hartley Museum, 108 E 5th St, P.O. Box 730 • Dalhart, TX 79022 • (806) 249-5390 • http://www.xitmuseum.com

Dallas
African American Museum Archives • 3536 Grand Ave, P.O. Box 150157 • Dallas, TX 75315 • (214) 565-9026 • http://www.aamdallas.org • *African American Museum Newsletter*

Age of Steam Railroad Museum Archives • Fair Park, 1105 Washington St, P.O. Box 153259 • Dallas, TX 75315 • (214) 428-0101 • http://www.dallasrailwaymuseum.com • *Clearance Card*

Basham Clearinghouse • 10352 White Rock Cr • Dallas, TX 75238 • (214) 348-1403 • *Basham Family*

Beadles Genealogy • 4037 Northview Ln • Dallas, TX 75229

Biblical Arts Center Museum Archives • 7500 Park Ln, P.O. Box 12727 • Dallas, TX 75225 • (214) 691-4752 • http://www.biblicalarts.org • *Creation of a Masterpiece*

Burleson Family Association • 10555 Le Mans Dr • Dallas, TX 75238-3667 • (214) 348-0668 • *Burleson Family Bulletin*

Christlieb-Chrislip-Crislip Family Association • 12016 Midlake Dr • Dallas, TX 75318 • (214) 341-0598 • *Jacob's Ladder*

Clan MacDuff Society of North America • 9902 Shoreview Rd • Dallas, TX 75238 • http://www.crimson.com/scots_austin/macduff.htm

Clan McLaren Society of North America • 5843 Royal Crest Dr • Dallas, TX 75230 • *Clan McLaren Society, USA Newsletter*

Cornelius Reunion • 7727 Village Trail Dr • Dallas, TX 75240 • (972) 385-9511

Cultural Heritage Center Archives • Davy Crockett School, 401 N Carroll • Dallas, TX 75246 • (214) 841-5355

Dallas County East Genealogical Society • 7637 Mary Dan Dr, P.O. Box 17704 • Dallas, TX 75217 • *Texas Kin*

Dallas County Heritage Society & Archives • Heritage Village Museum, 1717 Gano St • Dallas, TX 75215-1211 • (214) 421-5141 • http://www.dallasheritagevillage.org • *Legacies*; *Heritage News*

Dallas County Historical Church and Cemetery Association & Archives • Historical Museum, 1433 N Westmoreland Rd • Dallas, TX 75211 • (214) 879-9727

Dallas Firefighter's Museum Archives • 3801 Parry Ave • Dallas, TX 75226 • (214) 821-1500 • http://www.dallasfirerescue.com

Dallas Genealogical Society & Library • P.O. Box 12648 • Dallas, TX 75225-0648 • (214) 670-7932 • http://www.dallasgenealogy.org • *Dallas Journal*; *Dallas Genealogical Society Newsletter*

Dallas Heritage Village Archives • 1515 S Harwood • Dallas, TX 75215 • (214) 421-5141 • http://www.dallasheritagevillage.org

Dallas Historical Society & Archives • Dealey Library and Museum, 3939 Grand Ave, P.O. Box 150038 • Dallas, TX 75226-0038 • (214) 421-4500 • http://www.dallashistory.org • *Dallas Historical Society Register*

Dallas Holocaust Museum Archives • 211 N Record St, Ste 100 • Dallas, TX 75202 • (214) 741-7500 • http://www.dallasholocaustmuseum.org • *Dallas Holocaust Museum Newsletter*

Dallas Jewish Historical Society & Library • Center for Holocaust Studies, 7900 Northaven Rd • Dallas, TX 75230 • (214) 369-8373 • *Today Is Tomorrow's History*

Dallas Jewish Historical Society, Genealogy Division • 7900 Northaven Rd • Dallas, TX 75230 • (972) 739-2737 • http://www.dvjcc/DJHS.html • *Journal of the Dallas Jewish Historical Society*

Dallas Public Library • 1515 Young St • Dallas, TX 75201-5499 • (214) 670-1433 • http://www.dallaslibrary.org

DeGolyer Library of Special Collections • Southern Methodist Univ, 6404 Hilltop Dr, P.O. Box 750396 • Dallas, TX 75275 • (214) 768-3231 • http://www.smu.edu/~cul/degolyer/

Farrington Families of the South • 13822 Methuen Green • Dallas, TX 75240-5829 • (972) 690-1312

Flippin-Estep Family Association • 12206 Brisbane Ave • Dallas, TX 75234 • (972) 241-2739 • http://www.homestead.com/flippinfiles/ • *Flipping Flippins*; *Estep Family Journal*

Fondren Library • Southern Methodist Univ • Dallas, TX 75222 • (214) 768-2323

Frontiers of Flight Museum Archives • 6911 Lemmon Ave • Dallas, TX 75209 • (214) 350-3600 • http://www.flightmuseum.com • *Frontiers of Flight Museum Newsletter*

Ira Seth Arnold Family Organization • 6908 La Manga • Dallas, TX 75248 • (214) 387-2623

Martin Family Research • 8755 Rexford Dr • Dallas, TX 75214

Meyercord Library • Highland Park Presbyterian Church, 3821 University Blvd • Dallas, TX 75205 • (214) 526-7457 • http://www.hppc.org

Miltenberger Family Association • 10820 Colbert Wy • Dallas, TX 75214 • (214) 349-5318 • *Miltenberger Family Association Quarterly*

Muntzell Ancestors • 4250 Cedarbush • Dallas, TX 75229 • (214) 352-7093

National Odom Assembly • 13123 Roaring Springs • Dallas, TX 75240 • (972) 239-4901

Ogle-Ogles Family Association • 10119 Chimney Hill Ln • Dallas, TX 75243-2308 • *Ogle Genealogist*; *Ogling for Ogles*

Ousley Genealogical Society • 725 Bluegrass, P.O. Box 4305 • Dallas, TX 75208 • (214) 330-1635 • *Ousley Newsletter*

Preservation Dallas • 2922 Swiss Ave • Dallas, TX 75204 • (214) 821-3290

Sixth Floor Museum at Dealey Plaza Archives • 411 Elm St, Ste 120 • Dallas, TX 75202 • (214) 747-6660 • http://www.jfk.org • *Sixth Floor Museum at Dealey Plaza Newsletter*

Southern Methodist University Central Library • 6414 Hilltop Dr • Dallas, TX 75205 • (214) 768-2326 • http://www.smu.edu/cul

Southwest Railroad Historical Society & Archives • Age of Steam Railroad Museum, Fair Park, 1105 Washington St, P.O. Box 153259 • Dallas, TX 75315-3259 • (214) 428-0101 • http://www.dallasrailwaymuseum.com

Street Family Association • 4538 Hockaday Dr • Dallas, TX 75229 • (214) 351-3843

Texas African American Photography Archives • 5427 Columbia Ave • Dallas, TX 75214 • (214) 823-8824

Toler Research • 9103 Stone Creek Pl • Dallas, TX 75243 • *Toler Trails*

Truett Memorial Library • First Baptist Church of Dallas, 510 N Ervay • Dallas, TX 75201 • (214) 969-2442 • http://www.firstdallas.org • *Truett Memorial Library Newsletter*

USFR Media Group • 6688 N Central Expwy, Ste 650 • Dallas, TX 75206 • (214) 750-8222 • *Cowboys & Indians*

Wallace Library • Criswell College, 4010 Gaston Ave • Dallas, TX 75246 • (214) 818-1348 • http://www.criswell.edu

Wiley A Smart Family Organization • 5102 Vickery Blvd • Dallas, TX 75206

Zale Library • Paul Quinn College, 3837 Simpson Stuart Rd • Dallas, TX 75241 • (214) 302-3565 • http://www.pqc.edu

Dayton

Linck and Ragatz Families • 121 Northwood Dr • Dayton, TX 77535

Decatur

Decatur Public Library • 1700 Hwy 51 S • Decatur, TX 76234-9292 • (940) 627-5512 • http://www.decaturpubliclibrary.com

Wise County Historical Society & Archives • Heritage Museum, 1602 S Trinity St, P.O. Box 427 • Decatur, TX 76234 • (940) 627-5586 • *Wise County Historical Commission and Society Newsletter*

Deer Park

Calvin Family Association • 2317 Louisiana Ave • Deer Park, TX 77536-3811 • (281) 476-4715 • Calvin Connections Past and Present

Deer Park Public Library • 3009 Center St • Deer Park, TX 77536-5099 • (281) 478-7208 • Off the Shelf

Del Rio

McQuade-Cooper-McGinn-Irons-Cilley-Bastable Surname Organization • 207 E 1st • Del Rio, TX 78840-4603 • (830) 775-4556

Val Verde County Genealogy Society • 110 King John's Pl • Del Rio, TX 78840

Val Verde County Library • 300 Spring St • Del Rio, TX 78840 • (830) 774-7595 • http://www.vvcl.org

Whitehead Memorial Museum Archives • 1308 S Main St • Del Rio, TX 78840 • (830) 774-7586 • http://www.whitehead.museum.com

Denison
Blassingame Family Archive • 501 W Gandy St, P.O. Box 131 • Denison, TX 75020 • (903) 465-5005

Denison Historical and Genealogical Society • 2621 Brookhollow • Denison, TX 75020-7117 • (903) 465-7170

Denison Library Genealogy Group & Archives • c/o Denison Public Library, 300 W Gandy St • Denison, TX 75021 • (903) 465-1797 • *Grayson Gateway*

Denison Public Library • 300 W Gandy St • Denison, TX 75020-3153 • (903) 465-1797 • http://www.barr.org

Eisenhower Birthplace Historic Site Archives • 609 S Lamar Ave • Denison, TX 75021 • (903) 465-8908 • http://www.eisenhowerbirthplace.org • *Commander's Post*

Denton
Alexander Allen Foley Family Organization • 605 Chisholm Tr • Denton, TX 76201

Bayless-Selby House Museum Archives • 317 W Mulberry St • Denton, TX 76201 • (940) 349-2865

DAR-First Ladies of Texas • Historic Costume Collection, Texas Women's Univ, P.O. Box 425707 • Denton, TX 76204 • (940) 898-3644 • http://www.twu.edu

Denton County Genealogical Society & Library • P.O. Box 424707 • Denton, TX 76204-4707 • (940) 382-0464 • http://www.iglobal.net/pub/dcgs/ • Denton County Genealogical Society News

Denton County Historical Commission & Archives • Historical Museum, 5800 N I-35, Ste 308, P.O. Box 2800 • Denton, TX 76202 • (940) 565-8697 • http://www.dentoncountyhistoricalmuseum.com • *Museum Musings*

Denton Public Library • 502 Oakland • Denton, TX 76201 • (940) 349-8569

Denton Public Library-North Branch • 3020 N Locust St • Denton, TX 76209 • (940) 349-8756 • http://www.dentonlibrary.com

Historical Society of Denton County • P.O. Box 50503 • Denton, TX 76206-0503 • (940) 387-0995 • http://www.iglobal.net/mayhouse/hsdc.html

Mary Evelyn Blagg-Huey Library • Texas Women's Univ, 1200 Frame St, P.O. Box 425528, TWU Sta • Denton, TX 76204 • (940) 898-3701 • http://www.twu.edu

Military History of the West • Dept of History, Univ of North Texas, P.O. Box 13016 • Denton, TX 76203-6016 • (940) 565-2288 • *Military History of the West*

National Registry of the Family of Evert and Elizabeth S DeHaven • 913 Chasewood • Denton, TX 76205 • (940) 387-9993 • http://www.dehavenclub.org • *DeHaven Club Newsletter*

Taylor-Armstrong Family Association • 9100 Hwy 2181 #38K • Denton, TX 76205 • (940) 566-6605 • *Taylor-Armstrong Treasures*

University of North Texas Library • P.O. Box 305190 • Denton, TX 76203-5190 • (940) 565-3245 • http://www.library.unt.edu • *Friends of the Libraries Newsletter, Friday Fragments*

Denver City
McFarlane Surname Organization • 315 Mustang Dr • Denver City, TX 79323

Desoto
Lackey Family Association • 1316 Mosslake Dr • Desoto, TX 75115 • (214) 383-8824 • *Lackey Family Association Newsletter*

Wilt Surname Organization • 427 Newcastle • Desoto, TX 75115 • (214) 780-2836

Detroit
Turk Reunion • Route 2, Box 327 • Detroit, TX 75436 • (903) 982-5309

Devine
Thurman's Quest Online Surname Repository • 609 Hickory Hwy • Devine, TX 78016 • (830) 663-9410 • http://www.megabits.net/~lthurman

Diboll
T L L Temple Memorial Library • 300 Park St • Diboll, TX 75941 • (936) 829-5497

Dickinson
Griggs Surname Organization • 3406 Ash Dr • Dickinson, TX 77539

Grothaus, Morris Family Organization of VA and MO • P.O. Box 93 • Dickinson, TX 77539

Dodd City
Fort Inglish Archives • P.O. Box 29 • Dodd City, TX 75438 • (903) 583-3943

Donna
Donna Public Library • 301 S Main • Donna, TX 78537 • (956) 464-2221 • http://www.donna.lib.tx.us • *Donna Public Library Newsletter*

Dripping Springs
Harbor Ranch Museum Archives • US 290 W • Dripping Springs, TX 78620 • (512) 469-0716

Dublin
Dublin Public Library • 206 W Blackjack • Dublin, TX 76446 • (254) 445-4141

Dumas
Dumas Genealogical and Historical Society • 127 Oak Ave • Dumas, TX 79029

Killgore Memorial Library • 124 S Bliss Ave • Dumas, TX 79029-3889 • (806) 935-4941 • http://www.mocolib.net

Moore County Historical Museum Archives • Window on the Plains, 1820 S Dumas Ave, P.O. Box 851 • Dumas, TX 79029 • (806) 935-3113 • http://www.dumasmuseumandartcenter.org

Duncanville
Duncanville Genealogical Society • 622 W Camp Wisdom Rd, P.O. Box 381147 • Duncanville, TX 75188-1147 • (972) 296-4697 • *Duncanville Genealogical Society Newsletter*

Duncanville Public Library • 201 James Collins Blvd • Duncanville, TX 75116 • (972) 780-5050 • http://www.ci.duncanville.tx.us

Eagle Pass
Eagle Pass Public Library • 589 Main St • Eagle Pass, TX 78852 • (830) 773-2516 • http://www.eaglepass.lib.tx.us

Eastland
Cloud Family Association • 508 Crestwood • Eastland, TX 76448 • (805) 965-7423 • *Cloud Family Association Newsletter, Cloud Family Journal*

Eastland Centennial Memorial Library • 210 S Lamar St • Eastland, TX 76448-2794 • (254) 629-2281

Eastland County Genealogical Society • P.O. Box 6 • Eastland, TX 76448

Edgewood
Edgewood Historical Society • 103 E Elm St • Edgewood, TX 75117 • (903) 896-1940

Edinburg
Edinburg Public Library • 401 E Cano St • Edinburg, TX 78539-4596 • (956) 383-6246 • http://www.edinburg.lib.tx.us

Museum of South Texas History Archives • 121 E McIntyre • Edinburg, TX 78540 • (956) 383-6911 • http://www3.hiline.net/~mosthistory/homepage.html • *Museum of South Texas History Newsletter*

Musson Surname • P.O. Box 3035 • Edinburg, TX 78540 • (956) 381-0132

Porciones Genealogical Society • P.O. Box 392 • Edinburg, TX 78540-0392 • *Porciones Genealogical Society Journal*

Rio Grande Valley Historical Collection • Univ of Texas, 1201 W University Dr • Edinburg, TX 78539-2999 • (210) 381-2726 • http://www.lib.panam.edu

University of Texas-Pan American Library • 1201 W University Dr • Edinburg, TX 78541-2999 • (956) 381-2752 • http://www.lib.panam.edu • *Reflections/ Reflecciones*

Edna

Texana Museum and Library • 403 N Wells • Edna, TX 77957 • (361) 782-5431

Edom

Edom Historical Society • 8282 FM 279 • Edom, TX 75754

El Campo

El Campo Museum Archives • 2350 N Mechanic, P.O. Box 23 • El Campo, TX 77437-0023 • (979) 541-5092

El Paso

Americana Museum Archives • 11232 leo Collins Dr • El Paso, TX 79936-4632 • (915) 542-0394

Casa Magoffin Companeros • 1120 Magoffin Ave • El Paso, TX 79901 • (915) 533-5222

Chamizal National Memorial Archives • 800 S San Marcial • El Paso, TX 79905 • (915) 532-7273 • http://www.nps.gov/cham

Clan MacLellan in America • P.O. Box 640468 • El Paso, TX 79404 • http://www.clanmaclellan.org • *Think On*

El Paso County Historical Society & Library • 603 W Yandell Dr, P.O. Box 28 • El Paso, TX 79940 • (915) 533-3603 • *Password*

El Paso Genealogical Library • 3651 Douglas • El Paso, TX 79903

El Paso Genealogical Society & Archives • c/o El Paso Public Library, 501 N Oregon St • El Paso, TX 79901-1103 • (915) 543-5474 • *Rio Grande Researcher*

El Paso Holocaust Museum Archives • 715 N Oregon • El Paso, TX 79902 • (915) 351-0048 • http://www.elpasoholocaustmuseum.org

El Paso Museum of History Archives • 12901 Gateway W • El Paso, TX 79927 • (915) 858-1928 • *El Paso Museum of History Newsletter*

El Paso Public Library • 6501 N Oregon St • El Paso, TX 79901 • (915) 543-5401

Hipps-Hipp Clearinghouse • 1601 Rim Rd • El Paso, TX 79902

James Hanes and Jemina Calloway Family • 921 Thunderbird Dr • El Paso, TX 79912

Lucky Mee Family Association • P.O. Drawer 4487 • El Paso, TX 79914 • (915) 751-7233 • *Lucky Mee Family Association News and Notes*; *Lucky Mee Family Association Yearbook*

Magoffin Home State Historic Site Archives • 1120 Magoffin Ave • El Paso, TX 79901 • (915) 533-5147

National Border Patrol Museum Archives • 4315 Transmountain Rd • El Paso, TX 79924 • (915) 759-6060 • http://www.borderpatrolmuseum.com

Rio Grande Researchers • c/o El Paso Public Library, 5501 N Oregon • El Paso, TX 79901 • (915) 543-5474

University of Texas at El Paso Library • 500 W University Ave • El Paso, TX 79968-0582 • (915) 747-5643 • http://www.libraryweb.utep.edu

World Proudfoot Genealogical Society • 8702 Galena Dr • El Paso, TX 79904 • (915) 755-6684 • *Proudfoot Genealogical Press*

Wren Family Association • 5809 Tautago • El Paso, TX 79924 • (915) 755-0083 • *Wren Kin Newsletter*

Eldorado

Schleicher County Public Library • 201 SW Main St, P.O. Box 611 • Eldorado, TX 76936-0611 • (915) 853-3767

Electra

Clopton Family Association • 14246 SH 240 W • Electra, TX 76360 • http://www.cloptonfamily.org • *Clopton Family Newsletter*

Electra Public Library • 401 N Waggoner • Electra, TX 76360 • (940) 495-2208

Ennis

Ennis Public Library • 501 W Ennis Ave • Ennis, TX 75119-3803 • (972) 875-5360 • http://www.ennis-texas.com/library/

Euless

Euless Public Library • 201 N Ector Dr • Euless, TX 76039-3595 • (817) 685-1489 • http://www.ci.euless.tx.us/library/library.html

Granbury Depot Archives • 109 Ewell St • Euless, TX 76040 • (817) 573-2557

Fabens

El Paso County Library • 1331 N Fabens St, P.O. Drawer 788 • Fabens, TX 79838-0788 • (915) 764-3635

Fairfield

Fairfield Library Association • 350 W Main St • Fairfield, TX 75840 • (903) 389-3574

Freestone County Genealogical Society & Library • P.O. Box 14 • Fairfield, TX 75840 • (903) 389-2292 • *Freestone Frontiers*

Freestone County Historical Museum Archives • 302 E Main St, P.O. Box 524 • Fairfield, TX 75840 • (903) 389-3738 • http://www.fairfieldtx.com

Moody-Bradley House Museum Archives • 390 Moody St, P.O. Box 875 • Fairfield, TX 75840 • (903) 389-3164

Falfurrias

Brooks County Historical Commission & Archives • Heritage Museum, 415 N St Mary's St, P.O. Box 86 • Falfurrias, TX 78355 • (361) 325-2907 • http://www.heritagemuseum-falfurias.com

Brooks County Library • 203 S Calixto Mora Ave • Falfurrias, TX 78355 • (361) 325-2144

Brush Country Genealogical Society • P.O. Box 291 • Falfurrias, TX 78355

Farmers Branch

Farmers Branch Historical Park Archives • 2540 Farmers Branch Ln, P.O. Box 819010 • Farmers Branch, TX 75234 • (972) 406-0184 • http://www.farmersbranch.info • *Farmers Branch Historical Park Newsletter*

Farmers Branch Public Library • 13613 Webb Chapel St • Farmers Branch, TX 75234 • (972) 247-2511 • http://www.farmersbranch.info/

Lambeth Family from Virginia to Texas • 13319 Belfield Dr • Farmers Branch, TX 75234 • (972) 243-5444

Fayetteville

Round Top Historical Society • 304 N Washington St • Fayetteville, TX 78940 • (979) 249-5758

Ferris

Ferris Public Library • 514 S Mable • Ferris, TX 75125 • (972) 544-3696

Gullick Family Association • P.O. Box 33 • Ferris, TX 75125 • (214) 544-3988

Flint

National Icarian Heritage Society • 18433 Falls Creek Dr • Flint, TX 75762 • *National Icarian Heritage Society Newsletter*

Floresville

Charles Lewis Hillman Family Organization • general delivery • Floresville, TX 78114 • (512) 393-2417

Wilson County Public Library • 1 Library Ln • Floresville, TX 78114 • (830) 393-7361 • http://wilsoncounty.lib.tx.us

Floydada

Creed Surname Organization • Route 2, Box 175 • Floydada, TX 79235 • (806) 983-2633

Floyd County Historical Museum Archives • 105 E Missouri St, P.O. Box 304 • Floydada, TX 79235-0304 • (806) 983-2415

Forney

Forney Heritage Society • 98 FM 2757, P.O. Box 1292 • Forney, TX 75126 • (214) 552-3681 • *Timekeeper*

Fort Bliss
Fort Bliss Museum Archives • Bldg 1735, Marshall Rd, ATZC-GC-M • Fort Bliss, TX 79916-5300 • (915) 568-6940 • http://www.bliss.army.mil

Mickelsen Community Library • Bldg 2E, Sheridan Rd • Fort Bliss, TX 79916-3802 • (915) 568-6156 • http://www.blissmwr.com/Family/Library.htm

Sergeants Major Academy Library • Bldg 11291 Biggs Field • Fort Bliss, TX 79918-8002 • (915) 568-8451 • http://usasma.bliss.army.mil/LRC

US Army Air Defense Artillery Museum Archives • Bldg 1735, Marshall Rd • Fort Bliss, TX 79916-5300 • (915) 568-5412 • http://www.bliss.army.mil/museum/fort_bliss_museum.htm

Fort Davis
Fort Davis National Historic Site Library • 101 Lt Flipper Dr, P.O. Box 1379 • Fort Davis, TX 79734-0015 • (432) 426-2315 • http://www.nps.gov/foda

Neill Museum Archives • 7th & Court, P.O. Box 1034 • Fort Davis, TX 79734 • (915) 426-3838

Fort Hood
1st Cavalry Division Museum Archives • Bldg 2218, 56th & 761st Tank Batallion Ave, P.O. Box 5187 • Fort Hood, TX 76545 • (817) 287-3626 • http://pao.hood.army.mil/lcd_museum

4th Infantry Division Museum Archives • Bldg 418, 761st Tank Batallion Ave & 27th St, P.O. Box 5917 • Fort Hood, TX 76544 • (254) 287-8811

Fort McKavett
Fort McKavett State Historic Site Archives • P.O. Box 68 • Fort McKavett, TX 76841 • (325) 396-2358 • http://www.tpwd.state.tx.us • *Fort McKavett State Historic Site Newsletter*

Fort Sam Houston
Fort Sam Houston Library • 2601 Harney Rd, Suite 29 • Fort Sam Houston, TX 78234-5029 • (210) 221-4702

Fort Sam Houston Museum Archives • 1210 Stanley Rd • Fort Sam Houston, TX 78234-5002 • (210) 221-1886 • http://www.cs.amedd.army.mil/ribc

Mary Magdelena Kissinger Family Organization • HQ 5th USA DCST TR E • Fort Sam Houston, TX 78234-5000

US Army Medical Department Museum Archives • Bldg 1046, Stanley Rd, P.O. Box 244 • Fort Sam Houston, TX 78234 • (210) 221-6358 • http://www.amedicmuseumfoundation.com • *US Army Medical Department Museum Newsletter*

Fort Stockton
Fort Stockton Historical Society & Archives • Annie Riggs Museum, 301 S Main St • Fort Stockton, TX 79735 • (432) 336-2167 • *Fort Stockton Historical Society Newsletter*

Fort Stockton Public Library • 500 N Water St • Fort Stockton, TX 79735 • (432) 336-3374 • http://www.fort-stockton.lib.tx.us

Historic Fort Stockton Museum Archives • 301 E 3rd • Fort Stockton, TX 79735 • (432) 336-2400

Fort Worth
A Webb Roberts Library • Southwestern Baptist Theological Seminary, 2001 W Seminary Dr, P.O. Box 22490 • Fort Worth, TX 76122-2490 • (817) 923-1921 • http://www.swbts.edu/libraries

Amon Carter Museum Library • 3501 Camp Bowie Blvd • Fort Worth, TX 76107-2695 • (817) 738-1933 • http://www.cartermuseum.org

Ball-Eddleman-McFarland House Archives • 1110 Penn St • Fort Worth, TX 76102 • (817) 332-5875

Bazeltown Reunion • 6824 Beertwood Stair Rd • Fort Worth, TX 76112-3319

Buie Exchange • 3828 Heywood • Fort Worth, TX 76107

Cattle Raisers Museum Archives • 1301 W 7th St • Fort Worth, TX 76102 • (817) 332-8551 • http://www.cattleraisersmuseum.org • *Cattleman*

Clan MacDuff Society • 3524 Slade Blvd • Fort Worth, TX 76116-6910 • http://www.scotclans.com/clans/csmacduff.htm

Clan MacNeil Association of America, Texas • 4012 Harlanwood • Fort Worth, TX 76109

Culberson-Culbertson Family Association • 6428 Arthur Dr • Fort Worth, TX 76134

Fort Worth Genealogical Society • 1000 Macon St, P.O. Box 9767 • Fort Worth, TX 76107 • (817) 338-4426 • http://www.chrysalis.org/business/fwgen/ • *Footprints Quarterly Journal*; *Fort Worth Genealogical Society Bulletin*; *Fort Worth Genealogical Society Newsletter*

Fort Worth Museum of Science and History Archives • 1501 Montgomery St • Fort Worth, TX 76107 • (254) 225-9305 • http://www.fortworthmuseum.org

Fort Worth Public Library • 500 W 3rd St • Fort Worth, TX 76102 • (817) 871-7701 • http://www.fortworthlibrary.org

Frost-Blackwood-Buckland-Bucklin Family Association • 3708 Grady St • Fort Worth, TX 76119 • (817) 535-7207

Gold Family Reunion • 8105 Chapin Rd • Fort Worth, TX 76116 • (817) 244-7878 • http://homepages.rootsweb.com/~gold/ • *Gold Nugget*

Gresham-Grisham-Grisson-Grishem Family Organization • 2109 Skyline Dr • Fort Worth, TX 76114 • (817) 626-0014 • *Gresham-Any-Way-You-Spell-It*

Hinckley: Heritage and History • 6049 Wrigley Wy • Fort Worth, TX 76133-3533 • (817) 292-3942

Historic Fort Worth • 1110 Penn St • Fort Worth, TX 76102 • (817) 336-2344

Johnson-Caston-Allen Reunion • 10405 Lone Pine Ln • Fort Worth, TX 76108 • (817) 367-3609

Knebel Family Reunion • 1600 Texas St #504 • Fort Worth, TX 76102 • http://www.hcnews.com/knebel/

Lambirth-Murphey-Hughes-Bowers-James-Briggs-Despain Surname Organization • 2413 Lofton Terr • Fort Worth, TX 76109 • (817) 924-7990

Log Cabin Village Archives • 2100 Log Cabin Village Ln • Fort Worth, TX 76109 • (817) 926-5881 • http://www.logcabinvillage.org

Lokrig Family Association • 4913 Reynolds Rd • Fort Worth, TX 76180-7941 • (817) 498-2423 • http://www.geocities.com/Heartland/Hills/8593/ • *Lock On: Lokrig Family Record*

Mary Couts Burnett Library • Texas Christian Univ, 2913 Lowden St, TCU Box 298400 • Fort Worth, TX 76129 • (817) 257-7117 • http://www.library.tcu.edu • *Windows*

Mathes Cunningham Family Organization • 3925 Thistle Ln • Fort Worth, TX 76109

Matney Family Organization • 1307 Maxine • Fort Worth, TX 76117

Morse Family Society • 5208 Mallory Dr • Fort Worth, TX 76117 • (817) 834-0074 • http://www.morsesociety.org • *Morse Society Newsletter*

National Archives & Records Administration-Southwest Region • 501 W Felix St Bldg I, P.O. Box 6216 • Fort Worth, TX 76115-0216 • (817) 334-5515 • http://www.archives.gov/facilities/tx/fort_worth.html

Naval Air Station Library • 1500 Desert Storm Rd, NAS Fort Worth JRB • Fort Worth, TX 76127 • (817) 782-7735

North Fort Worth Historical Society & Library • 131 E Exchange Ave, Ste 110 • Fort Worth, TX 76106-8213 • (817) 625-5082 • *Cowtown Dispatch*

Pruitt-Black Family Reunion • 7929 Hulen Park Cr • Fort Worth, TX 76123-1349 • (817) 295-6938

Seagull Productions • 4833 Collinwood #4 • Fort Worth, TX 76107 • *Cummings and Goings*

Stovall Family Association • 1717 Druid Ct • Fort Worth, TX 76112-3707 • (817) 457-5383 • http://www.geocities.com/tommy~stovall/sfa/ • *Stovall Journal*

Tarrant County Black Historical and Genealogical Society • 1004 Illinois Ave, P.O. Box 50483 • Fort Worth, TX 76105 • (817) 332-6049 • *Tarrant County Black Historical and Genealogical Society Newsletter*

Thistle Hill House Museum Archives • 1509 Pennsylvania Ave • Fort Worth, TX 76104 • (817) 336-1212

Vintage Flying Museum Archives • Meacham Intl Airport, 505 NW 38th St, Hangar 33S • Fort Worth, TX 76182 • (817) 624-1935

Frankston
Frankston Depot Library and Museum Archives • 102 E Railroad St, P.O. Box 639 • Frankston, TX 75763-0639 • (903) 876-4463

Fredercksburg
Fredericksburg Genealogical Society • 108 N Edison St • Fredercksburg, TX 78624-3220 • (830) 990-4045

Admiral Nimitz National Museum of the Pacific War Archives • 328 E Main St • Fredericksburg, TX 78624 • (830) 997-4379 • http://www.nimitz-museum.org

Atwood Descendants • 310 Heritage Hills Dr • Fredericksburg, TX 78624-5430 • (830) 648-8608

Denny Research • 2853 Ranch Rd 965 • Fredericksburg, TX 78624-6746 • http://www.bdonline.com • *Discovering Denny Descendents*

Gillespie County Historical Society and Commission & Library • 312 W San Antonio St, P.O. Box 765 • Fredericksburg, TX 78624 • (830) 997-2835 • http://www.pioneermuseum.com • *Der Trompeter*

Pioneer Museum and Vereins Kirche • 309 W Main St • Fredericksburg, TX 78624 • (830) 997-2835 • http://www.pioneermuseum.com • *Pioneer Museum Newsletter*

Freer
Alamo Defender Descendants • P.O. Box 856 • Freer, TX 78357 • (361) 394-5556

Friendswood
Friendswood Historical Society • 108 Skyview Terr • Friendswood, TX 77546 • (281) 482-7390

William Franklin Bennett Family Organization • 303 Westfield Ln • Friendswood, TX 77546 • (281) 482-7147

Friona
Ellis Cousins Nationwide • 1201 Maple Ave • Friona, TX 79035 • (806) 247-3053 • http://www.wtrt.net/~case/ • *Ellis Cousins Newsletter*

Fulton
Fulton Mansion State Historic Site Archives • 317 Fulton Beach Rd, P.O. Box 1859 • Fulton, TX 78358 • (361) 729-0386 • http://www.tpwd.state.tx.us/park/fulton/fulton.htm • *Fulton Mansion State Historic Site Newsletter*

Gainesville
Cooke County Heritage Society & Archives • Historical Museum, 210 S Dixon St, P.O. Box 150 • Gainesville, TX 76240 • (940) 668-8900 • http://www.mortonmuseum.org • *Heritage Highlights*

Cooke County Library • 200 S Weaver St • Gainesville, TX 76240-4790 • (940) 665-2401

Cross Timbers Genealogical Society & Library • P.O. Box 197 • Gainesville, TX 76240 • *Cross Timbers Post*

Gainesville Genealogical Group • c/o Cook County College • Gainesville, TX 76200

Galveston
Ashton Villa and Heritage Visitor's Center Archives • 2328 Broadway • Galveston, TX 77550 • (409) 762-3933 • http://www.galvestonhistory.org

Bishop's Palace Museum Archives • 1402 Broadway • Galveston, TX 77550 • (409) 762-2475

David Glenn Hunt Memorial Library • Galveston College, 4015 Avenue Q • Galveston, TX 77550 • (409) 763-6551 • http://www.gc.edu/library

Galveston County Genealogical Society & Archives • c/o Rosenburg Library, 2310 Sealy, P.O. Box 1141 • Galveston, TX 77550-1141 • (409) 763-8854 • http://129.109.166.17 • *Galveston County Genealogical Society Quarterly*

Galveston County Historical Society & Archives • Historical Museum, 2219 Market St • Galveston, TX 77550-1503 • (409) 766-2340 • http://www.galvestonhistory.org

Galveston Historical Foundation & Archives • Historical Museum, 502 20th St • Galveston, TX 77550 • (409) 765-7834 • http://www.galvestonhistory.org • *Galveston Historical Foundation Membership Update*

Jack K Williams Library • Texas A&M Univ, P.O. Box 1675 • Galveston, TX 77553 • (409) 740-4560

John Sydnor's 1847 Powhatan House Museum Archives • 3427 Avenue A • Galveston, TX 77550 • (409) 763-0077

Lone Star Flight Museum Archives • 2002 Terminal Dr • Galveston, TX 77554 • (409) 740-7722 • http://www.lsfm.org • *Lone Star Flight Museum Newsletter*

Moody Mansion Museum Archives • 2618 Broadway, P.O. Box 1300 • Galveston, TX 77553 • (409) 762-7668 • http://www.moodymansion.org • *Moody Mansion Museum Newsletter*

Ocean Star Offshore Drilling Rig and Museum Archives • 20th St & Harborside Dr, 2002 Wharf C • Galveston, TX 77553 • (281) 679-8040 • http://www.oceanstarvec.com • *Star*

Rosenberg Library and Museum • 2310 Sealy Ave • Galveston, TX 77550 • (409) 763-8854 • http://www.rosenberg-library.org

Texas Seaport Museum Archives • Pier 21, No 8 • Galveston, TX 77550-1631 • (409) 763-1877 • http://www.tsm-elissa.org • *Elissa Log*

Texas State Genealogical Society • 2505 Beluche Dr • Galveston, TX 77551

Garland
Early Family Association • 525 Ivy Way • Garland, TX 75043

Garland Genealogical Society • P.O. Box 461882 • Garland, TX 75046-1882 • http://www.geocities.com/TheTopics/1926/society.html • *Garland Genealogical Society Quarterly*; *Garland Genealogical Society Newsletter*

Grizzle Family Organization • 1229 Tanager • Garland, TX 75042

Nicholson Memorial Library • 625 Austin St • Garland, TX 75040-6365 • (972) 205-2500 • http://www.nmls.lib.tx.us • *Access*

Gatesville
Coryell County Genealogical Society & Archives • c/o Gatesville Public Library, 811 Main St • Gatesville, TX 76528 • (254) 865-5367 • *Coryell Kin*; *Coryell County Genealogical Society Quarterly*

Gatesville Public Library • 111 N 8th St • Gatesville, TX 76528 • (254) 865-5367 • http://gatesvillecitylibrary.org

George West
Grace Armantrout Museum Archives • Hwy 281 S, P.O. Box 248 • George West, TX 78022 • (361) 449-3325 • http://www.the-t.net/~armant

Live Oak County Library • 402 Houston St • George West, TX 78022 • (361) 449-1124 • http://www.bclib.org/liveoak/

Georgetown
Georgetown Public Library • 808 Martin Luther King St • Georgetown, TX 78626-5527 • (512) 930-3551 • http://www.georgetowntex.org

Giddings
Giddings Public Library • 276 N Orange St • Giddings, TX 78942-3317 • (979) 542-2716

Lee County Historical Commission • 282 S Grimes • Giddings, TX 78942

Texas Wendish Heritage Society & Library • Route 2, Box 311 • Giddings, TX 78942 • (979) 366-2441

Gilmer
Gilmer Genealogical Society • W Pine St • Gilmer, TX 75644

Upshur County Library • 702 W Tyler St • Gilmer, TX 75644 • (903) 843-5001

Gladewater
Lee Public Library • 312 W Pacific, P.O. Box 1753 • Gladewater, TX 75647-1753 • (903) 845-2640

Glen Rose
Bates Family of Old Virginia • P.O. Box 2640 • Glen Rose, TX 76043 • http://www.halcyondays.com • *Bates Booster*

Descendants of John Witt and Ann Daux • P.O. Box 2640 • Glen Rose, TX 76043 • http://www.witts-end.org • *Witt's End*

Floyd Research • P.O. Box 2640 • Glen Rose, TX 76043 • http://www.halcyondays.com • *Floyd Folks*

Halcyon Days • P.O. Box 2640 • Glen Rose, TX 76043 • http://www.halcyondays.com • *Harbour Light Newsletter*

Somervell County Historical Society & Archives • Somervell County Museum, Vernon & Elm Sts, P.O. Box 669 • Glen Rose, TX 76043 • (254) 897-2739

Goliad
Goliad County Library • 320 S Commercial St, P.O. Box 1025 • Goliad, TX 77963-1025 • (361) 645-2291

Goliad State Historical Park Archives • 108 Park Rd 6 • Goliad, TX 77963 • (361) 645-3405 • http://www.tpwd.state.tx.us

Presidio La Bahia Archives • Refugio Hwy 1, P.O. Box 57 • Goliad, TX 77963 • (512) 645-3752 • http://www.presidiolabahia.org

Gonzales
Gonzales County Archives • Hwy 90A, P.O. Box 80 • Gonzales, TX 78629

Gonzales County Historical Commission • P.O. Box 114 • Gonzales, TX 78629-0114

Gonzales Memorial Museum Archives • 414 Smith • Gonzales, TX 78629 • (830) 672-6350

Gonzales Public Library • 415 St Matthew, P.O. Box 220 • Gonzales, TX 78629-0220 • (830) 672-6315

Hallmark Reunion • 216 S Fair St • Gonzales, TX 78629-4317 • (830) 672-9830 • *Hallmark Historical Quarterly*

South Texas Genealogical Society • P.O. Box 768 • Gonzales, TX 78629-0768 • *Yesterdays*

Graham
Fort Belknap Genealogical Association • HC 60, Box 409 • Graham, TX 76046 • (940) 549-1856 • *Fort Belknap Genealogical Association Bulletin*

Graham Public Library • 910 Cherry St • Graham, TX 76450-3547 • (940) 549-0600 • http://www.libraryofgraham.org

Main Street Graham • 458 Oak St • Graham, TX 76450 • (940) 549-0401

Young County Historical Society • P.O. Box 218 • Graham, TX 76046

Granbury
Historic Granbury • 116 1/2 N Crockett St • Granbury, TX 76048 • (817) 573-2636

Historic Granbury Merchants Association • 109 W Pearl St • Granbury, TX 76048 • (817) 573-5299

Hood County Genealogical Society & Library • Granbury Depot, 109 Ewell St, P.O. Box 1623 • Granbury, TX 76048-8623 • (817) 573-2557 • http://www.hcnews.com/~ancestor • *Hood County Genealogical Society Newsletter*

Hood County Public Library • 222 N Travis • Granbury, TX 76048 • (817) 573-3569

Jackson Research • 4623 E Holiday Est Cr • Granbury, TX 76049 • *Jackson Cousins Newsletter*

Grand Prairie
Brixey Research • 2662 Carrington Ln • Grand Prairie, TX 75052-4006 • (972) 206-2723 • *Brixey Bulletin: A Family History Quarterly*

Dorman-McDorman Family Association • 14 W Mountain Ln • Grand Prairie, TX 75051

Duncan-Butler Family Association • 1410 Chester Dr • Grand Prairie, TX 75050 • (214) 262-4425

Grand Prairie Genealogical Society • P.O. Box 532026 • Grand Prairie, TX 75053-2036

Grand Prairie Historical Organization • 1516 W Main St • Grand Prairie, TX 75050 • (972) 237-0389

Grand Prairie Memorial Library • 901 Conover Dr • Grand Prairie, TX 75051 • (972) 237-5700

Witherspoon Family Association • 402 Campo Dr • Grand Prairie, TX 75051-4908 • (214) 264-5220 • *Tie That Binds Newsletter*

Grand Saline
Grand Saline Public Library • 201 E Pacific Ave • Grand Saline, TX 75140 • (903) 962-5516

Grapevine
Grapevine Historic Preservation • 200 S Main St • Grapevine, TX 76051 • (817) 410-3197

Grapevine Historical Society • P.O. Box 99 • Grapevine, TX 76099

Grapevine Name Droppers • c/o Grapevine Public Library, 1201 S Main • Grapevine, TX 76051 • (817) 481-0339

Grapevine Public Library • 1201 Municipal Wy • Grapevine, TX 76051 • (817) 410-3400 • http://www.grapevine.lib.tx.us

Greenville
American Cotton Museum Archives • 600 E I-30, P.O. Box 347 • Greenville, TX 75403 • (903) 454-1990 • http://www.cottonmuseum.com • *Compress*

Hunt County Genealogical Society • P.O. Box 398 • Greenville, TX 75401 • (903) 886-8690

W Walworth Harrison Public Library • 1 Lou Finney Ln • Greenville, TX 75401-5988 • (903) 457-2992

Groesbeck
Maffett Memorial Library • 601 W Yeagua St • Groesbeck, TX 76642-1697 • (254) 729-3667 • http://198.213.140.253

Groves
Master Copy Printing • 3522 Twin City Hwy • Groves, TX 77619 • (409) 963-2679 • Gilmore, Gilmer, Gilmour, Gillmore Genealogical Newsletter

Hale Center
Hale Center Public Library • 609 Main St, P.O. Box 214 • Hale Center, TX 79041-0214 • (806) 839-2055

Hallettsville
French Simpson Memorial Library • 705 E 4th St • Hallettsville, TX 77964-2828 • (361) 798-3243

Haltom City
Birdville Historical Society • P.O. Box 14246 • Haltom City, TX 76117

Haltom City Public Library • 3201 Friendly Ln, P.O. Box 14277 • Haltom City, TX 76117-0277 • (817) 222-7786 • http://www.haltomcitytx.com • *Booknotes*

Hamilton
Central Texas Research Center • 209 W Henry • Hamilton, TX 76531 • (254) 386-4566 • http://207.17.189.3:80/hcgs

Hamilton County Genealogical Society & Archives • c/o Central Texas Research Center, 209 W Henry St, P.O. Box 20 • Hamilton, TX 76531 • (254) 386-4566 • http://207.17.189.3:80/hcgs • *Hamilton County Genealogical Society Family Circle Journal*

Harlingen
Harlingen Public Library • 410 76th Dr • Harlingen, TX 78550 • (956) 430-6650 • http://www.ci.harlingen.tx.us/library/htm

Mitchell Family Association • 2619 Cypress St • Harlingen, TX 78550-8525 • *Mitchell Family Association Newsletter*

Rio Grande Valley Museum Archives • Boxwood & Raintree • Harlingen, TX 78550 • (956) 430-8500 • http://www.hiline.net/rgvmuse/

Tip O'Texas Genealogical Society & Archives • c/o Harlingen Public Library, 410 76th Dr • Harlingen, TX 78550-5072 • (956) 430-6650 • *Genealogical Tips*

Haskell

Haskell County Genealogical Society • 300 N Avenue E • Haskell, TX 79521

Haskell County Library • 412 N 1st St • Haskell, TX 79521 • (940) 864-2747

Helotes

Helotes Historical Society • 14418 Old Bandera Rd • Helotes, TX 78023-3702 • (210) 695-3686

Hemphill

J R Huffman Public Library • Hwy 87 N, Rte 5 Box 2140 • Hemphill, TX 75948-9695 • (409) 787-4829 • http://www.toledo-bend.net/library

Virgie Speights Memorial Library & Museum Archives • 1 Hwy 83 • Hemphill, TX 75948 • (409) 787-4757

Hempstead

Waller County Library • 2331 11th St • Hempstead, TX 77445-6724 • (979) 836-7658

Henderson

Rusk County Genealogical Society • P.O. Box 1314 • Henderson, TX 75653

Rusk County Historical Association & Archives • Howard-Dickinson House Museum, 501 S Main St, P.O. Box 2434 • Henderson, TX 75652 • (903) 657-6925

Rusk County Historical Commission • Depot Museum, 514 N High St • Henderson, TX 75652 • (903) 657-2261 • http://www.depotmuseum.com • *Telegram*

Rusk County Memorial Library • 106 E Main St • Henderson, TX 75652 • (903) 657-8557 • http://www.rclib.org • *County Line*

Henrietta

Clay County Historical Society • 100 N Bridge St • Henrietta, TX 76365

Hereford

Deaf Smith County Genealogical Society • c/o Deaf Smith County Library, 211 E 4th St • Hereford, TX 79045 • (806) 364-1206

Deaf Smith County Historical Society & Archives • Historical Museum, 400 Sampson, P.O. Box 1007 • Hereford, TX 79045 • (806) 363-7070 • *Deaf Smith County Historical Society Newsletter*

Deaf Smith County Library • 211 E 4th St • Hereford, TX 79045 • (806) 364-1206 • http://www.hlc-lib.org/hereford

Deaf Smith County Museum Archives • 400 Sampson, P.O. Box 1007 • Hereford, TX 79045 • (806) 363-7070 • http://www.deafsmithcountymuseum.org • *Deaf Smithsonian*

Hidalgo

Old Hidalgo Pumphouse Archives • 902 S 2nd St • Hidalgo, TX 78557 • (956) 843-8686 • http://www.hidalgotexas.com

Hillsboro

Hill College Library • 112 Lamar, P.O. Box 619 • Hillsboro, TX 76645-0619 • (254) 582-2555 • http://www.hill-college.cc.tx.us/library

Hill County Genealogical Society • 1019 E Elm • Hillsboro, TX 76645

Hill County Genealogical Society & Archives • c/o Hillsboro City Library, 118 S Waco St, P.O. Box 636 • Hillsboro, TX 76645 • (254) 582-7385 • *Hill County Crossroads*

Hillsboro City Library • 118 S Waco St • Hillsboro, TX 76645 • (254) 582-7385

Hood's Texas Brigade Association & Archives • Heritage Museum, 112 Lamar Dr, P.O. Box 619 • Hillsboro, TX 76645 • (254) 582-2555 • http://www.hillcollege.edu • *Valor*

Jennings Surname Organization • 200 Walnut Hill Ave #4 • Hillsboro, TX 76645-9521 • (254) 582-8988

Hooks

Hooks Public Library • 108 W 1st St, P.O. Box 1540 • Hooks, TX 75561-1540 • (903) 547-3365

Houston

Afro-American Historical and Genealogical Society, Houston Chapter • P.O. Box 750877 • Houston, TX 77275-0877

Asa Lafitte Stark Family Association • 239 Deerfield • Houston, TX 77022-6103 • (713) 697-7874

Athy Tribe of Galway • 3834 Overbrook Ln • Houston, TX 77027 • (713) 622-1480 • *Newsletter of the Athy Tribe of Galway*

Barton-Cornell-Couch-Deroun-Dillard-Donley-Graf(f)-Harrison-Hefner Research • 12600 Bissonnet A4-407 • Houston, TX 77099 • *Barton Banner*; *Cornell Crier*; *Couch Genealogist*; *Deroun Diplomat*; *Dillard Doorways*; *Donley Directory*; *Graf(f) Gazette*; *Harrison Herald*; *Hefner Handbook*

Baul Reunion • 2210 Wavell St • Houston, TX 77088 • (281) 448-6036

Bear Creek Genealogical Society • 1438 Crescent Green Dr • Houston, TX 77094 • (713) 465-2483

Bellaire Genealogical Society • 6445 Sewanee • Houston, TX 77006

Breeding-Breeden Genealogical Exchange • 8311 Braesview Ln • Houston, TX 77071-1231 • (713) 777-8920 • Breeding-Breeden Genealogical Exchange Newsletter

Buffalo Soldiers National Museum Archives • 1834 Southmore • Houston, TX 77004 • (713) 942-8920 • http://www.buffalosoldiermuseum.com

Cantor Rubin Kaplan Memorial Library • Congregation Beth Yeshurun, 4525 Beechnut Blvd • Houston, TX 77096 • (713) 666-1884

Chapman Family Association • 770 S Post Oak Ln #435 • Houston, TX 77056-1913 • http://www.chapman family.com • *Chapman Family Association Newsletter*

Clan Brodie Association • 2601 S Braeswood #701 • Houston, TX 77025

Clan MacLeod Society USA • 7618 Twin Hills Dr • Houston, TX 77071-1418 • (713) 772-1492 • *Clan MacLeod Newsletter*; *Clan MacLeod Magazine*

Clan Matheson Society • 12126 Rhett Dr • Houston, TX 77024 • (713) 465-8519 • *Clan Matheson Society Newsletter*

Clayton Library for Genealogical Research • 5300 Caroline • Houston, TX 77004 • (713) 284-1999 • http://sparc.hpl.lib.tx.us/hpl/clayton.html

Clayton Library Friends • 5300 Caroline, P.O. Box 271078 • Houston, TX 77277-1078 • (713) 284-1999 • http://sparc.hpl.lib.tx.us/hpl/clayton.html • *Clayton Library Friends Fact Sheet*

Crocheron Family Organization • 4114 Woodhaven • Houston, TX 77025 • *Crocheron Family Newsletter*

DeArman, De Arman Family Organization • 2525 Nantucket #4 • Houston, TX 77057 • (713) 782-1557

Dennard Heritage • 5422 Fairdale Ln • Houston, TX 77056-6607 • (713) 621-8886 • *Dennard Newsletter*

Doctor Edwin E Lehr Library • San Jacinto College North, 5800 Uvalde Rd • Houston, TX 77049-4589 • (281) 459-7116

Edler-Morosini Research • 12402 Woodthorpe Ln • Houston, TX 77024-4109 • (713) 461-7437 • *Edler-Morosini Newsletter*

Fambrough Family Society of America • 4411 Ram Ct • Houston, TX 77072 • *Fambrough Family Society of America Newsletter*

Fite Database • 2525 Nantucket #4 • Houston, TX 77057 • (713) 782-1557

Fondren Library • Rice Univ, 6100 S Main St-MS-44, P.O. Box 1892 • Houston, TX 77251-1892 • (713) 348-5113 • http://riceinfo.rice.edu/fondren/

Greater Houston Jewish Genealogical Society • 7115 Belle Park Dr • Houston, TX 77072-2417 • (281) 495-9211

Hames Heritage • 14515 Wunderlich Dr #211 • Houston, TX 77069 • (281) 583-8878

Harris County Heritage Society & Archives • Historical Museum, 1100 Bagby St • Houston, TX 77002 • (713) 655-1912 • http://www.heritagesociety.org • *Panorama*

Harris County Public Library • 8080 El Rio St • Houston, TX 77054-4195 • (713) 749-9000 • http://www.hcpl.net

Hiner Reunion Association of TX • 11811 S Willowdale Cr • Houston, TX 77071 • *Hiner News Bulletin*

Hispanic Genealogical Society • 2932 Barksdale, P.O. Box 231271 • Houston, TX 77223-1271 • http://www.brokersys.com/~joguerra/ • *Hispanic Genealogical Journal*

Hollinquest-Stinson Family Organization • 14334 Lourdes Dr • Houston, TX 77049 • (281) 458-2650

Holocaust Museum Houston Archives • 5401 Caroline St • Houston, TX 77004 • (713) 942-8000 • http://www.hmh.org • *Holocaust Museum Houston Newsletter*

Houston Academy of Medicine Historical Research Center Archives • Texas Medical Center, 1133 M.D. Anderson Blvd • Houston, TX 77030-2809 • (713) 795-5183

Houston Fire Museum Archives • 2403 Milam St • Houston, TX 77066 • (713) 524-2526 • http://www.houstonfiremuseum.org • *Leather Bucket*

Houston Genealogical Forum & Library • P.O. Box 271466 • Houston, TX 77277-1466 • (281) 481-3636 • *Genealogical Bulletin*; *Genealogical Record*

Houston Metropolitan Research Center • c/o Houston Public Library, 500 McKinney Ave • Houston, TX 77002 • (713) 247-3557 • *Houston Review: History and Culture of the Gulf Coast*

Houston Police Museum Archives • 17000 Aldine Westfield Rd • Houston, TX 77073 • (281) 230-2360

Houston Polish Genealogical Society • 3606 Maroneal • Houston, TX 77025

Houston Public Library • 500 McKinney Ave • Houston, TX 77002-2534 • (832) 393-1313 • http://www.houstonlibrary.org

Hull Family Register • 4411 Ram Ct • Houston, TX 77072 • *Hull Family Register*

International Society of Family History Writers and Editors • 1001 W Loop North • Houston, TX 77055 • (713) 684-4633 • http://www.rootsweb.com/~cgc/ • *CGC Columns*

John P McGovern Museum of Health and Medical Science • 1515 Hermann Dr • Houston, TX 77004 • (713) 942-7364 • http://www.mhms.org • *John P McGovern Museum Newsletter*

Jouett Family Reunion • 2518 Peppermill • Houston, TX 77080 • (713) 973-8262

Ladd-Landry-Lewis-Mallory-McNair-Mercer-Moon-Morey-Oliver- Praters-Pulliam-Reece-Reed Research • 12600 Bissonnet A4-407 • Houston, TX 77099 • *Ladd Leads*; *Landry Leader*; *Lewis Listings*; *Mallory Memorabilia*; *McNair Memories*; *Mercer Family Historian Newsletter*; *Moon Tribune*; *Morey Maximum Reader*; *Oliver Orator*; *Praters in my Pocket*; *Pulliam Point*; *Reece's Pieces*; *Reed Review*

Lockhart Family Association • 2476 Bolsover St #295 • Houston, TX 77005-2518 • *Lockhart Letters*

M D Anderson Library • University of Houston, 114 University Libraries • Houston, TX 77204-2000 • (713) 743-9800 • http://www.uh.edu

Martin-Barnett Genealogical Co • 4314 Nenana Dr • Houston, TX 77035-3624 • *Genealogical Compendium of Books and Articles in Print*

McAllister-Carson-Harvey-Lindsay Family Association • 2306 Westgate • Houston, TX 77019 • (713) 529-2333

Moody Memorial Library • Houston Baptist University, 7502 Fondren Rd • Houston, TX 77074-3298 • (281) 649-3435 • http://moody.hbu.edu

National Grigsby Family Society • 10138 Valley Forge • Houston, TX 77042 • (713) 789-5766 • http://www.grigsby.org • *National Grigsby Family Society Newsletter*

National Museum of Funeral History Archives • 233 Barren Springs Dr • Houston, TX 77090 • (281) 876-2063 • http://www.nmfh.org

Noxon Family Association • 5810 Windsong Trails Dr • Houston, TX 77084 • *Noxontalk*

Parker Williams Library • San Jacinto College South, 13735 Beamer Rd • Houston, TX 77089-6099 • (281) 922-3416

Rothko Chapel Museum Archives • 1409 Sul Ross • Houston, TX 77006 • (713) 524-7461 • http://www.rothkochapel.org

Rugeley Family Association • 7614 River Point Dr • Houston, TX 77063 • (713) 465-8228 • *RUGFAN: Rugeley Family Association Newsletter*

Scott-Shoemaker-Shurtliff Research • 12600 Bissonnet A4-407 • Houston, TX 77099 • *Scott Searcher*, *Shoemaker Signpost Family Newsletter*, *Shurtliff Signatures*

Southern Historical Association • Rice Univ, 6100 Main St, P.O. Box 1892 • Houston, TX 77251 • (713) 348-6039 • http://www.jastor.org • *Journal of Southern History*

Space Center Houston Archives • 1601 NASA Road 1 • Houston, TX 77058 • (281) 244-2105 • http://www.spacecenter.org

Spire Historic Building Archives • 820 Fannin St • Houston, TX 77002 • (713) 227-1650

Tejas Publications and Research • 2507 Tannehill Dr • Houston, TX 77008-3052 • (713) 864-6862 • *Beverly Family Records Newsletter*, *Tejas Gazette*

Texas State Afro-American Genealogical Society • P.O. Box 670045 • Houston, TX 77267-0045

Weese Research • 1901 Driscoll St • Houston, TX 77019-6101 • *Weese Family Newsletter*

Weese Research • 6602 Westchester • Houston, TX 77005-3756 • (713) 664-3429 • *Weese Family Newsletter*

Whitworth Reunion • 1838 Cheshire Ln • Houston, TX 77018-4014 • (713) 688-1060

Zilliox-Marshall Family of Clearfield, Pennsylvania • 4063 Heathersage • Houston, TX 77084

Huffman

Childress-Childers Family Organization • 1321 Gum Tree • Huffman, TX 77336 • (281) 324-3797 • *Childress Chatter*

Johnson-Rogers-Bell Research • 1321 Gum Tree • Huffman, TX 77336 • (281) 324-3797 • *Johnson Quarterly*, *Rogers Roots*; *Three Bells*

Jonathon Milton Long Family Association • 1514 Fall Creek • Huffman, TX 77336 • (281) 324-2698

Humble

Castor Association of America • 2711 Eagle Nest Ln • Humble, TX 77396-1887 • *News Caster*

Humble Genealogical Society • 1700 Mustang Tr, P.O. Box 2723 • Humble, TX 77347-2723 • (281) 358-3062 • *Humble Genealogist*

James Herbert Bradley Family Organization • 2731 Golden Leaf Dr • Humble, TX 77339-1911

Huntsville

H.E.A.R.T.S. Veterans Museum of Texas Archives • 1600 Financial Plaza, Ste 200, P.O. Box 6060 • Huntsville, TX 77342 • (936) 295-5959 • http://www.heartsmuseum.com

Huntsville Public Library • 1216 14th St • Huntsville, TX 77340 • (936) 291-5470 • http://www.huntsville.lib.tx.us

Newton Gresham Library • Sam Houston State University, 1830 Bobby K Marks Dr, P.O. Box 2281 • Huntsville, TX 77341-2281 • (936) 294-1614 • http://www.shsu.edu/~lib_www/

Sam Houston Memorial Museum Archives • 1836 San Houston Ave, P.O. Box 2057 SHSU • Huntsville, TX 77341 • (936) 294-1832 • http://www.samhouston.memorial.museum

Texas Prison Museum Archives • 491 State Hwy 75 N • Huntsville, TX 77320

Walker County Genealogical Society • c/o Huntsville Public Library, 1216 14th St, P. O. Box 1295 • Huntsville, TX 77342-1295 • (936) 291-5472

Walker County Genealogical Society • 254 Willowbend, P.O. Box 1295 • Huntsville, TX 77342-1295

Hurst
Hackleman Reunion • 729 Grapevine Hwy, Ste 204 • Hurst, TX 76054-2805 • *Hackleman Newsletter*

Hurst Public Library • 901 Precinct Line Rd • Hurst, TX 76053 • (817) 788-7300 • http://www.hurst.lib.tx.us

McKenzie-McKenzie Reunion • 401 Mayfair Ct • Hurst, TX 76054 • (817) 268-2121

Richard Pratt Family of AL • P.O. Box 582 • Hurst, TX 76053 • (817) 282-5293

Ingleside
Ingleside Public Library • 2775 Waco St, P.O. Drawer 400 • Ingleside, TX 78362-0400 • (361) 776-5355

Ingram
Shelby Research • HCR 78, Box 234 • Ingram, TX 78025-9704 • *Shelby Exchange*

Iowa Park
Tom Burnett Memorial Library • 400 W Alameda • Iowa Park, TX 76367 • (940) 592-4981

Iraan
Iraan Museum Archives • 1000 Park Side St, P.O. Box 183 • Iraan, TX 79744 • (915) 639-2522

Irving
Irving Genealogical Society • P.O. Box 170881 • Irving, TX 75017-0881 • (972) 264-5183 • http://www.rootsweb.com/~txigs/ • *Irving Genealogical Society Newsletter*

Irving Public Library • 801 W Irving Blvd, P.O. Box 152288 • Irving, TX 75015-2288 • (972) 721-2639 • http://www.irvinglibrary.org

Ledford Clearinghouse • 702 Fouts Ave • Irving, TX 75061 • (2972 790-9030

Matilda Talbert-DeLaney-Perkins International • P.O. Box 167365 • Irving, TX 75016-7365

National Scouting Museum Archives • 1329 W Walnut Hill Ln • Irving, TX 75015 • (972) 580-2100 • http://www.bsamuseum.org • *Bridges & Trails*

Jacksboro
Fort Richardson State Historical Park Archives • 228 Park Rd 61 • Jacksboro, TX 76458 • (940) 567-3506 • http://www.tpwd.state.tx.us

Jack County Historical Society • 100 N Main St • Jacksboro, TX 76056

Jacksonville
Cherokee County Genealogical Society • P.O. Box 1332 • Jacksonville, TX 75766 • (903) 586-9067 • *Tree Talk*

Jacksonville Public Library • 502 S Jackson St • Jacksonville, TX 75766 • (903) 586-7664 • http://www.jacksonvillelibrary.com

Simon & Louise Henderson Library • Lon Morris College, 800 College Ave • Jacksonville, TX 75766 • (903) 589-4027 • http://library.lonmorris.edu

Jasper
Franklin Family Researchers United • 736 Dogwood St • Jasper, TX 75951-5826 • (409) 543-2883 • *Franklin Family Researchers United Newsletter*

Pace Society of America • 699 W Verna • Jasper, TX 75951 • *Pace Bulletin*

Jayton
Clark Family Organization • Route 3, Box 86 • Jayton, TX 79528

Harrison-Pounds Reunion • Route 3, Box 67 • Jayton, TX 79528

Kent County Genealogical Society • P.O. Box 414 • Jayton, TX 79528

Jefferson
Excelsior House Museum Archives • 211 W Austin St • Jefferson, TX 75657 • (903) 665-2513

Historic Jefferson Foundation • 305 W Lafayette St • Jefferson, TX 75657 • (903) 665-7064

Historic Jefferson Railway • 400 E Austin St • Jefferson, TX 75657 • (903) 665-6400

Jefferson Historical Society & Archives • Historical Museum, 223 W Austin St • Jefferson, TX 75657 • (903) 665-2775

Marion County Genealogical Society • 301 W Lafayette St, P.O. Box 224 • Jefferson, TX 75657-0224 • *Marion County Genealogical Society Quarterly*

Johnson City
Johnson City Library • 209 Nugent St, P.O. Box 332 • Johnson City, TX 78636-0332 • (830) 868-4469 • http://www.moment.net/~jclib/

Lyndon B Johnson National Historical Park Library • 390 Lady Bird Ln, P.O. Box 329 • Johnson City, TX 78636-0329 • (830) 868-7128 • http://www.nps.gov/lyjo • *LBJ Country*

Jourdanton
Jourdanton Community Library • 1101 Campbell St • Jourdanton, TX 78026 • (830) 769-3087

Junction
Kimble County Historical Museum Archives • 101 N 4th St, P.O. Box 271 • Junction, TX 76849 • (915) 446-4219 • http://www.junctiontexas.net/museum.htm

Kimble County Library • 208 N 10th St • Junction, TX 76849 • (915) 446-2342

Katy
Boggess Family Association • 23302 Fairbranch Dr • Katy, TX 77494 • (281) 395-1136 • *Boggess Family Association Newsletter*

Keene
Chan Shun Centennial Library • Southwestern Adventist University, 101 W Magnolia St • Keene, TX 76059 • (817) 645-3921 • http://www.library.swau.edu

Keller
Keller Public Library • 640 Johnson Rd • Keller, TX 76248 • (817) 431-9011 • http://www.kellerlib.org

Kenedy
Karnes County Library • 303 W Main St • Kenedy, TX 78119 • (830) 583-3313

Kermit
Winkler County Library • 307 S Poplar St • Kermit, TX 79745-4300 • (915) 586-3841

Kerrville
Butt-Holdsworth Memorial Library • 505 Water St • Kerrville, TX 78028 • (830) 257-8422 • http://www.bhmlibrary.org

Hill Country Preservation Society & Archives • Hill Country Museum, 226 Earl Garrett St, P.O. Box 107 • Kerrville, TX 78029 • (830) 896-8633

Kerrville Genealogical Society & Archives • c/o Butt-Holdsworth Memorial Library, 505 Water St • Kerrville, TX 78028 • (830) 257-8422 • http://www.ktc.net/kgs/ • *Kerr Trails*

MacEacain Family Association of North America • 703 Tanglewood Ln • Kerrville, TX 78028 • (830) 895-5419 • *Our Family*

Ribble of NY, VA and KY Descendants • 108 Wood Dr • Kerrville, TX 78029 • (210) 257-8249

W M Logan Library • Schreiner University, 2100 Memorial Blvd • Kerrville, TX 78028-5697 • (830) 792-7312 • http://library.schreiner.edu

Kilgore
Daniel McKinney-Valentine Corley Family Organization • 608 Hunter • Kilgore, TX 75662 • (903) 984-7564

East Texas Oil Museum Archives • Kilgore College, Hwy 259 & Ross St • Kilgore, TX 75062 • (903) 983-8295 • http://www.easttexasoilmuseum.com

Henson-Cartwright Cousins • 3321 Danville Dr #106 • Kilgore, TX 75662-5723

Randolph C Watson Library • Kilgore College, 1100 Broadway • Kilgore, TX 75662 • (903) 983-8237 • http://blc1.kilgore.cc.tx.us/kclibrary

Stokely National Reunion • 100 Parkview • Kilgore, TX 75662

Killeen
Jacques Emanuel Deroques Family Organization • 1404 Leader Dr • Killeen, TX 76542

Killeen Public Library • 205 E Church Ave • Killeen, TX 76541-4898 • (254) 501-8991 • http://www.ci.killeen.tx.us/publiclibrary

West Bell Genealogical Society • P.O. Box 851 • Killeen, TX 76540 • (254) 699-2143 • *Bel County Genealogist*

Kingsland
Kingsland Genealogical Society • P.O. Box 952 • Kingsland, TX 78639

Kingsville
James C Jernigan Library • Texas A&M Univ, 700 University Blvd, MSC 197 • Kingsville, TX 78363-8202 • (361) 593-3416 • http://www.tamuk.edu • *Jernigan Journal*

John E Conner Museum Archives • Texas A&M Univ, P.O. Box 2172, Sta 1 • Kingsville, TX 78363 • (361) 593-2810 • *John E Conner Museum Newsletter*

Naval Air Station Library • 904 Dealy Ave, Suite 110 • Kingsville, TX 78363-5034 • (361) 516-6271

Robert J Kleberg Public Library • 220 N 4th St • Kingsville, TX 78363-6309 • (361) 592-6381

Kountze
Big Thicket Genealogical Club • P.O. Box 1260 • Kountze, TX 77625

Genealogical Research Center and Library of Southeast Texas • Route 1, Box 405 • Kountze, TX 77625 • *International Genealogical Exchange*

Piney Woods Pioneer Genealogical Society • c/o Genealogical Research Center and Library of Southeast Texas, Route 1, Box 405 • Kountze, TX 77625

La Grange
Fayette Heritage Museum Archives • 855 S Jefferson • La Grange, TX 78945 • (979) 968-6418 • http://lagrange.fais.net/library/museum.html

Fayette Public Library • 855 S Jefferson • La Grange, TX 78945 • (979) 968-3765 • http://lagrange.fais.net/library/library.html

Nathaniel W Faison Home Museum Archives • 440 N Jefferson • La Grange, TX 78945 • (979) 968-8567

La Porte
Battleship Texas State Historic Park Archives • 3527 Battleground Rd, 3527 Hwy 134 • La Porte, TX 77571 • (281) 479-2411 • http://www.ipwd.state.tx.us • Dreadnought

La Porte Library • 600 S Broadway St • La Porte, TX 77571 • (281) 471-4022

San Jacinto Museum of History Archives • 1 Monument Cr • La Porte, TX 77571-9585 • (281) 479-2421 • http://www.sanjacinto-museum.org • *San Jacinto Museum of History Newsletter*

La Vernia
La Vernia Historical Association • P.O. Box 513 • La Vernia, TX 78221

Lackland AFB
History and Traditions Museum Archives • 37 TRW/MU, Bldg 5206, 2051 George Ave • Lackland AFB, TX 78236-5218 • (210) 671-3055

Ladonia
Ladonia Historical Preservation Society • 101 S Depot St • Ladonia, TX 75449-1411 • (903) 367-7216

Lake Jackson
Brazosport Genealogical Society • 500 College Dr, P.O. Box 813 • Lake Jackson, TX 77566 • http://www.brazosport.cc.tx.us/~gensoc

Lake Jackson Historical Museum Archives • 249 Circle Wy, P.O. Box 242 • Lake Jackson, TX 77566 • (979) 297-1570 • http://www.lakejacksonmusem.org • *Lake Jackson Historical Museum Newsletter*

Lake Kiowa
Bogan Family Association • 107 Noweta • Lake Kiowa, TX 76240

Lamesa
Dal-Paso Musuem Archives • 310 S 1st St, P.O. Box 1445 • Lamesa, TX 79331 • (806) 872-5007

Dawson County Public Library • 511 N 3rd St, P.O. Box 1264 • Lamesa, TX 79331-1264 • (806) 872-6502 • http://www.dclib.lib.tx.us

Lamesa Area Genealogical Society & Archives • c/o Dawson County Public Library, 511 N 3rd St, P.O. Box 1264 • Lamesa, TX 79331-1264 • (806) 872-6502 • *Lamesa Area Genealogical Society Bulletin*; *Threads of Life*

Mountjoy Data Base • P.O. Box 459 • Lamesa, TX 79331 • (806) 872-3603

Sprayberry-Spraberry-Sprabary Family Association • P.O. Box 1204 • Lamesa, TX 79331 • (806) 872-5503

Lancaster
Lancaster Genealogical Society • 220 Main St • Lancaster, TX 75146

Lancaster Public Library • 1600 Veterans Memorial Pkwy • Lancaster, TX 75134 • (972) 227-1080 • http://www.lancastertxlib.org

Langtry
Judge Roy Bean Visitor Center Archives • Hwy 93 W, Loop 25, P.O. Box 160 • Langtry, TX 78871 • (432) 291-3340 • http://www.dot.state.tx.us

Laredo
Harold R Yeary Library • Laredo Community College, West End Washington St • Laredo, TX 78040-4348 • (956) 721-5274 • http://www.laredo.edu • *Yeary Library Tidings Newsletter*

Laredo Public Library • 1120 E Calton Rd • Laredo, TX 78041 • (956) 795-2400 • http://laredolibrary.org

Webb County Heritage Foundation & Library • 500 Flores Ave, P.O. Box 446 • Laredo, TX 78042-0046 • (956) 727-0977 • *Heritage Register*

League City
JewishGen • 2951 Marina Bay Dr, Ste 130-472 • League City, TX 77573 • (713) 940-0605 • http://www.jewishgen.org

League City Genealogical Society • 302 Oak Forest Dr • League City, TX 77573 • (281) 554-7355

Leakey
Hassell Family Research Association • FM 1120 Saddle Mountain Rd, P.O. Box 1184 • Leakey, TX 78873-1184 • (830) 232-5038

Ledbetter
Lee County Genealogical Society • Route 1, Box 8 D • Ledbetter, TX 78946

Leon Valley
Leon Valley Public Library • 6425 Evers Rd • Leon Valley, TX 78238-1453 • (210) 684-0720 • http://www.leonvalley.lib.tx.us

Leonard
Tri-County Genealogical Society & Library • Connett & Thomas Sts, P.O. Box 107 • Leonard, TX 75452-0107 • (903) 587-2246 • *Tri-County Newsletter*

Levelland
Hockley County Memorial Library • 811 Austin St • Levelland, TX 79336 • (806) 894-6750

Lewisville
Lewisville Public Library • 1197 W Main, P.O. Box 299002 • Lewisville, TX 75029-9002 • (972) 219-3570 • http://www.library.cityoflewisville.com/

Liberty
Atascosito Historical Society & Library • P.O. Box 4003 • Liberty, TX 77575-4003 • (936) 336-7542 • *Sam Houston Regional Library and Research Center News*

Liberty Municipal Library • 1710 Sam Houston Ave • Liberty, TX 77575-4741 • (936) 336-8901

Sam Houston Regional Library • Texas State Library & Archives Commission, 650 FM 1011, P.O. Box 310 • Liberty, TX 77575-0310 • (936) 336-8821 • http://www.tsl.state.tx.us

Sam Houston Regional Library and Research Center • 1011 Governors Rd, P.O. Box 310 • Liberty, TX 77575 • (936) 336-8821 • http://link.tsl.state.tx.us

Lindale

Wilson, Sunderhaus and Trugstad Families of Ohio and Michigan • P.O. Box 893 • Lindale, TX 75771-0893 • (903) 886-5915

Littlefield

Lamb County Library • 232 Phelps • Littlefield, TX 79339 • (806) 385-5223

Llano Estacado Genealogical Society • 1313 W 9th St • Littlefield, TX 79339

Livingston

Hardwick-Hornbeck Hunting • 101 Rainbow Drive, #643 Route 5, Box 310-0677-643 • Livingston, TX 77351 • *Hardwick Hunting; Hornbeck Hunting*

Murphy Memorial Library • 601 W Church St • Livingston, TX 77351 • (409) 327-4252 • http://www.murphymemlib.org

Polk County Heritage Society • 120 Mockingbird Lane • Livingston, TX 77351 • (936) 327-3336

Polk County Historical Commission & Archives • Memorial Museum, 514 W Mill St • Livingston, TX 77351 • (936) 327-8192 • http://www.livingston.net/museum

Llano

Llano County Public Library • 102 E Haynie • Llano, TX 78643 • (915) 247-5248 • http://www.llano-library-system.net

Lockhart

Dr Eugene Clark Library • 217 S Main St, P.O. Box 209 • Lockhart, TX 78644-0209 • (512) 398-3223 • http://www.library.ci.lockhart.tx.us

Longview

Beall Family • 416 Delano • Longview, TX 75604 • (903) 297-3470 • http://www.rootsweb.com/~auntjean/families/beallfam.htm

Comer-Bowater-John Allen-Wagley-Scarlett Surname Organization • P.O. Box 8072 • Longview, TX 75607-8072 • (903) 757-8474

Dent Family Research Center • 416 Delano • Longview, TX 75604 • (903) 297-3470 • http://www.rootsweb.com/~auntjean/dent/

Gregg County Genealogical Society • c/o Longview Public Library, 222 W Cotton, P.O. Box 2985 • Longview, TX 75606-2985 • (903) 237-1350 • http://www.chrysalis.org/DallasGen.So/gcgs.htm • *Gregg County Genealogical Society Newsletter*

Gregg County Historical and Genealogical Society & Archives • Historical Museum, 214 N Fredonia, P.O. Box 2985 • Longview, TX 75606-2985 • (903) 753-5840 • http://www.gregghistorical.org • *Gregg County Historical Museum Newsletter*

Longview Public Library • 222 W Cotton St • Longview, TX 75601-6348 • (903) 237-1354 • http://www.longview.lib.tx.us

Shivers Research • 802 Camille Dr • Longview, TX 75605 • *Shivers Newsletter*

Lubbock

Gowen Research Foundation • 5708 Gary Ave • Lubbock, TX 79413 • (806) 795-8758 • http://freepages.genealogy.rootsweb.com/~gowenrf/netscape.html • *Gowen Research Foundation Newsletter*

Harbour-Witt Family Association • 7904 Joliet Ave • Lubbock, TX 79423-1720 • (806) 795-5136 • *Harbour-Witt Family Association Bulletin*

Lubbock Heritage Society • P.O. Box 5443 • Lubbock, TX 79417

Lubbock Public Library • 1306 9th St • Lubbock, TX 79401 • (806) 775-2834 • http://www.lubbocklibrary.com • *Between the Stacks*

Museum of Texas Tech University Archives • 3301 4th St, P.O. Box 43191 • Lubbock, TX 79409 • (806) 742-2442 • http://www.museum.ttu.edu • *MuseNews*

Silent Wings Museum Archives • 6202 N I-27 • Lubbock, TX 79423 • (806) 775-2047 • http://www.silentwingsmuseum.com • *Museum News*

South Plains Genealogical Society & Library • 4215 University Ave, P.O. Box 6607 • Lubbock, TX 79493-6607 • (806) 747-1319 • *Family Research Directory; South Plains Genealogical Society Newsletter*

Texas Data Books • 2410 47th St • Lubbock, TX 79412 • *Benson Magazine of Research*

Texas State Genealogical Society • 2107 54th St • Lubbock, TX 79412-2610 • (254) 778-2073 • http://www.rootsweb.com/~txsgs/tsgs.html • *Stirpes*

Texas Tech University Library • Southwest Collection Special Collections Library, P.O. Box 41041 • Lubbock, TX 79409-1041 • (806) 742-3676 • http://www.lib.ttu.edu; swco.ttu.edu • *Southwest Chronicle*; *Library News*

Lufkin

Angelina County Genealogical Society • P.O. Box 150631 • Lufkin, TX 75915-0631 • *Echoes Through the Pines*

Kurth Memorial Library • 706 S Raguet • Lufkin, TX 75904 • (936) 630-0560 • http://www.kurthmemoriallibrary.com

Lufkin Genealogical and Historical Society • 1008 Reen, P.O. Box 150631 • Lufkin, TX 75915-0631

Museum of East Texas Archives • 503 N 2nd St • Lufkin, TX 75901 • (936) 639-4434 • *Museum of East Texas Newsletter*

Texas Forestry Museum Archives • 1905 Atkinson Dr • Lufkin, TX 75901 • (936) 632-9535 • http://www.treetexas.com • *Crosscut*

Luling

Genealogical and Historical Society of Caldwell County • c/o Luling Public Library, 215 S Pecan Ave • Luling, TX 78648 • (830) 875-9466 • *Plum Creek Almanac*

J B Nickells Memorial Library • 215 S Pecan St • Luling, TX 78648 • (830) 875-2813

Lumberton

Lumberton Public Library • 130 E Chance Cut-Off • Lumberton, TX 77657 • (409) 755-7400 • http://www.cityoflumberton.com

Mabank

Root Seekers Genealogical Society • P.O. Box 1770 • Mabank, TX 75147

Madisonville

Madison County Genealogical Society • P.O. Box 26 • Madisonville, TX 77864 • (713) 247-0209 • *Family Historian*

Malakoff

Red Waller Community Library • 109 Mitcham St, P.O. Box 1177 • Malakoff, TX 75148-1177 • (903) 489-1818 • *Library Journal*

Mansfield

Fenton International Genealogy • 718 Kensington Ln • Mansfield, TX 76063-2819 • http://ligtree.cwru.edu • *Fig Tree News*

Mansfield Historical Society • 101 E Broad St • Mansfield, TX 76063 • (817) 473-4250

Mansfield Historical Society & Archives • Historical Museum 100 N Main St, P.O. Box 304 • Mansfield, TX 76063 • (817) 473-4250

Marble Falls

Blackmore Clearinghouse • 2508 Crider Rd • Marble Falls, TX 78654 • (512) 693-2532

Marfa

Marfa and Presidio County Museum Archives • 110 W San Antonio St • Marfa, TX 79843 • (432) 729-4140 • http://www.margamuseum.org

Marfa Public Library • 115 E Oak St, P.O. Drawer U • Marfa, TX 79843-0609 • (915) 729-4631

Marshall
Harrison County Genealogical Society • 300 S Alamo • Marshall, TX 75670

Harrison County Historical Society & Archives • Old Courthouse Museum, 707 N Washington, P.O. Box 1987 • Marshall, TX 75671 • (903) 938-2680 • http://www.rootsweb.com/~txharrison • *Harrison County Historical Society Newsletter*

Jarrett Library • East Texas Baptist University, 1209 N Grove St • Marshall, TX 75670-1498 • (903) 923-2262 • http://www.etbu.edu/library/

Marshall Public Library • 300 S Alamo Blvd • Marshall, TX 75670 • (903) 935-4465 • http://www.marshallpubliclibrary.org

Starr Family Home State Historic Site Archives • 407 W Travis St • Marshall, TX 75670 • (903) 935-3044

Thomas Winston Cole, Sr Library • Wiley College, 711 Wiley Ave • Marshall, TX 75670-5151 • (903) 927-3275 • http://www.wileyc.edu

Mason
Mason County Historical Society & Archives • Historical Museum, 321 Moody, P.O. Box 303 • Mason, TX 76856 • (915) 347-6411

Matador
Motley County Genealogical and Historical Society • c/o Motley County Library, 1105 Main St, P.O. Box 557 • Matador, TX 79244 • (806) 347-2717

Motley County Library • 1105 Main St, P.O. Box 557 • Matador, TX 79244-0557 • (806) 347-2717

McAllen
Goins Family • P.O. Box 3336 • McAllen, TX 78502 • (956) 687-2609

Hidalgo Pump House Heritage and Discovery Center Archives • 900 S 2nd St • McAllen, TX 78501 • (956) 843-8686

McAllen Genealogical Society & Archives • c/o McAllen Memorial Library, 601 N Main St, P.O. Box 4714 • McAllen, TX 78502-4714 • (956) 682-4531 • *Palm Breezes Newsletter*

McAllen Memorial Library • 601 N Main St • McAllen, TX 78501-4666 • (956) 682-4531 • http://mcallen.lib.tx.us

McCamey
Upton County Public Library • 212 W 7th St, P.O. Box 1377 • McCamey, TX 79752-1377 • (915) 652-8718

McDade
McDade Historical Society & Archives • Historical Museum, Main St, P.O. Box 817 • McDade, TX 78650 • (512) 273-0044

McGregor
Kelley Clan: Descendants of John Kelley • 811 S Harrison • McGregor, TX 76657 • (254) 840-3194

McKinney
Collin County Farm Museum Archives • 7117 County Rd 166 • McKinney, TX 75070 • (972) 542-9457 • http://www.co.collin.tx.us • *Collin County Farm Museum Newsletter*

Collin County Historical Society & Archives • Historical Museum, 105 Chestnut St • McKinney, TX 75069 • (972) 542-9457 • http://www.collincountyhistory.org • *Collin County History*

McKinney Memorial Public Library • 101 E Hunt St • McKinney, TX 75069 • (972) 547-7323

Moser: North Carolina Pioneers • 4904 East View Ct • McKinney, TX 75070 • (972) 540-2596

McLean
McLean Historical Society & Archives • McLean-Alanreed Area Museum, Main St, P.O. Box 354 • McLean, TX 79057 • (806) 779-2731

Medina
Medina Community Library • 13948 State Hwy 16 N, P.O. Box 300 • Medina, TX 78055-0300 • (830) 589-2825

Memphis
Hall County Genealogical Society • 915 Cleveland • Memphis, TX 79245

Menard
Menard Genealogical Society • P.O. Box 714 • Menard, TX 76859-0714

Mercedes
Mercedes Memorial Library • 434 S Ohio • Mercedes, TX 78570 • (956) 565-2371

Meridian
Bosque County Collection • P.O. Box 534 • Meridian, TX 76665

Mesquite
Alexander-Bain-Baine-Cantrell Research • 1221 Candice Ct • Mesquite, TX 75149 • *Alexander Family Association Newsletter*, *Bain-Baine Newsletter*, *Cantrell Cousins*; *Gray-Grey Lines*; *Hodgin-Hodges Newsletter*, *House Hunting*; *Glass Newsletter*, *Skeen-Skeins-Skenes Newsletter*, *Owen-Owens Newsletter*, *Tussey Newsletter*, *Thornton Newsletter*

Florence Ranch Homestead Archives • 1424 Barnes Bridge Rd, P.O. Box 850137 • Mesquite, TX 75150 • (972) 216-6468 • http://www.historicmesquite.org

Mesquite Historical and Genealogical Society • 600 Grubb Dr, P.O. Box 850165 • Mesquite, TX 75149-0165 • (972) 216-6229 • http://members.aol.com/dstuart101/mesquite/page1.htm • *Mesquite Tree*; *Mesquite Historical and Genealogical Society Newsletter*

Mesquite Public Library • 300 W Grubb Dr • Mesquite, TX 75149 • (972) 216-6220 • http://www.library.mesquite.tx.us

Wragg Exchange • 2523 Karla Dr • Mesquite, TX 75150

Mexia
Gibbs Memorial Library • 305 E Rusk St • Mexia, TX 76667-2398 • (254) 562-3231 • http://www.gibbslibrary.com

Limestone County Genealogical Society & Archives • c/o Gibbs Memorial Library, 350 E Rusk St, P.O. Box 1437 • Mexia, TX 76667 • (254) 562-3231 • *Gusher*

Miami
Roberts County Historical Commission & Archives • Roberts County Museum, 120 E Commercial, P.O. Box 306 • Miami, TX 79059 • (806) 868-3291 • http://www.robertscountymuseum.org

Midland
American Airpower Heritage Museum Archives • 9600 Wright Dr, P.O. Box 62000 • Midland, TX 79711 • (432) 567-3009 • http://www.airpowermuseum.org • *Co-Pilot Communique*

Bowman-Baumann Family Association • P.O. Box 141 • Midland, TX 79702-0141 • (915) 682-0509 • *Bowman-Baumann Family Newsletter*

Cauble Reunion • 2905 Sentinel Dr • Midland, TX 79701 • (915) 697-4955 • http://www.studiosr.com/cauble/ • Bulletin of the Cauble and Rotan Families

Chaffin-Allmon Family Organization • 4500 Neeley • Midland, TX 79707

Clan Donnachaidh Society, Texas • 2700 Kessler Ave • Midland, TX 79701 • (915) 697-2476 • *Donnaichaidh Dispatch: The Newsletter of the Clan Donnachaidh Society of the South*

Commemorative Air Force • P.O. Box 62000 • Midland, TX 79711-2000 • (432) 563-1000 • *Dispatch: American Airpower*

Hudnall Family Association • 4805A Dentcrest • Midland, TX 79707-5247 • http://www.hudnall-family.com • *Hudnall Family Association Newsletter*

Hudson Family Association, South • 1421 Ainslee • Midland, TX 79701 • (915) 684-7524 • http://Hudson-FamilyAssoc.rootsweb.com • *Hudsoniana*

Joseph Ray and Mary Fouts Reunion • 2606 Culver • Midland, TX 79705 • (915) 694-0101 • *Joseph and Mary Ray Reunion Newsletter*

Mendenhall Family Association • 1908 Sparks St • Midland, TX 79705-8529 • (915) 682-9986 • http://www.mendenhall.org • *Mendenhall Matters*

Midland County Historical Society & Archives • Historical Museum, 301 W Missouri • Midland, TX 79701 • (915) 682-2931 • *Staked Plains*

Midland County Public Library • 301 W Missouri • Midland, TX 79702-1191 • (432) 688-8991 • http://www.co.midland.tx.us/library • *Friends of the Library Newsletter*

Midland Genealogical Society & Archives • c/o Midland County Public Library, 301 W Missouri, P.O. Box 1191 • Midland, TX 79702 • (915) 688-8991 • *Midland Genealogical Society Magazine*; *Thorny Trail*; *Midland Genealogical Society Newsletter*

Museum of the Southwest Archives • 1705 W Missouri • Midland, TX 79701 • (915) 683-2882 • http://www.museumsw.org • *Museum of the Southwest Newsletter*

Nita Stewart Haley Memorial Library • J Evetts Haley History Center, 1805 W Indiana St • Midland, TX 79701 • (915) 682-5785 • http://www.haleylibrary.com • *Haley Library Newsletter*

Petroleum Museum Archives • 1500 I-20 W • Midland, TX 79701 • (432) 683-4403 • http://www.petroleummuseum.org • *Haley Library Newsletter*

Richard Ratcliff Genealogical Society • 1201 W Missouri • Midland, TX 79701 • http://don.ratcliff.net/tree/ • *Richard Ratcliff Genealogical Society Bulletin*

Smith Research • 2606 McClintic • Midland, TX 79705 • *Smith Digest*

Van Aersdalen Family Association • 505 N Big Springs #105 • Midland, TX 79701 • *Van Aersdalen Vanguard*

Z Taylor Brown-Saray Dorsey House Museum Archives • 213 N Weatherly • Midland, TX 79701 • (915) 682-2931

Milford
Nelson Research • P.O. Box 537 • Milford, TX 76670-0537 • *Nelson Family Newsletter*

Mineral Wells
Br(e)ashe(a)r(s) Research • 3110 NE 11th St • Mineral Wells, TX 76067-4128 • (940) 325-7631 • *Br(e)ashe(a)r(s) Family Branches*

Mingus
W K Gordon Center for Industrial History of Texas Archives • 65258 I-20 • Mingus, TX 76463 • (254) 968-1886 • http://www.tarleton.edu/~gordoncenter/

Mission
Speer Memorial Library • 801 E 12th St • Mission, TX 78572 • (956) 580-8750 • http://www.mission.lib.tx.us

Missouri City
Morrison Reunion • 3319 Bedford Forrest Dr • Missouri City, TX 77459 • (713) 438-4808 • *Morrisons*

Monahans
Ward County Genealogical Society & Library • 400 E 4th St • Monahans, TX 79756 • (915) 943-6312 • *Ward County Heritage*

Mont Belvieu
Chambers County Heritage Society • P.O. Box 870 • Mont Belvieu, TX 77580 • (281) 576-2594

Montague
Montague County Historical Society • P.O. Box 77 • Montague, TX 76251

Montgomery
Montgomery Historical Society • FM 149 Rd S • Montgomery, TX 77356 • (936) 597-4899

Polish Genealogical Society of Texas • 329 Harbor Cr • Montgomery, TX 77356-4739 • (281) 444-7579 • http://www.pgst.org • Polish Footprints

Mount Pleasant
Cypress Basin Genealogical and Historical Society • P.O. Box 403 • Mount Pleasant, TX 75455 • *Cypress Basin Genealogical Bulletin*; *Cypress Basin Genealogical and Historical Society Reporter*, *Cypress Basin Genealogical and Historical Society Quarterly*

Modern Western Museum Archives • 2747 Old Paris Rd • Mount Pleasant, TX 75455 • (903) 572-9416 • http://www.legendsandlawless.com

Mount Pleasant Public Library • 213 N Madison • Mount Pleasant, TX 75455 • (903) 575-4180 • http://www.ci.mount-pleasant.tx.us/library/library.htm • *Pleasant Reading*

Mount Vernon
Franklin County Genealogical Society & Library • 110 E Main St • Mount Vernon, TX 75457 • (903) 537-3931 • http://www.mt-vernon.com

Franklin County Historical Museum Archives • 201 S Kaufman • Mount Vernon, TX 75457 • (903) 537-4760 • http://www.mt-vernon.com/~chbrewer/museum.htm

Franklin County Historical Society • 701 Kaufman St S • Mount Vernon, TX 75457 • (903) 537-4760

Muleshoe
Muleshoe Area Public Library • 322 W 2nd • Muleshoe, TX 79347 • (806) 272-4707

Surnames, Ltd • RR3, Box 59 • Muleshoe, TX 79347-9208 • *Bailey Lines*; *Brantley Bandwagon*; *Clark Connection*; *Hints on Hintons*; *Huston Newsletter*, *Johnson Newsletter (Southern)*; *McNatt Ancestry*, *Searching for Searcy's*; *Woodworth Journal*

Nacogdoches
Burr Research • 613 Bostwick • Nacogdoches, TX 75961 • (936) 564-7478

Center for East Texas Studies • Stephen F Austin State Univ, P.O. Box 6134, Austin Sta • Nacogdoches, TX 75962 • (936) 468-1392 • http://www.sfasu.edu

East Texas Historical Association • P.O. Box 6223, SFA Sta • Nacogdoches, TX 75962 • (936) 468-2407 • http://leonardo.sfasu.edu/etha/ • *East Texas Historical Journal*

Herndon Family of VA • 613 Bostwick • Nacogdoches, TX 75961 • (936) 564-7478

Nacogdoches Genealogical Society & Library • P.O. Box 4634, SFA Sta • Nacogdoches, TX 75962 • (936) 564-5544 • *Yesterday*

Partin Publications • 230 Wedgewood • Nacogdoches, TX 75961-5523 • *Partin Family Archives*; *King Family Newsletter*, *Martin Historian*; *Vaughan-Vaughn Family Annals*

Ralph W Steen Library • Stephen F Austin State University, P.O. Box 13055, SFA Sta • Nacogdoches, TX 75962-3055 • (936) 468-4636 • http://libweb.sfasu.edu

Sterne-Hoya Library & Museum Archives • 211 S Lanana St, P.O. Box 635030 • Nacogdoches, TX 75963 • (936) 560-5426 • http://www.ci.nacogdoches.tx.us

Stone Fort Museum Archives • Stephen F Austin State Univ, Alumni & Griffith Blvd, P.O. Box 6075 SFASU • Nacogdoches, TX 75962 • (936) 468-2408

Navasota
Grimes County Heritage Association • 1215 E Washington Ave, P.O. Box 546 • Navasota, TX 77868

Horlock History Center Archives • 1215 E Washington Ave • Navasota, TX 77868 • (936) 825-7055

Navasota Public Library • 1411 E Washington Ave • Navasota, TX 77868-3240 • (936) 825-6744

Nederland
Marion and Ed Hughes Public Library • 2712 Mederland Ave • Nederland, TX 77627-7015 • (409) 722-1255

New Boston
New Boston Genealogical Society • c/o New Boston Public Library, 127 N Ellis, P.O. Box 104 • New Boston, TX 75570-2905 • (903) 628-5414 • *New Bostonian*

New Boston Public Library • 127 N Ellis St • New Boston, TX 75570-2905 • (903) 628-5414

New Braunfels
Comal County Genealogical Society & Archives • Sophienburg Musuem, 401 W Coll St • New Braunfels, TX 78131-0160 • (830) 629-1572 • http://www.nbtx.com/sophienburg • *Family Footsteps Magazine*

New Braunfels Conservation Society & Archives • Historical Museum, 1300 Church Hill Dr, P.O. Box 310933 • New Braunfels, TX 78130 • (210) 629-2943 • http://www.nbconservation.org • *New Braunfels Conservation Society Newsletter*

New Braunfels Historical Railroad and Modelers Society • 302 W San Antonio St • New Braunfels, TX 78130 • (830) 627-2447

New Braunfels Public Library • 700 E Common St • New Braunfels, TX 78130-5689 • (830) 608-2150 • http://www.nbpl.lib.tx.us

Newcastle
Fort Belknap Genealogical Association • Fort Belknap Museum, 110 Fort Circle • Newcastle, TX 76372-3210 • (940) 846-3504 • *Fort Belknap Genealogical Association Bulletin*

Newton
Newton County Historical Commission & Library • P.O. Box 1383 • Newton, TX 75966 • (409) 379-2109 • http://www.jas.net/~newton/links.htm

North Richland Hills
Florence Percy Merrill-Lucy E Holcomb-Percy Harvey Mason-Milton Crockett Mills-George H and William Buck-Sophia Lewis Family Organization • 7712 Buck St • North Richland Hills, TX 76180 • (817) 485-3792

North Richland Hills Public Library • 6720 NE Loop 820 • North Richland Hills, TX 76180 • (817) 427-6814 • http://www.library.nrhtx.com • *Off the Shelf*

North Zulch
Frederick Stuart Family Organization • Route 1, Box 52 • North Zulch, TX 77872 • (936) 399-2718

Nursery
Words from the Woods • P.O. Box 9 • Nursery, TX 77976 • (361) 575-0860 • *Buckelew Traces*

Odessa
Association des Familles Gosselin • 600 W 22nd St • Odessa, TX 79761 • *Newsletter of the Association des familles Gosselin*

Bushong Family Association • 1504 E 52nd St • Odessa, TX 79762-4457 • (915) 366-6861 • *Bushong Bulletin*

Ector County Library • 321 W 5th St • Odessa, TX 79761-5066 • (915) 332-0633 • http://www.ector.lib.tx.us

Finnerty Family • 1600 Century Ave • Odessa, TX 79762 • (915) 362-6290

J Conrad Dunagan Library • Univ of Texas, 4901 E University Blvd • Odessa, TX 79762 • (432) 552-2370 • http://www.utpb.edu/library/index

Library of the Presidents • Presidential Museum, 4919 E University • Odessa, TX 79762 • (915) 363-7737 • http://www.presidentialmuseum.org • *Library of the Presidents Newsletter*

Permian Basin Genealogical Society & Archives • c/o Ector County Library, 321 W 5th St • Odessa, TX 79763 • (915) 332-0633 • *Treeshaker, Permian Basin Genealogical Society Newsletter*

Permian Historical Society & Archives • Univ of Texas, 4901 W University • Odessa, TX 79762-8301 • (915) 552-2370 • *Permian Historical Annual*

Presidential Museum Archives • 622 N Lee • Odessa, TX 79761 • (915) 332-7123 • http://www.presidentialmuseum.org • *Presidential Museum Newsletter*

Olney
Olne Community Library • 807 W Hamilton, P.O. Box 67 • Olney, TX 76374 • (940) 564-5513

Olney Community Library & Arts Center • 807 W Hamilton, P.O. Box 67 • Olney, TX 76374-0067 • (940) 564-5513

Onalaska
Adams Association • 218 Kickapoo Forest • Onalaska, TX 77360 • *Adams Addenda*

Orange
Heritage House Museum of Orange County Archives • 905 W Division St • Orange, TX 77630 • (409) 886-5385 • http://www.heritagehouseoforange.org • *Nostalgic News*

Orange Public Library • 220 N 5th St • Orange, TX 77630 • (409) 883-1053

W H Stark House Archives • 610 W Main Ave, P.O. Box 909 • Orange, TX 77631 • (409) 883-0871 • http://www.whstarkhouse.org

Orchard
Rowell Foundation • 645 Sabine • Orchard, TX 77464 • (979) 478-7190 • *Rowell Quarterly*

Ozona
Crockett County Historical Society & Archives • Historical Museum, 404 11th St, P.O. Box 1444 • Ozona, TX 76943 • (325) 392-2837

Paducah
Bicentennial City-County Public Library • Courthouse, 8th St, P.O. Drawer AD • Paducah, TX 79248-1197 • (806) 492-2006

Cottle County Genealogical Society • P.O. Box 1005 • Paducah, TX 79248

Palestine
Anderson County Genealogical Society • P.O. Box 2045 • Palestine, TX 75802 • (903) 723-2285 • *Tracings*

Palestine Public Library • 1101 N Cedar St • Palestine, TX 75801 • (903) 729-4121 • http://www.palestine.lib.tx.us

Pampa
Lovett Memorial Library • 111 N Houston St, P.O. Box 342 • Pampa, TX 79066-0342 • (806) 669-5780 • http://www.lovettlibrary.org

Pampa Genealogical and Historical Society • 430 N Summer St • Pampa, TX 79065 • *Coronado Heritage*

White Deer Land Museum Archives • 112-116 S Cuyler, P.O. Box 1556 • Pampa, TX 79065 • (806) 669-8041 • http://www.museuminpampa.com

Panhandle
Carson County Historical Survey Committee & Library • Carson County Square, Hwy 207 & 5th St, P.O. Box 276 • Panhandle, TX 79068-0276 • (806) 537-3524 • http://www.squarehousemuseum.org

Carson County Public Library • 401 Main St, P.O. Box 339 • Panhandle, TX 79068-0339 • (806) 537-3742

Paris
AM and Welma Akin Jr Regional Archives • Paris Junior College, 2400 Clarksville St • Paris, TX 75460 • (903) 782-0415 • http://www.parisjc.edu

Genealogical Society of Northeast Texas & Archives • c/o Paris Junior College Library, 2400 Clarksville St, P.O. Box 187 • Paris, TX 75460 • (903) 782-0415 • *Northeast Texas Genealogy and History*

James and Mary Mackey Family Association • P.O. Box 459 • Paris, TX 75460

Lamar County Genealogical Society & Archives • c/o Paris Junior College, 2400 Clarksville St, P.O. Box 187 • Paris, TX 75460 • (903) 782-0415 • http://gen.1starnet.com • *Lamar County History and Genealogy*

Paris Public Library • 326 S Main St • Paris, TX 75460-9998 • (903) 785-8531 • http://www.paristexaslibrary.com

Sam Bell Maxey House State Historic Structure Library • 812 S Church St • Paris, TX 75460 • (903) 785-5716 • http://www.maxeyhouse.org

Pasadena
Gray-Posey Family Organization • 1107 W Thomas • Pasadena, TX 77506 • (713) 472-3582

Harris County Genealogical Society & Library • P.O. Box 391 • Pasadena, TX 77501-0391 • *Living Tree News*; *Harris County Genealogical Society Annual Seminar Surname Index*

Johann Jacob Trautman Family Organization • 4231 Hait Ln • Pasadena, TX 77505 • (713) 487-6173

Lee Davis Library • San Jacinto College, 8060 Spencer Hwy • Pasadena, TX 77505 • (281) 476-1850 • http://www.sjcd.edu

Pasadena Public Library • 1201 Jeff Ginn Memorial Dr • Pasadena, TX 77506-4875 • (713) 477-0276 • http://www.ci.pasadena.tx.us/library/home.html • *Booklets, Brochures & Bookmarks*

Pecos
Reeves County Library • 505 S Park St • Pecos, TX 79772 • (915) 445-5340

West of the Pecos Museum Archives • 1st & Cedar Sts, P.O. Box 1784 • Pecos, TX 79772 • (915) 445-5076 • http://www.westofthepecosmuseum.com • *West of the Pecos Museum Newsletter*

Perryton
Bagwell Family Association • 1009 Loyola • Perryton, TX 79070 • (806) 435-2323

Museum of the Plains Archives • 1200 N Main • Perryton, TX 79070 • (806) 435-6400 • http://www.museumoftheplains.com

Perry Memorial Library • 22 SE 5th Ave • Perryton, TX 79070 • (806) 435-5801

TX-OK Panhandle Genealogical Society & Archives • c/o Perry Memorial Library, 22 SE 5th Ave • Perryton, TX 79070 • (806) 435-5801 • *TX-OK Panhandler*

Pflugerville
Pflugerville Community Library • 102 10th St • Pflugerville, TX 78660 • (512) 251-9185 • http://www.cityofpflugerville.com

Pharr
Pharr Memorial Library • 121 E Cherokee St • Pharr, TX 78577-4826 • (956) 787-3966 • http://www.pharr.lib.tx.us

Pilot Point
Pilot Point Community Library • 324 S Washington St, P.O. Box 969 • Pilot Point, TX 76258-0969 • (940) 686-5004

Pipe Creek
Petter Abrahamson Lindberg Family Organization • P.O. Box 63263 • Pipe Creek, TX 78063-3263 • (830) 510-6049

Pittsburg
Camp County Genealogical Society • 102 Quitman St, P.O. Box 1083 • Pittsburg, TX 75686 • (903) 856-2062 • *News-Rear View Notes*

Northeast Texas Rural Heritage Museum Archives • 204 W Marshall, P.O. Box 157 • Pittsburg, TX 75686 • (903) 856-1200 • http://www.pittsburgtxmuseum.com • *Museum News*

Pittsburg-Camp County Library • 613 Quitman St • Pittsburg, TX 75686-1035 • (903) 856-3302

The Reynolds Family Circle • 405 Mount Pleasant St • Pittsburg, TX 75686-1121 • (903) 856-5186 • http://www.narnet.com/rfc/

Plains
Tsa Mo Ga Memorial Museum Archives • 1109 Avenue H, P.O. Box 718 • Plains, TX 79355 • (806) 456-8855

Yoakum County Library • 901 Ave East, P.O. Box 419 • Plains, TX 79355-0419 • (806) 456-8725

Plainview
Hi Plains Genealogical Society & Archives • c/o Unger Memorial Library, 825 Austin St • Plainview, TX 79072 • (806) 296-1148

Museum of the llano Estacado Archives • Wayland Univ • Plainview, TX 79072 • (806) 296-4735

Unger Memorial Library • 825 Austin St • Plainview, TX 79072-7235 • (806) 296-1148 • http://www.texasonline.net/unger • *Unger Ululations*

Plano
Barnett Research • 3025 Princess Ln • Plano, TX 75074 • *Barnett Banner*

Collin County Genealogical Society & Library • P.O. Box 865052 • Plano, TX 75086-5052 • (972) 596-3567 • http://www.staubase2l.com/PSGenealogy/ • *Collin Chronicles*; *Collin County Genealogical Society Newsletter*

Genealogy Friends Of Plano Libraries • c/o Plano Public Library, 2501 Coit Rd, P.O. Box 860477 • Plano, TX 75086-0477 • (972) 964-4208

Gladys Harrington Public Library • 1501 18th St • Plano, TX 75074 • (972) 461-7175 • http://www.ci.plano.tx.us/library/genealgy.htm

Heritage Farmstead Association of Collin County & Library • 1900 W 15th St • Plano, TX 75075 • (972) 881-0140 • http://www.heritage.farmstead.museum • *Heritage Today*

Interurban Railway Station Museum Archives • 901 E 15th St, P.O. Box 861810 • Plano, TX 75086 • (972) 941-2117

Irish Family Names Society • P.O. Box 861656 • Plano, TX 75086-1656 • (972) 424-1270

Plano Public Library • 2501 Coit Rd • Plano, TX 75075 • (972) 964-4208 • http://www.planolibrary.org

Plano Public Library-Gladys Harrington Library • 1501 E 18th St • Plano, TX 75074 • (972) 941-7175

Pleasanton
Longhorn Musem Archives • 1959 Hwy 97 E, P.O. Box 601 • Pleasanton, TX 78064 • (512) 569-6313

Pleasanton Public Library • 321 N Main • Pleasanton, TX 78064 • (830) 569-3622 • http://www.world-net.net/home/dguthrie

Port Arthur
Gates Memorial Library • Lamar State College, 317 Stilwell Blvd, P.O. Box 310 • Port Arthur, TX 77641-0310 • (409) 984-6220 • http://libnt4.lamarpa.edu

Port Arthur Historical Society & Archives • Museum of the Gulf Coast, 700 Procter St • Port Arthur, TX 77640 • (409) 982-7000 • http://www.museumofthegulfcoast.org • *Mosquito Bytes*

Port Arthur Public Library • 4615 9th Ave • Port Arthur, TX 77642-3136 • (409) 985-8838 • http://www.pap.lib.tx.us • *Friends Newsletter*

Port Lavaca
Calhoun County Genealogical Society • P.O. Box 1150 • Port Lavaca, TX 77979-0299 • (361) 552-2588 • *Karankawa Kountry*

Calhoun County Museum Archives • 301 S Ann St • Port Lavaca, TX 77978 • (361) 553-4689 • http://www.calhouncountymuseum.org

Port Neches
Effie and Wilton Hebert Public Library • 2025 Merriman St • Port Neches, TX 77651 • (409) 722-4554 • http://www.ptn.lib.tx.us

Portland
Bell-Whittington Public Library • 2400 Memorial Pkwy • Portland, TX 78374 • (361) 777-0921

Post
Garza County Historical Museum Archives • 111 N Avenue N • Post, TX 79356 • (806) 495-2207

Post Public Library • 105 E Main St • Post, TX 79356-3299 • (806) 495-2149

Poteet
Atascosa County Genealogical Society & Library • P.O. Box 93 • Poteet, TX 78065 • (830) 276-4684 • http://members.aol.com/poteetlib/gen

Poteet Public Library • 500 Avenue H, P.O. Box 380 • Poteet, TX 78065-0380 • (830) 742-8917

Prairie View
John B Coleman Library • Prairie View A&M University, P.O. Box 519 • Prairie View, TX 77446-0519 • (936) 857-2012 • http://www.tamu.edu/pvamu/library

Presidio
Fort Leaton State Historic Site Archives • River Rd, FM 170, P.O. Box 2439 • Presidio, TX 79845 • (432) 229-3613 • http://www.tpwd.state.tx.us

Quinlan
Pacer-Hunt County Genealogical Society • P.O. Box 2306 • Quinlan, TX 75474 • (903) 356-2789 • *Jackson Journal*

Tawakoni Area Public Library • 340 W Hwy 276 • Quinlan, TX 75474-2644 • (903) 447-3445

Quitman
Glasco: La Colline • Route 4, Box 4819 • Quitman, TX 75783

Governor Hogg Shrine State Park Archives • 100 Gov Hogg Pkwy • Quitman, TX 75783 • (903) 763-2701 • *Hogg Shrine News*

Quitman Public Library • 202 E Goode St, P.O. Box 1677 • Quitman, TX 75783-1677 • (903) 763-4191 • http://www.quitmanlibrary.org

Wood County Genealogical Society & Library • P.O. Box 832 • Quitman, TX 75783 • (903) 763-4191 • Wood County Genealogical Society Newsletter

Ralls
Ralls Historical Museum Archives • 801 Main St, P.O. Box 384 • Ralls, TX 79357 • (806) 253-2425

Randolph AFB
Randolph Air Force Base Library • 12 SPTG/SVMG, Bldg 598 Fifth St E • Randolph AFB, TX 78150-4405 • (210) 652-2617 • http://rafblibrary.org

Ranger
Central Texas Historical and Genealogical Society • 1505 W Loop 254 • Ranger, TX 76470-3213 • (254) 657-5353

Ranger Historical Preservation Society • P.O. Box 320 • Ranger, TX 76470

Rankin
Rankin Museum Archives • 101 W Main St, P.O. Box 82 • Rankin, TX 79778 • (915) 693-2758 • http://www.rootsweb.com/~txupton/

Upton County Genealogical Society • P.O. Box 6 • Rankin, TX 79778 • Trails and Tails

Reagan
Railsback Descendants Association • Route 1, Box 222 • Reagan, TX 76680 • *Railsback Lines*

Red Oak
Pounders-Cain Reunion • 221 Overlook • Red Oak, TX 75154

Refugio
Dennis M O'Connor Public Library • 815 S Commerce St • Refugio, TX 78377 • (361) 526-2608 • http://www.tsl.org

Refugio County Historical Society & Archives • Refugio County Museum, 102 W West St • Refugio, TX 78377 • (512) 526-4943 • *Refugio County Historical Society Newsletter*

Rhome
Wise County Genealogical Society • P.O. Box 86 • Rhome, TX 76078 • Wise Ancestry

Richardson
Bolling Family Association • P.O. Box 835490 • Richardson, TX 75083-5490 • *Bolling Family Newsletter*

Chaffin-Chafin-Chalfin-Chalfant-Chapin Families • 1408 N Cheyenne Dr • Richardson, TX 75080 • *Chaffin-Chafin-Chalfin-Chalfant-Chapin Newsletter*

Descendants of Mexican War Veterans • 1114 Pacific Dr, P.O. Box 830482 • Richardson, TX 75081-0482 • (972) 699-8823 • *American Eagle: A Newsletter of the Descendants of Mexican War Veterans*; *Mexican War Journal*

Eugene McDermott Library • University of Texas at Dallas, 2601 N Floyd Rd, P.O. Box 830643, MC33 • Richardson, TX 75083-0643 • (972) 883-2950 • http://www.utdallas.edu/library

Henry Haley Millard Family Organization • 331 Ridgehaven Pl • Richardson, TX 75080

James G Murphey Family Organization • 1432 Dumont Dr • Richardson, TX 75080 • (972) 239-0934

Maiorca-Maiorka Family Association • P.O. Box 831038 • Richardson, TX 75083-1083 • (972) 907-9215 • http://rampages.onramp.net/~wordwork/maiorka.htm • *Maiorca-Maiorka Family News*

National Museum of Communications Archives • 2001 Plymouth Rock • Richardson, TX 75081 • (972) 690-3636 • http://www.yesterdayusa.com • *Transcription*

Richardson Historical and Genealogical Society • P.O. Box 831676 • Richardson, TX 75080-1676

Richardson Public Library • 900 Civic Center Dr • Richardson, TX 75080-5210 • (972) 744-4355 • http://www.cor.net/library/

Sanders-Sanderson-Saunderson-Saunders Research • 1408 N Cheyenne Dr • Richardson, TX 75080 • *Sanders Newsletter*; *Sanderson-Saunderson Quarterly*; *Saunders Newsletter*

Shapley Family Association • P.O. Box 832130 • Richardson, TX 75083-2130 • (972) 562-1058 • *Shapley Connection*

Stibbens Family Reunion • 315 Ridgehave Pl • Richardson, TX 75080 • (972) 783-8484

Tolson-Toalson Surname Organization • 1204 Dunbarton Dr, P.O. Box 852245 • Richardson, TX 75085 • (972) 783-9211 • *Tolson-Toalson Family History*

Richland Hills
Richland Hills Public Library • 6724 Rena Dr • Richland Hills, TX 76118 • (817) 299-1860

Richmond
Boggess Family Association • 1410 Lamar Dr • Richmond, TX 77469 • (832) 341-5257 • *Boggess Family Association Newsletter*

Castor Association of America • 2103 Plantation Dr • Richmond, TX 77469 • (832) 342-5033 • *News-Caster*

Fort Bend County Genealogical Society & Library • P.O. Box 274 • Richmond, TX 77469-0274 • (281) 341-2608 • http://www.georgeranch.org • *Around the Bend*

Fort Bend Museum Association & Archives • Historical Museum, 500 Houston St, P.O. Drawer 460 • Richmond, TX 77406 • (281) 342-6478 • http://www.fortbendmuseum.org

George Foundation • 215 Morton St • Richmond, TX 77469 • (281) 232-3013

George Memorial Library of Fort Bend County • 1001 Golfview Dr • Richmond, TX 77469 • (281) 342-4455 • http://www.fortbend.lib.tx.us/lib.html

Rio Hondo
Texas Air Museum Archives • FM 106, P.O. Box 70 • Rio Hondo, TX 78583 • (956) 748-2112 • http://www.texasairmuseum.com • Airspeed

Roanoke
Roanoke Public Library • 308 S Walnut St • Roanoke, TX 76262-8635 • (817) 491-2691 • http://roanoke.lib.tx.us

Robstown
Bradshaw in America • 5380 Wagon Tr • Robstown, TX 78380-9792 • *Bradshaw in America Newsletter*

Rochelle
Heart of Texas Genealogical Society • P.O. Box 1837 • Rochelle, TX 76872

Rockdale
Lucy Hill Patterson Memorial Library • 201 Ackerman St • Rockdale, TX 76567 • (512) 446-3410 • http://www.main.org/patlib/library.htm

Milam County Genealogical Society & Archives • c/o Lucy Hill Patterson Memorial Library, 201 Ackerman St • Rockdale, TX 76567 • (512) 446-3410 • http://www.aisi.net/GenWeb/MilamCo/mcgs.htm • *Legacy*

Rockport
Arkansas County Public Library • 701 E Mimosa St • Rockport, TX 78382 • (361) 790-0153 • http://www.acplibrary.org

Texas Maritime Museum Archives • 1202 Navigtion Circle • Rockport, TX 78382 • (361) 729-1271 • http://www.texasmaritimemuseum.org • *Log Line*

Texas

Rockwall
Badger Research • 215 Joe White St • Rockwall, TX 75087 • *Badger Family Newsletter*

Rockwall County Genealogical Society • P.O. Box 471 • Rockwall, TX 75087-0471 • (972) 771-9018 • http://www.geocities.com/Heartland/Ranch/7757 • *Rockwall County Genealogical Society Quarterly*

Rockwall County Historical Foundation • general delivery • Rockwall, TX 75087 • (972) 722-1507

Rockwall County Library • 105 S 1st St • Rockwall, TX 75087 • (972) 882-0340 • http://www.rocklib.org

Rosanky
Central Texas Museum of Automotive History • 2502 Hwy 304 • Rosanky, TX 78953 • (512) 237-2635 • http://www.ctmab.org

Rotan
Rotan Public Library • 404 E Sammy Baugh • Rotan, TX 79546-3820 • (915) 735-3362

Round Rock
Round Rock Public Library • 216 E Main St • Round Rock, TX 78664-5245 • (512) 218-7006 • http://www.ci.round-rock.tx.us

Umhauer Family Association • P.O. Box 1464 • Round Rock, TX 78680 • (512) 255-5603

Williamson County Genealogical Society & Library • 3601 Arrowhead Cr, P.O. Box 585 • Round Rock, TX 78680-0585 • (512) 255-7057 • http://www.flash.net/~hmwalden/wcgs.htm • *Chisholm Trail*

Round Top
Round Top Family Library • 206 W Mill St, P.O. Box 245 • Round Top, TX 78954-0245 • (979) 249-2700 • http://ilovetoread.org

Windale Historical Center Library • FM Rd 2714, P.O. Box 11 • Round Top, TX 78954-0011 • (979) 278-3530 • http://www.cah.utexas.edu • *Quid Nuc*

Rowlett
Rowlett Historical Society • 3913 Main St • Rowlett, TX 75088 • (972) 475-8915

Runge
Runge Public Library • 311 N Helena, P.O. Box 37 • Runge, TX 78151-0037 • (830) 239-4192 • http://www.runge.lib.tx.us

Rusk
Singletary Memorial Library • 207 E 6th St • Rusk, TX 75785 • (903) 683-5916

Saginaw
Saginaw Public Library • 355 W McLeroy Blvd, P.O. Box 79070 • Saginaw, TX 76176-0070 • (817) 232-2100

Salado
Central Texas Area Museum Archives • 1 Main St, P.O. Box 36 • Salado, TX 76571 • (254) 947-5232 • http://www.ctam-salado.org

San Angelo
Fort Concho National Historic Landmark Museum Library • 630 S Oakes • San Angelo, TX 76903-7099 • (915) 481-2646 • http://www.fortconcho.com • *Fort Concho Guidon*

Genealogy of the Elder Clan • 1636 Utah Ave • San Angelo, TX 76904 • (915) 942-9499

Gilstrap Family Association • 1921 N Harrison • San Angelo, TX 76901 • (915) 949-0792

Porter Henderson Library • Angelo State Univ, 2025 S Johnson, P.O. Box 11013, ASU Sta • San Angelo, TX 76909-0001 • (915) 942-2141 • http://www.angelo.edu/services/library

Railway Museum of San Angelo Archives • 703 S Chadbourne • San Angelo, TX 76903 • (325) 486-2140 • http://www.railwaymuseumsanangelo.homestead.com

San Angelo Genealogical and Historical Society • 902 N Main St, P.O. Box 3453 • San Angelo, TX 76902 • (915) 949-3223 • http://www.rootsweb.com/saghs • *Stalkin' Kin*; *San Angelo Genealogical and Historical Society Newsletter*

Tom Green County Library • 113 W Beauregard St • San Angelo, TX 76903-5834 • (915) 655-7321 • http://www.co.tom-green.tx.us

San Antonio
Afro-American Historical and Genealogical Society, San Antonio Chapter • P.O. Box 200784 • San Antonio, TX 78220-0784 • (210) 223-1119

Alamo Archives • 300 Alamo Plaza, P.O. Box 2599 • San Antonio, TX 78205 • (210) 225-1391 • http://www.thealamo.org

Ancestors Are Just Somewhere In Time • 9511 Perrin Beitel Rd, #710 • San Antonio, TX 78217-3547

Bellard-Ballard Family: Descendants of John Ballard and Sarah Heston • 7214 Harlow Dr #3E • San Antonio, TX 78218

Benigno and Severiano Gomez Family Organization • 2326 Hiawatha St • San Antonio, TX 78210-5318 • (210) 534-0263

Bolivar Hall Archives • 418 Villita • San Antonio, TX 78205 • (210) 224-5711 • http://www.saconservation.org

Buckhorn Saloon and Museum Archives • 318 E Houston St • San Antonio, TX 78205 • (210) 247-4002 • http://www.buckhornmuseum.com

Burney Family Reunion • 7202 Glen Tr • San Antonio, TX 78239 • (210) 653-6054 • *Burney Gazette*

Cain-Winegar Research • 318 Jamaica Dr • San Antonio, TX 78227 • (210) 674-2535 • Cain Newsletter; Winegar Family Newsletter

Casa Navarro State Historical Park Museum Archives • 228 S Laredo St • San Antonio, TX 78207 • (210) 226-4801 • http://www.tpwd.state.tx.us/park/jose/jose.htm

Catholic Diocese of San Antonio Archives • 2718 W Woodlawn, P.O. Box 24810 • San Antonio, TX 78228-0410 • (210) 734-2620 • *Archival Outlook*; American Archivist

Chenault Family National Association • 2915 Burnside Dr • San Antonio, TX 78209-3012 • (210) 826-3323 • http://chenault.org • *Chenault Family National Association Newsletter*

Cleaver Family Reunion • P.O. Box 701628 • San Antonio, TX 78270-1628 • (210) 545-5533

Coates Library • Trinity University, 1 Trinity Pl, No 56 • San Antonio, TX 78212-7200 • (210) 999-7213 • http://www.trinity.edu/departments/library/library.html

Daughters of the Republic of Texas & Library • 300 Alamo Plaza, P.O. Box 1401 • San Antonio, TX 78295-1401 • (210) 225-8155 • http://www.drtl.org

Edith Roxy Grant-George Oliver Boldway Family Organization • 4302 Hollow Hill • San Antonio, TX 78217 • (210) 653-2542

Foppes Reunion • 3630 Ridge Cluster • San Antonio, TX 78247-3422 • (210) 496-8921

GenServ-Family History • P.O. Box 3393 • San Antonio, TX 78265 • (210) 946-4808 • http://www.genserv.com/CliffManis

Graham Family Association • 118 Yosemite Dr • San Antonio, TX 78232-1323 • (210) 494-2772

Heston Family Association: Descendants of Zebulon Heston and Dorothy Hutchinson • 7214 Harlow Dr #3E • San Antonio, TX 78218

Hoelscher-Buxkemper Family Heritage Association • 1811 Forest Park • San Antonio, TX 76901 • (915) 653-9491 • http://www.hostville.com/hoelscher/ • *Hoelschler/Buxkemper Family Newsletter*

HQ Air Force Services Agency, Directorate of Programs • Air Force Libr & Info Syst HQ-AFSVA/SVPAL, 10100 Reunion Pl Suite 502 • San Antonio, TX 78216-4138

Institute of Texan Cultures Archives • Univ of Texas, 801 S Bowie St • San Antonio, TX 78205-3296 • (210) 458-2300 • http://www.texancultures.utsa.edu

Ives-Green(e) Research • 2118 Goliad Rd #109A • San Antonio, TX 78223-3220 • Ives Index; Greenleaves

Jarrell-Beard Research • 2810 Thousand Oaks Dr #163 • San Antonio, TX 78232-4108 • *Jarrell Newsletter*

Kelly Branch Library • Lackland Airforce Base, 250 Goodrich Dr, Suite E6, 37 MSG/SVMGK • San Antonio, TX 78236 • (210) 925-3214

Kight Research • P.O. Box 790274 • San Antonio, TX 76279-0274 • *Kight Newsletter*

King William Association • 1032 S Alamo St • San Antonio, TX 78210-1100 • (210) 227-8786

Las Casas Foundation • 222 E Houston St • San Antonio, TX 78205 • (210) 223-4343

Los Bexarenos Genealogical Society • 203 Belvidere, P.O. Box 1935 • San Antonio, TX 78297 • (210) 822-1526 • *Los Bexarenos Genealogical Register*

McCarroll-Robert Brough Longbotham-William Christian Bower Surname Organization • 214 Middlebury • San Antonio, TX 78217

McCraw Family Reunion • 7400 Crestway #917 • San Antonio, TX 78239

Monte Vista Historical Association • 233 Bushnell Ave • San Antonio, TX 78212-5206 • (210) 737-8212

NARFE Chapter 1320 Genealogy Group • 11327 Chaco Canyon • San Antonio, TX 78245-2808 • (210) 673-6614

Pioneers, Trail Drivers and Former Texas Rangers Association Archives • 3805 Broadway • San Antonio, TX 78209 • (210) 822-9011

Polk-Abell Family • 5139 Hacienda Dr • San Antonio, TX 78233-5424 • *Bridges and Trails*; *Branches and Twigs*

Saint Mary's University Academic Library • 1 Camino Santa Maria • San Antonio, TX 78228-8608 • (210) 436-3508 • http://www.stmarytx.edu/acadlib

San Antonio Central Library • 600 Soledad • San Antonio, TX 78205 • (210) 207-2500 • http://www.sanantonio.gov/library

San Antonio College Library • 1001 Howard St • San Antonio, TX 78212 • (210) 733-2482 • http://www.accd.edu/sac/lrc/

San Antonio Genealogical and Historical Society • 911 Melissa Dr, P.O. Box 17461 • San Antonio, TX 78217-0461 • (210) 342-5242 • http://saghs.home.texas.net • *Our Heritage*; *San Antonio Genealogical and Historical Society Newsletter*

San Antonio Library, San Pedro Branch • 1300 San Pedro Ave • San Antonio, TX 78212 • (210) 733-1454

San Antonio Missions National Historic Park Library • 6701 San Jose Dr • San Antonio, TX 78210 • (210) 534-8833 • http://www.nps.gov/saan

Sociedad de Familias Fajardo • 259 Liverly Dr • San Antonio, TX 78213 • (210) 377-2892

Southwest Genealogical Society • c/o San Antonio County Library, San Pedro Branch, 1300 San Pedro Ave • San Antonio, TX 78212 • (210) 733-1454

Spanish Governor's Palace Archives • 105 Military Plaza • San Antonio, TX 78205 • (210) 224-0601 • http://www.sanantoniocvb.com/things/attract.htm

Steves Homestead Archives • 509 King William St • San Antonio, TX 78204 • (210) 225-6924 • http://www.saconservation.org • *San Antonio Conservation Newsletter*

Sueltenfuss Library • Our Lady of the Lake University, 411 SW 24th St • San Antonio, TX 78207-4689 • (210) 434-6711 • http://www.ollusa.edu

Teachout-Crull Family Association: Descendants of Alfred Jacob Teachout and Esther York Crull • 7214 Harlow Dr #3E • San Antonio, TX 78218 • *Teachout-Cross Family Newsletter*

Texas State Genealogical Society • 204 Glentower • San Antonio, TX 78213 • (210) 341-8372 • http://www.rootsweb.com/~txsgs/tsgs.html • *Stirpes*

Texas Transportation Museum Archives • 11731 Wetmore Rd • San Antonio, TX 78247 • (210) 490-3554

University of Texas-San Antonio Library • 6900 N Loop 1604 W • San Antonio, TX 78249-0671 • (210) 458-4573 • http://www.lib.utsa.edu/Special_Collections/lib

US Daughters of 1812 • 223 Savannah • San Antonio, TX 78213-3550

Wallace Library • San Antonio First Baptist Church, 515 McCullough St • San Antonio, TX 78215 • (210) 226-0363

Witte Museum Library • 3801 Broadway, P.O. Box 2601 • San Antonio, TX 78209 • (210) 357-1900 • http://www.witemuseum.org

Wooden Nickel Historical Museum Archives • 345 Old Austin Rd • San Antonio, TX 78209 • (210) 829-1291 • http://www.wooden-nickel.net

Yturri-Edmunds Historic Site Archives • 128 Mission Rd • San Antonio, TX 78210 • (210) 534-8237 • http://www.saconservation.org

San Augustine
Cullen House Archives • 205 S Congress St • San Augustine, TX 75972 • (936) 275-5110

San Augustine Public Library • 413 E Columbia St • San Augustine, TX 75972-2111 • (936) 275-5367

San Benito
Cooley Family Association of America • 1400 Zillock Rd, Fun N Sun #W1273 • San Benito, TX 78586

San Marcos
Albert B Alkek Library • Texas State University-San Marcos, Comanche & Talbot St • San Marcos, TX 78666 • (512) 245-2685 • http://www.library.swt.edu

Bartee Association • 2841 Paso Del Robles • San Marcos, TX 78666 • (512) 396-6182 • *Bartee News*

Calaboose African American History Museum Archives • 200 W Martin Luther King Jr Dr • San Marcos, TX 78666 • (512) 393-8421 • http://www.sanmarcostarts.com/calaboose.htm

San Marcos Public Library • 625 E Hopkins • San Marcos, TX 78666 • (392) 393-8200 • http://ci.san-marcos.tx.us/library.htm

San Marcos-Hays County Genealogical Society • P.O. Box 503 • San Marcos, TX 78666 • (512) 353-5823

Sanger
Sanger Public Library • 501 Bolivar, P.O. Box 1729 • Sanger, TX 76266-0017 • (940) 458-3257

Santa Anna
Santa Anna Library • 606 Wallas Ave • Santa Anna, TX 76878-2031 • (325) 348-3395

Schertz
Schertz Public Library • 608 Schertz Pkwy • Schertz, TX 78154-1911 • (210) 658-6011 • http://www.schertz.lib.tx.us

Schulenburg
Stanzel Model Aircraft Museum Archives • 311 Baumgarten St • Schulenburg, TX 78956 • (979) 743-6559 • http://www.stanzelmuseum.org

Seabrook
Bay Area Genealogy Study Club • 914 Forest Lake • Seabrook, TX 77586

Seabrook
Bay Area Museum Archives • 5000 Nasa Rd 1 • Seabrook, TX 77598-8686 • (281) 326-5950 • *Bay Area Museum Newsletter*

Seagraves
Seagraves-Loop Museum Archives • Seagraves Loop Dr, 201 Main, P.O. Box 1387 • Seagraves, TX 79359 • (806) 546-2810

Seguin
Guadalupe County Genealogical Society & Archives • c/o Seguin-Guadalupe County Public Library, 707 E College St • Seguin, TX 78155-3217 • (830) 401-2422 • *Guadalupe Valley Trails*

Harry Hugh Frazier-Sidney Levi Gipson Family Association • P.O. Box 1306 • Seguin, TX 78156-1306 • *Gipson Gazette*; *Frazier Footnotes*

Seguin Conservation Society & Archives • Los Nogales Museum, 415 S River, P.O. Box 245 • Seguin, TX 78156 • (830) 372-2649

Seguin-Guadalupe County Public Library • 707 E College St • Seguin, TX 78155-3217 • (830) 401-2422 • http://www.seguin.lib.tx.us

Stoffel Reunion • 520 N River • Seguin, TX 78155 • (210) 379-2373

Seminole
Gaines County Library • 704 Hobbs Hwy • Seminole, TX 79360 • (915) 758-4007

Seymour
Baylor County Historical Society • P.O. Box 689 • Seymour, TX 76380

Sheridan
Sheridan Memorial Library • 5805 Logan Park Dr, P.O. Box 274 • Sheridan, TX 77475-0274 • (979) 234-5154

Sherman
George T & Gladys H Abell Library • Austin College, 900 N Grand Ave, Suite 6L • Sherman, TX 75090-4402 • (903) 813-2556 • http://abell.austincollege.edu/Abell/uc

Grayson County Genealogical Society & Library • c/o Sherman Public Library, 421 N Travis • Sherman, TX 75090 • (903) 892-7240 • Bulletin of the Grayson County Genealogical Society

Red River Historical Museum Archives • 301 S Walnut St • Sherman, TX 75090 • (903) 893-7623 • http://www.texoma.net/rrhms

Sherman Preservation League • 915 S Crockett St • Sherman, TX 75090-7927 • (903) 893-4067

Sherman
Sherman Public Library • 421 N Travis • Sherman, TX 75090-5975 • (903) 892-7240 • http://www.barr.org

William Newton Morris Family Organization • 705 S Burdette Ave • Sherman, TX 75090-8309 • (903) 893-2497

Shiner
Edwin Wolters Museum Archives • 306 S Avenue 1, P.O. Box 308 • Shiner, TX 77984 • (361) 594-3774

Silsbee
Hardin County Genealogical Society • 335 Santa Fe • Silsbee, TX 77656

Historical and Genealogical Society of Hardin County • 790 Myrtle • Silsbee, TX 77656 • Hardin County Connections

Sinton
San Patricio County Library • 313 N Rachal, Rm 226 • Sinton, TX 78387 • (361) 364-6199

Sinton Public Library • 100 N Pirate Blvd • Sinton, TX 78387 • (361) 364-4545

Smithville
Smithville Public Library • 508 Main St • Smithville, TX 78957 • (512) 237-2707 • http://www.ci.smithville.tx.us/library.htm

Snyder
Scurry County Genealogical Society • c/o Scurry County Library, 1916 23rd St, P.O. Box 195 • Snyder, TX 79549 • (915) 573-5572 • *White Buffalo Tales*

Scurry County Library • 1916 23rd St • Snyder, TX 79549 • (325) 573-5572

Scurry County Museum Genealogical Group & Archives • Scurry County Museum, 6200 College Ave • Snyder, TX 79549-6105 • (915) 573-6107 • *Scurry County Museum Newsletter*

Western Texas College Library • 6200 College Ave • Snyder, TX 79549 • (325) 573-8511 • http://www.wtc.edu

Western Texas Genealogical Association • c/o Scurry County Library, 1916 23rd St • Snyder, TX 79549

Sonora
Cauthorn Memorial Depot and Sutton County Jail Archives • Oak St, P.O. Box 1045 • Sonora, TX 76950 • (915) 387-2880

Sutton County Historical Society • Historical Museum, 307 E Oak St, P.O. Box 885 • Sonora, TX 76950 • (325) 387-5084

Sourlake
Alma M Carpenter Public Library • 300 S Ann, P.O. Box 536 • Sourlake, TX 77659-0536 • (409) 287-3592 • http://www.sourlaketexas.com

Spearman
Hansford County Library • 122 Main St • Spearman, TX 79081 • (806) 659-2231

Spring
Clan Ewing in America • 26222 Oakhurst • Spring, TX 77386-1258 • (281) 367-2908 • *Journal of the Clan Ewing*

Fimpel-Fimple Family Factor • 6503 Darby Wy Rd • Spring, TX 77389

Redford Research • 19110 Doveton • Spring, TX 77388 • *Redford Family Newsletter*

Stanton
Martin County Historical Museum Archives • 207 Broadway, P.O. Box 929 • Stanton, TX 79782 • (915) 756-2722 • *Martin County Historical Museum Newsletter*

Stephenville
Datatrace Systems • P.O. Box 1587 • Stephenville, TX 76401-1587 • (254) 965-6979 • *Genealogymagazine.com*

Dick Smith Library • Tarleton State University, 201 Saint Felix, Box T-0450 • Stephenville, TX 76402 • (254) 968-9246 • http://www.tarleton.edu/~library • *General Stacks*

Erath County Genealogical Society • c/o Stephenville Public Library, 174 N Columbia • Stephenville, TX 76401

Stephenville Historical Museum Archives • 525 E Washington, P.O. Box 899 • Stephenville, TX 76401 • (817) 965-5880

Stephenville Public Library • 174 N Columbia St • Stephenville, TX 76401-3492 • (254) 918-1240

Stratford
Sherman County Public Library • 719 N Main, P.O. Box 46 • Stratford, TX 79084-0046 • (806) 366-2200

Sudan
Parrott Research • P.O. Box 446 • Sudan, TX 79371 • (806) 227-2563 • *Parrott Talk*

Sugarland
Metherell Surname Organization • 2808 Grants Lake Blvd, #703 • Sugarland, TX 77479 • (713) 980-4513

Museum of Southern History Archives • 14080 Southwest Fwy • Sugarland, TX 77478 • (281) 269-7171 • http://www.museumofsouthernhistory.org • *Museum of Southern History Newsletter*

Sugarland Genealogical Society • 302 Oyster Creek • Sugarland, TX 77478

Sulphur Springs
First Families of Hopkins County • 201 N Davis St, P.O. Box 624 • Sulphur Springs, TX 75482-0624 • http://gen.1starnet.com/hopkins

Hopkins County Genealogical Society & Library • 212 Main St, P.O. Box 624 • Sulphur Springs, TX 75482-0624 • (903) 885-8523 • http://gen.1starnet.com/hopkins • *Hopkins County Heritage*

Pioneer Families of Hopkins County • 201 N Davis St, P.O. Box 624 • Sulphur Springs, TX 75482-0624 • (903) 885-8523 • http://gen.1starnet.com/hopkins

Rainey Reunion • Route 4, Box 56 • Sulphur Springs, TX 75482 • (903) 885-3523 • http://www2.1starnet.com/mbryant/rainey.htm • *Rainey Times*

Samuel Brooks Family Organization • 823 S Davis • Sulphur Springs, TX 75428 • (214) 885-8715

Southwest Dairy Museum Archives • 1210 Houston, P.O. Box 936 • Sulphur Springs, TX 75492 • (903) 439-6455

Thomas K Hardister Family Organization • 823 S Davis • Sulphur Springs, TX 75428 • (214) 885-8715

Sunset

Old West Museum Archives • 11838 Hwy 287, Access Rd S • Sunset, TX 76270 • (940) 872-9698 • http://www.cowboymuseum.net • *International Barbwire Gazette*

Sweetwater

Fambrough Family Society • 1 Lakewood Dr • Sweetwater, TX 79556-1709 • http://www.tffs.com

Nolan County Genealogical Association • c/o Sweetwater County-City Library, 206 Elm St • Sweetwater, TX 79556 • (915) 235-4978

Pioneer Museum Archives • 610 E 3rd • Sweetwater, TX 79556-4643 • (915) 235-8547

Sweetwater County-City Library • 206 Elm St • Sweetwater, TX 79556 • (915) 235-4978

Taft

Taft Public Library • 501 Green Ave, P.O. Box 416 • Taft, TX 78390-0416 • (361) 528-3512

Taylor

Taylor Heritage Society & Library • P.O. Box 385 • Taylor, TX 76574 • (512) 352-7230

Teague

Burlington-Rock Island Museum Archives • 208 S 3rd St, P.O. Box 604 • Teague, TX 75860 • (254) 739-2645 • http://www.therailroadmuseum.com

Teague Public Library • 400 Main St • Teague, TX 75860 • (254) 739-3311

Temple

East Bell County Genealogical Society & Library • 3219 Meadow Oaks Dr • Temple, TX 76502-1752 • (254) 778-2073

East Bell Genealogical Society • 2902 Oaklawn • Temple, TX 76502

Hoelscher-Buxkemper Family Heritage Association • 4090 Mountain Laurel Loop • Temple, TX 76502 • (254) 986-8353

Michael Reed Family Association • 316 N 8th St • Temple, TX 76501

Railroad and Heritage Museum Archives • 315 West Ave B • Temple, TX 76501 • (254) 298-5172 • http://www.rrhm.org • *RRHM Newsletter*

Slavonic Benevolent Order of the State of Texas & Archives • Spjst Museum, 520 N Main St, P.O. Box 100 • Temple, TX 76503-0100 • (254) 773-1575 • http://www.spjst.com • *Spjst Vestnik*

Slavonic Benevolent Order of the State of Texas Archives • Historical Museum, 520 N Main St, P.O. Box 100 • Temple, TX 76503 • (254) 773-1575

Temple Public Library • 100 W Adams Ave • Temple, TX 76501-7641 • (254) 770-5702 • http://library.ci.temple.tx.us

Terrell

Kaufman County Genealogical Society & Library • P.O. Box 337 • Terrell, TX 75160-0337 • (214) 524-5605 • *Kaufman Kounty Konnections*

Military Glider Pilots Association Museum Archives • 119 Silent Wings Blvd, P.O. Box 775 • Terrell, TX 75160 • (214) 563-0402

Terrell Public Library • 301 N Rockwall St • Terrell, TX 75160-2618 • (972) 551-6663 • http://www.terrellpl.org

Texarkana

Ace of Clubs House Museum Archives • 420 Pine St, P.O. Box 2343 • Texarkana, TX 75504 • (903) 793-4831 • http://www.texarkanamuseums.org • *Artifacts*

Texarkana Genealogical Society • 1605 E 29th St, P.O. Box 2323 • Texarkana, TX 75504-2323 • (903) 832-7419 • *Texarkana Quarterly*

Texarkana Historical Society & Archives • Historical Museum, 219 State Line Ave, P.O. Box 2243 • Texarkana, TX 75504-2343 • (903) 793-4831 • http://www.texarkanamuseums.org • *Artifacts*

Texarkana Museums System Archives • 219 N State Line Ave, P.O. Box 2343 • Texarkana, TX 75504-2343 • (903) 793-4831 • http://www.texarkanamuseums.org • *Artifacts*

Texarkana Public Library • 600 W 3rd St • Texarkana, TX 75501-5054 • (903) 794-2149 • http://www.txar-publib.org

Texarkana USA Genealogy Society • 2404-A Briar Rose Dr, P.O. Box 2323 • Texarkana, TX 75504-2323 • (870) 772-3955 • *Texarkana USA Genealogical Society Quarterly*

Texas City

College of the Mainland Library • 1200 Amburn Rd • Texas City, TX 77591-2499 • (409) 938-1211 • http://www.com.edu/library

Hightower Research • 9213 Gettysburg • Texas City, TX 77591-2909 • http://home.switchboard.com/hightowerquest • *Hightower Quest*

Moore Memorial Library • 1701 9th Ave N • Texas City, TX 77590 • (409) 643-5979 • http://www.texascity.library.org

Texas City Ancestry Searchers & Archives • c/o Moore Memorial Library, 1701 9th Ave N, P.O. Box 3301 • Texas City, TX 77592-3301 • (409) 643-5979 • *Through the Spyglass*

Texas City Museum Archives • 409 6th St N • Texas City, TX 77592 • (409) 948-9570 • http://www.texas-city-tx.org

Timpson

Timpson Area Genealogical and Heritage Society • P.O. Box 726 • Timpson, TX 75975 • (936) 254-3500 • *Tap Root*

Tomball

Chaparral Genealogical Society & Library • 310 N Live Oak, P.O. Box 606 • Tomball, TX 77377-0606 • (281) 255-9081 • http://www.chaparraltx.org • *Chaparral Genealogical Society Newsletter*

Spring Creek County Historical Association & Archives • Tomball Museum, 510 N Pine St, P.O. Box 457 • Tomball, TX 77377-0457 • (281) 444-2449 • *Spring Creek County Historical Association Newsletter*

Trinity

Blanche K Werner Public Library • Hwy 19 N, P.O. Box 1168 • Trinity, TX 75862-1168 • (936) 594-2087

Tulia

Swisher County Archives and Museum Archives • 127 SW 2nd St, P.O. Box 445 • Tulia, TX 79088 • (806) 995-2819

Swisher County Library • 127 SW 2nd St • Tulia, TX 79088 • (806) 995-3447

Vaugh'a'n Family Association • 735 N Dallas • Tulia, TX 79088 • (806) 995-3308 • *Vaugh'a'n Family Association Newsletter*

Tyler

Clark-Jones Family Reunion • 509 Hyde Park • Tyler, TX 75701 • (903) 595-0671

East Texas Genealogical Society & Library • P.O. Box 6967 • Tyler, TX 75711 • (903) 561-3830 • *East Texas Family Records*; *East Texas Genealogical Society Newsletter: The Bulletin*

Fitzgerald House Archives • 815 S Broadway Ave • Tyler, TX 75701 • (903) 597-8869

Goodman Museum Archives • 624 N Broadway, P.O. Box 2039 • Tyler, TX 75702 • (903) 531-1286

Historic Tyler • 815 S Broadway Ave • Tyler, TX 75701 • (903) 595-1960

Loughmiller Family Genealogy Organization • 13715 CR 2216 • Tyler, TX 75707-9619 • (903) 566-1842

McClendon House Archives • 806 W Houston St • Tyler, TX 75702 • (903) 592-3533

Smith County Historical Society & Archives • Carnegie History Center, 125 S College Ave • Tyler, TX 75702-7216 • (903) 592-5993 • http://www.smithcountyhistory.org • *Chronicles of Smith County Texas*

Tyler Public Library • 201 S College Ave • Tyler, TX 75702-7381 • (903) 593-7323 • http://www.tylerlibrary.com/

Vaughn Library • 1327 S Baxter St, P.O. Box 9020 • Tyler, TX 75711-9020 • (903) 510-2549 • http://www.tjc.edu/library

Universal City
Randolph Area Genealogical Society & Library • P.O. Box 2134 • Universal City, TX 78148-1134 • (210) 659-7881 • *Rag Sheet*

Samuel Nash Family Organization • 114 Rimdale • Universal City, TX 78148

Uvalde
El Progreso Memorial Library • 129 W Nopal St • Uvalde, TX 78801 • (830) 278-2017 • http://www.elprogreso.org

Garner Memorial Museum Archives • 333 N Park St • Uvalde, TX 78801 • (830) 278-5018 • http://www.cah.utexas.edu

Southwest Texas Genealogical Society & Library • 120 W Nopal St, P.O. Box 295 • Uvalde, TX 78802 • (512) 563-2976 • *Branches and Acorns*

Will C Miller Memorial Library • Southwest Texas Junior College, 2401 Garner Field Rd • Uvalde, TX 78801 • (830) 591-7367 • http://library.swtjc.cc.tx.us

Valley Mills
Bosque Valley Heritage Society • P.O. Box 168 • Valley Mills, TX 76689

Van Alstyne
Van Alstyne Public Library • 117 N Waco St, P.O. Box 629 • Van Alstyne, TX 75495-0629 • (903) 482-5991 • http://www.vanalstynepl.lib.tx.us

Van Horn
Clark Hotel Museum Archives • 112 W Broadway • Van Horn, TX 79855 • (915) 283-8028 • *Clark Hotel Museum Newsletter*

Culberson County Historical Museum Archives • 212 W Broadway, P.O. Box 231 • Van Horn, TX 79855 • (915) 283-2043

Van Vleck
Meadows Family: Footprints on the James • P.O. Box 504 • Van Vleck, TX 77482 • (979) 245-4885

Vernon
Carnegie City-County Library • 2810 Wilbarger St • Vernon, TX 76384 • (940) 552-2462

Red River Valley Museum Archives • 4600 College Dr W, P.O. Box 2004 • Vernon, TX 76384 • (940) 553-1848 • http://www.rrvm.org

Wilbarger County Historical Society • 1700 Wilbarger St • Vernon, TX 76384

Victoria
McNamara House Museum Archives • 502 N Liberty • Victoria, TX 77901 • (361) 575-8227 • http://www.viptx.net/museum/ • *YRMA Newsletter*

Swanger Research • 505 Cambridge • Victoria, TX 77901 • *Swanger Family Helper*

Victoria College Library • University of Houston, 2602 N Ben Jordan St • Victoria, TX 77901-5699 • (361) 572-6421 • http://lois.vic.uh.edu

Victoria County Genealogical Society • c/o Victoria Public Library, 302 N Main St • Victoria, TX 77901-6505 • (361) 572-2704 • *Victoria-Crossroads of South Texas*

Victoria Preservation • 205 W Goodwin Ave • Victoria, TX 77901-6520 • (361) 573-1878

Victoria Public Library • 302 N Main St • Victoria, TX 77901 • (361) 572-2704

Vidor
Vidor Public Library • 440 E Bolivar St • Vidor, TX 77662 • (409) 769-7148

Waco
Baylor University Library • 1312 S 3rd, P.O. Box 97148 • Waco, TX 76798-7148 • (254) 710-2112 • http://www.baylor.edu/Library

Brown-Stanton-Evans-Sherman-Neville-Jones-Giles-Spencer-Harrison Families • 2620 MacArthur • Waco, TX 76708 • (254) 776-0330

Central Texas Genealogical Society & Archives • c/o McLellan County Library, 1717 Austin Ave • Waco, TX 76701-1741 • (254) 750-5941 • http://aisi.net/GenWeb/McLennanCo/ • *Heartlines*; *Heart of Texas Records*

Dr Pepper Museum Archives • 300 S 5th • Waco, TX 76701 • (254) 757-1025 • http://www.drpeppermuseum.com • *Bottlecaps*

Earle-Harrison House Museum Archives • 1901 N 5th St • Waco, TX 76708 • (254) 753-2032 • http://www.carleharrison.com • *Columns*

Hamilton House Archives • 1521 Austin Ave • Waco, TX 76701 • (254) 754-2823

Helen Marie Taylor Museum of Waco History Archives • 701 Jefferson Ave • Waco, TX 76701-1353 • (254) 752-4774

Historic Waco Foundation & Archives • Historical Museum, 810 S 4th St, P.O. Box 3222 • Waco, TX 76706-1036 • (254) 753-5166 • http://www.historicwaco.org • *Waco Heritage and History*

IC Anderson Library • First Baptist Church, 500 Webster St • Waco, TX 76706 • (254) 752-3000 • http://www.fbcwaco.org

Masonic Grand Lodge & Library • 715 Columbus St, P.O. Box 446 • Waco, TX 76703-0446 • (254) 753-7395 • http://www.grandlodgeoftexas.org

Texas Collection • Baylor University, 1429 S 5th St, P.O. Box 97142 • Waco, TX 76798-7142 • (254) 710-1268 • http://diogenes.baylor.edu/wwwproviders/Library/home.html

Texas Oral History Association • 1 Bear Place #97271, Baylor Univ • Waco, TX 76798-7271 • (254) 710-6285 • *Texas Oral History Association Newsletter*; *Sound Historian: Journal of the Texas Oral History Association*

Texas Ranger Hall of Fame and Museum Archives • 100 Texas Ranger Trail, P.O. Box 2570 • Waco, TX 76702-2570 • (254) 750-8639 • http://www.texasranger.org • *Dispatch*

Waco-McLennan County Library • 1717 Austin Ave • Waco, TX 76701-1794 • (254) 750-5944 • http://www.waco-texas.com

Waco-McLennan County Library System-East Waco • 901 Elm • Waco, TX 76704-2659 • (254) 750-8412 • http://www.waco-texas.com/library

Wake Village
Burket(t)-Burkitt Research • 104 Quail Ln • Wake Village, TX 75501-5784 • Burket(t)-Burkitt Newsletter

Wallisville
Gulf Coast Ancestry Researchers & Library • P.O. Box 16 • Wallisville, TX 77597 • (409) 389-2486 • *Newsletter of the Gulf Coast Ancestry Researchers*

Wallisville Heritage Society & Library • P.O. Box 16 • Wallisville, TX 77597 • (409) 389-2252 • *Age*

Washington
Barrington Living History Farm Archives • 23100 Barrington Ln • Washington, TX 77880 • (936) 878-2213 • http://www.tpwd.state.tx.us/park/washingt/

Star of the Republic Museum Library • 23200 Park Rd 12, P.O. Box 317 • Washington, TX 77880-0317 • (936) 878-2461 • http://www.starmuseum.org • *Star of the Republic Museum Newsletter*

Waxahachie
Dameron-Damron Family Association • 1111 Culbertson • Waxahachie, TX 75165

Ellis County Genealogical Society • P.O. Box 479 • Waxahachie, TX 75165-0479 • (972) 617-0028 • *Searchers and Researchers*

Ellis County Museum Archives • 201 S College St, P.O. Box 706 • Waxahachie, TX 75165 • (972) 937-0681 • http://www.elliscountymuseum.org • *Ellis County Museum Newsletter*

Nicholas P Sims Library • 515 W Main St • Waxahachie, TX 75165-3235 • (972) 937-2671

Winton Family Reunion • 209 Virginia Ave • Waxahachie, TX 75165-2417 • (972) 625-5098

Weatherford

Eidson Research • 607 W Columbia • Weatherford, TX 76086 • (817) 594-4740 • *Eidson Newsletter*

Jelly's Works of Memories • 322 W Columbia St • Weatherford, TX 76086-4052 • (817) 599-0874

Parker County Genealogical Society & Archives • c/o Weatherford Public Library, 1214 Charles St, P.O. Box 201 • Weatherford, TX 76086 • (817) 594-2767 • *Trails West*

Stone Research • 1214 Julie St • Weatherford, TX 76086-6039 • *Stone Newsletter*

Weatherford College Library • 225 College Park Dr • Weatherford, TX 76086 • (817) 594-5471 • http://www.wc.edu/library • *Library Lamplighter*

Weatherford Public Library • 1014 Charles St • Weatherford, TX 76086-5098 • (817) 598-4150 • http://www.weatherford.lib.tx.us

Wellington

Bowen Family Reunion • P.O. Box 309 • Wellington, TX 79095

Collingsworth County Museum Archives • 1404 15th St, P.O. Box 495 • Wellington, TX 79095 • (806) 447-5327 • http://www.collingsworthcountymuseum.org

Weslaco

Wedmore Clan • 20 Siesta Village • Weslaco, TX 78596 • (956) 969-1103 • *Wedmore Clan Newsletter*

Weslaco Museum Archives • 515 S Kansas, P.O. Box 8062 • Weslaco, TX 78599 • (956) 968-9142 • http://www.texasescapes.net • *Weslaco Museum Newsletter*

Weslaco Public Library • 525 S Kansas Ave • Weslaco, TX 78596-6215 • (956) 968-4533 • http://www.weslaco.lib.tx.us

West Columbia

Varner-Hogg Plantation State Historic Site Archives • 1702 N 13th St, P.O. Box 696 • West Columbia, TX 77486 • (979) 345-4656 • http://www.tpwd.state.tx.us

Wharton

Wharton County Historical Museum Archives • 3615 N Richmond Rd, P.O. Box 349 • Wharton, TX 77488 • (979) 532-2600 • http://www.whartoncountymuseum.com • *Wharton County Historical Museum Newsletter*

Wharton County Library • 1920 N Fulton • Wharton, TX 77488 • (409) 532-8080 • http://www.wharton.lib.tx.us

Whitesboro

Whitesboro Public Library • 308 W Main St • Whitesboro, TX 76273 • (903) 564-5432

Wichita Falls

George Moffett Library • Midwestern State Univ, 3410 Taft Ave • Wichita Falls, TX 76308-2099 • (940) 397-4758 • http://library.mwsu.edu

North Texas Genealogical and Historical Association • P.O. Box 4602 • Wichita Falls, TX 76309 • (940) 692-7089 • http://www.wf.net/~fmaier/ • *North Texas Trail Tracers*

Ogden Database • 1801 Ardath • Wichita Falls, TX 76301 • (940) 767-6658

Wichita County Heritage Society & Archives • Kell House Museum, 900 Bluff St • Wichita Falls, TX 76301 • (940) 723-0623 • http://www.wichitaheritage.org • *Heritage Review*

Wichita County Historical Society • 900 7th St • Wichita Falls, TX 76301

Wichita Falls Museum Library • 2 Eureka Cr • Wichita Falls, TX 76308 • (940) 692-0923

Wichita Falls Public Library • 600 11th St • Wichita Falls, TX 76301-4604 • (940) 767-0868 • http://www.wfpl.net • *Check It Out*

Wills Point

Pope Research • 1492 Creek Crossing Tr • Wills Point, TX 75169 • *Pope Historian*

Wimberley

Pioneer Town Archives • 333 Wayside Dr • Wimberley, TX 78676 • (512) 847-3289

Wimberley Valley Genealogical Society • P.O. Box 2102 • Wimberley, TX 78878-2102 • (512) 847-2722

Wimberley Village Library • 400 FM 2325, P.O. Box 1240 • Wimberley, TX 78676-1240 • (512) 847-2188 • http://www.wimberleylibrary.org

Winnie

East Chamber Agriculture Historical Society • 327 E Leblanc Rd • Winnie, TX 77665 • (409) 296-3571

Winnsboro

Carl and Augusta Malluege Organization • 400 N Church St • Winnsboro, TX 75494 • (903) 342-5598

Winters

Genealogical Society of Winters High School • P.O. Box 125 • Winters, TX 79567

Robert Paris Derington Family Organization • 308 Paloma • Winters, TX 79567 • (915) 754-5313

Winters Public Library • 120 N Main • Winters, TX 79567 • (915) 754-4251 • http://www.winterspl.org

Woodville

Allan Shivers Museum Archives • 302 N Charlton • Woodville, TX 75979 • (409) 283-3709 • http://www.allanshiverslibrary.com

Heritage Village Museum Archives • Hwy 190 W, P.O. Box 888 • Woodville, TX 75979 • (409) 283-2272 • http://www.heritage-village.org

Tyler County Genealogical Society • Whitmeyer Genealogy Library, Hwy 190 W, P.O. Box 888 • Woodville, TX 75979 • (409) 283-3253 • http://www.angelfire.com/tx/TCGS/

Tyler County Heritage Society & Archives • Whitmeyer Genealogy Library, Hwy 190 W, P.O. Box 888 • Woodville, TX 75979 • (409) 283-2272 • *Sketches of Tyler County*

Woodway

Dopp Research • 9337 Hill Ln • Woodway, TX 76712-3328 • *Dopp Family Newsletter*

Yorktown

Yorktown Historical Society & Archives • Historical Museum, 144 W Main St, Route 2, Box 123cl • Yorktown, TX 78164 • (361) 564-2174

Zapata

Zapata County Public Library • 901 Kennedy St, P.O. Box 2806 • Zapata, TX 78076-2806 • (956) 765-5351

Alpine
Reinhart Jared Walz-James Albert Johnson Family Organization • 580 N Grove Dr • Alpine, UT 84003 • (801) 756-5761

Seth Alvin Johnson-Joseph Smith Fuller-Eldridge-Dugard-Price-Richard Joseph Healey Family Organization • 310 East 100 South • Alpine, UT 84002 • (801) 756-4726

American Fork
American Fork City Library • 64 S 100 E • American Fork, UT 84003 • (801) 763-3070 • http://www.americanforklibrary.com

Andreas Christiansen Family Organization • 444 Thornwood Dr • American Fork, UT 84003 • (801) 756-3240

Arnold Custer-Victor Moses Iverson-Hyatt-Wheeler-Albert Alexander McCain-Cundiff Surname Organization • 5892 West 10620 North Highland • American Fork, UT 84003-9591 • (801) 756-0155

Bells-Piedmont-John Daniel Malan Family Organization • 388 South 460 East • American Fork, UT 84003 • (801) 492-7993 • http://homepages.rootsweb.com/~waldense/ • *Malan Monitor*; *Bells-Piedmont Families Organization Report*

Phillip Nell Family Organization • 873 North 610 East • American Fork, UT 84003 • (801) 756-2176 • *Phillip Nell Family Biannual Publication*

William Gallimore Dunn Family Organization • 712 East 672 North • American Fork, UT 84003 • (801) 756-7584

Bennion
Albert Clements-Samuel Jackson Family Organization • 2261 Ledgewood Dr • Bennion, UT 84084 • (801) 966-2134

Blanding
John Kilpatrick McDonald Family • 821 North 100 West • Blanding, UT 84511-3465 • (435) 678-3821

Bluffdale
Drugge-Carl Richard Holmqvist Family Organization • 2555 West 15000 South • Bluffdale, UT 84065 • (801) 254-1095

Jenny Fredrika Hedlund Family Organization • 2555 West 15000 South • Bluffdale, UT 84065 • (801) 254-1095

Bountiful
Abraham Marchant Family Organization • 301 East 1050 North • Bountiful, UT 84010

American Genealogical Lending Library • 593 West 100 North, P.O. Box 244 • Bountiful, UT 84011-0329 • (801) 298-5358 • http://www.agll.com

Augustus Rich Family Organization • 731 North 700 East • Bountiful, UT 84010

Clarence Edmund Hyatt Family Organization • 261 West 1200 North • Bountiful, UT 84010 • (801) 295-2670

Farnes, Isacke, Shackleton Association • 1451 S Main St • Bountiful, UT 84010-5135 • (801) 295-1916

Frank and Ada Jardine Family Organization • 1020 S Davis Boulevard • Bountiful, UT 84010 • (801) 295-8115

Hunt Family Foundation International • 150 West 1950 South • Bountiful, UT 84010

James Ellison Family Organization • 499 North 200 West #14 • Bountiful, UT 84010-6922

Niels Christensen Iverson Family Organization • 517 South 100 East #28 • Bountiful, UT 84010-5075

Peter Michael Hansen Family Organization • 1041 North 200 West • Bountiful, UT 84010 • (801) 292-5247

Robert Moore Family Organization • 2025 Chokecherry Dr • Bountiful, UT 84010 • (801) 292-7783

Thomas Tolman Family Organization • 2937 S Orchard Dr • Bountiful, UT 84010 • (801) 292-7745 • http://www.genealogy.tolman.com • *Thomas Tolman Family Magazine*; *Thomas Tolman Family Organization Newsletter*

Thomsens Genealogical Center • 833 W 3600 S • Bountiful, UT 84010 • (801) 294-5105

William Charles Mann Family Organization • 320 West 1600 North • Bountiful, UT 84010 • (801) 295-0817

Brigham City
Box Elder County Historic Courthouse Archives • general delivery • Brigham City, UT 84302 • (435) 734-3394

Brigham City Library • 26 E Forest • Brigham City, UT 84302-2198 • (435) 723-5850 • http://bcpl.lib.ut.us

Brigham City Museum Archives • 24 N 300 W, P.O. Box 583 • Brigham City, UT 84302 • (435) 723-6769 • http://www.brigham-city.org

Draper Family Organization • 528 E Forest • Brigham City, UT 84302 • (435) 723-2535 • *Down Draper Lane*

Golden Spike National Historic Site Archives • Promontory Summit, P.O. Box 897 • Brigham City, UT 84302 • (435) 471-2209 • http://www.nps.gov/gosp

Hendrik Molenaar Family Organization • 438 East 5th South • Brigham City, UT 84302 • (435) 723-7453

James Henry Howarth Family Organization • 474 North 5th East • Brigham City, UT 84302 • (435) 734-2384

Jens Christian Jensen Family Organization • 944 Hillview Rd • Brigham City, UT 84302 • (435) 723-7405

John Franklin Haws Family Ancestral Organization • 165 N 9th St • Brigham City, UT 84302 • (435) 723-8069

Castle Dale
Museum of San Rafael Archives • 96 N 100 E • Castle Dale, UT 84720 • (435) 381-5252 • http://www.museumsanrafael.org

Cedar City
Cedar City Public Library • 303 N 100 E • Cedar City, UT 84720 • (435) 586-6661 • http://cedarcitylibrary.org

Culver-Colver Research • 1675 E Sunset Rd • Cedar City, UT 84720 • (435) 586-4507 • *Culver-Colver Crossings*

Edward Burgoyne Family Organization • 694 South 300 East • Cedar City, UT 84720 • (435) 586-3036

Ernest James May Family Organization • 2561 West 3550 North • Cedar City, UT 84720 • (435) 586-2349

Gerald R Sherratt Library • Southern Utah State College, 351 W Center St • Cedar City, UT 84720 • (435) 865-8040 • http://www.li.suu.edu

Iron County Historical Society • c/o Gerald R Sherratt Library, Southern Utah State College, 351 W Center St • Cedar City, UT 84720 • (435) 586-7933

Iron Mission State Park Museum Archives • 635 N Main • Cedar City, UT 84720 • (435) 586-9290 • http://www.stateparks.utah.gov

Peter Petersen Siggard-William Henry Grimshaw Family Organization • 485 E Churchfield Ln • Cedar City, UT 84720

Clifford James Quittner Family Organization • 4463 W Summerplace Cr • Cedar Hills, UT 84062 • (801) 492-4274 • *Quittner Family Organization*

Southworth Family Organization • 9869 N Deep Creek Dr • Cedar Hills, UT 84062 • http://users.aol.com/sforg/ • *Southworth Chronicles*

Centerville
Clan MacPhail Society in North America • 585 North 400 East • Centerville, UT 84014 • http://www.geocities.com/Heartland/Prairie/9803/phail/

Maher-Gauge-Thynne Surname Organization • 1247 N Main St • Centerville, UT 84014-1107 • (801) 298-1029

Utah

Clearfield
Duncan C Crolley Family Organization • 941 Hilltop Dr • Clearfield, UT 84015 • (801) 773-5667

Gilberth Haws and Hannah Whitcomb Family Organization • 448 Barlow • Clearfield, UT 84015 • (801) 776-2551

Croydon
Utah Genealogical Association, Morgan Valley Chapter • 1950 North 6900 East • Croydon, UT 84018-9707 • (801) 829-3295

Delta
Great Basin Historical Society & Archives • Historical Museum, 328 W 100 N, P.O. Box 550 • Delta, UT 84624 • (435) 864-5013

Joseph Smith Black-Peter Thompson Black-Greenlaw-Pineo-Caroline Petersen-Isabella Jane Holt-Joshua Bennett-Isabella Jane Bennett Family Organization • 2230 North 4000 West • Delta, UT 84624 • (435) 864-3674

Draper
Draper Historical Society & Library • 12441 South 900 East • Draper, UT 84020 • (801) 495-3476

Forbes Surname Organization • 846 East 13685 South • Draper, UT 84020 • (801) 571-4558

James Bevan Family Organization • 526 Ringneck Cr • Draper, UT 84020-8906

Utah Cornish Association • P.O. Box 703 • Draper, UT 84020

William Hayes Family Organization • 636 East 11900 South • Draper, UT 84020 • (801) 572-0736

Duchesne
Janney Research • P.O. Box 413 • Duchesne, UT 84021-0413 • (208) 233-8642 • *Janney Journal*

Eagle Mountain
Daniel Quimby Dennett Family Organization • 1403 Osprey Wy • Eagle Mountain, UT 84043-4207 • (801) 266-3361

Elmo
Hugh Marshall Murray Family Organization • P.O. Box 21 • Elmo, UT 84521 • (435) 653-2963

Ephraim
Lucy A Phillips Library • Snow College, 150 E College Ave, P.O. Box 1008 • Ephraim, UT 84627-2700 • (435) 283-7362 • http://www.library.snow.edu

Erda
Ransom Tracy Phelps-William Cicero Bailey Family Organization • 4172 N Palmer Rd • Erda, UT 84074 • (435) 882-5235

Eureka
Tintic Mining Museum Archives • P.O. Box 218 • Eureka, UT 84628 • (435) 433-6842

Fairfield
Camp Floyd-Stagecoach Inn State Park Archives • 18035 W 1540 N • Fairfield, UT 84013 • (801) 768-8932 • http://www.parks.state.ut.us

Fairview
Fairview Museum of History and Art Archives • 85 N 100 E, P.O. Box 157 • Fairview, UT 84629 • (435) 427-9216 • http://www.sanpete.com

Joseph Leslie Shelley Family Organization • Route 1, Box 259 • Fairview, UT 84629 • (435) 462-2794

William Arlof Bohne Family Organization • RR 1, Box 301 • Fairview, UT 84629

Farmington
Davis County Library • 38 S 100 E, P.O. Box 115 • Farmington, UT 84025-0115 • (801) 451-2322 • http://www.co.davis.ut.us/library

Huckstep-Greer-Dumford-Ator Surname Organization • 11 West 300 South • Farmington, UT 84025 • (801) 451-2904 • *Ater-Ator Family Newsletter*

Pioneer Village Archives • 375 N Lagoon Ln, P.O. Box 696 • Farmington, UT 84025 • (801) 451-8050

Ferron
Benjamin Howard May Family Organization • P.O. Box 788 • Ferron, UT 84523 • (435) 384-2642

Fillmore
Family of William Speakman • 135 West 300 South • Fillmore, UT 84631-2553 • (435) 743-6217

Territorial Statehouse State Park Archives • 50 W Capitol Ave • Fillmore, UT 84631 • (435) 743-5316

Fort Douglas
Fort Douglas Military Museum Library • 32 Potter St, Bldg 32 • Fort Douglas, UT 84113 • (801) 588-5188 • http://www.fortdouglas.org

Fort Duschesne
Ute Indian Tribe Museum Archives • Hwy 40, P.O. Box 190 • Fort Duschesne, UT 84026 • (801) 722-4992

Fountain Green
George Coombs Family Organization • P.O. Box 84 • Fountain Green, UT 84632 • (435) 445-3430

Jacob Barben Family Organization • P.O. Box 84 • Fountain Green, UT 84632 • (435) 445-3430

Genola
David Beynon-Anders Eric Lundholm Family Organization • 135 North 400 West • Genola, UT 84655 • (801) 754-3239

Grantsville
Abraham Fawson Family Organization • 647 E Main St • Grantsville, UT 84029 • (435) 884-5572

Utah Genealogical Association, Tooele Chapter • P.O. Box 148 • Grantsville, UT 84029 • (435) 884-6120

Heber
Albert Andrew Bahr Family Organization • 3505 Cobble Creek Ln • Heber, UT 84032 • (435) 654-3623 • *Bahr Newsletter*

Herriman
Ludwig Koelsch Family Organization • 6775 W Rose Canyon Rd • Herriman, UT 84065 • (801) 254-4629

Highland
Gralla Surname Organization • 5663 West 11200 North • Highland, UT 84003 • (801) 756-2713 • *Gralla Family Newsletter*

Ozias Goodwin Family Organization • 10328 N Oak Creek Ln • Highland, UT 84003 • (801) 756-4775

Hill AFB
Hill Aerospace Museum Archives • 7961 Wardleigh Rd • Hill AFB, UT 84506 • (801) 777-6868 • http://www.hill.af.mil/museum

Huntington
David Bruner-Joshua Atchley Holmes-John Monroe-Solomon Lyon-Samuel Drew Family Organization • P.O. Box 612 • Huntington, UT 84528 • (435) 687-9109

Huntsville
Cox Surname Organization • 6800 East 400 North • Huntsville, UT 84317 • (801) 745-2035

Hurricane
Hans Christian Hansen Family Organization • 1350 West 100 North 63-11 • Hurricane, UT 84737 • (435) 638-2411

Hurricane Valley Heritage Park Museum Archives • 112 E 200 N, P.O. Box 91 • Hurricane, UT 84737 • (435) 635-0360

Mary Evans-Elizabeth Draper-Robert and Judith Gibson Family Organization • 125 East 600 North #31-2 • Hurricane, UT 84737 • (435) 635-2474

Samuel Jesse Workman Family Organization • 181 South 100 West #88-15 • Hurricane, UT 84737-1917

Washington H Brown Family Organization • 66 North 3910 West #31611 • Hurricane, UT 84737-2798

William Robinson Crawford Family Organization • 60 North 100 East • Hurricane, UT 84737 • (435) 635-2221

Hyrum

Early Mormon Research Institute • 433 East 300 South • Hyrum, UT 84110 • (801) 575-6535 • http://www.n1.net/mcward/nj.htm • *Nauvoo Journal*

Hyrum City Museum Archives • 83 W Main St • Hyrum, UT 84319 • (435) 245-6850

Maxfield Surname Organization • 250 South 100 East • Hyrum, UT 84319 • (801) 245-6984

Uriah Bickers Memorial Association • 407 West 200 South • Hyrum, UT 84319 • (801) 245-6726

Kaysville

Family Heritage Resources • 178 E 600 S • Kaysville, UT 84037-2589

William S Clay Family Organization • 208 East 600 North • Kaysville, UT 84037 • (801) 546-1415

Kearns

Eli Morris Family Organization • 4956 South 4300 West • Kearns, UT 84118 • (801) 968-0440

Jeremiah Mott Family Organization • 4891 S Forest Cr • Kearns, UT 84118 • (801) 969-5730

Lydia Moser Family Organization • 5241 South 5200 West • Kearns, UT 84118-7024 • (801) 968-5916

La Verkin

Hatfield and Lichfield • P.O. Box 925 • La Verkin, UT 84775 • (435) 635-4575

Layton

Charles Madison Scriven-William Benjamin Bowater-Julian Emil Bernhard Jacobsen Family Organization • 427 Sweet Briar Cr • Layton, UT 84041-5700

Coates Research • 820 Sapphire Dr • Layton, UT 84041 • *Coates Cousins Newsletter*

John Bartlett Family Organization • 302 Harriger Wy • Layton, UT 84041 • (801) 773-4251

Mormon History Association • 2470 North 1000 West • Layton, UT 84041-1236 • (801) 378-4048 • *Journal of Mormon History*

Richard J Jackson Family Organization • 345 East 1150 North • Layton, UT 84041 • (801) 546-0412

Thomas Cott Griggs Family Organization • 427 Sweet Briar Cr • Layton, UT 84041-5700

Utah State Historical Society • 1972 E. Daniel Dr • Layton, UT 84040 • (801) 533-3500 • http://www.utahpreservation.org • Utah Preservation

Victor Hough James Family Organization • 2767 E Brinton Wy • Layton, UT 84041 • (801) 546-3828

Lehi

James McBride Family Organization • 473 West 1800 North • Lehi, UT 84043 • (801) 768-8248

Mary Ann Rostron-Frances Harriet Townsden-John Moroni Blackham-Adam Craik Smyth Family Organization • P.O. Box 383 • Lehi, UT 84043 • (801) 968-1740

William Ashby Family Database • 979 East 500 North • Lehi, UT 84043 • (801) 768-9666

Liberty

John Morse (Moss) Family Organization • 2954 East 4800 North • Liberty, UT 84310

Logan

Descendants of William Hawk-James Brinkerhoff Family Organization • 454 West 6th North • Logan, UT 84321 • (435) 753-0736

Ernest Merrill Morrison Family Organization • 370 North 150 West • Logan, UT 84321 • (435) 752-1795

Everton Publishers • P.O. Box 368 • Logan, UT 84321 • (800) 443-6325 • http://www.everton.com • *Everton's Genealogical Helper*

Family History Network • P.O. Box 368 • Logan, UT 84323-0368 • (435) 752-6022 • *Family History Magazine*

Finchum-Flinchum-Fincham Family Association • 278 West 870 North • Logan, UT 84321 • (435) 753-8233 • *Fincham-Flinchum-Finchum Newsletter*

Frank Poulson Family Organization • 1675 East 1460 North • Logan, UT 84341 • (435) 752-3364

Franqois Kalanquin-Temperance Westwood-Thomas Jefferson King-Elizabeth Jane Shaw-Henry Moon-Henry Huntington-Rebecca Englesby Olin Family Organization • 1774 Country Club Dr • Logan, UT 84321 • (435) 753-6924

James Lackey Turman Family Organization • 158 North 200 West • Logan, UT 84321 • (435) 752-8330

John Robinson and Ann Gregson Family Organization • 825 West 600 South • Logan, UT 84321 • (435) 753-5108 • *Mountain Robin*

Jonathan Earl Family Organization • 385 North 150 West • Logan, UT 84321 • (435) 752-4919

Logan Public Library • 255 N Main St • Logan, UT 84321-3914 • (435) 716-9120 • http://www.logan.lib.ut.us

Merrill Library • Utah State University, 3000 Old Main Hill • Logan, UT 84322-3000 • (435) 797-2678 • http://www.usu.edu/library/

Mochelbost Surname Organization • 155 South 300 East • Logan, UT 84321 • (435) 753-0078

Nathan Williams Packer Family Organization • 1360 East 9th North • Logan, UT 84321 • (435) 752-6466 • *Grist Mill Builders*; *Bridge Builder*, *Family Builder*

Shupe Family Organization • 1117 North 600 East • Logan, UT 84341 • (435) 787-1944

Thornton Research • 962 East 2100 North • Logan, UT 84341-1841 • *Thomas Thornton Family Bulletin*

Western History Association • Main 321, Utah State Univ • Logan, UT 84322-0740 • (435) 750-1301 • http://www.usu.edu/~history/text/whq.htm • *Western Historical Quarterly*

Lynndyl

John Greathouse Family Organization • P.O. Box 205 • Lynndyl, UT 84640

Magna

Bellon Family Organization • 3150 South 7700 West • Magna, UT 84044 • (801) 250-5603

Manti

Manti Public Library • 2 S Main St • Manti, UT 84642-1349 • (435) 835-2201 • http://www.manti.com

Temple Area Genealogical Library • general delivery • Manti, UT 84642

William and Ann Sly Parsons-Samuel and Phebe Wilkinson Mackey Family Organization • 295 W Union • Manti, UT 84642 • (435) 835-9872 • *Mackey Family Newsletter*, *Parsons Family Newsletter*

Mapleton

Henn-Haines Family Organization • 1000 South 1000 East • Mapleton, UT 84663

Richard Pessner Family Organization • 915 East 1600 South • Mapleton, UT 84663 • (801) 489-9877

Midvale

Mazuran-Burkinshaw Surname Organization • 67 E Carlson Ave • Midvale, UT 84047 • (801) 255-2494

Sloan Family • 325 W Wasatch St • Midvale, UT 84047 • (801) 568-2589 • http://hometown.aol.com/sloan473/

William Boyer Family Organization • 7010 South 840 East • Midvale, UT 84047 • (801) 566-8186

Midway

Heber City Regional Branch Genealogical Library • 160 W Main St, P.O. Box 611 • Midway, UT 84049-0611 • (435) 654-2760 • Heber Region Family History Center Newsletter

Jim Mar Publications • 1130 Pine Canyon Rd, P.O. Box 430 • Midway, UT 84049-0430 • (435) 654-4336 • *Bailey Connections*; *Gardner-Gardener-Gardiner-Garner Family Newsletter*

Moab

Dan O'Laurie Museum of Moab Archives • 118 E Center St • Moab, UT 84532 • (801) 259-7985 • *Canyon Legacy*

Darbonne Surname Organization • 1156 Murphy Ln • Moab, UT 84532 • (435) 259-5001

Monroe

Casto-Golden Surname Organization • 53 North 100 West • Monroe, UT 84754-4113 • (435) 527-4475

Monticello

Lemuel Hardison Redd Family Organization • P.O. Box 306 • Monticello, UT 84535 • (801) 587-2576

Morgan

Morgan County Library • 50 W 100 N, P.O. Box 600 • Morgan, UT 84050-0600 • (801) 829-3481

Shupe Family Organization • P.O. Box 39 • Morgan, UT 84050 • (801) 829-3295

Mount Green

Charles Carter Flanary Family Organization • 5655 Monte Verde Dr • Mount Green, UT 84050

Mount Pleasant

William Hamlin Freeman Family Organization • 186 South 300 West #49 • Mount Pleasant, UT 84647

Murray

Broschinsky Surname Organization • 835 E Willowood Ave • Murray, UT 84107 • (801) 262-6087

John Nokes Family Organization • 645 Lasalle Dr • Murray, UT 84123-6827 • (801) 266-2575 • *Newsletter of the John Nokes Family Organization*

Murray Public Library • 166 E 5300 S • Murray, UT 84107-6075 • (801) 264-2580 • http://www.murray.lib.ut.us

Powell Surname Organization: James Quaintance Powell • 6262 S Westridge • Murray, UT 84107 • (801) 266-4904

Thomas Sunderland Hawkins Family Organization • 656 Lasalle Dr • Murray, UT 84123 • (801) 262-4218

New Harmony

George Wadsworth Family Organization • P.O. Box 627 • New Harmony, UT 84757

Kerr Database; Baggs Database; Broadbent Database; Hollingshead Database; Free Database • Harmony Heights • New Harmony, UT 84757

Nibley

Everton Publisher's Library • 3223 S Main • Nibley, UT 84321

Sidwell, Hufstetler-Hufstutler, Gordy, Frazee Research • 162 Quarter Cr Dr • Nibley, UT 84321 • (435) 753-3409

North Logan

Flatt Surname Organization • 1016 East 2050 North • North Logan, UT 84341 • (435) 752-8439

Orin Hatch and Maria Thompson-William Edmund Gooch and Anne Burkinsham-Andrew Lee Allen and Ciarinda Knapp-Andrew Bickmore Allen and Susannah Preece Allen-William Bickmore and Christena Bagley Family Organization • 2015 North 1000 East • North Logan, UT 84321 • (435) 753-1458

North Ogden

Albert Arthur Furse Family Organization • 3125 North 575 East • North Ogden, UT 84414 • (801) 782-5302

MacDuff-McDuff Surname Organization • 639 East 3100 North • North Ogden, UT 84414 • (801) 782-4432

North Salt Lake

Alfred Brady Dooley Family Organization • 105 South 350 East • North Salt Lake, UT 84054 • (801) 936-3161

Heritage Quest Library • 669 West 900 North, P.O. Box 540670 • North Salt Lake, UT 84054 • (801) 298-5446 • http://www.heritagequest.com • *Heritage Quest Magazine; Heritage Quest Genealogy Bulletin*

Hinman-Humphrey Family Association • 337 North 725 East • North Salt Lake, UT 84054-3130 • *Hinman Newsletter; Humphrey Family Quarterly*

Ogden

Carn Surname Organization • 803 Bel Mar Dr • Ogden, UT 84403 • (801) 392-0154

Charles Clark and Henry Uriah Burr Family Organization • 428 20th St • Ogden, UT 84401 • (801) 394-9030

Child(e) Family History Organization • 3787 Jackson Ave • Ogden, UT 84403 • (801) 392-5384

Cowdery Family Association • 4851 South 600 West • Ogden, UT 84405-6008 • (801) 476-0723

Fort Buena Ventura Archives • 2450 A Avenue • Ogden, UT 84401 • (801) 399-8099

Fredrich and Ann M Peterson Family Organization • 938 North 450 East • Ogden, UT 84404 • (801) 782-9538

Harshbarger Association • 975 East 6000 South #64 • Ogden, UT 84405-9702 • (801) 476-9633

Hatch Surname Organization • 795 Bel Mar Dr • Ogden, UT 84403 • (800) 393-0278

Henry and Martha Elizabeth Brackley Bateman Family Organization • 4045 Liberty Ave • Ogden, UT 84403-2942 • (801) 393-7459

Irish-Irishe-Iryshe Surname Association • 4375 Weber River Dr #35 • Ogden, UT 84405 • (801) 392-8726 • *Irish Inquirer: A Surname Genealogical Periodical*

James Winterbottom-Mary Ridgeway-John Welsh-Matthews-Misner-James William Creager-Amaziah Church-Ann Fortesque-Johan Matthias George-Hollingshead-Hollinshead-Rollins-Rawlins Surname Organization • 6154 South 2900 East • Ogden, UT 84403 • (801) 479-4244

John A Thurgood Family Organization • 1225 West 4575 South • Ogden, UT 84405 • (801) 627-2115

John Lloyd Family Organization • 1943 East 6600 South • Ogden, UT 84405 • (801) 479-6057

Nebeker Family Association • 2765 Jefferson Ave • Ogden, UT 84403 • (801) 393-5714

Ogden Union Station Museum Archives • 25th & Wall Sts, Union Station • Ogden, UT 84401 • (801) 629-8444 • http://www.theunionstation.org • *All Aboard*

Purley Louis Reeder Family Organization • 4851 South 600 West • Ogden, UT 84405-6008 • (801) 479-7625

Robert Berrett Family Organization • 2461 North 525 East • Ogden, UT 84414 • (801) 782-9662

Shupe Family Organization • 1523 Lake St • Ogden, UT 84401 • *Shupe Family Organization Bulletin*

Those Utah Dopps • 4045 Liberty Ave • Ogden, UT 84403 • (801) 393-7459

Weber County Library • 2464 Jefferson Ave • Ogden, UT 84401-2464 • (801) 337-2617 • http://www.weberpl.lib.ut.us • *Friends of the Library*; *Rough Draft*

William Lemon Family Organization • 3429 North 950 East • Ogden, UT 84414-1727

Orem

Allison Family Research • 11 West 1780 North • Orem, UT 84057 • (801) 224-9315

Bernhard-Dickinson Family Organization • P.O. Box 2127 • Orem, UT 84059-2127 • (801) 221-0603

Cassell Family Organization • 1572 South 50 West • Orem, UT 84058 • (801) 225-3153 • *Cassell Family Newsletter*

David and Elizabeth Dorwart Sabin Family Organization • 1937 S Main St • Orem, UT 84058 • (801) 225-7218

David Clyde Campbell Family Organization • 1449 South 200 East • Orem, UT 84058

Edward Durtschi Family Organization • 383 East 1800 South • Orem, UT 84058 • (801) 224-1609

Fonville Research • 1937 S Main St • Orem, UT 84058 • (801) 225-7218 • *Fonville Family Findings*

Franklin Thomas Wisdom Family Organization • 612 N Main St • Orem, UT 84057-3922

Johannes Class Family Organization • 313 East 1165 North • Orem, UT 84057 • (801) 225-0056 • *Class Act*

Markham Family Organization • 490 East 600 South • Orem, UT 84058 • (801) 224-1167

Mormon Miner Family Organization • 529 West 1600 South • Orem, UT 84058-7319 • (801) 224-2297

My Family.com • 360 West 4800 North, P.O. Box 990 • Orem, UT 84059 • (801) 705-7000 • http://www.ancestry.com • *Ancestry Magazine*

Orem Public Library • 56 N State St • Orem, UT 84057-5596 • (801) 229-7050 • http://www.oremlibrary.org

Posey Family of America • 275 West 1200 North • Orem, UT 84057-2610

Prince Wing-Sarah Basford-Avery Hall Family Organization • 497 West 120 North • Orem, UT 84057-1940

Thomas Chamberlain Family Organization • 147 N 200 E • Orem, UT 84057-5516 • (801) 225-2598

Thomas Guthrie Family Organization • 39 South 300 East • Orem, UT 84058 • (801) 225-4161

Utah Valley PAF Users Group • 490 E 600 S • Orem, UT 84097 • (801) 224-1167 • http://www.uvpafug.org • *PAFology*

Walter Muir-William Golding Family Organization • 1895 North 285 East • Orem, UT 84057 • (801) 225-7375

Panquitch

Mary Moyer Family Organization • 142 West 2nd North, P.O. Box 361 • Panquitch, UT 84759 • (801) 676-8035

Park City

Park City Historical Society & Archives • Historical Museum, 528 Main St, P.O. Box 555 • Park City, UT 84060 • (435) 649-7457 • http://www.parkcityhistory.org • *Park City Historical Society Quarterly*

Park City Library • 1255 Park Ave, P.O. Box 668 • Park City, UT 84060-0668 • (435) 615-5600

Parowan

Parowan Public Library • 16 S Main St, P.O. Box 427 • Parowan, UT 84761-0427 • (435) 477-3491

Payson

Payson City Library • 66 S Main St • Payson, UT 84651-2223 • (801) 465-5220

Peter Davis-Matthew Duke Family Organization • 739 East 400 North • Payson, UT 84651 • (801) 465-3155

Perry

David Henry Toyn Family Organization • 1805 South 225 West • Perry, UT 84302

Jacob Elsasser-George Mackey-Hedrick Surname Organization • 2425 South 500 West • Perry, UT 84302 • (435) 723-2554

Wallace Kendall Burnham Family Organization • 2240 Highway 89 • Perry, UT 84302 • (435) 723-2543

Pleasant Grove

Busker Surname Organization • 323 W Center • Pleasant Grove, UT 84062

John William Gilson Family Organization • 895 North 200 West • Pleasant Grove, UT 84062 • (801) 785-1002 • *Gilson Family History Report*

Pleasant Grove Public Library • 30 E Center St • Pleasant Grove, UT 84062-2234 • (801) 785-3950 • http://www.plgrove.org/library/

Price

College of Eastern Utah Library • 451 E 400 N • Price, UT 84501 • (435) 613-5616 • http://www.library.ceu.edu

Price City Library • 159 E Main St • Price, UT 84501-3046 • (435) 636-3188 • http://www.pricecityutah.com

Providence

Thomas Clemens Foley-Adele Louise Franke-Mary Frances Daglan Family Organization • 555 Spring Creek Rd • Providence, UT 84332 • (435) 753-1537

Provo

Ancestry Publications • 360 West 4800 North • Provo, UT 84604 • (800) 262-3787 • http://www.ancestry.com • *Ancestry Magazine*

Armstrong Research • 1746 West 220 South • Provo, UT 84601-3822 • *Armstrong Bulletin Board*

Baggerly Surname Organization • P.O. Box 1594 • Provo, UT 84604 • (801) 377-6301

Charles E C Musig Family Organization • 44 South 700 East • Provo, UT 84601

Charles Redd Center for Western Studies • Brigham Young Univ • Provo, UT 84602 • (801) 378-4048

David Henry Toyn Family Organization • 560 E Sumac • Provo, UT 84604-1828 • (801) 375-5333

Erastus Snow Family Organization • Dept of Mathematics, BYU • Provo, UT 84602 • (801) 378-2366

Graham Family Organization • 965 E 2680 N • Provo, UT 84604-4105

Harold B Lee Library and Genealogy Dept • Brigham Young Univ, 2720 HBLL • Provo, UT 84602 • (801) 378-2927 • http://www.lib.byu.edu/dept/uvrfhc

Hopper Researchers Clearinghouse • P.O. Box 7324, Univ Sta • Provo, UT 84602 • *Hopper Journal*

Isiah Guyman-Chunn Surname Organization • 1785 North 1500 East • Provo, UT 84604 • (801) 374-1777

James Bean Family Organization • 313 East 2020 North • Provo, UT 84601 • (801) 374-5328

John Wood Family Organization • 1286 Apple Ave • Provo, UT 84604 • (801) 373-9897

My Family.com • 360 West 4800 North • Provo, UT 84604 • (801) 705-7000 • http://www.ancestry.com • *Genealogical Computing*; *Ancestry's Guide to Research and Vital Record Catalog*

Phineas Walcott Cook Family Organization • 1334 Maple Ln • Provo, UT 84604 • *Phineas Wolcott Cook Family Organization Newsletter*

Provo City Public Library • 550 N University Ave • Provo, UT 84601-1618 • (801) 852-6661 • http://www.provocitylibrary.com

Reimschussel Surname Organization • 495 South 900 East • Provo, UT 84606 • (801) 377-2662

Robert Edgar Family Organization • P.O. Box 7107 • Provo, UT 84602

Thomas Minor Family Society • 815 North 300 West • Provo, UT 84604 • (801) 377-8294 • *Minor Mirror*

Thomas Thorn and Mary Ann Dowman-John Hall and Sarah Edge and Mary Bates-William Hutchison and Jane Penman Organization • 2421 North 750 East • Provo, UT 84604-4014 • (801) 375-4390 • *William Hutchison and Jane Penman Organization Newsletter*

Titus Billings Family Organization • 706 North 970 West • Provo, UT 84601 • (801) 373-4605

Utah Genealogical Association, Utah Valley Chapter • P.O. Box 7227 • Provo, UT 84602 • (801) 224-1728

Vernon Carniehan Jamison Family Organization • 1245 Blair Ave • Provo, UT 84604

Richfield

George Franklin Carroll-Johannes Jonsson Family Organization • 555 West 600 North • Richfield, UT 84701 • (801) 896-6982

George Mills Family Association • 905 West 740 South • Richfield, UT 84701 • (801) 896-8600 • *George Mills Family Newsletter*

Riverton

Joseph Callison-Thomas Sasson Smith-Charles Hardesty-Horace Nokes Family Organization • 2644 West 12420 South • Riverton, UT 84065

Roosevelt

Frank Frederick Meyer Family Organization • Route 2, Box 63 • Roosevelt, UT 84066 • (435) 722-3740

Roy

James Johnston-Ellen E Pinney Family Organization • 5246 South 2150 West • Roy, UT 84067 • (801) 773-4568

Saint George

Benjamin Frederick Blake Family Organization • 165 East 200 South • Saint George, UT 84770 • (435) 628-6284

Brigham Young's Winter Home Museum Archives • 67 W 200 N • Saint George, UT 84770 • (435) 673-2517 • http://www.stgeorgetemplevisitorcenter.org/byounghome.html

Clair L Hawes Family Organization • 3019 S Birch Cr • Saint George, UT 84770 • (435) 673-8366

David Milne Family Organization • 211 South 100 East • Saint George, UT 84770 • (435) 673-2283

Evenson-Knudsen-West-Powell Family Organization • 2941 S Palmetto Cr • Saint George, UT 84770 • (435) 628-0215

Institute of Genealogy and History for Latin America • 316 West 500 North • Saint George, UT 84770 • (435) 656-1129

James Hearknett Wallis Family Organization • 3642 South 1730 West • Saint George, UT 84790 • (435) 674-5285

James Simkins and Mary Walker Family Association • 1090 East 700 South #8 • Saint George, UT 84770 • (435) 628-3449

John and Mary Willey-Ernst Ludwig Reinbold-Hopkin-Jubb-Cliff-Johnson-Lane-Fike-Richardson-Trachsel-Troxell-McKitrick Family Database • 998 Bloomington Dr S • Saint George, UT 84770-7500 • (435) 673-6314

John Rowlandson Robinson Family Organization • 454 South 100 East #11 • Saint George, UT 84770 • (435) 674-2136

Kreitzer Surname Organization • 149 East 300 South • Saint George, UT 84770 • (435) 673-2927

Porritt Surname Organization • 2045 South 1400 East #14 • Saint George, UT 84770-6841

Val A Browning Library • Dixie College, 225 S 700 E • Saint George, UT 84770 • (435) 652-7714 • http://www.library.dixie.edu/library/

Washington County Library • 50 S Main St • Saint George, UT 84770-3490 • (435) 634-5737 • http://www.washco.lib.ut.us • *Washington County Library Newsletter*

Salt Lake City

Abbey Surname Organization • 453 6th Ave • Salt Lake City, UT 84103 • (801) 359-8409

Accelerated Indexing Systems International • P.O. Box 2127 • Salt Lake City, UT 84110-2127 • *Genealogy Times and Seasons*

American Research Bureau • 2386 E Heritage Wy • Salt Lake City, UT 84109

Association of Professional Genealogists • P.O. Box 11601 • Salt Lake City, UT 84147 • *Association of Professional Genealogists Quarterly*; *Association of Professional Genealogists List of Professional Genealogists and Related Services Quarterly*

Azariah Elswood Family Organization • 1057 Princeton Ave • Salt Lake City, UT 84105 • (801) 363-8754

Basil Archabald Jackson Family Organization • 643 Bunbury Cove #907 • Salt Lake City, UT 84104-3191

Beehive House Archives • 67 E South Temple • Salt Lake City, UT 84131 • (801) 240-2681

Brit'n Genealogy Clearing House • 2751 E Wilshire Dr • Salt Lake City, UT 84109 • (801) 485-4249 • *Brittain-Britton Newsletter*

Burningham Surname Organization • 4231 Marquis Wy • Salt Lake City, UT 84124

Charles Allen Foster Family Organization • 3850 Bobwhite Wy • Salt Lake City, UT 84120 • (801) 967-1257

Chippendale Surname Organization • 2701 Milo Wy • Salt Lake City, UT 84117 • (801) 277-1453

Classic Cars International Museum Archives • 355 W 700 S • Salt Lake City, UT 84101 • (801) 322-5509 • http://www.classiccarmuseumsales.com

Cuban Genealogical Society • 2552 Tamara Dr, P.O. Box 2650 • Salt Lake City, UT 84110-2650 • (801) 968-7312 • *Revista*

Daughters of the American Revolution, Utah Society • 6855 S Willow Wy • Salt Lake City, UT 84121

Doss Surname Organization • 718 North 900 West #206 • Salt Lake City, UT 84116 • (801) 531-2529

Faatz Family Association • 2143 Blair St • Salt Lake City, UT 84115

Federation of East European Family History Societies & Library • P.O. Box 510898 • Salt Lake City, UT 84151-0898 • (801) 278-4586 • http://feefhs.org • *FEEFHS: Newsletter of the Federation of East European Family History Societies*

Francis Millan Family Organization • 1364 East 1300 South • Salt Lake City, UT 84105 • (801) 581-1718

Franklin Raymond Farr Family Organization • 1202 McClelland St • Salt Lake City, UT 84105

Genealogical Institute & Library • 162 I Street • Salt Lake City, UT 84122 • (801) 328-2305 • *Genealogical Institute Research News*; *Immigration Digest*

Genealogical Library of the Church of Jesus Christ of Latter Day Saints • 50 East North Temple • Salt Lake City, UT 84150 • (801) 240-2745 • http://www.lds.org/churchhistory/askalibrarian

George Edwin Woolley Family Association • 3722 South 1880 East • Salt Lake City, UT 84106 • (801) 277-9930 • *George Edwin Woolley Association Newsletter*

German Genealogical Digest • 245 N Vine St, Ste 106, P.O. Box 112054 • Salt Lake City, UT 84147 • http://feefhs.org/pub/frg-ggdp.html • *German Genealogical Digest: A Quarterly Journal for German Researchers*

German Genealogical Society • 544 E Wilmington Ave • Salt Lake City, UT 84106

Gillie-Gilley-George Carson Family History Association • 1480 Edison St • Salt Lake City, UT 84115 • (801) 485-0976 • http://www.wolsi.com/~gnat/carson/carson.html • *George Carson Family History Association Bulletin*

Giovale Library • Westminster College, 1840 S 1300 E • Salt Lake City, UT 84105-3697 • (801) 832-2251 • http://www.westminstercollege.edu/library

Graff-Luken Research • 927 E 7th St • Salt Lake City, UT 84102 • *Graff Newsletter, Luken Family History*

Halsell Family Research • 846 Garfield Ave • Salt Lake City, UT 84105 • (801) 485-4782 • *Halsells and Their Families*

Hans Jensen Family Organization • 731 Wall St • Salt Lake City, UT 84103 • (801) 359-3117

Heber Chase Kimball -Fitch Family Collection • 1387 Emery St • Salt Lake City, UT 84104 • (435) 872-2341 • *Heber Chase Kimball Family News*

Henry Willis Family Organization • 531 C Street • Salt Lake City, UT 84103

International Society for British Genealogy and Family History • P.O. Box 3115 • Salt Lake City, UT 84110-3115 • (801) 272-2178 • http://homestart.com/isbgfh/ • *International Society for British Genealogy and Family History Newsletter, International Genealogical Directory*

James and Agnes Erwin Family Organization • 391 Trolley Sq • Salt Lake City, UT 84102 • (801) 521-6248

James Godfrey and Fannie Alice Jones Family Organization • 1064 West 13th South • Salt Lake City, UT 84104

James Ritter Hebdon Family Organization • 70 N Street • Salt Lake City, UT 84103

Jared Green-Deloretta Harris Family Association • 947 McClelland • Salt Lake City, UT 84105 • (801) 359-5762

Jensen Publications • P.O. Box 112054 • Salt Lake City, UT 84147 • (801) 225-8661 • http://www.german-digest.com • *German Genealogical Digest*

Jewish Genealogical Society of Salt Lake City • 3510 Fleetwood Dr • Salt Lake City, UT 84109 • (801) 277-8752

John Benion Family Organization • 2166 Parley's Terr • Salt Lake City, UT 84109 • (801) 968-7848

John Gooley-Peter Morgan Maughan Family Organization • 109 East South Temple #3M • Salt Lake City, UT 84111-1106

John Ross Browne-Thomas Craven-Levi Collins Frisbie-Whittlesey Surname Organization • P.O. Box 26183 • Salt Lake City, UT 84126 • (801) 272-3928 • *Whittlesey Family Newsletter*

John Walter Neal-William Bateman Family Organization • 1071 N Topaz Dr • Salt Lake City, UT 84116 • (801) 595-6325

John William Roper Database • 4392 South 1300 West • Salt Lake City, UT 84123 • (801) 261-4414

Joseph Toronto Family Organization • 7969 Top of the World Drive • Salt Lake City, UT 84121 • (801) 942-5070

Justine Kolb Family Organization • 4565 Jarrah St • Salt Lake City, UT 84123

Lelia Tuckett Whiting Family Organization • 6460 Tanner Ln • Salt Lake City, UT 84121-2766 • (801) 278-2405

Marriott Library • Univ of Utah, 295 S 1500 E • Salt Lake City, UT 84112-0860 • (801) 581-6273 • http://www.lib.utah.edu/spc/spc.html • *Friends of the Libraries Newsletter*

Martin Isaac Bushman Family Organization • 1434 Roxbury Rd • Salt Lake City, UT 84108-2843 • (801) 582-8700

McCormick-Reid-Casebolt-Wooldridge-Haymore-Cook-McConnell-Douglas-Bottoms Family Organization • 241 N Vine St #1104E • Salt Lake City, UT 84103-1945 • (801) 278-4800 • *Casebolt Quarterly*

Moody-Joyner -McCune Family Association • 5243 Carpell Ave, P.O. Box 18044 • Salt Lake City, UT 84118-8044 • (801) 964-2825 • *McCune Family Association Newsletter*

Moses Martin Sanders-William Hurst Family Organization • 1441 Yale Ave • Salt Lake City, UT 84105 • (801) 583-0604

Museum of Church History Archives • 45 N West Temple St • Salt Lake City, UT 84150 • (801) 240-5342 • http://www.lds.org/churchhistory/museum

National Society, Daughters of Utah Pioneers & Library • 300 N Main St • Salt Lake City, UT 84103-1699 • (801) 538-1050 • http://www.dupinternational.org • *Legacy Newsletter*

National Society, Sons of Utah Pioneers & Library • 3301 East 2920 South • Salt Lake City, UT 84109 • (801) 484-4441 • http://www.sonsofutahpioneers.org • *Pioneer Magazine*

Nils Nilson-George Done Smith Family Organization • 2905 Craig Dr • Salt Lake City, UT 84109 • (801) 277-6107

Orlando Hopkins Carr Family Organization • 2015 Sycamore Ln • Salt Lake City, UT 84117

Rasmus Jorgensen Family Organization • 3847 Lares Wy • Salt Lake City, UT 84124 • (801) 278-1444

Registry of American Black Ancestry • P.O. Box 417 • Salt Lake City, UT 84110

Robert Marshall Family Organization • 4231 Helaman Cr • Salt Lake City, UT 84124 • (801) 278-5245

Salt Lake City Public Library • 210 E 400 S • Salt Lake City, UT 84111-3280 • (801) 524-8211 • http://www.slcpl.lib.ut.us • Images

Salt Lake County Library System • 2197 East 7000 South • Salt Lake City, UT 84121-3188 • (801) 943-4636

Stephen Smith McCann Family Organization • 1330 Diane Dr • Salt Lake City, UT 84123 • (801) 266-1182

Stow(e) Surname Associates • 57 W Guest Ave • Salt Lake City, UT 84115 • (801) 262-2894

Swen Backman Family Organization • 1852 E Zenda Wy • Salt Lake City, UT 84121 • (801) 277-0440

Swope Family Association • 2609 Keddington Ln • Salt Lake City, UT 84117-4562 • (801) 278-2230

Taylor Family Association • 2065 East 9060 South • Salt Lake City, UT 84093 • *Taylor Times*

This is the Place Heritage Park Archives • 2601 Sunnyside Ave • Salt Lake City, UT 84108 • (801) 582-1847 • http://www.thisistheplace.org

Thomas Barclay John Family Organization • 1748 Garfield Ave • Salt Lake City, UT 84108 • (801) 467-0056

Thomas Crowton-John Fidkin Family Organization • 45 East 500 North • Salt Lake City, UT 84103 • (801) 363-3272

Thomas Franklin Fussell Family Organization • 518 Driggs Ave • Salt Lake City, UT 84106 • (801) 466-6785

Thomas Harris-John Edmond Baker Family Organization • 1310 Phillips Ln • Salt Lake City, UT 84123 • (801) 262-1492

Thomas Jones and Letitia Thomas Family Organization • 470 6th Ave • Salt Lake City, UT 84103 • (801) 359-5300

Thomas Thorn-Thomas Courtney-Thomas Hall-Thomas Glisson-Thomas McDonough Family Organization • 1599 Monaco Cr • Salt Lake City, UT 84121 • (801) 278-7708

Utah Genealogical Association & Library • 35 North West Temple, P.O. Box 1144 • Salt Lake City, UT 84150-3400 • (801) 240-2331 • http://www.familysearch.org • *Genealogical Journal; Utah Genealogical Association News*

Utah Genealogical Association, Salt Lake Valley Chapter • 1131 South 1100 East • Salt Lake City, UT 84105 • (801) 582-3157

Utah Preservation Society • 300 Rio Grande • Salt Lake City, UT 84101-1182 • (801) 533-3500 • *Utah Preservation*

Utah State Archives • Archives Bldg, State Capitol • Salt Lake City, UT 84114-1021 • (801) 538-3013 • http://www.archives.state.ut.us

Utah State Historical Society & Library • 300 Rio Grande • Salt Lake City, UT 84101-1182 • (801) 533-3535 • http://www.history.state.ut.us • *Beehive History*; *Utah Historical Quarterly*; *News of the Utah State Historical Society*

Utah State Library • 250 N 1950 W, Suite A • Salt Lake City, UT 84116-7901 • (801) 715-6777 • http://www.state.lib.ut.us

Wheeler Historic Farm Archives • 6351 S 900 E • Salt Lake City, UT 84121 • (801) 264-2241 • http://www.wheelerfarm.com

Whitfield-John Hurst-Abraham Shepard Lane-Jeremiah Exum-Margaret Murphy-John Kirkland Family Organization • 532 Millcreek Wy • Salt Lake City, UT 84106-1104

Wilford Woodruff Family Association • 57 W South Temple, Ste 300, P.O. Box 11980 • Salt Lake City, UT 84147 • (801) 531-0920

Willard James Jones Family Organization • 2432 Wilson Ave • Salt Lake City, UT 84108 • (801) 583-1838

William Capell Family Organization • 3035 E Lajoya Dr • Salt Lake City, UT 84117 • (801) 277-7617

William Robert Jenkins-David Alma Brown Family Organization • 4275 White Wy • Salt Lake City, UT 84124 • (801) 277-4783

William Thomas Butler Family Organization • 1616 West 700 North • Salt Lake City, UT 84116 • (801) 359-1396

William W Bibee Family Organization • 1174 Glorieta Dr • Salt Lake City, UT 84106 • (801) 485-0584

Woolley-Hampton-Foster-Olpin-Dunbar-Ashbridge-Samuel Rose Parkinson-Chandler Research • 2069 E Yale Ave • Salt Lake City, UT 84108-1905 • (801) 582-3668

Sandy

Knick-Christie Surname Organization • 1020 Eastridge Rd • Sandy, UT 84094 • (801) 572-7807

Lorenzo Snow Whiting-Moses Fannin-John Elmer Brimhall Family Organization • 1257 E Cedar Ridge Rd • Sandy, UT 84094

Thomas Lunnen Family Organization • 1780 Siesta Dr • Sandy, UT 84093-6247 • (801) 942-6414

Santa Clara

Jacob Hamblin Home Museum Archives • US Hwy 91 • Santa Clara, UT 84770 • (435) 652-9589

Santaquin

Dyckman-Dikeman-Dykeman Family Association • P.O. Box 674 • Santaquin, UT 84655 • (508) 754-3560 • *Dyckman-Dikeman-Dykeman Family Newsletter*

Smithfield

McKenzie Family • 252 North 200 East • Smithfield, UT 84335 • (435) 563-5614

Stephen Elliot Byington Family Organization • 174 North 200 West • Smithfield, UT 84335 • (435) 563-9004

South Jordan

Huntsman-Weirick-Weyrick Surname Organization • 10315 South 1540 West • South Jordan, UT 84095 • (801) 254-3532

William Gill Family Organization • 2614 N Forty Wy • South Jordan, UT 84065 • (801) 254-1814

Spanish Fork

Heaer Christian Christiensen Family Organization • P.O. Box 768 • Spanish Fork, UT 84660-0768

James Parkinson Family Organization • 430 North 200 East • Spanish Fork, UT 84660 • (801) 798-2995

National Gorby Association • 8165 S Mill Rd • Spanish Fork, UT 84660 • (801) 798-2651 • *Gorby Roots*

William Goates Family Organization • 2411 East 1370 South • Spanish Fork, UT 84660 • (801) 968-3442

Springville

Albert Miner Family Organization • 545 South 200 East • Springville, UT 84663 • (801) 489-4126

Dup Museum and Historical Society • 175 S Main St • Springville, UT 84663 • (801) 491-2076

Elizabeth Freeman Family Organization • 130 West 400 North • Springville, UT 84663 • (801) 489-8158

Joseph Hepworth and Mary Hirst-Lorin Elias Bassett-Caroline Geneva Jenkins-John William Dutson Family Organization • 1055 E Hillcrest Dr • Springville, UT 84663 • (801) 489-6298 • *Dutson Family Research Report*; *Hepworth-Hirst Family Newsletter*; *Hepworth Research Report*; *Lorin Elias Bassett Family Organization Research Report*; *Newsletter of the Caroline Geneva Jenkins Family Organization*

Martin Harris Family Organization • 101 North 1300 East • Springville, UT 84663 • (801) 489-6567

Niels Hansen Family Organization • 360 North 200 East • Springville, UT 84663 • (801) 489-7871

Springville Public Library • 50 S Main St • Springville, UT 84663 • (801) 489-2720

Sunset

Alfred Cordon Family Organization • 816 North 250 West • Sunset, UT 84015 • (801) 776-1219

Syracuse

James Thomas Family Organization • 1178 Bluff Rd • Syracuse, UT 84075 • (801) 773-0531

Marlin Gailey Family Organization • 3333 South 1000 West • Syracuse, UT 84075 • (801) 776-2461

Reber-Grasser-John and Amelia Mitchell Croft-Benjamin Waldron-James Gray Willie Family Organization • 3385 S Bluff Rd • Syracuse, UT 84075 • (801) 773-0531 • James Gray Willie Family Organization Newsletter

Taylorsville

Bellingham Family History Association • 4798 S Settlers Wy #11 • Taylorsville, UT 84123 • (801) 313-1478

George Gidney Family Organization • 4214 S Morris St • Taylorsville, UT 84119 • (801) 967-8957

Hugh Jordan Moore Family Association • 3374 W Brigarade Ln • Taylorsville, UT 84118 • (801) 968-4326

Tooele

Cornelius Maxwell Family Organization • 495 East 500 North • Tooele, UT 84074 • (435) 882-4851

Hans Christian Mortensen-Daniel James Family Organization • 389 South 360 West • Tooele, UT 84074 • (435) 882-2204

Lothropp Family Foundation • 271 Julie Ann Ct • Tooele, UT 84074 • *Lothropp Family Foundation Newsletter*

Tooele Public Library • 148 W Vine St • Tooele, UT 84074-2059 • (435) 882-2182 • http://www.tooelecity.org

Tremonton

Family History World • P.O. Box 129 • Tremonton, UT 84337 • (801) 250-6717 • *Immigration Digest*

Genealogical Institute • 375 N 300 E, P. O. Box 129 • Tremonton, UT 84337-1340 • (435) 257-3185 • http://www.genealogicalinstitute.com • *Research News*

George Sterling Mason-John Peacock Wood Family Organization • P.O. Box 352 • Tremonton, UT 84337 • (435) 257-6197

Trenton
Descendants of Fielding Steele and Jane Brooks of IL • 25 N Center • Trenton, UT 84338

Fields Jarvis Family Association of Westmoreland, VA • 25 North Center • Trenton, UT 84338

Venice
Charles Cowley Family Organization • 155 East 100 South • Venice, UT 84701

Vernal
Dolan and Charles Augustus Davis Family Organization • 950 West 500 South • Vernal, UT 84078 • (801) 789-4882

John H Broadaway Family Organization • 1147 West 1500 South • Vernal, UT 84078 • (801) 789-5768

Linschoten Family Organization • 177 West 650 North • Vernal, UT 84078 • (801) 781-1179

Uintah County Library • 155 E Main St • Vernal, UT 84078-2695 • (435) 789-0091 • http://www.catalog.uintah.lib.ut.us

Washington
John Nock Hinton Family Organization • 155 North 200 East • Washington, UT 84780 • (435) 628-1043

Wellsville
Ronald V Jensen Living Historical Farm Archives • 4025 S Hwy 89-91 • Wellsville, UT 84339 • (801) 245-4064 • http://www.awhc.org • *Hay Derrick*

West Bountiful
Hans Christian Svendsen-Henry Bockholdt Christensen-Hans Peter Hansen Miller-Olsen Family Organization • 936 W Pages Ln • West Bountiful, UT 84087-1803 • (801) 292-5830 • *Miller Monitor*

West Jordan
Alexander Hamilton Hutton Family Organization • 6945 South 3420 West • West Jordan, UT 84084-1713 • (801) 966-6585

Clan Graham Society • 7378 S Lona Cr • West Jordan, UT 84084

Dutch Family Heritage Society • 2463 Ledgewood Dr • West Jordan, UT 84084 • (801) 967-8400 • *Dutch Family Heritage Society Newsletter*, *Dutch Family Heritage Society Quarterly*

Henry William Davis Family Organization • 7472 Silver Cr • West Jordan, UT 84084 • (801) 566-1083

Isaiah Goodman Family Organization • 2353 W Buena Vista • West Jordan, UT 84084 • (801) 561-3724 • *Goodman 'Treesearch' Notes*

Joel Allen Smith Family Organization • 1192 West 8680 South • West Jordan, UT 84088 • (801) 569-0155

Lot Smith Family Organization • 1192 West 8680 South • West Jordan, UT 84088 • (801) 569-0155

Sons of the American Revolution, Utah Society • 5539 Capital Reef Dr • West Jordan, UT 84084

William Flack-Hugh Bodkin-Molen-Johanne Sophia Dahl-William Bull-Mette Jespersen-Helene and Karen Jensen-Jacob and Laurany Huffaker-Kari Christensen Family Organization • 2644 Toni Lee St • West Jordan, UT 84084 • (801) 561-2464

West Point
Banz Family Organization • 2140 West 300 North • West Point, UT 84015 • (801) 773-4388 • *Banz Bunch*

George Farnworth Family Organization • 136 South 3000 West • West Point, UT 84105 • (801) 773-5791

West Valley City
Anders Mortensen Family Organization • 4218 Ben View Dr • West Valley City, UT 84120 • (801) 969-3670

Cigarroa-Yanez Family Organization • 4249 S 3290 W • West Valley, UT 84119 • (801) 864-9374

Clan MacLeod Society USA • P.O. Box 70928 • West Valley City, UT 84170-0928 • (801) 532-7840 • http://www.clan-macleod.com

Ewell Family National Historical and Genealogical Society • 3654 West 3965 South • West Valley City, UT 84120 • (801) 968-9976 • *Roots and Branches*

Ferrin Research • 3857 South 3660 West • West Valley City, UT 84120 • (801) 967-0392 • *Ferrin Family Newsletter*

Johnson Surname Organization • 4726 Palmer Dr • West Valley City, UT 84120 • (801) 969-5113

Molina-Gamboa-Gardea Surname Organization • 4249 South 3290 West • West Valley City, UT 84119 • (801) 964-9374

Rufus Edwards Family Organization • 4150 Westlake Ave • West Valley City, UT 84120 • (801) 968-3834

William and Hannah Maria Byington Burrup-John Carver-William Geddes Family Organization • 6602 W King Valley Rd • West Valley City, UT 84120 • (801) 250-9017 • *Geddes Gazette*; *Carver Crier*, *William and Hannah Maria Byington Burrup Family Organization Newsletter*

Willard
Abraham Braegger Family Organization • 36 North 200 West, P.O. Box 304 • Willard, UT 84340 • (435) 723-7658

VERMONT

Addison
Chimney Point State Historic Site Archives • 7305 VT Rte 125 • Addison, VT 05491 • (802) 759-2412 • http://www.historicvermont.org

Daughters of the American Revolution • John Strong Mansion Museum, 6656 VT Rte 17 W • Addison, VT 05491 • (802) 759-2309 • http://www.northshirecomputer.com/VTDAR

Alburgh
Alburgh Historical Society • P.O. Box 453 • Alburgh, VT 05440

Arlington
Martha Canfield Memorial Free Library • 528 E Arlington Rd, P.O. Box 267 • Arlington, VT 05250-0267

Ascutney
Proctor Library • 5181 Rte 5, P.O. Box 519 • Ascutney, VT 05030-0519 • (802) 674-2863 • http://www.weathersfield.org

Barnard
Barnard Historical Society & Archives • c/o Charles Danforth Public Library, P.O. Box 204 • Barnard, VT 05031 • (802) 234-9183

Charles Danforth Public Library • Rt 12, P.O. Box 204 • Barnard, VT 05031-0204 • (802) 234-6375

Barnet
Barnet Historical Society & Archives • Goodwille House Museum, P.O. Box 26 • Barnet, VT 05821 • (802) 633-2611

Barnet Public Library • 147 Church St, P.O. Box 34 • Barnet, VT 05821-0034 • (802) 633-4436

Barre
Aldrich Public Library • 6 Washington St • Barre, VT 05641-4227 • (802) 476-7550 • http://www.aldrich.lib.vt.us

Barre Historical Society • 46 Granite St • Barre, VT 05641 • (802) 476-0567

Vermont Historical Society & Library • 60 Washington St • Barre, VT 05641 • (802) 479-8500 • http://www.vermonthistory.org

Barton
Crystal Lake Falls Historical Association & Archives • Pierce House Museum, 97 Water St, P.O. Box 253 • Barton, VT 05822 • (802) 525-3583 • *Crystal Lake Falls Historical Association Newsletter*

Bellows Falls
Bellows Falls Historical Society & Archives • Adams Grist Mill Museum, Mill St • Bellows Falls, VT 05101 • (802) 463-3706

Rockingham Free Public Library and Museum • 65 Westminster St • Bellows Falls, VT 05101 • (802) 463-4270 • http://www.rockingham.lib.vt.us

Belmont
Mount Holly Historical Society & Archives • Historical Museum, Tarbelville Rd, P.O. Box 17 • Belmont, VT 05730 • (802) 259-2460 • http://www.vermonthistory.org

Mount Holly Library • P.O. Box 93 • Belmont, VT 05730-0093 • (802) 259-3707

Bennington
Bennington Covered Bridge Museum Archives • West Rd, P.O. Box 260 • Bennington, VT 05201 • (802) 442-7158 • http://www.benningtoncenterforthearts.org

Bennington Free Library • 101 Silver St • Bennington, VT 05201 • (802) 442-9051 • http://bennington.lib.vt.us

Bennington Historical Society & Archives • Bennington Museum, W Main St • Bennington, VT 05201 • (802) 447-1571 • http://www.benningtonmuseum.com

Genealogy & History Research Library • Bennington Museum, 75 Main St • Bennington, VT 05201 • (802) 447-1571 • http://www.benningtonmuseum.com

Robert Dunbar Family Reunion • 123 McKinley St • Bennington, VT 05201-1824 • (802) 442-4081 • http://www.hometown.aol.com/BillBudde/ • *Dunbar Notes*

Bethel
Bethel Historical Society & Library • Church St • Bethel, VT 05032 • (802) 234-9413

Bradford
Bradford Historical Society & Archives • Historical Museum, Town Hall, Main St, P.O. Box 301 • Bradford, VT 05033 • (802) 222-4727 • *Bradford Historical Society Newsletter*

Bradford Public Library • 21 S Main St, P.O. Box 619 • Bradford, VT 05033-0619 • (802) 222-4536

Brandon
Brandon Free Public Library • 4 Franklin St • Brandon, VT 05733 • (802) 247-8230

Brattleboro
Brattleboro Historical Society & Library • 230 Main St, P.O. Box 6392 • Brattleboro, VT 05302 • (802) 258-4957 • *Newsletter of the Brattleboro Historical Society*

Brattleboro Museum Archives • 10 Vernon St • Brattleboro, VT 05301-2623 • (802) 257-0124 • http://www.brattleboromuseum.org • *Brattleboro Museum Newsletter*

Brooks Memorial Library • 224 Main St • Brattleboro, VT 05301 • (802) 254-5290 • http://www.brooks.lib.vt.us

Guilford Historical Society • RR2, Box 18A • Brattleboro, VT 05301 • (802) 257-7306 • *Guilford Slate*

Halifax Historical Society & Library • RR4, Box 531 • Brattleboro, VT 05301 • (802) 368-7490

Jewett-Pearl Family Reunion • 248 Meetinghouse Ln • Brattleboro, VT 05301

Bridgport
Bridport Historical Society & Library • RR1, Box 656 • Bridgport, VT 05734 • (802) 758-2654

Bristol
Bristol Historical Society & Library • Howden Hall, Main St • Bristol, VT 05443 • (802) 453-6029

Burbank-Burbanck Family • 80 East St • Bristol, VT 05443-1316 • (802) 453-2907 • *Burbank Banner*

Brookfield
Brookfield Free Public Library • 40 Ralph Rd • Brookfield, VT 05036 • (802) 276-3358

Brookfield Historical Society & Archives • Marvin Newton House Museum, 1133 Ridge Rd, P.O. Box 447 • Brookfield, VT 05036 • (802) 276-3959 • *Brookfield Historical Society Newsletter*

Brownington
Orleans County Historical Society & Archives • Old Stone House Museum, 109 Old Stone House Rd • Brownington, VT 05860 • (802) 754-2022 • http://www.oldstonehousemuseum.org • *Orleans County Historical Society Bulletin*

Brownsville
West Windsor Historical Society • P.O. Box 12 • Brownsville, VT 05037 • (802) 484-7474

Burlington
Bailey-Howe Memorial Library • University of Vermont, 538 Main St • Burlington, VT 05405-0036 • (802) 656-2020 • http://library.uvm.edu • *Newsletter for Friends of Special Collections*

Burlington Genealogical Group • 36 Franklin Square • Burlington, VT 05401

Fletcher Free Library • 235 College St • Burlington, VT 05401 • (802) 865-7217 • http://www.fletcherfree.org • *BiblioFile*

Miller Library • Champlain College, 83 Summit St • Burlington, VT 05401-0670 • (802) 865-6486 • http://campus.champlain.edu/library

Vermont French-Canadian Genealogical Society • P.O. Box 65128 • Burlington, VT 05402

Vermont

Cabot
Cabot Historical Society & Archives • Historical Museum, 193 McKinistry • Cabot, VT 05647 • (802) 563-2547

Canaan
Alice M Ward Memorial Library • 27 Park St, P.O. Box 134 • Canaan, VT 05903-0134 • (802) 266-7135

Canaan Historical Society & Library • P.O. Box 371 • Canaan, VT 05903 • (802) 266-8845

Castleton
Calvin Coolidge Library • Castleton State College, 178 Alumni Dr • Castleton, VT 05735 • (802) 468-1255 • http://www.castleton.edu/library/

Castleton Historical Society & Archives • Higley Homestead Museum, Main St, P.O. Box 219 • Castleton, VT 05735 • (802) 468-5523

Hubbardton Historical Society • 5568 Monument Hill Rd • Castleton, VT 05735 • (802) 273-3901

Cavendish
Cavendish Historical Society & Library • Main St, P.O. Box 110 • Cavendish, VT 05142 • (802) 484-7498 • http://www.web-home.com/vt-genealogy/cavendish.htm

Chelsea
Chelsea Historical Society • Main St, P.O. Box 206 • Chelsea, VT 05038

Chelsea Public Library • Main St, P.O. Box 67 • Chelsea, VT 05038-0067 • (802) 685-2188

Chester
Chester Historical Society • Main St • Chester, VT 05143 • (802) 875-3767

Whiting Library • 117 Main St, P.O. Box 68 • Chester, VT 05143-0068 • (802) 875-2277

Colchester
Burnham Memorial Library • 898 Main St • Colchester, VT 05446 • (802) 879-7576 • http://www.burnham/~bumeli/burnham.htm

Durick Library • Saint Michael's College, 1 Winooski Pk, Box L • Colchester, VT 05439-2525 • (802) 654-2405 • http://www.smcvt.edu/library

Cornwall
Cornwall Free Public Library • 2629 Rte 30 • Cornwall, VT 05753-9340 • (802) 462-2606

Craftsbury
Craftsbury Public Library • Craftsbury Common, P.O. Box 74 • Craftsbury, VT 05827-0074 • (802) 586-9683 • http://www.craftsburypubliclibrary.org

John Woodruff Simpson Library • RR1, Box 1034 • Craftsbury, VT 05826 • (802) 586-9692

Danville
Pope Memorial Library • 121 Park St, P.O. Box 260 • Danville, VT 05828-0260 • (802) 684-2256

Derby
Dailey Memorial Library • P.O. Box 30 • Derby, VT 05829 • (802) 766-5063

Derby Historical Society & Library • Main St, P.O. Box 357 • Derby, VT 05829 • (802) 766-5324

Derby Line
Haskell Free Library • 93 Caswell Ave, P.O. Box 337 • Derby Line, VT 05830-0337 • (802) 873-3022 • http://www.haskellopera.org

Dorset
Dorset Historical Society • Main St, P.O. Box 52 • Dorset, VT 05251 • (802) 867-0331

East Dover
Dover Historical Society • P.O. Box 53 • East Dover, VT 05341-0053

East Poultney
East Poultney Historical Society & Archives • Historical Museum, The Green • East Poultney, VT 05741 • (802) 287-5268

Enosburgh Falls
Enosburgh Historical Society • Over Town Offices, Main St, P.O. Box 98 • Enosburgh Falls, VT 05450 • (802) 933-2102

Essex Junction
Brownell Library • 6 Lincoln St • Essex Junction, VT 05452-3154 • (802) 878-6957 • http://www.essexjunction.org/library/brownell.shtml

Essex Community Historical Society • 3 Browns River Rd • Essex Junction, VT 05452

Fair Haven
Fair Haven Free Public Library • 107 Main St • Fair Haven, VT 05743 • (802) 265-8011

Sleeper Queries • P.O. box 81 • Fair Haven, VT 05743 • *Sleeper Queries*

Fairfax
Fairfax Community Library • 75 Hunt St • Fairfax, VT 05454 • (802) 849-2420

Fairfax Historical Society • 1181 Main St, Route 104, P.O. Box 415 • Fairfax, VT 05454 • (802) 849-6638 • *Fairfax News*

Fairfield
Fairfield Historical Society • Fairfield Town Clerk • Fairfield, VT 05455 • (802) 827-6160

President Chester A Arthur Historic Site Archives • general delivery • Fairfield, VT 05455 • (802) 828-3206 • http://www.historicvermont.org

Fairlee
Fairlee Historical Society & Library • P.O. Box 95 • Fairlee, VT 05045 • (802) 333-9729

Ferrisburgh
Rokeby Estate Museum Archives • 4334 Rte 7 • Ferrisburgh, VT 05456 • (802) 877-3406 • http://www.rokeby.org • *Rokeby Messenger*

Franklin
Franklin Historical Society • 1389 Richard Rd • Franklin, VT 05457

Glover
Glover Historical Society • Municipal Bldg • Glover, VT 05839 • (802) 525-6227

Grafton
Grafton Historical Society & Archives • Historical Museum, 147 Main St, P.O. Box 202 • Grafton, VT 05146 • (802) 843-2584 • http://www.graftonhistory.org

Greensboro
Greensboro Historical Society • RR1, Box 1290 • Greensboro, VT 05841 • (802) 472-3381 • *Hazen Road Dispatch*

Town of Greensboro Historical Society • Breezy Ave • Greensboro, VT 05841 • (802) 533-2457

Greensboro Bend
Stannard Historical Society • 9 Willey Rd • Greensboro Bend, VT 05842 • (802) 533-2561

Groton
Groton Historical Society • Route 302, Main St, P.O. Box 89 • Groton, VT 05046 • (802) 584-3417

Guilford
Guilford Free Library • 4024 Guilford Center Rd • Guilford, VT 05301 • (802) 257-4603 • Guilford Free Library Newsletter

Hardwick
Hardwick Historical Society • 47 Depot • Hardwick, VT 05843 • (802) 472-8555

Jeudevine Memorial Library • P.O. Box 536 • Hardwick, VT 05843 • (802) 472-5948

Hartford
Hartford Historical Society • 187 Route 14, P.O. Box 547 • Hartford, VT 05047 • (802) 296-3132

Hartford Library • 1587 Maple, P.O. Box 512 • Hartford, VT 05047-0512 • (802) 296-2568

Hartland
Hartland Historical Society & Library • 14 Route 12 • Hartland, VT 05048 • (802) 436-1703 • *Newsletter of Hartland Historical Society*

Hartland Public Library • 153 Rte 5, P.O. Box 137 • Hartland, VT 05048-0137 • (802) 436-2473

Hinesburg
George Mills Family Organization • Route 1, Box 2168 • Hinesburg, VT 05461 • (802) 482-3797 • *Mills Ancestry*

Sarah Carpenter Memorial Library • Ballards-Corner Rd P.O. Box 127 • Hinesburg, VT 05461 • (802) 482-2878

Holland
Holland Historical Society & Archives • Historical Museum, Gore Rd • Holland, VT 05830 • (802) 895-4440 • *Holland Historical Society Newsletter*

Hubbardton
Hubbardton Battlefield Museum Archives • Monument Hill Rd • Hubbardton, VT 05620-0501 • (802) 759-2412 • http://www.historicvermont.org/hubardton

Huntington
Huntington Historical Society • P.O. Box 147 • Huntington, VT 05462

Huntington Library • P.O. Box 98 • Huntington, VT 05462 • (802) 434-4583

Hyde Park
Lanpher Memorial Library • 141 Main St, P.O. Box 196 • Hyde Park, VT 05655-0196 • (802) 888-4628

Island Pond
Island Pond Historical Society • Canadian National Railway Station, P.O. Box 408 • Island Pond, VT 05846 • (802) 482-3923

Island Pond Public Library • Main St, P.O. Box 422 • Island Pond, VT 05846-0422 • (802) 723-6134

Isle la Motte
Isle la Motte Historical Society & Archives • Historical Museum, 283 School St • Isle la Motte, VT 05463 • (802) 928-3422 • *Isle la Motte Historical Society Newsletter*

Isle La Motte Library • 2238 Main St • Isle La Motte, VT 05463 • (802) 928-4113

Jacksonville
Whitingham Historical Society & Archives • Historical Museum, P.O. Box 125 • Jacksonville, VT 05342 • (802) 368-2448

Jamaica
Jamaica Memorial Library • 17 Depot St, P.O. Box 266 • Jamaica, VT 05343-0266 • (802) 874-4901

Jeffersonville
Hubbard Families Association • Upper Valley Rd, P.O. Box 34 • Jeffersonville, VT 05464 • (802) 644-2995 • *Hubbard Families Association Newsletter*

Jericho
Deborah Rawson Memorial Library • 8 River Rd • Jericho, VT 05465 • (802) 899-4962

Jericho Historical Society & Archives • Chittenden Mills Museum, Route 15, P.O. Box 35 • Jericho, VT 05465 • (802) 899-3225 • http://www.jerichohistoricalsociety.org • *Jericho Reporter*

Killington
Sherburne Memorial Library • P.O. Box 73 • Killington, VT 05751 • (802) 422-9765

Lincoln
Chase Purinton Family Association • 1986 W River Rd • Lincoln, VT 05443 • (802) 453-3154 • *Chase Purinton Family Association Newsletter*

Lincoln Historical Society • Town Clerk, Quaker St • Lincoln, VT 05443 • (802) 453-3628

Lower Waterford
Davies Memorial Library • P.O. Box 64 • Lower Waterford, VT 05848-0064 • (802) 748-1742

Ludlow
Black River Historical Society & Archives • Black River Academy Museum, 14 High St, P.O Box 73 • Ludlow, VT 05149 • (802) 228-5050

Fletcher Memorial Library • 88 Main St • Ludlow, VT 05149 • (802) 228-8921

Lyndon Center
Lyndon Historical Society • P.O. Box 85 • Lyndon Center, VT 05850 • (802) 626-8746 • http://www.sover.net/boerad/historical • *Lyndon Legacy*

Shores Memorial Museum Archives • Main St, P.O. Box 85 • Lyndon Center, VT 05850 • (802) 626-5742

Lyndonville
Cobleigh Public Library • 14 Depot St, P.O. Box 147 • Lyndonville, VT 05851-0147 • (802) 626-5475 • http://cobleighlibrary.org

Manchester
Hildene Museum Archives • 1005 Hildene Rd, P.O. Box 377 • Manchester, VT 05254 • (802) 362-1788 • http://www.hildene.org • *News from Historic Hildene*

Manchester Historical Society • c/o Mark Skinner Library, P.O Box 363 • Manchester, VT 05254 • (802) 362-2607

Marlboro
Marlboro Historical Society & Archives • Historical Museum, 364 South Rd, P.O. Box 242 • Marlboro, VT 05344 • (802) 257-9265 • http://www.marlboro.vt.us • *Marlboro Historical Society Newsletter*

Marshfield
Cabot Historical Society • RFD, Lower Cabot • Marshfield, VT 05658 • (802) 563-2558

Jaquith Public Library • Old Schoolhouse Common, 122 School St, P.O. Box 227 • Marshfield, VT 05658-0227 • (802) 426-3581

Middlebury
Egbert Starr Library • Middlebury College, 15 Old Chapel Rd • Middlebury, VT 05753-6007 • (802) 443-5496 • http://www.middlebury.edu/library.html • *Friends of the Library Newsletter*

Henry Sheldon Museum Archives • 1 Park St • Middlebury, VT 05753 • (802) 388-2117 • http://www.henrysheldonmuseum.org • *Henry Sheldon Museum Newsletter*

Isley Public Library • 75 Main St • Middlebury, VT 05753 • (802) 388-4095 • http://www.ilsleypubliclibrary.org • *Ilsley Inklings*

Vermont Folklife Center Archives • Masonic Hall, 3 Court St, P.O. Box 442 • Middlebury, VT 05753 • (802) 388-4964 • http://www.vermontfolklifecenter.org • *Visit'N*

Middlesex
Middlesex Historical Society • RR3, Box 3395 • Middlesex, VT 05602 • (802) 223-2201

Middletown Springs
Chittenden Family • 2 Buxton Ave • Middletown Springs, VT 05757 • (802) 235-2302 • *Chittenden Family Newsletter; Crittenden Family Reunion Reminder*

Middletown Springs Historical Society & Library • On the Green, P.O. Box 1001 • Middletown Springs, VT 05757 • (802) 235-2144 • *Middletown Springs Historical Society Newsletter*

Milton

Milton Historical Society & Archives • Historical Museum, 13 School St, P.O. Box 2 • Milton, VT 05468 • (802) 893-1604 • *Milton Historical Society Newsletter*

Milton Public Library • 39 Bombadier Rd • Milton, VT 05468 • (802) 893-4644

Montgomery

Montgomery Historical Society & Library • Montgomery Village, P.O. Box 47 • Montgomery, VT 05470 • (802) 326-4404

Montpelier

Berlin Historical Society • RR4, Box 2210 • Montpelier, VT 05602 • (802) 223-1203

Kellogg-Hubbard Library • 135 Main St • Montpelier, VT 05602 • (802) 223-3338 • http://www.khl.lib.vt.us

State of Vermont Historic Preservation Office • general delivery • Montpelier, VT 05601 • (802) 828-3226

Vermont Department of Libraries • 109 State St • Montpelier, VT 05609-0601 • (802) 828-3261 • http://dol.state.vt.us

Vermont Historical Society & Archives • Historical Museum, Pavilion Office Bldg, 109 State St • Montpelier, VT 05609-0901 • (802) 828-2291 • http://www.vermonthistory.org • *Vermont History*; Vermont History News; *Green Mountaineer*, *In Context*

Vermont State House Museum Archives • 115 State St • Montpelier, VT 05609 • (802) 828-2228 • http://www.leg.state.vt.us • *Friends Proceedings*

Morrisville

Morristown Centennial Library • 7 Richmond St, P.O. Box 727 • Morrisville, VT 05661-0727 • (802) 888-3853

Morristown Historical Society & Archives • Noyes House Museum, Main St, P.O. Box 1299 • Morrisville, VT 05661-1299 • (802) 888-7617 • *Morristown Two Times*

New Haven

New Haven Community Library • 50 North St • New Haven, VT 05472-0085 • (802) 453-4015

Newbury

Tenney Memorial Library • 4886 Main St S, P.O. Box 85 • Newbury, VT 05051-0085 • (802) 866-5366

Newfane

Historical Society of Windham County & Library • P.O. Box 246 • Newfane, VT 05345 • (802) 365-4148 • *Vermont Life*; *News and Views*

Moore Free Library • 23 West St, P.O. Box 208 • Newfane, VT 05345-0208 • (802) 365-7948

Newport

Goodrich Memorial Library • 202 Main St • Newport, VT 05855 • (802) 334-7902 • http://www.state.vt.us/libraries/n47

Memphremagog Historical Society • c/o Goodrich Memorial Library, 70 Main St • Newport, VT 05855 • (802) 334-7902 • http://www.state.vt.us/libraries/n47

North Bennington

John G McCullough Free Library • 2 Main St, P.O. Box 339 • North Bennington, VT 05257-0339 • (802) 447-7121 • http://www.mccullough.lib.vt.us

Park-McCullough House Archives • 1 Park St, P.O. Box 388 • North Bennington, VT 05257 • (802) 442-5441 • http://www.parkmccullough.org

North Concord

Concord Historical Society & Library • HCR 60, Box 40 • North Concord, VT 05858 • (802) 695-2289

North Hero

North Hero Public Library • P.O. Box 187 • North Hero, VT 05474 • (802) 372-5458

North Troy

Missisquoi Valley Historical Society & Archives • Historical Museum, E Main St, P.O. Box 237 • North Troy, VT 05859 • (802) 988-4323

William and Lucy Rand Memorial Library • 160 Railroad St, P.O. Box 509 • North Troy, VT 05859-0509 • (802) 988-4741

Northfield

Brown Public Library • 93 S Main St • Northfield, VT 05663 • (802) 485-4621 • http://www.tds.net/brownpubliclibrary

Northfield Historical Society • 75 Main St, P.O. Box 88 • Northfield, VT 05663 • (802) 485-4792 • *Dog River Crier*

Sullivan Museum and History Center • 158 Harmon Dr • Northfield, VT 05663 • (802) 485-2379 • http://www.norwich.edu

Norwich

Norwich Historical Society & Archives • Historical Museum, 27 Main St, P.O. Box 1680 • Norwich, VT 05055 • (802) 649-2711 • *Norwich Historical Society Newsletter*, *Museum Muse*

Norwich Public Library • 368 Main St, P.O. Box 290 • Norwich, VT 05055-0290 • (802) 649-1184 • http://www.norwichlibrary.org • *Book Mark*

Sons of the American Revolution, Vermont Society • RFD, Box 18 • Norwich, VT 05055

Old Bennington

Bennington Battle Monument Archives • 15 Monument Cr • Old Bennington, VT 05201 • (802) 828-3051 • http://www.historicvermont.org/bennington

Orleans

Orleans County Historical Society & Archives • Brownington Village, Old Stone House Museum, Route 1, Box 500 • Orleans, VT 05860 • (802) 754-2022 • http://homepages.together.net/~osh/ • *Old Stone House Museum Bulletin*

Orwell

Mount Independence Historic Site Archives • Mount Independence Rd • Orwell, VT 05760 • (802) 828-3051 • http://www.historicvermont.org/mountindependence

Pawlet

Pawlet Public Library • P.O. Box 98 • Pawlet, VT 05761 • (802) 325-3123

Pawlett Historical Society • 79 School St • Pawlet, VT 05761 • (802) 325-2406

Perkinsville

Weathersfield Historical Society & Archives • Rev Dan Foster House, 2656 Center Rd • Perkinsville, VT 05151 • (802) 263-5230

Pittsfield

Pittsfield Historical Society • Town Hall, P.O. Box 808 • Pittsfield, VT 05762 • (802) 746-8147

Pittsford

Genealogical Society of Vermont & Library • P.O. Box 422 • Pittsford, VT 05763-0422 • (802) 483-2957 • *Branches and Twigs*

Maclure Library • P.O. Box 60 • Pittsford, VT 05763-0060 • (802) 483-2972

New England Maple Museum Archives • US Rte 7 • Pittsford, VT 05763 • (802) 775-1650 • http://www.maplemuseum.com

Pittsford Historical Society & Archives • Eaton Hall Museum, Route 7, P.O. Box 423 • Pittsford, VT 05763 • (802) 483-6623 • http://www.pittsford-historical.org • Pittsford Historical Society Newsletter

Plymouth

Calvin Collidge Memorial Foundation Archives • Route 100A, Grandview Rd, P.O. Box 97 • Plymouth, VT 05056 • (802) 672-3389 • http://www.calvin-coolidge.org • *Plymouth Notch Newsletter*

Calvin Coolidge Memorial Foundation • P.O. Box 97 • Plymouth, VT 05056 • (802) 672-3389 • *Plymouth Notch News*; *Calvin Coolidge Memorial Foundation Newsletter*

Poultney
Griswold Library • Green Mountain College, 1 College Cr • Poultney, VT 05764-1199 • (802) 287-8225

Poultney Historical Society • RFD 1, Box 177 • Poultney, VT 05764 • (802) 287-5268

Poultney Public Library • 205 Main St • Poultney, VT 05764 • (802) 287-5556

Welsh-American Genealogical Society & Library • 60 Norton Ave, Box 516 • Poultney, VT 05764 • (802) 287-5744 • http://www.rootsweb.com/~vtwags • Welsh-American Genealogical Society Newsletter

Proctor
Pittsford Historical Society • Main St • Proctor, VT 05765 • (802) 483-2040

Proctor Free Library • 4 Main St • Proctor, VT 05765 • (802) 459-3539

Vermont Marble Museum Archives • 52 Main St, P.O. Box 607 • Proctor, VT 05765 • (802) 459-2300 • http://www.vermont-marble.com

Wilson Castle Museum Archives • W Proctor Rd • Proctor, VT 05765 • (802) 773-3284

Putney
Putney Historical Society & Archives • Historical Museum, Town Hall, Main St, P.O. Box 233 • Putney, VT 05346 • (802) 387-5862 • http://www.putneyvt.org/history • *Putney Historical Society Newsletter*

Randolf Center
Randolf Historical Society • P.O. Box 15 • Randolf Center, VT 05091 • (802) 457-1822

Randolph
Braintree Historical Society & Library • RFD 1, Thayer Brook Rd • Randolph, VT 05060 • (802) 728-5272 • Braintree Historical Society Newsletter

Kimball Public Library • 67 Main St • Randolph, VT 05060 • (802) 728-5073

Randolph Historical Society • Historical Museum, Salisbury St • Randolph, VT 05060 • (802) 728-6677

Randolph Center
Randolph Historical Society & Archives • Historical Museum, Salisbury St, P.O. Box 15 • Randolph Center, VT 05061 • (802) 728-5398

Reading
Reading Historical Society & Archives • Historical Museum, Main St, Route 106, P.O. Box 252 • Reading, VT 05062 • (802) 484-5005

Readsboro
Readsboro Historical Society & Archives • Historical Museum, Main St, P.O. Box 158 • Readsboro, VT 05350 • (802) 423-5432

Richford
Arvin A Brown Public Library • 88 Main St • Richford, VT 05476-1133 • (802) 848-3313 • http://www.aabrown.org

Richford Historical Society • 186 S Main St • Richford, VT 05470

Rochester
Rochester Historical Society • P.O. Box 7 • Rochester, VT 05767 • (802) 767-4453

Rochester Public Library • P.O. Box 256 • Rochester, VT 05767 • (802) 767-3927

Royalton
Royalton Historical Society & Archives • Historical Museum, 4184 Route 14 • Royalton, VT 05068 • (802) 828-3051

Rutland
Rutland Free Library • 10 Court St • Rutland, VT 05701-4058 • (802) 773-1860 • http://rutlandfree.org

Rutland Historical Society & Library • 96 Center St, P.O. Box 6473 • Rutland, VT 05701-4023 • (802) 775-2006 • *Rutland Historical Society Quarterly*; *News from Nickawackett*

Tuttle Antiquarian Books • 28 S Main St • Rutland, VT 05701 • (802) 773-8229 • *Genealogy and Family History*

Saint Albans
Genealogical Society of Vermont • P.O. Box 1553 • Saint Albans, VT 05478-1006 • (802) 254-9554 • http://www.rootsweb.com/~vtgsv/ • *Vermont Genealogy*; *Genealogical Society of Vermont Newsletter*

Georgia Historical Society • RD3 • Saint Albans, VT 05478 • (802) 524-3318

Saint Albans Free Library • 11 Maiden Lane • Saint Albans, VT 05478 • (802) 524-1507 • *Bookworm*

Saint Albans Historical Society & Archives • Historical Museum, 9 Church St, P.O. Box 772 • Saint Albans, VT 05478 • (802) 527-7933 • http://www.stalbansmuseum.org • *Saint Albans Historical Society Newsletter*

Saint Johnsbury
Fairbanks Museum Archives • 1302 Main St • Saint Johnsbury, VT 05819 • (802) 748-2372 • http://www.fairbanksmuseum.org • *Fairbanks Museum Newsletter*

Saint Johnsbury Athenaeum • 1171 Main St • Saint Johnsbury, VT 05819-2289 • (802) 748-8291 • http://www.stjathenaeum.org

Saxtons River
Saxtons River Historical Society & Library • P.O. Box 18 • Saxtons River, VT 05154 • (802) 869-2657

Shaftsbury
Reverend Elijah Bump Family Organization • Route 1, Box 141 A • Shaftsbury, VT 05262 • (802) 442-6037

Shaftsbury Historical Society & Archives • Historical Museum, P.O. Box 401 • Shaftsbury, VT 05262 • (802) 447-7488

Shelburne
Pierson Library • 5376 Shelburne Rd • Shelburne, VT 05482 • (802) 985-5124 • http://www.pierson.lib.vt.us

Shelburne Museum Archives • 5555 Shelburne Rd, P.O. Box 10 • Shelburne, VT 05482-0010 • (802) 985-3348 • http://www.shelburnemuseum.org • *Shelburne Museum Newsletter*

Shoreham
Shoreham Historical Society • Route 22A • Shoreham, VT 05770 • (802) 897-2600

South Burlington
Oviatt Family Association • 23 Forest St • South Burlington, VT 05401 • *Ovi(a)tt Newsletter*

South Hero
South Hero Bicentennial Museum Archives • 2 Hill Rd • South Hero, VT 05486 • (802) 372-6615

South Londonderry
Londonderry Historical Society • P.O. Box 114 • South Londonderry, VT 05155

South Londonderry Free Library • 15 Old School St, P.O. Box 95 • South Londonderry, VT 05155-0095 • (802) 824-3371

South Pomfret
Wardner Family Historical Association • P.O. Box 41 • South Pomfret, VT 05067 • (802) 457-4938 • *Words on Wardners*; *Wardners in America*

South Ryegate
Christian Marks Society • 1979 North Rd • South Ryegate, VT 05069 • (802) 429-2346 • *Christian Marks Society Newsletter*

South Ryegate Public Library • 140 Church St • South Ryegate, VT 05069 • (802) 584-3675

Springfield
Eureka School House Archives • State Rte 11 • Springfield, VT 05156 • (802) 828-3051 • http://www.historicvermont.org

Pierce Research-Clan Bell Descendants • 79 Elm Hill St • Springfield, VT 05156-2420 • (802) 885-3151 • *Franklin Pierce Times*; *Bell Chimes*

Springfield Historical Society & Library • 9 Elm St, P.O. Box 313 • Springfield, VT 05156 • (802) 885-2415 • *News and Reviews*

Springfield Town Library • 43 Main St • Springfield, VT 05156 • (802) 885-3108

Wethersfield Historical Society & Library • Rev Dan Foster House, RR2, Box 457 • Springfield, VT 05156 • (802) 263-5230

Stowe
Stowe Free Library • School & Pond Sts, P.O. Box 1029 • Stowe, VT 05672-1029 • (802) 253-4808

Stowe Historical Society • Akeley Memorial Bldg, Main St • Stowe, VT 05672 • (802) 253-6133

Strafford
Justin Smith Morrill Homestead Archives • 214 Justin Morrill Memorial Hwy • Strafford, VT 05072 • (802) 828-3051 • http://www.historicvermont.org/morrill

Strafford Historical Society & Library • 1 Brook Rd • Strafford, VT 05072 • (802) 765-4379

Swanton
Stebbins Ancestral Society • 1845 Carter Hill Rd • Swanton, VT 05488 • (802) 868-7863 • http://www.sover.net/~neills/Stebbins.html

Swanton Historical Society • 11 Lake St • Swanton, VT 05488

Swanton Public Library • 1 1st St • Swanton, VT 05488 • (802) 868-7657

Thetford
Thetford Historical Society & Library • Bicentennial Bldg, 16 Library Rd, P.O. Box 33 • Thetford, VT 05074 • (802) 785-2068 • *Thetford Historical Society Newsletter*

Thetford Town Library • P.O. Box 240 • Thetford, VT 05074 • (802) 785-4361

Tinmouth
Tinmouth Historical and Genealogical Society • 43 Chipmunk Crossing Dr • Tinmouth, VT 05773-1179 • (802) 446-3587

Townshend
Townshend Public Library • 1971 Rte 30, P.O. Box 252 • Townshend, VT 05353-0252 • (802) 365-4039

Tunbridge
Historical Publications • 234 Monarch Hill Rd • Tunbridge, VT 05077-9707 • (802) 889-3500 • http://www.civilwarnews.com • *Civil War News*; *Artilleryman*

Tunbridge Public Library • 289 Vt Rte 110, P.O. Box 9 • Tunbridge, VT 05077-0009 • (802) 889-9404

Vergennes
Addison Town Historical Society • RD 1, Box 1348 • Vergennes, VT 05491 • (802) 759-2406

Bixby Memorial Free Library • 258 Main St • Vergennes, VT 05491 • (802) 877-2211 • http://www.vetc.usc.edu/vuhs/bixby

Daughters of the American Revolution, Vermont Society & Library • RD1 • Vergennes, VT 05491-9529 • (802) 545-2153

Lake Champlain Maritime Museum Archives • 4472 Basin Harbor Rd • Vergennes, VT 05491 • (802) 475-2022 • http://www.lcmm.org • *LCMM News*

Vernon
Vernon Historians • Historical Museum, 4388 Bridgman Rd, P.O. Box 282 • Vernon, VT 05354 • (802) 257-0292 • *Vernon Historians Newsletter*

Waitsfield
Joslin Memorial Library • 4391 Main St, P.O. Box 359 • Waitsfield, VT 05673-0359 • (802) 496-4205 • http://www.waitsfield.lib.vt.us

Waitsfield Historical Society • General Wait House Museum, Route 100 • Waitsfield, VT 05673 • (802) 496-2218 • http://www.waitsfieldhistoricalsociety.org • *Waitsfield Historical Society Newsletter*

Wallingford
Gilbert Hart Library • 14 S Main, P.O. Box 69 • Wallingford, VT 05773 • (802) 446-2685

Wallingford Historical Society & Archives • Town Hall Museum, P.O. Box 327 • Wallingford, VT 05773 • (802) 446-2336

Waterbury
Waterbury Historical Society & Library • c/o Waterbury Village Public Library, 28 N Main St • Waterbury, VT 05676 • (802) 244-7036

Waterbury Village Public Library • 28 N Main St • Waterbury, VT 05676 • (802) 244-7036 • http://www.waterburypubliclibrary.com

Waterbury Center
Green Mountain Club Archives • 4711 Waterbury Stowe Rd • Waterbury Center, VT 05677 • (802) 244-7037 • http://www.greenmountainclub.org • *Long Trail News*

Weathersfield
Weathersfield Historical Society • Rev Dan Foster House Museum, 2656 Weathersfield Center Rd • Weathersfield, VT 05156 • (802) 263-5230 • http://www.weathersfield.net • *Weathersfield Historical Society Newsletter*

Wells
Wells Historical Society • RR 1, Box 37 • Wells, VT 05774 • (802) 645-0435

West Charleston
Charleston Historical Society & Library • RR1, Box 710 • West Charleston, VT 05872 • (802) 895-4329

West Danville
Walden Community Library • 135 Cahoon Farm Rd • West Danville, VT 05873 • (802) 563-3000

West Dover
Dover Historical Society • RR 100 • West Dover, VT 05356 • (802) 464-7351

West Hartford
West Hartford Library • 5133 Rte 14, P.O. Box 26 • West Hartford, VT 05084-0026 • (802) 295-7992

Westfield
Hitchcock Memorial Museum and Library • 1252 Rte 100, P.O. Box 87 • Westfield, VT 05874-0087 • (802) 744-8258

Westford
Westford Library • 1718 Vermont Rte 128, P.O. Box 86 • Westford, VT 05494-0086 • (802) 878-5639 • http://www.westford.lib.vt.us

Westminster
Westminster Historical Society & Archives • Historical Museum, Main St, P.O. Box 2 • Westminster, VT 05158 • (802) 387-5778

Weston
Weston Historical Society & Archives • Farrar-Mansur House Museum, On the Green, P.O. Box 247 • Weston, VT 05161 • (802) 824-6781 • *Weston Historical Society Newsletter*

Whitingham
Whitingham Historical Society • Historical Museum, 13 Stimpson Hill Rd • Whitingham, VT 05361 • (802) 368-2586 • *Sadawga Springs*

Williamstown
Ainsworth Public Library • P.O. Box 236 • Williamstown, VT 05679 • (802) 433-5887

Williamstown Historical Society • RFD 1, Box 612 • Williamstown, VT 05679

Williston
Dorothy Alling Memorial Library • 21 Library Ln • Williston, VT 05495 • (802) 878-4918 • http://www.williston.lib.vt.us

Williston Historical Society & Library • P.O. Box 995 • Williston, VT 05495 • (802) 878-3742 • *Williston Historical Society Bulletin*

Wilmington
Living History Association • P.O. Box 578 • Wilmington, VT 05363-0578 • (802) 464-0535 • *Living Historian*; *Living History Journal*

Pettee Memorial Library • P.O. Box 896 • Wilmington, VT 05363 • (802) 464-8557

Windsor

American Precision Museum Association Archives • 196 Main St, P.O. Box 679 • Windsor, VT 05089 • (802) 674-5781 • http://www.americanprecision.org

Old Constitution House Museum Archives • N Main St • Windsor, VT 05089 • (802) 672-3773 • http://www.historicvermont.org/constitution

Windsor Public Library • 43 State St • Windsor, VT 05089 • (802) 674-2556 • http://www.together.net/~windsorl

Winooski

Winooski Historical Society • 21 Park St • Winooski, VT 05404

Wolcott

Glee Merritt Kelley Community Library • P.O. Box 179 • Wolcott, VT 05680 • (802) 472-6551

Woodstock

Billings Farm and Museum Archives • River Rd & Rte 12, P.O. Box 489 • Woodstock, VT 05091-0489 • (802) 457-2355 • http://www.billingsfarm.org

Norman Williams Public Library • 10 S Park St • Woodstock, VT 05091 • (802) 457-2295

Robert Williams of Roxbury Association • Route 4 West, Box 110 • Woodstock, VT 05091-1241 • (802) 457-2206 • *Root and Branch*

Woodstock Historical Society & Library • Historical Museum, 26 Elm St • Woodstock, VT 05091 • (802) 457-1822 • http://www.woodstockhistsoc.org

VIRGINIA

Abingdon
Historic Society of Washington County, Virginia & Library • Old Courthouse, E Main St, P.O. Box 484 • Abingdon, VA 24210-0484 • (276) 628-2813 • *Historic Society of Washington County, Virginia Newsletter*; *Historic Society of Washington County, Virginia Bulletin*

Historical Society of Washington County • 306 Depot Sq SW • Abingdon, VA 24210 • (276) 623-8337

Washington County Public Library • 205 Oak Hill St • Abingdon, VA 24210 • (276) 676-6222 • http://www.wcpl.net

Wilson Family Reunion • 359 Augusta Dr • Abingdon, VA 24210 • (276) 628-9059

Accomac
Eastern Shore Public Library • 23610 Front St, P.O. Box 360 • Accomac, VA 23301-0360 • (757) 787-3400 • http://www.espl.org

Alberta
Brunswick County Historical Society • 86 Lew Jones Rd • Alberta, VA 23621

Alexandria
Alexandria Black History Resource Center Archives • 638 N Alfred St • Alexandria, VA 22314 • (703) 838-4356 • http://www.alexblackhistory.org

Alexandria Historical Society & Library • 201 S Washington St • Alexandria, VA 22314 • (703) 548-1776

Alexandria Library • 5005 Duke St • Alexandria, VA 22304 • (703) 519-5900 • http://www.alexandria.lib.va.us

Alexandria Library-Ellen Coolidge Burke Branch • 4701 Seminary Rd • Alexandria, VA 22304 • (703) 370-6000

Alexandria Public Library-Kate Waller Barrett • 717 Queen St • Alexandria, VA 22314 • (703) 838-4577 • http://www.alexandria.lib.va.us/lhsc/special_collections_home.html/ • *Doorway Quarterly Newsletter*

Ancestors and Descendants of Warren Gerade and Pearl Eva Gibson • 5222 Mitchell St • Alexandria, VA 22312 • (703) 354-3830

Carlyle House Historic Park Archives • 121 N Fairfax St • Alexandria, VA 22314 • (703) 549-2997 • http://www.carlylehouse.org

Clan Arthur • 6430 Princeton Dr • Alexandria, VA 22307-1347 • (703)765-6593 • *Round Table*

Clan Forbes Society • P.O. Box 1118 • Alexandria, VA 22313 • *Clan Forbes Newsletter*

Clan Henderson Society of the US and Canada • 8500 Wendell Dr • Alexandria, VA 22308 • (703) 780-1068 • http://msnhomepages.talkcity.com:6010/NonProfit Blvd/clanhenderson/ • *An Canach (The Cottongrass): Newsletter of the Clan Henderson Society*

Clans of Scotland USA • P.O. Box 411 • Alexandria, VA 22313 • http://www.clansofscotland.org

Cobb Research • 1208 Tatum Dr • Alexandria, VA 22307-2007 • *Cobb Chronicles*

Collingwood Library and Museum on Americanism Archives • 8301 E Boulevard Dr • Alexandria, VA 22308 • (703) 765-1652 • http://www.collingwoodlibrary.com • *Collingwood Library and Museum Newsletter*

Duckstein Surname Organization • 6103 Marilyn Dr • Alexandria, VA 22310 • (703) 971-8769

Fort Ward Museum and Historic Site Archives • 4301 W Braddock Rd • Alexandria, VA 22304-1008 • (703) 838-4848 • http://www.fortward.org • *Fort Ward Museum Newsletter*

Friendship Firehouse Museum Archives • 107 S Alfred St • Alexandria, VA 22314 • (703) 838-3891 • http://www.friendshipfirehouse.org

Gadsby's Tavern Museum Library • 134 N Royal St • Alexandria, VA 22314 • (703) 838-4242 • http://www.gadsbytavern.org

George Washington Masonic National Memorial Archives • 101 Callahan Dr • Alexandria, VA 22301 • (703) 683-2007 • http://www.gwmemorial.org • *George Washington Masonic National Memorial Newsletter*

Gum Springs Historical Society • 8100 Fordson Rd • Alexandria, VA 22306 • (703) 799-1198

Higdon Family Association • 911 Croton Dr • Alexandria, VA 22308 • (703) 360-4776 • *Higdon Family Newsletter*

Jewish Historical Society • 600 1st St • Alexandria, VA 22314 • (703) 789-0900

Lee-Fendall House Museum Archives • 614 Oronoco St • Alexandria, VA 22314 • (703) 548-1789 • http://www.leefendallhouse.org • *Lee-Fendall House Museum Newsletter*

Lyceum-Alexandria's History Museum Archives • George Washington Bicentennial Center, 201 S Washington St • Alexandria, VA 22314 • (703) 838-4994 • http://www.alexandriahistory.org • *Alexandria Observer*, *Historic Alexandria Quarterly*

Mount Vernon Genealogical Society & Library • Hollin Hall Senior Center, 1500 Shenandoah Rd • Alexandria, VA 22308-1120 • (703) 360-4986 • http://www.mindspring.com/~mvgs • *Mount Vernon Genealogical Society Newsletter*

National Association of Hans Jacob 'Honegger' Honaker Families • P.O. Box 3636 • Alexandria, VA 22302-0636 • (703) 751-7321 • *Honaker Family Newsletter*

National Preservation Institute • P.O. Box 1702 • Alexandria, VA 22313 • (703) 765-0100

Nichols Professional Library • 2000 N Beauregard St • Alexandria, VA 22311 • (703) 824-6670

Office of Historic Alexandria • City Hall Museum, P.O. Box 178 • Alexandria, VA 22313 • (703) 838-4554 • http://www.ci.alexandria.va.us/oha/ • *Historic Alexandria Quarterly*

Palatines to America, Virginia Chapter • 1121 Gladstone Pl • Alexandria, VA 22308-1738 • (703) 768-0451 • *Wagon Road*

Pope-Leighey House Museum Archives • 9000 Richmond Hwy • Alexandria, VA 22309 • (703) 780-4000 • http://www.popeleighey1940.org

Ramsay House Museum Archives • 221 King St • Alexandria, VA 22314 • (703) 838-5005 • http://www.funside.com

Reynolds Family Association • 4004 Javins Dr • Alexandria, VA 22310 • (703) 960-1782 • http://www.narnet.com/rfc/rfa.htm • *Reynolds Recollections*

Stabler-Leadbeater Apothecary Museum Archives • 105-107 S Fairfax St • Alexandria, VA 22314 • (703) 836-3713 • http://www.apothecarymuseum.org

US Patent and Trademark Office Museum Archives • Madison Bldg, 600 Delany St, W #1C65 • Alexandria, VA 22314 • (571) 272-0095 • http://www.uspto.gov

Woodlawn Museum Archives • 9000 Richmond Hwy • Alexandria, VA 22309 • (703) 780-4000 • http://www.woodlawn1805.org

Altavista
Avoca Museums and Historical Society • 1514 Main St • Altavista, VA 24517 • (434) 369-1076

Amelia
Amelia Historical Society & Library • Jackson Bldg, P.O. Box 113 • Amelia, VA 23002-0113 • (804) 561-3180

Amherst
Amherst County Historical Society & Archives • Historical Museum, 154 S Main, P.O. Box 741 • Amherst, VA 24521 • (434) 946-9068 • http://members.aol.com/achmuseum/achmhis.htm • *Newsletter of ACHM*

Amherst County Public Library • 382 S Main St, P.O. Box 370 • Amherst, VA 24521-0370 • (434) 946-9388 • http://www.acpl.us

Monacan Indian Tribe • 114 Indian Mission Rd • Amherst, VA 24521 • (434) 946-0389

Virginia

Amissville

Schauf-Hommell Reunion • 459 Viewtown Rd • Amissville, VA 20106

Annandale

Annandale Family History Center Library • 3900 Howard St • Annandale, VA 22003-0089 • (703) 256-5518

Clan MacInnes Society • 8232 Kay Ct • Annandale, VA 22003 • (703) 560-4371 • http://www.clanmacinnes.org • *Thistle and the Bee*

Downen Family Exchange • 4009 Terrace Dr • Annandale, VA 22003 • *Downen Family Exchange Newsletter*

Appomattox

Appomattox Courthouse National Historic Park Library • P.O. Box 218 • Appomattox, VA 24522-0218 • (434) 352-8987 • http://www.nps.gov/apco/

Wilson Family Historial Society • P.O. Box 1058 • Appomattox, VA 24522 • (434) 352-2539 • *Wilson Clan Newsletter*

Arlington

American Battle Monuments Commission • 5119-5120 Pulaski Building Courthouse, 2300 Clarendon Blvd • Arlington, VA 22201 • (703) 696-6897 • http://www.usabmc.com

Arlington County Department of Libraries • 2100 Clarendon Blvd • Arlington, VA 22201 • (703) 228-3348 • http://www.co.arlington.va.us/lib/

Arlington County Department of Libraries-Central Library • 1015 N Quincy St • Arlington, VA 22201-4661 • (703) 228-5990

Arlington Historical Society & Archives • Historical Museum, 1805 S Arlington Ridge Rd, P.O. Box 100402 • Arlington, VA 22210-0402 • (703) 892-4204 • http://www.arlingtonhistoricalsociety.org • Arlington Historical Magazine

Bluemont Historical Railroad Junction • Bluemount Junction Park, 601 N Manchester St • Arlington, VA 22203 • (703) 525-0294

Hoster Family Club • 1600 S Eads St #134 S • Arlington, VA 22202 • (703) 521-9156 • *Acorns to Oak Leaves: Hoster Family Newsletter*

Mechling-Mechlin-Macklin Family • 3456 N 13th St • Arlington, VA 23103 • *Mechling-Mechlin-Macklin Newsletter*

National Genealogical Society & Library • 4527 N 17th St • Arlington, VA 22207-2399 • (703) 525-0050 • http://www.ngsgenealogy.org • *National Genealogical Society Quarterly; National Genealogical Society Newsletter; National Genealogical Society, Computer Interest Group Digest*

Newseum Archives • 1101 Wilson Blvd • Arlington, VA 22209 • (703) 284-3700 • http://www.newseum.org

Ortstadt-Ottstadt-Otstot(t) Organization • 5124 N 33rd St • Arlington, VA 22207-1854 • (703) 538-5446 • *Ortstadt-Ottstadt-Otstot(t) Organization Annual*

Owen Family Association • 2111 Jefferson Davis Hwy • Arlington, VA 22202 • (703) 415-1473 • *Owen Newsletter*

Pentagon Library • Taylor Bldg, Rm 9N14, 2531 Jefferson Davis Hwy • Arlington, VA 22202-3905 • (703) 602-6345 • http://www.hqda.army.mil/library

Robert E Lee Memorial Museum Archives • Arlington House, National Park Service, Arlington National Cemetery • Arlington, VA 22211 • (703) 557-0613 • http://www.nps.gov/arho

Samuel Adams Society • 2507 N Harrison • Arlington, VA 22207

Wooten-Wooton and Related Families • 3517-A S Stafford • Arlington, VA 22206 • (703) 379-1092 • Wooten/Wooton Newsletter

Nelson City Historical Society • 5365 Thomas Nelson Hwy • Arrington, VA 22922 • (434) 263-8400

Ashburn

Rhode Island Families Association • P.O. Box 1414 • Ashburn, VA 20146-1414 • *Rhode Island Genealogical Register*

Ashland

Hanover County Historical Society & Archives • Historical Museum, 8516 E Patrick Henry Rd • Ashland, VA 23005 • (804) 537-5815

McGraw-Page Library • Randolph-Macon College, 305 Henry St, P.O. Box 5005 • Ashland, VA 23005-5505 • (804) 752-7323 • http://www.rmc.edu/library

Bassett

Blue Ridge Regional Library-Bassett Branch • 3969 Fairystone Park Hwy • Bassett, VA 24055 • (276) 629-2426

Henry County Historical Society • Historical Center, 3964 Fairyston • Bassett, VA 24055 • (703) 629-2426

Bastian

Bland County Historical Society • Route 1, Box 1530 • Bastian, VA 24314

Beaverdam

Scotchtown Museum Archives • 16120 Chiswell Ln • Beaverdam, VA 23015 • (804) 227-3500 • http://www.scotchtown.com

Bedford

Bedford City-County Museum Archives • 201 E Main St • Bedford, VA 24523 • (540) 586-4520 • http://www.bedfordvmuseum.org • *Museum Report*

Bedford County Genealogical Society • 201 E Main St • Bedford, VA 24523

Bedford Historical Society • 149 W Main St, P.O. Box 602 • Bedford, VA 24523 • (540) 586-8188

Bedford Public Library • 321 N Bridge St • Bedford, VA 24523-1924 • (540) 586-8911 • http://www.library.bedford.va.us

Berryville

Civil War Society • P.O. Box 770 • Berryville, VA 22611 • (540) 955-1176 • http://www.civilwarsociety.com • *Civil War Magazine*

Clarke County Historical Association & Archives • Historical Museum, 32 E Main St, P.O. Box 306 • Berryville, VA 22611 • (540) 955-2600 • http://www.clarkehistory.org • *Clarke County Proceedings*

Pocahontas Foundation • P.O. Box 431 • Berryville, VA 22611 • (540) 955-1428

Big Stone Gap

Southwest Virginia Museum Historical State Park Archives • 30 W 1st St N • Big Stone Gap, VA 24219 • (276) 523-1322 • http://www.dcr.state.va.us/parks/swvamus.htm

Blacksburg

Historic Smithfield • Historical Museum, 1000 Smithfield Plantation Rd • Blacksburg, VA 24060 • (540) 231-3947 • http://www.civic.bev.net/smithfield • *Smithfield Review*

Newman Library • Virginia Polytechnic Institute, Drill Field Dr, P.O. Box 90001 • Blacksburg, VA 24062-9001 • (540) 231-9232 • http://www.lib.vt.edu

Smithfield Plantation Archives • 1000 Smithfield Plantation Rd • Blacksburg, VA 24060 • (540) 231-3947

Virginia Technical University Library • P.O. Box 90001 • Blacksburg, VA 24062-9001 • (540) 231-5595 • http://www.lib.vt.edu

Bluefield

Graham Historical Society • general delivery • Bluefield, VA 24605 • (276) 326-6680

Bowling Green

Caroline County Genealogical Society • P.O. Box 9 • Bowling Green, VA 22427

Caroline Historical Society • P.O. Box 324 • Bowling Green, VA 22427

Boydton

Southside Regional Library • 316 Washington St, P.O. Box 10 • Boydton, VA 23917-0010 • (434) 738-6580 • http://www.srlib.org

Bridgewater

Alexander Mack Memorial Library • Bridgewater College, E College St • Bridgewater, VA 22812 • (540) 828-5415 • http://www.bridgewater.edu/departments/library/

Kirshop-Caracoff-Caricoff-Karacoff-Kiracoff Family Reunion • Bridgewater Home • Bridgewater, VA 22812

Mason Family: Our Family Books • 115 E Rainbow Dr • Bridgewater, VA 22812-1733 • (540) 828-4617

Reuel B Pritchett Museum Archives • Bridgewater College, E College St, Box 147 • Bridgewater, VA 22812 • (540) 828-5482 • http://www.bridgewater.edu

Bristol
Bristol Genealogical Society • P.O. Box 433 • Bristol, VA 24203

Bristol Public Library • 701 Goode St • Bristol, VA 24201-4199 • (276) 645-8788 • http://www.bristol-library.org

Holston Territory Genealogical Society • P.O. Box 433 • Bristol, VA 24203-0433 • (276) 669-6839 • http://members.aol.com/Seesie260/index.HTGS.html • *Holston Pastfinder*

Sullivan County Genealogical Society • P.O. Box 433 • Bristol, VA 24203

William Strother Society • 15181 Big Knob • Bristol, VA 24202 • (276) 645-7052 • http://www.wmstrother.org • *Houses of Strother*

Bristow
Hite Family Association • 9345 Linton Hall Rd • Bristow, VA 20136 • *Hite Family Association Newsletter*

Brookneal
Patrick Henry National Memorial Archives • Red Hill Home, 1250 Red Hill Rd • Brookneal, VA 24528 • (434) 376-2044 • http://www.redhill.org • *Red Hill Quarterly*

Buena Vista
Von Canon Library • Southern Virginia University, 1 University Hill Dr • Buena Vista, VA 24416 • (540) 261-4241 • http://www.southernvirginia.edu

Burke
Clan Donald, Mid-East • 9921 Marquand Dr • Burke, VA 22015 • (703) 978-7155

Selma-Sanders Reunion • 5405 Crossrail Dr • Burke, VA 22015

Sweet-Wallace-Wright-Zimmerman-Hitt-Galbraith-Cooksey-Lawson-Brisbin-Morrow-Horn-Kenton-Lansdowne-Barney-Bookout-McClurg-Henderson-Russell Roots • 9503 Burning Bush Rd • Burke, VA 22015 • http://www.rootsweb.com/~daisy/russell.htm • *Kenton Kin Association Quarterly*; *Most Wanted: Frank and Jesse James*; *Daisy's Balleau Page*; *Lucky Family Tree*

Carson
Appomattox Regional Library-Carson Branch • P.O. Box 428 • Carson, VA 23830-0428 • (434) 246-2900

Catharpin
Carper Family Association • 4918 Sudley Rd • Catharpin, VA 22018 • (703) 754-2665

Centreville
Bates Family of Old Virginia • 5817 Stone Ridge Dr • Centreville, VA 20120-2888 • (703) 266-2427 • http://www.halcyondays.com/bbates.htm • *Bates Booster*

Chantilly
Bruce International USA Branch • P.O. Box 223452 • Chantilly, VA 20153-3452 • (703) 934-8183 • http://www.brucefamily.com • *Blue Lion*

National Railway Historical Society • general delivery • Chantilly, VA 20151 • (703) 273-8440

Walney Visitor Center Archives • Ellanor C Lawrence Park, 5040 Walney Rd • Chantilly, VA 20151 • (703) 631-0013 • http://www.co.fairfax.va.us/parks/parks.htm • *Walney Visitor Center Newsletter*

Charles City
Berkeley Plantation Archives • 12602 Harrison Landing Rd • Charles City, VA 23030 • (804) 829-6018 • http://www.berkeleyplantation.com

Charles City County Historical Society • 16530 The Glebe Lane • Charles City, VA 23030

Sherwood Forest Plantation Archives • 14501 John Tyler Memorial Hwy, P.O. Box 8 • Charles City, VA 23030 • (804) 829-5377 • http://www.sherwoodforest.org

Shirley Plantation Archives • 501 Shirley Plantation Rd • Charles City, VA 23030 • (804) 829-5121 • http://www.shirleyplantation.com

Charlotte Court House
Taylor Tracing Tribe-Fore Reunion • 9501 Thomas Jefferson Hwy • Charlotte Court House, VA 23923-3014 • (434) 248-5754 • *Taylor Talk*; *Fore Front: History and News for and About Fores with Virginia Roots*

Charlottesville
1784 Michie Tavern Museum Archives • 683 Thomas Jefferson Pkwy • Charlottesville, VA 22902 • (434) 977-1234 • http://www.michietavern.com

Albemarle County Historical Society & Library • 220 Court Sq • Charlottesville, VA 22902-5245 • (434) 296-1492 • http://monticello.avenue.gen.va.us/community/agencies/achs • *Magazine of Albemarle County History*; *Bulletin of the Albemarle County Historical Society*

Alderman Library • Univ of Virginia, P.O. Box 400114 • Charlottesville, VA 22904-4114 • (434) 924-3021 • http://www.virginia.edu/speccol/ • *Libra*

Ash Lawn-Highland Museum Archives • 1000 James Monroe Pkwy • Charlottesville, VA 22902 • (434) 293-9539 • http://www.ashlawnhighland.org

Central Virginia Genealogical Association • 303 Farm Ln, P.O. Box 5583 • Charlottesville, VA 22905-5583 • (434) 295-1523 • http://avenue.org/cvga/ • Central Virginia Heritage

Culpeper Genealogical Society • P.O. Box 1791 • Charlottesville, VA 22902

Jefferson-Madison Regional Library • 201 E Market St • Charlottesville, VA 22902-5287 • (434) 979-7151 • http://www.jmrl.org

Rotunda Museum Archives • Univ of VA, P.O. Box 400305 • Charlottesville, VA 22904 • (434) 924-7969 • http://www.virginia.edu/~urelat/Tours/rotunda/rotunda.html

Samuel Nettleton Family Organization • 142 W Park Dr • Charlottesville, VA 22901-2504

Thomas Jefferson Memorial Foundation & Library • Monticello Plantation, P.O. Box 316 • Charlottesville, VA 22902-0316 • (434) 984-7543 • http://www.monticello.org

Chase City
MacCallum More Museum Archives • 603 Hudgins St, P.O. Box 104 • Chase City, VA 23924 • (434) 372-0502 • http://www.nmmg.org

Chatham
Pittsylvania Historical Society • 320 Whitehead St • Chatham, VA 24531 • (434) 432-2790

Pittsylvania Historical Society & Library • 112 N Main St, P.O. Box 1206 • Chatham, VA 24531 • (434) 432-5031 • *Quill Pen*; *Pittsylvania Packet*

Chesapeake
Chesapeake Public Library • 298 Cedar Road • Chesapeake, VA 23320-5598 • (757) 382-6579 • http://www.chesapeake.lib.va.us

Norfolk County Historical Society of Chesapeake, VA & Archives • c/o Chesapeake Public Library, 298 Cedar Rd • Chesapeake, VA 23320-5512 • (757) 382-6579

Chester
Face Family of America • 12517 Petersburg St • Chester, VA 23831 • (804) 748-2414

John Bosher Family Organization • P.O. Box 1314 • Chester, VA 23831-8314 • (804) 748-6456

Chesterfield
Chesterfield County Historical Society & Archives • Historical Museum, 10201 Ironbridge Rd, P.O. Box 40 • Chesterfield, VA 23832 • (804) 777-9663 • http://www.chesterfieldhistory.com • *Messenger*, *Journal of the Chesterfield Historical Society*

Chesterfield County Public Library • 9501 Lori Rd, P.O. Box 297 • Chesterfield, VA 23832-0297 • (804) 784-1603 • http://library.co.chesterfield.va.us

Chincoteague
Oyster and Maritime Museum of Chincoteague Archives • 7125 Maddox Blvd, P.O. Box 352 • Chincoteague, VA 23336 • (757) 336-6117

Christiansburg
Montgomery Museum Archives • 300 S Pepper St • Christiansburg, VA 24073 • (540) 382-5644 • http://www.montgomerymuseum.org • *Montgomery Museum Newsletter*

Montgomery-Floyd Regional Library • 125 Sheltman St • Christiansburg, VA 24073 • (540) 382-6965 • http://www.mfrl.org

Phillips-Hollandsworth Annual Reunion • P.O. Box 162 • Christiansburg, VA 24073-0162 • (540) 382-3256

Phillips-Quesenberry Families • 910 N High Street NE • Christiansburg, VA 24073 • (540) 382-7783

Clarksville
Prestwould Foundation Museum Archives • 429 Preswould Dr, P.O. Box 872 • Clarksville, VA 23927 • (434) 372-8672

Clifton Forge
Chesapeake and Ohio Historical Society & Library • 312 E Ridgeway St, P.O. Box 79 • Clifton Forge, VA 24422-0079 • (540) 862-2210 • http://www.cohs.org

Colonial Beach
Colonial Beach Historical Society & Archives • Historical Museum, 128 Hawthorne St • Colonial Beach, VA 22443 • (804) 224-3379

George Washington Birthplace National Monument Archives • 1732 Popes Creek Rd • Colonial Beach, VA 22443 • (804) 224-1732 • http://www.nps.gov/gewa

Colonial Heights
Francis Epes Family Organization • 235 Dunlop Farms Blvd #144 • Colonial Heights, VA 23834-1753

Courtland
Walter Cecil Rawls Library and Museum • 22511 Main St • Courtland, VA 23837-1030 • (757) 653-2821 • http://www.blackwaterlib.org

Covington
Alleghany Highlands Genealogical Society • 1011 N Rockbridge St • Covington, VA 24426-1136 • (703) 962-4683 • *Alleghany Highlands Genealogical Society Newsletter*

Charles Pinckney Jones Memorial Library • 406 W Riverside St • Covington, VA 24426 • (540) 962-3321 • http://www.cpjones.org

Crewe
Harden, Hardin, Harding Family Association • Route 1, Box 2290 • Crewe, VA 23930 • (434) 645-8595 • *Harden, Hardin, Harding Newsletter*

Nottoway County Historical Association • RDF 1, Box 56 • Crewe, VA 23930

Nottoway County Public Libraries • 414 Tyler St • Crewe, VA 23930 • (434) 645-9310 • http://www.nottlib.org

Critz
Reynolds Homestead Museum Archives • 463 Homestead Ln • Critz, VA 24082 • (276) 694-7181 • http://www.reynoldshomestead.vt.edu

Culpeper
Culpeper County Library • 271 Southgate Shopping Center • Culpeper, VA 22701-3215 • (540) 825-8691 • http://www.tlc.library.net/culpeper

Culpeper Historical Society • P.O. Box 785 • Culpeper, VA 22701

Ford Stoud Historical Foundation • general delivery • Culpeper, VA 22701 • (540) 825-7355

Memorial Foundation of the Germanna Colonies • P.O. Box 693 • Culpeper, VA 22701-0693 • (540) 825-1496 • http://www.germanna.org • *Germanna*; *Germanna Record*; *Gottschee Tree*

Cumberland
Cumberland County Historical Society • P.O. Box 88 • Cumberland, VA 23040 • (804) 492-4533 • Cumberland County Virginia Historical Bulletin

Daleville
Crotty Family Organization • 2342 Coventry Ln • Daleville, VA 24083 • (540) 992-1292

Danville
Danville Museum of Art and History Archives • 975 Main St • Danville, VA 24541 • (434) 793-5644 • http://www.danvillemuseum.org • *Danville Museum of Art and History Newsletter*

Danville Public Library • 511 Patton St • Danville, VA 24541 • (434) 799-5195 • http://www.danvillelibrary.org

Griffin Family • 333 Chadwyck Dr • Danville, VA 24541-3306 • (434) 793-1744

Mary B Blount Library • Averett University Library, 344 W Main St • Danville, VA 24541-2849 • (434) 791-5692 • http://www.averett.edu/library

VA-NC Piedmont Genealogical Society & Archives • c/o Danville Public Library, 511 Patton St, P.O. Box 2272 • Danville, VA 24541-0272 • (434) 799-5195 • *Bulletin of the VA-NC Piedmont Genealogical Society*; *Piedmont Lineages*

Whittington W Clement Library • Danville Community College, 1008 S Main St • Danville, VA 24541-4004 • (434) 797-8555 • http://www.dcc.vccs.edu/lrc/lrc/lrchome.htm

Dayton
Harrisonburg-Rockingham Historical Society & Library • Heritage Center, 382 High St, P.O. Box 716 • Dayton, VA 22821-0716 • (540) 847-2616 • http://www.heritagecenter.com • *Harrisonburg-Rockingham Historical Society Newsletter*; *Rockingham Recorder*

Dugspur
Turman Annual Reunion • Route 1, Box 170 • Dugspur, VA 24325 • (276) 728-3657

Dumfries
Alton-Allton-Aulton Family Association • 15510 Laurel Ridge Rd • Dumfries, VA 22026 • (703) 670-4842 • http://members.aol.com/altonnews/aaaafn.htm • *Alton-Allton-Aulton Association Family Newsletter*

Historic Dumfries Virginia & Archives • Weems-Botts Museum, 3944 Cameron St, P.O. Box 26 • Dumfries, VA 22026 • (703) 221-3346 • http://www.geocities.com/HDVINC • *Historic Dumfries Virginia Newsletter*

Sons of The American Revolution, Virginia Society • 15762 Edgewood Dr • Dumfries, VA 22025 • (703) 897-4875

Edinburg
Shenandoah County Historical Society & Archives • c/o Shenandoah County Library, 514 Stoney Creek Blvd, Route 1, Box 1-B • Edinburg, VA 22824 • (540) 984-8200 • *Shenando News*

Shenandoah County Library • 514 Stoney Creek Blvd • Edinburg, VA 22824 • (540) 984-8200 • http://www.shenandoah.co.lib.va.us • *Stoney Creek Current*

Elk Creek
Grayson County Historical Society • Route 1, Box 293 • Elk Creek, VA 24326

Emory
Frederick T Kelly Library • Emory & Henry College, 30480 Armbrister Dr, P.O. Box 948 • Emory, VA 24327-0948 • (276) 944-6208 • http://www.ehc.edu

Fairfax
Carpatho-Rusyn American • P.O. Box 192 • Fairfax, VA 22030-0192 • (703) 691-8585 • *Carpatho-Rusyn American Newsletter*

Carper Family Association • 10110 Farmington Dr • Fairfax, VA 22030

Crowl-John and Eleanor Cusick-James and Esther Swartz McCue Family Association • 9603 Bel Glade St • Fairfax, VA 22031-1105 • (703) 281-9562 • *Crowl Connections*

Fairfax County Public Library • 3915 Chain Bridge Rd • Fairfax, VA 22030 • (703) 293-6227 • http://s70itw0l.dit.co.fairfax.va.us/library/va_room/htm

Fairfax County Public Library • 12000 Government Ctr Pkwy • Fairfax, VA 22035 • (703) 324-3100 • http://www.fairfaxcounty.gov/library

Fairfax Museum Archives • 10209 Main St • Fairfax, VA 22030 • (703) 385-8414 • http://www.ci.fairfax.va.us

Fenwick Library • George Mason Univ, 4400 University Dr • Fairfax, VA 22030-4444 • (703) 993-2210 • http://www.gmu.edu/library/specialcollections/

Garrigues Assemblee • 3781 Center Wy • Fairfax, VA 22033 • (703) 278-8747 • *Branches and Roots*

Historical Society of Fairfax County, Virginia & Library • P.O. Box 415 • Fairfax, VA 22030 • (703) 246-2123 • *Yearbook of the Historical Society of Fairfax County*

National Firearms Museum Archives • 11250 Waples Mill Rd • Fairfax, VA 22030 • (703) 267-1620 • http://www.nrahq.org

Rathbun-Rathbone-Rathburn Family Association • 11308 Pope's Head Rd #B • Fairfax, VA 22030-4614 • (703) 278-8512 • *Rathbun-Rathbone-Rathburn Family Historian*

Palatines to America, Virginia Chapter • 3249 Cambridge Ct • Fairfax, VA 22032-1942 • (703) 591-3656 • *Wagon Road*

Fairfax Station
Clan Donnachaidh Society, Mid-Atlantic States • 7506 Willowbrook • Fairfax Station, VA 22039 • (703) 978-7268 • *Robertson's Rant*

Falls Church
Agnew Association of America • 2910 Madison Pl • Falls Church, VA 22042

Golden Family Association • P.O. Box 742 • Falls Church, VA 22046

Kerr Family Association of North America • P.O. Box 1099 • Falls Church, VA 22041 • http://www.tartans.com/clans/Kerr/kerr.html • *Borderline*

Mary Riley Styles Public Library • 120 N Virginia Ave • Falls Church, VA 22046 • (703) 248-5030 • http://www.falls-church.lib.va.us

Pardue Family Historical Association • 7534 Willow Ln • Falls Church, VA 22042 • *Pardue Times & Historical Gazette*

Trail Dust • 407 W Rosemary Ln • Falls Church, VA 22046-3847 • *Trail Dust*

Farmville
Central Virginia Regional Library • 217 W 3rd St • Farmville, VA 23901 • (434) 392-6924

Ferrum
Blue Ridge Institute and Museum Archives • Ferrum College, 20 Museum Dr, P.O. Box 1000 • Ferrum, VA 24088 • (540) 365-4416 • http://www.blueridgeinstitute.org

Franklin County Genealogical Society • P.O. Box 316 • Ferrum, VA 24088

Fincastle
Botetourt County Historical Society • P.O. Box 468 • Fincastle, VA 24090-0468

Presley-Pressley Family Society • P.O. Box 75 • Fincastle, VA 24090 • http://egroups.com/group/presley-pressley

Fishersville
Augusta County Library • 1759 Jefferson Hwy • Fishersville, VA 22939 • (540) 949-6354 • http://www.lib.co.augusta.va.us • *Augusta County Library Newsletter*

Floyd
Ira Slusher Hylton Descendants • Route 2, Box 506 • Floyd, VA 24091 • (540) 745-2314

Forest
Thomas Jefferson's Poplar Forest Archives • Rte 661, Bateman Bridge Rd, P.O. Box 419 • Forest, VA 24551 • (434) 525-1806 • http://www.poplarforest.org • *Poplar Forest Newsletter*

Fork Union
Fluvanna County Library • 8880 James Madison Hwy, P.O. Box 548 • Fork Union, VA 23055-0548 • (434) 842-2230 • http://www.fcplva.org

Fort Belvoir
Silvers-Rogers Family Association • 9120 Belvoir Woods Pkwy #H409 • Fort Belvoir, VA 22060 • (703) 799-4874

US Army Center for Army Analysis • Bldg 1839, 6001 Goethals Rd • Fort Belvoir, VA 22060 • (703) 806-5191

US Army-Institute of Heraldry Library • 9325 Gunston Rd, Suite S112 • Fort Belvoir, VA 22060-5579 • (703) 806-4967 • http://www.perscom.army.mil/tagd/tioh/tioh.htm

US Army-Van Noy Library • 5966 12th St, Suite 101 • Fort Belvoir, VA 22060-5554 • (703) 806-3323

Fort Eustis
Fort Eustis Historical and Archaeological Association • P.O. Box 4408 • Fort Eustis, VA 23604 • (757) 878-3480

US Army Groninger Library • Bldg 1313, Army Transportation Ctr • Fort Eustis, VA 23604-5107 • (757) 878-5017

US Army Transportation Museum Library • Besson Hall, 300 Washington Blvd • Fort Eustis, VA 23604-5260 • (757) 878-1182 • http://www.eustis.army.mil/dptmsec/museum.htm

US Army-Transportation School Library • Bldg 705 Rm 36 • Fort Eustis, VA 23604-5450 • (757) 878-5563 • http://www.lic.eustis.army.mil • US Army-Transportation School LibraryQuarterly Newsletter

Fort Lee
US Army Quartermaster Museum Archives • 4218 A Avenue • Fort Lee, VA 23801 • (804) 734-4203 • http://www.qmmuseum.lee.army.mil

US Army Women's Museum Archives • 2100 Adams Ave • Fort Lee, VA 23801 • (804) 734-4327 • http://www.awm.lee.army.mil • US Army Women's Museum Newsletter

Fort Monroe
Casemate Museum Archives • 20 Bernard Rd, P.O. Box 51341 • Fort Monroe, VA 23651-0341 • (757) 727-3935 • http://www.tradoc.monroe.army.mil/museum/

US Army Headquarters, US Army Fort Monroe Technical Library • Bldg 7 • Fort Monroe, VA 23651-5124 • (757) 788-2821 • http://www.tradoc.monroe.army.mil/library

Fort Myer
Council on America's Military Past • P.O. Box 1151 • Fort Myer, VA 22211-0151 • (703) 912-6124 • *Headquarters Heliogram*; *Council on America's Military Past Periodical*

Old Guard Museum Archives • Commander, 3rd US Infantry, 204 lee Ave • Fort Myer, VA 22211 • (703) 696-6670 • http://www.mdw.army.mil/oldguard/

US Army Fort Myer Post Library • 210 McNair Rd, Bldg 469 • Fort Myer, VA 22211-1101 • (703) 696-3555

Fredericksburg
Bowen-Woolard-Lilley Family Association • 10509 Running Cedar Ln #502 • Fredericksburg, VA 22407 • (540) 898-6529

Boyd Society • 5 Little Creek Ln • Fredericksburg, VA 22405-3643 • http://www.tartans.com/clans/Boyd/society/nasociety.html • *Boyd Family: Kilmarnock*

Central Rappahannock Heritage Center Archives • Fredericksburg Battlefield, 300 Central Rd, P.O. Box 8533 • Fredericksburg, VA 22404 • (540) 373-3704 • http://www.crhcarchives.org

Central Rappahannock Regional Library • 1201 Caroline St • Fredericksburg, VA 22401-3761 • (540) 372-1144 • http://www.librarypoint.org

Civil War Life-Soldier's Museum Archives • 4712 Southpoint Pkwy • Fredericksburg, VA 22407 • (540) 834-1859 • http://www.civilwar-life.com

Clell Miller's Cousins • 808 Charlotte St • Fredericksburg, VA 22401 • (540) 371-3253

Fredericksburg and Spotsylvania National Military Park Library • 120 Chatham Ln • Fredericksburg, VA 22405 • (540) 371-0802 • http://www.nps.gov/ffrsp

Virginia

Fredericksburg Area Museum Archives • 907-911 Princess Anne St, P.O. Box 922 • Fredericksburg, VA 22404 • (540) 371-3037 • http://www.famcc.org • *Fredericksburg Area Museum Newsletter*

Fredericksburg Regional Genealogical Society • P.O. Box 42013 • Fredericksburg, VA 22404-2013 • (540) 371-3906 • *Fredericksburg Regional Genealogical Society Newsletter*

Historic Fredericksburg Foundation • 604 William St #A • Fredericksburg, VA 22401 • (540) 371-4504 • *Preservation Notes*

Hugh Mercer 1761 Apothecary Shop Museum Archives • 1020 Caroline St • Fredericksburg, VA 22401 • (540) 373-3362 • http://www.apva.org

James Monroe Museum and Memorial Library • 908 Charles St • Fredericksburg, VA 22401-5810 • (540) 654-2113 • http://www.umw.edu/jamesmonroemuseum

Kenmore Plantation and Washington's Ferry Farm Archives • 1201 Washington Ave • Fredericksburg, VA 22401 • (540) 373-3381 • http://www.kenmore.org

Mary Washington House Museum Archives • 1200 Charles St • Fredericksburg, VA 22401 • (540) 373-1569 • http://www.apva.org

McAtee Surname Association • 5057 MacNamara Dr • Fredericksburg, VA 22407

Rising Sun Tavern Museum Archives • 1304 Caroline St • Fredericksburg, VA 22401 • (540) 371-1494 • http://www.apva.org

Saint James' House Museum Archives • 1300 Charles St • Fredericksburg, VA 22401 • (540) 373-1569 • http://www.apva.org

Simpson Library • Mary Washington College, 1801 College Ave • Fredericksburg, VA 22401-4664 • (540) 654-1147 • http://www.library.mwc.edu

Front Royal

Samuels Public Library • 538 Villa Ave • Front Royal, VA 22630 • (540) 635-3153 • http://www.shentel.net/library/samuels/

Warren Rifles Confederate Museum Archives • 95 Chester St, P.O. Box 1304 • Front Royal, VA 22630 • (540) 636-6982

Galax

Galax-Carroll Regional Library • 610 W Stuart Dr • Galax, VA 24333 • (276) 236-2042 • http://galaxcarroll.lib.va.us

Hackler-Comer Reunion • 144 Wildwood Ln • Galax, VA 24333 • (276) 236-2012

Jeff Matthews Memorial Museum Archives • 606 W Stuart Dr • Galax, VA 24333 • (540) 236-7874

Glen Allen

Henrico County Museum Archives • Mountain & Courtney Rds • Glen Allen, VA 23060 • (804) 501-5100

Gloucester

Toney Genealogy Exchange • 5998 Ladysmeade Ln • Gloucester, VA 23061 • http://www.toneyweb.com/exchange/

Walter Reed Birthplace Museum Archives • Hwy 614 & 616, P.O. Box 160 • Gloucester, VA 23061 • (804) 693-3663

Warner Hall Graveyard Archives • Rte 629 & 614, P.O. Box 335 • Gloucester, VA 23061 • (804) 725-9250

Goochland

Goochland County Historical Society & Archives • Historical Museum, 2875 River Rd W, P.O. Box 602 • Goochland, VA 23063 • (804) 556-3966 • http://www.goochlandhistory.org • *Goochland County Historical Society Magazine*

Gordonsville

Exchange Hotel Civil War Museum Archives • 400 S Main St, P.O. Box 542 • Gordonsville, VA 22942 • (540) 832-2944 • http://www.hgiexchange.org • *Exchange Hotel Civil War Museum Newsletter*

Historic Gordonsville • 400 S Main St • Gordonsville, VA 22942 • (540) 832-2944

Grafton

Kirkham Research • 405 Cockletown Rd • Grafton, VA 23692 • (757) 898-5692 • Kirkham Family Newsletter

Great Falls

Bell Family Association of the United States • 12147 Holly Knoll Cr • Great Falls, VA 22066 • (703) 430-6745 • http://www.clanbell.org • *Bell-a-Peal*

Hoy Research • 718 Gouldman Ln • Great Falls, VA 22055 • (703) 759-0473 • *Hoy Family Newsletter*

Grundy

Buchanan County Historical Society • c/o Buchanan County Public Library, Route 2, Box 3 • Grundy, VA 24614

Buchanan County Public Library • Route 2, Box 3 • Grundy, VA 24614-9613 • (276) 935-6581 • http://www.bcplnet.org

Halifax

Halifax-South Boston Regional Library • 177 S Main St, P.O. Box 1729 • Halifax, VA 24558-1729 • (434) 476-3357 • http://www.halifax.com/library

Hampden Sydney

Eggleston Library • Hampden Sydney College, 12 Via Sacra, HSC Box 7 • Hampden Sydney, VA 23943 • (434) 223-6190 • http://www.hsc.edu

Esther Thomas Atkinson Museum Archives • College Rd, P.O. Box 745 • Hampden Sydney, VA 23943 • (434) 223-6134 • http://www.hsc.edu/museum/ • *Esther Thomas Atkinson Museum Newsletter*

Hampton

Air Power Park Museum Archives • 413 W Mercury Blvd • Hampton, VA 23666 • (757) 727-1163

Hampton History Museum Archives • 120 Old Hampton Ln • Hampton, VA 23669 • (757) 727-1610 • http://www.hampton.gov/history_museum • *Hampton History Museum Newsletter*

Hampton Public Library • 4207 Victoria Blvd • Hampton, VA 23669-4243 • (757) 727-1312 • http://www.hamptonpubliclibrary.org

Hampton University Museum Archives • Hampton Univ • Hampton, VA 23668 • (757) 727-5308 • http://www.hamptonu.edu

Howes Family Association • 504 White Hall Cr • Hampton, VA 23669 • (434) 851-2963 • *Howes Family Association Newsletter*

Saint John's Church and Parish Museum Archives • 100 W Queensway • Hampton, VA 23669 • (757) 722-2567 • http://www.stjohns-hampton.org

Tidewater Genealogical Society • 131 Wilderness Rd, P.O. Box 7650 • Hampton, VA 23666 • (804) 484-3800 • *Virginia Tidewater Genealogy*

Virginia Air and Space Center Museum Archives • 600 Settlers Landing Rd • Hampton, VA 23669 • (757) 727-0900 • http://www.vasc.org • CenterLine

William and Norma Harvey Library • Hampton Univ, 130 E Tyler St • Hampton, VA 23668 • (757) 727-5371 • http://www.hamptonu.edu

Hanover

Hanover County Historical Society & Archives • Hanover County Courthouse, P.O. Box 91 • Hanover, VA 23069 • (804) 537-6262 • *Hanover County Historical Society Bulletin*; *Highlights*

Pamunkey Regional Library • 7527 Library Dr, P.O. Box 119 • Hanover, VA 23069-0119 • (804) 537-6211 • http://www.pamunkeylibrary.org

Hardy

Booker T Washington National Monument Archives • 12130 Booker T Washington Hwy • Hardy, VA 24101 • (540) 721-2094 • http://www.nps.gov/bowa

Harrisonburg

Carrier Library • James Madison Univ, 800 S Main St • Harrisonburg, VA 22807-0001 • (540) 568-6267 • http://www.lib.jmu.edu

Harrisonburg-Rockingham Historical Society • 301 S Main St • Harrisonburg, VA 22801

Massanutten Regional Library • 174 S Main St • Harrisonburg, VA 22801 • (540) 434-4475 • http://www.mrlib.org • *Check-It-Out*

Menno Simons Historical Library and Archives • Eastern Mennonite College, 1200 Park Rd • Harrisonburg, VA 22802-2462 • (540) 432-4178 • http://www.emu.edu/library

Rockingham County Historical Society • 301 S Main St • Harrisonburg, VA 22801

Roudabush Family • Route 10, Box 28 • Harrisonburg, VA 22801 • (540) 867-5257

Heathsville
Genealogical Society of the Northern Neck of Virginia & Library • P.O. Box 511 • Heathsville, VA 22473-0511 • (804) 438-6327 • *Genealogical Society of the Northern Neck of Virginia Newsletter*

Northumberland County Historical Society • general delivery • Heathsville, VA 22473 • (804) 580-8581

Herndon
Carpathian Connection • P.O. Box 1087 • Herndon, VA 20172 • *Carpathian Connection-Ohio Page*

Claffey Surname Organization • 13405 Running Pump Ct • Herndon, VA 22071

Kidwell Farm at Frying Pan Park Archives • 2709 W Ox Rd • Herndon, VA 20171 • (703) 437-9101 • http://www.fairfaxcounty.gov/parks/fpp

Ong Surname Organization • 2221 Christy Pl • Herndon, VA 22070 • (703) 481-0143

Sovereign Media Co • 453 Carlisle Dr • Herndon, VA 22071 • (703) 964-0361 • *WW II History*

Hillsville
Carroll County Genealogy Club • P.O. Box 395 • Hillsville, VA 24343

Carroll County Historical Society & Archives • Historical Museum, 307 N Main St, P.O. Box 937 • Hillsville, VA 24343 • (276) 728-2125 • *Carroll County Chronicles*

Hood
Roaring Twenties Antique Car Museum Archives • Rte 230 W • Hood, VA 22723 • (540) 948-6290 • http://www.roaring-twenties.com

Hopewell
Appomattox Regional Library • 245 E Cawson St • Hopewell, VA 23860 • (804) 458-0110 • http://www.arls.org

Flowerdew Hundred Foundation & Archives • 1617 Flowerdew Hundred Rd • Hopewell, VA 23860 • (804) 541-8897 • http://www.flowerdew.org

Hot Springs
Bath Company Historical Society • P.O. Box 279 • Hot Springs, VA 24445 • (540) 839-2566

Independence
Grayson County Historical Society • P.O. Box 529 • Independence, VA 24348 • *Glimpses of Grayson*

Wythe-Grayson Regional Library • 147 S Independence Ave, P.O. Box 159 • Independence, VA 24348-0159 • (276) 773-3018 • http://wythegrayson.lib.va.us

Irvington
Foundation for Historic Christ Church & Library • Routes 646 & 709, P.O. Box 24 • Irvington, VA 22480 • (804) 438-6855 • http://www.christchurch1735.org

Jamestown
Jamestown National Historic Site Archives • Colonial National Pkwy • Jamestown, VA 23081 • (804) 648-1889 • http://www.historicjamestowne.org

Jonesville
Claiborne County Historical Society • Route 1, Box 589 • Jonesville, VA 24263

Lee County Historical and Genealogical Society • P.O. Box 231 • Jonesville, VA 24263

Keswick
Arcadia Preservation • general delivery • Keswick, VA 22947 • (434) 293-7772

Kilmarnock
Lancaster Community Library • 235 School St, P.O. Box 850 • Kilmarnock, VA 22482-0850 • (804) 435-1729 • http://www.lancasterlibrary.org

King George
King George County Historical Society • 9483 Kings Hwy, P.O. Box 424 • King George, VA 22485 • (540) 775-9477

Lewis Egerton Smoot Memorial Library • 9533 Kings Hwy • King George, VA 22485 • (540) 775-7951 • http://www.smoot.org

King William
Pamunkey Indian Museum Archives • Rte 1, Box 2220 • King William, VA 23086 • (804) 843-4792

Lancaster
Mary Ball Washington Museum and Library • Lancaster House, 8346 Mary Ball Rd, P.O. Box 97 • Lancaster, VA 22503-0097 • (804) 462-7280 • http://www.mbwm.org • *Mary Ball Washington Museum Newsletter*

Langley AFB
Langley Air Force Base Library FL4800 • 1 SVS/SVMG, 42 Ash Ave • Langley AFB, VA 23665 • (757) 764-2906 • *Tales of Air Warriors*

Lawrenceville
Meherrin Regional Library • 133 W Hicks St • Lawrenceville, VA 23868 • (434) 848-2418 • http://www.meherrinlib.org

Lebanon
Russell County Public Library • 203 NW Main St, P.O. Box 247 • Lebanon, VA 24266-0247 • (276) 889-8044 • http://www.russell.lib.va.us • *Friends of the Library Newsletter*

Leesburg
Loudoun Genealogy Society • P.O. Box 254 • Leesburg, VA 20176 • (703) 779-1328 • *Loudoun: The 1757 Legacy*

Loudoun Museum Archives • 14-16 Loudoun St SW • Leesburg, VA 22075 • (703) 777-7427 • http://www.loudonmuseum.org • *Heritage Review*

Morven Park Museum Archives • 17263 Southern Planter Ln, P.O. Box 6228 • Leesburg, VA 22017 • (703) 777-6034 • http://www.morvenpark.com

Oatlands Plantation Museum Archives • 20850 Oatlands Plantation Ln • Leesburg, VA 20175 • (703) 777-3174 • http://www.oatlands.org • *Oatlands Plantation Museum Newsletter*

Primedia Enthusiast Group • 741 Miller Dr SE, Ste D2 • Leesburg, VA 20175-8994 • (703) 771-9400 • http://www.thehistorynet.com/WorldWarII • *American History; Civil War Times Illustrated; Military History; Quarterly Journal of Military History; Columbiad: a Journal for Amateur Historians Interested in the Civil War, World War II; America's Civil War; Wild West*

Ralph Blaisdell Family Organization • 110 Mayfair Dr NE • Leesburg, VA 22075-2423 • (703) 771-8957

Lexington
Air Force Historical Foundation • Virginia Military Institute, George C Marshall Research Library, P.O. Box 1600 • Lexington, VA 24450 • (540) 464-7468 • *Air Power History*

American Work Horse Museum Archives • 487 Maury River Rd • Lexington, VA 224450 • (540) 464-2950 • http://www.horsecenter.org

George C Marshall Foundation & Archives • Historical Museum, VMI Parade Ground, P.O. Box 1600 • Lexington, VA 24450-1600 • (540) 463-7103 • http://www.marshallfoundation.org • *George C Marshall Foundation Topics*

J T L Preston Library • Virginia Military Institute • Lexington, VA 24450 • (540) 464-7228 • http://www.vmi.edu/library/ • *Friends of Preston Library Newsletter*

James Graham Leyburn Library • Washington & Lee Univ • Lexington, VA 24450 • (540) 458-8644 • http://library.wlu.edu

Lee Chapel Museum Archives • Washington & Lee Univ • Lexington, VA 24450 • (504) 463-8768 • http://www.leechapel.slu.edu

Rockbridge Historical Society & Archives • Historical Museum, 101 E Washington St, P.O. Box 514 • Lexington, VA 24450 • (540) 464-1058 • http://www.rockhist.org • *Rockbridge Historical Society Proceedings*

Rockbridge Regional Library • 138 S Main St • Lexington, VA 24450-2316 • (540) 463-4324 • http://www.rrlib.net • *Library News*

Stonewall Jackson House Library • Garland Gray Research Center, 8 E Washington St • Lexington, VA 24450 • (540) 463-2552 • http://www.stonewalljackson.org

Virginia Military Institute Museum Archives • Jackson Memorial Hall • Lexington, VA 24450 • (540) 464-7232 • http://www.vmi.edu/museum

Lightfoot

House of Gordon, United States Branch • P.O. Box 422 • Lightfoot, VA 23090 • (757) 565-2271 • http://www.tartans.com/clans/Gordon/gordon.html • *House of Gordon Newsletter*; *Gordon Gazette*

Locust Grove

Germanna Community College-Locust Grove Campus Library • 2130 Germanna Hwy • Locust Grove, VA 22508 • (540) 727-3120 • http://www.gcc.vccs.edu

Orange County Library-Wilderness • 6421 Flat Run Rd • Locust Grove, VA 22508 • (540) 972-1675

Lorton

Heimbach Reunion • 9501 4th Pl • Lorton, VA 22079 • (703) 883-8231 • Heimbach Herald

Pohick Episcopal Church Archives • 9301 Richmond Hwy • Lorton, VA 22079 • (703) 339-5472 • http://www.pohick.org

Society of the Old Creek Cross • 9501 4th Pl • Lorton, VA 22079 • (703) 883-8231

Louisa

Louisa County Historical Society & Archives • Historical Museum, 200 Church Ave, P.O. Box 1172 • Louisa, VA 23093 • (703) 967-2794 • http://www.trevilians.com • *Louisa County Historical Magazine*

Lovettsville

Barner Research • 23 Mills Ct • Lovettsville, VA 20180 • *Barner Family Newsletter*

Lovettsville Historical Society & Archives • Historical Museum, 4 E Pennsylvania Ave • Lovettsville, VA 20180 • (540) 822-5499

Willow Bend Books • 39475 Tollhouse Rd • Lovettsville, VA 20180-1817 • (540) 822-5292 • http://www.mediasoft.net/scottc • *Northern Virginia Genealogy*

Luray

Genealogical Society of Page County • 5651 Mill Creek Road, P.O. Box 734 • Luray, VA 22835 • (540) 743-6867 • *Genealogical Society of Page County Newsletter*

Lynchburg

Anne Spencer Memorial Foundation & Archives • Historic Home Museum, 1313 Pierce St • Lynchburg, VA 24501 • (804) 845-1313 • http://www.lynchburgmuseum.org

Central Virginia Community College Library • 3506 Wards Rd • Lynchburg, VA 24502-2498 • (434) 832-7750 • http://www.cvcc.vccs.edu/library

George M Jones Library Association • 2311 Memorial Ave • Lynchburg, VA 24501 • (434) 846-0501 • http://www.jmlibrary.org • *JML Report*

Lynchburg Museum Archives • 901 Court St, P.O. Box 60 • Lynchburg, VA 24505 • (434) 847-1459 • http://www.lynchburgmuseum.org

Lynchburg Public Library • 2315 Memorial Ave • Lynchburg, VA 24501 • (434) 455-6310 • http://www.lynchburgva.gov/publiclibrary

Point of Honor Archives • 112 Cabell St, P.O. Box 60 • Lynchburg, VA 24505 • (434) 847-1459 • http://www.pointofhonor.org

South River Meeting House Archives • 5810 Fort Ave, P.O. Box 4056 • Lynchburg, VA 24502 • (434) 239-2548

Thienemann Reunion • 1205 Regency Woods Pl • Lynchburg, VA 24503-1983 • (434) 384-9636 • *Thienemann Newsletter*

Madison

Madison County Historical Society • 124 N Main St • Madison, VA 22727 • (540) 948-5488

Madison County Library • 402 N Main St, P.O. Box 243 • Madison, VA 22727-0243 • (540) 948-4720

Madison Heights

Lee Family • 108 Worley Dr • Madison Heights, VA 24572

Maidens

Bonnet(t)e and Kin Family Association • 2200 Sheppard Town Rd • Maidens, VA 23102-2507 • (804) 556-4757 • Bonnett-Bonnettes and Kin

Manassas

Association of Descendants of John and Grace Smith of Milford, Connecticut • 10547 River Run Ct • Manassas, VA 20112-3007 • (703) 257-2990 • *Association of John and Grace Smith Newsletter*

Balderson-Balderston-Balderstone International Family Reunion Association • P.O. Box 1151 • Manassas, VA 20108-1151 • *Balder Dashes*

Historic Manassas • 9431 West St • Manassas, VA 20110 • (703) 361-6599

Manassas Museum Archives • 9101 Prince William St, P.O. Box 560 • Manassas, VA 20108 • (703) 368-1873 • http://www.manassasmuseum.org • *Word from the Junction*

Manassas National Battlefield Park Archives • 6511 Sudley Rd • Manassas, VA 20109-2005 • (703) 361-1339 • http://www.nps.gov/mana

Prince William County Genealogical Society • 9029 Center St, P.O. Box 2019 • Manassas, VA 22110-0812 • (703) 754-2234 • http://www.pwcgs.org • *Kindred Spirits: Newsletter of the Prince William County Genealogical Society*

Prince William Public Library System-Bull Run Regional • 8051 Ashton Ave • Manassas, VA 20109 • (703) 792-4500 • http://www.co.prince-william.va.us

Marion

Smyth County Historical and Museum Society & Archives • Historical Museum, 105 E Strother St, P.O. Box 710 • Marion, VA 24354 • (276) 783-7067

Smyth-Bland Regional Library • 118 S Sheffey St • Marion, VA 24354 • (276) 783-2323 • http://www.sbrl.org

Veselik Historical Society • 354 College St • Marion, VA 24354-2441

Marshall

Farquier Heritage Society & Library • 8266 E Main St, P.O. Box 548 • Marshall, VA 22115 • (540) 364-3440 • *Farquier Heritage Society News*

Martinsville

Blue Ridge Regional Library • 310 E Church St, P.O. Box 5264 • Martinsville, VA 24115-5264 • (540) 532-7125 • http://www.brrl.lib.va.us

John Waddey Carter House Museum Archives • 324 E Church St, P.O. Box 472 • Martinsville, VA 24112 • (540) 632-3463

Lester Library • Patrick Henry Community College, 645 Patriot Ave, P.O. Box 5311 • Martinsville, VA 24115-5311 • (276) 638-8777 • http://www.ph.vccs.edu/library

Martinsville-Henry County Historical Society • P.O. Drawer 432 • Martinsville, VA 24114

Mason Neck

Gunston Hall Plantation Library • 10709 Gunston Rd • Mason Neck, VA 22079-3901 • (703) 550-9220 • http://www.gunstonhall.org

Mathews

Mathews County Historical Society • 1001 Brickbat, P.O. Box 885 • Mathews, VA 23109 • (804) 725-2614

McDowell

Highland County Museum and Heritage Center Archives • 161 Mansion House Rd, P.O. Box 63 • McDowell, VA 24458 • (540) 396-4478 • http://www.highlandhistoricalsociety.com • *Highland County Museum Newsletter*

McLean

Ankers of Virginia • 5941 Oakdale Rd • McLean, VA 22101 • (703) 536-5875

Archer Association • P.O. Box 6233 • McLean, VA 22106 • (703) 264-1372 • *Archer Quarterly*

Clan Ross Association of the US • 6351 Old Dominion Dr #177 • McLean, VA 22101-4805 • (703) 533-0767 • http://www.ClanRossAssociation.org • *Clan Ross News Quarterly*

Gentry Research • 6151 Tompkins Dr • McLean, VA 22101 • (703) 356-9370 • *Gentry Family Gazette and Genealogy Exchange*

Mechanicsville

Lineage Search Associates • 6419 Colts Neck Rd • Mechanicsville, VA 23111-4233 • (804) 730-7414 • http://www.mindspring.com/~mpollock.com • *Morgan Migrations*; *Frederick Findings*; *Pollock Potpourri*

Merrifield

Fairfax Genealogical Society • P.O. Box 2290 • Merrifield, VA 22116-2290 • (703) 569-3469 • *Fairfax Genealogical Society Newsletter*

Hull Family Association • P.O. Box 2066 • Merrifield, VA 22116-2066 • (703) 280-5627 • *Hull Family Newsletter*, *Hull Family Association Journal*; *Hull Family Association Book of Member Lineages*

Pratuch Family • P.O. Box 178 • Merrifield, VA 22116-0178

Middletown

Belle Grove Plantation Archives • 336 Belle Grove Rd, P.O. Box 537 • Middletown, VA 22645 • (540) 869-2028 • http://www.bellegrove.org • *Belle Grove Plantation Newsletter*

Midlothian

Hatevil Nutter of Dover, New Hampshire and his Descendants • 3309 Fox Chase Ct • Midlothian, VA 23112 • (804) 744-2141 • http://resources.rootsweb.com/sumames/n/ u/NUTTER/

Huguenot Society of Manakin Library • 981 Huguenot Trail • Midlothian, VA 23113 • (804) 794-5702

Taylor-Kellum-Kellam-Webb-Loving-Goodman-Hale Family Association • 14333 Aldengate Rd • Midlothian, VA 23113 • *Hale Family Newsletter*, *Goodman Family Gazette*

Millboro

Arbogast Reunion • HCR03, Box 1A • Millboro, VA 24460

Millwood

Clarke County Historical Association & Archives • Burwell-Morgan Hill Museum, 15 Tannery Ln, P.O. Box 306 • Millwood, VA 22646 • (540) 837-1799 • http://www.clarkehistory.org • *CCHA Newsletter*

Mineral

North Anna Nuclear Information Center Archives • 1022 Haley Dr • Mineral, VA 23117 • (804) 771-3200 • http://www.dorn.com

Monterey

Highland County Public Library • 10 Water St, P.O. Box 519 • Monterey, VA 24465 • (540) 468-2363 • http://highlandlibrary.com

Highland Maple Museum Archives • US 220 S, P.O. Box 223 • Monterey, VA 24465 • (540) 468-2550 • http://www.highlandcounty.org

Montpelier Station

James Madison's Montepelier Archives • 11407 Constitution Hwy, P.O. Box 67 • Montpelier Station, VA 22957 • (540) 672-2728 • http://www.montpelier.org • *James Madison's Montepelier Newsletter*

Montross

Northern Neck Historical Society & Library • 247 Polk St, P.O. Box 716 • Montross, VA 22520 • (804) 493-1862 • *Northern Neck of Virginia Historical Magazine*

Reynolds Family Association • 200 Starboard Ct • Montross, VA 22520

Moon

Mathews Maritime Foundation • Highway 708 • Moon, VA 23119 • (804) 725-4444

Mount Vernon

Mount Vernon Ladies' Association of the Union & Library • Mount Vernon, GW Pkwy, P.O. Box 110 • Mount Vernon, VA 22121-0110 • (703) 780-2000 • http://www.mountvernon.org

Woodlawn Plantation Archives • P.O. Box 37 • Mount Vernon, VA 22121 • (703) 780-4000 • http://www.nthp.org/main/sites/woodlawn.htm

Nellysford

Leftwich Family History Association • P.O. Box 277 • Nellysford, VA 22958-0277 • (434) 361-1055 • http://www.leftwich.org • *Leftwich Heritage Newsletter*

New Castle

Craig County Historical Society & Library • 223 Main St, P.O. Box 206 • New Castle, VA 24127-0206 • (540) 864-7023 • *Our Proud Heritage*

New Market

New Market Battlefield Park Library • P.O. Box 1864 • New Market, VA 22844 • (703) 740-3101 • http://www.vmi.edu/newmarket

Newbern

New River Historical Society & Archives • Wilderness Road Museum, State Rt 611, P.O. Box 373 • Newbern, VA 24126 • (540) 674-4835 • *Journal of the New River Historical Society*, *Benchmarks*

Radford City Historical Society • P.O. Box 373 • Newbern, VA 24126

Wenrich Family Association of America • P.O. Box 491 • Newbern, VA 24126-0941 • (540) 674-2636 • http://www.wenrich.net/history/other/

Newport News

Afro-American Historical and Genealogical Society, Hampton Roads Chapter • P.O. Box 2448 • Newport News, VA 23609-2448 • (757) 827-7522

Burkett Family Organization • 201 Maxwell Ln • Newport News, VA 23606

Descendants of Valentine Hollingsworth Society • 18 Westover Rd • Newport News, VA 23601-3928 • (757) 596-3064 • *Hollingsworth Heritage*

John Thomas Martin Family Organization • 327 Thalia Dr • Newport News, VA 23608-2718 • (757 877-1190

Lee Hall Mansion Museum Archives • 163 Yorktown Rd • Newport News, VA 23603 • (757) 888-3373 • http://www.leehall.org

Mariners' Museum Archives • 100 Museum Dr • Newport News, VA 23606-3759 • (757) 596-2222 • http://www.mariner.org/library.html • *Mariners' Museum Newsletter*

Newport News Library • 110 Main St • Newport News, VA 23601-4105 • (757) 591-4858

Newport News Public Library System • 700 Town Center Dr, Suite 300 • Newport News, VA 23607 • (757) 926-1350 • http://www.nngov.com/library

Newsome House Museum Archives • 2903 Oak Ave • Newport News, VA 23602 • (757) 247-2360 • http://www.newsomehouse.org

Tidewater Genealogical Society • 14415 Old Courthouse Way • Newport News, VA 23608 • (757) 988-1055

Virginia Society for Black Historical and Genealogical Research • P.O. Box 2448 • Newport News, VA 23609-2448 • (757) 827-7522 • *Virginia Society for Black Historical and Genealogical Research News*

Virginia War Musuem Archives • Major George B Collings Memorial Library, 9285 Warwick Blvd • Newport News, VA 23607 • (757) 247-8523 • http://www.warmuseum.org • *Dufflebag*

Nickelsville

Addington Family • Route 2, Box 90 • Nickelsville, VA 24271 • (276) 479-2490

Nokesville

Historical Evaluation and Research Organization Library • 13140 Lakehill Rd • Nokesville, VA 20181-3328 • (703) 791-5005

Virginia

Norfolk

General Douglas Macarthur Memorial Archives • MacArthur Sq • Norfolk, VA 23510 • (757) 441-2965 • http://www.macarthurmemorial.org

Hampton Roads Naval Museum Archives • 1 Waterside Dr, Suite 248 • Norfolk, VA 23510-1607 • (757) 444-8971 • http://www.hmm.navy.mil • *Hampton Roads Naval Museum Newsletter*

Hull Family Association • 1214 N Fairwater Dr • Norfolk, VA 23508

Hunter House Victorian Museum Archives • 240 W Freemason St • Norfolk, VA 23510 • (757) 623-9814 • http://www.hunterhousemuseum.org

Jewish Genealogical Society of Tidewater Virginia & Library • 7300 Newport Ave • Norfolk, VA 23505 • (757) 489-1371 • http://www.jewishgen.org/jgsgw/ • *Jewish Genealogical Society of Tidewater Newsletter*

Kirn Norfolk Public Library • 301 E City Hall Ave • Norfolk, VA 23510-1776 • (757) 664-7323 • http://www.npl.lib.va.us

Lois E Woods Museum Archives • Norfolk State Univ, 2401 Corfew Ave • Norfolk, VA 23504 • (757) 823-2006 • http://www.nsu.edu/resources/woods/

Moses Myers House Museum Archives • 331 Bank St • Norfolk, VA 23510 • (757) 441-1526 • http://www.chrysler.org

Nauticus Maritime Center Archives • 1 Waterside Dr • Norfolk, VA 23510 • (757) 664-1000 • http://www.nauticus.org • *Signals*

Norfolk Genealogical Society • P.O. Box 12813, Thomas Corner Sta • Norfolk, VA 23502-5309 • *Navigator, Key*

Norfolk Historical Society & Archives • Historical Museum, 810 Front St, P.O. Box 6367 • Norfolk, VA 23508-0367 • (757) 625-1720 • http://www.norfolkhistorical.org • *Norfolk Courier*

Ohef Sholom Temple Archives • 530 Raleigh Ave • Norfolk, VA 23507 • (757) 625-4295 • http://www.ohefsholom.org

Perry Library • Old Dominion Univ, 4427 Hampton Blvd • Norfolk, VA 23529 • (757) 683-4178 • http://www.odu.edu/special.collections/

Sources Publishing • P.O. Box 6282 • Norfolk, VA 23508 • *Hale Heritage Newsletter*

US Navy-Naval Amphibious Base Library • Bldg 3004, Little Creek, 1432 Hewitt Dr NABLC • Norfolk, VA 23521-2522 • (757) 462-7691

Willoughby-Baylor House Archives • 601 E Freemason St • Norfolk, VA 23510 • (757) 441-1526 • http://www.chrysler.org

Nottoway

Nottoway County Library • State Rte 625 • Nottoway, VA 23955 • (434) 645-9310

Oakton

John McDonald Family Organization • 10303 Conejo Ln • Oakton, VA 22124 • (703) 938-0073

Occoquan

Historic Occoquan & Archives • Historical Museum, 413 Mill St, P.O. Box 65 • Occoquan, VA 22125 • (703) 491-7525 • *Historic Occoquan Newsletter*

Onancock

Eastern Shore Of Virginia Historical Society • 69 Market Street • Onancock, VA 23417

Eastern Shore of Virginia Historical Society & Library • Kerr Place Museum, 69 Market St, P.O. Box 193 • Onancock, VA 23417 • (757) 787-8012 • http://www.kerrplace.org • *Eastern Shore of Virginia Historical Society Newsletter*

Orange

James Madison Museum Archives • 129 Caroline St • Orange, VA 22960 • (540) 672-1776 • http://www.jamesmadisonmus.org • *James Madison Museum Newsletter*

Orange County Historical Society & Library • 130 Caroline St, P.O. Box 591 • Orange, VA 22960-1533 • (540) 672-5366 • http://home.rica.net/tel26/orange/orange.htm • *Orange County Historical Society Newsletter*

Orange County Public Library • 146A Madison Rd • Orange, VA 22960 • (540) 672-3811 • http://tlc.library.net/orange

Palmyra

Fluvanna County Historical Society & Archives • Old Stone Jail Musuem, 14 Stone Jail St • Palmyra, VA 22963 • (434) 589-7910 • *Fluvanna County Historical Society Bulletin*

Pamplin

South Central Virginia Genealogical Society • Route 1, Box 66-G • Pamplin, VA 23958

Pearisburg

Giles County Historical Society & Library • 208 N Main St, P.O. Box 404 • Pearisburg, VA 24134 • (540) 921-1050 • *Giles County Historical Society Newsletter*

Pearisburg Public Library • 209 Fort Branch Rd • Pearisburg, VA 24134 • (540) 921-2556 • http://www.library.pearisburg.org

Petersburg

Archibald Graham McIlwaine House Archives • 423 Cockade Alley • Petersburg, VA 23803 • (804) 733-2400 • http://www.petersburg.va.org

Battersea House Museum Archives • Upper Appomattox St • Petersburg, VA 23803 • (804) 733-2400 • http://www.petersburg.va.org

Blandford Church Museum Archives • 321 S Center Rd • Petersburg, VA 23803 • (804) 733-2400 • http://www.petersburg.va.org

Centre Hill Museum Archives • Hill Ave • Petersburg, VA 23803 • (804) 733-2400 • http://www.petersburg-va.org

Farmers Bank Museum Archives • Bradford St • Petersburg, VA 23803 • (804) 733-2400 • http://www.petersburg-va.org

Harris-Butler-Bassard Reunion • 26203 Smith Grove • Petersburg, VA 23803-7771 • (804) 732-5329

Landmark Resource Center Archives • 25 W Old St • Petersburg, VA 23803 • (804) 732-9155

Pamplin Park Civil War Site Archives • 6125 Boylton Plank Rd • Petersburg, VA 23803 • (804) 861-2408 • http://www.pamplinpark.org

Petersburg National Battlefield Library • 1539 Hickory Hill Rd • Petersburg, VA 23803-4721 • (804) 732-3531 • http://www.nps.gov/pete/

Petersburg Public Library • 137 S Sycamore St • Petersburg, VA 23803 • (804) 733-2387 • http://www.ppls.org

Richard Bland College Library • 11301 Johnson Rd • Petersburg, VA 23805 • (804) 862-6227 • http://www.rbc.edu/library/ • *Library Bookmarks*

Siege Museum Archives • 15 W Bank St • Petersburg, VA 23803 • (804) 733-2404 • http://www.petersburg-va.com

Toone, Toon and Tune of America Family Association • 1375 Baxter Rd • Petersburg, VA 23803 • (804) 861-2704

Portsmouth

Clifton Research • 901 Jewell Ave • Portsmouth, VA 23701-1911 • http://www.pilot.infi.net/~nkcliftn/cccpage.htm • *Clan Clifton Chronicle*

Marshall W Butt Library • Portsmouth Naval Shipyard Museum, 2 High St, P.O. Box 248 • Portsmouth, VA 23705-0248 • (757) 393-8591

Portsmouth Genealogical Society & Archives • c/o Portsmouth Public Library, 601 Court St, P.O. Box 7062 • Portsmouth, VA 23707-7062 • (757) 393-8501 • *Portsmouth Genealogical Society Newsletter*

Portsmouth Historical Association & Archives • Historical Museum, 221 North St • Portsmouth, VA 23704 • (757) 393-0241

Portsmouth Museum Archives • 420 High St, P.O. Box 850 • Portsmouth, VA 23705 • (757) 393-8983

Portsmouth Museum of Military History Archives • 700 Court St • Portsmouth, VA 23704 • (757) 393-2773 • *Victory Garden*

Portsmouth Public Library • 601 Court St • Portsmouth, VA 23704-3604 • (757) 393-8501 • http://www.portsmouth.va.us/ppl

Powhatan

Powhatan County Historical Society • 3880 Old Buckingham Rd • Powhatan, VA 23139 • (804) 598-1139

Prince William

Historic Prince William • P.O. Drawer 2086 • Prince William, VA 22193

Prince William Public Library System • 13083 Chinn Park Dr • Prince William, VA 22192-5073 • (703) 792-6100 • http://www.pwcgov.org/library

Providence Forge

Charles City-New Kent Heritage Foundation & Library • 9001 Blvd, P.O. Box 8 • Providence Forge, VA 23140-0008 • (804) 966-2480

New Kent Historical Society • 12007 Courthouse Cir • Providence Forge, VA 23140 • (804) 966-1376

Pulaski

Cox Reunion • Route 2, Box 83 • Pulaski, VA 24301 • (703) 980-1208

Pulaski County Library • 60 W 3rd St • Pulaski, VA 24301 • (540) 980-7770 • http://www.pclibs.org

Quantico

US Marine Corps Air-Ground Museum Archives • 2014 Anderson Ave • Quantico, VA 22134 • (703) 784-2606

US Marine Corps James Carson Breckinridge Library • 2040 Broadway St • Quantico, VA 22134-5207 • (703) 784-4409 • http://www.mcu.usmc.mil

US Marine Corps Quantico Family Library • 2040 Broadway St • Quantico, VA 22134 • (703) 784-4348 • http://www.mcu.usmc.mil/mcrcweb/library6.html

Quicksburg

Zirkle Family Historical Association • 3691 S Middle Rd • Quicksburg, VA 22847-1222 • (703) 740-8652 • *Zirkle Family Historical Association Newsletter*

Radford

Granville Carell Thompson Descendants • HC-66, Box 79, Indian Valley Rd • Radford, VA 24141 • (540) 789-4444

John Preston McConnell Library • Radford University, 801 E Main St, P.O. Box 6881 • Radford, VA 24142-6881 • (540) 831-5696 • http://lib.radford.edu

New River Historical Society • P.O. Box 711 • Radford, VA 24141

Radford Public Library • 30 W Main St • Radford, VA 24141 • (540) 731-3621 • http://www.radford.va.us/library

Rapidan

Peyton Society of Virginia • P.O. Box 128 • Rapidan, VA 22733-0128 • (540) 672-2943 • *Peyton Society of Virginia Newsletter*

Reedville

Reedville Fishermen's Museum Archives • 504 Main St • Reedville, VA 23539 • (804) 453-6529 • http://www.rfmuseum.org • *Starry Banner*

Reston

Hayner Family Association • P.O. Box 3523 • Reston, VA 22090 • *Hayner Family News*

US Geological Survey Library • 950 National Center, 12201 Sunrise Valley • Reston, VA 20192 • (703) 648-4302 • http://library.usgs.gov/reslib.html

Richmond

Agecroft Hall Museum Archives • 4305 Sulgrave Rd • Richmond, VA 23221 • (804) 353-4241 • http://www.agecrofthall.com • *Agecroft Hall Newsletter*

Allen E Roberts Masonic Museum Archives • 4115 Nine Mile Rd • Richmond, VA 23223-4926 • (804) 222-3110 • http://www.grandlodgeofvirginia.org • *Virginia Masonic Herald*

American Historical Foundation & Archives • Historical Museum, 1142 W Grace St • Richmond, VA 23220 • (804) 353-1812 • http://www.ahfrichmond.com • *Military Chronicle*

Association for the Preservation of Virginia Antiquities & Library • 204 W Franklin St • Richmond, VA 23220-5091 • (804) 648-1889 • http://www.apva.org • *Association for the Preservation of Virginia Antiquities Discovery Newsletter, Preservation Virginia Journal*

Beth Ahabah Museum and Archives • 1109 W Franklin St • Richmond, VA 23235 • (804) 353-2668 • http://www.bethahabah.org • *Generations*

Black History Museum and Cultural Center Archives • Clay St • Richmond, VA 23219 • (804) 780-9093 • http://www.blackhistorymuseum.org

Blanks-Beale-Ferguson-Clements Family History • 8529 Spalding Dr • Richmond, VA 23229 • (804) 741-1836

Bledsoe Family Historical Society • 1810 Aisquith Rd • Richmond, VA 23229 • (804) 282-1544

Boatwright Memorial Library • University of Richmond, 28 Westhampton Way • Richmond, VA 23173 • (804) 289-8669 • http://www.richmond.edu/is/library

Byerly Family of the Valley of Virginia • 8503 Spring Hollow Dr • Richmond, VA 23227-1227 • (804) 262-8855

Children of the Confederacy & Library • Memorial Bldg, 328 North Blvd • Richmond, VA 23220 • (804) 355-1636 • *Courier*

Clan Barclay International • 7844 Lake Forest Dr • Richmond, VA 23235 • (804) 745-0902 • http://www.clanbarclay.com

Colonial Dames in Virginia & Library • Wilton House, 215 S Wilton Rd • Richmond, VA 23226-2212 • (804) 282-5936

Corson-Colson Family History Association • 9311P Golden Wy Ct • Richmond, VA 23294 • (804) 747-8180 • *Corson Cousins*

County of Henrico Public Library • 1001 N Laburnum Ave • Richmond, VA 23223 • (804) 222-1643 • http://www.co.henrico.va.us/library

Descendants of Georg Conrad Bloss • 9939 Palmerston Rd • Richmond, VA 23236 • (502) 245-7114 • *Descendants of Georg Conrad Bloss Family Newsletter*

Edgar Allan Poe Museum Archives • 1914-16 E Main St • Richmond, VA 23223 • (804) 648-5523 • http://www.poemuseum.org • *Poe Messenger, Evermore*

First Baptist Church Library • 2709 Monument Ave • Richmond, VA 23220 • (804) 355-8637 • http://www.fbcrichmond.org

Genealogical Research Institute of Virginia • P.O. Box 29178 • Richmond, VA 23229-0178 • (804) 272-4240 • http://www.cvco.org/sigs/genealogy/ • *Genealogical Research Institute of Virginia News 'N Notes*

Grand Lodge of Virginia & Library • 4115 9 Mile Rd, P.O. Box 27345 • Richmond, VA 23261 • (804) 222-3110

Hammer Reunion • 6232 Derwent Rd • Richmond, VA 23225

Henrico County Historic Preservation • Historical Museum, 8600 Dixon Powers Dr, P.O. Box 27032 • Richmond, VA 23273 • (804) 501-5736 • http://www.co.henrico.va.us/rec

Henrico County Historical Society • 1590 E Parham Rd • Richmond, VA 23228 • (804) 501-5682

James Branch Cabell Library • Virginia Commonwealth Univ, 901 Park Ave, P.O. Box 842033 • Richmond, VA 23284-2033 • (804) 828-1101 • http://www.library.vcu.edu/jbc/

JERLS Incorporated • P.O. Box 3551 • Richmond, VA 23235 • *Kib's Kousins Newsletter*

John Marshall Foundation • c/o Virginia Bar Association 701 E Franklin St #1120 • Richmond, VA 23219 • (804) 644-0041

John Marshall House Museum Archives • 818 E Marshall St • Richmond, VA 23219 • (804) 648-7998 • http://www.john-marshall.org

Library of Virginia • 800 E Broad St • Richmond, VA 23219-8000 • (804) 692-3777 • http://www.lva.lib.va.us • *Library of Virginia News*

Maggie I Walker National Historic Site Archives • 602 N 2nd St • Richmond, VA 23219 • (804) 771-2017 • http://www.nps.gov/malw/

Mayflower Quarterly • 3800 Montrose Ave • Richmond, VA 23222-1137 • *Mayflower Quarterly*

Maymont Museum Archives • 1700 Hampton St • Richmond, VA 23220 • (804) 358-7166 • http://www.maymont.org • *Maymont Newsletter*

McGraw Family Reunion: Francis McGraw Descendants • Route 1, Box 11 • Richmond, VA 23321-9801 • (203) 998-4615

Museum of the Confederacy Archives • Eleanor S Brockenbrough Library, 1201 E Clay St • Richmond, VA 23219 • (804) 649-1861 • http://www.moc.org • *Museum of the Confederacy Journal*; *Museum of the Confederacy Newsletter*

Old Dominion Railway Museum Archives • 102 Hull St • Richmond, VA 23224 • (804) 233-6237 • http://www.odenrhs.org • *Highball*

Organ Historical Society • 2401 Westwood Ave • Richmond, VA 23230 • (804) 353-9226

Presbyterian Church Archives • Union Theological Seminary, 3401 Brook Rd • Richmond, VA 23227 • (804) 355-0671

Richmond National Battlefield Park Library • 3215 E Broad St • Richmond, VA 23223 • (804) 226-1981 • http://www.nps.gov/rich

Saint John's Episcopal Church Museum Archives • 2401 E Broad St • Richmond, VA 23223 • (804) 648-5015 • http://www.historicstjohnschurch.org

Sons of the American Revolution, Virginia Society • 3600 W Broad, Ste 446 • Richmond, VA 23230-4918

Southern Baptist Convention Archives Center • 3806 Monument Ave, P.O. Box 6767 • Richmond, VA 23230-0767 • (804) 219-1296 • http://www.imb.org

Southside Virginian • 2236 Cedar Crest Rd, P.O. Box 3684 • Richmond, VA 23235-7684 • (804) 272-4875 • *Southside Virginian: A Journal of Genealogy and History*

United Daughters of the Confederacy & Library • Memorial Bldg, 328 North Blvd • Richmond, VA 23220-4057 • (804) 355-1636 • http://www.hqudc.org • *United Daughters of the Confederacy Magazine*

United States Historical Society • 7431 Whitepine Rd • Richmond, VA 23237 • (804) 648-4736

United States Historical Society • 4019 MacArthur Ave • Richmond, VA 23227 • (804) 262-9403

University of Richmond Museum Archives • Univ of Richmond • Richmond, VA 23173 • (804) 289-8276 • http://www.museums.richmond.edu

Valentine Richmond History Center Archives • 1015 E Clay St • Richmond, VA 23219-1590 • (804) 649-0711 • http://www.richmondhistorycenter.com • *Valentine Richmond History Center Newsletter*

Virginia Aeronautical Historical Society • 5701 Huntsman Rd • Richmond, VA 23250 • (804) 222-8690

Virginia Association of Museums • 200 S 3rd St • Richmond, VA 23219 • (804) 788-5821 • http://www.vamuseums.org • *VAM Quarterly Newsletter*; *Directory of Virginia Museums*; *VAM Membership Directory*

Virginia Aviation Museum Archives • 5701 Huntsman Rd • Richmond, VA 23250 • (804) 236-3620 • http://www.vam.smv.org • *Virginia Aviation Museum Newsletter*

Virginia Baptist Historical Society & Archives • Univ of Richmond, Boatwright Library, P.O. Box 34 • Richmond, VA 23173 • (804) 289-8434 • http://www.baptistheritage.org • *Virginia Baptist Register*

Virginia Department of Conservation and Preservation • 203 Governor's St • Richmond, VA 23219 • (804) 786-9200 • http://www.state.va.us/~dcr/cler_home.htm

Virginia Department of Historic Resources Archives-Research Library • 2801 Kensington Ave • Richmond, VA 23221 • (804) 367-2323 • http://www.dhr.state.va.us

Virginia Genealogical Society • 5001 W Broad St, Ste 115, P.O. Box 7469 • Richmond, VA 23221-3023 • (804) 285-8954 • http://www.vgs.org • *Magazine of Virginia Genealogy*; *Virginia Genealogical Society Newsletter*

Virginia Historical Society & Library • 428 North Blvd, P.O. Box 7311 • Richmond, VA 23221-0311 • (804) 358-4901 • http://www.vahistorical.org • *Virginia Historical Society Occasional Bulletin*; *Virginia Magazine of History and Biography*; *Virginia Historical Society Documents*; *Virginia Historical Society History Notes*

Virginia Holocaust Museum Archives • 2000 E Cary St • Richmond, VA 23223 • (804) 257-5400 • http://www.va-holocaust.com • *De Malyene*

Virginia State Library and Archives • 1101 Capitol Square • Richmond, VA 23219-3491 • (804) 786-2306 • http://leo.vsla.edu/lva.html

Virginia War Memorial Archives • 621 S Belvedere St • Richmond, VA 23220 • (804) 786-2060 • http://www.vawarmemorial.org

Wilton House Museum Archives • 215 S Wilton Rd, P.O. Box 8225 • Richmond, VA 23226 • (804) 282-5936 • http://www.wiltonhousemuseum.org

Woodlief-Woodliff Family Association • 5826-C Willow Oaks Dr • Richmond, VA 23225-2434 • http://members.home.net/teylu/woodlief/assn/

Roanoke

Botetourt County Library • 28 Avery Row • Roanoke, VA 24012 • (540) 324-3433 • http://www.co.botetourt.va.us

Catholic Historical Society of the Roanoke Valley & Archives • Historical Museum, 400 W Campbell Ave • Roanoke, VA 24013 • (540) 982-0152 • *Catholic Historical Society of the Roanoke Valley Newsletter*

Clan MacLaine of Lochbuie • 1713 Jerome St SE • Roanoke, VA 24014-3813 • (540) 362-4706 • *Battleaxe*

Doolittles of America • 7015 Greenway Dr • Roanoke, VA 24019 • (703) 362-0329 • http://home.att.net/~edoolittle/

Elliott Research • 815 Hartsook Blvd • Roanoke, VA 24014-4321 • (540) 427-1535 • *Elliott n' Kin*

Harrison Museum of African American Culture Archives • 523 Harrison Ave NW • Roanoke, VA 24016 • (540) 345-4818 • http://www.harrisonmuseum.org

Historical Society of Western Virginia & Archives • Historical Museum, 1 Market Square, P.O. Box 1904 • Roanoke, VA 24008-1904 • (540) 342-5770 • http://www.history-museum.org • *Roanoke Valley Historical Society Journal*; *Roanoke Valley Historical Society Newsletter*

Maier-Avril-Herrold-Zeltner-Vogel-Schwoder Exchange • 2609 Hillcrest Ave NW • Roanoke, VA 24012 • (540) 362-2245

Mayberry-Maberry-Mabry Reunion • 2123 10th St NW • Roanoke, VA 24012 • (540) 982-1648

National Railway Historical Society, Roanoke Chapter • 303 Norfolk Ave SW • Roanoke, VA 24016 • (540) 982-3595

Norfolk and Western Historical Society • 2101 Salem Ave SW • Roanoke, VA 24016 • (540) 342-0575

O Winston Link Photography Museum Archives • 101 Shenandoah Ave • Roanoke, VA 24016 • (540) 982-5465 • http://www.linkmuseum.org • *Link News*

Patrick Henry Allied Families of Virginia • 2866 Summit Ridge Rd • Roanoke, VA 24012 • (540) 977-3848

Roanoke City Public Library • 706 S Jefferson St • Roanoke, VA 24016-5104 • (540) 853-2473 • http://www.roanokegov.com

Roanoke City Public Library System-Gainsboro • 15 Patton Ave NW • Roanoke, VA 24016 • (540) 853-2540

Roanoke County Public Library • 3131 Electric Rd SW • Roanoke, VA 24018-6496 • (540) 772-7507 • http://www.co.roanoke.va.us/library

Roanoke Valley Historical Society • P.O. Box 1904 • Roanoke, VA 24008

Southwestern Virginia Genealogical Society • 1716 Colgate St NE, P.O. Box 12485 • Roanoke, VA 24026-2486 • (540) 345-8709 • *Virginia Appalachian Notes*

Virginia Museum of Transportation Archives • P.O. Box 2611 • Roanoke, VA 24010 • (540) 342-5670 • http://www.vmt.org • *MUSE News*

Wade Reunion • 3403 Ashmeade Dr SW • Roanoke, VA 24018 • (540) 774-2887

Rockbridge
Rockbridge Area Genealogical Society • P.O. Box 75 • Rockbridge, VA 24473

Rocky Mount
Franklin County Heritage Society • 65 E Court St • Rocky Mount, VA 24151

Franklin County Historical Society & Library • 95 Floyd Ave, P.O. Box 905 • Rocky Mount, VA 24151-0905 • (540) 483-1890

Franklin County Public Library • 138 E Court St • Rocky Mount, VA 24151 • (540) 483-3098 • http://www.franklincountyva.org

Rural Retreat
Rural Retreat Historical Society • 113 N Main St • Rural Retreat, VA 24368 • (276) 686-4470

Rustburg
Campbell County Historical Society • P.O. Box 560 • Rustburg, VA 24588

Campbell County Public Library • 684 Village Hwy, P.O. Box 310 • Rustburg, VA 24588-0310 • (434) 332-9560 • http://tlc.library.net/campbell • *Campbell County Public Library Newsletter*

Ruther Glen
American Indian Society • 22226 Cool Water Dr • Ruther Glen, VA 22546-3309 • (804) 448-3707 • *American Indian Society Newsletter*

Saint Stephens Church
King and Queen Historical Society • P.O. Box 10 • Saint Stephens Church, VA 23148

Salem
Salem Historical Society & Archives • Historical Museum, 801 E Main St, P.O. Box 201 • Salem, VA 24153 • (540) 389-6760 • http://www.salemmuseum.org • *Salem Historical Society Newsletter*

Tickle Reunion • 1603 Frosty Ln • Salem, VA 24153 • (540) 389-0435

Saltville
Museum of the Middle Appalachians Archives • 123 Palmer Ave, P.O. Box 910 • Saltville, VA 24370 • (276) 496-3633 • *Museum of the Middle Appalachians Newsletter*

Scottsville
Scottsville Museum Archives • 290 Main St, P.O. Box 15 • Scottsville, VA 24590 • (434) 286-2247

Smithfield
Blackwater Regional Library-Isle of Wight County Public • 255 James St • Smithfield, VA 23430 • (757) 357-2264

Isle of Wight County Historical Society • P.O. Box 121 • Smithfield, VA 22431

Isle of Wight Courthouse Museum Archives • 130 Main St • Smithfield, VA 23430 • (804) 357-3502 • http://www.apva.org

South Boston
South Boston-Halifax County Museum of Fine Arts and History Archives • 1540 Wilborn Ave, P.O. Box 383 • South Boston, VA 24592 • (434) 572-9200 • http://www.sbhcmuseum.org • *South Boston-Halifax County Museum Newsletter*

Spotsylvania
Clan Cochrane in North America • 503 Ronnie Ct • Spotsylvania, VA 22553

Spotsylvania Historical Association & Archives • Historical Museum, 8956 Courthouse Rd, P.O. Box 64 • Spotsylvania, VA 22553-0064 • (540) 582-7167

Springfield
Barney Family Historical Association • 7503 Ridgebrook Dr • Springfield, VA 22153-1931 • (703) 451-3916 • http://www.barneyfamily.org • *Barney Family News*

Miller Reunion • 5917 Atteentee Rd • Springfield, VA 22150 • (703) 866-4510

Ryker-Riker Family • 8326 Garfield Ct • Springfield, VA 22152

Stafford
George Washington's Ferry Farm Archives • 268 Kings Hwy • Stafford, VA 22405 • (540) 370-0732 • http://www.kenmore.org • *Rosette*

Hack Family Association • 52 Anita Dr • Stafford, VA 22554 • (540) 657-5859

Standardsville
Greene County Historical Society • P.O. Box 185 • Standardsville, VA 22973 • *Greene County Magazine*

Staunton
Augusta County Historical Society & Library • 12 Taylor St, P.O. Box 686 • Staunton, VA 24402-0686 • (540) 886-1479 • *Augusta Historical Bulletin*

McCutchen Trace Association • 25 Troxell Ln • Staunton, VA 24401 • (540) 886-5032 • *McCutchen Newsletter*

Museum of American Frontier Culture Archives • 1250 Richmond Rd, P.O. Box 810 • Staunton, VA 24402-0810 • (540) 332-7850 • http://www.frontier.virginia.gov • *News from the Frontier*

Statlers Museum Archives • 501 Thornrose Ave, P.O. Box 2703 • Staunton, VA 24402 • (540) 885-7297 • http://www.statlerbrothers.com

Staunton Public Library • 1 Churchville Ave • Staunton, VA 24401-3229 • (540) 332-3902 • http://www.stauntonlibrary.org

Woodrow Wilson Birthplace Foundation & Library • 18 N Coalter St, P.O. Box 24 • Staunton, VA 24401-4332 • (540) 886-0897 • http://www.woodrowwilson.org • *Woodrow Wilson Birthplace Foundation Newsletter*

Steeles Tavern
Cyrus H McCormick Memorial Museum Archives • 128 McCormick Farm Cr, P.O. Box 100 • Steeles Tavern, VA 24476 • (540) 377-2255 • http://www.vaes.vt.edu/steeles/history.html

Stephens City
Historic Stephensburg Museum Archives • 5408 Main St, P.O. Box 143 • Stephens City, VA 22655 • (540) 869-1700 • http://www.newtownhistorycenter.org • *Museum Musings*

Sterling
Clan Mackintosh of North America • 46715 Lynn Haven Sq • Sterling, VA 20165-6478 • http://www.tartans.com/clans/MacKintosh/mackintosh.html • *Mists of Moigh*

Clan MacLachlan Association of North America • 119 Wrightwood Pl • Sterling, VA 20164 • http://www.shirenet.com/MacLachlan

Doane Family Association of America • 1044 S Ironwood Rd • Sterling, VA 20164-5111 • (703) 430-2255 • http://www.doane.edu/dfa/dfa2.htm • *Newsletter of the Doane Family Association of America*

Loudoun Heritage Farm Museum Archives • 21668 Heritage Farm Ln • Sterling, VA 20164 • (703) 421-5322 • http://www.loudounfarmmuseum.org • *Windmill*

Porter-Anderson-Robinson-Capers Reunion • 147 1/2 Magnolia Rd • Sterling, VA 20164-5305 • (703) 430-4225

Strasburg
Jeane Dixon Museum and Library • 132 N Massanutten St • Strasburg, VA 22657 • (540) 465-5884 • http://www.waysideofva.com • *By the Wayside*

Museum of American Presidents Archives • 130 N Massanutten St, P.O. Box 31 • Strasburg, VA 22657 • (540) 465-5999 • http://www.waysideofva.org

Stonewall Jackson Museum at Hupp's Hill • 33239 Valley Pike • Strasburg, VA 22657 • (540) 465-5884 • http://www.waysideofva.org

Strasburg Museum Archives • 440 E King St • Strasburg, VA 22657 • (540) 465-3428 • http://www.esonner.net/museum.htm

Stratford
Robert E Lee Memorial Association & Library • Stratford Hall Plantation • Stratford, VA 22558 • (804) 493-8572

Robert E Lee Memorial Association Archives • Stratford Hall Plantation, 485 Great House Rd • Stratford, VA 22558 • (804) 493-8572 • http://www.stratfordhall.org

Stuart
Patrick County Genealogical Society • P.O. Drawer 1016 • Stuart, VA 24171

Patrick County Historical Society & Archives • Historical Museum, Blue Ridge St, P.O. Box 1045 • Stuart, VA 24171 • (276) 694-2840

Suffolk
Riddick's Folly Archives • 510 N Main St, P.O. Box 1722 • Suffolk, VA 23439 • (757) 934-1390 • http://www.riddicksfolly.org • *Riddick's Folly Newsletter*

Suffolk Museum Archives • 118 Bosley Ave • Suffolk, VA 23434 • (757) 923-2371 • http://www.city.sufolk.va.us • *Suffolk Museum Quarterly*

Surry
Bacon's Castle Archives • 465 Bacon's Castle Trail • Surry, VA 23883 • (804) 648-1889 • http://www.apva.org • *Bacon's Castle Newsletter*

Blackwater Regional Library-Surry Public • 11640 Rolfe Hwy, P.O. Box 337 • Surry, VA 23883-0337 • (757) 294-3949

Chippokes Farm and Forestry Museum Archives • 695 Chippokes Park Rd • Surry, VA 23883 • (804) 786-7950 • http://www.dcr.state.ud.us • *Plantation Quarterly*

Smith's Fort Plantation Archives • 217 Smith's Fort Ln, P.O. Box 240 • Surry, VA 23883 • (757) 294-3872

Surry County Historical Society & Archives • Historical Museum, 16 Academy St, P.O. Box 262 • Surry, VA 23883 • (757) 294-0404

Sweet Briar
Sweet Briar Museum Archives • Sweet Briar College • Sweet Briar, VA 24595 • (434) 381-6246 • http://www.museum.sbc.edu

Tazewell
Historic Crab Orchard Museum Archives • Route 1, Box 194 • Tazewell, VA 24651 • (276) 988-6755 • http://www.craborchardmuseum.com • *Pisgah Pathfinder*

Tazewell County Historical Society • 100 E Main St, P.O. Box 916 • Tazewell, VA 24651-0916 • (276) 988-4069 • *Tazewell County Historical Society Newsletter*

Tazewell County Public Library • 310 E Main St, P.O. Box 929 • Tazewell, VA 24651-0929 • (276) 988-2541 • http://www.tcplweb.org

The Plains
African American Historical Association • 4243 Loudoun Ave • The Plains, VA 20198-2237 • (540) 253-7488 • http://www.afro-americanofva.org

Toms Brook
Hottel-Keller Memorial • P.O. Box 33 • Toms Brook, VA 22660-0033 • (540) 984-8881 • *Hottel-Keller Voice*

Unionville
Ramsay Clan Society • 7493 Zachary Taylor Hwy • Unionville, VA 22567 • (540) 854-5645 • *Clan Ramsay Newsletter*

Urbanna
Middlesex County Public Library • 150 Grace St, P.O. Box 189 • Urbanna, VA 23175-0189 • (804) 758-5717 • http://www.mcplva.org

Robinson Registry • Hewick Plantation, P.O. Box 82 • Urbanna, VA 23175-0082 • (804) 758-4214 • *Robinson Family Journal*

Verona
Augusta County Historical Society • general delivery • Verona, VA 24482 • (540) 248-4151

Vienna
Fiero-Fero Family Association • 2534 Rambling Ct • Vienna, VA 22180 • (703) 938-3158

History of the William Buckminster Lindsay Family • P.O. Box 1746 • Vienna, VA 22183-1746 • (703) 255-5263 • http://www.wardell.org/gen/

Larkin Database • 9029 Timberwolf Ct • Vienna, VA 22182

Snodgrass Clan Society • 8221 Stonewall Dr • Vienna, VA 22180-6947 • (703) 560-6631 • *Mace*

Vinton
Vinton Historical Society • 210 E Jackson Ave • Vinton, VA 24179 • (540) 342-8634

Virginia Beach
Adam Thoroughgood House Archives • 1636 Parish Rd • Virginia Beach, VA 23455 • (757) 664-6200 • http://www.whro.org/cl/cmhh

Afro-American Historical and Genealogical Society, Tidewater Chapter • P.O. Box 10522 • Virginia Beach, VA 23450

Cape Henry Lighthouse Museum Archives • 583 Atlantic Ave • Virginia Beach, VA 23459 • (757) 422-9421 • http://www.apva.org

Clan Barclay International • 2509 Placid Pl • Virginia Beach, VA 23456 • (757) 468-5829 • http://www.clanbarclay.com

Delano Kindred • 521 Buffer Dr • Virginia Beach, VA 23462 • http://www.delanoye.org

Edward and John Harrison Family • 1400 Linlier Dr • Virginia Beach, VA 23451 • (757) 425-1852

Francis Land House Historic Site Archives • 3131 Virginia Beach Blvd • Virginia Beach, VA 23452 • (757) 431-4000

Gant-Gaunt Clearinghouse • 444 Cold Springs Rd • Virginia Beach, VA 23454

Historic Naval Ships Association • 5245 Cleveland St, #207 • Virginia Beach, VA 23462 • (757) 499-1044 • *Anchor Watch*

Lynnhaven House Museum Archives • 4405 Wishart Rd • Virginia Beach, VA 23455 • (757) 456-0351 • http://www.apva.org

Marois Genealogy • 3425 Daisy Crescent • Virginia Beach, VA 23456 • (757) 468-5416

Nesbitt-Bryant-Mitchell-Guest Reunion • 3966 Kiwanis Loop • Virginia Beach, VA 23456 • (757) 471-1935

Nims Family Association • 5344 Hickory Ridge • Virginia Beach, VA 23455-6680 • (757) 499-9991

Princess Anne County Historical Society • 2040 Potters Rd • Virginia Beach, VA 23454 • (757) 491-3490 • *Princess Anne County Historical Society Newsletter*

Tidewater Afro-American Historical and Genealogical Society • 2200 Crossroad Tr • Virginia Beach, VA 23456

Virginia Beach Central Library • 4100 Virginia Beach Blvd • Virginia Beach, VA 23452 • (757) 437-6450 • http://www.vbgov.com/dept/library/

Virginia Beach Department of Public Libraries • 2416 Courthouse Dr • Virginia Beach, VA 23456 • (757) 427-4321 • http://www.vbgov.com/libraries • Virginia Beach Department of Public Libraries Update

Virginia Beach Maritime Museum Archives • 24th & Atlantic Ave • Virginia Beach, VA 23458 • (757) 422-1587 • http://www.oldcoastguardstation.com • *Keeper*

W S Dawson Company • P.O. Box 62823 • Virginia Beach, VA 23466 • *Goode Quarterly*

Warm Springs
Bath County Historical Society & Archives • Historical Museum, Courthouse Hill Rd, P.O. Box 212 • Warm Springs, VA 24484 • (540) 839-2543 • *Bath County Heritage; Newsletter of the Bath County Historical Society*

Warrenton
Farquier Historical Society & Archives • Old Jail Museum, Courthouse Sq & Ashby St, P.O. Box 675 • Warrenton, VA 22186 • (540) 347-5525 • *Fauquier Historical Society News & Notes*

Fauquier County Public Library • 11 Winchester St • Warrenton, VA 22186-2825 • (540) 347-8750 • http://www.library.fauquiercounty.gov/

Warrenton Historical Society • general delivery • Warrenton, VA 22186

Warsaw
Rappahannock Community College Library • 52 Campus Dr • Warsaw, VA 22572 • (804) 333-6710 • http://www.rcc.vccs.edu

Richmond County Public Library • 52 Campus Dr • Warsaw, VA 22572 • (804) 333-6710

Washington
Featherstone Research • Falls Church • Washington, VA 22042 • (703) 736-1726 • *Featherstone Families*

Rappahannock Historical Society • 328 Gay St • Washington, VA 22747 • (540) 675-1163

Washington's Birthplace
George Washington Birthplace National Monument Archives • 1732 Popes Creek Rd • Washington's Birthplace, VA 22443 • (804) 224-1732 • http://www.nps.gov/gewa

Waterford
Sutton Research • 40544 Browns Ln • Waterford, VA 20197-1204 • *Sutton Quarterly*

Waynesboro
Augusta County Genealogical Society • 2002 Lyndhurst Rd • Waynesboro, VA 22980-5226

Humpback Rocks Mountain Farm Museum Archives • Blue Ridge Pkwy • Waynesboro, VA 24483 • (540) 377-2377 • http://www.nps.gov/blri

Redmond Family Reunion • 413 Lake Rd • Waynesboro, VA 22980 • (540) 949-7075

Waynesboro Public Library • 600 S Wayne Ave • Waynesboro, VA 22980 • (540) 942-6746 • http://www.waynesboro-online.com/departments/publiclibrary • *Bookmark*

Weyers Cave
Houff Library • Blue Ridge Community College, 1 College Lane, P.O. Box 80 • Weyers Cave, VA 24486-0080 • (540) 453-2309 • http://www.br.vccs.edu

Williamsburg
Bassett Hall Museum Archives • 522 E Francis St • Williamsburg, VA 23185 • (757) 220-7453 • http://www.history.org

Carter's Grove Museum Archives • 8797 Pocahontas Tr • Williamsburg, VA 23185 • (757) 229-1000 • http://www.history.org

Clan Sutherland Society • 207 Buford Rd • Williamsburg, VA 23188

Colonial Williamsburg Foundation • 313 1st St, P.O. Box 17766 • Williamsburg, VA 23187-1776 • (757) 565-8510 • http://www.colonialwilliamsburg.org • *Foundations of America Series*

Colonial Williamsburg Foundation & Library • 134 N Henry St, P.O. Box 1776 • Williamsburg, VA 23185 • (757) 220-7284 • http://www.colonialwilliamsburg.org • *Colonial Williamsburg*; *Foundations of America Series*

Earl Greg Swem Library • College of William and Mary, P.O. Box 8794 • Williamsburg, VA 23187-8794 • (757) 221-3067 • http://www.swem.wm.edu

Jamestown-Yorktown Foundation & Library • Route 31 S, P.O. Box 1607 • Williamsburg, VA 23187 • (757) 253-4838 • http://www.historyisfun.org

Omohundro Institute of Early American History and Culture & Library • 109 Cary St, P.O. Box 8781 • Williamsburg, VA 23187-8781 • (757) 221-1126 • http://www.wm.edu/oieahc • *Institute of Early American History and Culture Newsletter*; *William and Mary Quarterly: A Magazine of Early American History and Culture*; *Uncommon Sense*

Pace Society of America • 128 Riviera • Williamsburg, VA 23188 • *Pace Society of America Bulletin*

Tidewater Virginia Families • 316 Littletown Quarter • Williamsburg, VA 23185-5519 • (757) 220-4888 • http://www.tidewatervirginiafamilies.com • *Tidewater Virginia Families: a Magazine of History and Genealogy*

Williamsburg Regional Library • 7770 Croaker Rd • Williamsburg, VA 23188-7064 • (757) 259-7720 • http://www.wrl.org • *Library Letter*

Winchester
Alson H Smith Jr Library • Shenandoah University, 1460 University Dr • Winchester, VA 22601 • (540) 665-5421 • http://www.su.edu/library/

Handley Library • 100 W Piccadilly St, P.O. Box 58 • Winchester, VA 22601-0058 • (540) 662-9041 • http://www.hrl.lib.state.va.us

Shenandoah Valley Discovery Museum Archives • Downtown Walking Mall • Winchester, VA 22604 • (540) 722-2020 • http://www.discoverymuseum.net

Winchester-Frederick County Genealogical Society • c/o Handley Library, 100 W Piccadilly St, P.O. Box 97 • Winchester, VA 22601 • (540) 662-9041 • http://www.shentel.net/handley-library/

Winchester-Frederick County Historical Society & Library • 1340 S Pleasant Valley Rd • Winchester, VA 22601-4447 • (540) 662-6550 • http://www.winchesterhistory.org • *Winchester-Frederick County Historical Society Journal*; *Winchester-Frederick County Historical Society Newsletter*

Wise
Historical Society of Southwest Virginia • P.O. Box 3877 • Wise, VA 24293 • *Historical Sketches of Southwest Virginia*

John Cook Wyllie Library • University of Virginia's College at Wise, 1 College Ave • Wise, VA 24293 • (276) 328-0157 • http://www.lib.uvawise.edu

Lonesome Pine Regional Library • 124 Library Rd SW • Wise, VA 24293-5907 • (276) 328-8325 • http://www.lprlibrary.org

Wise County Historical Society & Library • Main St, P.O. Box 368 • Wise, VA 24293 • (276) 328-6451 • *Wise County Historical Society Bulletin*; *Wise County News*; *Appalachian Quarterly*

Woodbridge
Hairston-Gallant Reunion • 15080 Catbrier Ct • Woodbridge, VA 22193-5339 • (202) 878-4195

Woodstock
Woodstock Museum of Shenandoah County Archives • 137 W Court St, P.O. Box 88 • Woodstock, VA 22664 • (540) 459-2452

Wytheville
Descendants of Hans Jacob Rippas and Anna Gerber • P.O. Box 505 • Wytheville, VA 24382 • (276) 228-2258 • http://www.repass.net • *Repass Family Newsletter*

Kegley Library • Wytheville Community College, 1000 E Main St • Wytheville, VA 24382 • (276) 223-4700

Thomas J Boyd Museum Archives • 295 Tazwell St, P.O. Box 533 • Wytheville, VA 24382 • (540) 223-3330

Wythe County Historical Society & Archives • Rock House Musuem, 205 Tazewell St, P.O. Box 730 • Wytheville, VA 24382 • (276) 228-6061 • http://www.wytheville.org • *Wythe County Historical Review*

Wythe-Grayson Regional Library-Wythe County Public • 300 E Monroe St • Wytheville, VA 24382-2367 • (276) 228-4951

Wytheville Community College Library • 1000 E Main St • Wytheville, VA 24382 • (276) 223-4743 • http://www.wcc.vccs.edu/visitors/library

Wytheville Historical Society • 155 W Spiller St • Wytheville, VA 24382 • (276) 228-6061

Yorktown
Colonial National Historical Park Library • Colonial Pkwy & Rte 238, P.O. Box 210 • Yorktown, VA 23690-0210 • (757) 898-3400 • http://www.nps.gov/colo/

Fulgham Reunion • 207 Lakewood Cr • Yorktown, VA 23692-3034 • (757) 898-6114

Pobst-Richardson Family Reunion • 105 Thornrose Dr • Yorktown, VA 23692 • (757) 833-1295

Watermen's Museum Archives • 309 Water St • Yorktown, VA 23690 • (757) 887-2641 • http://www.watermens.org

Virginia

York County Public Library • 8500 George Washington Pkwy • Yorktown, VA 23692 • (757) 890-3377 • http://www.yorkcounty.gov/library

Aberdeen
Aberdeen Genealogical Society • 111 E 3rd St, #D • Aberdeen, WA 98520 • (360) 538-7079

Aberdeen Museum of History Archives • 111 E 3rd St • Aberdeen, WA 98520 • (360) 533-1976 • http://www.aberdeen.museum.org

John Spellman Library • Grays Harbor College, 1620 Edward P Smith Dr • Aberdeen, WA 98520-7599 • (360) 538-4054 • http://spellman.ghc.ctc.edu

Sanford Families Association • P.O. Box 843 • Aberdeen, WA 98550 • (360) 533-0781 • http://techline.com/~franki/ • *Sanford Et All*

Timberland Regional Library-Aberdeen Branch • 121 E Market St • Aberdeen, WA 98520-5292 • (360) 533-2360

Anacortes
Anacortes Museum Archives • 1305 8th St • Anacortes, WA 98221 • (360) 293-1915 • http://www.anacorteshistorymuseum.org • *Anacortes Museum Newsletter*

Arlington
Brennand Family Association • P.O. Box 3447 • Arlington, WA 98223-3447 • (360) 658-1000

Mattaliano-Lumpkin-Heiderer-Shoe Exchange • 16315 Jim Creek Rd • Arlington, WA 98223

Roots Dugout • 3328 SR 530 NE • Arlington, WA 98223 • Hunt Heritage

Stillaguamish Valley Genealogical Society & Library • 135 S Olympic Ave, P.O. Box 34 • Arlington, WA 98223-0034 • (360) 435-4838 • Stillaguamish Star Newsletter

Whetnall Family Association • P.O. Box 3447 • Arlington, WA 98223-3447 • (360) 658-1000

Auburn
Kadunc-Krompel-Stibemik-Jamnik-Hribar-Gregorcik Surname Organization • 33516 170th Ave SE • Auburn, WA 98092 • (253) 833-7229

King County Library System-Auburn Branch • 1102 Auburn Way S • Auburn, WA 98002 • (253) 931-3018

White River Valley Historical Society & Archives • Historical Museum, 918 H Street SE • Auburn, WA 98002 • (253) 288-7433 • http://www.wrvmuseum.org • *White River Valley Historical Society Newsletter*

Wilfred Joseph Gabrio Family Organization • 2940 17th Street SE • Auburn, WA 98092-6456 • (253) 833-8723

Bainbridge Island
Bainbridge Island Historical Society & Archives • Historical Museum, 215 Ericksen Ave NE • Bainbridge Island, WA 98110 • (206) 842-2773 • http://www.bainbridgehistory.org

International Molyneux Family Association • P. O. Box 10306 • Bainbridge Island, WA 98110 • (206) 842-6636 • http://homepages.rootsweb.com/~imfa/home.html • *MX World: Newsletter of the International Molyneux Family Association*

Ramsey-Ramsay Repository • 11702 NE Sunset Loop • Bainbridge Island, WA 98110-1219 • (206) 842-4896

Belfair
William Sutherland Clan Association • NE 24170 Hwy 3, #18 • Belfair, WA 98528

Bellevue
Austin-Larkins Family Association • 3065 NE 124th • Bellevue, WA 98005

Bellevue Regional Library • 1111 110th Ave NE • Bellevue, WA 98004 • (425) 450-1765 • http://www.kcls.org

Clever Research • 10540 SE 28th St • Bellevue, WA 98004-7459 • *Clever Newsletter*

Eastside Genealogical Society & Archives • c/o Bellevue Regional Library, 1111 110th Ave NE, P.O. Box 374 • Bellevue, WA 98009-0374 • (425) 885-2012 • http://www.rootsweb.com/~wakcegs • *East Side Genealogical Society Bulletin Board*

Eastside Genealogical Society, Italian Interest Group • P.O. Box 374 • Bellevue, WA 98009-0374

Eastside Heritage Center Archives • 2102 Bellevue Way SE, P.O. Box 40535 • Bellevue, WA 98015 • (425) 450-1049 • http://www.eastsideheritagecenter.org

Jewish Genealogical Society of Washington State • 14222 NE 1st Ln • Bellevue, WA 98007-6941 • (425) 562-0533 • *Jewish Genealogical Society of Washington State Newsletter*

Kidd Family Heritage Publication • 14130 SE 17th, Ste C1 • Bellevue, WA 98007 • (425) 643-6650 • *Kidd Family Heritage*

Midkiff Family Names • 1837-184th NE • Bellevue, WA 98008 • (425) 747-4516

Mowreader-Robinson-Cox-McCoughey Family Organization • 15248 SE 49th St • Bellevue, WA 98006

Rosalie Whyel Museum of Doll Art • 1116 108th Ave NE • Bellevue, WA 98004 • (425) 455-1116 • http://www.dollart.com • *Rosalie Whyel Museum of Doll Art Newsletter*

Rowe Family Names • 1837 - 184th NE • Bellevue, WA 98008 • (425) 747-4516

State of Washington Archaeology and Historic Preservation • general delivery • Bellevue, WA 98004 • (425) 586-3064

Vance Family Association • 612 155th Pl NE • Bellevue, WA 98007-4822 • (425) 746-9907 • http://homepages.rootsweb.com/~rtr89/Vance/ • *Vance Family Association Newsletter*

Bellingham
American Museum of Radio and Electricity Archives • 1312 Bay St • Bellingham, WA 98225 • (360) 738-3886 • http://www.americanradiomuseum.org • *American Museum of Radio and Electricity Newsletter*

Bellingham Public Library • 210 Central St, P.O. Box 1197 • Bellingham, WA 98227-1197 • (360) 676-6860 • http://www.bellinghampubliclibrary.org

Mabel Zoe Wilson Library • Western Washington Univ, 516 High St • Bellingham, WA 98225 • (360) 650-3050 • http://www.library.wwu.edu

Whatcom County Public Library • 5205 Northwest Rd • Bellingham, WA 98226-9092 • (360) 384-3150 • http://www.wcls.org

Whatcom Genealogical Society • P.O. Box 1493 • Bellingham, WA 98225-1493 • (360) 734-9835 • http://www.rootsweb.com/~wawhatco/ • *Bulletin of the Whatcom Genealogical Society*

Whatcom Museum of History and Art Archives • 121 Prospect St • Bellingham, WA 98225 • (360) 676-6981 • http://www.whatcommuseum.org

Benton City
Dorsey Reunion • P.O. Box 959 • Benton City, WA 99320-9772 • *Dorsey Reunion Newsletter*

Beverly
Wanapum Dam Heritage Center Archives • Hwy 243 • Beverly, WA 99321 • (509) 754-2500

Bonney Lake
Fitt Surname Organization • 20103 Cascade Dr E • Bonney Lake, WA 98390 • (253) 862-7803

Bothell
Clan MacIntyre Society • 11936 NE 153rd Pl • Bothell, WA 98011-4133 • http://clanmacintyre.org

Everard Reunion • 22413 14th Pl W • Bothell, WA 98021 • (425) 485-5543

Bremerton
Bremerton Naval Museum Archives • 402 Pacific Ave • Bremerton, WA 98337 • (360) 479-7447

Washington

Cory National Family Association • 1123 N Cambrian • Bremerton, WA 98310 • (564) 377-1512 • *Cory Family Newsletter*

Kitsap County Historical Society & Archives • Historical Museum, 280 4th St, P.O. Box 903 • Bremerton, WA 98337-0903 • (360) 479-6226 • http://www.kitsaphistory.org • *Kitsap County Historical Society Newsletter*

Kitsap Regional Library • 1301 Sylvan Wy • Bremerton, WA 98310-3498 • (360) 405-9100 • http://www.krl.org • *KRL News*

US Navy Resource Center • Naval Station Bremerton, 120 S Dewey St • Bremerton, WA 98314-5000 • (360) 476-3178 • http://www.psnsmwr.org

Buckley

Foothills Historical Society • general delivery • Buckley, WA 98321 • (360) 829-1291

Burbank

Clan Maclaine Association • 19 Maple St • Burbank, WA 99323-8521 • (509) 545-4301 • http://www.nano.bc.ca/local/ethnic/celtic/maclaine.html • *Battleaxe*

Burlington

Burlington Public Library • 900 E Fairhaven St • Burlington, WA 98233-1998 • (360) 755-0760 • http://www.burlington.lib.wa.us

Camas

Camas Public Library • 625 NE Fourth Ave • Camas, WA 98607 • (360) 834-4692 • http://www.ci.camas.wa.us/library

Cashmere

Chelan County Historical Society & Archives • Historical Museum, 600 Corlets Wy, P.O. Box 22 • Cashmere, WA 98815 • (509) 782-3230 • http://www.cashmeremuseum.com • *Pioneer Messenger*

Castle Rock

Castle Rock Public Library • 137 Cowlitz St W, P.O. Box 1350 • Castle Rock, WA 98611-1350 • (360) 274-6961

Cathlamet

Wahkiakum County Historical Society & Archives • Historical Museum, 65 River St, P.O. Box 541 • Cathlamet, WA 98612 • (360) 795-3954

Centralia

Kirk Library • Centralia College, 600 W Locust St • Centralia, WA 98531 • (360) 736-9391 • http://library.centralia.ctc.edu

Chehalis

Lewis County Genealogical Society • 599 NW Front St, P.O. Box 782 • Chehalis, WA 98532 • (360) 748-0831 • *Lewis County Genealogical Society Newsletter*

Lewis County Historical Society & Archives • Historical Museum, 599 NW Front St, P.O. Box 782 • Chehalis, WA 98532 • (360) 748-0831 • http://www.lewiscountymuseum.org • *Lewis County Log*; *Lewis County Genealogical Society Newsletter*

Chelan

Chelan Valley Genealogical Society & Library • P.O. Box Y • Chelan, WA 98816-1396 • (509) 682-5131 • *Apple Orchard*

Lake Chelan Historical Society & Library • 204 E Woodin Ave, P.O. Box 1948 • Chelan, WA 98816 • (509) 682-5644 • *Lake Chelan History Notes*

Cheney

John F Kennedy Memorial Library • Eastern Washington University, 816 F St, 100 LIB • Cheney, WA 99004 • (509) 359-2263 • http://www.library.ewu.edu

Chewelah

Chewelah Public Library • E 301 Clay Ave, P.O. Box 87 • Chewelah, WA 99109-0087 • (509) 935-6805

Chinook

Fort Columbia State Park Museum Archives • Hwy 101, P.O. Box 488 • Chinook, WA 98624 • (360) 777-8221

Clarkston

Asotin County Library • 417 Sycamore St • Clarkston, WA 99403-2666 • (509) 758-5454 • http://users.clarkston.com/acpublib

Cle Elum

Carpenter Home Museum Archives • 221 E 1st St • Cle Elum, WA 98922 • (509) 674-5702

Carpenter Memorial Library • 302 Pennsylvania Ave • Cle Elum, WA 98922-1196 • (509) 674-2313 • http://www.cm-library.org

Northern Kittitas County Genealogical Society • P.O. Box 535 • Cle Elum, WA 98922

Colfax

Berner-Burner-Bernard Family Association • 281 SR 23 • Colfax, WA 99111 • (509) 397-3751 • *Berner Bridge*

Joseph Leinweber and Elizabeth Gerlitz Family Association • 281 SR 23 • Colfax, WA 99111 • (509) 397-3751

Whitman County Historical Society & Library • 623 N Perkins Ave • Colfax, WA 99111 • (509) 397-2555 • *Bunchgrass Historian*

Whitman County Library • S 102 Main St • Colfax, WA 99111-1892 • (509) 397-4366 • http://www.whitco.lib.wa.us

Colville

Colville Public Library • 195 S Oak St • Colville, WA 99114 • (509) 684-6620

Northeast Washington Genealogical Society & Archives • c/o Colville Public Library, 195 S Oak St • Colville, WA 99114-2845 • (509) 684-6620 • http://www.newgs.org • *Pioneer Branches*

Stevens County Historical Society & Archives • Historical Museum, 700 N Wynne St, P.O. Box 25 • Colville, WA 99114 • (509) 684-5968 • *In-Review*

Skagit Valley Genealogical Society • P.O. Box 715 • Conway, WA 98238-0715 • (360) 424-6528 • *Skagit Valley Genealogical Society Newsletter*

Cosmopolis

Grays Harbor Genealogical Society • P.O. Box 867 • Cosmopolis, WA 98537-0867 • (360) 249-4632 • *Grays Harbor Genealogical Society News*; *Family Tree Searcher*

Coulee Dam

Benjamin Gwynne and Maria Cobb Descendants Reunion • 605 Fir St • Coulee Dam, WA 99116 • (509) 633-2208

Daley-Crawford Surname Exchange • 605 Fir St • Coulee Dam, WA 99116 • (509) 633-2208

Nathaniel C and Lucy Ann Sandefur Taylor Descendants Reunion • 605 Fir St • Coulee Dam, WA 99116 • (509) 633-2208

Coupeville

Fort Casey Interpretetive Center Archives • Fort Casey State Park, Engle Rd • Coupeville, WA 98239 • (360) 679-7391

Island County Historical Society & Archives • Historical Museum, 908 NW Alexander St, P.O. Box 305 • Coupeville, WA 98239 • (360) 678-3310 • http://www.islandhistory.org • Island Heritage

Covington

KARD Files • 19305 SE 243rd Pl • Covington, WA 98042-4820 • (425) 432-1659 • *Karow Knowledge*; *Dye Data*; *Barnes Bulletin*; *Todd Times*; *Billingsley Yesterday and Today*

Davenport

Davenport Public Library • 411 Morgan St, P.O. Box 1169 • Davenport, WA 99122-1169 • (509) 725-4355

Fort Spokane Museum Archives • 44180 Office Ln N, P.O. Box 51 • Davenport, WA 99122 • (509) 725-2715 • http://www.nps.gov/laro/

Lincoln County Historical Society & Archives • Historical Museum, Park & 7th Sts, P.O. Box 585 • Davenport, WA 99122 • (509) 725-6711 • *Lincoln County Historical Society Newsletter*

Dayton
Columbia County Genealogical and Historical Society • P.O. Box 74 • Dayton, WA 99328-0074

Dayton Historical Depot Society & Archives • Historical Museum, 222 E Commercial, P.O. Box 316 • Dayton, WA 99328 • (509) 382-2026 • http://www.daytonhistoricdepot.org

Deer Park
Elwood-Hanna Research • W 5917 Crosscut Rd • Deer Park, WA 99006 • (509) 276-2550 • *Elwood Echoes*; *Hanna Herald*

Deming
Blockley Surname Organization • 5546 North Fork Rd • Deming, WA 98244 • (564) 592-5693

Des Moines
Greater Des Moines-Zenith Historical Society • 730 S 225th St, P.O. Box 98055 • Des Moines, WA 98188 • (206) 824-5226 • Timber, Tides and Tales

Highline Community College Library • 2400 S 240th St • Des Moines, WA 98198 • (206) 878-3710 • http://www.flightline.highline.ctc.edu/library/

DuPont
DuPont Historical Society • Historical Museum, 207 Barksdale Ave • DuPont, WA 98327 • (253) 964-2399 • http://www.dupontmuseum.com

Pierce County Genealogical Society • P.O. Box 189 • DuPont, WA 98327-0189

Duvall
Duvall Historical Society • 26526 NE Cherry Valley Rd • Duvall, WA 98019 • (425) 844-1976 • *Wagon Wheel Newsletter*

Eastsound
Orcas Island Historical Society & Archives • Historical Museum, 5 North Beach Rd, P.O. Box 134 • Eastsound, WA 98245 • (360) 376-4849

Eatonville
Pioneer Farm Museum and Ohop Indian Village • 7716 Ohop Valley Rd E • Eatonville, WA 98328 • (360) 832-6300 • http://www.pioneerfarmmuseum.org

South Pierce County Historical Society • P.O. Box 537 • Eatonville, WA 98328

Edmonds
Edmonds-South Snohomish County Historical Society & Archives • Historical Museum, 118 5th Ave N, P.O. Box 52 • Edmonds, WA 98020 • (425) 774-0900 • http://www.historicedmonds.org • *Museum Light*

Ellensburg
Ellensburg Genealogical Group • 507 E Tacoma St • Ellensburg, WA 98926

Ellensburg Public Library • 209 N Ruby St • Ellensburg, WA 98926-3397 • (509) 962-7250 • http://www.epl.eburg.com

Frame-Scribner Database • P.O. Box 1299 • Ellensburg, WA 98926-1299

Kittitas County Genealogical Society • 413 N Main, Ste D, P.O. Box 1342 • Ellensburg, WA 98926-1342 • (509) 925-5951 • *Kittitas County Kinfolk*

Olmstead Place State Park Archives • 921 N Ferguson Rd • Ellensburg, WA 98926 • (509) 925-1943 • http://www.parks.gov

Washington State Archives, Central Regional Branch • Central Washington Univ MS 7547, 400 E 8th Ave • Ellensburg, WA 98926-7547 • (509) 963-2136

Enumclaw
Enumclaw Public Library • 1700 1st St • Enumclaw, WA 98022 • (360) 825-2938 • http://www.enumclaw.lib.wa.us

Harmer Research • 18115 SE 416th St • Enumclaw, WA 98022 • *Harmer Family Newsletter*

Ephrata
Ephrata Genealogical Society • c/o Ephrata Public Library, 45 Alder St NW • Ephrata, WA 98823-1663 • (509) 754-3971 • *Big Bend Register*

Grant County Genealogical Society • c/o Ephrata Public Library, 45 Alder NW • Ephrata, WA 98823 • (509) 754-3971

Grant County Historical Society & Archives • Historical Museum, 742 Basin St NW, P.O. Box 1141 • Ephrata, WA 98823 • (509) 754-3334 • *Grant County Historical Society Newsletter*

Kroet(s)ch Family Association • 143 Crest Dr • Ephrata, WA 98823

North Central Regional Library-Ephrata Public Library • 45 AlderSt NW • Ephrata, WA 98823-1663 • (509) 754-3971

Everett
Bozarth Family • P.O. Box 5354 • Everett, WA 98206 • (425) 353-2540 • http://www.bozarth.org

Edward Carrell Family Organization • 9617 Belmont Dr • Everett, WA 98208-2713 • (425) 355-1128

Everett Public Library • 2702 Hoyt Ave • Everett, WA 98201-3556 • (425) 257-8000 • http://www.epls.org

Maybee Society • 10020 23rd Dr SE • Everett, WA 98208 • (425) 337-1369 • *Communicator*

Snohomish County Historical Association & Archives • Heritage Center Museum, 2911 1/2 Jewitt Ave, P.O. Box 5203 • Everett, WA 98206 • (425) 259-8849

Everson
Miller-Kimble Research • 7149 Sutton Dr • Everson, WA 98247 • *Miller Pursuit*; *Kimble Pursuit*

Fairchild AFB
Fairchild Base Library • 2 W Castle St • Fairchild AFB, WA 99011-9401 • (509) 247-5556

Federal Way
Clan Donald, North Pacific • 33513 18th Ave S • Federal Way, WA 98023 • (253) 838-2925

Historical Society of Federal Way • 31805 7th Ave SW • Federal Way, WA 98023 • (253) 945-7842

Ford
Pioneer Publications • P.O. Box 40 • Ford, WA 98013-0040 • (509) 276-9841 • *Batchelder Review; Berry By-Lines; Bricker Branches; Campbell Connections; Gates Gazette; Lewis Unlimited; Oakes Acorns; Page Pedigree; Small Siblings; Tucker Times; Williams Wandering*

Forks
Forks Genealogical Society • c/o Forks Memorial Library, 171 Forks Ave • Forks, WA 98331

Fort Lewis
Fort Lewis Library System • Bldg 2109, Box 339500 • Fort Lewis, WA 98433-9500 • (253) 966-1300 • http://www.lewis.army.mil/dpca/library

Fort Lewis Military Museum Archives • Bldg 4320, P.O. Box 331001 • Fort Lewis, WA 98433-1001 • (253) 967-7206 • http://www.lewis.army.mil/dptms/pomfi/museum • *Banner*

Fox Island
Fox Island Historical Society & Archives • Historical Museum, 1017 9th Ave, P.O. Box 242 • Fox Island, WA 98333-0242 • (253) 549-2461 • http://www.foxisland.net

FPO Seattle
Brammer Research • MEU Box 20 • FPO Seattle, WA 98762 • Brammer Branches

Freeland
South Whidbey Genealogical Group • general delivery • Freeland, WA 98249

Friday Harbor
San Juan Historical Society & Archives • Historical Museum, 405 Price St, P.O. Box 441 • Friday Harbor, WA 98250 • (360) 378-3949 • http://www.sjmuseum.org • *San Juan Historical Society Newsletter*

San Juan Island National Historic Site Archives • 650 Mullis St, Ste 100, P.O. Box 429 • Friday Harbor, WA 98250 • (360) 378-2240 • http://www.nps.gov/sajh

San Juan Island Public Library • 1010 Guard St • Friday Harbor, WA 98250-9612 • (360) 378-2798

Gig Harbor
Edward Norris Family Organization • 4502 Garden Place NW • Gig Harbor, WA 98335-1426 • (206) 851-7742

Gig Harbor Peninsula Historical Society & Archives • Historical Museum, 4218 Harborview Dr, P.O. Box 744 • Gig Harbor, WA 98335 • (253) 858-6722 • http://www.gigharbormuseum.org • *Gig Harbor Peninsula Historical Society Newsletter*

Goldendale
Klickitat County Historical Society & Library • Presby Mansion, 127 W Broadway, P.O. Box 86 • Goldendale, WA 98620-0086 • (509) 773-4303 • *Klickitat Heritage*

Grandview
Bleyhl Community Library • 311 Division St • Grandview, WA 98930-1398 • (509) 882-9217

Flora, Flory, Fleury Research • 300 Birch St • Grandview, WA 98930 • (509) 882-3973 • *Flora, Flory, Fleury Family Newsletter*

Harrah
Yakima Valley Regional Library-Harrah Library • 21 E Pioneer • Harrah, WA 98933 • (509) 848-3458

Hoodspont
Mason County Genealogical Society • P.O. Box 333 • Hoodspont, WA 98548

Hoquiam
Polson Park and Museum Historical Society & Archives • Historical Museum, 1611 Riverside Ave, P.O. Box 432 • Hoquiam, WA 98550 • (360) 533-5862 • http://www.polsonmuseum.org • *Polson Museum News*

Ilwaco
Ilwaco Heritage Foundation & Archives • Heritage Museum, 115 SE Lake St, P.O. Box 153 • Ilwaco, WA 98624 • (360) 665-3446 • http://www.ilwacoheritagemuseum.org • *Ilwaco Heritage Foundation Newsletter*

Lewis & Clark Interpretive Center Archives • Fort Canby State Park, P.O. Box 488 • Ilwaco, WA 98624 • (360) 642-3029 • http://www.fortcanby.org

Issaquah
Issaquah Historical Society • Historic Depot, 50 Rainier Blvd N • Issaquah, WA 98027 • (425) 392-2322

Issaquah Historical Society & Archives • Gilman Town Hall Museum, 165 SE Andrews St, P.O. Box 695 • Issaquah, WA 98027 • (425) 392-3500 • http://www.issaquahistory.org • *Issaquah Historical Society Newsletter*

King County Library System • 960 NW Newport Way • Issaquah, WA 98027-2702 • (425) 462-9600 • http://www.kcls.org

Kalama
Kalama Public Library • 312 N 1st, P.O. Box 576 • Kalama, WA 98625-0600 • (360) 673-4568

Kelso
Cowlitz County Historical Society & Archives • Historical Museum, 405 Allen St • Kelso, WA 98626 • (360) 577-3119 • http://www.co.cowlitz.wa.us/museum • *Cowlitz Historical Quarterly*

Kennewick
Crum Reunion • 6 W 6th Ave #606 • Kennewick, WA 99336-5663

East Benton County Historical Society & Library • 205 Keewaydin Dr, P.O. Box 6710 • Kennewick, WA 99336 • (509) 582-7704 • *Courier of the East Benton County Historical Society*

Mid-Columbia Library District • 405 S Dayton • Kennewick, WA 99336 • (509) 582-4745 • http://www.mcl-lib.org

Mid-Columbia Library District-Kennewick Branch • 1620 S Union • Kennewick, WA 99338 • (509) 783-7878

Pankaskie Family • 5403 W Tucannon • Kennewick, WA 99336-1337

Robert L DeCoursey Family Organization • 1819 S Polouse St • Kennewick, WA 99337-3547 • (509) 586-0219

Kent
Finefrock Clearinghouse • 28411 59th Ave S • Kent, WA 98031 • (253) 852-4557

Lehnher Research • 3631 S 257th St • Kent, WA 98032-5669 • *Lehnherr of Swiss Origins and Their Collateral Ties*

Olsen Enterprises • 3931 S 238th St • Kent, WA 98032 • (253) 824-4989 • *Smith Families of England and New England*; *Copeland Cuzzins*

Rush Family Association • 20834 103rd Ct SE • Kent, WA 98031-2075 • *Rush Family Association Newsletter*

Slagle Family Organization • 23516 156th Ave SE • Kent, WA 98042 • (253) 630-5899 • *Slagle World*

South King County Genealogical Society & Library, Computer Interest Group, German Interest Group • P.O. Box 3174 • Kent, WA 98032-3174 • http://www.rootsweb.com/~waskcgs • *South King Newsletter*

Swasey-Swesey Family Society • 25100 180th Ave SE • Kent, WA 98042 • (253) 630-8659 • *Swasey-Swesey Family Society Newsletter*

Wells Family Research Association • P.O. Box 5427 • Kent, WA 98064-5427 • *Wells Chronicles*

Kettle Falls
Fisher Research • 3960 E German Rd, Route 3, Box 545 • Kettle Falls, WA 99141-9402 • (509) 738-6731 • Fisher Families

Kettle Falls Public Library • 605 Meyers St, P.O. Box 478 • Kettle Falls, WA 99141-0478 • (509) 738-6817

Keyport
Naval Undersea Museum Archives • Garnett Wy • Keyport, WA 98345 • (360) 396-4148 • http://www.undersea.museum • *Undersea Quarterly*

Kingston
Davis Research • 9935 Kingston Farm Rd • Kingston, WA 98346 • *Days of Our Davis*

Kirkland
Kirkland Heritage Society • 203 Market St • Kirkland, WA 98033 • (425) 827-3446

Robbins Research • 701 8th Ave, P.O. Box 2361 • Kirkland, WA 98083 • (425) 823-0200 • *Robbins Journal*

La Conner
Skagit County Historical Museum Library • 501 S 4th St, P.O. Box 818 • La Conner, WA 98257-0818 • (360) 466-3365 • http://www.skagitcounty.net/museum

Skagit County Historical Society & Archives • Historical Museum, 501 S 4th St, P.O. Box 818 • La Conner, WA 98257 • (360) 466-3365 • http://www.skagitcounty.net/museum • *Skagit County Historical Society Quarterly Newsletter*

Lacey
Rusk Family Organization • 3802 Goldfinch Dr SE • Lacey, WA 98503 • (564) 493-2065 • *Rusk Roundup*

Lakebay
Anderson Island Historical Society • general delivery • Lakebay, WA 98349 • (253) 884-2135

Lakewood
Nicodemus Family Reunion • 8710 Moreland SW • Lakewood, WA 98498

Langley
Adkins Family Organization • P.O. Box 549 • Langley, WA 98260 • http://www.adkinsfamily.org

Genealogical Society of South Whidbey Island • P.O. Box 976 • Langley, WA 98260 • (360) 331-5715 • http://www.rootsweb.com/~wagsswi/ • *Genealogical Society of South Whidbey Island Newsletter*

South Whidbey Historical Society • 314 2nd St • Langley, WA 98260 • (360) 221-2101

Liberty Lake
McGowan Reunion • P.O. Box 219 • Liberty Lake, WA 99019 • (509) 255-5737

Lind
Adams County Historical Society & Archives • Historical Museum, 1st St, P.O. Box 526 • Lind, WA 99341 • (509) 677-3393

Longview
City of Longview Historic Preservation Committee • general delivery • Longview, WA 98632 • (360) 442-5081

Longview Public Library • 1600 Louisiana St • Longview, WA 98632-2993 • (360) 442-5315 • http://www.longviewlibrary.org • *In Review*

Lower Columbia Genealogical Society & Archives • c/o Longview Public Library, 1600 Louisiana St, P.O. Box 472 • Longview, WA 98632-7306 • (360) 423-1388 • *Lower Columbia Genealogical Society Newsletter*, *Key*

Loon Lake
Loon Lake Historical Society • 4000 Colville Rd • Loon Lake, WA 99148 • (509) 233-2222

Lopez Island
Lopez Island Historical Society & Archives • Historical Museum, 28 Washburn Pl, P.O. Box 163 • Lopez Island, WA 98261 • (360) 468-3447 • http://www.rockisland.com/~lopezmuseum • *Lopez Island Historical Society Newsletter*

Lopez Island Library • 2225 Fisherman Bay Rd, P.O. Box 770 • Lopez Island, WA 98261-0770 • (360) 468-2265

Lynden
Lynden Pioneer Museum Archives • 217 W Front St • Lynden, WA 98264 • (360) 354-3675 • http://www.lyndenpioneermuseum.com • *Museum Musings*; *Whatcom Moments & Memoirs*

Lynnwood
Thomas Duce Family Organization • 20125 28 Ave W • Lynnwood, WA 98036 • (425) 672-7188

Malo
Gard Research • 9 Apache Ln, P.O. Box 336 • Malo, WA 99150-0336 • (509) 779-4984 • http://www.geocities.com/Heartland/Fields/4106/ • *Gard Guardian*

Maple Valley
Maple Valley Historical Society & Archives • Historical Museum, 23015 SE 216 Way, P.O. Box 123 • Maple Valley, WA 98038 • (425) 432-3470 • http://www.maplevalley.com/community/historical • *Maple Valley Bugle*

Marysville
Family Publications • 5628 60th Dr NE • Marysville, WA 98270-9509 • (360) 653-8394 • *Bilyen by You*; *Military Queries and Reviews*; *Missouri Sources, Queries and Reviews*; *Oregon Trail Sources, Queries and Reviews*; *Reed, Read, Reid Roots Surname Booklets*; *Terry Tracings*; *Vilyeu-Workman Blood Lines Quarterly Newsletter*, *Workman Branches*

Frederick William Passey Family Organization • 12618 Marine Dr • Marysville, WA 98271-6011

Snow-Isle Regional Library • 7312 35th Ave NE • Marysville, WA 98271-7417 • (360) 659-8447 • http://www.sno-isle.org

Medina
Huyck-Howk-Houck-David Yeaw Family Organization • P.O. Box 11 • Medina, WA 98039 • (425) 454-3714

Mercer Island
Jewish Genealogical Society of Washington State • 3633 86th St SE • Mercer Island, WA 98040-3612 • (206) 232-2666 • http://members.tripod.com/~JGSWS

Mill Creek
Beyerlein Family Association • 15800 Village Green Dr #3 • Mill Creek, WA 98012 • (425) 337-6778 • *Beyerlein Beginnings*

Clan Moffat Society • 14614 26th Dr SE • Mill Creek, WA 98012-5730 • http://www.tartans.com/clans/Moffat/moffat.html • *Moffatana*

Moclips
Moclips by The Sea Historical Society & Archives • Historical Museum, 4658 State Route 109 • Moclips, WA 98562 • (360) 276-4441

Moses Lake
Big Bend Community College Library • 7662 Chanute St • Moses Lake, WA 98837 • (509) 762-6247 • http://library.bbcc.ctc.edu

Moses Lake Museum Archives • 228 W 3rd, P.O. Drawer 1579 • Moses Lake, WA 98837 • (509) 360-9395 • http://www.moses-lake.com • *MAChappenings*; *MACline*

Mount Vernon
Love Research-Gathering of Ketchum Kindred • 1743 Blodgett Rd • Mount Vernon, WA 98273 • (564) 428-0319 • *Love Is Love Forevermore*

Mount Vernon City Library • 315 Snoqualmie St • Mount Vernon, WA 98273 • (360) 336-6209 • http://www.ci.mount-vernon.wa.us

Norwood Cole Library • Skagit Valley College, 2405 E College Way • Mount Vernon, WA 98273 • (360) 416-7850 • http://library.skagit.edu

Ruhlman(n) Family Association • 18314 Beaver Marsh Rd • Mount Vernon, WA 98273 • (564) 424-5783

Mountlake Terrace
Williamite Branch, Scotch-Irish Bryans • 6003 233rd Pl SW • Mountlake Terrace, WA 98043 • *Ardseanchai*

Mukilteo
Mukilteo Historical Society • 604 Front St • Mukilteo, WA 98275 • (425) 356-2778

Naches
International Molyneux Family Association • 91 Fontaine Ln • Naches, WA 98937-9418 • (206) 842-6636 • *World Newsletter of the International Molyneux Family Association*

Napavine
McNeill Enterprises • 323 Cedarcrest Ct, P.O. Box 779 • Napavine, WA 98565-0779 • (360) 262-3300 • *Rogers Research Data*

Newport
Pend Oreille County Historical Society & Library • 402 N Washington Ave, P.O. Box 1409 • Newport, WA 99156 • (509) 447-5388 • *Big Smoke*

Pend Oreille County Library District • 116 S Washington Ave • Newport, WA 99156 • (509) 447-2111 • http://www.pocld.org

Nine Mile Falls
Spokane House Interpretative Center Archives • 9711 W Charles • Nine Mile Falls, WA 99026 • (509) 465-5064 • http://www.riversidestatepark.org

North Bend
Snoqualmie Valley Historical Society & Archives • Historical Museum, 320 N Bendigo Blvd S, P.O. Box 179 • North Bend, WA 98045 • (425) 888-3200 • http://www.snowqualmievalleymuseum.org • *Snoqualmie Valley Historical Society Quarterly*

North Seattle
Erath Surname Organization • 15714 Greenwood Ave • North Seattle, WA 98133

Oak Harbor
Whidbey Island Genealogical Searchers • P.O. Box 627 • Oak Harbor, WA 98277-0627

Oakville
Chehalis Valley Historical Society & Library • 268-11 Oak Meadows Rd • Oakville, WA 98568 • (360) 273-8044 • *Chehalis Valley Historian*

Ocean Park
Pacific County Genealogical Society & Library • P.O. Box 843 • Ocean Park, WA 98640 • (360) 665-6293 • http://www.pacifier.com/~unighorn • *Clan Digger*

Ocean Shores
North Beach Genealogical Society • P.O. Box 2007 • Ocean Shores, WA 98569

Ocean Shores Public Library • 573 Point Brown Ave NW, P.O. Box 669 • Ocean Shores, WA 98569-0669 • (360) 289-3919 • http://www.osgov.com/library.html

Okanagan
Gard Research • 985 Mill St • Okanagan, WA 98840 • *Gard Gardian*

Olympia
Badgett Family Depository • 2103 Harrison Ave NW #2 • Olympia, WA 98502 • (564) 439-9934 • *Badgett Family Depository*

Bale Family Organization • 1620 Ethridge NE • Olympia, WA 98506

Bigelow House Museum Archives • 918 Glass Ave NE, P.O. Box 1821 • Olympia, WA 98507 • http://www.bigelowhouse.org

Jeremiah Greene Family Organization • 6002 Tolmie Dr NE • Olympia, WA 98516 • (564) 456-0271

Norum Family Reunion • 7344 Marvin Rd NE • Olympia, WA 98516

Olympia Genealogical Society • c/o Olympia Public Library, 8th & Franklin Sts, P.O. Box 1313 • Olympia, WA 98507-1313 • (360) 943-5209 • *Olympia Genealogical Society Quarterly*

Olympic Flight Museum Archives • 7637 A Old Hwy 99 SE • Olympia, WA 98501 • (360) 705-3025 • http://www.olympicflightmuseum.com • *Flight Line*

Penland Historical Society • 9623 Glory Dr SE • Olympia, WA 98513-4804 • (564) 456-3509 • *Penland Historical Society Quarterly*

State Capitol Historical Association • 211 W 21st Ave • Olympia, WA 98501 • (206) 753-2580 • *Musings*; *Washington Heritage Bulletin*

Stephen Cantrall-George Elvis Fraim Family Organization • 2607 Timber C SE • Olympia, WA 98503 • (564) 491-5321

Timberland Regional Library • 415 Airdustrial Way SW • Olympia, WA 98501 • (360) 943-5001

Timberland Regional Library-Olympia Branch • 313 Eighth Ave SE • Olympia, WA 98501-9300 • (360) 352-0595

Washington State Capital Museum Archives • 211 21st Ave SW • Olympia, WA 98501 • (360) 753-2580 • http://www.wshs.org

Washington State Division Archives & Records Management • 1129 Washington St SE • Olympia, WA 98504-0238 • (360) 586-1492 • http://www.secstate.wa.gov/

Washington State Genealogical Society • P.O. Box 1422 • Olympia, WA 98507-1422 • (360) 352-0595 • http://www.rootsweb.com/~wasgs/ • Washington State Genealogical Society Newsletter

Washington State Historical Society • Heritage Resource Center, 211 21st Ave SE • Olympia, WA 98501 • (360) 753-2580 • http://www.wshs.org • *Washington Heritage Bulletin*

Washington State Library • 6880 Capitol Blvd S, P.O. Box 42460 • Olympia, WA 98504-2460 • (360) 704-5221 • http://www.statelib.wa.gov/

Omak
North Central Regional Library-Omak Community • 30 S Ash St, P.O. Box J • Omak, WA 98841-0969 • (509) 826-1820

Okanogan County Genealogical Society & Library • Okanogan County Historical and Genealogical Research Center, 263 Old Riverside Hwy • Omak, WA 98841 • (509) 826-1686

Onalaska
Hoopingarner Family Research • P.O. Box 84 • Onalaska, WA 98570-0084 • http://landru.i-link-2.net/misha327/hoopies.htm • *Hoopie Virtual Front Porch*

Orcas Island
Orcas Island Historical Museum Archives • 181 N Beach Rd • Orcas Island, WA 98245 • (360) 376-4849 • http://www.orcasisland.org/~history/ • *Orcas Islander*

Oroville
Molson Historical Society • 539 Molson Rd • Oroville, WA 98844 • (509) 485-3266

Old Oroville Depot Historical Society • general delivery • Oroville, WA 98844 • (509) 476-2666

Othello
McCrary-Eslinger-Wallace Surname Organization • 845 S Hummingbird Dr • Othello, WA 99344 • (509) 346-9307

Pasco
Franklin County Historical Society & Archives • Historical Museum, 305 N 4th St, P.O. Box 1033 • Pasco, WA 99301 • (509) 547-3714 • http://www.franklincountyhistoricalsociety.org • *Franklin Flyer*

John Lowell Family Organization • 1136 W Lincoln Dr • Pasco, WA 99301-3551 • (509) 545-6596

Sacajawea Interpretive Center Archives • 2503 Sacajawea State Park Rd • Pasco, WA 99301 • (509) 545-2361

Pateros
Fort Okanogan Inerpretive Center Archives • 1B Otto Rd • Pateros, WA 98846 • (509) 923-2473 • http://www.parks.wa.gov

Point Roberts
Fuerst Family Association • P.O. Box 1113 • Point Roberts, WA 98281

Pomeroy
William Graham and Mary Puckett Association • Route 3, Box 14 • Pomeroy, WA 99347

William Trescott Family Organization • Route 1, Box 48 • Pomeroy, WA 99347

Port Angeles
Clallam County Genealogical Society • 931 W 9th St, #13270 • Port Angeles, WA 98363 • (360) 417-5000

Clallam County Genealogical Society & Archives • c/o Genealogical Library, Clallam County Museum, 223 E 4th St, P.O. Box 1327 • Port Angeles, WA 98362-3098 • (360) 417-1284 • http://www.olypen.com/ccgs • *Clallam County Genealogical Society Bulletin*

Clallam County Historical Society & Archives • Historical Museum, 205 S Lincoln St, P.O. Box 1327 • Port Angeles, WA 98362-3098 • (360) 452-2662 • *Strait News*

Clallam County Museum Library • 223 E 4th St, P.O. Box 1024 • Port Angeles, WA 98362 • (360) 417-1284

North Olumpic Library System • 2210 S Peabody • Port Angeles, WA 98362-6536 • (360) 417-8501 • http://www.nols.org

Pierre Chastain Family Association • 356 Lawrence Rd • Port Angeles, WA 98363 • (360) 938-3154 • http://www.kopower.com/~jimchstn/hugsrcs2.htm • *Chestnut Tree*

Port Gamble
Port Gamble Historic Museum Archives • 3 Rainier Ave, P.O. Box 85 • Port Gamble, WA 98364 • (360) 297-8074 • http://www.portgamble.com

Port Orchard
Crossman Society • 2984 SE Aspen St • Port Orchard, WA 98366 • (360) 871-5694

Julia Ann Breyfoggel-Boyce-David Houck-Marx Surname Organization • 3176 SE Villa Carmel Dr • Port Orchard, WA 98366 • (360) 876-0833

McNees Family • 3362 Beach Dr E • Port Orchard, WA 98366-8116 • *Family Ties from McNees to Menees*

Puget Sound Genealogical Society • 2501 SE Mile Hill Dr • Port Orchard, WA 98366-4298 • (360) 874-8813 • http://www.rootsweb.com/~wapsgs/homepage.htm • *Family Backtracking*

Port Townsend
Jefferson County Genealogical Society & Library • 13692 Airport Cutoff Rd • Port Townsend, WA 98368 • (360) 379-6673 • http://www.rootsweb.com/~wajcgs • Jefferson County Genealogical Society Newsletter

Jefferson County Historical Society & Archives • Historical Museum, 540 Water St • Port Townsend, WA 98368-5725 • (360) 385-1003 • http://www.jchsmuseum.org • *Jefferson County Historical Society Newsletter*

Port Townsend Public Library • 1220 Lawrence St • Port Townsend, WA 98368-6527 • (360) 385-3181 • http://www.ptpl.lib.wa.us

Puget Sound Coast Artillery Museum Archives • Bldg 201 Fort Worden State Park, 200 Battery Wy • Port Townsend, WA 98368 • (360) 385-3295 • http://www.fortworden.org

Rothschild House State Park Archives • Franklin St • Port Townsend, WA 98368 • (360) 385-7248 • http://www.fortworden.org

Poulsbo
Suquamish Museum Archives • 15838 Sandy Hook Rd • Poulsbo, WA 98370 • (360) 598-3311 • http://www.suquamish.msn.us • *Suquamish Museum Newsletter*

Vincent Reunion • 1754 NE Mesford #35 • Pouslbo, WA 98370

Preston
Dunbar Research • P.O. Box 909 • Preston, WA 98050 • (425) 222-6940

Prosser
Benton County Historical Society & Archives • Historical Museum, 1000 Patterson Rd, P.O. Box 591 • Prosser, WA 99350 • (509) 786-3842

East Benton County Historical Society • P.O. Box 591 • Prosser, WA 99350

Pullman
Francis Simpson and America Reed and Mary Ann Corum Family Organization • 1652 S Grand Ave #166 • Pullman, WA 99163-4906 • (509) 276-6429 • *Simpson Family Newsletter*

Holland Library • Washington State Univ, P.O. Box 645610 • Pullman, WA 99164-5610 • (509) 335-9671 • http://www.wsulibs.wsu.edu

Neill Public Library • 210 N Grand Ave • Pullman, WA 99163-2693 • (509) 334-3595 • http://www.neill-lib.org

Palouse Publications • 310 SE Camino St • Pullman, WA 99163-2206 • (509) 334-1732 • *Cox Heritage; Morton Heritage; Hollowell Heritage*

Treffry-Trefry Family Reunion • NW 225 Ann St • Pullman, WA 99163 • (509) 332-0711

Whitman County Genealogical Society & Library • Gladish Community Center, 115 W Main St, P.O. Box 393 • Pullman, WA 99163-0393 • (509) 332-2386 • http://www.completebbs.com/simonsen/wcgsindex.html • *Whitman County Genealogical Society Newsletter*

Whitman County Historical Society & Archives • Gladish Community Center, 115 W Main St • Pullman, WA 99163 • (509) 332-2386

Puyallup
Ezra Meeker Historical Society • Meeker Mansion, 312 Spring St, P.O. Box 103 • Puyallup, WA 98371 • (253) 848-1770 • http://www.meekermansion.org • *Puyallup Valley Heritage*

Nancy Jane Buskirk Family Organization • 2616 31st St SE • Puyallup, WA 98374-5114

Nixon & Baccus Family Association Clearinghouse • 5817 144th St E • Puyallup, WA 98375-5221 • (253) 537-8288

Puyallup Public Library • 324 S Meridian St • Puyallup, WA 98371-5914 • (253) 841-5454 • http://www.ci.puyallup.wa.us

Quincy
Appling-Greenlee-Turner- Whiteside Research • 2130 Rd 12 NW • Quincy, WA 98848 • *Appling Herald; Greenlee Gazette; Turner Trails Newsletter; Whiteside Whisperings*

Boodry Family Organization • 15388 Rd 4 NW • Quincy, WA 98848

Raymond
Northwest Carriage Museum Archives • 314 Alder St, P.O. Box 534 • Raymond, WA 98577 • (360) 942-4150 • http://www.nwcarriagemuseum.org

Pacific Coast Historical Association & Archives • Historical Museum • Raymond, WA 98577 • (360) 875-5224

Raymond Public Library • 507 Duryea St • Raymond, WA 98577

Willapa Harbor Genealogical Society • c/o Raymond Public Library, 507 Duryea St • Raymond, WA 98577 • (360) 942-2408

Willapa Seaport Museum Archives • 310 Alder St • Raymond, WA 98577 • (360) 942-5666 • http://www.visit.willapabay.org

Reardan
Reardan Memorial Library • 120 S Oak, P.O. Box 227 • Reardan, WA 99029-0227 • (509) 994-9997

Redmond
Ephraim Elsbree Family Association • 2330 259th Ave NE • Redmond, WA 98053-9009 • (425) 836-8110

Marymoor Museum Archives • 6046 W Lake Sammamish Pkwy, P.O. Box 162 • Redmond, WA 98073-0162 • (425) 885-3684

Redmond Historical Society & Archives • Old Redmond Schoolhouse, 16600 NE 80th St, P.O. Box 464 • Redmond, WA 98073-0464 • (425) 885-2919 • *Redmond Historical Society Newsletter*

Moses Lamb Family Association • 16934 NE 131st Pl • Redmont, WA 98052 • (425) 881-1785

Renton
Hargrove-Hargrave-Harden-Hardin Research • 7600 129th Ave SE #40 • Renton, WA 98055 • *Harden-Hardin Family Quarterly; Hargrove Newsletter*

Nexus Publications • 2207 NE 12th St • Renton, WA 98056 • *Donahoe Nexus; Mooney Nexus; Thompson Nexus; Cassidy Nexus; Hendrickson Nexus*

Parrish Research • 3719 Meadow Ave N • Renton, WA 98055 • *Parrish Family Exchange*

Renton Historical Society & Archives • Historical Museum, 235 Mill Ave S • Renton, WA 98055-2133 • (425) 255-2330 • http://www.rentonhistory.org • *Renton Historical Society and Museum Newsletter; Renton Historical Quarterly*

Renton Public Library • 100 Mill Ave S • Renton, WA 98055-2126 • (425) 430-6610 • http://www.ci.renton.wa.us

Richland
Mock Reunion • 309 Catskill • Richland, WA 99352 • (509) 943-3776

Richland Public Library • 955 Northgate St • Richland, WA 99352-3539 • (509) 943-7457 • http://richland.lib.wa.us

Tri-City Genealogical Society & Library • P.O. Box 1410 • Richland, WA 99352-1410 • (509) 783-4262 • http://www.cbvcp.com/tcgs/ • *Tri-City Genealogical Society Bulletin*

Ritzville
Ritzville Library District Two • 302 W Main • Ritzville, WA 99169 • (509) 659-1222 • http://www.ritzcom.net/ritzlib/

Roslyn
Roslyn Historical Museum Society • P.O. Box 281 • Roslyn, WA 98941 • (509) 649-2776

Roslyn Public Library • 201 S 1st St, P.O. Box 451 • Roslyn, WA 98941-0451 • (509) 649-3420

Washington

Seattle

Allen Library • Univ of Washington, P.O. Box 352900 • Seattle, WA 98195-2900 • (206) 543-1760 • http://www.washington.edu

Autry Genealogy and History • 323 Queen Anne Ave N, Apt. 412 • Seattle, WA 98109 • http://homepages.rootsweb.com/~autry/ • *Autrey Genealogical Quarterly*

Barnard Research • 19033 46th Ave S • Seattle, WA 98188 • Barnard Lines

Barringer Family Association • 15035 29th Ave S • Seattle, WA 98188 • (206) 243-8057

Brooks-Cowles Research • 1717 S Angeline St • Seattle, WA 98108 • (206) 762-0957 • *Brooks Family Bulletin*

Burrell-Burrill Family Association • P.O. Box 31402 • Seattle, WA 98103-1402 • (206) 782-9250 • *Burrill-Burrill News*

Center for Wooden Boats Archives • 1010 Valley St • Seattle, WA 98109 • (206) 382-2628 • http://www.cwb.org • Shavings & Sawdust

Clan MacLean Association • 4536 20th NE • Seattle, WA 98105 • (206) 522-4557

Craig Clan Association of America • 10002 Aurora Ave N #4423 • Seattle, WA 98133 • (206) 527-8532 • http://www.tartans.com/clans/Craig/craig.html • *Clan Craig Connections*

Davee Surname Organization • 7558 45th Ave SW • Seattle, WA 98136

Descendants of the Staten Island-Pennsylvania Corsons • 5510 38th Avenue NE • Seattle, WA 98105 • (206) 525-2412

Descendants of William Buell who came to America from England about 1631 • 14203 6th Ave S • Seattle, WA 98168 • (206) 243-0609

Drescher-Hoeft-Hertges-Ferber Surname Organization • 15714 Greenwood Ave N • Seattle, WA 98133

Earnest-Ernest-Earnist-Arnest Family Exchange • 44075 1st Ave NE • Seattle, WA 98105-4932 • (206) 522-9269

English Stout Family Association • 8507 Inverness Dr NE • Seattle, WA 98115 • (206) 524-0216

Filipino American National Historical Society • 810 18th Ave, Rm 100 • Seattle, WA 98122 • (206) 322-0203 • http://www.fanhs-national.org

Fiske Genealogical Foundation & Library • 1644 43rd Ave E • Seattle, WA 98112-3222 • (206) 328-2716 • http://www.fiske.lib.wa.us • Fiske Genealogical Foundation Newsletter

Fleck Family Descendants • 9746 61st Ave S • Seattle, WA 98118 • (206) 722-8771

Francis Grant Dunbar Family Organization • 11310 15th NE • Seattle, WA 98125

George Merritt Descendants Association • 8542 19th Ave NW • Seattle, WA 98117-3518

Grinnell Family Association of America • 2122 N 63rd St • Seattle, WA 98103

Gross and Fessler Families • 9719 Mary Ave NW • Seattle, WA 98117-2334 • (206) 784-8403

Historic Seattle Preservation • 1117 Minor Ave • Seattle, WA 98101 • (206) 622-6952

Historical Society of Seattle and King County & Archives • Historical Museum, 2700 24th Ave E • Seattle, WA 98112 • (206) 324-1126 • http://www.seattlehistory.org

Holland America Club of the Pacific Northwest • 17122 25th Ave NE • Seattle, WA 98155-6134 • (425) 827-1969 • *Ye Old Dutch Mill*

Howard Reunion • 7410 S 127th St • Seattle, WA 98178-4353

Instructional Resources Center • South Seattle Community College, 6000 16th Ave SW • Seattle, WA 98106 • (206) 768-5395

Jewish Genealogical Society of Washington • 2917 NE Blakeley St • Seattle, WA 98115 • (206) 443-1903

John Phelps and Nathaniel Swingley Descendants • 8552 19th Ave NW • Seattle, WA 98117-3518

Judkins Family Association • 1538 NW 60th St • Seattle, WA 98107-2328 • (206) 784-3644 • http://geocities.com/Heartland/Oaks/1781/ • *Judkins Journal*

King County Office of Historic Preservation • Alaska Bldg # 805, 618 2nd Ave • Seattle, WA 98104 • (206) 296-4858

Klondike Gold Rush National Historical Park-Seattle Archives Unit • 117 S Main St • Seattle, WA 98104 • (206) 553-7220 • http://www.nps.gov/klse

Korean American Historical Society • 10303 Meridian Ave N, Ste 200 • Seattle, WA 98133-9483 • (206) 528-5784 • http://www.kahs.org

Melrose Family Association • 3555 27th Pl W #225 • Seattle, WA 98199-2161 • (206) 294-9304 • *Who's Who in American Melroses*

Museum of Flight Archives • 9404 E Marginal Way S • Seattle, WA 98108 • (206) 764-5720 • http://www.museumofflight.org • *Aloft*

Museum of History Archives • 2700 24th Ave E • Seattle, WA 98112 • (206) 324-1126 • http://www.seattlehistory.org • *MOHAI; Old News*

National Archives & Records Administration-Pacific Alaska Region • 6125 Sand Point Way NE • Seattle, WA 98115-7999 • (206) 526-6501 • http://www.archives.gov/facilities/wa/seattle.html

Nordic Heritage Museum Library • 3014 NW 67th St • Seattle, WA 98117 • (206) 789-5707 • http://www.nordicmuseum.com • *Nordic News*

Odyssey Maritime Discovery Center Archives • 2205 Alaskan Wy, Pier 66 • Seattle, WA 98121 • (206) 374-4000 • http://www.ody.org • *Voyages*

Pacific Northwest Cornish Association • 4676-41 Ave NE • Seattle, WA 98105

Philip Schuyler Green Family Organization • 1102 SW Trenton • Seattle, WA 98106-2423 • (206) 767-3413

Rainier Valley Historical Society • 3515 S Alaska St • Seattle, WA 98118 • (206) 723-1663

Scottish Blue Families in America • 2625 38th Ave W • Seattle, WA 98199-3107 • (206) 282-6342 • http://members.tripod.com/Whblue/scottish_blue.html

Scripture-Crumley-Van Cleave-Cleve-Cleff et al • 8036 11th Ave NW • Seattle, WA 98117-4123

Seattle Genealogical Society • 6200 Sand Point Way NE • Seattle, WA 98115 • (206) 522-8658

Seattle Genealogical Society & Library • 8511 15th Ave NE, P.O. Box 75388 • Seattle, WA 98111-0388 • (206) 682-1410 • http://www.seattlegenealogicalsociety.com • *Seattle Genealogical Society Bulletin*; *Seattle Genealogical Society Newsletter*

Shoreline Historical Museum Archives • 749 N 175th, P.O. Box 55594 • Seattle, WA 98133 • (206) 542-7111 • http://www.shorelinehistoricalmuseum.org • *Shoreline Memories*

Sons of the American Revolution, Washington Society • 12233 9th Ave NW • Seattle, WA 98177

Southwest Seattle Historical Society & Library • Log House Museum, 3003 61st Ave SW • Seattle, WA 98116 • (206) 338-5293 • http://www.loghousemuseum.org • *Footprints in the Sands of Time*

Swedish-Finn Historical Society & Library • 5410 17th Ave NW, Rm 329, P.O. Box 17264 • Seattle, WA 98107-0964 • (206) 706-0738 • http://sfhs.eget.net • *Swedish Finn Historical Society Newsletter*

Temple De Hirsch Sinai Library • 1511 E Pike • Seattle, WA 98122 • (206) 315-7398 • http://www.tdhs-nw.org

Univ of Washington • 4045 Brooklyn Ave NE, JA-15 • Seattle, WA 98105-6261 • (206) 543-2992 • http://www.washington.edu/uwired/outreach/cspn • *Pacific Northwest Quarterly*

Washington State Jewish Historical Society • 2031 3rd Ave #200 • Seattle, WA 98121-2429 • (206) 774-2277 • Jewish Transcript

William Henry Inglis Family Organization • 818 SW 120th St • Seattle, WA 98146 • (206) 244-1331

Sequim

Sequim Museum Archives • 175 W Cedar St • Sequim, WA 98383-3318 • (360) 683-8110

Shaw Island

Our Lady of the Rock Library • Order of Saint Benedict, P.O. Box 425 • Shaw Island, WA 98286-0425 • (360) 468-2321

Shaw Island Library and Historical Society & Archives • Historical Museum, Blind Bay Rd • Shaw Island, WA 98286 • (360) 468-4068

Shelton

Mason County Genealogical Society • P.O. Box 1535 • Shelton, WA 98584

Mason County Historical Society & Archives • Historical Museum, 427 Railroad Ave, P.O. Box 1366 • Shelton, WA 98584 • (360) 426-1020 • Mason County Historical Society Newsletter

Silverdale

Horton Family Association Gathering • 7151 NW Bogard Rd • Silverdale, WA 98383-9709

Skamokawa

Skamokawa Library • 11 Schoolhouse Rd, P.O. Box 83 • Skamokawa, WA 98647 • (360) 795-8605

Snohomish

Online Pioneers • P.O. Box 1571 • Snohomish, WA 98291-1571 • (425) 776-7978 • *Online Pioneers*

Snohomish Historical Society & Archives • Blackman House Museum, 118 Avenue B, P.O. Box 174 • Snohomish, WA 98290 • (360) 568-5235 • http://www.snohomishhistoricalsociety.com

Snoqualmie

Northwest Railway Museum Archives • 38625 SE King St, P.O. Box 459 • Snoqualmie, WA 98065 • (425) 888-3030 • http://www.trainmuseum.org • *Sounder*

Soap Lake

Shepherd Research • 191 Ephrata Ave NW • Soap Lake, WA 98851 • Shepherd Flock

Week-Weeks-Weekes Family Organization • 191 Ephrata Ave NW • Soap Lake, WA 98851 • *Weak Link: Week-Weekes-Weeks*

South Bend

Pacific County Historical Society & Archives • Historical Museum, 1008 W Robert Bush Dr, P.O. Box P • South Bend, WA 98586 • (360) 875-5224 • http://www.pacifcohistory.org • *Sou'wester*

South Cle Elum

Northeast Kittias County Genealogical Society • P.O. Box 303 • South Cle Elum, WA 98943

South Kent

Segler Family Organization • 28411 59th Ave • South Kent, WA 98032 • (253) 852-4557 • *Segler, Seagler, Siegler, Sigler Researchers Exchange*

Spanaway

Bunnell-Bonnell Research • 32717 41st Ave, P.O. Box 4282 • Spanaway, WA 98387 • (253) 847-3357 • *Bunnell-Bonnell Newsletter*

Markwell Family Association • 1921 E 208th St #60 • Spanaway, WA 98387 • *Markwell Newsletter*

Spanaway Historical Society • 812 176th St S • Spanaway, WA 98387 • (253) 536-6655

Spokane

Alexander Research • 6812 E 3rd • Spokane, WA 99212 • (509) 928-1808 • *All About Alexander*

Barton-Higgs Research • S 2707 Rhyolite Rd • Spokane, WA 99203 • (509) 747-6969 • *Barton Newsletter; Higgs Heritage*

Bell Enterprises • W 2418 Wellesley, P.O. Box 10328 • Spokane, WA 99209-1328 • (509) 327-7958 • Howell Lines; Dalton Data; Henderson Highlights; McCoy Material; Van Zandt Ancestors; Becker Banner; Lee Lines; Wilcox Excerpts

Bill(s) Family Research • 511 S Park Rd #133 • Spokane, WA 99212-0551 • (509) 891-9577

Brotherton-Hunters Family Association • 2727 E 53rd Ave #H207 • Spokane, WA 99223-7999 • (509) 448-4541 • Brotherton Family Tie

Catholic Diocese of Spokane Archives • 1023 W Riverside Ave, P.O. Box 48 • Spokane, WA 99210-0048 • (509) 358-7349

Cobb-Hobby-McMillan-Love-McAlpin Family Researchers • 511 S Park Rd #133 • Spokane, WA 99212-0551 • (509) 891-9577

Eastern Washington Genealogical Society • W 906 Main Ave, P.O. Box 1826 • Spokane, WA 99210-1826 • (509) 483-1257 • http://www.rootsweb.com/~waewgs/ • *Eastern Washington Genealogical Society Bulletin*

Eastern Washington State Historical Society & Archives • Northwest Museum, W 2316 1st Ave • Spokane, WA 98204-1099 • (509) 456-3931 • http://www.northwestmuseum.org • *Museum Notes*

Foley Center Library • Gonzaga Univ, E 502 Boone Ave • Spokane, WA 99258-0095 • (509) 323-5931 • http://www.foley.gonzaga.edu

Genealogy of the Kemble (Kimble) Family • 10419 N Mayberry Dr #9 • Spokane, WA 99218-1508 • (509) 464-4186

Harriet Cheney Cowles Memorial Library • Whitworth College, 300 W Hawthorne Rd, MS 0901 • Spokane, WA 99251-0001 • (509) 777-4491 • http://www.whitworth.edu/library

Jesuit Oregon Province Archives & Library • Gonzaga University, Special Coll, Foley Ctr • Spokane, WA 99258-0001 • (509) 323-3814 • http://www.foley.gonzaga.edu/spcoll/jopa.html

Kendall Research • P.O. Box 9265 • Spokane, WA 99209 • *Kendall Kin*

Lauri-Lines • S 2827 Ivory • Spokane, WA 99203 • (509) 624-0533 • *Ross Records and Lines; Fish Families Records and Lines; Layman-Lehman Records and Lines*

Lewis-McClure-Sutton Research • E 13124 Nixon • Spokane, WA 99216 • *Lewis Lineages; McClure Memento; Sutton Seeker*

Museum of Native American Cultures Library • 2316 W 1st Ave • Spokane, WA 99204-1099 • (509) 456-3931 • http://www.northwestmuseum.org

Name Game Enterprises • S 4204 Conklin St • Spokane, WA 99203-6235 • (509) 747-4903 • *Parker Papers; Hastings Herald; New York Wills: Richmond Co, Staten Island; Tennessee-Kentucky Queries; Robertson Report; Wade World*

Pence Publications • 11009 E 3rd Ave #67 • Spokane, WA 99206-5294 • (509) 235-8614 • *Brand(t) Names; Barnes Bulletin; Walker Footprints; Scottish Queries*

Perkins Research • N 5803 Ash • Spokane, WA 99205-6807 • (509) 325-5919 • *Perkins Press*

Potter-Oswald-Gilbert Family Association • 8002 W Mission Rd • Spokane, WA 99224-9572 • (509) 624-4118 • *Potter Profiles; Gilbert Gallery; Oswald Outlines*

Ryan Family • 10419 N Mayberry Dr #9 • Spokane, WA 99218-1508 • (509) 464-4186

Spokane County Historic Preservation Office • general delivery • Spokane, WA 99201 • (509) 625-6983

Spokane County Library District • 4322 N Argonne Rd • Spokane, WA 99212-1868 • (509) 924-4122

Spokane Public Library • 906 W Main St • Spokane, WA 99201-0976 • (509) 444-5336 • http://www.spokanelibrary.org

Washington

Topp of the Line • W 1304 Cliffwood Ct • Spokane, WA 99218-2917 • (509) 467-2299 • http://www.members.home.com/toppline/homepage • *Bush Branches; Carpenter Chronicles; Virginia-West Virginia Queries; Butcher Block; Baldwin By-Lines*

Weidner Words • W 2206 Borden Rd • Spokane, WA 99204-9668 • (509) 448-9263 • http://www.cet.com/~weidnerc/ • *Chamberlain Chain; New York State Queries*

Woodworth Ancestral Lines • 5905 W Bedford Ct • Spokane, WA 99208-9023 • http://homepages.rootsweb.com/~wdwrth/wdwrthlinks/Lines.html

Zeimantz Family Association • 920 E 26th St • Spokane, WA 99203 • (509) 838-6800

Sprague
Southeastern Lincoln County Historical Society • general delivery • Sprague, WA 99032

Stanwood
Camwood Genealogical Group • P.O. Box 41 • Stanwood, WA 98292

Stanwood Area Historical Society • 27112 102nd Ave NW • Stanwood, WA 98292 • (360) 629-6110

Steilacoom
Steilacoom Historical Museum Association & Library • 122 Main St, P.O. Box 88016 • Steilacoom, WA 98388 • (253) 584-4133 • *Steilacoom Historical Museum Quarterly*

Stevenson
Columbia George Interpretive Center Archives • 990 SW Rock Creek Dr, P.O. Box396 • Stevenson, WA 98648 • (509) 427-8211 • http://www.columbiagorge.org • *Explorations*

Sultan
Sky Valley Genealogical Society • 912 1st St • Sultan, WA 98294

Sumner
Heritage Quest Research Library & Bookstore • 909 Main St, Suite 5 • Sumner, WA 98390 • (253) 863-1806 • http://members.aol.com/hqrl/

Julia Keane-Otto Edwin Larson-Harmon Franklin Havener-Katherine Eugenia Cooper Family Organization • 323 Wood Ave • Sumner, WA 98390

Sumner Genealogical Group • c/o Sumner Public Library • Sumner, WA 98390

Sunnyside
Sunnyside Museum and Historical Association & Library • 704 S 4th St, P.O. Box 782 • Sunnyside, WA 98944 • (509) 837-6010 • http://www.ci.sunnyside.wa.us/parksandrec/museum.htm

Suquamish
Suquamish Tribal Cultural Center Archives • 15838 Sandy Hook Rd, P.O. Box 498 • Suquamish, WA 98392 • (360) 598-3311 • http://www.suquamish.nsn.us

Tacoma
Camp 6 Logging Museum Archives • Point Defiance Park, P.O. Box 340 • Tacoma, WA 98407 • (253) 752-0047 • http://www.camp-6-museum.org

Case Research • P.O. Box 98234 • Tacoma, WA 98499 • (253) 531-2520 • *Brief Case: Case Family*

City of Tacoma Historic Preservation Office • general delivery • Tacoma, WA 98401 • (253) 591-5220

Clan Donnachaidh Society, Pacific Northwest States • 262 E 68th St • Tacoma, WA 98404 • (253) 472-2044

Dr Martin Luther King, Jr Library • 1902 S Cedar St • Tacoma, WA 98405 • (253) 591-5166

Fort Misqually Historic Site Archives • 5400 N Pearl St #11 • Tacoma, WA 98407 • (253) 591-5339 • http://www.fortnisqually.org • Occurences

Genealogical Society of Pierce County • P.O. Box 98634 • Tacoma, WA 98498

Helland Reunion • 10625 S Broadway • Tacoma, WA 98444 • (253) 535-9404

Historic Fort Steilacoom Archives • 9601 Steilacoom Blvd SW • Tacoma, WA 98498 • (253) 756-3923 • http://www.fortsteilacoom.com • Historic Fort Steilacoom Newsletter

James Happy Family Organization • 11617 Gravelly Lake Dr • Tacoma, WA 98499 • (253) 588-2585

Longmire Family Organization • 1718 N Mildred St • Tacoma, WA 98406 • (253) 752-1496

Major(s) Productions • P.O. Box 7357 • Tacoma, WA 98407

McChord Air Museum Archives • AFB, P.O. Box 4205 • Tacoma, WA 98438 • (253) 982-2485 • http://www.mcchordmuseum.org • *Rip Chord*

Morgan Eli Asbury Lasley Family Organization • 2904 Sunset Dr W • Tacoma, WA 98466 • (253) 564-2755

Pacific Northwest Conference Depository, United Methodist Church • Collins Memorial Library, 1500 N Warner • Tacoma, WA 98416 • (253) 627-0700

Pearl A Wanamaker Library • Tacoma Community College, 6501 S 19th St • Tacoma, WA 98466-6100 • (253) 566-5134 • http://www.tacoma.ctc.edu/library

Pierce County Library System • 3005 112th St E • Tacoma, WA 98446-2215 • (253) 536-6500 • http://www.pcl.lib.wa.us

Points Northeast Historical Society • general delivery • Tacoma, WA 98401 • (253) 927-2536

Region 1 Archives, Evangelical Lutheran Church in America • Mortvedt Library, Pacific Lutheran Univ, Park & 121st St • Tacoma, WA 98447-0013 • (253) 535-7500 • http://www.plu.edu/~libr

Shelburn(e) Surname Organization • 8653 Zircon Dr SW • Tacoma, WA 98498

Sinex Reunion • 3631 N Mullen St • Tacoma, WA 98407-4124 • http://www.fortunecity.com/millenium/savannah/252/homepage.htm • *Sinex Reunion Newsletter*

Tacoma Family History Center • 5915 S 12th • Tacoma, WA 98465 • (253) 564-1103 • http://www.familysearch.org

Tacoma Historical Society • 3712 S Cedar St • Tacoma, WA 98409 • (253) 472-3738 • *City of Destiny Newsletter*

Tacoma Public Library • 1120 Tacoma Ave S • Tacoma, WA 98402-2098 • (253) 591-5622 • http://www.tpl.lib.wa.us

Tacoma Public Library-Fern Hill Branch • 765 S 84th St • Tacoma, WA 98444 • (253) 591-5620

Tacoma Public Library-Kobetich Branch • 212 Brown's Point Blvd NE • Tacoma, WA 98422 • (253) 591-5630

Tacoma Public Library-Moore Branch • 215 S 56th St • Tacoma, WA 98408 • (253) 591-5650

Tacoma Public Library-Mottet Branch • 3523 East G Street • Tacoma, WA 98404 • (253) 591-5660

Tacoma Public Library-South Tacoma • 3711 S 56th St • Tacoma, WA 98409 • (253) 591-5670

Tacoma Public Library-Swasey Branch • 7001 6th Ave • Tacoma, WA 98406 • (253) 591-5680

Tacoma Public Library-Wheelock Branch • 3722 N 26th St • Tacoma, WA 98407 • (253) 591-5640

Tacoma-Pierce County Genealogical Society & Library • 4507 N 27th St, P.O. Box 1952 • Tacoma, WA 98401-1952 • (253) 572-6650 • http://www.rootsweb.com/~watpcgs/tpcgs.htm • *Researcher*

Washington State Historical Society • 315 N Stadium Way • Tacoma, WA 98403 • (253) 798-5914

Washington State Historical Society & Archives • Historical Museum, 1911 Pacific Ave • Tacoma, WA 98402 • (253) 272-9747 • http://www.washingtonhistory.org • *Columbia: Magazine of Northwest History; History Highlights; Pacific Northwest Quarterly*

Zurial Hall Family Organization • 1610 S Highland • Tacoma, WA 98465 • (253) 565-4564

Tenino
South Thurston County Historical Society & Archives • Depot Museum, 399 W Park St, P.O. Box 339 • Tenino, WA 98589 • (360) 264-4321 • *South Thurston County Historical Society Newsletter*

Thorp
Thorp Mill Town Historical Preservation Society • P.O. Box 7 • Thorp, WA 98946 • (509) 964-9640

Tonasket
Tonasket Genealogical Society • P.O. Box 84 • Tonasket, WA 98855 • (509) 826-0837

Toppenish
Northern Pacific Railway Museum Archives • 10 Asotin Ave, P.O. Box 889 • Toppenish, WA 98948 • (509) 930-7210 • http://www.nprymuseum.org • *Northern Pacific Railway Museum Newsletter*

Toppenish Museum Archives • 1 S Elm • Toppenish, WA 98948 • (509) 865-4510 • *Toppenish Museum Newsletter*

Yakima National Museum Archives • Hwy 97, P.O. Box 151 • Toppenish, WA 98948 • (509) 865-2800 • http://www.wolfenet.com/~yingis/hert.html

TumTum
Pioneer Publications • P.O. Box 1179 • TumTum, WA 99034-1179 • (509) 276-9841 • *Farr Footnotes*

Tumwater
Timberland Regional Library • 415 Tumwater Blvd SW • Tumwater, WA 98501-5717 • (360) 943-5001 • http://www.trlib.org

Union Gap
Central Washington Agricultural Museum Archives • 4508 Main St, P.O. Box 3008 • Union Gap, WA 98903 • (509) 457-8735 • *Central Washington Agricultural Museum Newsletter*

Isaac Wells Family Organization • 1802 S 18th St • Union Gap, WA 98903 • (509) 248-3082

Vancouver
Clark County Genealogical Society & Library • 711 Grand Blvd, P.O. Box 2728 • Vancouver, WA 98668-2728 • (360) 750-5688 • http://www.ccgs-wa.org • *Trail Breakers*; *Newsletter of the Clark County Genealogical Society*; *Clark County Genealogical Society Quarterly Directory*

Clark County Historical Society & Archives • Historical Museum, 1511 Main St, P.O. Box 1834 • Vancouver, WA 98663 • (360) 695-4681 • *Clark County History*

Fort Vancouver Historical Society of Clark County • 1511 Main Street, P.O. Box 1834 • Vancouver, WA 98663

Fort Vancouver National Historic Site Library • 612 E Reserve St • Vancouver, WA 98661-3897 • (360) 696-7659 • http://www.nps.gov/fova

Fort Vancouver Regional Library • 1007 E Mill Plain Blvd • Vancouver, WA 98663 • (360) 695-1566 • http://www.fvrl.org

Neeley's Seedlings • 2114-B NE Stapleton Rd • Vancouver, WA 98661 • (564) 694-1826

Pearson Air Museum Archives • 1115 E 5th St • Vancouver, WA 98661 • (360) 694-7026 • http://www.pearsonairmuseum.org

Stevens Database • 6609 Montana Ln • Vancouver, WA 98661-7436 • (206) 694-1509

William McCalley Moultrie Family Organization • 12009 SE 11th St • Vancouver, WA 98664 • (564) 892-8704

Womack Family • 2415 E Mill Plain Blvd #31 • Vancouver, WA 98661-4369 • (564) 694-1276 • http://freepages.genealogy.rootsweb.com/~rgwomack/index3.htm

Vashon
Vashon Maury Island Heritage Association & Archives • Historical Museum, P.O. Box 723 • Vashon, WA 98070 • (206) 567-4462 • *Vashon Maury Island Heritage Association Newsletter*

Walla Walla
Penrose Memorial Library • Whitman College, 345 Boyer Ave • Walla Walla, WA 99362 • (509) 527-5915 • http://www.whitman.edu/departments/penrose/

Thomas John Harrison Family Organization • 1420 Garfield • Walla Walla, WA 99362

Walla Walla Public Library • 238 E Alder • Walla Walla, WA 99362 • (509) 527-4550 • http://www.ci.walla-walla.wa.us

Walla Walla Valley Genealogical Society • P.O. Box 115 • Walla Walla, WA 99362-0115 • *Blue Mountain Heritage*

Walla Walla Valley Pioneer and Historical Society & Library • Fort Walla Walla Musuem, 755 Myra Rd, P.O. Box 1616 • Walla Walla, WA 99362 • (509) 525-7703 • http://www.fortwallawallamuseum.org

Whitman Mission National Historic Site Library • 328 Whitman Mission Rd • Walla Walla, WA 99362 • (509) 522-6360 • http://www.nps.gov/whmi

Washougal
Croswell Surname Organization • 5909 W Street • Washougal, WA 98671

Waterville
Douglas County Genealogical Society • P.O. Box 580 • Waterville, WA 98858

Douglas County Historical Society • 113 W Locust • Waterville, WA 98858 • (509) 745-8800

Wellpinit
Spokane Tribe of Indians Tribal Council • P.O. Box 359 • Wellpinit, WA 99040-0359 • (509) 258-7320 • *Rawhide Press*

Wenatchee
Genealogical Society of North Central Washington & Library • 133 S Mission St, P.O. Box 5280 • Wenatchee, WA 98807-5280 • (509) 664-3346 • *Appleland Bulletin*

John A Brown Library • Wenatchee Valley College, 1300 5th St • Wenatchee, WA 98801 • (509) 682-6710 • http://wvc.ctc.edu/library

North Central Regional Library • 238 Olds Station Rd • Wenatchee, WA 98801-8103 • (509) 663-1117 • http://www.ncrl.org

Robert Fitzhugh Family Organization • 3318 Burch Mountain Rd • Wenatchee, WA 98801 • (509) 663-1254

Rocky Beach Dam Museum Archives • P.O. Box 1231 • Wenatchee, WA 98807 • (509) 663-8121 • http://www.chelandpud.org

Wenatchee Area Genealogical Society & Library • 113 S Mission, P.O. Box 5280 • Wenatchee, WA 98807-5280 • (509) 664-3346 • http://www.crcwnet.com/~wags/ • *Appleland Bulletin*

Wenatchee Valley Museum Archives • 127 S Mission • Wenatchee, WA 98801 • (509) 664-3340 • http://www.wenatcheevalleymuseum.com • *Wenatchee Valley Museum Newsletter*

West Richland
Mid-Columbia Library • 4101 E Lattin Rd • West Richland, WA 99353 • (509) 627-0285

Westport
Westport-South Beach Historical Society & Archives • Maritime Museum, 2201 Westhaven Dr, P.O. Box 1074 • Westport, WA 98595-1074 • (360) 268-0078 • http://www.westportwa.com/museum • *Foghorn*

White Swan
Fort Simcoe Museum Archives • 5150 Fort Simcoe Rd • White Swan, WA 98952 • (509) 874-2372

Wilbur
Hesseltine Public Library • 14 NW Division, P.O. Box 185 • Wilbur, WA 99185-0185 • (509) 647-5828

Washington

Winlock

John R Jackson House Museum Archives • 4583 Jackson Hwy • Winlock, WA 98596 • (360) 864-2643

Winthrop

Shafer Historical Museum Archives • 285 Castle Ave, P.O. Box 46 • Winthrop, WA 98862 • (509) 996-2712

Woodinville

Chenoweth-Laprath Family in America • P.O. Box 1188 • Woodinville, WA 98072 • http://www.accessone.com/~jegge/laprath.htm

Woodland

Cedar Creek Grist Mill Archives • P.O. Box 1404 • Woodland, WA 98674 • (360) 225-5832

Guild Reunion • 1620 Guild Rd • Woodland, WA 98674 • (564) 225-8752

Yacolt

Pomeroy Living History Museum Archives • 20902 NE Lucia Falls Rd • Yacolt, WA 98675 • (360) 686-3537 • http://www.pomeroyfarm.org • *Down on the Farm*

Yakima

Case-Walden Reunion • 782 Code Rd • Yakima, WA 98908

English-Schlegel-Schlagel-Linse-Schlager Family Organization • 731 Firing Center Rd • Yakima, WA 98901 • (509) 248-3672

King Research • 1602 E Beech • Yakima, WA 98901 • *King Quarterly*

Purviance Research • 105 Washington Ave #29 • Yakima, WA 98903 • (509) 575-0776 • *Purviance Family News and Notes*

Yakima Valley Genealogical Society & Library • 221 East B St, P.O. Box 445 • Yakima, WA 98907-0445 • (509) 248-1328 • http://www.rootsweb.com/~wayvgs/ • *Yakima Valley Genealogical Society Bulletin*

Yakima Valley Historical Association & Archives • Historical Museum, 2105 Tieton Dr • Yakima, WA 98902 • (509) 248-0747 • http://www.yakimavalleymuseum.org • *Museum Musette*

Yakima Valley Regional Library • 102 N 3rd St • Yakima, WA 98901-2759 • (509) 452-8541 • http://www.yvrl.lib.org

Yelm

Yelm Prairie Historical Society • general delivery • Yelm, WA 98597 • (360) 458-5909

WEST VIRGINIA

Alma
Dragoo Family Association • HC 74, Box 61 • Alma, WV 26320 • *Dragoo Family News*

Alum Creek
Hamlin-Lincoln County Public Library-Alum Creek Public • P.O. Box 530 • Alum Creek, WV 25003-0530 • (304) 756-9211

Anstead
Hawks Nest State Park Archives • Route 60, P.O. Box 857 • Anstead, WV 25812 • (304) 658-5212 • http://www.hawksnestsp.com

Arthurdale
Arthurdale Heritage & Archives • Historical Museum, P.O. Box 850 • Arthurdale, WV 26520 • (304) 864-3959 • http://www.arthurdaleheritage.org • *Arthurdale Heritage Newsletter*

Athens
Mercer County Genealogical and Historical Society • 101 Caldwell St • Athens, WV 24712 • (304) 384-9661

Beckley
Raleigh County Public Library • 221 N Kanawha St • Beckley, WV 25801-4716 • (304) 255-0511 • http://rcpl.lib.wv.us

Beech Bottom
Brooke County Genealogical Society • P.O. Box 144 • Beech Bottom, WV 26030

Belington
Belington Public Library • 512 Elliott Ave, P.O. Box 878 • Belington, WV 26250-0878 • (304) 823-1026

Berkeley Springs
Morgan County Historical and Genealogical Society • c/o Morgan County Public Library, 204 N Washington, P.O. Box 52 • Berkeley Springs, WV 25411 • (304) 258-3350 • *Morgan County Historical and Genealogical Society Newsletter*

Morgan County Public Library • 105 Congress St • Berkeley Springs, WV 25411 • (304) 258-3350

Museum of the Berkeley Springs Archives • P.O. Box 99 • Berkeley Springs, WV 25411 • (304) 258-3743 • *Museum of the Berkeley Springs Newsletter*

Shockey Family Memorial Fellowship • Route 2, Box 126D • Berkeley Springs, WV 25411 • (304) 258-5616 • *Shockey Newsletter*

Bethany
Historic Bethany • Bethany College, P.O. Box 478 • Bethany, WV 26022 • (304) 829-4258 • http://www.historicbethanywv.com • *Campbell Light*

Beverly
Randolph County Museum • Main St, P.O. Box 1164 • Beverly, WV 26253 • (304) 636-0841

Bluefield
Craft Memorial Library • 600 Commerce St, P.O. Box 4297 • Bluefield, WV 24701 • (304) 325-3943

Bradley
John Van Puffelen Library • Appalachian Bible College, 5701 Robert C Byrd Dr, P.O. Box ABC • Bradley, WV 25818 • (304) 877-6428 • http://www.abc.edu

Bridgeport
Bridgeport Public Library • 1200 Johnson Ave • Bridgeport, WV 26330 • (304) 842-8248 • http://www.bridgeportwv.com

Mullenuex Family Reunion • 406 Forest Dr • Bridgeport, WV 26330 • (304) 8420-2215

Buckhannon
Annie Merner Pfeiffer Library • West Virginia Wesleyan College, 59 College Ave • Buckhannon, WV 26201 • (304) 473-8059 • http://www.wvwc.edu/lib/

Upshur County Genealogical Society • P.O. Box 753 • Buckhannon, WV 26201

Upshur County Historical Society • P.O. Box 753 • Buckhannon, WV 26201 • http://www.msys.net/uchs • *Upshur County Historical Society Newsletter*

Burlington
Mineral County Historical Landmark Commission • Route 1, Box 94 • Burlington, WV 26710

Mineral County Historical Society • Route 1, Box 94 • Burlington, WV 26710

Ceredo
Ceredo Historical Society & Archives • Historical Museum, 601 Main St • Ceredo, WV 25507 • (304) 453-3025

Chapmanville
Chapmanville Public Library • 299 Vance St • Chapmanville, WV 25508 • (304) 855-3405 • *Library Paper*

Charles Town
Hansard-Brobeck-Brubeck Family of Virginia • RR 2 Box 166 • Charles Town, WV 25414-9643

Jefferson County Museum Archives • 200 E Washington St • Charles Town, WV 25414 • (304) 725-8628

Old Charles Town Library • 200 E Washington St • Charles Town, WV 25414 • (304) 725-2208

Charleston
Division of Archives and Records, City of Charleston • Cultural Center, Capitol Complex, 1900 Kanawha Blvd E • Charleston, WV 25305-0620 • (304) 558-0230 • http://www.wvculture.org/history

Kanawha County Public Library • 123 Capitol St • Charleston, WV 25301 • (304) 343-4646 • http://kanawha.lib.wv.us

Kanawha Valley Historical and Preservation Society • P.O. Box 2283 • Charleston, WV 25328 • (304) 342-7676 • *Up and Down the Valley*

Lilly Historical and Genealogical Society • 5267 Big Tyler Rd • Charleston, WV 25313 • *Lilly Letter*

Mining Your History Foundation • Cultural Center,1900 Kanawha Blvd E • Charleston, WV 25305-0009 • (304) 269-7091 • http://www.rootsweb.com/~myhf • *Mountain News*

Schoenbaum Library • University of Charleston, 2300 MacCorkle Ave SE • Charleston, WV 25304-1099 • (304) 357-4913 • http://www.ucwv.edu/library • *Library Leaves*

Sunrise Museum Archives • 746 Myrtle Rd • Charleston, WV 25314 • (304) 344-8035

Tazewell County Historical Society • 100 E Main St • Charleston, WV 25301 • (304) 988-4069

Tompkins Family of Washington County, Georgia • 1995 Parkwood Rd • Charleston, WV 25314 • (304) 346-2093 • http://www.mindspring.com/~jburval/genealogy/tompkins.htm

West Virginia Historical Society & Archives • Historical Museum, 1900 Kanawha Blvd E • Charleston, WV 25305-0300 • (304) 558-0220 • http://www.wvculture.org • *West Virginia Historical Society Newsletter*

Clarksburg
Casto-Eakle Family Gathering • 2000 Williams Ave • Clarksburg, WV 26301 • (304) 623-2674 • *Casto-Eakle Family Newsletter*

Clarksburg-Harrison Public Library • 404 W Pike St • Clarksburg, WV 26301 • (304) 627-2236 • http://www.clarksburglibrary.info/

Harrison County Genealogical Society • P.O. Box 387 • Clarksburg, WV 26302-0387 • *Harrison County Genealogical Society Newsletter*

Clifftop
West Virginia Camp Washington Museum Archives • Route 1, Box 5 • Clifftop, WV 25831 • (304) 438-3005 • http://www.svculture.org/sites/carver.html

Dunbar
Roose-Ruoss National Family Reunion (Ruse-Ruiz-Russ) • 2207 W Virginia Ave #A • Dunbar, WV 25064 • (304) 768-1647

West Virginia

Elizabeth
Beauchamp Newman House Museum Archives • Court St, P.O. Box 621 • Elizabeth, WV 26143 • (304) 275-6534

Dora Bee Woodyard Memorial Library • Mulberry St, P.O. Box 340 • Elizabeth, WV 26143-0340 • (304) 275-4295 • Book News

Elkins
Allegheny Regional Family Historical Society • P.O. Box 1804 • Elkins, WV 26241 • http://www.swcp.com/~dhickman/arfhs.html • *Allegheny Regional Journal*

Randolph County Historical Society & Archives • Historical Museum, P.O. Box 1164 • Elkins, WV 26241 • (304) 636-1959 • *Magazine of History and Biography*

Elkview
West Virginia Genealogy Society & Library • 5238 Elk River Rd N, P.O. Box 249 • Elkview, WV 25071 • (304) 965-1179 • *LOG: Ledger of Genealogy*

Fairmont
Fairmont Historical Society & Archives • Historical Museum, 200 Jackson St, Rm 403 • Fairmont, WV 26554 • (304) 367-5398

Marion County Genealogical Club & Archives • c/o Marion County Library, 321 Monroe St • Fairmont, WV 26554 • (304) 366-1210 • *Genealogy Gleanings*

Marion County Library • 321 Monroe St • Fairmont, WV 26554-2952 • (304) 366-1210 • http://www.marioncountypubliclibrary.org

Pricketts Fort Archives • Route 3, Box 407 • Fairmont, WV 26554 • (304) 363-3030 • http://www.prickettsfort.org • *Gatepost*

Falling Waters
Kershner-Seylar-Bucher Family Association • P.O. Box 1131 • Falling Waters, WV 25419-1131 • (304) 274-3104

Kump Klan • 210 Cliff Turn • Falling Waters, WV 25419-9530 • (304) 274-3104

Fayetteville
Fayette County Public Libraries-Fayetteville Branch • 200 W Maple Ave • Fayetteville, WV 25840 • (304) 574-0070

Franklin
Pendleton County Historical Society • Main St, P.O. Box 383 • Franklin, WV 26807 • (304) 358-7366

Glenville
Gilmer County Historical Society • 302 E Main St, P.O. Box 235 • Glenville, WV 26351 • (304) 462-4295 • *Gilmer County Historical Society Newsletter*

Gilmer County Historical Society & Library • 706 Mineral Rd • Glenville, WV 26351 • (304) 462-5620 • *Gilmer County Historical Society Newsletter*

Gilmer Public Library • 214 Walnut St • Glenville, WV 26351 • (304) 462-5620

Robert F Kidd Library • Glenville State College, 100 High St • Glenville, WV 26351 • (304) 462-4109 • http://www.glenville.edu/resources/rfk_library/

Grafton
Taylor County Historical and Genealogical Society • c/o Taylor County Library, 200 Beech St, P.O. Box 522 • Grafton, WV 26354 • (304) 265-6121 • *Taylor County in Profile*

Taylor County Public Library • 200 Beech St • Grafton, WV 26354 • (304) 265-6121 • http://taylor.clark.lib.wv.us

Grantsville
Calhoun County Historical and Genealogical Society • P.O. Box 242 • Grantsville, WV 26147 • (304) 354-7614 • *Calhoun County Lines and Links*; *Calhoun County Historical and Genealogical Society Newsletter*

Greenbank
Blackhurst Burner Reunion • P.O. Box 184 • Greenbank, WV 24944 • (304) 456-4815

Griffithsville
Lincoln County Genealogical Society • P.O. Box 92 • Griffithsville, WV 25521 • (304) 524-7326 • *Who, When and Where of Lincoln County, West Virginia*; *Lincoln Lineage*

Hamlin
Hamlin-Lincoln County Public Library • 7999 Lynn Ave • Hamlin, WV 25523 • (304) 824-5481 • http://www.cabell.lib.wv.us

Harpers Ferry
Bolivar-Harpers Ferry Public Library • 600 Polk St • Harpers Ferry, WV 25425 • (304) 535-2301 • http://www.youseemore.com/bhf

Harpers Ferry Center History Collection • Fillmore St, P.O. Box 50 • Harpers Ferry, WV 25425-0050 • (304) 535-6261 • http://www.nps.gov/hfc • *Courier*

Harrisville
Mullanix-Snider Family Reunion • RD 2, Box 128A • Harrisville, WV 26362 • (304) 643-2540

Ritchie County Public Library • 130 Court St • Harrisville, WV 26232 • (304) 643-2717 • http://www.park.lib.wv.us

Helvetia
Historical Society of Helvetia & Archives • Historical Museum, P.O. Box 42 • Helvetia, WV 26224 • (304) 924-6435

Henderson
Mason County Genealogical and Historical Society • general delivery • Henderson, WV 25106

Hillsboro
Pearl S Buck Birthplace Museum Archives • Route 219 N, P.O. Box 126 • Hillsboro, WV 24946 • (304) 653-4430 • http://www.pearlsbuckbirthplace.com

Hinton
Bluestone Museum Archives • Route 87, Box 10 • Hinton, WV 25951 • (304) 466-1454

Horner
Central West Virginia Genealogical and Historical Library • Abbotts Runn Rd, Old Rt 33, P.O. Box 56 • Horner, WV 26372-0056

Hacker's Creek Pioneer Descendants • c/o Central West Virginia Genealogical and Historical Library, Abbotts Runn Rd, Old Rt 33, P.O. Box 56 • Horner, WV 26372-0056

Huntington
Cabell County Public Library • 455 9th St Plaza • Huntington, WV 25701-1417 • (304) 528-5700 • http://www.cabell.lib.wv.us

Cabell-Wayne County Historical Society • 11th St & 2nd Ave, P.O. Box 9412 • Huntington, WV 25704 • *Cabell-Wayne Historical Society Newsletter*

Heritage Farm Museum and Village Archives • 3350 Harvey Rd • Huntington, WV 24704 • (304) 522-1244 • http://www.heritagefarmmuseum.com

Huntington Railroad Historical Society • 1323 8th Ave • Huntington, WV 25701 • (304) 523-0364

Huntington Railroad Museum Archives • 14th & Memorial Blvd • Huntington, WV 25705 • (304) 523-0364 • http://www.newrivertrain.com • *Gondolla Gazette*

James E Morrow Library • Marshall Univ, 400 Hal Greer Blvd • Huntington, WV 25705 • (304) 696-2343 • http://www.marshall.edu

KYOWVA Genealogical Society & Library • 232 Main St, P.O. Box 1254 • Huntington, WV 25715-1254 • (304) 525-4367 • http://www.rootsweb.com/~wvkgs/ • *KYOWVA Genealogical Society Newsletter*

Lineages • P.O. Box 1264 • Huntington, WV 25714 • *Hodges Family Newsletter*; *Allan-Allen Family Workbook*

Museum of Radio and Technology Archives • 1640 Florence Ave • Huntington, WV 25701 • (304) 525-8890 • http://www.mrtwv.org • *Radio Museum News*

Hurricane
Museum in the Community Archives • 3 Valley Park Dr, P.O. Box 423 • Hurricane, WV 25526 • (304) 562-0484 • http://www.museuminthecommunity.org • *Museum in the Community Newsletter*

Putnam County Library • 4219 State Route 34 • Hurricane, WV 25526 • (304) 757-7308 • http://putnam.lib.wv.us • *Putnam County Library Newsletter*

Iaeger
Roberts Reunion • general delivery • Iaeger, WV 24844 • (304) 938-2671

Institute
Drain-Jordan Library • West Virginia State College, Campus Box 166, P.O. Box 1002 • Institute, WV 25112-1002 • (304) 766-3135 • http://library.wvsc.edu

Inwood
Musselman-South Berkeley Community Library • 126 Excellence Way, Rte 11 S • Inwood, WV 25428 • (304) 229-2220 • http://www.youseemore.com/martinsburgberkeley/

Jane Lew
Hacker's Creek Pioneer Descendants • RR1, Box 238, P.O. Box 37 • Jane Lew, WV 26378-9755 • (304) 269-7091 • *Hacker's Creek Journal*

Kenova
Collis P Huntington Railroad Historical Society • 1429 Chestnut St • Kenova, WV 25530 • (304) 453-1641

Kerens
Arbogast Reunion • Route 1, Box 73A • Kerens, WV 26276 • (304) 745-4285

Keyser
Mary F Shipper Library • Potomac State College of West Virginia, 101 Fort Ave • Keyser, WV 26726 • (304) 788-6901 • http://www.potomacstatecollege.edu

Kingwood
Kingwood Public Library • 205 W Main St • Kingwood, WV 26537 • (304) 329-1499 • *Highlights*

Lahmansville
Grant County Genealogical and Historical Society • general delivery • Lahmansville, WV 26731

Lewisburg
Fort Savannah Museum Library • 204 N Jefferson St • Lewisburg, WV 24901 • (304) 645-3055

Greenbriar Valley Campus Library • New River Community & Technical College, 101 Church St • Lewisburg, WV 24901-0151 • (304) 647-6575

Greenbrier Historical Society & Library • 200 N Jefferson St • Lewisburg, WV 24901 • (304) 645-7746 • http://www.greenbrierhistorical.org • *Greenbrier Historical Society Journal*; *Appalachian Springs*

North House Museum Archives • 301 W Washington St • Lewisburg, WV 24901 • (304) 645-3398 • http://www.greenbrierhistorical.org • *Appalachian Springs*

Sons of the American Revolution, West Virginia Chapter • 132 N Court St • Lewisburg, WV 24901

Logan
Aracoma High School Historical Society • Cole St • Logan, WV 25601 • (304) 752-6500

Logan County Genealogical Society • P.O. Box 1959 • Logan, WV 25601 • Logan County Ancestree

Lost Creek
Watters Smith Memorial State Park Archives • Duck Creek Rd, P.O. Box 296 • Lost Creek, WV 26385 • (304) 745-3081

Madison
Boone County Genealogical Society & Library • P.O. Box 306 • Madison, WV 25130-0306 • (304) 369-2769 • *Kith and Kin of Boone County, West Virginia*; *Boone Genealogical Quarterly*

Boone-Madison Public Library • 375 Main St • Madison, WV 25130-1295 • (304) 369-7842 • http://boone.lib.wv.us

Marlinton
Pocahontas County Historical Society & Archives • Historical Museum, 810 2nd Ave • Marlinton, WV 24954 • (304) 799-4973 • *Pocahontas County Newsletter*

Martinsburg
Berkeley County Genealogical and Historical Society & Archives • Belle Boyd House, 126 E Race St, P.O. Box 1624 • Martinsburg, WV 25401 • (304) 267-7735 • *Berkeley Journal*

General Adam Stephen Memorial Association & Library • Stephen House Museum, 309 E John St, P.O. Box 1496 • Martinsburg, WV 25401 • (304) 267-4434 • http://www.orgsites.com/wv/adam-stephen

Martinsburg-Berkeley County Public Library • Public Square, 101 W King St • Martinsburg, WV 25401 • (304) 267-8933 • http://www.youseemore.com/martinsburgberkeley

Mathias
Lost River State Park Archives • 321 Park Dr • Mathias, WV 26812 • (304) 897-5325 • http://www.lostriversp.com

Middlebourne
Tyler County Heritage and Historical Society • P.O. Box 317 • Middlebourne, WV 26149 • (304) 758-4288 • *Heritage Windows*

Montgomery
Vining Library • West Virginia University Institute of Technology, 405 Fayette Pike • Montgomery, WV 25136-2436 • (304) 442-3321 • http://www.wvit.wvnet.edu/library

Moorefield
Hardy County Genealogical and Historical Society • general delivery • Moorefield, WV 26836

Hardy County Public Library • 102 N Main St • Moorefield, WV 26836 • (304) 538-6560 • http://hardycountymartin.lib.wv.us

Morgantown
Comer Museum Archives • 325 A Comer Bldg, West Virginia Univ, Box 6070 • Morgantown, WV 26506 • (304) 293-4211 • *Comer Museum Newsletter*

Morgantown Public Library • 373 Spruce St • Morgantown, WV 26505 • (304) 291-7425 • http://www.clark.lib.wv.us/morg/morg.html

Palatines to America, West Virginia Chapter • 500 Grove St • Morgantown, WV 26505-4709 • (304) 292-4828 • *Pal-Am Mountaineer*

Swecker Family Reunion • 309 Elmhurst St • Morgantown, WV 26505 • (304) 599-0368

Thomas Thorn Family Organization • 617 Grand St • Morgantown, WV 26505

West Virginia & Regional History Collection • West Virginia University, P.O. Box 6069 • Morgantown, WV 26506-6069 • (304) 293-3536

West Virginia and Regional History Association & Archives • c/o Wise Library, West Virginia Univ, P.O. Box 6069 • Morgantown, WV 26506-6069 • (304) 293-3536 • http://www.libraries.wvu.edu/wvcollection • *West Virginia and Regional History Collection Newsletter*

Wise Library • West Virginia Univ, 1549 University Ave, P.O. Box 6069 • Morgantown, WV 26506-6069 • (304) 293-4040 • http://www.libraries.wvu.edu

Moundsville
Anna B Smith House Museum Archives • 6th St & Tomlinson Ave, P.O. Box 826 • Moundsville, WV 26041 • (304) 845-9188

Miracle Valley Regional Library System • 700 5th St • Moundsville, WV 26041-1993 • (304) 845-6911 • *Miracle Valley Regional Library System Newsletter*

Mount Gay
Harless Library • Southern West Virginia Community & Technical College, Dempsey Branch Rd, P.O. Box 2900 • Mount Gay, WV 25637-2900 • (304) 792-7098 • http://www.southern.wvnet.edu

West Virginia

Mullens
Twin Falls State Park Museum Archives • Hwy Route 97, P.O. Box 667 • Mullens, WV 25882 • (304) 294-4000 • http://www.twinfallsresort.com

New Cumberland
Hancock County Historical Society • c/o Swaney Memorial Library, 601 Court St, P.O. Box 608 • New Cumberland, WV 26047 • (304) 564-3471

Swaney Memorial Library • 201 Court St, P.O. Box 608 • New Cumberland, WV 26047-0608 • (304) 564-3471 • http://www.weirton.lib.wv.us

New Martinsville
New Martinsville Public Library • 160 Washington St • New Martinsville, WV 26155 • (304) 455-4545

Wetzel County Genealogical Society & Library • P.O. Box 464 • New Martinsville, WV 26155-0464 • *Wetzel County Ggenealogical Society Newsletter*

Newell
Tri-State Genealogical and Historical Society • 707 Washington St, P.O. Box 454 • Newell, WV 26050-0454 • (304) 387-2467

Nitro
Lazarus and Mary Secoy Descendants Family Association • 438 Woodland Dr • Nitro, WV 25143-1060 • (304) 755-4728 • *Descendants of Lazarus and Mary Secoy Newsletter*

Wingo Research • 15 Barrington Rd • Nitro, WV 25143 • Wingo Watchers

Oak Hill
Fayette County Public Libraries • 531 Summit St • Oak Hill, WV 25901 • (304) 465-0121 • http://www.fayette.lib.wv.us

Genealogical Society of Fayette and Raleigh Counties • P.O. Box 68 • Oak Hill, WV 25901-0068 • *Genealogical Society of Fayette and Raleigh Counties News Notes*

Parkersburg
Parkersburg-Wood County Public Library • 3100 Emerson Ave • Parkersburg, WV 26104-2414 • (304) 420-4587 • http://parkersburg.lib.wv.us

Rogers-Rodgers Research • P.O. Box 4705 • Parkersburg, WV 26104-4705 • (304) 485-0921 • http://www.members.aol.com/jodewebb/rogersnewsletter.html • *Rogers-Rodgers Family Newsletter*

West Augusta Historical and Genealogical Society • 2515 10th Ave • Parkersburg, WV 26101 • *Newsletter of the West Augusta Historical and Genealogical Society*

Pennsboro
Ritchie County Historical Society • 410 Myles Ave • Pennsboro, WV 26415 • (304) 643-2738 • *Ritchie County Historical Society Newsletter*

Philippi
Barbour County Genealogical Society • c/o Philippi Public Library, 102 S Main St • Philippi, WV 26416 • (304) 457-3495

Philippi Public Library • 102 S Main St • Philippi, WV 26416-1317 • (304) 457-3495

Pickett Library • Alderson-Broaddus College, College Hill Rd • Philippi, WV 26416 • (304) 457-6229 • http://blue.ab.edu

Pine Grove
Pine Grove Public Library • Main St, P.O. Box 416 • Pine Grove, WV 26419-0416 • (304) 889-3288

Pineville
Wyoming County Genealogical Society • P.O. Box 1186 • Pineville, WV 24874

Wyoming County Library System • Castle Rock Ave, P.O. Box 130 • Pineville, WV 24874 • (304) 732-6228 • http://wyoming.lib.wv.us

Point Pleasant
Mason County Library Board • 508 Viand St • Point Pleasant, WV 25550-1199 • (304) 675-0894

Tu-Endie-Wei State Park Archives • 1 Main St, P.O. Box 486 • Point Pleasant, WV 25550 • (304) 674-0869 • http://www.tu-endie-weistatepark.com

West Virginia State Farm Museum Archives • Route 1, Box 479 • Point Pleasant, WV 25550 • (304) 675-5737 • http://www.farmmuseum.org

Princeton
Born Belcher Bunch • RR 9 Box 67 • Princeton, WV 24740 • *Belcher Bulletin*

Mercer County Genealogical and Historical Society & Library • P.O. Box 5012 • Princeton, WV 24740-5012 • (304) 425-4990 • *Mercer Dateline*

Princeton Public Library • 205 Center St • Princeton, WV 24740 • (304) 487-5045

Proctor
Tri-County Researcher • P.O. Box 196 • Proctor, WV 26055-0196 • (304) 455-3203 • *Tri-County Researcher*

Ravenswood
Jackson County Historical Society & Archives • Washington's Lands Museum, Sayre Log House, 200 Henrietta St • Ravenswood, WV 26164 • (304) 273-4160 • http://www.rootsweb.com/~wvjackso/jack.htm

Richwood
West Virginia Hillbilly • P.O. Box 430 • Richwood, WV 26261-0430 • (304) 846-2666 • *West Virginia Hillbilly*

Ripley
Jackson County Historical Society & Library • P.O. Box 22 • Ripley, WV 25271 • (304) 372-2541 • *Jackson County History*

Jackson County Public Library • 208 N Church St • Ripley, WV 25271-1204 • (304) 372-5343 • http://jackson.park.lib.wv.us

Romney
Hampshire County Public Library • 153 W Main St • Romney, WV 26757 • (304) 822-3185 • http://www.hampshirecopubliclib.com

Shepherdstown
Historic Sheperdstown Commission & Archives • Historical Museum, 129 E German St, P.O. Box 1786 • Shepherdstown, WV 25443 • (304) 876-0910 • *Historic Sheperdstown Commission Newsletter*

Scarborough Library • Shepherd College, 301 King St, P.O. Box 3210 • Shepherdstown, WV 25443-3210 • (304) 876-5420 • http://www.shepherd.edu/libweb

Shepherdstown Public Library • German & Kings Sts, P.O. Box 278 • Shepherdstown, WV 25443-0278 • (304) 876-2783 • http://www.lib.shepherdstown.wv.us

Sistersville
Caraher Family History Society • 142 Rexford St • Sistersville, WV 26175-1628 • *Caraher Family History Society Journal*

South Charleston
Kanawha Valley Genealogical Society & Library • 1330 Myers Ave, P.O. Box 8555 • South Charleston, WV 25303-0555 • (304) 776-1037 • http://www.rootsweb.com/~wvkvgs • *Journal of the Kanawha Valley Genealogical Society*

South Charleston Museum Archives • 312 4th Ave • South Charleston, WV 25303 • (304) 744-9711 • http://www.geocities.com/semuseum

South Charleston Public Library • 312 4th Ave • South Charleston, WV 25303-1297 • (304) 744-6561 • http://www.scpl.wvnet.edu

William Bean Family Organization • 286 Kenna Dr • South Charleston, WV 25309-2650 • (304) 727-6533

Spencer
Roane County Historical Society • P.O. Box 161 • Spencer, WV 25276

Roane County Public Library • 110 Parking Plaza • Spencer, WV 25276 • (304) 927-1130 • http://www.roanecountylibrary.org

Summersville
Carnifex Ferry Battlefield State Park Museum Archives • State Hwy 129 • Summersville, WV 26651 • (304) 872-0825 • http://www.wvweb.com/www/carifax.ferry.html

Nicholas County Historical and Genealogical Society • P.O. Box 443 • Summersville, WV 26651

Summersville Public Library • 6201 Webster Rd • Summersville, WV 26651 • (304) 872-0844

Terra Alta
Americana Museum Archives • 401 Aurora Ave • Terra Alta, WV 26764 • (304) 789-2361

Nine: 9's in America • 206 2nd St • Terra Alta, WV 26764-1406 • (304) 789-6888 • *Nine: 9's in America Newsletter*

Preston County Historical Society • 109 E Washington St • Terra Alta, WV 26764 • (304) 789-6990

Terra Alta Public Library • 701-B E State Ave • Terra Alta, WV 26764 • (304) 789-2724

Union
Monroe County Historical Society • P.O. Box 465 • Union, WV 24983 • *Monroe County Historical Society Newsletter*

Vienna
Vienna Public Library • 2300 River Rd • Vienna, WV 26105-1398 • (304) 295-7771 • http://vienna.park.lib.wv.us

Wayne
Wayne County Genealogical And Historical Society • P.O. Box 787 • Wayne, WV 25570

Webster Springs
Webster-Addison Public Library • 331 S Main St • Webster Springs, WV 26288 • (304) 847-5764

Weirton
Hancock County Genealogical and Historical Society • 103 Bell St • Weirton, WV 26067

Mary H Weir Public Library • 3442 Main St • Weirton, WV 26062-4590 • (304) 797-8510 • http://www.weirton.lib.wv.us

Welch
Hulda Jane Rose Lester Family Organization • P.O. Box 1084 • Welch, WV 24801 • (304) 436-6677

McDowell Public Library • 90 Howard St • Welch, WV 24801 • (304) 436-3070 • http://www.raleigh.lib.wv.us/mcdowell

Wellsburg
Brooke County Public Library • 945 Main St • Wellsburg, WV 26070 • (304) 737-1551 • http://www.brooke.lib.wv.us

West Liberty
Women's History Museum Archives • 108 Walnut St, P.O. Box 209 • West Liberty, WV 26074 • (304) 336-7159 • http://www.womens-history-museum.com

West Union
Doddridge County Historical Society • 201 Grand Ave, P.O. Box 23 • West Union, WV 26456

Doddridge County Public Library • 117 Court St • West Union, WV 26456 • (304) 873-1941 • Booklines

Weston
Jackson's Mill Historic Area Archives • 160 WVU Jackson Mill Rd • Weston, WV 26452 • (800) 287-8206 • http://www.jacksonsmill.wvu.edu

Lewis County Genealogical and Historical Society • 252 Main Ave • Weston, WV 26452

Louis Bennett Public Library • 148 Court Ave • Weston, WV 26452 • (304) 269-5151 • http://louisbennett.lib.wv.us

Wheeling
Bishop Hodges Library • Wheeling Jesuit University, 316 Washington Ave • Wheeling, WV 26003-6295 • (304) 243-2226 • http://library.wju.edu

Kruger Street Toy & Train Museum Archives • 144 Kruger St • Wheeling, WV 26003 • (304) 242-8133 • http://www.toyandtrain.com

Oglebay Institute & Archives • Mansion Museum, Oglebay Park • Wheeling, WV 26003 • (304) 242-7272 • http://www.nionline.com

Ohio County Public Library • 52 16th St • Wheeling, WV 26003-3696 • (304) 232-0244 • http://wheeling.weirton.lib.wv.us • OCPL Newsletter

Vitus Keller Family of Talheim, Baden • 183 Springdale Ave • Wheeling, WV 26003-5515 • (304) 242-5176 • http://www.hgo.net/~drwackes/

West Virginia Independence Hall Archives • 1528 Market St • Wheeling, WV 26003 • (304) 238-1300 • http://www.wvculture.org • *Goldenseal*

West Virginia Northern Community College Museum • 1704 Market St • Wheeling, WV 26006 • (304) 233-5900 • http://www.wvnorthern.edu • *WVNCC Newsletter*

Wheeling Area Genealogical Society • 2237 Marshall Ave • Wheeling, WV 26003 • (304) 242-1648 • *Upper Ohio Valley Historical Review*

White Sulphur Springs
President's Cottage Archives • The Greenbrier, 300 W Main St • White Sulphur Springs, WV 24986 • (304) 536-1110 • http://www.greenbrier.com

Williamson
Mingo County Genealogical Society • P.O. Box 2581 • Williamson, WV 25661 • (606) 237-4646 • *Mingo Heritage*

Williamson Campus Library • Southern West Virginia Community & Technical College, 1601 Armory Dr • Williamson, WV 25661 • (304) 235-6046 • http://www.southern.wvnet.edu

Winfield
Cartmill Reunion • P.O. Box 173 • Winfield, WV 25213 • (304) 586-9463

WISCONSIN

Albany
Albany Historical Society & Archives • Historical Museum, P.O. Box 464 • Albany, WI 53502

Algoma
Algoma Public Library • 406 Fremont St • Algoma, WI 54201 • (920) 487-2295

Kewaunee County Research Center Archives • 207 Steele St • Algoma, WI 54201 • (920) 487-2516

Alma
Alma Historical Society & Archives • Alma Area Museum, 407 S 2nd St • Alma, WI 54610 • (608) 685-4437

Buffalo City-Cochrane Area Historical Society • S 2178 County Rd N, P.O. Box 394 • Alma, WI 54610 • http://www.bchsonline.com

Almond
Almond Historical Society & Archives • Old Bank Building Historical Museum • Almond, WI 54909 • (715) 366-7341

Amery
Amery Historical Society • general delivery • Amery, WI 54001

Amherst Junction
Grosnick Family History • 1370 County Rd T • Amherst Junction, WI 54407

Seefeldt Family History • 1534 County Rd T North • Amherst Junction, WI 54407-8901

Antigo
Langlade County Historical Society & Archives • Deleglise Cabin Museum, 404 Superior St, P.O. Box 219 • Antigo, WI 54409 • (715) 623-3631 • http://www.langladehistory.com • *Langlade County Historical Society Newsletter*

Appleton
Appleton Public Library • 225 N Oneida St • Appleton, WI 54911-4780 • (920) 832-6173 • http://www.apl.org

Dobberstein Reunion Associates • P.O. Box 194 • Appleton, WI 54912-0194 • (920) 731-7181 • *Dobberstein Reunion Digest*

Fox Valley Genealogical Society & Library • P.O. Box 1592 • Appleton, WI 54913-1592 • (414) 233-3014 • *Genealogical Gems*; *Nuggets*

Hearthstone Historic House Museum Archives • 625 W Prospect Ave • Appleton, WI 54911 • (920) 730-8204 • http://www.hearthstonemuseum.org • *Upstairs & Downstairs*

High Cliff Historical Society • 3405 W Capitol Dr • Appleton, WI 54914 • (920) 734-0673

Outagamie County Historical Society & Archives • Houdini Historical Center, 330 E College Ave • Appleton, WI 54911 • (920) 735-9370 • http://www.foxvalleyhistory.org • *History Today*

Seeley G Mudd Library • Lawrence University, 113 S Lawe St, P.O. Box 599 • Appleton, WI 54912-0599 • (920) 832-6750 • http://www.lawrence.edu/library

Wisconsin Genealogical Council • 2308 W Applegate Dr • Appleton, WI 54911-2272 • (920) 739-3758 • *Wisconsin Genealogical Council Newsletter*

Arcadia
Arcadia Area Historical Society • 106 N 1st St • Arcadia, WI 54612 • (608) 323-7143

Argyle
Argyle Public Library • 401 E Milwaukee, P.O. Box 250 • Argyle, WI 53504-0250 • (608) 543-3113 • http://www.swls.org/member.ar.html

Ashland
Ashland County Historical Society & Archives • Historical Museum, 509 W Main, P.O. Box 906 • Ashland, WI 54806-0906 • (715) 682-4911 • http://www.ashlandhistory.com • Garland City Gazette

Dexter Library • Northland College, 1411 Ellis Ave • Ashland, WI 54806-3999 • (715) 682-1279 • http://library.northland.edu

Moquah Heritage Society • 27800 Cozy Corner Rd • Ashland, WI 54806 • (715) 373-5868

Northern Wisconsin Heritage • P.O. Box 347 • Ashland, WI 54806 • (715) 685-2646 • http://www.heritageconnection.org

Vaughn Public Library • 502 W Main St • Ashland, WI 54806 • (715) 682-7060 • http://www.ci.ashland.wi.us/dept/library/

Augusta
Augusta Memorial Public Library • 113 N Stone St, P.O. Box 474 • Augusta, WI 54772-0474 • (715) 286-2070

Balsam Lake
Polk County Historical Society & Archives • Historical Museum, Old Courthouse, P.O. Box 4 • Balsam Lake, WI 54810-0311 • (715) 483-3979 • http://www.co.polk.wi.us/history

Polk County Museum Archives • Main St, P.O. Box 41 • Balsam Lake, WI 54810-0041 • (715) 485-3292 • http://www.co.polk.wi.us/history

Bangor
Bangor and Area Historical Society & Archives • Historical Museum, 1525 Commercial St, P.O Box 15 • Bangor, WI 54614

Baraboo
Circus World Museum Archives • 550 Water St • Baraboo, WI 53913 • (608) 356-8341 • http://www.circusworldmuseum.com • *Center Ring*

Sauk County Historical Society & Archives • Historical Museum, 531 4th Ave, P.O. Box 651 • Baraboo, WI 53913-0651 • (608) 356-1001 • http://www.saukcounty.com/schs • *Sauk Trails*

Barkers Island
S S Meteor Maritime Museum Archives • 300 Marina Dr • Barkers Island, WI 54880 • (715) 394-5712 • http://www.superiorpublicmuseums.org

Bay City
River Bluffs History Center • Main St • Bay City, WI 54723 • (715) 273-6611

Bay View
Bay View Historical Society • 2590 S Superior St • Bay View, WI 53207 • http://www.bayviewhistoricalsociety.org

Bayfield
Apostle Islands National Lakeshore Library • 415 Washington Ave, Rte 1, Box 4 • Bayfield, WI 54814-0004 • (715) 779-3397 • http://www.nps.gov/apis • *Around the Archipelago*

Bayfield Heritage Association & Archives • Historical Museum, 30 N Broad St, P.O. Box 137 • Bayfield, WI 54814 • (715) 779-5958 • http://www.bayfieldheritage.org

Beaver Dam
Beaver Dam Community Library • 311 N Spring St • Beaver Dam, WI 53916-2043 • (920) 887-4631 • http://www.beaverdam.lib.wi.us

Dodge County Historical Society & Archives • Historical Museum, 105 Park Ave • Beaver Dam, WI 53916-2107 • (920) 887-1266 • http://www2.powercom.net/~dchs • *Dodge County Historical Society Newsletter*

Belleville
Belleville Area Historical Society • general delivery • Belleville, WI 53508

Belleville Public Library • 130 S Vine St, P.O. Box 140 • Belleville, WI 53508-0140 • (608) 424-1812 • http://www.scls.lib.wi.us/blv

Beloit
Beckman Mill Archives • 11600 S County Rd H, P.O. Box 74 • Beloit, WI 53511 • (608) 368-1435 • http://www.beckmanmill.org

Beloit Historical Society & Archives • Hanchett-Bartlett Homestead Museum, 845 Hackett St • Beloit, WI 53511-5742 • (608) 365-3811 • http://www.ticon.net/~beloiths/ • *Lincoln in Beloit*

Beloit Historical Society & Library • Lincoln Center, 845 Hackett St • Beloit, WI 53511 • (608) 365-7835 • http://www.ticon.net/~beloiths • *Pioneer Beloit*; *Confluence*

Beloit Public Library • 409 Pleasant St • Beloit, WI 53511 • (608) 364-2905 • http://www.als.lib.wi.us/BPL

Dunnagan Research • 1969 Pioneer Dr • Beloit, WI 53511 • *Dunnagans of All Spellings*

Ephraim Levi Moody Family Organization • 1347 White Ave • Beloit, WI 53511 • (608) 362-2283

Walworth County Genealogical Society, German Interest Group • 1742 Chapman Ave • Beloit, WI 53511 • (608) 363-0554

Benton
Benton Public Library • 48 W Main St, P.O. Box 26 • Benton, WI 53803-0026 • (608) 759-2665 • http://www.ci.benton.wi.us/web.bpl.htm

Robert Bruce Bradley-Joseph Goodbrake Montgomery Family Organization • P.O. Box 183 • Benton, WI 53803 • (608) 759-2755

Swindler's Ridge Museum Archives • 25 W Main St, P.O. Box 226 • Benton, WI 53803 • (608) 759-5182

Berlin
Berlin Historical Society & Archives • Historical Museum, 111 S Adams Ave, P.O. Box 24 • Berlin, WI 54923-2023 • (920) 361-4343

Berlin Public Library • 121 W Park Ave • Berlin, WI 54923-1594 • (920) 361-5420 • http://www.berlinlibrary.org

Clark School Museum Archives • 253 Water St • Berlin, WI 54923

Markofski Reunion • 623 SW Ceresco St • Berlin, WI 54923 • (920) 361-4103

Big Bend
Big Bend Village Library • W 230 S 90175 Nevins St, P.O. Box 40 • Big Bend, WI 53103-0040 • (262) 662-3571 • http://www.wcfls.lib.wi.us/bigbend

Big Bend-Vernon Historical Society • P.O. Box 68 • Big Bend, WI 53103-0068

Birchwood
Birchwood Area Historical Society • 2953 Stout St • Birchwood, WI 54817 • (715) 354-7300

Black Earth
Black Earth Historical Society & Archives • Depot Museum, P.O. Box 214 • Black Earth, WI 53515 • (608) 767-2667

Black River Falls
Black River Falls Public Library • 222 Fillmore St • Black River Falls, WI 54615 • (715) 284-4112

Jackson County Footprints Genealogy Club • W 11770 County Rd P • Black River Falls, WI 54615-5926

Jackson County Historical Society & Archives • Historical Museum, 13 S 1st St, P.O. Box 37 • Black River Falls, WI 54615-1721 • (715) 284-5314 • http://www.blackriverfalls.com

Monroe, Juneau, and Jackson Counties Genealogy Workshop & Library • 1488 Aqua Rd • Black River Falls, WI 54615-7609 • (608) 378-4388 • *Monroe, Juneau, and Jackson Counties Genealogy Workshop Newsletter*

Blanchardville
Blanchardville Historical Society • 101 S Main St • Blanchardville, WI 53516

Blanchardville Public Library • 208 Mason St, P.O. Box 104 • Blanchardville, WI 53516-0104 • (608) 523-2055 • http://www.swls.org

Blue Mounds
Blue Mounds Area Historical Society • general delivery • Blue Mounds, WI 53517

Little Norway Museum Archives • 3576 Hwy JG North • Blue Mounds, WI 53517 • (608) 437-8211 • http://www.littlenorway.com

Bonduel
Bonduel Community Archives • 108 S 1st St, P.O. Box 205 • Bonduel, WI 54107 • (715) 758-2687

Boscobel
Boscobel Historical Society • Boscobel Hotel, Gideon Room, Wisconsin Ave • Boscobel, WI 53805 • (608) 872-2429

Hildebrand Memorial Library • 1033 Wisconsin Ave • Boscobel, WI 53805-1597 • (608) 375-5723 • http://www.swls.org/member.bw.html

Boulder Junction
Boulder Junction Area Historical Society • P.O. Box 447 • Boulder Junction, WI 54512 • (715) 385-7567

Boulder Junction Public Library • 5386 Park St, P.O. Box 9 • Boulder Junction, WI 54512-0009 • (715) 385-2050 • http://merlin.nwls.lib.wi.us

Brantwood
Knox Creek Historical Society • N 4233 W Knox Rd • Brantwood, WI 54513 • (715) 564-2525

Brillion
Brillion Historical Society & Archives • Brillion History House, 110 N Francis St, P.O. Box 35 • Brillion, WI 54110 • (920) 756-3139 • http://www.BrillionHistoricalSociety.com

Brodhead
Brodhead Historical Society & Archives • Historical Museum, 805 1st Center Ave • Brodhead, WI 53520 • (608) 897-4150

Brookfield
Brookfield Public Library • 1900 Calhoun Rd • Brookfield, WI 53005 • (262) 782-4140 • http://www.ci.brookfield.wi.us/library.cfm • *BrookBytes*

Clausings Reunion • 855 Appletree Ln • Brookfield, WI 53005

Cornish Society Of Greater Milwaukee • 2405 N Brookfield Road • Brookfield, WI 53045

Elmbrook Historical Society & Archives • Dousman Stagecoach Inn Museum, 1075 Pilgrim Pkwy, P.O. Box 292 • Brookfield, WI 53005 • (262) 782-4057 • http://www.elmbrookhistoricalsociety.org

Johann Horkheimer and Mary Gaus(s) Family Organization • 18980 Glen Kerry Dr • Brookfield, WI 53045 • (262) 782-1329

Robert McElroy Descendants Organization • 17825 Continental Dr • Brookfield, WI 53045 • (262) 781-8215

Wisconsin Lineage Links • 2655 Fairview Lane • Brookfield, WI 53045-4117

Brown Deer
Brown Deer Historical Society & Archives • 1884 Little White Schoolhouse Museum, 4800 W Green Brook Dr • Brown Deer, WI 53223 • (414) 354-4116 • *Brown Deer Historical Society Newsletter*

Bruce
Bruce Area Historical Society & Archives • Historical Museum and Genealogical Library, River Ave, P.O. Box 155 • Bruce, WI 54819 • (715) 868-5475

Burlington
1840 Whitman School Museum Archives • 401 W Beloit St • Burlington, WI 53105

1850 Log Cabin Museum Archives • 416 N Perkins Blvd • Burlington, WI 53105

Burlington Genealogical Society • P.O. Box 593 • Burlington, WI 53105-0593 • http://www. rootsweb.com/~wiburlgs • *Burlington Genealogical Society Newsletter*

Burlington Historical Society & Archives • Historical Museum, 232 N Perkins Blvd • Burlington, WI 53105-1927 • (262) 767-2884 • http://www.burlingtonhistory.org

Burlington Public Library • 166 E Jefferson St • Burlington, WI 53105-1491 • (414) 763-7623 • http://www.burlington.lib.wi.us • *Friend to Friend*

Cable
Forest Lodge Library • 13450 County Hwy M, P.O. Box 176 • Cable, WI 54821-0176 • (715) 798-3189 • http://www.airstreamcomm.net/~cablelib

Iron River Historical Society • P.O. Box 416 • Cable, WI 54821-0416

Cadott
Cadott Area Historical Society & Archives • Histoircal Museum, 630 N Hwy 27, P.O. Box 1 • Cadott, WI 54727-0001

Caledonia
Caledonia Historical Society • general delivery • Caledonia, WI 53108

Cambria
Cambria-Friesland Historical Society & Archives • Wagener House, P.O. Box 501 • Cambria, WI 53923

Jane Morgan Memorial Library • 109 W Edgewater St, P.O. Box 477 • Cambria, WI 53923-0477 • (920) 348-4030

Cambridge
Cambridge Community Library • 200 Spring St, P.O. Box 490 • Cambridge, WI 53523-0490 • (608) 423-3900

Koshkonong Prairie Historical Society • South St, P.O. Box 190 • Cambridge, WI 53523 • http://www.koshkonong.org

Cameron
Barron County Historical Society & Archives • Pioneer Village Museum, 1870 13 1/2 Ave • Cameron, WI 54822-9511 • (715) 458-2841 • http://www.barroncountymuseum.com • *Pioneer Village Gazette*

Camp Douglas
Wisconsin National Guard Memorial Archives • 101 Independence Dr • Camp Douglas, WI 54618 • (608) 427-1280 • *Wisconsin National Guard Memorial Newsletter*

Cassville
Stonefield State Historic Site Archives • 12195 County Rd V V, P.O. Box 125 • Cassville, WI 53806 • (608) 725-5210 • http://www.wisconsinhistory.org/stonefield

Cataract
Paul and Matilda Wegner Grotto Archives • Hwys 71 & 27 • Cataract, WI 54620 • (608) 269-8680

Cedar Grove
Cedar Grove Public Library • 131 Van Altena • Cedar Grove, WI 53013-0287 • (920) 668-6834 • http://www.cedargrove.lib.wi.us

Cedarburg
Cedarburg Cultural Center Archives • W 62 N 546 Washington Ave, P.O. Box 84 • Cedarburg, WI 53012-1926 • (262) 375-3676 • http://www.cedarburgculturalcenter.org

Cedarburg Public Library • W 63 N 583 Hanover Ave • Cedarburg, WI 53012 • (262) 375-7640

General Store Museum Archives • W 61 N 480 Washington Ave • Cedarburg, WI 53012

Kuhefuss House Museum Archives • W 63 N 627 Washington Ave • Cedarburg, WI 53012

Ozaukee County Historical Society & Library • W 63 N 643 Washington Ave, P.O. Box 206 • Cedarburg, WI 53012 • (262) 377-4510 • http://www.co.ozaukee.wi.us/ochs • Ozaukee County Historical Society Newsletter

Chetek
Barron County Genealogical Society • 1122 Knapp St • Chetek, WI 54728

Chilton
Chilton Public Library • 221 Park St • Chilton, WI 53014 • (920) 849-4414 • http://www.chilton.lib.wi.us

Chippewa Falls
Chippewa County Genealogical Society & Library • 123 Allen St • Chippewa Falls, WI 54729-2898 • (715) 723-4399 • *Chippewa County (Wisconsin) Newsletter*

Chippewa County Historical Society & Library • 123 Allen St • Chippewa Falls, WI 54729-2802 • (715) 723-4399

Chippewa Falls Museum of Industry and Technology Archives • 21 E Grand Ave, P.O. Box 711 • Chippewa Falls, WI 54729 • (715) 720-9206 • http://cfmit.org

Chippewa Falls Public Library • 105 W Central • Chippewa Falls, WI 54729-2397 • (715) 723-1146 • http://www.chippewafallslibrary.org • *CFPL Highlights*

Cook Rutledge Mansion Archives • 505 W Grand Ave • Chippewa Falls, WI 54729 • (715) 723-7181

Clear Lake
Clear Lake Area Historical Society & Archives • Historical Museum, 450 5th Ave, P.O. Box 242 • Clear Lake, WI 54005 • (715) 263-3050

Clintonville
Clintonville Area Historical Society • 38 S Main St, P.O. Box 606 • Clintonville, WI 54929 • (715) 823-4680

Griepp Reunion • 207 N Main St • Clintonville, WI 54929 • (715) 828-3471

Columbus
Columbus Public Library • 223 W James • Columbus, WI 53925-1572 • (920) 623-5910 • http://www.scls.lib.wi.us/columbus

Sanks Family Association • 137 N Birdsey St • Columbus, WI 53925 • (262) 623-2251 • *Sanks Connection*

Winn, Wynn, Wynne, Wynns Research • 221 N Spring St • Columbus, WI 53925 • *Winn, Wynn, Wynne, Wynns Newsletter*

Cottage Grove
Cottage Grove Area Historical Society • P.O. Box 46 • Cottage Grove, WI 53527 • http://www.cottagegroveonline.com/community/cgahs

Crandon
Forest County Historical and Genealogical Society & Archives • Historical Museum, 103 W Jackson St, P.O. Box 432 • Crandon, WI 54520-1457 • (715) 478-5900

Crivitz
Crivitz Area Heritage Society • Oak & South Sts • Crivitz, WI 54114

Crivitz-Stephenson Historical Society & Archives • Crivitz Area Museum, P.O Box 776 • Crivitz, WI 54114 • (715) 854-3278

Cross Plains
Cross Plains-Berry Historical Society & Archives • Historical Museum, 2204 Brewery Rd, P.O. Box 219 • Cross Plains, WI 53528 • (608) 798-2760

Cuba City
Blackburn-Blackbourn Reunion • 413 N Jackson St • Cuba City, WI 53807 • (608) 744-2724

Cudahy
Cudahy Family Library • 3500 Library Dr, P.O. Box 100450 • Cudahy, WI 53110-6107 • (414) 769-2244 • http://www.ci.cudahy.wi.us/library/

Cudahy Historical Society & Library • Cudahy Depot, 4647 S Kinnickinnic Ave, P.O. Box 332 • Cudahy, WI 53110-1467 • (414) 747-1892 • http://www.ci.cudahy.wi.us

Wisconsin Slovak Historical Society & Library • P.O. Box 100164 • Cudahy, WI 53110-0164 • (262) 513-4981 • http://pages.prodigy.net/jhos/ • *Wisconsin Slovak*

Cumberland
Cumberland Public Library • 1305 2nd Ave, P.O. Box 97 • Cumberland, WI 54829-0097 • (715) 822-2767

Danbury
Burnett County Historical Society • 8500 County Rd U, P.O. Box 153 • Danbury, WI 54830-0159 • (715) 866-8890

Forts Folle Avoine Historic Park Archives • 8500 County Rd U • Danbury, WI 54830 • (715) 866-8890 • http://www.mwd.com/burnett/

Darlington
Johnson Public Library • 131 E Catherine St • Darlington, WI 53530 • (608) 776-4171 • http://www.swls.org/darlingtonlibrary/darlington.html

Lafayette County Historical Society & Archives • c/o Darlington Public Library, 525 Main St • Darlington, WI 53530 • (608) 776-8340 • *Looking Backwards*

De Forest

DeForest Area Historical Society & Archives • Hansen-Newell-Bennett House Museum, 119 E Elm St, P.O. Box 124 • De Forest, WI 53532 • (608) 846-5519 • *News and Notes*

Lyster House Archives • 201 DeForest St • De Forest, WI 53532

De Pere

Augustine Library • Saint Norbert Abbey, 1016 N Broadway • De Pere, WI 54115-2697 • (920) 337-4354

De Pere Historical Society & Archives • White Pillars Museum, 403 N Broadway • De Pere, WI 54115-2511 • (920) 336-3877 • *Pillars*

Oneida Nation Museum Archives • W892 County Trunk EE • De Pere, WI 54115 • (920) 869-2768 • http://www.museum.oneidanation.org

Delafield

Hawks Inn Historical Society & Archives • Historical Museum, 426 Wells St, P.O. Box 180104 • Delafield, WI 53018 • (262) 646-4794 • http://www.hawksinn.org • *Hawks Inn Newsletter*

Saint John's Northwestern Military Academy Archives • 1101 N Genessee St • Delafield, WI 53018 • (262) 646-3311 • http://www.sjnma.org • *Beacon*

Delavan

Aram Public Library • 404 E Walworth Ave • Delavan, WI 53115-1208 • (262) 728-3111

Delavan Historical Society • general delivery • Delavan, WI 53115

Walworth County Genealogical Society, Writer's Group • P.O. Box 159 • Delavan, WI 53115-0159 • (262) 728-3719 • http://www.rootsweb.com/~wiwalwor • Walworth County Genealogical Society Newsletter

Dodgeville

Dodge Mining Camp Cabin Museum Archives • 205 E Fountain St • Dodgeville, WI 53533 • (608) 935-5557

Iowa County Genealogical Society • P.O. Box 321 • Dodgeville, WI 53533-0321 • http://www.friendsnfamily.net/wiiowagensoc/ • *Iowa County Genealogical Society Newsletter*

Iowa County Historical Society & Archives • Historical Museum, 1301 N Bequette St, P.O. Box 38 • Dodgeville, WI 53533 • (608) 935-7694

Downsville

Empire in Pine Logging Museum Archives • general delivery • Downsville, WI 54735 • (715) 232-8685

Drummond

Drummond Historical Society & Archives • Drummond Museum, P.O. Box 8 • Drummond, WI 54832 • (715) 739-6500 • http://www.drummondwi.com

Durand

Durand Public Library • 604 7th Ave E • Durand, WI 54736 • (715) 672-8730 • http://www.cityofdurand.com

Ellenberger Family History • N6188 Dorwins Mill Rd • Durand, WI 54736 • http://members.1stnetusa.com/a/ellenberger/

Pepin County Historical Society • Washington Square, P.O. Box 74 • Durand, WI 54736 • (715) 672-8673

Eagle

Eagle Historical Society & Archives • Historical Museum, 217 W Main St, P.O. Box 454 • Eagle, WI 53119 • (262) 594-8961 • http://www.eaglehs.org

Old World Wisconsin Archives • S 103 W 37890 Hwy 67 • Eagle, WI 53119 • (262) 594-6300 • http://www.oldworldwisconsin.org

Eagle River

Eagle River Historical Society & Archives • Historical Museum, 519 Sheridan St, P.O. Box 2011 • Eagle River, WI 54521 • (715) 479-2396

East Troy

East Troy Area Historical Society • P.O. Box 722 • East Troy, WI 53120 • (262) 642-3491 • Walk Around the Square

East Troy Electric Railroad Museum Archives • P.O. Box 943 • East Troy, WI 53120 • (252) 642-3263 • http://www.easttroyrr.org • *Trolley Gazette*

East Troy Lions Public Library • 3094 Graydon Ave • East Troy, WI 53120 • (262) 642-6262 • http://www.easttroy.k12.wi.us/library

Eau Claire

Chippewa Valley Museum Archives • 1204 Carson Park, P.O. Box 1204 • Eau Claire, WI 54702-1204 • (715) 834-7871 • http://www.cvmuseum.com • *Chippewa Valley Museum Newsletter*

Genealogical Research Society of Eau Claire & Archives • Chippewa Valley Museum, 1204 Carson Park, P.O. Box 1204 • Eau Claire, WI 54702 • (715) 834-7871 • http://www.cumuseum.com

L E Phillips Memorial Public Library • 400 Eau Claire St • Eau Claire, WI 54701 • (715) 839-1648 • http://www.eauclaire.lib.wi.us

Paul Bunyan Logging Camp Museum Archives • 1110 Carson Park Dr • Eau Claire, WI 54702 • (715) 835-6200 • http://www.paulbunyancamp.org

Schlegelmilch-McDaniel House Archives • 517 S Farwell • Eau Claire, WI 54701 • (715) 832-7028

William D McIntyre Library • Univ of Wisconsin-Eau Claire, 105 Garfield Ave • Eau Claire, WI 54702-4004 • (715) 836-3858 • http://www.uwec.edu/admin/library/speccol.html • *Off the Shelf*

Edgerton

Albion Academy Historical Musuem Archives • 605 Campus Ln, P.O. Box 171 • Edgerton, WI 53334-0171 • (608) 884-4809

Edgerton Public Library • 101 Albion St • Edgerton, WI 53534-1836 • (608) 884-4511 • http://www.als.lib.wi.us/EPL

Rock River Thresheree • 51 Cox Rd • Edgerton, WI 53534 • (608) 868-2814 • http://www.thresheree.org

Sterling North Society & Archives • Historic Home Museum, 409 W Rollin St, P.O. Box 173 • Edgerton, WI 53534-1121 • (608) 884-3074 • http://www.sterlingnorth.com

Egg Harbor

Cupola House Museum Archives • 7836 Hwy 42 • Egg Harbor, WI 54209 • (920) 868-1871

Eland

Eland Area Historical Society & Archives • Depot Museum, P.O. Box 27 • Eland, WI 54427

Elkhorn

Doris M Reinke Resource Center • 210 S Washington St • Elkhorn, WI 53121 • (262) 723-7848

Walworth County Historical Society & Library • Webster House, 9 E Rockwell St, P.O. Box 273 • Elkhorn, WI 53521 • (262) 723-4248 • http://www.geocities.com/walcohistory • *Webster House Museum Newsletter*

Ellison Bay

Liberty Grove Historical Society • P.O. Box 94 • Ellison Bay, WI 54210 • (920) 854-1926

Ellsworth

Ellsworth Public Library • 312 W Main • Ellsworth, WI 54011 • (715) 273-3209 • http://www.ellsworthlibrary.org • *Booklist*

Pierce County Historical Association & Archives • Courthouse, 414 W Main, P.O. Box 148 • Ellsworth, WI 54011 • (715) 273-6611 • *Pierce County's Heritage*

Elm Grove

Elm Grove Public Library • 13600 W Juneau Blvd • Elm Grove, WI 53122-1679 • (262) 782-6717 • http://www.wcfls.lib.wi.us/elmgrove

Elroy
Elroy Area Historical Society & Archives • Historical Museum, Main St, P.O. Box 35 • Elroy, WI 53929 • http://www.elroywi.com/museum.htm

Endeavor
Endeavor Historical Society • 413 Academy Blvd, P.O. Box 12 • Endeavor, WI 53930-0012

Ephraim
Anderson Barn (1880) Museum Archives • Anderson Ln & Hwy 42 • Ephraim, WI 54211

Anderson Store (1858) Museum Archives • 10049 Water St • Ephraim, WI 54211

Door County Library-Ephraim Branch • 9996 Water St, P.O. Box 150 • Ephraim, WI 54211-0150 • (920) 854-2014

Ephraim Foundation Museum Archives • 3060 Anderson Ln, P.O. Box 165 • Ephraim, WI 54211 • (920) 854-9688 • http://www.ephraim.org • Ephraim Foundation Newsletter

Ephraim Historical Foundation • P.O. Box 165 • Ephraim, WI 54211 • (920) 854-9688 • http://www.ephraim.org

Ephraim Village Hall Archives • Hwy 42 • Ephraim, WI 54211

Iverson House Archives • 9966 Moravia St • Ephraim, WI 54211

Evansville
Eager Free Public Library • 39 W Main St • Evansville, WI 53536 • (608) 882-2260 • http://www.als.lib.wi.us/efpl

Evansville Grove Society & Library • P.O. Box 234 • Evansville, WI 53536 • (609) 882-5657

Exeland
Exeland Public Library • 1563 N Hwy 40 • Exeland, WI 54835 • (715) 943-2723

Fairwater
Fairwater Historical Society • P.O. Box 151 • Fairwater, WI 53931 • (920) 346-8346 • http://www.wlhn.org/fairwater_histsoc

Fennimore
Fennimore Railroad Historical Society & Archives • Historical Museum, 610 Lincoln Ave • Fennimore, WI 53809 • (608) 822-6144

Jacob H Wagner Annual Family Reunion • 1424 Ebenezer Rd • Fennimore, WI 53809 • (608) 943-6812

Southwest Wisconsin Library System • 1775 4th St • Fennimore, WI 53809-1137 • (608) 822-3393 • http://www.swls.org

Fifield
Price County Historical Society & Archives • Town Hall Museum, W 7213 Pine, P.O. Box 156 • Fifield, WI 54524 • (715) 339-2254 • http://www.pricecountyhistoricalsociety.com • *Price County Historical Society Newsletter*

Fish Creek
Eagle Bluff Lighthouse Museum Archives • Peninsula State Park, P.O. Box 218 • Fish Creek, WI 54212 • (920) 839-2377

Gibraltar Historical Association • P.O. Box 323 • Fish Creek, WI 54212 • (920) 868-2091

Fitchburg
Fitchburg Historical Society • Fitchburg City Hall, 5520 Lacy Rd • Fitchburg, WI 53711 • (608) 219-5421

Florence
Cornish Connection of Michigan • P. O. Box 639 • Florence, WI 54121

Florence County Historical Society • Old Florence County Jail, 501 Lake St, P.O. Box 162 • Florence, WI 54121 • (715) 528-3597

Fond du Lac
Adams House Resource Center Archives • 336 Old Pioneer Rd • Fond du Lac, WI 54936-1284 • (920) 922-0991

Fond du Lac County Historical Society & Library • Galloway House, 336 Old Pioneer Rd, P.O. Box 1284 • Fond du Lac, WI 54935-1284 • (920) 922-1166 • http://www.fdl.com/history/ • *Fond du Lac County Historical Society Newsletter*

Fond du Lac Public Library • 32 Sheboygan St • Fond du Lac, WI 54935 • (920) 929-7080 • http://www.fdlpl.org

Galloway House and Village-Blakely Museum Archives • 336 Old Pioneer Rd, P.O. Box 1284 • Fond du Lac, WI 54936 • (920) 922-0991 • http://www.fdl.com/history • *Galloway House and Village Newsletter*

Fontana
Fontana Public Library • 166 2nd Ave, P.O. Box 437 • Fontana, WI 53125-0437 • (262) 275-5107 • http://www.lakeshores.lib.wi.us/fontana/fontana.htm

Footville
Footville Telephone Company Museum Archives • 115 W Centre St • Footville, WI 53545 • (608) 754-3135

Luther Valley Historical Society & Archives • Footville State Bank Museum, 158 Depot St, P.O. Box 253 • Footville, WI 53537-0253

Forest Junction
Haese Memorial Village Historical Society • P. O. Box 146 • Forest Junction, WI 54123 • (920) 989-1322

Fort Atkinson
Dwight Foster Public Library • 102 E Milwaukee Ave • Fort Atkinson, WI 53538-2049 • (920) 563-7790 • http://www.fort.lib.wi.us

Fort Atkinson Historical Society & Archives • Hoard Historical Museum, 407 Merchant Ave • Fort Atkinson, WI 53538-2249 • (920) 563-7769 • http://www.hoardmuseum.org

Fort McCoy
Fort McCoy Post Library • B 2000 11th Ave • Fort McCoy, WI 54656-5161 • (608) 388-2410

Fountain City
Fountain City Area Historical Society & Archives • Historical Museum, 7 S Main St, P.O. Box 114 • Fountain City, WI 54629 • (608) 6887-7541

Fox Lake
Fox Lake Historical Society & Archives • Historical Museum, 211 Cordelia St • Fox Lake, WI 53933 • (920) 928-3754

Franklin
Franklin Historical Society • 9220 W Drexel, P.O. Box 245 • Franklin, WI 53132 • (414) 425-0903

Frederic
Frederic Historical Society & Archives • Depot Museum, 210 Oak St W, P.O. Box 1 • Frederic, WI 54837 • (715) 327-5653

Fredonia
Stony Hill School Museum Archives • 5595 Hwy I • Fredonia, WI 53021 • (262) 377-4510

Fremont
Fremont Area Historical Society • 410 S River Rd, P.O. Box 377 • Fremont, WI 54940 • (920) 446-3326

Friendship
Adams County Historical Society & Archives • McGowan House, 507 Main St, P.O. Box 264 • Friendship, WI 53934 • (608) 339-7732 • http://www.AdamsHistory.com

Galesville
Trempealeau County Historical Society & Archives • One Room Schoolhouse Museum, P.O. Box 444 • Galesville, WI 54630 • (608) 582-2908

Gay Mills
Crawford County Historical Society • Log Cabin Heritage Park, P.O. Box 63 • Gay Mills, WI 54631 • (608) 735-4863

Wisconsin

Genesee Depot
Genesee Heritage Society • P.O. Box 52 • Genesee Depot, WI 53127-0052 • (262) 968-3166

Germantown
Germantown Historical Society • Dheinsville Settlement, Holy Hill Rd & Hwy 145, P.O. Box 31 • Germantown, WI 53022-1451 • (262) 628-3170 • *Germantown Historical Society Newsletter*

Pommerscher Verein Freistadt & Library • P.O. Box 204 • Germantown, WI 53022-0204 • (414) 353-8949 • http://www.execpc.com/~pommem • *Pommerscher Verein Freistadt Rundschreiben*

Sila Lydia Bast Bell Museum Archives • Holy Hill Rd, P.O. Box 31 • Germantown, WI 53022-1451 • (262) 628-3170

Gills Rock
Door County Maritime Museum Archives • Wisconsin Bay Rd • Gills Rock, WI 54210 • (920) 854-1844 • http://www.dcmm.org • *Door County Maritime Museum Newsletter*

Gilman
Gilman Area Historical Society • 410 S 9th Ave • Gilman, WI 54433-9398 • (715) 447-5777

Glenwood City
Glenwood Area Historical Society • 224 E Oak St, P.O. Box 55 • Glenwood City, WI 54013 • (715) 256-4696

Gordon
Gordon Wascott Historical Society & Archives • Historical Museum, 9672 E Cty Trk Y, P.O. Box 222 • Gordon, WI 54838 • (715) 376-4649

Grafton
Treleven Reunion • 1678 Dellwood Ct • Grafton, WI 53024 • (262) 377-5826

Grantsburg
Grantsburg Area Historical Society & Archives • Historical Museum, 133 W Wisconsin Ave, P.O. Box 35 • Grantsburg, WI 54840 • (715) 463-2573 • http://www.grantsburgareahistoricalsociety.com

Grantsburg Public Library • 415 S Robert • Grantsburg, WI 54840-7423 • (715) 463-2244 • http://www.nwls.lib.wi.us

Green Bay
Ashwaubenon Historical Society & Archives • Heritage Center Museum, 737 Cormier Rd • Green Bay, WI 54304 • (920) 429-2863

Bay Area Genealogical Society • 253 Little Rd, P.O. Box 283 • Green Bay, WI 54305-0283 • (920) 494-9286 • *Gems of Genealogy*

Brown County Historical Society • 710 S Monroe, P.O. Box 8085 • Green Bay, WI 54308-8085 • (920) 465-2446 • http://www.browncohistoricalsoc.org • *Voyageur: Northeast Wisconsin's Historical Review; Brown County Historical Society Newsletter*

Brown County Library • 515 Pine St • Green Bay, WI 54301 • (920) 448-4400 • http://www.browncountylibrary.org • *Brown County Library Newsletter*

David A Cofrin Library • Univ of Wisconsin-Green Bay, 2420 Nicolet Dr • Green Bay, WI 54301-7001 • (920) 465-2303 • http://www.uwgb.edu/~library/

Dodge Memorial Society • 301 Roselawn Blvd • Green Bay, WI 54301

Hazelwood Historic House Archives • 1008 S Monroe Ave, P.O. Box 1411 • Green Bay, WI 54305 • (920) 437-1840 • http://www.browncohistoricalsoc.org/hazelwood/

Heritage Hill State Park Archives • 2640 S Webster Ave • Green Bay, WI 54301 • (920) 448-5150 • http://www.heritagehillgb.org

Howard Suamico Historical Society • 1871 Maplewood Ave • Green Bay, WI 54303 • (920) 499-5778

National Railroad Museum Archives • 2285 S Broadway • Green Bay, WI 54304 • (920) 437-7623 • http://www.nationalmuseum.org • *National Railroad Museum Newsletter*

Nevill Public Museum of Brown County Library • 210 Museum Pl • Green Bay, WI 54303-2780 • (920) 448-4460 • http://www.nevillepublicmuseum.org • *Nevill Public Museum Newsletter*

Society of Automotive Historians, Wisconsin Chapter • 3765 Spring Green Rd • Green Bay, WI 54313-7565 • (920) 865-4004

Green Lake
Dartford Depot Museum Archives • 554 Mill St • Green Lake, WI 54941

Dartford Historical Society & Library • 501 Mill St, P.O. Box 638 • Green Lake, WI 54941 • (920) 294-6194 • *Dartford News*

Greenbush
Wade House Stagecoach Inn Museum Archives • W7747 Plank Rd, P.O. Box 34 • Greenbush, WI 53026 • (920) 526-3271 • http://www.wisconsinhistory.org/sites/wade

Greendale
Buchan Clan Association • 5334 Lakeside Dr • Greendale, WI 53129 • (414) 421-3021 • *Buchan Clan Association Newsletter*

Greendale Historial Society • 5650 Parking St • Greendale, WI 53129 • (414) 421-8163 • http://www.greendale.org/history.htm

Greendale Public Library • 5647 Broad St • Greendale, WI 53129-1887 • (414) 423-2136 • http://www.greendale.org

Greenfield
Greenfield Historical Society • Finan-Gabel-Bodamer Log Cabin, 5601 W Layton Ave • Greenfield, WI 53220 • (262) 679-5016 • http://www.greenfieldlibrary.org/greenfield_history.htm • *Greenfield Historical Society Newsletter*

Partee-Purtee Family Organization • 6151 W Howard Ave #27 • Greenfield, WI 53220-1934 • (414) 604-0646

Greenwood
Greenwood Public Library • 102 N Main St, P.O. Box 100 • Greenwood, WI 54437-0100 • (715) 267-7103

Gresham
Hoffman Family Organization • P.O. Box 17 • Gresham, WI 54128 • (715) 787-3788

Hales Corners
French Canadian-Acadian Genealogists of Wisconsin • P.O. Box 414 • Hales Corners, WI 53130-0414 • http://www.fcgw.org • *French Canadian-Acadian Genealogists of Wisconsin Quarterly*

Hales Corners Historical Society • Ben Hunt Cabin, 5885 S 116th St • Hales Corners, WI 53130 • (414) 529-6150 • http://www.historichalescorners.org

Leo Dehon Library • Sacred Heart School of Theology, 7335 S Hwy 100, P.O. Box 429 • Hales Corners, WI 53130-0429 • (414) 425-8300

Hancock
Hancock Public Library • 114 S Main St, P.O. Box 217 • Hancock, WI 54943-0217 • (715) 249-5817 • http://www.hancocklibrary.org

Harshaw
James and Martha Pelham Thompson Database • 8675 Art Thompson Rd • Harshaw, WI 54529 • (952) 894-5970 • *Thompson Family Tree*

Hartford
Hartford Area Genealogical Society • c/o Hartford Public Library, 115 N Main St • Hartford, WI 53027 • (262) 673-8240

Hartford Public Library • 115 N Main St • Hartford, WI 53027-1596 • (262) 673-8240 • http://www.hnet.net/~hpl

Wisconsin Automotive Museum Archives • 147 N Rural St • Hartford, WI 53027 • (262) 673-7999 • http://www.wisconsinautomuseum.com • *Kissel Kar Klub*

Hartland
Hartland Historical Society • Hartland Depot, 22 Pawling Ave, P.O. Box 54 • Hartland, WI 53029

Hartland Public Library • 110 E Park Ave • Hartland, WI 53029 • (262) 367-3350 • http://www.hartlandlibrary.org

Wisconsin Postal Historical Society • N 95 W 32259 County Line Rd • Hartland, WI 53029-9735 • (262) 966-7096

Hayward
Hayward Carnegie Library • 10538 Main, P.O. Box 917 • Hayward, WI 54843-0917 • (715) 634-2161

Sawyer County Historical Society & Archives • Historical Museum, 15715 W County Hwy B, P.O. Box 384 • Hayward, WI 54843 • (715) 634-8053 • http://www.sawyercountyhist.org

Hewitt
Cook County Historical Society • general delivery • Hewitt, WI 54441 • (715) 387-2883

Hilbert
Endries Family Reunion • 11 W Barbie Rand Blvd • Hilbert, WI 54129

Hillsboro
Cheyenne Settlers Heritage Society • 123 Mechanic St, P.O. Box 447 • Hillsboro, WI 54634

Hillsboro Area Historical Society & Archives • Pioneer Log Cabin Museum, 532 Water Ave, P.O. Box 9 • Hillsboro, WI 54634 • (608) 489-3192

Holmen
Holmen Area Historical Society • P.O. Box 535 • Holmen, WI 54636 • http://www.holmenhistory.org

La Crosse County Library • 103 State St, P.O. Box 220 • Holmen, WI 54636-0220 • (608) 526-9600 • http://www.lacrossecountylibrary.com

Horicon
Horicon Historical Society & Archives • Satterlee Clark House Museum, 322 Winter St, P.O. Box 65 • Horicon, WI 53032 • (920) 485-4028

Houlton
Ostrem-Reierson Family Organization • Jente Ln, 1420 Hwy 35/64 • Houlton, WI 54082 • (310) 533-8243 • *Ostrem-Reierson Family Organization Newsletter*

Hudson
Saint Croix County Historical Society & Library • Octagon House, 1004 3rd St • Hudson, WI 54016 • (715) 386-2654 • http://www.pressenter.com/~octagon/ • *Saint Croix County Historical Society Bulletin*

Hurley
Iron County Historical Society & Archives • Historical Museum, 303 Iron St, P.O. Box 4 • Hurley, WI 54534 • (715) 561-2244 • http://www.HurleyWI.com/IronCountyHistory/

Old Iron County Courthouse Museum Archives • 303 Iron St • Hurley, WI 54534 • (715) 561-2244 • http://www.hurleywi.com/ironcountyhistory

Hustisford
Hustisford Historical Society & Archives • John Hustis House Museum, 134 N Ridge St, P.O. Box 44 • Hustisford, WI 53034-0044 • (920) 349-3501 • *Hustisford Historical Society Newsletter*

Iola
Iola Historical Society & Archives • Iola Railroad Depot & Museum, 300 N Main St • Iola, WI 54945 • (715) 445-3184

Simonis Family Association • E 2753 County Hwy C • Iola, WI 54945 • (715) 445-3148

Iron River
Western Bayfield County Historical Society • 68245 S Main St • Iron River, WI 54847 • (715) 372-8792

Jackson
Jackson Historical Society & Archives • Mill Road Church Museum, 1860 Mill Rd • Jackson, WI 53037 • (262) 677-2464

Janesville
Campbell Research • 416 JF Townline Rd • Janesville, WI 53545 • (608) 756-2495 • *Campbell Contacts in America*

Dutton-Davis-Jackson-Doane Memorial Association • 521 Caroline St • Janesville, WI 53545 • (608) 754-8067 • *Newsletter of the Davis Family: For the Descendants of Daniel Davis*; *Jackson Family Newsletter*

Frances Willard Schoolhouse Archives • Rock County 4-H Fairgrounds • Janesville, WI 53545 • (608) 756-4509

Hedberg Public Library • 316 S Main St • Janesville, WI 53545 • (608) 758-6581 • http://www.hedbergpubliclibrary.org • *Library Matters*

Helen Jeffris Wood Museum Center Archives • 426 N Jackson St • Janesville, WI 53548 • (608) 756-4509

Lincoln-Tallman Museum Archives • 440 N Jackson St, P.O. Box 8096 • Janesville, WI 53545 • (608) 756-4509 • http://www.rchs.us

Rock County Genealogical Society & Library • 10 S High St, P.O. Box 711 • Janesville, WI 53547-0711 • (608) 756-4509 • *Rock County Genealogical Society Member's Newsletter*

Rock County Historical Society & Archives • Historical Museum, 426 N Jackson St, P.O. Box 8096 • Janesville, WI 53547-8096 • (608) 756-4509 • http://www.rchs.us • *Rock County Recorder*

Rockwell Reunion • P.O. Box 8003 • Janesville, WI 53547 • (608) 752-8816

Seventh Day Baptist Historical Society & Library • 3120 Kennedy Rd, P.O. Box 1678 • Janesville, WI 53547-1678 • (608) 752-5055 • http://www.seventhdaybaptist.org • *Sabbath Recorder*; *Seventh Day Baptist Historical Society Annual Report*

Wilkinson Research • P.O. Box 8003 • Janesville, WI 53547-8003 • (608) 756-3759 • *Cemetery Q's and A's Newsletter*; *Wilkinson Connection*

Jefferson
Aztalan Museum Archives • N 6264 Hwy Q • Jefferson, WI 53549 • (920) 648-4362

Jefferson Historical Society • 1035 W Racine Rd • Jefferson, WI 53549 • (920) 674-5306

Juneau
Dodge Centre Historical Society & Archives • Historical Museum, Fair & E Oak Grove Sts • Juneau, WI 53039 • (920) 386-4915

Kaukauna
Charles A Grignon Mansion Archives • 1313 Augustine St • Kaukauna, WI 54130 • (920) 766-3122 • http://www.foxvalleyhistory.org • *History Today*

Kaukauna Public Library • 111 Main Ave • Kaukauna, WI 54130-2436 • (920) 766-6340 • http://www.owls.lib.wi.us/kau/

Outagamie County Historical Society • Grignon Mansion, 1313 Augustine St • Kaukauna, WI 54130 • (920) 766-3122

Kenosha
Clan MacMillan, Appalachian Branch • 1314 40th Ave • Kenosha, WI 53144 • (262) 552-7075 • *MacMillan Newsletter*

Gilbert Simmons Branch Library • 711 59th Pl, P.O. Box 1414 • Kenosha, WI 53141-1414 • (262) 564-6100 • http://www.kenosha.lib.wi.us

Kenosha County Genealogical Society • 4902 52nd St; P.O. Box 25 • Kenosha, WI 53141-0025 • (262) 652-2410 • *Southport Echo*

Kenosha County Historical Society & Archives • Historical Museum, 220 51st Pl • Kenosha, WI 53140 • (262) 654-5770 • http://www.kenoshahistorycenter.org • Southport Newsletter

Kenosha Public Library • 812 56th St, P.O. Box 1414 • Kenosha, WI 53141-1414 • (262) 564-6300 • http://www.kenosha.lib.wi.us

Kenosha Public Museum Archives • 5500 1st Ave • Kenosha, WI 53140 • (262) 653-4140 • http://www.kenoshapublicmuseum.org • FOM Newsletter

Nafzger Research • 3603 28th Ave #3 • Kenosha, WI 53140 • *Nafzger Heritage News*

Parkside Library • Univ of Wisconsin, 900 Wood Rd, P.O. Box 2000 • Kenosha, WI 53141-2000 • (262) 595-2360 • http://www.uwp.edu/info-services/library

Sebastian Heeter Family Organization • 7519 15th Ave • Kenosha, WI 53140 • *Heeter Connections*

Kewaskum
Kewaskum Historical Society & Archives • Log Cabin Museum, 1202 Park View Dr • Kewaskum, WI 53040 • (262) 626-4656

Roe Cousins Family Reunion • 9240 Werner Dr • Kewaskum, WI 53040 • (262) 626-2696

Kewaunee
Kewaunee County Historical Museum Archives • Courthouse Sq, 813 Dodge St • Kewaunee, WI 54216-1213 • (920) 388-7176 • http://www.rootsweb.com/~wikewaun • *Kewaunee County Historical Museum Newsletter*

Kewaunee County Historical Society • 630 Vliet St • Kewaunee, WI 54216 • (920) 388-0117 • http://www.rootsweb.com/~wikewaun/

Pannebakker Family Association • N 202 County Rd B • Kewaunee, WI 54216-9520 • (920) 776-1082 • http://www.sover.net/~rutins/

Kiel
Kiel Area Historical Society & Archives • Historic House, 227 Fremont St • Kiel, WI 53042

Kiel Public Library • 511 3rd St • Kiel, WI 53042-1496 • (920) 894-7122 • http://www.kiel.lib.wi.us

King
Waupaca Area Genealogical Society • P.O. Box 42 • King, WI 54946-0042

Wisconsin Veterans Museum Archives • Wisconsin Veterans Home, 30 W Mifflin St, Suite 300 • King, WI 53703 • (608) 267-1790 • http://museum.dva.state.wi.us/researchcenter.asp

La Crosse
Catholic Diocese of La Crosse Archives • 3710 East Ave S, P.O. Box 4004 • La Crosse, WI 54602-4004 • (608) 788-7700 • http://www.dioceseoflacrosse.com

Hixon House Museum Archives • 429 N 7th St, P.O. Box 1272 • La Crosse, WI 54602 • (608) 782-1980 • http://www.lchsweb.org • *Past, Present & Future*

La Crosse Area Genealogical Society Chapter • P.O. Box 1782 • La Crosse, WI 54602-1782 • (608) 788-1738 • *La Crosse Area Genealogical Society Quarterly*

La Crosse County Historical Society & Archives • Swarthout Museum, 112 S 9th St, P.O. Box 1272 • La Crosse, WI 54602-1272 • (608) 782-1980 • http://www.lchsweb.org • *Past, Present and Future*

La Crosse County Historical Society & Archives • Hixon House, 429 7th St N, P.O. Box 1272 • La Crosse, WI 54601-3301 • (608) 782-1980

La Crosse Heritage Association • 600 3rd St N • La Crosse, WI 54601-6299

La Crosse Public Library • 800 Main St • La Crosse, WI 54601-4122 • (608) 789-7122 • http://www.lacrosselibrary.org

Murphy Library • Univ of Wisconsin-LaCrosse, 1631 Pine St • La Crosse, WI 54601-3792 • (608) 785-8508 • http://www.uwlax.edu/murphylibrary/ • *Fine Print*

Riverside Museum Archives • 410 E Veterans Memorial Dr • La Crosse, WI 54601 • (608) 782-1980 • http://www.lchsweb.org

Todd Wehr Memorial Library • Viterbo University, 900 Viterbo Dr • La Crosse, WI 54601 • (608) 796-3270 • http://www.viterbo.edu/library

La Farge
Lawton Memorial Library • 118 N Bird St, P.O. Box 38 • La Farge, WI 54639-0038 • (608) 625-2015

La Pointe
Madeline Island Historical Museum Archives • Woods Ave & Main St, P.O. Box 9 • La Pointe, WI 54850 • (715) 747-2415 • http://www.wisconsinhistory.org/madelineisland

Lac du Flambeau
Lac du Flambeau Historical and Cultural Society & Archives • Chippewa Museum, P.O. Box 729 • Lac du Flambeau, WI 54538 • (715) 588-3333 • http://www.studiods.com/ojibwemuseum/museum.html

Ladysmith
Rusk County Historical Society & Archives • Historical Museum, W 8323 Fairground Rd • Ladysmith, WI 54848 • (715) 532-4208 • http://www.ruskcounty.org

Lake Geneva
Geneva Lake History Buffs & Archives • Historical Museum, 255 Mill St, P.O. Box 522 • Lake Geneva, WI 53147 • (262) 248-6060

Lake Geneva Public Library • 918 W Main St • Lake Geneva, WI 53147-1890 • (262) 249-5299 • http://www.lakegeneva.lib.wi.us • *Lakeside Reader*

Lake Mills
L D Fargo Public Library • 120 E Madison St • Lake Mills, WI 53551-1644 • (920) 648-2166 • http://www.lakemills.lib.wi.us

Lake Mills-Aztalan Historical Society & Archives • Aztalan Museum, N 6264 Hwy Q, P.O. Box 122 • Lake Mills, WI 53551 • (920) 648-4632

Lake Tomahawk
Lake Tomahawk Historical Society & Archives • Hofman House Museum, 7247 Kelly Dr, P.O. Box 325 • Lake Tomahawk, WI 54539 • (715) 277-2629 • *Deacon's Bench*

Lancaster
Grant County Historical Society & Archives • Cunningham Museum, 129 E Maple St • Lancaster, WI 53813 • (608) 723-4925 • *Here and There in Grant County*

Sutter-Ulrich-Plank Family Association • 132 W Nathan St • Lancaster, WI 53813 • (563) 568-3802 • *Sutter-Ulrich-Plank Family History*

Land O'Lakes
Land O'Lakes Historical Society & Archives • Northern Waters Museum, 6490 Chippewa Dr, P.O. Box 541 • Land O'Lakes, WI 54540 • (715) 547-6979 • http://www.landolakeshistory.org

Laona
Camp Five Museum Archives • 5480 Camp 5 Rd • Laona, WI 54541 • (715) 674-3414 • http://www.camp5museum.org

Larsen
Winchester Area Historical Society • P.O. Box 84 • Larsen, WI 54947

Lebanon
Lebanon Historical Society • P.O. Box 23 • Lebanon, WI 53047 • (920) 925-3439

Little Chute
Little Chute Historical Society • 506 E Lincoln Ave • Little Chute, WI 54140 • (920) 788-2566

Lodi
Lodi Valley Historical Society & Archives • Jolivette Historic House, 173 S Main St • Lodi, WI 53555 • (608) 592-4392

Lomira
Lomira Public Library • 1038 Main St • Lomira, WI 53048 • (920) 269-4115

Luck
Luck Public Library • 21 2nd Ave W, P.O. Box 500 • Luck, WI 54853-0500 • (715) 472-2770

Luxemburg
Wisconsin Genealogical Council • N 9307 Abitz Ln • Luxemburg, WI 54217

Madison
Barrett Research • 7657 Carrington Dr Apt A • Madison, WI 53719-2044 • *Grin and Barrett*

Computer Assisted Genealogists of Southern Wisconsin • P.O. Box 44627 • Madison, WI 53744-4627 • (608) 222-4591

Culinary History Enthusiasts of Wisconsin • 3550 Anderson St • Madison, WI 53704 • (608) 244-2342 • http://chew.wisconsincooks.org

Dane County Historical Society & Library • Lussier Family Heritage Center, 3101 Lake Farm Rd, P.O. Box 5003 • Madison, WI 53705 • http://www.danenet.org/dchs • *Dane County Historical Society Newsletter*

Edwards-Sahnow-Borchardt-Duxbury-Blackburn-Blackbourn Research • 202 S Segoe Rd • Madison, WI 53705-4939 • (608) 233-1506 • *Blackburn-Blackbourn Family Updated Report*

Emmert Family Association • 2820 Marshall Ct #1 • Madison, WI 53705-2270

Historic Madison • P.O. Box 2721 • Madison, WI 53701-2721 • (608) 249-7920 • http://www.danenet.org/hmi • *Journal of the Four Lakes Region*

Jacob Schultheiss Family Association • Route 2, 2491 S Seminole Hwy • Madison, WI 53711 • (608) 271-3577

Madison Public Library • 201 W Mifflin St • Madison, WI 53703 • (608) 266-6350 • http://www.madisonpubliclibrary.org

South Central Wisconsin Genealogical Society • P.O. Box 5652 • Madison, WI 53705 • (608) 233-0584

State Historical Museum of Wisconsin Archives • 30 N Carroll St • Madison, WI 53703-2707 • (608) 264-6555 • http://www.shsw.wisc.edu

State Historical Society of Wisconsin & Library • 816 State St • Madison, WI 53706-1488 • (608) 264-6482 • http://www.wisconsinhistory.org/library/ • *Columns: Wisconsin Then and Now; Wisconsin Magazine of History; Wisconsin Preservation: National Register of Historic Places Newsletter; Exchange: A Newsletter for County and Local Historical Societies*

University of Wisconsin-Madison Library • 728 State St • Madison, WI 53706 • (608) 262-3242 • http://www.library.wisc.edu

Vesterheim Genealogical Society & Library • Naeseth Library, 415 W Main St • Madison, WI 53703-3116 • (608) 255-2224 • http://www.vesterheim.org/genealogy/ • *Norwegian Tracks*

Wisconsin Historical Museum Archives • 30 S Carroll St • Madison, WI 53703 • (608) 266-6865 • http://www.wisconsinhistory.org • *Wisconsin Magazine of History*

Wisconsin State Genealogical Society • 2109 20th Ave, P.O. Box 5106 • Madison, WI 53705-0106 • (608) 325-2609 • http://www.wsgs.org • *Wisconsin State Genealogical Society Newsletter*

Wisconsin Veterans Museum Research Center Archives • 30 W Mifflin St • Madison, WI 53707 • (608) 267-1790 • http://badger.state.wi.us/agencies/dva/museum/wvmmain.html

Manawa
Sturm Memorial Library • 130 N Bridge St, P.O. Box 20 • Manawa, WI 54949-0020 • (920) 596-2252 • http://www.owls.lib.wi.us/main

Manitowish Waters
Frank B Koller Memorial Library • Hwy 51, P.O. Box 100 • Manitowish Waters, WI 54545-0100 • (715) 543-2700 • http://koller.nwls.lib.wi.us

Manitowoc
Henry Schuette Archives • Wisconsin Maritime Museum, 75 Maritime Dr • Manitowoc, WI 54220 • (920) 684-0218 • http://www.wisconsinmaritime.org

International Submariners Memorial Museum Archives • USS Cobia WWII, 75 Maritime Dr • Manitowoc, WI 54220 • (920) 684-0218

Manitowoc County Genealogical Society • P.O. Box 345 • Manitowoc, WI 54221-1745 • (920) 682-1046 • Family Vines

Manitowoc County Historical Society & Library • Pinecrest Historical Village, 1701 Michigan Ave • Manitowoc, WI 54220-0574 • (920) 684-4445 • http://www.mchistsoc.org • *Manitowoc County Historical Society Pinecrest Spirit*; *Manitowoc County Historical Society Monographs*; *Heritage Center News*

Manitowoc Public Library • 707 Quay • Manitowoc, WI 54220 • (920) 683-4863 • http://www.manitowoc.lib.wi.us • *Manitowoc Public Library Newsletter*

Watkins Family History Society • P.O. Box 518 • Manitowoc, WI 542210-0518 • http://www.ourworld.compuserve.com/ homepages/watkins-fhs • *Journal of the Watkins Family*

Maple
Old-Brule Heritage Society • P.O. Box 24 • Maple, WI 54854 • (715) 364-2500 • http://www.oldbrule.org

Marinette
Forest History Association of Wisconsin • P.O. Box 1001 • Marinette, WI 54143-1001 • (906) 863-6850

Marinette County Consolidated Public Library Services • 1700 Hall Ave • Marinette, WI 54143-1799 • (715) 732-7570 • http://www.nfls.lib.wi.us/mrt

Marinette County Historical Society & Archives • Historical Museum, Stephenson Island, US Hwy 41, P.O. Box 262 • Marinette, WI 54143-0262 • (715) 732-0831 • *Marinette County Historian*

White Pine Genealogical Society • P.O. Box 512 • Marinette, WI 54143

Marion
Marion Area Historical Society & Archives • Northwestern Railroad Depot Museum, 620 E Ramsdell St, P.O. Box 321 • Marion, WI 54950 • (715) 754-2118

Markesan
Markesan Historical Society & Archives • Grand River Valley Museum, 214 E John St • Markesan, WI 53946 • (920) 398-3554 • http://come.to/markesan

Marshall
Marshall Area Historical Society • general delivery • Marshall, WI 53559

Marshall Community Library • 605 Waterloo Rd • Marshall, WI 53559 • (608) 655-3123 • http://www.scls.lib.wi.us/mar

Marshfield
Marshfield Area Genealogy Group & Library • P.O. Box 337 • Marshfield, WI 54449 • *Kith and Kin*

Marshfield Public Library • 211 E 2nd St • Marshfield, WI 54449 • (715) 387-8494 • http://marshfieldlibrary.org

North Wood County Historical Society & Archives • Gov Upham Mansion, 212 W 3rd St, P.O. Box 142 • Marshfield, WI 54449-2706 • (715) 387-3322 • http://www.uphamansion.com • *Mansion News*

Mason
Bayfield County Genealogical Society • Route 1, Box 139 • Mason, WI 54856 • (715) 765-4597

Bayfield County Historical Society & Archives • Mason Depot Museum • Mason, WI 54856 • (715) 765-4554

Dahler-Daehler Reunion • Route 1, Box 139 • Mason, WI 54856 • (715) 765-4597 • *Dahler Family Newsletter*

Mauston
Juneau County Historical Society & Archives • Boorman House Museum, 211 N Union St, P.O. Box 321 • Mauston, WI 53948 • (608) 462-5931 • *Juneau County Historical Society Quarterly Bulletin*; *Juneau County History News*

Mayville
Mayville Historical Society & Archives • Historical Museum, 1 N German St, P.O. Box 82 • Mayville, WI 53050 • (920) 387-2420 • http://www.mayvillecity.com/organizations/historical_society.html • *Mayville Historical Society Newsletter*

Mayville Limestone School Museum Archives • P.O. Box 102 • Mayville, WI 53050-0102 • http://www.mayvillecity.com/organizations/whitelime.htm

Mazomanie
Mazomanie Free Library • 102 Brodhead St • Mazomanie, WI 53560-0458 • (608) 795-2104 • http://www.scls.lib.wi.us/maz

Mazomanie Historical Society & Archives • Historical Museum, 118 Brodhead St, P.O. Box 248 • Mazomanie, WI 53520 • (608) 795-2992 • http://www.mazoarea.com/ypahist.htm • *Local Sheaves; Mazomanie Historical Society Newsletter*

McFarland
McFarland Historical Society & Archives • Historical Museum, 5814 Main St, P.O. Box 94 • McFarland, WI 53558 • (608) 838-3992 • *McFarland Historical Society Newsletter*

Medford
Taylor County Historical Society & Archives • Log Cabin Museum, 845 E Broadway Ave, Apt A • Medford, WI 54451 • (715) 747-3808 • *Log Cabin News*

Mellen
Mellen Area Historical Society & Archives • Historical Museum, P.O. Box 134 • Mellen, WI 54546

Menasha
Elisha D Smith Public Library • 440 1st St • Menasha, WI 54952-3191 • (920) 967-5166 • http://www.menashalibrary.org

Menasha Historical Society • 233 Sunset Dr • Menasha, WI 54592 • (920) 722-8969

Menasha Historical Society Resource Center • 640 Keyes St • Menasha, WI 54952 • (920) 722-8969

Menomonee Falls
Maud Shunk Public Library • W 156th N, 8446 Pilgrim Rd • Menomonee Falls, WI 53051-0347 • (262) 532-8900 • http://www.mf.lib.wi.us

Menomonee Falls Historical Society & Archives • Old Falls Village Museum, N 96 W 15791 County Line Rd, P.O. Box 91 • Menomonee Falls, WI 53032 • (262) 250-5096 • http://www.oldfallsvillage.com • *Menomonee Falls Historical Society Newsletter*

Menomonie
Dunn County Genealogical Society • P.O. Box 633 • Menomonie, WI 54751 • *Quest*

Dunn County Historical Society & Archives • Heritage Museum, 1820 Wakanda St, P.O. Box 437 • Menomonie, WI 54751 • (715) 232-8685 • http://www.discover-net.net/~dchs

Robert L Pierce Library • Univ of Wisconsin-Stout, 315 10th St • Menomonie, WI 54751-0790 • (715) 232-1353 • http://www.uwstout.edu/lib

Mequon
Frank L Weyenburg Library • 11345 N Cedarburg Rd • Mequon, WI 53092-1998 • (262) 242-2593 • http://www.flwlib.org • *Columns*

Mequon Historical Society • 6100 W Mequon Rd 112N • Mequon, WI 53092 • (262) 242-3107

Wisconsin State Old Cemetery Society • 6100 W Mequon Rd • Mequon, WI 53092 • (262) 242-3290

Mercer
Mercer Area Historical Society & Archives • Historical Museum, P.O. Box 638 • Mercer, WI 54547 • (715) 476-9191

Merrill
Brickyard School Museum Archives • Fairgrounds, Sales St • Merrill, WI 54452 • (715) 536-5652

Kaiser-Weber Research • N 629 Hilly Rd • Merrill, WI 54452 • *Kaiser-Weber Family Newsletter from Freudenbrug, Germany; Kissinger Konnection; Laessig Newsletter*

Merrill Historical Society & Archives • Pinery Logging Museum, 804 E 3rd St, P.O. Box 64 • Merrill, WI 54452 • (715) 536-5652 • *Northwoods Historian*

T B Scott Library • 106 W 1st St • Merrill, WI 54452-2398 • (715) 536-7191 • http://ucat.wvls.lib.wi.us/webpac.html

Merrillan
Thunderbird Museum Archives • N 9517 Thunderbird Ln • Merrillan, WI 54754-8033 • (715) 333-5841

Middleton
Middleton Area Historical Society & Archives • Historical Museum, 7410 Hubbard Ave • Middleton, WI 53562-3118 • (608) 836-7614 • http://www.ci.middleton.wi.us/history/ • *Middleton Area Historical Society Newsletter*

Middleton Public Library • 7425 Hubbard Ave • Middleton, WI 53562-3117 • (608) 831-5564 • http://www.scls.lib.wi.us/middleton

Milton
Goodrich House Archives • 742 E Madison • Milton, WI 53563 • (608) 868-7772

Milton Historical Society & Library • Milton House, 18 S Janesville St, P.O. Box 245 • Milton, WI 53563 • (608) 868-7772 • http://www.miltonhouse.org • *Herald*

Milwaukee
Afro-American Genealogical Society of Milwaukee • 2620 W Center St • Milwaukee, WI 53206

America's Black Holocaust Museum Archives • 2233 N 4th St • Milwaukee, WI 53212 • (414) 264-2500 • http://www.blackholocaustmuseum.org • *Vision*

Brown Family Reunion • 3902 W Galena • Milwaukee, WI 53208 • (414) 344-0563

Cornish Society of Greater Milwaukee • 3753 85th St • Milwaukee, WI 53228 • *Cornish Immigrant*

Gleason Reunions and Research • 5721 W Washington Blvd • Milwaukee, WI 53208 • (414) 258-9340 • *Gleesheet*

Golda Meir Library • Univ of Wisconsin, 2311 E Hartford Ave P.O. Box 604 • Milwaukee, WI 53201-0604 • (414) 229-4659 • http://www.uwm.edu/library/

Historic Milwaukee • 828 N Broadway, Ste 110 • Milwaukee, WI 53202 • (414) 277-7795 • http://www.historicmilwaukee.org

Irish Genealogical Society of Wisconsin • P.O. Box 13766 • Milwaukee, WI 53213-5564

Jewish Genealogical Society of Milwaukee • 9280 N Fairway Dr • Milwaukee, WI 53217 • (414) 351-2190 • *Family Finding*

Milwaukee County Genealogical Society • 1728 N 51st St, P.O. Box 270326 • Milwaukee, WI 53227-0326 • http://www.execpc.com/~mcgs • *Milwaukee County Genealogical Society Reporter*

Milwaukee County Historical Society & Library • 910 N Old World 3rd St • Milwaukee, WI 53203 • (414) 273-1731 • http://www.milwauikeecountyhistsoc.org • *Milwaukee History; Magazine of the Milwaukee County Historical Society; Newsletter of the Milwaukee County Historical Society*

Milwaukee Public Library • 814 W Wisconsin Ave • Milwaukee, WI 53233-2385 • (414) 286-3000 • http://www.mpl.org

Milwaukee Public Museum Archives • 800 W Wells St • Milwaukee, WI 53233 • (414) 278-2736 • http://www.mpm.edu/collect/libmenu.html

Milwaukee Schools Historical Society • general delivery • Milwaukee, WI 53201 • http://www.milwschools.org

Mitchell Gallery of Flight Archives • Gen Mitchell Intl Airport, 5300 S Howell Ave • Milwaukee, WI 53207 • (414) 747-4503 • http://www.mitchellgallery.org • *Flightlines*

Mount Carmel Lutheran Church Library • 8424 W Center St • Milwaukee, WI 53222 • (414) 771-1270 • http://www.execpc.com/~mcarmel/

Mount Mary College Historic Costume Collection • 2900 N Menomonee River Pkwy • Milwaukee, WI 53222 • (414) 256-0164 • http://www.mtmary.edu

North Point Lighthouse Friends • general delivery • Milwaukee, WI 53211 • (414) 332-6754

Parke Society • P.O. Box 590 • Milwaukee, WI 53201-0590 • (414) 332-9984 • http://www.parke.org • *Newsletter of the Parke Society*

Pellien-Jaeger-Loretan-Steiner-Ross Society • 10435 W Concordia Ave • Milwaukee, WI 53222 • (414) 259-1315 • *Buffalo Root News*

Polish Genealogical Society of Wisconsin • P.O. Box 342341 • Milwaukee, WI 53237 • (262) 628-3742 • http://feefhs.org/pol/frgpgswi.html • *Korzenie Roots*

Raynor Memorial Library • Marquette University, 1355 W Wisconsin Ave, P.O. Box 3141 • Milwaukee, WI 53233 • (414) 288-7556 • http://www.marquette.edu/library

Sons of the American Revolution, Wisconsin Society • 5677 N Consaul Pl • Milwaukee, WI 53217

Swiss Connection, a Genealogical and Cultural Newsletter • 2845 N 72nd St • Milwaukee, WI 53210-1106 • (414) 778-1224 • http://www.feefhs.org/tsc/frg-tsc.html • *Swiss Connection, a Genealogical and Cultural Newsletter*

Wauwatosa Historical Society • 7406 Hillcrest Cr • Milwaukee, WI 53213-2226

Wellauer-Winz-Wintz-Buel Surname Organization • 2845 N 72nd St • Milwaukee, WI 53210 • (414) 778-1224

Wendler-Guetzke Family Organization • 4103 S Logan Ave • Milwaukee, WI 53207 • (414) 481-6697

Wilhelmine Dorothea Buss-Hans Friedrich Mintzlaff-Franz August Friedrich Ehlers-Peter Brendemuhl-Abertine Friedericke Brewer Family Organization • 4035 N 82nd St • Milwaukee, WI 53222 • (414) 462-4250

Wisconsin Black Historical Society & Archives • Historical Museum, 2620 W Center St • Milwaukee, WI 53206-1155 • (414) 372-7677

Wisconsin Jewish Genealogical Society • 9280 N Fairway Dr • Milwaukee, WI 53217-1317 • (414) 351-2190 • *Family Finding*

Wisconsin Labor History Society • Wisconsin Workers Memorial, N 4th & W Michigan Sts • Milwaukee, WI 53201 • http://www.wisconsinlaborhistory.org

Wisconsin Marine Historical Society • c/o Milwaukee Public Library, 814 W Wisconsin Ave • Milwaukee, WI 53233-2385 • (414) 286-3074 • http://www.wmhs.org • *Soundings*

Mineral Point

Mineral Point Historical Society & Library • Gundy House, 234 Madison St, P.O. Box 188 • Mineral Point, WI 53565 • (608) 987-2884

Mineral Point Public Library • 137 High St • Mineral Point, WI 53565 • (608) 987-2447 • http://www.swls.org/member.mi.html

Pendarvis State Historic Site Archives • 114 Shake Rag St • Mineral Point, WI 53565 • (608) 987-2122 • http://www.pendarvis.wisconsinhistory.org

Southwest Wisconsin Cornish Society • 23073 Sunny Slope Rd • Mineral Point, WI 53565

Minocqua

Lakeland Area Genealogical Society • P.O. Box 308 • Minocqua, WI 54548

Minocqua Museum Archives • 503 Flambeau St, P.O. Box 1007 • Minocqua, WI 54548 • (715) 356-7666

Monona

Celtic Cultural Center • P.O. Box 6646 • Monona, WI 53716

Historic Blooming Grove Historical Society & Archives • Dean House, 4718 Monona Dr, P.O. Box 6704 • Monona, WI 53716 • (608) 222-6127 • http://www.wlhn.org/daneco/hbg • Blooming Grove Courier

Monona Public Library • 1000 Nichols Rd • Monona, WI 53716-2531 • (608) 222-6127 • http://www.scls.lib.wi.us/monona

Monroe

Green County Historical Society & Archives • Historical Museum, 1218 17th Ave • Monroe, WI 53566 • (608) 325-2924 • http://www.fgs.org/~fgs/soc0203.htm

Monroe Public Library • 925 16th Ave • Monroe, WI 53566-1497 • (608) 325-3016 • http://www.scls.lib.wi.us/lud/

Wisconsin State Genealogical Society • 2109 20th Ave • Monroe, WI 53566-3426 • (608) 325-2609 • http://www.wsgs.org • *Wisconsin State Genealogical Society Newsletter; Chapter Chatter; Leaders' Letter*

Montello

Montello Historic Preservation Society • N 4577 County Rd Y • Montello, WI 53949

Monticello

Monticello Area Historical Society • P.O. Box 463 • Monticello, WI 53570 • http://www.monticellowi.com/mahs.htm

Moravia

Grenelle Family Association • Cayuga Lake MHP Box D6 • Moravia, WI 54929 • *Grenelle Family Association Official Newsletter*

Mount Horeb

Mount Horeb Area Historical Society & Library • 138 E Main • Mount Horeb, WI 53572-2195 • http://www.mounthoreb.org

Mount Horeb Area Museum Archives • 100 S 2nd St • Mount Horeb, WI 53572 • (608) 437-6486

Mount Horeb Public Library • 105 Perimeter Rd • Mount Horeb, WI 53572 • (608) 437-5021 • http://www.scls.lib.wi.us/mounthoreb • *Mount Horeb Reader*

Mount Sterling

Crawford County Historical Society • Hauge Norwegian History Center, P.O. Box 72 • Mount Sterling, WI 54645-0072 • (608) 734-3192

Mountain

Mountain Historical Society • P.O. Box 198 • Mountain, WI 54149 • (715) 276-6474

Mukwonago

Mukwonago Community Library • 300 Washington Ave • Mukwonago, WI 53149-1909 • (262) 363-6411 • http://www.wcfls.lib.wi.us/mukcom/

Mukwonago Historical Society • 103 Main St, P.O. Box 392 • Mukwonago, WI 53149

Muscoda

Muscoda Public Library • 206 N Wisconsin Ave, P.O. Box 138 • Muscoda, WI 53573-0138 • (608) 739-3182 • http://www.swls.org/member.mu.html

Muskego

Muskego Historical Society • Old Town Hall, W 180 S 7732 Pioneer Dr, P.O. Box 137 • Muskego, WI 53150 • (262) 679-5667 • Muskego Historical Society Newsletter

Nashotah

Nashotah House Library • 2777 Mission Rd • Nashotah, WI 53058-9793 • (262) 646-6535 • http://www.nashotah.edu/library

Neenah

Military Veterans Museum Archives • Park Plaza Mall, P.O. Box 511 • Neenah, WI 54957-0511 • (920) 426-8615

Neenah Historical Society & Archives • Octagon House Museum, 343 Smith St, P.O. Box 343 • Neenah, WI 54956-2425 • (920) 729-0244 • *Society Times*

Neenah Public Library • 240 E Wisconsin Ave, P.O. Box 569 • Neenah, WI 54957-0569 • (920) 886-6315 • http://www.neenahlibrary.org • *Neenah Public Library Newsletter*

Neillsville

Clark County Historical Society & Archives • Historical Museum, 215 E 5th St • Neillsville, WI 54456 • (715) 743-4799

Nekoosa

Historic Point Basse • P.O. Box 295 • Nekoosa, WI 54457 • (715) 886-4202 • http://www.historicpointbasse.com

Neosho

Neosho Historical Society & Archives • Old Village Hall Museum, 115 S Schuyler St, P.O. Box 105 • Neosho, WI 53059 • (920) 625-3632 • *Neosho Museum Researcher*

New Berlin

New Berlin Historical Society & Archives • Historical Museum, 19765 W National Ave • New Berlin, WI 53151 • (262) 679-1783 • *New Berlin Almanack*

New Berlin Public Library • 14750 W Cleveland Ave • New Berlin, WI 53151 • (262) 785-4980 • http://www.wcfls.lib.wi.us/newberlin

New Glarus

Chalet of the Golden Fleece Archives • 618 2nd St • New Glarus, WI 53574 • (608) 527-2614

New Glarus Historical Society • Swiss Historical Village, 612 7th Ave, P.O. Box 745 • New Glarus, WI 53574-0745 • (608) 527-2317 • http://www.swisshistoricalvillage.com

New Holstein

1892 Timm House Archives • 1600 Wisconsin Ave • New Holstein, WI 53061

Calumet County Historical Society & Archives • Historical Museum, 1704 Eisenhower St • New Holstein, WI 53061 • (920) 849-2084

New Holstein Historical Society & Archives • Pioneer Corner Museum, 2103 Main St, P.O. Box 144 • New Holstein, WI 53061 • (920) 898-5358 • http://www.geocities.com/nbhistorical • *New Holstein Historical Society Annual Newsletter*

New London

New London Heritage Historical Society & Library • 101 E Beckert Rd, Apt #204 • New London, WI 54961 • (920) 982-5186

New London Public Library and Museum • 406 S Pearl St • New London, WI 54961-1441 • (920) 982-8519 • http://www.owls.lib.wi.us/nlp; http://www.newlondonwi.org

Waupaca County Historical Society • N 4804 County Trunk B • New London, WI 54961

New Richmond

Carleton A Friday Memorial Library • 155 E 1st St • New Richmond, WI 54017 • (715) 246-2364

New Richmond Preservation Society • Heritage Center, 1100 Heritage Dr • New Richmond, WI 54017 • (715) 246-3276 • http://www.pressenter.com/~nrpsinc/

Niagara

Niagara Area Historical Society & Archives • Historical Museum, 1024 Main St, P.O. Box 114 • Niagara, WI 54151 • (715) 251-3348

North Fond du Lac

Fond du Lac County Genealogical Society • c/o Spillman Library, 715 Wisconsin Ave, P.O. Box 1264 • North Fond du Lac, WI 54936 • (608) 522-4571 • *Fond du Lac County Genealogical Society Newsletter*

Spillman Library • 719 Wisconsin Ave • North Fond du Lac, WI 54937-1335 • (608) 522-4571 • http://www.northfonddulaclibrary.org

North Freedom

Mid-Continent Railway Historical Society • P.O. Box 358 • North Freedom, WI 53951 • (800) 930-1385 • http://www.midcontinent.org

Mid-Continent Railway Museum Archives • F8948 Diamond Hill Rd • North Freedom, WI 53961 • (608) 522-4261 • http://www.midcontinent.org • *Mid-Continent Railway Gazette*

Oak Creek

Oak Creek Historical Society & Archives • Pioneer Village Museum, S 15th Ave & E Forest Hill Ave, P.O. Box 243 • Oak Creek, WI 53154 • (414) 764-0567 • http://www.ochistorical.freeservers.com

Oconomowoc

Oconomowoc Genealogical Club of Waukesha County & Library • 733 E Sherman Ave • Oconomowoc, WI 53066 • (262) 567-3197

Oconomowoc Historical Society & Archives • Historical Museum, 103 W Jefferson St, P.O. Box 563 • Oconomowoc, WI 53066 • (262) 569-0740 • http://www.oconomowoc.org/Library/Outreach.htm • *Coo-No-Mo-Wauk*

Oconto

Farnsworth Public Library • 715 Main St • Oconto, WI 54153-1795 • (920) 834-7730 • http://www.nfls.lib.wi.us/oco

Oconto County Historical Society & Archives • Beyer Home Museum, 917 Park Ave • Oconto, WI 54153-1641 • (920) 834-6206 • http://www.ocontocountyhistsoc.org • *News from the Northwoods*

Omro

Carter Memorial Library • 405 E Huron St • Omro, WI 54963-1405 • (920) 685-7016 • http://www.omrolibrary.org

Heritage Hall Archives • Masonic Temple, 160 E Main St • Omro, WI 54963 • (920) 685-3010

Omro Area Historical Society & Archives • Historical Museum, 114 E Main St, P.O. Box 133 • Omro, WI 54963 • (920) 685-6123

Onalaska

Onalaska Area Historical Society & Archives • Historical Museum, 741 Oak Ave S • Onalaska, WI 54650 • (608) 783-1586 • http://www.historyofonalaska.com

Oneida

Oneida Community Library • 201 Elm St, P.O. Box 365 • Oneida, WI 54155-0365 • (920) 869-2210

Oneida National Museum Archives • W 892 County Trunk EE, P.O. Box 365 • Oneida, WI 54155 • (920) 869-2768

Oregon

Oregon Area Historical Society & Archives • Historical Museum, 159 W Lincoln St, P.O. Box 262 • Oregon, WI 53575 • (608) 935-8961 • http://www.oregonareahistoricalsociety.org

Osceola

Osceola Depot Archives • 114 Depot Rd • Osceola, WI 54020 • (715) 755-3570

Osceola Historical Society & Archives • Historic Emily Olson House, 408 River St, P.O. Box 342 • Osceola, WI 54020 • (715) 294-2480

Oshkosh

EAA Airventure Museum Archives • 3000 Poberczny Rd • Oshkosh, WI 54903 • (920) 426-4800 • http://www.airventuremuseum.org

Forrest R Polk Library • Univ of Wisconsin-Oshkosh, 800 Algoma Blvd • Oshkosh, WI 54901 • (920) 424-4333 • http://www.uwosh.edu/library/ • *Polk Library News*

Military Veterans Museum Archives • 245 City Center • Oshkosh, WI 54901 • (920) 426-8615 • http://www.mvmwisconsin.com • *News from Home*

Oshkosh Public Library • 106 Washington Ave • Oshkosh, WI 54901-4985 • (920) 236-5200 • http://www.winnefox.org • *Library Lines*; *Tid Bits*

Oshkosh Public Museum Archives • 1331 Algoma Blvd • Oshkosh, WI 54901-2799 • (920) 424-4735 • http://www.publicmuseum.oshkosh.net • *Oshkosh Public Museum Newsletter*

Winnebago County Historical and Archaeological Society & Archives • Morgan House, 234 Church Ave, P.O. Box 401 • Oshkosh, WI 54902 • (920) 232-0260 • http://www.morganhouse.org

Winnebagoland Genealogical Society • c/o Oshkosh Public Library, 106 Washington Ave • Oshkosh, WI 54901-4985 • (920) 236-5226 • *Winnebagoland Roots*

Osseo

Osseo Historical Society • P. O. Box 124 • Osseo, WI 54758 • (715) 597-2269

Oulu

Bayfield County Historical Society, Oulu Chapter • general delivery • Oulu, WI 54758 • http://www.ouluwis.us

Palmyra

Palmyra Historical Society & Archives • Carlin House-Turner Museum, 112 N 3rd St, P.O. Box 265 • Palmyra, WI 53156 • (262) 495-4245 • http://www.palmyrahistoric.org • *Palmyra Historical Society Newsletter*

Powers Memorial Library • 115 Main St, P.O. Box O • Palmyra, WI 53156-0924 • (262) 495-4605 • http://www.palmyra.lib.wi.us

Pardeeville
Columbia County Historical Society & Archives • Myrtle Lintner Spear Museum, 112 N Main St • Pardeeville, WI 53954 • (608) 429-1447

Park Ave
Howard Morey House Archives • Park Ave • Park Ave, WI 54817 • (715) 354-3885

Park Falls
Old Town Hall Museum Archives • W 6925 Bush Rd • Park Falls, WI 54552 • (715) 762-4571

Park Falls Public Library • 121 N 4th St • Park Falls, WI 54552 • (715) 762-3121 • http://www.parkfallslibrary.org

Pepin
Laura Ingalls Wilder Memorial Society & Archives • Historical Museum, Hwy 35, P.O. Box 269 • Pepin, WI 54759 • (800) 442-3011 • http://www.pepinwisconsin.com

Peshtigo
Peshtigo Historical Society & Archives • Peshtigo Fire Museum, 400 Oconto Ave • Peshtigo, WI 54147 • (715) 582-3244 • *Peshtigo Fire Museum Newsletter*

Rhines Family History • N3291 River Bend Rd • Peshtigo, WI 54157-9502

Pewaukee
Pewaukee Area Historical Society & Archives • Historical Museum, 206 E Wisconsin Ave, P.O. Box 105 • Pewaukee, WI 53072-3519 • (262) 691-0233 • http://clarkhousemuseum.lakecountrybusiness.com

Phelps
Eleanor Ellis Public Library • Town Hall Rd, P.O. Box 8 • Phelps, WI 54554-0008 • (715) 545-2887 • http://www.nwls.lib.wi.us

Phillips
Jump River Valley Historical Society & Archives • Historical Museum, N 6882 The Loop • Phillips, WI 54555 • (715) 474-3408

Pine River
Leon-Saxeville Township Public Library • N4715 County Rd E, P.O. Box 247 • Pine River, WI 54965-0247 • (920) 987-5110 • http://www.pineriverlibrary.org

Plainfield
Plainfield Public Library • 126 S Main St, P.O. Box 305 • Plainfield, WI 54966-0305 • (715) 335-4523 • http://www.plainfieldlibrary.org

Platteville
Elton S Karrmann Library • Univ of Wisconsin-Platteville, 1 University Plaza • Platteville, WI 53818-3099 • (608) 342-1668 • http://www.uwplatt.edu/~library

Grant County Genealogical Society • 955 Williams St, P.O. Box 233 • Platteville, WI 53818 • *Grant County Heritage*

Mitchell-Rountree Stone Cottage Archives • Hwy 81 & W Madison St • Platteville, WI 53818 • (608) 723-2287

Platteville Mining Museum Archives • 385 E Main St, P.O. Box 780 • Platteville, WI 53818 • (608) 348-3301

Platteville Public Library • 65 S Elm St • Platteville, WI 53818 • (608) 348-7441 • http://www.platteville.net

Rollo Jamison Museum Archives • 405 E Main St, P.O. Box 780 • Platteville, WI 53818-0780 • http://www.platteville.org

Sprague Database • 45 Knollwood Wy • Platteville, WI 53818-3731 • (608) 348-4101

Pleasant Prairie
Kenosha Military Museum Archives • 11114 120th Ave • Pleasant Prairie, WI 53158 • (252) 857-3418 • http://www.kenoshamilitarymuseum.com

Plum City
Plum City Public Library • 611 Main St, P.O. Box 203 • Plum City, WI 54761-0203 • (715) 647-2373 • http://plumcitylibrary.org

Plymouth
John G Voigt House Archives • W 5639 Anokijig Ln • Plymouth, WI 53073 • (720) 893-0782

Plymouth Genealogical Society • c/o Plymouth Public Library, 130 Division St • Plymouth, WI 53073 • (920) 892-4416

Plymouth Historical Society & Archives • Plymouth Center Museum, 520 E Mill St • Plymouth, WI 53073 • http://www.plymouthhistoricalsociety.com

Plymouth Public Library • 130 Division St • Plymouth, WI 53073-1802 • (920) 892-4416

Port Washington
Letzebuerger Sprooch, Luxembourg Society of Wisconsin • P.O. Box 328 • Port Washington, WI 53074-0328

Port Washington Historical Society • 311 N Johnson St, P.O. Box 491 • Port Washington, WI 53074-1604 • (262) 284-7240 • http://www.PortWashingtonHistoricalSociety.org

Port Washington Historical Society Research Center • 101 E Grand Ave • Port Washington, WI 53074 • (262) 376-3190

Port Wing
Port Wing Historical Society • Heritage Hall, 8840 State Highway 13, P.O. Box 113 • Port Wing, WI 54865 • (715) 774-3949

Portage
Colonial Dames of America, Wisconsin Society & Archives • Indian Agency House, Hwy 33, P.O. Box 84 • Portage, WI 53211-3116 • (608) 742-6362 • http://www.nscda.org

Daughters of the American Revolution, Wisconsin Society & Library • Fort Winnebago Surgeon's Quarters, W 8687 St Hwy 33 E • Portage, WI 53901 • (608) 742-2949

Portage Historical Society & Archives • Historical Museum, 804 Macfarlane Rd, P.O. Box 727 • Portage, WI 53901 • (608) 742-6682

Portage Public Library • 253 W Edgewater St • Portage, WI 53901 • (608) 742-4959 • http://www.scls.lib.wi.us/portage

Poynette
Poynette Area Historical Society & Archives • Historical Museum, 114 N Main St, P.O. Box 162 • Poynette, WI 53955 • (608) 635-2336

Prairie du Chien
Prairie du Chien Historical Society & Archives • Fort Crawford Museum, 717 S Beaumont Rd, P.O. Box 298 • Prairie du Chien, WI 53821-0298 • (608) 326-6960 • http://www.fortcrawfordmuseum.com

Prairie du Chien Memorial Library • 125 S Wacouta Ave • Prairie du Chien, WI 53821-1632 • (608) 326-6211 • http://www.swls.org/member.so.html

Villa Louis Historic Site Archives • 521 Villa Louis Rd, P.O. Box 65 • Prairie du Chien, WI 53821 • (608) 326-2721 • http://www.wisconsinhistory.org/villalouis

Prairie du Sac
Prairie du Sac Public Library • 560 Park Ave • Prairie du Sac, WI 53578-1199 • (608) 643-8318 • http://www.scls.lib.wi.us/pds

Salem-Ragatz Church Museum Archives • S9515 Church Rd • Prairie du Sac, WI 53578

Sauk Prairie Area Historical Society & Archives • Tripp Memorial Museum, 565 Water St • Prairie du Sac, WI 53578 • (608) 644-8444 • http://www.saukprairiehistory.org

Prescott
Pierce County Historical Association • Heritage Center, 235 Broad St N • Prescott, WI 54021 • (715) 262-3284

Prescott Public Library • 800 Borner St N • Prescott, WI 54021-1703 • (715) 262-5555 • http://www.prescott-lib.org

Presque Isle
Presque Isle Heritage Society • P.O. Box 172 • Presque Isle, WI 54557 • (715) 686-2481

Wisconsin

Princeton
Princeton Historical Society & Library • Stone House, 632 W Water St • Princeton, WI 54968 • (920) 295-6949

Westside Center Museum Archives • 1009 W Main St • Princeton, WI 54968

Pulaski
Pulaski Area Historical Society • 129 W Pulaski St, P.O. Box 944 • Pulaski, WI 54162 • (920) 822-5856

Racine
Gradeless-Grayless-Mort Family of America • 1721 Edgewood Ave • Racine, WI 53404-2306 • (262) 634-2824 • http://www.execpc.com/~drg/mort.html • *Mort Newsletter*

Hentila Reunion • 5311 Twin Elms Dr • Racine, WI 53406 • (262) 634-4117

National Huguenot Society • 508 de Koven Ave • Racine, WI 53403-2754 • *Cross of Languedoc*

Racine County Historical Society & Archives • Heritage Museum, 701 S Main St, P.O. Box 1527 • Racine, WI 53401-1527 • (262) 636-3926 • http://www.spiritofinnovation.org • *Focus: Quarterly of the Racine County Historical Society*; *Outlook*

Racine Public Library • 75 7th St • Racine, WI 53403-1200 • (262) 636-9217 • http://www.racinelib.lib.wi.us

Randolph
Hutchinson Memorial Library • 228 N High St • Randolph, WI 53956 • (920) 326-4640

Lost Lake-Randolph Historical Society • N 7148 Hwy 73 • Randolph, WI 53956

Random Lake
Lakeview Community Library • 112 Butler St, P.O. Box 326 • Random Lake, WI 53075-0326 • (920) 994-4825 • http://randomlake.lib.wi.us

Reedsburg
Reedsburg Area Historical Society & Library • Reedsburg Log Village, P.O. Box 405 • Reedsburg, WI 53959 • (608) 727-2922 • *Reedsburg Area Historical Society Newsletter*

Rhinelander
Northwoods Genealogical Society • c/o Rhinelander District Library, 106 N Stevens St, P.O. Box 1132 • Rhinelander, WI 54501

Oneida County Genealogical Society • c/o Rhinelander District Library, 106 N Stevens St • Rhinelander, WI 54501 • (715) 369-1070

Rhinelander District Library • 106 N Stevens St • Rhinelander, WI 54501-3193 • (715) 369-1070

Rhinelander Historical Society & Archives • Historical Museum, 9 S Pelham St • Rhinelander, WI 54501-3458 • (715) 369-3833

Rhinelander Logging Museum Archives • Pioneer Park, Martin Lynch Dr • Rhinelander, WI 54501 • (715) 362-2193 • http://www.rhinelanderchamber.com

Rice Lake
Rice Lake Public Library • 2 E Marshall St • Rice Lake, WI 54868 • (715) 234-4861 • http://www.ricelakelibrary.org

Richfield
Polish Genealogical Society of Wisconsin • 3731 Turnwood Dr • Richfield, WI 53076-9635 • *Polish Genealogical Society of Wisconsin Newsletter*

Richfield Historical Park Archives • P.O. Box 268 • Richfield, WI 53076 • (262) 644-5857

Richfield Historical Society • 4399 Pleasant Hill Rd, P.O. Box 268 • Richfield, WI 53076 • (262) 628-4086

Richland Center
Brewer Public Library • 325 N Central Ave • Richland Center, WI 53581-1802 • (608) 647-6444 • http://www.brewerpubliclibrary.org

Ripon
Lane Library • Ripon College, 300 Seward St, P.O. Box 248 • Ripon, WI 54971-0248 • (920) 748-9751 • http://www.ripon.edu/library

Little White School House Archives • 303 Blackburn St • Ripon, WI 54971 • (920) 748-6764 • http://www.ripon-wi.com

Ripon Historical Society & Archives • Historical Museum, 508 Watson St, P.O. Box 274 • Ripon, WI 54797 • (920) 748-5354 • http://my.core.com/~riponhistsoc/

Ripon Public Library • 120 Jefferson St • Ripon, WI 54971-1395 • (920) 748-6160 • http://www.riponlibrary.org • *Ripon Public Library*

River Falls
Chalmer Davee Library • Univ of Wisconsin/River Falls, 410 S 3rd St • River Falls, WI 54022 • (715) 425-3343 • http://www.uwrf.edu/library

River Falls Public Library • 140 Union St, P.O. Box 45 • River Falls, WI 54022-0045 • (715) 425-0905 • http://www.rfcity.org/library

Saint Croix Valley Genealogical Society • 1010 Sunset Ln, P.O. Box 396 • River Falls, WI 54022-0396 • (715) 273-5239 • http://www.pressenter.com/~scvgs/ • *Pipost*

Roberts
Hazel Mackin Community Library • 107 W Main St, P.O. Box 88 • Roberts, WI 54023-0088 • (715) 749-3849 • http://www.robertspubliclibrary.org

Rock Springs
Rock Springs Public Library • 101 1st St, P.O. Box 56 • Rock Springs, WI 53961-0056 • (608) 522-5050

Rosendale
Rosendale Historical Society • P.O. Box 254 • Rosendale, WI 54974-0254 • (920) 872-2558

Saint Croix Falls
Polk County Historical Society, Saint Croix Falls Chapter • P.O. Box 281 • Saint Croix Falls, WI 54024 • (715) 483-3580 • http://www.scffwi.com/history.htm

Saint Croix Falls Public Library • 210 Washington St • Saint Croix Falls, WI 54024 • (715) 483-1777

Saint Francis
Saint Francis Historical Society • City Hall, 4235 S Nicholson Ave • Saint Francis, WI 53235

Salzmann Library • Saint Francis Seminary, 3257 S Lake Dr • Saint Francis, WI 53235-0905 • (414) 747-6476 • http://www.sfs.edu/salzmann.html

Saint Nazianz
Saint Nazianz Area Historical Society • P.O. Box 125 • Saint Nazianz, WI 54232

Sauk City
August Derleth Society • P.O. Box 481 • Sauk City, WI 53583-0481 • *August Derleth Society Newsletter*

Sauk City Public Library • 515 Water St • Sauk City, WI 53583-1159 • (608) 643-8346 • http://www.scls.lib.wi.us/skc/

Saukville
Ozaukee County Pioneer Village Archives • 4880 Hwy I • Saukville, WI 53080 • (262) 377-4510 • http://www.co.ozaukee.wi.us/ochs • *Timelines*

Saukville Area Historical Society • 200 N Mill St • Saukville, WI 53080 • (262) 268-9197 • http://www.saukvillehistory.org

Sayner
Plum Lake Public Library • 239 Hwy 155, P.O. Box 99 • Sayner, WI 54560 • (715) 542-2020

Vilas County Historical Society • Main St • Sayner, WI 54560

Schofield
Wisconsin Genealogical Council • 109 Summer St • Schofield, WI 54476-1282 • (608) 378-4388 • Quarterly Wisconsin Genealogical Council Newsletter

Seymour
Depot Museum Archives • 129 Depot St • Seymour, WI 54165 • (920) 833-2063

Seymour Community Historical Society & Archives • Historical Museum, 377 Washington St • Seymour, WI 54165 • (920) 833-2063

Seymour Community Museum Archives • Depot St • Seymour, WI 54165 • *Museum Muse*

Sharon

Sharon Historical Preservation Society • P.O. Box 109 • Sharon, WI 53585 • http://www.sharonwisconsin.com/HS/home.htm

Shawano

Selke-Holcomb Reunion • W5191 Lulu Lake Dr • Shawano, WI 54166 • (715) 745-4123

Shawano City-County Library • 128 S Sawyer St • Shawano, WI 54166-2496 • (715) 526-3829 • http://www.fnfls.lib.wi.us/sha

Shawano County Historical Society & Archives • Historical Museum, 524 N Franklin St • Shawano, WI 54166 • (715) 526-3323 • http://www.shawanohistorical.org

Sheboygan

John Esch Library • Lakeland College, P.O. Box 359 • Sheboygan, WI 53082-0359 • (920) 565-1238

Mead Public Library • 710 N 8th St • Sheboygan, WI 53081-4563 • (920) 459-3400 • http://www.sheboygan.lib.wi.us

Sheboygan County Historical Museum Archives • 3110 Erie Ave • Sheboygan, WI 53081 • (920) 458-1103 • http://www.co.sheboygan.wi.us/html/d_museum.html • *Sheboygan County Historical Museum Newsletter*

Sheboygan Falls

Sheboygan County Genealogical Society & Library • 518 Water St • Sheboygan Falls, WI 53085-1455 • (920) 467-4667 • *Sheboygan County Genealogist*

Sheboygan County Historical Research Center • 504 Broadway • Sheboygan Falls, WI 53085

Sheboygan County Historical Society & Archives • Historical Research Center, 518 Water St • Sheboygan Falls, WI 53085 • (920) 467-4667 • http://www.schrc.org • *Sheboygan County Historical Society Quarterly*

Sheboygan Falls Memorial Library • 330 Buffalo St, P.O. Box 140 • Sheboygan Falls, WI 53085-0140 • (920) 467-7908

Shell Lake

Shell Lake Public Library • 501 1st St, P.O. Box 318 • Shell Lake, WI 54871-0318 • (715) 468-2074

Washburn County Genealogical Society & Library • 102 W 2nd Ave, P.O. Box 366 • Shell Lake, WI 54871 • (715) 468-2982 • Roots in Washburn County

Washburn County Historical Society & Archives • Historical Museum, 102 2nd Ave W, P.O. Box 366 • Shell Lake, WI 54871 • (715) 468-2982 • http://www.rootsweb.com/~wiwashbu/

Sherwood

High Cliff Historical Society & Archives • Historical Museum, 7526 N Lower Cliff Rd, P.O. Box 1 • Sherwood, WI 54169 • (920) 989-1636 • http://www.historical-sctyatwebtv.net

Timmers Dutch Family Society • Springhill Dr • Sherwood, WI 54952

Shorewood

Shorewood Historical Society • Village Hall, 3930 N Murray Ave • Shorewood, WI 53211 • (414) 332-4437 • http://www.shorewoodhistory.org

Shullsburg

Badger Historical Society • 113 E Church St, P.O. Box 186 • Shullsburg, WI 53586 • (608) 965-3481

Badger Mine and Museum Archives • 279 Estey, P.O. Box 3 • Shullsburg, WI 53586 • (608) 965-4860 • http://www.shullsburg.com/mine/mine.htm

Lafayette County Genealogical Workshop • 226 W Church St, P.O. Box 443 • Shullsburg, WI 53586 • (608) 776-2755 • *Ancestral Diggin's of Lafayette County, Wisconsin*

Sister Bay

Sister Bay Historical Society & Archives • Old Anderson House Museum, P.O. Box 34 • Sister Bay, WI 54234 • (920) 854-7680

Solon Springs

Solon Springs Historical Society & Archives • John Beck Log House, 10732 S Rocky Hill Rd • Solon Springs, WI 54873 • (715) 798-4480

Somerset

Somerset Public Library • 208 Hud St, P.O. Box 129 • Somerset, WI 54025-0129 • (715) 247-5228

South Milwaukee

Breitbach Reunion • 730 Menomonee Ave • South Milwaukee, WI 53172

South Milwaukee Historical Society • Historical Museum, 717 Milwaukee Ave • South Milwaukee, WI 53172 • (414) 768-8790 • http://www.southmilwaukee.org • *South Milwaukee Historical Society Quarterly*

South Wayne

Schliem-Schlem Family Reunion • 302 E Psospect St, P.O. Box 238 • South Wayne, WI 53587 • (608) 439-5418

Sparta

Deke Slayton Memorial Space and Bike Museum Archives • 200 W Main St • Sparta, WI 54656 • (888) 200-5302 • http://www.DekeSlayton.com

Monroe County Historical Society & Archives • History Museum, 200 W Main St, P.O. Box 422 • Sparta, WI 54656-0422 • (608) 269-8680 • *Historical Time Capsules of Monroe County; Monroe County Historical Society Newsletter*

Monroe County Local History Room & Library • 200 W Main St • Sparta, WI 54656-2141 • (608) 269-8680 • http://www.rootsweb.com/~wimonroe/

Spring Green

House on the Rock Museum Archives • 5754 Hwy 23 • Spring Green, WI 53588 • (608) 935-3639 • http://www.thehouseontherock.com

Spring Green Community Library • 230 E Monroe St, P.O. Box 520 • Spring Green, WI 53588-0520 • (608) 588-2276 • http://www.scls.lib.wi.us/sgr

Springbrook

Springbrook Church Museum Archives • N 8582 Andrews Rd, P.O. Box 91 • Springbrook, WI 54875 • (715) 766-3876

Stanley

Historical Society of Stanley & Archives • Historical Museum, 228 Helgerson St • Stanley, WI 54768 • (715) 644-0464 • *Stanley Historical Society Newsletter*

Stevens Point

Portage County Historical Society & Archives • Historial Museum 1475 Water St, P.O. Box 672 • Stevens Point, WI 54481 • (715) 344-4423 • http://www.pchswi.org • *Pinery; Portage County Historical Society Newsletter*

Portage County Public Library • 1001 Main St • Stevens Point, WI 54481-2860 • (715) 346-1545 • http://library.uwsp.edu/pcl/

Stevens Point Area Genealogical Society & Archives • c/o Portage County Library, 1001 Main St • Stevens Point, WI 54481-2860 • (715) 346-1548 • *Pedigree Pointers*

University Library • Univ of Wisconsin-Stevens Point, 900 Reserve St • Stevens Point, WI 54481-1985 • (715) 346-3038 • http://library.uwsp.edu

Stone Lake

Stone Lake Area Historical Society & Archives • Historical Museum, Old Stone Lake Township Town Hall, P.O. Box 95 • Stone Lake, WI 54876

Stoughton

Stoughton Historical Society & Archives • Historical Museum, 324 S Page St • Stoughton, WI 53589-2166 • (608) 873-3162

Stratford

Stratford Area Historical Society & Archives • Historical Museum, Klemme Park • Stratford, WI 54484

Sturgeon Bay
Door County Historical Society • 120 N Madison Ave • Sturgeon Bay, WI 54235-3416 • (920) 743-4045 • http://www.CrossRoadsAtBigCreek.org

Door County Library • 107 S 4th Ave • Sturgeon Bay, WI 54235 • (920) 743-6578 • http://www.dcl.lib.wi.us

Door County Maritime Museum Archives • 120 N Madison Ave • Sturgeon Bay, WI 54235 • (920) 743-5958 • http://www.dcmm.org • *Door County Maritime Museum Newsletter*

Door County Museum Archives • 18 N 4th • Sturgeon Bay, WI 54235 • (262) 743-5809

Farm Museum Archives • 4285 Hwy 57, P.O. Box 44 • Sturgeon Bay, WI 54235 • (920) 743-6666 • http://www.thefarmindoorcounty.com • *Down on the Farm*

Jacksonport Historical Society • 4768 Hwy 57 • Sturgeon Bay, WI 54235 • (920) 823-2540 • http://www.doorbell.net/jhs

Sullivan
Concord Historical Society • N 5863 Hickory Hill Rd • Sullivan, WI 53178 • (262) 593-8099 • http://www.concordwisconsin.org/Concord_Historical_Society.html

Sun Prairie
Historical Library and Archives, Wisconsin United Methodist Conference Center • 750 Windsor St, P.O. Box 220 • Sun Prairie, WI 53590-0220 • (608) 837-7328

Sun Prairie Historical Library and Museum Archives • 115 E Main St • Sun Prairie, WI 53590 • (608) 837-2511

Sun Prairie Historical Society & Archives • Historical Museum, 115 E Main St, P.O. Box 313 • Sun Prairie, WI 53590 • (608) 837-2915 • http://www.sunprairie.com • *Sun Prairie Historical Society Newsletter*

Sun Prairie Public Library • 1350 Linnerud Dr • Sun Prairie, WI 53590-2631 • (608) 825-7323 • http://www.scls.lib.wi.us/sunprairie/home.html

Superior
Douglas County Historical Society & Archives • Historical Museum, 1101 John Ave • Superior, WI 54880 • (715) 392-8449 • http://www.douglashistory.org

Fairlawn Mansion Museum Archives • 906 E 2nd • Superior, WI 54880 • (715) 394-5712 • http://www.fairlawnmansion.org • *Whaleback Log*

Jim Dan Hill Library • Univ of Wisconsin-Superior, Belknap & Catlin Sts, P.O. Box 2000 • Superior, WI 54880 • (715) 394-8341 • http://www.uwsuper.edu

Richard I Bong WWII Heritage Center Archives • 305 Harbor View Pkwy • Superior, WI 54880 • (715) 392-7151 • http://www.bongheritagecenter.org • *Bong Flyer*

Superior Public Library • 1530 Tower Ave • Superior, WI 54880-2532 • (715) 394-8860 • http://ci.superior.wi.us

Tyomies Society • P.O. Box 549 • Superior, WI 54880-0549 • (715) 394-4961 • *Finnish American Reporter-Tyomies-Eteenpain*

Suring
Oconto County Genealogical Society • P.O. Box 114 • Suring, WI 54174 • (920)842-4274

Sussex
Sussex-Lisbon Area Historical Society • N 63 W 23791 Main St • Sussex, WI 53089 • (262) 820-9164 • http://www.slahs.org

Theresa
John Schiefer Historic Home Archives • general delivery • Theresa, WI 53091

Theresa Public Library • 290 Mayville St • Theresa, WI 53091-0307 • (920) 488-2342

Thiensville
Mequon Historical Society • 6100 W Mequon Rd 112N • Thiensville, WI 53092 • (262) 242-3107

Thorp
Thorp Area Historical Society • N 14945 Gorman Ave • Thorp, WI 54771 • (715) 669-7286

Thorp Area Historical Society & Archives • Historical Museum, 312 W Franklin St • Thorp, WI 54771 • (715) 669-7140

Three Lakes
Three Lakes Historical Society & Archives • Historical Museum, 1798 Huron St, P.O. Box 250 • Three Lakes, WI 54562 • (715) 546-2295 • *Pine, the Plow and the Pioneer, Echo*

Tigerton
Tigerton Area Historical Society • Swanke & Chestnut Sts • Tigerton, WI 54486

Tomah
Monroe, Juneau, Jackson County Wisconsin Genealogy Workshop • 723 Packard St • Tomah, WI 54660 • (608) 372-5810 • *Monroe, Juneau, Jackson County Wisconsin Genealogy Workshop Newsletter*

Tomah Area Historical Society & Archives • Historical Museum, 1112 S Superior Ave • Tomah, WI 54660-2608 • (608) 372-1880

Tomahawk
Tomahawk Historical Society & Archives • Log Cabin Museum, 18 E Washington Ave, P.O. Box 655 • Tomahawk, WI 54487 • (715) 453-3628

Trempealeau
Trempealeau Community Heritage Society • P.O. Box 109 • Trempealeau, WI 54661

Trevor
Western Kenosha County Historical Society & Archives • Twin Oaks Schoolhouse, 25905 114th St, P.O. Box 232 • Trevor, WI 53179-0232 • (262) 843-4673

Two Rivers
Lester Public Library • 1001 Adams • Two Rivers, WI 54241 • (920) 793-8888 • http://www.tworivers.lib.wi.us

Two Rivers Historical Society & Archives • Hamilton Wood Type Museum, 1619 Jefferson St • Two Rivers, WI 54241 • (920) 794-6272 • http://www.woodtype.org

Two Rivers Historical Society & Library • Historic Washington House, 1622 Jefferson St • Two Rivers, WI 54241-3017 • (920) 793-2490 • *Two Rivers Historical Society Newsletter*

Two Rivers History Museum Archives • 1810 Jefferson St • Two Rivers, WI 54241 • (920) 793-1103

Union Grove
Graham Public Library • 1215 Main St • Union Grove, WI 53182-1303 • (262) 878-2910 • http://www.uniongrove.lib.wi.us

Verona
Verona Public Library • 130 N Franklin St • Verona, WI 53593-1202 • (608) 845-7180 • http://www.ci.verona.wi.us/library

Vesper
Vesper Public Library • 6553 Cameron St • Vesper, WI 54489-9999 • (715) 569-4669

Viola
Viola Public Library • 137 S Main St • Viola, WI 54664-7037 • (608) 627-1850 • http://www.swls.org/member.vi.html

Viroqua
Banta Research • Route 4, Box V118 • Viroqua, WI 54665 • (608) 637-2003 • *Banta Pioneers*

Vernon County Historical Museum Archives • 410 S Center St, P.O. Box 444 • Viroqua, WI 54665 • (608) 637-7396 • http://www.frontiernet.net/~vcmuseum/ • *Museum Notes*

Vernon County Historical Society & Archives • Historical Museum, 410 S Center, P.O. Box 444 • Viroqua, WI 54665 • (608) 637-7396 • http://www.frontiernet.com/~vcmuseum/

Washburn
Bayfield County Historical Society & Archives • Historical Museum, 1 E Bayfield St, P.O. Box 272 • Washburn, WI 54891 • (715) 373-5591 • *Historical Happenings*

Washburn Historial Society • 1 E Bayfield • Washburn, WI 54891

Washburn Historical Museum Archives • 1 E Bayfield St, P.O. Box 725 • Washburn, WI 54891 • (715) 373-5591 • *Brownstone Notes*

Washington Island
Washington Island Farm Museum Archives • RR1 Jackson Harbor Rd • Washington Island, WI 54246 • (920) 847-3336 • http://www.washingtonisland.com/washingtonislandfarmmuseum/

Waterford
Rochester Area Historical Society • 2441 Beck Dr • Waterford, WI 53185-5101 • (262) 534-2071

Waterloo
Karl Junginger Memorial Library • 625 N Monroe St • Waterloo, WI 53594-1183 • (920) 478-3344 • http://www.waterloo.lib.wi.us • *Off the Shelves*

Waterloo Area Historical Society & Archives • Historical Museum, 136 Polk St, P.O. Box 52 • Waterloo, WI 53594 • (920) 478-2428 • *Timescape*

Watertown
Dodge and Jefferson Counties Genealogical Society • 504 S 4th St, P.O. Box 91 • Watertown, WI 53094-0091 • (920) 262-2362 • http://www.DodgeJeffGen.com • *Out on a Limb*

Heritage Military Music Foundation, 1st Brigade Band • 504 S 4th St • Watertown, WI 53094 • (920) 262-1864 • http://www.1stbrigadeband.org

Watertown Historical Society & Library • Octagon House, 919 Charles St • Watertown, WI 53094 • (920) 261-2796 • http://www.watertownhistory.org • *Historical Review*

Watertown Public Library • 100 S Water St • Watertown, WI 53094-4320 • (920) 262-4090 • http://www.watertown.lib.wi.us

Waukesha
Mich Family • S69 W24535 Longview Ct • Waukesha, WI 53186 • (262) 662-2252

Todd Wehr Memorial Library • Carroll College, 100 N East Ave • Waukesha, WI 53186 • (262) 524-7175 • http://www.marian.cc.edu/library

Waukesha County Genealogical Society • 551 W 25257 Glendale Rd, P.O. Box 1541 • Waukesha, WI 53187-1541 • *Waukesha County Genealogical Society Newsletter*

Waukesha County Historical Society & Archives • Historical Museum, 101 W Main St • Waukesha, WI 53186-4811 • (262) 521-2859 • http://www.waukeshacountymuseum.org • *Waukesha County Historical Society News*; Landmark

Waukesha Engine Historical Society • 1000 W St Paul Ave • Waukesha, WI 53188 • (262) 542-3930

Waukesha Public Library • 321 Wisconsin Ave • Waukesha, WI 53186-4786 • (262) 524-3682 • http://www.waukesha.lib.wi.us

Waunakee
Friends of Schumacher Farm • Schumacher Farm County Park, 5682 Hwy 19 • Waunakee, WI 53597 • (608) 849-4559 • http://www.madison.com/communities/fsf/

Waunakee Public Library • 710 South St • Waunakee, WI 53597-1638 • (608) 849-4217 • http://www.scis.lib.wi.us/wau/home.html

Waupaca
Rural Historical Society • E 1449 Main St • Waupaca, WI 54981

Waupaca Area Public Library • 107 S Main St • Waupaca, WI 54981-1521 • (715) 258-4414 • http://www.owls.lib.wi.us/wau/

Waupaca Historical Society & Genealogy Center • Hutchison House Museum, 321 S Main St, P.O. Box 313 • Waupaca, WI 54981 • (715) 256-9980 • http://www.waupacahistory.org • Waupaca Historical Society Newsletter

Wisconsin State Genealogical Society, Waupaca County Chapter • c/o Waupaca Free Public Library, 321 S Main St • Waupaca, WI 54981 • (715) 258-4414

Waupun
Waupun Historical Society & Archives • Heritage Museum, 22 S Madison St • Waupun, WI 53963 • (920) 324-7931

Waupun Public Library • 120 S Mill St, P.O. Box 391 • Waupun, WI 53963-0391 • (920) 324-7925 • http://www.waupunpubliclibrary.org

Wausau
Marathon County Genealogical Society • P.O. Box 1512 • Wausau, WI 54401-1512 • (715) 359-3305 • http://home.att.net/~mcgs/ • *Pinery Pedigree*

Marathon County Historical Society & Archives • Yawkey House Museum, 403 McIndoe St • Wausau, WI 54403-4746 • (715) 848-6143 • http://www.marathoncountyhistory.com • *Wanigan*

Marathon County Public Library • 300 N 1st St • Wausau, WI 54403-5405 • (715) 261-7230 • http://www.mcpl.lib.wi.us

University of Wisconsin-Wausau Library • 518 S 7th Ave • Wausau, WI 54401-5396 • (715) 261-6218 • http://www.uwmc.uwc.edu

Zdroik-Zdojewski-Belongia-Champau Family Reunion • 1208 N 10th Ave • Wausau, WI 54401 • (715) 675-6836

Wautoma
Waushara County Historical Society • 221 Sault Sainte Marie St, P.O. Box 886 • Wautoma, WI 54982 • (920) 787-7584 • *Waushara County Historical Society Newsletter*

Waushara County Historical Museum, 304 Valley View Dr • Wautoma, WI 54982 • (920) 787-7584

Wauwatosa
Irish Genealogical Society of Wisconsin • 2476 Lefeber Ave, P.O. Box 13766 • Wauwatosa, WI 53213-0766 • *Irish Genealogical Quarterly*

Lowell Damon House Museum Archives • 2107 Wauwatosa Ave • Wauwatosa, WI 53213 • (414) 273-8288 • http://www.milwaukeecountyhistsoc.org

Wauwatosa Historical Society & Library • Kneeland-Walker House, 7406 Hillcrest Dr • Wauwatosa, WI 53213-2226 • (414) 774-8672 • http://www.wauwatosahistoricalsociety.org • *Historic Wauwatosa*

Wauwatosa Public Library • 7635 W North Ave • Wauwatosa, WI 53212-1718 • (414) 471-8484 • http://tpublib.fp.execpc.com

Wauzeka
Lower Wisconsin River Genealogical and Historical Society • P.O. Box 202 • Wauzeka, WI 53826-0202 • (608) 326-2739 • *Looking for Yesterday*

West Allis
Longley Family in America • 2236 S 77th St • West Allis, WI 53219 • *Longley Family in America*

West Allis Historical Society & Archives • Historical Museum, 8405 W National Ave • West Allis, WI 53227 • (414) 541-6970 • http://www.westallishistory.org • *Historic Buzz*

West Bend
Descendants of George Hunt and Mary Ogilvie Allen • 5886 Scenic Dr • West Bend, WI 53095

Schweppe Family Association • 3661 Blue Goose Rd • West Bend, WI 53095

Seideman Reunion • 7185 Shady Ln • West Bend, WI 53090 • (262) 675-6364

Shanks Family Association • 4085 Pleasant Valley Rd • West Bend, WI 53095-9271 • (262) 644-6562 • *Shanks Newsletter*

Washington County Historical Society & Archives • Courthouse Museum, 340 S 5th Ave • West Bend, WI 53095-3333 • (262) 335-4678 • http://www.historyisfun.com • *Court Reporter*

West Milwaukee
West Milwaukee Historical Society & Library • 4755 W Beloit Rd • West Milwaukee, WI 53214 • (414) 321-9059

West Salem
Palmer-Gullickson Octagon House Archives • 360 N Leonard St, P.O. Box 884 • West Salem, WI 54669 • (608) 786-1399 • *Palmer-Gullickson Octagon House Newsletter*

West Salem Historical Society & Archives • Hamlin Garland Homestead Museum, 257 W Garland St, P.O. Box 884 • West Salem, WI 54669-1146 • (608) 786-1399 • *West Salem Historical Society Newsletter*

Westby
Westby Area Historical Society & Archives • Thoreson House, 101 Black River Ave, P.O. Box 42 • Westby, WI 54667 • (608) 634-4101

Westfield
Marquette County Historical Society & Library • Cochrane-Nelson House, 125 Lawrence St, P.O. Box 172 • Westfield, WI 53964 • (608) 296-3182 • *Imprints on the Sands of Marquette County*

Westfield Public Library • 117 E 3rd St, P.O. Box 355 • Westfield, WI 53964-0355 • (608) 296-2544 • http://westfieldlibrary.org

Weyauwega
Little Red School House Museum Archives • 411 W High St, P.O. Box 531 • Weyauwega, WI 54983 • (920) 867-2500 • http://www.weyauwegachamber.com

Weyerhaeuser
Finland Minnesota Historical Society • general delivery • Weyerhaeuser, WI 54895 • (715) 353-7380

Whitefish Bay
Whitefish Bay Public Library • 5420 N Marlborough Dr • Whitefish Bay, WI 53217 • (414) 964-4380 • http://www.wfblibrary.org • *Whitefish Bay Public Library Newsletter*

Whitewater
Godfrey Cousins Family Reunion • 124 N Franklin • Whitewater, WI 53190

Harold Anderson Library • Univ of Wisconsin-Whitewater, 800 W Main St, P.O. Box 900 • Whitewater, WI 53190 • (262) 472-1032 • http://library.uww.edu

Irvin L Young Memorial Library • 431 W Center St • Whitewater, WI 53190-1915 • (262) 473-0530 • http://www.whitewater.lib.wi.us

Whitewater Historical Society & Archives • Historical Museum, Whitewater St • Whitewater, WI 53190 • (262) 473-6820

Wild Rose
Patterson Memorial Library • 500 Wisconsin St, P.O. Box 305 • Wild Rose, WI 54984-0305 • (920) 622-3835

Pioneer Museum Archives • Main St, P.O. Box 63 • Wild Rose, WI 54984 • (262) 622-4355

Wild Rose Historical Society & Archives • Pioneer Museum, Main St, P.O. Box 63 • Wild Rose, WI 54984 • (920) 622-3555

Willard
Willard Historical Society • N 8311 Bachelors Ave • Willard, WI 54493 • (715) 267-6193

Wind Lake
Norway Historical Society • Colonel Heg Memorial Park, 6300 Heg Park Rd • Wind Lake, WI 53185 • (262) 895-2700

Winneconne
Winneconne Historical Society & Archives • Historical Museum and Kay Wilde Doll Cottage, 611 W Main St • Winneconne, WI 54986 • (920) 582-4132 • http://www.winneconne.org/Historical/historical.html

Winneconne Public Library • 31 S 2nd St, P.O. Box 5002 • Winneconne, WI 54986-5002 • (920) 582-7091 • http://www.winneconnelibrary.org

Wisconsin Dells
Dells County Historical Society & Archives • Bowman House, 714 Broadway, P.O. Box 177 • Wisconsin Dells, WI 53965 • (608) 254-2254

Kilbourn Public Library • 620 Elm St • Wisconsin Dells, WI 53965 • (608) 254-2146 • http://www.scls.lib.wi.us/wid

Wisconsin Rapids
Heart O'Wisconsin Genealogical Society & Archives • c/o MacMillan Memorial Library, 490 E Grand Ave • Wisconsin Rapids, WI 54494-4867 • (715) 423-1040 • Heart O'Wisconsin Genealogical Society Newsletter

McMillan Memorial Library • 490 E Grand Ave • Wisconsin Rapids, WI 54494-4898 • (715) 423-1040 • http://www.scls.lib.wi.us/mcm • Genealogical Resources At McMillan

South Wood County Historical Society & Archives • Historical Museum, 540 3rd St S • Wisconsin Rapids, WI 54494-4352 • (715) 423-1580 • http://www.swch-museum.com • *South Wood County Historical Corporation Newsletter*; *River City Memoirs*; *Artifacts*

Withee
Withee Public Library • 504 Division, P.O. Box 147 • Withee, WI 54498-0147 • (715) 229-2010

Wittenberg
Wittenberg Area Historical Society & Archives • Historical Museum, Vinal & Home Sts, P.O. Box 242 • Wittenberg, WI 54499 • (715) 253-3003

Wonewoc
Historical Society of the Upper Baraboo Valley & Archives • Painted Forest Folk Art Museum, E 940 Painted Forest Dr • Wonewoc, WI 53968 • (608) 983-2352

Wonewoc Public Library • 305 Center St, P.O. Box 116 • Wonewoc, WI 53968-0116 • (608) 464-7625 • http://www.mwt.net/~wonewocpl

Woodruff
Woodruff Historical Society & Archives • Dr Kate Newcomb Museum, 932 2nd Ave, P.O. Box 851 • Woodruff, WI 54568 • (715) 356-5562

Woodville
Woodville Community Library • 124 Main St, P.O. Box 204 • Woodville, WI 54028-0204 • (715) 698-2430

WYOMING

Afton
Lincoln County Historical Society • P.O. Box 242 • Afton, WY 83110

Star Valley Historical Society • P.O. Box 921 • Afton, WY 83110

Banner
Fort Phil Kearney Museum Archives • 528 Wagon Box Rd • Banner, WY 82832 • (307) 684-7629 • http://www.philkearney.vcn.com

Basin
Big Horn County Library • 430 West C St, P.O. Box 231 • Basin, WY 82410-0231 • (307) 568-2388 • http://wyld.state.wy.us/bighorn

Bedford
John Michael Maurer-Martin Brill-Charles Geissinger-Henry Mower Family Organization • P.O. Box 311 • Bedford, WY 83112 • (307) 883-2730

Big Horn
Bradford Brinton Memorial Museum Library • 239 Brinton Rd, P.O. Box 460 • Big Horn, WY 82833 • (307) 672-3173 • http://www.bradfordbrintonmemorial.com

Big Piney
Green River Valley Museum Archives • 206 N Front St, P.O. Box 12 • Big Piney, WY 83113 • (307) 276-5343 • http://www.grvm.com

Bondurant
John Tweed-Jacob Henry Siedenburg Family Organization • P.O. Box 39 • Bondurant, WY 82922-0172

Buffalo
Jim Gatchell Museum Archives • 10 Fort St, P.O. Box 596 • Buffalo, WY 82834 • (307) 684-9331 • http://www.jimgatchell.com • *Sentry*

Johnson County Genealogical Society • P.O. Box 103 • Buffalo, WY 82834

Johnson County Historical Society • P.O. Box 103 • Buffalo, WY 82834

Johnson County Library • 171 N Adams St • Buffalo, WY 82834 • (307) 684-5546 • http://www.will.state.wy.us/johnson/

Museum of the Occidental Archives • 10 N Main St • Buffalo, WY 82834 • (307) 684-0847

Casper
Dewitt and Bartlett Reunion • 146 N Lennox • Casper, WY 82601

Doyle Research • P.O. Box 4477 • Casper, WY 82604 • *Doyle Diary*

Fort Caspar Museum Library • 4001 Fort Caspar Rd • Casper, WY 82604 • (307) 235-8462 • http://www.fortcasparwyoming.com

Goodstein Foundation Library • Casper College, 125 College Dr • Casper, WY 82601 • (307) 268-2269 • http://caspercollege.edu/library

Natrona County Genealogical Society • P.O. Box 9244 • Casper, WY 82601 • (307) 265-0206

Natrona County Public Library • 307 E 2nd St • Casper, WY 82601 • (307) 237-4935 • http://www.library.natrona.net • *Natrona County Public Library Newsletter*

Society of Rocky Mountain Archivists • Casper College Library, 125 College Dr • Casper, WY 82601 • (720) 865-1906 • Rocky Mountain Archivist

Thompson G Bates Family Organization • 2315 Crescent Ave • Casper, WY 82604 • (307) 237-3966

Centennial
Centennial Valley Historical Association & Archives • Historical Museum, Hwy 130, P.O. Box 200 • Centennial, WY 82055-0130 • (307) 742-7158

Cheyenne
Cheyenne Frontier Days Old West Museum Archives • 4610 N Carey Ave, P.O. Box 2720 • Cheyenne, WY 82003 • (800) 778-7290 • http://www.cfdrodeo.com • *Stageline*

Cheyenne Genealogical Society & Archives, Computer Interest Group • c/o Laramie County Library, 2800 Central Ave • Cheyenne, WY 82001 • (307) 634-3561 x44 • http://www.wyomingweb.net/genealogy/ • *Cheyenne Genealogy Journal*; *Cheyenne Genealogical Society Membership Roster and Research Source Directory*

Clan MacNeil Association of America, Wyoming-Nebraska • 5304 Eastview St • Cheyenne, WY 82001

Evenson Surname Organization • 1918 East 18th St • Cheyenne, WY 82001 • (307) 635-6681

Grand Lodge of Ancient Free and Accepted Masons & Library • 1820 Capitol Ave • Cheyenne, WY 82001-4025 • (307) 634-1655

Historic Governors' Mansion Museum Archives • 300 E 21st St • Cheyenne, WY 82001 • (307) 777-7878 • http://www.wyoparks.state.wy.us

Knudsen Surname Organization • 1918 E 18th St • Cheyenne, WY 82001 • (307) 635-6681

Laramie County Community College Library • 1400 E College Dr • Cheyenne, WY 82007-3204 • (307) 778-1206 • http://www.lccc.cc.wy.us/library

Laramie County Library • 2800 Central Ave • Cheyenne, WY 82001-2799 • (307) 634-3561 • http://www.lclsonline.org • *Library News*

Union Pacific Historical Society • Univ of WY, P.O. Box 4006 • Cheyenne, WY 82003 • (307) 766-4114 • http://www.uphs.org

Union Pacific Historical Society • 1111 E Lincolnway • Cheyenne, WY 82001 • (307) 635-5197

Watson Clark Seward-Hiram Rose (Rowell) Descendants Association • 400 W 6th Ave • Cheyenne, WY 82001-1254

Wyoming State Archives • Barrett Bldg, 2301 Central Ave • Cheyenne, WY 82002 • (307) 777-7826 • http://wyoarchives.state.wy.us

Wyoming State Historical Society & Library • Barrett Bldg, 604 E 25th St, P.O. Box 4256 • Cheyenne, WY 82002 • (307) 766-5101 • Wyoming History News

Wyoming State Library • Supreme Court Library Bldg, 2301 Capitol Ave • Cheyenne, WY 82002-0060 • (307) 777-6333 • http://www.wsl.state.wy.us

Wyoming State Museum Archives • 2301 Central Ave • Cheyenne, WY 82002 • (307) 77-7022 • http://wyomuseum.state.sy.us

Wyoming Transportation Museum Archives • 1 Depot Sq, 115 W 15th • Cheyenne, WY 82001 • (307) 637-3376

Chugwater
Chugwater Historical Society • 315 1st St • Chugwater, WY 82210

Cody
Buffalo Bill Historical Center Archives • 720 Sheridan Ave, P.O. Box 1000 • Cody, WY 82414-1000 • (307) 578-4059 • http://www.bbhc.org/hmrl/

Park County Genealogy Society • P.O. Box 3056 • Cody, WY 82414

Park County Historical Society & Library • 1002 Sheridan Ave • Cody, WY 82414 • (307) 527-8530

Park County Library • 1057 Sheridan Ave • Cody, WY 82414 • (307) 587-8820

Douglas
Converse County Genealogical Society • 119 N 9th St • Douglas, WY 82633

Converse County Library • 300 Walnut St • Douglas, WY 82633 • (307) 358-3644 • http://will.state.wy.us/converse; conversecountylibrary.com • *Bridges*

Fort Fetterman State Historic Site Archives • 752 Hwy 93 • Douglas, WY 82633 • (307) 358-2864

Wyoming Pioneer Historical Society • P.O. Drawer 10 • Douglas, WY 82633

Wyoming Pioneer Memorial Musuem Archives • 400 W Center St, P.O. Box 911 • Douglas, WY 82633 • (307) 358-9288 • http://www.spacr.state.wy.us

Dubois
Dubois Museum Archives • 909 W Ramshorn, P.O. Box 896 • Dubois, WY 82513 • (307) 455-2284 • http://www.duboismuseum.org

Wyoming

Fremont County Library System-Dubois Branch • 202 N 1st, P.O. Box 787 • Dubois, WY 82513-0787 • (307) 455-2992

Wind River Historical Center • P.O. Box 896 • Dubois, WY 82513

Encampment
Grand Encampment Historical Society • P.O. Box 395 • Encampment, WY 82325

Grand Encampment Museum Archives • 807 Barnett Ave, P.O. Box 43 • Encampment, WY 82325-0043 • (307) 327-5308 • http://encampment.1wyo.net/gemuseum.html • *Encampment Museum News*

Evanston
Jean Bodine-Champe Surname Organization • 333 Center St • Evanston, WY 82930 • (307) 789-2893

Johnson Family Organization • 600 Palomino Dr • Evanston, WY 82930 • (307) 789-9436

Uinta County Historical Society • 36 10th St • Evanston, WY 82930

Uinta County Library • 701 Main St • Evanston, WY 82930 • (307) 789-1328 • http://www.uintalibrary.org

Evansville
Reshaw Exhibit Archives • 235 Curtis, P.O. Drawer 158 • Evansville, WY 82636 • (307) 234-6530

Fort Bridger
Fort Bridger Historical Association & Archives • Historical Museum, 37000 Business Loop I-80, P.O. Box 35 • Fort Bridger, WY 82933 • (307) 782-3842 • http://www.wyobest.org

Fort Laramie
Fort Laramie Historical Association & Archives • Historical Museum, 965 Gray Rocks Rd • Fort Laramie, WY 82212 • (307) 837-2221 • http://www.nationalparks.org/guide/parks/fort-laramie-1986.htm

Fort Washakie
Shoshone Tribal Cultural Center Archives • 90 Ethete Rd, P.O. Box 1008 • Fort Washakie, WY 82514 • (307) 332-9106

Frannie
Bond Family Tales and Trails • P.O. Box 34 • Frannie, WY 82423 • *Bond, a Newsletter By and For the Families and Branches of the Bond Family*

Gillette
Branches of Campbell County • 602 W 3rd St • Gillette, WY 82716-3517

Campbell County Historical Society • 900 W 2nd St • Gillette, WY 82716

Campbell County Public Library • 2101 S 4-J Rd • Gillette, WY 82718-5205 • (307) 687-0009 • http://www.ccpls.org • *Newsline*

Campbell County Rockpile Musuem Archives • 900 W 2nd St • Gillette, WY 82716 • (307) 682-5723 • http://www.gillettewyoming.com/rockpile/ • *Campbell County Rockpile Musuem Newsletter*

Joseph Walden Crowder Family Organization • 408 S Gurley Ave • Gillette, WY 82716 • (307) 687-0171

Glendo
Glendo Historical Historical Society • 204 S Yellowstone • Glendo, WY 82213

Green River
Sweetwater County Historical Museum Archives • 80 W Flaming Gorge Wy • Green River, WY 82935 • (307) 872-6435

Sweetwater County Historical Society & Archives • Historical Museum, 80 W Flaming Gorge Wy • Green River, WY 82935 • (307) 872-6435 • http://www.sweetwatermuseum.org • *Overland and Underground*

Sweetwater County Library • 300 N 1st St E • Green River, WY 82935 • (307) 875-3615 • http://wyldweb.state.wy.us/swtr • Library Link

Greybull
Greybull Historical Society • P.O. Box 348 • Greybull, WY 82426

Greybull Museum Archives • 325 Greybull Ave • Greybull, WY 82426 • (307) 765-2444

Guernsey
Lake Guernsey Museum Archives • US 26 & State Hwy 317, P.O. Box 429 • Guernsey, WY 82214 • (307) 836-2334

Hanna
Hanna Basin Historical Society • P.O. Box 144 • Hanna, WY 82327

Hillsdale
McWilliams Historical Project • P.O. Box 92 • Hillsdale, WY 82060 • (307) 547-3424 • http://members.aol.com/mcwmshist/ • *Now and Then*

Jackson
Andrea Bracchitta-Charles Dilday Family Organization • P.O. Box 2856 • Jackson, WY 83001 • (307) 733-5647

Teton County Historical Society & Archives • Historical Museum, 105 Mercill Ave, P.O. Box 1005 • Jackson, WY 83001 • (307) 733-2414 • http://www.jacksonholehistory.org • *Teton County Historical Society Quarterly*

Teton County Library • 320 S King St, P.O. Box 1629 • Jackson, WY 83001 • (307) 733-2164

Teton County Library-Huff Memorial Library • 125 Virginian Lane, P.O. Box 1629 • Jackson, WY 83001-1629 • (307) 733-2164 • http://tclib.org

Kaycee
Hoofprints of the Past Museum Archives • 344 Nolan Ave • Kaycee, WY 82639 • (307) 738-2381 • *Hoofprints of the Past Museum Newsletter*

Kemmerer
Fossil Country Museum Archives • 400 Pine, P.O. Box 854 • Kemmerer, WY 83101 • (307) 877-6551 • http://www.hamsfork.net/~museum

Lincoln County Historical Society • general delivery • Kemmerer, WY 83101

Lincoln County Library • 519 Emerald St • Kemmerer, WY 83101 • (307) 877-6961 • http://www.wsl.state.wy.us/lincoln

Lander
Fremont County Historical Society • 630 Lincoln • Lander, WY 82520

Fremont County Library • 451 N 2nd St • Lander, WY 82520-2316 • (307) 332-5194 • http://fremontcountylibraries.org

Fremont County Pioneer Museum Archives • 636 Lincoln St • Lander, WY 82520 • (307) 332-4137 • *Wind River Mountaineer*

Lander Genealogical Society • 1015 Black Blvd • Lander, WY 82520

Laramie
Albany County Genealogical Society • P.O. Box 6163 • Laramie, WY 82070

Albany County Historical Society • 1409 Downey St • Laramie, WY 82070 • (307) 742-5988

Albany County Public Library • 310 S 8th St • Laramie, WY 82070-3969 • (307) 721-2580 • http://acpl.lib.wy.us

American Heritage Center Library • Univ of Wyoming, 2111 Willet Dr, P.O. Box 3924 • Laramie, WY 82071-3924 • (307) 766-2565 • http://www.uwyo.edu/ahc/depts/toppan/toppan.htm

Archibald Surname Organization • 1103 E Canby St • Laramie, WY 82070

Clan Donald, Northwest • 4511 Bluebird Ln • Laramie, WY 82070 • (307) 745-8645

Laramie Plains Museum Association Library • 603 Ivinson Ave • Laramie, WY 82070-3299 • (307) 742-4448 • http://www.laramiemuseum.org

University of Wyoming Library • 15th & Lewis Sts, P.O. Box 3374, Univ Sta • Laramie, WY 82071-3334 • (307) 766-2035 • http://www.lib.uwyo.edu

Wyoming Territorial Prison and Old West Park Archives • 975 Snowy Range Rd • Laramie, WY 82070 • (307) 745-3733 • http://www.wyoprisonpark.org

Lusk
Niobara County Historical Society & Archives • Stagecoach Museum, 322 S Main, P.O. Box 367 • Lusk, WY 82225 • (307) 334-3444

Lyman
Trona Mining Museum of Bridger Valley Archives • Town Hall, P.O. Box 184 • Lyman, WY 82937 • (307) 787-6916

Meeteetse
Meeteetse Museum Archives • 1946 State St, P.O. Box 248 • Meeteetse, WY 82433 • (307) 868-2423 • *Meeteetse Museum Newsletter*

Moorcroft
Moorcroft Historical Society • 220 S Big Horn • Moorcroft, WY 82721 • (307) 756-9300

Moose
Grand Teton National Park Library • P.O. Box Drawer 170 • Moose, WY 83012-0170 • (307) 739-3399 • http://www.nps.gov/grte

Moran
Schaarschmidt Family Association • P.O. Box 75 • Moran, WY 83013 • (307) 543-2420

Newcastle
Weston County Genealogical Society • c/o Weston County Public Library, 23 W Main St • Newcastle, WY 82701

Weston County Historical Society & Archives • Anna Miller Museum, 401 Delaware, P.O. Box 698 • Newcastle, WY 82701 • (307) 746-4188

Weston County Public Library • 23 W Main St • Newcastle, WY 82701 • (307) 746-2206 • http://will.state.wy.us/weston/

Pinedale
Sublette County Genealogy Society • P.O. Box 1186 • Pinedale, WY 82941

Sublette County Historical Society & Archives • Historical Museum, 700 E Hennick, P.O. Box 909 • Pinedale, WY 82941 • (307) 367-4101 • http://www.pinedaleonline.com/mmmuseum • *Beaver Plew*

Sublette County Library • 1555 S Tyler Ave, P.O. Box 489 • Pinedale, WY 82941-0489 • (307) 367-4115 • http://pinedaleonline.com/library

Powell
Harney Family Association • 1269 Road 9 • Powell, WY 82435 • http://freepages.genealogy.rootsweb.com/~harney2/ • Harney Update

Homesteaders Museum Archives • 133 S Clark St, P.O. Box 54 • Powell, WY 82435 • (307) 754-9481

Powell Valley Genealogical Club • 830 N Day, P.O. Box 184 • Powell, WY 82435 • (307) 754-2848

Ranchester
Ranchester Historical Society • P.O. Box 666 • Ranchester, WY 82839

Rawlins
Carbon County Historical Society • P.O. Box 52 • Rawlins, WY 82301

Carbon County Museum Archives • 904 W Walnut St, P.O. Box 52 • Rawlins, WY 82301 • (307) 328-2740 • http://www.carboncountymuseum.org

Carbon County Public Library • 215 W Buffalo St • Rawlins, WY 82301 • (307) 328-2618

Riverton
Central Wyoming College Library • 2660 Peck Ave • Riverton, WY 82501 • (307) 855-2141 • http://www.cwc.edu/student-services/library/

Fremont County Genealogical Society & Archives • c/o Riverton Branch Library, 1330 W Park Ave • Riverton, WY 82501-3249 • (307) 856-5310 • *Fremont County Nostalgia News*

Fremont County Library System-Riverton Branch • 1330 W Park • Riverton, WY 82501 • (307) 856-3556

Riverton Historical Society • Riverton Museum, 700 E Park Ave • Riverton, WY 82501 • (307) 856-2665 • *Wind River Mountaineer*

William Tanner Family Organization • 222 E Sunset • Riverton, WY 82501 • (307) 856-0950

Winfield Family Association • 124 Two Valley • Riverton, WY 82501 • *Winfield Family Association Newsletter*

Rock River
Rock River Historical Society • P.O. Box 52 • Rock River, WY 82083

Rock Springs
George Cato Family Organization • 1025 Maple Wy • Rock Springs, WY 82901 • (307) 362-6365

Hay Library • Western Wyoming Community College, 2500 College Dr, P.O. Box 428 • Rock Springs, WY 82902-0428 • (307) 382-1701 • http://www.wwcc.cc.wy.us/library

Rock Springs Historical Museum Archives • 201 B Street • Rock Springs, WY 82901 • (307) 362-3138

Rock Springs Historical Society • 212 D Street • Rock Springs, WY 82901

Saint Stephens
Stephens Indian Mission Foundation • P.O. Box 278 • Saint Stephens, WY 82524-0278 • (307) 856-6797 • *Wind River Rendezvous*

Saratoga
Saratoga Historical and Cultural Association & Archives • Historical Museum, 106 Constitution Ave, P.O. Box 1131 • Saratoga, WY 82331 • (307) 326-5511 • http://members.xoom.com/kaikin/welcome

Savery
Little Snake River Museum Archives • Route 70, P.O. Box 81 • Savery, WY 82332 • (307) 383-7262

Sheridan
Cloniger-Kloniger-Gloniger Research • 1311 LaClede • Sheridan, WY 82801 • *Cloniger-Kloniger-Gloniger Newsletter*

Rench Research • 2068 Coffeen Ave #20 • Sheridan, WY 82801-5761 • *Rench Roundup Report*

Sheridan County Fulmer Public Library • 335 W Alger St • Sheridan, WY 82801-3899 • (307) 674-8585 • http://www.sheridanwyolibrary.org

Sheridan County Historical Society & Archives • Historical Museum, 429 W Alger St • Sheridan, WY 82801 • (307) 673-0644

Sheridan Genealogical Society & Archives • c/o Sheridan County Fulmer Library, 335 W Alger St, P.O. Box 6503 • Sheridan, WY 82801 • (307) 674-8585 • *Newsletter of the Sheridan Genealogical Society*; *Dusty Trails*

Sons of the American Revolution, Wyoming Society • 1040 S Thurmond • Sheridan, WY 82801

Trail End Historic Center • 400 S Clarendon Ave • Sheridan, WY 82801 • (307) 674-4589 • http://www.trailend.org • *End Notes*

Shoshoni
Herbst-Escalle-Desdier-Mazet Surname Organization • P.O. Box 117 • Shoshoni, WY 82649

Sinclair
Parco-Sinclair Historical Society • P.O. Box 247 • Sinclair, WY 82334

South Pass City
South Pass City State Historic Site Archives • 125 S Pass Main • South Pass City, WY 82520 • (307) 332-3684 • http://www.southpasscity.com

Story
Fort Fetterman State Museum Archives • 752 Hwy 93, P.O. Box 520 • Story, WY 82842 • (307) 358-2864

Fort Phil Kearney Archives • Hwy 87 P.O. Box 520 • Story, WY 82842 • (307) 684-7629

Sundance
Crook County Historical Society • P.O. Box 63 • Sundance, WY 82729

Wyoming

Crook County Library • 414 Main St, P.O. Box 910 • Sundance, WY 82729-0910 • (307) 283-1006 • http://will.state.wy.us/crook

Crook County Museum Archives • 309 Cleveland, P.O. Box 63 • Sundance, WY 82729 • (307) 283-3666 • http://www.geocities/heartland/park/9867

Thermopolis

Dancing Bear Folk Center Archives • 119 S 6th • Thermopolis, WY 82443 • (307) 864-9396 • http://www.dancing-bear-folk-center.org

Hot Springs County Historical Society • Hot Springs County Musuem, 700 Broadway • Thermopolis, WY 82443 • (307) 864-5183 • http://www.tnb.com/~history • *Broadway Pilot*

Hot Springs County Library • 344 Arapahoe, P.O. Box 951 • Thermopolis, WY 82443-0951 • (307) 864-3104 • http://will.state.wy.us/hotsprings

Wyoming Pioneer Home Library • 141 Pioneer Home Dr • Thermopolis, WY 82443-2451 • (307) 864-3151

Torrington

Goshen County Public Library • 2001 East A St • Torrington, WY 82240-2898 • (307) 532-3411 • http://wyldweb.state.wy.us/gosh

Warren AFB

Warren Heritage Museum Archives • 7405 Marne Loop, 90 MW/PACM • Warren AFB, WY 82005 • (307) 773-2980 • http://www.pawnee.com/fewmuseum

Wheatland

Laramie Peekers Genealogy Society of Platte County • 1108 21st St • Wheatland, WY 82201

Platte County Public Library • 904 9th St • Wheatland, WY 82201-2699 • (307) 322-2689 • http://www.wsd.state.wy.us/platte/

Worland

Washakie County Historical Society • Washakie Musuem, 1115 Obie Sue • Worland, WY 82401 • (307) 347-4102 • http://www.trib.com/~wmuseum

Wright

Wright Centennial Museum Archives • 104 Ranch Court • Wright, WY 82732 • (307) 444-1222

CANADA

Acme
Acme Municipal Library • 1610 Walsh Ave, POB 326 • Acme, Alberta T0M 0A0

Airdrie
Airdrie Public Library • 704 Main St, POB 3310 • Airdrie, Alberta T4B 2B6 • (403) 948-0600 • http://www.airdriepubliclibrary.ca/

Nose Creek Valley Museum Archives • POB 3351 • Airdrie, Alberta T4B 2B6 • (403) 946-6685

Alberta Beach
Alberta Beach Museum Archives • 4523-50 Ave • Alberta Beach, Alberta T0E 0A0 • (780) 924-2140

Garden Park Farm Museum Archives • POB 639 • Alberta Beach, Alberta T0E 0A0 • (780) 924-3391

Alix
Wagon Wheel Regional Museum Archives • 4912 50th St, POB 157 • Alix, Alberta T0C 080 • (403) 747-2462

Alliance
Alliance and District Museum Archives • POB 101 • Alliance, Alberta T0B 0A0

Andrew
Andrew and District Local History Museum Archives • POB 180 • Andrew, Alberta T0B 0C0 • (780) 365-3687

Athabasca
Alice B Donahue Library & Archives • POB 2099 • Athabasca, Alberta T9S 2B6 • (780) 675-2735

Banff
Cave and Basin National Historic Site Archives • Parks Canada, 311 Cave Av • Banff, Alberta T1L 1K2 • (403) 762-1566 • http://www.worldweb.com/parkscanada-banff/cave.html

Whyte Museum of the Canadian Rockies & Archives • 111 Bear St, POB 160 • Banff, Alberta T1l 1A3 • (403) 762-2291 • http://www.whyte.org

Barrhead
Barrhead and District Centennial Museum Archives • 5629 49th St, POB 4122 • Barrhead, Alberta T7N 1A1 • (780) 674-5203

Barrhead Public Library • 5103 53rd Ave • Barrhead, Alberta T7N 1N9 • (780) 674-8519 • http://www.phrd.ab.ca/bhdpublib/

Beaverlodge
South Peach Centennial Museum • Hwy 43 • Beaverlodge, Alberta T0M 0C0 • (780) 754-8869

Bonnyville
Bonnyville and District Historical Society & Archives • Historical Museum, 4401 54 Ave, POB 6995 • Bonnyville, Alberta T9N 1H4 • (780) 826-4925

Bonnyville Municipal Library • 4804 49th Ave, POB 8058 • Bonnyville, Alberta T9N 2J3 • (780) 826-3071

Long Lake (Kehewin) Cree Nation • POB 6218 • Bonnyville, Alberta T9N 2G8

Bowden
Bowden Pioneer Museum Archives • 2011 20th Ave • Bowden, Alberta T0M 0K0 • (403) 224-2122

Brocket
Oldman River Cultural Centre Archives • POB 70 • Brocket, Alberta T0K 0H0 • (403) 965-3939

Brooks
Alberta Genealogical Society, Brooks and District Library • POB 1538 • Brooks, Alberta T0J 0J0 • (403) 328-9564

Brooks and District Museum Archives • 568 Sutherland Dr, POB 2078 • Brooks, Alberta T0J 0J0 • (403) 362-4073

Brownvale
Brownvale North Peace Agricultural Museum Archives • POB 3 • Brownvale, Alberta T0H 0L0 • (780) 597-3950

Calgary
Aero Space Museum of Calgary • 4629 McCall Wy NE • Calgary, Alberta T2E 8A5 • (403) 250-3752 • http://www.asmac.ab.ca

Alberta Bible College Library • 635 Northmount Dr NW • Calgary, Alberta T2K 3J6 • (403) 282-2994 • http://www.abc-ca.org

Alberta Family Histories Society • 405-4510 Valiant Dr NW, POB 30270, Sta B • Calgary, Alberta T2M 4P1 • (403) 214-1447 • http://www.calcna.ab.ca/afhs/; www.freenet.calgary.ab.ca/science/genealogy/afs.html • *Alberta Family Histories Society Quarterly*; *Chinook*

Alberta Wheat Pool Grain Museum Archives • POB 2700 • Calgary, Alberta T2P 2P5 • (403) 290-4701

Archibald-Thomson Library • Canadian Bible College-Canadian Theological Seminary, 630-833 4th Ave • Calgary, Alberta T2P 3T5 • (403) 410-2946 • http://www.cbccts.ca/

Bearspaw Historical Society • 253253 Bearspaw Rd • Calgary, Alberta T3L 2P7 • (403) 208-2599

Beebe Research • 4610 Marbank Dr NE • Calgary, Alberta T2A 3JS • *Beebe Connection*

Calgary Chinese Cultural Centre Archives • 197 1st St SW • Calgary, Alberta T2P 4M4 • (403) 262-5071 • http://www.culturalcentre.ab.ca

Calgary Highlanders Museum Archives • 4520 Crowchild Tr SW • Calgary, Alberta T1Y 6J7 • (403) 974-2855 • http://db.mucleus.com/highmus

Calgary Police Service Interpretive Centre Archives • 316 7th Ave SE • Calgary, Alberta T2G 0J4 • (403) 206-4566

Calgary Public Library • 616 Macleod Trail SE • Calgary, Alberta T2G 2M2 • (403) 260-2600 • http://www.calgarypubliclibrary.com

Chinook Country Historical Society • 311-223 12 Avenue SW • Calgary, Alberta T2R 0G9 • (403) 261-4667

City of Calgary Archives • 33 7th Ave SE, POB 2100 Sta M • Calgary, Alberta T2P 2M5 • (403) 268-8180 • http://www.gov.calgary.ab.ca/cityclerks/archives

Fort Calgary Museum Archives • 750 9th Ave SE • Calgary, Alberta T2P 2M5 • (403) 290-1875 • http://www.fortcalgary.com

Glenbow Museum Library and Archives • 130 9th Ave SE • Calgary, Alberta T2G 0P3 • (403) 268-4197 • http://www.glenbow.org

Glenbow-Alberta Institute • 130 9th Ave SE • Calgary, Alberta T2G 0P3 • (403) 264-8300 • *Glenbow - Occasional Papers*; *Glenbow Museum Archives Series*

Heritage Park - Historical Village Archives • 1900 Heritage Park Dr SW • Calgary, Alberta T2V 2X3 • (403) 268-8500 • http://www.heritagepark.ab.ca

Historical Society of Alberta • 95 Holmwood Ave NW, POB 4035, Sta C • Calgary, Alberta T2T 5M9 • (403) 261-3662 • *Alberta History*; *History Now*

Jewish Genealogical Society of Southern Alberta • 914 Royal Ave SW • Calgary, Alberta T2T 0L5

Lord Strathcona's Horse Museum Archives • 4520 Crowchild Tr SW • Calgary, Alberta T2T 5J4 • (403) 242-6610 • http://www.strathconas.ca

Mennonite Historical Society of Alberta • 2946 32 Street NE • Calgary, Alberta T1Y 6J7 • (403) 250-1121

Museum of the Regiments Archives • 4520 Crowchild Tr SW • Calgary, Alberta T2T 5J4 • (403) 974-2853 • http://www.mucleus.com/~regiments

Naval Museum of Alberta Archives • 1820 24th St SW • Calgary, Alberta T2T 0G6 • (403) 242-0002 • http://www.lexicom.ab.ca/~navalmuseum/

Princess Patricia's Canadian Light Infantry Regimental Museum Archives • 4520 Crowchild Tr SW • Calgary, Alberta T2T 5J4 • (403) 974-2860 • http://www.ppcli.com

Saint Volodymyr's Ukranian Orthodox Cultural Centre Library and Archives • 404 Meredith Rd NE • Calgary, Alberta T2E 5A6 • (201) 768-4713

Sarcee People's Museum Archives • 3700 Anderson Rd SW • Calgary, Alberta T2W 3C4 • (403) 238-2677

Alberta

Society for German Genealogy in Eastern Europe • POB 905 • Calgary, Alberta T2P 2J3 • http://www.sggee.org

Ukrainian Genealogical and Historical Society of Canada • 2021 17th Ave SW • Calgary, Alberta T2T 0G2

Camrose
Augustana University College Library • 4901 46th Ave • Camrose, Alberta T4V 2R3 • (780) 679-1592 • http://elvis.augustana.ca

Camrose Public Library • 4710 50th Ave • Camrose, Alberta T4V 0R8 • (780) 672-4214

Canmore
Centennial Museum of Canmore Archives • 907 7th Ave • Canmore, Alberta T1W 2A9 • (403) 678-2462

Cardston
C O Card Home and Museum Archives • 337 Main St, POB 1830 • Cardston, Alberta T0K 0K0 • (403) 653-3366

Cardston & District Public Library • 25 3rd Ave W, POB 1560 • Cardston, Alberta T0K 0K0 • (403) 653-4775

Remington Carriage Museum Archives • 623 Main St • Cardston, Alberta T0K 0K0 • (405) 653-5139 • http://www.remingtoncentre.com

Carstairs
Museum Carstairs Historical Society • 1138 Nanton St • Carstairs, Alberta T0M 0N0 • (403) 337-3710

Roulston Museum Archives • 1138 Nanton St, POB 1067 • Carstairs, Alberta T0M 0N0 • (403) 337-3710

Castor
Castor and District Museum Archives • 5101 49th Ave, POB 92 • Castor, Alberta T0C 0X0 • (403) 882-3435

Cereal
Cereal Prairie Pioneer Museum Archives • Old Railway Station, POB 131 • Cereal, Alberta T0J 0N0 • (403) 326-3899

Claresholm
Claresholm Museum Archives • 5126 1st St, Hwy 2, Box 3970 • Claresholm, Alberta T0L 0T0 • (403) 625-3869

Claresholm Public Library • 5018 2nd St W, POB 548 • Claresholm, Alberta T0L 0T0 • (403) 625-4168 • http://www.town.claresholm.ab.ca/publiclibrary.htm

Cochrane
Alberta Genealogical Society, Cochrane and District Branch • 54 McDougall Rd W • Cochrane, Alberta T0L 0W4

Ukranian Genealogical and Historical Society of Canada • RR2 • Cochrane, Alberta T0L 0W0 • (403) 932-6811

Coleman
Crowsnest Museum Archives • 7701 18th Ave • Coleman, Alberta T0K 0M0 • (403) 563-5434 • http://www.telusplanet.net/public/cnmuseum

Colinton
Kinnoull Historical Museum Archives • general delivery • Colinton, Alberta T0G 0K0

Coutts
Belmore's Museum Archives • POB 176 • Coutts, Alberta T0K 0N0 • (403) 344-3888

Crowsnest Pass
Frank Slide Interpretive Centre • Hwy 3, POB 959 • Crowsnest Pass, Alberta T0K 0E0 • (403) 562-7388 • http://www.franklside.com

Leitch Collieries • Hwy 3, POB 959 • Crowsnest Pass, Alberta T0K 0E0 • (403) 562-7388 • http://www.frankslide.com

Czar
Prairie Panorama Museum Archives • Shorncliffe Park • Czar, Alberta T0B 0Z0 • (780) 857-2155

DeBolt
DeBolt and District Pioneer Museum Archives • Virginia Ave, POB 447 • DeBolt, Alberta T0H 1B0 • (780) 957-3957

Delburne
Anthony Henday Historical Society • 2603 20 Street • Delburne, Alberta T0M 0V0 • (403) 749-2711

Anthony Henday Museum Archives • POB 374 • Delburne, Alberta T0M 0V0 • (403) 749-2711

Dewberry
Dewberry Valley Museum Archives • 22 Centre St • Dewberry, Alberta T0B 1G0 • (780) 847-3053

Didsbury
Didsbury and District Museum Archives • POB 1175 • Didsbury, Alberta T0M 0W0 • (403) 335-9295

Donalda
Donalda and District Museum Archives • POB 40 • Donalda, Alberta T0B 1H0 • (403) 363-2100

Donnelly
Societe Historique et Genealogique de Smoky River • CP 224 • Donnelly, Alberta T0H 1G0

Drayton Valley
Alberta Genealogical Society, Drayton Valley Branch • 5138 52nd Ave • Drayton Valley, Alberta T0E 1Z0 • (780) 542-4628

Drayton Valley Museum Archives • POB 5099 • Drayton Valley, Alberta T7A 1R3

Drumheller
Drumheller and District Society Museum Archives • 335 1st St E, POB 2135 • Drumheller, Alberta T0J 0Y0 • (403) 823-2593

Drumheller Municipal Library • 224 Centre St, POB 1599 • Drumheller, Alberta T0J 0Y0 • (403) 823-5382 • http://www.drumhellerlibrary.ca

Homestead Antique Museum Archives • 901 Dinosaur Tr, POB 3154 • Drumheller, Alberta T0J 0Y0 • (403) 823-2600

Duffield
Paul Indian Band • POB 89 • Duffield, Alberta T0E 0N0

East Coulee
East Coulee School Museum Archives • POB 539 • East Coulee, Alberta T0J 1B0 • (403) 822-3970 • http://www.virtuallydrumheller.com

Historic Atlas Coal Mine Museum Archives • 110 Century Ave • East Coulee, Alberta T3J 1B0 • (403) 822-2220 • http://www.atlascoalmine.ab.ca

Edgerton
Edgerton and District Museum Archives • POB 64 • Edgerton, Alberta T0B 1K0 • (780) 755-3963

Edmonton
Alberta Association of Registered Nurses • Historical Museum, 11620 158th St • Edmonton, Alberta T5M 4A6 • (780) 453-0534 • http://www.nurses.ab.ca

Alberta Aviation Museum Archives • 11410 Kingsway Ave • Edmonton, Alberta T5C 3R6 • (780) 453-1078 • http://www.discoveredmonton.com/AviationMuseum

Alberta Genealogical Society, Edmonton Branch & Library • Prince of Wales Armouries Heritage Centre, 10440 108th Ave, Rm 116 • Edmonton, Alberta T5J 3L2 • (780) 496-8710 • http://www.agsedm.admonton.ab.ca • *Alberta Genealogical Society Ancestor Index*; *Relatively Speaking*; *Alberta Genealogical Society Newsletter*, *Clandigger*

Alberta Historical Resources Foundation & Library • 8820 112th St • Edmonton, Alberta T6G 2P8 • (780) 431-2305 • *Cornerstone*

Arnold Guebert Library • Concordia University College, 7100 Ada Blvd • Edmonton, Alberta T5B 4E4 • (780) 479-9338 • http://www.concordia.ab.ca

Calgary and Edmonton Railway Museum Archives • 10447 86th Ave • Edmonton, Alberta T6E 2M4 • (780) 433-9739 • http://www.canderailway.museum.com

Canadian Association of Slavists • Univ of Alberta, 347 Arts Bldg • Edmonton, Alberta T6G 2E6 • (780) 492-2566 • *Canadian Association of Slavists Newsletter*

City of Edmonton Archives • 10440 108th Ave • Edmonton, Alberta T5H 3Z9 • (780) 496-8711 • http://www.edmonton.ca/archives

Confederacy of Treaty 6 First Nations • 10621 100th Ave, Ste 350 • Edmonton, Alberta T5J OB3

Dental Museum Archives • Univ of Alberta, 89th Ave • Edmonton, Alberta T6G 2N8 • (780) 492-5194

Edmonton and District Historical Society • POB 1013, Main Sta • Edmonton, Alberta T5J 2M1 • (780) 439-2797

Edmonton Public Library • 7 Sir Winston Churchill Sq • Edmonton, Alberta T5J 2V4 • (780) 496-7020 • http://www.epl.ca

Edmonton Public Schools Museum Archives • 10425 99th Ave • Edmonton, Alberta T5K 0E5 • (780) 422-1970 • http://museum.epsb.net

Edmonton Telephone Historical Centre Archives • 10437 83rd Ave, POB 4459 • Edmonton, Alberta T6E 4T5 • (780) 433-1010 • http://www.telephonehistoricalcentre.com

Fort Edmonton Park Archives • Fox & Whitemond Drs • Edmonton, Alberta T5J 2R7 • (780) 496-8787 • http://www.edmonton.ca/fort

Genealogical Research Center • 10530 93rd Ave • Edmonton, Alberta T5R 5H2 • (780) 484-2132 • http://www.jgrc.net

Indian Association of Alberta • 11630 Kingsway Ave • Edmonton, Alberta T5G OX5

Loyal Edmonton Regiment Military Museum Archives • Prince of Wales Armoury, 10440 108th Ave, Ste 118 • Edmonton, Alberta T5H 3Z9 • (780) 421-9943

Prairie Treaty Nations Alliance • 11630 Kinssway Ave • Edmonton, Alberta T5G OX5

Provincial Archives of Alberta • 12845 102nd Ave • Edmonton, Alberta T5N 0M6 • (780) 427-1750 • http://www.gov.ab.ca/~mcd/mhs/paa/paa.htm

Provincial Museum of Alberta Archives • 12845 102nd Ave • Edmonton, Alberta T5N 0M6 • (780) 453-9100 • http://www.pna.edmonton.ab.ca

Rutherford House Archives • 11153 Saskatchewan Dr • Edmonton, Alberta T6G 2S1 • (780) 427-3995 • http://www.gov.ab.ca/~mcd/mcd.htm

Schalm Memorial Library • Taylor University College & Seminary, 11525 23rd Ave • Edmonton, Alberta T6J 4T3 • (780) 431-5237

Societe Genealogigue du Nord-Ouest • 10008 109th St, Ste 200 • Edmonton, Alberta T5J 1M4

Stephanson House Museum Archives • 8820 112th St • Edmonton, Alberta T6G 2P8 • (780) 427-3995

Ukrainian Catholic Women's League • Historical Museum, 10825 97th St • Edmonton, Alberta T5H 2M4 • (780) 474-0846

Ukrainian Cultural Heritage Village Archives • Trans Canada Hwy 16 • Edmonton, Alberta T6G 2P8 • (780) 662-3640 • http://www.cd.gov.ab.ca/uchv

Ukrainian Museum of Canada - Alberta Branch • 10611 110th Ave • Edmonton, Alberta T5H 1H7 • (780) 483-5932

Ukranian Canadian Archives and Museum • 10611 110th Ave • Edmonton, Alberta T5H 1H7 • (780) 424-7580

University of Alberta Archives • Books & Records Depository, 100 8170 50th St • Edmonton, Alberta T6G 2E2 • (780) 466-6123 • http://www.ualberta.ca/ARCHIVES

University of Alberta Museum Archives • Ring House 1 • Edmonton, Alberta T6G 2E1 • (780) 492-5834 • http://www.museums.ualberta.ca

Victoria School Museum and Archives • 10210 108th Ave • Edmonton, Alberta T5H 1A8 • (780) 498-8715

Victorian Studies Association of Western Canada • University of Alberta, 3-5 Humanities Ctr • Edmonton, Alberta T6G 2E5 • (780) 492-3258 • *Victorian Review*

Edson

Edson and District Public Library • 4726 8th Ave, POB 249 • Edson, Alberta T7E 1S8 • (780) 723-6691 • http://www.townofedson.ca/library.htm

Galloway Station Museum Archives • 5425a 3rd Ave • Edson, Alberta T7E 1L5 • (780) 723-5696

Elk Point

Fort George Museum Archives • POB 66 • Elk Point, Alberta T0A 1A0 • (780) 724-3654

Etzikom

Museum of South East Alberta Archives • POB 585 • Etzikom, Alberta T0K 0W0 • (403) 666-3737

Evansburg

Pembina Lobstick Historical Museum Archives • 48th St, POB 87 • Evansburg, Alberta T0E 0T0 • (780) 727-2211

Fairview

RCMP Centennial Celebration Museum Archives • POB 326 • Fairview, Alberta T0H 1L0 • (780) 835-2467

Forestburg

Forestburg Historical Society • Forestburg and District Museum, 4703 50th St • Forestburg, Alberta T0B 1N0 • (780) 582-2298

Fort Chipewyan

Fort Chipewyan Bicentennial Museum Archives • POB 203 • Fort Chipewyan, Alberta T0P 1B0 • (780) 697-3844

Fort Macleod

Fort Macleod Museum Archives • 219 25th St, POB 776 • Fort Macleod, Alberta T0L 0Z0 • (403) 553-4703

Head-Smashed-In Buffalo Jump Museum • POB 1977 • Fort Macleod, Alberta T0L 0Z0 • (480) 553-2731

Fort McMurray

Alberta Genealogical Society, Fort McMurray Branch • 10011 Franklin Ave, POB 6253 • Fort McMurray, Alberta T9H 4W1 • (780) 791-5663

Fort McMurray Public Library • 9907 Franklin Ave • Fort McMurray, Alberta T9H 2K4 • (780) 743-7800 • http://www.woodbuffalo.ab.ca/library

Heritage Park Archives • 1 Tolen Dr • Fort McMurray, Alberta T9B 1G7 • (780) 791-7575 • http://www.fortmcmurrayhistory.com

Historical Society of Fort McMurray • 1 Tolen Dr • Fort McMurray, Alberta T9H 1G7 • (780) 791-7575

Keyano College Library • 8115 Franklin Ave • Fort McMurray, Alberta T9H 2H7 • (780) 791-4917 • http://www.keyano.ca/

MicMac Historical Cultural Arts Society • 11-6 Riedel St • Fort McMurray, Alberta T9M 3E1

Oil Sands Discovery Centre • 515 MacKenzie Blvd • Fort McMurray, Alberta T9H 4X3 • (780) 743-7167 • http://www.oilsanddiscovery.com

Fort Saskatchewan

Fort Saskatchewan Historical Society & Archives • Historical Museum, 10104 101st St • Fort Saskatchewan, Alberta T8L 1V9 • (780) 998-1750

Fort Vermilion

Rocky Lane School Museum Archives • POB 9000 • Fort Vermilion, Alberta T0H 1N0 • (780) 927-3297

Frog Lake

Frog Lake Indian Band • general delivery • Frog Lake, Alberta T0A 1M0

Alberta

Girouxville
Musee Girouxville Archives • CP 276 • Girouxville, Alberta T0H 1S0 • (403) 323-4252

Goodfish Lake
Whitefish Lake Indian Band 128 • POB 271 • Goodfish Lake, Alberta T0A 1R0

Grand Center
Cold Lake First Nations • POB 1769 • Grand Center, Alberta T0A 1T0

Grande Prairie
Alberta Genealogical Society, Grand Prairie and District Branch • POB 1257 • Grande Prairie, Alberta T8V 4Z1 • (780) 538-0009 • http://www.terranet.ab.ca/~turmbl/gpbranch.html • *Heritage Seekers*

Grande Prairie Pioneer Museum Archives • 102nd St & 102nd Ave, POB 687 • Grande Prairie, Alberta T8V 3A8 • (403) 532-5482 • http://www.telusplanet.net/public/amassee/gpmuseum.html

Grande Prairie Public Library • 9910 99th Ave • Grande Prairie, Alberta T8V 0R5 • (780) 532-3580, Ext 225 • http://www.gppl.ab.ca/

Grimshaw
Lac Cardinal Regional Pioneer Village Museum Archives • POB 325 • Grimshaw, Alberta T0H 1W0 • (780) 332-4863

Hanna
Hanna Municipal Library • POB 878 • Hanna, Alberta T0J 1P0 • (403) 854-3865 • http://www.hanna.ca/library

Hanna Pioneer Museum Archives • POB 1528 • Hanna, Alberta T0J 1P0 • (403) 854-4244

Hay Lakes
Hay Lakes Municipal Public Library • POB 69 • Hay Lakes, Alberta T0B 1W0 • (780) 878-2665

High Prairie
High Prairie and District Centennial Museum Archives • POB 1442 • High Prairie, Alberta T0G 1E0 • (780) 523-2601 • http://www.inetnorth.net/org/museum

High Prairie and District Historical Society & Archives • Historical Museum, 5301 49 St • High Prairie, Alberta T0G 1E0 • (780) 523-2601

High River
High River Centennial Library • 909 1st St W • High River, Alberta T1V 1A5 • (403) 652-2917

Museum of the Highwood Archives • 408 1st St SW • High River, Alberta T1V 1R9 • (403) 652-7156

Hines Creek
End of Steel Heritage Museum Archives • POB 686 • Hines Creek, Alberta T0H 2A0 • (780) 494-3522

Hinton
Alberta Forestry Service Museum Archives • 1176 Switzer Dr • Hinton, Alberta T7V 1V3 • (780) 865-8200

Hinton Municipal Library • 803 Switzer Dr • Hinton, Alberta T7V 1V1 • (780) 865-2363 • http://www.hintonlibrary.org

Hobbema
Ermineskin Indian Band • POB 219 • Hobbema, Alberta T0C 1N0

Four Nations • POB 279 • Hobbema, Alberta T0C 1N0

Louis Bull Indian Band • POB 130 • Hobbema, Alberta T0C 1N0

Maskwachees Cultural College • POB 360 • Hobbema, Alberta T0C 1N0

Montana Indian Band • POB 70 • Hobbema, Alberta T0C 1N0

Samson Cree Indian Band • POB 159 • Hobbema, Alberta T0C 1N0

Holden
Holden Historical Society & Archives • Historical Museum, 4928 50 Holden Ave • Holden, Alberta T0B 2C0 • (780) 688-2464

Iddesleigh
Rainy Hills Historical Society • Historical Museum, general delivery • Iddesleigh, Alberta T0J 1T0 • (306) 898-2270

Innisfail
Innisfail Historical Museum Archives • general delivery • Innisfail, Alberta T0M 1A0 • (403) 227-2906

Innisfall and District Historical Museum Archives • 52nd Ave & 42nd St, POB 6042 • Innisfall, Alberta T0M 1A0 • (403) 227-2906

Irvine
Twenty Mile Post Historical Society • 55 S Railway Ave • Irvine, Alberta T0J 1V0 • (403) 834-2646

Islay
Morrison Museum of the Country School Archives • POB 120 • Islay, Alberta T0B 2J0 • (780) 744-2271

Jasper
Jasper-Hellowhead Museum and Archives • 400 Pyramid lake Rd • Jasper, Alberta T0E 1E0 • (780) 852-3013 • http://jasper-alberta.com/Museum&Arch/Index1.htm

Jasper-Yellowhead Historical Society & Library • 400 Pyramid Lake Rd, POB 42 • Jasper, Alberta T0E 1E0 • (780) 852-3013

Lac La Biche
Beaver Lake Indian Band • POB 960 • Lac La Biche, Alberta T0A 2C0

Heart Lake Indian Band • POB 447 • Lac La Biche, Alberta T0A 2C0

Lac La Biche Mission Historical Society • POB 1622 • Lac La Biche, Alberta T0A 2C0 • (780) 623-3274

Lacombe
Canadian University College Library • 5410 Ramona Ave • Lacombe, Alberta T4L 2B7 • (403) 782-3381, Ext 4102 • http://www.neoslibraries.ca/

Parkland Regional Library • 5404 56th Ave • Lacombe, Alberta T4L 1G1 • (403) 782-3850 • http://www.prl.ab.ca

Lancaster Park
Canadian Airborne Forces Museum Archives • Canadian Forces Base Edmonton • Lancaster Park, Alberta T0A 2H0

Leduc
Dr Woods House Museum Archives • 4801 49th Ave • Leduc, Alberta T9E 6L6 • (780) 986-1517

Leduc and District Historical Society • 4801 49 Ave • Leduc, Alberta T9E 7G6 • (780) 986-1517

Leduc Public Library • 2 Alexandra Park • Leduc, Alberta T9E 4C4 • (780) 986-2637 • http://www.leduc.ab.ca

Lethbridge
Alberta Genealogical Society, Lethbridge Branch • 909 3rd Ave N • Lethbridge, Alberta T1H 0H5 • (403) 328-9564

Fort Whoop-Up Centre • Indian Battle Park, 3rd Ave S, POB 1074 • Lethbridge, Alberta T1J 4A2 • (403) 329-0444 • http://www.fortwhoopup.com

Lethbridge Family Center Archives • 1912 10th Ave S • Lethbridge, Alberta T1K 0B7

Lethbridge Public Library • 810 5th Ave S • Lethbridge, Alberta T1J 4C4 • (403) 380-7310 • http://www.lethbridgelibrary.ab.ca/

Sir Alexander Galt Museum Archives • 910 4th Ave S • Lethbridge, Alberta T1J 0P6 • (403) 320-3898 • http://www.galtmuseum.com

University of Lethbridge Library • 4401 University Dr • Lethbridge, Alberta T1K 3M4 • (403) 329-2261 • http://www.home.uleth.ca/lib/

Lloydminster
Lloydminster Public Library • 5010 49th St • Lloydminster, Alberta T9V 0K2 • (780) 875-0877 • http://www.lloydminster.lib.sk.ca/

Saskatchewan Genealogical Society, Border Branch • 2615 53rd Ave • Lloydminster, Alberta T9V 2L6

Lougheed
Iron Creek Museum Archives • POB 294 • Lougheed, Alberta T0B 2V0 • (780) 386-3984

Markerville
Historic Markerville Creamery Archives • POB 837 • Markerville, Alberta T0M 1M6 • (403) 728-3006 • http://www.touralberta.com/creamery

Medicine Hat
Medicine Hat Municipal Library • 414 1st St SE • Medicine Hat, Alberta T1A 0A8 • (403) 527-5528 • http://www.shortgrass-lib.ab.ca/mhpl

Medicine Hat Museum Archives • 1302 Bomford Crescent SW • Medicine Hat, Alberta T1A 5E6 • (403) 507-8580 • http://www.medicine-hat.ab.ca/cityservices/museum/

Millet
Millet and District Museum Archives • 5120 50th St • Millet, Alberta T0C 1Z0 • (780) 387-5558

Mirror
Mirror and District Museum Archives • POB 246 • Mirror, Alberta T0B 3C0 • (403) 788-3828

Morinville
Alexander Tribal Government • POB 3419 • Morinville, Alberta T8R 1S3

Mundare
Basilian Fathers Museum Archives • 5420 Sawchuk St • Mundare, Alberta T0B 3H0 • (780) 764-3882 • http://www.basilianmuseum.org

Nampa
Nampa Municipal Library • 10203 99th Ave, POB 509 • Nampa, Alberta T0H 2R0 • (780) 322-3805

Nanton
Nanton Lancaster Air Museum Archives • POB 1051 • Nanton, Alberta T0L 1R0 • (403) 646-2270 • http://www.lancastermuseum.ca

Neerlandia
Neerlandia School Public Library • POB 10 • Neerlandia, Alberta T0G 1R0 • (780) 674-5384

Olds
Mountain View Museum Archives • 5038 50th St, POB 3882 • Olds, Alberta T4H 1P6 • (403) 558-8464

Olds Historical Society • Historical Museum, 5038 50 St • Olds, Alberta T4H 1S1 • (403) 556-8464

Oyen
Crossroads Museum Archives • 1st Ave, POB 563 • Oyen, Alberta T0J 2J0 • (403) 664-3850

Peace River
Lubicon Lake Indian Nation • POB 6731 • Peace River, Alberta T8S 1S5

Peace River Centennial Museum Archives • 10302 99th St, POB 747 • Peace River, Alberta T8S 1K1 • (780) 624-4261 • http://www.telusplanet.net/public/prcma

Pincher Creek
Kootenai Brown Pioneer Village Archives • 1037 Bridge Ave • Pincher Creek, Alberta T0K 1W0 • (403) 627-3684 • http://telusplanet.net/public/kootenai

Plamondon
Plamondon and District Museum Archives • 9735 99th St • Plamondon, Alberta T0A 2T0 • (780) 798-3896

Plamondon Municipal Library • POB 119 • Plamondon, Alberta T0A 2T0 • (780) 798-3840

Ponoka
Alberta Hospital Museum Archives • POB 1000 • Ponoka, Alberta T0C 2H0 • (403) 783-7600

Fort Ostell Museum Archives • 5320 54th St • Ponoka, Alberta T4J 1L8 • (403) 763-5224

Raymond
Raymond and District Historical Society • 10 Broadway N • Raymond, Alberta T0K 2S0 • (403) 752-4799

Red Deer
Alberta Genealogical Society, Red Deer Branch • POB 922 • Red Deer, Alberta T4N 1T9 • (403) 343-6842

Fort Normandeau Museum Archives • 6300 45th Ave • Red Deer, Alberta T4N 3M4 • (403) 347-7550 • http://www.city.red-deer.ab.ca/kerry/

Red Deer and District Museum and Archives • 4550-47 A Ave, POB 5008 • Red Deer, Alberta T4N 5H2 • (403) 309-8403 • http://www.museum_red-deer.ab.ca

Red Deer Public Library • 4818 49th St • Red Deer, Alberta T4N 1T9 • (403) 346-4576 • http://www.rdpl.red-deer.ab.ca

Redcliff
Redcliff Museum and Historical Society • 1 3rd St NE, POB 75B • Redcliff, Alberta T0J 2P0 • (403) 548-6260

Redwater
Redwater and District Museum Archives • POB 355 • Redwater, Alberta T0A 2W0 • (780) 942-2512

Rimbey
Rimbey Historical Society & Archives • Pas-Ka-Poo Historical Park • Rimbey, Alberta T0C 2J0 • (403) 843-2084

Rochester
Rochester Community Library • POB 309 • Rochester, Alberta T0G 1Z0 • (780) 698-3970

Rocky Mountain House
O'Chiese Indian Band • POB 1570 • Rocky Mountain House, Alberta T0M 1T0

Rocky Mountain House National Historic Park Archives • POB 2130 • Rocky Mountain House, Alberta T0L 1T0 • (403) 845-2412

Sunchild First Nations • POB 747 • Rocky Mountain House, Alberta T0M 1T0

Rockyford
Rockyford Municipal Library • Community Center, POB 277 • Rockyford, Alberta T0J 2R0 • (403) 533-9904

Rosebud
Rosebud Centennial Museum Archives • POB 601 • Rosebud, Alberta T0J 2T0 • (403) 677-2208

Rowley
Yester-Year Artifacts Museum Archives • general delivery • Rowley, Alberta T0J 2X0 • (403) 368-3816

Saddle Lake
Saddle Lake Indian Band • POB 100 • Saddle Lake, Alberta T0A 1N0

Saint Albert
Musee Heritage Museum Archives • 5 Saint Anne St • Saint Albert, Alberta T8N 3Z9 • (780) 459-1528 • http://www.compusmart.ab.ca/museum

Saint Albert Public Library • 5 St Anne St • Saint Albert, Alberta T8N 3Z9 • (780) 459-1530 • http://www.sapl.ab.ca/

Saint Paul
Fort George and Buckingham House Archives • 5025 49th Ave, Ste 318 • Saint Paul, Alberta T0A 3A4 • (780) 645-6256

History Museum of Saint Paul Archives • POB 1925 • Saint Paul, Alberta T0A 3A0 • (780) 645-4800

Tribal Chief's Association • POB 248 • Saint Paul, Alberta T0A 3A0

Sangudo
Lec Sainte-Anne and District Pioneer Museum Archives • POB 525 • Sangudo, Alberta T0E 2A0 • (708) 785-2338

Alberta

Sedgewick
Sedgewick Museum Archives • POB 808 • Sedgewick, Alberta T0B 4C0 • (780) 384-3741

Sherwood Park
Alberta Italian Times • 504 Alder Ave • Sherwood Park, Alberta T8A 1S9 • (780) 472-6397 • *Alberta Italian Times*

Strathcona County Heritage Museum Archives • 913 Ash St • Sherwood Park, Alberta T8A 2G3 • (780) 467-8189

Strathcona County Library • 104 Sherwood Park Mall, 2020 Sherwood Dr • Sherwood Park, Alberta T8A 5P7 • (780) 449-5801 • http://www.sclibrary.ab.ca/

Siksika
Siksika Cultural Centre • POB 1730 • Siksika, Alberta T0J 3W0

Siksika Nation Museum Archives • POB 1730 • Siksika, Alberta T0J 3W0 • (403) 734-5361

Spirit River
Spirit River and District Historical Society & Archives • Historical Museum, 4403 48 St • Spirit River, Alberta T0H 3G0 • (780) 864-2180

Spruce Grove
Spruce Grove Public Library • 420 King St, No 15 • Spruce Grove, Alberta T7X 2C6 • (780) 962-4423 • http://www.sgpl.sprucegrove.ab.ca/

Spruce View
Dickson Store Museum Archives • POB 146 • Spruce View, Alberta T0M 1V0 • (403) 728-3331

Standoff
Ninastako Cultural Centre • POB 232 • Standoff, Alberta T0L 1Y0

Stettler
Stettler Town and Country Museum Archives • 44th Ave W, POB 2118 • Stettler, Alberta T0C 2L0 • (403) 742-4534

Stirling
Stirling Historical Society • general delivery • Stirling, Alberta T0K 2E0

Stony Plain
Multicultural Heritage Centre Archives • 5411 51st St, POB 908 • Stony Plain, Alberta T0E 2G0 • (780) 963-2777 • http://www.heritage.ab.ca

Stony Plain and District Pioneer Museum Archives • 5120 43rd Av • Stony Plain, Alberta T7Z 1X2 • (780) 963-9825

Strome
Sodbuster Archives Museum Archives • 5029 50th St, POB 151 • Strome, Alberta T0B 4H0 • (780) 376-3688

Sundre
Historical Museum and Pioneer Village • POB 314 • Sundre, Alberta T0M 1X0 • (403) 638-3233

Taber
Taber and District Museum Archives • 4702 50th St • Taber, Alberta T1G 2B6 • (403) 223-5708

Three Hills
Kneehill Historical Museum Archives • POB 653 • Three Hills, Alberta T0M 2A0 • (403) 443-5348

Tofield
Tofield Historical Museum Archives • 5020 46th Av • Tofield, Alberta T0B 4J0 • (780) 662-3191 • http://www.tenap.tofield.ab.ca

Ukranian Cultural Heritage Village • Hwy 16 E • Tofield, Alberta T0B 4J0 • (780) 662-3640

Trochu
Trochu and District Museum Archives • POB 538 • Trochu, Alberta T0M 2C0 • (403) 442-2220

Trochu Municipal Library • POB 396 • Trochu, Alberta T0M 2C0 • (403) 442-2458

Two Hills
Two Hills and District Museum Archives • POB 566 • Two Hills, Alberta T0B 4K0 • (780) 657-2224

Vegreville
Vegreville Regional Museum Archives • POB 328 • Vegreville, Alberta T9C 1R3 • (780) 632-7650 • http://www.vegreville.com

Vermilion
Vermilion Heritage Museum Archives • POB 3612 • Vermilion, Alberta T9X 2B6

Vermilion Public Library • 5001 49th Ave • Vermilion, Alberta T9X 1B8 • (780) 853-4288

Viking
Viking Historical Museum Archives • 5024 58th Ave, POB 232 • Viking, Alberta T0B 4N0 • (780) 336-3066

Viking Historical Society • 5108 61 Ave, POB 232 • Viking, Alberta T0B 4N0 • (780) 336-3066

Vulcan
Vulcan and District Historical Society • 303 Centre St • Vulcan, Alberta T0L 2B0 • (403) 485-2168

Wainwright
Wainwright Museum Archives • POB 2994 • Wainwright, Alberta T9W 1S9 • (780) 842-3115

Wetaskiwin
Alberta Central Railway Museum Archives • RR2 • Wetaskiwin, Alberta T9A 1W9 • (780) 352-2257

Alberta Genealogical Society, Wetaskiwin Branch • 5320 47th Ave • Wetaskiwin, Alberta T9A 0K8

Canada's Aviation Hall of Fame • Hwy 13 W, POB 6360 • Wetaskiwin, Alberta T8A 2G1 • (780) 361-1351

Reynolds Museum Archives • 4110 57th St • Wetaskiwin, Alberta T9A 2B8 • (780) 352-6201

Wetaskiwin and District Museum Archives • 5010 53rd Ave • Wetaskiwin, Alberta T9A 0Y7 • (780) 352-0226

Willingdon
Historical Village and Pioneer Museum Archives • general delivery • Willingdon, Alberta T0B 4R0 • (780) 367-2428

Winterburn
Enoch Cree Nations • RR1, Site 2, POB 2 • Winterburn, Alberta T0E 2N0

Yellowhead Tribal Council • RR1, Site 2, POB 146 • Winterburn, Alberta T0E 2N0

BRITISH COLUMBIA

108 Mile Ranch
100 Mile and District Historical Society • 5206 Davis • 108 Mile Ranch, British Columbia V0K 2Z0 • (250) 791-5288

Abbotsford
Abbotsford Campus Library • University College of the Fraser Valley, 33844 King Rd • Abbotsford, British Columbia V2S 7M8 • (604) 504-7441 • http://www.ucfv.bc.ca/library

Abbotsford Genealogical Group • POB 672 • Abbotsford, British Columbia V2S 6R7

Columbia Resource Centre • Columbia Bible College, 2940 Clearbrook Rd • Abbotsford, British Columbia V2T 2Z8 • (604) 853-3567 • http://www.columbiabc.edu/library

Fraser Valley Regional Library • 34589 Delair Rd • Abbotsford, British Columbia V2S 5Y1 • (604) 859-7141 • http://www.fvrl.bc.ca

Lorne Philip Hudson Memorial Library • Western Pentecostal Bible College, 35235 Straiton Rd, POB 1700 • Abbotsford, British Columbia V2S 7E7 • (604) 851-7230

Matsqui-Sumas Abbotsford Museum Society & Library • Historical Museum, 2313 Ware St • Abbotsford, British Columbia V2S 3C6 • (604) 853-0313 • http://www.abbotsford.net/msamuseum

Sumas Indian Band • 3092 Sumas Mountain Road, RR4 • Abbotsford, British Columbia V2S 4N4

Agassiz
Agassiz-Harrison Historical Museum Archives • 6347 Lougheed Hwy • Agassiz, British Columbia V0M 1A1 • (604) 796- 3545

Agassiz-Harrison Historical Society • 7011 Pioneer Ave • Agassiz, British Columbia V0M 1A0 • (604) 796-3545

Chehalis Indian Band • RR1, Comp 66 • Agassiz, British Columbia V0M 1A0

Seabird Island Band • POB 650 • Agassiz, British Columbia V0M 1A0

Skawahlook Indian Band • POB 388 • Agassiz, British Columbia V0M 1A0

Ahousaht
Ahousaht First Nation • general delivery • Ahousaht, British Columbia V0R 1A0

Ainsworth Hot Springs
Silver Ledge Hotel Museum Archives • POB 1314 • Ainsworth Hot Springs, British Columbia V0G 1A0 • (403) 243-6302 • http://members.home.net/silverledge/

Aldergrove
Alder Grove Heritage Society • 3190 271st St • Aldergrove, British Columbia V4W 3H7

Alert Bay
Alert Bay Public Library and Museum Archives • 118 Fir St, POB 440 • Alert Bay, British Columbia V0N 1A0 • (250) 974-5721 • http://www.alertbay.com/library/

Musgamagw Tribal Council • POB 90 • Alert Bay, British Columbia V0N 1A0

Namgis First Nation • POB 210 • Alert Bay, British Columbia V0N 1A0

Tanakteuk Indian Band • POB 330 • Alert Bay, British Columbia V0N 1A0

Tlatlasikwala Indian Band • POB 270 • Alert Bay, British Columbia V0N 1A0

Tlowitsis-Mumtagila Band & Whe-la-la-u Area Indian Council • POB 150 • Alert Bay, British Columbia V0N 1A0

U'Mista Nation • U'Mista Cultural Centre Archives • POB 253 • Alert Bay, British Columbia V0N 1A0 • (250) 974-5403 • http://www.swifty.com/umista/

Alexis Creek
Anaham Indian Band • general delivery • Alexis Creek, British Columbia V0L 1A0

Anahim Lake
Ulkatcho Indian Band • general delivery • Anahim Lake, British Columbia V0L 1C0

Armstrong
Armstrong Museum Archives • 3415 Pleasant Valley Rd, POB 308 • Armstrong, British Columbia V0E 1B0 • (250) 546-6318

Ashcroft
Ashcroft Indian Indian Band • POB 440 • Ashcroft, British Columbia V0K 1A0

Ashcroft Museum Archives • 404 4th St • Ashcroft, British Columbia V0K 1A0 • (250) 453-4222

Oregon Jack Creek Indian Band • POB 940 • Ashcroft, British Columbia V0K 1A0

Atlin
Atlin Historical Museum Archives • 3rd & Trainor Sts, POB 111 • Atlin, British Columbia V0W 1A0 • (250) 651-7422

Atlin Historical Society • POB 111 • Atlin, British Columbia V0W 1A0

Dax Ka Nation • POB 132 • Atlin, British Columbia V0W 1A0

Taku River Tlingit First Nation • POB 132 • Atlin, British Columbia V0W 1A0

Bamfield
Huu-ay-aht First Nations • POB 70 • Bamfield, British Columbia V0R 1B0

Barkerville
Barkerville Historic Town Library & Archives • POB 19 • Barkerville, British Columbia V0K 1B0 • (250) 994-3332 • http://www.heritage.gov.bc.ca/

Lac La Roche Museum Archives • POB 252 • Barkerville, British Columbia V0H 1T0 • (250) 396-7332

Barriere
North Thompson Indian Band • POB 220 • Barriere, British Columbia V0E 1E0

North Thompson Museum Archives • POB 228 • Barriere, British Columbia V0E 1E0 • (250) 652-5583

Thompson-Nicola Regional District Library System-Barriere Library • 643 Barriere Town Rd • Barriere, British Columbia V0E 1E0 • (250) 672-5811 • http://www.tnrdlib.bc.ca/

Bella Coola
Bella Coola Indian Band • POB 65 • Bella Coola, British Columbia V0T 1C0

Bella Coola Museum Archives • POB 726 • Bella Coola, British Columbia V0T 1C0 • (250) 799-5767

Nuxalk Indian Band • POB 65 • Bella Coola, British Columbia V0T 1C0

Oweekeno-Kitasoo-Nuxalk Tribal Council • POB 760 • Bella Coola, British Columbia V0T 1C0

Boston Bar
Boothroyd Indian Band • POB 295 • Boston Bar, British Columbia V0K 1C0

Boston Bar Indian Band • SS1 • Boston Bar, British Columbia V0K 1C0

Bowen Island
Bowen Island Historians • POB 97 • Bowen Island, British Columbia V0N 1G0

Bralorne
Bralorne Pioneer Museum Archives • SS1 Goldbridge • Bralorne, British Columbia V0K 1P0 • (250) 238-2240

Brentwood Bay
Pauquachin Indian Band • POB 517 • Brentwood Bay, British Columbia V0S 1K0

Saanich Nation • Saanich Cultural Education Centre, POB 28 • Brentwood Bay, British Columbia V8M 1R3

Britannia Beach
British Columbia Museum of Mining Archives • Hwy 99 N, POB 188 • Britannia Beach, British Columbia V0N 1J0 • (604) 896-2233 • http://www.bcmuseumofmining.org

Buick Creek
Blueberry River Indian Band • POB 3009 • Buick Creek, British Columbia V0C 2R0

British Columbia

Burnaby

Burnaby Historical Society • 6501 Deer Lake Ave • Burnaby, British Columbia V5G 3T6 • (604) 434-6828

Burnaby Village Museum Archives • Deer Lake Park, 6501 Deer Lake Av • Burnaby, British Columbia V5G 3T6 • (604) 294-1231

Slovak Heritage and Cultural Society of British Columbia • 3804 Yale St • Burnaby, British Columbia V5C 1P6 • (604) 291-8065 • *Slovak Heritage Live*

W A C Bennett Library • Simon Fraser University, 8888 University Dr • Burnaby, British Columbia V5A 1S6 • (604) 291-5735 • http://www.lib.sfu.ca/

Burns Lake

Broman Lake Indian Band • POB 760 • Burns Lake, British Columbia V0J 1E0

Burns Lake Indian Band • Bag 9000 • Burns Lake, British Columbia V0J 1E0

Cheslatta Carrier Nation • POB 909 • Burns Lake, British Columbia V0J 1E0

Lake Babine Nation • POB 879 • Burns Lake, British Columbia V0J 1E0

Lakes District Museum Archives • POB 266 • Burns Lake, British Columbia V-J 1E0 • (250) 692-7450

Nee-Tahi-Buhn Indian Band • RR2, Box 28 • Burns Lake, British Columbia V0J 1E0

Cache Creek

Bonaparte Indian Band • POB 669 • Cache Creek, British Columbia V0K 1H0

Historic Hat Creek Ranch Archives • POB 878 • Cache Creek, British Columbia V0K 1H0 • (250) 457-9722 • http://www.heritage.gov.bc.ca

Pavilion Indian Band • POB 609 • Cache Creek, British Columbia V0K 1H0

Campbell River

Campbell River and District Historical Society • POB 70, Sta A • Campbell River, British Columbia V9W 2C7 • (250) 287-3103

Campbell River and District Museum and Archives • 470 Island Hwy, Box 70, Sta A • Campbell River, British Columbia V9W 4Z9 • (250) 287-3103 • http://www.crmuseum.ca

Campbell River Genealogy Club & Library • POB 884 • Campbell River, British Columbia V9W 6Y4 • (250) 286-8042 • http://www.rootsweb.com/bccrgc

Campbell River Indian Band • 1400 Weiwaikum Rd • Campbell River, British Columbia V9W 5W8

Campbell River Museum Archives • 470 Island Hwy • Campbell River, British Columbia V9W 4Z9 • (250) 287-3103 • http://www.crmuseum.ca

Campbell River Optical Maritime Museum Archives • 250 Dogwood St • Campbell River, British Columbia V9W 2X8 • (250) 287-2052

Ehattesaht Indian Tribe • POB 716 • Campbell River, British Columbia V9W 6J3

Homalco Indian Band • POB 789 • Campbell River, British Columbia V9W 6Y4

Kwiakah Indian Band • 1440 Island Hwy • Campbell River, British Columbia V9W 2E3

Mamaleleqala Qwe'Qwa'Sot'Enox Indian Band • 1400 Weiwaikum Rd • Campbell River, British Columbia V9W 5W8

Canim Lake

Canim Lake Indian Band • POB 1030 • Canim Lake, British Columbia V0K 1J0

Castlegar

Castlegar and District Public Library • 1005 3rd St • Castlegar, British Columbia V1N 2A2 • (250) 365-6611 • http://www.castlegarlibrary.com

Railway Station Museum Archives • 400 13th Ave • Castlegar, British Columbia V1N 1G2

Selkirk College Archives and Local History Collection • 301 Frank Beinder Wy, POB 1200 • Castlegar, British Columbia V1N 3J1 • (250) 365-7292 • http://www.library.selkirk.bc.ca

Celista

North Shuswap Historical Society • POB 22 • Celista, British Columbia V0E 1L0

Chase

Adams Lake Indian Band • POB 588 • Chase, British Columbia V0E 1M0

Chase and District Museum Archives • 1042 Shuswap Ave • Chase, British Columbia V0E 1M0 • (250) 679-8847

Little Shuswap Indian Band • POB 1100 • Chase, British Columbia V0E 1M0

Neskonlith Indian Band • POB 608 • Chase, British Columbia V0E 1M0

Chemainus

Chemainus Valley Historical Society • POB 172 • Chemainus, British Columbia V0R 1K0

Halalt Indian Band • RR1 • Chemainus, British Columbia V0R 1K0

Penelakut Indian Band • POB 360 • Chemainus, British Columbia V0R 1K0

Chetwynd

Little Prairie Heritage Museum Archives • POB 1777 • Chetwynd, British Columbia V0C 1J0 • (250) 788-3358

Saulteaux Indian Band • POB 414 • Chetwynd, British Columbia V0C 1J0

Chilanko Forks

Alexis Creek Indian Band • POB 69 • Chilanko Forks, British Columbia V0L 1H0

Chilliwack

Canadian Military Engineers Museum Archives • Canadian Force Base, Keith Wilson Rd • Chilliwack, British Columbia V0X 1Z0

Chilliwack Historical Society & Archives • Historical Museum, 45820 Spadina Ave • Chilliwack, British Columbia V2P 4A6 • (604) 795-5210 • http://www.chilliwack.museum.bc.ca

Kwaw Kwaw Apilt Indian Band • POB 412 • Chilliwack, British Columbia V2P 6J7

Popkum Indian Band • 62 - 45185 Wolfe Rd • Chilliwack, British Columbia V2P 1V5

Skwah Indian Band • POB 178 • Chilliwack, British Columbia V2P 6H7

Skway Indian Band • POB 364 • Chilliwack, British Columbia V2P 6J4

Squiala Indian Band • POB 392 • Chilliwack, British Columbia V2P 6J7

Clinton

High Bar Indian Band • POB 45 • Clinton, British Columbia V0K 1K0

South Cariboo Historical Museum Archives • 1419 Cariboo Hwy, POB 75 • Clinton, British Columbia V0K 1K0 • (250) 459-2442

Coal Harbour

Quatsino Indian Band • POB 100 • Coal Harbour, British Columbia V0N 1K0

Cobble Hill

British Columbia Folklore Society • POB 312 • Cobble Hill, British Columbia V0R 1L0

Coquitlam

Coquitlam Public Library • 575 Poirier St • Coquitlam, British Columbia V3J 6A9 • (604) 937-4144 • http://www.library.coquitlam.bc.ca/

Cortes Island

Klahoose Indian Band • Squirrel Cove, POB 9 • Cortes Island, British Columbia V0P 1K0

Courtenay

Comox Indian Band • 3320 Comox Rd • Courtenay, British Columbia V9N 3P8

Courtenay and District Museum Archives • 207 4th St • Courtenay, British Columbia V9N 1G7 • (250) 334-0686 • http://www.courtenaymuseum.ca

Cowichan Bay
Cowichan Bay Maritime Centre • POB 22 • Cowichan Bay, British Columbia V0R 1N0 • (250) 746-4955 • http://www.classicboats.org

Cranbrook
Canadian Museum of Rail Travel Archives • 57 Van Horne St S, POB 400 • Cranbrook, British Columbia V1C 4H9 • (250) 489-3918 • http://www.trainsdeluxe.com

East Kootenay Historical Association • POB 74 • Cranbrook, British Columbia V1C 4H6

Ktunaxa-Kinbasket Tribal Council • RR3, Site 15, Comp 14, Mission Rd • Cranbrook, British Columbia V1C 6H3

Learning Resource Centre • College of the Rockies, 2700 College Way, POB 8500 • Cranbrook, British Columbia V1C 5L7 • (250) 489-8293 • http://www.cotr.bc.ca/

Saint Mary's Indian Band • RR3, Site 15, Comp 55 • Cranbrook, British Columbia V1C 6H3

Creston
Creston and District Museum Archives • 219 Devon St • Creston, British Columbia V0B 1G3 • (250) 428-9262 • http://www.creston.museum.bc.ca

Lower Kootenay Indian Band • POB 1107 • Creston, British Columbia V0B 1G0

Crofton
Old Crofton School Museum Archives • POB 159 • Crofton, British Columbia V0R 1R0 • (250) 246-3804

Cultus Lake
Soowahlie Indian Band • 4070 Soowahlie Rd • Cultus Lake, British Columbia V0X 1H0

Cumberland
Cumberland Museum Archives • 2680 Dunsmuir Ave • Cumberland, British Columbia V0R 1S0 • (250) 336-2445 • http://www.cumberland.museum.bc.ca

D'Arcy
Anderson Lake Indian Band • POB 88 • D'Arcy, British Columbia V0N 1L0

Dawson Creek
Dawson Creek Municipal Public Library • 1001 McKellar Ave • Dawson Creek, British Columbia V1G 4W7 • (250) 782-4661

Dawson Creek Station Museum Archives • 900 Alaska Ave, POB 2033 • Dawson Creek, British Columbia V1G 4K8 • (250) 782-9595 • http://www.prls.bc.ca.dcsm

Northern Lights College Library • 11401 8th St • Dawson Creek, British Columbia V1G 4G2 • (250) 784-7533 • http://www.nlc.bc.ca

South Peace Historical Society & Archives • 1017 105 Ave, POB 2033 • Dawson Creek, British Columbia V1G 4K8 • (250) 782-4565

Walter Wright Pioneer Village Archives • 900 Alaska Ave • Dawson Creek, British Columbia V1G 4T6

Delta
Alliance Tribal Council • 130 N Tsawwassen Dr • Delta, British Columbia V4K 3N2

Delta Museum and Archives • 4858 Delta St • Delta, British Columbia V4K 2T8 • (604) 946-4781

Tsawwassen First Nation • N Tsawwassen Dr, Bldg 132 • Delta, British Columbia V4K 3N2

Denman Island
Denman Island Museum Archives • 1111 Northwest Rd • Denman Island, British Columbia V0R 1T0 • (250) 335-0880

Deroche
Lakahahmen Indian Band • RR2, 41290 Lougheed Hwy • Deroche, British Columbia V0M 1G0

Dog Creek
Canoe Creek Indian Band • general delivery • Dog Creek, British Columbia V0L 1J0

Duncan
B C Forest Discovery Centre Archives • 2892 Drinkwater Rd • Duncan, British Columbia V9L 6C2 • (250) 715-1113

Cowichan Historical Society • POB 1014 • Duncan, British Columbia V9L 3Y2

Cowichan Indian Band • 5760 Allenby Rd • Duncan, British Columbia V9L 5J1

Cowichan Valley Museum Archives • Duncan Train Station, POB 1014 • Duncan, British Columbia V9L 3W2 • (250) 746-6612

Mid-Island Tribal Council • POB 1000 • Duncan, British Columbia V9L 3Y2

Slovenian Genealogical Society, Canadian Chapter • 1383 Maple Bay Rd, RR5 • Duncan, British Columbia V9L 4T6

Enderby
Enderby and District Museum Archives • 901 George St • Enderby, British Columbia V0E 1V0 • (250) 838-7170 • http://www.enderbymuseum.ca

Spallumcheen Indian Band • POB 430 • Enderby, British Columbia V0E 1V0

Fernie
Fernie and District Historical Museum Archives • POB 1527 • Fernie, British Columbia V0B 1M0 • (250) 423-7016

Fernie and District Historical Society • 362 2nd Ave • Fernie, British Columbia V0B 1M0 • (250) 423-7016

Fernie Centennial Library • 592 3rd Ave, POB 448 • Fernie, British Columbia V0B 1M0 • (250) 423-4458 • http://www.elkvalley.net/library

Fort Fraser
Nadleh Whut'en Indian Band • POB 36 • Fort Fraser, British Columbia V0J 1N0

Fort Langley
British Columbia Farm Machinery and Agricultural Museum Archives • 9130 King St • Fort Langley, British Columbia V0X 1J0 • (604) 638-2273

Fort Langley National Historic Site Archives • 23433 Mavis Ave • Fort Langley, British Columbia V1M 2R5 • (604) 513-4777 • http://www.parkscanada.bc/ca/langley

Kwantlen First Nation • POB 117 • Fort Langley, British Columbia V0X 1J0

Langley Centennial Museum Archives • 9135 King St, POB 800 • Fort Langley, British Columbia V1M 2S2 • (604) 888-3922 • http://www.langleymuseum.org

Fort Nelson
Fort Nelson Heritage Museum Archives • POB 716 • Fort Nelson, British Columbia V0C 1R0 • (250) 774-3536

Fort Nelson Historical Society • 5603-50th Ave • Fort Nelson, British Columbia V0C 1R0 • (250) 774-3536

Fort Nelson Indian Band • RR1 • Fort Nelson, British Columbia V0C 1R0

Prophet River Band • POB 3250 • Fort Nelson, British Columbia V0C 1R0

Fort Saint James
Fort Saint James National Historic Park Library • Kwah Rd • Fort Saint James, British Columbia V0J 1P0 • (250) 996-7191

Nak'azdli Indian Band • POB 1329 • Fort Saint James, British Columbia V0J 1P0

Takla Lake Indian Band • general delivery • Fort Saint James, British Columbia V0J 2T0

Tl'azt'en Nation • POB 670 • Fort Saint James, British Columbia V0J 1P0

Fort Saint John
Fort Saint John Public Library Association • 10015 100th Ave • Fort Saint John, British Columbia V1J 1Y7 • (250) 785-3731 • http://www.pris.bc.ca/library

Fort Saint John-North Peace River Museum • 3323 100th St • Fort Saint John, British Columbia V7J 4N4 • (250) 787-0430 • http://collections.lc.qc.ca/north_peace

Treaty 8 Tribal Association • 10233 - 100th Ave • Fort Saint John, British Columbia V1J 1Y8

Fort Steele
Fort Steele Heritage Town Museum • Heritage Town, 9851 Hwy 93-95 • Fort Steele, British Columbia V0B 1N0 • (250) 417-6006 • http://www.fortsteele.bc.ca

Fraser Lake
Fraser Lake Museum Archives • POB 430 • Fraser Lake, British Columbia V0J 1S0 • (250) 699-6257 • http://www.village.fraserlk.bc.ca

Stella'ten First Nation • POB 760 • Fraser Lake, British Columbia V0J 1S0

Galiano
British Columbia Historical Federation, Gulf Islands Branch • RR1, Site 22, Comp 1 • Galiano, British Columbia V0N 1P0

Ganges
Salt Spring Island Museum Archives • POB 961 • Ganges, British Columbia V0S 1E0 • (250) 537-9567

Garibaldi Heights
Squamish Valley Museum Archives • POB 166 • Garibaldi Heights, British Columbia V0N 1T0 • (604) 898-3273

Gibsons
Sunshine Coast Museum Archives • 716 Winn Rd, POB 766 • Gibsons, British Columbia V0N 1V0 • (604) 886-8232 • http://www.gibsonslibrary.bc.ca/museum

Gitwinksihlkw
Gitwinksihlkw Indian Band • POB 1 • Gitwinksihlkw, British Columbia V0J 3T0

Gold River
Mowachaht-Muchalaht Indian Band • POB 459 • Gold River, British Columbia V0P 1G0

Golden
Golden District Historical Society & Archives • Historical Museum, 1302 11th Ave, POB 992 • Golden, British Columbia V0A 1H0 • (250) 344-5169 • http://www.rockies.net/~museum

Good Hope Lake
Dease River Band Council • general delivery • Good Hope Lake, British Columbia V0C 2Z0

Grand Forks
Boundary Historical Society • 12th St SE, POB 580 • Grand Forks, British Columbia V0H 1H0 • (250) 442-3283 • Boundary Historical Society Report

Boundary Museum Archives • 108 SE 9th St, POB 817 • Grand Forks, British Columbia V0H 1H0 • (250) 442-3737

Mountain View Doukhobor Museum Archives • Hardy Mountain Rd • Grand Forks, British Columbia V0H 1H0 • (250) 442-8855

Grasmere
Tobacco Plains Band • POB 76 • Grasmere, British Columbia V0B 1R0

Greenville
Laxqalts'ap Indian Band Council • general delivery • Greenville, British Columbia V0J 1X0

Greenwood
Greenwood Museum Archives • 214 Copper St, POB 399 • Greenwood, British Columbia V0H 1J0 • (250) 445-6355 • http://www.greenwoodmuseum.com

Groundbirch
Groundbirch Museum Archives • POB 149 • Groundbirch, British Columbia V0C 1T0 • (250) 780-2383

Hanceville
Stone Indian Band • general delivery • Hanceville, British Columbia V0L 1K0

Harrision Hot Springs
Douglas Indian Band • POB 339 • Harrision Hot Springs, British Columbia V0M 1K0

Harrison Mills
Kilby Historic Store and Farm Archives • 215 Kilby Rd • Harrison Mills, British Columbia V0M 1L0 • (604) 796-9576

Hartley Bay
Hartley Bay Indian Band • general delivery • Hartley Bay, British Columbia V0V 1A0

Hazelton
Gitanmaax Indian Band • POB 440 • Hazelton, British Columbia V0J 1Y0

Gitxsan Local Services Society • POB 335 • Hazelton, British Columbia V0J 1Y0

Glen Vowell Indian Band • POB 157 • Hazelton, British Columbia V0J 1Y0

Hazelton District Public Library • 4255 Government St, POB 323 • Hazelton, British Columbia V0J 1Y0 • (250) 842-5961 • http://www.hazletonlibrary.bc.ca/

Ksan Historical Village and Museum Archives • Hwy 62, Highlevel Rd, POB 326 • Hazelton, British Columbia V0J 1Y0 • (250) 842-5544

Hedley
Hedley Heritage Society • POB 218 • Hedley, British Columbia V0X 1K0

Hope
Chawathil Indian Band • POB 1659 • Hope, British Columbia V0X 1L0

Hope Museum Archives • 919 Water St, POB 26 • Hope, British Columbia V0X 1L0 • (604) 869-7322

Ohamil Indian Band • RR2, Site 22, Comp 4 • Hope, British Columbia V0X 1L0

Peters Indian Band • RR2, 16650 Peters Rd • Hope, British Columbia V0X 1L0

Union Bar Indian Band • POB 788 • Hope, British Columbia V0X 1L0

Yale First Nation • POB 1869 • Hope, British Columbia V0X 1L0

Horsefly
Jack Lynn Memorial Museum Archives • POB 71 • Horsefly, British Columbia V0L 1L0 • (604) 620-3304

Hudson's Hope
Hudson's Hope Museum Archives • 9510 Beattie Dr, POB 98 • Hudson's Hope, British Columbia V0C 1V0 • (250) 783-5735

Invermere
Shuswap Indian Band • POB 790 • Invermere, British Columbia V0A 1K0

Windermere District Historical Museum Archives • 7th Ave & 9th St, POB 2315 • Invermere, British Columbia V0A 1K0 • (250) 342-6859

Windermere Valley Museum Archives • 622 3rd St, POB 2315 • Invermere, British Columbia V0A 1K0 • (250) 342-9769

Iskut
Iskut Indian Band • POB 30 • Iskut, British Columbia V0J 1K0

Kamloops
Kamloops Family History Society • POB 1162 • Kamloops, British Columbia V2C 6H3

Kamloops Indian Band • 315 Yellowhead Hwy • Kamloops, British Columbia V2H 1H1

Kamloops Museum Association & Archives • Historical Museum, 207 Seymour St • Kamloops, British Columbia V2C 2E7 • (250) 828-3576

Rocky Mountain Rangers Museum Archives • 1221 McGill Rd • Kamloops, British Columbia V2C 6B8 • (250) 851-4890

Secwepemc Cultural Education Society • 345 Yellowhead Hwy • Kamloops, British Columbia V2H 1H1

Secwepemc Museum and Heritage Park Archives • 311-355 Yellowhead Hwy • Kamloops, British Columbia V2H 1H1 • (250) 828-9801 • http://www.secwepemc.org

Shuswap Nation Tribal Council • 355 Yellowhead Hwy • Kamloops, British Columbia V2H 1H1

Thompson-Nicola Regional District Library • 465 Victoria St, Suite 100 • Kamloops, British Columbia V2C 2A9 • (250) 374-8866 • http://www.trndlib.bc.ca

Whispering Pines Indian Band • RR1, Site 8, Comp 4 • Kamloops, British Columbia V2C 1Z3

Kaslo
Kootenay Lake Historical Society & Library • 312 4th St, POB 537 • Kaslo, British Columbia V0G 1M0

Langham Cultural Centre Archives • 447 A Avenue • Kaslo, British Columbia V0G 1M0 • (250) 353-2661 • http://www.kin.bc.ca/langham

SS Moyle National Historic Site Archives • 324 Front St, POB 537 • Kaslo, British Columbia V0G 1M0 • (250) 353-2525 • http://www.kin.bc.ca/moyle/moylehome1.html

Kelowna
British Columbia Orchard Industry Museum Archives • 1304 Ellis St • Kelowna, British Columbia V1Y 1Z8 • (250) 763-0433

Father Pandosy Mission Archives • 3685 Behvoulin Rd, POB 1532 • Kelowna, British Columbia V1Y 7V8 • (250) 860-8369

Kelowna and District Genealogical Society • POB 501, Sta A • Kelowna, British Columbia V1Y 7A1

Kelowna Centennial Museum Archives • 470 Queensway Ave • Kelowna, British Columbia V1Y 6S7 • (604) 763-2417

Westbank Indian Band • 301-515 Hwy 97 S • Kelowna, British Columbia V1Z 3J2

Keremeos
Grist Mill Museum Archives • Upper Bench Rd, RR1 • Keremeos, British Columbia V0X 1N0 • (250) 499-2888

Lower Similkameen Indian Band • POB 100 • Keremeos, British Columbia V0X 1N0

South Similkameen Museum Archives • POB 135 • Keremeos, British Columbia V0X 1N0 • (250) 499-5445

Upper Similkameen Indian Band • POB 310 • Keremeos, British Columbia V0X 1N0

Kimberley
Kimberley Heritage Museum Archives • POB 144 • Kimberley, British Columbia V1A 2Y5 • (250) 427-7510

Kincolith
Kincolith Indian Band • general delivery • Kincolith, British Columbia V0V 1B0

Kingcome Village
Tsawataineuk Indian Band • Kingcome Inlet • Kingcome Village, British Columbia V0N 2B0

Kispiox
Kispiox Indian Band • RR1, POB 25 • Kispiox, British Columbia V0J 1Y0

Kitamaat Village
Haisla Indian Band • POB 1101 • Kitamaat Village, British Columbia V0T 2B0

Kitamaat Village Council • POB 1101 • Kitamaat Village, British Columbia V0T 2B0

Kitimat
Kitimat Centennial Museum Association & Library • 293 City Centre • Kitimat, British Columbia V8C 1T6 • (250) 632-8950 • http://www.sno.net/kitmuse

Kitimat Public Library Association • 940 Wakashan Ave • Kitimat, British Columbia V8C 2G3 • (250) 632-8995 • http://www.kitimatpubliclibrary.org

Kitkatla
Kitkatla Indian Band • general delivery • Kitkatla, British Columbia V0V 1C0

Kitwanga
Gitanyow Indian Band • POB 340 • Kitwanga, British Columbia V0J 2A0

Gitwangak Indian Band • POB 400 • Kitwanga, British Columbia V0J 2A0

Meanskinisht Museum Archives • Cedarvale, POB 183 • Kitwanga, British Columbia V0J 2A0 • (250) 849-5732

Klemtu
Kitasoo Indian Band • general delivery • Klemtu, British Columbia V0T 1L0

Koksilah
Koksilah School Historical Society • 5213 Trans Canada Hwy • Koksilah, British Columbia V0R 2C0

Ladysmith
Black Nugget Museum Archives • 12 Gatacre St • Ladysmith, British Columbia V0R 2E0 • (250) 245-2846

Chemainus Indian Band • RR1 • Ladysmith, British Columbia V0R 2E0

Ladysmith Railway Museum Archives • POB 777 • Ladysmith, British Columbia V0R 2E0 • (250) 245-4454

Lake Cowichan
Cowichan Lake First Nations • POB 1376 • Lake Cowichan, British Columbia V0R 2G0

Kaatza Station Museum Archives • 125 S Shore Rd • Lake Cowichan, British Columbia V0R 2G0 • (250) 749-6142

Lake Errock
Scowlitz Indian Band • POB 76 • Lake Errock, British Columbia V0M 1N0

Langley
Canadian Museum of Flight Archives • 5333 216th St, Ste 200 • Langley, British Columbia V2Y 2N3 • (604) 532-0035 • http://www.canadianflight.org

Lantzville
Lantzville Historical Society • POB 274 • Lantzville, British Columbia V0R 2H0

Nanoose First Nation • 209 Mallard Wy • Lantzville, British Columbia V0R 2H0

Lasqueti Island
Lasqueti Island Historical Society • general delivery • Lasqueti Island, British Columbia V0R 2J0

Lazo
Comox Air Force Museum Archives • CFB • Lazo, British Columbia V0R 2K0 • (250) 339-8162 • http://mars.ark.com/~camuseum

Lillooet
Bridge River Indian Band • POB 190 • Lillooet, British Columbia V0K 1V0

Cayoose Creek Indian Band • POB 484 • Lillooet, British Columbia V0K 1V0

Fountain Indian Band • POB 1330 • Lillooet, British Columbia V0K 1V0

Lillooet Indian Band • POB 615 • Lillooet, British Columbia V0K 1V0

Lillooet Museum Archives • Main St, POB 441 • Lillooet, British Columbia V0K 1V0 • (250) 256-4556

Lillooet Tribal Council • POB 1420 • Lillooet, British Columbia V0K 1V0

Xaxli'p Indian Nation • POB 1330 • Lillooet, British Columbia V0K 1V0

Lytton
Fraser Canyon Tribal Administration • POB 400 • Lytton, British Columbia V0K 1Z0

Kanaka Bar Indian Band • POB 400 • Lytton, British Columbia V0K 1Z0

Lytton Indian Band • POB 20 • Lytton, British Columbia V0K 1Z0

Lytton Museum Archives • 420 Fraser St • Lytton, British Columbia V0K 1Z0 • (250) 455-2254

Nicomen Indian Band • POB 328 • Lytton, British Columbia V0K 1Z0

Nlaka'Pamux Nation Tribal Council • POB 430 • Lytton, British Columbia V0K 1Z0

British Columbia

Siska Indian Band • POB 358 • Lytton, British Columbia V0K 1Z0

Skuppah Indian Band • POB 116 • Lytton, British Columbia V0K 1Z0

Mackenzie
Mackenzie and District Museum Archives • POB 934 • Mackenzie, British Columbia V0J 2C0 • (250) 997-4323

Maple Ridge
Maple Ridge Museum Archives • 22520 116th Ave • Maple Ridge, British Columbia V2K 0S4 • (604) 463-5311

Thomas Haney House Museum Archives • 11012 224th St • Maple Ridge, British Columbia V2X 5Z7 • (604) 463-1377

Masset
Council of the Haida Nation • POB 589 • Masset, British Columbia V0T 1M0

Masset Haida Gwaii
Old Massett Village Council • POB 189 • Masset Haida Gwaii, British Columbia V0T 1M0

Matsqui
Matsqui Indian Band • RR1, POB 229 • Matsqui, British Columbia V0X 1S0

Mayne Island
Mayne Island Museum Archives • general delivery • Mayne Island, British Columbia V0N 2J0 • (250) 539-2283

McBride
Valley Museum Archives • POB 775 • McBride, British Columbia V0J 2E0 • (250) 569-2411

McLeod Lake
McLeod Lake Indian Band • general delivery • McLeod Lake, British Columbia V0J 2G0

Merrit
Nicola Valley Museum Archives • 2202 Jackson Ave • Merrit, British Columbia V1K 1B8 • (250) 378-4145

Coldwater Indian Band • POB 4600 • Merritt, British Columbia V0K 2B0

Lower Nicola Indian Band • RR1, Site 17, Comp 18 • Merritt, British Columbia V0K 2B0

Nicola Valley Museum Archives Association • 2202 Jackson Ave, POB 1262 • Merritt, British Columbia V0K 2B0 • (250) 378-4145 • *Nicola Valley Historical Quarterly*

Nicola Valley Tribal Council • POB 188 • Merritt, British Columbia V0K 2B0

Nicole Valley Museum Archives Association • 2202 Jackson Ave., POB 1262 • Merritt, British Columbia V1K 1B8 • (250) 378-4145 • *Nicole Valley Historical Quarterly*

Nooaitch Indian Band • POB 6000 • Merritt, British Columbia V0K 2B0

Shackan Indian Band • POB 6000 • Merritt, British Columbia V0K 2B0

Upper Nicola Indian Band • POB 3700 • Merritt, British Columbia V0K 2B0

Midway
Kettle River Museum Archives • POB 149 • Midway, British Columbia V0H 1M0 • (250) 449-2614

Mill Bay
First Nations of South Island Tribal Council • POB 62 • Mill Bay, British Columbia V0R 2P0

Malahat Indian Band • POB 111 • Mill Bay, British Columbia V0R 2P0

Mission
Mission Community Archives • 33215 2nd Ave, POB 3522 • Mission, British Columbia V2V 4L1 • (604) 820-2621 • http://www.missionarchives.com

Mission Museum Archives • 33201 2nd Ave • Mission, British Columbia V2V 1J9 • (604) 826-1011 • http://www.mission.museum.bc.ca

Samahquam Indian Band • POB 3068 • Mission, British Columbia V2V 4J3

Moberly Lake
West Moberly Lake Indian Band • general delivery • Moberly Lake, British Columbia V0X 1X0

Moricetown
Moricetown Indian Band Council • RR1, Box 1, Site 15 • Moricetown, British Columbia V0J 2N0

Mount Currie
Mount Currie Indian Band • POB 165 • Mount Currie, British Columbia V0N 2K0

Nakusp
Arrow Lakes Historical Society & Archives • Nakusp Museum, 92 7th Ave NW, POB 584 • Nakusp, British Columbia V0G 1R0 • (604) 265-4518

Nanaimo
Bastion Museum Archives • Front St • Nanaimo, British Columbia V9R 5S5 • (250) 753-1821

Centennial Museum of the Nanaimo Regional General Hospital • 1200 Dufferin Cres • Nanaimo, British Columbia V9W 2B7 • (250) 756-7637

Malaspina University College Library • 900 5th St • Nanaimo, British Columbia V9R 5S5 • (250) 753-3245 • http://www.mala.ca/www.discover/library/

Nanaimo and District Museum Society & Library • 100 Cameron Rd • Nanaimo, British Columbia V9R 2X1 • (250) 753-1821 • http://www.nanaimomuseum.bc.ca

Nanaimo Family History Society • POB 1027 • Nanaimo, British Columbia V9R 5Z2

Nanaimo First Nations • 1145 Totem Rd • Nanaimo, British Columbia V9R 1H1

Nanaimo Historical Society • POB 933, Sta A • Nanaimo, British Columbia V9R 5N2

Vancouver Island Regional Library • 6250 Hammond Bay Rd, POB 3333 • Nanaimo, British Columbia V9R 5N3 • (250) 758-4697 • http://www.virl.bc.ca

Naramata
Naramata Museum Archives • POB 95 • Naramata, British Columbia V0H 1N0 • (250) 498-5866

Nelson
Nelson Municipal Library • 602 Stanley St • Nelson, British Columbia V1L 1N4 • (250) 352-6333 • http://www.library.nelsonbc.net

Nelson Museum Association and Historical Society & Library • 402 Anderson St • Nelson, British Columbia V1L 3Y3 • (250) 352-9813 • http://www.kics.bc.ca/~museum/

Nemaiah Valley
Nemaiah Valley Indian Band • general delivery • Nemaiah Valley, British Columbia V0L 1X0

New Aiyansh
Gitlakdamix Indian Band • POB 233 • New Aiyansh, British Columbia V0J 1A0

Nisga'a Tribal Council • general delivery • New Aiyansh, British Columbia V0J 1A0

New Denver
Sandon Museum Archives • POB 52 • New Denver, British Columbia V0G 1S0 • (250) 358-2607

Silvery Slocan Historical Society • POB 301 • New Denver, British Columbia V0G 1S0

Silvery Slocan Museum Archives • 202 Main St • New Denver, British Columbia V0G 1S0 • (250) 358-2201

New Hazelton
Hagwilget Indian Band • POB 460 • New Hazelton, British Columbia V0J 2J0

New Westminster
Douglas College Library • 700 Royal Ave, POB 2503 • New Westminster, British Columbia V3L 5B2 • (604) 527-5182 • http://www.library.douglas.bc.ca

Irving House Historic Centre Archives • 302 Royal Ave • New Westminster, British Columbia V3L 1H7 • (604) 527-4640 • http://www.city.new-westminster.bc.ca

New Westminster Public Library • 716 6th Ave • New Westminster, British Columbia V3M 2B3 • (604) 527-4660 • http://www.nwheritage.org

Royal Westminster Regiment Historical Society & Library • Armoury Museum, 530 Queens Ave • New Westminster, British Columbia V3L 1K3 • (604) 526-5116

Samson V Maritime Museum Archives • 1005 Columbia St • New Westminster, British Columbia V3M 6H5 • (604) 522-6894

Vancouver Cornish Association • 419 Buchanan Ave • New Westminster, British Columbia V3L 3Z6

North Vancouver
Burrard Indian Band • 3082 Ghumlye Dr • North Vancouver, British Columbia V7H 1B3

Canadian Indian Voice Society • 429 E 6th St • North Vancouver, British Columbia V7L 1P8 • Indian Voice

North Shore Historical Society • 1541 Merlynn Crescent • North Vancouver, British Columbia V7J 2X9

North Vancouver City Library • 121 W 14th St • North Vancouver, British Columbia V7M 1P2 • (604) 998-3490 • http://www.cnv.org/nvcl

North Vancouver Museum Archives • 209 W 4th St • North Vancouver, British Columbia V7J 1S1 • (604) 987-5618 • http://www.drv.org/nvma

Pacific Great Eastern Station Archives • Lonsdale Ave • North Vancouver, British Columbia V7M 1H8 • (604) 987-5818 • http://www.drv.org/nvma

Squamish Nation • 320 Seymour Blvd • North Vancouver, British Columbia V7L 2J3

Okanagan
Lake Country Museum Archives • 11255 Okanagan Centre Rd • Okanagan, British Columbia V4V 2J7

Okanagan Falls
Bassett House Museum Archives • 1145 Main St • Okanagan Falls, British Columbia V0H 1R0 • (250) 497-5445

Oliver
Osoyoos Indian Band • RR3, Site 25, Comp 1 • Oliver, British Columbia V0H 1T0

Osoyoos
Osoyoos Museum Archives • Main St, Community Park, POB 791 • Osoyoos, British Columbia V0H 1V0 • (604) 495-2582

Parksville
Craig Heritage Park Museum Archives • Franklin Gull Rd & Island Hwy • Parksville, British Columbia V9P 2H4 • (250) 248-6966

District 69 Historical Society • POB 145 • Parksville, British Columbia V9P 2H4

Parksville and District Historical Society • 1245 Island Highway E • Parksville, British Columbia V9P 2E5 • (250) 248-6966

Peachland
Peachland Museum Archives • 5890 Beach Ave • Peachland, British Columbia V0H 1X0 • (250) 767-3441

Pemberton
Pemberton Museum Archives • POB 267 • Pemberton, British Columbia V3N 2L0 • (604) 894-6765

Skookumchuck Indian Band • POB 190 • Pemberton, British Columbia V0N 2L0

Penticton
Okanagan Tribal Council • RR2, Site 80, Comp 20 • Penticton, British Columbia V2A 6J7

Penticton Indian Band • RR2, Site 80, Comp 19 • Penticton, British Columbia V2A 6J7

Penticton Public Library • 785 Main St • Penticton, British Columbia V2A 5E3 • (250) 492-0024 • http://www.library.penticton.bc.ca

South Okanagan Genealogical Society & Archives • R N Atkinson Museum Archives, 785 Main St • Penticton, British Columbia V2A 5E3 • (250) 489-2451

Pitt Meadows
Katzie Indian Band • 10946 Katzie Rd • Pitt Meadows, British Columbia V3Y 2G6

Pitt Meadows
Pitt Meadows Museum Archives • 12294 Harris Rd • Pitt Meadows, British Columbia V3Y 2E9 • (604) 465-4322

Port Alberni
Alberni District Historical Society & Library • Echo 67 Centre, POB 284 • Port Alberni, British Columbia V9Y 7M7 • (604) 724-1833

Alberni Valley Museum Archives • 4255 Wallace St • Port Alberni, British Columbia V9Y 3Y6 • (604) 723-2181 • http://www.alberniheritage.com

Ditidaht Indian Band • POB 340 • Port Alberni, British Columbia V9Y 7M8

McLean Mill Museum Archives • 5633 Smith Rd • Port Alberni, British Columbia V9Y 7L5 • (250) 723-8284 • http://www.alberniheritage.com

Nuu-chan-nulth Tribal Council • POB 1383 • Port Alberni, British Columbia V9Y 7M2

Opetchesaht First Nation • POB 211 • Port Alberni, British Columbia V9Y 7M7

Tseshaht Indian Band • POB 1218 • Port Alberni, British Columbia V9Y 7M1

Uchucklesant Indian Band • POB 157 • Port Alberni, British Columbia V9Y 7M7

Port Clements
Port Clements Historical Society • 45 Bayview • Port Clements, British Columbia V0T 1R0 • (250) 557-4576

Port Clements Museum Archives • POB 417 • Port Clements, British Columbia V0T 1R0 • (250) 557-4576

Port Coquitlam
Coquitlam Indian Band • 65 Colony Farm Rd • Port Coquitlam, British Columbia V3C 3V4

Port Edward
North Pacific Cannery Village Museum Archives • 1889 Skeena Dr • Port Edward, British Columbia V0V 1G0 • (250) 628-3538

Port Hardy
Kwakiutl District Council • POB 2490 • Port Hardy, British Columbia V0N 2P0

Kwakiutl Indian Band • POB 1440 • Port Hardy, British Columbia V0N 2P0

Oweekeno Nation • POB 3500 • Port Hardy, British Columbia V0N 2P0

Port Hardy Museum Archives • POB 2126 • Port Hardy, British Columbia V0N 2P0 • (250) 949-8143

Port McNeill
Kwa-Wa-Aineuk Indian Band • POB 344 • Port McNeill, British Columbia V0N 2R0

Port Moody
Burrard-Fraser Heritage Society • Port Moody Station Museum, 2734 Murray St • Port Moody, British Columbia V3H 1X2 • (604) 939-1648 • http://www.bcn.bc.ca/prn/museum

Port Renfrew
Pacheenaht Indian Band • general delivery • Port Renfrew, British Columbia V0S 1K0

Port Simpson
Lax-Kw'alaams Indian Band • 206 Shashaak St • Port Simpson, British Columbia V0V 1H0

British Columbia

Pouce Coupe
Pouce Coupe Museum Archives • 5006 49th Ave • Pouce Coupe, British Columbia V0C 2C0 • (604) 786-5555

Powell River
Powell River District Library • 4411 Michigan Ave • Powell River, British Columbia V8A 2S3 • (604) 485-4796 • http://www.powellriverlibrary.ca

Powell River Historical Museum Archives • Centennial Bldg, Marine Ave, POB 42 • Powell River, British Columbia V8A 4Z5 • (604) 485-2222 • http://armourtechn.com/~museum

Sliammon Nation • Sliammon Cultural Center, RR2, Sliammon Rd • Powell River, British Columbia V8A 4Z3

Prince George
Carrier-Sekani Tribal Council • 1460 6th Ave, 2nd Fl • Prince George, British Columbia V2L 3N2

College of New Caledonia Library • 3330 22nd Ave • Prince George, British Columbia V2N 1P8 • (250) 452-2131 • http://www.cnc.bc.ca

Fort George Regional Museum Archives • 333 Becott Pl • Prince George, British Columbia V2L 4V7 • (250) 562-1612 • http://www.theexplorationplace.com

Fort Ware Indian Band • 3 - 1257 4th Ave • Prince George, British Columbia V2L 3J5

Lheit Lit'en Nation • RR1, Site 27, Comp 60 • Prince George, British Columbia V2N 2H8

Prince George Genealogy Society • POB 1056 • Prince George, British Columbia V2L 4V2

Prince George Public Library • 887 Dominion St • Prince George, British Columbia V2L 5L1 • (250) 563-9251 • http://www.lib.pg.bc.ca

Railway and Forestry Museum Archives • 850 River Rd • Prince George, British Columbia V2L 5S8 • (250) 563-7351 • http://www.pgrfm.bc.ca

Tsay Keh Dene Indian Band • 3845 15th Ave • Prince George, British Columbia V2N 1A4

Prince Rupert
Kwinitsa Station Railway Museum Archives • Waterfront, POB 669 • Prince Rupert, British Columbia V8J 3S1 • (250) 627-1915 • http://www.museumofnorthernbc.com

Metlakatla Indian Band • POB 459 • Prince Rupert, British Columbia V8J 3R2

Museum of Northern British Columbia Archives • 100 1st Ave • Prince Rupert, British Columbia V8J 3S1 • (250) 624-3207 • http://www.museumofnorthernbc.com

North Coast Tribal Council • 100 W 1st Ave • Prince Rupert, British Columbia V8J 1A8

Prince Rupert Fire Museum Archives • 200 1st Ave W • Prince Rupert, British Columbia V8J 1A8 • (250) 624-2211

Prince Rupert Library • 101 6th Ave W • Prince Rupert, British Columbia V8J 1Y9 • (250) 627-1345 • http://www.princerupertlibrary.ca/

Tsimshian Tribal Council • 737 2nd Ave W • Prince Rupert, British Columbia V8J 1H4

Princeton
Princeton and District Museum Archives • 167 Vermilion Ave • Princeton, British Columbia V0X 1W0 • (604) 295-7588

Qualicum Beach
Qualicum Beach Historical Society & Archives • Historical Museum, 587 Beach Rd • Qualicum Beach, British Columbia V9K 1K7 • (250) 752-5533

Qualicum Indian Band • 5850 River Rd • Qualicum Beach, British Columbia V9K 1Z5

Quathiaski Cove
Cape Mudge Indian Band • POB 220 • Quathiaski Cove, British Columbia V0P 1N0

Kwagiulth Museum Archives • POB 8 • Quathiaski Cove, British Columbia V0P 1N0 • (250) 285-3733 • http://www.island.net/~kmccchin/

Queen Charlotte
Kitwanga Fort Museum Archives • POB 37 • Queen Charlotte, British Columbia V0T 1S0 • (250) 559-8818

Quesnel
Alexandria Indian Band • RR2, POB 4 • Quesnel, British Columbia V2J 3H6

Kluskus Indian Band • 4 - 651 Wade Ave • Quesnel, British Columbia V5T 1E2

Nazko Indian Band • 1954 Hilborn Rd • Quesnel, British Columbia V21 3P7

Quesnel and District Museum Archives • 705 Carson Ave • Quesnel, British Columbia V2J 2B6 • (250) 992-9580 • http://www.city.quesnel.bc.ca

Quesnel Library • 593 Barlow Ave • Quesnel, British Columbia V2J 2C5 • (250) 992-7912 • http://www.cariboord.bc.ca/network.htm

Red Bluff Indian Band • POB 4693 • Quesnel, British Columbia V2J 5H8

Revelstoke
Revelstoke Court House Museum Archives • 1100 2nd St W • Revelstoke, British Columbia V0E 2S0 • (250) 837-7636

Revelstoke Museum Archives • 315 1st St W, POB 1908 • Revelstoke, British Columbia V0E 2S0 • (604) 837-3067

Revelstoke Railway Museum Archives • 719 Track St W • Revelstoke, British Columbia V0E 2S0 • (250) 837-6060 • http://www.railwaymuseum.com

Richmond
12th Vancouver Service Battalion Museum • Sherman Armoury, 5500 4th Rd • Richmond, British Columbia V6X 3L5 • (604) 666-4086

Britannia Heritage Shipyard Archives • 3811 Moncton St • Richmond, British Columbia V7E 3A0 • (604) 241-9453

British Columbia Genealogical Society & Library • POB 88054, Lansdowne Mall • Richmond, British Columbia V6X 3T6 • (604) 502-9119 • http://www.npsnet.com/bcgs/ • *British Columbia Genealogical Society Quarterly*; *British Columbia Genealogist*; *British Columbia Genealogical Society Newsletter*

Gulf of Georgia Cannery Museum Archives • 12138 4th Ave • Richmond, British Columbia V7E 3J1 • (604) 664-9009 • http://www.netlink2000.com/villager

Richmond Museum Archives • 7700 Minoru Gate • Richmond, British Columbia V6Y 1R9 • (604) 231-6457 • http://www.city.richmond.bc.ca

Steveston Historical Society • 3811 Moncton • Richmond, British Columbia V7E 3A5 • (604) 271-6868

Riske Creek
Toosey Indian Band • POB 80 • Riske Creek, British Columbia V0L 1T0

Rose Prairie
Doig River Indian Band • POB 55 • Rose Prairie, British Columbia V0C 2H0

Rosedale
Cheam Indian Band • 10704 Hwy 9 • Rosedale, British Columbia V0X 1X0

Rossland
Rossland Historical Museum Association & Library • POB 26 • Rossland, British Columbia V0G 1Y0 • (250) 362-7722 • http://www.rosslandmuseum.ca

Saanichton
Saanich Historical Artifacts Society • Historical Museum, 7321 Lochside Dr • Saanichton, British Columbia V8M 1W4 • (250) 652-5522

Saanich Pioneer Log Cabin Museum Archives • 7910 E Saanich Rd • Saanichton, British Columbia V8M 1T4 • (250) 656-4506 • http://victoria.bc.ca

Tsawout Indian Band • POB 121 • Saanichton, British Columbia V0S 1M0

Salmo
Salmo Museum Archives • 104 4th St • Salmo, British Columbia V0G 1Z0 • (250) 357-2200

Salmon Arm
Salmon Arm Museum Archives • POB 7642 • Salmon Arm, British Columbia V0E 2T0 • (250) 832-5243

Salt Spring Island
Salt Spring Island Historical Society • 129 McPhillips Ave • Salt Spring Island, British Columbia V8K 2T6

Sandon
Sandon Historical Society & Archives • Historical Museum, Slocan Star Rd • Sandon, British Columbia V0G 1R0

Sardis
Aitchelitz Indian Band • RR1, 8150 Aitken Rd • Sardis, British Columbia V2R 1A9

Skowkale Indian Band • POB 159 • Sardis, British Columbia V2R 1A7

Tzeachten Indian Band • POB 278 • Sardis, British Columbia V2R 1A6

Yakweakwioose Indian Band • RR2, 7176 Chilliwack River Rd • Sardis, British Columbia V2R 1B1

Savona
Skeetchestn Indian Band • POB 178 • Savona, British Columbia V0K 2J0

Sechelt
Sechelt Indian Band • POB 740 • Sechelt, British Columbia V0N 3A0

Trans-Swiya Museum Archives • POB 740 • Sechelt, British Columbia V0N 3A0 • (604) 885-8981

Shalalth
Seton Lake Indian Band • Site 3, Box 76 • Shalalth, British Columbia V0N 3C0

Shawnigan Lake
Shawnigan Lake Historical Museum Archives • POB 331 • Shawnigan Lake, British Columbia V0R 2W9 • (250) 748-5707

Sicamous
Sicamous and District Historical Society & Archives • Historical Museum, Trans-Canada Hwy • Sicamous, British Columbia V0E 2V0 • (250) 836-4456

Sicamous and District Museum Archives • POB 944 • Sicamous, British Columbia V0E 2V0 • (250) 836-4456

Sidney
British Columbia Aviation Museum Archives • Victoria Airport, 1910 Norseman Rd • Sidney, British Columbia V8L 5V5 • (250) 655-3300 • http://www.bcam.net

Sidney and North Saanich Historical Society • POB 2402 • Sidney, British Columbia V8L 3Y3

Sidney Historical Museum Archives • 2423 Beacon Av • Sidney, British Columbia V8L 1X5 • (250) 655-6355 • http://www.sidneymuseum.ca

Sidney Marine Historical Museum Archives • 9801 Seaport Pl • Sidney, British Columbia V8L 4X3 • (250) 656-1322 • http://www.sidneymuseum.ca

Tseycum Indian Band • Totem Ln, POB 1210 • Sidney, British Columbia V8L 5S4

West Coast Museum of Flying Archives • 10137 W Saanich Rd • Sidney, British Columbia V8L 5T6 • (250) 656-9339

Silverton
Frank Mills Outdoor Mining Museum • POB 69 • Silverton, British Columbia V0G 1S0 • (250) 358-2485

Simoon Sound
Kwicksutaineuk-Ah-Kwaw-Ah-Mish Indian Band • general delivery • Simoon Sound, British Columbia V0P 1S0

Skidegate
Queen Charlotte Islands Museum Society & Library • Halda Gwaii Museum at Qay 'ilnagaay, 2nd Beach • Skidegate, British Columbia V0T 1S0 • (250) 559-4643 • *Charlottes: a Journal of the Queen Charlotte Islands*

Skidegate Haida Gwaii
Skidegate Indian Band • POB 1301 • Skidegate Haida Gwaii, British Columbia V0T 1S1

Smithers
Bulkley Valley Museum Archives • POB 2615 • Smithers, British Columbia V0J 2N0 • (250) 847-5322

Smithers Public Library • 3817 Alfred Ave, POB 55 • Smithers, British Columbia V0J 2N0 • (250) 847-3043 • http://www.smitherslibrary.ca/

Sooke
Beecher Bay Indian Band • RR6, 3843 E Sooke Rd • Sooke, British Columbia V0S 1N0

Sooke Region Museum Library • 2070 Phillips Rd, POB 774 • Sooke, British Columbia V0S 1N0 • (604) 642-6351 • http://www.island.net/~scm_chin

T'Sou-ke Indian Nation • RR3, POB 5 • Sooke, British Columbia V0S 1N0

South Hazelton
Gitsegukla Indian Band • RR1 • South Hazelton, British Columbia V01 2R0

Sparwood
Sparwood Public Library • 110 Pine Ave, POB 1060 • Sparwood, British Columbia V0B 2G0 • (250) 425-2299 • http://www.elkvalley.net/sparwoodlibrary

Spences Bridge
Cook's Ferry Indian Band • POB 130 • Spences Bridge, British Columbia V0K 2L0

Squamish
Squamish Public Library • 37907 2nd Ave, POB 1039 • Squamish, British Columbia V0N 3G0 • (604) 892-3110 • http://www.squamishlibrary.bc.ca/

Squamish Valley Museum Archives • 2nd Ave • Squamish, British Columbia V0N 1T0

Stewart
Stewart Historical Museum Archives • Columbia & 6th Ave, POB 690 • Stewart, British Columbia V0T 1W0 • (250) 636-2568

Stewart Historical Society & Archives • Historical Museum, 603 Columbia St • Stewart, British Columbia V0T 1W0 • (250) 636-2568

Summerland
Summerland Museum and Arts Society & Archives • Historical Museum, 9521 Wharton St, POB 1491 • Summerland, British Columbia V0H 1Z0 • (250) 494-9395 • http://www.chin.qc.ca

Surrey
British Columbia Genealogical Society • 211-12837 76 Ave • Surrey, British Columbia V3W 2V3 • (604) 502-9119

British Columbia Genealogical Society • Landsdowne Mall, 12837 76th Ave, POB 88054 • Surrey, British Columbia V3W 2V3 • (604) 502-9119 • http://www.bcgs.ca/

Historic Stewart Farmhouse Archives • 13723 Crescent Rd • Surrey, British Columbia V4A 2W3 • (604) 574-5744

Kwantlen University College Library • 12666 72nd Ave • Surrey, British Columbia V3@ 2M8 • (604) 599-2105 • http://www.kwantlen.ca/library

Surrey Historical Society • POB 34003 • Surrey, British Columbia V3S 8C4

Surrey Museum Archives • 6022 176th St • Surrey, British Columbia V3S 4E8 • (604) 502-6459

Surrey Public Library • 13742 72nd Ave • Surrey, British Columbia V3W 2P4 • (604) 572-8269 • http://www.spl.surrey.bc.ca

Surrey Public Library, Guildford Branch • 15105-105th Ave • Surrey, British Columbia V3R 7G8 • (604) 588-5015 • http://www.spl.surrey.bc.ca

Surrey Public Library-Cloverdale • 5642-176A St • Surrey, British Columbia V3S 4G9 • (604) 574-1384 • http://www.sp1.surrey.bc.ca/referencelinks

British Columbia

Telkwa
Telkwa Museum Archives • POB 595 • Telkwa, British Columbia V0J 2X0 • (250 846-9656

Terrace
Heritage Park Museum Archives • 4113 Sparks St • Terrace, British Columbia V8G 4B5 • (250) 635-4546

Kitselas Indian Band • 4562 Queensway Dr • Terrace, British Columbia V8G 3X6

Kitsumkalum Indian Band-House of Sim-Oi-Ghes • POB 544 • Terrace, British Columbia V8G 4B5

Northwest Community College Library • 5331 McDonnell Ave, P.O Box 726 • Terrace, British Columbia V8G 4C2 • (250) 638-5407 • http://www.nwcc.bc.ca

Terrace Public Library • 4610 Park Ave • Terrace, British Columbia V8G 1V6 • (250) 638-8177 • http://www.tpl.monarch.net

Tofino
Hesquiaht Indian Band • POB 2000 • Tofino, British Columbia V0R 2Z0

Tla-o-qui-aht First Nation • POB 18 • Tofino, British Columbia V0R 2Z0

West Coast Maritime Museum Archives • POB 249 • Tofino, British Columbia V0R 2Z0 • (250) 725-3346

Trail
Trail and District Public Library • 1051 Victoria St • Trail, British Columbia V1R 3T3 • (250) 364-1731 • http://www.traillibrary.com

Trail Historical Society • POB 405 • Trail, British Columbia V1R 4L7

Trail Museum Archives • 1051 Victoria St • Trail, British Columbia V1R 4L7 • (250) 364-1262

Ucluelet
Toquaht Indian Band • POB 759 • Ucluelet, British Columbia V0R 3A0

Ucluelet Indian Band • POB 699 • Ucluelet, British Columbia V0R 3A0

Union Bay
Union Bay Historical Society • 5527 S Island Hwy • Union Bay, British Columbia V0R 3B0 • (250) 335-9155

Valemount
Valemount and Area Museum Archives • POB 850 • Valemount, British Columbia V0E 2Z0 • (250) 566-4177

Vancouver
15th Field Artillery Regiment Museum Archives • 2025 11th Ave W • Vancouver, British Columbia V8J 2C7 • (604) 666-4370

Bible Holiness Movement Library • 207, 850 W Hastings St, POB 223 • Vancouver, British Columbia V6C 2M3 • (250) 492-3376

Biblical Museum of Canada • 4800 University Bovd • Vancouver, British Columbia V5R 5A8 • (804) 432-6122

British Columbia Historical Association • 3450 W 20th Ave • Vancouver, British Columbia V6Y 1A8

British Columbia Regiment Museum Archives • 620 Beatty St • Vancouver, British Columbia V6B 2L9 • (504) 987-1358 • http://www.bcregiment.com

Flag and Banner • 1755 W 4th Ave • Vancouver, British Columbia V6J 1M2 • (604) 736-8161 • http://www.flagshop.com • Flag and Banner

H H MacMillan Space Centre Museum • 1100 Chestnut St • Vancouver, British Columbia V6J 3J9 • (604) 738-7827 • http://www.hrmacmillanspacecentre.com

Heritage Vancouver Society • POB 3336 • Vancouver, British Columbia V6B 3Y3

Jewish Genealogical Institute of British Columbia • 950 W 41st Ave • Vancouver, British Columbia V5Z 2N7 • (604) 257-5199 • http://www.geocities.com/Heartland/hills

Marpole Museum and Historical Society • 8743 Marine Drive SW • Vancouver, British Columbia V6P 6A5 • (604) 261-0131

Musqueam Indian Band • 6370 Salish Dr • Vancouver, British Columbia V6N 2C6

Native Fishing Association • 102-1500 Howe St • Vancouver, British Columbia V6Z 2N1

New Westminster Indian Band • 105-3680 Rae Ave • Vancouver, British Columbia V5R 2P5

Old Hastings Mill Store Museum Archives • 1575 Alma Rd • Vancouver, British Columbia V6R 3P3 • (604) 734-1212

Roedde House Museum Archives • 1415 Barclay St • Vancouver, British Columbia V6G 1J6 • (604) 684-7040 • http://www.roeddehouse.org

Seaforth Highlanders Regimental Museum Archives • Seaforth Armoury, 1650 Burrard St • Vancouver, British Columbia V6J 3G4 • (604) 738-9510

Swedish Press • 1294 W 7th Ave • Vancouver, British Columbia V6H 1B6 • (604) 731-6381 • http://www.norticway.com • *Swedish Press*

Ukrainian Museum of Canada Archives • 154 E 10th Ave • Vancouver, British Columbia V5T 1Z4 • (604) 327-7725

Union of British Columbia Indian Chiefs • 440 W Hastings St • Vancouver, British Columbia V6B 1L1

United Native Nations • 736 Granville St, 8th Fl • Vancouver, British Columbia V6Z 1G3

University of British Columbia • 164 - 1855 W Mall, C.K. Choi Building • Vancouver, British Columbia V6T 1Z2 • (604) 822-3727 • http://www.bcstudies.com • BC Studies

University of British Columbia Library • 1956 Main Mall • Vancouver, British Columbia V6T 1Z1 • (604) 822-6375 • http://www.library.ubc.ca

Vancouver Historical Society • POB 3071 • Vancouver, British Columbia V6B 3X6 • (604) 878-9140 • Vancouver Historical Society Newsletter

Vancouver Holocaust Education Centre • 950 W 41st Av, Ste 50 • Vancouver, British Columbia V5Z 2N7 • (604) 264-0499 • http://www.vhec.org

Vancouver Maritime Museum Archives • 1905 Ogden Av • Vancouver, British Columbia V6J 1A3 • (604) 257-8300 • http://www.vmm.bc.ca

Vancouver Museum Archives • Vanier Park, 1100 Chestnut St • Vancouver, British Columbia V6J 3J9 • (604) 736-5417 • http://vanmuseum.bc.ca

Vancouver Museum Library • 1100 Chestnut St • Vancouver, British Columbia V6J 3J9 • (604) 736-4431 • http://www.vanmuseum.bc.ca

Vancouver Police Centennial Museum Archives • 240 Cordova St E • Vancouver, British Columbia V6A 1L3 • (604) 665-3346 • http://www.city.vancouver.bc.ca/police/museum/

Vancouver Public Library • 350 W Georgia St • Vancouver, British Columbia V6B 6B1 • (604) 331-3600 • http://www.vpl.vancouver.bc.ca

Vanderhoof
Stoney Creek Elders Cultural Society • RR1, Site 12, Comp 15 • Vanderhoof, British Columbia V0J 3A0

Stoney Creek Indian Band • RR1, Site 12, Comp 2G • Vanderhoof, British Columbia V0J 3A0

Vanderhoof Community Museum Archives • POB 1515 • Vanderhoof, British Columbia V0J 3A0 • (250) 567-2991

Vernon
Greater Vernon Museum Archives • 3009 32nd Av • Vernon, British Columbia V1T 2L8 • (250) 542-3142

Historic O'Keefe Ranch Archives • Hwy 97 • Vernon, British Columbia V1T 6M8 • (250) 542-7868 • http://www.okeeferanch.bc.ca

Okanagan Historical Society • POB 313 • Vernon, British Columbia V1T 6M3 • (250) 832-5345 • *Okanagan History*

Okanagan Indian Band • RR7, Site 8, Comp 20 • Vernon, British Columbia V1T 7Z3

Tophan Brown Gallery Archives • 3009 32nd Ave • Vernon, British Columbia V1T 2L8 • (250) 545-3173

Vernon and District Family History Society • POB 1447 • Vernon, British Columbia V1T 6N7

Victoria

British Columbia Historical Federation • POB 5254, Sta B • Victoria, British Columbia V8R 6N4 • (604) 254-1429 • http://www.bchistory.ca • *British Columbia Historical News*

Canadian Scottish Regiment Museum Archives • Bay Street Armoury, 715 Bay St • Victoria, British Columbia V8T 1R1 • (250) 363-8753 • http://www.islandnet.com/~csrmuse

Carr House Museum Archives • 207 Government St • Victoria, British Columbia V8V 2T3 • (250) 383-5843

CFB Esquimalt Naval and Military Museum • POB 17000 Stn Forces • Victoria, British Columbia V6T 7N2 • (250) 363-4312

Craigdarroch Castle Historical Society & Archives • Historical Museum, 1050 Joan Crescent • Victoria, British Columbia V8S 3L5 • (250) 592-1225

Esquimalt Indian Band • 1000 Thomas Rd • Victoria, British Columbia V9A 7K7

Fort Rodd Hill Museum Archives • 501 Belmont Rd • Victoria, British Columbia V9C 1B5 • (250) 380-4662

Goldstream Region Museum Archives • 697 Goldstream Av • Victoria, British Columbia V9B 2X2 • (250) 474-6113

Greater Victoria Public Library • 735 Broughton St • Victoria, British Columbia V8W 3H2 • (250) 382-7241 • http://www.gvpl.bc.ca

Helmcken House Pioneer Doctor's Residence Museum • 638 Elliott St • Victoria, British Columbia V8V 1W1 • (250) 387-4697

Heritage Society of British Columbia • 660 Michigan St • Victoria, British Columbia V8V 4Y7

Lieutenant General Ashton Armoury Museum • 724 Vanalman Av • Victoria, British Columbia V8Z 3B5 • (250) 477-1117

Maritime Museum of British Columbia • 28 Bastion Sq • Victoria, British Columbia V8W 1H9 • (250) 385-4222 • http://mmbc.bc.ca

Metchosin School Museum Archives • 4475 Happy Valley Rd • Victoria, British Columbia V9C 4B1 • (250) 478-3451

Ministry of Aboriginal Affairs • POB 9100 • Victoria, British Columbia V8W 9B1

Point Ellice House Museum Archives • 2616 Pleasant St • Victoria, British Columbia V8T 4V3 • (250) 385-3837

Provincial Archives of British Columbia • 655 Belleville St, POB 9419 • Victoria, British Columbia V8V 9V1 • (250) 387-5885 • http://www.bcarchives.gov.bc.ca

Royal British Columbia Museum Archives • 675 Belteville St, POB 9815 • Victoria, British Columbia V8W 9W2 • (250) 356-7226 • http://www.royalbcmuseum.bc.ca

Songhees Indian Band • 1500A Admirals Rd • Victoria, British Columbia V9A 2R1

Victoria Cornish Association • 619 Oliver St • Victoria, British Columbia V8S 4W2

Victoria Genealogical Society • 947 Alston St, POB 45031 • Victoria, British Columbia V8Z 7G9 • (250) 360-2808 • *Journal of the Victoria Genealogical Society*

Victoria Heritage Foundation • 1 Centennial Sq • Victoria, British Columbia V8W 1P6

Victoria Historical Society • POB 43035 • Victoria, British Columbia V8X 3G2

Waglisla

Heiltsuk Indian Band • POB 880 • Waglisla, British Columbia V0T 1Z0

Wells

Wells Museum Archives • 2323 Pooley St • Wells, British Columbia V0K 2R0 • (250) 994-3342 • http://www.wellsbc.com

West Vancouver

Vancouver Naval Museum Archives • POB 91339 • West Vancouver, British Columbia V7V 3P1 • (604) 913-3363

West Vancouver Museum Archives • 680 17th St • West Vancouver, British Columbia V7V 3T2 • (604) 925-7295 • http://www.westvancouver.net

White Rock

Semiahmoo Indian Band • RR7, 16010 Beach Rd • White Rock, British Columbia V4B 5A8

White Rock Museum Archives • 14970 Marine Dr • White Rock, British Columbia V4B 1C4 • (604) 541-2222 • http://www.whiterock.museum.bc.ca

Williams Lake

Alkali Lake Indian Band • POB 4479 • Williams Lake, British Columbia V2G 2V5

Cariboo Tribal Council • POB 4333 • Williams Lake, British Columbia V2G 2V4

Carrier-Chilcotin Tribal Council • 59 1st Ave S • Williams Lake, British Columbia V2G 1H4

Museum of the Cariboo Chilcotin Archives • 113 N 4th Av • Williams Lake, British Columbia V2G 2C8 • (250) 392-7404 • http://www.cowboy-museum.com

Soda Creek Indian Band • RR4, Site 15, Comp 2 • Williams Lake, British Columbia V2G 4M8

Ts'ilhqot'in Tribal Council • 102 - 383 Oliver St • Williams Lake, British Columbia V2G 1M4

Williams Lake Indian Band • RR 3, Box 4, Sugarcane • Williams Lake, British Columbia V2G 1M3

Williams Lake Library • 180 N 3rd St, Suite A • Williams Lake, British Columbia V2G 2A4 • (250) 392-3630 • http://www.cariboard.bc.ca

Williams Lake Museum Archives • Cariboo Hwy S, RR2, Fox Mountain • Williams Lake, British Columbia V2G 2P2 • (250) 392-5573

Windermere

Columbia Lake Indian Band • POB 130 • Windermere, British Columbia V0B 2L0

Wonowon

Halfway River Indian Band • POB 59 • Wonowon, British Columbia V0C 2N0

Yale

Historic Yale Museum Archives • 31187 Douglas St • Yale, British Columbia V0K 2S0 • (604) 863-2324

Spuzzum Indian Indian Band • RR1 • Yale, British Columbia V0K 2S0

Ymir

Ymir Museum Archives • POB 65 • Ymir, British Columbia V0G 2K0 • (250) 357-9600

Zeballos

Nuchatlaht Tribes • POB 40 • Zeballos, British Columbia V0P 2A0

MANITOBA

Altona
Schwartz Heritage House Museum Archives • POB 1391 • Altona, Manitoba R0G 080 • (207) 324-5921

Anola
Anola and District Community Museum Archives • POB 153 • Anola, Manitoba R0E 0A0 • (204) 866-2922

Ashern
Ashern Pioneer Museum Archives • 1st St SW, POB 642 • Ashern, Manitoba R0C 0E0 • (204) 768-3147

Ashville
Drifting River Museum Archives • Farm in Gilbert Plains, RR2 • Ashville, Manitoba R0L 0A0

Austin
Manitoba Agricultural Museum Archives • Hwys 1 & 34 • Austin, Manitoba R0H 0C0 • (204) 637-2354

Beausejour
Pioneer Village Museum Archives • Brokenhead Centennial Park, POB 310 • Beausejour, Manitoba R0E 0C0 • (204) 268-1835

Belmont
Belmont and District Museum Archives • POB 69 • Belmont, Manitoba R0K 0C0 • (204) 537-2252

Evergreen Firearms Museum Archives • general delivery • Belmont, Manitoba R0K 0C0 • (204) 537-2647

Binscarth
Binscarth and District Gordon Orr Memorial Museum Archives • 152 2nd Ave • Binscarth, Manitoba R0J 0G0 • (204) 532-2217

Boissevain
Beckoning Hills Museum Archives • 425 Mill Rd, POB 670 • Boissevain, Manitoba R0K 0E0 • (204) 534-6544

Boissevain and Morton Regional Library • 436 S Railway, POB 340 • Boissevain, Manitoba R0K 0E0 • (204) 534-6478 • http://www.boissevain.ca/

Bowsman
McKays Museum Archives • RR1 • Bowsman, Manitoba R0L 0H0 • (204) 238-4412

Brandon
26th Field Artillery Regimental Museum Archives • 116 Victoria Ave • Brandon, Manitoba R7A 1B2 • (204) 728-2559

Assiniboine Historical Society • Historical Museum, 609 McDiarmid Dr • Brandon, Manitoba R7A 0K9

Chapman Museum Archives • RR2 • Brandon, Manitoba R7A 5Y2 • (204) 728-7396

Commonwealth Air Training Plan Museum Archives • Group 520, RR5 • Brandon, Manitoba R7A 5Y5 • (204) 727-2444 • http://www.airmuseum.ca

Dakota Ojibway Tribal Council • 702 Douglas St • Brandon, Manitoba R7A 5V2

Manitoba Agricultural Hall of Fame Archives • 1129 Queens Av • Brandon, Manitoba R7A 1L9 • (204) 728-3736 • http://www.mts.net/~agrifame

Manitoba Genealogical Society, Southwest Branch • 53 Almond Crescent, POB 1332 • Brandon, Manitoba R7A 6N2 • (204) 728-2857 • *Leaf of the Branch*

Oaly House Museum Archives • 122 18th St • Brandon, Manitoba R7A 5A4 • (204) 727-1722

Western Manitoba Regional Library • 710 Rosser Ave, Unit 1 • Brandon, Manitoba R7A 0K9 • (204) 727-6648 • http://www.wmrlibrary.mb.ca/

Carberry
Carberry Plains Museum Archives • 520 4th Ave • Carberry, Manitoba R0K 0H0 • (204) 834-2195

Seton Centre Archives • 116 Main St • Carberry, Manitoba R0K 0H0 • (204) 834-2059

Carman
Dufferin Historical Museum Archives • 44 King's Park Rd • Carman, Manitoba R0G 0J0 • (204) 745-3597

Heaman's Antique Autorama Archives • Hwy 3, POB 105 • Carman, Manitoba R-G 0J0 • (204) 745-2981

Cartwright
Badger Creek Museum Archives • 350 Broadway Ave • Cartwright, Manitoba R0K 0O0 • (204) 529-2363

Churchill
Eskimo Museum Archives • 242 La Verendrye • Churchill, Manitoba R0B 0E0 • (204) 675-2030

Prince of Wales Fort Archives • POB 127 • Churchill, Manitoba R0B 0E0 • (204) 675-8863

Crystal City
Crystal City Community Museum Archives • 218 Broadway • Crystal City, Manitoba R0K 0N0 • (204) 873-2293

Darlingford
Darlingford School Heritage Museum Archives • 197 Bradburn St • Darlingford, Manitoba R0G 0L0 • (204) 246-2015

Dauphin
Fort Dauphin Museum Archives • 140 Jackson Ave, POB 181 • Dauphin, Manitoba R7N 2V1 • (204) 638-6630 • http://www.city.dauphin.mb.ca

Manitoba Genealogical Society, Dauphin Branch • 25 Kirby Ave E, POB 855 • Dauphin, Manitoba R7N 3B3

Manitoba Heritage Federation • general delivery • Dauphin, Manitoba R7N 1H1

McCallum's Museum Archives • Hwy 5 • Dauphin, Manitoba R7N 2V1

Trembowla Cross of Freedom Museum Archives • 121 7th Ave SE • Dauphin, Manitoba R7N 2E3 • (204) 638-9641

West Region Tribal Council • 21 4th Ave NW • Dauphin, Manitoba R7N 1H9

Deloraine
Deloraine Museum • POB 227 • Deloraine, Manitoba R0M 0M0

Dufresne
Aunt Margaret's Museum of Childhood Archives • Trans-Canada Hwy • Dufresne, Manitoba R0A 0J0 • (204) 422-8426

Dugald
Cook's Creek Heritage Museum Archives • Hwy 212, RR2, Cook's Creek • Dugald, Manitoba R0E 0K0 • (204) 444-4448 • http://www.blazenet.com/st-micheels

Costume Museum of Canada Archies • POB 38 • Dugald, Manitoba R0E 0K0 • (204) 853-2166 • http://www.costumemuseum.com

Elkhorn
Manitoba Automobile Museum Archives • POB 477 • Elkhorn, Manitoba R0M 0N0 • (204) 845-2604

Erickson
Rolling River Band • Rolling River Cultural Centre, POB 145 • Erickson, Manitoba R0J 0P0

Eriksdale
Creamery Museum Archives • Creamery Rd • Eriksdale, Manitoba R0C 0W0 • (204) 739-2140

Eriksdale Museum Archives • Railway Ave S, POB 13 • Eriksdale, Manitoba R0C 0W0 • (204) 739-5408

Fairford
Interlake Reserves Tribal Council • Pineimuta Pl • Fairford, Manitoba R0C 0X0

Manitoba

Flin Flon
Flin Flon Museum Archives • 529a S Hudson St • Flin Flon, Manitoba R8A 1J8 • (204) 687-2946

Flin Flon Public Library • 58 Main St • Flin Flon, Manitoba R8A 1J8 • (204) 687-3397

Gilbert Plains
Wasyl Negrych Pioneer Homestead Archives • general delivery • Gilbert Plains, Manitoba R0L 0X0

Gillam
Gillam Community Museum Archives • 236 Mattonnabee Ave • Gillam, Manitoba R0B 0L0 • (204) 652-2206

Gimli
Evergreen Regional Library • 63 1st Ave, POB 1140 • Gimli, Manitoba R0C 1B0 • (204) 642-7912

Gimli Historical Museum Archives • 108-94 1st Ave, POB 1200 • Gimli, Manitoba R0C 1B0 • (204) 642-5317

Icelandic Nation League of North America • 103-94 1st Ave • Gimli, Manitoba R0C 1B1

Gladstone
Gladstone Museum Archives • Williams Park, 6th St, POB 651 • Gladstone, Manitoba R0J 0T0 • (204) 385-2551

Glenboro
Western Manitoba Regional Library-Glenboro Branch • 105 Broadway St, POB 429 • Glenboro, Manitoba R0K 0X0 • (204) 827-2874

Glenora
Claude Crayston Museum Archives • POB 95 • Glenora, Manitoba R0K 0Y0 • (204) 535-2283

Grandview
Watson Crossley Community Museum Archives • Railway Ave N, POB 396 • Grandview, Manitoba R0L 0Y0 • (204) 546-2661

Hamiota
Clegg's Museum of Horse-Drawn Vehicles • Lilac Residence, Ste 1 • Hamiota, Manitoba R0M 0T0 • (204) 764-2791

Hamiota Pioneer Club Museum Archives • Centennial Park, POB 577 • Hamiota, Manitoba R0M 0T0 • (204) 764-2222

Hartney
Hart-Cam Museum Archives • general delivery • Hartney, Manitoba R-M 0X0 • (204) 858-2590 • http://www.techplus.com/towns/towns.htm

Hodgson
Peguis Nation • Peguis Cultural Centre, POB 219 • Hodgson, Manitoba R0C 1N0

Inglis
Saint Elie Pioneer Church Museum Archives • POB 203 • Inglis, Manitoba R0J 0X0 • (204) 564-2228

Killarney
J A Victor David Museum Archives • 414 Williams Ave, POB 584 • Killarney, Manitoba R0K 1G0 • (204) 523-7325

La Broquerie
Musee Saint-Joachim • Baie Normandau, BP 314 • La Broquerie, Manitoba R0A 0W0 • (204) 424-9442

La Riviere
Archibald Historical Museum Archives • POB 97 • La Riviere, Manitoba R0G 1A0 • (204) 242-2825

Langruth
Heritage Museum Archives • general museum • Langruth, Manitoba R0H 0N0

Leaf Rapids
Leaf Rpaids National Exhibition Centre • POB 220 • Leaf Rapids, Manitoba R0B 1W0 • (204) 473-8682

Lundar
Lundar Museum Archives • POB 265 • Lundar, Manitoba R0C 1Y0 • (204) 762-5689

Lynn Lake
Lynn Lake Mining Town Museum Archives • 470 Cobalt Pl • Lynn Lake, Manitoba R0B 0W0 • (204) 356-8302

Melita
Antler River Historical Society • Historical Museum, Ash St • Melita, Manitoba R0M 1L0 • (204) 522-3919

Miami
Miami Station Museum Archives • POB 153 • Miami, Manitoba R0G 1H0 • (204) 435-2305

Miniota
Miniota Municipal Museum Archives • RR1, POB 189 • Miniota, Manitoba R0M 1M0 • (204) 567-3675

Minnedosa
Minnedosa and District Museum Archives • 100 Heritage Crescent • Minnedosa, Manitoba R0J 1E0 • (204) 867-5963

Moosehorn
Moosehorn Museum Archives • 1st St N & Railway Ave, POB 28 • Moosehorn, Manitoba R0C 2E0 • (204) 768-2542

Morden
Morden and District Museum Archives • 2nd St & Gilmour Ave • Morden, Manitoba R0G 1J0 • (204) 822-3406

Morris
Morris and District Centennial Museum Archives • POB 344 • Morris, Manitoba R0G 1K0 • (204) 746-2169

Neepawa
Beautiful Plains Museum Archives • 80 Hamilton St W • Neepawa, Manitoba R0J 1H0 • (204) 476-3866 • http://www.town.neepawa.nb.ca/museum

Margaret Laurence Home Museum Archives • 312 1st Ave • Neepawa, Manitoba R0J 1H0 • (204) 476-3612 • http://www.town.neepawa.mb.ca/mlh

Murray's Museum of History • POB 489 • Neepawa, Manitoba R0J 1H0 • (204) 476-2460

Norway House
Norway House Band • POB 250 • Norway House, Manitoba R0B 1B0

Notre-Dame-de-Lourdes
Museum Dom Benoit • general delivery • Notre-Dame-de-Lourdes, Manitoba R0G 1M0 • (204) 248-2372

Pilot Mound
Marringhurst Pioneer Park Museum Archives • RR2 • Pilot Mound, Manitoba R0G 1P0 • (204) 825-2697

Pilot Mound Centennial Museum Archives • Centennial Bldg, 219 Broadway Ave W • Pilot Mound, Manitoba R0G 1P0 • (204) 825-2784

Plum Coulee
Plum Coulee and District Museum Archives • 277 Main Ave, POB 36 • Plum Coulee, Manitoba R0G 1R0 • (204) 829-3419

Portage la Prairie
Fort La Reine Museum and Pioneer Village Archives • Hwys 1a & 26, POB 744 • Portage la Prairie, Manitoba R1N 3C2 • (204) 857-3259

Manitoba Genealogical Society, Prior Relations Branch • 306-615 6th St NW • Portage la Prairie, Manitoba R1N 2K3

Portage La Prairie City Library • 40-B Royal Rd N • Portage la Prairie, Manitoba R1N 1V1 • (204) 857-4271

Rapid City
Rapid City Museum Archives • 4th Ave • Rapid City, Manitoba R0K 1W0 • (204) 826-2597

Reston
Reston and District Historical Museum Archives • Reston Park, 9th St, POB 304 • Reston, Manitoba R0M 1X0 • (204) 877-3960

Riverton
Hecla Island Heritage Home Museum Archives • POB 70 • Riverton, Manitoba R0C 2R0 • (204) 279-2056

Roblin
Keystone Pioneer Museum Archives • Hwy 5 • Roblin, Manitoba R0L 10O • (204) 937-2935

Rossburn
Rossburn Museum Archives • POB 487 • Rossburn, Manitoba R0J 1V0 • (204) 859-2762

Saint Boniface
La Societe Historique de Saint Boniface & Library • 340 Provencher Blvd, CP 125 • Saint Boniface, Manitoba R2H 0G7 • (204) 233-4888 • http://www.shsb.mb.ca/ • *Societe Historique de Saint Boniface Bulletin*

Musee de Saint Boniface Archives • 494 av Tache • Saint Boniface, Manitoba R2H 2B2 • (204) 237-4500

Saint Claude
Saint Claude Museum Archives • POB 131 • Saint Claude, Manitoba R0G 1Z0 • (204) 379-2405

Saint George
Saint George Historical Society • 19 Baie Caron S • Saint George, Manitoba R0E 1V0 • (204) 367-8801

Sainte-Anne
Musee Pointe des Chenes • 208 Av Centrale • Sainte-Anne, Manitoba R5H 1C9 • (204) 422-5639

Saint-Joseph
Musee Saint-Joseph • CP 47 • Saint-Joseph, Manitoba R0G 2C0 • (204) 737-2241

Saint-Malo
Musee le Pionnier • general delivery • Saint-Malo, Manitoba R0A 1T0 • (204) 347-5767

Saint-Pierre-Jolys
Musee de Saint-Pierre-Jolys • 432 Rue Joubert • Saint-Pierre-Jolys, Manitoba R0A 1V0 • (204) 433-7226

Sandy Lake
Ukrainian Cultural Heritage Museum • general delivery • Sandy Lake, Manitoba R0J 1X0 • (204) 585-2168

Scanterbury
Brokenhead Ojibway Cultural Program • general delivery • Scanterbury, Manitoba R0E 1W0

Selkirk
Kennedy House Museum Archives • 1 Keystone Dr • Selkirk, Manitoba R1A 2H5 • (204) 334-2496

Lower Fort Garry Museum Archives • Hwy 9, RR3, POB 37-343 • Selkirk, Manitoba R1A 2A5 • (204) 785-6050 • http://parkscanada.pch.qc.ca/garry

Marine Museum of Manitoba Archives • Sekirk Park, Eveline St • Selkirk, Manitoba R1A 2B1 • (204) 482-7761 • http://www.marinemuseum.ca

Seven Sisters Falls
Nutimik Lake Museum Archives • general delivery • Seven Sisters Falls, Manitoba R0E 1Y0 • (2104) 348-2203

Shilo
Royal Canadian Artillery Museum Archives • Canadian Forces Base Shilo, POB 5000 • Shilo, Manitoba R0K 2A0 • (204) 765-3000 • http://www.artillery.net

Shoal Lake
Police and Pioneer Museum Archives • Lakeside Park • Shoal Lake, Manitoba R0J 1Z0

Shoal Lake Historical Society & Archives • Spruce Haven Museum, Lakeside Park • Shoal Lake, Manitoba R0J 1Z0

Snowflake
Star Mound School Museum Archives • general delivery • Snowflake, Manitoba R0G 2K0 • (204) 876-4749

Souris
Hillcrest Museum Archives • 26 Crescent E, POB 492 • Souris, Manitoba R0K 2C0 • (204) 483-2008

Steinbach
Mennonite Heritage Village Archives • Hwy 12, POB 1136 • Steinbach, Manitoba R0A 2A0 • (204) 326-9661 • http://www.mennoniteheritagevillage.com

Strathclair
Strathclair Museum Archives • Main St • Strathclair, Manitoba R0J 2C0 • (204) 365-5201

Swan River
Manitoba Genealogical Society, Swan Valley Branch • POB 6 • Swan River, Manitoba R0L 1Z0

Swan River Valley Historical Society & Archives • Historical Museum, POB 2078 • Swan River, Manitoba R0L 1Z0 • (204) 734-3585

Teulon
Teulon and District Museum Archives • Owen Acres Park • Teulon, Manitoba R0C 3B0 • (204) 886-2792

The Pas
Sam Waller Museum Archives • 306 Fischer Ave, POB 185 • The Pas, Manitoba R9A 1K4 • (204) 623-3802 • http://www.cancom.net/~museum

The Pas Public Library • 53 Edwards Ave, POB 4100 • The Pas, Manitoba R9A 1R2 • (204) 623-2023 • http://www.cancom.net/~books

Thompson
Thompson Public Library • 81 Thompson Dr N • Thompson, Manitoba R8N 0C3 • (204) 677-3717 • http://www.thompsonlibrary.com

Treherne
Treherne Museum Archives • 183 Van Zile St • Treherne, Manitoba R0G 2V0 • (204) 723-2621

Virden
Border Regional Library • 312 7th Ave • Virden, Manitoba R0M 2C0 • (204) 748-3862 • http://www.escape.ca/~vwinernet/library

Curahee Military Museum Archives • POB 729 • Virden, Manitoba R0M 2C0 • (204) 748-2454

River Valley School Museum Archives • POB 729 • Virden, Manitoba R0M 2C0 • (204) 748-2454

Virden Pioneer Museum Archives • 390 King St W • Virden, Manitoba R0M 2C0 • (204) 748-1659 • http://town.virden.mb.ca

Wabowden
Waboden Historical Museum Archives • general delivery • Wabowden, Manitoba R0B 1S0 • (204) 689-2362

Waskada
Waskada Museum Archives • Railway Ave, POB 27 • Waskada, Manitoba R0M 2E0 • (204) 673-2503 • http://www.techplus.com/was/history/museum.html

Wawanesa
Spipweske Museum Archives • general delivery • Wawanesa, Manitoba R0K 2J0 • (204) 824-2244

Manitoba

Whitemouth
Whitemouth Municipal Museum Archives • Community Grounds • Whitemouth, Manitoba R0E 2G0 • (204) 348-2641

Winkler
Pembina Threshermen's Museum Archives • POB 1103 • Winkler, Manitoba R6W 4B2 • (204) 822-5369

Winnipeg
Aboriginal Centre of Winnipeg • 181 Higgins Ave • Winnipeg, Manitoba R3B 3G1

Air Force Heritage Museum and Air Park • 1 Canadian Air Division Hqts • Winnipeg, Manitoba R3J 3Y5 • (204) 833-2500 • http://www.airforce.dnd.ca

Canada's National History Society • 478-167 Lombard Ave • Winnipeg, Manitoba R3B 0T6 • (204) 988-9300 • http://www.thebeaver.ca • *Beaver: Canada's History Magazine*

Canadian Federation of Genealogical and Family History Societies • 227 Parkville Bay • Winnipeg, Manitoba R2M 2J6 • http://www.geocities.com/Athens/Troy/2274/

Canadian Mennonite University Library • 500 Shaftesbury Blvd • Winnipeg, Manitoba R3P 2N2 • (204) 487-3300 • http://www.cmu.ca/library

Center for Mennonite Brethren Studies in Canada • 169 Riverton Ave • Winnipeg, Manitoba R2L 2E5 • (204) 669-6575 • http://www.mbconf.ca/mb/cmbs.htm • *Mennonite Historian*

City of Winnipeg Libraries • 251 Donald St • Winnipeg, Manitoba R3C 3P5 • (204) 986-6462 • http://www.wpl.city.winnipeg.mb.ca

East European Genealogical Society • POB 2536 • Winnipeg, Manitoba R3C 4A7 • (204) 989-3292 • http://www.eegsociety.org/member.html

Elizabeth Dafoe Library • Univ of Manitoba, 25 Chancellor's Circle • Winnipeg, Manitoba R3T 2N2 • (204) 474-9881 • http://www.umanitoba.ca

Father Harold Drake Library-St Pauls College • University of Manitoba, 70 Dysart Rd • Winnipeg, Manitoba R3T 2M6 • (204) 474-8585

First Nations Confederacy • 274 Garry St • Winnipeg, Manitoba R3C 1H3

Fort Garry Historical Society & Library • 650 Riverwood Ave • Winnipeg, Manitoba R3T 1K4 • (204) 284-6567

Fort Garry Horse Museum Archives • 551 Machray Ave • Winnipeg, Manitoba R2W 1A8 • (204) 586-6298 • http://www.escape.ca/~fgh

German Society of Winnipeg • 121 Charles St • Winnipeg, Manitoba R2W 4A6 • (204) 589-7724 • *Deutsche Vereinigung von Winnipeg: Mitteilungen*

Historical Museum of Saint James-Assinboia Archives • 3180 Portage Ave • Winnipeg, Manitoba R3K 0Y5 • (204) 888-8706

Ivan Franko Museum Archives • 595 Pritchard Av • Winnipeg, Manitoba R2W 2K4 • (204) 589-4397

Jewish Historical Society of Western Canada & Library • 365 Hargrave St., Rm. 404 • Winnipeg, Manitoba R3N 2B2 • (204) 942-4822 • http://www.concentric.net/~lkessler/geninst.html • *Jewish Life and Times*; *Jewish Historical Society of Western Canada Annual*

Logberg-Heimskringla • 206-900 St James St • Winnipeg, Manitoba R3G 3J7 • (866) 564-2374 • *Logberg-Heimskringla*

Manitoba Genealogical Society & Library • 1045 Saint James St #E • Winnipeg, Manitoba R3H 1B1 • (204) 783-9139 • http://www.mts.net/~mgsi • *Generations*

Manitoba Genealogical Society, East European Branch • 885 Notre Dame Ave, POB 2536 • Winnipeg, Manitoba R3C 4A7

Manitoba Historical Museum Archives • 190 Rupert Ave • Winnipeg, Manitoba R3B 0N2 • (204) 988-0692 • http://www.manitobamuseum.ca/

Manitoba Historical Society • 304-250 McDermot Ave • Winnipeg, Manitoba R3B 1G4 • (204) 947-0559 • http://www.mhs.mb.ca • *Manitoba History*; *Manitoba Historical Society Newsletter*; *Keywords*; *Time Lines*

Manitoba Mennonite Historical Society • 169 Riverton Ave • Winnipeg, Manitoba R2L 2E5

Masonic Grand Lodge & Library • 420 Corydon Ave • Winnipeg, Manitoba R3L 0N8 • (204) 284-2423

Mennonite Heritage Centre • 600 Shaftesbury Blvd • Winnipeg, Manitoba R3P 0M4 • (204) 888-6781

Ogniwo Polish Museum Archives • 1417 Main St • Winnipeg, Manitoba R2W 3V3 • (204) 586-5070

Provincial Archives of Manitoba • 200 Vaughan St • Winnipeg, Manitoba R3C 1T5 • (204) 945-3971 • http://www.gov.mb.ca/chc/archives/

Queen's Own Cameron Highlanders Museum Archives • Minto Armoury, 969 St Mathews's St • Winnipeg, Manitoba R3G 0J7 • (204) 786-4330

Riel House Museum Archives • 330 River Rd • Winnipeg, Manitoba R2M 3Z8 • (204) 257-1783

Ross House Museum Archives • 140 Meade St N • Winnipeg, Manitoba R2W 3K5 • (204) 943-2835 • http://www.nhs.mb.ca

Royal Canadian Mint Museum Archives • 520 Lagimodiere Blvd • Winnipeg, Manitoba R2J 3E7 • (204) 983-6400 • http://www.rcmint.ca

Royal Winnipeg Rifles Museum Archives • 208 Minto Armoury, 969 Saint Matthews Av • Winnipeg, Manitoba R3G 0J7 • (204) 786-4300

Saint Andrew's College Library • University of Manitoba, 29 Dysart Rd • Winnipeg, Manitoba R3T 2M7 • (204) 474-8901

Saint Norbert Provincial Heritage Park Museum Archives • 40 Turnbull Dr • Winnipeg, Manitoba R3J 3W3 • (204) 945-4375 • http://manitobaparks.com

Seven Oaks House Museum Archives • 115 Rupertsland Av, POB 25176 • Winnipeg, Manitoba R2V 4C8 • (204) 339-7429

Transcona Historical Museum Archives • 141 Regent Ave W • Winnipeg, Manitoba R2C 1R1 • (204) 222-0423

Ukrainian Museum of Canada Library • 1175 Main St • Winnipeg, Manitoba R2W 3S4 • (204) 582-7346

Ukrainian National Home Association Library • 582 Burrows Ave • Winnipeg, Manitoba R2W 2A6 • (204) 582-4528

Ukrainian Public Library of Ivan Franko • 200 McGregor St • Winnipeg, Manitoba R2W 5L6 • (204) 586-4136

Ukranian Cultural and Education Centre Library • 184 Alexander Ave E • Winnipeg, Manitoba R3B 0L6 • (204) 942-0218

University of Winnipeg Library • 515 Portage Ave • Winnipeg, Manitoba R3B 2E9 • (204) 786-9815 • http://cybrary.uwinnipeg.ca

UVAN Historical Museum Archives • 205-456 Main St • Winnipeg, Manitoba R3B 1B6 • (204) 942-5095

Western Canada Aviation Museum Archives • Hangar T-2, 858 Ferry Rd • Winnipeg, Manitoba R3H 0Y8 • (204) 786-5503 • http://www.wcam.mb.ca

Winnipeg Police Museum Archives • 130 Allard Av • Winnipeg, Manitoba R3K 0T4 • (204) 986-3976

Winnipegosis
Winnipegosis Historical Society & Archives • Historical Museum, POB 4 • Winnipegosis, Manitoba R0L 2G0 • (204) 656-4791

Woodlands
Woodlands Pioneer Museum Archives • general delivery • Woodlands, Manitoba R0C 3H0 • (204) 383-5584

NEW BRUNSWICK

Au Lac
Fort Beausejour National Historic Site Archives • 111 Fort Beausejour Rd • Au Lac, New Brunswick E4L 2W5 • (506) 364-5080 • http://www.parkscanada.qc.ca

Bathurst
Memorial War Museum Archives • Royal Canadian Legion Branch 18, 575 Saint Peters Av • Bathurst, New Brunswick E2A 2Y5 • (506) 546-3135

Pabineau Indian Band • RR5, Site 26, POB 1 • Bathurst, New Brunswick E2A 3Y8

Bedford
Atlantic Canada Aviation Museum Archives • 1658 Bedford hwy • Bedford, New Brunswick E4S 4J7 • (302) 873-3772

Blackville
Blackville Historical Museum Archives • Route 8 • Blackville, New Brunswick E0C 1C0 • (506) 543-7761

Boiestown
Central New Brunswick Woodmen's Museum Archives • 6342 Route 8 • Boiestown, New Brunswick E6A 1Z5 • (509) 369-5081 • http://www.woodsmenmuseum.com

Buctouche
Buctouche Micmac Band • RR2, Box 9, Site 1 • Buctouche, New Brunswick E0E 1G0

Caraquet
Federation des Caisses Populaires Acadiennes • 295 boul Saint Pierre ouest, POB 5554 • Caraquet, New Brunswick E1W 1B7 • (506) 726-4530

Le Musee Acadien • 15 Blvd Saint-Pierre E • Caraquet, New Brunswick E1W 1B6 • (506) 727-2727

Village Historique Acadien • 14311 Route 11, CP 5626 • Caraquet, New Brunswick E1W 1B7 • (506) 726-2600 • http://www.villagehistoriqueacadien.com

Chatham
New Brunswick Genealogical Society, Miramichi Branch • POB 403, Sta B • Chatham, New Brunswick E1N 3A8

Saint Michael's Historical Museum Archives • 12 Alexandra St • Chatham, New Brunswick E1N 1V2 • (506) 773-3277 • http://www.nibc.nb.ca/st-mikes/

Clair
Petit Musee • POB 401 • Clair, New Brunswick E0L 1B0 • (506) 992-3637

Connors
Connors Museum Archives • 3614 Rte 205 • Connors, New Brunswick E7A 1S3 • (506) 992-2500

Pioneer Historical Connors Museum Archives • 1352 Rte 205 • Connors, New Brunswick E7A 1S3 • (506) 992-2500

Dalhousie
Chaleur Area History Museum Archives • Courthouse Sq, POB 1717 • Dalhousie, New Brunswick E0K 1B0 • (506) 684-4685

Eel River Bar Indian Band • POB 1660 • Dalhousie, New Brunswick E0K 1B0

New Brunswick Genealogical Society, Restigouch Branch • POB 179 • Dalhousie, New Brunswick E0K 1B0

Restigouche Regional Museum Archives • 115 George St • Dalhousie, New Brunswick E8C 1R6 • (506) 684-7490

Dorchester
Fort Folly Indian Band • POB 21 • Dorchester, New Brunswick E0A 1M0

Keillor House Museum Archives • 4974 Main St • Dorchester, New Brunswick E4K 2M2 • (509) 379-6633 • http://www.keillorhousemuseum.com

Douglastown
Miramichi Historical Society & Archives • Rankin House • Douglastown, New Brunswick E0C 1H0 • (506) 773-3448

Edmundston
Bibliotheque Rhea-Larose • University de Moncton, 165 boul Hebert • Edmundston, New Brunswick E3V 2S8 • (506) 737-5058 • http://www.cuslm.ca/biblio/

Societe Historique du Madawaska & Archives • Historical Museum, 165 Blvd Hebert • Edmundston, New Brunswick E3V 3L1 • (506) 739-9357 • *Societe Historique du Madawaska Revue*

Le Centre d'Etudes Madawaska • 165 boul Herbert • Edmunston, New Brunswick E3V 2S8

Societe Historique de Madawaska • POB 474 • Edmunston, New Brunswick E3V 3L1

Fredericton
Aboriginal Peoples Council • 320 Saint Mary's St • Fredericton, New Brunswick E3A 2S4

Acadiensis: Journal of the History of the Atlantic Region • Univ of New Brunswick, Hist Dept, POB 4400 • Fredericton, New Brunswick E3B 5A3 • (506) 453-4978 • http://www.cmpa.ca/sl1.html • *Acadiensis: Journal of the History of the Atlantic Region*

Archives and Special Collections • Univ of New Brunswick, POB 7500 • Fredericton, New Brunswick E3B 5H5 • (506) 453-4748

Guard House and Soldiers Barracks Museum Archives • Carleton St, Fredercton Military Compound, POB 6000 • Fredericton, New Brunswick E3N 5H1 • (506) 460-2041 • http://www.city.fredericton.ab.ca

House of International Dolls Archives • 214 Cedar Ave • Fredericton, New Brunswick E3A 2C6 • (902) 658-2449

Kings Landing Historical Museum Archives • POB 522 • Fredericton, New Brunswick E3B 5A6 • (506) 363-3081

Kingsclear Indian Band • RR6, Comp 19, Site 6 • Fredericton, New Brunswick E3B 4X7

New Brunswick Genealogical Society & Library • POB 3235, Sta B • Fredericton, New Brunswick E3A 5G9 • http://degaulle.hil.unb.ca/genealogy/society.html • Generations

New Brunswick Healthcare Museum Archives • 384 Smythe St • Fredericton, New Brunswick E3B 3E4 • (506) 453-0747

Old Government House Archives • 51 Woodstock Rd • Fredericton, New Brunswick E3B 5H1 • (505) 453-2505

Provincial Archives of New Brunswick • 23 Dineen Dr, POB 6000 • Fredericton, New Brunswick E3B 5H1 • (506) 453-2122 • http://www.gov.nb.ca/supply/archives/

Saint Mary's Indian Band • 247 Paul St • Fredericton, New Brunswick E3A 2V7

Union of New Brunswick Indians • 35 Dedam St • Fredericton, New Brunswick E3A 2V2

University of New Brunswick Library • 5 Macaulay Dr, POB 7500 • Fredericton, New Brunswick E3B 5H5 • (506) 453-4740 • http://www.lib.unb.ca/

Wulastock Museum Archives • 105 Queen St • Fredericton, New Brunswick E3B 5B4 • (506) 451-7777

York Regional Library • 4 Carleton St • Fredericton, New Brunswick E3B 5P4 • (506) 453-5380 • http://www.gnb.ca/0003/york.html

York-Sunbury Historical Society & Archives • Historical Museum, 500 Block Queen St, POB 1312 • Fredericton, New Brunswick E3B 5C8 • (506) 455-6041

Fredericton Junction
Sunbury West Historical Society • general delivery • Fredericton Junction, New Brunswick E0G 1T0 • (506) 368-2818

Gagetown
Queens County Tilley House Museum Archives • Front St • Gagetown, New Brunswick E0G 1V0 • (506) 488-2926 • http://www.geocities.com/heartland/lake/334

New Brunswick

Gloucester
Musee Acadien Archives • Caraquet • Gloucester, New Brunswick E0B 1K0 • (506) 727-3269

Grand Falls
Grand Falls Historical Museum Archives • 142 Court St, POB 1572 • Grand Falls, New Brunswick E0J 1M0 • (506) 473-7160

Grand Manan
Grand Manan Museum Archives • 1141 Rte 776 • Grand Manan, New Brunswick E5G 4E9 • (506) 662-3524

Grand Sault
Haut-Saint-Jean Regional Library-Grand Sault Public • 131 Rue Pleasant, Suite 201 • Grand Sault, New Brunswick E3Z 1G6 • (506) 475-7781

Grand-Anse
Musee des Papes • 184 Rue Acadie • Grand-Anse, New Brunswick E8N 1A6 • (506) 732-3003

Hampton
Kings County Historical Society & Archives • Dalling Sussex Corner, 27 Centennial Rd • Hampton, New Brunswick E5N 6N3 • (506) 832-6009 • http://www3.nbnet.nb.ca/kingcan • Kings County Historical Society Newsletter; Kings County Memories

Hartland
New Brunswick Genealogical Society, Carleton County Branch • POB 514 • Hartland, New Brunswick E0J 1N0

Hillsborough
Hillsborough Railway Museum Archives • 2847 Main St • Hillsborough, New Brunswick E4H 2X7 • (506) 734-3195 • http://www.shrr.ca

William Henry Steeves House Museum Archives • 40 Mill St • Hillsborough, New Brunswick E4H 2Z8 • (506) 734-3102 • http://www.steeveshousemuseum.ca

Kingston
John Fisher Memorial Museum Archives • 3950 Rte 845 • Kingston, New Brunswick E5N 1E9 • (506) 763-2101

Legaceville
Burnt Church First Nation • RR2 • Legaceville, New Brunswick E0C 1K0

Memramcook
Monument Lefebvre • 480 Rue Centrale • Memramcook, New Brunswick E4K 3S6 • (506) 758-9783

Minto
Minto Museum Archives • 71 Main St • Minto, New Brunswick E0E 1J0 • (506) 327-3383

Miramichi
Rankin House Museum Archives • 2224 King George Hwy • Miramichi, New Brunswick E1V 6N3 • (506) 773-3448

Moncton
Albert-Westmoreland-Kent Regional Library • 644 Main St, Suite 201 • Moncton, New Brunswick E1C 1E2 • (506) 869-6032

Bibliotheque Champlain • Universite de Moncton • Moncton, New Brunswick E1A 3E9 • (506) 858-4012 • http://www.umoncton.ca/champ/

Centre D'Edutis Acadiennes • Universite de Moncton • Moncton, New Brunswick E1A 3E9

Centre d'Etudes Acadiennes • Musee Acadien, Universite de Moncton • Moncton, New Brunswick E1A 3E9 • (506) 858-4085 • http://www.umoncton.ca • *Contact-Acadie*

Lutz Mountain Meeting House Archives • 3030 Mountain Rd, POB 2952 • Moncton, New Brunswick E1C 8T8 • (506) 384-4967 • http://personal.nbnet.nb.ca/lutzmtn

Moncton Museum Archives • 20 Mountain Rd • Moncton, New Brunswick E1C 2J8 • (506) 854-1001 • http://www.moncton.org

New Brunswick Genealogical Society, Southeastern Branch • POB 4321 • Moncton, New Brunswick E1A 6E9

Societe Historique Acadienne • L'Universite de Moncton, CP 632 • Moncton, New Brunswick E1C 8M7 • (506) 383-7991 • *Cahiers de la Societe Historique Acadienne*

New Denmark
New Denmark Historical Society • Historical Museum, 710 Rte 380 • New Denmark, New Brunswick E7G 2T6 • (506) 553-6464

Newcastle
Eel Ground Indian Band • RR1, Box 9, Site 23 • Newcastle, New Brunswick E1V 3L8

Miramichi Historical Society & Archives • Historical Museum, 225 Mary St • Newcastle, New Brunswick E1V 1Z3 • (506) 622-0453

Oromocto
CFB Gagetown Military Museum Archives • Base Gagetown, POB 17000 • Oromocto, New Brunswick E0G 2P0 • (506) 357-8401 • http://www.brumnet.net/museum_gagetown

Fort Hughes Military Blockhouse Archives • Wharf Rd, POB 37 • Oromocto, New Brunswick E2V 2G4

Oromocto Nation • RR1, POB 417 • Oromocto, New Brunswick E2V 2J2

Perth
Tobique Indian Band • RR3, POB 840 • Perth, New Brunswick E0J 1V0

Petit-Rocher
New Brunswick Mining Museum • Route 134 • Petit-Rocher, New Brunswick E0B 2E0 • (506) 783-8714

Plaster Rock
Plaster Rock Museum Archives • 157 Main St • Plaster Rock, New Brunswick E7G 2H2 • (506) 356-6077

Prince William
Kings Landing Historical Settlement Museum Archives • 20 Kings Landing Service Rd • Prince William, New Brunswick E6K 3W3 • (506) 363-4999 • http://www.kingslanding.nb.ca

Red Bank
Red Bank Indian Band • POB 120 • Red Bank, New Brunswick E0C 1W0

Richibucto
Richibucto River Museum Archives • Old Post Office, Town Hall • Richibucto, New Brunswick E0A 2M0 • (506) 523-4408

Riverside-Albert
Old Bank of New Brunswick Museum Archives • 5985 Rte 114 • Riverside-Albert, New Brunswick E4H 2B8 • (506) 882-2015 • http://personal.nbnet.nb/ca/maryspt/ACHT/

Sackville
Ralph Pickard Bell Library • Mount Allison Univ, 49 York St • Sackville, New Brunswick E0A 3C0 • (506) 364-2562 • http://www.mta.ca/library

Sackville and District Assistance Center • 5 Willow Ln • Sackville, New Brunswick E0A 3C0

Saint Andrews
Charlotte County Genealogy Society • POB 595 • Saint Andrews, New Brunswick E0G 2X0

Saint Andrews Blockhouse Archives • 23 Joes Point Rd, Town Hall • Saint Andrews, New Brunswick E0G 2X0 • (506) 529-1829

Saint Basile
Chapel Museum Archives • Saint Basile Parish, POB 150 • Saint Basile, New Brunswick E0L 1H0

Haunt-Saint-Jean Regional Library • 540 rue Principale • Saint Basile, New Brunswick E7C 1J5 • (506) 263-3423 • http://www.gnb.ca/0003/nbpls.htm

Saint John
Barbour's General Store Museum Archives • City Hall, King St E & Carmarthen • Saint John, New Brunswick E2L 4L1 • (506) 658-2939

Biblioteque Le Cormoran • 67 Ragged Point Rd • Saint John, New Brunswick E2K 5C3 • (506) 658-4610

Loyalist House Museum Library • 120 Union St • Saint John, New Brunswick E2L 1A3 • (506) 652-3590

New Brunswick Genealogical Society, Saint John Branch • POB 2423 • Saint John, New Brunswick E2L 3V9

New Brunswick Museum Archives • 277 Douglas Ave • Saint John, New Brunswick E2K 1E5 • (506) 643-2322 • http://www.grb.ca/0130/

Saint John Jewish Historical Museum • 29 Wellington Row • Saint John, New Brunswick E2L 3H4 • (506) 633-1833

Saint John Regional Library • 1 Market Sq • Saint John, New Brunswick E2L 4Z6 • (506) 643-7220 • http://www.gnb.ca/0003/nbpls.htm

Saint Martins
Quaco Historical and Library Society & Archives • Quaco Museum, 236 Main St • Saint Martins, New Brunswick E0G 2Z0 • (506) 833-4740 • http://www.fundytrailparkway.com • Quaco Signal

Saint Stephen
Charlotte County Museum Library • 443 Milltown Blvd • Saint Stephen, New Brunswick E3L 1J9 • (506) 466-3295

Saint-Basile
Saint-Basile Chapel Museum Archives • Saint-Basile Parish • Saint-Basile, New Brunswick E7C 1H7 • (506) 263-5971

Saint-Jacques
Musee Automobile • Les Jardins, CP 1567 • Saint-Jacques, New Brunswick E7B 1H3 • (506) 735-2525

Shippagan
Societe Historique Nicolas-Denys & Archives • Centre Universitaire Shippagan • Shippagan, New Brunswick E0B 2P0 • (506) 336-4761 • *Revue d'Histoire de la Societe Historique Nicolas-Denys*

Sussex
Agricultural Museum of New Brunswick • Rte 1 • Sussex, New Brunswick E0E 1P0 • (506) 433-6799

Tabusintac
Tabusintac Centennial Museum Archives • 4490 Route 11 • Tabusintac, New Brunswick E9H 1J3 • (508) 779-8045

Taylor Village
Westmorland Historical Society • 1225 Taylor Rd • Taylor Village, New Brunswick E4K 2T5 • (506) 758-9355 • *Westmorland Historical Society Newsletter*

Upper Woodstock
Carleton County Historical Society Archives • 128 Connell, POB 898 • Upper Woodstock, New Brunswick E0J 2B0

Welshpool
Campobello Island Museum • general delivery • Welshpool, New Brunswick E0G 3H0 • (506) 752-2268

Roosevelt Campobello International Park • Campobello Island • Welshpool, New Brunswick E5E 1A4 • (506) 752-2922 • http://www.fdr.net

Woodstock
Carleton County Historical Society & Archives • Old Carleton County Court House, 128 Connell St • Woodstock, New Brunswick E7M 1L5 • (506) 328-9706

NEWFOUNDLAND

Baie Verte
Baie Verte peninsula Miners' Museum Archives • POB 122 • Baie Verte, Newfoundland A0K 1B0 • (709) 532-4166

Bonavista
Bonavista Museum Archives • POB 882 • Bonavista, Newfoundland A0C 1B0 • (709) 468-2575

Cape Bonavista Lighthouse Museum Archives • Hwy 230 • Bonavista, Newfoundland A0C 1B0 • (709) 728-0562

Mockbeggar Plantation Museum Archives • Mockbeggar Rd • Bonavista, Newfoundland A0C 1B0 • (709) 728-6592

Bonne Bay
Wiltondale Pioneer Village Archives • Woody Point • Bonne Bay, Newfoundland A0K 1P0 • (709) 453-2470

Botwood
Botwood Heritage Centre Archives • 12 Airbase Pl, POB 490 • Botwood, Newfoundland A0H 1E0 • (709) 257-2839 • http://town.botwood.nf.ca

Boyd's Cove
Beothuk Interpretation Centre • Hwy 340, POB 8700 • Boyd's Cove, Newfoundland A0G 1G0 • (709) 729-0592 • http://www.ndmuseum.com

Burin
Burin Heritage House Archives • POB 326 • Burin, Newfoundland A0E 1G0 • (709) 891-2217

Carbonear
Carbonear Railway Station Archives • POB 64 • Carbonear, Newfoundland A0A 1T0 • (709) 596-2267

Shades of the Past Archives • POB 496 • Carbonear, Newfoundland A0A 1T0 • (709) 596-1977

Channel-Port-aux-Basques
Channel-Port-aux-Basques Museum Archives • 118 Main St • Channel-Port-aux-Basques, Newfoundland A0M 1C0 • (709) 695-7604 • http://www.gatewaytonewfoundland.com

Corner Brook
Corner Brook City Library • Sir Richard Squires Bldg • Corner Brook, Newfoundland A2H 6J8

Humber-Bay of Islands Museum Archives • 65 Central St • Corner Brook, Newfoundland A2H 2M7 • (709) 634-7907

Sticks and Stones House Archives • 12 Riverhead Rd • Corner Brook, Newfoundland A2H 1J6 • (709) 834-3275

Cow Head
Dr Henry H Payne Community Museum Archives • POB 47 • Cow Head, Newfoundland A0K 2A0 • (709) 243-2023

Cupids
Cupids Museum Archives • Seaforest Dr • Cupids, Newfoundland A0A 2B0 • (709) 528-3500 • http://www3.nf.sympatico.ca/cupidshistorical

Deer Lake
Roy Whalen Regional Heritage Centre Archives • 44 Trans Canada Hwy • Deer Lake, Newfoundland A8A 2E4 • (709) 635-4440 • http://www.town.deerlake.nf.ca

Durrell
Durrell Museum Archives • Arm Lads' Brigade Armoury, 17 Museum Rd • Durrell, Newfoundland A0S 1V0 • (709) 884-5637

Ferryland
Ferryland Historical Society • POB 7 • Ferryland, Newfoundland A0A 2H0

Historic Ferryland Museum Archives • Old Courthouse • Ferryland, Newfoundland A0A 2H0 • (709) 432-2711

Flat Rock
Flat Rock Museum Archives • 663 Windpeg Rd • Flat Rock, Newfoundland A1K 1C7 • (709) 437-6312

Fogo Island
Bleakhouse Museum Archives • general delivery • Fogo Island, Newfoundland A0B 2B0 • (709) 266-2237

Gander
North Atlantic Aviation Museum Archives • Trans-Canada Hwy, POB 234 • Gander, Newfoundland A1V 1W6 • (709) 256-2923 • http://naam1.tripod.com

Goose Bay
Northern Lights Military Museum Archives • Hamilton River Rd • Goose Bay, Newfoundland A0P 1E0 • (709) 896-5939

Grand Bank
Southern Newfoundland Seamen's Museum Archives • Marine Dr • Grand Bank, Newfoundland A0E 1W0 • (709) 832-1484 • http://www.nfmuseum.com

Grand Falls-Windsor
Beothuck Village Museum Archives • Saint Catherine St • Grand Falls-Windsor, Newfoundland A2A 1W9 • (709) 489-9629 • http://www.grandfallswindsor.com

Mary March Regional Museum and Logging Exhibition • 24 Catherine St • Grand Falls-Windsor, Newfoundland A2A 1W9 • (709) 292-4522 • http://www.delweb.com/nfmuseum

Greenspond
Greenspond Museum Archives • POB 99 • Greenspond, Newfoundland A0G 2H0 • (709) 289-3591

Happy Valley
Labrador Heritage Museum Archives • POB 729, Sta B • Happy Valley, Newfoundland A0P 1E0 • (709) 896-2762

Harbour Grace
Conception Bay Museum Archives • Water St, POB 298 • Harbour Grace, Newfoundland A0A 2M0 • (709) 596-5465

Heart's Content
Heart's Content Cable Station Museum Archives • Hwy 80 • Heart's Content, Newfoundland A0B 1Z0 • (706) 729-0592 • http://www.nfmuseum.com

Labrador City
Labrador Institute of Northern Studies Information Centre • Memorial University of Newfoundland, Sta B, POB 490 • Labrador City, Newfoundland A0P 1E0 • (709) 896-6210

Lamaline
Lawn Heritage Museum Archives • POB 39 • Lamaline, Newfoundland A0E 2C0 • (709) 857-2555

L'Anse-au-Loup
Labrador Straights Museum Archives • POB 98 • L'Anse-au-Loup, Newfoundland A0K 3L0 • (709) 827-5659

Lewisporte
By the Bay Museum Archives • Women's Institute Bldg • Lewisporte, Newfoundland A0G 3A0 • (709) 535-2844

Marystown
Marystown Museum Archives • POB 688 • Marystown, Newfoundland A-E 2M0 • (708) 279-1507 • http://www.schooner.nf.ca

Moreton's Harbour
Moreton's Harbour Museum • POB 28 • Moreton's Harbour, Newfoundland A0G 3H0 • (709) 684-2355

Musgrave Harbour
Fisherman's Museum Archives • 4 Marite Dr • Musgrave Harbour, Newfoundland A0G 3J0 • (709) 684-2355

Nain
Piulimatsivik-Nain Museum Archives • POB 247 • Nain, Newfoundland A0P 1L0 • (709) 922-2821

Newfoundland

Old Pelican
Howard House of Artifacts Archives • POB 100 • Old Pelican, Newfoundland A0A 3G0 • (709) 587-2172

Placentia
Castle Hill National Historic Park Archives • Jerseyside • Placentia, Newfoundland A0B 2G0 • (709) 227-2401

Placentia Area Museum Archives • O'Reilly House, 48 Riverside Dr • Placentia, Newfoundland A0B 2Y0 • (709) 227-5568

Port Union
Port Union Museum Archives • POB 98 • Port Union, Newfoundland A0C 2J0 • (709) 484-3315

Port-au-Port
Our Lady of Mercy Museum Archives • POB 239 • Port-au-Port, Newfoundland A0N 1T0 • (709) 648-2632

Port-aux-Basques
Gulf Museum Archives • POB 1299 • Port-aux-Basques, Newfoundland A0M 1C0 • (709) 695-7604

Port-aux-Basques Railway Heritage Centre • POB 1299 • Port-aux-Basques, Newfoundland A0M 1C0 • (709) 695-7560 • http://www.gatewaytonewfoundland.com

Port-de-Grace
Fishermen's Museum Archives • Porter House and School • Port-de-Grace, Newfoundland A0A 3J0 • (709) 786-3912

Pouch Cove
Pouch Cove Museum Archives • POB 59 • Pouch Cove, Newfoundland A0A 3L0 • (709) 335-2848

Red Bay
Red Bay Historic Site Archives • POB 103 • Red Bay, Newfoundland A0K 4K0 • (709) 920-2142 • http://parkscanada.pch.qc.ca/parks/newfoundland/red_bay

Saint Anthony
Grenfell Historical Society • general delivery • Saint Anthony, Newfoundland A0K 4S0 • (709) 454-4010

Greybill House Museum Archives • POB 93 • Saint Anthony, Newfoundland A0K 4S0 • (709) 454-3333

Saint John's
Anglican Cathedral Museum Archives • 68 Queen's Rd • Saint John's, Newfoundland A1C 2A8 • (709) 725-5677 • http://www.infonet.st-johns.nf.ca

Association of Newfoundland and Labrador Archives • Colonial Bldg, Military Rd • Saint John's, Newfoundland A1C 2C9 • (709) 726-2876 • *Association of Newfoundland and Labrador Archives Newsletter, ANLA Bulletin*

Cape Spear National Historic Site • POB 1268 • Saint John's, Newfoundland A1C 5M9 • (709) 772-5367

Commissariat House Museum Archives • Kings Bridge Rd, POB 8700 • Saint John's, Newfoundland A1B 4J6 • (709) 729-0592

Heritage Foundation of Newfoundland and Labrador • POB 5171 • Saint John's, Newfoundland A1C 5V5

James J O'Mara Pharmacy Museum • Apothecary Hall, 488 Water St • Saint John's, Newfoundland A1E 1B3 • (709) 753-5877

Lillian Stevenson Nursing Archives Museum • Dr Miller Centre, Forest Rd • Saint John's, Newfoundland A1A 1E5 • (709) 777-7682

Memorial University • 232 Elizabeth Ave, POB 4200 • Saint John's, Newfoundland A1C 5S7 • (709) 737-8983 • Newfoundland Studies

Memorial University of Newfoundland • Maritime Studies Research Center • Saint John's, Newfoundland A1C 5S7 • (709) 737-8424 • *International Journal of Maritime History*

Newfoundland and Labrador Genealogical Society • Colonial Bldg, Military Rd • Saint John's, Newfoundland A1C 3C7 • (709) 754-9525 • http://ifonet.st-johns.nf.ca/Community/Providers/NHGS/nlgs.html • *Newfoundland Ancestor*

Newfoundland Historical Society & Library • Colonial Bldg, Rm 115, Military Road • Saint John's, Newfoundland A1C 3C9 • (709) 777-3191 • http://www.infonet.st-johns.nf.ca/providers/nfldhist

Newfoundland Naval and Military Museum Archives • Confederation Bldg, 281 Duckworth St • Saint John's, Newfoundland A1C 1G9

Point Amour Lighthouse Museum Archives • L'Anse Amour Rd, Hwy 510, POB 8700 • Saint John's, Newfoundland A1B 4L6 • (709) 729-0592 • http://www.nfmuseum.com

Provincial Archives of Newfoundland and Labrador • Colonial Bldg, Military Rd • Saint John's, Newfoundland A1C 5E2 • (709) 729-3065

Provincial Museum of Newfoundland and Labrador Archives • 285 Duckworth St • Saint John's, Newfoundland A1C 1G9 • (709) 729-2355 • http://www.nfmuseum.com

Provincial Public Library Services • 125 Allandale Rd • Saint John's, Newfoundland A1B 3A3 • (709) 737-3964

Provincial Resource Library • Arts & Culture Centre • Saint John's, Newfoundland A1B 3A3 • (709) 737-3946 • http://www.publib.nf.ca/

Queen Elizabeth II Library • Memorial University of Newfoundland • Saint John's, Newfoundland A1B Y1 • (709) 737-7428 • http://www.mun.ca/library

Quidi Vidi Battery Museum Archives • Cuckhold's Cove Rd, POB 8700 • Saint John's, Newfoundland A1B 4J6 • (709) 729-6745 • http://www.nfmuseum.com

Royal Newfoundland Constabulary Museum Archives • POB 7247 • Saint John's, Newfoundland A1E 3Y4 • (709) 729-7247

Royal Saint John's Regatta Museum Archives • POB 214 • Saint John's, Newfoundland A1C 5J3 • (709) 753-9448

Saint Thomas' Old Garrison Church Museum • 8 Military Rd • Saint John's, Newfoundland A1C 2C4 • (709) 576-6632 • http://www3.nf.sympatico.ca/st.thomas/

Signal Hill National Historic Site Museum Archives • Signal Hill Rd, POB 1268 • Saint John's, Newfoundland A1C 5M9 • (709) 772-5367 • http://www.parkscanada.qc.ca

Saint Lawrence
Saint Lawrence Memorial Miner's Museum • Rte 220, POB 128 • Saint Lawrence, Newfoundland A0E 2V0 • (709) 873-2222

Saint-Lunaire-Griquet
L'Anse aux Meadows National Historic Site • POB 70 • Saint-Lunaire-Griquet, Newfoundland A0K 2X0 • (709) 623-2608 • http://parkscanada.pch.ac.ca/parks/newfoundland/anse_meadows

Salvage
Salvage Fisherman's Museum Archives • Bishop Dr • Salvage, Newfoundland A0B 5X0 • (709) 677-2414

Seal Cove
Seal Cove Campus Library • College of the North Atlantic, Conception Bay Hwy, POB 10 • Seal Cove, Newfoundland A0A 3T0 • (709) 744-6829

Sheshatshiu
Innu Indian Nation • POB 119 • Sheshatshiu, Newfoundland A0P 1M0

Springdale
Harvey Grant Heritage Centre Archives • POB 57 • Springdale, Newfoundland A0L 1T0 • (709) 673-4313

Stephenville
Bay Saint George Campus Library • College of the North Atlantic, POB 5400 • Stephenville, Newfoundland A2N 2Z6 • (709) 643-7786

Port-au-Port-Bay St George Heritage Association & Library • 16 Glendale St, POB 314 • Stephenville, Newfoundland A2N 2Z5 • (709) 643-4262

Provincial Information and Library Resources Board • 48 St George's Ave • Stephenville, Newfoundland A2N 1K9 • (709) 643-0902 • http://www.public.nf.ca

Torbay
Torbay Museum Archives • 1288 Torbay Rd • Torbay, Newfoundland A1K 1K4 • (709) 437-6571 • http://www.torbay.public.ng.ca

Trepassey
Trepassey Area Museum Archives • POB 63 • Trepassey, Newfoundland A0A 4B0 • (709) 436-2044

Trinity
Hiscock House Museum Archives • Church St • Trinity, Newfoundland A0C 2S0 • (709) 729-0870

Lester-Garland Premesis Museum Archives • West St • Trinity, Newfoundland A0C 2S0 • (709) 729-0592 • http://www.nfmuseum.com

Trinity Historical Society • general delivery • Trinity, Newfoundland A0C 2S0

Trinity Interpretation Centre Archives • West St • Trinity, Newfoundland A0C 2S0 • (709) 729-0592 • http://www.nfmuseum.com

Trinity Museum and Archives • POB 32 • Trinity, Newfoundland A0C 2S0 • (709) 464-3706

Twillingate
Twillingate Museum Association & Library • Historical Museum, Saint Peter's Church Rd, POB 369 • Twillingate, Newfoundland A0G 4M0 • (709) 884-2825 • http://www.tmaca.tripod.ca

Wesleyville
Bonavista North Regional Museum Archives • Memorial Dr • Wesleyville, Newfoundland A0B 4B0 • (709) 536-2110

Whitbourne
Whitbourne Museum Archives • general delivery • Whitbourne, Newfoundland A0B 3K0 • (709) 759-2346

NORTHWEST TERRITORIES

Aklavik
Aklavik First Nation • POB 118 • Aklavik, Northwest Territories X0E OA0

Arctic Bay
Sod House Museum Archives • general delivery • Arctic Bay, Northwest Territories X0A 0A0 • (867) 439-9918

Arviat
Arviat Historical Society • general delivery • Arviat, Northwest Territories X0C 0E0 • (867) 857-2806

Fort Good Hope
Dene Museum Archives • general delivery • Fort Good Hope, Northwest Territories X0E 0H0 • (867) 598-2331

Fort Liard
Acho Dene Koe Indian Band • general delivery • Fort Liard, Northwest Territories X0G OA0

Fort Smith
Northern Life Museum and National Exhibition Centre • 110 King St • Fort Smith, Northwest Territories X0E 0P0 • (867) 872-2859 • http://www.northernlifemuseum.org

Hay River
Dene Cultural Institute • POB 570 • Hay River, Northwest Territories X0E 0R0

Northwest Territories Public Library Services • 75 Woodland Dr, POB 1100 • Hay River, Northwest Territories X0E 0R0 • (867) 874-6531 • http://www.nwtpls.gov.net.ca

Inuvik
Inuvik Centennial Library • 100 Mackenzie Rd, POB 1640 • Inuvik, Northwest Territories X0E 0T0 • (867) 777-8620 • http://www.inuvik.net/icl

Iqaluit
Iqaluit Centennial Library • Bag 189A • Iqaluit, Northwest Territories X0A 0H0 • (867) 979-5400

Nuantta Sunakkutaangit Museum Archives • Bldg 212, POB 1900 • Iqaluit, Northwest Territories X0A 0H0 • (867) 979-5537

Nunavut Arctic College Library • Tunnganaqsarvik Bldg, 1st Flr, POB 600 • Iqaluit, Northwest Territories X0A 0H0 • (867) 979-7220 • http://www.nac.nu.ca/

Norman Wells
Colville Lake Museum Archives • general delivery • Norman Wells, Northwest Territories X0E 1L0 • (867) 709-2500

Norman Wells Historical Centre • POB 56 • Norman Wells, Northwest Territories X0E 0V0 • (867) 587-2415

Pangnirtung
Spialaseequtt Museum Archives • Angmarlik Visitor Centre • Pangnirtung, Northwest Territories X0A 0R0 • (867) 473-8737

Sachs Harbour
Sachs Harbour Museum Archives • general delivery • Sachs Harbour, Northwest Territories X0E 0Z0 • (867) 690-4361

Yellowknife
Archives of the Northwest Territories • Prince of Wales Northern Heritage Centre, POB 1320 • Yellowknife, Northwest Territories X1A 2L9 • (867) 873-7551 • http://www.pwnhc.learnnet.nt.ca

Dene Indian Nation • POB 2338 • Yellowknife, Northwest Territories X1A 2P7

Metis Association of the Northwest Territories • POB 1375 • Yellowknife, Northwest Territories X0E 1H0

Northwest Territories Genealogical Society • POB 1715 • Yellowknife, Northwest Territories X1A 2P3

Yellowknife Public Library • Center Square Mall, 5022 49th St, 2nd Flr, POB 694 • Yellowknife, Northwest Territories X1A 2N5 • (867) 920-5642 • http://www.city.yellowknife.nt.ca

NOVA SCOTIA

Amherst
Amherst Township Historical Society • 51 A LaPlanche • Amherst, Nova Scotia B4H 3Y6

Atlantic Policy Congress of First Nation Chiefs • POB 36 • Amherst, Nova Scotia B4H 3Y7

Cumberland County Historical Society & Archives • Historical Museum, 150 Church St • Amherst, Nova Scotia B4H 3C3 • (902) 667-2561

Annapolis Royal
Annapolis Valley Historical Society • general delivery • Annapolis Royal, Nova Scotia B0S 1A0

Annapolis Valley Regional Library • Saint George St, POB 579 • Annapolis Royal, Nova Scotia B0S 1A0 • (902) 532-2226 • http://avrl.library.ns.ca/

Fort Anne National Historic Park Archives • POB 9 • Annapolis Royal, Nova Scotia B0S 1A0 • (902) 532-5197

Historic Restoration Society of Annapolis County • 158 St George St, POB 503 • Annapolis Royal, Nova Scotia B0S 1A0 • (902) 532-7754

O'Dell Inn Museum Archives • POB 503 • Annapolis Royal, Nova Scotia B0S 1A0 • (902) 532-2041

Port Royal National Historic Park Archives • POB 9 • Annapolis Royal, Nova Scotia B0S 1A0 • (902) 532-2898

Antigonish
Antigonish Heritage Museum Archives • 20 E Main St • Antigonish, Nova Scotia B2G 2E9 • (902) 863-6160

Saint Francis Xavier University Archives • West St, POB 5000 • Antigonish, Nova Scotia B2G 2W5 • (902) 867-2242 • http://libmain.stfx.ca/newlib/ • *Forward*

Arichat
Le Noir Forge • general delivery • Arichat, Nova Scotia B0E 1A0 • (902) 226-8364

Baddeck
Alexander Graham Bell National Historic Site Reference Archives • 559 Chebucto St, POB 159 • Baddeck, Nova Scotia B0E 1B0 • (902) 295-2069 • http://www.parkscanada.gc.ca/

Highland Pioneers Museum Archives • POB 9 • Baddeck, Nova Scotia B0E 1B0 • (902) 295-3411

Victoria County Library Museum and Archives • Gilbert Grosvenor Bldg, POB 75 • Baddeck, Nova Scotia B0E 1B0 • (902) 295-3397

Barrington
Barrington Woolen Mill Museum Archives • Hwy 103 • Barrington, Nova Scotia B0W 1E0 • (902) 637-2185

Cape Sable Historical Society • general delivery • Barrington, Nova Scotia B0W 1E0 • (902) 637-2185

Old Meeting House Museum Archives • Hwy 103 • Barrington, Nova Scotia B0W 1E0 • (902) 632-2165

Seal Island Light Museum Archives • Hwy 103 • Barrington, Nova Scotia B0W 1E0 • (902) 637-2185

Barrington Passage
Cape Sable Historical Society & Library • RR1, POB 134 • Barrington Passage, Nova Scotia B0W 1G0 • (902) 637-2185

Barss Corner
Parkdale-Maplewood Community Museum Archives • 3008 Barss Corner Rd, RR1 • Barss Corner, Nova Scotia B0P 1A0 • (902) 644-3288

Bridgetown
Annapolis Valley Regional Library • POB 640 • Bridgetown, Nova Scotia B0S 1C0 • (902) 665-2995 • http://www.valleylibrary.ca/

Bridgetown and Area Historical Society & Library • POB 645 • Bridgetown, Nova Scotia B0S 1C0 • (902) 665-4530

James House Museum Archives • POB 373 • Bridgetown, Nova Scotia B0S 1C0 • (902) 665-4530

Tupperville School Museum Archives • RR3 • Bridgetown, Nova Scotia B0S 1C0 • (902) 665-2427

Bridgewater
DesBrisay Museum Archives • 130 Jubilee Rd, POB 353 • Bridgewater, Nova Scotia B4V 2W9 • (902) 543-4033

Wile Carding Mill Museum Archives • 242 Victoria Rd • Bridgewater, Nova Scotia B4V 2W9 • (902) 543-8233 • http://www.cardingmill.museum.gov.ns.ca

Caledonia
North Queens Heritage Society • Route 8, Box 88 • Caledonia, Nova Scotia B0T 1B0

Canso
Canso Museum Archives • Union St • Canso, Nova Scotia B0H 1H0 • (902) 366-2170 • http://www.schoolnet.ca/collections/canso/

Cape Sable Island
Archelaus Smith Museum Archives • 915 Hwy 330 • Cape Sable Island, Nova Scotia B0W 1P0 • (902) 745-3361

Centerville
Cape Sable Historical Society, Archelaus Smith Branch & Archives • Archelaus Smith Museum • Centerville, Nova Scotia B0W 2G0 • (902) 745-2478

Chester
Chester Municipal Heritage Society • general delivery • Chester, Nova Scotia B0J 1J0

Cheticamp
Musee Acadien Archives • 114 Main St, CP 98 • Cheticamp, Nova Scotia B0E 1H0 • (902) 224-2170

Church Point
Louis R Comeau Bibliotheque • Universite Sainte Anne, POB 40 • Church Point, Nova Scotia B0W 1M0 • (902) 769-2114 • http://www.ustanne.ednet.ns.ca/biblio

Musee Sainte-Marie • POB 28 • Church Point, Nova Scotia B0W 1M0 • (902) 769-2832

Societe Historique Acadienne de la Baie Sainte-Marie • Saint Ann's College • Church Point, Nova Scotia B0W 1M0

Clementsport
Old Saint Edward's Anglican Church Archives • RR2, Annapolis Royal • Clementsport, Nova Scotia B0S 1E0

Cole Harbour
Cole Harbour Heritage Farm Museum Archives • 471 Poplar Dr • Cole Harbour, Nova Scotia B2W 4L2 • (902) 462-0154 • http://www3.ns.sympatico.ca/farmmuseum/

Dartmouth
Black Cultural Centre For Nova Scotia Library • 1149 Main St • Dartmouth, Nova Scotia B2Z 1A8 • (902) 434-6223 • http://www.bccns.com

Cole Harbour Rural Heritage Society • 471 Poplar Dr • Dartmouth, Nova Scotia B2W 4L2

Dartmouth Heritage Museum Archives • 100 Wyse Rd • Dartmouth, Nova Scotia B3A 1M1 • (902) 464-2300 • http://www.dartmouthheritagemuseum.ns.ca

Dartmouth Regional Library • 60 Alderney Dr • Dartmouth, Nova Scotia B2Y 4P8 • (902) 490-5744 • http://www.halifax.library.ns.ca

Evergreen Historic House Archives • 26 Newcastle St • Dartmouth, Nova Scotia B2Y 3M5 • (902) 464-2301

Regional Museum of Cultural History Library • 100 Wyse Rd • Dartmouth, Nova Scotia B3A 1M1 • (902) 464-2300 • http://www.region.halifax.ns.ca

Royal Nova Scotia Historical Society • POB 2097 • Dartmouth, Nova Scotia B2W 3X8 • (902) 423-9115 • *Genealogical Newsletter of the Royal Nova Scotia Historical Society*

William Ray House Archives • 57 Qutterloney St • Dartmouth, Nova Scotia B2Y 1C3 • (902) 464-2253

Denmark
Sutherland Steam Mill Archives • Rte 326 • Denmark, Nova Scotia B3H 3A6 • (902) 657-3365 • http://www.museum.gov.ns.ca

Digby
Admiral Digby Library and Historical Society & Library • Historical Museum, 95 Montague Row, POB 1644 • Digby, Nova Scotia B0V 1A0 • (902) 245-6322 • http://www3.ns.sympatico.ca/admuseum

Dingwall
North Highland Community Museum Archives • RR1 • Dingwall, Nova Scotia B0C 1G0 • (902) 383-2579 • http://www.nhighlandsmuseum.com

Fort Lawrence
Fort Lawrence Heritage Association • 106 Cumberland Loop • Fort Lawrence, Nova Scotia B4H 4V6 • (902) 667-1756

Freeport
Island Historical Society • general delivery • Freeport, Nova Scotia B0V 1B0

Glace Bay
Cape Breton Miners' Museum Library • 42 Birkley St • Glace Bay, Nova Scotia B1A 5T8 • (902) 849-4522 • http://www.cbnet.ns/ca/cbnet/mainmenu.html

Glace Bay Historical Society • general delivery • Glace Bay, Nova Scotia B1A 5T8

Grand-Pre
Fort Edward Museum Archives • POB 150 • Grand-Pre, Nova Scotia B0P 1M0 • (902) 542-3631

Grand-Pre Historical Society • POB 20 • Grand-Pre, Nova Scotia B0P 1M0 • (902) 542-2659

Grand-Pre National Historic Site Archives • 2242 Grand-Pre Rd • Grand-Pre, Nova Scotia B0P 1M0 • (902) 542-3631 • http://www.grand-pre.com

Granville Ferry
North Hills Museum Archives • 5055 Granville Rd • Granville Ferry, Nova Scotia B0S 1K0 • (902) 532-2168 • http://museum.gov.ms.ca

Greenwood
Greenwood Military Aviation Museum Archives • Ward Rd • Greenwood, Nova Scotia B0P 1N0 • (902) 765-1494 • http://gmam.ednet.ns.ca

Guysborough
Guysborough Historical Society & Archives • Old Courthouse Museum, Church St, POB 232 • Guysborough, Nova Scotia B0H 1N0 • (902) 533-4008 • http://www.chebucto.ns.ca/Recreation/GANS/consult.html

Halifax
Atlantic School of Theology Library • 624 Francklyn St • Halifax, Nova Scotia B3H 3B5 • (902) 423-7986 • http://astheology.ns.ca/library.htm

Cambridge Military Library • Royal Artillery Park, 1575 Queen St, Bldg 3 • Halifax, Nova Scotia B3J 2H9 • (902) 427-7193 • http://www3.ns.sympatico.ca/library

Cavalier Block Halifax Citadel Museum Archives • Nova Scotia Museum, 1747 Summer St • Halifax, Nova Scotia B3H 3A6

Clansman Publishing Ltd • 50 Bluewater Rd, POB 8805, Sta A • Halifax, Nova Scotia B3K 5M4 • (902) 835-6244 • http://www.celticheritage.ns.ca • *Celtic Heritage*

Federation of Museums, Heritage and Historical Societies • 5516 Spring Garden Rd, Ste 305 • Halifax, Nova Scotia B3J 1G6 • (902) 423-4677

Fisherman's Life Museum Archives • Jeddore Oyster Ponds 58 Navy Pool Loop • Halifax, Nova Scotia B0J !W0 • (902) 889-2053

Genealogical Association of Nova Scotia • POB 641, Sta M • Halifax, Nova Scotia B3L 4K5 • (902) 454-0322 • http://www.ccn.cs.dal.ca/Recreation/GANS/gans_homepage.html • *Nova Scotia Genealogist*

Halifax Citadel National Historic Park Library • POB 3666 • Halifax, Nova Scotia B3J 3K6 • (902) 422-5979 • http://www.parkscanada.pcn.qc.ca/citadel

Halifax Police Museum Archives • City Police Headquarters, 1975 Gottigen St • Halifax, Nova Scotia B3J 2H1 • (902) 421-6840

HMCS Sackville Museum Archives • POB 99000, STN Forces • Halifax, Nova Scotia B3K 5X5 • (902) 429-7955 • http://www.hmcssackville-cnmt.ns.ca

Killam Memorial Library • Dalhousie University, 6225 University Ave • Halifax, Nova Scotia B3H 4H8 • (902) 494-3601 • http://www.library.dal.ca/

Maritime Command Museum Archives • Admiralty House, 2725 Gottingen St, POB 99000 • Halifax, Nova Scotia B3K 2X0 • (902) 427-0550 • http://www.pspmembers.com/marcommuseum

Maritime Museum of the Atlantic Archives • 1675 Lower Water St • Halifax, Nova Scotia B3J 1G3 • (902) 424-7490 • http://maritime.museum.gov.ns.ca

Nova Scotia Archives and Records Management • 6016 University Ave • Halifax, Nova Scotia B3H 1W4 • (902) 424-6060 • http://www.gov.ns.ca/nsarm

Nova Scotia Historical Society • POB 1102 • Halifax, Nova Scotia B3J 2X1

Nova Scotia Museum Library • 1747 Summer St • Halifax, Nova Scotia B3H 3A6 • (902) 424-7198 • http://museum.gov.ns.ca

Nova Scotia Provincial Library • 3770 Kempt Rd • Halifax, Nova Scotia B3K 4X8 • (902) 424-2457 • http://www.library.ns.ca

Patrick Power Library • Saint Mary's University, 5429 Inglis St • Halifax, Nova Scotia B3H 3C3 • (902) 420-5534 • http://www.smu.ca/library

Prince of Wales Martello Tower Museum Archives • POB 9080, St A • Halifax, Nova Scotia B3K 5M7 • (902) 426-5080 • http://parkscanada.pch.qc.ca

Public Archives of Nova Scotia • 6016 University Ave • Halifax, Nova Scotia B3H 1W4 • (902) 424-6060

Rockingham Heritage Society • 35 Montgomery Ct • Halifax, Nova Scotia B3M 4M5

Ross Thompson Museum Archives • 1747 Summer St • Halifax, Nova Scotia B3H 1Z9 • (902) 875-2698

Telephone Historical Collection Museum Archives • Maritime Centre • Halifax, Nova Scotia B3J 2W3

University of King's College Archives • 6350 Coburg Rd • Halifax, Nova Scotia B3H 2A1 • (902) 422-1271 • http://www.ukings.ns.ca/kings/library

William D Lawrence House Museum Archives • 1747 Summer St • Halifax, Nova Scotia B3H 3A6 • (902) 429-4610

Hall's Harbour
Hall's Harbour Historical Society • 3586 Highway 359 • Hall's Harbour, Nova Scotia B0P 1J0 • (902) 678-7001

Hants County
Avon River Heritage Museum Archives • POB 17 • Hants County, Nova Scotia B0N 2A0 • (902) 757-1869

Hantsport
Hantsport and Area Historical Society • POB 525 • Hantsport, Nova Scotia B0P 1P0

Inverness
Inverness Miners Museum Archives • 62 Lower Railway St, POB 598 • Inverness, Nova Scotia B0E 1N0 • (902) 258-3822

Iona
Highland Village Archives • 4119 Route 223, Hector's Point • Iona, Nova Scotia B0A 1L0 • (902) 725-2272

Jeddore Oyster Ponds
Fishermen's Life Museum Archives • general Delivery • Jeddore Oyster Ponds, Nova Scotia B0A 1W0 • http://museum.gov.ns.ca

Kentville
Blair House Museum Archives • Agricultural Centre • Kentville, Nova Scotia B4N 1J5 • (902) 678-1093

Kings County Historical Society • 37 Cornwallis St • Kentville, Nova Scotia B4N 2E2 • (902) 678-6237 • Kings County Memories

Kings Historical Society & Archives • Historical Museum, 37 Cornwallis St • Kentville, Nova Scotia B4N 2E2 • (902) 678-6237 • http://www.okcm.ca

La Have
Fort Point Museum Archives • POB 99 • La Have, Nova Scotia B0R 1C0 • (902) 688-2696

La Have Islands Marine Museum Archives • RR1, Bldg 100, Bell's Island • La Have, Nova Scotia B0R 1C0 • (902) 688-2565 • http://www.lunco.com/heritage/lehaveist.htm

Lake Charlotte
Lake Charlotte Area Heritage Society • general delivery • Lake Charlotte, Nova Scotia B0J 1Y0 • (902) 845-2211

Little River
Society for the Preservation of the Eastern Head, Digby Neck and Islands Genealogical Division • Scenic Dr • Little River, Nova Scotia B0V 1C0

Liverpool
Queens County Historical Society & Archives • Historical Museum, 109 Main St, POB 1078 • Liverpool, Nova Scotia B0T 1K0 • (902) 354-4058 • http://www.geocities.com/Paris/2669/

Queens County Museum Library • 115 Main St, POB 1078 • Liverpool, Nova Scotia B0T 1K0 • (902) 354-4058

Simeon Perkins Museum Archives • 105 Main St • Liverpool, Nova Scotia B0T 1K0 • (902) 354-4058

Lockeport
Little School Museum Archives • Locke St • Lockeport, Nova Scotia B0T 1L0 • (902) 656-2238 • http://museum.ocatch.com

Londonderry
Londerry Mines Museum Archives • RR1 • Londonderry, Nova Scotia B0M 1M0 • (902) 668-2043

Louisbourg
Atlantic Statiquarium Marine Museum Archives • POB 316 • Louisbourg, Nova Scotia B0A 1M0 • (902) 783-2721

Fortress of Louisbourg National Historic Park Library • 259 Park Service Rd, POB 160 • Louisbourg, Nova Scotia B0A 1M0 • (902) 733-3534 • http://fortress.uccb.ns.ca

Sydney and Louisburg Railway Museum • 7330 Main St • Louisbourg, Nova Scotia B1C 1P5 • (902) 733-2720 • http://fortress.uccb.ns.ca/historic/s_1.html

Lower Sackville
Fultz House Museum Archives • POB 124 • Lower Sackville, Nova Scotia B4C 2S8 • (902) 865-3794 • http://users.andara.com/~zx2

Lunenburg
Lunenburg County Historical Society • general delivery • Lunenburg, Nova Scotia B0J 2C0

South Shore Genealogical Society • 68 Bluenose Dr, POB 901 • Lunenburg, Nova Scotia B0J 2C0 • (902) 634-4794 • http://www.rootsweb.com/~nslssgs

South Shore Genealogical Society • 120 Townsend St, POB 901 • Lunenburg, Nova Scotia B0J 2C0 • (902) 634-8768

Mabou
James Saint Clair, Mabou Gaelic and Historical Society • general delivery • Mabou, Nova Scotia B0E 1X0

Mabou Gaelic and Historical Society & Library • An Drochaid, POB 175 • Mabou, Nova Scotia B0E 1X0 • (902) 945-2311

Mahone Bay
Mahone Bay Founders Society & Archives • Settlers' Museum and Cultural Centre, 578 Main St • Mahone Bay, Nova Scotia B0J 2E0 • (902) 624-6263

Maitland
East Hants Historical Museum Archives • RR1 • Maitland, Nova Scotia B0N 1T0 • (902) 261-2627

East Hants Historical Society • Lower Selma • Maitland, Nova Scotia B0N 1T0 • (902) 261-2796

Lawrence House Museum Archives • 8660 Rte 215, RR1 • Maitland, Nova Scotia B0N 1T0 • (902) 424-6478

Maplewood
Parkdale-Maplewood Community Museum Archives • RR1, Barss Corners • Maplewood, Nova Scotia B0R 1A0 • (902) 644-2893

Middelton
Annapolis Valley Macdonald Museum Library • 21 School St, POB 925 • Middelton, Nova Scotia B0S 1P0 • (902) 825-6116

Milton
Milton Blacksmith Shop Museum Archives • POB 572 • Milton, Nova Scotia B0T 1P0 • (902) 350-0268 • http://www.qcis.ns.ca

Mount Uniacke
Uniacke Estata Museum Archives • general delivery • Mount Uniacke, Nova Scotia B3H 3A6 • (902) 866-0032 • http://museum.gbv.ns.ca

Mulgrave
Eastern Counties Regional Library • 390 Murray St, POB 2500 • Mulgrave, Nova Scotia B03 2G0 • (902) 747-2597 • http://ecrl.library.ns.ca

Musquodoboit Harbour
Musquodoboit Harbour Heritage Society • general delivery • Musquodoboit Harbour, Nova Scotia B0J 2L0

Musquodoboit Railway Museum • POB 303 • Musquodoboit Harbour, Nova Scotia B0J 2L0 • (902) 889-2689

New Germany
Old Sydney Society & Archives • Parkdale-Maplewood Community Museum • New Germany, Nova Scotia B0R 1A0

New Glasgow
Carmichael-Stewart House Museum Archives • 100 Churchill Dr • New Glasgow, Nova Scotia B2M 1V2 • (902) 752-5583

MacPherson's Mill and Farm Homestead • POB 403 • New Glasgow, Nova Scotia B2H 5E5 • (902) 752-7828

Pictou County Historical Museum Archives • 88 Temperance St • New Glasgow, Nova Scotia B2H 3A7 • (902) 752-5582

Pictou County Historical Society • 86 Temperance St • New Glasgow, Nova Scotia B2H 3A7 • (902) 752-5583

New Ross
Ross Farm Museum Archives • 4568 Hwy 12 • New Ross, Nova Scotia B0J 2M0 • (902) 689-2210 • http://www.rossfarm.museum.gov.ns.ca

New Waterford
New Waterford and District Historical Society • 3696 Ellsworth Ave • New Waterford, Nova Scotia B1H 2H7 • (902) 862-1116

North East Margaree
Museum of Cape Breton Heritage • general delivery • North East Margaree, Nova Scotia B0E 2H0 • (902) 248-2551

North Sydney
North Sydney Historical Society • general delivery • North Sydney, Nova Scotia B2A 3B4 • (902) 794-2524

Nouvelle-Ecosse
Universite Saint-Anne • Pointe-de-l'Eglise • Nouvelle-Ecosse, Nova Scotia B0W 1M0

Nova Scotia

Orangedale
Orangedale Railway Museum Archives • general delivery • Orangedale, Nova Scotia B0E 2K0 • (902) 758-3384

Parrsboro
Parrsboro Shore Historical Society • POB 98 • Parrsboro, Nova Scotia B0M 1S0 • (902) 254-2376

Pictou
Northumberland Fisheries Museum Archives • POB 1489 • Pictou, Nova Scotia B0K 1H0 • (902) 485-4972

Pictou County Genealogy and Heritage Society • 100 Old Haliburton Rd, POB 1210 • Pictou, Nova Scotia B0K 1H0 • (902) 485-4563

Thomas McCulloch House and Hector National Exhibition Centre Archives • POB 1210 • Pictou, Nova Scotia B0K 1H0 • (902) 485-4563 • http://www.rootsweb.com/~spcghs

Plympton
Weymouth Historical Society • RR1 • Plympton, Nova Scotia B0W 1R0

Port Hastings
Port Hastings Historical Museum and Archives • 367 Church St, POB 115 • Port Hastings, Nova Scotia B0E 2T0 • (902) 625-1295

Port Hastings Historical Society • 9 Church St • Port Hastings, Nova Scotia B9A 1N5 • (902) 625-1295

Port Hood
Chestico Museum and Historical Society • Harborview, POB 144 • Port Hood, Nova Scotia B0E 2W0 • (902) 787-3104

Port Williams
Prescott House Museum Archives • Starr's Point • Port Williams, Nova Scotia B0P 1T0 • (902) 542-3984 • http://museum.gov.ns.ca

Pugwash
North Cumberland Historical Society • POB 353 • Pugwash, Nova Scotia B0K 1L0 • (902) 243-3348

River Herbert
King Seaman School Museum • RR2 • River Herbert, Nova Scotia B0L 1G0 • (902) 251-2041

Sackville
Sackville Heritage Society • 70 First Lake Dr • Sackville, Nova Scotia B4C 3E4

Saint Peters
Nicolas Denys Museum Library • POB 249 • Saint Peters, Nova Scotia B0E 3B0 • (902) 535-2379

Shag Harbor
Chapel Hill Museum Archives • general delivery • Shag Harbor, Nova Scotia B0W 3B0 • (902) 723-2830

Shearwater
Shearwater Aviation Museum Archives • Bocaventure Av • Shearwater, Nova Scotia B0J 3A0 • (902) 460-1083 • http://www.shearwateraviationmuseum.ns.ca

Shelburne
Dory Shop Museum Archives • Dock St • Shelburne, Nova Scotia B0T 1W0 • (902) 875-3141 • http://museu.gov.ns.ca

Nova Scotia Genealogy Network Association • POB 248 • Shelburne, Nova Scotia B0T 1W0

Shelburne County Genealogical Society & Library • 168 Water St, POB 248 • Shelburne, Nova Scotia B0T 1W0 • (902) 875-4299 • http://msgna.ednet.ns.ca/shelburne

Shelburne County Museum Archives • 8 Maiden Ln, POB 39 • Shelburne, Nova Scotia B0T 1W0 • (902) 875-3219 • http://www.historicshelburne.com

Shelburne Historical Society & Library • Ross Thomson House, 9 Charlotte Ln, POB 39 • Shelburne, Nova Scotia B0T 1W0 • (902) 875-3141 • http://www.historicshelburne.com

Sherbrooke
Sherbrooks Village Museum Archives • POB 285 • Sherbrooke, Nova Scotia B0J 3C0 • (902) 522-2400 • http://sherbrooke.museum.gov.ns.ca

Smith's Cove
Smith's Cove Historical Museum Archives • RR1 • Smith's Cove, Nova Scotia B0S 1S0

Smith's Cove Historical Society • RR1 • Smith's Cove, Nova Scotia B0S 1S0

South Rawdon
South Rawdon Museum Archives • 1761 S Rawdon Rd, Hwy 202 • South Rawdon, Nova Scotia B0N 1Z0 • (902) 757-2344 • http://www.rawdonmuseum.com

Springhill
Springhill Miner's Museum Archives • Black River Rd • Springhill, Nova Scotia B0M 1X0 • (902) 597-3449 • http://www.grtplaces.com/ac/mine

Stellarton
Museum of Industry Archives • 147 N Ford St • Stellarton, Nova Scotia B0K 1S0 • (902) 755-5425 • http://www.industry.museum.gov.ns.ca

Sydney
Beaton Institute University • University College of Cape Breton, 1250 Grand Lake Rd, POB 5300 • Sydney, Nova Scotia B1P 6L2 • (902) 563-1329 • http://beaton.uccb.ns.ca

Cape Breton Centre for Heritage Archives • Lyceum, 225 George St • Sydney, Nova Scotia B1P 1J5 • (902) 539-1572

Cape Breton Genealogical Society • POB 53 • Sydney, Nova Scotia B1P 6G9 • *Cape Breton Genealogical Society Newsletter*

Cape Breton Regional Library • 50 Falmouth St • Sydney, Nova Scotia B1P 6X9 • (902) 562-3279 • http://www.cbrl.ca/

Cossit House Museum Archives • 75 Charlotte St • Sydney, Nova Scotia B1P 1J5 • (902) 539-7973

Jost House Museum Archives • 54 Charlotte St, POB 912 • Sydney, Nova Scotia B1P 6J4 • (902) 539-0366

Micmac Association of Cultural Studies • POB 961 • Sydney, Nova Scotia B1P 6J4

Saint Patrick's Church Museum Archives • Esplanade St, POB 912 • Sydney, Nova Scotia B1P 6J4 • (902) 539-3115

Saint Patrick's Museum Archives • 89 Esplanade • Sydney, Nova Scotia B1P 1J5 • (902) 562-8237

Union of Nova Scotia Indians • POB 961 • Sydney, Nova Scotia B1P 6J4

University College of Cape Breton Library • 1250 Grand Lake Rd, POB 5300 • Sydney, Nova Scotia B1P 6L2 • (902) 563-1387 • http://www.uccb.ns.ca/library

Whitney Pier Historical Society • 88 Mt Pleasant St • Sydney, Nova Scotia B1N 2G1 • (902) 564-9819

Tatamagouche
Balmoral Grist Mill Museum Archives • RR4 • Tatamagouche, Nova Scotia B0K 1V0 • (902) 657-3016

Sunrise Trail Museum Archives • Main St • Tatamagouche, Nova Scotia B0K 1V0 • (902) 657-2423

Truro
Colchester Historical Museum Archives • 29 Young St, POB 412 • Truro, Nova Scotia B2N 5C5 • (902) 895-6284 • http://www.genealogynet.com/colchester/

Colchester Historical Society & Archives • Historical Museum, 29 Young St • Truro, Nova Scotia B2N 3W3 • (902) 895-6284 • http://www.shelburne.nscc.ns.ca/nsgna/col/col_main.html

Little White Schoolhouse Museum Archives • 20 Arthur St • Truro, Nova Scotia B2N 5N2 • (902) 895-5170 • http://www.lwsm.ednet.ns.ca

MacRae Library • Nova Scotia Agricultural College, 135 College Rd, POB 550 • Truro, Nova Scotia B2N 5E3 • (902) 893-6669 • http://www.nsac.ns.ca/lib/

Tusket
Argyle Municipality Historical and Genealogical Society • POB 101 • Tusket, Nova Scotia B0W 3M0

Wallace
Malagash and Area Heritage Association • general delivery • Wallace, Nova Scotia B0K 1E0

Wallace Bridge
Wallace Area Museum Archives • 13440 Route 6 • Wallace Bridge, Nova Scotia B0K 1Y0 • (902) 257-2191

Waverley
Waverley Heritage Society • general delivery • Waverley, Nova Scotia B0N 2S0

West Bay
Marble Mountain Community Museum • RR1 • West Bay, Nova Scotia B0E 3K0 • (902) 756-2638

West Pubnico
Musee Acadien du Pubnico Ouest • CP 92 • West Pubnico, Nova Scotia B0W 3S0 • (902) 762-3360 • http://www.sdrie.ns.ca/~museum

Whycocomagh
Whycocomagh and District Historical Society • general delivery • Whycocomagh, Nova Scotia B0E 3M0

Windsor
Haliburton House Museum Archives • 414 Clifton Av • Windsor, Nova Scotia B3M 3A6 • (902) 798-2915

Shand House Museum Archives • Avon St • Windsor, Nova Scotia B0N 2T0 • (902) 798-8213 • http://museum.gov.ns.ca

West Hants Historical Society & Library • 281 King St, POB 2335 • Windsor, Nova Scotia B0N 2T0 • (902) 798-4706 • http://www.glinx.com/users/whhs

Wolfville
Randall House Museum Archives • 259 Main St • Wolfville, Nova Scotia B4P 1C6 • (902) 542-9775

Vaughan Memorial Library • Acadia Univ, 50 Acadia St • Wolfville, Nova Scotia B4P 2R6 • (902) 585-1170 • http://library.acadiau.ca

Wolfville Historical Society & Archives • Randall House Museum, 171 Main St, POB 38 • Wolfville, Nova Scotia B0P 1X0 • (902) 542-9775

Yarmouth
Firefighters' Museum of Nova Scotia • 451 Main St • Yarmouth, Nova Scotia B5A 1G9 • (902) 742-5525

Western Counties Regional Library • 405 Main St • Yarmouth, Nova Scotia B5A 1G3 • (902) 742-2486 • http://www.westerncounties.ca/

Yarmouth County Historical Society & Archives • Historical Museum, 22 Collins St, POB 39 • Yarmouth, Nova Scotia B5A 3C8 • (902) 742-5539 • http://yarmouthcountymuseum.ednet.ns.ca • *Historiogram*

ONTARIO

Adulphustown
United Empire Loyalist Museum Archives • Adolphustown Park RR1 • Adulphustown, Ontario K0K 2T0

Agincourt
Generation Press • 172 King Henrys Blvd • Agincourt, Ontario M1T 2V6 • (416) 292-9845 • *Canadian Genealogist*

Ailsa Craig
Ailsa Craig and District Historical Society • 158 Church • Ailsa Craig, Ontario N0M 1A0 • (519) 293-9388

Ajax
Ajax Public Library • 65 Harwood Ave S • Ajax, Ontario L1S 2H8 • (905) 683-4000 • http://www.townofajax.com

Alexandria
Glengarry Historical Society & Archives • Pioneer Museum, RR1, POB 416 • Alexandria, Ontario K0C 1A0

Nor'Wester and Loyalist Museum Archives • POB 416 • Alexandria, Ontario K0C 1A0

Allanburg
Ball's Falls Historical Park • Vineland, Victoria Ave S • Allanburg, Ontario L0S 1A0 • (905) 788-1121 • http://www.conservation-niagara.on.ca/conservation-areas/ballsfalls.html

Alliston
New Tecumseth Public Library • 17 Victoria St E, POB 1199 • Alliston, Ontario L0M 1A0 • (705) 435-0250 • http://www.newtecumseth.library.on.ca

South Simcoe Pioneer Museum Archives • Riverdale Park, Fletcher Cres • Alliston, Ontario L9R 1A1 • (705) 435-0167

Almonte
Almonte Public Library • 155 High St, POB 820 • Almonte, Ontario K0A 1A0 • (613) 256-1037

North Lanark Regional Museum Archives • POB 218 • Almonte, Ontario K0A 1A0 • (613) 256-1905

Ameliasburg
Seventh Town Historical Society • 528 County Road 19 • Ameliasburg, Ontario K0K 1A0 • (613) 967-6291

Ameliasburgh Historical Museum Archives • Main St • Ameliasburgh, Ontario K0K T4O • (513) 962-1514

Ontario Genealogical Society, Quinte Branch • POB 35 • Ameliasburgh, Ontario K0K 1A0

Amherstburg
Fort Malden Historic Park Library • 100 Laird Ave, POB 38 • Amherstburg, Ontario N9V 2Z2 • (519) 736-5416 • http://www.parkscanada.gc.ca/malden

North American Black Historical Museum • 277 King St • Amherstburg, Ontario N9V 2O7 • (519) 738-5433

Ancaster
Fieldcode Museum • 300 Wilson St E • Ancaster, Ontario L9G 2B9 • (905) 548-8144

Hermitage Gatehouse Museum Archives • 838 Mineral Springs Rd • Ancaster, Ontario L9G 3L3 • (905) 648-4427

Valens Log Cabin Museum Archives • 838 Mineral Springs Rd, POB 7099 • Ancaster, Ontario L9N 3L3 • (905) 525-2183

Appin
Eidrid Township Museum Archives • general delivery • Appin, Ontario N0L 1A0

Arnprior
Arnprior and District Museum Archives • 35 Madawaska St • Arnprior, Ontario K7S 3B5 • (613) 623-4902

Astra
Royal Canadian Air Force Memorial Museum Archives • 8 Wing Trenton, POB 1000 Sm Forces • Astra, Ontario K0K 3W0 • (613) 965-2140 • http://www.rcafmuseum.on.ca

Atikokan
Atikokan Centennial Museum Archives • Civic Centre • Atikokan, Ontario P0T 1C0 • (807) 597-6585

Quetico Provincial Park Museum Library • Dawson Tr Campground, Quetico Park • Atikokan, Ontario P0T 1C0 • (807) 929-2571

Atitokan Centennial Museum and Historical Park Archives • POB 849 • Atitokan, Ontario P0T 1C0 • (807) 597-6585

Aurora
Aurora and District Historical Society & Archives • Historical Museum, 22 Church St, POB 356 • Aurora, Ontario L4G 3H4 • (416) 727-8991

Aurora Public Library • 15145 Young St • Aurora, Ontario L4G 1M1 • (905) 727-9494 • http://www.library.aurora.on.ca

Hillary House and Koffler Museum of Medicine Archives • 15372 Strange St • Aurora, Ontario L4G 1N8 • (905) 727-4015

Babcaygeon
Kewartha Settlers' Village • 85 Duran St • Babcaygeon, Ontario K0M 1A0 • (705) 738-6153

Bancroft
North Hastings Heritage Museum Archives • Station St, POB 238 • Bancroft, Ontario K0L 1C3 • (513) 332-1884

Barrie
Barrie Area Native Advisory Circle • 29 Victoria St • Barrie, Ontario L4N 2H5

Barrie Native Friendship Center • 175 Bayfield St • Barrie, Ontario L4M 3B4

Barrie Public Library • 60 Worley St • Barrie, Ontario L4M 1L6 • (705) 728-1010 • http://www.library.barrie.on.ca

Huronia Area Aboriginal Management Board • 175 Bayfield St • Barrie, Ontario L4M 3B4

Ontario Genealogical Society, Simcoe County Branch • POB 892 • Barrie, Ontario L4M 4Y6 • Simcoe County Ancestors' News

Rama and Area Native Women's Association • 29 Victoria St • Barrie, Ontario L4N 2H5

Simcoe County Historical Association & Genealogy Branch • POB 144 • Barrie, Ontario L4M 4S9

Simcoe County Museum Archives • Hwy 26, RR2 • Barrie, Ontario L0L 1Y0

Wiingashk Kwek Women's Group • 175 Bayfield St • Barrie, Ontario L4M 3B4

York Region Native Women's Association • 29 Victoria St • Barrie, Ontario L4N 2H5

Bath
Loyalist Cultural Centre • Adolphstown Park, Box 112 • Bath, Ontario K0H 1G0 • (613) 378-2196

Bayfield
Huron County Historical Society • RR1, Box 16 • Bayfield, Ontario N0M 1G0 • (519) 565-2000 • Huron Historical Notes

Beachville
Beachville District Museum Archives • S84371 Beachville Rd • Beachville, Ontario N0J 1A0 • (519) 423-6497

Beamsville
Lincoln Public Library • 4996 Beam St, POB 460 • Beamsville, Ontario L0R 1B0 • (905) 563-7014 • http://www.lincoln.library.on.ca

Beardmore
Beardmore Public Library • 185 Main St, POB 240 • Beardmore, Ontario P0T 1G0 • (807) 875-2212 • http://town.beardmore.on.ca

Ontario

Beaverton
Beaverton Thorah and Eldon Historical Society & Archives • Beaver River Museum, 284 Simcoe St • Beaverton, Ontario L0K 1A0 • (705) 426-9641

Brock Township Public Library System • 401 Simcoe St, POB 310 • Beaverton, Ontario L0K 1A0 • (705) 426-9283 • http://www.accessbrockap.com/beavlibrary.html

Belleville
Belleville Public Library • 223 Pinnacle St • Belleville, Ontario K8N 3A7 • (613) 968-6731 • http://www.bellevillelibrary.com

Glanmore National Historic Site Archives • 257 Bridge St E • Belleville, Ontario K8N 1P4 • (613) 962-2329

Hastings County Museum Archives • 157 Bridge St E • Belleville, Ontario K8N 1P4 • (613) 962-2329

Blind River
Timber Village Museum Archives • Hwy 17, 13 Michigan Ave • Blind River, Ontario P0R 1B0 • (705) 356-7544

Bloomfield
Quinta Educational Museum Archives • POB 190 • Bloomfield, Ontario K0K 1G0 • (613) 393-3752

United Empire Loyalist Museum Library • POB 215 • Bloomfield, Ontario K0K 1G0 • (613) 393-2869

Borden
Basse Borden Military Museum Archives • Worthington Park, Canadian Forces Base • Borden, Ontario L0M 1C0 • (705) 423-3531

Bothwell
Fairfield Museum Archives • 14878 Longwoods Rd • Bothwell, Ontario N0P 1C0 • (519) 692-4397

Bowmanville
Bowmanville Museum Archives • 37 Silver St, POB 188 • Bowmanville, Ontario L1C 3K9 • (905) 623-2734 • http://www.bowmanville-museum.org

Darlington Province Park Pioneer Home Archives • RR2 • Bowmanville, Ontario L1C 3K3 • (416) 723-4341

Bracebridge
Bracebridge Historical Society • Woodchester Villa, 15 King St • Bracebridge, Ontario P1L 1H4 • (705) 645-5501

Woodchester Ville • 15 King St • Bracebridge, Ontario P1L 1W1 • (705) 645-6111 • http://www.octagonalhouse.com

Bradford
Bradford-West Gwillimbury Public Library • 100 Holland Ct, POB 130 • Bradford, Ontario P0B 1C0 • (905) 775-3328 • http://www.bradford.library.on.ca

Brampton
Brampton Public Library • 65 Queen St E • Brampton, Ontario L6W 3L6 • (905) 453-2444 • http://www.bramlib.on.ca

Lorne Scots Regimental Museum Archives • 48 John St • Brampton, Ontario L6W 2H1 • (416) 451-5724

Peel Heritage Complex Archives • 9 Wellington St E • Brampton, Ontario L6W 1Y1 • (905) 791-4045 • http://www.region.peel.on.ca/heritage/hcomplex.htm

Brantford
Baptist Federation of Canada • POB 1298 • Brantford, Ontario N3T 5T6

Bell Homestead Museum Archives • 94 Tutela Heights Rd • Brantford, Ontario N3T 1A1 • (519) 756-6220 • http://www.city.brantford.on.ca

Brant Historical Society & Archives • Brandt County Museum, 57 Charlotte St • Brantford, Ontario N3T 1A1 • (519) 752-2483 • http://www.blres.on.ca/comdir/musgal/bcma

Brantford Public Library • 173 Colborne St • Brantford, Ontario N3T 2G8 • (519) 756-2220 • http://www.brantford.library.on.ca

Myrtleville House Museum Archives • 34 Myrtlesville Dr • Brantford, Ontario N3V 1C2 • (519) 752-3216 • http://www.bfree.on.ca/comdir/musgal/myrtle

Ontario Genealogical Society, Brant County Branch • 34 Market St, POB 23030 • Brantford, Ontario N3T 6K4 • (519) 753-4140 • *Newsletter of the Brant County Branch, OGS*

Brighton
Presqu'ile Provincial Park Museum Archives • Presqu'ile Provincial Park, RR4 • Brighton, Ontario K0K 1H0 • (613) 475-4324

Proctor House Museum Archives • 96 Young St • Brighton, Ontario K0K 1H0 • (613) 475-2144 • http://www.3.sympatico.ca/proctorhousemuseum

Britt
Magnetawan First Nation Public Library • RR1, Box 15 • Britt, Ontario P0G 1A0 • (705) 383-2477

Brockville
Brockville Museum Archives • 5 Henry St • Brockville, Ontario K6V 6M4 • (613) 342-4397 • http://www.cybertap.com/bmchin

Ontario Genealogical Society, Leeds and Grenville Branch • POB 536 • Brockville, Ontario K6V 5V7 • News n' Views

Bruce Mines
Bruce Mines Museum Archives • Hwy 17 • Bruce Mines, Ontario P0R 1C0 • (705) 785-3426

Burgessville
Thames Valley Museum School Archives • 656 Main St N, POB 37 • Burgessville, Ontario N0J 1C0 • (519) 424-9964 • http://www.countrycousins.org

Burlington
Ireland House Museum Archives • 2168 Guelph Line • Burlington, Ontario L7P 4M3 • (905) 332-9888

Joseph Brant Museum Archives • 1240 North Shore Blvd E • Burlington, Ontario L7S 1C5 • (905) 634-3556 • http://www.geocities.com/burlington_museums

Caledonia
Edinburgh Square Heritage and Cultural Centre Archives • 80 Caithness St E • Caledonia, Ontario N3W 2G6 • (905) 765-3134 • http://www.headstartcomp.on.ca.heritage/square

Callander
Callander Bay Heritage Museum Archives • 107 Lansdowne St E • Callander, Ontario P0H 1H0 • (705) 752-2282 • http://www.township.callander.ca/museum

Cambellcroft
Dorothy's House Museum Archives • 3632 Ganaraska Rd • Cambellcroft, Ontario L0A 1B0 • (905) 979-1170 • http://www.nhb.com/edhs.htm

Cambridge
Cambridge Libraries and Galleries • 1 North Sq • Cambridge, Ontario N1S 2K6 • (519) 621-0460 • http://www.library.cambridge.on.ca

Ontario Genealogical Society, Guerin Dit la Fontaine Chapter • 119 Pollack Ave • Cambridge, Ontario N1R 2C2

Campbellford
Campbellford-Seymour Heritage Centre Archives • 113 Front St N • Campbellford, Ontario K0L 1L0 • (705) 653-2634

Cannington
Cannington and Area Historical Society • McLeod Park • Cannington, Ontario L0E 1E0 • (705) 432-3136

Cannington Centennial Museum Archives • MacLeod Park, Peace St • Cannington, Ontario L0E 1E0 • (705) 432-3136

Carleton Place
Victoria School Museum Archives • 267 Edmund St • Carleton Place, Ontario K7C 3E8 • (613) 253-1395

Cayuga
Haldimand County Museum Archives • 8 Echo St • Cayuga, Ontario N0A 1E0 • (905) 772-5880 • http://www.haldimandcounty.on.ca

Ontario Genealogical Society, Haldimand County Branch • POB 38 • Cayuga, Ontario N0A 1E0

Chapleau
Chapleau Centennial Museum Archives • Monk St, POB 129 • Chapleau, Ontario P0M 1K0 • (705) 864-1211 • http://www.township.chapleau.on.ca

Chatham
Chatham Railroad Museum Archives • 2 McLean St • Chatham, Ontario N7M 5K5 • (5190 352-3097

Chatham-Kent Black Historical Society • 177 King Street E • Chatham, Ontario N7M 3N1 • (519) 352-3565

Chatham-Kent Museum Archives • 75 William St N • Chatham, Ontario N7M 4L4 • (519) 354-8338 • http://www.city.chatham-kent.on.ca./ccc

Chatham-Kent Public Library • 120 Queen St • Chatham, Ontario N7M 2G6 • (519) 365-2940 • http://city.chatham-kent.on.ca

Firefighting Museum Archives • 5 2nd St • Chatham, Ontario K7M 5X2 • (519) 436-3295

Milner House Museum • 75 William St N • Chatham, Ontario N7M 4L4 • (519) 360-1998 • http://www.city.chatham-kent.on.ca/ccc

Ontario Genealogical Society, Kent County Branch • POB 964 • Chatham, Ontario N7M 5L3 • *Roots Branches and Twigs*

Cheltenham
Great War Flying Museum Archives • Brampton Airport, RR1 • Cheltenham, Ontario L0P 1C0 • (905) 838-1400

Clinton
Huron County Library • RR5, Hwy 4 S • Clinton, Ontario N0M 1L0 • (519) 482-5457 • http://www.huroncap.org/hurlib

Cloyne
Cloyne Pioneer Museum Archives • POB 228 • Cloyne, Ontario K0N 1K0 • (613) 336-2203

Cobalt
Cobalt Historical Society • 21 Silver St • Cobalt, Ontario P0J 1C0 • (705) 679-5070

Cobalt's Northern Ontario Mining Museum Archives • 24 Silver St, POB 215 • Cobalt, Ontario P0J 1C0 • (706) 679-8301 • http://www.nt.net/cobalt

Cobourg
Clan Colquhoun Association of Canada • 448 Burnham St • Cobourg, Ontario K9A 2W7 • (416) 372-9446

Cobourg And District Historical Society & Archives • c/o Cobourg Public Library, 200 Ontario St • Cobourg, Ontario K9A 5P4 • (905) 377-0413

Cobourg Public Library • 200 Ontario St • Cobourg, Ontario K9A 5P4 • (905) 372-9271 • http://www.cobourg.library.on.ca

Northumberland County Public Library • 860 William St • Cobourg, Ontario K9A 3A9 • (905) 372-3329

Cochrane
Cochrane Railway and Pioneer Museum Archives • 210 Railway St • Cochrane, Ontario P0L 1C0 • (705) 272-4361 • http://www.town.cochrane.on.ca

Colborne
Township of Cramahe Public Library • 6 King St, P.O Box 190 • Colborne, Ontario K0K 1S0 • (905) 355-3722 • http://www.colbornecap.com

Coldwater
Coldwater Canadiana Heritage Museum Archives • 1474 Woodrow Rd, POB 125 • Coldwater, Ontario L0K 1E0 • (705) 835-5032

Collingwood
Colingwood Museum Archives • Memorial Park, 1 St Paul St, POB 566 • Collingwood, Ontario L9Y 3B9 • (705) 445-4811 • http://www.town.collingwood.on.ca

Collingwood Public Library • 100 2nd St • Collingwood, Ontario L9Y 1E5 • (705) 445-1571

Comber
Comber and District Historical Society • Historical Museum, 8840 Hwy 77 • Comber, Ontario N0P 1J0 • (519) 687-3332

Combermere
Madonna House Pioneer Museum Archives • general delivery • Combermere, Ontario K0J 1L0 • (613) 756-0103

Commanda
Commanda General Store Museum Archives • 4077 Hwy 552 • Commanda, Ontario P0H 1J0 • (705) 729-5121

Cornwall
Canadian Heritage-Parks Canada, Ontario Region Library • 111 Water St E • Cornwall, Ontario K6H 6S3 • (613) 938-5787

Museum of the North American Indian Travelling College • RR3 • Cornwall, Ontario K6H 5R7 • (613) 832-9454

Societe Franco-Ontarienne d'Histoire et de Genealogie, Region Saint-Laurent • CP 1894 • Cornwall, Ontario K6H 6N6

Stormont, Dundas and Glengarry Historical Society & Library • POB 773 • Cornwall, Ontario K6H 5T5 • (613) 932-2381

United Counties Museum Archives • 731 2nd St W, POB 773 • Cornwall, Ontario K6H 5T5 • (613) 932-2281

Cornwall Island
North American Indian Travelling College • RR3 • Cornwall Island, Ontario K6H 5R7

Cumberland
Cumberland Township Heritage Museum Archives • 2940 Queen St, POB 159 • Cumberland, Ontario K4C 1E6 • (613) 833-3059

Delhi
Delhi Ontario Tobacco Museum and Heritage Centre • 200 Talbot Rd • Delhi, Ontario N4B 2A2 • (519) 582-0278

Delhi Township Public Library • 192 Main St • Delhi, Ontario N4B 2M2 • (519) 582-1791 • http://www.simcom.on.ca/~delpub

Teeterville Pioneer Museum Archives • 200 Talbot Rd • Delhi, Ontario N4B 2A2 • (519) 582-0278

Delphi
Ontario Genealogical Society, Norfolk County Branch • POB 145 • Delphi, Ontario N4B 2W9

Delta
Delta Mill and Old Stone Mill Museum Archives • POB 172 • Delta, Ontario K0E 1G0 • (613) 928-2584 • http://www.rideau-info.com/delta/stonemill.html

Deseronto
Deseronto Public Library • 309 Main St W, POB 302 • Deseronto, Ontario K0K 1X0 • (613) 395-2744

Dresden
Uncle Tom's Cabin Historic Site Archives • 29251 Uncle Tom's Rd • Dresden, Ontario N0P 1M0 • (519) 583-2978 • http://www.uncletomscabin.org

Dryden
Dryden and District Museum Archives • 15 Van Horne Ave • Dryden, Ontario P8N 2A5 • (807) 223-4671

Dryden Public Library • 36 Van Horne Ave • Dryden, Ontario P8N 2A7 • (807) 223-1475 • http://www.dryden.virtual-library.org

Ontario

Dundas

Dundas Historical Society & Archives • Historical Museum, 139 Park St W • Dundas, Ontario L9H 5G1 • (905) 627-7412

Dundas Public Library • 18 Ogilvie St • Dundas, Ontario L9H 2S2 • (905) 627-3507

Dunvegan

Glengarry Pioneer Museum Archives • 1645 County Rd 30 • Dunvegan, Ontario K0C 1J0 • (613) 527-5230 • http://www.glen-net.ca/museums

Durham

West Gray Public Library • 240 Garafraxa St N, POB 706 • Durham, Ontario N0G 1R0 • (519) 369-2107

Ear Falls

Ear Falls District Museum Archives • Hwy 105, POB 309 • Ear Falls, Ontario P0W 1T0 • (807) 222-3198 • http://www.town.earfalls.on.ca

East York

Canadian Macedonian Historical Society • 850 O'Connor Dr • East York, Ontario M4B 3L6 • (416) 755-3117

Elgin

Kingston Mills Blockhouse Museum Archives • POB 10 • Elgin, Ontario K0G 1E0 • (613) 359-5377

Rideau Lakes Union Library • Halladay St, POB 89 • Elgin, Ontario K0G 1E0 • (613) 359-5334 • http://www.king.igs.net/~elgin

Elk Lake

Elk Lake Heritage Museum Archives • Rosedale, POB 70 • Elk Lake, Ontario P0J 1G0 • (705) 678-2237

Elliot Lake

Elliot Lake Nuclear and Mining Museum Archives • Lester B Pearson Civic Center, Hwy 108 • Elliot Lake, Ontario P5A 2T1 • (705) 848-2084

Elliot Lake Public Library • Algo Centre Mall, 151 Ontario Ave • Elliot Lake, Ontario P5A 2T2 • (705) 461-7204

Emo

Rainy River District Women's Institute Museum Archives • POB 511 • Emo, Ontario P0W 1E0 • (807) 482-2007

Englehart

Englehart and Area Historical Museum Archives • 67 6th Ave • Englehart, Ontario P0J 1H0 • (705) 544-2400 • http://www.museumnorth.org

Englehart and Area Public Library • 71 4th Ave, POB 809 • Englehart, Ontario P0J 1H0 • (705) 544-2100

Espanola

Espanola Public Library • 245 Avery Dr, POB 1187 • Espanola, Ontario P0P 1C0 • (705) 869-2940 • http://www.etown.net/library

Etobicoke

Clan Mackay Association of Canada • 52 Mendota Rd • Etobicoke, Ontario M8Y 1G2 • (416) 251-3894 • http://www.clanmackayusa.org

Montgomery's Inn Museum Archives • 4709 Dundas St W • Etobicoke, Ontario M9A 1A8 • (416) 394-8113 • http://www.montgomerysinn.com

Fenelon Falls

Fenelon Falls Museum Archives • 50 Oak St • Fenelon Falls, Ontario K0M 1N0 • (705) 887-3343

Fergus

Wellington County Historical Society • POB 5 • Fergus, Ontario N1M 2W7

Wellington County Museum and Archives • Wellington Pl, RR1 • Fergus, Ontario N1M 2W3 • (519) 846-0916 • http://www.wcm.on.ca

Wellington County Public Library • 522 Wellington Rd 18, RR1 • Fergus, Ontario N1M 2W3 • (519) 846-0918 • http://www.county.wellington.on.ca

Flesherton

Flesherton Public Library • 10 Elizabeth St • Flesherton, Ontario N0C 1E0 • (519) 924-2241 • http://www.bmts.com/~fletub

South Grey Museum and Historical Library • Memorial Park, 40 Syderham St • Flesherton, Ontario M0C 1E0 • (519) 924-2843 • http://www.greycounty.on.ca/museum/southgrey.html

Forest

Forest Lambton Museum Archives • 59 Broadway, RR1, POB 707 • Forest, Ontario N0N 1J0 • (519) 786-3239

Fort Erie

Fort Erie Public Library • 136 Gilmore Rd • Fort Erie, Ontario L2A 2M1 • (905) 871-2546

Fort Erie Railroad Museum Archives • Central Ave • Fort Erie, Ontario L2A 3S2 • (905) 871-1412

Fort Frances

Fort Frances Museum Archives • 259 Scott St • Fort Frances, Ontario P9A 1G8 • (807) 274-7891 • http://www.fort-frances.com/museum

Fort Saint Pierre Museum Archives • Pither's Point Park • Fort Frances, Ontario P9A 1G8 • (807) 274-7391 • http://www.fort-frances.com/museum

Frankford

Frankford Public Library • 12 Trent St N, POB 550 • Frankford, Ontario K0K 2C0 • (613) 398-7572

Frankford

Orval Berry Museum Archives • 46 Belleville St • Frankford, Ontario K0K 2C0 • (613) 398-6531

Gananoque

Gananoque Historical Museum Archives • 10 King St, POB 293 • Gananoque, Ontario K7G 2T7 • (613) 382-4663

Gananoque Public Library • 100 Park St • Gananoque, Ontario K7G 2Y5 • (613) 382-2436

Georgetown

Esquesing Historical Society • POB 51 • Georgetown, Ontario L7G 4T1

Halton Hills Public Libraries • 9 Church St • Georgetown, Ontario L7G 2A3 • (905) 873-2681 • http://www.library.hhpl.on.ca

Glencoe

Glencoe Historical Society • 247 Main • Glencoe, Ontario N0L 1M0 • (519) 287-3897

Gloucester

Gloucester Historical Society & Archives • Historical Museum, 4550 Bank St • Gloucester, Ontario K1G 3N4 • (613) 822-2076

Goderich

Huron County Museum Archives • 110 N Street • Goderich, Ontario N7A 2T8 • (519) 524-2686 • http://www.odyssey.on.ca/~hcm-chin

Ontario Genealogical Society, Huron County Branch • POB 469 • Goderich, Ontario N7A 5C7

Golden Lake

Algonquin Culture and Heritage Centre Archives • 1674 Mishomis Inamo • Golden Lake, Ontario K0J 1X0 • (613) 625-2823

Gore Bay

Western Manitoulin Historical Society & Archives • Historical Museum, Dawson St, POB 145 • Gore Bay, Ontario P0P 1H0 • (705) 282-2114

Gormley

Whitchurch-Stouffville Museum Archives • 14732 Woodbine Ave • Gormley, Ontario L0H 1G0 • (905) 727-8954 • http://www.townd.ws.com/museum.php

Gowganda

Gowganda and Area Museum Archives • general delivery • Gowganda, Ontario P0J 1J0 • (705) 624-3171

Gow-Ganda
Gow-Ganda and Area Museum Archives • general delivery • Gow-Ganda, Ontario P0J 1J0

Grafton
Barnum House Museum Archives • Hwy 2, Cherry Hill Rd • Grafton, Ontario K0K 2G0 • (905) 349-2656

Grand Bend
Lambton Heritage Museum Archives • RR2 • Grand Bend, Ontario N0M 1T0 • (519) 243-2600

Gravenhurst
Bethune Memorial House Museum Archives • 235 John St N • Gravenhurst, Ontario P1P 1G4 • (705) 687-4261 • http://www.parkscanada.qc.ca/bethune

Muskoka Steamship and Historical Society • 821 Bay St • Gravenhurst, Ontario P1P 1G7 • (705) 687-2115

Segwun Heritage Centre Archives • Gravenhurst Bay, POB 1283 • Gravenhurst, Ontario P0C 1G0 • (705) 687-6667

Grimsby
Grimsby Museum Archives • 6 Murray St • Grimsby, Ontario L3M 4G5 • (905) 945-5292

Stone Shop Museum Archives • 271 Main St W • Grimsby, Ontario L3M 1G3

Guelph
Guelph Museum Archives • 6 Dublin St S • Guelph, Ontario N1H 4L5 • (519) 836-1221 • http://www.museum.guelph.on.ca

Guelph Public Library • 100 Norfolk St • Guelph, Ontario N1H 4J6 • (519) 824-6220 • http://www.library.guelph.on.ca

Hagarsville
Mississaugas of the New Credit Indian Reserve • RR6 • Hagarsville, Ontario N0A 1H0

Haileybury
Haileybury Public Library • 545 Lakeshore Rd, POB 2090 • Haileybury, Ontario P0J 1K0 • (705) 672-3707 • http://www.haileyburylibrary.com

Hamilton
Dundurn Catle Museum Archives • 610 York Blvd • Hamilton, Ontario L8R 3H1 • (906) 522-5313 • http://www.city.hamilton.on.ca

Hamilton Military Museum Archives • Dundurn Park, York Blvd • Hamilton, Ontario L8R 3H1 • (905) 546-4974 • http://www.hamilton.ca

Hamilton Public Library • 55 York Blvd, POB 2700 • Hamilton, Ontario L8R 3K1 • (905) 546-3200 • http://www.hpl.ca

Head-of-the-Lake Historical Society • POB 896, LCD1 • Hamilton, Ontario L8N 3P6

Ontario Genealogical Society, Hamilton Branch • 155 Macassa Ave, POB 904 • Hamilton, Ontario L8N 3P6 • (905) 318-8086 • http://www.ogs.on.ca • *Hamilton Branch, Ontario Genealogical Society Newsletter*

Royal Hamilton Light Infantry Heritage Museum Archives • 200 James St N • Hamilton, Ontario L8R 2L1 • (905) 528-2945

Saint Joseph's Mountain Site Museum Archives • 100 W 5th St • Hamilton, Ontario L8N 3K7 • (905) 388-2511

Wentworth Library • 70 Frid St, Suite 1 • Hamilton, Ontario L8P 4M4 • (905) 546-4126 • http://www.wentworth.library.on.ca

Westfield Heritage Centre Archives • Hwy 52, POB 910 • Hamilton, Ontario L0R 1X0 • (519) 621-8851

Whitehorn Historic House Archives • 41 Jackson St W • Hamilton, Ontario L8P 1L3 • (905) 546-2018

Hanmer
Valley East Public Library • 4100 Elmview Dr • Hanmer, Ontario P3P 1J7 • (705) 969-5565 • http://www.atbs.com/velib.html

Hanover
Hanover Public Library • 341 10th St • Hanover, Ontario N4N 1P5 • (519) 364-1420

Harrow
Harrow Early Immigrant Research Society & Library • POB 53 • Harrow, Ontario N0R 1G0 • (519) 738-2500

John R Park Homestead Museum Archives • 915 Cty Rd 50 E • Harrow, Ontario N0R 1G0 • (519) 738-2029 • http://www.erca.org

Hawkesbury
Hawkesbury Public Library • 550 Higginson St • Hawkesbury, Ontario K6A 1H1 • (613) 632-0106 • http://www.bibliotheque.hawkesbury.on.ca

Hilton Beach
Hilton Union Public Library • 3085 Marks St, RR1 • Hilton Beach, Ontario P0R 1G0 • (705) 246-2557

Holland Centre
Comber Pioneer Village Museum Archives • Rte 3 • Holland Centre, Ontario N0H 1R0 • (519) 794-3467

Hull
Canadian Heritage Library • 15 rue Eddy, Rm 2E2 • Hull, Ontario K1A 0M5 • (819) 994-5478

Huntsville
Huntsville Public Library • 7 Minerva St E • Huntsville, Ontario P1H 1W4 • (705) 789-5232 • http://www.huntsville.publiclibraries.net

Muskoka Pioneer Village and Museum Archives • Huntsville Park, 88 Brunel Rd, POB 2802 • Huntsville, Ontario P0A 1K0 • (705) 789-7576 • http://www.muskokaheritageplace.org

Ignace
Ignace Heritage Centre Archives • 36 Hwy 17 W • Ignace, Ontario P0T 1T0 • (807) 934-2280

Ingersoll
Oxford County Library • 130 Oxford St • Ingersoll, Ontario N5C 2V5 • (519) 485-7394 • http://www.ocl.net

Innisville
Innisville and District Museum Archives • Hwy 7 N • Innisville, Ontario K0A 1J0 • (613) 253-1604

Iroquois
Carman House Museum Archives • Carman Rd S • Iroquois, Ontario K0E 1K0 • (613) 652-4422

Iroquois Falls
Iroquois Falls Pioneer Museum Archives • 245 Devonshire Ave • Iroquois Falls, Ontario P0K 1E0 • (705) 258-3730 • http://www.iroquoisfallsmuseum.com

Jarvis
Nanticoke Public Library • 2 Monson St, POB 399 • Jarvis, Ontario N0A 1J0 • (519) 587-4293

Jordan
Jordan Historical Museum of the Twenty Archives • 3802 Main St • Jordan, Ontario L0R 1S0 • (905) 562-5242 • http://tourismniagara.com/jordan.museum

Kakabeka Falls
Hymers Museum Archives • RR1 • Kakabeka Falls, Ontario P0T 1W0

Kapuskasing
Ron Morel Memorial Museum Archives • 88 Riverside Dr • Kapuskasing, Ontario P5N 1B3 • (705) 335-5443

Keene
Lang Pioneer Village Archives • general delivery • Keene, Ontario K0L 2G0 • (705) 295-6694 • http://www.langpioneerviolage.ca

Ontario

Keewatin
Keewatin Public Library • 812 Ottawa St, POB 602 • Keewatin, Ontario P0X 1C0 • (807) 547-2145

Kenora
Grand Council Treaty Number 3 • POB 1720 • Kenora, Ontario P9N 3X7

Kenora Public Library • 24 Main St S • Kenora, Ontario P9N 1S7 • (807) 467-2081 • http://www.library.kenora.com

Lake of the Woods Museum Archives • 300 Main St S • Kenora, Ontario P9N 3X5 • (807) 467-2105 • http://www.lakeofthewoodsmuseum.ca

Ojibway Nation • Lake of the Woods Ojibway Cultural Centre, POB 159, Airport Rd • Kenora, Ontario P9N 3X3

Keswick
Georgina Pioneer Museum Archives • Civic Centre Rd • Keswick, Ontario L4P 3E9 • (905) 476-4301 • http://www.town.georgina.on.ca

Killarney
Killarney Centennial Museum Archives • 32 Commissioners St • Killarney, Ontario P0M 2A0 • (705) 287-2424

King City
King Township Historical Museum Archives • 2920 King Rd • King City, Ontario L7B 1L6 • (905) 727-6322

King Township Public Library • 190 King Rd, POB 399 • King City, Ontario L7B 1A6 • (905) 833-5101 • http://www.king-library.on.ca

Kingston
Bellevue House Museum Archives • 35 Centre St • Kingston, Ontario K7L 4E5 • (613) 545-8666 • http://parkscanada.pch.qc.ca

Canada's Penitentiary Museum Archives • 555 King St W • Kingston, Ontario K7L 4Y6 • (513) 530-3122

Canadian Forces Communications Museum Archives • Vimy Barracks, Canadian Forces Base • Kingston, Ontario K7L 5L0 • (613) 541-5395

Fort Henry Museum Archives • Hwys 2 & 15, POB 213 • Kingston, Ontario K7L 4V8 • (613) 542-7388 • http://www.forthenry.com

Frontenac County Schools Museum Archives • 559 Bagot St • Kingston, Ontario K7K 3E1 • (613) 544-9113

Kingston Fire Department Museum Archives • 271 Brock St • Kingston, Ontario K7L 1S5 • (613) 542-9727

Kingston Frontenac Public Library • 130 Johnson St • Kingston, Ontario K7L 1X8 • (613) 549-8888 • http://www.kfpl.library.on.ca

Kingston Historical Society • POB 54 • Kingston, Ontario K7L 4V6 • (613) 531-8948 • Historic Kingston

Marine Museum of the Great Lakes • 55 Ontario St • Kingston, Ontario K7L 2Y2 • (613) 542-2261 • http://www.marmuseum.ca

Military Communications and Electronics Museum Archives • Canadian Forces Base, POB 17000 • Kingston, Ontario K7K 7B4 • (613) 541-5395 • http://www.c-and-a-museum.org

Murrey Tower Museum Archives • King & Barrie Sts • Kingston, Ontario K7L 1X0 • (613) 544-9925

Museum of Health Care Archives • Ann Baillie Bldg, George St • Kingston, Ontario K7L 2V7 • (613) 548-2419 • http://www.museumofhealthcare.ca

Ontario Genealogical Society, Kingston Branch • POB 1394 • Kingston, Ontario K7L 5C6 • (416) 489-0734 • *Ontario Genealogical Society, Kingston Branch Newsletter*; *Kingston Relations*

Pump House Steam Museum Archives • 23 Ontario St • Kingston, Ontario K7L 2Y2 • (613) 546-4896 • http://www.marmus.ca

Royal Military College of Canada Museum Archives • 4 Point Frederick Dr, RMC Campus • Kingston, Ontario K7L 7B4 • (613) 541-6000 • http://www.rmc.ca/museum

Stauffer Library • Queen's University • Kingston, Ontario K7L 5C4 • (613) 533-2527 • http://www.stauffer.queensu.ca

Kingsville
Southern Ontario Heritage Village Archives • general delivery • Kingsville, Ontario N9Y 2E5 • (519) 776-6909 • http://www.cnis.com/swo_heritage_village

Kirkland Lake
Moose Factory Centennial Museum Archives • general delivery • Kirkland Lake, Ontario P2N 3H6 • (705) 567-4500

Museum of Northern History Archives • Sir Henry Oakes Chateau, 2 Chateau Dr, POB 966 • Kirkland Lake, Ontario P2N 3L1 • (705) 568-8800

Ontario Library Service • 11 Station Rd S • Kirkland Lake, Ontario P2N 3H2 • (705) 567-3341 • http://www.library.on.ca

Teck Centennial Library • 10 Kirkland St E • Kirkland Lake, Ontario P2N 1K1 • (705) 567-7966 • http://www.nt.net/teck

Kitchener
Doon Heritage Crossroads Archives • 10 Huron Rd • Kitchener, Ontario N2P 2R7 • (519) 748-1914 • http://www.region.waterloo.on.ca/doon

Joseph Schneider Haus Museum Archives • 466 Queen St S • Kitchener, Ontario N2G 1W7 • (519) 742-7752 • http://www.region.waterloo.on.ca

Kitchener Public Library • 85 Queen St N • Kitchener, Ontario N2H 2H1 • (519) 743-0271 • http://www.kpl.org

Ontario Genealogical Society, Waterloo-Wellington Branch • POB 43030, RPO Eastwood Sq • Kitchener, Ontario N2H 6S9 • Branch Notes

Waterloo Historical Society & Library • 85 Queen Street N • Kitchener, Ontario N2H 2H1 • (416) 743-0271 • http://www.ist.uwaterloo.ca • *Waterloo Historical Society Annual Volume*

Woodside National Historic Site Archives • 528 Wellington St N • Kitchener, Ontario N2H 5L5 • (519) 571-5684 • http://parkscanada.pch.qc.ca/parks/ontario/woodside

Komoka
Komoka Railway Museum Archives • 133 Queen St • Komoka, Ontario N0L 1R0 • (519) 657-1912 • http://www.komokarail.ca

Lakefield
Christ Church Community Museum Archives • POB 1542 • Lakefield, Ontario K0L 2H0

Lakefield Public Library • 2 Queen St, POB 2200 • Lakefield, Ontario K0L 2H0 • (705) 652-8623 • http://www.kawartha.net/~caplake

Lanark
Middleville Museum Archives • RR2 • Lanark, Ontario K0G 1K0 • (613) 259-5462

Lancaster
Glengarry and Area Genealogial Library • 20342 Arlington Rd, RR1 • Lancaster, Ontario K0C 1N0 • (613) 347-3180

Glengarry Genealogical Society • RR1 • Lancaster, Ontario K0C 1N0

Latchford
House of Memories • POB 82 • Latchford, Ontario P0J 1N0 • (705) 676-2417

Leamington
Leamington Public Library • 1 John St • Leamington, Ontario N8H 1H1 • (519) 326-3441

Limehouse
Canadian Military Studies Museum Archives • RR1 • Limehouse, Ontario L0P 1H0 • (905) 877-6522

Lindsay
City of Kawartha Lakes Library • 190 Kent St W, POB 9000 • Lindsay, Ontario K9V 5R8 • (705) 324-9411 • http://www.city.kawarthalakes.on.ca

Victoria County Historical Society • Historical Museum, 322 Kent St W • Lindsay, Ontario K9V 4R8 • (705) 324-6756

Listowel
Northperth Public Library • 260 Main St W • Listowel, Ontario N4W 1A1 • (519) 291-4621 • http://www.northperth.library.on.ca

Lively
Walden Public Library • 15 Kin Dr, POB 189 • Lively, Ontario P3Y 1M3 • (705) 692-4749

London
Association of Iroquois and Allied Indians • 920 Commissioners Rd E • London, Ontario N5Z 3J1

Dadswell Research • 1310 Brydges St • London, Ontario N5W 2C4 • (519) 451-7594 • *Dadswell Family Bulletin*

Eldon House Museum Archives • 421 Ridout St N • London, Ontario N6A 2P8 • (519) 672-4580 • http://www.londonmuseum.on.ca

Fanshawe Pioneer Village • 2609 Fanshawe Park Rd E • London, Ontario N5X 4A1 • (519) 457-1296 • http://www.pioneer.wwdc.com

First Hussars Citizen Soldiers Museum Archives • 399 Ridout St N • London, Ontario N6A 2P1 • (519) 471-1538

Grosvenor Lodge Museum Archives • 1017 Western Rd • London, Ontario N6G 1G5 • (519) 645-2845

London and Middlesex Historical Society & Archives • Historical Museum, 1017 Western Rd, POB 303, Sta B • London, Ontario N6A 4W1 • (519) 661-5165 • *Transactions of the London and Middlesex Historical Society*

London Public Libraries • 305 Queens Ave • London, Ontario N6B 3L7 • (519) 661-4600 • http://www.discover.lpl.london.on.ca

Ontario Genealogical Society, London and Middlesex Branch • c/o Grosvenor Lodge Museum, 1017 Western Rd • London, Ontario N6G 1G5 • (519) 679-3398 • *London Leaf*

Royal Canadian Regiment Museum Archives • Wolseley Hall, 750 Elizabeth St • London, Ontario N5Y 4T7 • (519) 679-5773 • http://www.army.dnd.ca/rcr_rhq/english/museum

Lucan
Donelly Homestead Museum Archives • 34937 Roman Line, RR3 • Lucan, Ontario N0M 2J0 • (519) 227-1244 • http://www.quadro.net/~donnelly

Magnetawan
Magnetawan Historical Museum Archives • Hwy 520 at Biddy St, POB 130 • Magnetawan, Ontario P0A 1P0 • (705) 387-3308

Manitoulin
Ojibwe Cultural Foundation • POB 278 • Manitoulin, Ontario P0P 1G0

Manitowaning
Assiginack Historical Society & Archives • Historical Museum, Arthur St, Norisle Park • Manitowaning, Ontario P0P 1N0 • (705) 859-3905

Manotick
Watson's Mill Museum Archives • 5525 Dickinson St • Manotick, Ontario K4M 1A2 • (613) 682-6455

Markdale
Walter Harris Memorial Library • 75 Walker St, POB 499 • Markdale, Ontario N0C 1H0 • (519) 986-3436 • http://www.bmts.com/~library

Markham
Markham Museum and Historic Village Archives • 9350 Hwy 48 • Markham, Ontario L3P 3J3 • (905) 294-4576 • http://www.markham.on.ca

Markham Public Libraries • 445 Apple Creek Blvd, Suite 100 • Markham, Ontario L3R 9X7 • (905) 513-7977 • http://www.city.markham.on.ca/mpl/

Marten River
Marten River Logging Museum Archives • general delivery • Marten River, Ontario P0H 1T0 • (705) 892-2200

Martintown
Cornwall Township Historical Society • RR2 • Martintown, Ontario K0C 1S0

Massey
Massey Area Museum Archives • 160 Sauble St • Massey, Ontario P0P 1P0 • (705) 865-2268

Matheson
Thelma Miles Museum Archives • POB 601 • Matheson, Ontario P0K 1N0 • (705) 273-2325

Mattawa
Mattawa and District Museum Archives • 285 1st St • Mattawa, Ontario P0H 1V0 • (705) 744-5495

Mattawa District Historical Society • 285 1st St • Mattawa, Ontario P0H 1V0

Voyageur Heritage Centre Archives • Samuel de Champlain Provincial Park, Hwy 17 • Mattawa, Ontario P0H 1V0 • (705) 744-2276

Meaford
Meaford Museum Archives • 111 Bayfield St • Meaford, Ontario N4L 1H1 • (519) 538-5974 • http://www.meaford.com

Meldrum
Mississagi Strait Lighthouse Museum Archives • general delivery • Meldrum, Ontario P0P 1R0 • (705) 283-3011

Meldrum Bay
Ned Shed Museum Archives • Water St • Meldrum Bay, Ontario P0P 1R0 • (705) 283-3385

Merrickville
Blockhouse Museum Archives • St Lawrence & Main Sts, POB 294 • Merrickville, Ontario K0G 2B4 • (613) 269-3614

Mersea
Leamington And Mersea Historical Society • Con 9 • Mersea, Ontario N0R 1B0 • (519) 326-7252

Midland
Georgian Bay Nation • Georgian Bay Native Friendship Centre, 175 Younge St • Midland, Ontario L4R 2A7

Historic Naval and Military Establishments Archives • POB 160 • Midland, Ontario L4R 4K8 • (705) 526-7838

Huronia Museum Archives • 549 Little Lake Park, POB 638 • Midland, Ontario L4R 4P4 • (705) 526-2844 • http://www.huroniamuseum.com

Martyrs' Shrine Archives • 16163 Hwy 12 W • Midland, Ontario L4R 4K5 • (705) 526-3788 • http://www.jesuits.ca/martyrs-shrine

Milford
Corporation of the County of Prince Edward Island Library • 3053 County Rd 10, POB 77 • Milford, Ontario K0K 2P0 • (613) 476-4130 • http://www.pec.on.ca/library/

Mariners' Park Museum Archives • Cty 1349 & RR2 • Milford, Ontario K0K 2P0 • (613) 476-4695

Millbrook
Millbrook and Cavan Historical Society • POB 334 • Millbrook, Ontario L0A 1G0

Milton
Association of Philipps du Trieux Descendants • 55 Ontario St S, POB 23074 • Milton, Ontario L9T 5B4 • (905) 878-4205 • *Association of Philipps du Trieux Descendants Newsletter*

Halton Museum Archives • Kelso Park, RR3 • Milton, Ontario L9T 2X7 • (416) 878-3232 • http://www.region.halton.on.ca/museum

Milton Historical Society • Waldie Black-Smith Shop, 16 James St • Milton, Ontario L9T 2P4 • (905) 875-4156

Ontario Agricultural Museum Archives • general delivery • Milton, Ontario L9T 2V3 • (905) 878-8151

Streetcar and Electric Railway Museum Archives • 13629 Guelph Line Rd, POB 578 • Milton, Ontario L9T 5A2 • (519) 856-9802 • http://www.hcry.org

Ontario

Minesing
Simcoe County Archives • 1149 Hwy 26, RR 2 • Minesing, Ontario L0L 1Y0 • (705) 726-9331 • http://www.county.simcoe.on.ca

Simcoe County Museum Archives • RR2 • Minesing, Ontario L0L 1Y0 • (705) 728-3721 • http://www.county.simcoe.on.ca

Mississauga
Benares Historic House Museum Archives • 1507 Clarkson Rd N • Mississauga, Ontario L5J 2W8 • (905) 822-2347 • http://www.museumsofmississauga.com

Bradley Museum Archives • 1620 Orr Rd • Mississauga, Ontario L5J 4T2 • (905) 822-1569 • http://www.museumsofmississauga.com

Lithuanian Museum-Archives of Canada • 2185 Stavebank Rd • Mississauga, Ontario L5C 1T3 • (905) 566-8755 • http://daryl.chin.qc.ca

Mississauga Library System • 301 Burnhamthorpe Rd W • Mississauga, Ontario L5B 3Y3 • (905) 615-3500 • http://www.city.mississiauga.on.ca/library

Mooretown
Moore Museum Archives • 94 Moore Ln • Mooretown, Ontario N0N 1M0 • (519) 867-2020 • http://www.timewellspent.ca

Morrisburg
Ontario Genealogical Society, Saint Lawrence United Empire Loyalist Branch • POB 607 • Morrisburg, Ontario K0C 1X0

Upper Canada Village Archives • 13740 Cty Rd 2 • Morrisburg, Ontario N0C 1Z3 • (513) 543-3704 • http://www.uppercanadavillage.ca

Mount Hope
Canadian Warplane Heritage Museum Archives • Hamilton Airport, 9280 Airport Rd • Mount Hope, Ontario L0R 1W0 • (906) 679-4183 • http://www.warplane.com

Napanee
Alan Macpherson House Archives • 180 Elizabeth St • Napanee, Ontario K7R 3M3 • (613) 354-5982 • http://www.horizons.net/macpherson

Lennox and Addington County Museum Library • 97 Thomas St E, POB 1000 • Napanee, Ontario K7R 3S9 • (613) 354-3027 • http://home.fox.nstn.ca/~museum

Lennox and Addington County Public Library • 97 Thomas St E • Napanee, Ontario K7R 3S9 • (613) 354-2525

Navan
Cumberland Township Historical Society • 4560 Ruissellet Rd • Navan, Ontario K1E 2N7

Nepean
Algonquin College Museum Archives • 1385 Woodoffe Ave • Nepean, Ontario K2G 1V8 • (613) 727-4723

Log Farm Museum Archives • 670 Cedarview Rd • Nepean, Ontario K2G 1E2 • (613) 825-4362

Nepean Central Library • Ben Franklin Pl, 101 Centrepointe Dr • Nepean, Ontario K2G 5K7 • (613) 727-6646

Nepean Museum Archives • 16 Rowley Ave • Nepean, Ontario K2G 1L9 • (613) 723-7936

New Liskeard
Temiskaming Genealogy Group • POB 1568 • New Liskeard, Ontario P0J 1P0

Newmarket
Elman W Campbell Museum Archives • 134 Main St S • Newmarket, Ontario L3V 3Y7 • (905) 953-5314 • http://www.town.newmarket.on.ca

Gillespie Research Foundation • 266 Maciver Blvd • Newmarket, Ontario L3X 1Y5

Niagara Falls
Laura Secord Homestead Museum Archives • 7556 Montrose Rd • Niagara Falls, Ontario L2H 2E9

Lundy's Lane Historical Museum Library • 5810 Ferry St • Niagara Falls, Ontario L2G 1S9 • (905) 358-5082 • http://www.lundyslanemuseum.com

McFarland House Museum Archives • Niagara Pkwy, POB 150 • Niagara Falls, Ontario L2E 6T2 • (905) 371-0254 • http://www.niagaraparks.com

Niagara Falls Public Library • 4848 Victoria Ave • Niagara Falls, Ontario L2E 4C5 • (905) 356-8080 • http://www.nfpl.library.on.ca

Old Fort Erie Museum Archives • Niagara River Pkwy, POB 150 • Niagara Falls, Ontario L2E 6T2 • (905) 871-0540

Willoughby Historical Museum Archives • 9935 Niagara Pkwy • Niagara Falls, Ontario L2E 6S6 • (905) 295-4036 • http://niagara.becon.org/~willomus

Niagara-on-the-Lake
Fort George National Historic Park Archives • POB 787 • Niagara-on-the-Lake, Ontario L0S 1J0 • (905) 468-4257

Niagara Apothecary Archives • 5 Queens St • Niagara-on-the-Lake, Ontario L0S 1J0 • (416) 962-4861 • http://www.ocpharma.com

Niagara Fire Museum Archives • POB 498 • Niagara-on-the-Lake, Ontario L0S 1J0 • (905) 468-7279

Niagara Historical Society & Archives • Historical Museum, 43 Castlereagh St, POB 208 • Niagara-on-the-Lake, Ontario L0S 1J0 • (905) 468-1728 • http://www.niagara.com/~nhs

Niagara-on-the-Lake Public Library • Rear 26 Queen St, POB 430 • Niagara-on-the-Lake, Ontario L0S 1J0 • (905) 468-2023 • http://www.vaxxine.com/fa/notlpl/

Nipigon
Nipigon Museum Archives • POB 208 • Nipigon, Ontario P0T 2J0 • (807) 887-2727

Nipigon Township Public Library • 25 3rd St, POB 728 • Nipigon, Ontario P0T 2J0 • (807) 887-3142 • http://nipigon.lakeheadu.ca/~niplib/nnpl.html

Nipissing
Nipissing Township Museum • general delivery • Nipissing, Ontario P0H 1W0 • (705) 724-2938

North Bay
Dionne Homestead Museum Archives • POB 747 • North Bay, Ontario P1B 8J8 • (705) 472-8480

North Bay Historical Society and Area Museum Archives • 171 Main St W • North Bay, Ontario P1B 8J5 • (705) 476-2323

North Bay Public Library • 271 Worthington St E • North Bay, Ontario P1B 1H1 • (705) 495-3271 • http://www.city.north-bay.on.ca

Ontario Genealogical Society, Nipissing District Branch • POB 93 • North Bay, Ontario P1B 8G8

North Buxton
Buxton Museum Archives • 21975 AD Shadd Rd • North Buxton, Ontario N0P 1Y0 • (519) 352-4799 • http://www.buxtonmuseum.com

North York
Black Creek Pioneer Village Archives • 1000 Murray Ross Pkwy • North York, Ontario M3J 2P3 • (416) 736-1733 • http://www.blackcreek.ca

Gibson House Museum Archives • 5172 Yonge St • North York, Ontario M2N 5P6 • (416) 395-7432

Irving E and Ray Kanner Heritage Museum Archives • 3580 Bathurst St • North York, Ontario M6A 2E1 • (416) 789-2500

Ontario Genealogical Society & Library • 5120 Yonge St • North York, Ontario M2N 5N9 • (416) 395-4523 • http://www.interlog.com/~dreed/ogs_home.htm

Ontario Historical Society • 34 Parkview Ave • North York, Ontario M2N 3Y2 • (416) 226-9011

University of Toronto Press • 5201 Dufferin St • North York, Ontario M3H 5T8 • (416) 667-7810 • *Canadian Historical Review*

Norwich
Norwich and District Historical Society Archives & Library • 91 Stover St N, RR3 • Norwich, Ontario N0J 1P0 • (519) 863-3638

Norwich and District Museum Archives • RR3 • Norwich, Ontario N0J 1P0 • (519) 863-3101 • http://www.ocl.net/projects/norwich_historical/museum/

Oakville
Bronte Historical Society • 7 W River St • Oakville, Ontario L6L 6N9 • (905) 825-5552

Oakville Historical Society & Archives • Erchless Estate, 8 Navy St • Oakville, Ontario L6J 2Y5 • (905) 338-4400 • http://www.oakvillemuseum.com

Oakville Public Library • 120 Navy St • Oakville, Ontario L6J 2Z4 • (905) 815-2042 • http://www.opl.on.ca

Ontario Genealogical Society, Halton-Peel Branch • 2441 Lakeshore Rd W, POB 70030 • Oakville, Ontario L6L 6M9

Odessa
Historic Babcock Mill Museum Archives • 100 Bridge St • Odessa, Ontario K0H 2H0 • (613) 389-8314 • http://www.loyalist-township.on.ca

Ohsweken
Chiefwood Museum Archives • POB 5000 • Ohsweken, Ontario N0A 1M0 • (518) 752-5005

Oil Springs
Oil Museum of Canada Archives • RR2 • Oil Springs, Ontario N0N 1P0 • (519) 834-2940

Orangeville
Orangeville Public Library • 1 Mill St • Orangeville, Ontario L9W 2M2 • (519) 941-0610 • http://www.orangeville.library.on.ca

Orillia
Couchiching Association for Native Services • 38 James St E • Orillia, Ontario L3V 6S1

Orillia Museum of Art and History • 30 Peter St S • Orillia, Ontario L3V 6A9 • (705) 326-2159

Orillia Public Library • 36 Mississauga St W • Orillia, Ontario L3V 3A6 • (705) 324-2338 • http://www.inserv.bconnex.net

Stephen Leacock Memorial Library Museum Archives • 50 Museum Dr, POB 625 • Orillia, Ontario L3V 6K5 • (705) 329-1908 • http://www.transdata.ca/leacock.html

Orono
Clarke Museum Archives • Church & Centre Sts, POB 150 • Orono, Ontario L0B 1M0 • (905 983-9425

Oshawa
Canadian Automotive Museum Archives • 99 Simcoe St S • Oshawa, Ontario L1H 4G7 • (905) 576-1222

Oshawa Historical Society Archives & Library • 1450 Simcoe St S • Oshawa, Ontario L1H 8S8 • (905) 435-7624 • http://www.worldsites.net/oshawamuseum/

Oshawa Public Library • 65 Bagot St • Oshawa, Ontario L1H 1N2 • (905) 579-6111 • http://www.oshawalibrary.on.ca

Oshawa Sydenham Museum Archives • Lakeview Park, 7 Henry St • Oshawa, Ontario L1H 7V5 • (905) 436-7624

Ottawa
Assembly of First Nations • One Nicholas St, Ste 1002 • Ottawa, Ontario K1N 7B7

Association of Canadian Archivists • 395 Wellington St, POB 2596, Sta D • Ottawa, Ontario K1P 5W6 • (613) 443-0251 • http://www.archives.ca/aca/publicat/archivar/ • *Association of Canadian Archivists Bulletin*; *Archivaria*

Billings Estate Museum Archives • 2100 Cabot St • Ottawa, Ontario K1H 6K1 • (613) 563-3075

Brian O'Regan Memorial Library • 330 Kent St • Ottawa, Ontario K2C 3Y7

British Isles Family History Society of Greater Ottawa • POB 38026 • Ottawa, Ontario K2C 1N0 • (613) 224-9868 • http://www.cyberus.ca/~bifhsgo • *Anglo-Celtic Roots*; *Anglo-Celtic Annals*

Cameron Highlanders of Ottawa Regimental Museum Archives • Drill Hall, Cartier Sq • Ottawa, Ontario K1A 0K2 • (613) 990-3507 • http://www.cameronsottawa.net

Canada Agriculture Museum Archives • Prince of Wales Dr, POB 9724, Sta T • Ottawa, Ontario K1G 5A3 • (613) 991-3044 • http://www.agriculture.nmstc.ca

Canada Aviation Museum Archives • Aviation & Rockcliffe Pkwy S, POB 9724, Sta T • Ottawa, Ontario K1G 5A3 • (613) 993-2010 • http://www.aviation.mus.ca

Canadian Historical Association • 395 Wellington St • Ottawa, Ontario K1A 0N3 • (613) 233-7885 • http://www.yorku.ca/research/chalcha.shc.html • *Historical Papers*; *Canadian Historical Society Newsletter*; *Canadian Historical Association Historical Booklets*; *Archivaria*; *Journal of the Canadian Historical Association*

Canadian War Museum Library • 330 Sussex Dr • Ottawa, Ontario K1A 0M8 • (613) 776-8652 • http://www.warmuseum.ca

Governor General's Foot Guards Regimental Museum Archives • 2 Queen Elizabeth Dr • Ottawa, Ontario K1A 0K2 • (613) 990-0620

Heraldry Society of Canada-Societe Heraldique du Canada • POB 8467, Sta T • Ottawa, Ontario K1G 3H9 • *Gonfanon*

Heritage Canada • 306 Metcalfe St, POB 1358, Sta B • Ottawa, Ontario K1P 5R4 • (613) 237-1066 • http://heritagecanada.org/eng/mag.html • *Canadian Heritage*

Historical Society of Canada • Ottawa Locks • Ottawa, Ontario K1N 9J7

Historical Society of Ottawa & Library • Bytown Historical Museum, POB 523, Sta B • Ottawa, Ontario K1P 5P6 • (613) 234-4570

Laurier House Archives • 335 Laurier Ave E • Ottawa, Ontario K1N 6R4 • (613) 992-8142

Mackenzie King Estate Archives • 40 Elgin St, Ste 202 • Ottawa, Ontario K1P 1C7 • (819) 827-6026 • http://www.capcan.ca

National Aboriginal Forestry Association • 875 Bank St • Ottawa, Ontario K1S 3W4

National Archives of Canada • 395 Wellington St • Ottawa, Ontario K1A 0N3 • (613) 996-7458 • http://www.archives.ca

National Capital Genealogy Club • POB 33006 • Ottawa, Ontario K2C 3X9

National Indian Arts and Crafts Corporation • 141 Laurier Ave W, Ste 604 • Ottawa, Ontario K1P 5J3

National Library of Canada • 395 Wellington St • Ottawa, Ontario K1A 0N4 • (613) 995-9481 • http://www.nlc-bnc.ca/services/genealogy/gnlogy-e.htm

Native Council of Canada • 450 Rideau St, 4th Fl • Ottawa, Ontario K1N 5Z4

Native Women's Association of Canada • 9 Melrose Ave • Ottawa, Ontario K1Y 1T8

Ontario Genealogical Society, Ottawa Branch • POB 8346, Sta J • Ottawa, Ontario K1G 3H8 • (613) 224-9015 • http://www.cyberus.ca/~ogsottawa/ogsottawa.htm • Ottawa Branch News

Ottawa Public Library • 120 Metcalfe St • Ottawa, Ontario K1P 5M2 • (613) 236-0303 • http://www.library.ottawa.on.ca

Canadian Jewish Congress • 100 Sparks St, Ste 650 • Ottowa, Ontario K2C 3Y7 • (514) 931-7531 • *National Archives Newsletter*

Owen Sound
Billy Bishop Heritage Museum Archives • 948 3rd Ave W • Owen Sound, Ontario N4K 4P6 • (519) 371-0031 • http://www.billybishop.org

Grey County Museum Archives • 975 6th St E • Owen Sound, Ontario N4K 1G9 • (519) 376-3690 • http://www.greycounty.on.ca/museum

Ontario Genealogical Society, Bruce and Grey Branch • POB 66 • Owen Sound, Ontario N4K 5P1 • Branches of Bruce and Grey

Owen Sound Marine and Rail Museum Archives • 1155 1st Ave W • Owen Sound, Ontario N4K 4K8 • (519) 371-3333 • http://www.e-owensound.com/marinerail

Owen Sound Museum Archives • 975 6th St E • Owen Sound, Ontario N4K 1G9 • (519) 376-3690

Owen Sound Public Library • 824 1st Ave W • Owen Sound, Ontario N4K 4K4 • (519) 376-6623 • http://www.owensound.library.on.ca

Oxbridge
Thomas Foster Memorial Temple Museum • POB 1301 • Oxbridge, Ontario L9P 1N5 • (905) 852-5854 • http://www.uxlib.com/museum

Paris
Paris Historical Society & Archives • Historical Museum, 15 Curtis N • Paris, Ontario N3L 3W1 • (519) 442-9295

Parry Sound
West Parry Sound District Museum Archives • 17 George St • Parry Sound, Ontario P2A 2X4 • (705) 746-5365 • http://www.zeuter.com/wpschir/

Pembroke
Champlain Trail Museum Archives • 1032 Pembroke St E, POB 985 • Pembroke, Ontario K8A 7M5 • (613) 735-0517

Pembroke Public Library • 237 Victoria St • Pembroke, Ontario K8A 4K5 • (613) 732-8844 • http://www.pembroke.library.on.ca

Upper Ottawa Valley Genealogical Group • POB 972 • Pembroke, Ontario K8A 7M5

Penetanguishene
Beausoleil First Nation • Cedar Point Post Office • Penetanguishene, Ontario L0K 1C0

Discovery Harbour Museum Archives • 93 Jury Dr • Penetanguishene, Ontario L9M 1G1 • (705) 549-8064 • http://www.hhp.on.ca/discover

Penetanguishene Centennial Museum Archives • 13 Burke St, POB 389 • Penetanguishene, Ontario L0K 1P0 • (705) 549-2150 • http://www.town.penetanguishene.on.ca

Perth
Lanark County Genealogical Society • POB 512 • Perth, Ontario K7H 3K4

Perth Museum Archives • 11 Gore St E • Perth, Ontario K7H 1H9 • (613) 267-1947 • http://www.superaje.com/~perth.museum

Petawawa
Canadian Airborne Forces and CFB Petawawa Military Museum Archives • Canadian Forces Base Petawawa • Petawawa, Ontario K8H 2X3 • (613) 588-5886

Peterborough
Hope Water Powered Saw Mill Archives • 250 Milroy Dr • Peterborough, Ontario K9H 7M9 • (705) 745-5791 • http://www.otonabee.com/otonabee-hope.htm

Ontario Genealogical Society, Kawartha Branch & Library • POB 162 • Peterborough, Ontario K9J 6Y8 • (705) 743-ROOT

Perkins Bull Collection Archives • 361 Park St N • Peterborough, Ontario K9H 7M9 • (705) 742-0146

Peterborough Centennial Museum Archives • Hunter St E, POB 143 • Peterborough, Ontario K9J 6Y5 • (705) 743-5180

Peterborough Historical Society • 270 Brock St • Peterborough, Ontario K9H 2P9 • (705) 740-2600 • *Peterborough Historical Society Bulletin*

Peterborough Public Library • 345 Aylmer St N • Peterborough, Ontario K9H 3V7 • (705) 745-5382 • http://www.peterborough-library.com

Petrolia
Petrolia Discovery Museum • POB 1480 • Petrolia, Ontario N0N 1R0 • (519) 882-0897 • http://www.petroliadiscovery.com

Pickering
Pickering Museum Village Archives • 1 The Esplanade • Pickering, Ontario L1V 6K7 • (905) 420-4620

Pickering Public Library • 1 The Esplanade, POB 368 • Pickering, Ontario L1V 6K7 • (905) 831-6265 • http://www.picnet.org

Picton
Prince Edward County Museum Library • Macaulay Heritage Park, 35 Church St, POB 2150 • Picton, Ontario K0K 2T0 • (613) 476-3833 • http://www.pec.on.ca/macaulay

Picton Public Library • 208 Main St, POB 260 • Picton, Ontario K0K 2T0 • (613) 476-5962 • http://pec.library.org

Rose House Museum Archives • POB 3530 • Picton, Ontario K0K 2T0 • (613) 476-5439 • http://www.pec.on.ca

Port Carling
Mushoka Lakes Museum Archives • Island Park • Port Carling, Ontario P0B 1J0 • (705) 765-5367

Port Carling Pioneer Museum Archives • Island Park • Port Carling, Ontario P0B 1J0 • (705) 755-5367

Port Colborne
Port Colborne Historical and Marine Museum Archives • 280 King St, POB 572 • Port Colborne, Ontario L3K 5K8 • (905) 834-7604 • http://www.chin.qc.ca

Port Dover
Norfolk Public Library • 413 Main St • Port Dover, Ontario N0A 1N0 • (519) 583-0622 • http://www.kwic.com/~ptdoverlib

Port Dover Harbour Museum Archives • 44 Harbour St • Port Dover, Ontario N0A 1N0 • (519) 583-2660

Port Elgin
Bruce County Genealogical Society • POB 1083 • Port Elgin, Ontario N0H 2C0

Bruce County Historical Society • POB 1900 • Port Elgin, Ontario N0G 2T0 • (519) 934-2270 • *Bruce County Historical Society Yearbook*

Bruce County Public Library • 1243 MacKenzie Rd • Port Elgin, Ontario N0H 2C6 • (519) 832-6935 • http://www.brucecountylibraries.net

Port Hope
East Durham Historical Society & Library • POB 116 • Port Hope, Ontario L1A 3V9 • (416) 885-5044 • *Bulletin of the East Durham Historical Society*

Port Hope Public Library • 31 Queen St • Port Hope, Ontario L1A 2Y8 • (905) 885-4712 • http://www.porthope.on.ca

Port McNicoll
BeWabBon Metis Nation • BeWabBon Metis and Aboriginal Centre, 545 1st Street • Port McNicoll, Ontario L0K 1R0

Port Perry
Scugog Shores Historical Museum Archives • 16210 Island Rd • Port Perry, Ontario L9L 1B4 • (905) 985-3589 • http://www.durham.net/~ssh-chin

Port Rowan
Backus Heritage Village Museum Archives • general delivery • Port Rowan, Ontario N0E 1M0 • (519) 586-2201 • http://www.iprca.on.ca

Prescott
Fort Wellington National Historic Site Archives • 400 Dibble St, POB 479 • Prescott, Ontario K0E 1T0 • (613) 925-2896 • http://www.parkscanada.qc.ca/fortwellington

Forwarders' Museum Archives • POB 2179 • Prescott, Ontario K0E 1T0 • (613) 925-5788

Grenville County Historical Society & Library • 439 Edward • Prescott, Ontario K0E 1T0 • (613) 925-0489 • *Sentinel*; *Pioneer People and Places*; *Early Grenville*

Queenston
MacKenzie Heritage Museum Archives • 1 Queenston St • Queenston, Ontario L0S 1L0 • (905) 262-5676 • http://www.niagaraparks.com

Rainy River
Rainy River Public Library • 202 4th St, POB 308 • Rainy River, Ontario P0W 1L0 • (807) 852-3375 • http://www.rainyriver.lakehedu.ca/~librr/

Rama
M'Njikaning First Nation • Rama Rd, POB 35 • Rama, Ontario L0K 1T0

Red Lake
Red Lake Museum Archives • 55 Hwy 105, POB 64 • Red Lake, Ontario P0V 2M0 • (807) 727-3006

Red Rock
Red Rock Public Library • 42 Salls St, POB 285 • Red Rock, Ontario P0T 2P0 • (807) 886-2558

Renfrew
McDougall Mill Museum Archives • POB 544 • Renfrew, Ontario K7V 4B1 • (613) 432-2129

Renfrew Public Library • 13 Railway Ave E • Renfrew, Ontario K7V 3A9 • (613) 432-8151

Richards Landing
Fort Saint Joseph Museum Archives • POB 220 • Richards Landing, Ontario P0R 1J0 • (705) 246-2664 • http://www.parcsczaten.ge.ca

Saint Joseph Island Museum Village • RR2 • Richards Landing, Ontario P0R 1J0 • (705) 246-2672 • http://www.stjosephisland.net

Richmond
Richmond Hill Public Library • 1 Atkinson St • Richmond, Ontario L4C 0H5 • (905) 770-0310 • http://www.rhpl.richmondhill.on.ca

Richmond Hills
Doane Family Association of America • 9481 Leslie St • Richmond Hills, Ontario L4B 3Y5

Ridgetown
Ridge House Museum Archives • 53 Erie St S • Ridgetown, Ontario N0P 2C0 • (519) 674-2223

Ridgeville
Johnson Family Niagara Peninsula Region • RR1, 504 Kilman Rd • Ridgeville, Ontario L0S 1M0 • (905) 892-2390 • *Johnson Reporter: Relatively Speaking*

Ridgeway
Fort Erie Historical Museum Archives • 402 Ridge Rd • Ridgeway, Ontario L0S 1N0 • (905) 694-5322

Rockton
Westfield Heritage Village Archives • Regional Rd 552 • Rockton, Ontario L0R 1X0 • (519) 621-8851 • http://www.westfieldheritage.ca

Rosemont
Dufferin County Museum Archives • POB 120 • Rosemont, Ontario L0N 1R0 • (705) 435-1881 • http://www.dufferincounty.on.ca/departments

Saint Catharines
Mountain Mills Museum Archives • POB 3012 • Saint Catharines, Ontario L2R 7C2

Ontario Genealogical Society, Niagara Peninsula Branch • POB 2224, Sta B • Saint Catharines, Ontario L3M 6P6 • Notes from Niagara

Saint Catharines Historical Museum • 1932 Welland Canals Pkwy • Saint Catharines, Ontario L2R 7C2 • (905) 984-8880 • http://www.lock3.com

Saint Catharines Public Library • 54 Church St • Saint Catharines, Ontario L2R 7K2 • (905) 688-6103 • http://www.stcatherines.library.on.ca

Halfyard Research • 11 Timber Ln • Saint Catherines, Ontario L2N 7R7 • (416) 934-3651 • *Halfyard Heritage*

Historical Society of Saint Catharines • POB 23104 • Saint Catherines, Ontario L2R 7P6

Jordan Historical Museum of the Twenty Archives • Main St, POB 39 • Saint Catherines, Ontario L2R 7E4 • (416) 562-5242

Saint Catherines Historical Museum Archives • 343 Merritt St • Saint Catherines, Ontario L2T 1K7 • (416) 227-2962

Saint George
Adelaide Hunter Hoodless Homestead Archives • 359 Blue Lake Rd, RR1 • Saint George, Ontario N0E 1N0 • (519) 448-1130

Saint Jacobs
Maple Syrup Museum Archives • Princess St • Saint Jacobs, Ontario N0B 2M0 • (519) 669-2423

Saint Joseph Island
Fort Saint Joseph National Historic Park • Richmond's Landing • Saint Joseph Island, Ontario N0M 2T0

Saint Mary's
Saint Marys Museum Archives • 177 Church St S, POB 96 • Saint Mary's, Ontario N4X 1A9 • (519) 284-3556 • http://www.townofstmarys.com/museum

Saint Mary's Public Library • 15 Church St N, POB 700 • Saint Mary's, Ontario N4X 1B4 • (519) 284-3346

Saint Thomas
Elgin County Pioneer Museum Archives • 32 Talbot St • Saint Thomas, Ontario N5P 1A3 • (519) 631-6537 • http://www.execulink.com/~ecpmchin

Elgin County Public Library • 450 Sunset Dr • Saint Thomas, Ontario N5R 5V1 • (519) 631-1460 • http://www.library.elgin-county.on.ca

Elgin Military Museum Archives • 30 Talbot St • Saint Thomas, Ontario N5P 1A3 • (519) 633-7641

Ontario Genealogical Society, Elgin County Branch • POB 20060 • Saint Thomas, Ontario N5P 4H4

Saint Thomas Public Library • 153 Curtis St • Saint Thomas, Ontario N5P 3Z7 • (519) 631-6050 • http://www.st-thomas.library.on.ca

Sarnia
Lambton County Historical Society & Library • 1777 Lakeshore Rd • Sarnia, Ontario N7V 7Y1 • (519) 542-2373 • *Lambton County Historical Society Bulletin*

Ontario Genealogical Society, Lambton County Branch • POB 2857 • Sarnia, Ontario N7T 7W1

Sault Sainte Marie
Batchewana Indian Band • 236 Frontenac St, RR4 • Sault Sainte Marie, Ontario P6A 5K9

Ermatinger Old Stone House Archives • 831 Queen St E, POB 580 • Sault Sainte Marie, Ontario P6A 5N1 • (705) 759-5443

Metis Aboriginal Association • 452 Albert St, 2nd Fl • Sault Sainte Marie, Ontario P5A 2A4

Ontario Genealogical Society, Sault Sainte Marie and District Branch • 150 Churchill Rd, POB 20007 • Sault Sainte Marie, Ontario P6A 6W3

Sault Sainte Marie Museum Archives • 690 Queen St E • Sault Sainte Marie, Ontario P5A 2A4 • (705) 759-7278

Sault Sainte Marie Public Library • 50 East St • Sault Sainte Marie, Ontario P6A 3C3 • (705) 759-5242

Scarborough
Scarborough Historical Museum Archives • 1067 Bromley Rd • Scarborough, Ontario M1P 3E5 • (418) 431-3441

Schrieber
Schreiber Township Public Library • POB 39 • Schrieber, Ontario P0T 2S0 • (807) 824-2477 • http://www.schreiber.library.on.ca

Selkirk
Nanticoke Public Library, Selkirk Branch • POB 130 • Selkirk, Ontario N0A 1P0 • (905) 776-2127

Wilson MacDonald Memorial School Museum Library • RR 1 • Selkirk, Ontario N0A 1P0 • (905) 776-3319

Ontario

Sharon
Sharon Temple Historic Site Archives • 18974 Leslie St • Sharon, Ontario L0G 1V0 • (905) 478-2389 • http://www.sharontemple.ca

Sheguiandah
Little Current-Howland Centennial Museum Archives • Hwy 68 • Sheguiandah, Ontario P0P 1W0 • (705) 368-2367

Simcoe
Norfolk Historical Society & Archives • Eva Brook Donly Museum, 109 Norfolk St S • Simcoe, Ontario N3Y 2W3 • (519) 426-1583 • http://www.norfolklore.com • *Long Point Genealogist*; *Norfolklore*

Simcoe Public Library • 46 Colborne St S • Simcoe, Ontario N3Y 4H3 • (519) 426-3506 • http://www.simcoe.library.on.ca

Sioux Lookout
Sarah Vaughan Museum Archives • 5th Ave, POB 1028 • Sioux Lookout, Ontario P0V 2T0

Sioux Lookout Museum Archives • 75 Wellington St • Sioux Lookout, Ontario P8T 1B9 • (807) 737-1562 • http://www.municipalityofsiouxlookout.ca

Sioux Lookout Public Library • 21 5th Ave, POB 1028 • Sioux Lookout, Ontario P8T 1B3 • (807) 737-3660 • http://www.slpl.on.ca

Smiths Falls
Heritage House Museum Archives • Old Slys Rd • Smiths Falls, Ontario K7A 4T6 • (613) 283-8560 • http://www.town.smiths.falls.on.ca

Industrial Heritage Complex Archives • 34a Beckwith St S • Smiths Falls, Ontario K7A 2A8 • (613) 283-5170

Smiths Falls Public Library • 81 Beckwith St N • Smiths Falls, Ontario K7A 2B9 • (613) 283-2911

Smiths Falls Railway Museum of Eastern Ontario • 90 William St W • Smiths Falls, Ontario K7A 5A5 • (613) 283-5696 • http://www.magma.ca/~sfrm

Smithville
West Lincoln Historical Society • 288 Station • Smithville, Ontario L0R 2A0 • (905) 957-0138

Sombra
Sombra Township Museum Archives • 146 Saint Clair St, POB 99 • Sombra, Ontario N0P 2H0 • (519) 892-3672

South Dumfries
South Dumfries Historical Society & Archives • Saint George Museum, 36 Main S • South Dumfries, Ontario N0E 1N0 • (519) 448-3265

South Porcupine
Timmins Museum Archives • National Exhibition Centre, 70 Legion Dr • South Porcupine, Ontario P0N 1H0 • (705) 235-5066

South River
South River-Machar Union Public Library • 22 Marie St, POB 190 • South River, Ontario P0A 1X0 • (705) 386-0222

Southampton
Bruce County Museum Archives • 33 Victoria St N • Southampton, Ontario N0H 2L0 • (519) 797-2080 • http://museum.brucecounty.on.ca

Stayner
Clearview Public Library • 201 Huron St, POB 160 • Stayner, Ontario L0M 1S0 • (705) 428-3595 • http://www.geocities.com/athens/parthenon/1799

Stittsville
Goulbourn Township Public Library • 1637 Main St S, POB 760 • Stittsville, Ontario K0A 3G0 • (613) 836-3381 • http://www.opl.ottawa.on.ca

Stoney Creek
Battlefield House Museum Archives • 77 King St W • Stoney Creek, Ontario L8G 5E5 • (905) 682-8458 • http://www.battlefieldhouse.ca

Erland Lee Museum Archives • 552 Ridge Rd • Stoney Creek, Ontario L8J 2Y6 • (905) 662-2691 • http://www.fwio.on.ca

Stouffville
Whitchurch-Stouffville Public Library • 30 Burkholder St • Stouffville, Ontario L4A 4K1 • (905) 640-2395 • http://www.whitchurch-library.on.ca

Stratford
Brocksden County School Museum Archives • Vivian St, Lot 33-2 • Stratford, Ontario N5A 4C7 • (519) 271-0499

Ontario Genealogical Society, Perth County Branch & Library • 24 St Andrew St, POB 9 • Stratford, Ontario N5A 6S8 • (519) 273-0399 • *Perth County Profiles*

Perth Regiment Museum Archives • Stratford Armoury, 80 Waterloo St S • Stratford, Ontario N5A 4A9

Stratford Public Library • 19 St Andrew St • Stratford, Ontario N5A 1A2 • (519) 271-0220 • http://www.stratford.library.on.ca

Strathroy
A W Campbell House Museum Archives • 205 Mill Pond Crescent • Strathroy, Ontario N7G 3A5 • (519) 245-3710 • http://www.scrca.on.ca

Strathroy-Middlesex Museum Archives • 84 Oxford St • Strathroy, Ontario N7G 3A5 • (519) 245-0492

Sturgeon Falls
Sturgeon River House Museum Archives • 250 Chemin du Fort, POB 1390 • Sturgeon Falls, Ontario P0H 2G0 • (705) 753-4716 • http://www.sturgeonriverhouse.com

Sudbury
Centre Franco-Ontarien de Folklore • Maison d'Youville, 38 Rue Xavier • Sudbury, Ontario P3C 2B9 • (705) 675-8986

Copper Cliff Museum Archives • BP 5000, Sta A • Sudbury, Ontario P3A 5P3 • (705) 674-3141

Flour Mill Museum Archives • 514 Rue Notre Dame • Sudbury, Ontario P3A 5P3 • (705) 674-2391

Greater Sudbury Heritage Museum Archives • POB 6400 • Sudbury, Ontario P3A 3B7 • (705) 692-4448 • http://www.city.greatersudbury.on.ca

Ontario Genealogical Society, Sudbury District Branch • c/o Sudbury Public Library, 74 Mackenzie St, Bag 5000, Sta A • Sudbury, Ontario P3E 5P3 • (705) 673-1155 • *Sudbury Ancestor Hunting*

Sudbury Public Library • 74 Mackenzie St • Sudbury, Ontario P3C 4X8 • (705) 673-1155 • http://www.sudbury.library.on.ca

Sundridge
Maple Sugar Museum and Pioneer Home • general delivery • Sundridge, Ontario P0A 1Z0 • (705) 384-7764

Sundridge-Strong Union Public Library • 110 Main St, POB 429 • Sundridge, Ontario P0A 1Z0 • (705) 384-7311

Sutton
Eldon Hall Sibbald Memorial Museum Archives • Sibbald Provincial Park, RR2 • Sutton, Ontario L0E 1R0 • (905) 722-3268

Sutton West
Elm Grove School Heritage Society • 577 Catering Rd • Sutton West, Ontario L0E 1R0 • (905) 722-7230

Georgina Island First Nation • RR2 • Sutton West, Ontario L0E 1R0

Teeterville
Teeterville Pioneer Museum Archives • POB 85 • Teeterville, Ontario N0E 1S0 • (519) 443-4400

Tehkummah
Tehkummah Township Museum Archives • Municipal Office • Tehkummah, Ontario P0P 2C0 • (705) 859-3293

Terrace Bay
Terrace Bay Public Library • Selkirk & Hwy 7, POB 369 • Terrace Bay, Ontario P0T 2W0 • (807) 825-3819 • http://www.nwconx.net/~terpl

Thorold
Thorold Public Library • 14 Ormond St N • Thorold, Ontario L2V 1Y8 • (905) 227-2581 • http://www.thorold.com/library

Thunder Bay
Centennial Park 1910 Logging Museum Archives • 111 Syndicate Av S • Thunder Bay, Ontario P7E 6S4 • (807) 625-2113

Old Fort William Historical Park Archives • Vickers Heights Post Office, Kings Rd • Thunder Bay, Ontario P0T 2Z0 • (807) 577-8461 • http://www.oldfortwilliam.on.ca

Ontario Genealogical Society, Thunder Bay District Branch • POB 373, Sta F • Thunder Bay, Ontario P7C 4V9

Paipoonga Historical Museum Archives • RR6 • Thunder Bay, Ontario P7C 5N5 • (807) 839-1262

Thunder Bay Historical Museum Society & Library • 425 Donald St E • Thunder Bay, Ontario P7E 5V1 • (807) 623-0801 • *Thunder Bay Historical Museum Society Papers and Records*

Thunder Bay Military Museum Archives • Armoury, 317 Park Av • Thunder Bay, Ontario P7B 1C7 • (807) 343-5175

Thunder Bay Public Library • 285 Red River Rd • Thunder Bay, Ontario P7B 1A9 • (807) 344-3585 • http://www.thpl.thunder-bay.on.ca

Tillsonburg
Annandale National Historic Site Archives • 30 Tillson Av • Tillsonburg, Ontario N4G 2Z8 • (519) 842-2294 • http://www.town.tillsonburg.on.ca

Tillsonburg and District Historical Museum Archives • 8 Ross St • Tillsonburg, Ontario N4G 3N8

Timmins
Ojibway and Cree Cultural Centre Archives • 210 Spruce St S, Suite 101 • Timmins, Ontario P4N 2M5 • (705) 267-7911 • http://www.schoolnet.ca/aboriginal/occc/

Ojibway and Cree Nations • Ojibway and Cree Cultural Centre, 43 Balsalm St S • Timmins, Ontario P4N 2C7

Tobermory
Peninsula and Saint Edmunds Township Museum Archives • RR1 • Tobermory, Ontario N0H 2R0 • (519) 596-2479

Toronto
Angelican Church of Canada Archives • 600 Jarvis St • Toronto, Ontario M5S 2E6 • (416) 924-9199

Archives of Ontario • 300-77 Grenville St • Toronto, Ontario M7A 2R0 • (416) 965-4030 • http://www.archives.gov.on.ca

Bata Shoe Museum Archives • 327 Bloor St W • Toronto, Ontario M5S 1W7 • (416) 979-7799 • http://www.batashoemuseum.ca

Beth Tzedac Reuben and Helene Dennis Museum • 1700 Bathurst St • Toronto, Ontario N5P 3K3 • (416) 781-3514

Campbell House Museum Archives • 160 Queen St W • Toronto, Ontario M5H 3H3 • (416) 597-0227 • http://www.advsoc.on.ca/campbell

Canadian Friends Historical Association & Library • 60 Lowther Ave • Toronto, Ontario M5R 1C7 • (416) 839-4328 • *Canadian Quaker History Newsletter, Canadian Quaker History Journal*

Casa Loma Museum Archives • 1 Austin Terr • Toronto, Ontario M5R 1X8 • (416) 923-1171 • http://www.casaloma.org

Century Schoolhouse Museum Archives • 502 Sammon Av • Toronto, Ontario M4C 2V3 • (416) 396-2074

Champlain Society • 260 Adelaide St E, POB 60 • Toronto, Ontario M5A 1N1 • (416) 482-9635 • *Champlain Society Report*

Chiefs of Ontario • 22 College St, 2nd Fl • Toronto, Ontario M5G 1K2

City of Toronto Archives • 255 Spadina Rd • Toronto, Ontario M5R 2V3 • (416) 397-0778 • http://www.city.toronto.on.ca/archives

Clan Fraser Society of North America, Canadian Region • 71 Charles St E #1101 • Toronto, Ontario M4Y 2T3 • (416) 920-6851 • *Clan Fraser Society of North America, Canadian Explorer*

Colborne Lodge Museum Archives • 55 John St • Toronto, Ontario M5V 3C6 • (416) 392-6916 • http://www.toronto.ca/culture

Enoch Turner Schoolhouse Museum Archives • 106 Trinity St • Toronto, Ontario M5A 3C6 • (416) 863-0010

Estonian Central Archives in Canada • 958 Broadview Ave • Toronto, Ontario M4K 2R6 • (416) 465-2219

Fire Fighting Museum Archives • 895 Eastern Av • Toronto, Ontario M4L 1A2

German Canadian Historical Association • Box 1251, Sta K • Toronto, Ontario M4P 3E5 • (416) 488-3846 • *Canadiana Germanica*

Historic Fort York Archives • 100 Garrison Rd • Toronto, Ontario M5V 3K9 • (416) 392-6907 • http://www.toronto.ca/culture

History of Contraception Museum Archives • 19 Green Belt Dr • Toronto, Ontario M3C 1L9 • (416) 449-9444

HMCS Haida Museum Archives • 100-2 Bloor St W • Toronto, Ontario M4W 3E2 • http://www.hmcshaida.ca

Jewish Genealogical Society of Canada • 2901 Bayview Ave, POB 91006 • Toronto, Ontario M2K 2Y6 • *Shem Tov*

Latvian History Museum Archives • 125 Broadview Av • Toronto, Ontario M4M 2E9 • (416) 889-0472

Mackenzie House Museum Archives • 82 Bond St • Toronto, Ontario M5B 1T2 • (416) 392-6915 • http://www.city.toronto.on.ca/culture

Marine Museum of Upper Canada Archives • Exhibition Grounds • Toronto, Ontario M6K 3C3 • (416) 392-1765

Metropolitan Toronto Police Museum Archives • 40 College St • Toronto, Ontario M5G 2J3 • (416) 808-7020 • http://www.ntps.on.ca

Moorshead Magazines • 505 Consumers Rd #500 • Toronto, Ontario M2J 4V8 • (416) 491-3699 • http://www.familychronicle.com • *Family Chronicle: the Magazine for Families Researching their Roots*

Museum of the Royal Regment of Canada • Fort York Armoury, 660 Fleet St • Toronto, Ontario N5V L48 • (416) 755-1727

North York Public Library • 5120 Yonge St • Toronto, Ontario M2N 5N9 • (416) 395-5624

Ontario Black History Society • Ontario Heritage Center, 10 Adelaide St E, Ste 202 • Toronto, Ontario M5C 1J3

Ontario Genealogical Society & Library • 40 Orchard View, Ste 102, POB 66, Sta Q • Toronto, Ontario M4R 1B9 • (613) 489-0734 • http://www.ogs.on.ca • *Families; Ontario Genealogical Society Newsletter; Ontario Genealogical Society Membership*

Ontario Genealogical Society, Toronto Branch • POB 147, Sta Z • Toronto, Ontario M5N 2Z3

Ontario Genealogical Society, Toronto Branch (York County) • POB 518, Sta J • Toronto, Ontario M4P 2G9

Pontifical Institute of Medieval Studies • 59 Queen's Park Crescent E • Toronto, Ontario M5S 2C4 • (416) 926-7144 • Mediaeval Studies

Presbyterian Church of Canada Archives • 50 Wynford Dr • Toronto, Ontario M5C 1J7 • (416) 441-1111

Queen's Own Rifles of Canada Regimental Museum Archives • 1 Austin Terr • Toronto, Ontario M5R 1X8 • (905) 826-6138

Queen's York Rangers Regimental Museum • 660 Fleet St • Toronto, Ontario N5V 1A9 • (416) 203-4642 • http://www.connection.com/~qarang/

Royal Canadian Military Institute Museum Archives • 426 University Av • Toronto, Ontario M5G 1S9 • (416) 597-0286

Royal Ontario Museum Library • 100 Queen's Park • Toronto, Ontario M5S 2C6 • (416) 586-5595 • http://www.rom.on.ca

Ontario

Saint Vladimir Institute Library & Library • 620 Spadina Ave • Toronto, Ontario M5S 2H4 • (416) 923-3318

Salvation Army George Scott Railton Museum Archives • 2130 Bayview Av • Toronto, Ontario M4N 3K6 • (416) 481-4441 • http://www.salvationarmy.ca/heritage

Scadding Cabin Museum Archives • 2482 Yonge St, POB 45026 • Toronto, Ontario M4P 3E3 • (416) 494-0503

Sesquicentennial Museum Archives • 155 College St • Toronto, Ontario M5T 1P6 • (416(397-3680

Silverman Heritage Museum Archives • Baycrest Centre, 3560 Bathurst St • Toronto, Ontario M6A 2E1 • (416) 785-2500 • http://www.baycrest.org

Spadina Museum • 285 Spadina Rd • Toronto, Ontario M5R 2V5 • (416) 392-6910 • http://www.torontohistory.on.ca

Todmorden Mills Historic Site Archives • 67 Pottery Rd • Toronto, Ontario M4J 2H2 • (416) 396-2819 • http://www.city.toronto.on.ca/todmorden

Toronto Aerospace Museum Archives • 65 Carl Hall Rd • Toronto, Ontario M3K 2B6 • (416) 638-6078 • http://www.torontoaerospacemuseum.com

Toronto Cornish Association • 1 Ottawa St • Toronto, Ontario M4T 2B5

Toronto Public Library • 789 Yonge St • Toronto, Ontario M4W 2G8 • (416) 393-7131 • http://www.tpl.toronto.on.ca

Toronto Scottish Regimental Museum Archives • Fort York Armoury, 660 Fleet St • Toronto, Ontario M5V 1A9

Toronto's Waterfront Museum Archives • 245 Queen Quay W • Toronto, Ontario M5J 2K9 • (416) 392-6827 • http://www.torontohistory.on.ca

Ukrainian Museum of Canada Library • 620 Spadina Ave • Toronto, Ontario M5S 2H4 • (416) 923-3318

Union of Ontario Indians • 27 Queen St E, 2nd Fl • Toronto, Ontario M5C 1R2

United Church of Canada Central Archives • Victoria College, 73 Queen's Park Crescent E • Toronto, Ontario M5S 1R7 • (416) 585-4563 • http://vicu.utoronto.ca/archives/archives.html

United Empire Loyalists' Association of Canada & Library • George Brown House, 50 Baldwin St • Toronto, Ontario M5T 1L4 • (416) 923-7921 • *Loyalist Gazette*

University of Toronto Library • 130 St George St • Toronto, Ontario M5S 1A1 • (416) 978-6215 • http://www.library.utoronto.ca

Vietnamese Association • 1364 Dundas St W • Toronto, Ontario M6J 1Y2 • (416) 536-3611 • *Ban Viet*

West Toronto Junction Historical Society • 145 Annette St • Toronto, Ontario M6P 1P3 • (416) 763-3161

York Pioneer and Historical Society • 2482 Yonge St, POB 45026 • Toronto, Ontario M4P 3E3 • (416) 231-1829 • *York Pioneer*

Trenton
Quente West Public Library • 18 Albert St • Trenton, Ontario K8V 4S3 • (613) 394-3381 • http://www.library.quintewest.com

Tweed
Tweed and Area Heritage Centre Archives • 40 Victoria St N, POB 665 • Tweed, Ontario K0K 3J0 • (613) 478-3989

Uxbridge
Ontario Genealogical Society, Simcoe County Branch • RR2 • Uxbridge, Ontario L9P 1R2

Uxbridge-Scott Historical Society & Archives • Uxbridge-Scott Museum, 7239 Concession 6, POB 704 • Uxbridge, Ontario L0C 1K0 • (905) 852-5854 • http://www.uxlib.com/museum

Vernon
Osgoode Township Historical Society & Archives • Historical Museum, 7814 Lawrence • Vernon, Ontario K0A 3J0 • (613) 821-4062

Osgoode Township Museum Archives • POB 74 • Vernon, Ontario K0A 3J0 • (613) 821-4082 • http://www.magma.ca/~oths

Verona
Bell Rock Mill Museum Archives • general delivery • Verona, Ontario K0H 2W0 • (613) 374-1458

Wainfleet
Wainfleet Township Public Library • 19M9 Park St • Wainfleet, Ontario L0S 1V0 • (905) 899-1277 • http://www.go.to.wtpl

Ward
Smith Township-Ennismore Historical Society • general delivery • Ward, Ontario L0S 1V0 • (705) 292-9430

Wasaga Beach
Nancy Island Historic Site Archives • Wasaga Beach Provincial Park, Mosley St • Wasaga Beach, Ontario L0N 2P0 • (705) 429-2728

Waterford
Norfolk Public Library • 15 Main St S • Waterford, Ontario N0E 1Y0 • (519) 443-7682 • http://www.kwic.com/~watpublib

Spruce Row Museum Archives • 159 Nichol St • Waterford, Ontario N0E 1Y0 • (519) 443-4211

Waterloo
Armstrong Clan • 267 Roxton Dr • Waterloo, Ontario N2T 1R2

Brubacher House Museum Archives • Conrad Grebel College • Waterloo, Ontario N2L 3G6 • (519) 886-3855 • http://grebel.uwaterloo.ca/bhouse

Elliott Avedon Museum and Archives of Games • Univ of Waterloo, 200 University Av W • Waterloo, Ontario N2L 3G1 • (519) 888-4424 • http://www.ahs.uwaterloo.ca/~museum

Waterloo Public Library • 35 Albert St • Waterloo, Ontario N2L 5E2 • (519) 886-1310

Welland
Welland Historical Museum Archives • 65 Hooker St • Welland, Ontario L3C 5G9 • (905) 732-2215 • http://www.niagara.com/~whmchln

Wellington
Wellington Community Historical Museum Archives • 290 Main St • Wellington, Ontario K0K 3L0 • (613) 399-5015 • http://www.pecomity.on.ca/wellmuseum

Wendake
Musee Arouane • 10 Rue Alexandre-Duschesneau • Wendake, Ontario G0A 4V0 • (418) 845-1241

Westport
Rideau District Museum Archives • 29 Bedford St • Westport, Ontario K0G 1X0 • (613) 273-2502 • http://www.rideaulakes.net/museum

Whitby
Ontario Genealogical Society, Whitby-Oshawa Branch • POB 174 • Whitby, Ontario L1N 5S1 • (905) 668-1362 • Kindred Spirits

Town of Whitby Archives • 603 Harriet St • Whitby, Ontario L1N 1L4 • (905) 668-5570 • http://www.town.whitby.on.ca

Whitby Public Library • 405 Dundas St W • Whitby, Ontario L1N 6A1 • (905) 668-6541 • http://www.whitbylibrary.on.ca

White Lake
Waba Cottage Museum Archives • RR1, POB 167 • White Lake, Ontario K0A 1G0 • (613) 6523-4341

Whitney
Algonquin Park Logging Museum Archives • Hwy 60, POB 248 • Whitney, Ontario K0J 2M0 • (613) 637-2828 • http://www.algonquinpark.on.ca

Wiarton
Nawash First Nation • RR5 • Wiarton, Ontario N0H 2T0

Williamstown
Nor'Wester and Loyalist Museum Archives • 19651 John St • Williamstown, Ontario K0C 2J0 • (613) 347-3547

Willowdale
Canadian Jewish Historical Society • 4600 Bathurst St • Willowdale, Ontario M2R 3V2 • (416) 635-2883 • *Canadian Jewish Historical Society Journal*

Gibson House Archives • 5172 Yonge St • Willowdale, Ontario M2N 5P6

Jewish Genealogical Society of Canada • POB 446, Sta A • Willowdale, Ontario M2N 5T1 • (416) 638-3280 • *Shem Tov*

Ontario Historical Society • 34 Parkview Ave • Willowdale, Ontario M2N 3Y2 • (416) 226-9011 • *Ontario Historical Society Bulletin*; *Ontario History*

Serbian National Shield Society of Canada • 1900 Sheppard E #303 • Willowdale, Ontario M2J 4T4 • (416) 496-7881 • *Glas Kanadskih Srba: Voice of Canadian Serbs*

Windsor
Hiram Walker Historical Museum Library • 254 Pitt St W • Windsor, Ontario N9A 5L5 • (519) 253-1812

Italian Genealogy and Heraldry Society of Canada • 110 Eugenie St W, Ste 541 • Windsor, Ontario N8X 5C7

Ontario Genealogical Society, Windsor Branch • POB 2, Sta A • Windsor, Ontario N9A 6J5 • (519) 948-5092 • *Trails*

Serbian Heritage Museum of Windsor • 6770 Tecumseh Rd E • Windsor, Ontario N8T 1E6 • (519) 944-4884

Southwestern Ontario Heritage Village Archives • County Rd 23, POB 788 • Windsor, Ontario N9A 4H7

Tecumseh Area Historical Society • 12340 Tecumseh Rd E • Windsor, Ontario N8N 1M4 • (519) 735-5609

Willistead Manor House Museum • 1899 Niagara St • Windsor, Ontario N8Y 1K3 • (519) 253-2365 • http://www.willistead.city.windsor.on.ca

Windsor Public Library • 850 Ouellette Ave • Windsor, Ontario N9A 4M9 • (519) 255-6770 • http://www.windsorpubliclibrary.com

Windsor's Community Museum Archives • 254 Pitt St W • Windsor, Ontario N9A 5L5 • (519) 253-1812 • http://www.city.windsor.on.ca/wpl/museum

Wingham
Wingham District Heritage and History Society & Archives • Historical Museum, 275 Josephine St • Wingham, Ontario N0G 2W0 • (519) 357-1096

Woodstock
Ontario Genealogical Society, Oxford County Branch • POB 1092 • Woodstock, Ontario N4S 8P6 • *Oxford Tracer*

Woodstock Museum National Historic Site • 466 Dundas St • Woodstock, Ontario N4S 1C4 • (519) 537-8411 • http://www.city.woodstock.on.ca

Woodstock Public Library • 445 Hunter St • Woodstock, Ontario N4S 4G7 • (519) 539-4801 • http://www.woodstock.library.on.ca

Wyoming
Lambton County Library • 787 Broadway St, POB 3100 • Wyoming, Ontario N0N 1T0 • (519) 845-3324 • http://www.lanbtonlibrary.org

York
City of York Museum Archives • 2694 Eglinton Av W • York, Ontario M6M 1V1 • (416) 394-2513

PRINCE EDWARD ISLAND

Alberton
Alberton Museum Archives • 457 Church St, POB 285 • Alberton, Prince Edward Island C0B 1B0 • (902) 853-4048

Charlottetown
Confederation Centre Public Library • Queen & Richmond St, POB 7000 • Charlottetown, Prince Edward Island C1A 8G8 • (902) 368-4642 • http://www.library.pe.ca

Fort Amherst National Historic Park Archives • Rocky Point • Charlottetown, Prince Edward Island C1A 7L1

Green Gables House Museum Archives • 2 Palmers Ln • Charlottetown, Prince Edward Island C1A 5V6 • (902) 963-3370

Lord Selkirk Settlement Archives • Trans-Canada Hwy near Eldon • Charlottetown, Prince Edward Island C1A 7N7

Lucy Maud Montgomery Birthplace Museum Archives • New London • Charlottetown, Prince Edward Island C1A 4N6 • (902) 436-7329

Port-la-Joye-Fort Amherst Museum Archives • 2 Palmers Ln • Charlottetown, Prince Edward Island C1A 5V6 • (902) 566-8287 • http://www.parkscanada.pch.gc.ca

Prince Edward Island Genealogical Society & Library • 2 Kent St, POB 2744 • Charlottetown, Prince Edward Island C1A 8C4 • (902) 892-9127

Prince Edward Island Museum and Heritage Foundation & Library • Beaconsfield Historic House, 2 Kent St • Charlottetown, Prince Edward Island C1A 1M6 • (902) 368-6600 • http://www.peimuseum.com • *Island Magazine*; *Prince Edward Island Old and News*

Prince Edward Island Regiment Museum Archives • 3 Haviland St • Charlottetown, Prince Edward Island C1A 7N1 • (902) 368-0108

Province House Museum Archives • 165 Richmond St • Charlottetown, Prince Edward Island C1A 1J1 • (902) 560-7626

Public Archives of Prince Edward Island • POB 1000 • Charlottetown, Prince Edward Island C1A 7M4 • (902) 368-4290 • http://www.gov.pe.ca/educ/archives/

Robertson Library • University of Prince Edward Island, 550 University Ave • Charlottetown, Prince Edward Island C1A 4P3 • (902) 566-0696 • http://www.upei.ca/~library/info/dept/

Spoke Wheel Car Museum Archives • RR3 • Charlottetown, Prince Edward Island C1A 7J7

Cornwall
Abegweit First Nation • POB 220 • Cornwall, Prince Edward Island C0A 1H0

Eldon
Belfast Historical Society • general delivery • Eldon, Prince Edward Island C0A 1A0 • (902) 659-2209

Elmira
Elmira Railway Museum Archives • general delivery • Elmira, Prince Edward Island C-A 1K0 • (902) 357-7234

Kensington
Anne of Green Gables Museum Archives • Silver Bush Park, Cnr Route 20, POB 491 • Kensington, Prince Edward Island C0B 1M0 • (902) 436-7329 • http://www.annesociety.org/anne

Keir Memorial Museum Archives • POB 177 • Kensington, Prince Edward Island C0B 1M0 • (902) 836-3054

Veterans' Memorial Military Museum Archives • Legion Branch 9 • Kensington, Prince Edward Island C0B 1M0 • (902) 836-3600

Lennox Island
Lennox Island Museum Archives • general delivery • Lennox Island, Prince Edward Island C0B 1P0

Miscouche
Musee Acadien • 23 Main Dr • Miscouche, Prince Edward Island C0B 1T0 • (902) 432-2880

Morell
Prince Edward Island Provincial Library Service • Red Head Rd, POB 7500 • Morell, Prince Edward Island C0A 1S0 • (902) 961-7320 • http://www.library.pe.ca/

Murray Harbour
Log Cabin Museum Archives • general delivery • Murray Harbour, Prince Edward Island C0A 1V0 • (902) 962-2201

O'Leary
Prince Edward Island Potato Museum Archives • 1 Heritage Ln • O'Leary, Prince Edward Island C0V 1V0 • (902) 859-2639 • http://www.peipotatomuseum.com

West Point Lighthouse Museum Archives • POB 429 • O'Leary, Prince Edward Island C0B 1V0 • (902) 859-3605 • http://www.westpointlighthouse.com

Orwell
Orwell Garner Historic Village Museum • Vernon RR2 • Orwell, Prince Edward Island C0A 2E0 • (902) 651-8510 • http://www.orwellcorner.net

Port Hill
Green Park Shipbuilding Museum • Yeo House, Tyne Valley, RR1 • Port Hill, Prince Edward Island C0B 2C8 • (902) 831-7947

Rustico
Farmers Bank of Rustice Museum • Hunter River, RR3 • Rustico, Prince Edward Island C0A 1N0 • (902) 963-2304

Summerside
Eptek National Exhibition Centre • 130 Harbour Dr • Summerside, Prince Edward Island C1N 1A9 • (902) 888-8373

Rotary Regional Library • 192 Water St • Summerside, Prince Edward Island C1N 1B1 • (902) 436-7323

Tignish
Tignish Cultural Centre Museum Archives • 103 School St • Tignish, Prince Edward Island C0B 2B0 • (902) 882-1999 • http://www.tignish.com

Tyne Valley
Ellerslie Shellfish Museum Archives • POB 24 • Tyne Valley, Prince Edward Island C0B 2C0 • (902) 831-2933

Amos
Societe d'Histoire d'Amos & Bibliotheque • 222 Libre Avenue Est • Amos, Quebec J9T 1H3 • (819) 727-9935

Anse-au-Griffon
Manior Leboutillier • CP 37 • Anse-au-Griffon, Quebec G4X 6A4 • (418) 892-5150

Authier
Ecole du Rang II • 269 Rang II • Authier, Quebec J0Z 1C0 • (819) 782-7289

Aylmer
Bibliotheque Municipale d'Aylmer • 120 rue Principale • Aylmer, Quebec J9H 3M3 • (819) 685-5009 • http://www.ville.aylmer.qc.ca/biblio

Baie Comeau
Musee de Baie Comeau • 43 Rue Mance • Baie Comeau, Quebec G4Z 2H1 • (418) 296-2690

Baie-Sainte-Catherine
Pointe-Noire-Parc Marin du Saguencay • Rte 13B Est • Baie-Sainte-Catherine, Quebec G1N 4L8 • (418) 237-4383

Batiscan
Musee du Manoir du Presbytere de Batiscan Archives • 340 rue Principale, Route 138 • Batiscan, Quebec G0X 1A0 • (418) 362-2061

Beaconsfield
Beaconsfield Public Library • 303 Beaconsfield Blvd • Beaconsfield, Quebec H9W 4A7 • (514) 428-4473 • http://www.total.net/~beaclib/

Beauport
Biblioteque Municipale de Beauport • 3515 Clemenceau, CP 5187 • Beauport, Quebec G1E 6P4 • (418) 666-2231 • http://www.biblioteque.ville.beauport.qc.ca

Berthierville
Musee Gilles Villeneuve Archives • 960 ave Gilles Villeneuve • Berthierville, Quebec J0K 1A0

Bonaventure
Musee Acadien du Quebec • 95 Av Port Royal • Bonaventure, Quebec G0C 1E0 • (418) 534-4000

Boucherville
Bibliotheque Montarville-Boucher-de la Bruere • 501 Chemin du Lac • Boucherville, Quebec J4B 6V6 • (450) 463-7120

Maison Louis-Hippolyte Lafontaine • 314 Rue Marie Victorin • Boucherville, Quebec J4B 7J9 • (450) 449-8347

Brossard
Bibliotheque Municipale de Brossard • 7855 San Francisco • Brossard, Quebec J4X 2A4 • (450) 463-7130 • http://www.ville.brossard.qc.ca

Cap Sainte Ignace
Societe Historique des Bernier d'Amerique & Bibliotheque • 133 est du Manoir, CP 82 • Cap Sainte Ignace, Quebec G0R 1H0 • (418) 246-5383 • *Journal Historique des Bernier*

Chambly
Parc Historique National du Fort Chambly Archives • 2 Rue Richelieu, CP 115 • Chambly, Quebec J3L 2B9 • (450) 658-1585

Societe Monteregienne de genealogie • 251 rue Bonque • Chambly, Quebec J3L 1H1

Chateau-Richer
Centre D'Interpretation de la cote de Beaupre Archives • 7007 Av Royale • Chateau-Richer, Quebec G0A 1N0 • (418) 824-3677

Musee de l'Abeille • 8862 Blvd Sainte-Anne • Chateau-Richer, Quebec G0A 1N0 • (418) 824-4411 • http://www.musee-abeille.qc.ca

Chelsea
Historical Society Of The Gatineau • 4 chemin Sherrin • Chelsea, Quebec J9B 2E2 • (819) 827-4432

Chicoutimi
Centre d'Archives du Saguenay-Lac-Saint-Jean • 930 rue Jacques Chartier E Bureau C103 • Chicoutimi, Quebec G7H 2A9 • (418) 698-3516 • http://www.anq.gouv.qc.ca

La Pulperie de Chicoutimi • 300 Rue Duboc • Chicoutimi, Quebec G7J 4M1 • (418) 698-3100 • http://www.pulperie.com

Musee du Saguenay-Lac-Saint-Jean Archives • 534 rue Jacques-Cartier est • Chicoutimi, Quebec G7H 1Z6 • (418) 545-9400

Seminaire De Chicoutimi Bibliotheque • 679 rue Chabanel • Chicoutimi, Quebec G7H 1Z7 • (418) 693-8448

Societe Genealogique du Saguenay & Bibliotheque • Musee du Saguenay-Lac-Saint-Jean, 930 Jacques Cartier est, CP 814 • Chicoutimi, Quebec G7H 5E8 • (418) 549-2805 • *Saguenayensia*

Universite du Quebec a Chicoutimi Bibliotheque • 555 Boul de l'Universite E • Chicoutimi, Quebec G7H 2B1 • (418) 545-5011 • http://www.uqac.ca/

Chisasibi
Cree Nation of Chisasibi • general delivery • Chisasibi, Quebec J0M 1E0

James Bay Cree Nation • James Bay Cree Cultural Education Centre, POB 291 • Chisasibi, Quebec J0M 1M0

Coaticook
Musee Bealne Archives • Chateau Norton, 96 Rue Union • Coaticook, Quebec J1A 1Y9 • (819) 849-6560 • http://www.museebeaulne.qc.ca

Coteau-du-Lac
Lieu Historique National de Coteau-du-Lac Archives • 308 Ch du Fleuve • Coteau-du-Lac, Quebec J0P 1B0 • (450) 763-5631

Desbiens
Centre d'Interpretation de la Metabetchouane • 243 Rue Hebert • Desbiens, Quebec G0W 1N0 • (418) 346-5341

Dolbeau
Societe d'histoire et de genealogie de Maria Chapdeleine • CP 201 • Dolbeau, Quebec G8L 1G9

Dorval
Bibliotheque Municipale de Dorval • 1401 Chemin du Bord du Lac • Dorval, Quebec H9S 2E5 • (514) 633-4170

Drummondville
Bibliotheque Municipale Come-Saint-Germain • 545 rue Des Ecoles • Drummondville, Quebec J2B 1J6 • (819) 478-6573

Societe de genealogie de Drummondville • 545 des Ecoles • Drummondville, Quebec J2B 1J6

Village Ouebecois d'Antan • 1425 Rue Montplaisir • Drummondville, Quebec J2B 7T5 • (819) 478-1441

Eastmain
Cree Nation of Eastmain • general delivery • Eastmain, Quebec J0M 1W0

Eaton
Compton County Historical Society & Archives • Historical Museum, 374 Rte 253 • Eaton, Quebec J0B 1M0 • (819) 875-5256

Eaton Corner
Compton County Historical Museum Archives • 374 Rte 253 • Eaton Corner, Quebec J0B 1M0 • (819) 875-5256

Forestville
Petite Angelicane Museum Archives • 22e Rue • Forestville, Quebec G0T 1E0 • (418) 587-2109

Gaspe
Hyman and Sons General Store Museum • 122 Blvd de Gaspe • Gaspe, Quebec G4X 1A9 • (418) 368-5505 • http://www.parkscanada.qc.ca/forillon

Musee d'Histoire et de Traditions Populaires • Bale de Gaspe • Gaspe, Quebec G0C 1R0

Quebec

Societe Historique de la Gaspesie & Bibliotheque • Historical Museum, 80 Blvd Gaspe, POB 680 • Gaspe, Quebec G0C 1R0 • (418) 368-5710 • *Gaspesie*

Gatineau
Musee Canadien des Civilisations • 100 Rue Laurier • Gatineau, Quebec J8X 4H2 • (819) 776-7000 • http://www.civilization.ca

Societe de Genealogie de l'Outaouais & Bibliotheque • Historical Museum, 855 boul de la Gappe • Gatineau, Quebec J8T 8H9 • (819) 643-0888 • http://www.ville.gatineau.qc.ca/artimage

Granby
Bibliotheque du College • College de Grancy, 50 Saint Joseph St, CP 7000 • Granby, Quebec J2G 9H7 • (450) 372-6614 • http://www.cegepgranby.qc.ca/

Societe d'Histoire de Shefford & Bibliotheque • Maison Vittie, 135-1 Principale • Granby, Quebec J2G 4W7 • (450) 372-4500

Havre-Aubert
Musee de la Mer • general delivery • Havre-Aubert, Quebec G0B 1J0 • (418) 937-5711 • http://www.ilesdelamadeleine.com

Hinchinbrooke
Chateauguay Valley Historical Society • 745 Fairvew Rd • Hinchinbrooke, Quebec J0S 1H0 • (450) 264-3234 • *Chateauguay Valley Historical Society Journal*

Hull
Bibliotheque Municipale de Hull • Maison du Citoyen, 25 rue Laurier, CP 1970 Succ B • Hull, Quebec J8X 3Y9 • (819) 595-7460 • http://www.ville.hull.qc.ca/bibliotheque

Canadian Museum of Civilization Archives • 100 rue Laurier, POB 3100 Sta B • Hull, Quebec J8X 4H2 • (819) 776-7179 • http://www.civilization.ca/cmc/biblio/

Native Alliance of Quebec • 21 Brodeur • Hull, Quebec J8Y 2P6 • (819) 770-7763 • *Alliance*

Societe de Genealogie de L'Outaouais & Bibliotheque • 170 rue de l'Hotel de Ville, CP 2025, Succ B • Hull, Quebec J8X 3Z2 • (819) 663-3744 • *L'Outaouais genealogique*

Iles-de-la-Madelaine
Musee de la Mer Archives • Havre-Aubert, CP 60 • Iles-de-la-Madelaine, Quebec G0B 1J0 • (418) 937-5711

Musee de la Mer • 1023 Rte 199 • Iles-de-la-Madeleine, Quebec G0B 1J0 • (418) 937-5711

Inukjuak
Musee et Centre de Transmission de la Culture • general delivery • Inukjuak, Quebec J0M 1M0 • (819) 254-8277

Joliette
Societe de Genealogie de Lanaudiere • CP 221 • Joliette, Quebec J6E 3Z6 • Nos Sources

Jonquiere
Bibliotheque Municipale de Jonquiere • 2850 Place Davis, CP 2000 • Jonquiere, Quebec G7X 7W7 • (418) 699-6068 • http://www.jonquiere.biblio.qc.ca

Kahnawake
Kahnawake Economic Development Authority • general delivery • Kahnawake, Quebec J0L 1B0

Kanien'kehaka Raotitiohkwa Nation • Kanien'kehaka Raotitiohkwa Cultural Centre, POB 1988 • Kahnawake, Quebec J0L 1B0

Musee Kateri Tekakwitha • Mission Saint-Francois Xavier • Kahnawake, Quebec J0L 1B0 • (450) 632-6030

Kamouraska
Musee de Kamouraska • 69 Av Morel • Kamouraska, Quebec G0L 1M0 • (418) 492-3144

Kanesatake
Kanesatake Nation • Kanesatake Cultural Centre, 681 Sainte Philomene, POB 971 • Kanesatake, Quebec J0N 1E0

Kirkland
Kirkland Municipal Library • 17100 Hymus Blvd • Kirkland, Quebec H9J 2W2 • (514) 630-2726 • http://www.ville.kirkland.qc.ca.

Knowlton
Bibliotheque Commemorative Pettes • 276 rue Knowlton, POB 177 • Knowlton, Quebec J0E 1V0 • (450) 243-6128 • http://www.endirect.qc.ca/~pettes/

Brome County Historical Society & Archives • Historical Museum, 130 Lakeside, POB 690 • Knowlton, Quebec J0E 1V0 • (450) 243-6782 • *Brome County Historical Society Publication*; *Yesterdays of Brome County*

La Baie
Musee du Fjord • 3346 Blvd de la Grande-Baier S • La Baie, Quebec G7B 1G2 • (418) 697-5077 • http://www.museedufjord.com

La Macaza
Les Amis de la Genealogie du Quebec • 1104 Chemin du Lac Chaud • La Macaza, Quebec J0T 1R0

La Pocatiere
College de Sainte Anne de la Pocatiere Bibliotheque • 140 4th Ave • La Pocatiere, Quebec G0R 1Z0 • (418) 856-1525 • http://www.cglapocatiere.qc.ca/biblio/

Musee Francois-Pilote Archives • College de la Pocatiere, 100 av Painchaud • La Pocatiere, Quebec G0R 1Z0 • (418) 856-3145 • http://www.kam.qc.ca

Societe Historique de la Cote du Sud & Bibliotheque • 100 Ave Painchaud, CP 937 • La Pocatiere, Quebec G0R 1Z0 • (418) 856-2104 • http://www.shcds.org

La Salle
L'Octogone Centre de la Culture • 1080 Dollard • La Salle, Quebec H8N 2T9 • (514) 367-6488 • http://www.bpin.qc.ca/lasalle/

Moulin Fleming Museum Archives • 9675 Blvd LaSalle • La Salle, Quebec H8R 2W8 • (514) 367-6486

La Tuque
Conseil de la Nation Atikamekw • 317 Saint Joseph, CP 848 • La Tuque, Quebec G9X 3P6

Lac Megantic
Musee Namesokanjik • 5527 Rue Frontenac • Lac Megantic, Quebec G8B 1H6 • (819) 583-2441 • http://www.lac-megantic.qc.ca

Lac Simon
Centre Amikwan • 1011 Rue Amik-Awiche • Lac Simon, Quebec J0Y 3M0

Lac-au-Saumon
Societe d'histoire et de genealogie de la Matapedia • CP 224 • Lac-au-Saumon, Quebec G0J 1M0

Lachenaie
Societe d'Histoire Region Terrebonne • 230 Sainte-ThTrFse • Lachenaie, Quebec J6W 5L7

Lachine
Bibliotheque Municipale de Saul Bellow • 3100 rue St-Antoine • Lachine, Quebec H8S 4B8 • (514) 634-3471

Lieu Historique National du Commerce de la Fourrure • 1255 Saint-Joseph • Lachine, Quebec H8S 2M2 • (514) 637-7433

Musee de Lachine • 110 Chemin de LaSalle • Lachine, Quebec H8S 2X1 • (514) 634-3471 • http://www.cum.qc.ca/lachine/fr/musee.htm

Musee des Soeurs de Sainte-Anne • 1300 Blvd Saint-Joseph • Lachine, Quebec H8S 2M8 • (514) 637-4616

Lachute
Bibliotheque Municipale de Lachute • 378 Principale • Lachute, Quebec J8H 1Y2 • (450) 562-3781 • http://www.lachute.qc.ca/biblio

Societe genealogique d'Argenteuil • 378 rue Principale • Lachute, Quebec J8H 1Y2

Lafontaine
Jesuits Library • Compagnie de Jesus, 175 boul des Hauteurs • Lafontaine, Quebec J7Z 5T8 • (450) 438-3593

Lanoraie
Societe d'Histoire de Lanoraie D'Autray • 9 Louis-Joseph Doucet • Lanoraie, Quebec J0K 1E0

L'Assomption
Societe d'Histoire de MRC L'Assomption • CP 2305 • L'Assomption, Quebec J5W 1R7

Laval
Maison Andre-Benjamin-Papineau • 5475 Blvd Saint-Martin W • Laval, Quebec H7T 1C6 • (450) 681-1157

Service de la Bibliotheque de Ville de Laval • 1535 boul Chomedey • Laval, Quebec H7V 3Z4 • (450) 978-5990

Lavaltrie
Societe d'Histoire de Lavaltrie • 501 Notre-Dame • Lavaltrie, Quebec J0K 1H0

Lennoxville
Canadian Church Historical Society • Quebec Diocesan Archives, Bishop Univ • Lennoxville, Quebec J1M 1Z7 • (416) 924-9192 • Canadian Church Historical Society Journal

John Bassett Memorial Library • Bishop's University & Champlain Regional College, College St • Lennoxville, Quebec J1M 1Z7 • (819) 822-9600 • http://www.ubishops.ca/library_info

L'Epiphanie
Societe d'Histoire de L'Epiphanie • 682 Rang Petit Saint-Esprit • L'Epiphanie, Quebec J5X 2M4

Levis
Bibliotheque Alphonse-Desjardins • College de Levis, 9 rue Mgr Gosselin • Levis, Quebec G6V 5K1 • (418) 833-1249 • http://www.collegedelevis.qc.ca/biblio

Musee du College de Levis • 9 Rue M. Gosselin • Levis, Quebec G6V 5K1 • (418) 837-8600

L'Islet
Musee Maritime du Quebec • 55 Rue des Pionniers Est • L'Islet, Quebec G0R 2B0 • (418) 247-5001

Listuguj
Listuguj Mi'gmaq First Nation Government • 17 Riverside W, POB 298 • Listuguj, Quebec G0C 2R0

Longueuil
Bibliotheque Municipal de Longueuil • 100 rue St Laurent Ouest, CP 5000 • Longueuil, Quebec J4K 4Y7 • (450) 463-7180 • http://www.ville.longueuil.qc.ca/bibliotheque • *Bibliotheque Municipal de Longueuil Bulletin*

Bibliotheque Municipale de Longueuil-C H Grignon Branch • 1660 rue Bourassa • Longueuil, Quebec J4J 3A4 • (450) 463-7180

Musee Historique Charles le Moyne • 4 Rue Saint-Charles Est • Longueuil, Quebec J4H 1A9

Musee Marie-Rose Durocher • 80 Rue Saint-Charles E • Longueuil, Quebec J4H 1A9 • (450) 651-8104

Lorette
Conseil Attikamek-Montagnais • 80 Boulevard Bastien • Lorette, Quebec G0A 4V0

Loretteville
Association des Blais d'Amerique • 123 Mgr Dumas • Loretteville, Quebec G2B 2Z6

Musee Kio-Warini • Village Huron • Loretteville, Quebec G2B 3W5 • (418) 843-5515

Malartic
Musee Regional des Mines • 650 Rue de la Paix • Malartic, Quebec J0Y 1Z0 • (619) 757-4677

Maniwaki
Chateau Logue Museum Archives • 8 Rue Comeau • Maniwaki, Quebec J9E 2R8 • (819) 449-7999

Conseil de la Nation Algonquine Anishnabeg • 314 Hill St, Box 313 • Maniwaki, Quebec J9E 3C9

Kitigan Zibi Nation • Kitigan Zibi Cultural Education Centre, 41 Kikinamage Mikan • Maniwaki, Quebec J9E 3B1

Maria
Micmacs of Maria Band • POB 1280 • Maria, Quebec G0C 1Y0

Marieville
Bibliotheque Commemorative Desautels • 1801 duPont St • Marieville, Quebec J3M 1J7 • (450) 460-4988 • http://www.ville.marieville.qc.ca

Matane
Societe d'histoire et de genealogie de Matane • CP 608 • Matane, Quebec G4W 2E1

Societe d'Histoire et de Genealogie de Matane • 230 ave St-Jerome • Matane, Quebec G4W 3A2 • (418) 562-9766 • http://www.genealogie.org/club/shgmatame • *Revue: Au Pays de Matane*

Melbourne
Richmond County Historical Society & Archives • Historical Museum, 1296 Rte 243 • Melbourne, Quebec J0B 2B0 • (819) 845-2303 • http://www.interlinx.qc.ca/~e-dhealy

Mistissini
Cree Nation of Mistissini • general delivery • Mistissini, Quebec G0W 1C0

Mont Royal
Reginald J P Dawson Library • 1967 blvd Graham • Mont Royal, Quebec H3R 1G9 • (514) 734-2967

Montebello
Lieu Historique National du Manoir-Papineau • 500 Notre-Dame • Montebello, Quebec J0V 1L0 • (819) 423-6965

Montmagny
Societe genealogique de Montmagny • 188 rue Saint-Ignace • Montmagny, Quebec G2T 2Y1

Montreal
Archives Provinciales Capucins • 3650 boul de la Rousseliere • Montreal, Quebec H1A 2X9 • (514) 642-5391

Basilique Notre-Dame de Montreal • 110 Rue Notre-Dame W • Montreal, Quebec H2Y 1T2 • (514) 842-2925

Biblioteque Municipale de Montreal • Salle Gagnon, 1210 Sherbrooke E St • Montreal, Quebec H2L 1L9 • (514) 872-2900 • http://ville.montreal.qc.ca/biblio/biblio.htm

Bibliotheque de Pavillon Lalemant • College Jean-De-Brebeuf, 5625 rue Decelles • Montreal, Quebec H3T 1W4 • (514) 342-9342 • http://www.brebeuf.qc.ca/

Bibliotheque de Theologe • Compagnie de Jesus, 5605 av Decelles • Montreal, Quebec H3T 1W4 • (514) 737-1465

Bibliotheque du Musee du Chateau Ramezay Museum Library • 280 rue Notre Dame Est • Montreal, Quebec H2Y 1C5 • (514) 861-3708 • http://www.chateauramezay.qc.ca/

Bibliotheque Nationale du Quebec • 2275 rue Holt • Montreal, Quebec H2G 3H1 • (514) 873-1100 • http://www.bnquebec.ca/

Black Watch of Canada Regimental Memorial Museum Archives • 2067 Bleury St • Montreal, Quebec H3A 2K2 • (514) 496-1686 • http://www.blackwatchcanada.com

Quebec

Canadian Jewish Congress • 1590 McGregor Ave • Montreal, Quebec H3G 1C5 • (514) 931-0548 • *Canadian Jewish Archives, New Series*

Canadian Jewish Congress National Archives • 1590 Docteur Penfield Ave • Montreal, Quebec H3G 1C5 • (514) 931-7531 • http://www.cjc.ca/archives.html

Centre Commemoratif de l'Holocauste a Montreal • 1 Carre Cummings • Montreal, Quebec H3W 1M6 • (514) 345-2605

Centre d'Histoire de Montreal • 335 Pl d'Youville • Montreal, Quebec H2Y 3T1 • (514) 872-9645 • http://www.ville.montreal.qc.ca/chm

Chateau Ramezay • 280 E Notre Dame • Montreal, Quebec H2Y 1C5 • (514) 861-3708

College De Montreal Bibliotheque • 1931 Ouest rue Sherbrooke • Montreal, Quebec H3H 1E3 • (514) 933-7397 • http://www.college-montreal.qc.ca/

Direction des Archives Nationales de l'Ouest du Quebec • 1945 rue Mullins • Montreal, Quebec H3K 1N9 • (514) 873-3064

Institut d'histoire de l'Amerique Francaise • Fondation Lionel-Groulx, 261 Bloomfield Ave • Montreal, Quebec H2V 3R6 • (514) 278-2232 • *Revue D'Histoire de L'Amerique Francaise*

Italian Cultural Institute • 1200 Penfield Ave • Montreal, Quebec H3A 1A9 • (514) 849-3473

Jewish Genealogical Society of Montreal • 5599 Edgemore Ave • Montreal, Quebec H4W 1V4 • (514) 484-0100

Lake Saint Louis Historical Society • Historical Museum, POB 1024, Sta A • Montreal, Quebec H3C 2W9

Marguerite d'Youville Museum • 1185 Rue Saint-Mathieu • Montreal, Quebec H3H 2H6 • (514) 932-7724

Marianopolis College Library • 3880 Cote des Neiges • Montreal, Quebec H3H 1W1 • (514) 931-8792 • http://www2.marianopolis.edu

McGill University Libraries • 3459 McTavish St • Montreal, Quebec H3A 1Y1 • (514) 398-4677 • http://www.library.mcgill.ca/ • *Fontanus*

Musee David M Stewart Archives • The Old Fort St Helen's Island, CP 1200, Succ A • Montreal, Quebec H3C 2Y9 • (514) 861-6701 • http://www.stewart-museum.org • *4 M's Bulletin*

Musee de l'Eglise Notre-Dame • 424 Rue Saint-Sulpice • Montreal, Quebec H2Y 2Y5 • (514) 842-2925

Musee de l'Oratoire Saint-Joseph • 3800 CH Reine-Marle • Montreal, Quebec H3V 1H6 • (514) 733-8211

Musee des Soeurs Grises de Montreal • 1185 Rue Saint-Matthieu • Montreal, Quebec H3H 2H6 • (514) 937-9501

Musee du Frere Andre • Oratoire Saint-Joseph, 3800 Chemin Queen Mary • Montreal, Quebec H3V 1H6 • (514) 733-8211

Musee Maison Saint-Gabriel • 2145 Pl Dublin • Montreal, Quebec H3K 2A2 • (514) 935-9136 • http://www.maisonsaint-gabriel.qc.ca

Musee Marc-Aurele Fortin • 118 Rue Saint-Pierre • Montreal, Quebec H2Y 2L7 • (514) 845-6108

Musee Marguerite Bourgeoys • 400 Rue Saint-Paul Est • Montreal, Quebec H2Y 1H4 • (514) 282-8670 • http://www.marguerite-bourgeoys.com

Musee Stewart au Fort de Ile Sainte-Helene • 20 Chemin Tour de l'Iste • Montreal, Quebec H3C 4G5 • (514) 861-6701 • http://www.stewart-museum.org

Polish Library • McGill University, 3479 Peel St • Montreal, Quebec H3A 1W7 • (514) 398-6978 • http://www.biblioteka.info/

Redpath Museum Archives • 859 Sherbrooke St W • Montreal, Quebec H3A 2K6 • (514) 348-4086 • http://www.mcgill.ca/redpath

Royal Canadian Ordnance Corps Museum Archives • 6560 Rue Hochlega • Montreal, Quebec H1N 3R9 • (514) 252-2241

Societe Genealogique Canadienne-Francaise & Bibliotheque • 3440 rue Davidson • Montreal, Quebec H1W 2Z5 • (514) 527-1010 • http://www.sgcf.com • *Societe Genealogique Canadienne-Francaise Memoires*

Universite de Montreal Dept. d'Histoire • CP 6128, Sec Centre-Ville • Montreal, Quebec H3C 3J7 • (514) 343-6254 • Bulletin RCHTQ

MontrTal

Centre de recherches genealogiques du Quebec • 11440 54iFme Ave • MontrTal, Quebec H1E 2J1

Mutane

Musee du Vieu-Phare • 968 Av du Phare • Mutane, Quebec G4W 1V7 • (418) 562-1065

Nemaska

Cree Nation of Nemaska • general delivery • Nemaska, Quebec J0Y 3B0

New Richmond

Gaspesian British Heritage Village Archives • 351 Blvd Pardo W • New Richmond, Quebec G0C 2B0 • (418) 392-4487

Nicolet

Seminaire De Nicolet Library & Museum • 900 Blvd Louis Frechette, Bureau 110 • Nicolet, Quebec J3T 1V5 • (819) 293-4838 • http://www.archives-seminaire-nicolet.qc.ca/

Societe d'Histoire Regionale de Nicolet & Bibliotheque • 2705 du Fleuve ouest, RR1 • Nicolet, Quebec J0G 1E0 • (819) 293-2213 • *Les Cahiers Nicholetains*

Notre Dame du Nord

Algonquin Nation Programs and Services Secretariat • POB 367 • Notre Dame du Nord, Quebec J0Z 3B0

Nedelec

Societe du patrimoine et de genealogie du Canton Nedelec • 623 Route 101 • Nedelec, Quebec J0Z 2Z0

Odanak

Reserve Indienne d'Odanak • 102 rue Waban-aki • Odanak, Quebec J0G 1H0

Old Chelsea

Historical Society of the Gatineau • POB 485 • Old Chelsea, Quebec J0X 1N0 • (819) 827-4432 • *Up the Gatineau*

Ouje-Bougoumou

Cree Nation of Ouje-Bougoumou • general delivery • Ouje-Bougoumou, Quebec G0W 3C0

Outremont

Centre de Recherche Lionel-Groulx • 261 Bloomfield Ave • Outremont, Quebec H2V 3R6 • (514) 271-4759 • http://www.sdm.qc.ca/crlg

Pasbpebiac

Site-Historique du Banc-de-Paspebiac • 3e Rue Pte du Banc • Pasbpebiac, Quebec G0C 2K0 • (418) 752-6229

Perce

Centre d'Interpretation du Parc de l'Ile-Bonaventure-et-du Rocher-Perce • general delivery • Perce, Quebec G0C 2L0 • (418) 782-2721

Musee Le Chataud • 145 Rte 132 • Perce, Quebec G0C 2L0 • (418) 782-5100

Pierrefonds

La Societe Genealogique Des Martin Casier • CP 156, Succ Pierrefonds • Pierrefonds, Quebec H9H 4K9

Pointe Claire

Quebec Family History Society • POB 1026 • Pointe Claire, Quebec H9S 4H9

Pointe-a-la-Croix

Lieu Historique National du Canada de la Batalle-de-la-Ristigouche • Route 132 • Pointe-a-la-Croix, Quebec G0C 1L0 • (418) 788-5676 • http://www.parcscanada.qc.ca/ristigouche

Pointe-au-Pere
Musee de la Mer Rimouski • 1034 du Phare • Pointe-au-Pere, Quebec G5M 1L8 • (418) 724-6214

Pointe-au-Pic
Musee de Charlevois • 1 Chemin du Havre • Pointe-au-Pic, Quebec G0T 1M0 • (418) 665-4411

Musee Laure Conan Archives • 30 rue Saint-Andre • Pointe-au-Pic, Quebec G0T 1M0

Pointe-Claire
Quebec Family History Society & Library • POB 1026, Sta Pointe Claire • Pointe-Claire, Quebec H9S 4H9 • (845) 695-1502 • http://www.cam.org/~qfhs.index.html • *Connections*

Quebec
Cap aux Diamants • 1 Cote de la Fabrique, CP 26 Haute Ville, Quebec Quebec • G1R 4S2 • (418) 692-4242 • *Cap aux Diamants*

Fortifications-de-Quebec • 2 Rue d'Auteuil, Quebec Quebec • G1K 7R3 • (418) 648-7016 • http://www.parcscanada.qc.ca/fortifications

Fort-Numero-Un de la Pointe-de-Levy • 41 Ch du Gouvernement, Quebec Quebec • G1K 7R3 • (418) 835-5182 • http://www.parcscanada.qc.ca/levy

La Societe Historique de Quebec & Bibliotheque • 72 Cote de la Montagne, Quebec Quebec • G1K 4E3 • (418) 692-0556 • http://www.societehistoriquedequbec.qc.ca • *Cahier C'Histoire*

Les Archives de la Ville de Quebec • 350 rue Saint Joseph E, 4th Flr, Quebec Quebec • G1K 3B2 • (418) 691-7307 • http://www.ville.quebec.qc.ca/

Literary and Historical Society of Quebec & Library • 1080 rue de la Chevrotiere, Quebec Quebec • G1R 3J4 • (418) 694-9147

Literary and Historical Society of Quebec Library • 44 rue Saint Stanislas, Quebec Quebec • G1R 4H3 • (418) 694-9147

Musee Bon-Pasteur • 14 Rue Couillard, Quebec Quebec • G1R 3S9 • (418) 694-0243

Musee des Augustines de l'Hopital General de Quebec • Monastere des Augustines, 260 Blvd Langelier, Quebec Quebec • G1K 5N1

Musee des Ursulines • 12 Rue Donnacona, Quebec Quebec • G1R 4T1 • (418) 694-0694 • http://www.museocapitale.qc.ca

Musee Royal 22e Regiment Archives • Cote La Citadelle, Quebec Quebec • G1R 4V7 • (418) 694-2815 • http://www.lacitadelle.qc.ca

Parc de l'Artillerie • 2 Rue d'Auteuil, Quebec Quebec • G1K 7R3 • (418) 648-4205 • http://www.parcscanada.qc.ca/artillerie

Soeurs Ursulines De Quebec Archives • 18 Rue Donnacona, Quebec Quebec • G1R 4T1 • (418) 692-2523

Vieille Maison des Jesuites • 2320 Chemin des Foulons, Quebec Quebec • G1T 1X4

Restigouche
Confederacy of Indians of Quebec • POB 443 • Restigouche, Quebec G0C 2R0

Richmond
Centre d'Interpretation de l'Ardoise • 5 Rue Belmont • Richmond, Quebec J0B 2H0 • (819) 82603313

Rimouski
Maison Lamontagne Museum Archives • 707 Blvd du Rivage E • Rimouski, Quebec G5L 1E9 • (418) 722-4038

Musee Regional de Rimouski • 35 Rue Saint-Germain Ouest • Rimouski, Quebec G5L 4B4 • (418) 724-2272 • http://www.museerimouski.qc.ca

Societe Genealogique de l'Est du Quebec • 110 Rue de L'Eveche Est • Rimouski, Quebec G5L 1X9 • (418) 724-3242 • L'Estuaire Genealogique

Societe Genealogique de L'est du Quebec & Bibliotheque • 110 Rue de L'Eveche Ouest • Rimouski, Quebec G5L 1X9 • (418) 724-3242 • http://www.genealogie.org/club/sgar

Riviere-Du-Loup
Bibliotheque Municipale Francoise-Bedard • 67 rue de Rocher • Riviere-Du-Loup, Quebec G5R 1J8 • (418) 862-4252 • http://www.riviere-du-loup.qc.ca/biblio

Bibliotheques Publiques Du Bas-Saint-Laurent • 465 St Pierre • Riviere-du-Loup, Quebec G5R 4T6 • (418) 867-1682 • http://www.crsbp.net

Societe d'histoire et de genealogie de Riviere-du-Loup • 65 rue Hotel-de-Ville • Riviere-du-Loup, Quebec G5R 1L4

Rouyn-Moranda
Maison Dumulon Museum Archives • CP 242 • Rouyn-Moranda, Quebec J9X 5C3 • (819) 797-7125

Bibliotheque Universite du Quebec en Abitibi-Temiscamingue • 425 Blvd du College, BP 8000 • Rouyn-Noranda, Quebec J9X 5M5 • (819) 762-0931 • http://www.uqat.uquebec.ca/

Genealogie Abitibi-Temiscamingue • 27 du Terminus Ouest • Rouyn-Noranda, Quebec J9P 2P3

Societe du patrimoine et de genealogie de Rouyn-Noranda • 541 ave la Liberte • Rouyn-Noranda, Quebec J9X 3X7

Roxboro
Bibliotheque de Roxboro • 110 rue Cartier • Roxboro, Quebec H8Y 1G8 • (514) 684-8247

Saint Bruno-de Montarville
Bibliotheque Municipale de Saint Bruno-de-Montarville • 82 Seigneurial W • Saint Bruno-de Montarville, Quebec J3V 5N7 • (450) 441-8338

Saint Constant
Canadian Railroad Historical Association & Archives • Canadian Railway Museum, 120 St Pierre • Saint Constant, Quebec J5A 2G9 • (450) 638-1522 • http://www.exporail.org

Saint Eustache
Bibliotheque Municipale Guy-Belisle Saint Eustache • 80 boul Arthur Sauve • Saint Eustache, Quebec J7R 2H7 • (514) 974-5035 • http://www.ville.saint/qc.ca/biblio

Saint Hyacinthe
Bibliotheque a Saint Germain • 2720 rue Dessaulles • Saint Hyacinthe, Quebec J2S 2V7 • (450) 773-4865 • http://www.biblios.saint-hyacinthe.qc.ca/

Bibliotheque du Seminaire de Saint-Hyacinthe • 650 rue Girouard Est • Saint Hyacinthe, Quebec J2S 2Y2 • (450) 774-8977 • http://www.bibssh.qc.ca/

Cegep de Saint-Hyacinthe, Bibliotheque • 3000 rue Boulle • Saint Hyacinthe, Quebec J2S 1H9 • (450) 773-6800

Sisters Of Saint Joseph Of Saint Hyacinthe Bibliotheque • 805 Raymond • Saint Hyacinthe, Quebec J2S 5T9 • (450) 773-6067

Saint Laurent
Tekeyan Armenian Cultural Association • 825 Manoogian St • Saint Laurent, Quebec H4N 1Z5 • (514) 747-6680 • *Abaka*

Saint-Andre-Avelin
Musee des Pioneers • 20 Rue Bourgeois • Saint-Andre-Avelin, Quebec J0V 1W0 • (819) 983-2624

Saint-Andre-d'Argenteuil
Musee Regional d'Argenteuil • 44 Rue du Long-Sault • Saint-Andre-d'Argenteuil, Quebec J0V 1X0 • (514) 387-3861

Saint-Basile-le-Grand
Bibliotheque Municipale de Saint-Basile-le-Grand • 40 rue Avaria, CP 1010 • Saint-Basile-le-Grand, Quebec J3N 1M5 • (450) 653-0287

Saint-Calixte
Societe d'Histoire de Saint-Calixte • 3850 Route 335 • Saint-Calixte, Quebec J0K 1Z0

Saint-Denis
Maison des Chapais • 2 Rte 132, CP 70 • Saint-Denis, Quebec G0L 2R0 • (418) 498-2353 • http://www.mcq.qc.ca

Saint-Donat
Societe d'Histoire de Saint-Donat • CP 815 • Saint-Donat, Quebec J0T 2C0

Sainte Anne-de-Bellevue
John Abbott College Library • POB 2000 • Sainte Anne-de-Bellevue, Quebec H9X 3L9 • (514) 457-6610 • http://www.johnabbott.qc.ca

Sainte Anne-des-Monts
Societe d'histoire et d'Archeologie des Monts & Bibliotheque • 675 Blvd Saint Anne Ouest, CP 1192 • Sainte Anne-des-Monts, Quebec G4V 1T9 • (418) 763-7871

Sainte Therese-de-Blanville
Bibliotheque Municipale de Sainte-Therese • 150 Boul du Seminaire • Sainte Therese-de-Blanville, Quebec J7E 1Z2 • (450) 434-1442 • http://www.ville.sainte-therese.qc.ca

Sainte-Anne-de-Beaupre
Musee de Sainte-Anne • 9803 Blvd Sainte-Anne • Sainte-Anne-de-Beaupre, Quebec G0A 3C0 • (418) 827-6873

Sainte-Anne-des-Monts
Societe d'histoire et d'archeologie des Monts • CP 1192 • Sainte-Anne-des-Monts, Quebec G0E 2G0

Sainte-Foy
Archives Nationales du Quebec • 1210 ave du Seminaire, CP 10450 • Sainte-Foy, Quebec G1V 4N1 • (418) 644-4797 • http://www.anq.gouv.qc.ca

Bibliotheque Municipale de Sainte-Foy • 999 Ave Roland Beaudin • Sainte-Foy, Quebec G1V 4E1 • (418) 641-6277 • http://www.ville.sainte-foy.qc.ca

Federation des Societes d'histoire du Quebec • CP 9454 • Sainte-Foy, Quebec G1V 4B8

Federation Quebecoise des Societes de Genealogie • CP 9454 • Sainte-Foy, Quebec G1V 4B8

Maison Hamel-Bruneau • 2608 Ch Saint-Louis • Sainte-Foy, Quebec G1V 4E1 • (418) 654-4325

Societe de Genealogie de Quebec & Bibliotheque • 1210 ave du Seminaire, CP 9066 • Sainte-Foy, Quebec G1V 4A8 • (418) 651-9127 • http://www.sgq.qc.ca/ • L'Ancestre

Sainte-Julie
Club de Genealogie de Sainte-Julie • 391 du Roussillon • Sainte-Julie, Quebec J3E 1B4

Sainte-Julienne
Societe d'Histoire et Genealogie Sainte-Julienne • CP 429 • Sainte-Julienne, Quebec J0K 2T0

Societe historique et genealogique de Sainte-Julienne • 2482 place Rivet, CP 429 • Sainte-Julienne, Quebec J0K 2T0

Sainte-Marie
Maison J A Vachon • 343 Rue de la Cooperative • Sainte-Marie, Quebec G5E 3B6 • (418) 387-4052

Saint-Epiphane
Societe genealogique du KRT • 258 ave Sirois • Saint-Epiphane, Quebec G0L 2X0

Saint-Eustache
Moulin Legare • 232 Rue Saint-Eustache • Saint-Eustache, Quebec J7R 2L7 • (514) 472-4440

Musee Jean-Hotte • 405 Grande-Obte • Saint-Eustache, Quebec J7P 1H6 • (450) 473-4370

Nos Amis de la Genealogie • 107 25th Ave • Saint-Eustache, Quebec J7P 2V1

Saint-Evariste
Ecomusee de la Haute-Beauce • Musee Territoire, 325 Rue Principale • Saint-Evariste, Quebec G0M 1G0 • (418) 459-3195

Saint-Hubert
Societe de genealogie Saint-Hubert • CP 37036, CSP Comp Cousineau • Saint-Hubert, Quebec J3Y 8N3

Saint-Hyacinthe
Musee de Seminaire de Saint-Hyacinthe • 650 Rue Girard Est • Saint-Hyacinthe, Quebec J2S 7B7 • (450) 774-0203

Saint-Jean
Musee du Fort Saint-Jean Archives • 15 Jacques-Cartien Nord • Saint-Jean, Quebec J3B 8R8 • (450) 358-6777

Saint-Jean-de-Matha
Societe d'Histoire de St-Jean-de-Matha • CP 151 • Saint-Jean-de-Matha, Quebec J0K 2S0

Saint-Jean-Port-Joli
Maison Medard-Bourgault • 332 de Gaspe W • Saint-Jean-Port-Joli, Quebec G0R 3G0 • (418) 598-3880

Musee des Anciens Canadiens • 332 Av de Gaspe W • Saint-Jean-Port-Joli, Quebec G0R 3G0 • (418) 598-3392

Musee Les Retrouvailles • 248 Av de Gaspe • Saint-Jean-Port-Joli, Quebec G0R 3G0 • (418) 598-3531

Saint-Jean-sur-Richelieu
Bibliotheque Municipale Adelard-Berger • 180 rue Laurier, CP 1025 • Saint-Jean-sur-Richelieu, Quebec J3B 7B2 • (450) 357-2113 • http://www.ville.saint-jean-sur-richelieu.qc.ca

Musee de Haut-Richelieu • 182 Jacques-Cartier N • Saint-Jean-sur-Richelieu, Quebec J3B 7W3 • (450) 347-0649

Saint-Jerome
Societe de genealogie des Laurentides • CP 131 • Saint-Jerome, Quebec J7Z 5T7 • Echos Genealogiques

Saint-Joseph-de-Beauce
Musee Marius Barbeau • CP 1081 • Saint-Joseph-de-Beauce, Quebec G0S 2V0 • (418) 397-4039

Saint-Joseph-de-Sorel
Nusee du Nativageur Rottant • La Goeletta, 425 Port Desiree • Saint-Joseph-de-Sorel, Quebec J31 3E2

Saint-Lambert
Musee Marsil • 349 Riverside • Saint-Lambert, Quebec J4P 1A8 • (450) 671-3098

Saint-Laurent
Yorkshire Air Museum, Canada Branch • 470 Petit St • Saint-Laurent, Quebec H4N 2H6 • http://www.yorksairmuseum.freeserve.co.uk

Saint-Paul-de-Ile-aux-Noix
Fort Lennox Museum Archives • 1 61st Av • Saint-Paul-de-Ile-aux-Noix, Quebec J0J 1G0 • (450) 291-5700 • http://parkscanada.pch.qc.ca/parks/Quebec/Fortlennox

Saint-Paul-de-Joliette
Societe d'Histoire de Saint-Paul • 21 boul Brassard • Saint-Paul-de-Joliette, Quebec J0K 3E0

Saint-Polycarpe
Societe genealogique de la Presqu'ile • 137 rue Sainte-Catherine • Saint-Polycarpe, Quebec J0P 1X0

Saint-Prosper
Societe d'histoire et de genealogie de Saint-Prosper • CP 4 • Saint-Prosper, Quebec G0X 3A0

Saint-Roch de L'Achigan
Societe d'Histoire et Souvenirs Saint-Roch • 14 Impasse Roy • Saint-Roch de L'Achigan, Quebec J0K 3H0

Musee D'Histoire de Saint-Roch Archives • Roger Lemay, 437 Rang RiviFre Sud • Saint-Roch-de-L'Achigan, Quebec J0K 3H0

Sept Iles
Bibliotheque Louis-Ange-Santerre • 500 Ave Jolliet • Sept Iles, Quebec G4R 2B4 • (418) 964-3355 • http://www.verkuel.net

Bibliotheques Publiques de la Cote-Nord • 59 Napoleon • Sept Iles, Quebec G4R 5C5 • (418) 962-1020 • http://www.crsbpcn.qc.ca/

Mamit Innuat Nation • 700 boulevard Laure, Bureau 208 • Sept-Iles, Quebec G4R 1Y1

Musee Regional de la Cote-Nord • 500 Blvd Laure • Sept-Iles, Quebec G4R 4K9 • (418) 968-2070

Societe de genealogie de la Cote-Nord • 700 boul Laure, local 190 • Sept-Iles, Quebec G4R 1X1

Shawnigan
Cite de l'Energie • CP 156 • Shawnigan, Quebec G9N 5T9 • (819) 536-4992 • http://www.mauricie.net/citeenergie

Sherbrooke
Biliotheque Municipale Eva-Senecal • 450 Marquette St • Sherbrooke, Quebec J1H 1M4 • (819) 821-5861 • http://www.bibliotheque.ville.sherbrooke.qc.ca

La Societe d'Histoire de Sherbrooke & Bibliotheque • Centre d'Interpretation de l'Historie de Sherbrooke, 275 Rue Dufferin • Sherbrooke, Quebec J1H 4M5 • (819) 821-5406 • http://www.shs.ville.sherbrooke.qc.ca

Musee Regimentaire les Fusiliers de Sherbrooke • 64 Rue Belvidere S • Sherbrooke, Quebec J1H 4B4 • (819) 564-5940

Seminaire De Sherbrooke Bibliotheque • 195 rue Marquette • Sherbrooke, Quebec J1H 1L6 • (819) 563-2050

Societe de Genealogie des Cantons de l'Est & Bibliotheque • 275 Dufferin • Sherbrooke, Quebec J1H 4M5 • (819) 821-5414 • http://www.gencalogie.org/club/sgce • *L'Entraide Genealogique*

Sillery
Association of Pelletier Families • CP 6700 • Sillery, Quebec G1T 2W2 • (450) 467-1023

Domaine Cataraquai Musee • 2141 Ch Saint-Louis • Sillery, Quebec G1T 1P9 • (418) 681-3010 • http://www.cataraqui.qc.ca

Federation des Familles-Souches Quebecoises • CP 6700 • Sillery, Quebec G1T 2W2

Seminaire Des Peres Maristes Bibliotheque • 2315 Chemin St-Louis • Sillery, Quebec G1T 1R5 • (418) 651-4944

Villa Bagatelle • 1563 Ch Saint-Louis • Sillery, Quebec G1S 1G1 • (418) 688-8074 • http://www.cataraqui.qc.ca

Sorel
Societe genealogique Les Patriotes • 105 Prince Local 111 • Sorel, Quebec J3P 4J9

Sorel-Tracy
Bibliotheque Municipale de Sorel-Tracy • 145 rue George • Sorel-Tracy, Quebec J3P 1C7 • (450) 780-5750 • http://www.bbliotheque.sorel.qc.ca

Stanbridge East
Mississquoi Historical Society & Archives • Mississquoi Museum, 2 River St, POB 186 • Stanbridge East, Quebec J0J 2H0 • (450) 248-3153 • http://www.geocities.com/Heartland/lake/8392 • *Missisquoi Historical Society Reports*

Stanstead
Stanstead County Historical Society & Library • 535 rue Dufferin, POB 268 • Stanstead, Quebec J0B 3E0 • (819) 876-7322 • *Stanstead Historical Society Journal*

Tadoussac
Chapelle des Indiens • general delivery • Tadoussac, Quebec G0T 2A0 • (418) 235-4324

Poste de Traite Chauvin • 147 Rue du Bord-de-l'Eau • Tadoussac, Quebec G0T 2A0 • (418) 295-4857

Terrasse-Vaudreuil
Montreal Quebec Cornish Association • 29 9E Ave • Terrasse-Vaudreuil, Quebec J7V 3L5

Terrebonne
Bibliotheque Municipale • 855 Ile-des-moulins • Terrebonne, Quebec J6W 4N7 • (450) 471-4192

Societe de Developpement Culturel de Terrebonne • 867 Saint-Pierre • Terrebonne, Quebec J6W 1E6

Thetford Mines
Societe genealogique de la region de l'Amiante • 671 boul Smith Sud • Thetford Mines, Quebec G6G 1N1 • *Bercail*

Tracy
Bibliotheque de Tracy • 3025 Place de la Mairie • Tracy, Quebec J3R 1C2 • (450) 742-8321

Trois-Pistoles
Societe historique et genealogique de Trois-Pistoles • CP 1586 • Trois-Pistoles, Quebec G0L 4K0 • (418) 851-3144 • L'Echo des Basques

Trois-Rivieres
Archives du Seminaire de Trois-Rivieres • 858 rue Laviolette, Local 221 • Trois-Rivieres, Quebec G9A 5S3 • (819) 376-4459 • http://www.sites.cgocable.ca/crc

Bibliotheques de Trois-Rivieres, Bibliotheque Gatien-la Pointe • 1225 Place de l'Hotel de Ville, CP 1713 • Trois-Rivieres, Quebec G9A 5L9 • (819) 372-4617 • http://www.bibliomcq.qc.cq/trois-rivieres/

Centre d'Exposition sur l'Industrie des Pates et Papiers • 800 Parc Portuaire, CP 368 • Trois-Rivieres, Quebec G9A 5H3 • (819) 372-4633 • http://www.v3r.net

L'Arbre Historique • 610 Prevost • Trois-Rivieres, Quebec G8Y 4A5

Lieu Historique National des Forges du Saint-Maurice • 10000 Blvd des Forges • Trois-Rivieres, Quebec G9C 1B1 • (819) 378-5116

Musee des Ursulines • 734 Rue des Ursulines • Trois-Rivieres, Quebec G9A 5B5 • (819) 375-7922 • http://www.musee-ursulines.qc.ca

Musee Militaire du 12e Regiment Blinde du Canada • 574 Rue Saint-Francois-Xavier • Trois-Rivieres, Quebec G9A 1R6 • (819) 371-5290

Universite du Quebec a Trois-Rivieres Bibliotheque • 3351 Blvd des Forges • Trois-Rivieres, Quebec G9A 5H7 • (819) 376-5005 • http://www.uqtr.uquebec.ca/biblio/

Val d'Or
Grand Council of the Crees • 1500 Sullivan Rd • Val d'Or, Quebec J9P 1M1

Village Minier de Bourlamaque • La Cite de l'Or, 90 Av Perreault • Val d'Or, Quebec J9P 4P3 • (819) 825-7616 • http://www.citedelor.qc.ca

Valcourt
Musee J Armand Bombardier • 1001 Av J A Bombardier • Valcourt, Quebec J0E 2L0 • (514) 632-5300 • http://www.museebombardier.com

Valleyfield
Societe de genealogie Salaberry de Valleyfield • CP 164 • Valleyfield, Quebec J6S 2M2 • Au fil du Temps

Societe d'histoire et de genealogie de Salaberry • 75 rue St-Jean-Baptiste • Valleyfield, Quebec J6T 1Z6

Varennes
Club de Genealogie d'Hydro-Quebec • 51 de la Sarcelle • Varennes, Quebec J3X 2A2

Quebec

Vaudreuil-Dorion
Musee Regional de Vaudreuil-Soulanges • 431 Av Saint-Charles • Vaudreuil-Dorion, Quebec J7V 2N3 • (450) 455-2092 • http://www.mrvs.qc.ca

Verdun
Bibliotheque de Verdun • 5955 Bannantyne Ave • Verdun, Quebec H4H 1H6 • (514) 765-7170 • http://www.cum.qc.ca/verdun

Societe d'histoire et de genealogie de Verdun • 450 rue Bannantyne • Verdun, Quebec H4G 1E3

Victoriaville
Cegep de Victoriaville Centre de Documentation • 475 rue Notre Dame E • Victoriaville, Quebec G6P 4B3 • (819) 758-6401

Musee Laurier • 16 Rue Laurier Ouest • Victoriaville, Quebec G6P 6P3 • (819) 357-8655

Societe d'histoire et de genealogie des Bois-Francs • 4 Ave Laurier Ouest, no 1 • Victoriaville, Quebec G6P 6P3

Village des Hurons Wendake
Nation Huronne-Wendat • 225 Place Chef Michel Laveau • Village des Hurons Wendake, Quebec G0A 4V0

Ville de la Baie
Bibliotheque Municipale de Ville de la Baie • 1911 6th Ave • Ville de la Baie, Quebec G7B 1S1 • (418) 697-5085 • http://www.labaie.biblio.qc.ca/

Ville des Laurentides
Lieu Historique National de Sir Wilfrid Laurier • 12e Av Laurier • Ville des Laurentides, Quebec J0R 1C0 • (450) 439-3702

Waskaganish
Cree Nation of Waskaganish • general delivery • Waskaganish, Quebec J0M 1R0

Waswanipi
Cree Nation of Waswanipi • general delivery • Waswanipi, Quebec J0Y 3C0

Waterloo
Waterloo Public Library • 650 Rue de la Cour, CP 700 • Waterloo, Quebec J0E 2N0 • (450) 539-2268

Wemindji
Cree Nation of Wemindji • 16 Beaver Rd • Wemindji, Quebec J0M 1L0

Wendake
Institut Culturel et Educatif Montagnais • 40 rue Francois Gros-Louis #7 • Wendake, Quebec G0A 4V0

Westmount
Atwater Library • 1200 Atwater Ave • Westmount, Quebec H3Z 1X4 • (514) 935-7344

Westmount Historical Association & Bibliotheque • 4574 Sherbrooke St W • Westmount, Quebec H3Z 1G1

Westmount Public Library • 4574 rue Sherbrooke Ouest • Westmount, Quebec H3Z 1G1 • (514) 989-5300 • http://www.westlib.org

Whapmagoostui
Cree Nation of Whapmagoostui • general delivery • Whapmagoostui, Quebec J0M 1G0

Windsor
Centre Culturel et Patrimonial la Poudriere de Windsor • 342 Saint-Georges • Windsor, Quebec J1S 2Z5 • (819) 845-5284

SASKATCHEWAN

Abernethy
Motherwell Homestead Museum Archives • POB 247 • Abernethy, Saskatchewan SQA 040 • (306) 333-2116

Arcola
Arcola Museum Archives • POB 279 • Arcola, Saskatchewan S0C 0G0 • (306) 455-2480

Assinboia
Assiniboia and District Historical Society • Historical Museum, POB 1211 • Assinboia, Saskatchewan S0H 0B0

Saint Mary's Museum of Maxstone • POB 1693 • Assiniboia, Saskatchewan S0H 0B0

Avonlea
Avonlea and District Museum Archives • 201 Railway Av, POB 401 • Avonlea, Saskatchewan S0H 0C0 • (306) 666-2101 • http://www3.sk.sympatico.ca/avonlea

Balcarres
Okanese First Nation • POB 759 • Balcarres, Saskatchewan S0G 0C0

Peepeekisis First Nation • POB 518 • Balcarres, Saskatchewan S0G 0C0

Star Blanket First Nation • POB 456 • Balcarres, Saskatchewan S0G 0C0

Bateman
Bateman Historical Museum Archives • POB 89 • Bateman, Saskatchewan S0H 0E0 • (306) 648-3548

Batoche
Batoche National Historic Site Archives • POB 999 • Batoche, Saskatchewan S0M 0E0 • (306) 423-5400

Battleford
Battleford National Historic Park Archives • POB 70 • Battleford, Saskatchewan S0M 0E0 • (306) 937-2621 • http://parkscanada.pch.qc.ca

Fred Light Museum • POB 40 • Battleford, Saskatchewan S0M 0E0 • (306) 937-7111

Beauval
Frazer's Museum Archives • Hwy 155 N, POB 64 • Beauval, Saskatchewan S0M 0G0

Big River
Big River Memorial Museum Archives • POB 220 • Big River, Saskatchewan S0J 0E0 • (306) 469-2112

Biggar
Biggar Museum and Gallery Archives • 106 3rd Ave, POB 1598 • Biggar, Saskatchewan S0K 0M0 • (306) 948-3451 • http://www.sasktourism.com/biggarmuseum

Homestead Museum Archives • POB 542 • Biggar, Saskatchewan SoK 0M0 • (306) 348-3427

Saskatchewan Genealogical Society, Biggar Branch • POB 135 • Biggar, Saskatchewan S0K 0M0

Birch Hills
Muskoday First Nation • POB 9 • Birch Hills, Saskatchewan S0J 0G0

Black Lake
Black Lake Denesuline Nation • general delivery • Black Lake, Saskatchewan S0J OH0

Blaine Lake
Blaine Lake Museum Archives • POB 10 • Blaine Lake, Saskatchewan S0J 0L0

Briercrest
Briercrest and District Museum Archives • POB 216 • Briercrest, Saskatchewan S0H 0K0 • (306) 799-4406

Saskatchewan Genealogical Society, Moose Jaw Branch • POB 154 • Briercrest, Saskatchewan S0H 0K0

Broadview
Broadview Historical Association & Archives • Historical Museum, POB 556 • Broadview, Saskatchewan S0G 0K0 • (306) 696-2286 • http://townwelcome.to/broadview

Cowessess First Nation • POB 607 • Broadview, Saskatchewan S0G 0K0

Kahkewistahaw First Nation • POB 609 • Broadview, Saskatchewan S0G 0K0

Yorkton Tribal Council • POB 790 • Broadview, Saskatchewan S0G 0K0

Bulyea
Lakeside Museum Archives • RR1 • Bulyea, Saskatchewan S0G 0L0 • (306) 725-4558

Cabri
Cabri and District Museum Archives • 102 1st St • Cabri, Saskatchewan S0N 0J0 • (306) 587-2915

Cadillac
Cadillac Museum Archives • general delivery • Cadillac, Saskatchewan S0N 0K0 • (306) 785-2128

Cando
Mosquito Grizzly Bear Head First Nation • POB 177 • Cando, Saskatchewan S0K 0V0

Red Pheasant First Nation • POB 70 • Cando, Saskatchewan S0K 0V0

Red Pheasant Healing Lodge • POB 283 • Cando, Saskatchewan S0K 0V0

Canoe Narrows
Canoe Lake First Nation • general delivery • Canoe Narrows, Saskatchewan S0M 0K0

Canwood
Canwood Museum Archives • Village • Canwood, Saskatchewan S0J 0K0 • (306) 468-2676

Carlyle
Rusty Relics Museum Archives • Railway Av & 3rd St W • Carlyle, Saskatchewan S0C 0R0 • (306) 453-2812

White Bear First Nation • POB 700 • Carlyle, Saskatchewan S0G 0R0

Carnduff
Saskatchewan Genealogical Society, Southeast Branch • POB 460 • Carnduff, Saskatchewan S0C 0S0

Central Butte
Central Butte District Museum Archives • POB 165 • Central Butte, Saskatchewan S0H 0T0 • (306) 796-2146

Saskatchewan Genealogical Society, Central Butte Branch • POB 224 • Central Butte, Saskatchewan S0H 0T0

Climax
Climax Community Museum Archives • 1st E, POB 59 • Climax, Saskatchewan S0N 0N0 • (306) 293-2051

Cochin
Moosomin First Nation • POB 45 • Cochin, Saskatchewan S0M 0L0

Saulteaux First Nation • POB 159 • Cochin, Saskatchewan S0M 0L0

Coronach
Coronach District Museum Archives • 240 1st St W • Coronach, Saskatchewan S0H 0Z0 • (306) 267-5724

Craik
Prairie Pioneer Museum Archives • Old 11 Hwy • Craik, Saskatchewan S0G 0V0 • (306) 734-2480

Saskatchewan Genealogical Society, Craik Branch • POB 337 • Craik, Saskatchewan S0G 0V0

Cumberland House
Cumberland House Cree Nation • POB 220 • Cumberland House, Saskatchewan S0E 0S0

Saskatchewan

Cupar
Cupar and District Heritage Museum Archives • POB 164 • Cupar, Saskatchewan S0G 0Y0 • (306) 723-4324

Cutknife
Clayton McLain Memorial Museum Archives • general delivery • Cutknife, Saskatchewan S0M 0N0 • (306) 398-2590

Debden
Big River First Nation • POB 519 • Debden, Saskatchewan S0J OS0

Denare Beach
Northern Gateway Museum Archives • general delivery • Denare Beach, Saskatchewan S0P 0B0 • (306) 362-2054 • http://www.quantumlynx.com

Dillon
Buffalo River First Nation • general delivery • Dillon, Saskatchewan S0M 0S0

Dinsmore
Yester-Years Community Museum Archives • POB 216 • Dinsmore, Saskatchewan S0L 0T0

Dodsland
Dodsland Museum Archives • POB 203 • Dodsland, Saskatchewan S0L 0V0 • (306) 356-4700

Duck Lake
Beardy's and Okemasis First Nation • POB 340 • Duck Lake, Saskatchewan S0K 1J0

Duck Lake Regional Interpretive Centre • POB 328 • Duck Lake, Saskatchewan S0K 1J0 • (306) 467-2057

Fort Carlton Agency Council • POB 340 • Duck Lake, Saskatchewan S0K 1J0

Duff
Duff Community Heritage Museum • POB 57 • Duff, Saskatchewan S0M 0S0 • (306) 728-3682

Dysart
Dysart Historical Society • Qu'Appelle Ave • Dysart, Saskatchewan S0G 1H0 • (306) 432-2255

Eastend
Eastend School Museum Archives • 1st Ave, POB 214 • Eastend, Saskatchewan S0N 0T0 • (306) 295-3819

Edam
Harry S Washbrook Museum Archives • POB 182 • Edam, Saskatchewan S0M 0V0 • (306) 397-2260

Elbow
Elbow Museum Archives • POB 207 • Elbow, Saskatchewan S0H 1J0 • (306) 854-2285

Elrose
Elrose Heritage Museum Archives • 116 4th Ave E • Elrose, Saskatchewan S0L 0Z0 • (306) 378-2202

Esterhazy
Esterhazy Community Museum Archives • Hwy 22, POB 149 • Esterhazy, Saskatchewan S0A 1X0 • (306) 745-6761

Kaposvar Historic Site Archives • Our Lady of Assumption Church • Esterhazy, Saskatchewan S0A 0X0 • (306) 745-2715

Estevan
Estevan National Exhibition Centre Archives • 118 4th St • Estevan, Saskatchewan S4A 0T4 • (306) 634-7644 • http://www.cap.estevan.sk.ca/enec

Eston
Prairie West Historical Society & Archives • Historical Museum, 946 2nd St SE, POB 910 • Eston, Saskatchewan S0L 1A0 • (306) 962-3772

Saskatchewan Genealogical Society, West Central Branch • POB 1147 • Eston, Saskatchewan S0L 1A0

Foam Lake
Foam Lake Museum Archives • POB 1041 • Foam Lake, Saskatchewan S0A 1A0 • (306) 272-41292

Fond Du Lac
Fond Du Lac Denesuline Nation • general delivery • Fond Du Lac, Saskatchewan S0J 0W0

Fort Qu'Appelle
Fort Qu'Appelle Museum Archives • 198 Bay Ave N • Fort Qu'Appelle, Saskatchewan S0G 1S0 • (306) 332-6033

Muscowpetung First Nation • POB 1310 • Fort Qu'Appelle, Saskatchewan S0G 1S0

Pasqua First Nation 79 • POB 968 • Fort Qu'Appelle, Saskatchewan S0G 1S0

Standing Buffalo Dakota Nation • POB 128 • Fort Qu'Appelle, Saskatchewan S0G 1S0

Frenchman Butte
Frenchman Butte Museum Archives • POB 114 • Frenchman Butte, Saskatchewan S0M 0W0 • (306) 344-4478

Frobisher
Frobisher Thresherman's Museum Archives • POB 194 • Frobisher, Saskatchewan S0C 0V0 • (306) 486-2162

Gallivan
Sweetgrass First Nation • POB 147 • Gallivan, Saskatchewan S0M 0X0

Glen Ewen
Glen Ewen Community Antique Centre • general delivery • Glen Ewen, Saskatchewan S0C 1C0 • (306) 925-2221

Glentworth
Glentworth Museum Archives • POB 174 • Glentworth, Saskatchewan S0H 1V0

Goodeve
Little Black Bear First Nation • POB 40 • Goodeve, Saskatchewan S0A 1C0

Goodsoil
Goodsoil Historical Museum Archives • POB 57 • Goodsoil, Saskatchewan S0M 1A0 • (306) 238-2084

Govan
Govan and District Museum • general delivery • Govan, Saskatchewan S0G 1Z0

Parkland Regional Library-Govan Branch • POB 40 • Govan, Saskatchewan S0G 1Z0 • (306) 484-2122

Gravelbourg
Gravelbourg and District Museum Archives • POB 862 • Gravelbourg, Saskatchewan S0H 1X0 • (306) 648-2332

Grenfell
Grenfell Community Museum Archives • Wolseley Ave, POB 400 • Grenfell, Saskatchewan S0G 2B0 • (306) 697-2930

Sakimay First Nation • POB 339 • Grenfell, Saskatchewan S0G 0R0

Harris
Harris Heritage and Museum Archives • Railway Ave • Harris, Saskatchewan S0L 1K0 • (306) 652-2158

Hazenmore
Heritage Hazenmore Museum Archives • POB 103 • Hazenmore, Saskatchewan S0N 1C0 • (306) 264-5105

Hodgeville
Hodgeville Community Museum Archives • 3rd Rd NW • Hodgeville, Saskatchewan S0H 2B0 • (306) 677-2693

Hudson Bay
Hudson Bay Museum Archives • 512 Churchill St, POB 931 • Hudson Bay, Saskatchewan S0E 0Y0 • (306) 865-2170

Humboldt
Humboldt and District Museum Archives • Main St & 6th Ave, POB 2349 • Humboldt, Saskatchewan S0K 2A0 • (306) 682-5226

Imperial
Imperial and District Museum Archives • POB 269 • Imperial, Saskatchewan S0G 2J0 • (306) 963-2280

Indian Head
Indian Head Museum Archives • POB 155 • Indian Head, Saskatchewan S0G 2K0 • (306) 695-3800

Ituna
Ituna Cultural and Historical Museum Archives • POB 282 • Ituna, Saskatchewan S0A 1N0

Kamsack
Cote First Nation • POB 1659 • Kamsack, Saskatchewan S0A 1S0

Kamsack and District Museum Archives • POB 991 • Kamsack, Saskatchewan S0A 1S0 • (306) 542-4415

Kamsack Historical Society • Historical Society, Centennial Park • Kamsack, Saskatchewan S0A 1S0 • (306) 542-4415

Keeseekoose First Nation • POB 1120 • Kamsack, Saskatchewan S0A 1S0

Kelliher
Kelliher and District Heritage Museum Archives • POB 8 • Kelliher, Saskatchewan S0A 1V0 • (306) 675-4514

Kerrobert
Kerrobert and District Museum Archives • POB 401 • Kerrobert, Saskatchewan S0L 1R0 • (306) 834-2744

Kincaid
Kincaid Museum Archives • POB 177 • Kincaid, Saskatchewan S0H 2J0 • (306) 254-3910

Kindersley
Kindersley Plains Museum Archives • Baker Park, 1st St W & Princess Ave, POB 609 • Kindersley, Saskatchewan S01 1S0 • (306) 463-6620

Saskatchewan Genealogical Society, Kindersley Branch • POB 645 • Kindersley, Saskatchewan S0L 1S0

Kinistino
Kinistino District Pioneer Museum Archives • POB 10 • Kinistino, Saskatchewan S0J 1H0 • (306) 864-2838

Kipling
Kipling District Historical Society & Archives • Historical Museum, 4th St & Centennial Ave • Kipling, Saskatchewan S0G 2S0 • (306) 736-2488

Kisbey
Pheasant Rump Nakota First Nation • POB 238 • Kisbey, Saskatchewan S0C 1L0

La Loche
Clearwater River Dene Nation • POB 389 • La Loche, Saskatchewan S0M 1G0

La Ronge
Lac La Ronge Museum Archives • City Center • La Ronge, Saskatchewan S0J 1L0

Pahkisimon Nuye Ah Library • Bag Serv 6600 • La Ronge, Saskatchewan S0J 1L0 • (306) 425-4525 • http://www.lib.sk.ca/pnls

Lac La Rong
Lac La Ronge Indian Band • POB 480 • Lac La Rong, Saskatchewan S0J 1L0

Lancer
Lancer Centennial Museum Archives • POB 3 • Lancer, Saskatchewan S0N 1G0 • (306) 889-2925

Langham
Langham and District Heritage Village Museum Archives • POB 516 • Langham, Saskatchewan S0K 2L0 • (306) 283-4342

Lanigan
Lanigan and District Heritage Centre Archives • 75 Railway Ave • Lanigan, Saskatchewan S0K 2M0 • (306) 365-2569 • http://www3.sk.sympatico.ca/ldha

Lashburn
Lashburn Centennial Museum Archives • general delivery • Lashburn, Saskatchewan S0M 1H0 • (306) 285-3860

Leask
Mistawasis First Nations • POB 250 • Leask, Saskatchewan S0J 1M0

Lebret
Touchwood-File Hills-Qu' Appelle Tribal Council • POB 178 • Lebret, Saskatchewan S0G 2Y0

Leoville
Pelican Lake First Nation • POB 399 • Leoville, Saskatchewan S0J 1N0

Leross
Kellross Heritage Museum Archives • POB 46 • Leross • Sasketchewan • S0A 2C0 • (306) 675-6144

Leroy
Leroy and District Herigage Museum Archives • POB 47 • Leroy, Saskatchewan S0K 2P0 • (306) 286-3464

Lestock
Muskowekwan First Nation • POB 249 • Lestock, Saskatchewan S0A 2G0

Lloydminster
Barr Colony Cultural Centre • 4420 50th Ave • Lloydminster, Saskatchewan S9V 0W2 • (306(825-5655

Lloydminster Public Library • 5010 49th Ave • Lloydminster, Saskatchewan S9V 0T2 • (306) 875-0850

Loon Lake
Big Bear Trails Museum • general delivery • Loon Lake, Saskatchewan S0M 1L0 • (306) 837-2070

Island Lake First Nation • POB 460 • Loon Lake, Saskatchewan S0M 1L0

Makwa Sahgaiehcan First Nation • POB 340 • Loon Lake, Saskatchewan S0M 1L0

Lumsden
Lumsden Heritage Museum Archives • Qu'Appelle Dr • Lumsden, Saskatchewan S0G 3C0 • (306) 731-2905

Lumsden Historical Society & Archives • Historical Museum, 50 Qu'Appelle Dr W • Lumsden, Saskatchewan S0G 3C0 • (306) 731-2905

Luseland
Luseland and Districts Museum Archives • Grand Av • Luseland, Saskatchewan S0L 2A0 • (306) 372-4258

Macklin
Macklin and District Museum Archives • 5002 Herald St • Macklin, Saskatchewan S0L 2C0 • (306) 753-2610

Macrorie
Macrorie Museum Archives • POB 177 • Macrorie, Saskatchewan S0L 2E0 • (306) 243-4507

Main Centre
Main Centre Heritage Museum Archives • POB 42 • Main Centre, Saskatchewan S0H 2V0 • (306) 784-2953

Mankota
Saskatchewan Genealogical Society, Grasslands Branch • POB 272 • Mankota, Saskatchewan S0H 2W0

Manor
Manor Museum • Newcombe St • Manor, Saskatchewan S0C 1R0 • (306) 448-2055

Maple Creek
Antique Tractor Museum and Frontier Village • general delivery • Maple Creek, Saskatchewan S0N 1N0 • (306) 667-2964

Fort Walsh Museum Archives • Cypress Hills • Maple Creek, Saskatchewan S0N 1N0 • (306) 562-2645 • http://parkscanada.pch.qc.ca/parks/saskatchewan/fort_walsh

Jasper Cultural and Historical Centre Archives • POB 1504 • Maple Creek, Saskatchewan S0N 1N0 • (306) 562-2434

Nekaneet First Nation • POB 548 • Maple Creek, Saskatchewan S0N 1N0

Southwestern Saskatchewan Oldtimer's Museum Archives • 218 Jasper St, POB 1540 • Maple Creek, Saskatchewan S0N 1N0 • (306) 662-2474

Marcelin
Muskeg Lake First Nation • POB 248 • Marcelin, Saskatchewan S0J 1R0

Mayfield
Maryfield Museum Archives • POB 262 • Mayfield, Saskatchewan S0G 3K0 • (306) 646-2201

McCord
McCord and District Museum Archives • 1 Main St • McCord, Saskatchewan S0H 2T0 • (306) 478-2522 • http://www.virtualmuseum.ca

Meadow Lake
Flying Dust First Nation • POB 8001 • Meadow Lake, Saskatchewan S9X 1T8

Meadow Lake Museum Archives • POB 610 • Meadow Lake, Saskatchewan S0M 1V0 • (306) 236-3622

Meadow Lake Tribal Council • POB 8003 • Meadow Lake, Saskatchewan S9X 1T8

Melfort
James Smith First Nation • POB 1059 • Melfort, Saskatchewan S0E 1A0

Melfort and District Museum Archives • 401 Melfort St W • Melfort, Saskatchewan S0E 1A0 • (306) 752-5870 • http://collections.lc.qc.ca/melford

Saskatchewan Genealogical Society, North-East Branch • POB 1988 • Melfort, Saskatchewan S0E 1A0

Melville
Melville Heritage Museum Archives • Heritage Dr, POB 2528 • Melville, Saskatchewan S0A 2P0 • (306) 728-2070

Melville Railway Museum Archives • Melville Regional Park • Melville, Saskatchewan S0A 7P0 • (306) 728-4177

Meota
Saskatchewan Genealogical Society, Battlefords Branch • POB 138 • Meota, Saskatchewan S0M 1X0

Middle Lake
Middle Lake Museum Archives • POB 157 • Middle Lake, Saskatchewan S0K 2X0

Milden
Milden Community Museum Archives • general delivery • Milden, Saskatchewan S0L 2L0 • (306) 935-2199

Montreal Lake
Montreal Lake Cree Nation • general delivery • Montreal Lake, Saskatchewan S0J 1Y0

Moose Jaw
History of Transportation Museum • 50 Diefenbacker Dr • Moose Jaw, Saskatchewan S6J 1L9 • (306) 693-5989 • http://www.wdm.ca

Moose Jaw Museum and Exhibition Centre Archives • Crescent Park • Moose Jaw, Saskatchewan S6H 0X6 • (306) 692-4471

Palliser Regional Library • 366 Coteau St W, POB 2500 • Moose Jaw, Saskatchewan S6H 6Y2 • (306) 692-3669 • http://www.palliser.lib.sk.ca

Palliser Regional Library-Moose Jaw Branch • 461 Langdon Crescent • Moose Jaw, Saskatchewan S6H 0X6 • (306) 692-2787 • On Line

Pioneer Village and Museum of Saskatchewan • Hwy 2 • Moose Jaw, Saskatchewan S6H 7T2 • (306) 650-3505

Moosomin
Jamieson Museum Archives • 306 Gertie St, POB 236 • Moosomin, Saskatchewan S0G 3N0

Saskatchewan Genealogical Society, Pipestone Branch • POB 832 • Moosomin, Saskatchewan S0G 3N0

Morse
Morse Museum Archives • POB 308 • Morse, Saskatchewan S0H 3C0 • (306) 629-3230

Mossbank
Mossbank and District Museum Archives • 3rd St, POB 278 • Mossbank, Saskatchewan S0H 3G0 • (306) 354-2829

Muenster
Saint Peter's Abbey & College Library • 100 College Dr, POB 40 • Muenster, Saskatchewan S0K 2Y0 • (306) 682-7860 • http://www.stpeterscollege.ca/

Naicam
Naicam Museum Archives • POB 93 • Naicam, Saskatchewan S0K 2Z0 • (306) 874-2280 • http://www3.sk.sympatico.ca/mnaicam

Neiburg
Manitou Pioneer Museum Archives • POB 160 • Neiburg, Saskatchewan S0M 2C0

Nipawin
Nipawin and District Historical Museum Archives • 2nd Ave W & Hwy 35 E, POB 1917 • Nipawin, Saskatchewan S0E 1E0 • (306) 862-9299

Nokomis
Mokomis and District Museum • POB 56 • Nokomis, Saskatchewan S0G 3R0 • (306) 528-2979

Norquay
Key First Nation • POB 70 • Norquay, Saskatchewan S0A 2V0

North Battleford
Battleford's Tribal Council • 1022-102nd St • North Battleford, Saskatchewan S9A 1E6

Heritage Farm and Village Archives • Hwys 16 & 40 • North Battleford, Saskatchewan S9A 2V1 • (306) 445-8033 • http://www.wdm.ca

Lakeland Regional Library • 1302 100th St • North Battleford, Saskatchewan S9A 0V8 • (306) 445-6108 • http://www.lakeland.lib.sk.ca

Onion Lake
Onion Lake First Nation • POB 100 • Onion Lake, Saskatchewan S0M 2E0

Osler
Osler Historical Museum Archives • POB 54 • Osler, Saskatchewan S0K 3A0 • (306) 239-2155

Outlook
Outlook and District Heritage Museum Archives • 100 Railway Ave • Outlook, Saskatchewan S0L 2N0 • (306) 867-8265

Oxbow
Ralph Allen Memorial Museum Archives • 802 Railway Ave • Oxbow, Saskatchewan S0C 2B0 • (306) 483-5082

Pakwaw Lake
Shoal Lake Cree Nation • POB 51 • Pakwaw Lake, Saskatchewan S0E 1G0

Pangman
Saskatchewan Genealogical Society, Pangman Branch • POB 23 • Pangman, Saskatchewan S0C 2C0

Patuanak
English River First Nation • general delivery • Patuanak, Saskatchewan S0M 2H0

Payton
Bresaylor Heritage Museum Archives • POB 33 • Payton, Saskatchewan S0M 2J0 • (306) 895-4813

Little Pine First Nation • POB 70 • Payton, Saskatchewan S0M 2J0

Poundmaker First Nation • POB 220 • Payton, Saskatchewan S0M 2J0

Pelican Narrows
Peter Ballantyne Cree Nation • general delivery • Pelican Narrows, Saskatchewan S0P 0E0

Pelly
Fort Pelley and Livingston Museum Archives • POB 33 • Pelly, Saskatchewan S0M 2J0 • (306) 595-2030

Pierceland
Joseph Bighead First Nation • POB 309 • Pierceland, Saskatchewan S0M 2K0

Plenty
Carscadden's Museum Archives • POB 149 • Plenty, Saskatchewan S0K 2R0 • (306) 932-2226

Porcupine Plain
Porcupine Plain and District Museum Archives • Cultural Centre Bldg, Elm St, POB 98 • Porcupine Plain, Saskatchewan S0E 1H0 • (306) 278-2317

Prairie River
Prairie River Museum Archives • Railway Ave • Prairie River, Saskatchewan S0E 1J0 • (306) 889-4248

Prelate
Saint Angela's Museum Archives • Saint Angela's Convent • Prelate, Saskatchewan S0N 2B0 • (306) 673-2200 • http://www3.sk.sympatico.ca/stangela

Prince Albert
Diefenbaker House Archives • 10 River St E • Prince Albert, Saskatchewan S6V 8A9

Prince Albert Grand Council • POB 2350 • Prince Albert, Saskatchewan S6V 6Z1

Prince Albert Historical Society & Archives • Historical Museum, 10 River St E, • Prince Albert, Saskatchewan S6V 5R8 • (306) 764-2992

Rotary Museum of Police and Corrections Archives • POB 3008 • Prince Albert, Saskatchewan S6V 6J9 • (306) 922-3313

Saskatchewan Genealogical Society, Prince Albert Branch • POB 1464 • Prince Albert, Saskatchewan S6V 5T1

Wahpeton Dakota First Nation • POB 128 • Prince Albert, Saskatchewan S6V 5R4

Punnichy
Day Star First Nation • POB 277 • Punnichy, Saskatchewan S0A 3C0

Gordon First Nation • POB 248 • Punnichy, Saskatchewan S0A 3C0

Raymore
Kawacatoose First Nation • POB 640 • Raymore, Saskatchewan S0A 3J0

Raymore Pioneer Museum Archives • POB 453 • Raymore, Saskatchewan S0A 3J0

Readlyn
Thompson Museum Archives • POB 40 • Readlyn, Saskatchewan S0H 3N0

Red Earth
Red Earth First Nation • POB 109 • Red Earth, Saskatchewan S0E 1K0

Regina
Alex Youck School Museum Archives • 1600 4th Ave • Regina, Saskatchewan S4R 8C8 • (306) 791-8200

Cannington Manor Historic Park Archives • Dept of Historic Parks, Avord Tower • Regina, Saskatchewan S4P 0M8 • (306) 787-9571 • http://www.serm.gov.sk.ca/parks

Cumberland House Museum Archives • 3211 Albert St, Ste 530 • Regina, Saskatchewan S4S 5W6 • (306) 787-9571 • http://www.sarm.gov.sk.ca/parks

Diefenbaker Homestead House Museum Archives • 2900 Wascana Dr, POB 7111 • Regina, Saskatchewan S4P 2S7 • (306) 522-3661 • http://www.wascana.sk.ca

Dr John Archer Library • University of Regina, 3737 Wascana Pkwy • Regina, Saskatchewan S4S 0A2 • (306) 585-4134 • http://www.uregina.ca/library/

Fort Carlton Museum Archives • 3211 Albert St, Sta 530 • Regina, Saskatchewan S4S 5W6 • (306) 787-9571 • http://www.serm.gov.sk.ca/parks

Gabriel Dumont Institute Library • Educ Bldg, Univ Regina, Rm 311, 3737 Wascana Pkwy • Regina, Saskatchewan S4S 0A2 • (306) 347-4100 • http://www.gdinf.org

Government House Historical Society • 4607 Dewdney Ave • Regina, Saskatchewan S4T 1B7 • (306) 787-5363

Government House Museum and Heritage Site • 4607 Dewdney Ave • Regina, Saskatchewan S4P 3V7 • (306) 787-5773 • http://www.graa.gov.sk.ca/govhouse

Regina Firefighters Museum Archives • 1205 Ross Ave • Regina, Saskatchewan S4P 3C8 • (306) 777-7830

Regina Plains Museum Archives • 1835 Scarth St • Regina, Saskatchewan S4P 2G9 • (306) 780-9435 • http://www.reginaplainsmuseum.com

Regina Public Library • 2311 12th Ave, POB 2311 • Regina, Saskatchewan S4P 3Z5 • (306) 777-6000 • http://www.rpl.regina.sk.ca

Royal Canadian Mounted Police Museum Archives • POB 6500 • Regina, Saskatchewan S4P 3J7 • (306) 780-5558 • http://www.rcmpmuseum.com

Saskachewan Pharmacy Museum Archives • 4010 Pasqua St, Ste 700 • Regina, Saskatchewan S4S 7B9 • (306) 359-7277

Saskatchewan Archives • Univ of Regina • Regina, Saskatchewan S7N 0W0 • (306) 787-4068 • http://www.saskarchives.com

Saskatchewan Archives Board • University of Regina, 3303 Hillsdale St • Regina, Saskatchewan S4S 0A2 • (306) 787-4068 • *Saskatchewan History*

Saskatchewan Genealogical Society & Library • 1870 Lorne St, POB 1894 • Regina, Saskatchewan S4P 3E1 • (306) 780-9207 • http://www.saskgenealogy.com • *Saskatchewan Genealogical Society Bulletin*

Saskatchewan Genealogical Society, Regina Branch • 1119 Broadway Ave • Regina, Saskatchewan S4P 1E4

Saskatchewan History and Folklore Society • 1860 Lorne • Regina, Saskatchewan S4P 2L7

Saskatchewan Military Museum Archives • 1600 Elphinstone St • Regina, Saskatchewan S4T 3N1 • (306) 347-9349

Saskatchewan Provincial Library • 1352 Winnipeg St • Regina, Saskatchewan S4P 3V7 • (306) 787-2976 • http://www.lib.sk.ca

Societe historique de la Saskatchewan • 218 - 514 ave Victoria Est • Regina, Saskatchewan S4P 0N7

Wood Mountain Post Archives • 3211 Albert St • Regina, Saskatchewan S4K 5W6 • (306) 787-9571 • http://www.serm.gov.sk.ca/parks

Riverhurst
F T Hill Museum Archives • general delivery • Riverhurst, Saskatchewan S0H 3P0 • (306) 353-2112

Rocanville
Rocanville and District Museum Archives • Qu'Appelle Ave & Saint Albert St • Rocanville, Saskatchewan S0A 3L0 • (306) 645-2605 • http://www3.sk.sympatico.ca/tuccap

Rose Valley
Rose Valley and District Heritage Museum Archives • POB 232 • Rose Valley, Saskatchewan S0E 1M0

Saskatchewan Genealogical Society, Quill Plains Branch • POB 432 • Rose Valley, Saskatchewan S0E 1M0

Rosetown
Rosetown Museum and Art Center • Centennial Library • Rosetown, Saskatchewan S0L 2V0 • (305) 882-3556

Rosthern
Batoche National Historic Site Archives • POB 999 • Rosthern, Saskatchewan S0K 3R0 • (306) 423-6227 • http://parkscanada.pch.qc.ca/parks/saskatchewan/batoche

Mennonite Heritage Museum Archives • general delivery • Rosthern, Saskatchewan S0K 3R0 • (306) 232-5353

One Arrow First Nation • POB 1048 • Rosthern, Saskatchewan S0K 3R0

Rouleau
Rouleau and District Museum Archives • POB 132 • Rouleau, Saskatchewan S0G 4H6 • (306) 776-2363

Saint Victor
Beau Village Museum Archives • POB 58 • Saint Victor, Saskatchewan S0H 3T0 • (306) 642-4016

McGillis Pioneer Home Archives • general delivery • Saint Victor, Saskatchewan S0H 3T0 • (306) 642-3155

Saint Walburg
Saint Walburg and District Historical Museum • POB 336 • Saint Walburg, Saskatchewan S0M 2T0 • (306) 248-3359

Saint-Brieux
Musee Saint-Brieux • 300 Barbier Dr • Saint-Brieux, Saskatchewan S0K 3M0 • (396) 275-2229

Saskatoon
1910 Boomtown Museum Archives • 2610 Lorne Ave S • Saskatoon, Saskatchewan S7J 0S8 • (308) 931-1910 • http://www.sdn.ca

Diefenbaker Canada Centre • Univ of Saskatchewan, 101 Diefenbaker Pl • Saskatoon, Saskatchewan S7N 5B8 • (306) 956-8384 • http://www.usask.ca/diefenbaker

Federation of Saskatchewan Indian Nations • A Packham Ave, Ste 200-103 • Saskatoon, Saskatchewan S7N 4K4

Lucky Man First Nation • 103B Packham Ave, Ste 225 • Saskatoon, Saskatchewan S7N 2T7

Mennonite Historical Society of Saskatchewan • 110 La Ronge Rd • Saskatoon, Saskatchewan S7K 7H8 • (306) 242-6105

Saint Andrew's College Library • 1121 College Dr • Saskatoon, Saskatchewan S7N 0W3 • (306) 966-8983 • http://www.usask.ca/stu

Saskatchewan Archives • Univ of Saskatchewan • Saskatoon, Saskatchewan S7N 0W0 • (306) 933-5832

Saskatchewan Archives Board • Univ of Saskatchewan, 3 Campus Dr • Saskatoon, Saskatchewan S7N 5A4 • (306) 933-5832 • Saskatchewan History

Saskatchewan Genealogical Society, Saskatoon Branch • POB 8651 • Saskatoon, Saskatchewan S7K 6K8

Saskatoon Heritage Society • POB 7051 • Saskatoon, Saskatchewan S7K 4J1

Saskatoon Public Library • 311 23rd St E • Saskatoon, Saskatchewan S5K 0J6 • (306) 975-7555 • http://www.publib.saskatoon.sk.ca

Saskatoon Tribal Council • 200-203 Packham Ave • Saskatoon, Saskatchewan S7N 4K4

Shannon Library • Saint Thomas More College-University of Saskatchewan, 1437 College Dr • Saskatoon, Saskatchewan S7N 0W6 • (306) 966-8916 • http://www.usask.ca/stm/

Ukraine Museum Archives • 202 Av M South • Saskatoon, Saskatchewan S7M 2K4 • (306) 244-4212

Ukranian Museum of Canada Library • 910 Spadina Crescent E • Saskatoon, Saskatchewan S7K 3H5 • (306) 244-3800 • http://www.umc.sk.ca

Univ of Saskatchewan • History Dept, 9 Campus Dr • Saskatoon, Saskatchewan S7N 5A5 • (306) 966-5794 • http://www.usask.ca/history/cjh • *Canadian Journal of History-Annales Canadiennes d'Histoire*

University of Saskatchewan Library • Main Library, 3 Campus Dr • Saskatoon, Saskatchewan S7N 5A4 • (306) 966-6005 • http://library.usask.ca

Western Development Museum Archives • 2935 Melville St, POB 1910 • Saskatoon, Saskatchewan S7K 3S5 • (306) 934-1400 • http://www.wdmuseum.sk.ca/

Whitecap Dakota-Sioux First Nation • RR5, Site 507, Box 28 • Saskatoon, Saskatchewan S7K 3J8

Sceptre
Great Sandhills Museum • POB 29 • Sceptre, Saskatchewan S0W 2H0 • (306) 623-4345

Shamrock
Shamrock Museum Archives • POB 106 • Shamrock, Saskatchewan S0H 3W0 • (306) 648-2909

Shaunavon
Chinook Regional Library-Shaunavon Branch • Grand Coteau Heritage & Cultural Ctr, 440 Centre St, POB 1116 • Shaunavon, Saskatchewan S0N 2M0 • (306) 297-3844

Grand Coteau Heritage and Cultural Centre • Center St, POB 966 • Shaunavon, Saskatchewan S0N 2M0 • (306) 297-3882 • http://www.shaunavonmuseum.sk.ca

Shell Lake
Ahtahkakoop First Nation • POB 220 • Shell Lake, Saskatchewan S0J 2M0

Shell Lake Museum Archives • POB 280 • Shell Lake, Saskatchewan S0J 2G0 • (306) 427-2272

Young Chippewayan First Nation • POB 220 • Shell Lake, Saskatchewan S0J 2G0

Shellbrooke
Sturgeon Lake First Nation • RR1, Comp 5, Site 12 • Shellbrooke, Saskatchewan S0J 2E0

Sintaluta
Carry the Kettle First Nation • POB 57 • Sintaluta, Saskatchewan S0G 4N0

Somme
Saskatchewan Genealogical Society, Porcupine Plain Branch • POB 63 • Somme, Saskatchewan S0N 2N0

Southey
Southey and District Museum Archives • general delivery • Southey, Saskatchewan S0G 4P0

Spalding
Reynold Rapp Museum Archives • 1st St S • Spalding, Saskatchewan S0K 4C0 • (306) 287-4030

Spiritwood
Agency Chiefs Tribal Council • POB 32 • Spiritwood, Saskatchewan S0J 2M0

Witchekan Lake First Nation • POB 879 • Spiritwood, Saskatchewan S0J 2M0

Spruce Home
Buckland Heritage Museum Archives • Hwy 2 • Spruce Home, Saskatchewan S0J 2N0 • (306) 764-8470

Spy Hill
Spy Hill Museum Historical Society & Archives • Historical Museum, 108 Main St, POB 187 • Spy Hill, Saskatchewan S0A 3W0 • (306) 534-2252

Star City
Star City Heritage Museum Archives • 217 5th St • Star City, Saskatchewan S0E 1P0 • (306) 863-2309

Stoughton
Ocean Man First Nation • POB 157 • Stoughton, Saskatchewan S0G 4T0

Stoughton and District Museum Archives • 327 Main St • Stoughton, Saskatchewan S0G 4T0 • (306) 457-2662

Strasbourg
Strasbourg and District Museum Archives • CPR Station, Railway Ave, POB 446 • Strasbourg, Saskatchewan S0G 4V0 • (306) 725-3443

Sturgis
Sturgis Station House Museum Archives • POB 255 • Sturgis, Saskatchewan S0A 4A0 • (306) 548-5565

Swift Current
Saskatchewan Genealogical Society, Swift Current Branch • POB 307 • Swift Current, Saskatchewan S9H 3V8

Wright Historical Museum Archives • Hwy 4, POB 712 • Swift Current, Saskatchewan S9H 3W7

Tisdale
Kinistin First Nations • POB 2590 • Tisdale, Saskatchewan S0E 1T0

Tompkins
Buffalo Bean Museum Archives • near the Railroad • Tompkins, Saskatchewan S0N 2S0 • (306) 622-2024

Torquay
Saskatchewan Genealogical Society, Estevan Branch • POB 81 • Torquay, Saskatchewan S0C 2L0

Turnor Lake
Saskatchewan Genealogical Society, Turnor Lake Branch • general delivery • Turnor Lake, Saskatchewan S0M 3E0

Turtleford
Thunderchild First Nation • POB 340 • Turtleford, Saskatchewan S0M 2Y0

Unity
Unity and District Heritage Museum Archives • POB 12 • Unity, Saskatchewan S0K 4L0 • (306) 228-4464

Val Marie
Perrault's Museum Archives • 1st St N • Val Marie, Saskatchewan S0N 2T0 • (306) 298-2241

Vanguard
Vanguard Centennial Museum Archives • general delivery • Vanguard, Saskatchewan S0N 2V0 • (306) 582-2244

Verigin
Doukhoubor Society Museum Archives • general delivery • Verigin, Saskatchewan S0A 4H0

National Doukhobour Heritage Village • POB 99 • Verigin, Saskatchewan S0A 4H0 • (306) 542-4441

Verwood
Verwood Community Museum Archives • general delivery • Verwood, Saskatchewan S0H 4G0 • (306) 642-5767

Wadena
Fishing Lake First Nation • POB 508 • Wadena, Saskatchewan S0A 4J0

Wadena and District Museum Archives • POB 1208 • Wadena, Saskatchewan S0A 4J0 • (306) 338-3454 • http://wsd.inet.wadena.sk.ca/wadena

Wakaw
John G Diefenbaker Law Office Museum • POB 760 • Wakaw, Saskatchewan S0K 4P0 • (306) 233-5157

Wakaw Heritage Museum Archives • POB 475 • Wakaw, Saskatchewan S0K 4P0 • (306) 233-4257

Waterhen Lake
Waterhen Lake First Nation • POB 9 • Waterhen Lake, Saskatchewan S0M 3B0

Wawota
Wawota and District Museum Archives • general delivery • Wawota, Saskatchewan S0G 5A0 • (306) 739-2116

Weekes
Dunwell and Community Museum Archives • Weekes Recreation Centre • Weekes, Saskatchewan S0E 1V0 • (306) 278-2908

Weyburn
Saskatchewan Genealogical Society, Weyburn Branch • POB 1422 • Weyburn, Saskatchewan S4H 3J9

Sod Line Historical Museum Archives • 411 Industrial Ln • Weyburn, Saskatchewan S4H 2L2 • (306) 842-2922

White Fox
White Fox Museum • POB 68 • White Fox, Saskatchewan S0J 3B0 • (306) 276-2170

Whitewood
Ochapowace First Nation • POB 550 • Whitewood, Saskatchewan S0J 5C0

Old George's Authentic Collectibles Museum • POB 118 • Whitewood, Saskatchewan S0G 5C0 • (306) 735-2255

Southeast Treaty 4 Tribal Council • POB 550 • Whitewood, Saskatchewan S0G 5C0

Whitewood Historical Museum Archives • POB 752 • Whitewood, Saskatchewan S0G 5C0 • (306) 735-2210

Wilcox
Athol Murray College of Notre Dame Museum Archives • POB 100 • Wilcox, Saskatchewan S0G 5E0 • (306) 732-2080 • http://www.notredame.sk.ca

Wilkie
Wilkie and District Museum Archives • 209 1st St E • Wilkie, Saskatchewan S0K 4W0 • (306) 843-2717 • http://www.townofwilkie.com

Willow Bunch
Willow Bunch Museum Archives • 8 5th St E, POB 39 • Willow Bunch, Saskatchewan S0H 4K0 • (306) 473-2806 • http://www.quantumlynx.com/fts/musee

Wollaston Lake
Hatchet Lake Denesuline Nation • general delivery • Wollaston Lake, Saskatchewan S0J 3C0

Wolseley
Wolseley Community Museum Archives • general delivery • Wolseley, Saskatchewan S0G 5H0 • (306) 698-2543

Wood Mountain
Wood Mountain First Nation • POB 104 • Wood Mountain, Saskatchewan S0H 4L0

Wood Mountain Ranch and Rodeo Museum Archives • POB 53 • Wood Mountain, Saskatchewan S0H 4L0 • (306) 266-4539

Wynyard
Wynyard and District Museum • POB 734 • Wynyard, Saskatchewan S0A 4T0 • (306) 554-2898

Yellow Quill
Yellowquill First Nation • POB 40 • Yellow Quill, Saskatchewan S0A 3A0

Yorkton
Saskatchewan Genealogical Society, Yorkton Branch • 28 Dalewood Crescent • Yorkton, Saskatchewan S3N 2P7

Saskatchewan Western Development Museum Archives • Hwy 16 W • Yorkton, Saskatchewan S3N 2V6 • (306) 934-4467 • http://www.sdmuseum.sk.ca

Zehner
Piapot First Nation • general delivery • Zehner, Saskatchewan S0G 5K0

YUKON TERRITORY

Beaver Creek
Beaver Creek Historical Society • general delivery • Beaver Creek, Yukon Territory Y0B 1A0

Burwash Landing
Burwash Landing Historical Society • POB 20 • Burwash Landing, Yukon Territory Y0B 1V0

Carcross
Carcross Historical Society • POB 93 • Carcross, Yukon Territory Y0B 1B0

Carmacks
Carmacks Historical Society • POB 131 • Carmacks, Yukon Territory Y0B 1C0

Dawson City
Dawson City Community Library • POB 1410 • Dawson City, Yukon Territory Y0B 1G0 • (867) 993-5571 • http://www.users.yknet.yk.ca/dcpages

Dawson City Historical Society • Historical Museum, 595 5th Ave, POB 303 • Dawson City, Yukon Territory Y0B 1G0 • (867) 993-5291 • http://www.gold-rush.org

Dawson City Museum and Historical Society & Library • 595 5th Ave, POB 303 • Dawson City, Yukon Territory Y0B 1G0 • (867) 993-5291 • http://www.gold-rush.org

Klondike National Historic Sites Archives • POB 390 • Dawson City, Yukon Territory Y0B 1G0 • (867) 993-5462

Destruction Bay
Destruction Bay Historical Society • general delivery • Destruction Bay, Yukon Territory Y0B 1H0

Faro
Faro Historical Society • POB 279 • Faro, Yukon Territory Y0B 1K0

Haines Junction
Champagne and Aishihik First Nations • POB 5309 • Haines Junction, Yukon Territory Y0B 1L0

Haines Junction Historical Society • POB 5350 • Haines Junction, Yukon Territory Y0B 1L0

Keno City
Keno City Historical Society • Site 1, Box 17 • Keno City, Yukon Territory Y0B 1M0

Keno City Mining Museum Archives • general delivery • Keno City, Yukon Territory Y0B 1J0 • (867) 895-2792 • http://www.kenocity.yk.ca

Mayo
Mayo Historical Society • POB 158 • Mayo, Yukon Territory Y0B 1M0 • (403) 996-2550

Old Crow
Old Crow Historical Society • POB 101 • Old Crow, Yukon Territory Y0B 1N0

Vuntut Gwitch'in First Nation • POB 94 • Old Crow, Yukon Territory Y0B 1N0

Pelly Crossing
Pelly Crossing Historical Society • POB 108 • Pelly Crossing, Yukon Territory Y0B 1P0

Ross River
Ross River Historical Society • general delivery • Ross River, Yukon Territory Y0B 1P0

Tagish
Tagish Historical Society • general delivery • Tagish, Yukon Territory Y0B 1T0

Teslin
George Johnston Tlingit Indian Museum Archives • Mile 804, Alaska Hwy • Teslin, Yukon Territory Y0A 1B0 • (867) 390-2550

Teslin Historical Society • POB 161 • Teslin, Yukon Territory Y0A 1B0

Teslin Tlingit Council • POB 133 • Teslin, Yukon Territory Y0A 1B0

Watson Lake
Kaska Tribal Council • POB 530 • Watson Lake, Yukon Territory Y0A 1C0

Watson Lake Historical Society • POB 390 • Watson Lake, Yukon Territory Y0A 1C0

Whitehorse
Council for Yukon Indians • 22 Nisutlin Dr • Whitehorse, Yukon Territory Y1A 2S5

Fort Selkirk Museum Archives • POB 2703 • Whitehorse, Yukon Territory Y1A 2C6 • (867) 667-5386

MacBride Museum Archives • 1124 1st Ave • Whitehorse, Yukon Territory Y1A 3S9 • (867) 667-2709 • http://www.macbridemuseum.com

MacBride Museum Society & Archives • MacBride Museum, 1st Ave & Wood St, POB 4037 • Whitehorse, Yukon Territory Y1A 3S9 • (867) 667-2709

Whitehorse Historical Society • POB 2703 • Whitehorse, Yukon Territory Y1A 2C6

Yukon Heritage Resources Board • POB 4750 • Whitehorse, Yukon Territory Y1A 4N6

Yukon Historical and Museums Association & Library • 3126 3rd Ave • Whitehorse, Yukon Territory Y1A 1E7 • (867) 667-4704 • http://www.yukonalaska.com/yhma • *Yukon Historical and Museums Association Newsletter*, *Yukon Historical and Museums Association Occasional Papers*; *Borderlands*

Yukon Indian Cultural Education Society • 11 Nisutlin Dr • Whitehorse, Yukon Territory Y1A 3S5

Yukon Territory Archives • 2071 2nd Ave, POB 2703 • Whitehorse, Yukon Territory Y1A 4Z6 • (867) 667-3668 • http://www.gov.yk.ca

Yukon Transportation Museum Archives • 30 Electra Cres • Whitehorse, Yukon Territory Y1A 6E6 • (867) 668-4792 • http://www.yukontransportmuseum.homestead.com

INDEX

Symbols

@ the Library 123
@ Your Library 178, 189, 392
100 Mile and District Historical Society 647
100th Meridian Museum 350
103rd Ohio Volunteer Infantry Memorial Foundation & Archives 457
12th Vancouver Service Battalion Museum 654
15th Field Artillery Regiment Museum Archives 656
1719 Hans Herr House Archives 505
1719 William Trent House Museum Archives 379
1719 William Trent House Museum Newsletter 379
1768 Jeremiah Lee Mansion Archives 274
1784 Michie Tavern Museum Archives 585
1793 Col John Carson House Archives 431
1797 Ezekiel Harris House Archives 126
1840 Whitman School Museum Archives 618
1850 Log Cabin Museum Archives 618
1855 Missouri Town Archives 334
1855 Missouri Town Quarterly 334
1859 Jail Museum Archives 330
1880 Town Museum Archives 523
1881 Mueller-Schmidt House 213
1890 House Museum Archives 394
1892 Timm House Archives 628
1910 Boomtown Museum Archives 710
1st Cavalry Division Museum Archives 545
1st Michigan Museum of Military History Archives 293
20th Century Library Club 387
26th Field Artillery Regimental Museum Archives 659
369th Historical Society 406
3-D Data: Dyckman-Dikeman-Dykeman Newsletter 22
3M Club Genealogy Club 314
3rd Cavalry Museum Archives 85
4 M's Bulletin 700
442nd Veterans Club Archives 141
45th Infantry Division Museum Library 467
4-H Schoolhouse Museum Archives 199
4th Infantry Division Museum Archives 545
54th Mass Glory Brigade Foundation 272
5th Maine Regiment Center Archives 249
82nd Airborne Division War Memorial Museum Archives 427
82nd Historical Society 427

A

A C Clark Library, Newsletter 305
A C Gilbert's Discovery Village Museum Archives 479
A Friendly Word-Friends of the Library Newsletter 448
A H Brown Public Library 523
A J Eastwood Library 514
A J Snyder Estate Museum 414
A Journal of Georgia & the South 125
A Live Thing in the Whole Town 186
A Noble Witness 122
A Nossa Heranca (Our Portuguese Heritage) 142
A R Bowman Museum 479
A R Reddin Memorial Library 321
A R Wentz Library 488
A Tale of Mid-Cities 537
A W Campbell House Museum Archives 690
A Webb Roberts Library 545
A:Shiwi A:Wan Museum and Heritage Center 385
Aaron Cutler Memorial Library 362
Aaronsburg Historical Museum Association & Library 481
AASR Valley of Chicago 154
Abaka 701
Abbe Museum Library 243
Abbess Journal 237
Abbeville County Historical Society, Museum & Archives 511
Abbeville County Library 511
Abbeville County Museum Association 511
Abbeville Historic Preservation Commission 511
Abbeville Memorial Library 1
Abbey Family 570
Abbey of Gethsemani Library 233
Abbey of Regina Laudis Library 91
Abbie Greenleaf Library 361
Abbotsford Campus Library 647
Abbotsford Genealogical Group 647
Abbott Memorial Library 245
ABC-CLIO 70
Abegweit First Nation 695
Abel J Morneault Memorial Library 252
Aberdeen Area Genealogical Society & Library 521
Aberdeen District Library 145
Aberdeen Genealogical Society 319, 599
Aberdeen Museum of History Archives 599
Aberdeen Proving Ground Post Library 255
Abigail Adams Historical Society 276
Abigail Adams Smith Museum Library 406
Abigail S Timme Library 286
Abilene Free Public Library 211
Abilene Preservation League 535
Abilene Public Library 535
Abington Memorial Library 25
Abington Presbyterian Church Library 481
Abington Public Library 265
Abington Social Library 91
Ablah Library 223
Ables Family 527
Abney Family Researcher 186
Aboriginal Centre of Winnipeg 662
Aboriginal Peoples Council 663
About Alfords 329
About Towne 363
Abraham Lincoln Birthplace National Historic Site Library 229
Abraham Lincoln Institute 262
Abraham Lincoln Museum Archives 527
Abraham Lincoln Presidential Library and Museum 174
Absecon Historical Society 367
Abstract 390
Academy Chronicles 390, 396
Academy Hall Museum 98
Academy Museum 98, 396
Academy of American Franciscan History 105
Acadia National Park Archives 243
Acadia Parish Library 236
Acadia Ranch Museum 18
Acadian Archives 246
Acadian Cultural Society & Library 271
Acadian Genealogical and Historical Association 362

INDEX

Acadian Genealogy Exchange & Library 226
Acadian Village 252
Acadiensis: Journal of the History of the Atlantic Region 663
Access 546
Access Point 231
Accohannock Tribe 261
Accokeek Agricultural Museum 255
Accokeek Foundation, Newsletter & Archives 255
Accordian 387
Ace Genealogical Society 287
Ace of Clubs House Museum Archives 561
Acer-Acker Family 301
Acho Dene Koe Indian Band 671
Ackerson-Eckerson Newsletter 387
Acme Municipal Library 641
Acoma Pueblo Historical Society 381, 384
Acoma Tourist and Visitation Center Archives 384
Acorn 278
Acorn Hall House 374
Acorns to Oaks 287
Acree Foundation 248
Across the Border 314
Action Cadienne 238
Acton Historical Society, Newsletter 265
Acton Memorial Library 265
Acton Public Library 98
Acton-Shapleigh Historical Society 243
Acuff Family 528
Acworth Historical Society 359
Acworth Silsby Library 359
Ad Libs 468
Ada Community Library 145
Ada Public Library 441, 463
Ada Township Historical Society 285
Adair County Anquestors 202
Adair County Genealogical Society & Library 226
Adair County Historical Museum 333
Adair County Historical Society 202
Adair County Historical Society, Newsletter & Archives 333
Adair County Kentucky Review 226
Adair County Public Library 226, 333
Adair Family 16
Adair Historian 333
Adak Community Museum Archives 11
Adam Thoroughgood House Archives 596
Adams Addenda 130
Adams Banner 521
Adams County Genealogical Society 184
Adams County Genealogical Society & Library 207, 352, 460
Adams County Historical Museum 81, 182, 352, 603,
Adams County Historical Society 148
Adams County Historical Society & Archives 81, 182, 352, 603, 621
Adams County Historical Society & Library 460, 488
Adams County Historical Society Newsletter 488
Adams County History 488
Adams County Library 438
Adams County Library System 90, 488
Adams County Trumpeter 182
Adams Family 154, 169, 338, 529, 555
Adams Free Library 265
Adams Grist Mill Museum 575
Adams Historical Society, Newsletter & Library 265
Adams House Resource Center Archives 621
Adams Lake Indian Band 648
Adams Museum and House Archives 521
Adams National Historic Site Library 278
Adams Quarterly 119
Adams' Family 239
Adamson House 53
Adams-Powell Family 74
Aday to Remember 88
Addington Family 591
Addington Newsletter 257, 518
Addison Town Historical Society 580
Additon Family 247
Adee Family 242
Adelaide Hunter Hoodless Homestead Archives 689
Adena Mansion and Garden Archives 444
Adirondack Community College Library 412
Adirondack Genealogical-Historical Society 415
Adirondack Historical Association & Archives 390
Adirondack History Center 396
Adirondack Museum 390
Adkins Family 602
Adler Shinensky Library 117
ADLIB 417
Admiral Digby Historical Museum 674
Admiral Digby Library and Historical Society 674
Admiral Nimitz National Museum of the Pacific War Archives 546
Admiral Peary Monument Archives 485
Adobe de Palomares Museum Archives 60
Adobe House Museum 215
Adobe Trails 47
Adrian Public Library 285
Adsmore Musuem Archives 233
Advisory Council on Historic Preservation 105
Advocate 208, 359
Aero Space Museum of Calgary 641
Aeronotes 398
Affton Historical Society & Library 339
AFGNews 510
Afn Shvel 407
African American Genealogy Group & Archives 497
African American Historical Association 596
African American Historical Museum Archives 198
African American Museum 497
African American Museum & Library 57
African American Museum Archives 445, 541
African American Museum in Philadelphia Archives 497
African American Museum Newsletter 541
African American News 289
African Ancestored Genealogy 2
African Atlantic Genealogical Society 399
African Studies Center 266
African-American Cultural and Genealogical Society 157
African-American Family History Association, Newsletter 125
African-American Genealogical and Historical Society, Patricia Liddell Researchers 154
African-American Genealogical Society in Cleveland, Newsletter 445
African-American Genealogical Society of California & Archives 51

African-American Heritage Commission 513
African-American Historical and Genealogical Society 180
African-American Historical and Genealogical Society of Northern California, Newsletter 57
African-American National Capital Area Historical Genealogical Society 105
African-Atlantic Genealogical Society 398
AfriGeneas 2
Afrique Histoire U.S. 186
Afro-American Cultural Center Archives 424
Afro-American Family History Project 427
Afro-American Genealogical and Historical Society of Chicago Newsletter 154
Afro-American Genealogical Society of California & Archives 51
Afro-American Genealogical Society of Milwaukee 626
Afro-American Heritage Society of North Carolina 431
Afro-American Historical and Genealogical Society, Tidewater Chapter 596
Afro-American Historical and Genealogial Society, Prince George's County Chapter 259
Afro-American Historical and Genealogical Journal 153, 154
Afro-American Historical and Genealogical Society 105, 111
Afro-American Historical and Genealogical Society Journal 105
Afro-American Historical and Genealogical Society News 105, 153, 499
Afro-American Historical and Genealogical Society of Central Maryland 258
Afro-American Historical and Genealogical Society of New Jersey, Newsletter & Archives 371
Afro-American Historical and Genealogical Society, Arkansas Chapter 29
Afro-American Historical and Genealogical Society, Baltimore Chapter 255
Afro-American Historical and Genealogical Society, Central Florida Chapter 118
Afro-American Historical and Genealogical Society, Columbia Chapter 513
Afro-American Historical and Genealogical Society, Freedom Trail Chapter 334
Afro-American Historical and Genealogical Society, Hampton Roads Chapter 591
Afro-American Historical and Genealogical Society, Houston Chapter 548
Afro-American Historical and Genealogical Society, James Dent Walker Chapter 259
Afro-American Historical and Genealogical Society, Jean Sampson Scott Greater New York Chapter , Newsletter 391
Afro-American Historical and Genealogical Society, Landon Cheek Chapter 339
Afro-American Historical and Genealogical Society, Little Egypt Chapter 153
Afro-American Historical and Genealogical Society, MAGIC Chapter 332
Afro-American Historical and Genealogical Society, New England Chapter 279
Afro-American Historical and Genealogical Society, New Jersey Chapter 378
Afro-American Historical and Genealogical Society, Piedmont-Triad Chapter 427
Afro-American Historical and Genealogical Society, San Antonio Chapter 558
Afro-American Historical and Genealogical Society, Tucson Chapter 21
Afro-American Historical and Genealogical Society, Western Pennsylvania Chapter 499
Afro-American Historical Association of the Niagara Frontier 391
Afro-American Historical Museum 371
Afro-American Historical Society of Delaware 104
Afro-American Museum 51
Afro-Americans in New York Life and History 391
Afton Historical Society 388
Afton Historical Society & Library 305
Agassiz-Harrison Historical Museum Archives 647
Agassiz-Harrison Historical Society 647
Agawam Public Library 265
Age 562
Age of Johnson 406
Age of Steam Railroad Museum & Archives 541, 542
Agecroft Hall Museum Archives 593
Agecroft Hall Newsletter 593
Agency Chiefs Tribal Council 710
Agency Public Library 197
Agents House 413
Agness Community Library 473
Agnew Family 490
Agnew Family 587
Agricultural Heritage Museum Archives, Newsletter 411, 538
Agricultural Museum Archives 54
Agricultural Museum of New Brunswick 665
Agrirama Living History Museum Archives 138
AgriRamblins 138
AGS Quarterly 271
Agua Caliente Cultural Museum Archives 58
Agua Mansa Pioneer Cemetery Library 41
Aguilar Public Library 81
AHEPAN 106
AHHF Newsletter 492
Ahousaht First Nation 647
Ahtahkakoop First Nation 710
Ah-Tah-Thi-Ki Museum Archives 110
Ah-Tah-Thi-Ki Museum at Okalee 113
Ah-Tah-Thi-Ki Museum News 110
Ahtna Heritage Foundation 12
Aiken County Historical Commission & Archives 511
Aiken County Historical Museum, Archives, Newsletter 511
Aiken County Historical Society & Library 511
Aiken-Bamberg-Barnell-Edgefield Regional Library System 511
Aiken-Bamberg-Barnwell-Edgefield Regional Library System-Barnwell County 511
Aiken-Barnwell Genealogical Society Chapter, SCGS & Library 511
Ailsa Craig and District Historical Society 679
Ainger, Anger(s), Angier, Auger, Manter Family 112
Ainsworth Public Library 349, 580
Ainsworth Trading Post 242
Ainsworth-Gunter Family 242
Air Acres Museum Archives 128
Air Classic Museum of Aviation Archives 175
Air Force Armament Museum Archives, Quarterly 112
Air Force Flight Test Center Museum Archives 43
Air Force Heritage Museum and Air Park 662
Air Force Historical Foundation 255, 589
Air Mobility Command Museum Archives 103
Air Mobility Command, McConnell Air Force Base Library 218
Air Power History 255, 589
Air Power Park Museum Archives 588
Air University Library 6
Air Victory Museum Archives, Newsletter 372
Air Zoo Newsletter 295
Airborne and Special Operations Museum Archives 426
Airdrie Public Library 641
Airline History Museum Archives 332
Airmen Memorial Museum Archives 263
Airpower Museum Archives 206
Airpower Museum Bulletin 206
Aitchelitz Indian Band 655
Aitionn 506

INDEX

Aitkin County Historical Society 305
Ajax Public Library 679
Ajo Historical Museum 15
Ajo Historical Society & Archives 15
Akapath 63
Akin Free Library 410
Akin-Parker-Tripp Family 151
Akins Clan 6
Aklavik First Nation 671
Akron Carnegie Public Library 179
Akron Public Library 81
Akron-Summit County Public Library 441
Akron-Summit County Public Library-Tallmadge Branch 458
Akta Lakota Museum Archives 521
Akwesasne Library and Cultural Center Archives 400
Al Goin Historical Museum Archives 192
Alabama Agricultural Museum Archives 3
Alabama Archives and History Department Library 7
Alabama Baptist Historian 1
Alabama Baptist Historical Society 1
Alabama Constitution Village Archives 5
Alabama Department Of Archives And History 7
Alabama Department of Public Health Center for Health Statistics 7
Alabama Genealogical Society & Archives 1
Alabama Genealogical Society Magazine 1
Alabama Genealogical Society Newsletter 1
Alabama Heritage 9
Alabama Historical Association 7, 9
Alabama Historical Commission 7
Alabama Mining Museum Archives 3
Alabama Mining Museum Quarterly Newsletter 3
Alabama National Guard Historical Society 1
Alabama Preservation Alliance 7
Alabama Review 9
Alabama River Museum Archives 7
Alabama State Library 7
Ala-Benton Genealogical Society & Archives 1
AlaBenton Genealogy Quarterly 1
Alachua County Genealogical Society 113
Alachua County Library District 113
Alamance Battleground State Historic Site Archives 424
Alamance County Genealogical Society 424
Alamance County Historic Properties Commission & Library 427
Alamance County Historical Museum 424, 427
Alamance Genealogist 424
Alameda Architectural Preservation Society 35
Alameda County Historical Society, Quarterly 57
Alameda County Library 45
Alameda County Library-San Lorenzo Branch 68
Alameda Free Library 35
Alameda Historical Society 35
Alameda McCollough Library 188
Alameda Museum Archives 35
Alamo Archives 558
Alamo Defender Descendants 546
Alamo Township Museum Archives 295
Alamogordo Genealogical Society 381
Alamogordo Public Library 381
Alan Macpherson House Archives 686
Alaska Association for Historic Preservation 11
Alaska Association for Historic Preservation Quarterly 11
Alaska Federation of Natives 11
Alaska Federation of Natives Newsletter 11
Alaska Genealogical Society 11
Alaska Genealogical Society Newsletter 11
Alaska Genealogical Society Quarterly 11
Alaska Heritage Library and Museum Archives 11
Alaska Historical Commission 11
Alaska Historical Library 12
Alaska Historical Society & Library 11
Alaska History 11
Alaska in Perspective 11
Alaska Office of History and Archaeology 11
Alaska State Library 11, 12
Alaska State Museum Archives 12
Albany Civil Rights Movement Museum Archives 125
Albany County Genealogical Society 636
Albany County Historical Association & Library 387
Albany County Historical Society 636
Albany County Public Library 636
Albany Historical Museum 221, 617
Albany Historical Society 305
Albany Historical Society & Archives 221, 617
Albany Institute of History and Art Library 387
Albany Old Times 473
Albany Public Library 325, 387, 473
Albany Regional Museum Archives 473
Albany State University 125
Albany Township Historical Society 491
Albee Memorial Museum 201
Albemarle County Historical Society & Library 585
Albemarle Genealogical Society, Newsletter 425
Albemarle Regional Library 435
Albemarle-Stanley County Historic Preservation Commission & Archives 423
Albemarle-Stanley County Historical Museum 423
Alberni District Historical Society & Library 653
Alberni Valley Museum Archives 653
Albert B Alkek Library 559
Albert B Simpson Historical Library 82
Albert L Scott Library 1
Albert Lea Public Library 305
Albert P Brewer Library 3
Albert Wisner Public Library 419
Alberta Association of Registered Nurses 642
Alberta Aviation Museum Archives 642
Alberta Beach Museum Archives 641
Alberta Bible College Library 641
Alberta Central Railway Museum Archives 646
Alberta Family Histories Society, Quarterly 641
Alberta Forestry Service Museum Archives 644
Alberta Genealogical Society Ancestor Index 642
Alberta Genealogical Society Newsletter 642
Alberta Genealogical Society, Brooks and District Library 641
Alberta Genealogical Society, Cochrane and District Branch 642
Alberta Genealogical Society, Drayton Valley Branch 642
Alberta Genealogical Society, Edmonton Branch & Library 642
Alberta Genealogical Society, Fort McMurray Branch 643
Alberta Genealogical Society, Grand Prairie and District Branch 644
Alberta Genealogical Society, Lethbridge Branch 644
Alberta Genealogical Society, Red Deer Branch 645

Alberta Genealogical Society, Wetaskiwin Branch 646
Alberta Historical Resources Foundation & Library 642
Alberta History 641
Alberta Hospital Museum Archives 645
Alberta Italian Times 646
Alberta Wheat Pool Grain Museum Archives 641
Alberton Museum Archives 695
Albertsons Library 145
Albertville Public Library 1
Albert-Westmoreland-Kent Regional Library 664
Albin O Kuhn Library 257
Albin O Kuhn Museum Archives 255
Albion Academy Historical Musuem Archives 620
Albion Historical Society, Newsletter & Archives 285
Albion Public Library 145
Albion Public Library 285
Albion Town Historian 387
Album 113, 221
Album of the Ages 305
Albuquerque Historical Society 381
Albuquerque Museum Archives 381
Albuquerque Public Library-Special Collections 381
Albuquerque-Bernadillo County Library System 381
Alburgh Historical Society 575
Alburtis-Lockridge Historical Society 481
Alcatraz Island Museum Archives 66
Alcona County Historical Society 287
Alcona County Library 293
Alcorn County Genealogy Society 319
Alden B Dow Home Archives 297
Alden Community Historical Society & Library 305
Alden Family 270
Alden Historical Museum 387
Alden Historical Society & Library 387
Alden House Museum 270
Alder Grove Heritage Society 647
Alderman Library 585
Alderson Roots and Branches 66
Aldrich Family 416
Aldrich House Museum 509
Aldrich Public Library 575
Alert 69
Alert Bay Public Library and Museum Archives 647
Alex Youck School Museum Archives 709
Alexander & Baldwin Sugar Museum, Newsletter 143
Alexander County Ancestry Society 428
Alexander County Genealogical Society 428
Alexander County Library 433
Alexander Family 132, 607
Alexander Family Association Newsletter 553
Alexander Graham Bell National Historic Site Reference Archives 673
Alexander Grant House 377
Alexander Hamilton Memorial Free Library 504
Alexander M Bracken Library 190
Alexander Mack Memorial Library 584
Alexander Mitchell Public Library 521
Alexander Ramsey House Museum Archives 314
Alexander Tribal Government 645
Alexander-Crawford Historical Society, Newsletter & Library 243
Alexander-Smith Library 530
Alexandre Mouton House Museum Archives 238
Alexandria Black History Resource Center Archives 583
Alexandria Historical and Genealogical Society 235
Alexandria Historical Society & Library 583
Alexandria Indian Band 654
Alexandria Library 583
Alexandria Library-Ellen Coolidge Burke Branch 583
Alexandria Monroe Township Historical Society Newsletter 179
Alexandria Observer 583
Alexandria Public Library 441
Alexandria Public Library-Kate Waller Barrett 583
Alexandria Town Historian 387
Alexandria Township Historical Society 373
Alexandria-Monroe Public Library 179
Alexandria-Monroe Township Genealogy Society 179
Alexandria-Monroe Township Historical Society 179
Alexandrian Public Library 190
Alexis Creek Indian Band 648
Alfalfa County Historical Society, Museum, Newsletter & Archives 464
Alford American Family Association Action 329
Alfred P Sloan Museum Archives 291
Alfred Univ, Division of Human Studies 387
Alger County Heritage Center Archives 298
Alger County Historical Museum 298
Alger County Historical Society & Archives 298
Alger Footprints 298
Alger-Sullivan Historical Society 110
Algoma Public Library 617
Algoma Township Historical Society 302
Algona Public Library 197
Algonac Clay Historical Society 285
Algonquin Area Public Library District 151
Algonquin College Museum Archives 686
Algonquin Culture and Heritage Centre Archives 682
Algonquin Nation Programs and Services Secretariat 700
Algonquin Park Logging Museum Archives 692
Alhambra Historical Museum 35
Alhambra Historical Society & Archives 35
Alhambra Public Library 35
Alice Austen House Museum Archives, Newsletter 417
Alice B Donahue Library & Archives 641
Alice J Bickers Library 375
Alice L Pendleton Memorial Library 247
Alice M Farr Library 349
Alice M Ward Memorial Library 576
Alice Public Library 535
Alice T Miner Colonial Collection Archives 393
Alice's House Archives 452
Aliceville Historical Society 1
Aliceville Historical Society Museum 1
Aliceville Public Library 1
Alkali Lake Indian Band 657
All Aboard 568
All About It 171
Allagash Historical Society 250
Allamakee County Historical and Genealogical Society 209
Allan Shivers Museum Archives 563
Allan-Allen Family Workbook 612
Allegan County Historical Society & Archives 285
Allegan County Miscellany 285

INDEX

Allegan Public Library 285
Allegany College of Maryland Library 258
Allegany County Department of History & Archives 389
Allegany County Historical Society & Library 389
Allegany County Historical Society, Museum & Archives 258
Allegany County Library 258
Alleghany County Public Library 433
Alleghany Highlands Genealogical Society 586
Alleghany Highlands Genealogical Society Newsletter 586
Alleghany Historical and Genealogical Society, Bulletin & Archives 433
Allegheny Foothills Historical Society 499
Allegheny Portage Ralroad and Johnstown Flood Memorial Archives 488
Allegheny Regional Family Historical Society 612
Allegheny Regional Journal 612
Allegheny-Kiski Valley Historical Society & Library 503
Allen County Chapter, OGS, Newsletter 451
Allen County Genealogical Society 183, 216
Allen County Historical Museum 216
Allen County Historical Society & Archives 216
Allen County Historical Society, Newsletter & Archives 451
Allen County History Society 233
Allen County Lines 183
Allen County Museum 451
Allen County Public Library 183, 233
Allen County Reporter 451
Allen County-Fort Wayne Historical Society, Bulletin & Library 183
Allen County-Fort Wayne History Center 183
Allen E Roberts Masonic Museum Archives 593
Allen Family 59, 529
Allen Family Circle 332
Allen Family Newsletter 48
Allen Genealogical and Historical Society 238
Allen J Ellender Memorial Library 242
Allen Library 606
Allen Memorial Library 237, 439
Allen Parish Library 240
Allen Park Library 285
Allen-Braden Family 332
Allendale County Historical Society 511
Allendale-Hampton-Jasper Regional Library 511
Allenstown Public Library 359
Allentown Public Library 481
Allerton Family 274
Allerton Public Library 166
Alleyne Family 134
Allgor-Barkalow Homestead 379
Alliance 698
Alliance and District Museum Archives 641
Alliance Genealogical Society & Library 441
Alliance of Transylvania Saxons 445
Alliance Public Library 349
Alliance Rodman Public Library 441
Alliance Tribal Council 649
Allis-Bushnell House 95
Allison Family 569
Allison-Antrim Museum Archives, Annals 488
Allison-Blackburn(e)-Bruan(t)-Harper-Holley-Officer-Sharp(e)-Tabor-Tubb(s) Family 385
Alma Area Museum 617
Alma Clyde Field Library of Florida 110
Alma Historical Society & Archives 617
Alma M Carpenter Public Library 560
ALMA Matters 281
ALMA Newsletter 281
Almanac 208
Almanac Calendar 421
Almanzo and Laura Ingalls Wilder Association 392
Almond Historical Society & Archives 617
Almond Historical Society, Newsletter & Archives 387
Almonte Public Library 679
Alna Historical Society & Archives 243
Aloft 606
Along the River 273
Along the Saucony 491
Along Those Lines 271
Alpena County Library 285
Alpharetta Historical Society & Archives 125
Alpine County Free Library 53
Alpine County Historical Museum 53
Alpine County Historical Society & Archives 53
Alpine Historical Museum 35
Alpine Historical Park Archives 13
Alpine Historical Society & Archives 35
Alpine Public Library 535
ALSI Historical and Genealogical Society 480
Alson H Smith Jr Library 597
Alta District Historical Society 42
Altadena Heritage 35
Altadena Historical Society 35
Altadena Library District 35
Altama Museum of History Archives 139
Altamaha Echoes 129
Altamonte Springs City Library 109
Altmar Village Historian 387
Alton Area Historical Society & Library 151
Alton Museum of History and Art Archives 151
Alton Public Library 197
Altona Town Historian 387
Alton-Allton-Aulton Family 419, 586
Altoona Public Library 481
Altus Public Library 463
Alumni Library 21
Alutiiq Museum and Archaelogical Repository Archives 12
Alvah N Belding Library 286
Alvan Bolster Ricker Memorial Library 250
Alvarado Adobe & Blume House Museum Archives 69
Alverta Green Museum 452
Alvin S Okeson Library 13
AM and Welma Akin Jr Regional Archives 555
Amador County Archives 48
Amador County Genealogical Society 48, 74
Amador County Historical Society 60
Amador County Historical Society & Library 48
Amador County Library 48
Amador County Museum Archives 48
Amador-Livermore Valley Historical Museum 60
Amador-Livermore Valley Historical Society & Archives 60
Amana Heritage Museum 197
Amana Heritage Society & Archives 197
Amana Heritage Society Quarterly 197

Amarillo Genealogical Society & Archives 535
Amarillo Genealogical Society Newsletter 535
Amarillo Public Library 535
Amboy Town Historian 421
Amelia Earhart Birthplace Archives 211
Amelia Historical Society & Library 583
Amelia Island Genealogical Society 112
Amelia Island Museum of History Archives 112
Amelia Island Museum of History Newsletter 112
Amelia Island Museum of History Quarterly 112
Amelia S Givin Free Library 495
Amelia V Galucci-Cirio Library 271
Amelia V Galucci-Cirio Library Newsletter 271
Ameliasburgh Historical Museum Archives 679
America Italia Review 407
America Letter 201
America: History and Life 70
America's Black Holocaust Museum Archives 626
America's Civil War 589
America's Frierson's Ancestry Book Supplements 2
America's Friersons Ancestry Bureau 2
America's Ice Cream and Dairy Museum Archives 453
Americal Civic Center 281
American Airpower Heritage Museum Archives 553
American Antiquarian Historical Museum 283
American Antiquarian Society & Archives 283
American Antiquarian Society Newsletter 283
American Archivist 156
American Archivist 558
American Association for State and Local History 531
American Association of Museums 105
American Aviation Historical Society & Library 69
American Baptist Churches Historical Society & Research Library 504
American Baptist Churches of New Hampshire Archives 360
American Baptist Historical Society & Archives 413
American Baptist Quarterly 413
American Battle Monuments Commission 584
American Bulletin 157
American Catholic Historical Association 105
American Catholic Historical Association Quarterly Journal 105
American Catholic Historical Society & Archives 497
American Catholic Historical Society Records 497
American Cherokee Confederacy 125
American Cherokee Confederacy News 125
American Civil War Institute 226
American College of Heraldry 3, 9
American Congregational Library 266
American Congregational Library Bulletin 266
American Cotton Museum Archives 547
American Council for Polish Culture 120
American Croat: Americki Hrvat 35
American Decades 291
American Diner Museum Archives 509
American Eagle: A Newsletter of the Descendants of Mexican War Veterans 557
American Elm 280
American Eras 291
American Falls District Library 145
American Family History 376
American Family Records Association & Archives 332
American Family Records Association Member Directory & Ancestral Surname Registry 332
American Fork City Library 565
American Friends of Lafayette 486
American Friends of Lafayette Gazette 486
American Friends of the Hermitage Museum 406
American Genealogical Lending Library 565
American Genealogical Society & Depository 1
American Genealogical-Biographical Index 96
American Genealogist 130
American Helicopter Museum Archives 505
American Helicopter Museum Newsletter 505
American Heritage 406
American Heritage Center Library 636
American Heritage Fire Museum Archives 321
American Heritage Library 464
American Historical Association 105, 180
American Historical Association, Pacific Coast Branch 53
American Historical Association-Pacific Coast Branch 51
American Historical Foundation & Archives 593
American Historical Museum 353, 593
American Historical Review 105, 180
American Historical Society of Germans from Russia & Archives 353
American Historical Society of Germans from Russia Journal 353
American Historical Society of Germans from Russia, Arizona Sun Chapter 17, 20
American Historical Society of Germans from Russia, Central California Chapter & Library 45
American Historical Society of Germans from Russia, Colorado High Plains Chapter 90
American Historical Society of Germans from Russia, Colorado Springs Chapter 82
American Historical Society of Germans from Russia, Denver Metro Chapter 83
American Historical Society of Germans from Russia, Melon Valley Chapter 89
American Historical Society of Germans from Russia, Northern Colorado Chapter 86
American Historical Society of Germans from Russia, Northern Illinois Chapter 169, 177
American History 589
American History Illustrated 489
American Hungarian Foundation 374
American Hungarian Historical Museum 374
American Hungarian Historical Society & Library 406
American Independence Museum Archives 360
American Independence Museum Quarterly 360
American Indian 407
American Indian Community House 406
American Indian Community House Bulletin 406
American Indian Institute 467
American Indian Quarterly 353
American Indian Society 595
American Indian Society Newsletter 595
American Indian Studies Center 51
American Institute for Conservation of Historic and Artistic Works Newsletter 105
American Institute for the Conservation of Historic and Artistic Works 105
American Irish Historical Museum 406
American Irish Historical Society & Archives 406
American Irish Historical Society Recorder 406

INDEX

American Italian Heritage Association 387
American Italian Heritage Digest 387
American Jewish Archives 444
American Jewish Committee 105
American Jewish Historical Museum 406
American Jewish Historical Society 281, 406
American Jewish Historical Society & Library 276
American Jewish History 256, 281, 406
American Labor Museum Archives 370
American Legacy 406
American Legion National Headquarters Library 186
American Library Association, Genealogy Committee 155
American Maple Museum Archives 395
American Merchant Marine Museum Archives 402
American Military Museum Archives 512
American Museum of Nursing Archives 21
American Museum of Radio and Electricity Archives 599
American Museum of Radio and Electricity Newsletter 599
American Overseas Schools Historical Society 223
American Police Center and Museum Archives 155
American Precision Museum Association Archives 581
American Presbyterians: Journal of Presbyterian History 498
American Quarter Horse Heritage Center Museum Archives 535
American Red Cross Museum Archives 105
American Research Bureau 570
American Royal Museum Archives 332
American Saddlebred Horse Museum Archives 335
American Society for Croatian Migration 445
American Society of Genealogists 250
American Society of Military History & Library 73
American Society of Sephardic Studies 406
American Society of the French Legion of Honor 406
American Spirit Magazine 531
American Swedish Historical Foundation & Archives 497
American Swedish Historical Foundation and Museum Newsletter 497
American Swedish Historical Museum 497
American Swedish Institute & Archives 311
American Swedish Institute Museum 311
American Swedish Institute Posten 311
American Textile History Museum Archives 273
American Truck Historical Museum 332
American Truck Historical Society 332
American Veterans Historical Museum Archives 411
American Victorian Museum Archives 56
American Visions 105
American Waldensian Society 505
American Waldensian Society Newsletter 505
American West Research Center and Historical Society 445
American Wings Air Museum Archives 306
American Work Horse Museum Archives 589
Americana Manse Whitney-Halsey Home Archives 389
Americana Museum Archives 544, 615
American-Canadian Genealogical Society & Library 362
American-Canadian Genealogical Society, Father Leo E Begin Chapter & Library 247
American-Canadian Genealogist 362
American-French Genealogical Society & Library 508, 510
American-French Genealogical Society News 508
American-Portuguese Genealogical and Historical Society 280
Americans of Italian Origin Society 289
American-Scandinavian Foundation 406
American-Schleswig-Holstein Heritage Society & Library 204
American-Schleswig-Holstein Heritage Society Newsletter 204
American-Swedish Handbook 311
Amerikanski Srbobran 499
Amerind Foundation & Library 16
Amery Historical Society 617
Ames Free Library of Easton 276
Ames Public Library 197
Amesbury Public Library 265
Amherst Archives and Research Center 387
Amherst County Historical Museum 583
Amherst County Historical Society & Archives 583
Amherst County Public Library 583
Amherst Historical Society & Archives 265, 441
Amherst Historical Society Newsletter 441
Amherst Historical Society Quarterly 265
Amherst Museum Archives 387
Amherst Public Library 387
Amherst Township Historical Society 673
Amigos 382
Amigos de la Colina Heritage Hill Historical Park Archives 49
Amistad Research Center 239
Amite County Historical Society 320, 321
Amite Genealogical Club 235
Amity and Woodbridge Historical Society & Archives 101
Amityville Historical Society & Archives 387
Amon Carter Museum Library 545
Among Friends 508
Among the Coles 154
Amory Regional Museum Archives 319
Amos Herr House Foundation and Historical Society & Library 492
Amos J Blake House 361
Amos Memorial Public Library 457
AMPL News 521
AMS Studies in the Emblem 391
Amsterdam Free Library 388
Amy B Yerkes Museum 489
An Canach (The Cottongrass): Newsletter of the Clan Henderson Society 583
An Clerich 230
An Darach 512
Anaconda-Deer Lodge County Historical Museum 343
Anaconda-Deer Lodge County Historical Society & Archives 343
Anacortes Museum Archives 599
Anacortes Museum Newsletter 599
Anacostia Museum for African American History & Culture Archives 105
Anacostia Museum for African American History & Culture Archives Newsletter 105
Anadarko Heritage Museum Archives 463
Anadarko Public Library 463
Anaham Indian Band 647
Anaheim Historical Society 35
Anaheim Museum Archives 35
Anaheim Museum Archives Newsletter 35
Anaheim Museum Press 35
Anaheim Public Library 35
Anasazi Heritage Center Library 84
Ancestor Charts 353
Ancestor Hunt 449
Ancestor Seekers 77

Ancestor Seminars Library 56
Ancestor Trails 459
Ancestor Update 134
Ancestoring 126
Ancestors 460
Ancestors Are Just Somewhere In Time 558
Ancestors Unknown Newsletter 26
Ancestors Unlimited 132, 354
Ancestors West 46, 70
Ancestral Diggin's of Lafayette County, Wisconsin 631
Ancestral News 234
Ancestral Trails Genealogical Society 234
Ancestral Trails Historical Society 234
Ancestral Trails Historical Society News 234
Ancestral Tree 303
Ancestree 349
Ancestree Kinnection 219
Ancestry 124
Ancestry Magazine 569
Ancestry's Guide to Research and Vital Record Catalog 569
Anchor 232, 509
Anchor Watch 596
Anchorage Genealogical Society 11
Anchorage Genealogical Society Newsletter 11
Anchorage Genealogical Society Quarterly 11
Anchorage Municipal Libraries 11
Anchorage Museum of History and Art Archives 11
Ancient and Honorable Artillery Company of Massachusetts Museum Archives 266
Ancient Free and Accepted Masons & Archives 198
Ancient Free and Accepted Masons Museum 198
Ancient Free and Accepted Masons, Grand Lodge of Massachusetts & Library 266
Ancient Order of Hibernians 495
Ancient Order of Hibernians in America 388
Ancient Spanish Monastery of St Bernard de Clairvaux Cloisters 118
Ancient Times 95
Andalusia Public Library 1
Andaste Inquirer 394
Anderson Barn (1880) Museum Archives 621
Anderson Clan 44, 425
Anderson County Genealogical Society 214, 511, 555
Anderson County Historical Museum 214
Anderson County Historical Museum Archives 214
Anderson County Historical Society 511
Anderson County Historical Society & Archives 214
Anderson County Historical Society News 511
Anderson County Historical Society Newsletter 214
Anderson County Library 511
Anderson County Museum Archives 511
Anderson Falls Historical Society 401
Anderson Family Courier 239
Anderson Heritage 511
Anderson Homestead 480
Anderson House 106
Anderson Island Historical Society 602
Anderson Lake Indian Band 649
Anderson Marsh State Historic Park Archives 63
Anderson Public Library 179
Anderson Store (1858) Museum Archives 621
Anderson Township Historical Society 444
Anderson Valley Historical Museum 38
Anderson Valley Historical Society & Archives 38
Anderson-Abruzzo International Balloon Museum Archives 381
Anderson-Lee Library 416
Andersonville National Historic Site Archives 125
Andes Family 62
Andis Ancestry 77
Andover Historic Preservation Corporation 388
Andover Historical Museum 265
Andover Historical Society 151, 243
Andover Historical Society & Archives 265
Andover Historical Society & Library 91
Andover Historical Society Newsletter 265
Andrew and District Local History Museum Archives 641
Andrew Bayne Memorial Library 482
Andrew Carnegie Free Library 484
Andrew County Historical Museum 340
Andrew County Historical Society & Archives 340
Andrew Jackson Garrison Broken Branches 35
Andrew Johnson National Historic Site Library 527
Andrews County Library 535
Andrews Dallas Township Public Library 179
Androscoggin Historical Museum 243
Androscoggin Historical Society & Library 243
Androscoggin History 243
Angel Mounds State Historic Site Library 183
Angelican Church of Canada Archives 691
Angelina County Genealogical Society 552
Angels Attic Museum Archives 71
Angels Camp Museum & Carriage House Archives 35
Anglaize County Public District Library 459
Anglican and Episcopal History 536
Anglican Bush: A New England Species 223
Anglican Cathedral Museum Archives 668
Anglo-Celtic Annals 687
Anglo-Celtic Roots 687
Anglo-Saxon England 406
Angola-Carnegie Public Library 179
Animas Museum 84
Animas Museum Newsletter 84
Ankeny Area Historical Society 197
Ankeny Genealogical Society 197
Ankers Family 591
ANLA Bulletin 668
Ann Arbor District Public Library 285
Ann Arbor Historical Foundation & Library 285
Anna B Smith House Museum Archives 613
Anna Bemis Palmer Musem Archives 357
Anna Hazzard Museum 104
Anna Maria Island Historical Society 114
Anna Miller Museum 637
Anna Porter Public Library 527
Annals & Recollections 414
Annals of Edgefield District 514
Annals of Iowa 203
Annandale Family History Center Library 584
Annandale National Historic Site Archives 691
Annapolis Valley Historical Society 673
Annapolis Valley Macdonald Museum Library 675

INDEX

Annapolis Valley Regional Library 673
Anne Arundel County Historical Society & Archives 259
Anne Arundel County Public Library 255
Anne Arundel Genealogical Society & Archives 261
Anne Arundel Historical Society 260
Anne Arundel Speaks 261
Anne of Green Gables Museum Archives 695
Anne Parish Markham Library 231
Anne Spencer Memorial Foundation & Archives 590
Annenberg Family 497
Annie E Woodman Institute 360
Annie Halenbake Ross Library 493
Annie Merner Pfeiffer Library 611
Annie Porter Ainsworth Memorial Library 415
Annie Riggs Museum 545
Anniston Historical Society & Archives 1
Annotation 106, 435
Annual Bulletin of the Snyder County Historical Society 494
Annual Report of the Henry Wolcott Descendants Society 101
Annual Report of the Minnesota Historical Society 314
Annual Report of the Society of the Founders of Norwich Connecticut 97
Annual Summary of Programs 388
Ano Nuevo State Reserve Museum Archives 60
Anoka County Genealogical Society & Library 305
Anoka County Historical Museum 305
Anoka County Historical Society & Archives 305
Anoka County Historical Society Newsletter 305
Anoka County History Center & Library 305
Anoka County Library 306
Anoka County, Minnesota, Genealogical Society Newsletter 305
Anola and District Community Museum Archives 659
Anschutz Library 217
Anshe Hesed Temple Library 487
Ansley Family 512
Anson County Historical Museum 434
Anson County Historical Society & Archives 434
Anson County Historical Society Newsletter 434
Anson Wolcott Historical Society & Library 196
Anson Wolcott Historical Society News 196
Ansonia Library 91
Antelope County Historical Museum 354
Antelope County Historical Society & Archives 354
Antelope Valley African American Museum Archives 50
Antelope Valley Genealogical Society 50, 58
Antelope Valley Genealogical Society Surname Index 50
Antelope Valley Indian Museum 50, 77
Antepasados 65, 67
Anthemion 407
Anthonly Library Newsletter 211
Anthony Henday Historical Society 642
Anthony Henday Museum Archives 642
Anthony Public Library 211
Antietam Ancestors 504
Antigonish Heritage Museum Archives 673
Antioch Historical Society 35
Antioch Township Library 151
Antiquarian 411
Antiquarian and Historical Society of Culver Lake Maxinkuckee 182
Antiquarian and Landmarks Society 94
Antique Boat Museum Archives 393
Antique Boat Museum Gazette 393
Antique Gas and Steam Engine Museum Archives 76
Antique Tractor Museum and Frontier Village 708
Anti-Saloon League Museum Archives 460
Antler River Historical Museum 660
Antler River Historical Society 660
Antwerp Town Historian 418
Anubis Society 528
Anvik Historical Society 11
Any Amsbaugh Ancestors? 56
APA Newsletter 202
Apache County Historical Museum 20
Apache County Historical Society & Archives 20
Apache County Library District 20
Apache Cultural Center Museum Archives 16
Apache Genealogy Society of Cochise County 20
Apache Junction Public Library 15
Apalachicola Area Historical Society 109
Apathy Ancestors 112
Apellidos Familiares 389
Apex Museum Archives 125
APEX Times 125
Apgar Family 378
Apollo Area Historical Society 481
Apollo Memorial Library 481
Apollo Memorial Library Newsletter 481
Apopka Historical Society & Archives 109
Apostle Islands National Lakeshore Library 617
Appalachian Journal 423
Appalachian Journal: A Regional Studies Review 423
Appalachian Quarterly 597
Appalachian Regional Library 431
Appalachian Springs 613
Appaloosa Museum and Heritage Center Archives 148
Appanoose County Genealogy Society 198
Apple Orchard 600
Apple Press 72
Apple Trees Museum 198
Applebee Family 444
Applegate Ancestry 355
Appleland Bulletin 609
Appler Family Newsletter 116, 361
Appleton City Landmarks Restoration 325
Appleton Public Library 617
Appling County Heritage Center 127
Appling County Historical Society & Library 127
Appling-Greenlee-Turner- Whiteside Family 605
Appomattox Courthouse National Historic Park Library 584
Appomattox Regional Library 589
Appomattox Regional Library-Carson Branch 585
Aptucxet Trading Post Museum 267
Arab American National Museum Archives 289
Arab Historical Society 1
Arab Public Library 1
Aracoma High School Historical Society 613
Aragon Historical Society 125
Aram Public Library 620
Ararat 377
Arbogast Family 123, 522, 527, 591, 613
Arbor Lodge State Historical Park Archives 354

Arbuckle Historical Society 463
Arbuckle Historical Society & Library 464
Arcade Historical Museum 388
Arcade Historical Society & Archives 388
Arcade Historical Society News 388
Arcadia Area Historical Society 285, 617
Arcadia Historical Museum 35
Arcadia Historical Society 35, 408
Arcadia Historical Society 408
Arcadia Preservation 589
Arcadia Public Library 35
Arcadia Township Historical Commission & Library 285
Arcadia Township Historical Commission Newsletter 285
Arcadia Township Historical Museum 285
Arcata Historical Museum Archives 36
Archbishop Henry J O'Brien Library 91
Archbishop Ireland Memorial Library 314
Archbold Community Library 441
Archbold Community Library Update 441
Archdiocese for the Military Services 105
Archdiocese of the Evangelical Lutheran Church in America Archives 173
Archelaus Smith Museum 673
Archer County Historical Society 535
Archer County Museum Archives 535
Archer Family 591
Arches Museum of Pioneer Life 317
Archibald Clan Newsletter 215
Archibald Family 109, 636
Archibald Graham McIlwaine House Archives 592
Archibald Historical Museum Archives 660
Archibald Stevens Alexander Library 374
Archibald-Thomson Library 641
Archival 99
Archival Outlook 156, 558
Archivaria 687
Archives 8
Archives and Regional History Collection 295
Archives and Special Collections 663
Archives du Seminaire de Trois-Rivieres 703
Archives Library 298
Archives Nationales du Quebec 702
Archives Newsletter 110
Archives of J S G Boggs 110
Archives of Maryland 255
Archives of Ontario 691
Archives of the Catholic Central Union of America 339
Archives of the Czechs and Slovaks Abroad 155
Archives of the Episcopal Diocese of Honolulu 141
Archives of the Episcopal Diocese of Massachusetts 266
Archives of the Evangelical Lutheran Church in America 155, 159
Archives of the Kentucky-Indiana Synod, Lutheran Church of America 186
Archives of the Lutheran Church in America 155
Archives of the Maryland Synod, Lutheran Church of America 263
Archives of the Moravian Church 482
Archives of the Moravian Church in America, Southern Province 435
Archives of the New England Yearly Meeting of Friends 509
Archives of the Northwest Territories 671
Archives Provinciales Capucins 699
Archivist 373, 377
Archuleta County Genealogical Society & Library 88
Arcola Museum Archives 705
Ardenwood Historic Farm Museum Archives 45
Ardmore Public Library 463
Ardsley Historical Society 388
Ardsley Public Library 388
Area Footprints 337
Arehac County Historical Society & Library 286
Arey (Ihrig) Family 342
Argie Cooper Public Library 532
Argo Gold Mine & Mill Museum Archives 86
Argonauts Historical Society 67
Argonia and West Sumner County Historical Society & Archives 211
Argyle Municipality Historical and Genealogical Society 677
Argyle Public Library 617
Arizona and the West Library 21
Arizona Chapter, Ohio Genealogical Society 16, 18
Arizona Chapter, Ohio Genealogical Society Newsletter 16
Arizona City Community Library 15
Arizona Computer Interest Group 18
Arizona Cornish Society 15
Arizona Council of Professional Genealogists 15
Arizona First Families 18
Arizona Genealogical Advisory Board 17
Arizona Genealogical Advisory Board Newsletter 17
Arizona Genealogical Computer Interest Group 21
Arizona Hall of Fame Museum Archives 18
Arizona Historical Foundation & Archives 21
Arizona Historical Museum 21
Arizona Historical Society & Archives 16
Arizona Historical Society Downtown Museum Archives 21
Arizona Historical Society Historical Monographs 21
Arizona Historical Society Newsletter 16, 21
Arizona Historical Society, Central Arizona Division & Archives 21
Arizona Historical Society, Southern Arizona Division & Archives 21
Arizona Historical Society, Yuma (Rio Colorado) Branch & Archives 22
Arizona History Magazine 21
Arizona Jewish Historical and Genealogical Society 17
Arizona Jewish Historical Museum 18
Arizona Jewish Historical Society & Archives 18
Arizona Mayflower Society 20
Arizona Mining and Mineral Museum Archives 18
Arizona Pioneer 19
Arizona Pioneer's Historical Society 21
Arizona Railway Museum Archives 15
Arizona Society Children of the American Revolution 22
Arizona Society of Genealogists 21
Arizona State Capitol Museum Archives 18
Arizona State Genealogical Society & Library 21
Arizona State Library, Archives and Public Records 18
Arizona State Museum Archives 21
Arizona State University 21
Arizona Welsh Society 16
Arizona Western College Library 22
Ark Valley Crossroads 223
Arkansas Air Museum Archives 27
Arkansas Air Museum Newsletter 27
Arkansas City Historical Society & Library 211
Arkansas City Public Library 211
Arkansas County Public Library 557
Arkansas Department of Heritage Services 29

INDEX

Arkansas Family Historian 28, 29
Arkansas Family History Association 32
Arkansas Genealogical Research 32
Arkansas Genealogical Society 29
Arkansas Genealogical Society & Library 28
Arkansas Historical and Genealogical Magazine 26
Arkansas Historical Association 27
Arkansas Historical Association News 27
Arkansas Historical Quarterly 27
Arkansas Historical Society 33
Arkansas Historical Society Newsletter 27
Arkansas History Commission & Library 29
Arkansas Institute For Historical Building Trades 28
Arkansas Museum of Science and History Archives 29
Arkansas National Guard Museum Archives 31
Arkansas News 29
Arkansas Post Museum Archives 27
Arkansas Post National Memorial Archives 27
Arkansas Post National Memorial Newsletter 27
Arkansas Preservation Digest 29
Arkansas Railroad Museum Archives 31
Arkansas Records Center 31
Arkansas River Historical Society 464
Arkansas River Valley Regional Library System 26
Arkansas Smiley Public Library and Museum 61
Arkansas State Library 29
Arkansas State University Museum Archives 29
Arkansas Tech University Museum of History Archives 32
Arkansas Territorial Restoration Library 29
Ark-La-Tex Antique and Classic Vehicle Museum Archives 241
Ark-La-Tex Genealogical Association & Library 241
Ark-La-Tex Newsletter 241
Arledge-Aldridge Family 384
Arlene Cherry Memorial Library 26
Arlington County Department of Libraries 584
Arlington County Department of Libraries-Central Library 584
Arlington Genealogical Society & Archives 535
Arlington Heights Historical Museum 151
Arlington Heights Historical Society & Archives 151
Arlington Heights Memorial Library 151
Arlington Historical Magazine 584
Arlington Historical Museum 584
Arlington Historical Society 535
Arlington Historical Society & Archives 265, 584
Arlington House 584
Arlington Museum Archives 2
Arlington Public Library 535
Arm Lads' Brigade Armoury 667
Arma City Library 211
Armenian Cultural Foundation & Library 265
Armenian General Benevolent Union 377
Armenian General Benevolent Union Annual Report 377
Armenian Library and Museum of America Archives 281
Armenian Review 281
Armiger's News 9
Armoury Museum 653
Arms Family Museum of Local History 461
Armstrong Air & Space Museum Archives 459
Armstrong Chronicles 130
Armstrong Clan 130, 499, 535, 692
Armstrong County Historical and Genealogical Society & Archives 491
Armstrong County Historical Museum 491
Armstrong Family 569
Armstrong Museum Archives 647
Armstrong University Library 57
Armstrong-Lockett House 528
Army & Navy Club Library 105
Army Historian 107
Army Museum Memo 107
Arnold Ancestry 292
Arnold Bernhard Library 94
Arnold Expedition Historical Society & Archives 246
Arnold Family 542
Arnold Guebert Library 642
Arnold Missouri Historical Society 325
Arnold's Archives Library 290
Arnprior and District Museum Archives 679
Arnsparger Family 227
Arnulfo Oliviera Memorial Library 539
Arnulfo Oliviera Memorial Library Newsletter 539
Aroostook Historical Museum 247
Around the Archipelago 617
Around the Bend 557
Around the District 159
Around the Plantation 428
Arrow Lakes Historical Society & Archives 652
Arrow Rock Historical Museum 325
Arrow Rock State Historic Site Archives 325
Art Circle Public Library 526
Artesia Historical and Genealogical Society 381
Artesia Historical and Genealogical Society Newsletter 381
Artesia Historical Museum 381
Artesia Historical Society & Archives 381
Artesia Public Library 382
Arthur A Houghton Jr Library 394
Arthur and Elizabeth Schlesinger Library 268
Arthur Clan 583
Arthur County Historical Society 349
Arthur E Pomeroy Public Library 17
Arthur Family Newsletter 474
Arthur Hufnagel-Glen Rock Public Library 488
Arthur J Moore Methodist Museum Library 136
Arthur Johnson Memorial Library 384
Arthur Public Library 151
Arthurdale Heritage & Archives 611
Arthurdale Heritage Newsletter 611
Arthurdale Historical Museum 611
Artifact 131
Artifacts 84, 85, 403, 561 634
Artillery Company of Newport Military Museum Archives 508
Artilleryman 580
Art-N-Facts 526
Arvada Center for the Arts and Humanities Museum Archives 81
Arvada Historical Society 87
Arviat Historical Society 671
Arvin A Brown Public Library 579
Arvon Township Historical Society 302
As Time Goes By 316
Asa Packer Mansion Museum Archives 490
Asbill Family Newsletter 470

Asbury Park Historical Society 367
Ascension Heritage Association 237
Ascension Historical Committee 57
Ascension Parish Library-Gonzales Branch 237
Ascension Roots 237
Ash Hollow State Historical Park Archives 353
Ash Lawn-Highland Museum Archives 585
Ashantilly Center Archives 129
Ashaway Free Library 507
Ashby Family 567
Ashcroft Indian Indian Band 647
Ashcroft Museum Archives 647
Ashdown Community Library 25
Ashe County Historical Society 434
Ashe County Public Library 434
Ashern Pioneer Museum Archives 659
Ashland Area Historic Preservation Society 481
Ashland Community Library 243
Ashland County Chapter, OGS & Archives 441
Ashland County Historical Society & Archives 617
Ashland Historical Museum 265
Ashland Historical Society & Archives 265, 359
Ashland Historical Society Newsletter 265
Ashland Logging Museum Archives 243
Ashland Public Library 211, 441
Ashland Railroad Station Museum Archives 359
Ashley County Genealogical Society 26
Ashley County Library 28
Ashley-Evans-Lewis-Martin-Palmer-Turner Family 467
Ashtabula County Covered Bridges 450
Ashtabula County District Library 441
Ashtabula County Genealogical Society 449
Ashtabula County Historical Museum 449
Ashtabula County Historical Society & Archives 449
Ashtabula County Historical Society & Library 450
Ashtabula County History 449
Ashtabula Plantation 517
Ashton Villa and Heritage Visitor's Center Archives 546
Ashtree Echo 45
Ashville Free Library 388
Ashville Museum 1
Ashville Museum & Archives 1
Ashville-Bumcombe Library System 423
Ashwaubenon Historical Society & Archives 622
Asistencia San Gabriel Mission Outpost Museum Archives 61
Asotin County Library 600
Aspen Historical Society & Library 81
Aspen Historical Society Newsletter 81
Aspinock Newsletter 98
Assembly Call 457
Assembly of First Nations 687
Assiginack Historical Museum 685
Assiginack Historical Society & Archives 685
Assiniboia and District Historical Museum 705
Assiniboia and District Historical Society 705
Assiniboine Historical Museum 659
Assiniboine Historical Society 659
Associated American Jewish Museums 499
Associated Daughters of Early American Witches 18
Association des Blais d'Amerique 699
Association for Gravestone Studies 271
Association for Northern California Records and Research & Library 40
Association for Northern California Records and Research Newsletter 40
Association for the Advancement of Dutch-American Studies & Archives 292
Association for the Certification of Minnesota Genealogists 312
Association for the Preservation of Tennessee Antiquities & Library 531
Association for the Preservation of Tennessee Antiquities, Hamblen County Chapter & Archives 530
Association for the Preservation of Virginia Antiquities & Library 593
Association for the Preservation of Virginia Antiquities Discovery Newsletter 593
Association for the Study of Afro-American Life and History 262
Association for the Study of Connecticut History 266
Association for the Study of Connecticut History Newsletter 266
Association of Asian Indians in America 413
Association of Asian Indians in America Journal 413
Association of Boothe Descendants Newsletter 100
Association of Canadian Archivists 687
Association of Canadian Archivists Bulletin 687
Association of Hawaiian Civic Clubs 141
Association of Historical Societies of Los Angeles County 59
Association of Illinois Museums and Historical Societies 174
Association of Illinois Museums and Historical Societies News 174
Association of Iroquois and Allied Indians 685
Association of Jewish Genealogical Societies 58, 367
Association of Newfoundland and Labrador Archives 668
Association of Newfoundland and Labrador Archives Newsletter 668
Association of One-Name Studies 263
Association of Professional Genealogists 83, 105, 570
Association of Professional Genealogists List of Professional Genealogists and Related Services Quarterly 570
Association of Professional Genealogists Quarterly 83, 105, 570
Association of Professional Genealogists, Southern California Chapter 38
Association of Saint Louis Area Archivists 339
Assumption Abbey Library 439
Assumption Parish Library 239
Assumption Public Library 151
Assyrain American League 173
Assyrian Star 155
Assyrian-American Federation 155
Aston Historical Society 481
Astor House Museum Archives 85
Astoria Heritage Association 473
Astoria Heritage Museum 473
Astoria Public Library 473
Astors' Beechwood Mansion Museum Archives 508
Astrolabe 115
Astronaut Ellison S Onizuka Space Center 142
AT & SF Depot Museum Archives 211
At Home 111, 114
At Homewood 256
At the Front 169
Ataloa Lodge Museum Archives 467
Atascadero Historical Society & Library 36
Atascosa County Genealogical Society & Library 556
Atascosito Historical Society & Library 551
Atchison Connection 211
Atchison County Genealogical Society & Archives 211
Atchison County Historical Society 338
Atchison County Historical Society & Archives 211, 341

INDEX

Atchison County Library 338
Atchison Public Library 211
Athenaeum Annotations 497
Athenaeum Archives 526
Athenaeum of Philadelphia 497
Athens Area Historical Society 285
Athens County Chapter, OGS & Archives 441
Athens County Chapter, OGS Bulletin 441
Athens County Historical Museum 441
Athens County Historical Society & Archives 441
Athens Genealogical Organization & Archives 536
Athens Historical Society 125, 243
Athens Historical Society and Museum Bulletin 441
Athens Regional Library 125
Athens Regional Library System-Oconee County 139
Athens Regional Library System-Winterville Branch 140
Athens State University Library 1
Athens-Clarke Heritage Foundation 125
Athens-Limestone Public Library 1
Atherton Heritage Association 36
Athol Historical Society & Library 265
Athol Murray College of Notre Dame Museum Archives 711
Athol Public Library 265
Athy Family 548
Atikokan Centennial Museum Archives 679
Atkinson Family 186
Atkinson Historical Society 349
Atkinson Historical Society & Library 359
Atkinson Public Library 151
Atlanta Cyclorama Archives 125
Atlanta Historical Journal 125
Atlanta Historical Society & Library 125
Atlanta History 125
Atlanta History Center 125
Atlanta History Center News 125
Atlanta History Center Newsletter 125
Atlanta History: A Journal of Georgia and the South 125
Atlanta Library and Museum Archives 151
Atlanta Public Library 536
Atlanta-Fulton Public Library 125
Atlantic 1 Fire-Fighting Museum Archives 280
Atlantic Beach Historical Society 517
Atlantic Canada Aviation Museum Archives 663
Atlantic City Free Public Library 367
Atlantic City Historical Museum Archives 367
Atlantic County Historical Museum 378
Atlantic County Historical Society & Archives 378
Atlantic County Historical Society Newsletter 378
Atlantic County Historical Society Yearbook 378
Atlantic County Library 373
Atlantic Heritage 378
Atlantic Highlands Historical Society 371
Atlantic Highlands Historical Society & Library 367
Atlantic Policy Congress of First Nation Chiefs 673
Atlantic Public Library 197
Atlantic School of Theology Library 674
Atlantic Statiquarium Marine Museum Archives 675
Atlin Historical Museum Archives 647
Atlin Historical Society 647
Atmore Public Library 1
Atoka County Genealogical Society 463
Atoka County Historical Museum 463
Atoka County Historical Society & Archives 463
Attakpas Gazette 238
Attakpas Historical Association 238
Atterbury Family 467
Attica Historical Society 388
Attica Public Library 179
Attleboro Area Industrial Museum Archives 265
Attleboro Public Library 265
Attmore-Oliver House Museum Archives 430
Attmore-Oliver House Museum Newsletter 430
Atwater Historical Society 36
Atwater History Area Society 305
Atwater Kent Museum Archives 497
Atwater Library 704
Atwood Ancestors 314
Atwood Family 546
Atwood Public Library 211
Atwood-Hammond Public Library 151
Au Sable-Oscoda Historical Society 299
Aubrey R Watzek Library 478
Auburn Avenue Research Library on African-American Culture & History 125
Auburn Cord Duesenberg Museum Archives 179
Auburn Heritage Association 1
Auburn Hills Genealogical and Historical Society 286
Auburn Historical Society 265
Auburn Joss House Museum Archives 36
Auburn Public Library 243
Auburn Public Library 265
Auburn-Placer County Library 36
Audrain County Area Genealogical Society & Archives 335
Audrain County Area Genealogical Society Newsletter 335
Audrain County Historical Society & Archives 335
Audubon County Courthouse Museum 201
Audubon County Genealogical Society 197
Audubon County Historical Society & Library 201
Audubon House Museum Archives 115
Audubon Pilgrimage 241
Audubon Public Library 197
Audubon Regional Library 236
Audubon Regional Library-East Feliciana 236
Audubon State Historic Site Archives 241
Augeron, Sur le Bayou LaFourche 238
Auglaize County Genealogy Society & Library 459
Auglaize County Historical Museum 456
Auglaize County Historical Society 454, 459
Auglaize County Historical Society & Archives 456
Auglaize County Historical Society Newsletter 456
AuGlaize Village Museum 447
Augus 317
Augusta Canal Authority 126
Augusta County Genealogical Society 597
Augusta County Historical Society 596
Augusta County Historical Society & Library 595
Augusta County Library 587
Augusta County Library Newsletter 587
Augusta Genealogical Society & Library 126
Augusta Historical and Genealogical Society & Archives 211
Augusta Historical Bulletin 595

Augusta Historical Museum 211
Augusta Memorial Public Library 617
Augusta Museum of History Archives 126
Augustan Society & Library 42
Augustan Society Newsletter 42
Augustan Society Omnibus 42
Augustana College Library 172
Augustana Historian 172
Augustana Historical Society & Archives 172
Augustana Historical Society, Rock Island, Illinois Publications 172
Augustana University College Library 642
Augusta-Richmond County Historical Society 126
Augusta-Richmond County Public Library 126
Augustine Fathers, Province of Our Mother of Good Counsel 169
Augustine Library 620
Augustinian Historical Institute Library 504
Aunt Margaret's Museum of Childhood Archives 659
Aurand (Aurant) Family 431
Auraria Library 83
Aurelia Public Library 197
Aurora and District Historical Museum 679
Aurora and District Historical Society & Archives 679
Aurora Genealogical Society of Colorado & Archives 81
Aurora Genealogical Society of Colorado Newsletter 81
Aurora Historical Courier 396
Aurora Historical Museum 81, 151, 396, 441
Aurora Historical Society 81, 325
Aurora Historical Society & Archives 151, 396, 441
Aurora Historical Society Newsletter 81
Aurora Pioneer 441
Aurora Public Library 81, 151, 441, 679
Aurora Public Library District 179
Aurora Regional Fire Museum Archives 151
Austell City Museum Archives 127
Austell Historic Preservation Society 127
Austen K deBlois Library 506
Austerlitz Historical Society 388
Austerlitz Historical Society Quarterly 388
Austin Archives 536
Austin Dam Memorial Association 482
Austin Family 269, 444
Austin Genealogical Society & Library 536
Austin Genealogical Society Quarterly 536
Austin History Center 536
Austin Memorial Home Archives 326
Austin Memorial Library 540
Austin Public Library 305, 536
Austin Public Library-Carver 536
Austin-Larkins Family 475, 599
Austintown Historical Society 443
Austrian History Yearbook 311
Autauga Ancestry 8
Autauga County Heritage Association 8
Autauga Genealogical Society 8
Autauga-Pratville Public Library System 8
Auto Museum News 65
Auto Trail Blazer 22
Auto-Aviation Museum 445
Automotive Hall of Fame Archives 289
Autrey Genealogical Quarterly 606
Autry Genealogy and History 606
Auxier Family 530
Auxiliary to the Sons of Union Veterans of the Civil War, Ohio Department 455
Avalon Historical Museum 367
Avalon Historical Society & Archives 367
Averill Argas 291
Avery Advocate 97
Avery County Morrison Public Library 430
Avery County Museum Archives 430
Avery Family 173, 218, 442
Avery Institute of Afro-American History and Culture & Library 512
Avery Memorial Association 94
Avery Newsletter 94
Avery Review 512
Avery-Downer House 449
Avery-Mitchell-Yancey Regional Library System 424
Aviation Hall of Fame and Museum Archives 378
Aviation Museum of Kentucky Archives 229
Avila Adobe Historic House Museum Archives 51
Avisen 308
Avivot: Forefathers 51
Avoca Historical Society 197
Avoca Museums and Historical Society 583
Avon Free Public Library 91
Avon Historical Society 151
Avon Historical Society & Archives 91
Avon Living History Museum 91
Avon Park Library 109
Avon River Heritage Museum Archives 674
Avondale Historical Society 127
Avonlea and District Museum Archives 705
Avonmore Area Historical Society 482
Avonmore Area Historical Society Newsletter 482
Avon-Washington Township Public Library 179
Avotaynu: The International Review of Jewish Genealogy 367
Avoyelles Parish Library 239
Avoyelles Publishing Company 239
AWA Electronic-Communication Museum Archives 390
Await Ancestors 46
Axis 514
Axsom Association of America Newsletter 17, 114
Axtell Public Library 349
Ayars Heirs 502
Ayer Public Library District 158
Ayer y Hoy en Taos 385
Azle Public Library 537
Aztalan Museum 624
Aztalan Museum Archives 623
Aztec Museum Association & Library 382
Aztec Museum Association Newsletter 382
Azusa Historical Society 51
Azusa Historical Society & Library 36
Azuza City Library 36

B

B B Comer Memorial Library 9
B C Forest Discovery Centre Archives 649
B C Pearce Learning Resources Center 119
B D Owens Library 335
B D Phillips Memorial Library 218

INDEX

B L Fisher Library 234
B'man Family Newsletter 32
B'nai B'rith International 105
B'nai Brith Klutznick Museum Archives 105
B-26 Maruauder Historical Society 21
Babb Family 260
Babbitt Family 425
Babbitt Newsletter 311
Babbitt Public Library 305
Babby Family 40
Babcock Library 91
Baber(s) Family 69
Babylon Public Library 388
Baca House, Trinidad History Museum Archives 90
Bachiler-Batchelder Buttons 36
Backenstoss Family 380
Backman Family 571
Backstage 133
Back-tracking Pa's Roots 287
Backus Heritage Village Museum Archives 688
Bacon Families Association Quarterly 177
Bacon Free Library 279
Bacon Memorial Public Library 304
Bacon's Castle Archives, Newsletter 596
Bacone College Library 467
Bacon-Williams-Parker-Weatherly Family 494
Bad Axe Historical Society 286
Badger Creek Museum Archives 659
Badger Family 558
Badger Historical Society 631
Badger Mine and Museum Archives 631
Badgett Family 604
Baer Family 447
Baer Memorial Library 6
Bagby-Auton-Aughton Family 226
Bagg Bonanza Historical Farm Archives 439
Baggerly Family 569
Bagley Public Library 197
Bagwell Family 556
Bahr Family 566
Baie Verte peninsula Miners' Museum Archives 667
Bailey Connections 568
Bailey Family 270
Bailey House Museum 143
Bailey Lines 554
Bailey, Bayley Family 341
Bailey-Colvin Family 56
Bailey-Howe Memorial Library 575
Bailey-Marshall-McLain Family 296
Bailor-Baylor-De Witt-Julien Family 62
Bain-Baine Newsletter 553
Bainbridge House 376
Bainbridge House Museum 376
Bainbridge Island Historical Society, Museum & Archives 599
Bair Family 145
Baird Clan 83
Baird Family 120
Baiting Hollow Free Library 392
Baker Cabin Historical Society 477
Baker County Genealogy Group 473
Baker County Historical Society & Library 116
Baker County Public Library 473
Baker Family 160
Baker Family Newsletter 229
Baker Family Newsletter International 174
Baker Heritage Center 235
Baker Mansion 481
Baker Memorial Library 361
Baker University Archives 211
Baker-Cederberg Museum Archives 413
Baker-Cederberg Notebook 413
Baker-Yaple-Dumond-Coy-Comstock-Comfort-Smith-Brown-Davis-Cahill-Flavin-Hitchcock-Alexander-Dickensen Family 470
Bala-Cynwyd Library 482
Balbec Historical Club 181
Balboa Island Historical Museum 56
Balboa Island Historical Society & Archives 56
Balch Institute for Ethnic Studies & Library 497
Balch Institute for Ethnic Studies Library 497
Bald Eagle 217
Balderson-Balderston-Balderstone Family 590
Baldwin City Library 211
Baldwin County Genealogical Society & Archives 4
Baldwin County Genealogical Society & Library 6
Baldwin County Heritage Museum Archives 4
Baldwin County Heritage Museum Quarterly Newsletter 4
Baldwin County Historical Quarterly 9
Baldwin County Historical Society & Library 9
Baldwin Heritage Museum Association 4
Baldwin Historical Museum 388
Baldwin Historical Society, Newsletter & Archives 388
Baldwin Park Historical Society 36
Baldwin Public Library 287, 388
Baldwin-Lucas-Bridwell-Wallace Family 537
Baldwin-Reynolds House Museum Archives 493
Baldwinsville Public Library 388
Bale Family 604
Bale Grist Mill State Historic Park Archives 38
Bales Family 475
Balhinch Gazette 182
Balkan and Eastern European American Genealogical and Historical Society, Quarterly 66
Ball Beginnings 314
Ball Family 424
Ball's Falls Historical Park 679
Ballard-Carlisle County Historical and Genealogical Society 234
Ballard-Carlisle-Libingston County Public Library 225
Ball-Eddleman-McFarland House Archives 545
Ballentine-Huxford Family 541
Ballew Family 125
Ballew Family Journal 125
Ballston Spa Genealogy Club & Archives 389
Ballston Spa Public Library 389
Ballwin Historical Commission 325
Balmoral Grist Mill Museum Archives 676
Balthaser Family Newsletter 482
Baltimore & Ohio Railroad Historical Society 260
Baltimore & Ohio Railroad Museum Archives 255
Baltimore City Archives 255
Baltimore Civil War Museum Archives, Newsletter 255

Baltimore County Genealogical Society 263
Baltimore County Historical Museum 257
Baltimore County Historical Society, Newsletter & Archives 257
Baltimore County Public Library 263
Baltimore County Public Library-Reisterstown Branch 261
Baltimore Maritime Museum Archives, Quarterly 255
Baltimore Museum of Industry Archives 255
Baltimore Streetcar Museum Archives 255
Baltzer Meyer Historical Society 488
Balzekas Museum of Lithuanian Culture 156
Balzekas Museum of Lithuanian Culture and Genealogical Archives 155
Ban Viet 692
Bancroft Library 37
Band of Botsford Bulletin 96
Bandera County Library 537
Bandon Historical Society & Library 473
Bandon Public Library 473
Bangle-Bangall Family 222
Bangor and Area Historical Society & Archives 617
Bangor Historical Museum 243
Bangor Historical Society, Newsletter & Archives 243
Bangor Public Library 243, 482
Bankmule 234
Banks County Historical Society 132
Bankston Family 236
Banneker Journal 255
Banneker-Douglass Museum Archives 255
Banner 355, 601
Banner County Historical Museum 352
Banner County Historical Society, Newsletter & Archives 352
Banning and Company 78
Banning Public Library 36
Banning Residence Museum Archives 78
Bannock County Historical Society, Museum, Newsletter & Archives 149
Bannockburn 274
Banta Family 632
Bantam Historical Society & Library 91
Banz Family 573
Baptist Federation of Canada 680
Baptist General Conference History Center 314
Baptist Heritage Update 531
Baptist Historical Society 334
Baptist History and Heritage 531
Bar Harbor Historical Society, Museum, Newsletter & Archives 243
Baraga Bulletin 297
Baraga County Historical Museum 295
Baraga County Historical Society & Archives 295
Baranov Museum 13
Baranov Quarterly 13
Barbara Firtchie House Museum Archives 259
Barbed Wire Museum Archives 216
Barben Family 566
Barberton Public Library 441
Barbour County Genealogical and Local Historical Society 4
Barbour County Genealogical Society 614
Barbour House Museum Archives 289
Barbour's General Store Museum Archives 665
Barclay Clan 593, 596
Bard Family 255, 409
Bardstown Historical Museum Archives 225
Bare Cove Fire Museum Archives 272
Barfield Family Historical Review 155
Barker 503
Barker Free Library 389
Barker Historical Museum, Newsletter 397
Barker Mansion Archives 189
Barker-Joslyn Family Tree Climber 220
Barkerville Historic Town Library & Archives 647
Barkhamsted Historical Society 91, 98
Barkley Museum Archives 232
Barksdale Air Force Base Library 235
Barlow Family 301
Barnacle Historic State Park Archives 111
Barnard Community Historical Society 325
Barnard Family 149, 418, 606
Barnard Historical Society & Archives 575
Barnard Library 216
Barnegat Historical Society 367
Barnegat Light Historical Society & Library 367
Barner Family Newsletter 285, 489, 590
Barnes County Historical Society, Museum & Archives 439
Barnes County History 439
Barnes Family 41, 44, 600
Barnes Family Quarterly 459
Barnes Museum Archives 99
Barnes-Beghtol-Bechtel-Koeth-Kate Family 209
Barnesville Heritage Society 305
Barnesville Hutton Memorial Library 441
Barnesville-Lamar County Historical Museum 127
Barnesville-Lamar County Historical Society & Archives 127
Barnet Historical Society & Archives 575
Barnet Public Library 575
Barnett Family 556
Barnett Family Publication 213
Barnett Historic Preservation Society 114
Barney Family 595
Barngrover-Berngruber Newsletter 467
Barnhill Family 528
Barnsdall Public Library 463
Barnum Herald 91
Barnum House Museum Archives 683
Barnum Museum Archives 91
Barnwell County Museum and Historical Board 511
Barnwell County Museums Archives 511
Barnwell Family 475
Barr Colony Cultural Centre 707
Barr Memorial Library 227
Barratt's Chapel and Museum Archives 103
Barre Historical Society 575
Barre Historical Society, Museum & Archives 266
Barren County Historical Foundation 228
Barrett Family 624
Barrett House Museum Archives 363
Barrett Township Historical Society 495
Barrett(e) Family 266
Barrhead and District Centennial Museum Archives 641
Barrhead Public Library 641
Barrie Area Native Advisory Circle 679
Barrie Family 524
Barrie Native Friendship Center 679

INDEX

Barrie Public Library 679
Barrineau Park Historical Society 109
Barringer Family 606
Barrington Area Historical Museum 151
Barrington Area Historical Society & Library 151
Barrington Area Library 151
Barrington Living History Farm Archives 562
Barrington Preservation Society 507
Barrington Public Library 359
Barrington Public Library 507
Barrington Woolen Mill Museum Archives 673
Barron County Genealogical Society 619
Barron County Historical Society & Archives 619
Barron Family 448
Barron's Chesapeake and Ohio Canal Museum Library 262
Barron-Whitworth Family 298
Barrow County Historical Society & Library 139
Barry County Genealogical Society 327
Barry County Historical Society 293
Barry-Lawrence Library 335
Barry-Lawrence Regional Library 335
Barstow California Stake Branch Genealogical Library 36
Barstow Route 66 Mother Road Museum Archives, Newsletter 37
Bartee Family 559
Bartholomew County Ancestors 181
Bartholomew County Genealogical Society 181
Bartholomew County Historical Society & Library 181
Bartholomew County Public Library 181
Bartleson Family 463
Bartlesville Area History Museum Archives 463
Bartlesville Bookmark 463
Bartlesville Genealogical Society, Newsletter & Archives 463
Bartlesville Public Library 463
Bartlett Family 274, 278
Bartlett Family 567
Bartlett Historical Society 152
Bartlett Historical Society & Archives 525
Bartlett Museum 525
Bartlett Museum Archives 265
Bartlett Museum Quarterly 265
Bartlett-Carnegie Sapulpa Public Library 469
Bartlett-Hardesty Newsletter 219
Bartlett-Tittsworth Family 150
Barton Banner 548
Barton County Genealogical Society 214
Barton County Historical Society & Archives 214
Barton County Historical Society & Library 333
Barton County Village 214
Barton Library 27
Barton Library-Smackover Branch 32
Barton Library-Strong Branch 33
Barton Museum Archives 435
Barton-Higgs Family 607
Bartow County Genealogical Society & Family Research Library 128
Bartow County Historical Society & Library 128
Bartow County Library System 128
Bartow County Public Library System-Adairsville Branch 125
Bartow County Quarterly 128
Bartow History Center 128
Bartow Public Library 109
Bartow-Pell Mansion Museum Archives 390
Bartow-Pell Mansion Museum Newsletter 390
Bartram Trail Regional Library 139
Barwick Branches 113
Basalt Regional Library District 81
Basehor Historical Society 211
Basham Family 542
Bashlor Family 130
Bashore Family 40
Basileiad Library 490
Basilian Fathers Museum Archives 645
Basilique Notre-Dame de Montreal 699
Basin Research Associates 68
Basket Historical Society of the Upper Delaware Valley 403
Bass Family 135
Basse Borden Military Museum Archives 680
Bassett Family 572
Bassett Hall Museum Archives 597
Bassett House Museum Archives 653
Bassett-Walker-Puffer-Banbury Family 62
Bastion Museum Archives 652
Bastrop County Historical Museum 537
Bastrop County Historical Society & Archives 537
Bastrop Public Library 537
Bata Shoe Museum Archives 691
Batavia Depot Museum 152
Batavia Historical Society, Newsletter & Archives 152
Batavia Public Library District 152
Batchelder Family 601
Batchewana Indian Band 689
Bateman Family 406
Bateman Historical Museum Archives 705
Bater Surname Organization Newsletter 185
Bates County Genealogical Society & Library 326
Bates County Historical Society & Library 326
Bates County, Missouri Genealogical Quarterly 325
Bates Family 184, 279, 547, 585, 635
Bates-Scofield Homestead 92
Batesville Area Historical Society 179
Batesville Genealogical Society 25
Batesville Memorial Public Library 179
Bath Company Historical Society 589
Bath County Heritage 596
Bath County Historical Museum 596
Bath County Historical Society & Archives 596
Bath County Memorial Library 232
Bath Family 87
Bath Historical Society & Archives 243
Bath Historical Society Newsletter 243
Batoche National Historic Site Archives 705, 710
Baton Rouge Genealogical and Historical Society 235
Baton Rouge Genealogical and Historical Society: Membership and Surname Book 235
Baton Rouge Newsletter 235
Batsto Village Museum Archives 371
Batsto Village Newsletter 371
Battersea House Museum Archives 592
Battle of Lexington State Historic Site 334
Battleaxe 594
Battleaxe 600

Battlefield House Museum Archives 690
Battlefield Photographer 488
Battleford National Historic Park Archives 705
Battleford's Tribal Council 708
Battleground Historical Society & Library 369, 378
Battles for Chattanooga Museum Archives 529
Battles Museums of Rural Life Archives 488
Battleship Massachusetts Museum Archives 270
Battleship Massachusetts Quarterly 270
Battleship New Jersey Museum Archives 368
Battleship North Carolina Museum Archives 434
Battleship North Carolina Newsletter 434
Battleship South Dakota Museum Archives 523
Battleship Texas State Historic Park Archives 551
BATUN News 390
Baudouin Family 536
Bauer-Beissel Family 309
Baughman-Banks-Puckett-Talbert-Hanvey Family 391
Baul Family 548
Bax Axe Public Library 286
Baxter County Historical and Genealogical Society 31
Baxter County History 31
Baxter County Library 31
Baxter Family Chronicle 170
Baxter House Museum Archives 246
Baxter Springs Historical Museum 211
Baxter Springs Historical Society & Archives 211
Bay Area Genealogical Society 622
Bay Area Genealogy Study Club 559
Bay Area Heritage Society 537
Bay Area Historical Society 315
Bay Area Museum Archives 559
Bay Area Museum Newsletter 559
Bay Chronicle 251
Bay City Branch Library 286
Bay City Public Library 537
Bay County Genealogical Society 119, 286
Bay County Genealogical Society & Library 291
Bay County Historical Museum 286
Bay County Historical Society & Archives 286
Bay County Library System 286
Bay County Library System-Sage Branch 286
Bay County Library System-South Side Branch 286
Bay De Noc Community College Library 291
Bay Mills-Brimley Historic Research Society 287
Bay Minette Public Library 1
Bay of Pigs Museum Archives 117
Bay Saint George Campus Library 668
Bay Shore-Brightwaters Public Library 390
Bay State Historical League 281
Bay View Historical Society 617
Bay View Histrorical Museum Archives 286
Bay Village Historical Society & Archives 442
Bayard Public Library 349
Bayard Taylor Memorial Library 491
Bayard-Chimney Rock Historical Society 349
Bayfield County Genealogical Society 625
Bayfield County Historical Museum 633
Bayfield County Historical Society & Archives 625, 633
Bayfield County Historical Society, Oulu Chapter 628
Bayfield Heritage Association & Archives 617
Bayfield Historical Museum 617
Bayless-Selby House Museum Archives 543
Bayliss Public Library 302
Baylor County Historical Society 560
Baylor Townsend Memorial Library 538
Baylor University Library 562
Bayonne Free Public Library 367
Bayonne Free Public Library Newsletter 367
Bayou Branches 239
Bayport Public Library 305
Bayport-Blue Point Public Library 390
Bayport-Blue Point Public Library Newsletter 390
Bays Family 469
Baytown Genealogical Society & Archives 537
Baytown Genealogical Society Newsletter 537
Baytown Historical Museum Archives 537
Bazel-Johnson Family 446
Bazeltown Family 545
BCHS Newsletter 8, 10
Beach 413
Beach Family 293
Beach Haven Free Public Library 367
Beach-Danforth-Potter-Warren Family 433
Beaches Area Historical Society & Library 114
Beachville District Museum Archives 679
Beacon 157, 281, 405, 620
Beacon Falls Historical Commission 91
Beacon Falls Historical Commission Newsletter 91
Beacon Historical Museum 389
Beacon Historical Society & Archives 389
Beacon Historical Society Newsletter 389
Beaconsfield Public Library 697
Beadles Family 542
Beale Air Force Base Library 37
Beall Family 478, 552
Beall-Dawson House 262
Beals Family 214
Beals Memorial Library 282
Beaman Community Memorial Library 197
Beaman Museum 413
Bean Creek Valley Historical Society 294
Bean Family 530, 569, 614
Bear Creek Genealogical Society 548
Bear Family Newsletter 82
Bear Library 103
Bear Mountain Trailside Museum Archives 389
Bear Tracks 216
Beardmore Public Library 679
Beardslee Library 293
Beardsley & Memorial Library 101
Beardstown Public Library 152
Beardy's and Okemasis First Nation 706
Beargrass-Saint Matthews Historical Society 230
Bearspaw Historical Society 641
Beasley Family News 129
Beatley Family 73
Beatley Library 266
Beaton Institute University 676
Beatrice Public Library 349

INDEX

Beaty-Burlingame Newsletter 262
Beau Fort Plantation Home Archives 236
Beau Village Museum Archives 710
Beauchamp Newman House Museum Archives 612
Beaudet Family 370
Beaufort County Genealogical Society 434, 515
Beaufort County Historical Society 511
Beaufort County Library 511
Beaufort Genealogical Society 517
Beaufort Historic Site Museum 423
Beaufort Historical Association & Archives 423
Beaufort Museum Archives 511
Beaufort, Hyde, Martin Regional Library 434
Beaumont Branches 355
Beaumont Heritage Society & Archives 537
Beaumont Library District 37
Beaumont Public Library 537
Beauport Magazine 271
Beauport Sleeper-McCann House Archives 271
Beauregard Historical Society 236
Beauregard Parish Public Library 236
Beausoleil First Nation 688
Beautiful Plains Museum Archives 660
Beauvais Heritage Center 521
Beauvoir, Jefferson Davis Home Archives 319
Beaver Briefs 479
Beaver City Public Library 349
Beaver Countian 482
Beaver County Genealogical Society 482
Beaver County Historical Research and Landmarks Foundation 488
Beaver County, Pennsylvania Historical Research and Landmarks Foundation 482
Beaver Creek Historical Society 713
Beaver Dam Community Library 617
Beaver Island Historical Museum 286
Beaver Island Historical Society 301
Beaver Island Historical Society & Archives 286
Beaver Island Historical Society Journal 301
Beaver Island Preservation Association 286
Beaver Lake Indian Band 644
Beaver Paw Press 247
Beaver Plew 637
Beaver River Genealogical and Historical Society 466
Beaver River Museum 680
Beaver River News 466
Beaver: Canada's History Magazine 662
Beaverdale Community Library 482
Beaverhead County Historical Museum 344
Beaverhead County Historical Society & Archives 344
Beaverhead County Museum 344
Beaverhead County Museum Newsletter 344
Beaverhead Hunters 346
Beaverhead Hunters Genealogical Society 344
Beaverhead Hunters Genealogical Society News 344
Beaver-Head-Hunters Genealogical Society & Archives 344
Beavers-Riddle Family 350
Beavertail Lighthouse Museum Archives 507
Beavertail Lighthouse Museum Newsletter 507
Beaverton City Library 473
Beaverton Thorah and Eldon Historical Society & Archives 680
Beck Bookman Library 215
Beck Cultural Exchange Center Archives 528
Becker County Historical Museum 307
Becker County Historical Society & Archives 307
Becker County Historical Society Newsletter 307
Beckman Coulter Heritage Museum Archives 45
Beckman Mill Archives 617
Beckoning Hills Museum Archives 659
Bedford Bee 442
Bedford City-County Museum Archives 584
Bedford County Genealogical Society 584
Bedford County Pioneer Historical Society 482
Bedford Family 48
Bedford Free Library 389
Bedford Free Public Library 266
Bedford Historical Museum 389, 442
Bedford Historical Society 359, 584
Bedford Historical Society & Archives 389, 442
Bedford Park Public Library District 152
Bedford Park Public Library District Newsletter 152
Bedford Public Library 179, 197, 537, 584
Bedingfield Inn Museum 133
Bee County Public Library 537
Bee Line 138, 380
Beebe Family 334, 441, 641
Beech Grove Historical Society 179
Beech Grove Public Library 179
Beech Island Historical Society 511
Beecher Bay Indian Band 655
Beecher Community Historical Society & Archives 152
Beecher Community Library 152
Beeghly Library 447
Beehive History 572
Beehive House Archives 570
Beekman Library 412
Beekmantown Town Hall Archives 411
Beeland-Shine Family 139
Beers Bulletin 169
Beezley Family News 58
Begley Family 300
Behnke Family Newsletter 77
Behringer-Crawford Museum Library 226
Behringer-Crawford Museum Newsletter 226
Beinecke Rare Book & Manuscript Library 96
Beit Hashoah Museum Archives 51
Beith House Museum Archives 173
Beitzel Family 259
Bel County Genealogist 551
Belair Mansion Museum Archives 257
Belair Stable Museum Archives 257
Belcher Family 614
Belchertown Historical Association & Archives 266
Belchertown Historical Association Newsletter 266
Belcourt Banner 508
Belcourt Castle Archives 508
Belden Historical Society 449
Belding Area Historical Society 299
Belding Museum Archives 286
Belding Museum Quarterly 286
Belen Public Library 382

Belfast Free Library 243
Belfast Historical Museum 243
Belfast Historical Society 695
Belfast Historical Society & Archives 243
Belgian Lace 191
Belgian Laces 473
Belgian-American Heritage Association 473
Belgrade Community Library 343
Belhaven Memorial Museum Archives 423
Belhaven Memorial Museum Newsletter 423
Belington Public Library 611
Belk Library 423
Belknap Mill Historical Museum 362
Belknap Mill Society & Library 362
Belknap Mill Society Newsletter 362
Bell Clan 579
Bell County Historical Museum 231
Bell County Historical Society & Archives 231
Bell County Museum Archives 538
Bell County Museum Newsletter 538
Bell Family 35, 497, 549, 588
Bell Family 6
Bell Homestead Museum Archives 680
Bell Memorial Public Library 189
Bell Ringer 173
Bell Rock Mill Museum Archives 692
Bell Township Historical Preservation Society 501
Bella Coola Indian Band 647
Bella Coola Museum Archives 647
Bella Vista Historical Museum 25
Bella Vista Historical Society & Archives 25
Bella Vista Historical Society Newsletter 25
Bella Vista Public Library 25
Bella Vista Vision 25
Bellaire Area Historical Society 286
Bellaire Area Historical Society Newsletter 286
Bellaire City Library 538
Bellaire Genealogical Society 548
Bellamy Mansion Museum Archives 434
Bellamy Mansion News 434
Bellard-Ballard Family 558
Belle Alliance Plantation Archives 237
Belle Boyd House 613
Belle Fourche Public Library 521
Belle Grove Plantation Archives 591
Belle Grove Plantation Newsletter 591
Belle Meade Mansion 531
Belle Plaine Community Library 197
Belle Plaine Historical Society 197, 305
Belle Tree 125
Belleville Area Historical Society 617
Belleville Area Museum Archives 286
Belleville Historical Society & Archives 367
Belleville Public Library 152, 211, 617, 680
Belleville Township Free Public Library 367
Bellevue Area Historical Society 286
Bellevue Area Historical Society Newsletter 286
Bellevue House Museum Archives 684
Bellevue Library Times 349
Bellevue Public Library 349, 442
Bellevue Regional Library 599
Bellevue Valley Historical Society 326
Bellewood Public Library 152
Bellflower Genealogical and Historical Society 152
Bellflower Heritage Society 37
Bellflower Highlights 152
Bellflower Historical Museum 152
Bellingham Family 572
Bellingham Public Library 599
Bellmont Town Archives 404
Bellon Family 567
Bellows Falls Historical Society & Archives 575
Bellport-Brookhaven Historical Museum 389
Bellport-Brookhaven Historical Society & Archives 389
Bellport-Brookhaven Historical Society Newsletter 389
Bells-Piedmont-Malan Family 565
Bellville Historical Society 538
Bell-Whittington Public Library 556
Bellwood Public Library 152
Belmont and District Museum Archives 659
Belmont County Chapter, OGS 441
Belmont County Genealogy News 441
Belmont County Victorian Mansion Museum Archives 441
Belmont Historical Museum 37
Belmont Historical Society & Archives 37, 266
Belmont Historical Society Newsletter 266
Belmont Memorial Library 266
Belmore's Museum Archives 642
Beloit Historical Society & Archives 617
Beloit Historical Society & Library 617
Beloit Public Library 617
Belote Family 413
Belpre Area Historical Society 442
Belton Historical Society 325
Belton Historical Society Newsletter 325
Belton, Grandview and Kansas City Railroad Company 325
Beltrami County Historical Society & Archives 305
Beltrami County History Center 305
Belvedere Castle Museum Archives 406
Belvedere-Tiburon Landmarks Society & Library 37
Belvidere-Tiburon Public Library 75
Belview Depot School Museum Archives 305
Bement Public Library District 152
Bement-Billings Farmstead Museum 408
Bemidji Genealogical Society 305
Bemidji Public Library 305
Bemus Point Public Library 389
Ben Hunt Cabin 622
Benares Historic House Museum Archives 686
Benchmarks 591
Bend Genealogical Society 473
Bend of the River: a Magazine of the Historic Maumee Valley 452
Benderman Family 3
Beneath the Rafters 200
Benedict Family History News 71, 124
Benedict Family News 57
Be-Ne-Lux Genealogist 42
Benicia Capitol State Historic Park Archives 37
Benicia Fire Museum Archives 37
Benicia Historical Museum Archives 37

Benicia Historical Society 37
Benicia Public Library 37
Benion Family 571
Benjamin and Dr Edgar R Cofield Judaic Museum 391
Benjamin Banneker Park Museum Archives 255
Benjamin Harrison Presidential Library 186
Benjamin P Browne Library 159
Benjamin-Flournoy Family 155
Benn-Bain Family 41
Bennell Museum Archives 342
Benner Family 145
Bennett County Genealogical Society 521
Bennett D Katz Library 243
Bennett Exchange Newsletter 387
Bennett Family 236, 387, 546
Bennett Family News 532
Bennett Place State Historic Site Archives 425
Bennett Place State Historic Site Newsletter 425
Bennett Quarterly 418
Bennett School Museum Archives 209
Bennett-Thornton Family 483
Benning Family 125
Bennington Battle Monument Archives 578
Bennington Battlefield State Historic Site Archives 419
Bennington Bulletin 20
Bennington Covered Bridge Museum Archives 575
Bennington Free Library 575
Bennington Historical Society 359
Bennington Historical Society & Archives 575
Bennington Museum 575
Benny Gambaiani Public Library 207
Bensalem Historical Society 482
Bensenville Historical Society 152
Benson Family 552
Benson Hammond House 259
Benson Historical Society 355
Benson Memorial Library 503
Benson Public Library 15
Benson-Brown-Hunstock-Clark Family 60, 474, 476
Bent County Historical Society 87
Bent's Old Fort Historical Association 86
Bentheim - History of a Family Dispersed 155
Bentley Historical Library 285
Bentley House 416
Benton County Genealogical Society 474, 477, 525
Benton County Genealogical Society Newsletter 474
Benton County Historical Museum 477, 605
Benton County Historical Society 25, 184, 209, 319, 342
Benton County Historical Society & Archives 477, 605
Benton County Historical Society & Library 315
Benton County Historical Society Record 477
Benton County Pioneer 25
Benton County Preservation Society 25
Benton County Public Library 184, 525
Benton Harbor Public Library 286
Benton House 186
Benton Newsline 315
Benton Public Library 618
Benton Public Library District 152
Bentonville Battleground State Historic Site Archives 427
Bentonville Public Library 25
Benzie Area Historical Museum 286
Benzie Area Historical Society & Archives 286
Benzonia Public Library 286
Benzonia Public Library Newsletter 286
Beothuck Village Museum Archives 667
Beothuk Interpretation Centre 667
Bepko Family 93
Bercail 703
Berea Area Historical Society & Archives 442
Beresford Public Library 521
Bergen County Genealogical Society 373
Bergen County Genealogical Society Quarterly 373
Bergen County Historical Museum 377
Bergen County Historical Society & Archives 377
Bergen Historical Society & Archives 389
Bergen Museum of Local History 389
Bergenfield Free Public Library 367
Berkeley Architectural Heritage Association 37
Berkeley County Genealogical and Historical Society & Archives 613
Berkeley County Historical Museum 516
Berkeley County Historical Society 515
Berkeley County Historical Society & Archives 516
Berkeley County Library 516
Berkeley Historical Museum 37
Berkeley Historical Society & Archives 37
Berkeley Journal 613
Berkeley Plantation Archives 585
Berkeley Public Library 37, 152
Berkeley Township Historical Society 367
Berkler Family 208
Berkley Historical Society 266
Berks County Conservancy 500
Berks County Genealogical Society 492
Berks County Genealogical Society & Library 491, 500
Berks County Genealogical Society Journal 491
Berks of Old: The History and Genealogy of Berks County, PA 492
Berkshire Athanaeum 277
Berkshire County Historical Museum 277
Berkshire County Historical Society & Archives 277
Berkshire Family History Association & Library 277
Berkshire Genealogist 277
Berkshire History 277
Berkshire Museum Archives 277
Berkshire Scenic Railway Museum Archives 273
Berlin Area Historical Society 482
Berlin Art and Historical Collections Archives 266
Berlin Fortier Library 359
Berlin Heritage Foundation 256
Berlin Heritage Foundation Newsletter 256
Berlin Historian 266
Berlin Historical Museum 91, 618
Berlin Historical Society 266, 367, 482, 578
Berlin Historical Society & Archives 91, 618
Berlin Public Library 618
Berlin-Coos County Historical Society 359
Berlin-Peck Memorial Library 91, 95
Bernard Historical Museum 289
Bernard Historical Society & Archives 289
Bernard Historical Society Quarterly 289

Bernard Judaica Museum Archives 406
Bernards Township Library 367
Bernardsville Library Times 367
Bernardsville Public Library 367
Berne Public Library 179
Berner-Burner-Bernard Family 600
Bernhard Museum Archives 36
Bernhard-Dickinson Family 569
Bernice P Bishop Museum Library 141
Berrett Family 568
Berrien County Genealogical Society 286
Berrien County Historical Association & Library 286
Berrien County Historical Association Annual Report 286
Berrien Springs Community Library 286
Berry Family 181, 601
Berry Memorial Library 243
Berry Pickers 55
Berry-Harrison-Hardman-Edmondson Family 506
Bertha Historical Society & Library 306
Bertha Historical Society Newsletter 306
Berthoud Historical Society 81
Berthoud Public Library 81
Bertolet Memorial Library District 164
Berwick Family 312
Berwick Historical Society 243, 482
Berwick Public Library 244, 482
Berwyn Historical Society 152
Besancon Historical Society 89, 190
Bessemer Hall of History Archives 1
Bessemer Hall of History Newsletter 1
Bessie Boehm Moore Stone County Library 31
Best Friend 512
Best Friend of Charleston Museum Archives 512
Best of the Professional Genealogists of Arkansas Newsletter 26
Bestman House on Ballard Road 151
Betchtel Family Association Update 7
Beth Ahabah Museum and Archives 593
Beth Israel Synagogue Library 379
Beth Tzedac Reuben and Helene Dennis Museum 691
Bethany Cemetery Inscriptions 512
Bethany Historical Society 91
Bethel Courier 244
Bethel Historical Association 442
Bethel Historical Museum 244
Bethel Historical Society 103
Bethel Historical Society & Archives 244
Bethel Historical Society & Library 575
Bethel Library Association 244
Bethel Park Public Library 482
Bethel Public Library 91
Bethel Public Library Newsletter 91
Bethel Seminary Library 305
Bethelehem Area Public Library 482
Bethelehem Historical Association Museum 416
Bethelehem Public Library 395
Bethel-Tulpehocken Public Library 482
Bethesda United Methodist Church Library 256
Bethesda-Union Society 136
Bethlehem Historical Association-Genealogy Committee 416
Bethlehem Public Library 91
Bethune Memorial House Museum Archives 683
Betsey Williams Cottage Archives 509
Betsy Ross House and Flag Museum Archives 497
Bettendorf Public Library and Family Museum 197
Betts House Research Center Archives 444
Between the Bookends 138
Between the Lakes Newsletter 401
Between the Lines 149, 163, 279, 360
Between the Lions Newsletter 163
Between the Pages 120, 180
Between the Rivers 211
Between the Stacks 552
Beulah Williams Library 521
Bevan Family 566
Beverly Family Records Newsletter 549
Beverly Free Library 367
Beverly Hills Historical Society 37
Beverly Historical Museum 266
Beverly Historical Review 266
Beverly Historical Society & Archives 266
Beverly Shores Historical Society 180
Bevier-Etling Family 255, 424
BeWabBon Metis and Aboriginal Centre 688
BeWabBon Metis Nation 688
Bewley Family 539
Bexley Historical Museum 442
Bexley Historical Society & Archives 442
Beyer Home Museum 628
Beyerlein Family 603
Beynon-Lundholm Family 566
Beyond Words 106
Bezarn Family 435
Bezotte-Collins Family 40
Bibb County Heritage Association & Library 2
Bibee Family 572
Bible Holiness Movement Library 656
Biblical Arts Center Museum Archives 542
Biblical Museum of Canada 656
Biblical Resource Center Museum Archives 526
Bibliobits-Off the Shelf 278
Biblio-File 282
BiblioFile 509, 575
Biblion 408
Biblioteque Le Cormoran 665
Biblioteque Municipale de Beauport 697, 699
Bibliotheque a Saint Germain 701
Bibliotheque Alphonse-Desjardins 699
Bibliotheque Champlain 664
Bibliotheque Commemorative Desautels 699
Bibliotheque Commemorative Pettes 698
Bibliotheque de Pavillon Lalemant 699
Bibliotheque de Roxboro 701
Bibliotheque de Theologe 699
Bibliotheque de Tracy 703
Bibliotheque de Verdun 704
Bibliotheque du College 698
Bibliotheque du Musee du Chateau Ramezay Museum Library 699
Bibliotheque du Seminaire de Saint-Hyacinthe 701
Bibliotheque Louis-Ange-Santerre 703
Bibliotheque Montarville-Boucher-de la Bruere 697

INDEX

Bibliotheque Municipal de Longueuil 699
Bibliotheque Municipal de Longueuil Bulletin 699
Bibliotheque Municipale 703
Bibliotheque Municipale Adelard-Berger 702
Bibliotheque Municipale Come-Saint-Germain 697
Bibliotheque Municipale d'Aylmer 697
Bibliotheque Municipale de Brossard 697
Bibliotheque Municipale de Dorval 697
Bibliotheque Municipale de Hull 698
Bibliotheque Municipale de Jonquiere 698
Bibliotheque Municipale de Lachute 698
Bibliotheque Municipale de Longueuil-C H Grignon Branch 699
Bibliotheque Municipale de Saint Bruno-de-Montarville 701
Bibliotheque Municipale de Saint-Basile-le-Grand 701
Bibliotheque Municipale de Sainte-Foy 702
Bibliotheque Municipale de Sainte-Therese 702
Bibliotheque Municipale de Saul Bellow 698
Bibliotheque Municipale de Sorel-Tracy 703
Bibliotheque Municipale de Ville de la Baie 704
Bibliotheque Municipale Francoise-Bedard 701
Bibliotheque Municipale Guy-Belisle Saint Eustache 701
Bibliotheque Nationale du Quebec 699
Bibliotheque Rhea-Larose 663
Bibliotheque Universite du Quebec en Abitibi-Temiscamingue 701
Bibliotheques de Trois-Rivieres, Bibliotheque Gatien-la Pointe 703
Bibliotheques Publiques de la Cote-Nord 703
Bibliotheques Publiques Du Bas-Saint-Laurent 701
Bicentennial City-County Public Library 555
Bicentennial Historical Museum Archives 146
Bickers Family 567
Bickford Newsletter 105, 391
Bicknell Family 195
Bicknell-Vigo Township Public Library 180
Bicksler-Bixler Newsletter 482
Bicycle Museum of America Archives 454
Biddeford Historical Society 244, 253
Biddeford Historical Society Annual Report 244
Bidwell Family 444
Bidwell House Archives 275
Bidwell Mansion Association & Library 40
Bidwell Mansion News & Notes 40
Bidwell Mansion State Historic Park Archives 40
Biedenharn Coca-Cola Museum Archives 322
Biedenharn Museum Archives 239
Bielarus 75
Bienville Historical Society 236
Bienville Parish Library 235
Bierce Family 446
Bierce Library 441
Big Bear Trails Museum 707
Big Bear Valley Historical Society & Museum 37
Big Bend Community College Library 603
Big Bend Genealogical Society 535
Big Bend Register 601
Big Bend Village Library 618
Big Bend-Vernon Historical Society 618
Big Bone Lick State Park Museum Archives 233
Big Butte Historical Society 474, 475
Big Country News 535
Big Flats Historical Society & Library 389
Big Flats Historical Society Newsletter 389
Big Hole National Battlefield Archives 347
Big Horn County Genealogical Society 345
Big Horn County Historical Museum Archives 345
Big Horn County Historical Society 345
Big Horn County Library 635
Big Horn County Public Library 345
Big Lake Family History Society 118
Big Lake Family History Society Newsletter 118
Big Lake Public Library 11
Big River First Nation 706
Big River Memorial Museum Archives 705
Big Sandy Community & Technical College Library 232
Big Sky Newsletter 345
Big Sky Roundup 343
Big Smoke 603
Big Springs Museum Archives 392
Big Springs Public Library 349
Big Stone County Historical Society 312
Big Sur Historical Society 37, 39
Big Thicket Genealogical Club 551
Big Thunder Gold Mine Museum Archives 522
Big Timbers Museum 87
Big Valley Historical Museum Archives 37
Bigaouette-Thomas Family 309
Bigbie Family 383
Bigelow Genealogical Society 291
Bigelow House Museum Archives 604
Biggar Museum and Gallery Archives 705
Biggar-Conklin-Mills-Albertson Family 535
Biggerstaff Family 517
Biggs Family 465
Bigle Family 383
BIGWILL Newsletter 171
Biliotheque Municipale Eva-Senecal 703
Bill Baggs Cape Florida State Park Archives 115
Bill Memorial Library 94
Bill(s) Family 607
Billbrough Family 380
Billerica Historical Society 266
Billerica Public Library 266
Billie Creek Village Archives 192
Billie Holiday NYC Landmark Society 371
Billings County Historical Society 523
Billings Estate Museum Archives 687
Billings Family 570
Billings Farm and Museum Archives 581
Billings Preservation Society & Archives 343
Billings Preservation Society Newsletter 343
Billingsley Family 600
Billups Bulletin 163
Billy Bishop Heritage Museum Archives 687
Billy Graham Center 177
Billy the Kid Museum Archives 383
Biltmore Estate Museum Archives 423
Bilyen by You 603
Binder-Gearing-Carmichael Family 89
Bingham County Historical Museum Archives 145
Bingham Family 273
Bingham-Waggoner Historical Society 330

Binkley Family 495
Binnie Family 332
Binscarth and District Gordon Orr Memorial Museum Archives 659
Biography Index 390
Birch Family 149
Birchard Public Library 448
Birch-Harrison Family 76
Birch-Luck-Van Stewart Family 48
Birchwood Area Historical Society 618
Bird Branches 529
Bird Family 21, 457
Birds Family 382
Birdville Historical Society 547
Birlingmair Family 203
Birman-Rosenblatt-Bialac-Mathysee Family 134
Birmingham Genealogical Society 2
Birmingham Genealogical Society Newsletter 2
Birmingham Heritage 287
Birmingham Historical Museum 287
Birmingham Historical Society 287
Birmingham Historical Society & Library 2
Birmingham Public Library 2
Birmingham-Jefferson Historical Society 2
Birthplace Bound 137
Birthplace of John Wayne Museum Archives 209
Bisbee Family 200, 286
Bisbee Historical Society 15
Bisbee Mill Museum 269
Bisbee Mining and Historical Museum Archives 15
Biscayne Bay Campus Library 118
Bish Family 77
Bishop Baraga Association & Archives 297
Bishop Family 174, 301, 492
Bishop Hill Heritage Association & Archives 152
Bishop Hill Heritage Museum 152
Bishop Hill Old Settlers Association 152
Bishop Hodges Library 615
Bishop Library 481
Bishop Museum and Historical Society & Library 37
Bishop Museum and Historical Society Quarterly Bulletin 37
Bishop's Mill Historical Institute & Library 493
Bishop's Palace Museum Archives 546
Bishop-McCallum Family 343
Bismarck Public Library 437
Bismarck State College Library 437
Bismarck-Mandal Historical and Genealogical Society Quarterly 437
Bismarck-Mandan Historical and Genealogical Society 437
Biswell Family 469
Bit of Nostalgia 265
Bit Oh Roots 344
Bits and Bytes 122
Bits and Pieces 259, 437
Bits and Pieces of the Past 223
Bits of Bark from the Family Tree 25
Bitter Root Genealogical Society 344
Bitter Root Valley Historical Society & Archives 344
Bitter Root Valley Historical Society Newsletter 344
Bitterroot Public Library 345
Bitzer-Bizer-Haigis Family 96
Biuletyn Korzenie (Bulletin Roots) 276
Bixby Family 201
Bixby Memorial Free Library 580
Black American West Museum and Heritage Center Archives 83
Black Archives History Foundation 117
Black Archives of Mid-America 332
Black Archives Research Center and Museum 122
Black Brook Town Historian 388
Black Chronicle Newspaper 267
Black Creek Pioneer Village Archives 686
Black Cultural Centre For Nova Scotia Library 673
Black Earth Historical Society & Archives 618
Black Family Genealogy and History Society 17
Black Family History Society of Arizona 16
Black Genealogy Research Group Newsletter 83
Black Genealogy Research Group of Colorado 83
Black Hawk State Park 172
Black Heritage Museum Archives 117
Black Heritage Museum Newsletter 117
Black Heritage Museum of West Alabama Archives 9
Black Hills Mining Museum Archives 522
Black Hills Mining Museum Newsletter 522
Black Historical Society of Santa Clara 67
Black History Magazine 266
Black History Museum and Cultural Center Archives 593
Black History News & Notes 186
Black Horse Bulletin 283
Black in Rhode Island 509
Black Kettle Museum Archives 464
Black Lake Denesuline Nation 705
Black Nugget Museum Archives 651
Black River Academy Museum 577
Black River Falls Public Library 618
Black River Genealogists 451
Black River Historical Museum 451
Black River Historical Society & Archives 451, 577
Black River Historical Society Newsletter 451
Black Swamp Chanticleer 442
Black Watch of Canada Regimental Memorial Museum Archives 699
Blackberry Farm's Pioneer Village Archives 151
Blackbourne Family 44
Blackburn Beginnings 83
Blackburn Family 83
Blackburn Historical Society 325
Blackburn-Blackbourn Family 619
Blackburn-Watts-Carson-Challacombe Family 303
Blackfeet Community College Library 343
Blackfoot Public Library 145
Blackford County Historical Museum 185
Blackford County Historical Society & Archives 185
Blackford County Historical Society & Library 185
Blackford-Wells Genealogy Society 180
Black-Greenlaw-Pineo-Petersen-Holt-Bennett Family 566
Blackhawk Genealogical Society of Rock Island and Mercer County Illinois & Library 166, 172
Blackhawk Genealogical Society Quarterly 172
Blackhawk Museum Archives 42
Blackhawk Museum Newsletter 42
Blackhurst Family 612
Blackketter Family 463
Blackman Family 3

INDEX

Blackman House Museum 607
Blackmore Family 290, 552
Blackmur Memorial Library 323
Blacksmith Shop Museum Archives 245
Blacksmith: Wells Family Association Newsletter 169
Blackstock Family 113
Blackstone Valley Historical Museum 508
Blackstone Valley Historical Society & Archives 508
Blackville Area Historical Society 511
Blackville Historical Museum Archives 663
Blackwater Regional Library-Isle of Wight County Public 595
Blackwater Regional Library-Surry Public 596
Blackwell Genealogy Study Group 271
Blackwell Library 262
Blackwell Public Library 463
Blackwell Researcher's Newsletter 64
Bladen County Public Library 426
Bladenboro Historical Society 423
Blaine County Historical Museum 147, 343
Blaine County Historical Society 350
Blaine County Historical Society & Archives 147, 343
Blaine County Historical Society Newsletter 147
Blaine House Museum Archives 243
Blaine Lake Museum Archives 705
Blaine S Kern Library 239
Blair Bruidhinn 172
Blair Bruidhinn 53
Blair Clan 53, 172, 369, 497
Blair County Genealogical Society 481, 489
Blair County Genealogical Society Newsletter 481
Blair County Historical Society & Library 481
Blair Family 163, 266
Blair Family Magazine 154, 180
Blair House Museum Archives 675
Blair Public Library 349
Blairline and Blairtrees 369
Blaisdell Family 251, 253, 589
Blaisdell Papers 124
Blake Banner 529
Blake Family 570
Blake Library 246
Blakeley State Park Archives 9
Blakey-Blakley-White Family 338
Blakley Family 388
Blalock, Blaylock Clans 469
Blanc Family 17
Blancahard-Santa Paula Public Library District 71
Blanchardville Historical Society 618
Blanchardville Public Library 618
Blanche K Werner Public Library 561
Bland County Historical Society 584
Bland Family 193, 387
Blandford Church Museum Archives 592
Blandford Historical Society & Library 266
Blanding Public Library 278
Blandinsville-Hire Public Library 152
Blankenship Indian Association 1
Blanks-Beale-Ferguson-Clements Family 593
Blanton Family 233
Blanton Quarterly Bulletin 227
Blassingame Family 543
Blattenberger-Plattenberger Family Newsletter 496
Blauvelt Family 380
Blauvelt Free Library 390
Blauvelt News 90
Blazer Family 493
Bleakhouse Museum Archives 667
Bleckley County Historical Society & Archives 128
Bledsoe County Public Library 532
Bledsoe Family 593
Bledsoe's Lick Historical Association 525
Blegen Library 444
Blencowe Families Association Newsletter 73
Bleyhl Community Library 602
Bliss Family 476
Bliss Memorial Public Library 442
Blissfield Area Historical Society 287
Blithewold Mansion Archives 507
Blithewold Mansion Newsletter 507
Blockhouse Museum Archives 685
Blockley Family 601
Blockson Afro-American Collection 497
Blodgett Memorial Library 397
Blois Family 478
Bloom Mansion 90
Bloom Southwest Jewish Archives 21
Bloomfield Academy Museum Archives 390
Bloomfield Carnegie Public Library 180
Bloomfield Historical Museum 367
Bloomfield Public Library 197, 325, 367
Blooming Grove Courier 627
Blooming Grove Historical Society 485
Bloomingdale Free Public Library 367
Bloomingdale Historical Society 152
Bloomington Historical Museum 306
Bloomington Historical Society & Archives 306
Bloomington Historical Society Newsletter 306
Bloomington Public Library 152
Bloomington-Normal Genealogical Society & Library 168
Bloomsburg Public Library 483
Bloss Family 230, 593
Bloss-Pyles-Ross-Sellards-Jackson-Thompson-Lett-Copley-Wilson-Williamson Family 111
Blount County Archives 8
Blount County Genealogical and Historical Society 530
Blount County Historical Museum 8
Blount County Historical Society & Archives 8
Blount County Public Library 530
Blount Journal 530
Blount Library 397
Blount Mansion Archives 528
Blountsville Historical Society 2
Blountsville Public Library 2
Blue and Gray Magazine 446
Blue and Gray Museum Archives 131
Blue ButterFlyer 43
Blue Cloud Abbey Library 522
Blue Earth Community Library 306
Blue Earth County Historical Museum 310
Blue Earth County Historical Society & Archives 310

Blue Earth County Historical Society Newsletter 310
Blue Earth County Library 310
Blue Family 449, 606
Blue Farm News 423
Blue Grass Trust for Historic Preservation & Library 229
Blue Hill Historical Society & Archives 244
Blue Hill Public Library 244
Blue Hills Trailside Museum 275
Blue Island Historical Society & Archives 152
Blue Island Public Library 152
Blue Licks Battlefield Museum Archives 231
Blue Mounds Area Historical Society 618
Blue Mountain Genealogical Society 477
Blue Mountain Heritage 609
Blue Ridge Institute and Museum Archives 587
Blue Ridge Regional Library 590
Blue Ridge Regional Library-Bassett Branch 584
Blue Ridge Township Public Library 165
Blue Springs Historical Museum 325
Blue Springs Historical Society & Archives 325
Blue Water Family Backgrounds 300
Blueberry River Indian Band 647
Bluegrass Historian 230
Bluegrass Railroad Museum Archives 234
Bluegrass Roots 227
Bluemont Historical Railroad Junction 584
Blueprints 106
Bluestem Genealogical Society & Archives 213
Bluestem Root Diggers 213
Bluestone Museum Archives 612
Bluff Hall Antebellum Home 3
Bluffton Historical Preservation Society & Archives 511
Blunden Family 116
Bluster-Blewster Family 27
Blytheville Heritage Museum Archives 25
Blything Family 445
Boal Mansion Museum Newsletter 483
Board and Batten 58
Board for Certification of Genealogists 105
Boatwright Memorial Library 593
Boaz Public Library 2
Bob Bullock Texas State History Museum Archives 536
Bob Burns Museum and River Valley Museum of Van Buren 33
Bobo Family 57
Bobo Roots-Cellar 57
Boca Grande Historical Society 120
Boca Raton Historical Society & Library 109
Boca Raton Public Library 109
Boddie Family 241
Bodega Bay Historical Society 37
Bodensteiner Family 200
Bodie Island Museum Archives 433
Bodie State Historic Park Archives 38
Bodine-Champe Family 636
Bodison Family 18
Bodley-Bullock House Archives 229
Bodman Memorial Library and Museum Archives 411
Boerne Area Historical Society & Library 538
Boerne Public Library 538
Bogan Family 551
Bogardus Family 292, 460
Boggess Family 550, 557
Boggs Family 45, 280
Bohart Family 65
Bohne Family 566
Boise Basin Library District 147
Boise Basque Museum and Cultural Center Archives 145
Boise Bible College Library 145
Boise Public Library 145
Boissevain and Morton Regional Library 659
Bolduc House Archives 340
Boles-Bole-Boal-Boyle Record 9
Bolinas Museum Archives 38
Bolinas Museum News 38
Bolingbrook Historical Society & Library 153
Bolivar County Historical Society 319
Bolivar County Library 319
Bolivar Free Library 390
Bolivar Hall Archives 558
Bolivar-Hardeman County Public Library 525
Bolivar-Harpers Ferry Public Library 612
Boll Weevil Newsletter 32
Bolles Family 97
Bolling Air Force Base Library 105
Bolling Family 557
Bollinger County Historical Society 334
Bollinger County Library 334
Bollinger Mill State Historic Site Archives 326
Bolton Free Library 390
Bolton Hall Museum 75
Bolton Historical Society & Archives 266
Bolton Historical Society Newsletter 266
Bolton Public Library 266
Bonanza Bugle 295
Bonanzaville Museum 440
Bonanzaville Pioneer 440
Bonaparte Indian Band 648
Bonaventure Historical Society 136
Bonavista Museum Archives 667
Bonavista North Regional Museum Archives 669
Bond County Genealogical Society 161
Bond County Genealogical Society News 161
Bond County Historical Society & Library 161
Bond Family 274, 529, 636
Bond Library 177
Bonds Conway House Museum 512
Bonduel Community Archives 618
Bondurant Family Association Newsletter 125
Bone Rattler 424
Boney-Stutts Family 539
Bong Flyer 632
Bonham Family 333
Bonham Public Library 538
Bonita Historical Museum Archives 38
Bonita Spring Historical Society 109
Bonita Springs Genealogical Club 109
Bonita Springs Public Library 109
Bonne Terre Memorial Library 325
Bonner County Genealogical Society 146, 147
Bonner County Historical Museum 149

INDEX

Bonner County Historical Society & Archives 149
Bonnet House Museum Archives 112
Bonnet House Newsletter 112
Bonnett-Bonnette Family 590
Bonneville County Historical Society & Library 147
Bonneyville Mill Museum Archives 180
Bonnie Bell Wardman Library 77
Bonniebrook Historical Society 326
Bonnyville and District Historical Museum 641
Bonnyville and District Historical Society & Archives 641
Bonnyville Municipal Library 641
Boodry Family 605
Booher Library 536
Book Charger 382
Book Ends 180
Book Family 54
Book List 248
Book Mark 272, 450, 578
Book Remarks 208
Book Report 163
Book Shelf 499
Booked Up 334
Bookends 56, 93, 185, 375, 433
Booker Family 26
Booker T Washington National Monument Archives 588
Bookie 477
Bookings 518
Booklets, Brochures & Bookmarks 556
Booklist 248, 620
Bookmark 54, 99, 132, 190, 215, 226, 388, 428, 532, 597
Bookmarks Newsletter 399
Booknotes 547
Books & Beyond 167, 416
Books & Happenings 100
Books 'n More 492
BookSampler 538
Bookshelf 303
BookTalk 300
Bookworm 152, 291, 419, 579
Bookworm Bugle 482
Bookworm Express 159
Bookworm Notes 129
Boone County Genealogical Society 194, 197
Boone County Genealogical Society & Library 613
Boone County Genealogical Society Newsletter 197
Boone County Heritage Museum 28
Boone County Heritage Museum Archives 28
Boone County Historian 28
Boone County Historic Preservation 226
Boone County Historical and Genealogical Society & Archives 28
Boone County Historical Museum 152, 197, 327
Boone County Historical Society 188, 349
Boone County Historical Society & Archives 152, 197, 327
Boone County Historical Society Newsletter 188, 327
Boone County Public Library 28, 227
Boone Family 73, 82, 220, 327, 335
Boone Genealogical Quarterly 613
Boone Society 125
Boone Station State Historic Site Archives 229
Boone's Desert Sky 18
Boone's Lick State Historic Site Archives 325
Boone's Sierra Echoes 73
Boone-Duden Historical Society 336
Boone-Duden Historical Society Newsletter 336
Boone-Madison Public Library 613
Boone-Nance County Genealogical Society 349
Boonesborough Historical Society 514
Booneville Public Library 25
Boonsboro Historical Society 256
Boonsboro Museum of History Archives 257
Boonslick Historical Society of Cooper and Howard Counties 326
Boonslick Historical Society Quarterly 326
Boonslick Regional Library 340
Boonton Historical Museum 367
Boonton Historical Society & Archives 367
Boonton Holmes Public Library 367
Boonville-Warrick County Public Library 180
Boorman House Museum 625
Boose Family 263
Boot Hill Museum Archives 213
Boot Your Roots 18
Booth and Dimock Memorial Library 92
Booth Family 114
Booth Library 154
Boothbary Railway Village Archives 244
Boothbay Harbor Memorial Library 244
Boothbay Regional Historical Society 244
Boothe Family 100
Boothe Memorial Park Museum Archives 100
Bootheel Youth Museum Archives 334
Boothroyd Indian Band 647
Booze Family 466
Borden Genealogical Society 131
Bordentown Historical Society & Archives 368
Bordentown Historical Society & Library 368
Border Historical Society & Library 245
Border Regional Library 661
Border-Fifield Family 134
Borderlands 713
Borders Family 113, 475
Boreham Library 27
Boren Family 147
Borgo Family Histories 64
Borgstedt-Borgstadt-Erdwins-Cairer-Burrow-Clark-Buckmaster Family 328
Borland Family 89
Born Young Newsletter 315
Borror's Corners 192
Borthwick Clan 244
Boscawen Historical Society 360
Boscawen Public Library 359
Boscobel Historical Society 618
Boscobel Restoration House Museum 398
Bosher Family 585
Bosler Free Library 484
Bosque County Collection 553
Bosque Valley Heritage Society 562
Bossier Parish Central Library 236
Bossier Parish Community College Library 236
Bossier Restoration Foundation 236
Boston & Maine Railroad Historical Society 273

Boston Athenaeum 266
Boston Bar Indian Band 647
Boston Fire Museum Archives 266
Boston Historical Society 390
Boston National Historical Park Archives 266
Boston Public Library 266
Bostonian Society & Library 266
Bosun's Pipe 247
Boswell & Grant Township Public Library 180
Botetourt County Historical Society 587
Botetourt County Library 594
Botkins Historical Society & Archives 442
Botna Valley Genealogical Society News 206
Botna Valley Genealogical Society of East Pottawattamie County & Library 206
Botsford Family Historical Association 96
Bottineau County Genealogical Society 437
Bottineau Historical Museum 437
Bottineau Historical Society 437
Bottlecaps 562
Botwood Heritage Centre Archives 667
Boucher Family 446
Boulder Creek Historical Society 38
Boulder Genealogical Society & Archives 81
Boulder Genealogical Society Newsletter 81
Boulder Genealogical Society Quarterly 81
Boulder Historical Museum 81
Boulder Historical Society & Archives 81
Boulder Historical Society Newsletter 81
Boulder Junction Area Historical Society 618
Boulder Junction Public Library 618
Boulder Public Library 81
Bouligny Foundation Newsletter 239
Bound Brook Memorial Library 368
Boundary County Historical Museum 145
Boundary County Historical Society & Archives 145
Boundary County Library 145
Boundary Historical Society 650
Boundary Museum Archives 650
Bouquet (Bucket) Newsletter 262
Bouquet-Buckey Newsletter 262
Bourbon Public Library 180
Bourbonnais Grove Historical Society 153
Bourland Family 329
Bourland-Loving Family 161, 320
Bourne Historical Society 268
Bourne Historical Society & Archives 267
Bouton Family 97
Bovaird Research Cooperative Newsletter 114
Bovey Public Library 306
Bowden Pioneer Museum Archives 641
Bowdoin College Library 244
Bowdoinham Public Library 244
Bowdon Area Historical Society 127
Bowen Family 563
Bowen Family Newsletter 128
Bowen Island Historians 647
Bowen Library 189
Bowen-Woolard-Lilley Family 587
Bower Family Newsletter 327
Bower-Kimmel-Champion Family 327
Bowers Family Historical Review 155
Bowerston Public Library 442
Bowie Public Library 538
Bowie Railroad Station and Huntington Museum Archives 257
Bowlby Family 176
Bowlin Family 203
Bowling Green Public Library 225
Bowman County Genealogical Society 437
Bowman House 634
Bowman-Baumann Family 553
Bowmanville Museum Archives 680
Bowne House Historical Society & Archives 397
Bowne House Museum 397
Bowne Township Historical Society 285
Box Elder County Historic Courthouse Archives 565
Boxford Historical Society 274
Boyd Clan 65, 298
Boyd County Historical Society 353
Boyd County Historical Society & Archives 225
Boyd County Public Library 225
Boyd Family 430, 454, 587
Boyd T and Mollis Gattis Library 31
Boyd: the Dean Road 56
Boyden Library 271
Boyds 59
Boyer Family 445, 506, 568
Boyer Roots 260
Boyertown Area Historical Society 483
Boyertown Museum of Historic Vehicles Archives 483
Boyertown Museum of Historic Vehicles Newsletter 483
Boyle County Genealogical Association 226
Boyle County Public Library-Danville Library 226
Boyle Family 341
Boyle House-Hot Spring County Museum Archives 30
Boylston Historical Society & Library 267
Boylston Town Historian 402
Boyne City Public Library 287
Boynton Beach City Library 109
Boys Town Hall of History Archives 350
Boyt(e)-Boyet(t)(e) Newsletter 60
Bozarth Family 480, 601
Bozeman Public Library 343
Br(e)ashe(a)r(s) Family 554
Brabazon Family 190
Bracchitta-Dilday Family 636
Bracebridge Historical Society 680
Bracken County Historical Society 226
Brackett 203
Brackett Library 32
Brackley-Bateman Family 568
Bradburn Family 20
Braddock's Field Historical Society & Library 483
Bradford Area Public Library 483
Bradford Brinton Memorial Museum Library 635
Bradford Compact Newsletter 257
Bradford County Genealogical Society & Archives 503
Bradford County Historical Museum 503
Bradford County Historical Society & Archives 503
Bradford County Library 503

INDEX

Bradford County Public Library 122
Bradford Family 257
Bradford Family History Newsletter 69
Bradford Heritage Museum 244
Bradford Historical Museum 575
Bradford Historical Society & Archives 244, 575
Bradford Historical Society Newsletter 575
Bradford House 504
Bradford House Museum 60
Bradford Landmark Society 483
Bradford Memorial Library 213
Bradford Ohio Railroad Museum Archives 442
Bradford Public Library 442, 575
Bradford Village 206
Bradford-Shrout Family 154, 458
Bradford-West Gwillimbury Public Library 680
Bradlee Family 449
Bradley County Genealogical Society 33, 526
Bradley County Historical Museum Archives 33
Bradley County Historical Society & Library 526
Bradley County Roots 33
Bradley Family 42, 549
Bradley House Museum 29
Bradley Museum Archives 686
Bradley-Montgomery Family 618
Bradshaw Family 557
Bradt Family 404
Bradt Family News 109
Brady Family 118
Bradys Bend Historical Society 486
Braegger Family 573
Braffett Newsletter 361
Bragg Family 531
Bragg-Mitchell Mansion Archives 6
Brainard-Brainerd-Braynard Family 478
Brainers Memorial Library 94
Braintree Historical Museum 267
Braintree Historical Society & Archives 267
Braintree Historical Society & Library 579
Braintree Historical Society Newsletter 267, 579
Bralorne Pioneer Museum Archives 647
Bramble Bush 33
Brammer Family 601
Brammier-Morris-Lawrence Family 77
Brampton Public Library 680
Branch County Genealogical Society 288
Branch County Genealogical Society Newsletter 288
Branch County Historical Society & Library 288
Branch County Library 288
Brancheau-Branchaud Family 70
Branches 117
Branches and Acorns 562
Branches and Twigs 442, 578
Branches and Twigs Genealogical Society & Library 216
Branches of Berks 491
Branches of Bruce and Grey 687
Branches of Campbell County 636
Branches of Laurel 230
Branches off the Laurel 82
Branching Out 39, 286, 307
Branching Out from Saint Clair County Illinois 165
Branchville Railroad Shrine and Museum Archives 512
Brand Family 53
Brand(t)-Barnes-Walker Family 607
Brandeis University Library 281
Brandel Library 155
Branding Iron 43
Brandon Free Public Library 575
Brandon Historical Museum 473
Brandon Historical Society 473
Brandon Light 473
Brandon Public Library 319
Brandon Township Public Library 299
Brandt County Museum 680
Brandywine Battlefield Park Library 484
Brandywine Historical Society 103
Brandywine Hundred Branch 104
Brandywine River Museum Archives 484
Branford Historical Society & Library 91
Brant Historical Society & Archives 680
Brantford Public Library 680
Brantley Bandwagon 554
Brantley County Historical and Preservation Society 135
Brantly Family 135
Brasher Town Historian 390
Braswell Bookworm 432
Braswell Branches 37
Brattleboro Historical Society & Library 575
Brattleboro Museum Archives 575
Brattleboro Museum Newsletter 575
Bratton, Bretton, Braton, Britton, Brayton, Brotton, Bratten, Brattan, Brattin, Brittin and Brattain Family 131
Braun Research Library 51
Brawley Family 426
Bray Family 351
Brazasport Facts Library 540
Brazeau Historical Society 326
Brazelton Newsletter 441
Brazil Public Library 180
Brazoria County Historical Museum Library 535
Brazoria County Historical Museum Newsletter 535
Brazoria County Library System 535
Brazoria County Library System-Brazoria Branch Genealogical Library 538
Brazos Genealogical Advertiser 539
Brazos Genealogical Association 539
Brazosport Genealogical Society 551
Brea Historical Society 38
Breagh Burnett Gazette 45
Breakey-Brakey-Breakly-DeBrequet Family 388
Brearley House Archives 379
Breathitt County Genealogical and Historical Society 229
Breathitt County Public Library 229
Brec's Magnolia Mound Plantation Archives 235
Brec's Magnolia Mound Plantation Newsletter 235
Breckenridge Public Library 538
Breckinridge County Historical Society & Archives 228
Breckinridge County Public Library 228
Breckler-McCann Family 443
Breeding-Breeden Family 548
Brees Family 442

Brees-Harris-Phillips Family 464
Breillatt Family 167
Breitbach Family 631
Brellsford Newsletter 258
Bremen Libray Times 180
Bremen Public Library 180
Bremer County Browsings 206, 207
Bremer County Genealogical Society 206, 207
Bremer County Genealogical Society Newsletter 206
Bremerton Naval Museum Archives 599
Brennan Library 275
Brennand Family 599
Brenner Library 171
Brent-Centreville Public Library 2
Brentwood Historical Society 339
Brentwood Library 525
Brentwood Public Library 390
Bresaylor Heritage Museum Archives 709
Brethren Historical Library and Archives 159
Brethren Roots 458
Brevard Community College Library 110
Brevard Genealogical Society 110
Brevard Genealogical Society Newsletter 110
Brevard Museum of History and Science Archives 110
Brewer Family 33, 205, 526
Brewer Family 6
Brewer Family Redwood 84
Brewer Historical Society & Archives 244
Brewer Public Library 630
Brewer Researcher 216
Brewster Family 300
Brewster Historical Museum 267
Brewster Historical Society & Archives 267
Brewster Ladies' Library 267
Brewster Public Library 390
Brewster-Sugar Creek Township Historical Society & Library 442
Brewton Public Library 2
Breyfoggel-Boyce-David Houck-Marx Family 604
Brian O'Regan Memorial Library 687
Briar Patch Observer 278
Briarcliff Manor-Scarborough Historical Society 390
Brice's Crossroads Visitor-Interpretive Center Archives 319
Brick House Museum Archives 405
Brick House Museum Newsletter 405
Brick Store Ledger 247
Brick Store Museum Archives 247
Brick Township Historical Society 368
Bricker Family 601
Brickyard School Museum Archives 626
Bridesburg Historical Society 497
Bridge 49, 186, 390
Bridge Builder 408
Bridge River Indian Band 651
Bridge to Sweden 393
Bridgehampton Historical Museum 390
Bridgehampton Historical Society & Archives 390
Bridgehampton Historical Society Newsletter 390
Bridgehead Sentinel 177
Bridgeport Public Library 91, 350, 611
Bridger Public Library 343
Bridges 635
Bridges & Trails 550
Bridgeton Free Public Library 368
Bridgetown and Area Historical Society & Library 673
Bridgeview Public Library 153
Bridgeville Historical Society 103
Bridgeville Public Library 103
Bridgewater Historical Society 91
Bridgewater Library Association-Burnham Library 91
Bridgewater Public Library 267
Bridging the Years 398
Bridgman Public Library 287
Bridgton Historical Museum 244
Bridgton Historical Society & Archives 244
Bridgton Historical Society Newsletter 244
Bridgton Public Library 244
Bridport Historical Society & Library 575
Brielle Public Library 368
Brier Creek Banner 136
Briercrest and District Museum Archives 705
Brigantine Historical Society 368
Briggs Public Library 302
Briggs-Lawrence County Public Library 450
Brigham City Library 565
Brigham City Museum Archives 565
Brigham Young's Winter Home Museum Archives 570
Brighton Area Historical Society 287
Brighton District Library 287
Brighton Genealogical Society 81
Brighton Genealogical Society Newsletter 81
Brighton Memorial Library 413
Brighton-Allston Historical Society 268
Brightwell Beings 259
Brillion Historical Society & Archives 618
Brillion History House 618
Brimfield Historical Society 153
Brimfield Public Library 153, 268
Brimson Grow Library 165
Brimstone Historical Society & Archives 242
Brimstone Museum 242
Brin(c)kerhoff History 187
Brindley International Historical Foundation 1, 2, 38
Briner Library 218
Bringin' Home the Bacon 220
Brinser-Brentzer Family 491
Brinton Family 505
Brisco Family 209
Bristol Cultural and Historical Foundation 483
Bristol Family Association Newsletter 101
Bristol Genealogical Society 585
Bristol Historical and Preservation Society & Archives 507
Bristol Historical Museum 507
Bristol Historical Society 91
Bristol Historical Society & Library 575
Bristol Public Library 91, 585
Bristol-Washington Township Public Library 180
Bristow Genealogical Society 463
Bristow Public Library 463
Britannia Heritage Shipyard Archives 654
British Columbia Aviation Museum Archives 655

British Columbia Farm Machinery and Agricultural Museum Archives 649
British Columbia Folklore Society 648
British Columbia Genealogical Society 655
British Columbia Genealogical Society & Library 654
British Columbia Genealogical Society Newsletter 654
British Columbia Genealogical Society Quarterly 654
British Columbia Genealogist 654
British Columbia Historical Association 656
British Columbia Historical Federation 657
British Columbia Historical Federation, Gulf Islands Branch 650
British Columbia Historical News 657
British Columbia Museum of Mining Archives 647
British Columbia Orchard Industry Museum Archives 651
British Columbia Regiment Museum Archives 656
British Family Historical Society of Los Angeles 75
British Heritage Society 303
British Interest Group of Wisconsin and Illinois 171
British Isles Family History Society of Greater Ottawa 687
British Isles Family History Society of Los Angeles & Library 51
British Isles Family History Society of Los Angeles Newsletter 51
British Isles Genealogical Research Association 65
British Isles Genealogical Research Association Quarterly 65
British, Irish, Scottish and Welsh Journal 51
Brittain-Britton Newsletter 570
Brittingham Family 490
Britts Family 51
Brixey Family 547
Broad River Basin Historical Society 515, 518
Broad River Genealogical Society 515
Broad River Genealogical Society & Library 433
Broad River Genealogical Society Quarterly 515
Broad Top Area Coal Miners Historical Society & Archives 500
Broad Top Historical Museum 500
Broadaway Family 573
Broadhurst Library 332
Broadside 397, 408, 409
Broadview Historical Association & Archives 705
Broadview Historical Museum 705
Broadway Pilot 638
Brobst Family 429
Brock Family 36
Brock Township Public Library System 680
Brocksden County School Museum Archives 690
Brockton Historical Museum 268
Brockton Historical Quarterly 268
Brockton Historical Society & Archives 268
Brockton Public Library 268
Brockville Museum Archives 680
Brockway Area Historical Museum 483
Brockway Area Historical Society & Archives 483
Brockway-Wolston Family Information Exchange 117
Brodhead Family 411
Brodhead Historical Society 618
Brodhead Historical Society & Archives 618
Brodie Clan 548
Brodnax Family 235
Broida Family 339
Broken Arrow Genealogical Society & Library 463
Broken Arrow Historical Society 463
Broken Bow Public Library 350
Broken Mountains Genealogical Society & Archives 343
Broken Mountains Genealogical Society Newsletter 343
Brokenhead Ojibway Cultural Program 661
Brokenspear 134
Broman Lake Indian Band 648
Brome County Historical Museum 698
Brome County Historical Society & Archives 698
Brome County Historical Society Publication 698
Bronte Historical Society 687
Bronx County Historical Society & Archives 390
Bronx County Historical Society Journal 390
Bronx Historian Newsletter 390
Bronxville Public Library 390
BrookBytes 618
Brooke County Genealogical Society 611
Brooke County Public Library 615
Brookfield Free Public Library 575
Brookfield Historical Museum 575
Brookfield Historical Society 153
Brookfield Historical Society & Archives 575
Brookfield Historical Society & Library 91
Brookfield Historical Society Newsletter 91, 575
Brookfield Public Library 326, 618
Brookhaven Free Library 391
Brooking Family 453, 524
Brooking-Brookings Family 444
Brookings Area Genealogical Society & Library 521
Brookings Area Genealogical Society Newsletter 521
Brookings County Historical Museum 524
Brookings County Historical Society & Archives 524
Brookings Public Library 521
Brook-Iroquois Township Carnegie Public Library 180
Brookline Historical Society & Archives 268
Brookline Historical Society Proceedings 268
Brookline New Hampshire Historical Society & Library 359
Brookline Public Library 268
Brooklyn Genealogy Workshop 391
Brooklyn Historical Museum 391
Brooklyn Historical Society 198, 306, 311
Brooklyn Historical Society & Archives 391, 442
Brooklyn Historical Society & Library 91
Brooklyn Historical Society Newsletter 91, 391, 442
Brooklyn Public Library 391
Brooklyn Record 391
Brooklyn Town Library Association 91
Brooks Academy Museum 272
Brooks and District Museum Archives 641
Brooks County Genealogical Society 135
Brooks County Historical Commission & Archives 544
Brooks County Historical Museum 544
Brooks County Historical Society 135
Brooks County Library 544
Brooks County Public Library 135
Brooks Family 111, 560
Brooks Free Library 272
Brooks Historical Society 479
Brooks Memorial Library 575
Brooks-Cowles Family 606
Brookside Columns: Newsletter of the Saratoga County Museum 389
Brookston-Prairie Township Public Library 180

Brooksville Free Public Library 244
Brooksville Free Public Library Newsletter 244
Brooksville Historical Museum 244
Brooksville Historical Society & Archives 244
Brookville Historical Society & Library 443
Brookville Town-Township Library 180
Broome County Historical Museum 389
Broome County Historical Society & Library 389
Broome County History Bulletin 389
Broome County Public Library 389
Broschinsky Family 568
Brotherton Family Tie 607
Brotherton-Hunters Family 607
Brough Family 526
Brough-Malkin-Mielsen-Wilson-Willson Family 43
Broward County Division of Libraries 112
Broward County Division of Libraries-African-American Research Library & Cultural Center 112
Broward County Genealogical Society 112
Broward County Historical Commission & Archives 112
Broward County Historical Museum 112
Broward Legacy 112
Brown County Chapter, OGS & Library 449
Brown County Genealogical Society 190, 215, 227
Brown County Genealogical Society Newsletter 190
Brown County Historical Museum 190, 312
Brown County Historical Society 622
Brown County Historical Society & Archives 190, 312
Brown County Historical Society & Library 215, 349
Brown County Historical Society Newsletter 622
Brown County Library 622
Brown County Library Newsletter 622
Brown County Newsletter 215
Brown County Public Library 449
Brown Deer Historical Society & Archives 618
Brown Deer Historical Society Newsletter 618
Brown Family 13
Brown Family 77, 155, 409, 444, 567, 626
Brown Family Genealogical Society 229
Brown Family Helper 314
Brown Family News 362
Brown Genealogical Society 362
Brown House Museum Archives 136
Brown Mansion Archives 212
Brown Mansion Museum 391
Brown Memorial Library 245
Brown Public Library 578
Brown-Ash Family 488
Brown-Daniel Library 531
Browne-Craven-Frisbie-Whittlesey Family 571
Brownell Library 576
Brownell Research Center Library 337
Brownella Cottage Archives 448
Brownfield Gleanings 75
Brownfield Historical Society 244
Brownington Village 578
Brown-Murray Family 204
Brown-Probst Reunion 452
Browns Valley Historical Society & Library 306
Brownsburg Public Library 180
Brown-Stanton-Evans-Sherman-Neville-Jones-Giles-Spencer-Harrison Family 562
Brownstone Notes 633
Brownstown Public Library 180
Brownsville Community Library 474
Brownsville Historical Association & Library 539
Brownsville Historical Association Newsletter 539
Brownsville Historical Society 483
Brownsville Public Library 539
Browntown Museum Archives 515, 516
Brownvale North Peace Agricultural Museum Archives 641
Brownville Banner 350
Brownville Historical Museum 350
Brownville Historical Society 338
Brownville Historical Society & Archives 350
Brownville Historical Society Bulletin 350
Brownville Town Historian 395
Brownville-Glen Park Library 391
Brown-Warner Family 342
Brownwood Public Library 539
Browse 193
Browsing 158
Brubacher House Museum Archives 692
Brubaker Family 502
Bruce Area Historical Museum and Genealogical Library 618
Bruce Area Historical Society & Archives 618
Bruce County Genealogical Society 688
Bruce County Historical Society 688
Bruce County Historical Society Yearbook 688
Bruce County Museum Archives 690
Bruce County Public Library 688
Bruce Family 125
Bruce Family 274, 525, 585
Bruce Journal 125
Bruce Mines Museum Archives 680
Brucemore Museum Archives 198
Brucemore Museum Quarterly 198
Brucker Family 361
Brueckner Museum of Starr Commonwealth Archives 285
Bruggmeyer Memorial Library 55
Brumage-Brummage Family 55
Brumback Library 459
Bruner-Holmes-Monroe-Lyon-Drew Family 566
Brunner Family 334
Brunner Family 35
Brunner-Debrot Family 181
Brunswick and Glynn County Regional Library 127
Brunswick Area Historical Society 443
Brunswick Community College Library 433
Brunswick County Historical Society 583
Brunswick Historical Society 257, 395, 418
Brunswick Railroad Museum Archives 257
Brunswick Town State Historic Site Archives 435
Brunswick-Glynn County Regional Library-Brantley County 135
Brunswick-Glynn County Regional Library-Charlton County 131
Brunswick-Glynn County Regional Library-Ida Hilton Library 129
Brunswick-Glynn County Regional Library-Long County 133
Brunswick-Glynn County Regional Library-Wayne County 132
Brunwsick County Library 433
Brush and Palette Club 330

Brush Country Genealogical Society 544
Brush Country Museum Archives 541
Bryan & College Station Public Library 539
Bryan Clan 76
Bryan County Heritage Society 464
Bryan Family 4
Bryan Family 603
Bryan Wildenthal Memorial Library 535
Bryan-Bennett Library 173
Bryan-Lang Historical Library 140
Bryant Backtrails 183
Bryant Cottage Historic Home Museum Archives 152
Bryant County Heritage Association & Library 463
Bryant County Heritage Quarterly 463
Bryant Family 220
Bryant Library 414
Brymer Family 476
Bu Gao Ban 407
Buccleuch Mansion Archives 374
Buchan Clan 622
Buchanan Clan 134
Buchanan Clearinghouse Newsletter 179
Buchanan County Genealogical Society & Library 203
Buchanan County Genealogical Society Newsletter 203
Buchanan County Historical Society 588
Buchanan County Public Library 588
Buchanan District Library 287
Buchanan Family 131
Buchanan Genealogical Group 319
Buck Family 476
Buck Hill Archives 483
Buck Hill Associates 412
Buck Hill Associates Newsletter 412
Buck Surname Booklet 54
Buckeye Californian 51
Buckeye Furnace State Memorial Museum Archives 459
Buckeye Historical Society 15
Buckeye Public Library 15
Buckfield Historical Society 251
Buckhorn Saloon and Museum Archives 558
Buckland Heritage Museum Archives 710
Buckley Public Library 469
Bucklin Public Library 212
Buckner Family 271
Buckner Newsletter 459
Bucks County Civil War Library & Museum 486
Bucks County Civil War Roundtable 486
Bucks County Community College Library 495
Bucks County Free Library 486
Bucks County Genealogical Society & Library 486
Bucks County Genealogical Society Newsletter 486
Bucks County Historical Society & Archives 486
Bucksport Historical Museum 244
Bucksport Historical Society & Library 244
Buctouche Micmac Band 663
Bucyrus Historical Museum 443
Bucyrus Historical Society & Archives 443
Bucyrus Public Library 443
Bud Werner Memorial Library 89
Buechel Memorial Lakota Museum Archives 523
Buechele-Kirchner Family 297
Buell Family 606
Buena Park Historical Museum 38
Buena Park Historical Society & Archives 38
Buena Park Historical Society Newsletter 38
Buena Vista County Historical and Genealogical Society & Library 208
Buena Vista County Historical Society 208
Buena Vista Heritage Association & Archives 82
Buena Vista Historical Museum 82
Buena Vista Public Library 82
Buena Vista University Library 208
Buenger Memorial Library 314
Buffalo & Erie County Public Library-Lackawanna 402
Buffalo and Erie County Historical Museum 391
Buffalo and Erie County Historical Society & Archives 391
Buffalo and Erie County Historical Society Newsletter 391
Buffalo and Erie County Military Park Museum Archives 391
Buffalo and Erie County Public Library 391
Buffalo and Western New York Italian Genealogy Society 402
Buffalo Bean Museum Archives 711
Buffalo Bill Cody Homestead Archives 207
Buffalo Bill Historical Center Archives 635
Buffalo Bill Memorial Museum Archives 85
Buffalo Bill Museum of LeClaire Archives 204
Buffalo Bill Ranch State Historic Park Archives 354
Buffalo Chips 353
Buffalo City-Cochrane Area Historical Society 617
Buffalo County Historical Society & Library 353
Buffalo Fire Historical Society 391
Buffalo Gap Historic Village Archives 539
Buffalo Genealogical Society of The African Diaspora 391
Buffalo Genealogical Society of The African Diaspora News 391
Buffalo Historical Museum Archives 521
Buffalo Irish Genealogical Society & Library 391
Buffalo Irish Times 391
Buffalo National River Archives 28
Buffalo River First Nation 706
Buffalo Soldiers National Museum Archives 548
Buffalo Tales 353
Buffalo Trails Museum Library 437
Buffington Family 135
Buffum Family 408, 527
Buford Family 201, 262
Bugeye Times 263
Bugle 456
Bugle Call 500
Bugle Notes 214
Bugler 189
Buhl Public Library 145
Buie Family 545
Bukovina Society of the Americas 213
Bukovina Society of the Americas Newsletters 213
Buley Bulletin 96
Bulgaria National Front 155
Bulgarian Heritage Society 286
Bulkley Valley Museum Archives 655
Bull's Eye Bull-e-tin 167
Bullard Community Library 539
Bullard Family Newsletter 381
Bulletin from Johnny Cake Hill 275

Bulletin of the Albemarle County Historical Society 585
Bulletin of the Association for Gravestone Studies; Markers 271
Bulletin of the Avery Institute of Afro-American History and Culture 512
Bulletin of the Clearfield County Historical Society 485
Bulletin of the Cortland County Historical Society 395
Bulletin of the Delaware County Historical Society 483
Bulletin of the East Durham Historical Society 688
Bulletin of the Fort Ticonderoga Museum 418
Bulletin of the Genealogical Society of South Brevard County 116
Bulletin of the Gloucester County Historical Society 380
Bulletin of the Grayson County Genealogical Society 560
Bulletin of the Hanover-Horton Area Historical Society 293
Bulletin of the Historical Association of Greater Cape Girardeau 326
Bulletin of the Historical Society of Haddonfield 370
Bulletin of the Johnson County Historical Society 342
Bulletin of the Kentucky Historical Society 227
Bulletin of the Medfield Historical Society 274
Bulletin of the Rowe Historical Society 278
Bulletin of the Shawnee County Historical Society 222
Bulletin of the Underhill Society of America 410
Bulletin of the VA-NC Piedmont Genealogical Society 586
Bulletin of the Whatcom Genealogical Society 599
Bullitt County Genealogical Society 233
Bullitt County Public Library 233
Bulloch County Historical Society 137
Bulloch Hall 136
Bullock County Historical Society 10
Bullock Family 497
Bullrush 38
Bulow Plantation Ruins Historic State Park Archives 110
Bumgardner Family 118
Bump Family 282, 579
Bunchgrass Historian 600
Bundlet-May House Museum Archives 364
Bunker Family 379
Bunker Hill Museum 268
Bunker Hill Museum Archives 268
Bunnell Family 478
Bunnell-Bonnell Newsletter 607
Bunnett Family 70
Bunton Family 525
Bunyard-Fitzwater-Haseltine Family 48
Burbank Historical Society 38
Burbank-Burbanck Family 575
Burcham Family 22
Burdick International Ancestry Newsletter 121
Bureau County Genealogical Society 171
Bureau County Genealogical Society & Library 171
Bureau County Genealogical Society Newsletter 171
Bureau County Historical Museum 171
Bureau County Historical Society & Archives 171
Bureau County Historical Society Newsletter 171
Bureau of Historic Preservation & Archives 122
Bureau of Land Management 105
Bureau of the Census - Personal Search Unit 187
Burgess Family 145, 432
Burgoyne Family 565
Burgwin-Wright House 434
Burgwin-Wright Museum Archives 434
Burhans Family 403
Buried Treasures 118
Buried Treasures from Aceto Genealogical Files 121
Burin Heritage House Archives 667
Burkburnett Genealogical Society 539
Burkburnett Library 539
Burke County Genealogical Society 139
Burke County Genealogical Society & Archives 430
Burke County Historical Museum 439
Burke County Historical Museum Archives 437
Burke County Historical Society & Archives 430, 439
Burke County Historical Society Newsletter 439
Burke County Public Library 430
Burke Journal 430
Burket(t)-Burkitt Family 562
Burkett Family 199, 591
Burkhead Family 234
Burkholder Family 285
Burleson County Courthouse 539
Burleson County Historical Museum Archives 539
Burleson Family 3
Burleson Family 542
Burley Public Library 145
Burling Family 279
Burling Library 202
Burlingame Classic Toy Museum 38
Burlingame Classic Toy Museum Newsletter 38
Burlingame Historical Society 38
Burlington County College Library 376
Burlington County Genealogy Club & Library 374
Burlington County Historical Museum 368
Burlington County Historical Society & Archives 368
Burlington County Historical Society Newsletter 368
Burlington County Library 374, 380
Burlington County Library-Bordentown Branch 368
Burlington Genealogical Group 575
Burlington Genealogical Society 618
Burlington Genealogical Society Newsletter 618
Burlington Historical Commission & Archives 268
Burlington Historical Museum 268, 618
Burlington Historical Society & Archives 618
Burlington Library Company 368
Burlington Public Library 91, 198, 600, 618
Burlington Story 368
Burlington-Rock Island Museum Archives 561
Burlison Family 59
Burnaby Historical Society 648
Burnaby Village Museum Archives 648
Burnam Family of Northwest Missouri 329
Burnet County Genealogical Society & Archives 539
Burnet County Heritage Society & Archives 539
Burnett County Historical Society 619
Burnett Family 45, 481
Burnett-Anderson Family 35
Burnette Family 387
Burney Family 216, 340, 558
Burney Gazette 558
Burnham Family 569
Burnham Memorial Library 576
Burnham Tavern Museum Archives 248
Burnham-Earhart Family 499

Burnham-Martin Family 261
Burningham Family 570
Burns Family 423
Burns Lake Indian Band 648
Burnside Bulletin 83
Burnside Family 383
Burnside Plantation Museum Archives 482
Burnt Church First Nation 664
Burnt Hills-Ballston Lake Community Library 392
Burr Family 554
Burrard Indian Band 653
Burrard-Fraser Heritage Society 653
Burrell Family 82
Burrell-Burrill Family 606
Burress-Burrows-Burroughs Family 383
Burrillville Historical and Preservation Society & Library 508
Burritt Museum and Park Archives 5
Burroughs House Museum 477
Burroughs Library 530
Burrowes Mansion Museum 373
Burrup Family 573
Burt County Historical Society 357
Burt County Museum Library 357
Burt County Museum Newsletter 357
Burt Family 383
Burton Bits 'n Business 186, 234
Burton Families Quarterly 77
Burton Family 31, 332
Burton L Goddard Library 279
Burton Payne Library 207
Burton Public Library 443
Burton-Wilfong Family 186
Burwash Landing Historical Society 713
Burwell-Morgan Hill Museum 591
Bus Musings 489
Bush Memorial Library 314
Bush-Carpenter-Butcher-Baldwin Family 608
Bush-Hall-Meek Family 222
Bush-Holley House 92
Bushman Family 571
Bushnell Historical Society 153
Bushong Family 454, 555
Bushore-Bourchard-Trahan Family 353
Bushwhacker Museum 336
Bushwhacker Musings 336
Bushy Family 9
Bushy Run Battlefield Museum Archives 489, 490
Bushyaeger Branches Newsletter 38
Bushyeager Family 483
Business Connection 152
Business Newsletter Quarterly Newsletter 168
Busker Family 569
Buskirk Family 605
Buss-Mintzlaff-Ehlers-Brendemuhl-Brewer Family 627
Busti Historical Society 401
Bustins Island Historical Society & Library 251
Buswell Library 339
Butler Branches 207
Butler County Chapter, OGS & Archives 453
Butler County Genealogical Society 197, 199, 207, 483
Butler County Historian 483
Butler County Historical and Genealogical Quarterly 5
Butler County Historical and Genealogical Society 231
Butler County Historical and Genealogical Society & Library 5
Butler County Historical Museum 197, 213, 449
Butler County Historical Society 5, 351, 483
Butler County Historical Society & Archives 197, 213, 449
Butler County Historical Society & Library 337
Butler County Historical Society Quarterly Newsletter 337
Butler Family 17, 327, 363, 572
Butler House Museum 111
Butler Library 406
Butler Public Library 181
Butler-McDonnell Family 282
Butte and Silver Bow Public Library 343
Butte County Historical Society 58
Butte County Historical Society & Library 58
Butte County Historical Society Slickens 58
Butte County Library 58
Butte County Pioneer Memorial Museum Archives 58
Butte Historical Society 350
Butterfield Happenings 221
Butterfield Museum 71
Butterfield Trail Association and Logan County Historical Society, Newsletter & Archives 221
Butterworth Center Archives 166
Butt-Holdsworth Memorial Library 550
Buttonwoods Museum 272
Buttram Family 2, 5
Buttram Kith and Kin 5
Butts County Genealogical Society 132
Butts County Historical Society 131, 132
Butts Family 292
Buwalda Family 338
Buxton Museum Archives 686
Buzzard-Alt Family 68
By Sea By Land 135, 158
By the Bay Museum Archives 667
By the Wayside 595
Byberry Waltons Bulletin 103
Byelorussian Autocephalic Orthodox Church Archiles 445
Byelorussian-American Association 75
Byerly Family 593
Byers-Byars Family 540
Byers-Evans House Museum Archives 83
Bygone Times 480
Byington Family 572
Byrd Family 126
Byrnes-Quanbeck Library 438
Byron Area Historical Society 127
Byron G Merrill Library 364
Byron Historical Museum Archives 392
Byron Historical Society 306
Byron Historical Society & Library 392
Byron R Lewis Historical Collections Library 195
Byron-Bergen Public Library 389
Bytes & Books 486
Bytown Historical Museum 687
Byzantine Catholic Seminary of Saints Cyril & Methodius Library 499

C

C A Dana-Life Library 350
C E Brehm Memorial Library 167
C E Weldon Public Library 529
C E Weldon Public Library Newsletter 529
C F Lawrence Memorial Library 277
C F Lott Historic Home Museum Archives 58
C Grier Beam Truck Museum Archives 425
C H Moore Homestead Archives 157
C O Card Home and Museum Archives 642
C W Robbins Library 429
Cabarrus County Public Library 425
Cabarrus Genealogy Society 425
Cabbage Campbell Capps 529
Cabbage Head Gazette 109
Cabbage-Cabage Family 533
Cabell County Public Library 612
Cabell-Wayne County Historical Society 612
Cabell-Wayne Historical Society Newsletter 612
Cabin Chat 343
Cabin Chronicle 211
Cabot Historical Museum 576
Cabot Historical Society 26, 577
Cabot Historical Society & Archives 576
Cabot's Old Indian Pueblo Museum Archives 42
Cabri and District Museum Archives 705
Cabrillo Historical Association & Library 65
Cabrini College Library 500
Cactus on a Pine 19
Cade Books & Bytes 235
Cade Family 76
Cades Cove Open-Air Museum Archives 533
Cadillac Area Genealogical Society 287
Cadillac Museum Archives 705
Cadillac-Wexford Public Library 287
Cadott Area Historical Museum 619
Cadott Area Historical Society & Archives 619
Cagle Journal of Historical Inquiry 29
Cahier C'Histoire 701
Cahiers de la Societe Historique Acadienne 664
Cahill Cooperative Newsletter 209
Cahill Family 355
Cahokia Courthouse State Historic Site Archives 153
Cahokia Mounds Historic Site Archives 157
Cail-Cale-Kahl-Kale-Kehl Family 145
Cain Newsletter 558
Cairo Historical Association 153
Cairo Public Library 153, 392
Cairo Roots 350
Cajun Clickers Computer Club 235
Calabasas Historical Society 38
Calabasas Public Library 38
Calaboose African American History Museum Archives 559
Calais Free Library 244
Calaveras County Historical Museum 64
Calaveras County Historical Society & Archives 64
Calaveras County Library 64
Calaveras County Library-Angels Camp Branch 35
Calaveras County Museum & Archives 64
Calaveras Genealogical Society 35
Calcasieu Historical Preservation Society 238
Calcasieu Parish Public Library 238
Caldwell County Genealogical Society & Library 429
Caldwell County Genealogical Society Bulletin 429
Caldwell County Historical Railroad Society 233
Caldwell County Historical Society 233
Caldwell County Historical Society & Library 333
Caldwell County Public Library 429
Caldwell Genealogical Group 145
Caldwell Public Library 145, 368, 443
Caleb Lothrop House 269
Caledonia Historical and Genealogical Society 287
Caledonia Historical Society 619
Caledonia Public Library 306
Caledonia Township Historical Society 285
Caledonian Society of Arizona 20
Calgary and Edmonton Railway Museum Archives 643
Calgary Chinese Cultural Centre Archives 641
Calgary Highlanders Museum Archives 641
Calgary Police Service Interpretive Centre Archives 641
Calgary Public Library 641
Calhoun County Genealogical Society 285, 297, 556
Calhoun County Genealogical Society & Archives 207
Calhoun County Historical And Genealogical Society 322, 612
Calhoun County Historical and Genealogical Society Newsletter 612
Calhoun County Historical Society 1
Calhoun County Historical Society 28
Calhoun County Historical Society & Archives 207
Calhoun County Historical Society & Library 162
Calhoun County Historical Society Newsletter 162
Calhoun County Library 109
Calhoun County Lines and Links 612
Calhoun County Museum 207
Calhoun County Museum Archives 517, 556
Calhoun Family Research Society 1
Calico Ghost Town and Lane House Museum Archives 78
Califon Historical Society 368
Califon Story 368
California African-American Museum Archives 51
California Area Historical Society 484
California Area Public Library 484
California Association of Museums & Archives 69
California Christian College Library 45
California Chronicle 66
California Committee for the Promotion of History 63
California Council for the Promotion of History 42
California County Recorders 35
California County Recorders Source Book 42
California Folklore Society 40
California Genealogical Society 66
California Genealogical Society & Library 57
California Genealogical Society Newsletter 57, 66
California Heritage Council 66
California Heritage Museum Archives 71
California Hispanica 65
California Historian 73
California Historical Courier 66
California Historical Resources Commission, Office of Historic Preservation 63
California Historical Society & Library 66

INDEX

California History 66, 69
California History Action 63
California History Center Archives 42
California Indian 71
California Indian Museum and Cultural Center Archives 71
California Journal 484
California Living Museum Archives 36
California Memorial and Museum Archives 41
California Mennonite Historical Society 45
California Mennonite Historical Society Bulletin 45
California Mission Studies Association 36
California Newspaper Project 62
California Oil Museum Archives 71
California Pioneers of Santa Clara County 67
California Preservation Foundation 57
California Rodeo Heritage Collection Museum Archives 64
California Route 66 Museum Archives 76
California Society of Colonial Pioneers 66
California Star 67
California State Archives 63
California State Capitol Museum Archives 63
California State Genealogical Alliance 35, 42, 49
California State Genealogical Alliance Newsletter 35, 42
California State Genealogical Alliance Society Directory 42
California State Genealogical Alliance Speakers Directory 35, 42
California State History Museum Archives 63
California State Indian Museum Archives 63
California State Library 63
California State Library California History Room 63
California State Library, Sutro Branch 66
California State Military Museum 63
California State Mining and Mineral Museum Archives 53
California State Museum Resource Center Archives 63
California State Railroad Museum Library 63
California State University, Long Beach Library 50
California Supreme Court Historical Society 76
California's Couts Cousins 78
California-Nevada United Methodist Archives 37
Calk Family 341
Calkins Family 85
Calkins World 85
Call to Remember 151
Callahan County Pioneer Museum Archives 537
Callander Bay Heritage Museum Archives 680
Callaway Bulletin 533
Callaway Communique 533
Callaway Family 83, 533
Callaway Journal 126, 533
Call-Booth House Museum Archives 59
Callicott Family in America Newsletter 121
Calling Card 452
Callison-Smith-Hardesty-Nokes Family 570
Calloway County Public Library 232
Calmes Family 170
CAL-MONT News 220
CalState-Fullerton Oral History Program 45
Calumet City Historical Society & Library 153
Calumet County Historical Museum 628
Calumet County Historical Society & Archives 628
Calumet Regional Archives 184
Calvary Episcopal Church Library 327
Calvert Connections 355
Calvert County Genealogy Newsletter 263
Calvert County Genealogy Society 263
Calvert County Historical Society 261
Calvert County Historical Society & Library 261
Calvert County Historical Society News and Notes 261
Calvert County Public Library 261
Calvert Historian 261
Calvert Marine Museum Archives 263
Calvin Collidge Memorial Foundation Archives 578
Calvin Connections Past and Present 542
Calvin Coolidge Library 576
Calvin Coolidge Memorial Foundation 578
Calvin Coolidge Memorial Foundation Newsletter 578
Calvin Coolidge Presidential Library 276
Calvin Coolidge Presidential Museum 276
Calvin Family 542
Calvin-Colvin Family 73
Camanche Public Library 198
Camarena Memorial Library 38
Camas County Historical Society 146
Camas Public Library 600
Cambria County Area Community College Library 490
Cambria County Heritage 486
Cambria County Historical Museum 486
Cambria County Historical Society & Archives 486
Cambria County Library System 490
Cambria Historical Society 39
Cambria-Friesland Historical Society & Archives 619
Cambridge City Public Library 181
Cambridge Community Library 619
Cambridge Historical Commission & Library 268
Cambridge Historical Museum 268, 392
Cambridge Historical Society 153
Cambridge Historical Society & Archives 268, 392
Cambridge Libraries and Galleries 680
Cambridge Military Library 674
Cambridge Museum Archives 350
Cambridge Public Library 268
Cambridge Public Library District 153
Cambridge Springs Heritage Society 484
Camden County Genealogical Association 334
Camden County Historian 334
Camden County Historical Museum 368
Camden County Historical Society 334
Camden County Historical Society & Archives 368
Camden County Historical Society Bulletin 368
Camden County History Journal 368
Camden County Library 379
Camden County Library System 379
Camden Free Public Library 368
Camden Historical Society 244
Camden Museum Archives and DAR Collection 512
Camden Public Library 244, 392
Camden-Carroll Library 231
Camden-Jackson Township Public Library 181
Camden-Ouachita County Public Library 26
Camden-Rockport Historical Society & Library 244
Camden-Rockport Historical Society Newsletter 244

Camel Tracks 37
Cameron Clan 138, 424, 431, 455
Cameron County Historical Society 487
Cameron County Public Library-Barbara Moscato Brown Memorial 487
Cameron Highlanders of Ottawa Regimental Museum Archives 687
Cameron Historical Preservation Society 326
Cameron Historical Society 326
Cameron Parish Historical and Genealogical Society 236
Cameron Parish Library 236
Cameron Public Library 539
Camp 6 Logging Museum Archives 608
Camp Atterbury Museum Archives 182
Camp County Genealogical Society 556
Camp Curtin Historical Society 489
Camp Family 475
Camp Five Museum Archives 624
Camp Floyd-Stagecoach Inn State Park Archives 566
Camp Hancock State Historic Site Archives 437
Camp Roberts History Museum Archives 69
Camp Verde Historical Society 15, 19
Campaign for Buffalo History Architecture and Culture 391
Campbell Area Genealogical and Historical Society 326
Campbell Clan 116, 426
Campbell Clans 529
Campbell Countian 529
Campbell County Historical and Genealogical Society & Library 225
Campbell County Historical Museum 529
Campbell County Historical Society 529, 595, 636
Campbell County Historical Society & Archives 529
Campbell County History News 225
Campbell County Public Library 595, 636
Campbell County Public Library District-Newport Branch 232
Campbell County Public Library Newsletter 595
Campbell County Rockpile Musuem Archives 636
Campbell County Rockpile Musuem Newsletter 636
Campbell Family 83, 300, 339, 362, 417, 569, 601, 623
Campbell Historic Preservation Board 39
Campbell Historical Museum Archives 39
Campbell Historical Museum Newsletter 39
Campbell House Courier 339
Campbell House Museum Archives 339, 691
Campbell Light 611
Campbell River and District Historical Society 648
Campbell River and District Museum and Archives 648
Campbell River Genealogy Club & Library 648
Campbell River Indian Band 648
Campbell River Museum Archives 648
Campbell River Optical Maritime Museum Archives 648
Campbellford-Seymour Heritage Centre Archives 680
Campo de Cahuenga Museum Archives 56
Campobello Historical Museum 248
Campobello Island Museum 665
Campus Martius Museum 452
Camron-Stanford House Archives 57
Camron-Stanford House Newsletter 57
Camrose Public Library 642
Camwood Genealogical Group 608
Canaan Eagle 392
Canaan Historical Museum 392
Canaan Historical Society 396
Canaan Historical Society & Archives 392
Canaan Historical Society & Library 576
Canada Agriculture Museum Archives 687
Canada Aviation Museum Archives 687
Canada's Aviation Hall of Fame 646
Canada's National History Society 662
Canada's Penitentiary Museum Archives 684
Canadian Airborne Forces and CFB Petawawa Military Museum Archives 688
Canadian Airborne Forces Museum Archives 644
Canadian Association of Slavists 643
Canadian Association of Slavists Newsletter 643
Canadian Automotive Museum Archives 687
Canadian Church Historical Society 699
Canadian County Genealogical Society & Library 465
Canadian County Historical Museum Library 465
Canadian Federation of Genealogical and Family History Societies 662
Canadian Forces Communications Museum Archives 684
Canadian Friends Historical Association & Library 691
Canadian Genealogist 679
Canadian Heritage 687
Canadian Heritage Library 683
Canadian Heritage-Parks Canada, Ontario Region Library 681
Canadian Historical Association 687
Canadian Historical Association Historical Booklets 687
Canadian Historical Review 686
Canadian Historical Society Newsletter 687
Canadian Indian Voice Society 653
Canadian Jewish Archives 700
Canadian Jewish Congress 687, 700
Canadian Jewish Congress National Archives 700
Canadian Jewish Historical Society 693
Canadian Jewish Historical Society Journal 693
Canadian Journal of History-Annales Canadiennes d'Histoire 710
Canadian Macedonian Historical Society 682
Canadian Mennonite University Library 662
Canadian Military Engineers Museum Archives 648
Canadian Military Studies Museum Archives 684
Canadian Museum of Civilization Archives 698
Canadian Museum of Flight Archives 651
Canadian Museum of Rail Travel Archives 649
Canadian Quaker History Journal 691
Canadian Quaker History Newsletter 691
Canadian Railroad Historical Association & Archives 701
Canadian Scottish Regiment Museum Archives 657
Canadian University College Library 644
Canadian War Museum Library 687
Canadian Warplane Heritage Museum Archives 686
Canadian-American Genealogical Journal 308
Canadian-American Journal of History 308
Canajoharie Library 392
Canal Boat Primer 418
Canal Currents 486
Canal Fulton Heritage House 443
Canal Fulton Heritage Society & Library 443
Canal House 182
Canal Museum and Hugh Moore Historic Park Archives 486
Canal Society Historical Museum 418
Canal Society of Indiana 183
Canal Society of Indiana Newsletter 183
Canal Society of New Jersey & Archives 373

INDEX

Canal Society of New York State & Archives 418
Canal Winchester Historical Society 443
Canamore Family 289
Canawler 443
Canby Depot Museum 474
Canby Heritage Association 474
Candler County Historical Society 134
Caney Valley Historical Museum 212
Caney Valley Historical Society & Archives 212
Caney Valley Historical Society Quarterly 212
Canfield Exchange 409
Canfield Family Association Quarterly 223
Canfield Historical Society 443
Canim Lake Indian Band 648
Canisteo Historical Society 392
Cannelton Public Library 181
Cannington and Area Historical Society 680
Cannington Centennial Museum Archives 680
Cannington Manor Historic Park Archives 709
Cannon 251
Cannon Beach Historical Society 474
Cannon Falls Area Historical Museum 306
Cannon Falls Area Historical Society & Archives 306
Cannon Falls Library 306
Cannon Family 40
Cannon Free Library 395
Cannon Village Visitor Center Archives 429
Cannonball House Archives 133
Canoe Creek Indian Band 649
Canoe Lake First Nation 705
Canoga-Owensmouth Historical Museum 39
Canoga-Owensmouth Historical Society 39
Canon City Heritage Association 82
Canon City Public Library 82
Canonchet Farm 508
Canonchet Gazette 508
Canosia Historical Society 307
Canso Museum Archives 673
Canterbury Family 49
Canterbury Shaker Village Archives 359
Canterbury Shaker Village Newsletter 359
Canton Classic Car Museum Archives 443
Canton Crossroads 287
Canton Free Library 392
Canton Historical Museum 92, 268
Canton Historical Society & Archives 92, 268
Canton Historical Society & Library 92, 287
Canton Public Library 92, 326
Canton Town and Village Historian 392
Cantor Rubin Kaplan Memorial Library 548
Cantrall-Fraim Family 604
Cantrell Cousins 553
Cantwell Tapestry 161
Cantwell-Conteville Family Association Newsletter 161
Canwood Museum Archives 705
Canyon County Historical Museum 148
Canyon County Historical Society & Archives 148
Canyon Legacy 568
Cap aux Diamants 701
Cape Ann Historical Association & Archives 271
Cape Ann Historical Association Newsletter 271
Cape Ann Historical Family 271
Cape Bonavista Lighthouse Museum Archives 667
Cape Breton Centre for Heritage Archives 676
Cape Breton Genealogical Society 676
Cape Breton Genealogical Society Newsletter 676
Cape Breton Miners' Museum Library 674
Cape Breton Regional Library 676
Cape Cod Genealogical Society 270, 272, 277
Cape Cod Genealogical Society Bulletin 270, 277
Cape Cod Mariner 266
Cape Cod Pilgrim Memorial Association & Archives 277
Cape Coral Historical Museum 110
Cape Coral Historical Society & Archives 110
Cape Fear Community College Library 434
Cape Fear Museum Archives 434
Cape Fear Museum Newsletter 434
Cape Girardeau County Archive Center 331
Cape Girardeau County Genealogical Society & Archives 331
Cape Girardeau County Historical Society 331
Cape Girardeau Public Library 326
Cape Hatteras National Seashore Library 429
Cape Henry Lighthouse Museum Archives 596
Cape May County Crier 368
Cape May County Historical and Genealogical Society 368
Cape May County Historical and Genealogical Society & Library 368
Cape May County Historical Museum 368
Cape May County Magazine of History and Genealogy 368
Cape May County Public Library 368
Cape May Historical and Genealogical Society & Archives 368
Cape Mudge Indian Band 654
Cape River Heritage Museum Archives 326
Cape Sable Historical Society 673
Cape Sable Historical Society & Library 673
Cape Sable Historical Society, Archelaus Smith Branch & Archives 673
Cape Spear National Historic Site 668
Cape Vincent Historical Museum Archives 392
Capell Family 572
Capistrano Indian Council 68
Capital 413
Capital Area Genealogical Society & Library 489
Capital District Genealogical Society & Library 387
Capitol Area District Library 295
Capitol Chronicle 235
Capitol District Genealogical Society Newsletter 387
Capitola Historical Museum Archives 39
Caples House Museum Archives 474
Caplinger Family 457
Capoot Family 527
Cappon and Settlers House Museum Archives 294
Capps Family 529
Capt Charles H Hurley Museum Archives 268
Capt Forbes House Museum Archives 275
Capt Forbes House Museum Quarterly 275
Capt George Flavel House Archives 473
Capt John Wilson House Museum Archives 269
Capt Salem Avery House Museum 262
Captain John Curtis Memorial Library 244
Captain John Curtis Memorial Library Newsletter 244
Captain Nathaniel B Palmer House Museum 99

Caraher Family 614
Carberry Plains Museum Archives 659
Carbon County Historical Society 637
Carbon County Historical Society & Library 346
Carbon County Museum Archives 637
Carbon County Public Library 637
Carbondale Historical Museum 484
Carbondale Historical Society & Archives 484
Carbonear Railway Station Archives 667
Carcross Historical Society 713
Cardston & District Public Library 642
Carey Database 256
Carey-Cary Family 258
Caribbean Historical and Genealogical Journal 47
Cariboo Tribal Council 657
Caribou County Historical Society & Archives 150
Caribou Historical Society 244
Caribou Public Library 244
Carillon Historical Park Archives 447
Carl B Ylvisaker Library 311
Carl Family 489
Carl Johann Memorial Library 326
Carl M Reinert Library 355
Carl S Swisher Library 111, 114
Carl Sandburg College Library 160
Carl Sandburg Home National Historic Site Archives 426
Carl Sandburg State Historic Site Archives 160
Carlen House Museum Archives 6
Carleton A Friday Memorial Library 628
Carleton College-German Studies Association 312
Carleton County Historical Society & Archives 665
Carleton County Historical Society Archives 665
Carlin House-Turner Museum 628
Carlinville Public Library 153
Carlisle Historical Society 268
Carlisle Public Library 198
Carlsbad City Library 39
Carlsbad City Library-Georgina Cole Library 39
Carlsbad Historical Society 39, 382
Carlsbad Historical Society Archives 382
Carlsbad Museum 382
Carlsbad Public Library 382
Carlton County Historical Museum 306
Carlton County Historical Society & Archives 306
Carlton County Historical Society News 306
Carlton-Reed-Scott-Skaggs Family 467
Carlyle House Historic Park Archives 583
Carmacks Historical Society 713
Carman House Museum Archives 683
Carmel Clay Historical Society 181
Carmel Clay Public Library 181
Carmel Heritage 39
Carmel Heritage Society 39
Carmel Mission Basilica Archives 39
Carmel Preservation Foundation 39
Carmel Valley Historical Society 39
Carmichael Clan 134
Carmichael-Stewart House Museum Archives 675
Carminos 35
Carn Family 568
Carnegie Branch Library for Local History Research 81
Carnegie Center for History Archives 190
Carnegie City-County Library 562
Carnegie Clan Society International 193
Carnegie Free Library 482, 485
Carnegie Free Library Newsletter 485
Carnegie Historic Landmarks 190
Carnegie Historic Landmarks Preservation Society 190
Carnegie Historical Museum Archives 201
Carnegie Historical Society 484
Carnegie History and Cultural Arts Center Archives 58
Carnegie History Center 562
Carnegie Library 432
Carnegie Library of Pittsburgh 499
Carnegie Library of Pittsburgh-Squirrel Hill 499
Carnegie Public Library 27, 88, 90, 154. 343. 383, 437, 447, 459, 463, 521
Carnegie Public Library of Clarksdale & Coahoma County 319
Carnegie Regional Library 438
Carnegie Times 193
Carnegie Vincent Library 527
Carnegie-Evans Public Library 197
Carnegie-Stout Public Library 201
Carney Chronicles Newsletter 531
Carney Family 470
Carnifex Ferry Battlefield State Park Museum Archives 615
Carnotes 268
Carnrike Past Times 118
Carnton Plantation Association & Archives 527
Carnton Plantation Museum 527
Caro Area District Library 287
Carol Grotnes Belk Library 423, 426
Carol Stream Historical Society & Archives 153
Carolina Comments 431
Carolina Herald 513, 515
Carolina Trees and Branches 423, 426
Carolinas Aviation Museum Archives 424
Carolinas Genealogical Society & Library 430
Carolinas Genealogical Society Bulletin 430
Carolinas Genealogical Society Yearbook 430
Caroline County Genealogical Society 584
Caroline County Historical Society 261
Caroline County Public Library 258
Caroline Historical Society 584
Carolltonian 263
Carologue: A Bulletin of South Carolina History 512
Carolyn Floyd Library 12
Carondelet Historical Society & Library 339
Carondelet Historical Society Newsletter 339
Carousel 91
Carpathian Connection-Ohio Page 589
Carpatho-Rusyn American 586
Carpatho-Rusyn American Newsletter 586
Carpatho-Rusyn Society 499
Carpenter and Related Family Historical Journal 225
Carpenter Chronicles 355
Carpenter Family Courier 239
Carpenter Home Museum Archives 600
Carpenter Memorial Library 363, 600
Carpenter Memorial Library Newsletter 363
Carpenter Newsletter 82

INDEX

Carper Family 585, 586
Carpinteria Valley Historical Society & Library 39
Carr Family 571
Carr House Museum Archives 657
Carr Milestones 149
Carr Surname Newsletter 18
Carrell Family 601
Carriage and Western Arts Museum Archives 70
Carriage House Museum 392
Carriage House Museum Archives 82
Carrie M McLain Memorial Museum Archives 13
Carrier Family 160
Carrier Library 588
Carrier Mills Public Library 154
Carrier-Chilcotin Tribal Council 657
Carrier-Sekani Tribal Council 654
Carr-Kerr Chronicle 529
Carr-Kerr Family 377
Carroll Cables 292
Carroll Clan 125
Carroll County Chapter, NHSOG 361
Carroll County Chronicles 589
Carroll County District Library 443
Carroll County Farm Museum 264
Carroll County Genealogical Association 326
Carroll County Genealogical Society & Library 443, 198
Carroll County Genealogical Society 128
Carroll County Genealogical Society & Archives 173, 263
Carroll County Genealogical Society Newsletter 173
Carroll County Genealogical Society Quarterly 128
Carroll County Genealogy Club 589
Carroll County Genealogy Newsletter 198
Carroll County Genealogy Society 319
Carroll County Historical and Genealogical Society & Archives 25
Carroll County Historical Museum 182, 263, 589
Carroll County Historical Society 128, 167, 326
Carroll County Historical Society & Archives 182, 443, 530, 589
Carroll County Historical Society News 443
Carroll County Historical Society Newsletter 182
Carroll County Historical Society Quarterly 25
Carroll County History Journal 263
Carroll County Library 528
Carroll County Public Library 226, 263
Carroll Cousins 443
Carroll Family 511
Carroll Public Library 198
Carroll Reece Museum Archives 528
Carroll-Carson-Darnell-Kyle Family 467
Carroll-Jonsson Family 570
Carrollton Public Library 154, 326, 539
Carrolltonian 263
Carrousel Newsletter 409
Carrousel Society of the Niagara Frontier & Archives 409
Carry A Nation Home Archives 218
Carry the Kettle First Nation 710
Carscadden's Museum Archives 709
Carson City Public Library 287
Carson County Historical Survey Committee & Library 555
Carson County Public Library 555
Carter County and Its People 1796-1993 527
Carter County Genealogical Society 463
Carter County Historical and Genealogical Society 228
Carter County Library District 341
Carter Family 120, 345, 468
Carter Family 9
Carter G Woodson Library 155
Carter House Association & Archives 527
Carter House Museum 527
Carter Memorial Library 628
Carter Researcher 58
Carter's Grove Museum Archives 597
Carter-Coile Country Doctors Museum Archives 140
Carteret County Historical Museum 430
Carteret County Historical Society & Archives 430
Carteret County Public Library 423
Carterville Public Library 154
Carthage Free Library 392
Carthage Genealogical Society & Library 326
Carthage Historic Preservation & Archives 327
Carthage Public Library 154
Carthage Public Library 327
Carthage Village Historian 392
Cartmel-Cartmell-Cartmill Family 247
Cartmill Family 615
Caruthersville Public Library 327
Carver African American Historical and Genealogical Society 18
Carver County Historical Museum 316
Carver County Historical Society & Archives 316
Carver County Historical Society Quarterly 316
Carver County Library 306
Carver Crier 573
Carver Memorial Library 251
Carver Public Library 268
Carver-on-the-Minnesota 306
Cary Cottage Archives 444
Cary Grove Historical Society 154
Cary Historical Society 424
Cary Historical Society Newsletter 424
Cary Library 247
Cary Memorial Library 273
Cary-Fox River Grove Historical Society Of Illinois 154
Caryl House and Fisher Barn Museum Archives 270
Casa Adobe de San Rafael Archives 46
Casa Amesti Museum Archives 55
Casa de Rancho Cucamonga Archives 61
Casa del Herrero Foundation 70
Casa del Herrero Foundation Museum 70
Casa Grande Public Library 15
Casa Grande Valley Historical Museum 15
Casa Grande Valley Historical Society & Library 15
Casa Loma Museum Archives 691
Casa Magoffin Companeros 544
Casa Navarro State Historical Park Museum Archives 558
Casady Family 344
Cascade County Historical Society & Library 344
Cascade Locks Historical Society 474
Cascade Public Library 146
Case Family 608
Case Memorial Library 98
Case-Halstead Library 153

Case-Lee Family 378
Caselman Chronicle 502
Casemate Museum Archives 587
Case-Walden Family 146, 610
Casey County Bicentennial Heritage Association 230
Casey County Public Library 230
Casey Farm Museum Archives 509
Casey Jones Home and Railroad Museum Archives 528
Cashiers Historical Society 424
Casper College Library 635
Cass County Connections 536
Cass County Conservancy 536
Cass County Family History Guild 330
Cass County Genealogical Society 188, 197, 330, 536
Cass County Genealogical Society News 197
Cass County Genealogical Society Quarterly 536
Cass County Historical and Genealogical Society 176
Cass County Historical Museum 188, 356
Cass County Historical Society & Archives 188, 316 356, 440
Cass County Historical Society & Library 330
Cass County Historical Society Newsletter 356
Cass County Historical Society Quarterly Newsletter 440
Cass County Illinois Historian Newsletter 176
Cass County Library 287
Cass County Public Library 330
Cass District Library-Edwardsburg Branch 290
Cass District Library-Local History Room 287
Cassell Family 569
Cassia County Historical Museum 145
Cassia County Historical Society & Archives 145
Cassia Diary 145
Cassion Tracks 211
Cassoday Historical Museum Archives 212
Casteel-Linn House and Museum Archives 337
Casteel-Linn House and Museum Newsletter 337
Castillo de San Marcos National Monument Archives 121
Castillo Family Newsletter 48
Castine Historical Society 245
Castine Scientific Society & Archives 245
Castle Air Museum Archives 36
Castle Air Museum Quarterly Newsletter 36
Castle and Key 262
Castle Clinton National Monument Archives 406
Castle Family 262
Castle Genie 376
Castle Hill National Historic Park Archives 668
Castle Lite 376
Castle Museum 301, 452
Castle Piatt Mac-a-Cheek Archives 460
Castle Rock Historical Museum 82
Castle Rock Historical Society & Archives 82
Castle Rock Public Library 600
Castle Tucker Museum Archives 252
Castle View 235
Castlegar and District Public Library 648
Castleton Historical Society & Archives 576
Castleton Public Library 392
Casto House and Northfield Museum Archives 375
Casto-Eakle Family 611
Casto-Golden Family 568
Castor (Gerster) Family 400
Castor and District Museum Archives 642
Castor Canandensis 73
Castor Family 59, 549, 557
Castro Colonies Heritage Association 540
Castroville Public Library 540
Caswell County Historical Association & Library 435
Caswell County Historical Association Newsletter 435
Catahoula Parish Library 237
Catalina Island Museum Society Archives 36
Catalogue of Genealogical and Historical Material 397
Catasauqua Preservation Association 484
Catasauqua Public Library 484
Catawba County Genealogical Society 428
Catawba County Historic Museum Library 430
Catawba County Historical Association & Archives 430
Catawba County Library 431
Catawba County Library Newsletter 431
Catawba Cousins 428
Catawba Valley Scottish Society 428
Catawba-Wateree Genealogical Society & Library 512
Catawba-Wateree Messenger 512
Catawissa Railroad Company Museum Archives 484
Cathedral Cultural Center Archives 355
Cathedral of Saint John the Divine Museum Archives 406
Cathedral of Saint John the Divine Museum Newsletter 406
Catherine B Mitchell Museum 100
Catherine V Yost Museum Archives 171
Cathey Family 515
Catholic Archdiocese of Atlanta 126
Catholic Archdiocese of Boston Archives 266
Catholic Archdiocese of Detroit Archives 289
Catholic Archdiocese of Saint Paul and Minneapolis Archives 314
Catholic Center 391
Catholic Diocese of Austin 536
Catholic Diocese of Boise Archives 145
Catholic Diocese of Fairbanks Archives 12
Catholic Diocese of Honolulu 141
Catholic Diocese of Jackson Archives 320
Catholic Diocese of La Crosse Archives 624
Catholic Diocese of Ogdensburg Archives 409
Catholic Diocese of San Antonio Archives 558
Catholic Diocese of Savannah 137
Catholic Diocese of Spokane Archives 607
Catholic Historical Museum 594
Catholic Historical Society of the Diocese of Amarillo & Library 535
Catholic Historical Society of the Roanoke Valley & Archives 594
Catholic Historical Society of the Roanoke Valley Newsletter 594
Catholic Record Society 446
Catholic Record Society Bulletin 446
Catholic Southwest: A Journal of History and Culture 536
Catlin Family 173
Catlin House Museum 501
Catlow-Whitney Family 151
Cato Family 637
Caton Family 383
Catonsville Branch Library 257
Catonsville Historical Society and Genealogical Section & Archives 257
Catoosa County Historical Society 135
Catoosa County Historical Society Newsletter 135

INDEX

Cattaraugus Area Historical Society & Library 393
Cattaraugus County Historian Museum and Library 403
Cattle Raisers Museum Archives 545
Cattleman 545
Cauble-Rotan Family 553
Cauthorn Memorial Depot and Sutton County Jail Archives 560
Cavalier Block Halifax Citadel Museum Archives 674
Cavalier County Historical Society 438
Cavalry Armor Foundation 227
Cavalry Journal 214
Cave and Basin National Historic Site Archives 641
Cave Creek Historical Museum 15
Cave Creek Historical Society 15
Cave Spring Historical Society 128
Cavelier Family 162
Cavendish Historical Society & Library 576
Cavins-Cavens Newsletter 161
Cawker City Public Library 212
Cayce Historical Museum Archives 512
Caylor Family 209
Cayoose Creek Indian Band 651
Cayuga County Historian Library 388
Cayuga County Historical Society & Archives 388
Cayuga Gazette 388
Cayuga Museum Library 388
Cayuga Museum Newsletter 388
Cayuga-Owasco Lakes Historical Society 388
Cayuga-Owasco Lakes Historical Society & Archives 405
Cayuga-Owasco Lakes Historical Society Newsletter 405
Cazenovia Historic Preservation & Archives 393
Cazenovia Public Library Association 393
CCCM News 443
CCHA Newsletter 591
CDC/Global Health Odyssey 126
Cecil County Historical Museum 258
Cecil County Public Library 258
Cecil H Green Library 73
Cedar Bog Archives 458
Cedar City Public Library 565
Cedar County Genealogical Society 208
Cedar County Historical Museum 341
Cedar County Historical Review 208
Cedar County Historical Society 352
Cedar County Historical Society & Archives 341
Cedar County Historical Society & Library 208
Cedar Creek Grist Mill Archives 610
Cedar Falls Historical Museum 198
Cedar Falls Historical Society & Archives 198
Cedar Falls Historical Society Quarterly 198
Cedar Falls Public Library 198
Cedar Grove Historical Museum 368
Cedar Grove Historical Society & Archives 368
Cedar Grove Historical Society Newsletter 368
Cedar Grove Mansion Inn Archives 323
Cedar Grove Public Library 619
Cedar Key Historical Museum 110
Cedar Key Historical Society & Archives 110
Cedar Key Museum State Park Archives 110
Cedar Lake Historical Association & Archives 181
Cedar Mill Community Library 478
Cedar Park Public Library 540
Cedar Rapids Historical Archives 198
Cedar Rapids Public Library 198
Cedar Springs Historical Society 288
Cedar Springs Museum Archives 288
Cedar Tree Branches 209
Cedar Valley Memories Archives 206
Cedarburg Cultural Center Archives 619
Cedarburg Public Library 619
Cedarville Area Historical Society 154
Cegep de Saint-Hyacinthe, Bibliotheque 701
Cegep de Victoriaville Centre de Documentation 704
Celtic Cultural Center 627
Celtic Heritage 674
Celtic League, American Branch 406
Celtic Society of the Ozarks 340
Cemetery Q's and A's Newsletter 623
Centenary United Methodist Church-Missouri East Archives 339
Centennial Gazette 305
Centennial Library 443
Centennial Museum of Canmore Archives 642
Centennial Museum of the Nanaimo Regional General Hospital 652
Centennial Park 1910 Logging Museum Archives 691
Centennial Valley Historical Association & Archives 635
Centennial Valley Historical Museum 635
Center City Historical Society & Library 306
Center for Agricultural Heritage Archives 186
Center for Agricultural Heritage Quarterly 186
Center For American Archeology Archives 163
Center for American History 536
Center for American History Newsletter 536
Center for Appalachian Studies 423
Center for California Studies 63
Center for Civil War Photography Museum Archives 488
Center for East Texas Studies 554
Center for Historic Preservation 531
Center For History 193
Center for History Archives 177
Center for Holocaust Studies 542
Center for Immigrant Research 497
Center for Jewish History 406
Center for Judaic Studies 84
Center for Living History Preservation Archives 326
Center for Lowell History 273
Center for Medieval and Renaissance History 52
Center for Medieval and Renaissance Studies 51, 389, 446
Center for Mennonite Brethren Studies 215
Center for Mennonite Brethren Studies in Canada 662
Center for Migration Studies of New York 417
Center for Oral History Archives 141
Center for Photography at Woodstock Archives 421
Center for Reformation Research 339
Center for Reformation Research Newsletter 339
Center for Southern Folklore Archives 530
Center for the Advancement of Jewish Education 117
Center for Western Studies 523
Center for Wooden Boats Archives 606
Center Harbor Historical Society 359
Center Moriches Free Public Library 393
Center News 454

Center North Yarmouth Historical Society & Archives 245
Center of Scottish Heritage Archives 428
Center Ring 617
CenterLine 588
Centerpieces 448
Centerville and Center Township Public Library 181
Centerville Community Library 521
Centerville Historical Museum 268
Centerville Historical Society & Archives 268
Centerville-Wash Township Historical Society 447
Centerville-Washington Township Historical Museum 443
Centerville-Washington Township Historical Society & Archives 443
Centinel of the Northwestern Territory 460
Central Alabama Genealogical Society & Library 8
Central Alabama Genealogical Society Newsletter 8
Central Archives of Polonia 299
Central Arkansas Library System 29
Central Brevard Library and Reference Center 110
Central Butte District Museum Archives 705
Central California Jewish Heritage 52
Central City Opera House Association 82
Central City Public Library 350
Central Community Historical Society 200
Central Delta Depot Museum Archives 25
Central Delta Historical Society 25
Central European History 266
Central Falls Free Public Library 507
Central Florida Genealogical and Historical Society 118
Central Florida Railroad Museum Archives 124
Central Georgia Genealogical Society 139
Central Georgia Genealogical Society Newsletter 139
Central Georgia Genealogical Society Quarterly 139
Central Heritage Society 512
Central High School National Historic Site Archives 29
Central Illinois Genealogical Quarterly 158
Central Illinois Landmarks Foundation-Architectural Archives 170
Central Iowa Genealogical Society 205
Central Iowa Pioneer 205
Central Islip Public Library 393
Central Jersey Genealogical Club 371
Central Jersey Genealogical Club News, Notes, Tips and Quips 371
Central Kentucky Researcher 226
Central Lake District Library 288
Central Louisiana Genealogical Society 235
Central Louisiana Genealogical Society Quarterly 235
Central Louisiana Historical Society 235
Central Massachusetts Genealogical Society & Library 282
Central Minnesota Historical Center Library 314
Central Missouri State University Archives and Museum 341
Central Montana Historical Association & Archives 345
Central Montana Historical Museum 345
Central Montana Wagon Trails 345
Central New Brunswick Woodmen's Museum Archives 663
Central New York Genealogical Society 418
Central North Carolina Regional Library 424
Central North Dakota Genealogical Society 438
Central of Georgia Railway Historical Society 531
Central Ohio Fire Museum Archives 446
Central Pennsylvania Genealogical Pioneers 496, 502
Central Presbyterian Church Library 194
Central Rappahannock Heritage Center Archives 587
Central Rappahannock Regional Library 587
Central Sierra Historical Society 72
Central Square Library 393
Central Square Village Historian 393
Central States Scout Museum Archives 217
Central Susquehanna Valley Genealogy Society 496
Central Texas Area Museum Archives 558
Central Texas Genealogical Society & Archives 562
Central Texas Historical and Genealogical Society 557
Central Texas Museum of Automotive History 558
Central Texas Research Center 547
Central Union Church Archives 141
Central United Methodist Church Library 381
Central Virginia Community College Library 590
Central Virginia Genealogical Association 585
Central Virginia Heritage 585
Central Virginia Regional Library 587
Central Washington Agricultural Museum Archives 609
Central Washington Agricultural Museum Newsletter 609
Central West Virginia Genealogical and Historical Library 612
Central Wyoming College Library 637
Centralia Historical Society 327
Centralia Public Library 154, 327
Centre Amikwan 698
Centre Commemoratif de l'Holocauste a Montreal 700
Centre County Genealogical Society 502
Centre County Heritage 502
Centre County Historical Museum 502
Centre County Historical Society & Archives 502
Centre County Library and Historical Museum Archives 482
Centre County Roots 502
Centre Culturel et Patrimonial la Poudriere de Windsor 704
Centre d'Archives du Saguenay-Lac-Saint-Jean 697
Centre d'Etudes Acadiennes 664
Centre d'Exposition sur l'Industrie des Pates et Papiers 703
Centre d'Histoire de Montreal 700
Centre d'Interpretation de l'Ardoise 701
Centre d'Interpretation de l'Historie de Sherbrooke 703
Centre D'Interpretation de la cote de Beaupre Archives 697
Centre d'Interpretation de la Metabetchouane 697
Centre d'Interpretation du Parc de l'Ile-Bonaventure-et-du Rocher-Perce 700
Centre de Recherche Lionel-Groulx 700
Centre de recherches genealogiques du Quebec 700
Centre Franco-Ontarien de Folklore 690
Centre Hill Museum Archives 592
Century House Historical Society 414
Century Schoolhouse Museum Archives 691
Century Village 443
Cereal Prairie Pioneer Museum Archives 642
Ceredo Historical Museum 611
Ceredo Historical Society & Archives 611
Cerritos Public Library 40
Certified Copy 445
Ceylon Area Historical Society 306
CFB Esquimalt Naval and Military Museum 657
CFB Gagetown Military Museum Archives 664
CFPL Highlights 619
CGC Columns 549
Chaba-Hegedus-Szalay-Bressler-Meredith Family 391

INDEX

Chabot College Library 47
Chadbourne Family 249
Chadburn 459
Chadderdon, Chatterton, Chatterson Family 419
Chadds Ford Historical Society 484
Chadds Ford Historical Society Newsletter 484
Chadron Public Library 350
Chaffee Historical Museum 327
Chaffee Historical Society & Archives 327
Chaffee-Stewart Family 73
Chaffey Communities Cultural Center and Museum Archives 76
Chaffin's Early Easton Families 276
Chaffin-Allmon Family 553
Chaffin-Chafin-Chalfin-Chalfant-Chapin Family 557
Chagrin Falls Historical Museum 444
Chagrin Falls Historical Society & Archives 444
Chagrin Falls Historical Society Newsletter 444
Chaille Family 122
Chalet of the Golden Fleece Archives 628
Chaleur Area History Museum Archives 663
Chalmer Davee Library 630
Chalmette Battlefield Library 236
Chamberlain Area Historical Preservation Association 521
Chamberlain Association News 93
Chamberlain Family 569, 608
Chamberlain Index 51
Chamberlain Key 286, 300
Chamberlin-Schabowski Family 185
Chambers County Heritage Society 554
Chambers County Library 535
Chambers Helping Chambers 314
Chambers Library 464
Chamizal National Memorial Archives 544
Champ Clark Honey Shuck Restoration Archives 326
Champagne and Aishihik First Nations 713
Champaign County Chapter, OGS 459
Champaign County Genealogical Society & Archives 176
Champaign County Genealogical Society Newsletter 176
Champaign County Genealogical Society Quarterly 176
Champaign County Historical Archives Historical Publication Series 459
Champaign County Historical Archives Publication Series 176
Champaign County Historical Museum 459
Champaign County Historical Museum Archives 154
Champaign County Historical Museum Newsletter 154
Champaign County Historical Society 176
Champaign County Historical Society & Archives 459
Champaign County Library 459
Champaign Public Library 154
Champaign-Urbana Jewish Genealogy Society 154
Champion City 457
Champion Mill State Historical Park Archives 350
Champion Town Historian 392
Champlain Memorial Library 393
Champlain Society 691
Champlain Town Historian 393
Champlain Trail Museum Archives 688
Champlain Village Historian 393
Champlin Fighter Aircraft Museum Archives 17
Champoeg Gazette 479
Champoeg State Heritage Area Museum Archives 479
Chan Shun Centennial Library 550
Chancellor Robert R Livingston Masonic Library 406
Chandler Collections 146
Chandler Family Association Newsletter 115
Chandler Historical Museum 15
Chandler Historical Society 15
Chandler Public Library 15
Chandler-Cross-Grant-Green-Poe Family 146
Chaney Family 349, 458, 524
Channel-Port-aux-Basques Museum Archives 667
Chanticleer 492
Chanute Genealogy Society & Library 212
Chanute Public Library 212
Chapaign County Genealogical Society Newsletter 459
Chaparral Genealogical Society & Library 561
Chaparral Genealogical Society Newsletter 561
Chapel Hill Historical Society 424
Chapel Hill Museum Archives 676
Chapel Hill Public Library 424
Chapel Museum Archives 664
Chapelle des Indiens 703
Chapin Community Historical Society 154
Chapin Library of Rare Books 282
Chapin Memorial Library 516
Chapleau Centennial Museum Archives 681
Chaplin Public Library 92
Chapman Family 445, 548
Chapman Family Association Newsletter 69
Chapman Historical Museum 398
Chapman Library 212
Chapman Museum Archives 659
Chapmanville Public Library 611
Chappal Family 356
Chappell Hill Historical Museum 540
Chappell Hill Historical Review 540
Chappell Hill Historical Society & Archives 540
Chappell Historical Society 350
Chappell Public Library 350
Chapter Chatter 627
Chapter Notes 459
Chapter One 113
Charboneau Family 299
Charbonneau Family 300
Chardon Library 444
Chariton County Historical Museum 340
Chariton County Historical Society & Archives 340
Chariton County Newsletter 340
Chariton Free Public Library 198
Charles A Amble Library 293
Charles A Grignon Mansion Archives 623
Charles A Lindbergh Historic Site Archives 310
Charles Andrew Rush Library 2
Charles B Aycock Birthplace State Historic Site Archives 427
Charles B Phillips Library 151
Charles City County Historical Society 585
Charles City Public Library 199
Charles City-New Kent Heritage Foundation & Library 593
Charles County Historical Society 260
Charles County Public Library-La Plata Branch 260
Charles Danforth Public Library 575

Charles Dawson History Center 420
Charles Di Peso Library 15
Charles E Shain Library 97
Charles Evans Community Library 12
Charles F Curry Library 334
Charles H Wright Museum of African American History Archives 289
Charles Leaming Tutt Library 82
Charles Pinckney Jones Memorial Library 586
Charles Pinckney National Historic Site Archives 516, 518
Charles Ralph Holland Memorial Library 527
Charles Redd Center for Western Studies 569
Charles River Museum of Industry Archives 281
Charles S Miley Learning Resources Center 113
Charles Towne Landing 1620 & Archives 512
Charles W Bowers Museum Archives 70
Charleston Air Force Base Library 513
Charleston County Genealogical Society & Library 512
Charleston County Public Library 512
Charleston Historical Society & Library 580
Charleston Library Society 512
Charleston Museum Archives 512
Charleston Museum Newsletter 512
Charleston Public Library 26
Charleston Tea Garden Archives 518
Charlestown Historical Society 507
Charlestown Historical Society & Archives 268
Charlestown-Clark County Public Library 181, 193
Charlevoix County Genealogical Society 287
Charlevoix County Historical Society 287
Charlevoix Historical Society & Archives 288
Charlevoix Public Library 288
Charlotte Community Library 288
Charlotte County Genealogical Society 120
Charlotte County Genealogy Society 664
Charlotte County Historical Center 110
Charlotte County Museum Library 665
Charlotte E Hobbs Memorial Library 248
Charlotte Glades Library System 120
Charlotte Glades Library System Newsletter 120
Charlotte Glades Library System-Glades County Branch 117
Charlotte Glades Library System-Port Charlotte 120
Charlotte Glades Library System-Punta Gorda Branch 120
Charlotte Museum of History Archives 424
Charlotte Museum of History Newsletter 424
Charlotte-Genesee Lighthouse Historical Society 413
Charlotte-Mecklenburg Public Library 424
Charlottes: a Journal of the Queen Charlotte Islands 655
Charlton County Historical Society & Library 131
Charlton Historical Society 388
Charlton Historical Society & Library 268
Charlton Park Historic Village and Museum Library 293
Charnley-Persky House Museum Archives 155
Charter 138
Charter Connections 223
Charter-Pierce Memorial Internet Genealogical Society & Library 200
Chase and District Museum Archives 648
Chase County Genealogical Society 352
Chase County Historical Museum 213
Chase County Historical Society 352
Chase County Historical Society & Archives 213
Chase Newsletter: The Descendants of Aquila and Thomas Chase 250
Chase Purinton Family Association Newsletter 577
Chase-Pierce Family 261
Chaska Historical Society 306
Chastain Family 321, 463, 604
Chatard Family Journal 147
Chateau de Mores State Historic Site Archives 439
Chateau Logue Museum Archives 699
Chateau Ramezay 700
Chateauguay Valley Historical Society 698
Chateauguay Valley Historical Society Journal 698
Chatequgay Memorial Library 393
Chatfield College Library 456
Chatfield Historical Society 306
Chatfield Public Library 306
Chatham County Historical Association 431
Chatham County Historical Association Newsletter 431
Chatham Historical Journal 431
Chatham Historical Museum 268
Chatham Historical Society 359
Chatham Historical Society & Archives 268
Chatham Historical Society of East Hampton, Connecticut 93
Chatham Public Library 393
Chatham Railroad Museum Archives 681
Chatham Township Historical Society 457
Chatham Township Historical Society & Library 368
Chatham Village Historical Society 393
Chatham-Kent Black Historical Society 681
Chatham-Kent Museum Archives 681
Chatham-Kent Public Library 681
Chatillon-Demenil Mansion Museum Archives 339
Chatillon-Demenil Mansion Museum Newsletter 339
Chatsworth Historical Society 154
Chatsworth Historical Society & Library 40
Chattahoochee Tracings 4
Chattahoochee Valley Community College Library 8
Chattahoochee Valley Historical Society & Archives 10
Chattahoochee Valley Historical Society & Library 139
Chattan Clan 2
Chattan Clan 42, 54
Chattanooga African-American Heritage Museum Archives 525
Chattanooga Regional History Museum Archives 525
Chattanooga Regional History Museum Newsletter 525
Chattanooga-Hamilton County Bicentennial Library 525
Chattooga County Historical Society 138
Chattooga County Historical Society Newsletter 138
Chattooga County Library 138
Chaudoin Family 76
Chautauqua Association 81
Chautauqua County Genealogical Society 397
Chautauqua County Historical and Genealogical Society 221
Chautauqua County Historical Museum 421
Chautauqua County Historical Society & Archives 421
Chautauqua County History 421
Chautauqua Genealogist 397
Chautauqua-Cattaraugus Library 401
Chautauqua-Cattaraugus Library Newsletter 401
Chaves County Genealogical Society 384
Chaves County Historical Society & Library 384
Chaves County Roots and Branches 384

INDEX

Chavis Family 516
Chavous Family 133
Chawathil Indian Band 650
Chazy Public Library 393
Chazy Town Historian 393
Cheam Indian Band 654
Cheasapeake Bay Maritime Museum Archives 262
Cheatham County Historical and Genealogical Society 525
Cheatham County Public Library 525
Chebeague Island Historical Society 245
Chebeaque Island Library 245
Cheboygan County Genealogical Society & Library 288
Cheboygan Historical Museum 288
Cheboygan Public Library 288
Cheboygan Rivertown Roots 288
Check It Out 103, 151, 170, 195, 343, 563, 589
Check It Out! 169
Check Out 238
Check Us Out 66
Checking Out 164
Cheektowaga Historical Association 393
Cheesman-Cheeseman Family 151
Chehalis Indian Band 647
Chehalis Valley Historian 603
Chehalis Valley Historical Society & Library 603
Chelan County Historical Museum 600
Chelan County Historical Society & Archives 600
Chelan Valley Genealogical Society & Library 600
Chelmsford Historical Society & Library 279
Chelmsford Historical Society Newsletter 279
Chelmsford Public Library 268
Chelsea Area Historical Society 288
Chelsea District Library 288
Chelsea Historical Society 576
Chelsea Public Library 269, 576
Chemainus Indian Band 651
Chemainus Valley Historical Society 648
Chemung County Historical Society & Archives 396
Chemung County Historical Society Newsletter 396
Chemung Historical Journal 396
Chemung Valley History Museum 396
Chemung Valley History Museum Archives 396
Chenango County Historian's Newsletter 409
Chenango County Historical Museum 409
Chenango County Historical Society & Archives 409
Chenault Family 558
Chenault Family National Association Newsletter 558
Cheney Homestead Museum Archives 95
Chenoweth Family 225
Chenoweth-Laprath Family 610
Chequaquet Log 268
Cheraw Lyceum Museum Archives 513
Cherish 8
Cherish: Quarterly Journal of the St. Clair County Historical Society 1
Cherokee Advocate 470
Cherokee City-County Public Library 464
Cherokee County Genealogical and Historical Society 213
Cherokee County Genealogical Society 550
Cherokee County Genealogy Society 9
Cherokee County Genealogy Society Newsletter 9
Cherokee County Historical Museum Archives 430
Cherokee County Historical Society 127, 140, 430
Cherokee County Historical Society & Library 199
Cherokee County Historical Society Newsletter 199
Cherokee County Public Library 514
Cherokee County Tree Stumpers & Library 199
Cherokee Courthouse Archives 465
Cherokee Family Ties 17
Cherokee Heritage and Museum Association & Library 40
Cherokee Historic and Preservation Society 514
Cherokee Historical Society 2
Cherokee Museum Archives 58
Cherokee Nation of Oklahoma 470
Cherokee National Historical Society & Library 470
Cherokee National Museum Archives 468, 471
Cherokee One Feather 425
Cherokee Public Library 199
Cherokee Regional Library System 132
Cherokee Regional Library System-Chickamauga Public 128
Cherokee Regional Library System-Dade County Public Library 138
Cherokee Regional Library System-Rossville Public 136
Cherokee Strip Land Rush Museum Archives 211
Cherokee Strip Museum Archives 463, 469
Cherrington Family 448
Cherry County Genealogical Society 357
Cherry County Historical Museum 357
Cherry County Historical Society & Archives 357
Cherry Hill Historical Museum 387
Cherry Hill Public Library 369
Cherry Street Rag 117
Cherry Valley Memorial Library 393
Cherry Valley Museum Archives 393
Cherry Valley Public District Library 154
Cherryfield-Narraguagus Historical Society & Library 245
Cherryville Historical Society 425
Chesaning Area Historical Museum 288
Chesaning Area Historical Society & Archives 288
Chesaning Genealogical Society 288
Chesaning Public Library 288
Chesaning Public Library Newsletter 288
Chesapeake & Ohio Canal National Historical Park Library 259
Chesapeake and Ohio Historical Society & Library 586
Chesapeake Beach Railway Museum Archives 257
Chesapeake Beach Railway Museum Newsletter 257
Chesapeake Cousins 258
Chesapeake Dispatcher 257
Chesapeake Public Library 585
Chesebro Family 336
Cheshire County Historical Society 362
Cheshire County Historical Society Newsletter 362
Cheshire Historical Society & Archives 92
Cheshire Public Library 92
Cheslatta Carrier Nation 648
Chesnutt-Griffin Family 528
Chestatee Regional Library System-Dawson County Library 130
Chestatee Regional Library System-Lumpkin County Library 129
Chester C Corbin Public Library 281
Chester County Archives and Records Service 505
Chester County Historical Museum 513
Chester County Historical Society & Archives 513

Chester County Historical Society & Library 505
Chester County Historical Society Newsletter 505
Chester County Historical Society Quarterly Newsletter 513
Chester County Library 513
Chester County Library System 487
Chester District Genealogical Society & Library 517
Chester District Genealogical Society Bulletin 517
Chester Fritz Library 438
Chester Genealogy Club 40
Chester Historical Society 92, 269, 393, 576
Chester Historical Society & Library 359 369
Chester Historical Society Newsletter 369
Chester Municipal Heritage Society 673
Chester Public Library 92, 154, 393
Chester Springs Library 484
Chesterfield County Historic Preservation Commission 513
Chesterfield County Historical Museum 585
Chesterfield County Historical Society & Archives 585
Chesterfield County Library 513
Chesterfield County Public Library 586
Chesterfield District Chapter, SCGS & Library 513
Chesterfield District Chronicle 513
Chesterfield Historical Society & Archives 269
Chesterfield Public Library 269, 359
Chesterfield Town Historian 401
Chesterfield Township Historical Society 368
Chester-Lake Almanor Museum Archives 40
Chesterland Historical Foundation 444
Chesterwood Museum Archives 280
Chestico Museum and Historical Society 676
Chestnut Hill Historical Society 497
Chestnut Ridge Historical Society 491, 502
Chestnut Tree 321
Chetco Community Public Library 473
Chetco Valley Historical Society & Archives 473
Chetopa Historical Museum 212
Chetopa Historical Society & Archives 212
Chevy Chase Historical Society 257
Chewelah Public Library 600
Cheyenne County Genealogical Newsletter 356
Cheyenne County Genealogical Society & Library 356
Cheyenne County Historical Association & Archives 356
Cheyenne County Historical Society & Archives 221
Cheyenne County Historical Society Newsletter 221
Cheyenne County Museum 221
Cheyenne Frontier Days Old West Museum Archives 635
Cheyenne Genealogical Society & Archives 635
Cheyenne Genealogical Society Membership Roster and Research Source Directory 635
Cheyenne Genealogy Journal 635
Cheyenne Settlers Heritage Society 623
Chicago & East Illinois Railroad Historical Society 157
Chicago and Northwestern Historical Society 168
Chicago and Northwestern Railroad Historical Society & Library 159
Chicago Genealogical Society & Library 155
Chicago Genealogical Society Newsletter 155
Chicago Genealogist 155
Chicago Heights Free Public Library 156
Chicago Heights Free Public Library Newsletter 156
Chicago Heights Historical Society 156
Chicago Historical Museum 155
Chicago Historical Society & Library 155
Chicago History 155
Chicago Jewish Historical Society & Archives 155
Chicago Jewish History 155
Chicago Public Library 155
Chicago Public Library-Avalon 155
Chicago Public Library-Carter G Woodson Regional 155
Chicago Public Library-Conrad Sulzer Regional 155
Chicago Tribune Archives 155
Chickamauga and Chattanooga National Military Park Library 131
Chickasaw Council House Museum Archives 470
Chickasaw County Genealogical Society & Library 206
Chickasaw County Genealogical Society Quarterly 206
Chickasaw County Historical Society & Archives 206
Chickasaw County Historical Society Newsletter 206
Chickasaw Cultural Center 463
Chickasaw Nation Tribal Government 463
Chickasaw Regional Library System 463
Chickasaw Regional Library System-Atoka County Library 463
Chickasaw Times 463
Chickasaw Times Past 320
Chickasha Public Library 464
Chico Museum Archives 40
Chicopee Public Library 269
Chicora Foundation 513
Chicora Foundation Research 513
Chief Andrew J Blackbird Home Museum Archives 293
Chief John Ross House Museum Archives 136
Chief Plenty Coups State Monument Archives 346
Chief Plenty Coups State Monument Newsletter 346
Chief Wapello Memorial Park Association 197
Chief Wapello's Association Newsletter 197
Chiefs of Ontario 691
Chieftains Museum Archives 136
Chieftains Museum Newsletter 136
Chiefwood Museum Archives 687
Chilao Visitor Center Archives 35
Chilcote-Chilcoat Family 182
Child(e) Family 568
Childers-Childress Family 136, 340
Children of the American Revolution Magazine 106
Children of the Confederacy & Library 593
Children's Newsletter 404
Children's Toy and Doll Museum Archives 452
Childress Genealogical Society 540
Childress Heritage Museum Archives 540
Childress Public Library 540
Childress-Childers Family 549
Chili Public Library 413
Chillicothe and Ross County Public Library 444
Chillicothe Historical Society 156
Chillicothe Public Library District 157
Chilliwack Historical Museum 648
Chilliwack Historical Society & Archives 648
Chilson Chatter 72
Chilton County Historical Society & Archives 3
Chilton County Historical Society Quarterly 3
Chilton Public Library 619
Chimney Chatter 290

Chimney Point State Historic Site Archives 575
Chimney Rock Historical Society 349
China Camp State Park Archives 69
China Historical Society 251
Chinese America: History and Perspectives 66
Chinese American Museum Archives 51
Chinese Cultural Association 51
Chinese Cultural Association Journal 51
Chinese Cultural Center of San Francisco Archives 66
Chinese Historians in the US 398
Chinese Historical & Cultural Project 68
Chinese Historical and Cultural Project 74
Chinese Historical Society of America 66
Chinese Historical Society of America Bulletin 66
Chinese Historical Society of New England 266
Chinese Historical Society of Southern California 51
Chinese House-O.R & N Museum-St Peter's Catholic Church Museums 475
Chinese Museum Archives 44
Chinese Studies in History 388
Chino Valley Historical Society & Library 40
Chino's Old Schoolhouse Museum Archives 40
Chinook 641
Chinook Country Historical Society 641
Chinook Regional Library-Shaunavon Branch 710
Chinqua-Penn Plantation Museum Archives 432
Chipley Historic Center of Pine Mountain 135
Chipman Quarterly 66
Chipola Historical Trust 116
Chipola Junior College Library 116
Chippendale Family 570
Chippewa County (Wisconsin) Newsletter 619
Chippewa County Clippings 311
Chippewa County Genealogical Society 302
Chippewa County Genealogical Society & Library 311, 619
Chippewa County Historical Museum 311
Chippewa County Historical Society 302
Chippewa County Historical Society & Archives 311
Chippewa County Historical Society & Library 619
Chippewa Falls Museum of Industry and Technology Archives 619
Chippewa Falls Public Library 619
Chippewa Museum 624
Chippewa Valley Museum 620
Chippewa Valley Museum Newsletter 620
Chippokes Farm and Forestry Museum Archives 596
Chips From Many Trees and Growing Roots 121
Chiricahua National Monument Library 22
Chisago County Genealogical Group 306
Chisago County Historical Society 310
Chisago Heritage Newsletter 310
Chisholm Clan 362
Chisholm Trail 558
Chisholm Trail Heritage Center Archives 464
Chisholm Trail Historical Museum Archives 471
Chisholm Trail Museum Archives 466
Chisholm Trail Museum Library 223
Chism Family 353
Chispa 73
Chittenango Landing Canal Boat Museum Archives 393
Chittenden Family 577
Chittenden Mills Museum 577
Chivalry 42
Choate Family 274
Choctaw Community News 322
Choctaw County Genealogical Society 2
Choctaw County Genealogical Society 466
Choctaw County Historical Museum 466
Choctaw County Historical Museum 2, 5
Choctaw County Historical Society 2, 466
Choctaw County Historical Society & Archives 5
Choctaw County Public Library 2
Cholochwost-Holochwost Family 255
Chopp-Guibord Family 220
Choteau Society 220
Choteau-Teton Public Library 343
Chou OnLine 141
Chouteau County Free Library 344
Chouteau Memorial Museum Archives 469
Choyce Family 369
Choyce Family Reunion Newsletter 369
CHPS Quarterly Newsletter 445
Chrisman Public Library 157
Chrismon Family 424
Christ Church Community Museum Archives 684
Christ Church Parish Preservation Society 516
Christensen-Bjerg-Berg Family 65
Christian Bulletin 327
Christian C Sanderson Museum Archives 484
Christian County Genealogical Society & Archives 175, 229
Christian County Genealogical Society Newsletter 175
Christian County Genealogical Society Quarterly 175
Christian County Historical Museum 175, 336
Christian County Historical Society & Archives 336
Christian County Historical Society & Library 175
Christian County Library 336
Christian Marks Society 579
Christian Marks Society Newsletter 579
Christian Theological Seminary Library 186
Christiana Historical Society 484
Christianity Today 502
Christiansen Family 21, 565, 572
Christlieb-Chrislip-Crislip Family 542
Christmas Family 117, 476
Christmas History of Louisiana 237
Christopher Gist Historical Society & Archives 229
Chronica 40
Chronicle 22, 101, 158, 285, 288, 418, 503, 507
Chronicle of the Early American Industries Association 279
Chronicler 93, 110, 489
Chronicles 317
Chronicles of Christopher C Randall 22
Chronicles of Oklahoma 464, 468
Chronicles of Saint Mary's 260
Chronicles of Smith County Texas 562
Chronicle-Times 395
Chugiak-Eagle River Historical Society 11
Chugwater Historical Society 635
Chula Vista Genealogy Society 40
Chula Vista Historical Society 40
Chula Vista Public Library 40
Chumash Interpretive Center Archives 74

Chung Family 58
Church Family Chronicles 292
Church of Jesus Christ of Latter-Day Saints Family History Center 381
Church of Jesus Christ of Latter-Day Saints-Philadelphia Stake Family History Center 483
Church of the Nazarene Archives 332
Church Street Historic Foundation 512
Churchill Memorial Memo 329
Church-Waddel-Brumby House Museum Archives 125
Churchyard Family 41
Churubusco Public Library 181
Chute Family Newsletter 460
Cian Clan 63, 73
Cigarroa-Yanez Family 573
Ciletti Memorial Library 501
Cimarron Valley Railroad Museum Archives 464
Cimmaron Historical Society & Archives 382
Cincinnati Fire Museum Archives 444
Cincinnati Historical Society & Archives 444
Cincinnati Historical Society Bulletin 444
Cincinnati History Museum 444
Cincinnati Preservation Association & Library 444
Circa 321
Circle District Historical Museum 11
Circle District Historical Society & Library 11
Circle District Historical Society Newsletter 11
Circuit Rider 174, 227
Circular 186
Circus World Museum Archives 617
Citadel Archives and Museum 512
Cite de l'Energie 703
Citizen 291
Citizen Soldier's Museum Guard Historical Society 63
Citizens Library 504
Citizens' Committee for Historic Preservation 383
Citronelle Historical Preservation Society 3
Citrus County Genealogical Society 114
Citrus County Genealogical Society Newsletter 114
Citrus County Historical Society & Archives 111, 114
Citrus County Library System 109
City Hall Museum 49
City Island Historical Society & Archives 390
City Island Historical Society Newsletter 390
City Museum Archives 339
City of Burlington Historical Museum 368
City of Burlington Historical Society 368
City of Burlington Historical Society Newsletter 368
City of Calgary Archives 641
City of Destiny Newsletter 608
City of Edmonton Archives 643
City of Hazelwood Historic Preservation Commission 330
City of Inglewood Public Library 48
City of Kawartha Lakes Library 684
City of Las Vegas and Rough Riders Memorial Museum Archives 383
City of Longview Historic Preservation Committee 603
City of Mesa Library 17
City of Mobile Archives 6
City of Monte Sereno Historical Committee 55
City of Parkland Historical Society 119
City of Pueblo Municipal Reference Library 89
City of Rancho Cucamonga Historical Program 61
City of Reading Historic Preservation 500
City of Rensselaer Historical Society & Archives 413
City of San Bernardino Historical and Pioneer Society 64
City of San Juan Capistrano Cultural Heritage Commission 68
City of Tacoma Historic Preservation Office 608
City of Toronto Archives 691
City of Winnipeg Libraries 662
City of York Museum Archives 693
City Program Quarterly 509
Civil War and Underground Railroad Museum Archives 497
Civil War and Underground Railroad Museum Newsletter 497
Civil War Descendants Society-Confederate Descendants Society 1
Civil War History 450
Civil War Lady 313
Civil War Library 337
Civil War Life-Soldier's Museum Archives 587
Civil War Magazine 584
Civil War Museum 457
Civil War Museum of Lone Jack Archives 334
Civil War News 580
Civil War Round Table Associates 29
Civil War Round Table Digest 29
Civil War Round Table of Kansas City 217, 221
Civil War Round Table of NY 414
Civil War Round Table of Saint Louis 329
Civil War Round Table of the Ozarks 340
Civil War Round Table of the Trans Mississippi 330
Civil War Round Table Of Western Missouri 333
Civil War Society 75, 584
Civil War Soldiers Museum Archives 119
Civil War Times Illustrated 589
Clach A Choilich 245
Clackamas County Family History Society & Library 477
Clackamas County Historical Society 477
Clackamas County History Notes 477
Clackamas County Library-Oak Lodge 477
Clackamas Legacy 477
Claffey Family 589
Claiborne County Historical Society 533, 589
Claiborne Historical Association 237
Claiborne Parish Library 237
Claiborne Parish Trails 241
Clairton Public Library 484
Clallam County Genealogical Society 604
Clallam County Genealogical Society & Archives 604
Clallam County Genealogical Society Bulletin 604
Clallam County Historical Society & Archives 604
Clallam County Museum 604
Clallam County Museum Library 604
Clamage, Clenowich, Klemitz and Klimist Family Ties Newsletter 70
Clan Akins Journal 6
Clan Annual and Tonnochy 38
Clan Blackstock Society Newsletter 113
Clan Campbell Society (USA) Journal 116
Clan Chisholm Journal 362
Clan Chisholm Newsletter 362
Clan Clamor 346
Clan Colquhoun Newletter 134
Clan Connections 279

INDEX

Clan Coulthart: A Newsletter about the Coulthart Family and their Descendants in North America 169
Clan Digger 604
Clan Diggers Genealogical Society of the Kern River Valley 49
Clan Donnachaidh 38
Clan Forsyth 125
Clan Gleanings Newsletter 49
Clan Gunn Salute 72
Clan Lachlan Magazine 43
Clan Leask Newsletter 78
Clan MacDuff Newsletter 54
Clan MacLellan Quarterly Newsletter 233
Clan MacLeod Society USA 573
Clan MacTavish Association Newsletter 64
Clan MacThomas Society of Scotland, US Branch Newsletter 245
Clan McCubbin Society Newsletter 77
Clan Montgomery Society of North America Newsletter 170
Clan Register 83
Clandigger 642
Clanline: Jardine of Applegirth 54
Clans of Scotland USA 583
Clanton Public Library 3
Clara Barton Birthplace Museum Archives 276
Clara Barton National Historic Site Library 259
Clare Town Historian 414
Claremont Heritage 40
Claremont Historical Society & Library 359
Clarence Dillon Public Library 367
Clarence Historical Museum 393
Clarence Historical Society & Archives 393
Clarendon College Library 540
Clarendon County Archives 516
Clarendon County Historical Society 516
Clarendon Courier 434
Clarendon Hills Public Library 157
Claresholm Museum Archives 642
Claresholm Public Library 642
Clarion 291, 413
Clarion County Historical Society & Archives 484
Clarion Free Library 484
Clarion Historical Society 199
Clark Clan 230
Clark Clarion 225
Clark Connection 554
Clark County Chapter, OGS & Library 457
Clark County Friends of the Library Genealogical Research Group 457
Clark County Genealogical and Historical Society 25
Clark County Genealogical Newsletter 166
Clark County Genealogical Society & Library 166, 609
Clark County Genealogical Society Quarterly Directory 609
Clark County Heritage Center 457
Clark County Historical Association & Archives 25
Clark County Historical Association Journal 25
Clark County Historical Museum 166, 332, 609, 627
Clark County Historical Quarterly 25
Clark County Historical Society 234
Clark County Historical Society & Archives 166, 187, 211, 332, 457, 521, 609, 627
Clark County Historical Society Newsletter 457, 521
Clark County History 609
Clark County Iowa Genealogical Society Newsletter 206
Clark County Kin 457
Clark County Library 25
Clark County Museum Newsletter 166
Clark County Public Library 234, 457
Clark Family 471
Clark Family 81, 518, 550
Clark Historical Society & Archives 369
Clark Hotel Museum Archives 562
Clark Hotel Museum Newsletter 562
Clark House Herald 490
Clark Memorial Library 507, 509
Clark Memorial Library Newsletter 507
Clark Public Library 369
Clark School Museum Archives 618
Clark's Fork Valley Museum Archives 344
Clark-Burr Family 568
Clarke County Historical Association & Archives 584, 591
Clarke County Historical Museum 584
Clarke County Historical Society 5, 6
Clarke County Iowa Genealogical Society 206
Clarke County Proceedings 584
Clarke Family 239
Clarke Historical Library 298
Clarke House Museum Archives 155
Clarke Manse 454
Clarke May Museum Archives 445
Clarke Memorial Museum Archives 44
Clarke Museum Archives 687
Clarke-Oconee Genealogical Society of Athens 125
Clarke-Oconee Genealogical Society of Athens News 125
Clarkesville-Habersham County Library 128
Clark-Jones Family 561
Clark-Merlo-Jimenez-Breen Family 255
Clarks Grove Area Heritage Society 306
Clarksburg-Harrison Public Library 611
Clarkson Historical Museum 350
Clarkson Historical Society & Archives 350
Clarkson University Archives 412
Clarkston Community Historical Society 288
Clarkston Historical Society 288
Clarksville History Committee 181
Clarksville-Montgomery County Historical Museum Archives 526
Clarksville-Montgomery County Public Library 526
Clark-Williams Family 277
Class Family 569
Classen Family 350
Classic Car Museum Archives 420
Classic Cars International Museum Archives 570
Clatskanie Library District 474
Clatsop Community College Library 473
Clatsop County Genealogical Society & Archives 473
Clatsop County Heritage Museum 473
Clatsop County Historical Society & Archives 473
Clatsop County Historical Society Newsletter 473
Claude Crayston Museum Archives 660
Claude R Rickman Library 512
Clausen Memorial Museum Archives 13
Clausings Family 618
Claussville One-Room Schoolhouse Archives 485

Clawson Historical Commission & Archives 288
Clawson Historical Museum 288
Clay County Ancestral News 231
Clay County Archives and Historical Library 334
Clay County Genealogical and Historical Society 31
Clay County Genealogical and Historical Society & Archives 231
Clay County Genealogical and Historical Society Newsletter 31
Clay County Genealogical Society 113, 165
Clay County Genealogical Society & Library 181
Clay County Historic Sites 333
Clay County Historical Museum 212, 311, 328, 334
Clay County Historical Society 1
Clay County Historical Society 113, 180, 350, 548
Clay County Historical Society & Archives 212, 311, 328, 334
Clay County Historical Society Newsletter 311
Clay County Public Library 231
Clay County Researcher 181
Clay Family 442, 567
Clay Roots 165
Clay Township Historical Society 185, 443
Clayson House Museum 169
Clayton College & State University Library 134
Clayton County Genealogical Society & Library 201
Clayton County Library System 132
Clayton Historical Society 40, 327
Clayton House Archives 27
Clayton Library for Genealogical Research 548
Clayton Library Friends 548
Clayton Library Friends Fact Sheet 548
Clayton McLain Memorial Museum Archives 706
Clayton Town & County Library 3
Clayton-Liberty Township Public Library 181
Clayton-Thousand Islands Area Historical Society & Archives 393
Clear Creek History Park Archives 85
Clear Lake Area Historical Museum 619
Clear Lake Area Historical Society & Archives 619
Clearance Card 541
Clearfield County Historical Museum 485
Clearfield County Historical Society & Archives 485
Clearfield County Public Library 485
Clearlake State Park 48
Clearview Public Library 690
Clearwater County Historical Museum 148, 315
Clearwater County Historical Society 315
Clearwater County Historical Society & Archives 148
Clearwater County Historical Society & Library 305
Clearwater County History Museum Archives 315
Clearwater Historical Society 110, 212
Clearwater History News 305, 315
Clearwater Public Library System 110
Clearwater Public Library System-North Greenwood 110
Clearwater River Dene Nation 707
Clearwater United Church Library 110
Cleary News 419
Cleaver Family 558
Cleburne County Historical Quarterly 28
Cleburne County Historical Society 5, 28
Cleburne County Library 28
Cleburne Public Library 540
Clegg's Museum of Horse-Drawn Vehicles 660
Clement C Maxwell Library 267
Clement-Clemant-Clements-Clemmons-Clemens Newsletter 71
Clements Family 157
Clements-Jackson Family 565
Clendening History of Medicine Library and Museum 216
Cleo Redd Fisher Museum Archives 451
Clermont County (OH) Genealogical Society 139
Clermont County Genealogical Society & Archives 441
Clermont County Genealogical Society Newsletter 139, 441
Clermont County Public Library 442
Clermont Historical Society & Archives 199
Clermont State Historic Site Archives 394
Cleveland Area Genealogical Society 540
Cleveland Area Pioneer 540
Cleveland Community College Library 433
Cleveland County Genealogical Society 467
Cleveland County Genealogical Society & Library 467
Cleveland County Historical Association & Archives 433
Cleveland County Historical Association Newsletter 433
Cleveland County Historical Museum 433
Cleveland County Historical Society 32
Cleveland County Historical Society & Archives 26
Cleveland County Historical Society Newsletter 32
Cleveland County Memorial Library 433
Cleveland County, Oklahoma Genealogical Society Newsletter 467
Cleveland Family Chronicle 173
Cleveland Heights-University Heights Public Library 445
Cleveland Historical Center 306
Cleveland Historical Society 382
Cleveland Park Historical Society 105
Cleveland Police Historical Museum 445
Cleveland Police Historical Society 445
Cleveland Public Library 445, 526
Cleveland State Community College Library 526
Cleveland Village Historian 394
Clevenger Newsletter 180
Clever Newsletter 599
Clewiston Historical Society 110
Clewiston Museum Archives 110
Clewly Museum 244
Cliff Dwellings Museum Archives 88
Cliffs of the Neuse State Park Museum Archives 432
Clift Family 63
Clifton Clan 592
Clifton Community Library 395
Clifton Historical Museum 212
Clifton Historical Society & Archives 212
Clifton House Museum 487
Clifton M Miller Library 257
Clifton Public Library 15, 369
Clifton Springs Historical Society 394
Clifton Town Historian 395
Climax Community Museum Archives 705
Climax Historical Society & Archives 288
Cline Library 16
Clinkscale Family 122
Clinton Academy Museum Archives 396
Clinton Chronicle 460
Clinton County Chapter, OGS & Library 460
Clinton County Gateway Genealogical Society 198, 199

Clinton County Gateway Genealogical Society Newsletter 198
Clinton County Genealogical Society 184, 199, 302, 484
Clinton County Historian 411
Clinton County Historical and Genealogical Society 337
Clinton County Historical Association & Archives 411
Clinton County Historical Commission 295
Clinton County Historical Museum 153, 184, 199, 302, 460
Clinton County Historical Notes 184
Clinton County Historical Society 199
Clinton County Historical Society & Archives 153, 184, 302, 460, 493
Clinton County Historical Society Newsletter 199
Clinton County Historical Society Quarterly 153
Clinton County Museum Newsletter 153
Clinton County Public Library 225
Clinton County Trails 302
Clinton Historical Society & Library 269, 394
Clinton Historical Society Newsletter 394
Clinton House Museum 412
Clinton Lake Historical Society & Library 220
Clinton Public Library 181, 199, 526
Clinton Township Public Library 177
Clinton-Essex-Franklin Library System 411
Clinton-Macomb County Library 288
Clintonville Area Historical Society 619
Clintonville Town Historian 394
Clipboard-Friend of the Library 277
Cliveden House Museum Archives 497
Cliveden House Newsletter 497
Cloniger-Kloniger-Gloniger Family 637
Clopton Family 75, 411, 544
Closer Look 183
Closter Free Public Library 369
Cloud Comments 213
Cloud County Genealogical Society & Archives 213
Cloud County Genealogical Society Newsletter 213
Cloud County Historical Museum 213
Cloud County Historical Society & Archives 213
Cloud Family 543
Cloudas Family 355
Clover Historical Society 513
Clover Library District 178
Cloverdale Historical Society 40
Clovis Big Dry Creek Historical Museum Archives 41
Clovis Depot Model Train Museum Archives 382
Clovis-Carter Public Library 382
Cloyne Pioneer Museum Archives 681
Club de Genealogie d'Hydro-Quebec 703
Club de Genealogie de Sainte-Julie 702
Clues 353
Clyde Public Library 540
Coachella Valley Genealogical Society 48
Coachella Valley Historical Museum 48
Coachella Valley Historical Society 48
Coachwork Chronicle 494
Coal County Historical and Genealogical Society 464
Coal County News Letter 464
Coalinga-Huron Library District 41
Coarsegold Historical Museum 41
Coarsegold Historical Society & Archives 41
Coast Line 434
Coastal Bend Genealogical Society & Library 541
Coastal Discovery Museum Archives 515
Coastal Discovery Museum Newsletter 515
Coastal Genealogical Society 433
Coastal Genealogical Society Quarterly 433
Coastal Georgia Genealogical Society 136
Coastal Georgia Historical Society & Library 136
Coastal Heritage Museum 111
Coastal Heritage Society 137
Coastal Heritage Society Update 137
Coastal Plain Regional Library 138
Coastal Scottish Heritage Society 137
Coates Cousins Newsletter 567
Coates Library 558
Coatesville Area Public Library 485
Coatesville Public Library 181
Coatney-Courtney Family 160
Cobalt Historical Society 681
Cobalt's Northern Ontario Mining Museum Archives 681
Cobb County Genealogical Society 134
Cobb County Public Library System 134
Cobb Family 583
Cobb Landmarks and Historical Society & Archives 134
Cobb-Hobby-McMillan-Love-McAlpin Family 607
Cobblestone Museum 398
Coberly Family 84, 470
Coble Family 427, 493
Cobleigh Public Library 577
Cobleskill Public Library 394
Cobourg And District Historical Society & Archives 681
Cobourg Public Library 681
Coburn Free Library 410
Cobweb 158
Cocalico Valley Historical Museum 487
Cochise County Historical and Archaeological Society & Library 15
Cochise County Historical and Archaeological Society Newsletter 15
Cochise Genealogical Society & Library 19
Cochise Quarterly 15
Cochiti Lake Public Library 382
Cochran Family 223
Cochrane Clan 595
Cochrane Railway and Pioneer Museum Archives 681
Cochrane-Nelson House 634
Cochrane-Woods Library 353
Cochran-Lewis Family 53
Cocoa Beach Public Library 110
Coconino County Genealogical Society 22
Cocumscussoc Association 508
Codington County Historical Museum 524
Codington County Historical Society & Archives 524
Codington County Historical Society Newsletter 524
Codman Estate Museum Archives 273
Coe Hall Museum Archives 410
Coenen Family 241
Coen-Evans Family 166
Coeur d'Alene Public Library 146
Coffee County Historical Quarterly 529
Coffee County Historical Society & Library 529
Coffee County Lannom Memorial Public Library 533
Coffey County Footprints 212

Coffey County Genealogical Society & Library 212
Coffey County Historical Museum 212
Coffey County Historical Society & Archives 212
Coffey County Library 212
Coffey County Library-Waverly Branch 223
Coffey Family 331
Coffeyville Public Library 212
Coffin House Museum Archives 275
Coffin School 275
Coffman-Callahan Clan 452
Coggeshall Farm Museum Archives 507
Coggeshall Farmer 507
Cogswell Family 281
Cohasset Historical Society & Library 269
Cohen Family Ties 70
Cohen, Ostroff, Ostrov and Ostrow Family Ties Newsletter 70
Cohen-Bray House Museum Archives 57
Cohoes Public Library 394
Cokato Historical Society & Archives 307
Cokato Museum 307
Cokato Museum Archives 307
Cokato-Finnish American Society 307
Cokesbury Historical and Recreational Commission 515
Col Ashley House Archives 265
Col Timothy Pickering Museum 281
Colborne Lodge Museum Archives 691
Colby College Library 252
Colchester Area Historical Society 157
Colchester Historical Museum 92
Colchester Historical Museum Archives 676
Colchester Historical Society & Archives 92, 676
Cold Lake First Nations 644
Cold Spring Harbor Library 394
Cold Spring Harbor Whaling Museum Library 394
Coldwater Canadiana Heritage Museum Archives 681
Coldwater Indian Band 652
Coldwater Public Library 445
Cole Camp Area Historical Society & Archives 327
Cole County Historical Museum 331
Cole County Historical Society & Archives 331
Cole County Historical Society Newsletter 331
Cole Family 87, 404
Cole Harbour Heritage Farm Museum Archives 673
Cole Harbour Rural Heritage Society 673
Cole Land Transportation Museum Archives 243
Cole Memorial Library 246
Cole-Brion Family 355
Colebrook Historical Society & Library 92
Coleman Family 83
Coleman House 349
Coleman Public Library 540
Coleman-Hadley-Jackson-Smith Family 497
Coleraine Historical Society 445
Coleraine Pageant 445
Coleraine Public Library 307
Coles County Genealogical Society & Library 154
Coles County Historical Museum 154
Coles County Historical Society 166
Coles County Historical Society & Archives 154
Coles County Historical Society Newsletter 154
Colesville & Windsor Museum Archives 399
Coley Family 98
Coley Homstead Museum 101
Colfax Area Historical Society 41
Colfax Historical Society 199
Colfax Public Library 181
Colingwood Museum Archives 681
Collage of Cape County 331
Collections 94, 209
Collections & Connections 225
Collectors Club Museum Archives 406
Collectors Page 341
College De Montreal Bibliotheque 700
College de Sainte Anne de la Pocatiere Bibliotheque 698
College of Eastern Utah Library 569
College of New Caledonia Library 654
College of Saint Gertrude Library 146
College of Southern Idaho Library 150
College of Southern Maryland Library 260
College of the Albemarle Library 426
College of the Mainland Library 561
College Park Aviation Museum Archives 257
College Park Historical Society & Library 128
Colleton County Genealogical Society 518
Colleton County Historical and Preservation Society 518
Colleton County Memorial Library 518
Colleton Museum Archives 518
Colley Family 300
Collier County Genealogical Society 117
Collier County Historical Society & Library 118
Collier County Historical Society Membership Directory 118
Collier County Museum and Archives 118
Collier County Museum Archives 112
Collier County Public Library 118
Collier Library 4
Collier Memorial State Park Logging Museum Archives 474
Collin Chronicles 556
Collin County Farm Museum Archives 553
Collin County Farm Museum Newsletter 553
Collin County Genealogical Society & Library 556
Collin County Genealogical Society Newsletter 556
Collin County Historical Museum 553
Collin County Historical Society & Archives 553
Collin County History 553
Collings Family 168
Collingswood Free Public Library 369
Collingsworth County Museum Archives 563
Collingwood Family 69
Collingwood Library and Museum on Americanism Archives 583
Collingwood Public Library 681
Collins Caller 216
Collins Family 109, 232, 321
Collins Library 211
Collins-Callaway Library 126
Collins-Collings Family 235
Collinsville Depot Museum Archives 464
Collinsville Historical Association 3
Collinsville Memorial Public Library & Historical Museum Archives 157
Collins-Yarnall-Yarnell Family 216
Collis P Huntington Railroad Historical Society 613

Coloma Public Library 288
Colon Historical Society & Archives 288
Colon Museum 288
Colonel Allensworth State Historic Park Archives 43
Colonel Allenworth State Historic Park Archives 35
Colonel Davenport Historical Foundation 172
Colonel William Jones Home Museum Archives 188
Colonial Beach Historical Museum 586
Colonial Beach Historical Society & Archives 586
Colonial Burlington Foundation & Library 368
Colonial Burlington Historical Museum 368
Colonial Charlestown 257
Colonial Courier 106
Colonial Dames in Virginia & Library 593
Colonial Dames of America, Wisconsin Society & Archives 629
Colonial Genealogist 42
Colonial Hall Crier 305
Colonial Industrial Quarter Historic Site Archives 482
Colonial National Historical Park Library 597
Colonial Order of the Acorn & Library 406
Colonial Pemaquid State Historical Site Archives 248
Colonial Pennsylvania Plantation Archives 493
Colonial Society of Massachuesetts 266
Colonial Society of Massachusetts Publications 266
Colonial Spanish Quarter Museum Archives 121
Colonial Williamsburg 597
Colonial Williamsburg Foundation & Library 597
Colony House Museum Archives 508
Colorado Association of Professional Genealogists 81
Colorado Chapter, OGS 87
Colorado Collections 87
Colorado Committee for Women's History 83
Colorado Cornish Cousins 85, 87
Colorado Council of Genealogical Societies 83
Colorado Council of Genealogical Societies Newsletter 83
Colorado Department of Health and Environment Vital Records Division 83
Colorado Division of State Archives and Public Records Library 83
Colorado Genealogical Chronicles 87
Colorado Genealogical Society 87
Colorado Genealogical Society & Library 83
Colorado Genealogical Society Newsletter 83
Colorado Genealogist 83
Colorado Heritage 83, 85
Colorado Heritage Center 83
Colorado Historical Society 86
Colorado Historical Society & Library 83
Colorado History News 88
Colorado History Now 83, 89
Colorado Northwestern Community College Library 89
Colorado Pioneer 82
Colorado Rail Annual 85
Colorado Railroad Historical Foundation 85
Colorado Railroad Museum Archives 85
Colorado River Indian Tribes Museum 18
Colorado River-Blythe Quartzsite Genealogical Society 37
Colorado Ski Museum Archives 90
Colorado Ski Museum Quarterly 90
Colorado Springs Pioneer Museum Archives 82
Colorado Springs Pioneer Museum Newsletter 82
Colorado State Archives 84
Colorado State Library 83
Colquhoun Clan 134, 681
Colquitt County Historical Society 135
Colton Area Museum Archives 41
Colton Area Museum Newsletter 41
Colton Clarion 77
Colton Hall Museum Archives 55
Colton Historical Society 394
Colton Historical Society Newsletter 394
Columbia (Rhinebeck) 413
Columbia Chapter, SCGS & Library 513
Columbia Chronicle 513
Columbia College Library 73
Columbia County Genealogical and Historical Society 601
Columbia County Historical and Genealogical Society & Archives 483
Columbia County Historical and Genealogical Society Newsletter 483
Columbia County Historical Museum 115, 402
Columbia County Historical Society 115, 125
Columbia County Historical Society & Archives 402, 629
Columbia County Historical Society Archives & Archives 479
Columbia County Histories 479
Columbia County Library 30
Columbia County Library-Calhoun County Library 28
Columbia Fire Department Museum Archives 513
Columbia Fire Department Museum Newsletter 513
Columbia Genealogical Society 406
Columbia George Interpretive Center Archives 608
Columbia Gorge Genealogical Society 480
Columbia Gorge-Wasco County Museum Archives 480
Columbia Historic Preservation Society 485
Columbia Historical Society 157, 445
Columbia Lake Indian Band 657
Columbia Public Library 157, 485
Columbia Public Library Newsletter 157
Columbia Public Library Quarterly Newsletter 485
Columbia Repository Newsletter 402
Columbia Resource Centre 647
Columbia River Maritime Museum Archives 473
Columbia State Historic Park Archives 41
Columbia: Magazine of Northwest History 608
Columbian 483
Columbiana County Chapter, OGS & Library 456
Columbiana County Connection 456
Columbiana Library 3
Columbine Genealogical and Historical Society 86, 87
Columbine Genealogical and Historical Society Newsletter 87
Columbus and Lowndes County Historical Society & Archives 319
Columbus Chapel, Boal Mansion Museum Archives 483
Columbus County Public Library 434
Columbus Heritage Association & Archives 128
Columbus Historical Society 446
Columbus Historical Society & Library 382
Columbus Jewish Historical Society & Library 446
Columbus Metropolitan Library 446
Columbus Museum 128
Columbus Museum Archives 128
Columbus Museum Quarterly 128
Columbus Public Library 350, 619
Columbus-Belmont Civil War Museum Archives 226
Columbus-Lowndes Public Library 319

Column Inches 207
Columns 29, 450, 468, 470, 626
Columns Magazine 190
Columns: Wisconsin Then and Now 625
Colusa County Free Library 41
Colusa County Genealogical Society 77
Colusa County Historical Records Commission 41
Colusa County Historical Society 46, 78
Colville Lake Museum Archives 671
Colville Public Library 600
Comal County Genealogical Society & Archives 555
Comanche County Historical Society & Library 212
Comanche Crossing Historical Museum 90
Comanche Crossing Historical Society 90
Comanche Genealogical Society 540
Comanche Public Library 540
Combat Air Museum 222
Comber and District Historical Museum 681
Comber and District Historical Society 681
Comber Pioneer Village Museum Archives 683
Combined Arms Research Library 214
Comer Museum Archives 613
Comer Museum Newsletter 613
Comer-Bowater-Allen-Wagley-Scarlett Family 552
Comfort Public Library 541
Comfrey Area Historical Society 307
Comines Family 379
Comitatus; A Journal of Medieval and Renaissance Studies 51
Comite Lousiane Francaise 239
Commanda General Store Museum Archives 681
Commander's Post 543
Commemorative Air Force 553
Commerce Historical and Genealogical Society 328
Commerce Public Library 541
Commissariat House Museum Archives 668
Commission des Avoyelles & Library 237
Commission for the Preservation of Pioneer Jewish Cemeteries and Landmarks & Archives 37
Commission on Archives and History, Southern Illinois Conference of the United Methodist Church 167
Commission on Archives and History, United Methodist Church 152, 246
Commission on Archives and History, United Methodist Church Library 311
Committee of Carpenters 370
Common Quest 105
Commonwealth Air Training Plan Museum Archives 659
Commonwealth Museum Newsletter 266
Commonwealth of Kentucky Department for Health Vital Statistics Branch 227
Commonwealth of Massachusetts Museum Archives 266
Communal Agriculture Museum Archives 208
Communal Kitchen and Coopershop Museum Archives 205
Communicator 368
Communique 198, 314, 376
Community Calendar 411
Community Connections Newsletter 192
Community Free Library 400
Community Library Association 147
Community Library of Allegheny Valley-Tarentum Branch 503
Community Library on the Square 458
Community Memorial Museum of Sutter County 79
Community Memorial Museum of Sutter County Newsletter 79
Community News 152
Community of Christ Library 330
Community of Christ Museum Archives 330
Community United Methodist Church Library 168
Comox Air Force Museum Archives 651
Comox Indian Band 648
Compact 267
Compass 125, 132, 258, 528
Compass Rose 536
Complete Catalogue of Publications 255
Composite Columns 189
Compress 547
Compton County Historical Museum 697
Compton County Historical Museum Archives 697
Compton County Historical Society & Archives 697
Compton Family 335
Compton-Criqui Family 73
Compton-Frederick Family 117
Computer Assisted Genealogists of Southern Wisconsin 624
Computer Assisted Genealogy Group of the Cleveland Area 456
Computer Genealogy Society of San Diego 65
Computer History Museum Archives 55
Computer Interest Group Newsletter 414
Computer-Assisted Genealogy Group of Northern Illinois 173
ComputerRooters 63
Comstock Comments 311
Comstock Historic House Society & Archives 311
Comstock Township Library 288
Con Foster Museum Archives 303
Conant Library 270
Conant Library Newsletter 270
Conant Public Library 365
Conception Abbey & Seminary Library 328
Conception Bay Museum Archives 667
Concord Free Public Library 269
Concord Genealogical Roundtable 269
Concord Historical Society 41
Concord Historical Society 632
Concord Historical Society & Archives 417
Concord Historical Society & Library 578
Concord Historical Society Newsletter 417
Concord Museum Library 269
Concord Public Library 360
Concord Review 268
Concord Township Historical Society 485
Concordia Area Heritage Society 328
Concordia Historical Institute & Archives 339
Concordia Historical Institute Quarterly 339
Concordia Historical Museum 339
Concordia University Library 478
Conejo Valley Genealogical Society & Library 74
Conejo Valley Historical Society & Archives 56
Conejo Valley Historical Society & Library 74
Conemaugh Township Area Historical Society 491
Conemaugh Township Historical Society 486
Conestoga Area Historical Society 485
Conestoga Newsletter 331
Coney Island Museum Archives 391
Confederacy of Indians of Quebec 701
Confederacy of Treaty 6 First Nations 643

INDEX

Confederate Historical Institute 29
Confederate Historical Institute Dispatch 29
Confederate Historical Institute Journal 29
Confederate Memorial Hall Archives 528
Confederate Memorial Museum Newsletter 463
Confederate Memorial State Historic Site Library 330
Confederate Museum Archives 129, 240
Confederate Veteran 526
Confederated Tribes of Grand Ronde Museum 475
Confederation Centre Public Library 695
Confederation of South Carolina Local Historical Societies 513
Conference House Museum Archives 417
Conference House Museum Newsletter 417
Conference of California Historical Societies & Archives 73
Confluence 172, 383, 617
Confluence News 440
Conger Confab 174
Congregation Beth-El Zedeck 186
Congregation Mishkan Israel Library 94
Congregation Rodeph Shalom Museum Archives 497
Congregational Christian Historical Society & Library 266
Congress News 174
Congress of Illinois Historical and Genealogical Societies 174
Congressional Studies 107
Conneaut Area Historical Society 446
Conneaut Carnegie Library 446
Conneaut Railroad Museum Archives 446
Conneaut Valley Area Historical Society 485
Connecticut Aeronautical Historical Association 101
Connecticut Aeronautical Historical Association Newsletter 101
Connecticut Ancestry 99
Connecticut Ancestry Society & Archives 99
Connecticut Antiquarian 94
Connecticut Conference Archives 94
Connecticut Fire & Trolley Museum Archives 93
Connecticut Firemen's Historical Society 95
Connecticut Historical Commission 94
Connecticut Historical Society & Library 94
Connecticut Historical Society Bulletin 94
Connecticut Historical Society Notes & News 94
Connecticut History 266
Connecticut League of Historical Societies 92
Connecticut League of History Organizations 94
Connecticut Maple Leaf 100
Connecticut Nutmegger 93
Connecticut Professional Genealogists Council 94
Connecticut Professional Genealogists Council Newsletter 94
Connecticut Railroad Historical Association 91
Connecticut River Foundation & Archives 93
Connecticut River Historical Museum 93
Connecticut Society of Genealogists 93
Connecticut Society of Genealogists & Library 93
Connecticut Society of Genealogists Newsletter 93
Connecticut State Library 94
Connecticut Trolley Museum Quarterly 93
Connecticut Valley Historical Museum Archives 279
Connecticut Valley Historical Museum Library 280
Connecticut Valley Historical Museum Quarterly 279
Connecting Rod 234
Connections 277, 300, 507, 701
Connellsville Area Historical Society & Library 485
Connellsville Area Historical Society Newsletter 485
Connelly Chronicle 497
Connelly Library 497
Connelly Library Newsletter 497
Connely Family 258
Conner Prairie Library 183
Conner Prairie Museum Archives 183
Connestoga Area Historical Society 485
Connors Museum Archives 663
Conrad Mansion Archives 345
Conrad Public Library 199, 344
Conrad Weiser Homestead Museum Archives 505
Conrad Weiser Homestead Museum Newsletter 505
Conrad-Caldwell House Museum Archives 230
Conran Memorial Library 330
Conseil Attikamek-Montagnais 699
Conseil de la Nation Algonquine Anishnabeg 699
Conseil de la Nation Atikamekw 698
Conservancy of Montgomery County 481
Conserve 494
Conshokochen Historical Society 485
Constable Hall Association 394
Constable Town Historian 394
Constantia Town Historian 394
Constitution Convention Museum State Park Archives 120
Constitution Island Association & Archives 420
Constitution Island Historical Museum 420
Constitution Square State Historic Site Archives 226
Contact-Acadie 664
Continental Columns 106
Continental Society, Daughters of Indian Wars 21
Contra Costa County Genealogical Society 41
Contra Costa County Genealogical Society Surname Index 41
Contra Costa County Genealogical Society, Using Computers in Genealogy 41
Contra Costa County Historical Society 53
Contra Costa County Historical Society & Library 60
Contra Costa County Historical Society Bulletin 60
Convergence 52
Converse County Genealogical Society 635
Converse County Library 635
Conway County Genealogical Association 30
Conway County Historical Museum Archives 30
Conway County Library 30
Conway Historical Society 360
Conway Public Library 360
Conway Scenic Railroad Museum Archives 363
Conyers-Rockdale Library System 129
Cook County Historical Museum 308
Cook County Historical Society 125, 623
Cook County Historical Society & Archives 308
Cook Family 53, 206, 569
Cook Inlet Historical Society & Archives 11
Cook Memorial Library 164, 364
Cook Rutledge Mansion Archives 619
Cook's Creek Heritage Museum Archives 659
Cook's Crier 110
Cook's Ferry Indian Band 655
Cooke County Heritage Society & Archives 546

Cooke County Historical Museum 546
Cooke County Library 546
Cooke House Archives 457
Cooke Library 141
Cookeville Depot Museum Archives 526
Cook-Reid-Stalling Family Association Newsletter 49
Cooley Communique 203
Cooley Family 203, 559
Coolidge Historical Society 15
Coolspring Power Museum Archives 485
Coombs Family 431, 566
Coon Rapids Historical Society 307
Coonfield Connection 463
Coo-No-Mo-Wauk 628
Cooper Collection 292
Cooper County Historical Society 337
Cooper Landing Community Library 11
Cooper Regional History Museum Archives 76
Coopers of Izard County, Arkansas 25
Coopersville Area Historical Museum 288
Coopersville Area Historical Society 288
Coos Bay Genealogical Forum & Library 477
Coos Bay Public Library 474
Coos County Historical Museum 477
Coos County Historical Society & Archives 477
Coos Genealogical Bulletin 477
Coos Historical Journal 477
Coosa County Historical Society 8
Coosa Heritage 8
Coosa River Valley Historical and Genealogical Society 2
Co-Pal-Am 81, 87
Copeland Family 602
Copeland-Sewell-Morgan-Kendrick-Morphis Family 467
Copiah-Jefferson Regional Library-George W Covington Memorial Library 320
Co-Pilot Communique 553
Coppage Family 255
Coppage-Bilbrough Family 104
Copper Cliff Museum Archives 690
Copper Filings 21
Copper King Mansion Museum Archives 343
Copper Queen Library 15
Copper Range Historical Museum Archives 302
Copper State Bulletin 21
Copper State Journal 21
Copper Valley Historical Society & Archives 11
Copper Village Museum Archives 343
Copperas Cove Public Library 541
Coppertown USA Museum Archives 287
Coppertown USA Today 287
Coppock Family 74
Coquille River Lighthouse Museum 473
Coquitlam Indian Band 653
Coquitlam Public Library 648
Coraopolis Memorial Library 485
Corapolis Memorial Library 485
Corbin Family 230
Corbin Genealogical Society 31
Corbin Genealogy Society & Library 226
Corbin Public Library 226
Corbit-Calloway Memorial Library 104
Corbly Descendants News Letter 191
Cordele-Crisp County Historical Society 129
Cordelia A Greene Library 392
Cordelia B Preston Memorial Library 355
Cordon Family 572
Cordova Discoverer 11
Cordova Historical Museum 11
Cordova Historical Society & Archives 11
Cordova Public Library 11
Corew Family 531
Corinna Historical Society 245
Corinth Interpretive Center Archives 319
Corkery Genealogical Society 268
Corley Family 158
Corley Quarterly 62
Cornelius Family 542
Cornelius Low House 376
Cornell Crier 548
Cornell Museum 111
Cornell Plantations 401
Cornell Plantations Museum Archives 401
Corner Brook City Library 667
Cornerstone 42, 164, 353, 642
Cornerstone Clues 505
Cornerstone Genealogical Society & Library 505
Cornerstone Landmark Newsletter 414
Cornerstones 346
Cornett Family 341
Cornette Library 539
Cornette Library Newsletter 539
Corning Connection 87
Corning Library 26
Corning Public Library 199
Corning-Painted Post Historical Museum 394
Corning-Painted Post Historical Society & Archives 394
Corning-Painted Post Historical Society Newsletter 394
Cornish American Heritage Society 120, 164
Cornish Connection of Michigan 621
Cornish Crier 374
Cornish Heritage Society East 374, 375
Cornish Immigrant 626
Cornish Society Of Greater Milwaukee 618
Cornish Society of Greater Milwaukee 626
Cornish-American Heritage Society 291
Cornsilk from DeKalb County Illinois 175
Cornucopia 120, 172
Cornum Family 89
Cornwall Free Public Library 576
Cornwall Historical Society & Library 92
Cornwall Iron Furnace Museum Archives 485
Cornwall Public Library 394
Cornwall Township Historical Society 685
Corona Public Library 41
Coronach District Museum Archives 705
Coronado Heritage 555
Coronado Historical Association 41
Coronado Historical Association & Archives 41
Coronado Historical Museum 41
Coronado Public Library 41
Coronado-Quivira Museum 218

INDEX

Corporation of the County of Prince Edward Island Library 685
Corps of Engineers, Rock Island District Technical Library 172
Corpus Christi Museum of Science and History Archives 541
Corpus Christi Public Library 541
Corral Dust 539
Corrales Community Library 382
Corrales Historical Society 382
Corriher-Linn-Black Library 432
Corry Area Historical Museum 485
Corry Area Historical Society & Archives 485
Corry Public Library 485
Corsicana Public Library 541
Corson Family 606
Corson-Colson Family History 593
Corte Madera Public Library 41
Cortez Center Archives 82
Cortez Public Library 82
Cortland County Historical Society & Archives 395
Cortland Free Library 395
Cortland Free Library News 395
Corunna Public Library 289
Corvallis-Benton County Public Library 474
Cory Family 600
Corydon Capitol Historic Site Archives 182
Coryell County Genealogical Society & Archives 546
Coryell County Genealogical Society Quarterly 546
Coryell Kin 546
Coshocton County Chapter, OGS & Library 446
Coshocton Public Library 446
Cossit House Museum Archives 676
Cossitt Family 200
Cossitt-Goodwyn Library 530
Costa Mesa Historical Society & Library 41
Costales Family 82
Costilla County Library 89
Costume Museum of Canada Archives 659
Cosumnes River College Library 63
Cote First Nation 707
Coteau Heritage 313
Cottage Grove Area Historical Society 619
Cottage Grove Genealogical Society & Library 474
Cottage Grove Museum Archives 474
Cottage Grove Public Library 474
Cottage Lawn Historic House Museum 409
Cottle County Genealogical Society 555
Cottonlandia Communique 320
Cottonlandia Foundation 320
Cottonlandia Foundation Museum 320
Cottonwood Area Historical Society 307
Cottonwood County Historical Museum 317
Cottonwood County Historical Society & Archives 317
Cottonwood County Historical Society Newsletter 317
Cottonwood Public Library 15
Cottonwood-Jackson Genealogy Group 309
Couch Genealogist 548
Couchiching Association for Native Services 687
Couey Family 479
Coulter Family 334
Coulterville Public Library 157
Coulthart Family History Center 169
Council Bluffs Free Public Library 199
Council for Yukon Indians 713
Council News Coordinator 63
Council of Historic Institutions and Preservation Societies in Summit and Portage Counties 450
Council of Northeastern Illinois Genealogical Societies 165, 166
Council of Scottish Clans and Associations 424
Council of the Haida Nation 652
Council on America's Military Past 587
Council on America's Military Past Periodical 587
Country Doctor Museum Library 423
Country Relics Little Village Archives 208
Countryman-Wood Family Association 100
County Center Historical Museum 316
County Center Historical Society & Archives 316
County Line 119, 548
County Lines 351
County Mayo Chronicles 291
County of Henrico Public Library 593
County of Los Angeles Public Library-Central Regional Office 55
County of Los Angeles Public Library-Downey Branch 42
County Seat Genealogy Society 182
County Seat Scraps 182
Courier 8, 36, 95, 212, 375, 531, 593, 612
Courier Newsletter 230
Courier of the East Benton County Historical Society 602
Courson-Finten Family 77
Court Reporter 633
Court Reporter 70
Court Street Shuttle Newsletter 391
Courtenay and District Museum Archives 648
Courthouse Museum 492, 538
Courthouse Square Museum Archives 288
Courtney Chronicles 170
Cousins 470
Cousins et Cousines 308
Couts Family 78
Covenant Church Historical Archives 155
Coventry Family 17
Coventry Historical Society 507
Coventry Historical Society & Library 92
Coventry Public Library 507
Coventry Public Library Newsletter 507
Cover Family 476
Cover to Cover Newsletter 221
Covert Activities Newsletter 122
Covert Family 16, 122, 259
Covey Cousins 18
Covina Valley Historical Society 41
Covina Valley Historical Society & Archives 41
Covington County Historical Society 1
Cow Neck Peninsula Historical Journal 412
Cow Neck Peninsula Historical Society & Archives 412
Coward Family Newsletter 2
Cowboys & Indians 542
Cowdery Family 568
Cowessess First Nation 705
Coweta Chapter Genealogical and Historical Society 137
Coweta County Genealogical Society 135
Coweta County Genealogical Society Magazine 135

Cowgill Family 355, 443
Cowichan Bay Maritime Centre 649
Cowichan Historical Society 649
Cowichan Indian Band 649
Cowichan Lake First Nations 651
Cowichan Valley Museum Archives 649
Cowles Library 200
Cowley County Genealogical Society 211, 223
Cowley County Historical Museum 223
Cowley County Historical Society & Archives 223
Cowley County Historical Society Newsletter 223
Cowley Family 573
Cowlitz County Historical Museum 602
Cowlitz County Historical Society & Archives 602
Cowlitz Historical Quarterly 602
Cowpens National Battlefield Archives 513
Cowtown Dispatch 545
Cox Family 385, 566, 593, 605
Cox-Hayes Family 157
Cox-Phillips Family 433
Coyle Free Library 484
Coyote Point Museum Archives 69
Cozad Genealogy Club & Archives 350
Cozad Historical Society & Archives 350
Cozad Historical Society Newsletter 350
Cozard Memorial Library 521
Cozens Ranch Archives 90
Cozier Museum 423
CPM News 485
Crab Orchard Public Library District 165
Crabbe Library 233
Crabtree Family 35, 73
Cracker Country 122
Cracker Country Archives 122
Cracker Crumbs 109
Cracker Trail Museum Archives 124
Crackerbarrel 159
Cradle of Aviation Museum Archives 398
Craft and Folk Art Museum Archives 51
Craft Memorial Library 611
Craft-Hill-Haynes-Harris Family 476
Crafton Historical Society 499
Craftsbury Common 576
Craftsbury Public Library 576
Cragsmoor Free Library 395
Cragsmoor Historical Society 411
Craig Clan 289, 606
Craig County Historical Society & Library 591
Craig County Oklahoma Genealogical Society 470
Craig County Oklahoma Genealogical Society Newsletter 470
Craig Creatures 219
Craig Heritage Park Museum Archives 653
Craig Public Library 11
Craigdarroch Castle Historical Museum 657
Craigdarroch Castle Historical Society & Archives 657
Craighead County Historical Society & Library 29
Craighead County Jonesboro Public Library 29
Crailo State Historic Site Archives 413
Cramer-Kenyon Heritage Home Museum Archives 524
Cranberry Genealogy Club 485
Cranbrook House & Gardens Archives 287
Cranbury Historical and Preservation Society & Archives 369
Cranbury Historical and Preservation Society Newsletter 369
Cranbury Historical Museum 369
Cranbury Public Library 369
Crandall Family 400
Crandall Public Library 398
Crane and Tyler in New England and the Eastern US 311
Crane Family 305
Crane Family Newsetter 112
Crane Historical Society & Archives 147
Crane House 147
Crane-Craine Bulletin 327
Cranetown Crier 373
Cranford Free Public Library 369
Cranford Free Public Library Newsletter 369
Cranford Historical Museum 369
Cranford Historical Society 369
Cranford Historical Society & Archives 369
Cranston Family 44, 116
Cranston Historical Society 507
Cranston Public Library 507
Craven County Kinfolk Trackers 423
Cravens House Museum Archives 529
Craver-Harrington Family 420
Crawford Auto-Aviation Museum Archives 445
Crawford County Chapter, OGS 448
Crawford County Federated Library 493
Crawford County Genealogical Society 25, 172, 200, 208, 493
Crawford County Genealogical Society & Archives 220
Crawford County Genealogical Society Newsletter 172
Crawford County Genealogy 493
Crawford County Historical and Genealogical Society 188
Crawford County Historical Museum 220
Crawford County Historical Society 136, 328, 621, 627
Crawford County Historical Society & Archives 220, 528
Crawford County Historical Society & Library 33, 172, 493
Crawford County Iowa Genealogical Society Newsletter 200
Crawford County Library-Devereaux Memorial 293
Crawford County News 443
Crawford County Public Library 183
Crawford Exchange 48
Crawford Family 326, 567
Crawford Historical Society 350
Crawford Public Library 350
Crawford W Long Museum Archives 132
Crawford W Long Museum Newsletter 132
Crawfordsville District Public Library 182
Crazy Mountain Museum Archives 343
Creag Dhubh 99
Creamery Museum Archives 659
Creation of a Masterpiece 542
Cree Family 536
Cree Family History 257
Cree Nation of Chisasibi 697
Cree Nation of Eastmain 697
Cree Nation of Mistissini 699
Cree Nation of Nemaska 700
Cree Nation of Ouje-Bougoumou 700
Cree Nation of Waskaganish 704

INDEX

Cree Nation of Waswanipi 704
Cree Nation of Wemindji 704
Cree Nation of Whapmagoostui 704
Cree News 536
Creech Family 384
Creed Family 544
Creed Genealogy Newsletter 65
Creede Underground Mining Museum Archives 83
Creek Council House Museum 468
Creek Indian Memorial Association & Archives 468
Creekmore Cousins 181
Creekmore Family 230, 300
Crego Family 367
Creighton Historical Center 351
Creighton Public Library 351
Crenshaw County Historical Society 6
Crenshaw County Historical Society Quarterly Bulletin 6
Creole-American Genealogical Society 406
Cresap Society 398
Crescent Bend Museum Archives 528
Crescent Chronicle 127
Crescent Farm Historical Center 127
Crescent Historic House Museum Archives 139
Cresco Historical Society 485
Cresco Public Library 199
Cressman Family 485
Cressona Historical Society 485
Crest 491
Crested Butte Mountain Heritage Museum Archives 83
Crestline Historical Society & Archives 446
Crestline Public Library 446
Creston and District Museum Archives 649
Creswell Historical Society 474
Crete Public Library 351
Creve Coeur-Chesterfield Historical Society 339
Crew Family 148
Crews Family 424
Crews News 153
Creyts-Wait Family 290
Crickman Family 15
Crier 100
Cripe Family Newsletter 51
Crippen Family Newsletter 260, 297
Cripple Creek District Museum Archives 83
Crisp Newsletter 346
Crispell Family 402, 503
Crispin Family 441
Crispus Attucks Center Museum Archives 186
Crist Family 459
Crist-Caylor Family 154
Crittenden County Genealogical Society 231
Crittenden County Historical Museum 27
Crittenden County Historical Society 30
Crittenden County Historical Society & Library 33, 231
Crittenden County Public Library 231
Crittenden Family 164
Crivitz Area Heritage Society 619
Crivitz-Stephenson Historical Society & Archives 619
Croat-Croatt Family 207
Croatian Ethnic Institute 155
Croatian Genealogical and Heraldic Society 64
Croatian Genealogical Society Quarterly 64
Croatian Genealogy Network 42
Croatian Heritage Museum & Library 460
Croatian Heritage Museum Archives 448
Croatian Information Service 35
Croatian-American Academic Association and Croatian Genealogical Society Quarterly Bulletin 65
Croatian-Serbian-Slovenian Genealogical Society & Library 65
Crocheron Family 548
Crocker House Museum 298
Crockett County Historical Museum 555
Crockett County Historical Society & Archives 555
Crockett Memorial Library 525
Crockett Museum and Historical Society 42
Crockett Tavern Museum 530
Croghan Free Library 395
Croghan Town Historian 392
Crolley Family 566
Cromaine District Library 293
Cromwell Belden Public Library 92
Cromwell Historical Society 92
Cronn-Sears Family 212
Crook Clan 112
Crook County Genealogical Society & Library 479
Crook County Genealogical Society Newsletter 479
Crook County Historical Society 637
Crook County Historical Society & Library 479
Crook County Historical Society Newsletter 479
Crook County Library 638
Crook County Museum Archives 638
Cropp Family 499
Crosby County Historical Society 541
Crosby County Pioneer Memorial Museum Archives 541
Crosby Historical Society & Archives 437
Cross Collections 146
Cross County Historical Society & Library 33
Cross Family 54
Cross Mills Public Library 507
Cross Notebook 292
Cross of Languedoc 306, 630
Cross Paths 95
Cross Plains-Berry Historical Museum 619
Cross Plains-Berry Historical Society & Archives 619
Cross Timbers Genealogical Society & Library 546
Cross Timbers Post 546
Crosscut 552
Crossed Sabers Newsletter 214
Crossett Historical Society 26
Crossett Public Library 26
Crossing 315
Crossings 314
Crosslake Area Historical Society 307
Crosslake Area Historical Society Museum Newsletter 307
Crossman Family 604
Crossroad Trails 159
Crossroads Bible College Library 186
Crossroads Museum Archives 645
Crossroads of America Museum Archives 359
Crossroads: a Journal of Colton Area History 41

Crosswicks Public Library 369
Croswell Family 609
Crotty Family 586
Crouse-Krause Connection 332
Crouse-Krause Family 332
Crover Family 477
Crow Family 220
Crow River Genealogical Society 309
Crow Wing County Genealogical Society & Library 306
Crow Wing County Genealogy Newsletter 306
Crow Wing County Historical Museum 306
Crow Wing County Historical Society & Archives 306
Crowder Family 636
Crowl Family 458
Crowl-Cusick-Swartz-McCue Family 586
Crowley Historical Society & Archives 236
Crowley Museum Archives 121
Crowley Museum Quarterly 121
Crowley's Ridge Genealogical Society 33
Crown Garden and Archives, 129
Crown Hill Heritage Foundation 186
Crown Point Community Library 182
Crown Point State Historic Site Archives 395
Crownblock 213
Crowsnest Museum Archives 642
Crowton-Fidkin Family 571
Crum Family 602
Crumbaugh Memorial Public Library 164
Crumley-Van Cleave-Cleve-Cleff Family 606
Crusader 500
Crusan Family 501
Crystal 30
Crystal City Community Museum Archives 659
Crystal City Memorial Library 541
Crystal City Public Library 328
Crystal Lake Falls Historical Association & Archives 575
Crystal Lake Falls Historical Association Newsletter 575
Crystal Lake Historical Society 157
Crystal Lake Public Library 157
Crystal Rice Plantation Archives 236
Crystal-Chrystal-Christal Family 340
CSA Ledger 288
CSS Neuse State Historic Site Archives 429
CTC Families Association 521
CU Heritage Center Archives 81
Cub Reporter 493
Cuba Circulating Library 395
Cuba Public Library 382
Cuban Genealogical Society 570
Cuban Historical and Cultural Center Library 122
Cudahy Family Library 619
Cudahy Historical Society & Library 619
Cudworth Family 16
Cuero Public Library 541
Cuillard Family 72
Culberson County Historical Museum Archives 562
Culberson-Culbertson Family 545
Culbertson Mansion State Historic Site 190
Culbertson Museum Archives 344
Culbertson Museum Newsletter 344
Culbertson Newsletter 190
Culbertson Public Library 351
Culinary History Enthusiasts of Wisconsin 625
Cullen House Archives 559
Cullins Family Historical Review 155
Cullman County Historical Society 3
Cullman County Historical Society & Archives 3
Cullman County Public Library 3
Cullman Historical Museum 3
Cullom-Davis Library 170
Culpeper County Library 586
Culpeper Genealogical Society 585
Culpeper Historical Society 586
Culpepper Family 119, 321
Cultural Currents 475
Cultural Heritage Center Archives 542
Cultural Heritage Foundation of Southern California 51
Culver City Historical Society 42
Culver-Colver Family 565
Culver-Union Township Public Library 182
Cumberland and Coles County Genealogical Society 175
Cumberland County College Library 379
Cumberland County Genealogical Society & Library 426
Cumberland County Historical and Genealical Society 526
Cumberland County Historical and Genealogical Society 161
Cumberland County Historical Museum 673
Cumberland County Historical Society 586
Cumberland County Historical Society & Archives 673
Cumberland County Historical Society & Library 370, 484
Cumberland County History 484
Cumberland County Public Library 426
Cumberland County Virginia Historical Bulletin 586
Cumberland Gap National Historical Park Archives 231
Cumberland Historical Society 245
Cumberland House Cree Nation 705
Cumberland House Museum Archives 709
Cumberland Island National Seashore Museum Archives 136
Cumberland Museum Archives 649
Cumberland Patriot 370
Cumberland Presbyterian Church Birthplace Archives 525
Cumberland Public Library 507, 619
Cumberland Science Museum Archives 531
Cumberland Township Heritage Museum Archives 681
Cumberland Township Historical Society 686
Cumberland Trail Genealogical Society 445, 456
Cuming County Historical Society 357
Cumming Clan 124
Cummings Chronicles 196
Cummings Family 42, 57, 196, 545
Cummington Historical Commission & Archives 269
Cumston Public Library 248
Cumtux: Clatsop County Historical Society Quarterly 473
Cuneo Museum Archives 176
CuneoGram 176
Cunning Clan 200
Cunningham Clan 90
Cunningham Family 185, 545
Cunningham Lair 37
Cunningham Memorial Library 194
Cunningham Museum 624

Cupar and District Heritage Museum Archives 706
Cupertino Chronicle 42
Cupertino Historical Museum 42
Cupertino Historical Society & Museum 42
Cupids Museum Archives 667
Cupola 244
Cupola House Museum Archives 620
Curahee Military Museum Archives 661
Curator 443
Curlee House Archives 319
Curley Family 487
Curnalia Family of New York State and Michigan 92
Current Events & Information 455
Current River Heritage Museum 328
Currents 117, 125
Currie Clan 378
Currituck County Public Library 423
Curry County Echoes 475
Curry County Genealogy Society 382
Curry County Historical Museum 475
Curry County Historical Society 475
Curry Critters 166
Curry-Berry-Rogers-Lawrence-Killgore-Jones-McInvale Family 539
Curtis Family Journal 418
Curtis Memorial Library 209
Curtis-Curtiss Family 409
Curtiss Flyleaf 399
Curtiss-Wright Historical Association 75
Curwood Castle 299
Cushing Genealogical Society 464
Cushing Historical Museum 245
Cushing Historical Society & Archives 245
Cushing House Museum 275
Cushing Library 540
Cushing Public Library 464
Cushwa Center for the Study of American Catholicism 191
Custer Battlefield Historical and Museum Archives 344
Custer Battlefield Museum Archives 344
Custer County Genealogical Society & Library 350
Custer County Historical Museum 350
Custer County Historical Society 90
Custer County Historical Society & Archives 350, 521
Custer County Library 521
Custer County Times 350
Custer Museum Archives 146
Custer State Park Museum Archives 521
Custer-Iverson-Hyatt-Wheeler-McCain-Cundiff Family 565
Custom House Maritime Museum 275
Cutchogue Free Library 395
Cuttyhunk Historical Society 275
Cuyahoga County Archives Library 445
Cuyahoga County Public Library 455
Cuyahoga County-Greater Cleveland Chapter, OGS 445
Cuyahoga County-Parma Chapter, OGS 455
Cuyahoga Valley Chapter, OGS & Library 442
Cuyahoga West Chapter, OGS 448
Cuyuna Country Heritage Preservation Society 307, 309
Cuyuna Range Historical Museum 307
Cuyuna Range Historical Society & Archives 307
Cynthiana-Harrison County Public Library 226
Cypress Basin Genealogical and Historical Society 554
Cypress Basin Genealogical and Historical Society Quarterly 554
Cypress Basin Genealogical and Historical Society Reporter 554
Cypress Basin Genealogical Bulletin 554
Cypress Heritage Committee 42
Cyrenius H Booth Library 97
Cyrus H McCormick Memorial Museum Archives 595
Czech & Slovak Genealogical Society of Arizona 16
Czech and Slovak American Genealogy Society of Illinois 175
Czech and Slovak Genealogical Library 157
Czech and Slovak Genealogical Society of Arizona 18
Czech and Slovak Search Group 83
Czech Heritage Foundation 198
Czech Heritage Preservation Society 524
Czech Heritage Preservation Society Annual Newsletter 524
Czech Opera House Museum Archives 223
Czechoslovak Genealogical Society 314
Czechoslovak Heritage Museum Archives 168
Czechoslovak National Council of America 157

D

D A Hurd Library 249
D C Booth Historic Fish Hatchery Museum Archives 524
D C Booth Historic Fish Hatchery Museum Newsletter 524
D Hiden Ramsey Library 423
D Tenney Lamoreux Genealogical Organization 16
D'arcy McNickle Library 346
Da Lee Family 467
Dabney Family 529
Dacotah Prairie Museum Library 521
Dacotah Prairie Times 521
Dade Battlefield Historic State Park Archives 110
Dade County Genealogical Society 329
Dade County Historical Society 138
Dade County Historical Society & Library 329
Dade County Historical Society Newsletter 138
Dadswell Family 685
Dafft-Daft Family Newsletter 540
Dagenhart Family 76
Dagger 259
Daggett Family 281
Daggett House 508
Dahle Family 146
Dahler Family 625
Dahlonega Courthouse Gold Museum Archives 129
Dailey Memorial Library 576
Dakota City Heritage Village Archives 308
Dakota City Public Library 351
Dakota County Family Ties 351
Dakota County Genealogical Society 315, 351
Dakota County Genealogist 315
Dakota County Historical Society 351
Dakota County Historical Society & Archives 315
Dakota County Library System 307
Dakota Discovery Museum Archives 523
Dakota Discovery Museum Newsletter 523
Dakota Frontier Days 521
Dakota Homestead Historical Newsletter 437
Dakota Ojibway Tribal Council 659
Dakota Sunset Museum Archives 522

Dakota Sunset Newsletter 522
Dakota Territorial Museum 524
Dakota Territory Air Museum Archives 439
Dakotaland Museum Archives 522
Dale and Martha Hawk Museum Archives 438
Dale County Genealogical and Historical Society 8
Dale County Historical Society 8
Dale H Gramley Library 435
Daleville Historical Society 182
Daley-Crawford Family 600
Dallam-Hartley Counties Historical Association & Archives 541
Dallam-Hartley Museum 541
Dallas County East Genealogical Society 542
Dallas County Genealogical and Historical Society 27
Dallas County Genealogical and Historical Society & Archives 25
Dallas County Genealogical Society & Archives 199
Dallas County Genealogical Society & Library 326
Dallas County Genealogical Society News Bulletin 326
Dallas County Genealogical Society Newsletter 199
Dallas County Heritage Society & Archives 542
Dallas County Historical Church and Cemetery Association & Archives 542
Dallas County Historical Society 27
Dallas County Historical Society & Library 326
Dallas County Historical Society New Bulletin 326
Dallas County Library 27
Dallas Firefighter's Museum Archives 542
Dallas Genealogical Society & Library 542
Dallas Genealogical Society Newsletter 542
Dallas Heritage Village Archives 542
Dallas Historical Society & Archives 542
Dallas Historical Society Register 542
Dallas Holocaust Museum Archives 542
Dallas Holocaust Museum Newsletter 542
Dallas Jewish Historical Society & Library 542
Dallas Jewish Historical Society, Genealogy Division 542
Dallas Journal 542
Dallas Public Library 474, 542
Dalles City-Wasco County Public Library 480
Dallidet Adobe and Gardens Archives 68
Dal-Paso Musuem Archives 551
Dalton Community Library 485
Dalton Community Library Newsletter 485
Dalton Defenders Museum Archives 212
Dalton Free Public Library 269
Dalton Gang Letters 425
Dalton Genealogical Society 59
Dalton Historical Society 351
Dalton Public Library 351
Daly City Public Library 42
Dam-Damn Family 50
Dameron-Damron Family 332, 340, 445, 562
Dames of the Loyal Legion of the United States & Library 497
Damon Family Newsletter 48
Damon-Demming Family 265
Dan Nagle Walnut Grove Pioneer Village Archives 204
Dan O'Laurie Museum of Moab Archive 568
Dana Adobe Museum Archives 56
Dana Adobe Museum Newsletter 56
Dana Point Historical Society 42
Dana-Thomas House Foundation Newsletter 174
Dana-Thomas House State Historic Site Archives 174
Danbury Historical Society & Archives 92
Danbury Public Library 92
Danbury Railway Museum 92
Dance Family 21
Dancing Bear Folk Center Archives 638
Dandridge Memorial Library 526
Dane County Historical Society & Library 625
Dane County Historical Society Newsletter 625
Dane G Hansen Memorial Museum Archives 217
Dane G Hansen Memorial Museum Quarterly 217
Daniel A Reed Library 397
Daniel Benton Homestead Archives 100
Daniel Boone and Frontier Families Research Association 330
Daniel Boone Homestead Archives 483
Daniel Boone Regional Library 327
Daniel Discoverer and Documenter 49
Daniel Family 74, 372
Daniel Family Newsletter 128
Daniel Library 512
Daniel Tichenor Cemetery Club 327
Daniel-Daniels Newsletter 529
Daniel-Glawson-Pryor-Wilson-Carter-Reed-Reid-Simonton-Gardner-Bagley Family 129
Daniels County Museum and Pioneer Town Archives 346
Daniels County Museum Newsletter 346
Danish American Fellowship 311
Danish American Heritage Society 197
Danish Immigrant Archives 200
Danish Immigrant Museum Archives 201
Danish-American Heritage Society & Archives 200
Danish-American Historical Society of California 45
Dannenberg Staffeldt 20
Dannenmueller Family 342
Dannewitz Family 383
Dansville Area Historical Museum 395
Dansville Area Historical Society & Archives 395
Dansville Public Library 395
Danvers Archival Center 269
Danvers Historical Collections 269
Danvers Historical Museum 269
Danvers Historical Society 157
Danvers Historical Society & Archives 269
Danville Constitution 226
Danville Museum of Art and History Archives 586
Danville Museum of Art and History Newsletter 586
Danville Public Library 157, 182, 586
Danville Public Library News 157
Daphne Public Library 3
DAR State Library 467
Darbonne Family 568
Darby Borough Historical and Preservation Society 485
Darby Foundation Museum Archives 27
Darby Free Library 485
Dare County Library 429
DAR-First Ladies of Texas 543
Dar-Hervey Fly House Museum Archives 413
Darien Historical Society 157
Darien Historical Society & Library 92
Darien Historical Society Newsletter 157

INDEX

Darien Historical Society Quarterly 92
Darien Library 92
Darke County Chapter, OGS 449
Darke County Historical Society & Archives 449
Darling Family 344
Darlingford School Heritage Museum Archives 659
Darlington County Genealogical Research Library 515
Darlington County Genealogical Society 515
Darlington County Historical Commission & Library 514
Darlington County Historical Society 514
Darlington County Library 514
Darlington Flag 515
Darlington Province Park Pioneer Home Archives 680
Darlington Public Library 182
Darnall's Chance House Museum Archives 263
Darnall-Darnell-Dawn to Dusk 259
Darris Family 329
Dartford Depot Museum Archives 622
Dartford Historical Society & Library 622
Dartford News 622
Dartmouth College Library Bulletin 361
Dartmouth Heritage Museum Archives 673
Dartmouth Regional Library 673
Darwin R Barker Library 397
Das Deutsche Haus 186
Dassel Area Historical Society 307
Dates and Updates 72
Daub Family 491
Daubenspeck-Doverspike-Milliron-Millison-Muhleisen-Shreckengost Family 412
Daughers of the American Revolution & Library 467
Daughters of Charity Archives Albany 387
Daughters of Hawaii 141
Daughters of the American Revolution 517, 575
Daughters of the American Revolution Magazine 106
Daughters of the American Revolution, Abraham Coryelle Chapter 470
Daughters of the American Revolution, Allegheny County & Library 499
Daughters of the American Revolution, Aloha Chapter 141
Daughters of the American Revolution, Arizona Society 18
Daughters of the American Revolution, Arizona State 20
Daughters of the American Revolution, Arizona State Chapter 20
Daughters of the American Revolution, Arkansas Post Chapter 33
Daughters of the American Revolution, Covina California Chapter 41
Daughters of the American Revolution, Cullman County Chapter 3
Daughters of the American Revolution, Enoch Ashley Chapter 32
Daughters of the American Revolution, Faith Trumbull Chapter & Library 97
Daughters of the American Revolution, Georgia State Society Meadow Garden 126
Daughters of the American Revolution, Grand Prairie Chapter 26
Daughters of the American Revolution, Kansas Society 223
Daughters of the American Revolution, Louisiana Chapter 235
Daughters of the American Revolution, Lue R Spencer Chapter & Archives 352
Daughters of the American Revolution, Oregon Chapter & Archives 476
Daughters of the American Revolution, Oregon Chapter & Library 479
Daughters of the American Revolution, Pawtucket Chapter & Archives 508
Daughters of the American Revolution, Putnam Hill Chapter & Library 94
Daughters of the American Revolution, Rosalie Branch & Archives 321
Daughters of the American Revolution, Sibley House Association of the Minnesota Branch 311
Daughters of the American Revolution, Utah Society 570
Daughters of the American Revolution, Vermont Society & Library 580
Daughters of the American Revolution, Wisconsin Society & Library 629
Daughters of the Cincinnati 406
Daughters of the Republic of Texas & Archives 536
Daughters of the Republic of Texas & Library 558
Daughters of the Union Veterans of the Civil War & Library 174
Daughters of Union Veterans of the Civil War 17
Daughters of Union Veterans of the Civil War 1861-1865, Missouri Department 326
Daughters of Union Veterans of the Civil War, Iowa Dept 205
Daughters of Union Veterans of the Civil War, Ohio Department 449
Dauphin County Library 489
DAV Veterans History Project 146
Davee Family 606
Davenport Historical Society 395
Davenport House Museum Archives 137
Davenport House Museum Newsletter 137
Davenport Public Library 200, 600
Davenport Times 355
David & Lorraine Cheng Library 379
David & Lorraine Cheng Library Newsletter 379
David A Cofrin Library 622
David A Howe Public Library 420
David and Joyce Milne Public Library 282
David Bishop Skillman Library 486
David Bradford House Archives 504
David Browning Railroad Musuem 119
David Conklin Farmhouse Museum Archives 400
David Crawford House Museum 408
David Crockett Cabin Museum Archives 532
David Davis Mansion Archives 152
David Davis Mansion Newsletter 152
David Family 237
David Glenn Hunt Memorial Library 546
David H Townsend Library 381
David L Rice Library 183
David Library of the American Revolution 504
David M Hunt Library 93
David O McKay Library 149
Davids Family 149
Davidson Clan 31
Davidson County Historical Museum Archives 429
Davidson County Historical Museum Newsletter 429
Davidson County Public Library 429
Davidson County Public Library System-Thomasville Public 433
Davidson County, NC Genealogical Journal 429
Davie County Public Library 430
Davies County Library 329
Davies Family 83
Davies Memorial Library 577
Daviess County Genealogical Society 195
Daviess County Historical Museum 195
Daviess County Historical Quarterly 232
Daviess County Historical Society 329
Daviess County Historical Society & Archives 195, 232
Daviess County Public Library 232
Davis County Genealogical Society & Archives 197
Davis County Genealogical Society Newsletter 197
Davis County Historical Society 197

Davis County Library 566
Davis Family 100, 147, 165, 323, 333, 473, 573, 602
Davis Genealogy Club & Library 42
Davis Memorial Library 248
Davis Surname Newsletter 18
Davis-Duke Family 569
Davison County Genealogical Society 523
Davistown Museum Archives 247
Davisville Free Library 508
Davisville Historical Society 328
Dawes County Historical Museum 350
Dawes County Historical Society & Archives 350
Dawes County Historical Society Newsletter 350
Dawes Family 488
Dawkins Family 446
Dawson City Community Library 713
Dawson City Historical Museum 713
Dawson City Historical Society 713
Dawson City Museum and Historical Society & Library 713
Dawson County Genealogical Newsletter 353
Dawson County Genealogical Society 350
Dawson County Historical and Genealogical Society 130
Dawson County Historical Museum 353
Dawson County Historical Society & Archives 353
Dawson County Historical Society Newsletter 353
Dawson County Public Library 551
Dawson Creek Municipal Public Library 649
Dawson Creek Station Museum Archives 649
Dawson Family 36, 235
Dawson Springs Museum Archives 226
Dawson-Mercer-Cable-Davis Family 45
Dax Ka Nation 647
Day Family News 252
Day Quayle Museum Archives 185
Day Star First Nation 709
Daymark 405
Dayton Historical Depot Museum 601
Dayton Historical Depot Society & Archives 601
Dayton Memorial Library 83
Dayton Metro Library 447
Daytona Beach Community College Library 111
DBPLetter 216
DC Superior Court Marriage License Bureau 105
De Anza Heritage Society 35
De Anza Trek Lancers Society 42
De Halve Maen 407
de la Montagne Family 341
De Lay International Genealogical Foundation 50
De Malyene 594
De Montbrun Family 42
De Paul Library 217
De Pere Historical Society & Archives 620
De Saisset Museum Archives 70
De Saisset Museum Newsletter 70
De Smet Depot Museum Archives 521
De Soto Historical Society 328
De Soto Historical Society & Library 238
De Soto Parish Library 238
De Soto Plume 238
De Soto Public Library 328
De Soto Trail Regional Library 127
de Southworth Family 150
De Witt Public Library 289
Deacon's Bench 624
Dead River Area Historical Society 251
Deadwood Magazine 521
Deadwood Public Library 521
Deaf Smith County Genealogical Society 548
Deaf Smith County Historical Museum 548
Deaf Smith County Historical Society & Archives 548
Deaf Smith County Historical Society Newsletter 548
Deaf Smith County Library 548
Deaf Smith County Museum Archives 548
Deaf Smithsonian 548
Dealey Library and Museum 542
Dean & Creech Newsletter 231
Dean B Ellis Library 29
Dean Family 421
Dean House 627
Dean-Deane Family 406
Dear Cousins Newsletter 460
Dear Friends 85
Dear Myrtle 271
Dearborn County Historical Museum 188
Dearborn County Historical Society & Archives 188
Dearborn Genealogical Society & Archives 289
Dearborn Genealogical Society Newsletter 289
Dearborn Historian 289
Dearborn Historical Commission & Archives 289
Dearborn Historical Museum 289
Dearborn Historical Society & Archives 289
Dearborn Public Library 289
Dearing-Peterson(sen) Family 45
DeArman-De Arman Family 548
Dease River Band Council 650
Death Valley National Monument Library 42
Death Valley National Park Archives 42
Deaton Family 320
DeBolt and District Pioneer Museum Archives 642
Deborah Rawson Memorial Library 577
Debrot Family 184
Debs Historic Home 194
Decatur County Genealogical Society 127, 204
Decatur County Genealogical Society & Archives 219
Decatur County Genealogical Society Newsletter 219
Decatur County Historical Society 127, 185, 526
Decatur Genealogical Society & Library 158
Decatur Genealogical Society Newsletter 158
Decatur House Museum Archives 105
Decatur Public Library 3, 158, 182, 542
Decatur Public Library Connections 158
Decatur Township Historical Society 195
Deck Family 467
Deck Log 256
Decker Family 198
Deckerville Public Library 289
Decorah Area Diggers 200
Decorah Genealogy Association & Archives 200
Decorah Public Library 200
DeCou-DeCow-DeCoux-DeCew Family 164

DeCoursey Family 602
Dedham Historical Museum 269
Dedham Historical Society & Library 269
Dedham Historical Society Newsletter 269
Dedham Public Library 269
Dedmon Family 140
Deep Delta 242
Deep River Historical Society 92
Deep South Genealogical Quarterly 7
Deep South Genealogical Society Newsletter 7
Deer Isle-Stonington Historical Museum 245
Deer Isle-Stonington Historical Society & Library 245
Deer Isle-Stonington Historical Society Newsletter 245
Deer Lodge Abner Ross Memorial Center Library 526
Deer Lodge Historical Society 526
Deer Park Escondido Winery & Auto Museum Archives 43
Deer Park Escondido Winery & Auto Museum Quarterly Newsletter 43
Deere-Wiman House Archives 166
Deerfield Area Historical Society 158
Deerfield Beach Historical Society & Archives 111
Deerfield Beach Historical Society Quarterly 111
Deerfield Historical Museum 269
Deerfield Public Library 158
Dees Family 383
Defender 9, 285
Deferiet Village Historian 392
Defiance County Chapter, OGS & Library 447
Defiance County Historical Society & Archives 447
Defiance Public Library 447
DeForest Area Historical Society & Archives 620
Degenstein Community Library 502
DeGolyer Library of Special Collections 542
Degroat Family 45
DeHaas Family 441
DeHaven Club 124
DeHaven Family 543
Deiter Family 223
DeKalb County Genealogical Society 4
DeKalb County Genealogy Society 179
DeKalb County Heritage 335
DeKalb County Historical and Genealogical Society 175
DeKalb County Historical Society 4, 179, 181
DeKalb County Historical Society & Library 335
DeKalb County Public Library 4, 130
DeKalb Diggins 179
DeKalb Historical Association 395
DeKalb Historical Museum 130
DeKalb Historical Society & Library 130
DeKalb Historical Society Newsletter 130
DeKalb Legend 4
DeKalb Public Library 157
Deke Slayton Memorial Space and Bike Museum Archives 631
Dekker Huis and Zeeland Historical Museum Archives 304
Del E Webb Memorial Library 50
Del Mar Historical Society 42
Del Norte County Historical Museum 41
Del Norte County Historical Society & Library 41
Del Norte County Historical Society Bulletin 41
Del Norte County Library District 41
Del Norte Public Library 83
DeLacy, Lacey, Lacy Family 297
DeLand Public Library, Volusia County Branch 111
Delano Family 596
Delano Heritage Park 42
Delano Heritage Park Archives 42
Delano Heritage Park Quarterly Bulletin 42
Delano Historical Society & Archives 42
Delashaw-Dilleshaw Family 470
Delashmutt-Taliaferro Family 209
DeLaughter Family 29
Delavan Community Historical Society 158
Delavan Historical Society 620
Delaware Academy of Medicine Historical Archives 104
Delaware Agricultural Museum & Village Library 103
Delaware and Hudson Canal Historical Museum 400
Delaware and Hudson Canal Historical Society & Archives 400
Delaware and Hudson Canal Historical Society Newsletter 400
Delaware County Chapter, OGS & Library 447
Delaware County District Library 447
Delaware County Genealogical Society 204, 465
Delaware County Genealogist 190
Delaware County Historical Alliance & Archives 190
Delaware County Historical Association & Library 395
Delaware County Historical Society 203, 465, 466, 494
Delaware County Historical Society & Library 447, 483
Delaware County Historical Society Quarterly 447
Delaware Free Library 392
Delaware Genealogical Society & Library 104
Delaware Genealogical Society Journal 104
Delaware Genealogical Society Newsletter 104
Delaware Genealogist 447
Delaware History 104
Delaware Notes 103
Delaware Public Archives 103
Delaware State Archives 103
Delaware State Library 103
Delaware State Museum 103
Deleglise Cabin Museum 617
Delhi Ontario Tobacco Museum and Heritage Centre 681
Delhi Township Historical Society & Library 444
Delhi Township Public Library 681
Delia Biddle Pugh Library 368
Dells County Historical Society & Archives 634
Delmar T Oviatt Library, Center for Southern California Studies 56
DeLong-Cline-Benbow-Cunningham-Cartwright-Jones-McCloud-Powell-Black Family 75
Deloraine Museum 659
Delozier Times: Delosier, De Lozier, Delosure 71
Delphi Public Library 182
Delphos Public Library 447
Delray Beach Historical Society & Archives 111
Delray Beach Historical Society Quarterly Newsletter 111
Delray Beach Library 111
Delta County Genealogical Society 291
Delta County Historical Museum 83, 291
Delta County Historical Society 291
Delta County Historical Society & Archives 83
Delta County Historical Society & Library 290
Delta County Historical Society Quarterly 83
Delta County Public Library 83

Delta County Public Library District-Paonia Branch 88
Delta Cultural Center Archives 28
Delta Genealogical Society & Archives 136
Delta Historian 291
Delta Historical Society 11
Delta Mill and Old Stone Mill Museum Archives 681
Delta Museum and Archives 649
Delta Pedigree Press 291
Delta Review 31
Delvee Family 99
Delyte W Morris Library 153
DeMary Memorial Library 149
Dement Family 329, 331
Deming Historical Society & Archives 382
Deming Luna Membres Museum 382
Demopolis Public Library 3
Demott Data 138
Demotte Historical Society 182
Demski Family 297
Demuth-DeMuth-Damuth Family 317
Denali National Park & Preserve Library 12
Dene Cultural Institute 671
Dene Indian Nation 671
Dene Museum Archives 671
Denison Historical and Genealogical Society 543
Denison Library Genealogy Group & Archives 543
Denison Newsletter 96
Denison Public Library 543
Denison Society 96
Denman Island Museum Archives 649
Denmark Town Historian 394
Dennard Family 548
Dennett Family 566
Denney Family 241
Dennis Historical Society 270
Dennis M O'Connor Public Library 557
Dennis Memorial Library 270
Dennis Public Library 270
Dennis Township Historical Society 378
Dennison Railroad Depot Museum Archives 447
Denny Family 546
Dennys River Historical Museum 245
Dennys River Historical Society & Archives 245
Dennys River Historical Society Newsletter 245
Dent County Historical Society 340
Dent Family 552
Dental Museum Archives 643
Denton Community Historical Society 351
Denton County Genealogical Society & Library 543
Denton County Genealogical Society News 543
Denton County Historical Commission & Archives 543
Denton County Historical Museum 543
Denton Public Library 543
Denton Public Library-North Branch 543
Denver Firefighters Museum Archives 83
Denver Public Library 83
Denville Historical Society 369
Department of Health and Rehabilitative Services, Office of Vital Statistics 114
Department of Military Affairs 227
Department of the Treasury Museum Archives 105
DePaul University Libraries 155
Depot Dispatch 46
Depot Express 305
Depot House Museum 250
Depot Museum 115, 123, 288, 295, 426, 474, 548, 609, 621, 630
Depot Park Museum 73
Depot Review 303
Depreciation Lands Museum Archives 481
Depreciation Lands Museum Newsletter 481
Dept of Veterans Affairs, National Cemetery System 105
Der Ahnenforscher 402
Der Blumenbaum 64
Der Deutsch Amerikaner 155
Der Maubaum 330
Der Reggeboge 491
Der Trompeter 546
Der Uberlick 502
Derby Historical Society 92
Derby Historical Society & Archives 91
Derby Historical Society & Library 576
Derby Neck Library 92
Derby Public Library-Harcourt Wood Memorial 92
Derington Family 563
Derleth Family 630
Deroques Family 551
Deroun Diplomat 548
Derr Family 495
Derrell C Roberts Library 129
Derrow Family 105
Derry Area Historical Society 493
Derry Public Library 360
Derry Township Historical Society 489
Derstine Family 489
Des Moines County Genealogical Society 198
Des Moines County Genealogical Society Quarterly 198
Des Moines County Historical Society 198
Des Moines County Historical Society Newsletter 198
Des Plaines Genealogical Questers 158
Des Plaines Historical Museum 158
Des Plaines Historical Society & Archives 158
Des Plaines Valley Public Library District 165
DesBrisay Museum Archives 673
Descendants 277
Descendants of Andrew Pittser Newsletter 74
Descendants of Founders of New Jersey 372
Descendants of James Bingham of County Down, Northern Ireland Newsletter 327
Descendants of Mexican War Veterans 557
Descendants of Peter Johnson Newsletter 37
Descendants of Robert Bartlett Newsletter 278
Descendants of the Bishop Hill Colonists 152
Descendants of the East Wood 52
Descendants of the Founders of Ancient Windsor & Library 101
Descendants of the Founders of Ancient Windsor Newsletter 101
Descendants of the Knights of Bath 113, 431
Descendants of the Signers of the Declaration of Independence 497, 502
Descendants of Valentine Bloss Newsletter 230
Descendants of William Daniel Newsletter 74
Descendants of William Henry Brown of Effingham County 155
Descendants of William Morgan Jesse Newsletter 48

INDEX

Descendants of William Robertson of NH Newsletter 56
Descender 212
Deschutes County Historical and Genealogical Society 473
Deschutes County Historical and Genealogical Society Newsletter 473
Deschutes County Historical Museum 473
Deschutes County Library 473
Deseronto Public Library 681
Desert Caballeros Western Museum 22
Desert Diggins 48, 76
Desert Dwellers 15
Desert Hot Springs Historical Society & Library 42
Desert Museum Archives 61
Desert Tracker 20
Desha County Historical Society 27, 30
Desha County Museum Archives 27
DeShazo Newsletter 6, 50
Desher Edwin Wood Memorial Library 447
DeSoto Descendants 320
DeSoto National Memorial Archives 109
Desoto Parish Library-Logansport Branch 238
Destin Library 111
Destruction Bay Historical Society 713
Detillion Family 36
Detour Reef Light Preservation Society 290
Detroit Conference United Methodist Archives 285
Detroit Historical Museum 289
Detroit Historical Society & Archives 289
Detroit in Perspective: A Journal of Regional History 289
Detroit Public Library 289
Detroit Public Library-Municipal Reference Center 289
Detroit Society for Genealogical Research & Archives 289
Detroit Society for Genealogical Research Newsletter 289
Detroit Society for Genealogical Research Quarterly Magazine 289
Deutsche Vereinigung von Winnipeg: Mitteilungen 662
Deutschheim State Historic Site Library 330
Deutschheim Verein 330
Devine-Falvey-Sheehy-Stack Clan 154
DeVito Italian American Society 416
Dewald Newsletter 46
Dewberry Plantation Archives 539
Dewberry Valley Museum Archives 642
Dewees-Deweese Family 474
Deweese Family 455
Dewey County Library 524
Dewey Hotel Museum Archives 464
Dewey Hotel Museum Newsletter 464
DeWitt County Genealogical Society 157
Dewitt County Genealogical Society Quarterly 157
DeWitt County Historical Museum Archives 541
DeWitt County Museum Association Archives 157
Dewitt Historical Society 351
Dewitt Historical Society History Center 401
Dewitt Historical Society of Tompkins County & Library 401
Dewitt Historical Society of Tompkins County Newsletter 401
DeWitt Public Library 26
Dewitt Stetten Museum of Medical Research Archives 256
DeWitt Wallace Library 314
Dewitt-Bartlett Family 635
Dexter Area Historical Society & Archives 290
Dexter Area Historical Society Newsletter 290
Dexter Free Library 395
Dexter Historical Museum 245
Dexter Historical Society & Archives 245
Dexter Historical Society Newsletter 245
Dexter Library 617
Dexter Museum 290
Dexter Village Historian 395
Deyarmond-Peddie Family 359
Deyo-Terwilliger Family 406
Dheinsville Settlement 622
Diablo Descendants Newsletter 41
Diablo Valley College Library & Museum 60
Diamond Library 360
Diana Town Historian & Archives 399
Diana Town Historical Museum 399
Dick Documents 19
Dick Smith Library 560
Dick Surname Newsletter 18
Dickens Family 476
Dickerson-Landis Family 186
Dickerson-Mayo Family 329
Dickinson County Genealogical Society & Archives 294
Dickinson County Heritage Center 211
Dickinson County Heritage Center Gazette 211
Dickinson County Historical Society & Archives 211
Dickinson County Library 294
Dickinson Diggins 294
Dickinson Public Library 437
Dickson County Public Library 527
Dickson Store Museum Archives 646
Didsbury and District Museum Archives 642
Didymus Thompson Library 413
Die Neue Pennsylvanische Staatsbote 497
Die Shilgrut fun der Tulpehock 505
Die Tseiding 488
Diefenbaker Canada Centre 710
Diefenbaker Homestead House Museum Archives 709
Diefenbaker House Archives 709
Dieffenbach Family 486
Diego Sepulveda Adobe Estancia Archives 41
Dietrick Museum of Medical History Archives 445
Dietz Database 43
Diff Clan Family Newsletter 2
Diggin' for Davises 43
Diggin' History 340
Diggin's 58
Dighton Historical Society & Library 270
Dighton Public Library 270
Dillard Doorways 548
Dillard Family 125, 130
Diller Historical Society 351
Dillingham Public Library 12
Dillon County Historical Society 514
Dillon County Library 514
Dillon Family 52
Dilworth Family Letter 22
Dimmick Memorial Library 490
Dimmit Family 59
Dinand Library 283
Dinand Library Newsletter 283

Dinger Family Newsletter 488
Dinsmore Dispatch 226
Dinsmore Homestead Foundation Archives 226
Dionne Homestead Museum Archives 686
Diplomatic Pouch 388
Direction des Archives Nationales de l'Ouest du Quebec 700
Directory of Archival and Manuscript Repositories in California 37
Directory of Genealogical Society of Old Tyron County 426
Directory of Illinois Museums 174
Directory of Kentucky Historical Organizations 227
Directory of Museums and Historical Organizations in Pennsylvania 489
Directory of Oklahoma Sources 468
Directory of Virginia Museums 594
Directory: Historical Agencies, Museums and Local Historians 397
Disbrow Family 118, 523
Disciples of Christ Historical Society & Library 531
Discipliana 531
Discover New Mexico 384
Discover North 337
Discovery 65, 72, 479, 541
Discovery Harbour Museum Archives 688
Disney Chronicles from Colonial Time to the Present 68
Disney Family Bulletin 205
Dispatch 70, 125, 247, 387, 531, 562
Dispatch News 174
Dispatch: American Airpower 553
Dispatcher 184
Distant Crossroads 532
Distant Traits 480
Distinguished Flying Cross Society 65
District 69 Historical Society 653
District of Columbia Archives 105
District of Columbia Department of Human Services Vital Records Branch 105
District of Columbia Genealogical Society 105
District of Columbia Public Library-Georgetown 105
District of Columbia Public Library-Southeast 105
Ditidaht Indian Band 653
Dittmann Family 523
Divide County Historical Museum 439
Divide County Historical Society & Archives 439
Divide County Public Library 437
Division of Archives and Records, City of Charleston 611
Division of Historic Preservation 235
Dixfield Historical Society 245
Dixie Gun Works' Old Car Museum Archives 533
Dixie News 322
Dixie Regional Library System 322
Dixon County Historical Society 351
Dixon Family 263
Dixon Public Library 42, 158
Dixon-Dixson-Dickson Family 495
Doak House Museum Archives 527
Doane Family 67, 93, 272, 411, 525, 595, 689
Dob's and Data 212
Dobberstein Family 617
Dobbs Ferry Historical Society 395
Dobbs Ferry Public Library 395
Dobie Clan 445
Dochnahl Newsletter 58
Dock Museum 371
Dockery Family 428
Docket 286
Doctor Bodo Otto Association Newsletter 118
Doctor Edwin E Lehr Library 548
Doctor Samuel A Mudd Society 260
Doctor Samuel A Mudd Society Newsletter 260
Doctors' House Museum Archive 46
Dodd Diggings 259
Dodd Family 127
Dodd Research Center 99
Doddridge County Historical Society 615
Doddridge County Public Library 615
Dodenhoff Family 39
Dodge and Jefferson Counties Genealogical Society 633
Dodge Centre Historical Museum 623
Dodge Centre Historical Society & Archives 623
Dodge City Public Library 213
Dodge County Chronicle 310
Dodge County Genealogical Society 307
Dodge County Genealogical Society Newsletter 307
Dodge County Historical Museum 310, 617
Dodge County Historical Museum 617
Dodge County Historical Society & Archives 310, 351, 617
Dodge County Historical Society Newsletter 351, 617
Dodge Family 622
Dodge Family Journal 87
Dodge Historical Society 130
Dodge Library 420
Dodge Mining Camp Cabin Museum Archives 620
Dodsland Museum Archives 706
Doeckel-Schniger Family Reunion Newsletter 172
Doerfler Family 479
Dog River Crier 578
Dogtown Historical Society 339
Dogtown Territorial Quarterly 58
Dohner Family Newsletter 58
Doig River Indian Band 654
Dolan Area Historical Society 182
Dolgeville Manheim Historical Museum 395
Dolgeville Manheim Historical Society & Archives 395
Dolores Library District 84
Dolph Family 494
Dolphin 271, 420
Dolsen Family 286
Dolton Notes 158
Dolton Public Library District 158
Domaine Cataraquai Musee 703
Don F Pratt Museum Archives 227
Donahoe-Mooney-Thompson-Cassidy-Hendrickson Family 605
Donald Clan 5, 46, 75, 87, 135, 136, 158, 281, 291, 316, 375, 471, 585, 601, 636
Donald G Trayser Museum 266
Donalda and District Museum Archives 642
Donald-Dobson-Allen-Flower Family 51
Donelly Homestead Museum Archives 685
Doniphan County Historical Society & Archives 222
Doniphan County Library 222
Donkey Milk House Museum Archives 115
Donley County Genealogical Society 540
Donley Directory 548

Donna Public Library 543
Donna Public Library Newsletter 543
Donnachaidh Clan 15, 42, 56, 83, 114, 125, 165, 265, 289, 457, 469, 527, 553, 587, 608
Donnaichaidh Dispatch: the Newsletter of the Clan Donnachaidh Society of the South 125
Donnell House Museum 1
Donnellson Public Library 201
Donnelly Library 164
Donner Memorial State Park and Emigrant Trail Museum Archives 75
Donner Memorial State Park Archives 63
Donner to America 155
Donora Historical Society 486
Donovan Research Library 128
Donshea-Barry-White-Merget-Mohr-Brangan-McKinney-Mandel-Warren-Caufield-Geyer Family 73
Dooley Family 568
Dooley-Duley Family Newsletter 478
Doolittle Family 75, 383, 594
Doollittle-Calvert-Abernathy-Chenoweth Family 346
Doon Heritage Crossroads Archives 684
Door County Historical Society 632
Door County Library 632
Door County Library-Ephraim Branch 621
Door County Maritime Museum Archives 622, 632
Door County Maritime Museum Newsletter 622, 632
Door County Museum Archives 632
Doorway Quarterly Newsletter 583
Dooty-Duty-Rice Family 335
Dopp Family 563, 569
Dora Bee Woodyard Memorial Library 612
Dorcheat Historical Association of Webster Parish 239
Dorchester County Genealogical Magazine 257
Dorchester County Genealogical Society 261
Dorchester County Historical Society & Library 257
Dorchester County Library 517
Dorchester County Public Library 257
Dorchester Historical Society & Archives 270
Dordt College Library 208
Doric House Museum 370
Doris & Harry Vise Library 529
Doris M Reinke Resource Center 620
Doris Wood Branch Library 442
Dorland Newsletter 67
Dorman-McDorman Family 547
Dormann Library 389
Dorn Historical Restoration Association 516
Dorney (Turni) Newsletter 262
Dorot: The Journal of Jewish Genealogy 407
Dorothea B Hoover Historical Society 331
Dorothy Alling Memorial Library 580
Dorothy Bramlage Public Library 216
Dorothy Page Museum 13
Dorothy's House Museum Archives 680
Dorrill-Dorrell-Darrell Family File 131
Dorset Historical Society 576
Dorsey Dreams: Our Dorsey Family Newsletter 35
Dorsey Family 599
Dorwart-Sabin Family 569
Dory Shop Museum Archives 676
Doss Family 570
Dossin Great Lakes Museum Archives 289
Dostal Family 56
Dothage Family 339
Doty Family 277, 450
Douberly-Dubberly Family 133
Doud Family 392
Dougan-Scowden Family 482
Dougherty County Public Library 125
Doughty Family 373
Douglas & Judith Krupp Library 509
Douglas Clan 2
Douglas College Library 652
Douglas County Genealogical Society 130, 176, 305, 609
Douglas County Genealogical Society & Library 217
Douglas County Genealogical Society Newsletter 217
Douglas County Historical and Genealogical Society 325
Douglas County Historical and Genealogical Society Journal 325
Douglas County Historical Museum 354, 521, 632
Douglas County Historical Society 82, 305, 609
Douglas County Historical Society & Archives 217, 354, 355, 479, 521, 632
Douglas County Historical Society & Library 355
Douglas County Libraries 82
Douglas County Library 479
Douglas County Museum Archives 479
Douglas County Pioneer 479
Douglas County Public Library-Philip S Miller Branch 82
Douglas County Society Newsletter 217
Douglas Historical Society 270
Douglas Indian Band 650
Douglas Library of Hebron 95
Douglas Public Library 15
Douglas Trails and Traces 176
Douglas Williams House Museum 19
Douglass Family 162
Douglass Historical Museum Library 213
Douglass-Woofter Union 118
Doukhoubor Society Museum Archives 711
Dousman History 170
Dousman Stagecoach Inn Museum 618
Douthit Ancestry 88
Doutt Dialogues 339
Dover Historical Society 576, 580
Dover Historical Society & Archives 270
Dover Historical Society & Archives 447
Dover Historical Society Newsletter 447
Dover Public Library 103, 360
Dover Town Library 270
Dover-Foxcroft Historical Society 245
Dowagiac Public Library 290
Dowdell Library of South Amboy 378
Dowden Newsletter 262
Down on the Farm 610, 632
Downeast Ancestry 248
Downen Family 584
Downers Grove Historical Society & Archives 158
Downers Grove Park Museum 158
Downers Grove Public Library 158
Downey City Library 43
Downey Family 167

Downey Historical Society & Library 43
Downey Historical Society Newsletter 43
Downieville Museum Archives 43
Downing Family 295, 335
Downing House Museum Archives 335
Downington Historical Society & Library 486
Downingtown Library Company 486
Downriver Genealogical Society & Library 296
Downriver Seeker 296
Downs Carnegie Library 213
Downs Family 230
Downs Genealogical Society 213
Downstate Delaware Genealogical Society 103
Dows Community Library 201
Dows Depot Museum 201
Dows Historical Society 201
Doyle Family 369, 635
Doylestown Historical Society 488
Dr Daniel W Kissam House Museum Archives 400
Dr Eugene Clark Library 552
Dr Henry H Payne Community Museum Archives 667
Dr Howe Medical Museum 70
Dr Howe-Waffle Victorian House 70
Dr Increase Matthews House Museum 461
Dr John Archer Library 709
Dr John Burroughs House Museum 420
Dr John Harris Dental Museum Archives 441
Dr John Woodenlegs Memorial Library 345
Dr Kate Newcomb Museum 634
Dr Martin Luther King, Jr Library 608
Dr Pepper Museum Archives 562
Dr Samuel D Harris National Museum of Dentistry Archives 255
Dr W B Konkle Memorial Library 494
Dr William Robinson Plantation 369
Dr Woods House Museum Archives 644
Dracut Historical Society 270
Dragon, the Thistle and the Harp 340
Dragoo Family 611
Dragoo Family News 113
Drain-Jordan Library 613
Drake Family 340
Drake House Museum 376
Drake Well Museum 503
Draper Family 565
Draper Historical Society & Library 566
Drayton Hall Museum Archives 512
Drayton Valley Museum Archives 642
Dread Nought 78
Dreadnought 551
Dreibelbis Family 370
Drennan Family 139
Drescher-Hoeft-Hertges-Ferber Family 606
Dresden Brick School House 245
Dresden Historical Society & Archives 245
Drew County Historical Journal 30
Drew County Historical Museum 30
Drew County Historical Society & Archives 30
Drew County Historical Society and Museum Notes 30
Drew University Library 372
Drewry Family 114
Drifting River Museum Archives 659
Driftwood Gazette 476
Driftwood Public Library 476
Drips-Dripps Family 353
Droke Family Association Newsletter 51
Drover's Post 517, 518
Drugge-Holmqvist Family 565
Drum Barracks Civil War Museum and Research Library Archives 78
Drumheller and District Society Museum Archives 642
Drumheller Municipal Library 642
Drumlin Farm Education Center Archives 273
Drummer Boy 418
Drummond Historical Society & Archives 620
Drummond Home Archives 466
Drummond Island Historical Museum 290
Drummond Island Historical Society & Archives 290
Drummond Museum 620
Drummond Public Library 344
Drummons-McMorris-Shelly Family 47
Drury Family 161
Drury Family 368
Dry Tortugas National Park Archives 115
Dryden and District Museum Archives 681
Dryden Family 470
Dryden Historical Society 290, 395
Dryden Public Library 681
Du Quoin Public Library 158
Du Trieux Family 299, 685
Duane G Meyer Library 340
Duane Town Historian 404
Duarte Historical Museum 43
Duarte Historical Society & Archives 43
Dubh Ghlase 2
Dublin Historical Preservation Association & Archives 43
Dublin Historical Society & Library 360, 447
Dublin Historical Society Newsletter 360
Dublin House Museum 43
Dublin Public Library 182, 543
Dublin-Lauren Museum 130
Dubois Area Historical Society 486
Dubois County Genealogical Society 183
Dubois County Genealogical Society Newsletter 183
Dubois County Historical Society & Library 187
DuBois Family 406
Dubois Museum Archives 635
DuBois-Marble Family 74
Dubuque County Historical Society & Archives 201
Dubuque County Library 202
Dubuque County-Key City Genealogical Society & Library 201
Dubuque County-Key City Genealogical Society Newsletter 201
Ducas 374
Duce Family 603
Duck Lake Regional Interpretive Centre 706
Duckstein Family 583
Duckworth Library 140
Dudley Family 363
Dudley Knox Library 55
Dudley Township Public Library 221
Duelge-Diilge Family 38
Duesing Daze 219

Duff Community Heritage Museum 706
Dufferin County Museum Archives 689
Dufferin Historical Museum Archives 659
Dufflebag 591
Dufur Historical Society 474
Dugan Family Newsletter 48
Duggan Library 185
Dugger Coal Museum Archives 182
Duhan Family 389
Duke Homestead State Historic Site Archives 426
Duke University Special Collections Library 426
Dukes County Historical Museum 270
Dukes County Historical Society & Archives 270
Dukes County Inteligencer 270
Dulaney-Browne Library 467
Dulany Family 158
Dulany Library 340
Dulong Family 286
Duluth Public Library 307
Duman-Etling-Wilkerson-Wilkinson Family 352
Dumas Genealogical and Historical Society 543
Dumbarton House 106
Dumbarton House Archives 105
Dunbar Clan 232
Dunbar Family 271, 575, 605, 606
Dunbar House Archives 447
Dunbarton Public Library 360
Duncan Association Newsletter 186
Duncan Association Newsletter 222
Duncan Cottage Museum Library 13
Duncan Memorial Library 198
Duncan Public Library 464
Duncan Tavern Shrine Archives 232
Duncan Train Station 649
Duncan-Butler Family 547
Duncanville Genealogical Society 543
Duncanville Genealogical Society Newsletter 543
Duncanville Public Library 543
Dundalk-Patapsco Neck Historical Society & Library 258
Dundalk-Patapsco Neck Historical Society Newsletter 258
Dundas Historical Museum 682
Dundas Historical Society & Archives 682
Dundas Public Library 682
Dundee Area Historical Society 395
Dundee Library 395
Dundee Township Historical Museum 158
Dundee Township Historical Society & Archives 158
Dundee Township Public Library 158
Dundee Township Public Library Newsletter 158
Dundurn Catle Museum Archives 683
Dundy County Historical Museum 349
Dundy County Historical Society 349
Dundy County Historical Society & Library 349
Dundy County Historical Society Newsletter 349
Dunedin Historical Society & Museum 112
Dunedin Public Library 112
Duneland Historical Museum 181
Duneland Historical Society & Archives 181
Duneland Notes 181
Dunham Hall 151
Dunham Tavern Museum Bulletin 445
Dunham Tavern Museum Library 445
Dunkelberger Family 500
Dunkerton Family 473
Dunklin County Genealogical Society 333
Dunklin County Genealogical Society Newsletter 333
Dunklin County Library 333
Dunklin County Missouri Genealogical Society 333
Dunklin County Museum Archives 333
Dunlop-Dunlap Family 83, 89, 424
Dunn County Genealogical Society 626
Dunn County Heritage Museum 626
Dunn County Historical Society & Archives 626
Dunn County Historical Society & Library 437
Dunn Descendants 153
Dunn Family 50, 227, 565
Dunn House 399
Dunnagan Family 618
Dunrobin Piper 172, 273
Dunsmuir Historic Estate Museum Archives 57
Dunstable Free Public Library 270
Dunton Post 151
Dunwell and Community Museum Archives 711
Dup Museum and Historical Society 572
DuPage County Genealogical Society 165, 177
DuPage County Genealogical Society Newsletter 165
DuPage County Historical Museum 177
DuPage County Historical Society 172
DuPage County Historical Society & Archives 177
DuPage Roots 177
Duplin County Historical Society & Archives 432
Duplin County Library 429
DuPont Historical Museum 601
DuPont Historical Society 601
DuPont-Ball Library 111
Dupy Family Newsletter 198
Duquet(te) Family 281
Durand Public Library 620
Durango Public Library 84
Durant House Museum Archives 173
Durch Die Fensterscheibe (Through the Windowpane): Scheib, Shipe, Shive Family 154
Durham Center Museum Library 396
Durham County Library 426
Durham Family 218
Durham Historic Association & Library 360
Durham Historic Association Newsletter 360
Durham Historical Society 92, 245, 500
Durham Public Library 92
Durham Western Heritage Museum 355
Durham Western Heritage Museum Archives 355
Durham-Orange Genealogical Society 424
Durham-Orange Genealogical Society Newsletter 424
Durham-Phillips Newsletter 328
Durick Library 576
Durkee Family Newsletter 51
Durrell Museum Archives 667
Durst-Stanton Family 258
Durtschi Family 569
Dusable Museum 154

DuSable Museum of African-American History Archives 155
Dust & Cobwebs 240
Dustin-Anderson Family 149
Dusty Shelf 336
Dusty Trails 637
Dutch Church Transcripts 374
Dutch Family Heritage Society 573
Dutch Family Heritage Society Newsletter 573
Dutch Family Heritage Society Quarterly 573
Dutch Fork Chapter, SCGS 512
Dutch Fork Digest 512
Dutch Settlers Society of Albany 387
Dutch Settlers Society of Albany Yearbook 387
Dutch-American Genealogist 374
Dutcher-Perry Clan 121
Dutchess 412
Dutchess County Genealogical Society & Library 412
Dutchess County Historical Society & Archives 412
Dutchess County Historical Society Collections 412
Dutchess County Historical Society Yearbook 412
Dutchess Historian 412
Dutson Family 572
Dutton Family 100
Dutton-Davis-Jackson-Doane Family 623
Dutton-Jefferis Family 149
Duvall Family 258, 444
Duvall Historical Society 601
DuVernet Family 126
Duxbury Free Library 270
Duxbury Historical Museum 270
Duxbury Rural and Historical Society & Archives 270
Duxbury Rural and Historical Society Newsletter 270
Dvey-Baxter Family 476
Dwight B Waldo Library 295
Dwight D Eisenhower Library 211
Dwight Foster Public Library 621
Dwight Genealogical Society 158
Dwight Historical Society 158
Dwyer-Mercer County District Library 443
Dyar-Dyer Family 457
Dyckman Farmhouse Museum Archives 406
Dyckman Farmhouse Museum Newsletter 406
Dyckman Free Library 315
Dyckman-Dikeman-Dykeman Family 572
Dye Family 600
Dyer Family 262, 312
Dyer Historical Society 182
Dyer Library 250
Dyer Library Association Newsletter 250
Dyer Memorial Library 265
Dyersville Area Historical Society & Library 201
Dysart Historical Society 201, 706

E

E C Scranton Memorial Library 95
E Clampus Vitus, Sacramento Chapter 63
E H Butler Library 391
E H Little Library 425
E M Oboler Library 149
E M Violette Museum Archives 333
E P Foster Library 76
E S Bird Library 418
E St Julien Cox House Museum Archives 315
E T Roux Library 115
E W King Library 525
E Y Berry Library 524
EAA Airventure Museum Archives 628
Eager Free Public Library 621
Eagle Bend Historical Society 307
Eagle Bluff Lighthouse Museum Archives 621
Eagle County Historical Society & Library 84
Eagle Gate 134
Eagle Historical Museum 12, 620
Eagle Historical Society & Archives 620
Eagle Historical Society & Library 12
Eagle Historical Society Newsletter 12
Eagle Pass Public Library 543
Eagle Public Library 146
Eagle River Historical Museum 620
Eagle River Historical Society & Archives 620
Eagle Rock Cultural Center 43
Eagle Rock Railroad Historical Society 147
Eagle Rock Valley Historical Society & Library 43
Eagle Tavern Museum Archives 139
Eagle Valley Enterprise 84
Eagle Valley Library District 84
Eagle Wireless 12
Eagle's Nest 393
Eakin Family 475
Eames-Ames Family 199
Ear Falls District Museum Archives 682
Earl Family 567
Earl Greg Swem Library 597
Earl K Long Library 240
Earl Park Public Library 182
Earl Township Public Library 158
Earle-Harrison House Museum Archives 562
Earlville Community Historical Society 158
Earlville Free Library 396
Early American Industries Society 279
Early American Museum Archives 165
Early County Historical Society 127
Early Family 546
Early Grenville 688
Early Issues of the Publications of the Alabama Genealogical Society 1
Early Meredith 362
Early Mormon Research Institute 567
Earnest Family 486, 492
Earnest-Ernest-Earnist-Arnest Family 606
Earnst Family 195
Easey Newsletter 121
Easlick-Eastlick-Eslick Newsletter 74
East Alabama Genealogical Society 8
East Albemarle Regional Library 426
East Arkansas Community College Library 27
East Ascension Genealogical and Historical Society 237
East Baker Historical Society 135
East Baton Rouge Parish Library 235
East Baton Rouge Parish Library, Bluebonnet Regional Branc 235
East Baton Rouge Parish Library-Centroplex 235

East Bay Genealogical Society & Library 57
East Bell County Genealogical Society & Library 561
East Bell Genealogical Society 561
East Benton County Historical Society 605
East Benton County Historical Society & Library 602
East Berlin Historical Preservation Society 486
East Bonner County Free Public Library District 149
East Bridgewater Public Library 270
East Brunswick Museum Archives 369
East Brunswick Museum Newsletter 369
East Brunswick Public Library 369
East Carroll Parish Library 238
East CCC Historical Society 212
East Central Arkansas Regional Library 33
East Central Arkansas Regional Library-Woodruff County Library 25
East Central Florida Genealogical Society 116
East Central Georgia Regional Library-Burke County Library 139
East Central Regional Library 306
East Chamber Agriculture Historical Society 563
East Chicago Historical Society & Archives 182
East Chicago Public Library 182
East Contra Costa Historical Museum 38
East Contra Costa Historical Society & Archives 38
East Contra Costa Museum Archives 38
East Coulee School Museum Archives 642
East Cuyahoga County Chapter, OGS 451
East Detroit Historical Society 290
East Durham Historical Society & Library 688
East End Seaport Museum Archives 399
East European Genealogical Society 662
East Feliciana History Committee 236
East Fishkill Historical Society 400
East Florida Gazette 121
East Georgia College Library 138
East Georgia Genealogical Society 130, 139
East Granby Public Library 93
East Greenbush Community Library 396
East Greenwich Free Library 507
East Greenwich Historic Preservation Society 507
East Haddam Free Public Library 96
East Haddam Historical Society & Library 93
East Hampton Free Library 396
East Hampton Historical Society 387
East Hampton Historical Society & Archives 396
East Hampton Public Library 93
East Hampton Town Marine Museum Archives 387
East Hanover Historical Society 488
East Hants Historical Museum Archives 675
East Hants Historical Society 675
East Hartford Historical Society 93
East Hartford Public Library 93
East Haven Historical Society & Library 93
East Hillsborough Historical Society 120
East Hounsfield Free Library 420
East Islip Public Library 396
East Jersey Old Towne Museum Archives 376
East Jersey Old Towne Museum Newsletter 376
East Jordan Portside Historical Museum Archives 290
East Jordan Portside Historical Museum Newsletter 290
East Kentucky Museum And History Center Archives 229
East Kern Genealogical Society 56
East Kern Genealogical Society & Library 38
East Kern Genealogical Society Newsletter 38
East Kootenay Historical Association 649
East Lansing Historical Society 290
East Lansing Public Library 290
East Linn Historical Society 480
East Lyme Historical Society & Archives 93, 97
East Lyme Public Library 97
East Machias Historical Society 245
East Meadow Public Library 396
East Mississippi Regional Library System-Waynesboro Memorial Library 323
East Morgan County Library District 82
East of Islip 396
East Orange Public Library 369
East Otter Tail Historical Society 313
East Palestine Area Historical Society 447
East Palestine Memorial Public Library 447
East Parker County Library 535
East Point Historical Society 126
East Point Historical Society & Library 130
East Point Public Library 130
East Polk Heritage Center 308
East Poultney Historical Museum 576
East Poultney Historical Society & Archives 576
East Providence Historical Society 509
East Providence Historical Society & Archives 507
East Providence Public Library 507
East Providence Public Library Newsletter 507
East River Genealogical Forum 524
East River Genealogical Society 524
East Rockaway Public Library 396
East Saint Louis Public Library 158
East Santa Clara Street Revitalization Committee 67
East Side Genealogical Society Bulletin Board 599
East Side Historical Society 155
East Smithfield Public Library 507
East Syracuse Free Library 396
East Tennessee Heritage Foundation 531
East Tennessee Historical Center 528
East Tennessee Historical Museum 529
East Tennessee Historical Society & Archives 529
East Tennessee Historical Society's Publications 529
East Tennessee Roots 531
East Texas Family Records 561
East Texas Genealogical Society & Library 561
East Texas Genealogical Society Newsletter: The Bulletin 561
East Texas Historical Association 554
East Texas Historical Journal 554
East Texas Oil Museum Archives 550
East Troy Area Historical Society 620
East Troy Electric Railroad Museum Archives 620
East Troy Lions Public Library 620
East Williston Public Library 396
East Windsor Historical Society & Archives 93
East Windsor Historical Society Newsletter 93
East Yuma County Historical Society & Library 90
Eastchester Historical Society 390
Eastchester Historical Society & Library 396
Eastend School Museum Archives 706

Easter Family 178
Easterling Family 25
Easterling Family Genealogical Society 323
Easterling Family Newsletter 323
Eastern & Central European Genealogist 42
Eastern Arizona Museum 19
Eastern Band of Cherokee Indians 425
Eastern California Museum Archives 48
Eastern Cherokee Southern Iroquois and United Tribes 513
Eastern Counties Regional Library 675
Eastern Fresno County Historical Society 36
Eastern Genealogical PPQ 370
Eastern Kentucky Genealogical Society & Library 225
Eastern Mississippi Regional Library 322
Eastern Monroe Public Library 502
Eastern Nebraska Genealogical Society & Library 351
Eastern Nebraska Genealogical Society Newsletter 351
Eastern North Carolina Genealogical Society 430
Eastern Oregon Museum on the Old Oregon Trail Archives 475
Eastern Pennsylvania Conference of the United Methodist Church Historical Society & Library 497
Eastern Shore Of Virginia Historical Society 592
Eastern Shore of Virginia Historical Society & Library 592
Eastern Shore of Virginia Historical Society Newsletter 592
Eastern Shore Public Library 583
Eastern State Penitentiary Historic Site Archives 497
Eastern Washington Genealogical Society 607
Eastern Washington Genealogical Society Bulletin 607
Eastern Washington State Historical Society & Archives 607
Eastham Historical Museum 270
Eastham Historical Society & Archives 270
Eastham Public Library 270
Eastland Centennial Memorial Library 543
Eastland County Genealogical Society 543
Eastland Disaster Historical Society & Library 151
Easton Area Public Library 486
Easton Historical Society 93, 245
Easton Historical Society & Library 276
Easton Library 399
Eastpoint Memorial Library 290
Eastside Genealogical Society & Archives 599
Eastside Genealogical Society, Italian Interest Group 599
Eastside Heritage Center Archives 599
Easttown Township Library 482
Eastville Community Historical Society 414
East-West Center Archives 141
Eastwood-Guy-Coffey-Studer Family 188
Eaton County Genealogical Society & Archives 288
Eaton County Historical Commission 288
Eaton County Quest 288
Eaton Family 467
Eaton Hall Museum 578
Eatonton-Putnam County Historical Society & Library 130
Eau Claire District Library 290
Eaves Family 131
Eaves-Eves Family 122
Ebbott Family 316
Ebenezer Maxwell Mansion Museum Archives 497
Ebenezer Maxwell Mansion Newsletter 497
Ebensburg Free Public Library 486
Eberly Family 503, 505
Eccles-Lesher Memorial Library 500
Echo 306, 334, 398, 632
ECHO Diary 397
ECHO Newsletter 397
Echo Park Historical Society 43
Echoes 33, 446
Echoes of Old Shelby 193
Echoes of the Past 235
Echoes Through the Pines 552
Echols County Historical Society 132, 137
Echos Genealogiques 702
Eck Family Newsletter 50
Eckelberry Family 116
Eckhart Public Library 179
Eckles Memorial Library 206
Eckley Miners' Village Library 505
Eckley Miners' Village Museum Archives 486
Eckley Miners' Village Newsletter 486
Ecole du Rang II 697
Ecomusee de la Haute-Beauce 702
Ecorse Public Library 290
Ecoutez 241
ECSU Library Newsletter 101
Ector County Library 555
Ed and Hazel Richmond Public Library 535
Eddens Family 4
Eddy County Genealogical Society & Archives 382
Eddy Family 270
Eddy Homestead Association 275
Edelen Family Newsletter 241
Eden Historical Society & Library 396
Eden Prairie Historical Society 307
Edenfield Genealogical Society 139
Edenfield Genealogical Society Newsletter 139
Edens Family 241
Eden-Webster Library 339
Edgar Allan Poe Cottage Archives 390
Edgar Allan Poe House & Museum Archives 255
Edgar Allan Poe Museum Archives 593
Edgar Allan Poe National Historic Site Archives 497
Edgar County Genealogical Society 170
Edgar County Genealogical Society Quarterly 170
Edgar County Genealogy Library 170
Edgar County Historical Museum 170
Edgar County Historical Society & Archives 170
Edgar County Historical Society Newsletter 170
Edgar Family 326, 570
Edgecombe County Memorial Library 433
Edgecombe County Memorial Library Newsletter 433
Edgecome County Genealogical Society & Archives 433
Edgefield County Genealogical Society 514
Edgefield County Historical Society & Library 514
Edgemont Public Library 521
Edgerton and District Museum Archives 642
Edgerton Public Library 620
Edgewater Historical Society 155
Edgewood Historical Society 543
Edgings & Trimmings 238
Edina Historical Society & Library 307

Edina Historical Society Newsletter 307
Edinboro Area Historical Society 486
Edinburg Public Library 543
Edinburg Wright-Hageman Public Library 183
Edinburgh Square Heritage and Cultural Centre Archives 680
Edison & Ford Winter States Museum Archives 112
Edison Museum Archives 537
Edison National Historic Site Archives 380
Edison Township Free Public Library 369
Edisonian 200
Edisto Echoes 514
Edisto Island Historic Preservation Society & Archives 514
Edisto Island Historical Museum 514
Edith Abbott Memorial Library 352
Edith Belle Libby Memorial Library 249
Edith Garland Dupre Library 238
Edler-Morosini Newsletter 548
Edmond Genealogical Society 464
Edmond Historical Museum 465
Edmond Historical Society & Archives 465
Edmond Historical Society Newsletter 465
Edmonds-Harrison Family 146
Edmondson Family 307
Edmonds-South Snohomish County Historical Museum 601
Edmonds-South Snohomish County Historical Society & Archives 601
Edmonson County Public Library 226
Edmonton and District Historical Society 643
Edmonton Public Library 643
Edmonton Public Schools Museum Archives 643
Edmonton Telephone Historical Centre Archives 643
Edmore Historical Society 437
Edmund Fowle House 281
Edmund S Muskie Archives 247
Edmund Stanley Library 223
Edmunds Newsletter 311
Edna Historical Museum 213
Edom Historical Society 544
Edsel and Eleanor Ford House Museum Archives 293
Edson and District Public Library 643
Edson Family 338
Edward Devotion House 268
Edward Family Historical Review 155
Edward H Broadhead Library 89
Edward H White II Memorial Museum Archives 538
Edward H. Nabb Research Center for DelMarVa History and Culture 262
Edward Hopper Landmark Preservation Foundation & Archives 409
Edward Livingston Historical Association 238
Edward-Dean Museum and Gardens 40
Edwards County Genealogical Society 151
Edwards County Historical Museum 216, 219
Edwards County Historical Society & Archives 216, 219
Edwards County Historical Society & Library 151
Edwards County Historical Society Quarterly 151
Edwards Family 168, 416, 573
Edwards History Center 396
Edwards Journal 260
Edwards Museum 269
Edwards Public Library 279
Edwards-Sahnow-Borchardt-Duxbury-Blackburn-Blackbourn Family 625
Edwardsville Public Library 158
Edwin A Bemis Library 87
Edwin Carter Museum Archives 81
Edwin H Mookini Library 141
Edwin Wolters Museum Archives 560
Edythe L Dyer Community Library 246
Eel Ground Indian Band 664
Eel River Bar Indian Band 663
Eells Family 482
Eells-Stow House 96
Effie and Wilton Hebert Public Library 556
Effingham County Genealogical Society & Archives 159
Effingham County Genealogical Society Newsletter 159
Effingham Historical Society 360
Effingham Public Library 360
Effingham Regional Historical Society 159
Egan Institute of Maritime Studies Archives 275
Egbert Starr Library 577
Egerton-Calvert Family 260
Egg Harbor City Historical Society 369
Eggert Family 536
Eggleston Family 116
Eggleston Library 588
Eglin Air Force Base Library 112
Ehattesaht Indian Tribe 648
Ehrhart Museum Archives 441
Ehrhart Museum Newsletter 441
Ehrlicher Research Center 170
Ehrman Mansion Museum Archives 74
EHS Heritage Council 227
Eibl-Dichtl-Dichtel Family 81
Eichelman Family 29
Eider 251
Eidrid Township Museum Archives 679
Eidson Newsletter 563
Eighteenth-Century Life 426
Eighteenth-Century Studies 256
Ein Schnabel Fur Nachrichten (A Nose for News) 325
Einman, Eiman, Eyman Family 454
Eipper Kin-Ship 165
Eirich (Eyrich-Irick)-Henton-Irick (Erich, Eurich) Family 63
Eisenberg Family 495
Eisenhower Birthplace Historic Site Archives 543
Eisenhower National Historic Site Library 488
Eisenhower Public Library District 162
Eisloeffel Family Newsletter 152
Eiteljorg Museum of American Indians and Western Art Archives 186
Eitzen Historical Society 307
Ekalaka Public Library 344
Ekes Family 239
El Cajon Historical Society & Library 43
El Campo Museum Archives 544
El Centro Public Library 43
El Coqui de Ayer 389
El Dorado County Historical Society & Archives 60
El Dorado County Library 60
El Dorado County Museum Archives 60
El Dorado Research Society & Archives 43
El Escribano: The Journal of Saint Augustine History 121
El Molino Viejo Museum Archives 69
El Monte Historical Museum 43

El Monte Historical Society 43
El Morro National Monument Archives 384
El Palacio 385
El Paso County Historical Society & Library 544
El Paso County Library 544
El Paso De Robles Area Historical Society & Library 59
El Paso de Robles Area Pioneer Museum Archives 59
El Paso Genealogical Library 544
El Paso Genealogical Society & Archives 544
El Paso Holocaust Museum Archives 544
El Paso Museum of History Archives 544
El Paso Museum of History Newsletter 544
El Paso Public Library 159, 544
El Progreso Memorial Library 562
El Pueblo de los Angeles Historical Monument Archives 51
El Pueblo Museum Archives 89
El Rancho de las Golondrinas Museum Archives 384
El Reno Carnegie Library 465
El Segundo Public Library 43
Ela Historical Society 164
Eland Area Historical Society & Archives 620
Elbert County Historical Society & Library 130
Elbert County Library 86
Elbert Hubbard-Roycroft Historical Museum 396
Elbert Hubbard-Roycroft Historical Society & Archives 396
Elberton Granite Museum Archives 130
Elbow Museum Archives 706
Elbridge Free Library 396
Elburn and Countryside Historical Society 159
ELCA Archives Network News 159
Elder Brewster Press 395
Elder Brewster Society 395
Elder Clan 558
Elder Family 427
Elder Family Newsletter 260
Elder William Brewster Society 270
Eldon Hall Sibbald Memorial Museum Archives 690
Eldon House Museum Archives 685
Eldon Public Library 201
Eldora Public Library 201
Eldredge Public Library 268
Eldridge Family 444
Eldridge Family 58
Eldridge Street Project Museum Archives 406
Eleanor Daggett Memorial Public Library 382
Eleanor Ellis Public Library 629
Eleanor Roosevelt National Historic Site Archives 401
Eleanor S Brockenbrough Library 594
Electronic Railway Historical Association of Southern California 51
Elephant Hotel Museum 416
Eleutherian Hills-Hagley Foundation & Library 103
Eleventh Circuit Historical Society 126
Elfreth's Alley Association 497
Elfreth's Alley Museum 497
Elgin Area Historical Museum 159
Elgin Area Historical Society & Archives 159
Elgin County Pioneer Museum Archives 689
Elgin County Public Library 689
Elgin Genealogical Society & Library 159
Elgin Genealogical Society Newsletter 159
Elgin Historical Society 351
Elgin Military Museum Archives 689
Elgin Public Library 201, 475
Eli Whitney Museum Archives 94
Elihu Burritt Library 96
Elijah Clark Memorial Museum Archives 133
Elijah Gillespie-Locke-Holloway-Ralston Family 480
Elijah P Lovejoy Library 158
Eliot Historical Society 246
Elisabet Ney Museum Library 536
Elisha D Smith Public Library 626
Elisha Kent Kane Historical Society 406
Elissa Log 546
Eliza Cruce Hall Doll Collection Archives 463
Elizabeth Dafoe Library 662
Elizabeth J Johnson Pawtucket History Research Center 508
Elizabeth Public Library 369
Elizabeth Taber Library 274
Elizabeth Taber Library Newsletter 274
Elizabeth Township Historical Society & Library 483
Elizabethton Public Library 527
Elizabethtown Community College Library 227
Elizabethtown Historical Foundation 369
Elizabethtown Historical Society 486
Elizabethtown Library 396
Elk City Carnegie Library 465
Elk City Genealogical Society of Western Oklahoma 465
Elk County Historical Society & Library 214, 500
Elk Grove Historical Society 159
Elk Grove Historical Society Newsletter 159
Elk Grove Village Public Library 159
Elk Grove-The Peony Village Highlights 159
Elk Horn 500
Elk Lake Heritage Museum Archives 682
Elk Rapids Area Historical Society 290
Elkader Public Library 201
Elkhart County Genealogical Society 183
Elkhart County Historical Museum 180
Elkhart County Historical Society & Archives 180
Elkhart County Historical Society Newsletter 180
Elkhart Historical Society 159
Elkhart Public Library 183
Elkhorn City Public Library 227
Elkhorn Valley Genealogical Society 357
Elkhorn Valley Historical Society 354
Elkhorn Valley Historical Society Newsletter 354
Elkhorn Valley Museum Archives 354
Elkin Public Library 426
Elkins Public Library 359
Elkland Area Community Library 486
Ella Johnson Memorial Public Library District 162
Ella M Everhard Public Library 459
Ella Sharp Museum Archives 294
Ella Sharp Museum Quarterly 294
Ellen Payne Odom Genealogy Library 135
Ellenberger Family 620
Ellensburg Genealogical Group 601
Ellensburg Public Library 601
Ellenville Public Library and Museum 396
Eller Family 432, 541

Ellerslie Shellfish Museum Archives 695
Ellett Family 539
Ellicott City B&O Railroad Station Museum Archives 258
Ellicottville Historical Society 396
Ellingson Car Museum Archives 313
Elliot Clan 138
Elliot Lake Nuclear and Mining Museum Archives 682
Elliot Lake Public Library 682
Elliott Avedon Museum and Archives of Games 692
Elliott Clan 428
Elliott Empire 292
Elliott Family 17, 295, 594
Elliott Museum 122
Elliott Public Library 201
Ellis County Genealogical Society 562
Ellis County Historical Museum 215
Ellis County Historical Society & Archives 215
Ellis County Museum Archives 562
Ellis County Museum Newsletter 562
Ellis Family 546
Ellis Island Immigration Museum Archives 403
Ellis Newsletter 470
Ellis Public Library 213
Ellison Family 565
Ellison Library 433
Ellsinore Pioneer Museum Archives 328
Ellsworth County Historical Museum 213
Ellsworth County Historical Society & Archives 213
Ellsworth Historical Society 246
Ellsworth Public Library 201, 246, 620
Ellwood City Area Historical Society 486
Ellwood House Museum Archives 157
Elm Fork Echoes 540
Elm Grove Public Library 620
Elm Grove School Heritage Society 690
Elma Historical Society 396
Elma Public Library 201
Elma Ross Public Library 525
Elman W Campbell Museum Archives 686
Elmbrook Historical Society & Archives 618
Elmendorf Air Force Base Library 12
Elmer E Rasmuson Library 12
Elmer Ellis Library 327
Elmhurst Historical Museum 159
Elmhurst Historical Museum Archives 159
Elmhurst Historical Society 159
Elmira Railway Museum Archives 695
Elmont Public Library 397
Elmore Area Historical Society 307
Elmore County Historical Foundation & Archives 148
Elmore County Historical Museum 148
Elmore County Historical Society & Museum 10
Elmore County Historical Society Quarterly 10
Elmshaven-E G White Home Archives 64
Elmwood Historical Society & Archives 159
Elmwood Park Historical Society 159
Elmwood Park Public Library 159
Eloy Public Library 16
Elrose Heritage Museum Archives 706
Elroy Area Historical Museum 621
Elroy Area Historical Society & Archives 621
Elsah History 159
Elsasser-Mackey-Hedric Family 569
Elsbree Family 605
Elsebuch-Broderson Family 51
Elsey Family 296
Elsie Historical Society & Library 290
Elswick Family 387
Elswood Family 570
Elting Memorial Library 406
Elton S Karrmann Library 629
Elverhoj Museum Newsletter 72
Elwood Echoes 476
Elwood Family 601
Elwood Haynes Home Museum Archives 187
Elwood Pipecreek Genealogical Society 183
Elwood Pipecreek Historical Society 183
Ely Library 282
Ely Public Library 201
Elyria Public Library 448
Ely-Winton Historical Society & Library 307
Emanuel County Historic Society & Archives 138
Emanuel Family 5
Emblematica 391
Embodied Spirits 314
Emerich Family 447
Emerson Family 414
Emerson Public Library 201
Emery Family 145
Emfield Historical Society 146
Emigrant Trail Museum Archives 63
Emigrant Trails Historical Study Series 331
Emily Dickinson Museum Archives 265
Emily Dickinson Museum Newsletter 265
Emily Kimbrough House Archives 190
Emline Fairbanks Memorial Library 194
Emma Knox Kenan Public Library 5
Emma S Clark Memorial Library 416
Emma Waters Summar Library 528
Emmaus Historical Society 486
Emmaus Public Library 486
Emmert Family 625
Emmet County Genealogical Society 201, 300
Emmet County Historical Society & Archives 201
Emmetsburg Public Library 201
Emmett Kelly Historical Museum Archives 221
Emmitsburg Historical Society 259
Empire Area Heritage Group & Archives 290
Empire Area Historical Museum 290
Empire in Pine Logging Museum Archives 620
Empire Leader 290
Empire State Aerosciences Museum Archives 398
Emporia Public Library 213
Emsfield Historical Society Newsletter 146
Emsland Heritage Society 444
Encampment Museum News 636
Enchanted World Doll Museum Archives 523
Encinitas Historical Society 43, 50
Encino Historical Society 43
End Notes 637

End of Steel Heritage Museum Archives 644
Endeavor Historical Society 621
Enderby and District Museum Archives 649
Enderlin Municipal Library 437
Enders Family 502
Endnotes 132
End-O-Line Railroad Park Museum Archives 307
Endries Family 623
Endsley Family 467
Enfield Free Public Library 360
Enfield Historical Museum 360
Enfield Historical Society 93
Enfield Historical Society & Archives 360
Enfield Public Library 93
Enfield Shaker Museum Archives 360
Engelmann-Hilgard Family 291
Englandia 333
Englehart and Area Historical Museum Archives 682
Englehart and Area Public Library 682
Englewood Public Library 84, 369
Englewood Public Library Newsletter 369
English Genealogist 42
English Researcher 56
English River First Nation 709
English-Schlegel-Schlagel-Linse-Schlager Family 610
Ennis Public Library 544
Enoch Cree Nations 646
Enoch Harrington House 246
Enoch Pratt Free Library 255
Enoch Turner Schoolhouse Museum Archives 691
Enon Community Historical Society 448
Enos Mills Cabin Museum Archives 84
Enosburgh Historical Society 576
Enquirer Newsletter 417
Ensminger Family 301
Ensor Library 228
Enterprise Public Library 4, 475
Enumclaw Public Library 601
Epes Family 586
Ephemera 387
Ephraim Foundation Museum Archives 621
Ephraim Foundation Newsletter 621
Ephraim Historical Foundation 621
Ephraim Village Hall Archives 621
Ephrata Cloister Museum Archives 487
Ephrata Genealogical Society 601
Episcopal Church Center Records Office 406
Episcopal Church Diocese of Delaware Archives 103
Episcopal Church Historical Society & Library 536
Episcopal Church Home Archives 413
Episcopal Church, Diocesan Archives 141
Episcopal Diocese of Chicago Archives 155
Episcopal Diocese of Connecticut Diocesan Library 94
Episcopal Diocese of Missouri Archives 339
Episcopal Diocese of Western North Carolina Library 423
Epitaph 332
Epoch 296
Epping Historical Society 360
Eptek National Exhibition Centre 695
Epworth-by-the-Sea 136
Equinunk Historical Society 487
Erath County Genealogical Society 560
Erath Family 603
Ericson Public Library 197
Erie Canal Museum Archives 418
Erie Canal Village Museum Archives 414
Erie City Public Library 213
Erie County Chapter, OGS 457
Erie County Connection 457
Erie County Historical Society & Library 487
Erie County Public Library 487
Erie Historical Museum Archives 213
Erie Historical Museum Newsletter 213
Erie History Center 487
Erie Maritime Museum Archives 487
Erie Society for Genealogical Research & Archives 487
Eriksdale Museum Archives 659
Eriksen Family 43
Erikson Biographical Institute 509
Erkkila-Hautamaki Family 97
Erland Lee Museum Archives 690
Erlander Home Museum 172
Ermatinger Old Stone House Archives 689
Ermineskin Indian Band 644
Ernest Hemingway House Museum Archives 115
Ernest Miller White Library 230
Ernie Pyle State Historic Site Archives 182
Ernst Schowengerdt National Historic Site Archives 342
Errol Public Library 360
Erskine Caldwell Birthplace Museum Archives 134
Erskine Family 58
Erwin Family 571
Escabana Public Library 290
Escalon Historical Museum 43
Escalon Historical Society & Archives 43
Escambia County Genealogy Society 2
Escambia County Historical Society 119
Escambia County Historical Society & Library 2
Escambia County Historical Society Journal 2
Escanaba Public Library 291
Esch Family 44
Escondido Genealogial Society 43
Escondido Genealogical Society Newsletter 43
Escondido Historical Society & Archives 44
Escondido Public Library 44
Eskimo Museum Archives 659
Esko Historical Society 308
Espanola Public Library 382, 682
Esquatak Historical Society 392
Esquesing Historical Society 682
Esquimalt Indian Band 657
Essays and Monographs in Colorado History 83
Essential Club Free Library 392
E-ssentials Discoveries 158
Essex and Middle River Heritage Society 259
Essex Community Heritage Association & Library 397
Essex Community Historical Society 576
Essex County Historical Association 278
Essex County Historical Society & Archives 396
Essex Genealogist 274

Essex Historical Society & Archives 270
Essex Historical Society & Library 93
Essex Historical Society Quarterly Newsletter 93
Essex Institute & Library 278
Essex Institute Historical Collections 278
Essex Society of Genealogists 274
Essley-Noble Museum 151
Estacada Public Library 475
Estancia Public Library 382, 383
Estell Manor Historical Society 370
Estep Family Journal 542
Esterhazy Community Museum Archives 706
Estes Park Area Historical Museum 84
Estes Park Area Historical Society 84
Estes Park Genealogical Society 84
Estes Park Heritage Association 84
Estes Park Public Library 84
Estes Trails 322
Estes-Winn Antique Automobile Museum Archives 423
Estevan National Exhibition Centre Archives 706
Estey Family 409
Esther Swinkin Memorial Library 94
Esther Thomas Atkinson Museum Archives 588
Esther Thomas Atkinson Museum Newsletter 588
Estherville Public Library 201
Estill County Historical and Genealogical Society 233
Estill County Historical and Genealogical Society Newsletter 233
Estill County Public Library 229
Estill County Public Library Newsletter 229
Estonian American National Council & Archives 406
Estonian Central Archives in Canada 691
Estonian House 406
Estrella Warbird Museum Archives 59
Eswau Huppeday 433
Etched in Time 172
Etchingham-Van Trump-Trump-Heiney-Etchingham Family 87
Ethnic Heritage Museum Archives 172
Etiwanda Historical Society 44
Eton Family 268
Etowah Historical Society & Library 4
Etowah Valley Family Tree Climbers & Archives 128
Etowah Valley Historical Society & Archives 128
Euclid Public Library 448
Eudora Area Historical Society & Library 213
Eudora Area Newsletter 213
Eufaula Carnegie Library 4
Eufaula Heritage Association 4
Eugene Field House and Toy Museum Archives 339
Eugene Historical Society & Archives 475
Eugene McDermott Library 557
Eugene O'Neill National Historic Site Archives 42
Eugene Oregon Jewish Genealogy Study Group 475
Eugene P Watson Memorial Library 239
Eugene Public Library 475
Eugene V Debs Foundation & Library 194
Eugene V Debs Foundation Newsletter 194
Eula Dees Memorial Library 319
Euless Public Library 544
Eunice LeDoux Library 237
Eunice Public Library 382
Eureka California Senior Center Genealogy Group 44
Eureka Fire Museum Archives 373
Eureka Pioneer Museum Archives 521
Eureka Public Library District 159
Eureka School House Archives 579
Eureka Springs Historical Museum 27
Eureka Springs Historical Society & Archives 27
European History Quarterly 74
Eustis Historical Preservation Society 112
Eustis Historical Preservation Society Newsletter 112
Eustis Memorial Library 112
Eva B Dykes Library 5
Eva Brook Donly Museum 690
Eva K Bowlby Public Library 505
Eva K Bowlby Public Library Quarterly Newsletter 505
Evangelical and Reformed Historical Society & Archives 491
Evangelical Covenant Church Archives 155
Evangelical Lutheran Synod, Dept of Archives 310
Evangeline Genealogical & Historical Society Newsletter 242
Evangeline Genealogical and Historical Society 242
Evangeline Parish Library 242
Evans Ancestors 229
Evans Ancestry 340
Evans City Historical Museum 487
Evans City Historical Society & Archives 487
Evans County Historical Society 128
Evans Family 343, 345, 362, 446, 540
Evans Historical Society 388
Evans Mills Public Library 397
Evans Public Library 176
Evans-Draper-Gibson Family 566
Evansville Grove Society & Library 621
Evansville Historical Foundation 308
Evansville Museum of Arts and Science Archives 183
Evansville Museum of Arts and Science Newsletter 183
Evansville-Vanderburgh County Public Library 183
Evenson Family 635
Evenson-Knudsen-West-Powell Family 570
Events Calendar 477
Everaert Family 303
Everard Family 599
Everett Free Library 487
Everett Journal 11
Everett L Cattell Library 443
Everett Library 424
Everett Public Library 601
Evergreen Firearms Museum Archives 659
Evergreen Heritage Association 67
Evergreen Historic House Archives 673
Evergreen House Museum Archives 255
Evergreen Regional Library 660
Evergreen-Conecuh Public Library 4
Evermore 593
Everton Publisher's Library 568
Everton's Genealogical Helper 567
Evesham Historical Society 373
Evilsizer Family 381
Evitt Family 501
Ewell Family 573
Ewen Clan 468

Ewing Clan 560
Ewing Exchange 292
Ewing Reunion 235
Ewing Township Historical Preservation Society & Library 370
Ex Libris 168, 181, 285, 450
Excelsior House Museum Archives 550
Excelsior Springs Genealogical Society & Library 328
Excelsior-Lake Minnetonka Historical Society & Archives 308
Excelsior-Lake Minnetonka Historical Society News 308
Excerpts 223
Exchange 68
Exchange Hotel Civil War Museum Archives 588
Exchange Hotel Civil War Museum Newsletter 588
Exchange: A Newsletter for County and Local Historical Societies 625
Exeland Public Library 621
Exeter Historical Society & Library 360
Exeter Historical Society Newsletter 360
Exeter Public Library 360
Explorations 608
Express 478
Exum Exchange 89
Eye Openers 67
Eygner Family 394
Ezell Family 466
Ezra Meeker Historical Society 605

F

F T Hill Museum Archives 709
F Wilbur Gingrich Library 500
Faatz Family 570
Fabula Family Newsletter 49
Face Family 585
Factor's Walk Military Museum Archives 137
Facts and Findings 177
Facts and Traditions 384
Faded Genes 345
Fadner-Bovee-Trever Family 260
Fagan Clan Flyer 65
Fagan-Feagin-Fagon Family 333
Fahrney Family 257
Faigh Corrie 56
Fair Bluff Historical Society & Archives 426
Fair Grove Historical and Preservation Society 328
Fair Haven Free Public Library 576
Fair Haven Public Library 397
Fair Lane Estate Museum Archives 289
Fairbanks Family 269, 316
Fairbanks Genealogical Society & Library 12
Fairbanks Genealogical Society Newsletter 12
Fairbanks Historical Preservation Foundation 12
Fairbanks Museum Archives 579
Fairbanks Museum Newsletter 579
Fairbanks North Star Borough Public Library 12
Fairbury City Historical Society 351
Fairchild Base Library 601
Fairchild-Martindale Library 482
Fairfax Community Library 576
Fairfax County Public Library 586, 587
Fairfax Depot Restoration Association 308
Fairfax Genealogical Society 591
Fairfax Genealogical Society Newsletter 591
Fairfax Historical Society 44
Fairfax Historical Society 576
Fairfax Museum Archives 587
Fairfax News 576
Fairfax Public Library 201
Fairfax Public Library 465
Fairfield County Chapter, OGS 451
Fairfield County District Library 451
Fairfield County Genealogical Society 519
Fairfield County Genealogical Society Newsletter 519
Fairfield County Historical Society 519
Fairfield County Library 519
Fairfield County Museum and Genealogy Room 519
Fairfield Heritage Association & Archives 451
Fairfield Heritage Quarterly 451
Fairfield Historical Museum 93
Fairfield Historical Society 576
Fairfield Historical Society & Archives 93
Fairfield Historical Society & Library 246
Fairfield Historical Society Chronicle 93
Fairfield Library Association 544
Fairfield Museum Archives 680
Fairfield Public Library 93, 201
Fairfield Trace 451
Fairhope Public Library 4
Fairlawn Mansion Museum Archives 632
Fairlee Historical Society & Library 576
Fairmont Historical Museum 612
Fairmont Historical Society & Archives 612
Fairmount Historical Museum Archives 183
Fairmount Park Historic Preservation Trust 497
Fairmount Public Library 183
Fairmount-Jamaica Historical Society 160
Fairport Harbor Historical Museum 448
Fairport Harbor Historical Society & Archives 448
Fairport Harbor Historical Society Quarterly 448
Fairview Area Historical Society 487
Fairview City Library 465
Fairview Historic Society 368
Fairview Museum of History and Art Archives 566
Fairview Register 41
Fairview-Rockwood-Wilkes Historical Society 475
Fairwater Historical Society 621
Faith Presbyterian Church Library 255
Faith Public Library 426, 521
Fajardo Family 559
Falcon 444
Falconburg Family 90
Fales Family 118
Fall River County Historical Museum 522
Fall River County Historical Society & Archives 522
Fall River Historical Museum 270
Fall River Historical Society & Archives 270
Fall River Historical Society Quarterly Report 270
Fall River Public Library 270
Fallasburg Historical Society 296
Fallbrook Historical Society & Library 44
Fallen Timbers Ances-Tree 459
Fallingwater Historic Home Museum Archives 494

INDEX

Falls Newsletter 344
Falls Village-Canaan Historical Society & Library 93
Falls Village-Canaan Historical Society Quarterly 93
Fallsington Library Company 487
Falmouth Genealogical Society 270
Falmouth Genealogical Society & Library 280
Falmouth Genealogical Society Newsletter 280
Falmouth Historical Museum 271
Falmouth Historical Society 246
Falmouth Historical Society & Library 271
Falmouth Historical Society Newsletter 271
Falmouth Memorial Library 246
Falmouth Public Library 271
Falvey Memorial Library 504
Fambrough Family 548, 561
Familia Ancestral Research Association 77
Families 691
Families of Fayette County 503
Families of Wyoming County, WV 56
Families of Yancey County North Carolina 56
Family Backtracking 605
Family Branches 195
Family Chronicle: the Magazine for Families Researching their Roots 691
Family Connection of the Cothren-Cochrane Surname 60
Family Connection of the O'Nell-Nell-O'Neill 60
Family Connections 16, 18
Family Finder 388
Family Finders Genealogy Club 467
Family Finding 626, 627
Family Findings 528
Family Footsteps Magazine 555
Family Gathering 79
Family Gatherings 112
Family Heritage Resources 567
Family Historian 552
Family History and Genealogy Center 332
Family History Capers 285
Family History Library 19
Family History Magazine 567
Family History Newsletter 344, 400
Family History Society of Arizona 18
Family History Society of Arizona Newsletter 16, 18
Family History Society of Arizona, East Valley Chapter 17
Family History Society of Arizona, Fountain Hills Chapter 16
Family History Society of Arizona, Glendale Chapter 16
Family History Society of Arizona, Paradise Valley Chapter 20
Family History Society of Arizona, Scottsdale Chapter 18
Family History Society of Arizona, Tempe Chapter 21
Family History World 572
Family Museum Newsletter 197
Family Organization 608
Family Pathways 192
Family Pictorial and Biographical 247
Family Records Today: the Journal of American Family Records 332
Family Research Association of Mississippi 320
Family Research Association of Mississippi Membership Directory and Surname Index 320
Family Research Directory 552
Family Research Society of Northeastern North Carolina 423, 426
Family Scanner Chapter, IGS 146
Family Snoop 54
Family Ties 294
Family Ties: Newsletter of the Hoffman and Volvoski Families 70
Family Traces 360
Family Tree 135, 258, 447
Family Tree and Crests 186
Family Tree Climbers & Library 333
Family Tree Digest 459
Family Tree Genealogical Society 459, 524
Family Tree is Growing 389
Family Tree Magazine 444
Family Tree Magazine Yearbook 444
Family Tree Newsletter 134
Family Tree Quarterly 134
Family Tree Searcher 600
Family Tree Searchers 41
Family Tree Talk 298
Family Vines 625
Fan Light 502
Fankhauser-Funkhouser Family 215
Fannin County Genealogical and Historical Society 538
Fannin County Genealogical and Historical Society Quarterly 538
Fannin County Historical Museum 538
Fannin County Historical Society & Archives 538
Fannin Library 18
Fanshawe Pioneer Village 685
Fanwood Memorial Library 370
Far Westerner 73
Faraday Family 18
Fargo Air Museum Archives 437
Fargo Public Library 437
Faribault County Historical Society & Archives 306
Faribault County Historical Society Newsletter 306
Farley Library 505
Farm & Mill Gazette 374
Farm America Museum Archives 316
Farm and Ranch Museum Archives 352
Farm House Museum Archives 197
Farm House Museum Quarterly 197
Farmer City Genealogical and Historical Society 160
Farmer City Public Library 160
Farmer Township Community Library 212
Farmer's Log 261
Farmers Bank Museum Archives 592
Farmers Bank of Rustice Museum 695
Farmers Branch Historical Park Archives 544
Farmers Branch Historical Park Newsletter 544
Farmers Branch Public Library 544
Farmers Castle Journal 442
Farmers' Museum Archives 394
Farmersburg Public Library 202
Farmingdale Public Library 397
Farmington Community Library 291
Farmington Genealogical Society & Archives 291
Farmington Historic Home Archives 230
Farmington Historic Home Newsletter 230
Farmington Historical Society & Library 93, 291
Farmington Library 93
Farmington Museum Archives 93, 383
Farmington Pioneer History Society 383

Farmington Public Library 246, 328, 383
Farmland Public Library 183
Farmville Heritage Center 426
Farnes-Isacke-Shackleton Family 565
Farnsworth Public Library 628
Farnworth Family 573
Faro Historical Society 713
Farquier Heritage Society & Library 590
Farquier Heritage Society News 590
Farquier Historical Society & Archives 596
Farr Family 54, 570, 609
Farragut Folklife Museum Archives 527
Farragut Folklife Museum Newsletter 527
Farrar-Mansur House Museum 580
Farrelly Family 255
Farrington Family 542
Farsarotul Family 91, 100
Farson-Mills House 169
Farver-Arter Family 286
FASNY Museum of Fire Fighting Archives 400
Fast Family 454
Father Harold Drake Library-St Pauls College 662
Father Leonard Alvey Library 232
Father Marquette National Memorial Museum Archives 301
Father Pandosy Mission Archives 651
Faulconer Family 450
Faulk County Historical Society 521
Faulkner County Historical Museum 26
Faulkner County Historical Society & Archives 26
Faulkner County Historical Society Newsletter 26
Faulkner County Library 26
Faulkner County Library-Fairfield Bay Branch 27
Faulkner County Library-Van Buren County 26
Faulkner Facts and Fiddlings 26
Faulkner Family 342
Fauquier County Public Library 596
Fauquier Historical Society News & Notes 596
Faust Cultural Heritage Park Archives 327
Fawsler Family 285
Fawson Family 566
Fay Family Newsletter 48
Fayette Area Heritage Society 328
Fayette Connection 459
Fayette County Chapter, OGS 459
Fayette County Genealogical Society 230, 503
Fayette County Genealogical Society & Archives 176
Fayette County Genealogical Society & Library 209
Fayette County Genealogical Society Quarterly 176, 230
Fayette County Helpers & Historical Society 209
Fayette County Historical Museum 209
Fayette County Historical Society 4, 503
Fayette County Historical Society & Archives 459
Fayette County Historical Society & Library 130, 209
Fayette County Journal of Genealogy and History 459
Fayette County Memorial Library 4
Fayette County Public Libraries 614
Fayette County Public Libraries-Fayetteville Branch 612
Fayette County Public Library 181
Fayette Facts 176
Fayette Heritage Museum Archives 551
Fayette Historic State Park Archives 292
Fayette Public Library 551
Fayetteville Free Library 397
Fayetteville Public Library 27
Fayetteville-Lincoln County Public Library 527
Fearing Family 112
Fearing House Museum Archives 452
Fearless Flyer 44
Featherstone Family 597
Federal Bureau of Investigation Museum Archives 105
Federal Hall National Memorial Museum Archives 406
Federation Bulletin 431
Federation des Caisses Populaires Acadiennes 663
Federation des Familles-Souches Quebecoises 703
Federation des Societes d'histoire du Quebec 702
Federation of East European Family History Societies & Library 570
Federation of Genealogical Societies 177, 200, 536
Federation of Genealogical Societies Forum 200
Federation of Museums 512
Federation of Museums, Heritage and Historical Societies 674
Federation of North Carolina Historical Societies & Library 431
Federation of Oklahoma Genealogical Societies 468
Federation of Saskatchewan Indian Nations 710
Federation Quebecoise des Societes de Genealogie 702
Feeback Folks 325
FEEFHS: Newsletter of the Federation of East European Family History Societies 570
Fehler Newsletter 56
Feinberg Library 411
Felix Valle State Historic Site Archives 340
Feller-Felty-Feltz-Veltz-Velty-Valentine Family 184
Fellowship of Brethren Genealogists 193, 458
Fellowship of Brethren Genealogists & Library 159
Fellowship of Brethren Genealogists Newsletter 159
Felton Family 479
Fence Painter 330
Fendall Hall Archives 4
Fenelon Falls Museum Archives 682
Fenimore House Museum 394
Fennell Family 148, 532
Fennimore Railroad Historical Museum 621
Fennimore Railroad Historical Society & Archives 621
Fennville District Library 291
Fenstermaker-Cypherts: Our Family News Notes 50
Fenton Family 552
Fenton Historical Society 291, 329
Fenton Historical Society & Archives 401
Fenton History Center 401
Fentress County Genealogical Society 528
Fentress County Historical Society & Library 528
Fentress County Historical Society Newsletter 528
Fenwick Library 587
Ferdinand Historical Society 183
Ferguson Family 45
Ferguson Files 292
Ferguson Historical Society 329
Ferguson Library 99
Ferguson Municipal Public Library 329
Fergusson Clan 138
Fern Cottage Museum Archives 44

Fern Dell Historic Association 168
Fern Dell Historic Association Newsletter 168
Ferndale Historical Society 291
Ferndale Museum Archives 44
Fernie and District Historical Museum Archives 649
Fernie and District Historical Society 649
Fernie Centennial Library 649
Ferrell Family 122
Ferrin Family 573
Ferris Public Library 544
Ferryland Historical Society 667
Ferryman 395
Fesmire Family 321
Fesse Chequy 528
Fester Family 473
FGS Forum 536
FGS Membership Directory 536
FHSA Newsletter 21
Fidler Family 499
Field Library of Peekskill 411
Field Notes 466, 478
Fieldcode Museum 679
Fields Family Findings 63
Fiero-Fero Family 596
Fife Family 467
Fife Lake Historical Society 291
Fifield Family 364
Fifth Maine News 249
Fifth Meeting House Archives 273
Fig Tree News 552
Figh-Pickett-Barnes School House Museum 7
Filbert Family 448
Filby Newsletter 262
Filer Public Library 146
Filipino American Historical Society of Chicago 155
Filipino American National Historical Society 606
Filipino American National Historical Society, San Francisco Chapter 42
Fillingham Family 17
Fillingim-Fullingim-Fillingame-Fillingham Family 48
Fillmore County Historical Center 308
Fillmore County Historical Society 351
Fillmore County Historical Society & Archives 308
Fillmore Heritage Genealogical Society 351
Fillmore Historical Museum 44
Fillmore Historical Museum Archives 44
Fillmore Historical Museum Newsletter 44
Fillmore Historical Society & Archives 44
Filoli Center Archives 78
Filson 230
Filson Historical Museum 230
Filson Historical Society & Archives 230
Fimpel Family 470
Fimpel-Fimple Family 560
Finan-Gabel-Bodamer Log Cabin 622
Finchum-Flinchum-Fincham Family 567
Finders Keepers 540
Findlay-Hancock County Public Library 448
Fine Print 624
Fine Town Historian 417
Finefrock Family 602
Finer Points 258
Finest Hour 360
Finger Lakes Genealogical Society & Library 416
Finkelstein Memorial Library 417
Finland Historical Society 308
Finland Minnesota Historical Society 634
Finley Findings International 33
Finnam Newsletter 478
Finnell Family 306
Finnerty Family 555
Finney County Genealogical Society & Archives 214
Finney County Genealogical Society Newsletter 214
Finney County Historical Museum 214
Finney County Historical Society & Archives 214
Finney County Public Library 214
Finnish American Club of Saima 271
Finnish American Club of Saima Newsletter 271
Finnish American Reporter-Tyomies-Eteenpain 632
Finnish-American Heritage 91
Finnish-American Heritage Center 293
Finnish-American Heritage Society 91
Finnish-American Historical Archives 293
Finnish-American Historical Society 317
Finnish-American Historical Society of the West 478
Finnish-American Society of Santa Clara County 67
Finnish-American Society of Santa Clara County Newsletter 67
Fiorello H LaGuardia Museum Archives 403
Fire Fighting Museum Archives 691
Fire in the Hole 113
Fire Museum Archives 506
Fire Museum News 151
Fire Museum of Maryland Archives 260
Fire Museum of Maryland Newsletter 260
Fire Museum of Memphis Archives 530
Fire Museum of Memphis Quarterly 530
Fire Museum of Missouri Archives 342
Fire Museum of Texas Archives 537
Fire Museum of Texas Newsletter 537
Fire Warden 35
Fireback 260
Firefighters' Museum of Nova Scotia 677
Firefighting Museum Archives 681
Firehouse Jail Museum 41
Firehouse Museum 65
Firehouse Museum Archives 258
Firehouse News 320
Firelands Historical Museum 454
Firelands Historical Society & Archives 454
Firelands Pioneer 454
Fireman's Hall Museum Archives 497
Firestone Library 376
First African Baptist Church Museum Archives 137
First American Title Insurance Historical Library 70
First Americans and Early Settlers Foundation 117
First Baptist Church Archives 236
First Baptist Church in America Archives 509
First Baptist Church Library 593
First Baptist Church Library 9
First Christian Church Library 495
First Christian Reformed Church Library 304

First Church of Christ, Scientist, Church History Library 266
First Consolidated School in Minnesota Museum Archives 315
First Division Museum at Cantigny Archives 177
First Families of Clermont County, Ohio 442
First Families of Georgia, 1733-1797 126
First Families of Hopkins County 560
First Families of Ionia County Society 295
First Families of Licking County Ohio 454
First Families of Montana 343
First Families of Ohio & Archives 452
First Families of Pacific States Bulletin 78
First Families of Pacific States Society & Archives 78
First Families of SC 1670-1700 518
First Families of the Twin Territories 468
First Hussars Citizen Soldiers Museum Archives 685
First Missouri State Capitol Archives 338
First National Black Historical Society of Kansas 223
First Nations Confederacy 662
First Nations of South Island Tribal Council 652
First Presbyterian Church Library 381, 424
First Regional Library 320
First Regional Library-Batesville Public 319
First San Diego Courthouse Archives 65
First Territorial Capitol of Kansas 214
First White House of the Confederacy Archives 7
Fischer-Hanlon House Archives 37
Fisher Facts 62
Fisher Family 439, 602
Fisher Grove Country School Museum Archives 522
Fisher Martin House Archives 103
Fisher Museum of Forestry Archives 277
Fisherman's Life Museum Archives 674
Fisherman's Museum Archives 667
Fishermen's Life Museum Archives 674
Fishermen's Museum Archives 248, 668
Fishing Lake First Nation 711
Fisk(e) Family Association Newsletter 218
Fisk(e)-Russell Family 38
Fiske Family Association Newsletter 217
Fiske Free Library 359
Fiske Genealogical Foundation & Library 606
Fiske Genealogical Foundation Newsletter 606
Fiske Museum Archives 40
Fitch Family 268
Fitchburg Historical Museum 271
Fitchburg Historical Society 621
Fitchburg Historical Society & Archives 271
Fitchburg Historical Society Newsletter 271
Fitchburg Public Library 271
Fite Family 548
Fitt Family 599
Fitts-Fitz-Fittz-Getchell-Marden Project 363
Fitze Family 30
Fitzgerald Family 225
Fitzgerald House Archives 561
Fitzgerald Library 317
Fitzgerald-Ben Hill County Library 131
Fitzhugh Family 609
Fitzwilliam Historical Society & Library 361
Five Civilized Tribes Museum Archives 467
Five Civilized Tribes Museum Newsletter 467
Five Day Capitol 214
Flack-Bodkin-Molen-Dahl-Bull-Jespersen-Jensen-Huffaker-Christensen Family 573
Flag and Banner 656
Flag Family 283
Flag House and Star Spangled Banner Museum Archives 255
Flag House Star 255
Flagg Creek Historical Museum 153
Flagg Creek Historical Society 168, 177
Flagg Creek Historical Society & Archives 153
Flagg Township Historical Society 172
Flaggan 156
Flagg-Rochelle Public Library District 172
Flagler Community Library 84
Flagler County Historical Museum 110
Flagler County Historical Society & Archives 110
Flagler County Public Library 119
Flagstaff City-Coconino County Public Library System 16
Flake Family 184
Flanagan Family 100
Flanary Family 568
Flanningham Family 297
Flash Forward, Flashback 27
Flat River Community Library 293
Flat River Historical and Genealogical Society 293
Flat Rock Historical Society & Library 291
Flat Rock Historical Society Newsletter 291
Flat Rock Museum Archives 667
Flathead County Library 345
Flathead Indian Museum Archives 346
Flathead Valley Genealogical Society 345
Flatt Family 504, 568
Flatwater Genealogical Society 352
Fleck Family 606
Fleetwood Area Historical Society 487
Fleig Newsletter 201
Fleming County Public Library 227
Fleming Historical Society & Archives 85
Flemish-American Heritage 301
Flenniken Memorial Library 484
Flesh Public Library 455
Flesher Family Redwood 84
Flesherton Public Library 682
Fletcher Family 122
Fletcher Family Research Bulletin 30
Fletcher Free Library 575
Fletcher Memorial Library 577
Flickertail Village Museum Archives 439
Flight Journal 65
Flight Line 604
Flight Plan 71
Flightline 53
Flightlines 626
Flin Flon Museum Archives 660
Flin Flon Public Library 660
Flint Genealogical Quarterly 291
Flint Genealogical Society 291
Flint Genealogical Society Newsletter 291
Flint Hills Genealogy Club & Archives 213

INDEX

Flint Hills Genealogy Club Newsletter 213
Flint Hills Historical Museum 213
Flint House 416
Flint Memorial Library 276
Flint Public Library 291
Flint Ridge State Memorial Museum Archives 449
Flint Ridge State Memorial Ohio Historical Society 449
Flint River Regional Library 131
Flintlock and Powderhorn 46
Flippin-Estep Family 542
Flipping Flippins 542
Flora Area Historical Society 320
Flora-Flory-Fleury Family 376, 602
Flora-Flory-Fleury Family Newsletter 376
Floral Park Public Library 397
Florala Public Library 4
Flora-Monroe Public Library 183
Florence County Historical Society 514, 621
Florence County Library 514
Florence Griswold Museum 97
Florence Heritage Foundation 514
Florence Historical Society 370
Florence Historical Society & Archives 214
Florence Historical Society News 214
Florence McLeod Hazard Museum 319
Florence Museum Newsletter 514
Florence Museum of History Archives 514
Florence Price Pioneer Museum Archives 85
Florence Ranch Homestead Archives 553
Florence-Lauderdale Public Library 4
Florewood River Plantation Archives 320
Florewood State Park Archives 320
Florham-Madison Campus Library 372
Florida Agricultural Museum Archives 119
Florida Air Museum Archives 115
Florida Baptist Historical Society & Archives 111
Florida Baptist Historical Society Newsletter 111
Florida Chapter Quest 116
Florida Chapter, OGS & Library 116
Florida Chapter, Ohio Genealogical Society 120
Florida Division of Historical Resources 112
Florida Genealogical Society 122
Florida Genealogical Society Journal 122
Florida Genealogical Society Newsletter 122
Florida Genealogist 122
Florida Gulf Coast Railroad Museum Archives 119
Florida Heritage Museum Archives 121
Florida Historical Quarterly 110, 116
Florida Historical Society 110, 116, 124
Florida Historical Society Report 110, 116
Florida History Associates & Archives 122
Florida History Associates Newsletter 122
Florida Holocaust Museum Archives 121
Florida Holocaust Museum Newsletter 121
Florida Parishes Genealogical Society 238
Florida Sandspur 114
Florida Society for Genealogical Research & Library 120
Florida Society of Genealogical Research 122
Florida State Department of the Historic Preservation Board 122
Florida State Genealogical Society 122
Florida State Genealogical Society Newsletter 122
Florida State Library 122
Florida Supreme Court Historical Society & Library 122
Florissant Valley Historical Museum 329
Florissant Valley Historical Society 329
Florissant Valley Quarterly 329
Flour Mill Museum Archives 690
Flourishing Roots 381
Flower Memorial Library Genealogical Committee 420
Flower Pentecostal Heritage Center 340
Flowerdew Hundred Foundation & Archives 589
Flowers Family 381
Floyd County Heritage Newsletter 199
Floyd County Historical and Genealogical Society 225
Floyd County Historical Museum 199
Floyd County Historical Museum Archives 544
Floyd County Historical Society 190
Floyd County Historical Society & Archives 199
Floyd County Public Library 232
Floyd Family 547
Floyd Memorial Library 399
Floyd Memorial Library Newsletter 399
Flushing Area Historical Society & Library 291
Flushing Area Historical Society Newsletter 291
Fluvanna County Historical Society & Archives 592
Fluvanna County Historical Society Bulletin 592
Fluvanna County Library 587
Fluvanna Free Library 401
Flyer 508
Flying Dust First Nation 708
Flying Tigers Warbird Air Museum Archives 115
Flyleaf 53
Flynn Clan 410
Flynt-Flint Newsletter 513
Foam Lake Museum Archives 706
Focs' le News 402
Focus 283, 419, 504
Focus on Friends Newsletter 282
Focus on Indiana Libraries 186
Focus: Quarterly of the Racine County Historical Society 630
Foghorn 609
Foley Center Library 607
Foley Family 336, 543
Foley Findings 119
Foley Public Library 4
Foley-Franke-Daglan Family 569
Folger Newsletter 105
Folger Shakespeare Library 105
Folio 302
Folke Bernadette Memorial Library 315
Folklife Museum 488
Follett House Museum Archives 457
Folsom Family 117
Folsom Historical Museum 44
Folsom Historical Society 383
Folsom Historical Society & Archives 44
Folsom House Museum 315
Folsom Library 418
Folsom Memorial Library 25
Folsom Prison Museum Archives 62

FOM Newsletter 623
Fond du Lac County Genealogical Society 628
Fond du Lac County Genealogical Society Newsletter 628
Fond du Lac County Historical Society & Library 621
Fond du Lac County Historical Society Newsletter 621
Fond Du Lac Denesuline Nation 706
Fond du Lac Public Library 621
Fondren Library 542, 548
Fondulac Public Library District 158
Fontaine Family 529
Fontana Historical Society & Library 44
Fontana Public Library 621
Fontanus 700
Fonthill Museum Archives 486
Fonville Family 569
Foos Family 450
Foote Family 291, 373
Foote-Hardy Family 290
Foothills Genealogical Society & Library 87
Foothills Historical Society 600
Foothills Inquirer 87
Footnote 100
Footnotes 299, 372, 373, 395, 432, 482, 528
Footprints 26, 444
Footprints for Williamson County 165
Footprints in Marion County 173
Footprints in the Sands of Time 606
Footprints in Time 430
Footprints of Jefferson County 31
Footprints Of Our Past 44
Footprints of the Exiled 96
Footprints Past and Present 169
Footprints Quarterly Journal 545
Footprints through Idaho 145
Footsteps through Time 335
Footsteps to the Past 442
Footville State Bank Museum 621
Footville Telephone Company Museum Archives 621
Foppes Family 558
For the Eye of a Friend 376
For the Record 54, 64
Forbes Clan 583
Forbes Family 566
Forbes Library 276
Forbes Memorial Library 276
Forbestown Museum 38
Forbush Memorial Library 282
Forby Family History Society Newsletter 88
Ford City Public Library 487
Ford County Historical Museum 170
Ford County Historical Society & Archives 170, 213
Ford County Historical Society Newsletter 170, 213
Ford Genealogy Club 289
Ford House Museum Archives 53
Ford Stoud Historical Foundation 586
Ford's Theatre National Historic Site Archives 105
Fore Bears Paws 193
Forebears 473
Forebears In Your Maine Family Tree 247
Forecast 505
Fore-Kin Trails Genealogical Society 88
Fore-Kin Trails Quarterly 88
Forest Capital State Museum Archives 120
Forest County Historical and Genealogical Society & Archives 619
Forest County Historical Museum 619
Forest County Historical Society 503
Forest History Association of Wisconsin 625
Forest History Center Archives 308
Forest History Cruiser 426
Forest History Society & Library 426
Forest Lake Historical Society 308
Forest Lambton Museum Archives 682
Forest Lawn Museum Library 46
Forest Lodge Library 618
Forest Park Historical Society 160
Forest Park Library 160
Forest Park Museum Archives 207
Forest Park Museum Quarterly 207
Forest Public Library 320
Forestburg and District Museum 643
Forestburg Historical Society 643
Foresthill Divide Historical Museum 44
Foresthill Divide Historical Society 44
Foreward 446
Foreword 59
Forge 291
Forget Me Not 530
Forgotten Pathways of Hancock County Kentucky 228
Forgotten Voices 171
Forked Deer Regional Library Center 527
Forkner Newsletter 467
Forks Genealogical Society 601
Former Governors' Mansion State Historic Site Archives 437
Forney Heritage Society 544
Forney Museum of Transportation Archives 84
Forrest City Public Library 27
Forrest R Polk Library 628
Forrester Clan 130, 137
Forrester Family 250
Forster-Foster Family 535
Forsyth Clan 56
Forsyth County Genealogical Journal 435
Forsyth County Genealogical Society 435
Forsyth County Genealogical Society Newsletter 435
Forsyth County Public Library 129, 435
Forsyth Library 215
Forsyth Township Historical Society 293
Fort Abercrombie State Historic Site Archives 437
Fort Abercrombie State Historical Park 13
Fort Abraham Lincoln State Park Archives 438
Fort Amanda Archives 451
Fort Amherst National Historic Park Archives 695
Fort Anne National Historic Park Archives 673
Fort Apache Scout 22
Fort Assiniboine Genealogical Society & Archives 345
Fort Atkinson Historical Society & Archives 621
Fort Atkinson State Historical Park Archives 351
Fort Beausejour National Historic Site Archives 663
Fort Bedford Museum Archives 482
Fort Belknap College Library & Tribal Archives 345

Fort Belknap Genealogical Association 547, 555
Fort Belknap Genealogical Association Bulletin 547, 555
Fort Belle Fontaine Historical Society 339
Fort Bend County Genealogical Society & Library 557
Fort Bend Museum Association & Archives 557
Fort Benjamin Harrison Historical Society 186
Fort Benton Museum of the Upper Missouri Archives 344
Fort Bliss Museum Archives 545
Fort Boonesborough Museum Archives 233
Fort Bowie National Historic Site Archives 15
Fort Bragg Building Museum Archives 44
Fort Bragg-Mendocino Coast Historical Society 44
Fort Branch-Johnson Township Public Library 183
Fort Brewerton Historical Society & Library 390
Fort Brewerton Historical Society Newsletter 390
Fort Bridger Historical Association & Archives 636
Fort Bridger Historical Museum 636
Fort Brown Genealogical Society 539
Fort Buena Ventura Archives 568
Fort Buford State Historic Site Archives 440
Fort Calgary Museum Archives 641
Fort Campbell Historical Foundation 227
Fort Carlton Agency Council 706
Fort Carlton Museum Archives 709
Fort Caroline National Memorial Archives 112
Fort Casey Interpretetive Center Archives 600
Fort Caspar Museum Library 635
Fort Chipewyan Bicentennial Museum Archives 643
Fort Christmas Historical Park Archives 110
Fort Clark Historical Society & Archives 538
Fort Clark Trading Post State Historic Site Archives 437
Fort Clatsop National Memorial Archies Archives 473
Fort Clinch State Park Archives 112
Fort Collins Historical Society 85
Fort Collins Museum Archives 85
Fort Collins Public Library 85
Fort Columbia State Park Museum Archives 600
Fort Concho Guidon 558
Fort Concho National Historic Landmark Museum Library 558
Fort Covington Reading Center and Museum Archives 397
Fort Crawford Museum 629
Fort Croghan Museum 539
Fort Crook Historical Museum 44
Fort Crook Historical Society & Archives 44
Fort Dalles Museum Archives 480
Fort Dauphin Museum Archives 659
Fort Davidson State Historic Site Archives 337
Fort Davis National Historic Site Library 545
Fort de Chartres State Historic Site Archives 171
Fort Defiance Archives 429
Fort Delaware Historical Museum 103
Fort Delaware Museum of Colonial History Archives 405
Fort Delaware Newsletter 103
Fort Delaware Society & Archives 103
Fort Delaware Society & Library 103
Fort Dix Museum Archives 370
Fort Dobbs State Historic Site Archives 433
Fort Dodge & Frontier Village Archives 202
Fort Dodge Center Library 202
Fort Dodge Historical Foundation & Archives 202
Fort Dodge Public Library 202
Fort Dodge Public Library Newsletter 202
Fort Donelson National Battlefield Archives 527
Fort Douglas Military Museum Library 566
Fort Edmonton Park Archives 643
Fort Edward Historical Association & Archives 397
Fort Edward Museum Archives 674
Fort Erie Historical Museum Archives 689
Fort Erie Public Library 682
Fort Erie Railroad Museum Archives 682
Fort Eustis Historical and Archaeological Association 587
Fort Fairfield Public Library 246
Fort Fetterman State Historic Site Archives 635
Fort Fetterman State Museum Archives 637
Fort Fisher State Historic Site Archives 429
Fort Folly Indian Band 663
Fort Frances Museum Archives 682
Fort Francisco Museum Archives 87
Fort Francisco Museum Quarterly 87
Fort Frederica National Monument Archives 136
Fort Frederica National Monument Library 136
Fort Frederick State Park Archives 256
Fort Gaines Historical Society 131
Fort Garland Heritage Association 85
Fort Garry Historical Society & Library 662
Fort Garry Horse Museum Archives 662
Fort George and Buckingham House Archives 645
Fort George G Meade Museum Library 259
Fort George Museum Archives 643
Fort George National Historic Park Archives 686
Fort George Regional Museum Archives 654
Fort Gibson Genealogical and Historical Society 465
Fort Gibson Historic Site Archives 465
Fort Gordon Museum Archives 131
Fort Guijarros Museum Foundation Archives 65
Fort Hancock Museum Archives 370, 377
Fort Harker Museum Archives 216
Fort Hartsuff State Historical Park Archives 350
Fort Hays State Historic Site Archives 215
Fort Hays Studies 215
Fort Hays, Kansas Genealogical Society 215
Fort Henrietta Interpretive Park Archives 475
Fort Henry Museum Archives 684
Fort Hill Heritage Museum 167
Fort Hill Museum Archives 449, 513
Fort Huachuca Museum Archives 16
Fort Hughes Military Blockhouse Archives 664
Fort Humboldt State Historic Park Archives 44
Fort Hunter Mansion Museum Archives 489
Fort Industry Reflections 458
Fort Inglish Archives 543
Fort Inglish Courier 538
Fort Inglish Museum Archives 538
Fort Irwin Post Library 45
Fort Jackson Main Post Library 514
Fort Jackson Museum Library 514
Fort Jones Museum Archives 45
Fort Kearney Museum Archives 353
Fort Kearny Genealogical Society 353
Fort Kearny Genealogical Society & Archives 353

Fort Kearny State Historical Park Archives 353
Fort Kent Historical Society 246
Fort King George Historic Site Archives 129
Fort Klamath Historical Society 475
Fort Klock Historic Restoration 415
Fort Klock Historical Museum 415
Fort Knox State Historic Site Archives 250
Fort La Reine Museum and Pioneer Village Archives 660
Fort LaMotte Genealogical and Historical Society 169
Fort Langley National Historic Site Archives 649
Fort Laramie Historical Association & Archives 636
Fort Laramie Historical Museum 636
Fort Larned Historical Society & Archives 217
Fort Larned National Historic Site Library 217
Fort Lauderdale Historical Museum 112
Fort Lauderdale Historical Society & Library 112
Fort Laurens State Memorial Archives 442
Fort Lawrence Heritage Association 674
Fort Le Boeuf Historical Society 504
Fort Leaton State Historic Site Archives 556
Fort Leavenworth Historical Society & Archives 214
Fort Leboeuf Archives 504
Fort Leboeuf Museum 504
Fort Lee Historic Park Museum Archives 370
Fort Lennox Museum Archives 702
Fort Leonard Wood Museum Archives 329
Fort Lewis Library System 601
Fort Lewis Military Museum Archives 601
Fort Ligonier Association & Archives 492
Fort Ligonier Museum 492
Fort Loudon Historical Society 487
Fort Loudoun Regional Library Center 525
Fort Lowell Museum Archives 22
Fort MacArthur Museum Archives 69
Fort Macleod Museum Archives 643
Fort Macon State Park Archives 423
Fort Madison Public Libraries 202
Fort Malden Historic Park Library 679
Fort Mason Historical Society 493
Fort Massac State Park and Historic Site Archives 166
Fort Matanzas National Monument Archives 121
Fort McAllister Historic Park Archives 135
Fort McCoy Post Library 621
Fort McHenry National Monument and Historic Shrine Library 255
Fort McKavett State Historic Site Archives 545
Fort McKavett State Historic Site Newsletter 545
Fort McMurray Public Library 643
Fort Meade Public Library 112
Fort Meigs State Memorial Archives 455
Fort Miami Heritage Society & Library 302
Fort Mifflin Museum Archives 497
Fort Misqually Historic Site Archives 608
Fort Missoula Historical Museum 346
Fort Missoula Historical Society 346
Fort Morgan Museum Archives 5, 85
Fort Morgan Public Library 85
Fort Morris Historic Site Archives 134
Fort Moultrie Museum Archives 518
Fort Myers Beach Public Library 113
Fort Myers-Lee County Public Library 112
Fort Nashborough Museum Archives 531
Fort Necessity National Battlefield Archives 487
Fort Nelson Heritage Museum Archives 649
Fort Nelson Historical Society 649
Fort Nelson Indian Band 649
Fort Normandeau Museum Archives 645
Fort Oglethorpe Preservation Society 131
Fort Okanogan Inerpretive Center Archives 604
Fort Ontario State Historic Site Library 410
Fort Osage National Historic Landmark Archives 340
Fort Ostell Museum Archives 645
Fort Payne Depot Museum Archives 4
Fort Peck Community College-Tribal Library 346
Fort Pelley and Livingston Museum Archives 709
Fort Phil Kearney Archives 637
Fort Phil Kearney Museum Archives 635
Fort Pike State Park Museum Archives 240
Fort Pitt Museum Archives 499
Fort Plain Free Library 397
Fort Plain Museum Archives 397
Fort Point and Army Museum Association 66
Fort Point and Presidio Historical Association & Library 66
Fort Point Museum Archives 675
Fort Polk Military Museum Library 237
Fort Pulaski National Monument Archives 137, 138
Fort Qu'Appelle Museum Archives 706
Fort Quarterly 497
Fort Raleigh National Historic Site Archives 429
Fort Recovery Museum Archives 448
Fort Richardson Post Library 12
Fort Richardson State Historical Park Archives 550
Fort Ridgely History Site Archives 308
Fort Robinson Museum 351
Fort Robinson Museum Library 351
Fort Rock Valley Historical Society 480
Fort Rodd Hill Museum Archives 657
Fort Saint James National Historic Park Library 649
Fort Saint John Public Library Association 649
Fort Saint John-North Peace River Museum 650
Fort Saint Joseph Museum Archives 299, 689
Fort Saint Joseph National Historic Park 689
Fort Saint Pierre Museum Archives 682
Fort Sam Houston Library 545
Fort Sam Houston Museum Archives 545
Fort Saskatchewan Historical Museum 643
Fort Saskatchewan Historical Society & Archives 643
Fort Savannah Museum Library 613
Fort Scott Community College Library 214
Fort Scott National Historic Site Archives 214
Fort Scott Public Library 214
Fort Sedgewick Museum 86
Fort Sedgwick Historical Society 86
Fort Selden State Monument Library 384
Fort Selkirk Museum Archives 713
Fort Shafter Library 141
Fort Sidney Museum 356
Fort Sill National Historic Landmark Museum Library 465
Fort Simcoe Museum Archives 609
Fort Sisseton State Historic Park Archives 522
Fort Smith Historical Society & Library 27

Fort Smith Museum of History Archives 27
Fort Smith Museum of History Newsletter 27
Fort Smith National Historic Site Archives 27
Fort Smith National Historic Site Newsletter 27
Fort Smith Public Library 27
Fort Smith Trolley Museum Archives 27
Fort Snelling History Center Archives 314
Fort Spokane Museum Archives 600
Fort St Jean Baptiste State Historic Site Archives 239
Fort Stanwix National Monument Archives 414
Fort Steele Heritage Town Museum 650
Fort Stewart Main Post Library 131
Fort Stewart Museum Archives 131
Fort Stockton Historical Society & Archives 545
Fort Stockton Historical Society Newsletter 545
Fort Stockton Public Library 545
Fort Sumner State Monument Museum Archives 385
Fort Sumter National Monument Library 518
Fort Supply Historic Site Archives 465
Fort Tejon State Historic Park Archives 50
Fort Ticonderoga Archives 418
Fort Ticonderoga Museum Library 397
Fort Ticonderoga-Thompson-Pell Research Center 418
Fort Totten State Historic Site Archives 438
Fort Towson Military Park Archives 465
Fort Tyler Association 139
Fort Uncompahgre Living History Museum Archives 83
Fort Union National Monument Library 385
Fort Union Trading Post National Historic Site Library 440
Fort Vancouver Historical Society of Clark County 609
Fort Vancouver National Historic Site Library 609
Fort Vancouver Regional Library 609
Fort Vasquez Museum Archives 89
Fort Verde State Historic Park Library 15
Fort Wainwright Post Library 12
Fort Walla Walla Musuem 609
Fort Wallace Memorial Association 223
Fort Walsh Museum Archives 708
Fort Ward Museum and Historic Site Archives 583
Fort Ward Museum Newsletter 583
Fort Ware Indian Band 654
Fort Washington Park Museum Archives 259
Fort Washita Historic Site Archives 464
Fort Wayne Firefighters Museum Archives 183
Fort Wayne Railroad Historical Society 183, 190
Fort Wellington National Historic Site Archives 688
Fort Whoop-Up Centre 644
Fort Wilkins Historic Complex Archives 289
Fort William Henry Museum Archives 402
Fort Winnebago Surgeon's Quarters 629
Fort Worth Genealogical Society 545
Fort Worth Genealogical Society Bulletin 545
Fort Worth Genealogical Society Newsletter 545
Fort Worth Museum of Science and History Archives 545
Fort Worth Public Library 545
Fort Yargo State Park Archives 140
Fort Zachary Taylor State Historical Site Museum Archives 115
Fortifications-de-Quebec 701
Fortiter 46
Fortitudine 106
Fortney-Fortna-Fortineux Family 446
Fort-Numero-Un de la Pointe-de-Levy 701
Fortress of Louisbourg National Historic Park Library 675
Forts Folle Avoine Historic Park Archives 619
Fortuna Depot Museum Archives 45
Fortuna Historical Commission 45
Forty Acres 271
Forum 177
Forum: A Ukrainian Review; Narodna Volya 501
Forward 286, 673
Forwarders' Museum Archives 688
Foshee Families of America Newsletter 89
Fossil Country Museum Archives 636
Fossil Ridge Public Library 153
Fossil Station Museum 221
Foster Family 314, 451, 536, 570
Foster Preservation Society 507
Fosterfields Living Historical Farm Archives 374
Fostoria Area Historical Museum 448
Fostoria Area Historical Society & Archives 448
Fostoria Lineage Research Society & Archives 448
Foulke Family 506
Foundation 231
Foundation Flashes 235
Foundation for Historic Christ Church & Library 589
Foundation for Historical Louisiana 235
Foundation Historical Association & Archives 388
Foundation News 104
Foundation Stone 4
Foundations of America Series 597
Founders of Natchitoches 239
Founding Mother 273
Foundry School Museum 394
Fountain City Area Historical Museum 621
Fountain City Area Historical Society & Archives 621
Fountain County Genealogical Society 187
Fountain County Historical Society 187, 194
Fountain County War Museum Archives 194
Fountain Indian Band 651
Fountain Valley Historical Society 45
Fountain: Welch Family Newsletter 63
Fountaindale Public Library District-Romeoville Branch 172
Fountain-New Library 135
Four Corners Genealogy Society 84
Four Flags Area Genealogical Society & Library 299
Four Flags Tracer 299
Four Lines West 76
Four Mile Historic Park Archives 83
Four Nations 644
Four Rivers Cultural Center Archives 477
Four Rivers Cultural Center Newsletter 477
Four Rivers Genealogical Society 342
Four State Genealogy Club & Library 214
Foust-Faust-Fautz Family 342
Fowler Historical Museum 85
Fowler Historical Society & Archives 85
Fowler Museum of Cultural History Archives 51
Fowler: The Family Series 292
Fox Family Facts 56
Fox Island Historical Museum 601

Fox Island Historical Society & Archives 601
Fox Lake Area Historical Society 160
Fox Lake Historical Museum 621
Fox Lake Historical Society & Archives 621
Fox River Grove Public Library District 160
Fox River Grove Public Library District Newsletter 160
Fox River Lines 174
Fox River Trolley Museum Archives 174
Fox Tales: Newsletter of the Fox Valley Genealogical Society 168
Fox Valley Genealogical Society & Library 168, 617
Foxfire Fund & Museum 135
Fox-Smith Family 165
Frackville Area Historical Society 487
Frackville Free Public Library 487
Fraktor 496
Frame-Scribner Family 601
Frameworks 320
Framingham Historical Society & Archives 271
Framingham Historical Society Newsletter 271
Framingham Public Library 271
France-Jones-Brown-Craigo-Dillinger-Crane-Estes-Jeremiah Dale Harbour-Dale Family 379
Frances E Willard Memorial Library 159
Frances Willard Schoolhouse Archives 623
Frances Willson Thompson Library 291
Francestown Improvement and Historical Society & Library 361
Francesville-Salem Township Public Library 184
Francis A Drexel Library 497
Francis Land House Historic Site Archives 596
Francis Scott Key Foundation 105
Franciscus Family 16
Franco-American Genealogical Society of York County & Archives 244
Frank B Koller Memorial Library 625
Frank Buchman House Museum Archives 481
Frank Carlson Library 213
Frank G Ray House Museum Archives 209
Frank H McClung Museum Archives 529
Frank H Schepler Jr Memorial Library 40
Frank J Basloe Library 399
Frank L Weyenburg Library 626
Frank Lloyd Wright Home Museum Archives 169
Frank M Allara Library 232
Frank Melville Memorial Library 417
Frank Mills Outdoor Mining Museum 655
Frank Phillips Home Archives 463
Frank Slide Interpretive Centre 642
Frank's Place 309
Frank-Crookston Family 89
Frankenfield Family 488
Frankenmuth Historical Association & Archives 291
Frankenmuth Historical Association Newsletter 291
Frankenmuth Historical Museum 291
Frankford Historical Society 497
Frankford Public Library 103
Frankford Public Library 682
Frankfort Area Genealogy Society 177
Frankfort Area Historical Museum 177
Frankfort Area Historical Society & Archives 177
Frankfort Area Historical Society of Will County 160
Frankfort City Library 214
Frankfort Community Public Library 184
Frankfort Newsletter 160
Franklin Area Historical Museum 448
Franklin Area Historical Society & Archives 448
Franklin Area Historical Society Newsletter 448
Franklin County Footnotes 484
Franklin County Genealogical Society 177, 202, 446, 587
Franklin County Genealogical Society & Library 220, 554
Franklin County Genealogical Society Quarterly 220
Franklin County Heritage Society 595
Franklin County Historical Association 31
Franklin County Historical Museum 180, 404, 604
Franklin County Historical Museum Archives 554
Franklin County Historical Newsletter 202
Franklin County Historical Review 533
Franklin County Historical Society 128, 175, 341, 351, 554
Franklin County Historical Society & Archives 180, 220, 404, 533, 604
Franklin County Historical Society & Library 202, 446, 595
Franklin County Library 31, 429, 484, 533
Franklin County Old Jail Museum Archives 526, 533
Franklin County Public Library 595
Franklin County Seminary Museum 180
Franklin D Roosevelt Library 401
Franklin F Moore Library 372
Franklin Family 478, 550
Franklin Ferguson Memorial Library 83
Franklin Flyer 604
Franklin Grove Area Historical Society 167
Franklin Historical Museum 246
Franklin Historical Review 404
Franklin Historical Society 271, 291, 576, 621
Franklin Historical Society & Archives 180
Franklin Historical Society & Library 246
Franklin or Bust 336
Franklin Parish Genealogical and Historical Society 242
Franklin Parish Library 242
Franklin Park Public Library & Historical Museum Archives 160
Franklin Park Public Library & Historical Museum Archives Newsletter 160
Franklin Pierce Homestead 361
Franklin Public Library 271, 361, 487
Franklin Record 202
Franklin Township Free Public Library 378
Franklin Township Historical Society 186
Franklin Trask Library 276
Franklintonian 446
Franks Clan 493
Frankston Depot Library and Museum Archives 546
Frantz Clan Newslette 482
Frantz Family 50
Frary Family 369
Fraser Canyon Tribal Administration 651
Fraser Clan 40, 691
Fraser Historical Society 291
Fraser Lake Museum Archives 650
Fraser Valley Regional Library 647
Frasher-Frazier-Hatfield-Phillips Family 111
Fraternal Order of Alaska State Troopers Museum Archives 11
Fraunces Tavern Museum Archives 406
Frawley-Ferry-LaFlamme-Gildea-Gilday-Lahaye-Lepele-Caret-Carette-Brann-Brawn-Garner Family 475

Frazee Family 457
Frazer's Museum Archives 705
Frazier Family 18
Frazier Footnotes 560
Frazier Historical Arms Museum Archives 230
Fred C Kuehner Memorial Library 483
Fred Hart Williams Genealogical Society 289
Fred J Graham Library 437
Fred J Johnston House Museum 402
Fred L Matthews Library 290
Fred Light Museum 705
Frederic Historical Society & Archives 621
Frederic Remington Museum Archives 409
Frederick A Cook Newsletter 499
Frederick Andrews Kith and Kindred 235
Frederick C Robie House Archives 155
Frederick County Genealogical Society & Library 261
Frederick County Genealogical Society Newsletter 261
Frederick County Historical Museum 259
Frederick County Public Libraries 259
Frederick Douglass Library 261
Frederick Douglass National Historic Site Museum Archives 105
Frederick E Parlin Memorial Library 270
Frederick Family 591
Frederick Law Olmsted National Historic Site Archives 268
Frederick Madison Smith Library 204
Frederick Remington Area Historical Society & Library 223
Frederick T Kelly Library 586
Fredericksburg and Spotsylvania National Military Park Library 587
Fredericksburg Area Museum Archives 588
Fredericksburg Area Museum Newsletter 588
Fredericksburg Genealogical Society 546
Fredericksburg Regional Genealogical Society 588
Fredericksburg Regional Genealogical Society Newsletter 588
Fredericktown Historical Society 448
Free Albania Organization 279
Free and Accepted Masons of Pennsylvania Library 497
Free Library of New Hope and Solebury 495
Free Library of Philadelphia 497
Free Methodist Historical Society Newsletter 187
Free Public Library of the Borough of Pompton Lakes 376
Free State 238
Free State of Winston Historical Society 3
Freeborn County Genealogical Society & Library 305
Freeborn County Historical Museum 305
Freeborn County Historical Society & Archives 305
Freeborn County Historical Society Newsletter 305
Freeborn County Tracer 305
Freeborn Family 35
Freeburg Historical and Genealogical Society 160
Freeburg Historical and Genealogical Society Quarterly 160
Freedom Public Library 361, 370
Freeholder 410
Freelove Family 53
Freeman Academy Library 522
Freeman Family 44
Freeman Family 568, 572
Freeman Historical Society 329
Freeman Public Library 522
Freeport Historical Society & Archives 246
Freeport Historical Society Newsletter 246
Freeport Memorial Library 398
Freeport Memorial Library Newsletter 398
Freeport Public Library 160
Freer Family 487
Freestone County Genealogical Society & Library 544
Freestone County Historical Museum Archives 544
Freestone Frontiers 544
Freetown Historical Museum 265
Freetown Historical Society & Archives 265
Fremont 167
Fremont Area Historical Society 621
Fremont County Genealogical Society 82, 207
Fremont County Genealogical Society & Archives 637
Fremont County Historical Society 149, 636
Fremont County Historical Society & Library 207
Fremont County Library 636
Fremont County Library System-Dubois Branch 636
Fremont County Library System-Riverton Branch 637
Fremont County Nostalgia News 637
Fremont County Pioneer Museum Archives 636
Fremont Historical Society 357
Fremont Museum of Local History Archives 45
Fremont Public Library 184, 291
Fremont Public Library District 167
French and Canadian Heritage Society, Florida Group 116
French Azilum Historic Home Archives 503
French Cable Station Museum in Orleans Archives 277
French Canadian-Acadian Genealogists of Wisconsin 622
French Canadian-Acadian Genealogists of Wisconsin Quarterly 622
French Canadian-American Genealogy 280
French Family 68
French Genealogist 42
French Historical Studies 426
French History 424
French Institute-Alliance Francaise & Library 406
French Legation Museum 536
French Legation Museum Archives 536
French Library and Cultural Center 267
French Settlement Historical Register 237
French Settlement Historical Society 237
French Simpson Memorial Library 547
French-American Review 406
French-Belgian-Franco-Swiss Historical and Heritage Society of the Ozarks 340
Frenchboro Historical Society & Library 246
Frenchboro Historical Society Newsletter 246
French-Canadian Genealogical Society of Connecticut & Library 100
French-Canadian Heritage Society of Michigan 288
French-Canadian Heritage Society of Michigan & Archives 295, 298
French-Canadian Heritage Society of Michigan, Detroit Chapter 289
French-Canadian Heritage Society of Southern California 38
Frenchline 68
Frenchman Butte Museum Archives 706
Frensley Family Newsletter 227
Fresno City and County Historical Society & Archives 45
Fresno County Free Library 45
Fresno County Genealogical Society & Archives 45
Fresno Flats Gazette 57
Fresno Flats Historical Park Archives 57

Fresno-Past & Present 45
Fretz Family 492, 494
Freund Family 166
Frey Family 70
Frey-Fry, Harding-Harting-Hartung-Kress-Gress-Klapp-Clapp-Rupp-Weinhold-Wineholt-Grill-Krill-Sollenberger-Lorah-Hoster Family 493
Frey-Frye-Fry Family 490
Frick Art and Historical Center Archives 499
Friday Fragments 543
Fridley Historical Museum 311
Fridley Historical Society 308
Fridley Historical Society & Archives 311
Friedenberg Lutheran Historical Society 337
Friend Family 32, 259
Friend Genealogy Library 89
Friend to Friend 618
Friend's Newsletter 270, 273
Friendly Notes 514
Friends 121
Friends 305, 473, 514
Friends Favorites 221
Friends Footnotes 51, 326
Friends for Long Island's Heritage 417
Friends Free Library of Germantown 497
Friends Historical Association 489
Friends Historical Library of Swarthmore College 503
Friends Journal 460
Friends Meeting House Museum Archives 453
Friends News 352
Friends Newsletter 91, 92, 97, 112, 129, 195, 218, 269, 376, 416, 418, 419, 428, 443, 496, 507, 556
Friends of Abandoned Cemeteries of Staten Island 417
Friends of Abandoned Cemeteries of Staten Island Newsletter 417
Friends of Altadena Newsletter 35
Friends of Arizona Archives 18
Friends of Arrow Rock 325
Friends of Baldwin County Cemeteries 134
Friends of Bulloch Hall 136
Friends of Cabildo 240
Friends of Caleb Pusey House & Archives 503
Friends of Carrillo Ranch 39
Friends of Champanoeg & Library 479
Friends of Coolspring Presbyterian Church & Library 104
Friends of Firemen's Museum Archives 430
Friends of Florida 341
Friends of Genealogy & Library 241
Friends of Hearst Castle 69
Friends of Historic Augusta 325
Friends of Historic Boonville & Library 326
Friends of Historic Fort Osage 340
Friends of Historic Jekyll Island 132
Friends of Historic Kingston 402
Friends of Historic Kingston Newsletter 402
Friends of Historic Meridian 299
Friends Of Historic Northport 8
Friends of Historic Northport & Library 4
Friends of Historic Rochester 387
Friends of History in Fulton 398
Friends of Hollenberg Station & Archives 215
Friends of Jesse James Farm 334
Friends of John Jay Newsletter 401
Friends of Keytesville 333
Friends of Larchmont Public Library 402
Friends of Library 244
Friends of Library Bulletin 48
Friends of Library Newsletter 201, 274, 499
Friends of LPL Potpourri 296
Friends of Madera County Library Newsletter 53
Friends of Miami 335
Friends of Michigan History 295
Friends of Missouri Town 1855 325
Friends of Mitchell Library Research Committee & Archives 293
Friends of Mokuula 142
Friends of Murell Home Newsletter 468
Friends of Oheka 400
Friends of Old Annville 481
Friends of Old Saint Ferdinand Shrine 329
Friends of Old Saint Ferdinand Shrine Newsletter 329
Friends of Our House Committee & Archives 448
Friends of Pasco County Newsletter 114
Friends of Preston Library Newsletter 589
Friends of Rocheport & Archives 338
Friends of Rose Lawn 128
Friends of Schumacher Farm 633
Friends of the Adobes 69
Friends of the Archival Center 54
Friends of the Assinboines Foundation 347
Friends of the Blue Hills Quarterly 275
Friends of the Blue Hills Trust & Library 275
Friends of the Bronxville Library 390
Friends of the Carrillo Adobe 71
Friends of the Cornwall Public Library 394
Friends of the Dartmouth Library 361
Friends of the Delaware Canal 495
Friends of the Fenwick Island Lighthouse & Library 104
Friends of the Florence Stockade 244
Friends of the Hermitage & Archives 371
Friends of the Kingston Station 510
Friends of the Libraries Newsletter 543, 571
Friends of the Library 54, 95, 311, 369, 398, 415, 508, 532, 569
Friends of the Library Events Postcard 91
Friends of the Library Genealogical Research Group 457
Friends of the Library Information Paper 481
Friends of the Library News 476
Friends of the Library Newsletter 63, 116, 119, 354, 382, 388, 401, 424, 426, 526, 554, 477, 589
Friends of the Longfellow House Newsletter 268
Friends of the Museum 68
Friends of the Museum Newsletter 213, 486
Friends of the North Country 401
Friends of the Pendleton District Commission Newsletter 517
Friends of The Ridge Historical Society 399
Friends of the Robert Frost Farm Newsletter 360
Friends of the Socorro Public Library Newsletter 385
Friends of The Thumb 292
Friends of the Truman Farm Home 332
Friends of Timberline 478
Friends of Villa Aurora 58
Friends Proceedings 578
Friends' Newsletter 361

Friends' Quarterly 360
Friendscript 176
Friendship Fire Company Museum Archives 380
Friendship Firehouse Museum Archives 583
Friendship Hill National Historic Site Archives 500
Friendship News 259
Friendsletter 428
Friendswood Historical Society 546
Frisbie-Frisbee Family 204
Frisco Historical Museum 85
Frisco Historical Society 84, 85
Frisco Historical Society Newsletter 85
Frisco Native American Museum Archives 427
Frisian-Germanic Heritage 43
Frobisher Thresherman's Museum Archives 706
Froeschle-Uptegrove Family 479
Frog Lake Indian Band 643
From Harbor Hill 244
From Ireland 328
From the Boatyard 393
From the Bookshelf 388
From the Stacks 257
From the Trenches 449
Front Street Museum Archives 355
Frontenac County Schools Museum Archives 684
Frontenac Historical Museum 388
Frontenac Historical Society 418
Frontenac Historical Society & Archives 388
Frontier Army Museum 214
Frontier County Genealogical Society 351
Frontier County Historical Society 351
Frontier Gateway Museum Library 344
Frontier Gateway Museum Newsletter 344
Frontier Historical Museum 85
Frontier Historical Society & Archives 85
Frontier Historical Society Newsletter 85
Frontier Museum Archives 440
Frontier Researchers Genealogical Society & Library 27
Frontier Times 85
Frontier Times Museum Archives 537
Frontier Times Museum Newsletter 537
Frontier Village 202
Frontier Village Association Archives 438
Frontiers of Flight Museum Archives 542
Frontiers of Flight Museum Newsletter 542
Frost Family 529
Frost Free Library 362
Frost-Blackwood-Buckland-Bucklin Family 545
Fruitlands Museum Library 272
Fryar Family 427
Frye's Measure Mill Archives 365
Fryeburg Fair Farm Museum Archives 246
Fryeburg Historical Museum 246
Fryeburg Historical Society & Archives 246
Fryer Memorial Museum Archives 405
Fuerst Family 604
Fulbright Family 337
Fulcrum 504
Fulda Heritage Society 308
Fulda Heritage Society & Library 308
Fulgham Family 597
Fulgham-Fulghum Family 114, 427
Full'n By 65
Fuller Family 17, 134, 453, 491
Fuller Findings 149
Fuller Newsletter 46
Fuller Society Newsletter 246, 453
Fuller-Jackson-Cobb-Clinkscales Family 497
Fullerton Historic Theater Foundation 45
Fullerton Museum Center Archives 45
Fullerton Museum Center Newsletter 45
Fullerton Public Library 45
Fulton City Historian 398
Fulton County Chapter, OGS 458
Fulton County Folk Finder 192
Fulton County Genealogical and Historical Society & Library 228
Fulton County Genealogical Society 167
Fulton County Historical and Genealogical Society 153
Fulton County Historical and Genealogical Society Newsletter 153
Fulton County Historical Museum 192, 459
Fulton County Historical Society 32
Fulton County Historical Society & Archives 192, 459
Fulton County Historical Society & Library 398, 493
Fulton County Historical Society Quarterly 192
Fulton County Images 192
Fulton County Library 32, 493
Fulton County Museum Archives 399
Fulton County Pioneer 459
Fulton County Public Library 192
Fulton Family Letter 484
Fulton Footprints 458
Fulton Mansion State Historic Site Archives 546
Fulton Mansion State Historic Site Newsletter 546
Fulton Public Library 228, 398
Fulton-Hickman Genealogical Journal 228
Fultz House Museum Archives 675
Fundamenta 499
Fuqua Family Foundation 83
Fuqua Foundation News 83
Furbay Family 454
Furnace Town Living Heritage Museum Archives 263
Furnace Town Times 263
Furnas County Genealogical Society & Archives 349
Furnas County Genealogical Society Quarterly 349
Furnas-Gosper County Historical Museum 349
Furnas-Gosper County Historical Society 349
Furnas-Gosper Historical Society & Library 349
Furnell Family 331
Furrow 378
Furse Family 568
Fussell Family 571
Futcher Family 313
Futral-Clifford Family 525
Fyffe Family 455
FYI Newsletter 218
Fyler Family 101

G

G B Vick Memorial Library 340
G Lamar Harrison Library 466

Gabler Family Association Newsletter and Record 119
Gabriel Dumont Institute Library 709
Gabrio Family 599
Gadsby's Tavern Museum Library 583
Gadsden County Historical Society 120
Gadsden Museum Archives 384
Gadsden-Etowah County Library 4
Gadsen Historical Society 384
Gaffney Seanache 48
Gafford Clan 136
Gafford Family 536
Gage County Historical Museum 349
Gage County Historical Society & Archives 349
Gage Family Newsletter 124
Gagnebin Family 149
Gagnier-Gunter Newsletter 150
Gahanna Historical Society 446
Gail Borden Public Library 159
Gail Borden Public Library Newsletter 159
Gailey Family 572
Gaines County Library 560
Gaines Township Historical Society 292
Gainesville Genealogical Group 546
Gaineswood Historic Home Archives 3
Gaither Family 326, 428
Galax-Carroll Regional Library 588
Galbraigh Clan 266
Galbraith Clan 118, 266
Galbreath Family 154
Gale Free Library 272
Gale Library 363
Galen Historical Society 394
Galena Historical Museum 160
Galena Historical Preservation Society 329
Galena Mining and Historical Museum Association & Archives 214
Galena Public Library 160, 214
Galena-Jo Daviess County Historical Society & Archives 160
Galesburg Historical Society 160
Galesburg Memorial Library 292
Galesburg Public Library 160
Galeton Public Library 488
Galewood-Mount Claire Historical Society & Library 155
Galien Woods Historical Society 292
Galion Historical Museum 448
Galion Historical Society & Archives 448
Galitzianer 70
Gallagher Family 217
Gallant Graham Family 8
Gallatin County Historical Society 173
Gallatin County Historical Society & Archives 343
Gallatin County Historical Society Newsletter 343
Gallatin County History and Families 173
Gallatin County Pioneer Group 343
Gallatin Genealogy Society 343
Gallatin Public Library 234
Gallatin Trails 343
Galleries 50
Gallia County Historical and Genealogical Society & Library 448
Gallia County Historical and Genealogical Society Newsletter 448
Gallia County Historical Society 448
Gallia County Historical-Genealogical Society Newsletter 448
Gallier House Museum Archives 240
Gallier House Museum Quarterly 240
Galloping Goose Historical Society 88
Galloping Goose Historical Society of Dolores 84
Galloway Family 448
Galloway House 621
Galloway House and Village Newsletter 621
Galloway House and Village-Blakely Museum Archives 621
Galloway Station Museum Archives 643
Galt Area Historical Society 46
Galva Historical Society & Archives 161
Galva Public Library District 161
Galveston County Genealogical Society & Archives 546
Galveston County Genealogical Society Quarterly 546
Galveston County Historical Museum 546
Galveston County Historical Society & Archives 546
Galveston Historical Foundation & Archives 546
Galveston Historical Foundation Membership Update 546
Galveston Historical Museum 546
Gamble House Museum Archives 59
Gamble Plantation Historic State Park Archives 112
Gananoque Historical Museum Archives 682
Gananoque Public Library 682
Gann Gazette 84, 133
Gann Historical Society 133
Ganondagan State Historic Site Archives 419
Gant-Gaunt Family 596
Gantry Plaza State Park Archives 403
Ganttrees Newsletter 49
Ganz Family 296
GAR Memorial and Veterans' Military Museum Archives 151
GAR Memorial Museum 155
Gard Family 603, 604
Garden City Library 146
Garden City Public Library 5, 214, 398
Garden County Historical Museum 355
Garden Grove Historical Society & Archives 46
Garden Grove Historical Society Newsletter 46
Garden Park Farm Museum Archives 641
Garden Peninsula Historical Society 292
Garden Prairie Genealogical and Historical Society 161
Garden Valley District Library 146
Gard-Holt Family 63
Gardiner A Sage Theological Library 374
Gardiner Public Library 246
Gardner House Museum 285
Gardner House Museum Archives 285
Gardner Museum Archives 271
Gardner Museum Newsletter 271
Gardner-Bass Family 73
Gardner-Gardener-Gardiner-Garner Family Newsletter 568
Garfield County Genealogists 465
Garfield County Historical Society 350
Garfield County Historical Society & Archives 465
Garfield County Public Library System-New Castle Branch 88
Garfield Farm and Tavern Museum 163
Garfield Farm and Tavern Museum Newsletter 163
Garfield Free Public Library 370
Garfield Heights Historical Museum 445

Garfield Heights Historical Society & Archives 445
Garfield Heritage Society & Archives 163
Garibaldi and Meducci Museum Archives 417
Garland City Gazette 617
Garland County Historical Society 28
Garland County Historical Society & Library 28
Garland County Library 28
Garland Family 431, 528
Garland Gazette 529
Garland Genealogical Society 546
Garland Genealogical Society Newsletter 546
Garland Genealogical Society Quarterly 546
Garland Gray Research Center 590
Garmon Newsletter 44
Garnavillo Historical Museum 202
Garnavillo Historical Society & Archives 202
Garner Family 540
Garner Memorial Museum Archives 562
Garner Public Library 202
Garner-Thain Family 148
Garrard County Historical Society 229, 233
Garrard County Historical Society Bulletin 229
Garrard County Public Library 229
Garren Family 123
Garrett College Library 261
Garrett County Historical Museum 261
Garrett County Historical Society & Archives 261
Garrett Folklore and Fact 211
Garrett Heritage Park 184
Garrett Historic Home Archives 465
Garrett Historical Museum 184
Garrett Historical Museum Archives 184
Garrett Historical Society & Archives 184
Garrett Memorial Library 205
Garrigues Family 587
Garringer Family 459
Garrison Family 234
Garrison Gazette 234
Garrison-Selfridge Library 302
Garr-Young Family 327
Garst Museum 449
Garstin Family 476
Garvey Family 55
Garvin Family 205
Garwood Free Public Library 370
Gary Public Library 184
Garza County Historical Museum Archives 556
Gas City Historical Society 184
Gas City-Mill Township Public Library 184
GAS Lites 63
Gasconade County Historical Museum 336
Gasconade County Historical Society & Archives 336
Gasconade County Historical Society & Library 330
Gasconade County Historical Society Newsletter 330
Gaskill Ghosts 219
Gaslight 216
Gaspesian British Heritage Village Archives 700
Gaspesie 698
Gastineau Channel Historical Society 12
Gastineau Genealogical Society 12
Gastineau Newsletter 227
Gaston County Museum of Art and History Archives 425
Gaston County Public Library 427
Gaston T Gooch Library 541
Gaston-Lincoln Genealogical Society 427, 430
Gatekeepers Museum 74
Gatepost 612
Gates County Historical Society 427
Gates County Historical Society & Library 427
Gates County Historical Society Newsletter 427
Gates Family 601
Gates Historical Society 413
Gates Memorial Library 556
Gates Mills Historical Museum 448
Gates Mills Historical Society & Archives 448
Gates of Memory 71
Gates Public Library 413
Gatesville Public Library 546
Gateway 231, 234
Gateway 59
Gateway Diggers 198
Gateway Heritage 339
Gateway Military Historical Society 338
Gateway to the Panhandle Library 465
Gatherers 367
Gathering Gibsons 292
Gatherings 295, 361
Gathland State Park Archives 257
Gault-Galt Family 286
Gavin Family Newsletter 20
Gavitt Family Newsletter 96
Gay-Hoyt House Museum 99
Gay-Kimball Public Library 365
Gaylord Fact-Finders Genealogical Society & Library 292
Gaylord Family 73
Gaylordsville Historical Society 93, 97
Gazebo Gazette 404
Gazette 101
Geary County Historical Society & Library 216
Geary Genealogical Society 465
Geary Glimmers 216
Geauga County Genealogical Society & Archives 444
Geauga County Historical Society & Archives 443
Geauga County Historical Society Quarterly 443
Geauga County Public Library 444
Geauga West Library 444
Gebhart Family Society of America Newsletter 262
Geddes Gazette 573
Geddes Historic District Village Archives 522
Gee Family 30
Geer Family Association Newsletter 136
Geisel Library 362
Geisler Library 207
Gem County Historical Museum 146
Gem County Historical Society & Library 146
Gemini 396
Gems of Genealogy 622
Gen William Hart House 98
GenCAP ONLINE Newsletter 497
GENCOM PC User Group of Shreveport 241

Gene Autry Oklahoma Museum Archives 465
Gene Stratton-Porter Memorial Society Newsletter 192
Gene Stratton-Porter State Historic Site Archives 192
Gene View 169
Geneagram 120
Genealogia 331
Genealogical Aids Bulletin 447
Genealogical and Historical Council of Sacramento Valley 63
Genealogical and Historical Council of Sacramento Valley Newsletter 63
Genealogical and Historical Society of Caldwell County 552
Genealogical Association of English-Speaking Researchers in Europe 388
Genealogical Association of Nova Scotia 674
Genealogical Association of Sacramento & Library 63
Genealogical Association of Southwestern Michigan & Library 302
Genealogical Bulletin 549
Genealogical Center Library 123, 134
Genealogical Club of Sun City 74
Genealogical Club of the Montgomery County Historical Society & Library 262
Genealogical Compendium of Books and Articles in Print 549
Genealogical Computing 569
Genealogical Computing Association of Pennsylvania 497
Genealogical Council of Maryland Bible Records 259
Genealogical Council of Oregon 479
Genealogical Extraction Center 145
Genealogical Forum of Elmhurst Illinois & Archives 159
Genealogical Forum of Elmhurst Newsletter 159
Genealogical Forum of Oregon & Library 478
Genealogical Gems 617
Genealogical Goldmine 59
Genealogical Group of Oklahoma City LDS Stake 468
Genealogical Group of Seminole County 110
Genealogical Inquirer 268
Genealogical Institute 572
Genealogical Institute & Library 570
Genealogical Institute of Oklahoma 468
Genealogical Institute Research News 570
Genealogical Journal 571
Genealogical Journal of Essex County, NY 145
Genealogical Journal of Jefferson County, NY 145
Genealogical Library at Lidderdale 198
Genealogical Library of the Church of Jesus Christ of Latter Day Saints 570
Genealogical Library Quarterly 42
Genealogical Magazine of New Jersey 374
Genealogical Newsletter of the Royal Nova Scotia Historical Society 674
Genealogical Periodical Annual Index 257
Genealogical Record 360, 549
Genealogical Research Center 643
Genealogical Research Center and Library of Southeast Texas 551
Genealogical Research Institute of Virginia 593
Genealogical Research Institute of Virginia News 'N Notes 593
Genealogical Research Society of Durango 84
Genealogical Research Society of Eau Claire & Archives 620
Genealogical Research Society of New Orleans 240
Genealogical Research Society of Northeastern Pennsylvania 496
Genealogical Researchers & Archives 211
Genealogical Researchers Of Linn County 326
Genealogical Resources At McMillan 634
Genealogical Roots and Branches 515
Genealogical Roundtable 269
Genealogical Society of Allegany County 258
Genealogical Society of Allegany County & Library 260
Genealogical Society of Arizona 21
Genealogical Society of Arizona Quarterly 21
Genealogical Society of Bergen County, New Jersey 377
Genealogical Society of Broward County & Library 119
Genealogical Society of Broward County Newsletter 112
Genealogical Society of Butler County 337
Genealogical Society of Carleton County Quarterly 307
Genealogical Society of Carlton County & Library 307
Genealogical Society of Carter County Oklahoma & Library 463
Genealogical Society of Cass County 290
Genealogical Society of Cecil County 257
Genealogical Society of Cecil County Newsletter 257
Genealogical Society of Central Missouri & Archives 327
Genealogical Society of Central Missouri Newsletter 327
Genealogical Society of Central Missouri Reporter Quarterly 327
Genealogical Society of Chesterfield County 513
Genealogical Society of Davidson County & Library 429
Genealogical Society of Davidson County Newsletter 429
Genealogical Society of DeSoto County & Library 320
Genealogical Society of Douglas County & Archives 479
Genealogical Society of East Alabama 1
Genealogical Society of Fayette and Raleigh Counties 614
Genealogical Society of Fayette and Raleigh Counties News Notes 614
Genealogical Society of Flemish Americans & Library 301
Genealogical Society of Flemish Americans Newsletter 301
Genealogical Society of Greater Miami 117
Genealogical Society of Hancock County & Archives 228
Genealogical Society of Henry and Clayton Counties & Library 134
Genealogical Society of Henry and Clayton Counties Quarterly 134
Genealogical Society of Hispanic America 83
Genealogical Society of Hispanic America Newsletter 83
Genealogical Society of Hispanic America, Pueblo Chapter 89
Genealogical Society of Hispanic America, Southern California 71
Genealogical Society of Hispanic America, Southern California Chapter 38
Genealogical Society of Hispanic America, Trinidad Chapter 90
Genealogical Society of Iredell County & Library 433
Genealogical Society of Liberty & Library 334
Genealogical Society of Liberty Quarterly Newsletter 334
Genealogical Society of Linn County Iowa & Library 198
Genealogical Society of Madera 53
Genealogical Society of Monroe County 298
Genealogical Society of Monroe County Michigan Quarterly 298
Genealogical Society of Monroe County Record 298
Genealogical Society of Montgomery County 182
Genealogical Society of Morongo Basin & Library 79
Genealogical Society of New Jersey & Library 374
Genealogical Society of North Brevard 123
Genealogical Society of North Central Washington & Library 609
Genealogical Society of North Orange County California 78
Genealogical Society of North Orange County Newsletter 78
Genealogical Society of Northeast Texas & Archives 555
Genealogical Society of Okaloosa County, Florida Journal 113
Genealogical Society of Okeechobee 118
Genealogical Society of Okeechobee Newsletter 118
Genealogical Society of Old Tryon County & Library 426
Genealogical Society of Old Tryon County Bulletin 426
Genealogical Society of Original Muscogee County 128
Genealogical Society of Page County 590
Genealogical Society of Page County Newsletter 590

INDEX

Genealogical Society of Pennsylvania & Archives 497
Genealogical Society of Pennsylvania Historical Museum 497
Genealogical Society of Pierce County 608
Genealogical Society of Riverside 62
Genealogical Society of Rockingham and Stokes Counties 430
Genealogical Society of Rockland County & Library 405
Genealogical Society of Rockland County Newsletter 405
Genealogical Society of Rowan County 432
Genealogical Society of Salem County 380
Genealogical Society of Santa Cruz County & Library 70
Genealogical Society of Santa Rosa County 117
Genealogical Society of Sarasota 121, 123
Genealogical Society of Sarasota Newsletter 121, 123
Genealogical Society of Siskiyou County & Archives 78
Genealogical Society of South Brevard County 116
Genealogical Society of South Whidbey Island 603
Genealogical Society of South Whidbey Island Newsletter 603
Genealogical Society of Southeast Alaska 12
Genealogical Society of Southeast Alaska Newsletter 12
Genealogical Society of Southeast Volusia County 112, 118
Genealogical Society of Southwestern Pennsylvania & Archives 504
Genealogical Society of Stanislaus County & Library 54
Genealogical Society of the Big Spring 538
Genealogical Society of the Northern Neck of Virginia & Library 589
Genealogical Society of the Northern Neck of Virginia Newsletter 589
Genealogical Society of the West Fields & Archives 380
Genealogical Society of Van Zandt County & Library 539
Genealogical Society of Vermont 579
Genealogical Society of Vermont & Library 578
Genealogical Society of Vermont Newsletter 579
Genealogical Society of Washington County 3
Genealogical Society of Washtenaw County 285
Genealogical Society of Washtenaw County Newsletter 285
Genealogical Society of Watauga County 423
Genealogical Society of Westfield 380
Genealogical Society of Whitley County 181
Genealogical Society of Winters High School 563
Genealogical Society of Yuma, Arizona & Library 23
Genealogical Society of Yuma, Arizona Newsletter 23
Genealogical Speaker's Guild 105
Genealogical Speakers Guild Directory 105
Genealogical Tips 548
Genealogical Workshop of Mesa & Library 17
Genealogically Speaking 514
Genealogie Abitibi-Temiscamingue 701
Genealogija 155
Genealogist 20, 74, 250
Genealogists of the Clinton County Historical Society & Library 302
Genealogy & History Research Library 575
Genealogy and Family History 579
Genealogy and Family History Committee Newsletter 385
Genealogy and Historical Society of Pulaski County 342
Genealogy Annual 104
Genealogy Central 278
Genealogy Club Newsletter 381
Genealogy Club of Albuquerque Quarterly 381
Genealogy Club of Angel Fire 381
Genealogy Club of Osceola County 121
Genealogy Club of Putnam County 184
Genealogy Club of the Albuquerque Public Library 381
Genealogy Council of the Jewish Historical Society of Maryland & Archives 255
Genealogy for Canadian, French and Metis Study 308
Genealogy Friends Of Plano Libraries 556
Genealogy Friends of the Library 335
Genealogy Friends of the Library Newsletter 335
Genealogy Gleanings 612
Genealogy Guild of Wilkin County, MN and Richland County, ND 439
Genealogy Jottings 180, 193
Genealogy Research Center and Museum 136
Genealogy Society of Craighead County, Arkansas 29
Genealogy Society of Craighead County, Arkansas Newsletter 29
Genealogy Society of Hernando County 110
Genealogy Society of Pinal County 15
Genealogy Society of Pulaski County & Library 328
Genealogy Society of Southern Illinois & Archives 154
Genealogy Society of Southern Illinois Newsletter: the Saga of Southern Illinois 154
Genealogy Society of Vallejo & Archives 76
Genealogy Times and Seasons 570
Genealogy Unlimited Society Newsletter 139
Genealogy West Newsletter 240
Genealogy West, West Bank of the Mississippi River 240
Genealogy Workshop Bulletin 391
Genealogy-History of Yellow Medicine County News Letter 308
Genealogymagazine.com 560
Geneline 112
Geneline: Renville County Genealogical Society Newsletter 313
General Adam Stephen Memorial Association & Library 613
General Conference of Seventh Day Adventists 262
General Crook House Museum 355
General Crook House Museum Newsletter 355
General Daniel Bissell House Museum 339
General Douglas L McBride Museum Archives 384
General Douglas Macarthur Memorial Archives 592
General Grant National Memorial Museum Archives 406
General Henry Knox Museum 251
General Jacob Brown Historical Society & Archives 391
General John Burrows Historical Society 494
General John J Pershing Boyhood Home Archives 333
General Lew Wallace Museum Archives 182
General Lew Wallace Museum Newsletter 182
General Lewis B Hershey Museum Archives 179
General Order 266
General Patton Memorial Museum Archives 40
General Patton Memorial Museum Newsletter 40
General Society of Colonial Wars 406
General Society of the War of 1812 494
General Stacks 560
General Sterling Price Museum 333
General Store Museum Archives 619
General Sweeny's Civil War Museum Archives 337
General Wait House Museum 580
Generation After 391
Generation Seekers 214
Generations 255, 256
Generations 291, 297, 304, 339, 593, 662, 663
Generations Of Our Past! 47
Generator 260
Genesee Area Genealogists 389

Genesee County Historical Department Library 389
Genesee County Historical Museum 291
Genesee County Historical Society & Archives 291
Genesee County Village Museum Archives 405
Genesee District Library 291
Genesee District Library-Davison Area 289
Genesee Heritage Society 622
Genesee Public Library 403
Genesee Valley Indian Association 291
Geneseo Historical Association 161
Geneseo Public Library 214
Geneseo Public Library District 161
Geneva County Historical Society 5
Geneva Free Library 398
Geneva Historical and Genealogical Society 113
Geneva Historical Museum 161
Geneva Historical Society & Archives 161, 398
Geneva Historical Society Newsletter 398
Geneva Lake Historical Museum 624
Geneva Lake History Buffs & Archives 624
Geneva Public Library 184
Geneva Public Library District 161
Genie 241
Genie Bug 205
Genie Gems 204
Genie Gleaners 202
Genie's View 169
Genoa Historical Society 351
GenServ-Family History 558
GEN-TREE 475
Gentry County Genealogical Society 325
Gentry County Library 341
Gentry Family 591
Genz Newsletter 262
Geographical Center Historical Museum 439
Geographical Center Historical Society & Archives 439
Geographical Center Historical Society Newsletter 439
George & Helen Ladd Library 247
George A Smathers Library 113
George Ade House Museum Archives 180
George Ashby Memorial Museum 11
George Brown House 692
George Bush Presidential Library 540
George C Marshall Foundation & Archives 589
George C Marshall Foundation Topics 589
George C Marshall Museum 589
George C Ruhle Library 347
George Coon Public Library 233
George Eastman House Museum Archives 413
George Eastman House Museum Newsletter 413
George F Boyer Museum 380
George F Johnson Memorial Library 397
George Family 351, 557
George Gamble Library 360
George Gustav Heye Cente 407
George H and Laura E Brown Library 434
George H Stowell Free Library 360
George Hail Free Library and Museum 509
George Holmes Bixby Memorial Library 361
George Johnston Tlingit Indian Museum Archives 713
George Little Family Association Newsletter 40
George M Jones Library Association 590
George McCone Memorial County Library 344
George Meany Memorial Archives 262
George Memorial Library of Fort Bend County 557
George Moffett Library 563
George Peabody Library 255
George Rogers Clark Heritage Association 457
George Rogers Clark National Historical Park Archives 195
George S Patton Jr Historical Society & Library 65
George State Cotton Museum Archives 139
George T & Gladys H Abell Library 560
George Washington Bicentennial Center 583
George Washington Birthplace National Monument Archives 586, 597
George Washington Carver Museum Library 536
George Washington Carver National Monument Library 328
George Washington Masonic National Memorial Archives 583
George Washington Masonic National Memorial Newsletter 583
George Washington's Ferry Farm Archives 595
George Washington's Headquarters Archives 258
George-Lyon(s)-Line(s) Family 137
Georgetown County Historical Commission 514
Georgetown County Historical Society 514
Georgetown County Library System 514
Georgetown Energy Museum Archives 85
Georgetown Historical Museum 85
Georgetown Historical Society 103, 246
Georgetown Peabody Library 271
Georgetown Public Library 103, 546
Georgia Baptist Historical Society & Archives 133
Georgia Capitol Museum Archives 126
Georgia Civil War Heritage Trails 130
Georgia Department of Archives & History Library 134
Georgia Department of Archives and History 126
Georgia Department of Human Resources Vital Records Service 126
Georgia Genealogical Magazine 515
Georgia Genealogical Research 529
Georgia Genealogical Society 126
Georgia Genealogical Society Newsletter 126
Georgia Genealogical Society Quarterly 126
Georgia Historical Museum 137
Georgia Historical Quarterly 137
Georgia Historical Records Advisory Board 126
Georgia Historical Society 579
Georgia Historical Society & Archives 137
Georgia Historical Society Foot-Notes 137
Georgia Military Academy Archives 128
Georgia Music Hall of Fame Archives 133
Georgia Regional Library for the Blind and Physically Handicapped 126
Georgia Rural Telephone Museum 133
Georgia Salzburger Society 135
Georgia Salzburger Society Newsletter 135
Georgia Southern University Museum Archives 137
Georgia State Library 126
Georgia Trust for Historic Preservation 126
Georgia Veterans Memorial Museum Archives 129
Georgia's Antebellum Capital Museum Society 134
Georgia's Old Capital Museum Archives 134
Georgian Bay Nation 685
Georgian Bay Native Friendship Centre 685

Georgian Museum 451
Georgina Island First Nation 690
Georgina Pioneer Museum Archives 684
Gerade-Gibson Family 583
Gerald B James Library 434
Gerald Family 490
Gerald Ford Foundation Newsletter 285
Gerald J Ball Library 182
Gerald R Ford Library 285
Gerald R Ford Museum Archives 292
Gerald R Sherratt Library 565
Gerber-Garber Family 492
Gerberich Family 491, 495
Gerhard-Bergkamp Family 219
Gerhart Family 481, 505
Gering Public Library 352
German American Genealogy 38
German American Heritage Center 200
German American Heritage Society 339
German Baptist Brethren Meeting House 486
German Canadian Historical Association 691
German Connection 65
German Friendly Societ 512
German Genealogical Digest 571
German Genealogical Digest: A Quarterly Journal for German Researchers 570
German Genealogical Society 571
German Genealogy Group 402
German Historical Institute & Library 105
German Research Association & Library 65
German Research Association Newsletter 65
German Research Index 314
German Settlement 330
German Society of Pennsylvania & Library 497
German Society of Winnipeg 662
German Studies Review 312
German Village Society 446
German-Acadian Coast Historical and Genealogical Society 236
German-American Heritage Institute 160
German-American National Congress 155
German-Bohemian Heritage Society 312
Germanic Genealogist 42
Germanic Genealogy Society 314
Germanic Genealogy Society Newsletter 314
German-Jewish Families Society 406
Germanna 586
Germanna Community College-Locust Grove Campus Library 590
Germanna Record 586
Germans from Russia Heritage Society & Library 437
Germans from Russia Heritage Society Newsletter 437
German-Texan Heritage Society & Library 536
German-Texan Heritage Society Newsletter 536
Germantown Commission Association 239
Germantown Crier 497
Germantown Historical Museum 497
Germantown Historical Society 622
Germantown Historical Society & Archives 497
Germantown Historical Society Newsletter 622
Germantown Library 398
Germantown Public Library 449
Geronimo Springs Museum 385
Gerould Family 494
Gerow Family Newsletter 96
Gerrish Family 75
Gerry-Bryan-Clark Family 489
Gerth Family 47
Gertrude Kistler Memorial Library 501
Gertrude Smith House Museum Archives 430
Getting Gray 292
Gettysburg National Military Park Library 488
Getz Family 483
Geyer Newsletter 541
Gholston-Cason Family 61
Ghost Ranch Living Museum Library 381
Ghost Town Museum Archives 82
Giacchi-Kelly-Colter-Morelli-Elder-Hubbell-Mallory-Lawrence-McDonald-Boots-Johnston Family 428
Gibbon Heritage Center Associates & Library 352
Gibbons Family 499
Gibbs Family 231
Gibbs Family Newsletter 200
Gibbs Gathering 153
Gibbs Memorial Library 553
Gibbs Museum of Pioneer and Dakotah Life Archives 308
Gibbs Newsletter 208
Gibbs-Johnson Family Newsletter 81
Gibbs-Shadowens-Dawson-Richardson-Beard-Wilson-Boutwell Family 236
Gibraltar Historical Association 621
Gibson County Historical Society 192
Gibson County Lines 192
Gibson County Memorial Library 533
Gibson House Archives 693
Gibson House Museum 267
Gibson House Museum Archives 686
Gibson Island Historical Society 259
Gibson Society 267
Giddens Family 424
Gidder House 368
Giddings Family 17
Giddings Public Library 546
Gideon Family 446
Gideon's Trumpet 392
Gidney Family 572
Gig Harbor Peninsula Historical Museum 602
Gig Harbor Peninsula Historical Society & Archives 602
Gig Harbor Peninsula Historical Society Newsletter 602
Gila County Historical Museum 16
Gila County Historical Museum Archives 17
Gila County Historical Society & Archives 16
Gila Heritage 18
Gilbart Mercier Memorial Library 393
Gilbert Hart Library 580
Gilbert Historical Society 16
Gilbert Library 97
Gilbert Simmons Branch Library 623
Gilbert Stuart Museum Archives 509
Gilbertsville Free Library 398
Gilbertsville Library Historical Committee & Archives 398
Gilchrist County Genealogical Society 123
Gilchrist Family 147

Gilcrease Journal 470
Gilcrease Museum Archives 470
Giles County Historical Society & Library 532, 592
Giles County Historical Society Bulletin 532
Giles County Historical Society Newsletter 592
Giles County Public Library 532
Giles County Public Library Bulletin 532
Gilford Public Library 361
Gill Family 572
Gill Memorial Library 376
Gillam Community Museum Archives 660
Gillean Clan 535
Gillean Family 528
Gilleland Family 535
Gilleland, Gilliland Newsletter 50
Gillenwater-Balfour-Marshall Family 143
Gillespie Clan Newsletter 332
Gillespie County Historical Society and Commission & Library 546
Gillespie Family 686
Gillespie Public Library 161
Gillet, Gillette, Gillett Family 354
Gillette Gazette 73
Gillette Historical Society 73
Gilliam Communique 11
Gilliam County Historical Society & Archives 474
Gilliam County Historical Society Newsletter 474
Gilliam Family 430
Gillie-Gilley-Carson Family 571
Gilman Area Historical Society 622
Gilman Garrison House Museum Archives 360
Gilman Historic Ranch and Wagon Museum Archives 36
Gilman Museum Archives 489
Gilman Town Hall Museum 602
Gilmer County Historical Society 612
Gilmer County Historical Society & Library 612
Gilmer County Historical Society Newsletter 612
Gilmer Genealogical Society 546
Gilmer Public Library 612
Gilmore Car Museum Archives 293
Gilmore Car Museum Newsletter 293
Gilmore City Public Library 202
Gilmore-Dickinson Famil 137
Gilmore-Gilmer-Gilmour-Gillmore Family 547
Gilpin County Historical Society 85
Gilpin County Public Library 85
Gilpin History Museum Archives 82
Gilson Family 569
Gilstrap Family 558
Gimli Historical Museum Archives 660
Gingras Trading Post State Historic Site Archives 439
Giorgi Family 71
Giovale Library 571
Gipson Gazette 560
Girard Public Library 214
Girard Township Library 161
Girdner Family 464
Gish Family 39
Gitanmaax Indian Band 650
Gitanyow Indian Band 651
Gitlakdamix Indian Band 652
Gitsegukla Indian Band 655
Gitwangak Indian Band 651
Gitwinksihlkw Indian Band 650
Gitxsan Local Services Society 650
Given Memorial Library 431
Glace Bay Historical Society 674
Glacier County Library 344
Glade Star 261
Glades County Historical Society 117
Gladstone Area School and Public Library 292
Gladstone Museum Archives 660
Gladwin County Historical Society 292
Gladwin County Library 292
Gladwyne Free Library 488
Gladys Harrington Public Library 556
Glandon Family 20
Glanmore National Historic Site Archives 680
Glas Kanadskih Srba: Voice of Canadian Serbs 693
Glasco: La Colline 557
Glascow Area Historical and Preservation Society 329
Glasgow City County Library 344
Glasgow Family 515
Glass Family 161
Glass Museum 278
Glass Newsletter 553
Glassboro Public Library 370
Glastonbury Historical Museum 93
Glattfelder Family 506
Gleanings 55, 203, 482
Gleanings from the Heart of the Cornbelt 168
Gleanings from the West Fields 380
Gleason Family 626
Gleason Public Library 268
Gleaves Family 333
Glebe House Archives 412
Glebe House Museum Archives 102
Glee Merritt Kelley Community Library 581
Glen Cove Public Library 398
Glen Ellyn Historical Society & Archives 161
Glen Ewen Community Antique Centre 706
Glen Ridge Free Public Library 370
Glen Rock Historical Society 370
Glen Ullin Historical Society & Library 438
Glen Vowell Indian Band 650
Glenbow - Occasional Papers 641
Glenbow Museum Archives Series 641
Glenbow Museum Library and Archives 641
Glenbow-Alberta Institute 641
Glencairn Museum Archives 483
Glencairn Museum Journal 483
Glencairn Museum Newsletter 483
Glencoe Historical Museum 161
Glencoe Historical Society 161, 682
Glencoe Historical Society & Archives 161
Glendale Area Public Library 485
Glendale Arizona Historical Society 16
Glendale Historical Society 16, 46329
Glendale Historical Society 329
Glendale Historical Society 46
Glendale Public Library 16, 46, 344

INDEX

Glendo Historical Historical Society 636
Glendora Genealogy Group & Library 46
Glendora Genealogy Group Newsletter 46
Glendora Historical Museum 46
Glendora Historical Society & Archives 46
Glendora Historical Society Newsletter 46
Glendora Public Library 46
Glendower State Memorial Museum Archives 451
Glengarry and Area Genealogial Library 684
Glengarry Genealogical Society 684
Glengarry Historical Society & Archives 679
Glengarry Pioneer Museum Archives 682
Glenn A Jones Memorial Library 86
Glenn Family 259
Glenn G Bartle Library 389
Glenn Genealogy Group 58
Glenn H Curtiss Museum of Local History Library 399
Glenn House 326
Glenn L Martin Maryland Aviation Museum Archives 256
Glenns Ferry Historical Museum 146
Glenns Ferry Historical Society & Archives 146
Glens Falls-Queensbury Historical Association & Archives 398
Glensheen Historic Estate Archives 307
Glenside Free Library 488
Glentworth Museum Archives 706
Glenview Area Historical Museum 161
Glenview Area Historical Society & Archives 161
Glenview Area Historical Society Newsletter 161
Glenview Public Library 161
Glenview Public Library Newsletter 161
Glenwood Area Historical Society 622
Glenwood Public Library 202
Glerum Family 49
Glessner House Museum Archives 155
Glimpses of Grayson 589
Gloucester City Historical Society 370
Gloucester County College Library 377
Gloucester County Historical Society & Archives 380
Gloucester County Historical Society & Library 380
Gloucester County Library System-Swedesboro Public 378
Gloucester Heritage Society & Library 507
Gloucester Historical Museum 682
Gloucester Historical Society & Archives 682
Glover Family Association Newsletter 134
Glover Historical Society 576
Gloversville Free Library 398
Gluckstal Colonies Research Association Newsletter 61
Gluckstal Colony Research Association 61
Glyndon Area Historical Society 308
Gnadenhutten Historical Museum 449
Gnadenhutten Historical Society & Archives 449
Gnadenhutten Public Library 449
Gneiss News 277
Go West 211
Goates Family 572
Goble Family 493
Gochenour Family 536
Godbee Family 136
Goddard Historical and Genealogical Society 493, 526
Goddard Newsletter 223, 493, 526
Godfrey Family 634
Godfrey Memorial Library 96
Goff-Gough Family 529
Goff-Nelson Memorial Library 418
Goffstown Historical Society 361
Gogebic County Historical Society 294
Goingsnake District Heritage Association & Archives 471
Goingsnake Messenger 471
Goins Family 553
Golconda Public Library 161
Gold Coast Railroad Museum Archives 117
Gold Diggers 73
Gold Family 545
Gold Hill Historical Society 475
Gold Nugget 545
Gold Nugget Museum Archives 59
Golda Meir Library 626
Golden Age 148
Golden Age Courier 350
Golden Age of Trucking Museum Archives 95
Golden Ball Tavern Trust Library 282
Golden District Historical Museum 650
Golden District Historical Society & Archives 650
Golden Family 587
Golden Gate Baptist Theological Seminary Library 54
Golden Gate Genealogy Society 66
Golden Gate Railroad Museum Archives 62, 66
Golden Gate-Naples Genealogical Society 118
Golden Gazette 430
Golden Historical Society 161
Golden Notes 63, 64
Golden Nugget 425
Golden Nuggets 64
Golden Pioneer Museum Archives 85
Golden Roots of the Mother Lode 73
Golden Spike 199
Golden Spike National Historic Site Archives 565
Golden State Museum Archives 63
Golden Valley Historical Society 308
Goldenseal 615
Goldfield Historical Society 15
Goldfinch 203
Goldhahn Family Newsletter 173
Golding Family 25, 321, 322
Goldsberry Family 444
Goldstream Region Museum Archives 657
Goleta Valley Historical Society 46
Goleta Valley Historical Society Newsletter 46
Goleta Valley History 46
Goliad County Library 547
Goliad State Historical Park Archives 547
Golliher-Trent Family 332
Gomez Family 558
Gonce Family 355
Gondolla Gazette 612
Gonfanon 687
Gonsalus-Duk Family 211
Gonzales County Archives 547
Gonzales County Historical Commission 547
Gonzales Family 236

Gonzales Memorial Museum Archives 547
Gonzales Public Library 547
Gooch Family Quarterly 133
Goochland County Historical Museum 588
Goochland County Historical Society & Archives 588
Goochland County Historical Society Magazine 588
Good Old Days 180
Good Old Days Vintage Motorcar Museum Archives 28
Good Will Record 247
Good Word 265
Goodall City Library 355
Goode Family 596
Goode-Barren Historical Genealogical Society 173
Goodenow Family 259, 261
Goodenow Family 529
Good-Hames Family 425
Goodhue Area Historical Society 308
Goodhue County Family Tree Club 313
Goodhue County Historical Museum 313
Goodhue County Historical News 313
Goodhue County Historical Society & Library 313
Gooding County Genealogical Society 146
Gooding County Historical Society & Archives 146
Gooding Public Library 146
Goodland & Grant Township Public Library 184
Goodly Heritage 167
Goodman Family 573
Goodman Museum Archives 561
Goodnight Memorial Library 227
Goodnow House Museum and Historical Site Archives 218
Goodnow Library 280
Goodrich Family 154, 406
Goodrich Gospel 154
Goodrich House Archives 626
Goodrich Memorial Library 578
Goodridge Area Historical Society & Library 308
Goodsoil Historical Museum Archives 706
Goodstein Foundation Library 635
Goodwille House Museum 575
Goodwin Family 36, 384, 566
Goodwin Memorial Library 271
Goodwin News 384
Goold Family 390
Gooley-Maughan Family 571
Goolsby Family 200
Gorbett-Gorbet Family 383
Gorby Family 572
Gordo Public Library 5
Gordon Browning Museum and Genealogical Library 530
Gordon City Library 352
Gordon College Library 127
Gordon County Historical Society 127
Gordon Family 590
Gordon First Nation 709
Gordon Wascott Historical Museum 622
Gordon Wascott Historical Society & Archives 622
Gordon-Nash Library 363
Gore Family 384
Gore Family Newsletter 41
Gore Place Museum Archives 281
Gorgas House Museum Archives 9
Gorham Grandparents 47
Gorham Historical Society 361
Gorham Public Library 361
Gorham-MacBane Public Library 533
Gorley-Gourlay Family 130
Goschenhoppen Historians & Archives 488
Goschenhoppen Newsletter 488
Goshen County Public Library 638
Goshen Historical Museum 93
Goshen Historical Society 184, 449
Goshen Historical Society & Archives 93, 398
Goshen Historical Society Annual Letter 93
Goshen Historical Society Newsletter 184
Goshen Public Library 184, 398
Gosnell Family 378
Gosnell Feathers 11
Gospel Advocate Archives and Library 531
Gosport History Museum Archives 184
Gosselin Family 555
Gossler Family 478
Goth Family 51
Gotham Family 384
Gothenburg Historical Society & Library 352
Gottlob Family 115
Gottschee Tree 586
Goulbourn Township Public Library 690
Gould Family 21
Gould Memorial Library 127
Gouldsboro Historical Societ & Archives 246
Gourdin Family 258
Gouverneur Historical Association & Archives 398
Gouverneur Historical Museum 398
Gov Upham Mansion 625
Govan and District Museum 706
Gover Family 225
Government House Historical Society 709
Government House Museum and Heritage Site 709
Governor Barry Historical Association 288
Governor Bent Museum Archives 385
Governor General's Foot Guards Regimental Museum Archives 687
Governor Henry Lippitt House Museum Archives 509
Governor Henry Lippitt House Museum Newsletter 509
Governor Hogg Shrine State Park Archives 557
Governor John Langdon House Museum Archives 364
Governor Printz Park Archives 500
Governor Printz Park Museum Archives 487
Governor Ross Plantation 104
Governor Seay Mansion Archives 466
Governor Sprague Mansion 507
Governor Stephen Hopkins House Museum Archives 509
Governor Wolf Historical Society 482
Governor's Mansion Archives 227
Governor's Mansion Museum Archives 513
Governor's Mansion State Historical Park Archives 63
Gowen Family 552
Gower Family 528
Gowganda and Area Museum Archives 682
Gow-Ganda and Area Museum Archives 683
GPS News 216

Grabeal Family 229
Graber Oliver House Museum Archives 57
Grace & Roger Babson Learning Center 109
Grace A Dow Memorial Library 297
Grace and Holy Trinity Cathedral Archives 332
Grace Armantrout Museum Archives 546
Grace Balloch Memorial Library 524
Grace Doherty Library 226
Grace Hall Memorial Library 275
Grace Hudson Museum & Sun House Archives 75
Grace Lutheran Church Library 20
Grace M Pickens Public Library 466
Grace Museum Archives 535
Grace Van Dyke Bird Library 36
Graceland Gazette 335
Graceland Museum 335
Gracie Mansion Conservancy Museum Archives 406
Grad Family 281
Gradeless-Grayless-Mort Family 630
Grady C Hogue Library 538
Grady County Genealogical Society & Archives 464
Grady County Genealogical Society Newsletter 464
Grady County Historical Society 127
Grady County Historical Society & Library 464
Grady E Love Library 429
Graeme Park Museum Archives 490
Graf(f) Gazette 548
Graff Family 145
Graff Newsletter 571
Grafton Historical Museum 576
Grafton Historical Society 398
Grafton Historical Society & Archives 576
Grafton-Midview Public Library 449
Graham Clan 428, 573
Graham County Historical Museum 20, 21
Graham County Historical Society 20
Graham County Historical Society & Archives 20, 21
Graham County Historical Society & Library 215
Graham County Public Library 215
Graham Family 558, 569
Graham Group 292
Graham Historical Society 584
Graham Historical Society & Library 335
Graham Public Library 547, 632
Graham-Gill Family 298
Graham-Puckett Family 604
Grain Valley Historical Society 329
Grains of Research 343
Gralla Family 566
Gramse-Gramsey Family 18
Granada Historical Society 308
Granbury Depot 547
Granbury Depot Archives 544
Granby Free Public Library 271
Granby Historical Society 329
Granby Town Historian 398
Grand Army of the Republic & Archives 155
Grand Army of the Republic Museum Archives 497
Grand Army of the Republic Museum Newsletter 497
Grand Canyon National Park Museum Archives 16
Grand Coteau Heritage and Cultural Centre 710
Grand Council of the Crees 703
Grand Council Treaty Number 3 684
Grand County Historical Association & Archives 86
Grand County Journal 86
Grand County Library 85
Grand County Library District-Granby Branch 85
Grand County Library District-Juniper Library at Grand Lake 86
Grand County Museum 86
Grand Encampment Historical Society 636
Grand Encampment Museum Archives 636
Grand Falls Historical Museum Archives 664
Grand Forks County Historical Museum 438
Grand Forks County Historical Society & Archives 438
Grand Forks County Historical Society Library 438
Grand Forks Historic Preservation 438
Grand Forks Public Library 438
Grand Forks Public Library Newsletter 438
Grand Gulf Military Park Archives 322
Grand Haven Area Historical Society 292
Grand Haven Genealogical Society 292
Grand Island Historical Society 398
Grand Island Trader's Cabin 298
Grand Lake Area Historical Museum 86
Grand Lake Area Historical Society & Archives 86
Grand Lake Area Historical Society Newsletter 86
Grand Ledge Area Historical Museum 292
Grand Ledge Area Historical Society & Archives 292
Grand Ledge Public Library 292
Grand Lodge Bulletin 198
Grand Lodge of Ancient Free and Accepted Masons & Library 635
Grand Lodge of Masons Library 345
Grand Lodge of Virginia & Library 593
Grand Lodge Proceedings 498
Grand Manan Museum Archives 664
Grand Marais Public Library 308
Grand Portage National Monument Archives 308
Grand Prairie Genealogical Society 33, 547
Grand Prairie Historical Bulletin 28
Grand Prairie Historical Organization 547
Grand Prairie Historical Society 26, 33
Grand Prairie Historical Society & Library 28
Grand Prairie Historical Society Bulletin 26
Grand Prairie Memorial Library 547
Grand Rapids Area Library 308
Grand Rapids Historical Society & Archives 292
Grand Rapids Museum Magazine 292
Grand Rapids Public Library 292
Grand Rapids Public Museum Archives 292
Grand River Historical Museum 327
Grand River Historical Society & Archives 292, 327
Grand River Museum Archives 522
Grand River Museum Newsletter 522
Grand River Times 292
Grand River Valley Museum 625
Grand River Valley Review 292
Grand Saline Public Library 547
Grand Teton National Park Library 637
Grand Traverse Genealogical Society 303
Grand Traverse Pioneer and Historical Society 303

Grand View College Library 200
Grand Village of the Natchez Indians Archives 321
Grande Prairie Pioneer Museum Archives 644
Grande Prairie Public Library 644
Grandin Library Association 369
Grand-Pre Historical Society 674
Grand-Pre National Historic Site Archives 674
Grandview Heights Public Library 446
Grandview Historical Society 329
Grandville County Library System 431
Grandville Historical Association & Library 292
Grange - Order of Patrons of Husbandry 105
Grange Clan 56
Granger Historical Society & Library 453
Granger Homestead Society & Library 392
Granger House Museum Archives 205
Grangeville Centennial Library 146
Granite Falls Public Library 308
Grant Birthplace Archives 454
Grant Boyhood Home 449
Grant Clan 114, 421, 495
Grant Cottage Chronicles 421
Grant County Beacon 189
Grant County Courthouse Museum 352
Grant County Genealogical and Historical Society 613
Grant County Genealogical Society 474, 601, 629
Grant County Genealogical Society & Archives 189
Grant County Genealogical Society Newsletter 474
Grant County Genealogy Club 189
Grant County Heritage 629
Grant County Historical Museum 222, 307, 437, 467, 601
Grant County Historical Society & Archives 222, 307, 352, 437, 467, 601, 624
Grant County Historical Society & Library 189
Grant County Historical Society Newsletter 601
Grant County Library 32, 222
Grant County Museum Archives 32, 437, 467, 474
Grant County Museum Library 222
Grant County Public Library 234, 522
Grant Family 513
Grant Genealogical Society 236
Grant Gleanings 146
Grant Historical Society 181
Grant Homestead Association 449
Grant Library 85
Grant Parish Library 236
Grant Public Library 292
Grant's Birthplace State Memorial Archives 455
Grant-Boldway Family 558
Grant-Humphreys Mansion Archives 83
Grant-Kohrs Ranch National Historic Site Library 344
Grant-Lee Association 165
Grants and Historic Preservation Bureau 407
Grants Pass Genealogical Society 475
Grantsburg Area Historical Society & Archives 622
Grantsburg Public Library 622
Granville County Genealogical Society 431
Granville County Historical Museum 431
Granville County Historical Society & Archives 431
Granville County Historical Society Newsletter 431
Granville Museum Archives 527
Granville Ohio Historical Museum 449
Granville Ohio Historical Society & Archives 449
Granville Public Library 449
Grape Vine 69
Grape Vine Newsletter 45
Grapevine 35, 39, 91, 195, 291
Grapevine Historic Preservation 547
Grapevine Historical Society 547
Grapevine Name Droppers 547
Grapevine Public Library 547
Grass Lake Area Historical Society 292
Grass Roots Genealogical Group 46
Grass Valley Museum Archives 46
Grassroots 32
Grassroots Catalog 385
Grasty Family 41
Gratiot County Historical and Genealogical Society 294
Gratiot Genealogical Group Newsletter 294
Gratta Families Worldwide Newsletter 320
Gratta Family 320
Grattan Township Historical Society 301
Gratz Historical Society & Library 488
Graue Mill and Museum Archives 168
Gravelbourg and District Museum Archives 706
Graves County Genealogical Society 231
Graves County Library 231
Graves Family 283
Graves Memorial Public Library 221
Graves Researcher 157
Graves-Bewley Family 478
Graves-Hume Public Library District 166
Gravette Historical Museum Archives 28
Gray Court-Owing Historical Society 515
Gray Family 145
Gray Family Newsletter 70
Gray House Museum 450
Gray Public Library 246
Gray-Grey Lines 553
Gray-Hurd-Jenkins Family 538
Gray-Posey Family 555
Grays Harbor Genealogical Society 600
Grays Harbor Genealogical Society News 600
Grayslake Historical and Genealogical Society & Archives 161
Grayslake Historical Museum 161
Grayson County Genealogical Society & Library 560
Grayson County Historical Society 229, 586, 589
Grayson County Public Library 229
Grayson Family Newsletter 161
Grayson Gateway 543
Grayville Carnegie Public Library 161
Great Basin Historical Museum 566
Great Basin Historical Society & Archives 566
Great Bend Public Library 214
Great Expectations 258
Great Falls Genealogical Society & Library 344
Great Falls Public Library 344
Great Harbor Maritime Museum Archives 249
Great Lakes Historical Society & Archives 459
Great Lakes Museum of Military History Archives 189
Great Lakes Naval Memorial and Museum Archives 298

Great Lakes Naval Museum Archives 161
Great Lakes Shipwreck Historical Society 302
Great Lakes Shipwreck Museum Archives 299
Great Migration Newsletter 267
Great Neck Library 399
Great Neck Library Newsletter 399
Great Overland Station Museum Archives 222
Great Plains Black Museum Archives 355
Great Plains Dispatcher 223
Great Plains Journal 466
Great Plains Transportation Museum Archives 223
Great River Genealogical Society 171
Great River Regional Library 314
Great Sandhills Museum 710
Great Smoky Mountains National Park 533
Great Smoky Mountains National Park Library 527
Great War Flying Museum Archives 681
Greater Astoria Historical Society 388
Greater Brandon Genealogical Society 116
Greater Bristol Historical Society 91
Greater Cannonsburg Public Library 484
Greater Cape May Historical Society 368
Greater Clinton Township Historical Society 298
Greater Des Moines-Zenith Historical Society 601
Greater Harrington Historical Society & Library 103
Greater Harrington Historical Society Newsletter 103
Greater Harvard Area Historical Museum 162
Greater Harvard Area Historical Society & Archives 162
Greater Harvard Area Historical Society Newsletter 162
Greater Houston Jewish Genealogical Society 548
Greater Kansas City Cornish Society 332
Greater Loveland Historical Museum 451
Greater Loveland Historical Society & Archives 451
Greater Lowell Genealogy Club 273
Greater Miami Genealogical Society 117
Greater Monessen Historical Society 494
Greater New Orleans Archivists & Archives 240
Greater Octorara Valley Historical Society 496
Greater Omaha Genealogical Society 355
Greater Phoenix Jewish Genealogical Society 20
Greater Phoenix Jewish Genealogical Society Newsletter 20
Greater Portland Landmarks Library 250
Greater Ridgewood Historical Society & Library 413
Greater Ridgewood Historical Society Newsletter 413
Greater Sioux County Genealogical Society & Archives 208
Greater Sudbury Heritage Museum Archives 690
Greater Vernon Museum Archives 656
Greater Victoria Public Library 657
Greater Ville Historic Redevelopment 339
Greater Washington Area Historical Society 303
Greater West Bloomfield Historical Museum 299
Greater West Bloomfield Historical Society 304
Greater West Bloomfield Historical Society & Archives 299
Greater West Center Public Library District-Augusta Branch 151
Greater York Area Genealogical Society & Archives 357
Greater York Area Genealogical Society Newsletter 357
Greathouse Family 567
Greece Historical Society 413
Greece Public Library 413
Greek Family Heritage Committee & Library 397
Greek Orthodox Archdiocese, North and South America Archives 407
Greeley County Historical Society 352
Greeley County Historical Society & Library 222
Greeley Heritage Association & Archives 86
Greeley Heritage Association Museum 86
Greeley Heritage Association Newsletter 86
Green Country Quarterly 463
Green County Historical Society & Archives 627
Green County Historical Society & Library 228
Green County Public Library 228
Green County Review 228
Green Cove Springs Public Library 113
Green Eye 52
Green Family 606
Green Family Courier 239
Green Family Quarterly 235, 471
Green Free Library 505
Green Gables House Museum Archives 695
Green Grapevine 183
Green Group 153
Green Hills Genealogical Society 170
Green Hills Public Library District 170
Green Mountain Club Archives 580
Green Mountaineer 578
Green Oak Historian 287
Green Oak Township Historical Society 287
Green Park Shipbuilding Museum 695
Green River Museum Archives 234
Green River Valley Museum Archives 635
Green Tree Lore 499
Green Valley Genealogical Society 16
Green(e) Family 398
Green(e) Newsletter 225
Greenbelt Museum Archives 259
Greenbelt Museum Quarterly 259
Greenbriar Valley Campus Library 613
Greenbrier Historical Society & Library 613
Greenbrier Historical Society Journal 613
Greenburgh Public Library 397
Greenbush Bookmark 396
Greenbush Historical Society 293, 396
Greendale Historial Society 622
Greendale Public Library 622
Green-Durham Family 186
Greene County Chapter, OGS & Archives 460
Greene County District Library 460
Greene County Genealogical Society 180, 203, 527
Greene County Historical and Genealogical Society 31, 154
Greene County Historical and Genealogical Society Newsletter 31, 154
Greene County Historical and Genealogical Society Quarterly 31
Greene County Historical Journal 395
Greene County Historical Museum 395, 461, 505
Greene County Historical Society 4, 131, 180, 340, 595
Greene County Historical Society & Archives 395, 461, 505
Greene County Historical Society & Library 203
Greene County Historical Society Bulletin 340
Greene County Historical Society Newsletter 180
Greene County Library 31
Greene County Magazine 595
Greene County Pioneer 527

Greene County Public Library 527
Greene Family 604
Greene Gleanings 203
Greene Hills Echo 505
Greene Hills of Home 488
Greene Plantation Historical Society & Library 248
Greene Plantation Newsletter 248
Greene Public Library 202
Greene Township Historical Society 488
Greenfield Community College Library 271
Greenfield Community College Library Newsletter 271
Greenfield Historical Museum 271
Greenfield Historical Society 449, 622
Greenfield Historical Society Newsletter 622
Greenfield Public Library 185, 202, 271
Greenfield Public Library Newsletter 271
Green-Greene Genealogist 146
Greenhalgh Family 507
Green-Harris Family 571
Greenleaves 559
Greenlee County Historical Society 15
Greenmead Historic Site 296
Greensboro Historical Museum Archives 427
Greensboro Historical Museum Newsletter 427
Greensboro Historical Society 576
Greensboro Masonic Museum Library 427
Greensboro Public Library 427
Greensburg-Decatur County Public Library 185
Greensburg-Hempfield Area Library 488
Green-Searcy Family 128
Greenspond Museum Archives 667
Greentown Historical Society 185
Greentown Public Library 185
Greenup County Public Libraries-Flatwoods Branch 227
Greenup County Public Libraries-McKell Public 233
Greenup County Public Library 228
Greenup Depot Archives 161
Greenup Township Carnegie Library 161
Greenville Area Historical Society 488
Greenville Chapter Journal 515
Greenville County Genealogical Society & Library 515
Greenville County Genealogical Society Newsletter 515
Greenville County Historic Preservation Commission 515
Greenville County Historical Society & Library 515
Greenville County Historical Society Proceedings and Papers 515
Greenville County Library 515
Greenville County Library System-Hughes Main Library 515
Greenville Public Library 161, 449, 507
Greenville-Butler County Public Library 5
Greenway-Greenaway Family 273
Greenwell Family 426
Greenwich History 92
Greenwich Library 94
Greenwich Library-Byram Shubert Branch 94
Greenwich Village Society for Historic Preservation 407
Greenwood County Genealogical Society 515
Greenwood County Historical Museum 213
Greenwood County Historical Society & Archives 213, 515
Greenwood County Library 515
Greenwood County Pioneers 215
Greenwood Historical Society 352
Greenwood Military Aviation Museum Archives 674
Greenwood Museum Archives 515, 650
Greenwood Museum Newsletter 515
Greenwood Public Library 185
Greenwood Public Library 622
Greenwood-Leflore Public Library 320
Greer County Genealogical and Historical Society 466
Greer Family 233
Greer Frontier 466
Gregg County Genealogical Society 552
Gregg County Genealogical Society Newsletter 552
Gregg County Historical and Genealogical Society & Archives 552
Gregg County Historical Museum 552
Gregg County Historical Museum Newsletter 552
Gregg Family 221
Gregg M Sinclair Library 141
Gregg-Gragg-Holder-Curtis-Mobley and Sarah Meador-William Gregg-Gragg-Holder Family 75
Gregg-Graniteville Library 511
Gregor Clan 60, 119, 138, 263, 434, 456
Gregory Public Library 522
Greig Town Historian 403
Grenelle Family 627
Grenfell Community Museum Archives 706
Grenfell Historical Society 668
Grenola Historical Society 214
Grenville County Historical Society & Library 688
Gresham Historical Society & Archives 475
Gresham Historical Society Newsletter 475
Gresham Pioneer Group & Archives 475
Gresham-Grisham-Grisson-Grishem Family 545
Gretna Heritage Society 352
Gretna Historical Society 237
Gretna Museum 153
Gretna Station and Caboose Museum Archives 153
Grevemberg House Museum Archives 237
Grevious Family 447
Grey County Museum Archives 687
Greybill House Museum Archives 668
Greybull Historical Society 636
Greybull Museum Archives 636
Grice Family 61, 465
Grice Museum Historical Society 293
Gridley District Library 162
Gridley Historical and Wildlife Museum Archives 46
Griepp Family 619
Grier Musser Antiques Museum Archives 51
Griesemer Family 50, 481, 502
Griesmer-Griesemer Family 445
Griffee Family 290
Griffen Family 355
Griffen Family Newsletter 389
Griffin 125
Griffin Family 442, 586
Griffin Historical and Preservation Society & Library 131
Griffin Museum of Photography 283
Griffin-Lassiter Family 263
Griffin-Spalding Historical Society 131
Griffith Family 199, 222

Griffith Historical Museum 185
Griffith Historical Society & Archives 185
Griffith-Bowles Family 305
Griffith-Milbradt Line and Allied Families 215
Griggs County Genealogical Society & Archives 437
Griggs County Historical Museum Archives 439
Griggs County Public Library 437
Griggs Family 543, 567
Griggsville Area Genealogical and Historical Society 162
Grignon Mansion 623
Grigsby Family 549
Grigsby National Family Society Newsletter 26
Grigsby National Family Society, Southwest Chapter 26
Grimes Bulletin 478
Grimes County Heritage Association 554
Grimes Family 31
Grimsby Museum Archives 683
Grindstaff-Grandstaff Family 20
Grindstone Bluff Museum Library 241
Grindstone Island Research 393
Grinnell Family 606
Grinnell Historical Museum Archives 202
Grinter Place State Historic Sites Archives 216
Griogarach 60
Grip Fast 488
Grissom Air Museum 191
Grissom Air Museum Times 191
Grist Mill 389
Grist Mill Museum Archives 651
Grist: the Millbrook Society Journal 489
Griswold Family Association of America Newsletter 101
Griswold Historical Society 94, 95
Griswold Library 579
Griswold Linkage 121
Grizzle Family 546
Grizzly Creek Redwoods State Park Archives 39
Groberg Surname Organization 147
Grodno Genealogy Group 478
Groendyke-Shields Kuzzin's 65
Gropius House Museum Archives 273
Groseclose Family 238
Grosnick Family 617
Grospitch Family 445
Gross-Cargo Family 295
Grosse Ile Historical Museum 293
Grosse Ile Historical Society & Archives 293
Grosse Ile Historical Society Newsletter 293
Grosse Pointe Historical Society 293
Grosse Pointe Public Library 293
Gross-Fessler Family 606
Grosvenor Lodge Museum Archives 685
Grothaus-Morris Family 543
Groton Historical Museum 271
Groton Historical Society 576
Groton Historical Society & Archives 271
Groton Public Library 271
Groton Public Library 94, 399
Groundbirch Museum Archives 650
Ground-Grounds Family 48
GroupLetter 524
Grout Museum of History 209
Grout Museum of History and Science Archives 209
Grove City Area Historical Society 309, 488
Grove Farm Homestead Museum Archives 142
Grove Heritage Association 161
Grove Hill Public Library 5
Grove National Historic Landmark Archives 161
Grove Public Library 465
Grover Cleveland Birthplace Archives 368
Grover Museum 193
Grover-Andlauer-Dunnavant-Andlauer Family 330
Grudzinskas Family 56
Gruenewald Historic House Archives 179
Grumman Memorial Park Archives 392
Grundy County Genealogical Society 202, 341
Grundy County Genealogical Society & Library 207
Grundy County Historical Society 341
Grundy County Swiss Historical Society 532
Grundy County-Jewett Norris Library 341
Grundy Gleanings 341
Gryphon 120
Guadalupe County Genealogical Society & Archives 559
Guadalupe Historic Foundation 384
Guadalupe Valley Trails 559
Guale Historical Society 136
Guale News 136
Guard House and Soldiers Barracks Museum Archives 663
Guelph Museum Archives 683
Guelph Public Library 683
Guernsey County District Public Library 443
Guernsey County Genealogical Society 443
Guernsey County Genealogical Society & Library 443
Guernsey County Historical Society & Archives 443
Guernsey County Ohio Genealogy Association Newsletter 443
Guernsey Memorial Library 409
Guernsey Roots and Branches 443
Guess-Guest Newsletter 138
Guest House Museum Archives 45
Guggenheim Memorial Library 380
Guild Family 610
Guilderland Public Library 399
Guilford County Genealogical Society & Library 427
Guilford Courthouse National Military Park Library 427
Guilford Family 57
Guilford Free Library 94, 576
Guilford Free Library Newsletter 576
Guilford Genealogist 427
Guilford Historical Society 246, 575
Guilford Keeping Society & Archives 94
Guilford Keeping Society News 94
Guilford Slate 575
Guilford Township Historical Society 192
Gulf Beaches Public Library 116
Gulf Coast Ancestry Researchers & Library 562
Gulf Coast Historical Review 6
Gulf County Genealogical Society 120
Gulf Museum Archives 668
Gulf of Georgia Cannery Museum Archives 654
Gulf South Historical Review 6
Gulfport-Harrison County Public Library 320

Gulick Family Newsletter 8
Gulledge Family 429
Gulley Family 449
Gullick Family 544
Gulliver Historical Society 293
Gum Springs Historical Society 583
Gumm Family 444
Gunderson House 309
Gundy House 627
Gunn Clan 72, 125
Gunn Memorial Library 100
Gunn Memorial Public Library 435
Gunn Museum of Saline County 25
Gunn Salute 125
Gunnin Family 131
Gunnison County Historical Museum 86
Gunnison County Pioneer and Historical Society & Archives 86
Gunnison County Public Library 86
Gunnison Museum News 86
Gunston Hall Plantation Library 590
Guntersville Historical Society 5
Guntersville Public Library 5
Gurney Family 142
Gusher 553
Guss Family 85
Guss Lines 202
Gustavus Adolphus Pfeiffer Library 430
Gustine Museum Archives 47
Guthery Family 441
Guthrie Clan 277
Guthrie County Genealogical Society & Library 203
Guthrie County Genealogical Society Newsletter 203
Guthrie Family 569
Guy B. Woodward Museum 61
Guyman-Chunn Family 569
Guymon Gazette 172
Guysborough Historical Society & Archives 674
Guyton Historical Society 131
Gwaltney Family 468
Gwinnett County Historical Museum 133
Gwinnett County Historical Society & Archives 133
Gwinnett County Historical Society Quarterly 133
Gwinnett County Public Library 133
Gwinnett History Museum Archives 133
Gwinnett Muse 133
Gwynne-Cobb Family 600
Gypsy Lore Society 257

H

H B Stamps Memorial Library 532
H F Davis Memorial Library 212
H Grady Bradshaw-Chambers County Library 10
H H MacMillan Space Centre Museum 656
H Lee White Marine Museum Archives 410
H Leslie Perry Memorial Library 428
H Raymond Danforth Library 361
H V Manning Library 517
H.E.A.R.T.S. Veterans Museum of Texas Archives 549
Haas-Lilienthal House Museum Archives 66
Haas-Lilienthal House Museum Newsletter 66
Habersham County Historical Society 128, 129
Hack Family 595
Hacker's Creek Journal 613
Hacker's Creek Pioneer Descendants 612, 613
Hackett Heirlooms: The Hackett Family Newsletter 130
Hackettstown Free Public Library 370
Hackettstown Historical Museum 370
Hackettstown Historical Society & Library 370
Hackleman Newsletter 550
Hackler-Comer Family 588
Hackley Public Library 298
Haddam Historical Society & Library 94
Haddon Heights Historical Society 370
Haddon Heights Public Library 370
Haddonfield Historical Museum 370
Haddonfield Public Library 370
Hadley Farm Museum Archives 271
Hadley Genealogical Society of Southern California 53
Hadley Historical Society 271
Haese Memorial Village Historical Society 621
Haessig Family 53
Haff Family 397
Hagen Family 480
Hagenbush Family 486
Hagerman Family 310
Hagerman Valley Historical Society 147
Hagerstown Roundhouse Museum Archives 259
Hagerstown-Jefferson Township Public Library 185
Hagesher: the Bridge 447
Haggin Museum 73
Haggin Museum Archives 73
Hagley Museum and Library 104
Hagley Museum Quarterly 104
Hagwilget Indian Band 652
Hahira Historical Society 131
Hahn Family 482
Hahns Peak Are Historical Society & Archives 82
Hahns Peak Village Museum 82
Hailey Public Library 147
Haileybury Public Library 683
Haines Borough Public Library 12
Haines City Public Library 113
Haines Falls Free Library 399
Haines Junction Historical Society 713
Haines Museum 177
Hairston-Gallant Family 597
Haisla Indian Band 651
Halalt Indian Band 648
Halbert-Holbert Family 518
Halcyon Days 547
Haldimand County Museum Archives 681
Hale Center Public Library 547
Hale County Historical Society 5
Hale County Public Library 5
Hale Family 592
Hale Farm and Village Archives 442
Hale Library 218
Hales Corners Historical Society 622
Hales Newsletter-New Series 22
Haley Library Newsletter 554

Half Moon 495
Half-Shire Historical Society & Library 413
Halfway River Indian Band 657
Halfyard Family 689
Haliburton House Museum Archives 677
Halifax Citadel National Historic Park Library 674
Halifax County Genealogical Society 428
Halifax County Genealogical Society Newsletter 428
Halifax County Library 428
Halifax County Library Newsletter 428
Halifax County Library-Scotland Neck Memorial 432
Halifax Genealogical Society 119
Halifax Historical Herald 111
Halifax Historical Museum 111
Halifax Historical Society & Archives 111
Halifax Historical Society & Library 575
Halifax Historical Society Newsletter 111
Halifax Police Museum Archives 674
Halifax-South Boston Regional Library 588
Hall Clan 232
Hall County Genealogical Society 553
Hall County Historical Society 131
Hall County Historical Society 352
Hall County Library System 131
Hall Family 82, 123, 609
Hall Memorial Library 93, 363
Hall of Fame for Great Americans Archives 390
Hall of Flame Museum Newsletter 18
Hall of Flame Museum of Firefighting 18
Hall's Harbour Historical Society 674
Hallam-Hallum-Lopp-Laup-Lape Family 460
Hall-Fowler Memorial Library 294
Halliburton-Gassaway Family 334
Hallmark 136
Hallmark Family 547
Hallmarks 452
Hallock Family 262, 281
Hallockville Museum Farm Archives 413
Hall-Tallant Family 256
Hall-Wiedeman Family 152
Halsell Family 571
Halsey Newsletter 311
Halstead Historical Museum 214
Halstead Historical Society & Archives 214
Halstead Public Library 214
Haltom City Public Library 547
Halton Hills Public Libraries 682
Halton Museum Archives 685
Hamblen Connector 234
Hamblen County Chapter APTA Newsletter 530
Hamblen County Genealogical and Historical Society & Archives 530
Hamblen Heritage 530
Hamblen, Hamblin, Hamlin, Hanlen Family 234
Hamburg Area Historical Society 488
Hamburg Historical Society & Archives 399
Hamburg Public Library 202, 488
Hamburg State Park Museum Archives 134
Hamburg Township Library 293
Hamden Historical Museum 94
Hamden Historical Society & Library 94
Hamden Library 94
Hames Family 548
Hamill Heritage Newsletter 189
Hamilton Branch, Ontario Genealogical Society Newsletter 683
Hamilton Clan 512
Hamilton County Chapter Gazette 444
Hamilton County Genealogical Society 444
Hamilton County Genealogical Society & Archives 547
Hamilton County Genealogical Society Family Circle Journal 547
Hamilton County Historical Museum 114
Hamilton County Historical Society 166
Hamilton County Historical Society & Archives 114, 349
Hamilton County Historical Society & Library 191
Hamilton County Library 222
Hamilton County Museum Archives 222
Hamilton Family 336, 521
Hamilton Grange National Memorial Museum Archives 407
Hamilton Heritage Hunters Genealogical Society & Archives 209
Hamilton Heritage Hunters Newsletter 209
Hamilton House Archives 562
Hamilton House Museum Archives 251
Hamilton Library 141
Hamilton Library, Special Collections 141
Hamilton Military Museum Archives 683
Hamilton North Public Library-Atlanta Branch 179
Hamilton Public Library 399, 683
Hamilton Township Historical Museum 371
Hamilton Township Historical Society 371
Hamilton Township Public Library 371
Hamilton Wood Type Museum 632
Hamilton-Van Wagoner House Museum Archives 369
Hamilton-Wenham Public Library 279
Hamiota Pioneer Club Museum Archives 660
Hamlet Public Library 428
Hamlin Garland Homestead Museum 634
Hamlin Memorial Library 502
Hamlin-Lincoln County Public Library 612
Hamlin-Lincoln County Public Library-Alum Creek Public 611
Hamm Family 40
Hamman Family 1
Hammer Family 208, 477, 593
Hammermill Library 487
Hammond Castle Museum Archives 271
Hammond Family 205, 217
Hammond Herald 49
Hammond Historical Society 185
Hammond Library 155
Hammond Public Library 185
Hammondsport Public Library 399
Hammon-Hamann-Hammann Family 460
Hammon-Harwood House Museum Archives 255
Hampden Historical Society & Library 246
Hampden Historical Society Newsletter 246
Hampshire County Public Library 614
Hampstead Public Library 361
Hampt Family 468
Hampton Antiquarian and Historical Society & Library 94
Hampton B Allen Library 434
Hampton Bays Public Library 399
Hampton County Historical Museum 515

Hampton County Historical Society & Archives 515
Hampton Historical Association & Archives 361
Hampton Historical Society & Library 162
Hampton Historical Society News 162
Hampton History Museum Archives 588
Hampton History Museum Newsletter 588
Hampton Library 390
Hampton National Historic Site Archives 263
Hampton Plantation Museum Archives 516
Hampton Public Library 202, 588
Hampton Roads Naval Museum Archives 592
Hampton Roads Naval Museum Newsletter 592
Hampton University Museum Archives 588
Hampton-Preston Mansion 513
Hana Cultural Center and Museum Archives 141
Hanby House 460
Hance-Daly-Gage-Talbot-Talbert-Tolbert Family 59
Hanceville Library 5
Hanchett-Bartlett Homestead Museum 617
Hancock County Archives 228
Hancock County Chapter, OGS & Library 448
Hancock County Courthouse Museum 154
Hancock County Genealogical and Historical Society 615
Hancock County Genealogical and Historical Society & Library 154
Hancock County Genealogical and Historical Society Newsletter 154
Hancock County Genealogical Society 185
Hancock County Genealogical Society & Library 204
Hancock County Historical Society 319, 322, 614
Hancock County Historical Society & Archives 228
Hancock County Historical Society & Library 185
Hancock County Library 228, 319
Hancock Family 74, 416
Hancock Heritage 448
Hancock Historical Museum Association Library 448
Hancock Historical Society 246, 260, 361
Hancock Historical Society & Library 361
Hancock Historical Society News 361
Hancock House 418
Hancock House Museum Archives 371
Hancock Mansion Museum Archives 52
Hancock Public Library 622
Hancock Shaker Village Museum Archives 277
Hancock Shaker Village Museum Newsletter 277
Hancock Town Library 361
Hand County Library 522
Hand Family 135, 191
Hand Family Courier 239
Handbook Newsletter 169
Handley Library 597
Hanes-Calloway Family 544
Haney Family 367
Hanford Carnegie Museum Archives 47
Hanford Mills Museum Archives 396
Hanford Mills Museum Newsletter 396
Hangar Digest 103
Hangar Happenings 304
Hanks Family 453
Hanley House Museum Archives 327
Hanna Basin Historical Society 636
Hanna Family 601
Hanna Herald 601
Hanna Municipal Library 644
Hanna Pioneer Museum Archives 644
Hanna, Hannah, Hannay Clan 454
Hannibal Free Public Library 330
Hannibal Historical Society 399
Hannibal Town Historian 399
Hannum Family 186
Hanover Area Historical Society & Library 489
Hanover Area Historical Society News 489
Hanover County Historical Museum 584
Hanover County Historical Society & Archives 584, 588
Hanover County Historical Society Bulletin 588
Hanover Historian 272
Hanover Historical Society & Library 272
Hanover House Museum Archives 513
Hanover House Newsletter 513
Hanover Park Ontarioville Historical Commission 162
Hanover Public Library 489, 683
Hanover Town Library 360
Hanover Township Library 162
Hanover-Horton Area Historical Museum 293
Hanover-Horton Area Historical Society 293
Hansard-Brobeck-Brubeck Family 611
Hanscom Air Force Base Library 272
Hansen Family 16, 64, 565, 566, 572
Hansen-Newell-Bennett House Museum 620
Hansford County Library 560
Hanson House Museum 369
Hanson Public Library 272
Hanson-Henson-Hinson-Hynson Family 537, 541
Hantsport and Area Historical Society 674
Hapeville Historical Society 131
Happenings 124, 181, 189, 338
Happy Hunter 161
Haralson County Historical Society & Archives 127
Har-Ber Village Museum Archives 465
Harbin Newsletter 479
Harbinger 282
Harbor Church Historical Society 280
Harbor Defense Museum Archives 391
Harbor Ranch Museum Archives 543
Harbor Springs Area Historical Society 293
Harbour Light Newsletter 547
Harbour Village 290
Harbour-Witt Family 552
Hardeman-McClure Newsletter 63
Harden-Hardin-Harding Family 586
Hardin County Connections 560
Hardin County Genealogical Society 201, 560
Hardin County Genealogical Society Newsletter 201
Hardin County Genealogy Society 450
Hardin County Historical and Genealogical Society 159
Hardin County Historical Museum Archives 450
Hardin County Historical Quarterly 532
Hardin County Historical Society & Library 227, 532
Hardin County Library 532
Hardin County Library Newsletter 532
Hardin Family Courier 239
Harding Home and Museum Archives 452

INDEX

Harding Township Historical Society 374
Hardister Family 561
Hardwick Family 535, 552
Hardwick Historical Museum 272
Hardwick Historical Society 576
Hardwick Historical Society & Archives 272
Hardy County Genealogical and Historical Society 613
Hardy County Public Library 613
Hardy Historical Society 33
Hardy-Hice-McElrath Family 194
Hardy-Rush Family 2
Harford Community College Library 256
Harford County Genealogical Society & Library 255
Harford County Genealogical Society Newsletter 255
Harford County Historical Society & Archives 256
Harford County Historical Society Newsletter 256
Harford County Public Library-Aberdeen Branch 255
Harford County Public Library-Bel Air Branch 256
Harford County Public Library-Darlington Branch 258
Harford County Public Library-Edgewood Branch 258
Harford County Public Library-Fallston-Jarrettsville 259
Harford County Public Library-Havre de Grace Branch 260
Harford County Public Library-Joppa Branch 260
Harford County Public Library-Whiteford Branch 264
Harford Family 50
Harford Historical Bulletin 256
Harger Family 198, 295
Hargitt House Museum Archives 56
Hargrave Family Newsletter 536
Hargrett Library 125
Hargrove-Hargrave-Harden-Hardin Family 605
Harkness Family 395
Harkness Memorial State Park Museum Archives 100
Harlan Community Library 202
Harlan County Genealogical Society 228
Harlan County Historical Society 355
Harlan County Public Library 228
Harlan Footprints 228
Harlan Heritage Seekers 228
Harlan Mountain Roots 228
Harlan-Lincoln House Museum Archives 205
Harlem Historical Society 390
Harler Family 492
Harless Family Association Bulletin 51
Harless Library 613
Harlingen Public Library 547, 548
Harlow Family 280
Harlow's Wooden Man 297
Harmer Family 601
Harmison-Harmason Family 235
Harmon-Rudland-Hellstrom-Grann Family 241
Harmony Public Library 309
Harn Homestead and 1889er Museum Archives 468
Harnett County Genealogical Society 424
Harnett County Public Library 429
Harney County Genealogy Society 474
Harney County Historical Museum 474
Harney County Historical Society & Archives 474
Harney County Historical Society Newsletter 474
Harney County Library 474
Harney Family 637
Harney Historical Highlights 474
Harney Update 637
Harold and Wilma Good Library 184
Harold Anderson Library 634
Harold B Lee Library and Genealogy Dept 569
Harold B Strunk Library 233
Harold Bell Wright Museum Archives 337
Harold C Manor Library 115
Harold R Yeary Library 551
Harold S Colton Memorial Research Library 16
Harold Warp Pioneer Village Museum Archives 354
Harp Family 241
Harp Notes 241
Harper City Historical and Genealogical Society & Archives 215
Harper City Historical Museum 215
Harper County Genealogical Society 214
Harper County Genealogical Society Newsletter 214
Harper Family 337
Harper Public Library 215
Harpers Ferry Center History Collection 612
Harpole Family 323
Harpswell Historical Society 249, 251
Harr Family 525
Harrell Family News 535
Harriet Beecher Stowe Center Archives 94
Harriet Beecher Stowe Center Journal 94
Harriet Beecher Stowe House Archives 444
Harriet Cheney Cowles Memorial Library 607
Harrietstown Town Historian 415
Harriette Person Memorial Library 322
Harriman Family Association Newsletter 120, 244
Harriman Public Library 527
Harrington Family 397
Harrington Meeting House 249
Harriotte B Smith Library 424
Harris County Genealogical Society & Library 555
Harris County Genealogical Society Annual Seminar Surname Index 555
Harris County Heritage Society & Archives 549
Harris County Historical Museum 549
Harris County Public Library 549
Harris Family 46, 198, 321, 457, 572
Harris Heritage and Museum Archives 706
Harris-Baker Family 571
Harrisburg Chapter National Railway Historical Society 489
Harrisburg Public Library 162
Harris-Butler-Bassard Family 592
Harris-Cauthorne Family 105
Harris-Elmore Public Library 448
Harrison Area Genealogical Society 293
Harrison Community Library 293
Harrison County Genealogical Society 553, 611
Harrison County Genealogical Society & Archives 210
Harrison County Genealogical Society & Library 325, 443
Harrison County Genealogical Society Newsletter 611
Harrison County Genealogical Volunteers Chapter, IGS 210
Harrison County Happenings 210
Harrison County Historical Society 182, 325
Harrison County Historical Society & Archives 553
Harrison County Historical Society & Library 443

Harrison County Historical Society Newsletter 553
Harrison County Library System-Biloxi Public 319
Harrison County Public Library 182
Harrison County, Mississippi Historical Society 235
Harrison Family 596, 609
Harrison Herald 548
Harrison Heritage 59
Harrison Historical Society 247
Harrison House 91
Harrison Memorial Library 39
Harrison Museum of African American Culture Archives 594
Harrison Public Library 399
Harrison Township Historical Society & Library 374
Harrisonburg-Rockingham Heritage Center 586
Harrisonburg-Rockingham Historical Society 588
Harrisonburg-Rockingham Historical Society & Library 586
Harrisonburg-Rockingham Historical Society Newsletter 586
Harrison-Pounds Family 550
Harrisville-Bonaparte History Association 399
Harrodsburg Historical Society - Genealogy Committee Newsletter 228
Harrodsburg Historical Society & Archives 228
Harrodsburg Historical Society Newsletter 228
Harrodsburg Historical Society, Genealogy Committee 228
Harrow Early Immigrant Research Society & Library 683
Harry C Trexler Library 481
Harry Caudill Memorial Library 234
Harry Lee Waterfield Library 232
Harry S Truman Birthplace Archives 333
Harry S Truman Independence 76 Fire Company Historical Society 330
Harry S Truman Library 330
Harry S Truman Little White House Museum Archives 115
Harry S Truman Little White House Museum Newsletter 115
Harry S Truman National Historic Site Archives 331
Harry S Truman Office & Courtroom Museum 331
Harry S Washbrook Museum Archives 706
Harshbarger Family 568
Hart Area Public Library 293
Hart Company Historical Society 132
Hart County Historical Museum 132
Hart County Historical Society 126
Hart County Historical Society & Archives 132
Hart County Historical Society & Library 232
Hart County Historical Society Quarterly 232
Hart County Library 132
Hart County Public Library 232
Hart Family 148, 273, 337, 508
Hart-Cam Museum Archives 660
Hartford Area Genealogical Society 622
Hartford County Library 256
Hartford County Public Library 185
Hartford Historical Society 577
Hartford House Museum 218
Hartford Library 577
Hartford Public Library 94, 293, 622
Hartford Public Library District 162
Hartford Public Library District Newsletter 162
Hartford Public Library-Mark Twain Memorial Branch 94
Harting Across the USA 35
Hartland Historical Society 622
Hartland Historical Society 93
Hartland Historical Society & Library 577
Hartland Public Library 247, 577, 623
Hartley Bay Indian Band 650
Hartman House Archives 179
Hartmann Model RR & Toy Museum Archives 361
Hartpence Family 446
Hartselle Historical Society 5
Hartshorn Family 332, 425
Hartslog Heritage Museum Archives 481
Hartsville Genealogical Research Library 515
Hartsville Museum Archives 515
Harvard Album 280
Harvard Historical Museum 280
Harvard Historical Newsletter 272
Harvard Historical Society 280
Harvard Historical Society & Library 272
Harvard Public Library 272
Harvard University Library 268
Harvey County Historical Museum 219
Harvey County Historical Society & Archives 219
Harvey Family 70, 316
Harvey Grant Heritage Centre Archives 668
Harvey Helm Memorial Library 233
Harvey House Museum 214
Harvey J Higgins Historical Society 330
Harvey Public Library 162, 438
Harvey W Scott Memorial Library 475
Harvey-Baker House Museum Archives 64
Harvey-Mitchell Memorial Library 360
Harvin Clarendon County Library 516
Harwell Researcher 155
Harwich Historical Society & Archives 272
Harwinton Historical Society 95
Harwinton Public Library 95
Harwood Foundation & Library 385
Hasbrouck Family 406
Hasbrouck Heights Free Public Library 371
Hash Family Historian 46
Haskell County Genealogical Society 548
Haskell County Genealogy Society 469
Haskell County Historical Society & Archives 222
Haskell County Historical Society Journal 222
Haskell County Library 548
Haskell Family 263
Haskell Free Library 576
Haskell Journal 226
Hassebrock Family 163
Hassell Family 551
Hastings County Museum Archives 680
Hastings Family 183, 526, 607
Hastings Historian 399
Hastings Historical Society 113, 309, 352, 399
Hastings Public Library 293, 352
Hastings Town Historian 393
Hastings-on-Hudson Historian 399
Hastings-on-Hudson Historical Society & Library 399
Hatch Family 568
Hatchet Lake Denesuline Nation 711
Hatch-Thompson-Gooch-Burkinsham-Allen-Knapp-Allen-Preece-Bagley Family 568

Hatfield Family 478
Hatfield Public Library 272
Hatfield-Lichfield Family 567
Hathaway Family 140
Hathaway Ranch Museum Archives 71
Hathaway Ranch Museum Newsletter 71
Hatheway House Archives 100
Hatt Family 121
Hatten Family 323
Hattie Weber Museum of Davis Archives 42
Hattiesburg Area Historical Museum 320
Hattiesburg Area Historical Society & Archives 320
Hattiesburg Area Historical Society Newsletter 320
Hattiesburg Genealogical Society 320
Hattiesburg Public Library System 320
Hatton Family Newsletter 110
Hatton-Eielson Museum Archives 438
Hauberg Indian Museum Archives 172
Haubstadt Area Historical Society 185
Hauer Newsletter 262
Hauge Norwegian History Center 627
Hauger Family 258
Haun Herald 116
Haunt-Saint-Jean Regional Library 664
Haupt-Yehl House 167
Haury Family 381
Haus Family 61
Haut-Saint-Jean Regional Library-Grand Sault Public 664
Havana Public Library System 162
Have You Read 303
Havekost Family 298
Haven Family 384
Havens Family 68
Haverford Township Historical Society & Library 489
Haverford Township Historical Society Newsletter 489
Haverhill Historical Society & Archives 272
Haverhill Historical Society Quarterly 272
Haverhill Public Library 272
Haverstraw Kings Daughters Public Library 399
Haviland Family 456
Havre-Hill County Library 345
Haw River Historical Association 428
Hawaii Chinese History Center Library 141
Hawaii County Genealogical Society 142
Hawaii County Genealogical Society & Archives 141
Hawaii Maritime Center Library & Photo Archives 141
Hawaii Plantation Village Archives 143
Hawaii State Archives 141
Hawaii State Department of Health Research and Statistics Office Vital Records Section 141
Hawaii State Library 141
Hawaii State Public Library System 141
Hawaiian Historical Society & Library 141
Hawaiian Journal of History 141
Hawaiian Mission Children's Society Library 141
Hawaiian Scottish Association 142
Hawarden Public Library 203
Hawbaker-Erisman Family 489
Hawes Family 570
Hawk Family 213
Hawk-Brinkerhoff Family 567
Hawken House 342
Hawkes Family 133, 269
Hawkes Happenings 133
Hawkes Library 132, 139
Hawkesbury Public Library 683
Hawkeye Heritage 200
Hawkeye Log Cabin Archives 198
Hawkeye Log Cabin Newsletter 198
Hawkeye Public Library 203
Hawkins County Genealogical and Historical Society 532
Hawkins Family 402, 416, 568
Hawkins Heritage 48
Hawkins Memorial Library 204
Hawkins Newsletter 262
Hawk-Kresge-Schupp-Shupp-Shup Family 370
Hawks Inn Historical Museum 620
Hawks Inn Historical Society & Archives 620
Hawks Inn Newsletter 620
Hawks Nest State Park Archives 611
Hawk-Sherretts Family 448
Hawley Bulletin 101
Hawn Memorial Library 393
Haworth (Hayworth) Association Newsletter 355
Haworth Family Newsletter 194
Haworth Municipal Library 371
Haws Family 565
Hawsey-Higdon-Mixson Family 113
Haws-Luttrell-Templeton-Mayberry Family 13
Haws-Whitcomb Family 566
Hawthorne Public Library 371
Hay Clan 319, 506
Hay Derrick 573
Hay House Museum Archives 133
Hay Lake School Museums Archives 315
Hay Lakes Municipal Public Library 644
Hay Library 637
Haycraft Family 310
Hayden Heritage Association 86
Hayden Historical Museum 185
Hayden Historical Society 185
Hayden Library 21
Hayden-Downs Family 230
Hayes County Historical Society 352
Hayes Family 402, 566
Hayes Historical Journal 448
Hayes House 256
Hayes Presidential Center Library 448
Hayes-Harris Family 260
Hayman Family 255
Haymes Family 336
Haymon Grapevine 237
Haymore Family 541
Hayner Family 593
Hayner Family News 120
Hayner Public Library District 151
Hayner Public Library District Newsletter 151
Haynes Family 285
Haynes Memorial Library 359
Haynes-McDonald Heritage Quest 11

Hays Antique Truck Museum Archives 78
Hays Masonic Bodies (A F & A M) 215
Hays Public Library 215
Hays-Breeze Family 165
Haysville Community Library 215
Hayward Area Genealogical Society 47
Hayward Area Genealogical Society & Archives 68
Hayward Area Historical Museum 47
Hayward Area Historical Society & Archives 47
Hayward Carnegie Library 623
Hayward Public Library 47
Haywood County Genealogical Society 434
Haywood County Public Library 434
Haywood Hall & Gardens Archives 431
Hazard Community College Library 228
Hazard Library Association 411
Hazel M Lewis Library 479
Hazel Mackin Community Library 630
Hazelbaker Family 288, 465
Hazelrigg Family 331
Hazelrigg Family Association Newsletter 331
Hazelton Area Public Library 489
Hazelton District Public Library 650
Hazelton Historical Society & Archives 489
Hazelton Historical Society Newsletter 489
Hazelton Newsletter 480
Hazelwood Historic House Archives 622
Hazen Family Association Newsletter 282
Hazen Historical Society 28
Hazen Memorial Library 279
Hazen Road Dispatch 576
HCF Research Library Newsletter 49
HCL Pulse 370
He'eia Historical Society 142
Head End 420
Head Newsletter 84
Headen-Inman House Museum 70
Headley-Whitney Museum Archives 230
Headlight 220
Headlines & Happenings 256
Headlung House Museum 86
Head-of-the-Lake Historical Society 683
Headquarters Heliogram 587
Headquarters House Museum Archives 27
Head-Smashed-In Buffalo Jump Museum 643
Headwaters Heritage Museum Archives 346
Headwaters Heritage Museum Newsletter 346
Headway Recorder 263
Heagany Family 294
Heald Family 474
Healdsburg Historical Museum 47
Healdsburg Historical Society & Archives 47
Healdton Oil Museum Archives 465
Healey Family 65
Healy House-Dexter Cabin Museum Archives 87
Heaman's Antique Autorama Archives 659
Hear Ye Hear Ye 414
Heard and Scene 131
Heard County Historical Society & Library 131
Heard Museum Archives 18
Heard Museum Archives Newsletter 18
Hear-Saye 98
Hearst San Simeon State Historical Monument Staff Library 69
Heart Lake Indian Band 644
Heart O' Lakes Genealogical Society 306
Heart O' Lakes Genealogical Society & Library 307
Heart O'Lakes Genealogical Newsletter 307
Heart O'Wisconsin Genealogical Society & Archives 634
Heart O'Wisconsin Genealogical Society Newsletter 634
Heart of America Genealogical Society & Archives 332
Heart of America Library 439
Heart of Dixie Railroad Museum Archives 2
Heart of Texas Genealogical Society 557
Heart of Texas Records 562
Heart of West Texas Museum Archives 540
Heart's Content Cable Station Museum Archives 667
Hearthstone Historic House Museum Archives 617
Heartland Museum of Military Vehicles Archives 353
Heartlines 332, 562
Heath Family 129
Heavener Runestone State Park Archives 466
Hebdon Family 571
Heber City Regional Branch Genealogical Library 568
Heber Region Family History Center Newsletter 568
Hebert Family 237
Hebner Family 300
Hebrew Union College Skirball Museum & Cultural Center Archives 52
Hebron Historical Society 95, 185
Hebron Secrest Library 352
Heckman Library 292
Heckmann-Harding Family 78
Heckscher State Park Archives 396
Hecla Island Heritage Home Museum Archives 661
Hector National Exhibition Centre Archives 676
Hedberg Public Library 623
Heddalines 282
Heddon Museum Archives 290
Hedgepost 218
Hedley Heritage Society 650
Hedlund Family 565
Heeke Family 186
Heermance Memorial Library 395
Heeter Family 624
Heflin Family 233
Hefner Handbook 548
Hege Library 427
Heiby Family 458
Heidelberg Family 320
Heidelberger Family 65
Heiltsuk Indian Band 657
Heimbach Family 590
Heir Lines 78, 451
Heirlines 295
Heirloom 117
Heirs and Ancestors 424
Heisey Museum 493
Hejnal 339
Held-Poage Memorial Home 75
Helen A Ganser Library 494
Helen B Hoffman Plantation Library 120

Helen Jeffris Wood Museum Center Archives 623
Helen Marie Taylor Museum of Waco History Archives 562
Helen Mathes Library 159
Helena Modjeska Historic House Museum Archives 54
Helena Modjeska Historic House Newsletter 54
Heliotrope Communications 81
Helix Public Library 476
Helland Family 608
Hellenic Museum and Cultural Center Archives 155
Hellenic Museum and Cultural Center Newsletter 155
Heller Helper 154
Hellertown Historical Society 489
Helm(s)-Casey-Porterfield-Fenis-Phoenix Family 407
Helmcken House Pioneer Doctor's Residence Museum 657
Helm-Cravens Library 225
Helmer Family 481
Helotes Historical Society 548
Helsey Family 147
Helvetia Historical Museum 612
Hemet Area Museum Association 47
Hemet Museum Archives 47
Hemet Public Library 47
Hemet-San Jacinto Genealogical Society & Library 47
Hemingford Public Library 352
Hemingway Birthplace Museum Archives 169
Hemingway Dispatch 169
Hemingway Family 298
Hemphill County Historical and Genealogical Society 539
Hemphill County Library 539
Hemphill Historical Society 323
Hempstead County Genealogical Society 28
Hempstead County Historical Society 28
Hempstead County Historical Society Journal 28
Hempstead Public Library 399
Hempstead Trails 28
Hempsted House Archives 97
Henager Memories and Nostalgia Museum Archives 181
Hendershot Family 481
Henderson Clan 116, 119, 583
Henderson County District Library 152
Henderson County Genealogical and Historical Society 228, 428
Henderson County Historical Commission 536
Henderson County Historical Museum 169
Henderson County Historical Society 536
Henderson County Historical Society & Archives 169
Henderson County Library 536
Henderson County North Carolina Genealogical and Historical Society Journal 428
Henderson County Public Library 428
Henderson Free Library 399
Henderson Historical Museum 399
Henderson Historical Society & Archives 399
Henderson Memorial Public Library 450
Henderson Public Library 228
Henderson-Peck Family 515
Hendren Family 530
Hendricks County Genealogical Society 182
Hendricks County Historical Museum 182
Hendricks County Historical Society & Archives 182
Hendricks County Historical Society Bulletin 182
Hendricks Family 208
Hendricks Hill Museum Archives 251
Hendricks House 272
Hendrickson Family 476
Hendrickson House Museum 104
Henery Family 452
Henika Public Library 304
Henkel-Hinkle Newsletter 262
Henlein-Heinlein Family 186
Henneman Family 504
Hennepin County Historical Museum 311
Hennepin County Historical Society & Archives 311
Hennepin County History 311
Hennepin County Library 311
Hennepin Overland Railway Historical Society 311
Hennessey Public Library 466
Henn-Haines Family 567
Henniker Historical Society & Library 361
Henrich Family 343
Henrico County Historic Preservation 593
Henrico County Historical Museum 593
Henrico County Historical Society 593
Henrico County Museum Archives 588
Henrietta Public Library 413
Henry B Plant Museum Archives 123
Henry C Adams Memorial Library 171
Henry Clay-Ashland Mansion Museum Archives 230
Henry Clay-Ashland Mansion Museum Newsletter 230
Henry County Genealogical Society 163, 190, 205
Henry County Genealogical Society & Archives 447
Henry County Genealogical Society Newsletter 163, 205, 447
Henry County Genie 163
Henry County Historical and Genealogical Society & Archives 327
Henry County Historical Center 584
Henry County Historical Group 8
Henry County Historical Museum 152, 190, 327
Henry County Historical Society 232, 453, 584
Henry County Historical Society & Archives 1, 152, 190
Henry County Historical Society Newsletter 1
Henry County Public Library 327
Henry County Update 134
Henry F Schricker Library 187
Henry Family 594
Henry Ford Museum Archives 289
Henry Guest House Archives 374
Henry Henley Public Library 181
Henry Herald 476
Henry Historical and Genealogical Society 162
Henry Madden Library 45
Henry Morrison Flagler Museum Archives 119
Henry Overnoiser House Archives 468
Henry Pfeiffer Library 163
Henry Public Library 162
Henry Schuette Archives 625
Henry Sheldon Museum Archives 577
Henry Sheldon Museum Newsletter 577
Henry W Seymour Library 160
Henry Waldinger Memorial Library 419
Henry Whitfield State Historical Museum Archives 94
Henry Whittemore Library 271

Henry Wilson Coil Library & Museum 66
Henryetta Public Library 466
Henryetta Territorial Museum Archives 466
Henson-Cartwright Family 551
Hente Family 161
Hentila Family 630
Hepburn Family 393
Hepburn Library 403
Hepworth Family 572
Hepworth-Hirst Family 572
Herald 327, 494, 541, 626
Heraldic Register of America 9
Heraldry Society of Canada-Societe Heraldique du Canada 687
Herbert H Lehman College Library 390
Herbert Hoover Presidential Library 209
Herbert Hoover Presidential Library Association 209
Herbert Westcoat Memorial Library 452
Herbst-Escalle-Desdier-Mazet Family 637
Herd-Dierhing Family 216
Here and There in Grant County 624
Heredity Order of the First Families of Massachusetts 18
Hereford Inlet Lighthouse Archives 375
Hereford Inlet Lighthouse Newsletter 375
Heritage 18, 33, 43, 99, 117, 133, 220, 223, 228, 281, 338, 394, 473, 525, 537
Heritage and Genealogical Society of Montgomery County & Archives 397
Heritage and History 76
Heritage Association of El Dorado County & Library 60
Heritage Battle Creek 286
Heritage Canada 687
Heritage Center and Citrus Museum Archives 123
Heritage Center Archives 523
Heritage Center Museum 25, 601, 622
Heritage Center News 625
Heritage Center Newsletter 303
Heritage Center of Lancaster County Archives 491
Heritage Center of Lancaster County Newsletter 491
Heritage Commission Corporation 457
Heritage Commission Corporation Newsletter 457
Heritage Complex Farm Equipment Museum Archives 75
Heritage Conservancy & Archives 486
Heritage Conservancy Museum 486
Heritage Coordinating Council 45
Heritage Express 221
Heritage Farm and Village Archives 708
Heritage Farm Museum and Village Archives 612
Heritage Farmstead Association of Collin County & Library 556
Heritage Foundation of Newfoundland and Labrador 668
Heritage Foundation of Oswego County & Library 410
Heritage Genealogical Society 65, 260
Heritage Genealogical Society & Archives 219
Heritage Genealogical Society Quarterly 219
Heritage Hall 133, 629
Heritage Hall Archives 628
Heritage Hall Museum 522
Heritage Happenings 183
Heritage Hazenmore Museum Archives 706
Heritage Highlights 233, 546
Heritage HiLites 316
Heritage Hill State Park Archives 622
Heritage Horizons 523
Heritage House Archives 191
Heritage House Library 45
Heritage House Museum 36
Heritage House Museum Archives 115, 690
Heritage House Museum of Montgomery County Archives 30
Heritage House Museum of Montgomery County Newsletter 30
Heritage House Museum of Orange County Archives 555
Heritage Hunter 27
Heritage Hunters 415
Heritage Hunters Newsletter 415
Heritage League of Greater Kansas City 332
Heritage League of Northwest Illinois & Archives 175
Heritage Library 515
Heritage Military Music Foundation, 1st Brigade Band 633
Heritage Museum & Gardens Archives 278
Heritage Museum & Underhill Museum Archives 86
Heritage Museum Archives 87, 256, 328, 538, 660
Heritage Museum Foundaiton of Tate County Archives 322
Heritage Museum Newsletter 199, 538
Heritage Museum Park 85
Heritage News 40, 133, 266, 316, 542
Heritage News Bulletin 152
Heritage Newsletter 67, 528
Heritage of Craven County 430
Heritage of Fayette County 181
Heritage of Granby 94
Heritage of Marion County 5
Heritage of Stone 31
Heritage of the Americas Museum Archives 43
Heritage of the Americas Museum Newsletter 43
Heritage of the Hills 466
Heritage of the Plains Historical Society 211
Heritage of Vermilion County 157
Heritage Orange County 70
Heritage Park - Historical Village Archives 641
Heritage Park Archives 71, 643
Heritage Park Museum 278
Heritage Park Museum Archives 656
Heritage Place Archives 429
Heritage Preservation Archives 105
Heritage Press 311
Heritage Quest Genealogy Bulletin 568
Heritage Quest Library 568
Heritage Quest Magazine 568
Heritage Quest Research Library & Bookstore 608
Heritage Register 551
Heritage Resource Group 257
Heritage Review 326, 437, 563, 589
Heritage Sandy Springs 136
Heritage Searchers of Kandiyohi County 316
Heritage Seeker 325
Heritage Seekers 644
Heritage Seekers & Library 336
Heritage Seekers Genealogy Club 29
Heritage Seekers Genealogy Club & Library 31
Heritage Seekers Quarterly 31
Heritage Society of Austin 536
Heritage Society of British Columbia 657
Heritage Society of Northwest Indiana 180, 181

INDEX

Heritage Society of Pennsylvania 492
Heritage Square Museum Archives 52
Heritage Station Museum 477
Heritage Station Museum Archives 130
Heritage Timepiece 164
Heritage Today 556
Heritage Trail 175
Heritage Vancouver Society 656
Heritage Village Archives 312
Heritage Village Museum 542
Heritage Village Museum Archives 563
Heritage Walk Museum 44
Heritage Walk Quarterly 44
Heritage Windows 613
Heritage: the Yorker Scene 394
Heritage-Hjemkomst Interpretive Center Archives 311
Heritagepac: Dedicated to the Preservation of American Battlefields 29
Herkimer County Historical Crier 399
Herkimer County Historical Museum 399
Herkimer County Historical Society & Archives 399
Herkimer Home State Historic Site Archives 403
Herlacher Herald 88
Herman Brown Free Library 539
Hermann-Grima Historic House Library 240
Hermann-Grima Historic House Quarterly 240
Hermitage Gatehouse Museum Archives 679
Hermitage Historical Society 489
Hermitage Museum 371
Hermitage Museum Newsletter 371
Hermitage: Home of President Andrew Jackson Archives 527
Hermon Heritage Hall Archives 399
Hermon Town Historian 399
Hermon Village Historian 400
Hermosa Beach Historical Society 47
Hernandez-Ziegler Family 385
Hernando County Library System 110
Hernando Desoto Historical Society 109
Hernando Heritage Museum Archives 110
Herndon Family 554
Hero Library 263
Heroy Family 388
Herr House Foundation Newsletter 505
Herreshoff Marine Museum Archives 507
Herrick District Library 294
Herrick Memorial Library 459
Herrick Township Public Library 162
Herrin City Library 162
Herring Family 327
Herriott Heritage Association 154
Herrold Family 195
Herschell Carrousel Factory Museum 409
Hersey Family 282
Hershey Museum Archives 489
Hershey Public Library 489
Hertford County Library 435
Hesburgh Library 191
Hesper-Mabel Area Historical Society 310
Hesquiaht Indian Band 656
Hesseltine Public Library 609
Hesston Public Library 215
Hessville Historical Society 185
Heston Family 558
Hettinger County Historical Museum 439
Hettinger County Historical Society & Archives 439
Hettinger County Historical Society Library 439
Hetty Green Historical Society 275
Hewes Library 166
Hewett-Hewitt-Huit Family Ancestry 74
Hewick Plantation 596
Hewitt Historical Society 309
Hezekiah Alexander Homesite 424
Hi Plains Genealogical Society & Archives 556
Hialeah-John F Kennedy Library 113
Hibbing Historical Museum 309
Hibbing Historical Society & Archives 309
Hibbing Historical Society Newsletter 309
Hickam Air Force Base Library 141
Hickman County Historical and Genealogical Society 226
Hickman County Historical Society 525
Hickman County Memorial Library 226
Hickman County Public Library 525
Hickories Museum 448
Hickory County Historical Society & Archives 330
Hickory Grove Rural School Museum Archives 206
Hickory Hill Historic House Museum Archives 138
Hickory House 247
Hickory Landmarks Society & Archives 428
Hickory Leaves 448
Hickory Public Library 428
Hicksville Public Library 400
Hidalgo Pump House Heritage and Discovery Center Archives 553
Hidden Child 407
Hidden Child Foundation 407
Hidden Valley Journal 43
Hiddenite Center Archives 428
Hi-Desert Genealogical Society & Archives 76
Hiebert Library 45
Higbee Area Historical Society 330
Higdon Family 583
Higganbottom Family 340
Higgerson School Historic Site Archives 336
Higginbotham Family 539
Higgins Armory Museum Library 283
Higgins Armory Museum Quarterly 283
Higgins Museum Archives 206
Higginson Family 50
High Bar Indian Band 648
High Cliff Historical Museum 631
High Cliff Historical Society 617
High Cliff Historical Society & Archives 631
High Desert Museum Archives 473
High Desert Museum Newsletter 473
High Family 513
High Family Association Newsletter 513
High Library 486
High Plains Chronicles 344
High Plains Genealogical Society 539
High Plains Heritage Center 344
High Plains Heritage Society & Archives 524
High Plains Historical Association 212

High Plains Historical Museum 354, 524
High Plains Historical Museum 88
High Plains Historical Society & Archives 354
High Plains Historical Society & Archives 88
High Plains Museum Archives 214
High Plains News 524
High Plains Preservation Projects 216
High Point Museum and Historical Park Archives 428
High Point Public Library 428
High Prairie and District Centennial Museum Archives 644
High Prairie and District Historical Museum 644
High Prairie and District Historical Society & Archives 644
High River Centennial Library 644
High Tides 426
Highball 594
Highballer 526
Highland Beach Library 113
Highland Community College Library 215
Highland County District Library 449
Highland County Genealogy Society & Archives 450
Highland County Historical Society & Archives 450
Highland County Museum and Heritage Center Archives 590
Highland County Museum Newsletter 590
Highland County Public Library 591
Highland Echo 232
Highland Falls Library 400
Highland Historical Society 162, 185
Highland House Museum 450
Highland Maple Museum Archives 591
Highland Mills Historical Society 400
Highland Mission 215
Highland Park Historical Museum 162
Highland Park Historical Society & Archives 162
Highland Park Historical Society Newsletter 162
Highland Park Public Library 162
Highland Pioneers Museum Archives 673
Highland Rim Regional Library Center 531
Highland Village Archives 674
Highlander 77, 225, 431
Highlands County Genealogial Society 122
Highlands County Genealogical Society & Archives 109
Highlands County Genealogical Society Newsletter 109
Highlands County Historical Society 122
Highlands County Public Library System 122
Highlands Historical Society 428
Highlands House Museum Archives 487
Highlands House Museum Quarterly 487
Highlands Museum Archives 225
Highlands Ranch Genealogical Society 86
Highlights 352, 588, 613
Highline Community College Library 601
Highmiller Family 457
Hightower Family 561
Hightower News 194
Hightstown-East Windsor Historical Society & Library 371
Hightstown-East Windsor Historical Society Newsletter 371
Highway to History 475
Higley Homestead Museum 576
Hildebrand Family Organization Quarterly 151
Hildebrand Memorial Library 618
Hildene Museum Archives 577
Hildreth Family 407
Hi-Lites 189
Hill Aerospace Museum Archives 566
Hill College Library 548
Hill Country Museum 550
Hill Country Preservation Society & Archives 550
Hill County Crossroads 548
Hill County Genealogical Society 548
Hill County Genealogical Society & Archives 548
Hill Cumorah Visitors Center Archives 410
Hill Family 156
Hill Memorial Library 235
Hillary House and Koffler Museum of Medicine Archives 679
Hillcrest Museum Archives 661
Hillen-Hillon Family 417
Hiller Aviation Museum Archives 65
Hiller Aviation Museum Quarterly 65
Hillforest Historical Foundation & Library 179
Hillforest House 179
Hillforest House Quarterly 179
Hill-Hold House Museum Archives 405
Hillman Family 544
Hillman Library 499
Hills and Dales Historic House Museum Archives 132
Hills Memorial Library 361
Hillsboro Area Historical Society & Archives 623
Hillsboro City Library 548
Hillsboro Historical Society & Archives 215
Hillsborough County Historic Commission Library 123
Hillsborough County Historical Commission 123
Hillsborough Historical Society & Archives 361
Hillsborough Public Library 162
Hillsborough Railway Museum Archives 664
Hillsdale County Historical Society 293
Hillsdale Free Will Baptist College Library 467
Hillside Historical Society 371
Hill-Stead Museum Library 93
Hilltop Historical Society 446
Hill-Wilson-Foster-Bla(y)lock Family 467
Hillwood Museum Archives 105
Hilpert-Morgans-Downs Family 426
Hilton C Buley Library 96
Hilton Head Island Genealogical Society 515
Hilton Head Island Genealogical Society Newsletter 515
Hilton Head Island Historical Society 515
Hilton Union Public Library 683
Hinchman Family 225
Hinchman-Henchman Family 271
Hinckley Family 141, 147, 545
Hinckley Fire Museum Archives 309
Hinckley Foundation Museum Archives 401
Hinckley Historical Society 450
Hinckley Home Association 247
Hinckley Home-School-Farm 247
Hiner Family 549
Hines Haze 219
Hingham Historical Society 272
Hingham Public Library 272
Hinkle (Henkle) Newsletter 262

INDEX

Hinman Family 17
Hinman-Humphrey Family 568
Hinsdale County Historical Society 87
Hinsdale Historical Museum 162
Hinsdale Historical Society & Archives 162
Hinsdale Historical Society Newsletter 162
Hinsdale Public Library 272
Hinshaw Family 72
Hinterlander 507
Hinton Family 573
Hinton Municipal Library 644
Hints on Hintons 554
Hipps-Hipp Family 544
Hiram Walker Historical Museum Library 693
Hire Family 442
Hisak-Cisac Newsletter 155
Hisaw Family Newsletter 87
Hiscock Family 479
Hiscock House Museum Archives 669
Hise Newsletter 68
Hisell-Hysell (Barnhisle-Barnheiser) Newsletter 68
Hisle-Hysell Genealogy Group 369
Hispanic American Historical Review 426
Hispanic Family History Society 21
Hispanic Genealogical Journal 549
Hispanic Genealogical Research Center of New Mexico 381
Hispanic Genealogical Society 68, 549
Hispanic Genealogical Society of New York & Archives 407
Hispanic Historical and Ancestral Research Society 46
Hispanic Society Historical Museum 407
Hispanic Society of America & Archives 407
Histo-Report 500
Historia 503
Historian 159, 177, 290, 306, 310, 314, 398, 448, 491
Historian of Hancock County 319
Historian's Digest 372
Historic 1841Courthouse 398
Historic Aiken Foundation 511
Historic Albany Foundation 387
Historic Alexandria Quarterly 583
Historic Allaire Village Archives 367
Historic Annapolis Foundation & Library 255
Historic Annapolis Foundation Museum 255
Historic Archaeological Research 195
Historic Arkansas Museum Archives 29
Historic Arkansas Museum Newsletter 29
Historic Atlas Coal Mine Museum Archives 642
Historic Augusta & Library 127
Historic Augusta Newsletter 127
Historic Babcock Mill Museum Archives 687
Historic Batavia 152
Historic Bath State Historic Site Museum Archives 423
Historic Batsto Village Archives 367
Historic Beaufort Foundation & Library 511
Historic Beaufort Foundation Newsletter 511
Historic Bethabara Park Library 435
Historic Bethany 611
Historic Bethel German Colony 325
Historic Bethlehem & Library 482
Historic Bethlehem Newsletter 482
Historic Bethlehem Partnership Newsletter 482
Historic Blooming Grove Historical Society & Archives 627
Historic Bowens Mills and Pioneer Park Archives 297
Historic Brattonsville & Archives 516
Historic Brattonsville Museum 516
Historic Burlington County Prison Museum Archives 374
Historic Buzz 633
Historic Camden and Revolutionary War Site & Library 512
Historic Camden Museum 512
Historic Camden Newsletter 512
Historic Cannelton 181
Historic Carson House Museum Archives 430
Historic Centennial Village Museum Archives 86
Historic Centennial Village Museum Newsletter 86
Historic Centerville & Archives 181
Historic Charleston Foundation & Archives 512
Historic Charleston Museum 512
Historic Chattahoochee Commission & Library 4
Historic Chattahoochee Committee 132
Historic Cheraw 513
Historic Cherry Hill & Archives 387
Historic Columbia Foundation & Archives 513
Historic Columbus Foundation & Archives 128
Historic Columbus Foundation Museum 128
Historic Columbus Foundation Newsletter 128
Historic Connersville & Archives 182
Historic Costume & Textiles Collection Archives 446
Historic County 376
Historic Crab Orchard Museum Archives 596
Historic Cragfont Archives 525
Historic Daniel Boone Home and Boonesfield Village Archives 328
Historic Deepwood Estate Museum Archives 479
Historic Deerfield & Archives 269
Historic Deerfield Quarterly 269
Historic Denver 83
Historic Denver News 83
Historic Depot Museum Archives 427
Historic Dumfries Virginia & Archives 586
Historic Dumfries Virginia Newsletter 586
Historic Echoes 130
Historic Edenton State Historic Site Archives 426
Historic Effingham Society 137
Historic Elsah Foundation & Archives 159
Historic Emily Olson House 628
Historic Fallsington & Archives 487
Historic Fallsington Museum 487
Historic Ferryland Museum Archives 667
Historic Florida Keys Foundation 115
Historic Florissant 329
Historic Forks of the Wabash 185
Historic Fort Steilacoom Archives 608
Historic Fort Steilacoom Newsletter 608
Historic Fort Stockton Museum Archives 545
Historic Fort Worth 545
Historic Fort York Archives 691
Historic Foundation of the Presbyterian and Reformed Churches & Library 430
Historic Fredericksburg Foundation 588
Historic Gardner's Basin Museum Archives 367
Historic General Dodge House Museum 199

Historic General Dodge House Quarterly 199
Historic George Key Ranch Archives 60
Historic Georgetown 85
Historic Georgetown Quarterly 85
Historic Gordonsville 588
Historic Governors' Mansion Museum Archives 635
Historic Granbury 547
Historic Granbury Merchants Association 547
Historic Greenville Foundation 515
Historic Hagerstown & Archives 185
Historic Halifax State Historic Site Archives 428
Historic Harrisburg Association 489
Historic Hartwood Mansion Museum Archives 499
Historic Harvey House Museum 37
Historic Hat Creek Ranch Archives 648
Historic Hermann 330
Historic Hermann Museum 330
Historic Homes Foundation 230
Historic Homes Foundation Newsletter 230
Historic Hope Foundation & Archives 435
Historic Hope Foundation Newsletter 435
Historic House News 407
Historic House Trust of New York City 407
Historic Hudson Community Association 454
Historic Hudson Valley 418
Historic Hudson Valley Newsletter 418
Historic Huntsville Foundation 5
Historic Huntsville Foundation Quarterly of Local Architecture and Preservation 5
Historic Illinois 153, 156, 159, 174
Historic Ink 531
Historic Jefferson College Library 323
Historic Jefferson College Museum Archives 323
Historic Jefferson College Museum Newsletter 323
Historic Jefferson Foundation 550
Historic Jefferson Railway 550
Historic Jordan House 209
Historic Journal 493
Historic Kansas City Foundation & Library 332
Historic Kansas City Foundation Gazette 332
Historic Kern 36
Historic Ketchikan 12
Historic Key West Preservation Board 115
Historic Landmarks Foundation 181
Historic Landmarks Foundation of Indiana & Archives 186
Historic Landmarks Museum 186
Historic Langhorne Association & Library 492
Historic Langhorne Association Newsletter 492
Historic Latta Plantation Archives 428
Historic Liberty Jail Archives 334
Historic Lincoln Museum Archives 383
Historic Linwood Foundation 128
Historic Lyme Village Association & Archives 442
Historic Madison 625
Historic Madison & Archives 189
Historic Madison Journal 189
Historic Madison Museum 189
Historic Manassas 590
Historic Mann House Museum Archives 288
Historic Marion 479
Historic Markerville Creamery Archives 645
Historic Maury 526
Historic Mill Creek Museum Archives 296
Historic Milwaukee 626
Historic Mobile Preservation Society & Library 7
Historic Nantucket 275
Historic Nashville & Archives 531
Historic Nashville Museum 531
Historic Naval and Military Establishments Archives 685
Historic Naval Ships Association 596
Historic New Carlisle 190
Historic New England 267
Historic New England Magazine 267
Historic New England Museum 267
Historic New Harmony & Archives 190
Historic New Harmony Museum 190
Historic New Harmony Newsletter 190
Historic New Orleans Collection Library 240
Historic New Orleans Collections Quarterly 240
Historic New Richmond 456
Historic New Richmond Historical Society 454
Historic Newburgh 190
Historic Newton Home Archives 289
Historic O'Fallon Museum Archives 343
Historic O'Keefe Ranch Archives 656
Historic Oakland Cemetery Archives 126
Historic Oakland News 126
Historic Ocala-Marion County Genealogical Society 118
Historic Occoquan & Archives 592
Historic Occoquan Museum 592
Historic Occoquan Newsletter 592
Historic Oglethorpe County 133
Historic Palmyra & Archives 410
Historic Palmyra News 410
Historic Pensacola Preservation Board of Trustees & Library 120
Historic Pensacola Quarterly 120
Historic Pensacola Village 120
Historic Pipestone 313
Historic Pittsford & Archives 411
Historic Pittsford Newsletter 411
Historic Point Basse 627
Historic Preservation 156
Historic Preservation Alliance of Arkansas 29
Historic Preservation Association Museum 214
Historic Preservation Association of Bourbon County & Archives 214
Historic Preservation Center Archives 31
Historic Preservation Foundation of North Carolina & Archives 431
Historic Preservation League of Oregon & Library 478
Historic Preservation League of Oregon Newsletter 478
Historic Preservation of Big Horn County 345
Historic Preservation of Shreveport & Library 241
Historic Preservation Society of Durham 426
Historic Preservation Training Center 259
Historic Preservation Trust of Lancaster County & Library 491
Historic Price House Museum Archives 517
Historic Prince William 593
Historic Prophetstown Archives 179
Historic Pullman Foundation 155
Historic Pullman Foundation Update 155
Historic Red Clay Valley 104

Historic Register 531
Historic Renville Preservation Commission & Archives 313
Historic Renville Preservation Commission Newsletter 313
Historic Resources Management Program 62
Historic Restoration Society of Annapolis County 673
Historic Richmond Town Archives 417
Historic Richmondtown 417
Historic Rock Ford Plantation Museum Archives 491
Historic Rock Hill 517
Historic Rosary Cathedral 458
Historic Rosedale Foundation & Archives 425
Historic Rosedale Newsletter 425
Historic Roswell 136
Historic Rugby & Archives 532
Historic Rugby Museum 532
Historic Sahuaro Ranch Archives 16
Historic Sahuaro Ranch Newsletter 16
Historic Saint Augustine Preservation Board & Library 121
Historic Saint Mary's City 262
Historic Saint Mary's City Library 262
Historic Saint Mary's City Quarterly 262
Historic Saint Thomas Society 434
Historic Salisbury Foundation 432
Historic Saranac Lake & Archives 415
Historic Sauder Village Magazine 441
Historic Sauder Village Museum Archives 441
Historic Savannah Foundation 137
Historic Schaefferstown 494
Historic Schaefferstown & Library 501
Historic Schaefferstown Record 494, 501
Historic Seattle Preservation 606
Historic Sheperdstown Commission & Archives 614
Historic Sheperdstown Commission Newsletter 614
Historic Sheperdstown Museum 614
Historic Ship Nautilus-Submarine Force Museum Archives 94
Historic Smithfield 584
Historic Smithfield Museum 584
Historic Society of Old Randolph & Archives 377
Historic Society of Washington County, Virginia & Library 583
Historic Society of Washington County, Virginia Bulletin 583
Historic Society of Washington County, Virginia Newsletter 583
Historic Southwest Ohio Archives 457
Historic Southwest Ohio Newsletter 457
Historic Spanish Point Museum Archives 119
Historic Speedwell 374
Historic Stagville & Library 423
Historic Stagville Museum Archives 426
Historic Stephensburg Museum Archives 595
Historic Stewart Farmhouse Archives 655
Historic Takoma Park 263
Historic Times 119, 423
Historic Tyler 561
Historic Vance House Association 433
Historic Waco Foundation & Archives 562
Historic Waco Museum 562
Historic Walnford Museum Archives 379
Historic Ward-Meade Park 222
Historic Warrior Run Church Archives 503
Historic Warrior Run Church Museum Archives 504
Historic Washington House 632
Historic Wauwatosa 633
Historic Winslow House Association 274
Historic Wolcott House 196
Historic Yale Museum Archives 657
Historical and Genealogical Society of Carter County 463
Historical and Genealogical Society of Hardin County 560
Historical and Genealogical Society of Indiana Quarterly 490
Historical and Genealogical Society of Indiana County 490
Historical and Genealogical Society of Panola County 319
Historical and Genealogical Society of Randolph County Newsletter 196
Historical and Genealogical Society of Somerset County 502
Historical and Scientific Association & Archives 231
Historical Arms Society 482
Historical Association of Greater Cape Girardeau & Archives 326
Historical Association of South Jefferson County 387
Historical Association of Southern Florida & Archives 117
Historical Association of Southern Florida Museum 117
Historical Bulletin 372
Historical Bulletin of Miami County 191
Historical Center of the Nebraska Conference of the United Methodist Church 353
Historical Commission of the Southern Baptist Convention & Library 531
Historical Committee of the Mennonite Church & Library 184
Historical Confederation of Kentucky 227
Historical Crossroads Village Archives 291
Historical Diving Society 46
Historical Electronics Museum Archives 260
Historical Electronics Museum Quarterly 260
Historical Evaluation and Research Organization Library 591
Historical Footnotes 99, 339
Historical Foundation News 430
Historical Happenings 15, 62, 255, 459, 633
Historical Happenings in the Mahoning Valley 461
Historical Herald 442
Historical Highlights 129, 136, 167, 269, 374, 420
Historical Hi-lites 49
Historical Journal 406
Historical Journal of Massachusetts 282
Historical Library and Archives, Wisconsin United Methodist Conference Center 632
Historical Lynnfield 274
Historical Marker 109
Historical Messenger 152, 285
Historical Museum 180
Historical Museum 627
Historical Museum and Carriage House 274
Historical Museum and Genealogy Library 220
Historical Museum and Pioneer Village 646
Historical Museum at St Gertrude Archives 146
Historical Museum at the Fairgrounds 222
Historical Museum of Saint James-Assinboia Archives 662
Historical New Hampshire 360
Historical News 352
Historical Notes 219
Historical Notes: Newsletter Of the KCHS 178
Historical Observer 96
Historical Oregon Information Services 475
Historical Papers 687
Historical Preservation Society of Upper Township 375

Historical Publications Section, North Carolina Division of Archives and History 431
Historical Quarterly 113
Historical Reflections-Reflexions Historiques 387
Historical Register 455
Historical Research Center 11
Historical Review 343, 633
Historical Review of Berks County 500
Historical Shrine of San Diego County Museum 65
Historical Sketches of Southwest Virginia 597
Historical Society for the Preservation of the Underground Railroad 387
Historical Society Genealogical Committee Bulletin 445
Historical Society of Alberta 641
Historical Society of Alma-Bacon County & Library 125
Historical Society of Amherst, New Hampshire & Library 359
Historical Society of Amherst, New Hampshire Newsletter 359
Historical Society of Bamberg 511
Historical Society of Battle Creek & Archives 286
Historical Society of Berks County & Archives 500
Historical Society of Bloomfield & Archives 367
Historical Society of Bloomfield Newsletter 367
Historical Society of Boonton Township 368
Historical Society of Boonton Township, New Jersey Newsletter 368
Historical Society of Bridgeport & Library 287
Historical Society of Bridgeport Business Directory 287
Historical Society of Bridgeport News Letter 287
Historical Society of Canada 687
Historical Society of Carroll County & Archives 263
Historical Society of Caseville 287
Historical Society of Cecil County & Archives 258
Historical Society of Cecil County Bulletin 258
Historical Society of Centinela Valley & Library 52
Historical Society of Centinela Valley Newsletter 52
Historical Society of Cheboygan County 288
Historical Society of Chesterfield County 513
Historical Society of Cicero 157
Historical Society of Cocalico Valley & Archives 487
Historical Society of Columbiana and Fairfield Township & Library 445
Historical Society of Columbiana and Fairfield Township Quarterly 445
Historical Society of Dauphin County & Archives 489
Historical Society of Decatur County Bulletin 185
Historical Society of Delaware & Archives 104
Historical Society of Delaware Museum 104
Historical Society of Delaware Newsletter 104
Historical Society of Denton County 543
Historical Society of Douglas County 130
Historical Society of Douglas County & Archives 355
Historical Society of Early American Decoration 394
Historical Society of East Pennsboro 487
Historical Society of Elba 396
Historical Society of Fairfax County, Virginia & Library 587
Historical Society of Federal Way 601
Historical Society of Forsyth County 129
Historical Society of Fort McMurray 643
Historical Society of Fort Meade 112
Historical Society of Fort Washington & Archives 487
Historical Society of Fort Washington Bulletin 487
Historical Society of Frederick County & Archives 259
Historical Society of Frederick County Journal 259
Historical Society of Frederick County Newsletter 259
Historical Society of Garden County & Archives 355
Historical Society of Garden County & Library 353
Historical Society of Glastonbury 99
Historical Society of Glastonbury & Archives 93
Historical Society of Graham County & Archives 19
Historical Society of Greater Lansing 296
Historical Society of Greater Peotone & Library 170
Historical Society of Greater Port Jefferson & Archives 412
Historical Society of Green Tree 499
Historical Society of Greenfield & Archives 271
Historical Society of Haddonfield & Archives 370
Historical Society of Helvetia & Archives 612
Historical Society of Jews from Egypt 391
Historical Society of Jonesboro and Clayton County 132
Historical Society of Kent County & Archives 257
Historical Society of La Verne 49
Historical Society of Lawrence and Its People & Archives 273
Historical Society of Long Beach & Library 51
Historical Society of Mannsville 404
Historical Society of Maplewood 334
Historical Society of Maries County & Library 341
Historical Society of Marshall County & Library 205
Historical Society of Martin County 122
Historical Society of Michigan 290
Historical Society of Michigan & Library 285
Historical Society of Michigan Newsletter 285
Historical Society of Middletown and the Wallkill Precinct & Archives 405
Historical Society of Middletown and the Wallkill Precinct Newsletter 405
Historical Society of Millersburg and Upper Paxton Township & Library 494
Historical Society of Monterey Park & Library 55
Historical Society of Monterey Park Newsletter 55
Historical Society of Montgomery County & Library 162
Historical Society of Montgomery County Pennsylvania Bulletin 496
Historical Society of Moorestown & Library 373
Historical Society of Moreau & Archives 416
Historical Society of Mount Lebanon 499
Historical Society of New Mexico 384
Historical Society of Newburgh Bay and the Highlands & Archives 408
Historical Society of Newburgh Bay and the Highlands Newsletter 408
Historical Society of North Caddo 242
Historical Society of North Iowa 199
Historical Society of Oak Park and River Forest & Library 169
Historical Society of Ocean Grove 375
Historical Society of Ocean Grove, New Jersey & Archives 375
Historical Society of Ogden Dunes 192
Historical Society of Ogden Dunes & Archives 191
Historical Society of Okaloosa and Walton Counties & Archives 123
Historical Society of Oktibbeha County 322
Historical Society of Old Newbury & Archives 275
Historical Society of Old Northfield & Archives 454
Historical Society of Old Northfield Newsletter 454
Historical Society of Old Randolph & Library 377
Historical Society of Old Yarmouth & Archives 283
Historical Society of Old Yarmouth Newsletter 283
Historical Society of Oregon County 333
Historical Society of Ottawa & Library 687
Historical Society of Palm Beach County & Library 119, 124
Historical Society of Palm Desert 58
Historical Society of Palmer 13
Historical Society of Penns Grove and Carnes Point 376

INDEX

Historical Society of Pennsylvania & Archives 497
Historical Society of Perry County & Library 495
Historical Society of Plainfield and North Plainfield & Library 376
Historical Society of Pomona Valley 60
Historical Society of Pottawattamie County & Library 199
Historical Society of Princeton & Archives 376
Historical Society of Quaker Hill and Pawling & Archives 410
Historical Society of Quaker Hill and Pawling Newsletter 410
Historical Society of Quincy and Adams County & Archives 171
Historical Society of Red Hook 413
Historical Society of Rockaway 377
Historical Society of Rockaways & Archives 369
Historical Society of Rockland County & Archives 405
Historical Society of Saginaw County & Archives 301
Historical Society of Saint Catharines 689
Historical Society of Saint Clair Shores 301
Historical Society of Saint Louis County 327
Historical Society of Saint Marys and Benzinger Township & Library 501
Historical Society of Saint Marys and Benzinger Township Newsletter 501
Historical Society of Santuit and Cotuit & Archives 269
Historical Society of Sarasota County 121
Historical Society of Saratoga Springs & Archives 415
Historical Society of Schuylkill County & Library 500
Historical Society of Seattle and King County & Archives 606
Historical Society of Sleepy Hollow and Tarrytown & Archives 418
Historical Society of Smithfield 509
Historical Society of Southeast New Mexico 384
Historical Society of Southern California 52
Historical Society of Southwest Virginia 597
Historical Society of Stanley & Archives 631
Historical Society of Stanton County & Archives 356
Historical Society of Stanton County & Library 357
Historical Society of Tacony 497
Historical Society of Talbot County & Archives 258
Historical Society of Talbot County Quarterly 258
Historical Society of Temple City 74
Historical Society of the Bellmores 389
Historical Society of the Blairsville Area 483
Historical Society of the Downs Carnegie Library 213
Historical Society of the Fort Hill Country & Archives 167
Historical Society of the Fort Hill Country Newsletter 167
Historical Society of the Gatineau 697, 700
Historical Society of the Phoenixville Area 498
Historical Society of the Reformed Church in America & Archives 374
Historical Society of the Somerset Hills 367
Historical Society of the South Georgia Conference, United Methodist Church 136
Historical Society of the Tonawandas & Archives 418
Historical Society of the Town of Barnstable & Archives 266
Historical Society of the Town Of Bolton 390
Historical Society of the Town of East Bloomfield & Archives 396
Historical Society of the Town of Greenwich & Library 92
Historical Society of the Town of Greenwich Post 92
Historical Society of the Town of Hampden & Library 272
Historical Society of the Town of North Hempstead 404
Historical Society of the Town of North Hempstead & Library 421
Historical Society of the Town of Warwick & Archives 419
Historical Society of the United Methodist Church & Library 372
Historical Society of the Upper Baraboo Valley & Archives 634
Historical Society of the Upper Mojave Desert 62
Historical Society of the Upper Mojave Desert Bulletin 62
Historical Society of the Upper Mojave Desert Newsletter 62
Historical Society of Topsail Island 428
Historical Society of Trappe 485, 503
Historical Society of University City & Archives 341
Historical Society of Upper Saint Clair 499
Historical Society of Vandalia 459
Historical Society of Walden and Wallkill Valley & Archives 419
Historical Society of Walden and Wallkill Valley Newsletter 419
Historical Society of Walton County 134
Historical Society of Washington County 583
Historical Society of Washington DC 105
Historical Society of Watertown & Archives 281
Historical Society of Wells and Ogunquit & Archives 252
Historical Society of West Covina 77
Historical Society of Western Pennsylvania & Library 499
Historical Society of Western Virginia & Archives 594
Historical Society of Windham County & Library 578
Historical Society of Woodstock 421
Historical Society of York County & Library 506
Historical Society Polk County & Archives 479
Historical Tidings 533
Historical Time Capsules of Monroe County 631
Historical Times 356, 449
Historical Trails Library 322
Historical Village and Pioneer Museum Archives 646
Historical Village Newsletter 207
Historical Whisperings 315
Historically Speaking 55, 122, 177, 191, 305
Historicalog 190, 451
Historico 174
Historiogram 677
History Abounds 307
History and Genealogy Research Letter 330
History and Memory 180
History and Traditions Museum Archives 551
History Center News 305
History Happenings 296, 529
History Highlights 418
History Highlights 608
History House 51
History is Happening in Long Beach 51
History Journal 392
History Lives Here 48
History Museum of Saint Paul Archives 645
History Network of Washington County 315
History News 212
Hi-Story News 81
History News & Notes 308
History News Magazine 531
History Notes 316, 523
History Now 641
History of Contraception Museum Archives 691
History of Cranbrook House 287
History of Medicine Museum Archives 426
History of Pharmacy Museum Archives 22
History of the Library in Basking Ridge Newsletter 367
History of the Silverthorn Family Newsletter 70
History of Transportation Museum 708
History Place Archives 430

History Place Newsletter 430
History Research Center 294
History San Jose Archives 68
History Speaks 233
History Today 617, 623
History Trails 257
History Workshop Journal 424
Hitchcock County Historical Society & Library 357
Hitchcock County Historical Society Newsletter 357
Hitchcock Memorial Museum and Library 580
Hitchcock-Phillips House 92
Hite Family 456, 504, 585
Hite Newsletter 179
Hitt Family 112
Hively Family Newsletter 500
Hixon House Museum Archives 624
HMCS Haida Museum Archives 691
HMCS Sackville Museum Archives 674
Hoag Family 52
Hoard Historical Museum 621
Hoard-Derry-De Witt-Rounsville-Athuson Family 294
Hobart Historical Museum 185
Hobart Historical Society & Archives 185
Hobart History Advocate 185
Hobart History News 185
Hobart Public Library 466
Hoboken Historical Museum Archives 371
Hoboken Public Library 371
Hobson Family 128
Hochstetler Family 184
Ho-Chunk Historical Society 357
Hockessin Public Library 103
Hocking County Genealogical Society & Archives 456
Hocking County Historical Society 451
Hocking Sentinel 456
Hockley County Memorial Library 551
Hodge Family 97
Hodgeman County Genealogical Society & Library 216
Hodgeman County Historical Society 216
Hodges Family Newsletter 285, 612
Hodgeville Community Museum Archives 706
Hodgin-Hodges Newsletter 553
Hodgson Family 213
Hoefler Family 342
Hoehn-Arthur Family 456
Hoekstra Family 120
Hoelscher-Buxkemper Family 558, 561
Hoenstine Rental Library 490
Hoesch Memorial Public Library 349
Hoffer Family 486
Hoff-Julianna Seib Family 116
Hoffman Family 622
Hoffman Happenings 17
Hoffman Newsletter 262, 311
Hoffman Newsletter 311
Hoffses Family History 252
Hoffses Family Newsletter 124
Hofman House Museum 624
Hofwyl-Broadfield Plantation Museum Archives 127
Hogan Family 48, 285
Hogard Family 200
Hogg Family 471
Hogg Shrine News 557
Hoggatt Family 224
Hoggatt-Hockett Family 480
Hoggs Family Newsletter 418
Hoiles-Davis Museum Archives 161
Hoke O'Kelley Memorial Library 135
Holben Family 382
Holbert-Halbert Family 233
Holbrook Family 478
Holbrook Gazette 76
Holbrook Historical Society 272
Holbrook Library 521
Holbrook Report 99
Hold Fast! 417
Holden Family 75
Holden Historical Museum 644
Holden Historical Society & Archives 272, 644
Holden Historical Society Newsletter 272
Holden Public Library 330
Holder Family 291
Holderness Free Library 361
Holderness Historical Society 364
Holding The Fort 447
Holdrege Area Genealogy Club & Library 352
Holdrege Public Library 352
Hole Family 473
Holeman-Holman Newsletter 163
Holiday World Museum Archives 193
Holland America Club of the Pacific Northwest 606
Holland Area Historical Society 294
Holland Family 131, 427
Holland Genealogical Society & Archives 294
Holland Historical Museum 577
Holland Historical Society 400
Holland Historical Society & Archives 577
Holland Historical Society Newsletter 577
Holland Land Office Museum 389
Holland Library 387, 605
Holland Museum Archives 294
Holland Purchase Historical Society & Library 389
Holland Society of New York & Library 407
Hollandale Area Historical Society 309
Hollen Family Newsletter 200
Hollenberg Pony Express Station Museum 215
Holley-Manwaring Family 147
Hollidaysburg Area Public Library 490
Hollingsworth Family 591
Hollinquest-Stinson Family 549
Hollis and Helen Baright Public Library 356
Hollis Burke Frissell Library 9
Hollis Historical Society & Archives 361
Hollis Social Library 361
Hollister Adobe Museum Archives 68
Holliston Historical Society & Library 272
Hollowell Family 605
Holly Leaf Chronicle 167
Holly Township Library 294
Hollyhock House Museum Archives 52

INDEX

Hollywood Bowl Museum Archives 52
Hollywood Entertainment Museum Archives 47
Hollywood Guinness World of Records & Wax Museum Archives 47
Hollywood Heritage 47
Hollywood Heritage Quarterly 47
Hollywood Historical Museum 47
Hollywood Historical Society 113
Hollywood History Museum Archives 47
Holman Library 164
Holmen Area Historical Society 623
Holmes County Chapter, OGS & Library 453
Holmes County District Public Library 453
Holmes County Heirs 453
Holmes County Historical Museum 453
Holmes County Historical Society & Archives 453
Holmes Family 65, 320
Holmes Family Newsletter 81
Holmes-Crafts Homestead 249
Holmes-Greatorex Family 149
Holmes-Wetzel Family 303
Holocaust Center of Northern California Library 66
Holocaust Center of Northern California Library Newsletter 66
Holocaust Documentation and Education Center 113
Holocaust Library & Research Center 391
Holocaust Memorial 116
Holocaust Memorial Center Archives 291, 304
Holocaust Memorial Resource Center Archives 116
Holocaust Museum Houston Archives 549
Holocaust Museum Houston Newsletter 549
Holocaust Museum of Southwest Florida Archives 118
Holston Pastfinder 585
Holston Territory Genealogical Society 525, 585
Holt County Genealogical Society 355
Holt County Historical Society 328, 335
Holt County Historical Society & Library 355
Holt County Historical Society Newsletter 355
Holt Family 35, 276, 345
Holt Street Baptist Church Historical Society 7
Holter Family 456
Holton Family 475
Holt-Stanton Family 155
Holtz-Cordes-Sandau-Strippgen Family 339
Holtzhauer-Holzover Family 74
Holway Family 259
Holy Cross Romanian Orthodox Church 489
Holy Mission to Minnesota 305
Holy Terror Tattler 522
Holy Trinity Church Foundation Library 104
Holy Trinity Monastery Library 20
Holyoke Public Library and Museum Archives 272
Holyoke Public Library and Museum Archives Quarterly Newsletter 272
Homalco Indian Band 648
Home Cookin' 59
Home of Franklin D Roosevelt National Historic Site Archives 401
Home Pylon News 240
Home Quarter Newsletter 437
Home Sweet Home Museum Archives 396
Home-Hume Clan 118
Homepage/Hardcopy 285
Homer Historical Society & Library 162, 294
Homer Historical Society Newsletter 294
Homer-Hodges Family 52
Homerville Antique Fire Department Museum Archives 400
Homestead 40, 157, 169, 419
Homestead Acre and Hill-Palmer House Archives 40
Homestead and Mifflin Township Historical Society 490, 495
Homestead Antique Museum Archives 642
Homestead Courier 269
Homestead Happenings 415
Homestead Hoot 420
Homestead Museum Archives 705
Homestead National Monument Archives 349
Homestead Pennsylvania Historical Society 490
Homesteader 215, 349, 473
Homesteaders Museum Archives 637
Hometown Public Library 162
Homeville Museum Archives 400
Homewood Hi-Lites 163
Homewood Historical Museum 162
Homewood Historical Society & Archives 162
Homewood House Museum Archives 256
Homewood Public Library District 163
Homochitto Valley Library Service 321
Hom-Tom Family 68
Honaker Family 583
Honathan Hager House & Museum Archives 259
Honey Brook Community Library 490
Honey Creek Church Preservation Library 206
Honeywell-Hunnewell Family 118
Honnold Family 163
Honnold-Mudd Library 40
Honolulu Community College Library 141
Honolulu House Museum 297
Honolulu Police Department Law Enforcement Museum Archives 141
Hood County Genealogical Society & Library 547
Hood County Genealogical Society Newsletter 547
Hood County Public Library 547
Hood Newsletter 82
Hood River County Historical Museum 476
Hood River County Historical Society 476
Hood River County Library 476
Hood's Texas Brigade Association & Archives 548
Hood's Texas Brigade Museum 548
Hoofprints of the Past Museum Archives 636
Hoofprints of the Past Museum Newsletter 636
Hoo-Hoo International Forestry Museum Archives 28
Hooker County Genealogical Quarterly 354
Hooker County Genealogical Society & Archives 354
Hooker County Historical Society 354
Hooker County Library 354
Hooker Family 155, 529
Hook-Hooke-Hooks-Houck-Hux Family Chronicles 257
Hooks Family 4, 257
Hooks Public Library 548
Hoopa Tribal Museum Archives 47
Hoopes Family Newsletter 37
Hoopeston Historical Society 163
Hoopie Virtual Front Porch 604
Hoopingarner Family 604
Hoosick Township Historical Society & Library 400

Hoosier Genealogist 186
Hoosier Highlights 186
Hoosier Journal of Ancestry 188
Hoover Family 464
Hoover Historical Center Archives 454
Hoover Historical Society 5
Hoover Histories 43
Hope Community Historical Association 215
Hope Historical Museum 371
Hope Historical Society & Archives 371
Hope Lodge and Mather Hill Museum Archives 487
Hope Museum Archives 650
Hope Town Historian 409
Hope Water Powered Saw Mill Archives 688
Hopewell Culture National Historic Park Archives 444
Hopewell Museum Archives 232, 371
Hopewell Museum Post 232
Hopewell Public Library 371
Hopewell Valley Historical Society 376
Hopewell Valley Historical Society's Newsletter 376
Hopewell Village National Historic Site Library 486
Hopkins County Genealogical Society & Archives 231
Hopkins County Genealogical Society & Library 560
Hopkins County Heritage 560
Hopkins County-Madisonville Public Library 231
Hopkins Family 148
Hopkins Heritage 292
Hopkins Historical Society 330
Hopkins Historical Society & Library 309
Hopkinsville Community College Library 229
Hopkinsville-Christian County Public Library 229
Hopkinsville-Christian County Public Library Newsletter 229
Hopkinton Historical Group 400
Hopkinton Historical Society 272
Hopkinton Historical Society & Library 507
Hopkinton Public Library 203, 272
Hopper Family 135
Hopper Journal 569
Hopper Newsletter 82
Hopsewee Plantation Museum Archives 515
Horace Greeley House 393
Horace W Sturgis Library 132
Horan Family 169
Horatio Colony House Museum Archives 362
Horicon Historical Society & Archives 623
Horizons 391
Horkheimer-Gaus(s) Family 618
Horlock History Center Archives 554
Horn Family 77
Horn(e) Family 321
Hornbeck Hunting 552
Hornby Historical Museum 400
Hornby Historical Society & Archives 400
Hornby Historical Society Newsletter 400
Hornell Historical Society 400
Hornell Public Library 400
Horner Family 235
Horning Family 294
Horridge House Museum 209
Horry County Genealogical Society 516
Horry County Historical Society 514
Horry County Memorial Library 514
Horry County Museum Archives 514
Horse Cave Free Public Library 229
Horseless Carriage Foundation and Automotive Research Library 49
Horsepower 415
Horseshoe Bend District Library 147
Horseshoe Bend National Military Park Archives 3
Horsham Preserveration and Historical Association 490
Horton Family 454, 607
Horton Free Public Library 215
Hose 5 Fire Museum Archives 243
Hosfeld Heritage 167
Hoster Family 584
Hostetter Family 492, 496
Hostutler Clan 47
Hot Spring County Library 30
Hot Springs County Historical and Genealogical Society 30
Hot Springs County Historical Society 30
Hot Springs County Historical Society 638
Hot Springs County Library 638
Hot Springs County Musuem 638
Hot Springs National Park Archives 28
Hot Springs Public Library 522
Hot Springs Village Genealogical Society 29
Hotchkiss Family 417
Hotchkiss Family Association Newsletter 98
Hotchkiss Library of Sharon 99
Hotchkiss-Crawford Historical Museum 86
Hotchkiss-Crawford Historical Society & Archives 86
Hotel de Paris Museum Archives 85
Hottel-Keller Family 596
Hottenstein Family 101
Houdini Historical Center 617
Houdini Museum Archives 501
Houff Library 597
Houghmann Newsletter 262
Houghton County Historical Museum 295
Houghton County Historical Society & Archives 295
Houghton County Historical Society Newsletter 295
Houghton Lake Area Historical Society 294
Houghton Memorial Library 7
Hour Glass Museum 191
Hourglass 101
Hourglass 276
House Hunting 553
House in the Horseshoe State Historic Site Archives 432
House of a Thousand Dolls Museum Archives 345
House of Baillie USA 516
House of International Dolls Archives 663
House of Memories 684
House of Refuge Museum Archives 122
House of Roses Library 521
House of the Seven Gables Museum Archives 278
House of the Temple Museum 106
House of Usher 145
House of Wickersham Museum Archives 12
House on the Rock Museum Archives 631
House with the Eye Museum Archives 87
Houses of Strother 205

Houston Academy of Medicine Historical Research Center Archives 549
Houston County Historical Commission & Library 541
Houston County Historical Society 306, 527
Houston County Historical Society & Library 309
Houston County Historical Society Newsletter 309
Houston County Museum Archives 541
Houston County Public Library System 135
Houston Family 21, 463
Houston Fire Museum Archives 549
Houston Genealogical Forum & Library 549
Houston Metropolitan Research Center 549
Houston Police Museum Archives 549
Houston Polish Genealogical Society 549
Houston Public Library 549
Houston Review: History and Culture of the Gulf Coast 549
Houston-Love Memorial Library 3
Howard City Library 215
Howard County Center of African American Culture Archives 258
Howard County Genealogical Society 187, 191, 328
Howard County Genealogical Society & Library 258
Howard County Genealogical Society Newsletter 187, 191
Howard County Heritage Club 31
Howard County Historical Museum 187, 259
Howard County Historical Society 356
Howard County Historical Society & Archives 187, 259
Howard County Historical Society Archives 187
Howard County Library 538
Howard County Library-East Columbia 258
Howard Family 147, 228, 264, 467, 606
Howard House of Artifacts Archives 668
Howard Morey House Archives 629
Howard Steamboat Museum 187
Howard Steamboat Museum and Mansion 187
Howard Suamico Historical Society 622
Howard Thurman Home Archives 111
Howard Tilton Library 240
Howard Whitemore Memorial Library 96
Howard-Brenneman-Green Family 343
Howard-Dickinson House Museum 548
Howard-Hayward Family 478
Howard-Miami Heritage Society 185
Howard-Winneshieck Genealogy Society 199
Howarth Family 565
Howden Hall 575
Howel-Howell Family Newsletter 478
Howell Carnegie Library 294
Howell Family 470
Howell Heritage 371
Howell Historical Museum 371
Howell Historical Society & Archives 371
Howell Living History Farm Museum Archives 378
Howell Newsletter 77
Howell-Dalton-Henderson-McCoy-Van Zandt-Becker-Lee-Wilcox Family 607
Howells Historical Society 352
Howenstine Family 185
Howenstine Reunion Newsletter 185
Howes Family 588
Howitt Family 333
Howkins Family 301
Howland House Museum Archives 277
Howland Public Library 389
Howland Quarterly 253
Howlet Family 55
Hoxsey Family Connections 170
Hoy Family 588
Hoyt Family 147, 232
Hoyt Library 491
HQ Air Force Services Agency, Directorate of Programs 558
Hrenchir Family 212
Hrenchir News 212
Huachuca City Public Library 16
Hubbard County Historical Society 312
Hubbard Family 75, 473, 577
Hubbard Free Library 246
Hubbard Memorial Library 273
Hubbard Museum of the American West Archives 384
Hubbard Museum of the American West Newsletter 384
Hubbardton Battlefield Museum Archives 577
Hubbardton Historical Society 576
Hubbell Family 340
Hubbell Trading Post National Historic Site Archives 16
Huber Family 43, 488
Huckstep-Greer-Dumford-Ator Family 566
Huddleston Family 50
Huddleston Farmhouse Inn Museum 181
Hudlow-Marchell-Ronk-Showalter Family 223
Hudnall Family 553
Hudson Area Association Library 400
Hudson Bay Museum Archives 706
Hudson Chapter, OGS & Archives 450
Hudson Falls Free Library 400
Hudson Falls Free Library Newsletter 400
Hudson Family 553
Hudson Family Association Bulletin 242
Hudson Green 450
Hudson Heritage Association 450
Hudson Heritage Newsletter 450
Hudson Historical Museum 450
Hudson Historical Society & Archives 450
Hudson Historical Society & Library 272
Hudson Library 450
Hudson Mohawk Industrial Gateway Society 418
Hudson Public Library 272, 294
Hudson River Maritime Museum Archives 402
Hudson River Museum Archives 421
Hudson Valley Regional Review 388
Hudson's Hope Museum Archives 650
Hudsoniana 553
Huebotter Family 46
Huellas del Pasado 71
Huerfano County Historical Museum 90
Huerfano County Historical Society Archives & Archives 90
Huey Family 504
Hueytown Historical Society 5
Hueytown Public Library 5
Huffer Family 74
Hufford Museum 453
Hufnagle Family 501
Hugh J Phillips Library 259
Hugh Mercer 1761 Apothecary Shop Museum Archives 588

Hugh Torrance House & Store Archives 428
Hughes County Historical Society 466
Hughes Family 237, 454, 457
Hughes House Historical Society 149
Hughes News 139
Hughes-Johnson Family 139
Hughs Family 157
Huguenot Historical Museum 406
Huguenot Historical Society & Archives 406
Huguenot Historical Society Report 406
Huguenot Historical Society Yearbook 406
Huguenot Society of America & Library 407
Huguenot Society of Manakin Library 591
Huguenot Society of South Carolina & Library 512
Hulet Family 150
Hulihee Palace Archives 142
Hull Family 72, 81, 463, 490, 502, 549, 591, 592
Hull Public Library 203, 272
Hullett Herald: Hullett Family Newsletter 36
Hullinger-Hollinger Family 444
Hulmeville Historical Society & Library 496
Hulse Family 360
Hulsey Family 20
Hulsey-Horn-Cantrell-Bevard Family 60
Humber-Bay of Islands Museum Archives 667
Humble Genealogical Society 549
Humble Genealogist 549
Humboldt and District Museum Archives 707
Humboldt County Genealogical Society 44
Humboldt County Genealogical Society & Archives 203
Humboldt County Genealogical Society Newsletter 203
Humboldt County Historical Association 199
Humboldt County Historical Association & Library 203
Humboldt County Historical Museum 199
Humboldt County Historical Society & Library 44
Humboldt County Library 44, 203
Humboldt Historian 44
Humboldt Historical Museum 215
Humboldt Historical Society 47
Humboldt Historical Society & Archives 215
Humboldt Public Library 215
Humboldt State University Library 36
Hummel Family 369
Hummelstown Area Historical Society & Library 490
Humpback Rocks Mountain Farm Museum Archives 597
Humphrey Family 92
Humphrey Family Quarterly 10
Humphreys County Historical Society 533
Humphreys County Historical Society Publication 533
Humphreys County Library System 319
Humphreys Family 480
Humphreys House 91
Humphries Family 528
Hungarian Digest 406
Hungarian Genealogical Society 458
Hungarian Genealogical Society Newsletter 458
Hungarian Jewish Special Interest Group 445
Hungarian Studies Newsletter 374
Hungarian-American Friendship Society 46
Hungarian-American Friendship Society of Sacramento 63
Hungate Family Historical Society Journal 127
Hunsberger-Huntsberger Family 490
Hunt County Genealogical Society 547
Hunt Family 22, 28, 496, 505, 565, 599
Hunt Library 499
Hunt-Allen Family 633
Hunter Clan 136, 159
Hunter Coulter Museum 25
Hunter House Museum 503
Hunter House Victorian Museum Archives 592
Hunter Library 425
Hunter-Dawson Home State Historic Site Archives 336
Hunterdon County Historical Society & Archives 370
Hunterdon County Library 370
Hunterdon Historical Museum Archives 369
Hunterdon Historical Newsletter 370
Hunters' Horn 159
Huntertown Historical Society 185
Hunting Hall 292
Huntingburg Public Library 185
Huntingdon County Historical Museum 490
Huntingdon County Historical Society & Archives 490
Huntingdon County Library 490
Huntington Beach Central Library 47
Huntington Beach Historical Society & Archives 47
Huntington City-Township Public Library 185
Huntington County Courthouse 186
Huntington County Genealogical Society 185
Huntington County Historical Society 185
Huntington County Historical Society & Library 186
Huntington County Historical Society Newsletter 185, 186
Huntington Family Association Newsletter 153
Huntington Free Library and Reading Room 390
Huntington Historical Society 99, 577
Huntington Historical Society and Genealogical Workshop 400
Huntington Historical Society News 99
Huntington Library 69, 577
Huntington Memorial Library 409
Huntington Public Library 400
Huntington Railroad Historical Society 612
Huntington Railroad Museum Archives 612
Huntington Trade School Museum 400
Huntington Woods Public Library 294
Huntley Area Public Library District 163
Huntley Family 44, 96, 301
Hunt-Morgan House 229
Huntress Family 362
Huntsman-Weirick-Weyrick Family 572
Huntsville Historical Review 5, 56
Huntsville Historical Society 330
Huntsville Public Library 549, 683
Huntsville-Madison County Historical Society 5
Huntsville-Madison County Public Library 6
Hupp Family 346
Hurlburt Field Base Library 114
Hurlbut-Hurlburt Family 261
Hurley Library 400
Hurley Patentee Manor Archives 401
Hurleyville Historian 401
Huron City Museum Archives 300

Huron County Genealogical Society 300, 454
Huron County Historical Notes 454
Huron County Historical Society 293, 460, 679
Huron County Kinologist 454
Huron County Library 681
Huron County Museum Archives 682
Huron Historical Society 450
Huron Public Library 522
Huron Shores Genealogical Newsletter 299
Huron Shores Genealogical Society 299
Huron Valley Genealogical Society 297
Huron Valley Railroad Historical Society 290
Huronia Area Aboriginal Management Board 679
Huronia Museum Archives 685
Hurricane Valley Heritage Park Museum Archives 566
Hursh-Horst Newsletter 163
Hursh-Horst-Hurst Family Quarterly 149
Hurst Public Library 550
Hurst Ranch Historical Museum Archives 77
Hurston Adult Library 105
Huskey Family 423
Hussey-Mayfield Memorial Public Library 196
Hustisford Historical Society & Archives 623
Hustisford Historical Society Newsletter 623
Huston Newsletter 554
Huston-Pottenger-Steig Family 448
Hutchens-Hutchins Family 214
Hutcheson Family 313
Hutchins Library 225
Hutchinson County Genealogical Society 538
Hutchinson County Historical Museum Archives 538
Hutchinson County Historical Museum Newsletter 538
Hutchinson County Library 538
Hutchinson Memorial Library 630
Hutchinson Public Library 215
Hutchison House Museum 633
Hutton Family 345, 573
Huu-ay-aht First Nations 647
Huxford Genealogical Society & Library 132
Huxford Genealogical Society Magazine 132
Huxley Public Library 203
Huyck-Howk-Houck-Yeaw Family 603
Hyannis Public Library Association 272
Hyatt Family 565
Hyde County Historical and Genealogical Society 426, 522
Hyde Family 465
Hyde Hall House Museum Archives 394
Hyde Historical and Genealogical Society 355, 522
Hyde Park Historical Society 155
Hyde Park Historical Society & Library 272, 401
Hyde Park History 155
Hyer-Buehler Family 148
Hyland House Museum Archives 94
Hyland House Times 94
Hylton Family 184, 587
Hyman and Sons General Store Museum 697
Hymers Museum Archives 683
Hynton-Hinton-Stone-Reeder-Stevens-Castle-Adkins Family 231
Hyrum City Museum Archives 567
Hyser Rivers Museum Archives 286

I

I & M Canal National Heriage Corridor Civic Center Archives 175
I & R Newsletter 45
I D Weeks Library 524
Iberia Cultural Resources 239
Iberia Parish Library 239
Iberville Parish Library 240
IC Anderson Library 562
Icelandic Nation League of North America 660
Icelandic National League of the USA 229
Ida County Genealogical Society 203
Ida Dennie Willis Museum of Miniatures, Dolls and Toys 470
Ida Jane Dacus Library 517
Ida Long Goodman Memorial Library 221
Ida Public Library 152
Ida Rupp Public Library 455
Idabel Public Library 466
Idaho Black History Museum 145
Idaho Center for Vital Statistics and Health Policy 145
Idaho City Historical Museum 147
Idaho City Historical Society & Archives 147
Idaho County Chapter, Idaho Genealogical Society 146
Idaho Falls Public Library 147
Idaho Genealogical Library 145
Idaho Genealogical Society & Library 145
Idaho Genealogical Society Quarterly 145
Idaho Heartland Genealogists 146
Idaho Heritage Trust 145
Idaho Military History Museum Archives 145
Idaho Museum of Mining Archives 145
Idaho Springs Public Library 86
Idaho State Historical Museum Archives 145
Idaho State Historical Society 145
Idaho State Historical Society & Library 145
Idaho State Historical Society Newsletter 145
Idaho Yesterdays 145
Idaho Yesterdays: The Quarterly Journal of the Idaho Historical Society 145
Ignace Heritage Centre Archives 683
Ilasco Area Historical Preservation Society 330
Iliff Genealogist 257
Ilion Free Public Library 401
Illiana Digest 157
Illiana Genealogical and Historical Society 157
Illiana Genealogist 157
Illiana Jewish Genealogical Society 160, 170
Illiana Jewish Genealogical Society Newsletter 160, 170
Illinois and Michigan Canal Museum 165
Illinois Association for the Preservation of Historic Arms and Armaments 160
Illinois Citizen Soldier Museum Archives 160
Illinois Cornish Heritage Society 151
Illinois Department of Public Health, Division of Vital Records 174
Illinois Heritage Association & Library 154
Illinois Historic Preservation Agency & Library 160, 174
Illinois Historic Preservation Agency Library 174
Illinois Historical Preservation Agency 157
Illinois Historical Review 155
Illinois Historical Survey & Library 176
Illinois History 174
Illinois Labor History Society 155
Illinois Langlitz Researchers 172

Illinois Mennonite Heritage Newsletter 166
Illinois Mennonite Historical and Genealogical Society 166
Illinois Postal History Society 177
Illinois Prairie District Public Library 166
Illinois Railway Museum Archives 176
Illinois State Archives 174
Illinois State Genealogical Society 174
Illinois State Genealogical Society Newsletter 174
Illinois State Genealogical Society Quarterly 174
Illinois State Historical Library 174
Illinois State Library 174
Illinois State Museum Archives 174
Illinois Valley Historical Society & Archives 476
Illinois Veterans' Home Library 171
Illumination 212
Illuminator 178
Ilo-Vollmer Historical Society 146
Ilsley Inklings 577
Ilwaco Heritage Foundation & Archives 602
Ilwaco Heritage Foundation Newsletter 602
Ilwaco Heritage Museum 602
Images 448
Immaculate Conception Catholic Church Archives 239
Immanuel Baptist Church Library 104
Immanuel Episcopal Church on the Green Archives 104
Immigrant Genealogical Society and Library 38
Immigrant Genealogical Society Newsletter 38
Immigration and Ethnic History Society 378
Immigration and Naturalization Service 105
Immigration Digest 570, 572
Immigration History Newsletter 311, 497
Immigration History Research Center 311
Immigration History Society 311, 444
Immigration History Society & Archives 497
Immigration Museum of New Americans Post WWII Museum 65
Immigration Station Barracks Museum Archives 75
Imogene Herbert Historical Museum 297
Imperial and District Museum Archives 707
Imperial Calcasieu Museum Archives 238
Imperial County Free Library 43
Imperial County Free Library-Holtville Branch 47
Imperial County Genealogical Society 43
Imperial County Historical Society 48
Imperial German Military Collector's Association 371
Imperial Polk Genealogical Society 114, 115
Imperial Polk Genealogical Society Newsletter 114
Imperial Valley College Museum and Society 57
Imperial-Saint Landry Genealogy and Historical Society 240
Imprints 112
Imprints on the Sands of Marquette County 634
In Bergen's Attic; Bergen County History 377
In Context 258, 578
In Flight 381
In Review 603
In Search of the Chopp-Guibord Family 220
In the Midst 307
In the Spirit of Tradition 105
Ina Dillard Russell Library 134
Independece County Chronicle 25
Independence County Historical Society 25
Independence County Historical Society & Library 25
Independence Heritage Association 476
Independence Historical Museum Archives 216
Independence Historical Museum Newsletter 216
Independence National Historic Park Library 498
Independence Public Library 203, 216, 476
Independence Seaport Museum Library 498
Independent Order of Odd Fellows, Grand Lodge 435
Independent Presbyterian Church Archives 137
Independent Republic Quarterly 514
Independent Township Library 212
Index of Surnames 435
Indian Agency House 629
Indian and Colonial Research Center Library 97
Indian Association of Alberta 643
Indian Awareness Newsletter 192
Indian Creek Historical Museum 201
Indian Creek Historical Society & Archives 201
Indian Grinding Rock State Historic Park Archives 60
Indian Head Museum Archives 707
Indian Hill Historical Society & Library 444
Indian King Tavern Museum Archives 370
Indian Lake Town Historian 401
Indian Mill Museum State Memorial Archives 458
Indian Museum of North America Library 521
Indian Museum of the Carolinas Archives 429
Indian Pueblo Cultural Center 381
Indian River County Historical Society 123
Indian River County Historical Society Newsletter 123
Indian River County Library 123
Indian River Genealogical Society 123
Indian River Genealogical Society Newsletter 123
Indian Springs State Park Museum Archives 131
Indian Temple Mound Museum Archives 113
Indian Territory Genealogical and Historical Society 470
Indian Valley Public Library 503
Indian Wells Valley Genealogical Society 62
Indiana 186
Indiana Canals 183
Indiana Chapter OGS 188
Indiana County Heritage 490
Indiana County Historical Museum 490
Indiana Covered Bridge Society & Library 186
Indiana Covered Bridge Society Newsletter 186
Indiana Genealogical Society 179, 183
Indiana Genealogical Society Newsletter 179, 183
Indiana Genealogist 183
Indiana German Heritage Society 186
Indiana German Heritage Society Newsletter 186
Indiana Historian 186
Indiana Historical Bureau & Library 186
Indiana Historical Collections 186
Indiana Historical Museum 186
Indiana Historical Society 180
Indiana Historical Society & Archives 186
Indiana Historical Society Newsletter 186
Indiana History Bulletin 186
Indiana History Resource Series 186
Indiana Jewish Historical Society & Library 183
Indiana Jewish Historical Society Newsletter 183

Indiana Jewish History 183
Indiana Libraries 186
Indiana Magazine of History 180, 186
Indiana Medical History Museum Archives 186
Indiana Medical History Museum Quarterly 186
Indiana Province Archives Center, Congregation of Holy Cross 191
Indiana Religious History Association 186
Indiana Religious History Association Newsletter 186
Indiana State Archives 186
Indiana State Library 186
Indiana State Museum Archives 186
Indiana Transportation Museum Archives 191
Indiana University Bloomington Library 180
Indiana University Bookman 180
Indiana University Museum Archives 180
Indiana University-Purdue Indianapolis Library 186
Indiana War Memorials Archives 186
Indianapolis in the World of Books 186
Indianapolis-Marion County Public Library 186
Indianola Public Library 203
Industrial and Agricultural Museum Archives 506
Industrial Heritage Complex Archives 690
Info Exchange 291
Information Booth 154
Informer 158, 327, 409, 425
Ingalls Inquirer 289
Ingalls Memorial Library 364
Ingersoll Family 11, 302
Ingham County Genealogical Society & Library 297
Ingham Family 60
Ingleside Public Library 550
Inglis Family 606
Ingram Inklings 170
Ingram Library 128
Ingram-Ingrum-Bingham Family 327
Inklings and Idlings 160
Inklings Quarterly newsletter 411
Inkster Public Library 294
Inkwell 532
Inland Seas 459
Inland Seas Maritime Museum 459
Inlet Town Historian 401
Inman Family 21
Inman Family Association Newsletter 166
Inman Heritage Association 216
Inman Newsletter 18, 82
Inn Sider 112
Innes Clan 38
Innisfail Historical Museum Archives 644
Innisfall and District Historical Museum Archives 644
Innisville and District Museum Archives 683
Innovator 281
Innu Indian Nation 668
In-Review 600
INS & OUTS 164
Inside Angle 162
Inside the Library 301
Inside Track 191, 230
Inside Your Library 397
Insight 174, 246
Insight University Museum 490
Inspire to Victory: The Journal of the Clan Currie Society 378
Institut Canado-Americain & Bibliotheque 362
Institut Culturel et Educatif Montagnais 704
Institut d'histoire de l'Amerique Francaise 700
Institute for American Indian Studies 100
Institute for Boston Studies & Archives 269
Institute for Historical Review 56
Institute for Historical Studies 66
Institute for Jewish Research 407
Institute for Masonic Studies Library and Museum 66
Institute for Massachusetts Studies & Archives 282
Institute of Diving Newsletter 119
Institute of Early American History and Culture Newsletter 597
Institute of Genealogy and Historical Research 2
Institute of Genealogy and History for Latin America 570
Institute of Historical Survey Foundation & Library 383
Institute of Museum and Library Services 105
Institute of Texan Cultures Archives 558
Institute on World War II and the Human Experience 122
Instruc'ns 512
Instructional Resources Center 606
Intelligencer 460
Interboro Public Library 496
Interchurch Center Museum Archives 407
Intercom 531
Interlake Reserves Tribal Council 659
Interlaken Historical Museum 401
Interlaken Historical Society & Archives 401
Interlaken Public Library 401
Intermountain Genealogical Society 38
Internal & Patron Newsletters 162
International Abraham Lincoln Journal 241
International Annual of Oral History 101
International Association of Jewish Genealogical Societies 126
International Association of Sri Lanka Genealogical Societies 52
International Association of Tartan Studies 139
International Barbwire Gazette 561
International Blacksheep Society of Genealogists 64
International Center of Photography Museum Archives 407
International Churchill Society 360
International Falls Public Library 309
International Genealogical Directory 571
International Genealogical Exchange 551
International Journal of African Historical Studies 266
International Journal of Maritime History 668
International Lincoln Center 241
International Linen Registry Museum Archives 470
International Migration Review 417
International Museum of Surgical Science Archives 155
International Museum of Women 66
International Museum of Women Quarterly 66
International Printing Museum 39
International Society for British Genealogy and Family History 445, 571
International Society for British Genealogy and Family History Newsletter 445, 571
International Society of Family History Writers and Editors 549
International Society of Sons and Daughters of Slave Ancestry 155
International Society of the Descendants of Charlemagne 123
International Society of the Descendants of Charlemagne Newsletter 123

International Spy Museum Archives 106
International Submariners Memorial Museum Archives 625
International Women's Air and Space Museum Archives 445
Interurban Railway Station Museum Archives 556
Intikba 466
Intrepid Sea-Air-Space Museum Archives 407
Intrepid Times 407
Inuvik Centennial Library 671
Inverness Miners Museum Archives 674
Inyo County Free Library 48
Iola Historical Society & Archives 623
Iola Public Library 216
Iola Railroad Depot & Museum 623
Iolani Palace Archives 141
Iolani Palace Newsletter 141
Iolani School Archives 141
Ionia County Genealogical Society 295, 300
Ionia County Genealogy Society Newsletter 295
Ionia County Historical Society 294
Ionia County Historical Society & Archives 294
Ionic Columns 447
Iosco County Genealogical Society 299
Iosco County Historical Museum 290
Iosco County Historical Museum Association & Archives 290
Iosco County Historical Museum Association Newsletter 290
Iosco-Arenac District Library 290
Iosco-Arenac Regional Library 303
Iowa Aviation Museum Archives 202
Iowa City Genealogical Society 205
Iowa City Public Library 203
Iowa City-Johnson County Genealogical Society 203
Iowa City-Johnson County Genealogical Society Newsletter 203
Iowa County Byways 204
Iowa County Genealogical Society 620
Iowa County Genealogical Society & Archives 204
Iowa County Genealogical Society Newsletter 620
Iowa County Historical Museum 620
Iowa County Historical Society 204
Iowa County Historical Society & Archives 620
Iowa County Historical Society & Library 204
Iowa County Historical Society Vignette 204
Iowa Department of Public Health, Vital Records Bureau 200
Iowa Falls Historical Society 203
Iowa Genealogical Society & Library 200
Iowa Genealogical Society Newsletter 200
Iowa Genealogical Society Surname Index 200
Iowa Great Lakes Maritime Museum Archives 197
Iowa Heritage Illustrated 199, 203
Iowa Historian 203
Iowa Historic Preservation Alliance 209
Iowa Lakes Genealogical Society 201
Iowa Lakes Genealogical Society & Library 208
Iowa Lakes Genealogical Society Teaser 208
Iowa Quarterly Journal of History 200
Iowa Railroad Historical Society 197
Ipnatchiaq Public Library 11
Ipswich Historical Society & Archives 272
Ipswich Historical Society Quarterly 272
Ipswich Public Library 272
Ipswich Public Library Newsletter 272
Iqaluit Centennial Library 671
Ira C Reed Public Library 164
Iraan Museum Archives 550
Iredell County Public Library 433
Iredell County Tracks 433
Iredell Museum of Heritage Archives 433
Ireland Historical Society 187
Ireland House Museum Archives 680
Irene Black Genealogical Library 153
Irene Ingle Public Library 14
Ireton Newsletter 332
Irick Family Association Newsletter 63
Irish American Genealogical Society 19
Irish American Heritage Center Archives 155
Irish American Heritage Museum Archives 387, 396
Irish Ancestral Research Association 280
Irish Center 391
Irish Families Historical Society 378
Irish Family History Forum 411, 414
Irish Family Names Society 556
Irish Genealogical Foundation & Library 332
Irish Genealogical Quarterly 633
Irish Genealogical Society International & Library 314
Irish Genealogical Society of Michigan 289
Irish Genealogical Society of Wisconsin 626, 633
Irish Herald 66
Irish Roses Plus a Thorn 41
Irish-American Cultural Association & Library 374
Irish-Irishe-Iryshe Family 568
Irma Glatty Library 206
Iron & Oil Review 485
Iron and Steel Museum 6
Iron County Chronicle 484
Iron County Genealogical Society & Library 259
Iron County Genealogy Society 325
Iron County Historical and Museum Society 294
Iron County Historical and Museum Society & Archives 287
Iron County Historical Museum 623
Iron County Historical Society 565
Iron County Historical Society & Archives 623
Iron County Historical Society & Library 331
Iron County Historical Society Newsletter 331
Iron County Museum Archives 287
Iron Creek Museum Archives 645
Iron Hill Museum Archives 104
Iron Horse Historical Society 220
Iron Horse News 85
Iron Mission State Park Museum Archives 565
Iron Mountain Historical Society 325
Iron Mountain Iron Mine Archives 303
Iron Range Historical Society 316
Iron Range Historical Society & Library 308
Iron Range Research Center 306
Iron River Historical Society 618
Irondequoit Public Library 413
Ironwood Area Historical Museum 294
Ironwood Area Historical Society & Archives 294
Ironwood Area Historical Society Newsletter 294
Ironwood Carnegie Public Library 294
Iroquois County Genealogical Society & Archives 177

INDEX

Iroquois County Genealogical Society Newsletter 177
Iroquois County Historical Museum 177
Iroquois County Historical Society & Archives 177
Iroquois County Historical Society Newsletter 177
Iroquois Falls Pioneer Museum Archives 683
Iroquois Indian Musuem Archives 400
Iroquois Stalker 177
Irvin L Young Memorial Library 634
Irvine Family 487
Irvine Historical Museum 48
Irvine Historical Society & Archives 48
Irving E and Ray Kanner Heritage Museum Archives 686
Irving Genealogical Society 550
Irving Genealogical Society Newsletter 550
Irving House Historic Centre Archives 653
Irving Park Historical Society 156
Irving Public Library 550
Irving Rubenstein Memorial Library 168
Irvington Historical Society 186
Irvington Historical Society 401
Irvington Historical Society & Archives 186
Irvington Public Library 371, 401
Irwin Clan 167
Irwin Family 104
Irwin Library 186
Irwindale Public Library 48
Irwin-Painted Post Museum Library 410
Isaac Farrar Mansion Archives 243
Isaac Franck Jewish Archives 262
Isaac Winslow House 274
Isabel Anderson Comer Museum Archives 9
Isabel Anderson Comer Museum Newsletter 9
Isabel Miller Museum 13
Isabella County Genealogical Society 298
Isabelle Hunt Memorial Public Library 19
Isanti County Historical Museum 306
Isanti County Historical Society 309
Isanti County Historical Society & Archives 306
Isanti Cuttings 306
Isbell Inquirer 529
Ischua Valley Historical Museum 397
Ischua Valley Historical Society & Archives 397
Ischua Valley Historical Society Newsletter 397
Ish-Isch Family 474
Ishmael Family 524
Iskut Indian Band 650
ISL Connection 186
ISL Newsletter 145
Islamic Center of New York 407
Island County Historical Museum 600
Island County Historical Society & Archives 600
Island Falls Historical Society 247
Island Free Library 507
Island Heritage 600
Island Historical Society 674
Island Lake First Nation 707
Island Magazine 695
Island Pond Historical Society 577
Island Pond Public Library 577
Isle la Motte Historical Museum 577
Isle la Motte Historical Society & Archives 577
Isle la Motte Historical Society Newsletter 577
Isle La Motte Library 577
Isle of Wight County Historical Society 595
Isle of Wight Courthouse Museum Archives 595
Isle Royale National Park Library 294
Islesboro Historical Society & Library 247
Islesford Historical Museum Archives 247
Isley Public Library 577
Islip Public Library 401
Isom-Isham Newsletter 138
Isothermal Community College Library 433
Israel Family 357
Israel T Naamani Library 230
Israel T Naamani Library Newsletter 230
Israelite-Eisenstadt Family 112
Issaquah Historical Society 602
Issaquah Historical Society & Archives 602
Issaquah Historical Society Newsletter 602
It's About Time 99
Italian American Museum Archives 407
Italian Cultural Center Library 175
Italian Cultural Institute 700
Italian Genealogical and Heraldic Institute 388
Italian Genealogical Group 389
Italian Genealogical Group Newsletter 389
Italian Genealogical Group of New York 395
Italian Genealogical Group of New York Newsletter 395
Italian Genealogical Society of America 507
Italian Genealogy and Heraldry Society of Canada 693
Italian Historical Society of America 391
Itasca County Genealogical Club & Library 306
Itasca County Historical Society & Library 308
Itasca Genealogy Club Newsletter 306
Itasca Historical Depot Museum 163
Itasca Historical Society & Archives 163
Itasca History News 308
Itawamba County Historical Society & Library 321
Itawamba Settlers 321
It-Haw-Pe-Hah Ah-Num Pahle 463
Ituna Cultural and Historical Museum Archives 707
Itza Voice 216
Ivan Franko Museum Archives 662
IVC Desert Museum & Southeastern Information Center Archives 57
Iverhoj Museum Archives 72
Iverson Family 565
Iverson House Archives 621
Ives Index 559
Iveson Family Association Newsletter 136
Ivy House 243
Izard County Historian 26, 32
Izard County Historical and Genealogical Society 32
Izard County Historical Society & Library 26
Izard County Library 30
Izard County Library-Calico Rock Branch 26
Izard County, Arkansas Historical Society Quarterly 26

J

J A Victor David Museum Archives 660
J B Nickells Memorial Library 552

J C Holliday Memorial Library 425
J C Penney Library and Museum Archives 329
J Cloyd Miller Library 385
J Conrad Dunagan Library 555
J E Cobb Library 26
J E Reeves Home Museum 447
J Edgar & Louise S Monroe Library 240
J Eugene Smith Library 101
J H Robbins Memorial Library 213
J L Bedsole Library 7
J Lewis Crozer Library 484
J M Davis Arms and Historical Museum Archives 464
J Murrey Atkins Library 425
J R Huffman Public Library 548
J Raymond Chadwick Library 205
J Robert Van Pelt Library 294
J T L Preston Library 589
J V Fletcher Library 282
J V Fletcher Library e-News 282
J W Dillion House Museum Archives 514
J W Parmely Historical Museum Archives 522
J Y Joyner Library 427
Jacinto Foundation 319
Jacinto Foundation Museum 319
Jack & Sallie Corette Library 345
Jack County Historical Society 550
Jack K Williams Library 546
Jack London State Historic Park Archives 46
Jack Lynn Memorial Museum Archives 650
Jack McConnico Memorial Library 532
Jack Tarver Library 133
Jackson Assembly of the Felicianas 237
Jackson Barracks Military Library 240
Jackson City Library 450
Jackson Company Genealogical Society 433
Jackson County Chronicles 8
Jackson County Florida Library 116
Jackson County Footprints Genealogy Club 618
Jackson County Genealogical Chapter, IGS & Library 204
Jackson County Genealogical Society 180, 193, 294, 322, 331, 425, 450
Jackson County Genealogical Society & Library 331
Jackson County Heritage Museums and Programs 325
Jackson County Historical Association 8
Jackson County Historical Museum 215, 309, 618
Jackson County Historical Society 181, 294, 309
Jackson County Historical Society & Archives 132, 204, 215, 309, 322, 614, 618
Jackson County Historical Society & Library 31, 168, 331, 614
Jackson County Historical Society Jottings Newsletter 309
Jackson County Historical Society Journal 331
Jackson County Historical Society Newsletter 215
Jackson County History 614
Jackson County Library 31
Jackson County Public Library 90, 193, 231, 614
Jackson County Public Library System 116
Jackson District Library 294
Jackson Family 185, 337, 547, 567, 570
Jackson Genealogy 160
Jackson Heritage Association 331
Jackson Historical Society 363, 452
Jackson Historical Society & Archives 623
Jackson Homestead Archives 275
Jackson Homestead Newsletter 275
Jackson Journal 557
Jackson Library 189
Jackson Memorial Museum 77
Jackson Parish Library 237
Jackson Place Journal 105
Jackson Public Library 331
Jackson's Mill Historic Area Archives 615
Jackson-Cowley Family 372
Jackson-George Regional Library System 322
Jackson-Hinds Library System 320
Jacksonian Ventilator 168
Jackson-Madison County Library 528
Jacksonport Historical Society 632
Jacksonport State Park Courthouse Museum Archives 29
Jacksonville Area Genealogical and Historical Society 163
Jacksonville Area Genealogical and Historical Society Quarterly 163
Jacksonville Fire Museum Archives 114
Jacksonville Genealogical Society & Library 114
Jacksonville Genealogical Society Newsletter 114
Jacksonville Genealogical Society Quarterly 114
Jacksonville Historical Society 114
Jacksonville Illinois Genealogical Journal 163
Jacksonville Maritime Museum 114
Jacksonville Public Library 6, 114, 163, 550
Jacksonville State University Library 6
Jackson-Washabough County Historical Museum 522
Jackson-Washabough County Historical Society & Archives 522
Jacob & Bernard Hostert Log Cabins Museum 169
Jacob Edwards Library 279
Jacob Hamblin Home Museum Archives 572
Jacob Sears Memorial Library 270
Jacob-Dudek-Maxam Family 301
Jacobs Memorial Library 169
Jacobsburg Historical Society 495
Jacobsburg Record 495
Jacobsen Family 473
Jacoby-Goble-Gibson-Tiller Family 336
Jaffrey Historical Society & Library 361
Jaffrey Historical Society Newsletter 361
Jafrey Public Library 362
Jahnke Newsletter 262
Jail Museum 75
Jail Museum Archives 354
Jailhouse Journal 228
Jailhouse Key 165
Jamaica Memorial Library 577
Jamaica Plain Historical Society 272
Jamaica Public Library 203
Jambalaya 237
James A Garfield National Historic Site Archives 453
James A Glasgow Library 8
James A Michener Library 86
James A Rogers Library 514
James A Tuttle Library 359
James B Duke Library 515
James B Duke Memorial Library 425
James Bay Cree Nation 697

James Blackstone Memorial Library 91
James Branch Cabell Library 593
James Buchanan Foundation for the Preservation of Wheatland Mansion 491
James C Bolton Library 235
James C Jernigan Library 551
James C Kirkpatrick Library 342
James D Van Trump Library 499
James Dunklin House Museum 516
James E Morrow Library 612
James E Polk Memorial State Historic Site Archives 431
James E Shepard Memorial Library 426
James E Walker Library 531
James E Whalley Museum Library 364
James E Wickson Memorial Library 291
James E Wickson Memorial Library Newsletter 291
James Family 236, 338, 426, 467, 529, 567
James Farm Journal 334
James Gilliam Gee Library 541
James Graham Leyburn Library 589
James H Carson Library 423
James H Johnson Memorial Library 369
James H Thomason Library 513
James Herbert White Library 320
James Herbert White Library Newsletter 320
James House Museum Archives 673
James J Hill House Museum Archives 314
James J O'Mara Pharmacy Museum 668
James K Polk Ancestral Home Archives 526
James Madison Museum Archives 592
James Madison Museum Newsletter 592
James Madison's Montepelier Archives 591
James Madison's Montepelier Newsletter 591
James Memorial Library 338
James Mitchell Varnum House Museum Archives 507
James Monroe Museum and Memorial Library 588
James P Adams Library 509
James P Fitzgibbons Historical Museum Archives 156
James P Magill Library 489
James Predergast Library Association 401
James River Genealogy Club 437
James S Copley Newspaper Museum Archives 49
James Saint Clair, Mabou Gaelic and Historical Society 675
James Smith First Nation 708
James Surname Newsletter 18
James V Brown Library 505
James W Dowdy Memorial Library 124
James W Miller Library 314
James Whitcomb Riley Birthplace Museum Archives 185
James Whitcomb Riley Home Museum Archives 186
James White Library 286
James White Memorial Library 270
James White Memorial Library-G H Hathaway Library 265
Jameson Newsletter 101
Jamestown Fire Department Museum Archives 508
Jamestown Historical Museum 508
Jamestown Historical Society & Archives 508
Jamestown Historical Society Newsletter 508
Jamestown National Historic Site Archives 589
Jamestown Philomenian Library and Museum 508
Jamestown Public Library 428
Jamestowne Society 126
Jamestown-Yorktown Foundation & Library 597
Jamesville Historic Preservation 401
Jamieson Museum Archives 708
Jamison Family 570
Jamison-Austin Family 380
Jane Addams' Hull House Museum Archives 156
Jane Morgan Memorial Library 619
Janesville Public Library 203
Janney Journal 566
Japanese American History Archives 66
Japanese American National Museum Archives 52
Japanese American Resource Center 68
Japanese Cultural Center of Hawaii Archives 141
Jaques Family Genealogy 101
Jaquith Family 38
Jaquith Public Library 577
Jardine Clan 265
Jardine Family 54, 147, 565
Jarrell Newsletter 559
Jarrell Plantation State Historic Site Archives 132
Jarrett Library 553
Jarvis Family 19, 573
Jasonville Public Library 187
Jasper County Genealogical and Historical Society 168
Jasper County Genealogical Society & Library 206
Jasper County Gleaner 206
Jasper County Historical Society 192, 517
Jasper County Historical Society & Library 206
Jasper County Historical Society Newsletter 206
Jasper County Public Library 192
Jasper County Public Library-DeMotte Branch 182
Jasper Cultural and Historical Centre Archives 708
Jasper Historical Society 309
Jasper Public Library 6, 187
Jasper-Hellowhead Museum and Archives 644
Jasper-Yellowhead Historical Society & Library 644
Java Jottings 133
Jay County Genealogy Society 192
Jay County Historical Society & Library 192
Jay County Public Library 192
Jay Family 39
Jay Historical Society & Library 249
Jay Johnson Public Library 221
Jay Town Historian 401
Jay-Rollins Library 535
Je Me Souviens 508, 510
Jean & Charles Schulz Information Center 62
Jean Lafitte National Historic Park Archives 240
Jean Miller Memorial Library 114
Jeane Dixon Museum and Library 595
Jeannete Public Library Association 490
Jedediah Strong Smith Society & Archives 73
Jeff Matthews Memorial Museum Archives 588
Jefferson Barracks Historic Site Archives 339
Jefferson College Library 330
Jefferson County District Library, Hamer Branch 147
Jefferson County Genealogical Society 31, 117, 167, 181, 189, 202, 330, 351, 420, 457, 528
Jefferson County Genealogical Society & Archives 219

Jefferson County Genealogical Society & Library 605
Jefferson County Genealogical Society Journal 528
Jefferson County Genealogical Society Newsletter 219, 605
Jefferson County Historical and Genealogical Society 483
Jefferson County Historical Association & Archives 457
Jefferson County Historical Association Newsletter 457
Jefferson County Historical Commission 2
Jefferson County Historical Museum 420, 457, 605
Jefferson County Historical Quarterly 31
Jefferson County Historical Society 31, 133, 149, 351, 483, 526
Jefferson County Historical Society & Archives 167, 420, 605
Jefferson County Historical Society & Library 84, 189, 220
Jefferson County Historical Society Bulletin 420
Jefferson County Historical Society Newsletter 220, 605
Jefferson County Historical Society Quarterly 84
Jefferson County Historical Village and Museum 167
Jefferson County History Center 330
Jefferson County Library 133, 330, 476
Jefferson County Library System-Boulder Community Library 343
Jefferson County Lines 457
Jefferson County Museum Archives 611
Jefferson County Office of Historic Preservation and Archives 230
Jefferson County Public Library 87, 117
Jefferson County Public Library-Golden Branch 85
Jefferson County Public Library-Standley Lake 81
Jefferson Davis Monument State Park Archives 229
Jefferson Davis Parish Library 237
Jefferson Genealogical Society 239
Jefferson Genealogical Society Newsletter 239
Jefferson Genealogical Society Surname Index 239
Jefferson Historical Museum 550
Jefferson Historical Society 623
Jefferson Historical Society & Archives 550
Jefferson Landing State Historic Site Archives 331
Jefferson National Expansion Memorial Archives 339
Jefferson Parish Library 239
Jefferson Parish Library-Belle Terre 239
Jefferson Parish Library-West Bank Regional 237
Jefferson Patterson Park Museum Archives 262
Jefferson Public Library 203, 362, 476
Jefferson Township Historical Society 373
Jefferson Township Historical Society & Library 375
Jefferson Valley Historical Society 347
Jeffersonian 483
Jefferson-Madison Regional Library 585
Jeffersonville Township Public Library 187
Jefford Family 185
Jekyll Island Museum Archives 132
Jelly's Works of Memories 563
Jemez State Monument Archives 383
Jenkerson-Ellis Family 142
Jenkins County Historical Society 134
Jenkins Family 572
Jenkins-Brown Family 572
Jenkins-Horlacher-Clemmens Family 88
Jenkintown Library 490
Jenner Family 41
Jennie Huizenga Memorial Library 169
Jennings City Library 216
Jennings County Genealogical Society 191, 193
Jennings County Genealogical Society Newsletter 191
Jennings County Historical Society 193, 194
Jennings County Public Library 191
Jennings Family 548
Jennings Genealogical Society 237
Jennings Historical Society 331
Jennings Library 368
Jennings-Brown House Museum 511
Jensen Family 565, 571
Jensen Memorial Library 354
Jensen-Alvarado Ranch Historic Park Library 62
Jensen-Petersen-Elkjer Family 352
Jericho Historical Society & Archives 577
Jericho Public Library 401
Jericho Public Library Newsletter 401
Jericho Reporter 577
Jernigan Journal 551
Jerome County Historical Museum 147
Jerome County Historical Society & Archives 147
Jerome County Historical Society Newsletter 147
Jerome Historical Society 15
Jerome Public Library 147
Jerome State Historic Park Archives 17
Jersey Central Railway Historical Society 380
Jersey City Public Library 371
Jersey County Genealogical Society 163
Jersey County Genealogical Society Newsletter 163
Jersey County Historical Museum 163
Jersey County Historical Society & Archives 163
Jersey Journeys 374
Jersey Shore Historical Society & Archives 484
Jersey Shore Historical Society & Library 490
Jervis Public Library Association 414
Jervis Public Library Association Newsletter 414
Jessamine County Public Library 232
Jesse Besser Museum 285
Jesse Besser Museum Library 285
Jesse Family 43
Jesse James Bank Museum Archives 334
Jesse James Farm Museum 333
Jesse James Home-Pony Express Historical Association & Archives 338
Jesse M Smith Memorial Library 507
Jesse-Shuptrine Family 48
Jessie Ball duPont Library 532
Jessie C Eury Library 164
Jester Family 487
Jesuit Oregon Province Archives & Library 607
Jesuit-Krauss-McCormick Library 156
Jesuits Library 699
Jesup Memorial Library 243
Jeter Family 8
Jetmore Municipal Library 216
Jett Set Family Newsletter 442
Jeudevine Memorial Library 576
Jewell 68, 230
Jewell County Historical Society & Archives 218
Jewett Family 278, 529
Jewett Family of America Year Book 278
Jewett Family Organization Newsletter 278
Jewett-Pearl Family 575

Jewish Federation Council of Greater Los Angeles 52
Jewish Federation of Nashville and Middle Tennessee & Library 531
Jewish Folklore & Ethnology Review 467
Jewish Genealogical Institute of British Columbia 656
Jewish Genealogical Society 407
Jewish Genealogical Society of Austin 536
Jewish Genealogical Society of Bergen County 373
Jewish Genealogical Society of Bergen County New Jersey 367
Jewish Genealogical Society of Broward County & Library 112
Jewish Genealogical Society of Buffalo 421
Jewish Genealogical Society of Canada 691, 693
Jewish Genealogical Society of Capital District 387
Jewish Genealogical Society of Central Florida & Library 116
Jewish Genealogical Society of Cleveland & Library 449
Jewish Genealogical Society of Colorado 83
Jewish Genealogical Society of Colorado Newsletter 83
Jewish Genealogical Society of Connecticut 93, 99
Jewish Genealogical Society of Dayton 447
Jewish Genealogical Society of Georgia 126, 134
Jewish Genealogical Society of Greater Boston 276
Jewish Genealogical Society of Greater Buffalo 387
Jewish Genealogical Society of Greater Cincinnati 444
Jewish Genealogical Society of Greater Miami 117
Jewish Genealogical Society of Greater Orlando & Archives 116
Jewish Genealogical Society of Greater Washington 256
Jewish Genealogical Society of Hawaii 142
Jewish Genealogical Society of Illinois & Library 168
Jewish Genealogical Society of Indiana 186
Jewish Genealogical Society of Indiana Newsletter 186
Jewish Genealogical Society of Long Island & Library 395
Jewish Genealogical Society of Los Angeles 43
Jewish Genealogical Society of Los Angeles & Library 72
Jewish Genealogical Society of Louisville & Archives 230
Jewish Genealogical Society of Maryland 261
Jewish Genealogical Society of Michigan 291, 294, 301, 302, 304
Jewish Genealogical Society of Milwaukee 626
Jewish Genealogical Society of Montreal 700
Jewish Genealogical Society of New Hampshire 362
Jewish Genealogical Society of New Orleans 239
Jewish Genealogical Society of North Jersey & Library 376, 379
Jewish Genealogical Society of Orange County 45
Jewish Genealogical Society of Orange County & Library 49, 51
Jewish Genealogical Society of Orange County Newsletter 45
Jewish Genealogical Society of Oregon & Library 478
Jewish Genealogical Society of Palm Beach County 111
Jewish Genealogical Society of Palm Springs 58
Jewish Genealogical Society of Philadelphia 369, 490
Jewish Genealogical Society of Philadelphia & Library 486
Jewish Genealogical Society of Philadelphia Bulletin 486
Jewish Genealogical Society of Philadelphia Chronicles 486, 490
Jewish Genealogical Society of Pittsburgh 499
Jewish Genealogical Society of Rochester 413
Jewish Genealogical Society of Rochester Newsletter 413
Jewish Genealogical Society of Sacramento 63
Jewish Genealogical Society of Sacramento Newsletter 63
Jewish Genealogical Society of Saint Louis 339
Jewish Genealogical Society of Salt Lake City 571
Jewish Genealogical Society of San Diego 65
Jewish Genealogical Society of San Diego & Library 72
Jewish Genealogical Society of Southern Alberta 641
Jewish Genealogical Society of Southwest Florida 121
Jewish Genealogical Society of Tampa Bay 118
Jewish Genealogical Society of Tidewater Newsletter 592
Jewish Genealogical Society of Tidewater Virginia & Library 592
Jewish Genealogical Society of Washington 606
Jewish Genealogical Society of Washington State 599, 603
Jewish Genealogical Society of Washington State Newsletter 599
Jewish Genealogical Society, South Suburban Branch 169
Jewish Genealogy Society of Buffalo 402
Jewish Genealogy Society of Buffalo Newsletter 402
Jewish Genealogy Society of Orange County 49
Jewish Genealogy Society of Raleigh 431
Jewish Heritage 105
Jewish Historical and Genealogical Society of Delaware 104
Jewish Historical Society 583
Jewish Historical Society of Central Jersey & Library 374
Jewish Historical Society of Central Jersey Newsletter 374
Jewish Historical Society of Greater Stamford & Library 99
Jewish Historical Society of Greater Washington 106
Jewish Historical Society of Maryland & Archives 256
Jewish Historical Society of Metrowest & Library 380
Jewish Historical Society of Michigan 302, 304
Jewish Historical Society of New Haven & Library 96
Jewish Historical Society of South Carolina 512, 513
Jewish Historical Society of Southern Arizona 22
Jewish Historical Society of the North Shore 274
Jewish Historical Society of The Upper Midwest 311
Jewish Historical Society of the Upper Midwest & Archives 314
Jewish Historical Society of Western Canada & Library 662
Jewish Historical Society of Western Canada Annual 662
Jewish Life and Times 662
Jewish Museum Archives 407
Jewish Museum of Florida Archives 117
Jewish Museum of Maryland 256
Jewish Museum San Francisco Archives 66
Jewish Romanian Genealogy Special Interest Group 94
Jewish Special Interest Group 106, 124
Jewish Special Interest Group of the Saint Louis Genealogical Society 339
Jewish Special Interest Group, Gesher Galicia 257
Jewish Theological Seminary Library 407
JewishGen 551
Jewitt Family 289
Jews in New Haven 96
JFK Library Foundation Newsletter 267
JFK Special Warfare Museum Archives 427
Jicarilla Apache Tribe 382
Jicarilla Chieftan 382
Jillson House 94
Jim Beckworth Museum Archives 61
Jim Crow Museum Archives 286
Jim Dan Hill Library 632
Jim Gatchell Museum Archives 635
Jim Lucas Checotah Public Library 464
Jim Thorpe House Archives 471
Jimmy Carter Library 126
Jimmy Carter National Historic Site Archives 135
Jimmy Stewart Museum Archives 490
Jimtown Historical Society 183
JML Report 590
Joachim Regional Museum Archives 437

Joan Weill Library 410
Joao Family 142
Job(e) Journal 73
Jocko Valley Public Library 343
Joe T Smitherman Historic Building Archives 8
Joel Lane House Archives 431
Johannes Schwalm Historical Association 502
John A Brown Library 609
John A Logan College Museum Archives 154
John A Stahl Library 357
John Abbott College Library 702
John B Cade Library 235
John B Coleman Library 556
John B Curtis Free Public Library 244
John Baldwin House Archives 97
John Bassett Memorial Library 699
John Beck Log House 631
John Brown Farm State Historic Site Archives 402
John Brown State Historic Site Archives 219
John Bulow Campbell Library 130
John Burroughs Association 420
John Burroughs State Historic Site Archives 414
John C Blanchard House 294
John C Calhoun House 513
John C Clegg Public Library 198
John C Hodges Library 529
John C Pace Library 120
John Carter Brown Library 509
John Clayton Fant Memorial Library 319
John Cook Wyllie Library 597
John Crerar Library 156
John Curtis Free Library 272
John Davis Williams Library 322
John Deere Historic Site Archives 158
John Dennis Forte Library 7
John Dubois Maritime Museum Archives 370
John E And Walter D Webb Museum of Vintage Fashion Archives 247
John E Conner Museum Archives 551
John E Conner Museum Newsletter 551
John E Riley Library 148
John Esch Library 631
John F Henderson Public Library 471
John F Kennedy Library 52
John F Kennedy Memorial Library 234, 600
John F Kennedy Presidential Library 267
John F Magale Library 241
John F Reed Library 84
John Family 571
John Fisher Memorial Museum Archives 664
John Fitzgerald Kennedy National Historic Site Archives 268
John Ford Home 319
John Fox Memorial Library 232
John G Diefenbaker Law Office Museum 711
John G McCullough Free Library 578
John G Neihardt Center Museum Archives 349
John G Neihardt Corral of the Westerners 327
John G Snowden Memorial Library 505
John G Voigt House Archives 629
John Gorrie Museum Archives 109
John Graham Public Library 495
John H Wootters-Crocket Public Library 541
John Harrison Family Newsletter 76
John Harris-Simon Cameron Mansion 489
John Hay Library 509
John Hay Whitney Medical Museum Archives 96
John Heard House 272
John Humphrey House Museum 280
John Hunt House Museum 507
John Hustis House Museum 623
John J Burns Library 269
John Jay French House 537
John Jay Homestead State Historical Site Library 401
John K Mullen of Denver Memorial Library 106
John Kane House 410
John L Street Memorial Library 226
John L Throckmorton Library 427
John M Olin Library 401
John Marshall Foundation 593
John Marshall House Museum Archives 593
John Mosser Public Library 151
John Muir National Historic Site Archives 53
John Nicholas Brown Center for the Study of American Civilization 509
John P McGovern Museum Newsletter 549
John P McGovern Museum of Health and Medical Science 549
John Paul Jones House 364
John Philip Sousa Museum Archives 154
John Preston McConnell Library 593
John R Jackson House Museum Archives 610
John R Kauffman Jr Public Library 503
John R Park Homestead Museum Archives 683
John Ralston Historical Association & Library 373
John Reeder Family 505
John Rivers Communications Museum Archives 512
John S Barry Historical Museum 288
John S Barry Historical Society & Archives 288
John Schiefer Historic Home Archives 632
John Smart House Museum 453
John Spellman Library 599
John Stark Edwards House Museum 459
John Strong Mansion Museum 575
John Sydnor's 1847 Powhatan House Museum Archives 546
John Timon Reily Historical Society 489, 493
John Tomay Memorial Library-Georgetown Library 85
John Van Puffelen Library 611
John Vaughan Library 470
John Waddey Carter House Museum Archives 590
John Wesley Powell Memorial Museum Archives 18
John Whitman Historical Association Journal 204
John Whitmer Historical Association 332
John Whitmer Historical Association & Archives 204
John Wood Community College Library 171
John Woodruff Simpson Library 576
John Woolman Memorial Museum Archives 374
John Work Garrett Library 256
John Wornall House Museum Archives 332
John Wornall House Museum Newsletter 332
Johns Family 122
Johnson City Historical Society 528
Johnson City Library 550
Johnson City Public Library 528

Johnson Clan 326
Johnson County Genealogical and Historical Society 176
Johnson County Genealogical Society 635
Johnson County Genealogical Society & Archives 221
Johnson County Genealogical Society & Library 540
Johnson County Genealogist 221
Johnson County Historian 199
Johnson County Historical and Genealogical Society 232
Johnson County Historical and Genealogical Society & Archives 184
Johnson County Historical Museum 184, 199, 357
Johnson County Historical Society 140, 199, 530, 635
Johnson County Historical Society & Archives 357
Johnson County Historical Society & Library 26, 342
Johnson County Historical Society Journal 26, 342
Johnson County Historical Society Newsletter 342
Johnson County Library 26, 220, 221, 635
Johnson County Museum of History Archives 184, 221
Johnson County Public Library 184, 232
Johnson Family 37, 145, 235, 320, 391, 468, 479, 480, 486, 573, 636, 689
Johnson Ferry House Museum Archives 378
Johnson Free Public Library 370
Johnson Hall State Historic Site Archives 401
Johnson Newsletter (Southern) 554
Johnson Public Library 619
Johnson Quarterly 549
Johnsonburg Public Library 490
Johnson-Caston-Allen Family 545
Johnson-Fuller-Eldridge-Dugard-Price-Healey Family 565
Johnson-Humrick House Museum Archives 446
Johnson-Humrick House Museum Newsletter 446
Johnson-Johansson Family 268
Johnson-Johnston Family 513
Johnson-Matthews Family 29
Johnson-Saint Paris Library 456
Johnston County Genealogical Society & Archives 433
Johnston County Genealogical Society Newsletter 433
Johnston County Historical Society 470
Johnston Family 57
Johnston Historical Society 508
Johnston Journal 433
Johnston Public Library 211
Johnston(e) Clan 203
Johnston-Pinney Family 570
Johnstown Area Genealogical and Historical Society 491
Johnstown Area Heritage Association 491
Johnstown Area Heritage Association Newsletter 491
Johnstown Flood Museum Association Library 491
Johnstown Flood National Memorial Archives 501, 502
Johnstown Genealogical Society 505
Johnstown Genealogy Society 450
Johnstown Historical Museum 401, 491
Johnstown Historical Society 86
Johnstown Historical Society & Archives 401
Johnstown Historical Society Newsletter 401
Johnstown Public Library 401
Joint Archives of Holland 294
Joint Free Public Library of Morristown and Morris Township 374
Joint Free Public Library of the Chathams 369
Joliet Area Historical Museum Archives 163
Joliet Area Historical Society & Library 163
Joliet Public Library 163
Joliet Public Library Newsletter 163
Jolivette Historic House 624
Joll(e)y Family 475
Jonathan Bailey Home Museum Archives 77
Jonathan Bourne Public Library 267
Jones Company Historical Society 205
Jones County Genealogical and Historical Organization 321
Jones County Genealogical Society & Library 197
Jones County Historical Society 207
Jones Family 118, 355, 364, 373, 530, 571, 572
Jones Family Newsletter 48
Jones Genealogist 9
Jones House 171
Jones Journeys 62
Jones Library 265
Jones Newsletter 532
Jones Ridge Village Historical Society & Archives 273
Jones-Baldwin Family 156
Jonesboro Historical Society 187
Jonesboro Public Library 187
Jonesborough-Washington County History Museum Archives 528
Jones-Foster Research 7
Jones-McCall Family 126
Jones-Persons Family 364
Jones-Thomas Family 571
Jonesville-Arlington Public Library 428
Joplin Genealogical Society & Archives 331
Joplin Historical Museum 332
Joplin Historical Society & Archives 332
Joplin Public Library 332
Jordaan Memorial Library 217
Jordan Family 41
Jordan Family Newsletter 101
Jordan Historical Museum of the Twenty Archives 683, 689
Jordanville Public Library 401
Jorgensen Family 571
Josef Pilsudski Institute of America Bulletin 407
Joseph A Tallman Museum Archives 199
Joseph and Elizabeth Shaw Public Library 485
Joseph Bighead First Nation 709
Joseph Boggs Society for Historic Preservation 180
Joseph Brant Museum Archives 680
Joseph City Library 476
Joseph F Smith Library 142
Joseph H Plumb Memorial Library 278
Joseph Horner Memorial Library 497
Joseph Lines 194
Joseph Mark Lauinger Library 106
Joseph Meyerhoff Library 256
Joseph Priestley House Museum Archives 496
Joseph Regenstein Library 156
Joseph Schneider Haus Museum Archives 684
Joseph Smith Historic Center Archives 168
Joseph W Walt Library 159
Josephine County Historical Museum 475
Josephine County Historical Society & Library 475
Josephine County Library 475
Joshua Hyde Public Library 280
Joshua Tree and Southern Railroad Museum Archives 75

Josiah Quincy House Archives 278
Joslin Memorial Library 580
Jost House Museum Archives 676
Jots from the Point 499
Jotted Line 45
Jouett Family 549
Jourdanton Community Library 550
Journal Historique des Bernier 697
Journal into the Past 231
Journal of African American History 262
Journal of American Catholic Studies 497
Journal of American Ethnic History 311, 378
Journal of American History 180
Journal of American Indian Family Research 23
Journal of Arizona History 21
Journal of Beaver Island History 286
Journal of Bolivar County Historical Society 319
Journal of Cherokee Studies 425
Journal of Chickasaw History 463
Journal of Colonialism and Colonial History 256
Journal of East Tennessee History 529
Journal of Erie Studies 487
Journal of Family History 74
Journal of Forest History 426
Journal of Historical Review 56
Journal of History 1
Journal of Illinois History 174
Journal of Maritime History 278
Journal of Medieval History 407
Journal of Mississippi History 321
Journal of Missouri Baptist History 334
Journal of Mormon History 567
Journal of Muscle Shoals History 4, 9
Journal of Rockingham County History and Genealogy 434
Journal of San Diego History 65, 66
Journal of Southern History 549
Journal of Southwest Georgia History 125
Journal of Supreme Court History 107
Journal of Texas Catholic History and Culture 536
Journal of the Abraham Lincoln Association 154
Journal of the Afro-American Historical and Genealogical Society 499
Journal of the Aiken County Historical Commission 511
Journal of the Aiken County Historical Society 511
Journal of the Aiken-Barnwell Genealogical Society Chapter, SCGS 511
Journal of the American Portuguese Society 280
Journal of the Birmingham Historical Society 2
Journal of the Canadian Historical Association 687
Journal of the Cherokee Strip 465
Journal of the Chesterfield Historical Society 585
Journal of the Cumberland County Historical Society 484
Journal of the Dallas Jewish Historical Society 542
Journal of the Dalton Genealogical Society 59
Journal of the Early Republic 195
Journal of the Early Republic 498
Journal of the East Ascension Genealogical and Historical Society 237
Journal of the Four Lakes Region 625
Journal of the Friends of Genealogy 241
Journal of the Genealogical Society of Rowan County North Carolina 432
Journal of the German-Texan Heritage Society 536
Journal of the Historical Society of the Cocalico Valley 487
Journal of the Illinois Historical Society 174
Journal of the Jackson County Genealogical Society 322
Journal of the Johannes Schwalm Historical Association 502
Journal of the Kanawha Valley Genealogical Society 614
Journal of the Lancaster County Historical Society 491
Journal of the Lewis County Historical Society 403
Journal of the Lycoming County Historical Society 505
Journal of the Magoffin County Historical Society 233
Journal of the Malden Historical Society 274
Journal of the National Convention 174
Journal of the New River Historical Society 591
Journal of the Norwood Park Historical Society 156
Journal of the Old Wall Historical Society 379
Journal of the Peter Willcocks Society 219
Journal of the Riverside Historical Society 62
Journal of the Rocky Mountain Medieval and Renaissance Association 16
Journal of the Shaw Historical Society 476
Journal of the Sonoma County Historical Society 71
Journal of the Southwest 22
Journal of the Victoria Genealogical Society 657
Journal of the West 218
Journal of the Westchester County Genealogical Society 421
Journal of the Yadkin County Historical and Genealogical Society 435
Journal of Unitarian Universalist History 267
Journal of Wilkinson County History 323
Journeys 256
Joy Family 150
Joyner-Williams Family 512
Jozef Pilsudski Institute of America 407
JP Newsletter 339
JPL Pages 163
Juan Matias Sanchez Adobe Museum Archives 55
Judah L Magnes Memorial Museum 37
Judaica Museum at Riverdale 390
Judaica Museum Newsletter 390
Judaica Museum of Central Synagogue Archives 407
Judaica Society International 372
Judaica Society International Newsletter 372
Juday P Benjamin Confederate Memorial 112
Judge Roy Bean Visitor Center Archives 551
Judith Basin County Museum Archives 346
Judkins Family 606
Judy Garland Museum Archives 308
Jugville Museum Archives 438
Julia A Purnell Museum Archives 263
Julia Boyer-Reinstein Library 393
Julia Hull District Library 175
Julia L Butterfield Memorial Library 394
Julia Rogers Library 256
Julian Black Historical Society 48
Julian H Sleeper House Museum Archives 314
Julian Historical Society 48
Julian Historical Society Reporter 48
Julian Pioneer Museum Archives 48
Julie Tutwiler Learning Resources Center 6
Juliette Gordon Low Birthplace Archives 137
Julius E Farr Family Organization Newsletter 54
Jump River Valley Historical Museum 629
Jump River Valley Historical Society & Archives 629
Junction 307

Junction City Historical Museum 476
Junction City Historical Society & Archives 476
Junction City Historical Society Newsletter 476
Junction Express 415
Juneau County Historical Society & Archives 625
Juneau County Historical Society Quarterly Bulletin 625
Juneau County History News 625
Juneau Public Libraries 12
Juneau-Douglas City Museum Library 12
Juneau-Douglas City Museum Quarterly Newsletter 12
Juniata County Historical Society 494
Juniata County Historical Society Quarterly 494
Juniata County Library 494
Juniata Mennonite Historical Society 500
Juniper Branch of the Family Finders & Library 476
Juniper Branch of the Family Finders Newsletter 476
Junipero Serra Museum Library 65
Junk Breeze 183
Junk Family 183
Junkins Family Association Newsletter 253
Jurger-Jorger-Yerger-Yarger Family 186
Jurnpa Mountains Cultural Center Library 62
Just Between Friends 181
Just for Old Times Sake 421
Justin Smith Morrill Homestead Archives 580
Justis, Justus, Justice Family 433
Justus Family 69

K

Kaatza Station Museum Archives 651
Ka-Do-Ha Indian Village Museum Archives 31
Kadunc-Krompel-Stibemik-Jamnik-Hribar-Gregorcik Family 599
Kahkewistahaw First Nation 705
Kahler Clearinghouse Newsletter 166
Kahnawake Economic Development Authority 698
Kaiser-Ramaker Library 523
Kaiser-Weber Family 626
Kaiserzeit 371
Kake Tribal Heritage Foundation 12
Kalama Public Library 602
Kalamazoo Aviation History Museum Archives 295
Kalamazoo County Historical Society 295
Kalamazoo Model Railroad Historical Society 295
Kalamazoo Public Library 295
Kalamazoo Valley Community College Library 295
Kalamazoo Valley Family Newsletter 288
Kalamazoo Valley Genealogical Society 295
Kalamazoo Valley Genealogical Society & Library 288
Kalamazoo Valley Heritage 288, 295
Kalamazoo Valley Museum Archives 295
Kalamo Township Historical Society 303
Kalanquin-Westwood-King-Shaw-Moon-Huntington-Olin Family 567
Kalaupapa National Historical Park Archives 142
Kaleva Historical Society 295
Kalkaska County Historical Society & Library 295
Kalkaska County Library 295
Kalkaska County Museum Archives 295
Kalkaska Genealogical Society 295
Kalloch Family 265
Kalloch Family Society Newsletter 249
Kalona Historical Society 203
Kalona Public Library 203
Kalteich Family 75
Kamenah-Brinkmann Family 200
Kamiah Genealogical Society 147
Kaminski House Museum Archives 515
Kamloops Family History Society 650
Kamloops Indian Band 650
Kamloops Museum Association & Archives 650
Kamsack and District Museum Archives 707
Kamsack Historical Society 707
Kanabec County Historical Society & Archives 312
Kanabec County History Center 312
Kanabec News 312
Kanaka Bar Indian Band 651
Kanawha County Public Library 611
Kanawha Valley Genealogical Society & Library 614
Kanawha Valley Historical and Preservation Society 611
Kandi Express 316
Kandiyohi County Historical Society & Archives 316
Kane County Chronicle 161
Kane County Genealogical Society & Library 161
Kane County Historical Society 159
Kane Family 256
Kane Public Library 491
Kanesatake Cultural Centre 698
Kanesatake Nation 698
Kaneville Public Library 163
Kanien'kehaka Raotitiohkwa Cultural Centre 698
Kanien'kehaka Raotitiohkwa Nation 698
Kankakee County Historical Museum 163
Kankakee County Historical Museum Newsletter 163
Kankakee County Historical Society & Archives 163
Kankakee Public Library 163
Kankakee Valley Genealogical Society 153, 163
Kanne-Marzahn-Minske Family 311
Kansas African American Museum 223
Kansas Aviation Museum Archives 223
Kansas Aviation Museum Quarterly 223
Kansas City Area Archivists 332
Kansas City Branch Genealogical Library 332
Kansas City Fire Brigade Museum Archives 332
Kansas City Genealogist 332
Kansas City Landmarks Commission 332
Kansas City Museum Archives 332
Kansas City Posse of the Westerners 221
Kansas City Public Library 216, 332
Kansas Council of Genealogical Societies 222
Kansas Department of Health and Environment Office of Vital Statistics 222
Kansas Genealogical Society 213
Kansas Genealogical Society & Library 213
Kansas Heritage 222
Kansas Heritage Center Archives 213
Kansas History Center 222
Kansas History: a Journal of the Central Plains; Kansas State Historical Society Mirror 222
Kansas Journal of Military History 222
Kansas Kin 218
Kansas Review 222
Kansas State DAR Library 213

Kansas State Historical Society & Library 222
Kansas State Library 222
Kansas West Conference Archives of the United Methodist Church 223
Kansas Wire Collector 216
Kapiolani Community College Library 141
Kaposvar Historic Site Archives 706
Karankawa Kountry 556
Karl C Harrison Museum of George Washington Archives 3
Karl E Mundt Library and Museum 522
Karl Junginger Memorial Library 633
Karl Miles LeCompte Memorial Library 199
Karnes County Library 550
Karow Family 600
Karpatska Rus 421
Karrick-Kerrick Family 451
Kasdorf Family 312
Kasilof Public Library 12
Kaska Tribal Council 713
Kaskaskia College Library 154
Kass Judaic Library 262
Katahdin Public Library 247
Kate Chopin House and Bayou Folk Museum Archives 236
Kate Love Simpson Library 452
Kate Shelley Railroad Museum Archives 198
Kate Strong Historical Library 417
Kateri Galleries-National Shrine of the North American Martyrs Archives 388
Kates Family 103
Kates Kin 456
Kates-Cates Family 456
Katie Murrell Library 226
Kattermann Family Newsletter 121
Katy Railroad Historical Society 338
Katzie Indian Band 653
Katzung Family 314
Kaua'i Historical Society 142
Kauai Museum Association & Archives 142
Kaubisch Memorial Public Library 448
Kaufman County Genealogical Society & Library 561
Kaufman Kounty Konnections 561
Kaufman Museum Archives 219
Kaufman Museum Newsletter 219
Kaufmann-Ogilvie-Westbrook-Hull-Gatkie-Good-Roome-Roberts-Heacock Family 301
Kaukauna Public Library 623
Kaw City Public Library 466
Kaw Mission State Historic Site 213
Kawacatoose First Nation 709
Kawaiahao Church Archives 141
Kaweah Indian Nation 216
Kay Family 518
Ke Ku'Auhau: The Genealogist 142
Keane-Larson-Havener-Cooper Family 608
Kearney County Historical Museum 354
Kearney County Historical Society & Archives 354
Kearney Mansion Museum 45
Kearney Public Library 353
Kearny Cottage Historical Association & Archives 376
Kearny Cottage Museum 376
Kearny County Historical Society 217
Kearny County Library 217
Kearny Public Library 371
Keefer Family Newsletter 49
Keeler Tavern Museum Archives 98
Keene Family 245, 531
Keene Historical Society 362
Keene Public Library 362, 401
Keene Valley Library 401
Keener Family 198
Keener Kinfolk 529
Keep Family 101
Keeper 596
Keeper of the Plains 223
Keeper's Log 67
Keeping Track 197
Keepsake 101
Keeran Family 65, 468
Keesee, Kazee, Kezee, Kissee, Kozee Family 469
Keeseekoose First Nation 707
Keeton-Matthews-Berendsen-Culver-Lowrance Family 370
Keewatin Public Library 684
Kegley Library 597
Kegoayah Kozga Public Library 13
Keiffer Family Newsletter 37
Keillor House Museum Archives 663
Keily Family 535
Keir Memorial Museum Archives 695
Keister Family 6
Keith & Shirley Campbell Library 370
Keith and Kin 130
Keith Clan 126, 130, 323, 362, 427
Keith County Historical Society 355
Keith Family 139
Kell House Museum 563
Kell(e)y Kinsfolk 314
Keller Cousins 83
Keller Family 615
Keller Public Library 328, 550
Kellett Family 89
Kelley Clan 553
Kelley Family 112, 135
Kelley House Museum 53
Kelley House Museum Archives 53
Kelley Jacob House Museum Archives 515
Kelley Klan 149
Kelley Library 364
Kelley-Kelly Quarterly Newsletter 297
Kelleys Island Historical Association 450
Kelliher and District Heritage Museum Archives 707
Kellogg Enterprise 203
Kellogg Historical Museum 203
Kellogg Historical Society & Archives 203
Kellogg-Hubbard Library 578
Kellross Heritage Museum Archives 707
Kelly Branch Library 559
Kelly Family 39
Kelly Memorial Library 156
Kelly-Bruen-Carey-Gorman-Weidner-Widener-Widner-Wydner Clan 380
Kelly-Griggs House Association & Museum 61
Kelly-Kelley Newsletter 166
Kelowna and District Genealogical Society 651

Kelowna Centennial Museum Archives 651
Kelsey Family News Bulletin 91
Kelsey Newsletter 41
Kelso Correspondence 198
Kelso Courier 450
Kelso House Museum Archives 450
Keltic Fringe 503
Kelton House Museum Archives 446
Keltonian 446
Kelty-Davis Family 537
Kemble (Kimble) Family 607
Kemp Family 535
Kemp Family 98
Kemp Files 98
Kemp Memorial Library 426
Kemper-Newton Regional Library System 322
Kenai Community Library 12
Kenai Peninsula College Library 13
Kenai Totem Tracers & Archives 12
Kendall County Genealogical Society 169, 178
Kendall County Genealogical Society & Library 538
Kendall County Historical Society & Library 178
Kendall Family 607
Kendall Family Newsletter 48
Kendall Whaling Museum Library 279
Kendall Young Library 209
Kendallville Historical Society 187
Kendallville Public Library 187
Kendallville Public Library Newsletter 187
Kendrick Memorial Library 539
Kendrick-Dendig Newsletter 311
Kenilworth Historical Museum 163
Kenilworth Historical Society & Archives 163
Kenitzee Indian Tribe 12
Kenmore Plantation and Washington's Ferry Farm Archives 588
Kennard Historical Society 187
Kennebec Historical Society 243
Kennebunk Free Library 247
Kennebunkport Historical Society & Library 247
Kennedy Family 443
Kennedy House Museum Archives 661
Kennedy Klues 62
Kennesaw Civil War and Locomotive Museum 132
Kennesaw Civil War and Locomotive Museum Newsletter 132
Kennesaw Civil War and Locomotive Museum Quarterly 132
Kennesaw Historic Preservation Commission 132
Kennesaw Historical Society 132
Kennesaw Mountain National Battlefield Park Library 132
Kenneth J Shouldice Library 302
Kenney Family 62
Kenning-Floyd-Squires Family 84
Keno City Historical Society 713
Keno City Mining Museum Archives 713
Kenora Public Library 684
Kenosha County Genealogical Society 623
Kenosha County Historical Museum 623
Kenosha County Historical Society & Archives 623
Kenosha Military Museum Archives 629
Kenosha Public Library 623
Kenosha Public Museum Archives 623
Kensington Mansion Museum Archives 514
Kensington Runestone Museum Library 305
Kensington Times 514
Kent City Area Historical Society 295
Kent County Genealogical Society 550
Kent County Historical Society 257
Kent District Library-Caledonia Branch 287
Kent District Library-Cutlerville 292
Kent District Library-Grandville Branch 292
Kent District Library-Plainfield 292
Kent Family 148
Kent Free Library 450
Kent Historical Association 450
Kent Historical Association Newsletter 450
Kent Historical Museum 257
Kent Historical Society & Library 95
Kent Library 326
Kent Memorial Library 100
Kent State University Museum Archives 450
Kent-Delord House Museum Archives 411
Kent-Delord House Quarterly 411
Kenton Company Historical Society 229
Kenton County Historical Society 226
Kenton County Historical Society Review 226
Kenton County Public Library 226
Kentucky Ancestors 227
Kentucky Archivist 230
Kentucky Coal Mining Museum Archives 225
Kentucky Council on Archives 230
Kentucky Department for Libraries and Archives 227
Kentucky Derby Museum Archives 230
Kentucky Explorer 229
Kentucky Family Records 232
Kentucky Folk Art Center Archives 231
Kentucky Folk Art Center Newsletter 231
Kentucky Genealogical Society & Library 227
Kentucky Heritage 227
Kentucky Historical Society & Library 227
Kentucky Historical Society Chronicle 227
Kentucky Historical Society Register 227
Kentucky Kinfolk 230
Kentucky Library 225
Kentucky Library & Museum Archives 225
Kentucky Military History Museum Library 227
Kentucky Pioneer 233
Kentucky Railway Museum Archives 232
Kentucky Society of Pioneers 233
Kentucky State Capitol Museum Archives 227
Kentucky Traces 231
Kentucky Tree-Search 230
Kentucky Wesleyan College Library 232
Kenyon Area Historical Society & Archives 309
Keo Mah Genealogical Society & Library 206
Keo Mah Tracers 206
Keohane Family 123
Keokuk County Historical Society 207
Keokuk Public Library 203
Keokuk River Museum Archives 203
Keomah Genealogical Society 197
Keough Family 94

Kepple, Klingensmith, Staymates Family 493
Kerby Family 160
Kerchner-Laudenslager Family 486
Kern County Genealogical Society & Library 36
Kern County Historical Society 36
Kern County Library 36
Kern County Library Scuttlebutt 36
Kern County Library-Boron Branch 38
Kern County Museum Archives 36
Kern Grapevine 36
Kern River Valley Historical Society & Archives 48
Kern Valley Museum 48
Kern-Antelope Historical Society 63
Kerns-Kearns-Kearnes Family 356
Kerr Family 123, 313, 481, 527, 532, 587
Kerr Kinseekers 219
Kerr Place Museum 592
Kerr Trails 550
Kerr-Baggs-Broadbent-Hollingshead-Free Family 568
Kerrobert and District Museum Archives 707
Kerrville Genealogical Society & Archives 550
Kershaw County Historical Society & Archives 512
Kershaw County Library 512
Kershner Family 425
Kershner-Seylar-Bucher Family 612
Kessenich Family 39
Kessler Family 445
Kessler-Kesler Family 369
Kessler-Wing Newsletter 82
Ketchpen 468
Ketchum Family 603
Ketchum-Sun Valley Historical Society 147
Kettle Falls Public Library 602
Kettle River Museum Archives 652
Kettleson Memorial Library 13
Kewanee • Kewanee Historical Society & Library 163
Kewanee Public Library District 163
Kewanna Public Library 187
Kewartha Settlers' Village 679
Kewaskum Historical Society & Archives 624
Kewaunee County Historical Museum Archives 624
Kewaunee County Historical Museum Newsletter 624
Kewaunee County Historical Society 624
Kewaunee County Research Center Archives 617
Keweenaw County Historical Museum 290
Keweenaw County Historical Society & Archives 290
Keweenaw Kernewek 294
Key 426, 592, 603
Key Finder 471
Key First Nation 708
Key West Art and Historical Society & Library 115
Key West Lighthouse Museum Archives 115
Key West Maritime Historical Society 115
Key West Museum of Art & History Archives 115
Keya Paha County Historical Society 356
Keyano College Library 643
Keyhole to the West 504
Keyport Free Public Library 371
Keyport Historical Society & Archives 371
Keys to the Past 538
Keystone Area Historical Museum 522
Keystone Area Historical Society 523
Keystone Area Historical Society & Archives 522
Keystone Genealogical Society & Library 117
Keystone Kin 117
Keystone Kuzzins 487
Keystone Model Railroad Historical Society 493
Keystone Newsletter 292
Keystone Pioneer Museum Archives 661
Keystone Seekers 489
Keywords 662
Kiamichi Genealogical Society 471
Kib Family 593
Kib's Kousins Newsletter 593
Kid 'n Kaboodle 441
Kidd Family 599
Kidron Community Historical Society 447
Kidron Heritage Center 460
Kidwell Farm at Frying Pan Park Archives 589
Kidwell-Huffman Family 179
Kiefer Library 86
Kiel Area Historical Society & Archives 624
Kiel Family 119
Kiel Public Library 624
Kielce-Radom Special Interest Group 116
Kielce-Radom Special Interest Group Journal 116
Kiener Family 528
Kierstede House 415
Kight Newsletter 559
Kilbourn Public Library 634
Kilby Family 104
Kilby Historic Store and Farm Archives 650
Kilduff Family 53
Kilgore Clan 512, 518
Kilgore Family 63
Kilgore Kith and Kin Newsletter 529
Kilgore Memorial Library 357
Killam Memorial Library 674
Killarney Centennial Museum Archives 684
Killeen Public Library 551
Killgore Memorial Library 543
Killian Family 428
Killingly Historical and Genealogical Society 92
Killingly Public Library 92
Killoran Family 18
Killough Family in Ireland, Canada and the United States 82
Kilner Family 461
Kimball County Plains Historical Society 353
Kimball Family 247
Kimball -Fitch Family 571
Kimball House Museum 286
Kimball Public Library 353, 359, 579
Kimballton Public Library 204
Kimberley Heritage Museum Archives 651
Kimberly Crest House and Garden Archives 61
Kimberly Public Library 147
Kimble County Historical Museum Archives 550
Kimble County Library 550
Kimbro-Kimbrough Genealogical Quarterly 1
Kimmel Family 220

Kimmel Reunion 218
Kimmswick Historical Society & Library 333
Kin Foulkes 19
Kin in Linn 220
Kincaid Clan 285
Kincaid Letter International 65
Kincaid Museum Archives 707
Kinchafoonee Regional Library System-Calhoun County Library 130
Kinchafoonee Regional Library-Clay County 131
Kinchafoonee Regional Library-Randolph County 129
Kinchafoonee Regional Library-Terrell County Library 129
Kincolith Indian Band 651
Kindel Family 44
Kinderhook Memorial Library 402
Kinderhook Regional Library 333
Kindersley Plains Museum Archives 707
Kindred Spirits 405
Kindred Spirits: Newsletter of the Prince William County Genealogical Society 590
Kinfolks 238
Kinfolks and Connections 428
Kinfolks Search 328
King and Queen Historical Society 595
King County Library System 602
King County Library System-Auburn Branch 599
King County Office of Historic Preservation 606
King Family 64, 110, 514, 610
King Family Newsletter 554
King George County Historical Society 589
King Hooper Mansion Museum Archives 274
King Kamehameha History Center Archives 141
King Library 68
King Manor Museum Archives 401
King Quarterly 610
King Seaman School Museum 676
King Township Historical Museum Archives 684
King Township Public Library 684
King William Association 559
King-Debolt-Dozier Family 72
Kingdom of Callaway Historical Society 329
Kingfield Historical Society 247
Kingfisher Memorial Library 466
Kingman Army Airfield Historical Museum 17
Kingman Army Airfield Historical Society & Archives 17
Kingman Carnegie Public Library 216
Kingman County Historical Museum 216
Kingman County Historical Society & Archives 216
Kingman Public LIbrary 187
Kingman Tavern Historical Museum 269
Kings County Historical Society 675
Kings County Historical Society & Archives 664
Kings County Historical Society Newsletter 664
Kings County Library 47
Kings County Memories 664
Kings Historical Museum 675
Kings Historical Society & Archives 675
Kings Landing Historical Museum Archives 663
Kings Landing Historical Settlement Museum Archives 664
Kings Mountain National Military Park Library 429, 511
Kingsborough Community College Library 391
Kingsborough Historical Society & Archives 391
Kingsburg Historical Park 48
Kingsbury Genealogical Society 521
Kingsclear Indian Band 663
Kingsland Genealogical Society 551
Kingsland Homestead Museum 397
Kingsley Plantation Museum Archives 114
Kingsport Public Library 528
Kingston Area Library 402
Kingston City Library 528
Kingston Fire Department Museum Archives 684
Kingston Frontenac Public Library 684
Kingston Historical Society 684
Kingston Mills Blockhouse Museum Archives 682
Kingston Public Library 273
Kingston Relations 684
Kingsville Public Library 450
Kingwood Public Library 613
Kingwood Township Historical Society & Library 367
Kinistin First Nations 711
Kinistino District Pioneer Museum Archives 707
Kinney County Public Library 538
Kinney -David Family 381
Kinney Memorial Library 202
Kinney Pioneer Museum 199, 205
Kinney-Furrow Family 171
Kinney-Heath-Pierce Family 480
Kinnoull Historical Museum Archives 642
Kinross Heritage Society 295
Kinseekers Genealogical Society of Lake County 116
Kinseekers Quarterly 116
Kinsey's On the Move 82
Kinsey-Coskrey Reunion Quarterly 211
Kinship 413
Kinship Kronicle 361
Kinship Tales 303
Kinships 75
Kinsland Family 424
Kinsley House 246
Kinsley Public Library 216
Kinsman Courier 446
Kinston-Lenoir County Public Library 429
Kintigh Family 57
Kiowa County Genealogical Society 466
Kiowa County Genealogical Society Newsletter 466
Kiowa County Historical Society 466
Kiowa County Library 214
Kiowa Historical Museum 216
Kiowa Historical Society & Archives 216
Kipling District Historical Museum 707
Kipling District Historical Society & Archives 707
Kipp Family 198
Kirby Library 491
Kircher Family 459
Kirchner-French Memorial Library 207
Kirk Library 600
Kirkham Family 588
Kirkland Heritage Society 602
Kirkland Municipal Library 698
Kirkland Town Library 394

Kirklin Public Library 187
Kirkman Family 76
Kirkpatrick Family 398, 409
Kirkpatrick Science and Air Space Museum Archives 468
Kirkwood Historical Review 333
Kirkwood Historical Society 333, 402
Kirkwood Mansion Archives 4
Kirkwood Public Library 333
Kirland Temple Historic Center Archives 450
Kirn Norfolk Public Library 592
Kirshop-Caracoff-Caricoff-Karacoff-Kiracoff Family 584
Kirtland Air Force Base Library 383
Kirtland Public Library 450
Kirwin City Library 216
Kishacoquillas Valley Historical Society 481
Kishwaukee Genealogists 172
Kishwaukee Genealogists Newsletter 172
Kispiox Indian Band 651
Kissel Kar Klub 622
Kissinger Family 545, 626
Kistler Family 19
Kistner-Doan-Doane Family 478
Kit Carson Historic Museum 385
Kit Carson Historic Society & Archives 385
Kit Carson Historical Museum 86, 87
Kit Carson Historical Society & Archives 86
Kit Carson Historical Society & Library 87
Kit Carson Historical Society Archives & Archives 86
Kit Carson Museum Newsletter 87
Kitamaat Village Council 651
Kitasoo Indian Band 651
Kitch Travelling Notebook 454
Kitchell Memorial Library 167
Kitchener Public Library 684
Kitchigami Regional Library 313
Kite and Key 291
Kith 'n Kin 448
Kith and Kin 39, 625
Kith and Kin of Boone County, West Virginia 613
Kitigan Zibi Nation 699
Kitimat Centennial Museum Association & Library 651
Kitimat Public Library Association 651
Kitkatla Indian Band 651
Kitsap County Historical Museum 600
Kitsap County Historical Society & Archives 600
Kitsap County Historical Society Newsletter 600
Kitsap Regional Library 600
Kitselas Indian Band 656
Kitsumkalum Indian Band-House of Sim-Oi-Ghes 656
Kittanning Public Library 491
Kittery Historical and Naval Museum 247
Kittery Historical Society & Archives 247
Kittitas County Genealogical Society 601
Kittitas County Kinfolk 601
Kittle Family 450
Kittochtinny Historical Society & Library 484
Kittochtinny Newsletter 484
Kittson County Historical Museum 309
Kittson County Historical Society & Archives 309
Kittson County Historical Society Newsletter 309
Kitwanga Fort Museum Archives 654
Kives Family 237
Kiwanis Van Slyke Museum Archives 146
Kjierulf Family Association Newsletter 51
Klahoose Indian Band 648
Klamath Basin Genealogical Society 476
Klamath County Library 476
Klamath County Museum Library 476
Klaxon 349
Klee Newsletter 82
Klein Museum Archives 523
Klewer News 149
Klickitat County Historical Society & Library 602
Klickitat Heritage 602
Kliewer Family 22
Kling Memorial Library 202
Kloepfer Family 17
Klondike Gold Rush National Historic Park Archives 13
Klondike Gold Rush National Historical Park-Seattle Archives Unit 606
Klondike National Historic Sites Archives 713
Kluskus Indian Band 654
Klyne Esopus Museum Archives 418
Klyne Esopus Museum Newsletter 418
Klyte Burt Memorial Public Library 351
Knarr, Knerr, Knorr Family 444
Knebel Family 545
Knechtel-Dolan-Faupel-Rapelje-Remsen-Sharpin-Vezina Family 194
Kneehill Historical Museum Archives 646
Kneeland-Walker House 633
Knee-Von Black Archives and Museum Archives 338
Knick-Christie Family 572
Knickerbocker 415
Knickerbocker Historical Society 415
Knickerbocker Mansion Newsletter 415
Knife River Indian Villages Historic Site Archives 439
Kniffin-Sniffin Family 377
Knight Family 113, 120, 121, 239, 338, 465
Knight Letter 173
Knight Library 475
Knight Museum Library 349
Knights of Columbus 106
Knights of Columbus Historical Museum 96
Knights of Columbus Library 96
Knightstown Public Library 187
Knoedler Memorial Library 225
Knott County Historical and Genealogical Society & Library 229
Knott County Historical and Genealogical Society Journal 229
Knott County Public Library 229
Knott Family 537
Knott House Museum Archives 122
Knott Library 256
Knowles-Knoles-Noles Family 50, 77, 238
Knox County Chapter Newsletter 453
Knox County Chapter, OGS 453
Knox County Genealogical Society 448
Knox County Historical Commission & Archives 538
Knox County Historical Museum 163, 328
Knox County Historical Society 160, 225, 453
Knox County Historical Society & Archives 163, 328
Knox County History 195

Knox County Illinois Genealogical Society & Library 160
Knox County Illinois Genealogical Society Quarterly 160
Knox County Public Library 195, 225
Knox County Public Library System 529
Knox County Records Library 195
Knox Creek Historical Society 618
Knox Family 382
Knox Headquarters State Historic Site Archives 419
Knox House Museum Archives 43
Knox House Museum Quarterly Newsletter 43
Knox Memorial Association & Archives 251
Knoxville Public Library 204
Knoxville Public Library & Museum Archives 491
Knudsen Family 635
Knudt Salle Log Cabin Museum Archives 437
Koch Newsletter 262
Kochy Newsletter 262
Kodak Genealogical Club 414
Kodiac Public Library 13
Kodiak Historical Society & Archives 13
Kodiak Military History Museum Archives 13
Koehn Kindred 219
Koelsch Family 566
Kohlhagen Family 420
Kokkonen Family 291
Kokomo Public Library 187
Koksilah School Historical Society 651
Kolb Family 571
Kolker Family 465
Koloa Public & School Library 142
Kolomoki Mounds State Park Museum Archives 127
Komoka Railway Museum Archives 684
Kona Historical Society & Library 141
Kona Historical Society Newsletter 141
Koochiching Chronicle 309
Koochiching County Historical Museum 309
Koochiching County Historical Society & Archives 309
Koontz Family 441
Kootenai Brown Pioneer Village Archives 645
Kootenai County Genealogical Society & Library 147
Kootenai-Shoshone Area Libraries-Hayden Branch 147
Kootenay Lake Historical Society & Library 651
Korean American Historical Society 606
Korean American Museum Archives 52
Korean War Veterans National Museum Archives 171
Koreshan State Historic Site Archives 112
Korner's Folly Museum Archives 429
Kornerstone 429
Korzenie Roots 627
Kosciusko County Historical Society & Library 195
Kosciusko County Newsletter 195
Koshare Indian Museum Library 86
Koshare News 86
Koshkonong Area Historical Society 333
Koshkonong Prairie Historical Society 619
Kothe Family 468
Kothe Foundation Newsletter 468
Kotzebue Museum Library 13
Kraemer Family Library 82
Krans-Buckland Family 56
Krauth Memorial Library 498
Krefeld Immigrants and Their Descendants 63
Kregal-Willenbrock-Willenbrook Family 202
Kreitzer Family 570
Kremer House Library 311
Krenelka Family 311
Kresge Library 301
Kriegbaum Heritage 171
KRL News 600
Kroet(s)ch Family 601
Kruger Street Toy & Train Museum Archives 615
Kruse House Museum 177
Kruse House Museum Newsletter 177
Ksan Historical Village and Museum Archives 650
Ktunaxa-Kinbasket Tribal Council 649
Kuethe Library, Historical & Genealogical Research Center 259
Kuhefuss House Museum Archives 619
Kuhlman Family 475
Kuhlmann King Historical House and Museum Archives 538
Kuhn Kuzns 476
Kulp Family 496
Kultur Un Lebn 408
Kumbera Family Newsletter 327
Kump Family 612
Kuna School Community Library 147
Kunders-Conard-Cunnard-Conrad Newsletter 63
Kunkel-Kunkle-Conkle-Gunkel-Spindle Family Newsletter 41
Kurdish Museum Archives 391
Kurth Memorial Library 552
Kuser Farm Mansion Archives 371
Kuskokwim Consortium Library 11
Kutztown Area Historical Society & Library 491
Kutztown Area Historical Society Newsletter 491
Kuykendall Newsletter 115
Kwagiulth Museum Archives 654
Kwakiutl District Council 653
Kwakiutl Indian Band 653
Kwantlen First Nation 649
Kwantlen University College Library 655
Kwaw Kwaw Apilt Indian Band 648
Kwa-Wa-Aineuk Indian Band 653
Kwelth Tahlkie Cultural and Heritage Museum Archives 475
Kwiakah Indian Band 648
Kwicksutaineuk-Ah-Kwaw-Ah-Mish Indian Band 655
Kwinitsa Station Railway Museum Archives 654
Kyburz Family 301
Kylander, Kilander, Callendar Families of America Newsletter 531
KYOWVA Genealogical Society & Library 612
KYOWVA Genealogical Society Newsletter 612

L

L A Beeghly Library 490
L A Foster Library 330
L D Fargo Public Library 624
L E Phillips Memorial Public Library 620
L Zenobia Coleman Library 322
L'Ancestre 702
L'Anse aux Meadows National Historic Site 668
L'Arbre Historique 703
L'Chaim 256

L'Entraide Genealogique 703
L'Etoile D'Acadie 362
L'Heritage 236
L'Heritage Vivant - Living Heritage Society & Library 252
L'Octogone Centre de la Culture 698
L'Outaouais genealogique 698
La Campana 70
La Casa Primera de Rancho San Jose Museum Archives 60
La Crescent Area Historical Society 309
La Crescent Public Library 309
La Cronica de Nuevo Mexico 384
La Crosse Area Genealogical Society Chapter 624
La Crosse Area Genealogical Society Quarterly 624
La Crosse County Historical Society & Archives 624
La Crosse County Library 623
La Crosse Public Library 624
La Cygne Genealogical Society & Archives 216
La Fourche Heritage Society 242
La Grande Public Library 476
La Grange Area Historical Museum 163
La Grange Area Historical Society & Archives 163
La Grange Public Library 163
La Habra Old Settlers Historical Society 49
La Harpe Carnegie Public Library 163
La Harpe Historical and Genealogical Society 163
La Harpe Historical and Genealogical Society Newsletter 163
La Have Islands Marine Museum Archives 675
La Jolla Historical Society & Library 49
La Jolla Historical Society Quarterly Newsletter 49
La Mesa Depot Museum Archives 49
La Mesa Historical Society & Library 49
La Moille-Clarion District Public Library 163
La Peninsula 69
La Pine Genealogical Society 476
La Plata County Historical Society & Archives 84
La Plata Public Library 333
La Porte Library 551
La Puente Valley Historical Society 47
La Puente Valley Historical Society & Library 49
La Pulperie de Chicoutimi 697
La Purisima Mission State Historic Park Archives 50
La Quinta Historical Society 49
La Sierra University Library 62
La Societe d'Histoire de Sherbrooke & Bibliotheque 703
La Societe des Cajuns 237
La Societe Genealogique Des Martin Casier 700
La Societe Historique de Quebec & Bibliotheque 701
La Societe Historique de Saint Boniface & Library 661
La Verne Heritage Foundation 49
La Vernia Historical Association 551
La Veta Public Library 87
La Vista 69
La Voix des Prairies 242
LaBelle Heritage Museum Archives 115
Labette Community College Library 220
Labor's Heritage 262
Labrador Heritage Museum Archives 667
Labrador Institute of Northern Studies Information Centre 667
Labrador Straights Museum Archives 667
Lac Cardinal Regional Pioneer Village Museum Archives 644
Lac du Flambeau Historical and Cultural Society & Archives 624
Lac La Biche Mission Historical Society 644
Lac La Roche Museum Archives 647
Lac La Ronge Indian Band 707
Lac La Ronge Museum Archives 707
Lac Qui Parle County Historical Museum 310
Lac Qui Parle County Historical Society & Archives 310
Lac Qui Parle County Historical Society Bulletin 310
Lace Museum Archives 55
Lacey Township Historical Museum 370
Lacey Township Historical Society 370
Lackawanna County Historical Society & Library 501
Lackawanna County Library 501
Lackawanna Historical Society Journal 501
Lackey Family 543
Laclede County Genealogical Society 334
Laclede County Genealogical Society Newsletter 334
Laclede County Historical Museum 334
Laclede County Historical Society & Archives 334
Lacon Public Library 164
Lacona Village Historian 415
Laconia Historical Society & Archives 362
Laconia Historical Society Newsletter 362
Laconia Public Library 362
Lacy Genealogist Newsletter 119
Ladd Family 474
Ladd Leads 549
Ladies of the Grand Army of the Republic 500
Ladies of the Grand Army of the Republic, Ohio Department 450
Ladoga Historical Society 187
Ladoga-Clark Township Public Library 188
Ladoga-Clark Township Public Library Newsletter 188
Ladonia Historical Preservation Society 551
Ladson Genealogical and Historical Foundation & Library 139
Lady Lake Public Library 115
Ladysmith Railway Museum Archives 651
Laessig Newsletter 626
Lafayette County Genealogical Workshop 631
Lafayette County Heritage News 321
Lafayette County Historical Society 29, 32, 330
Lafayette County Historical Society & Archives 25, 620
Lafayette Genealogical Society 238
Lafayette Historical Society 238
Lafayette Historical Society & Archives 49
Lafayette Lookback 25, 29
Lafayette Miners Museum Archives 87
Lafayette Public Library 87, 238
Lafayette Square Restoration Committee 339
LaFayette: The History and Genealogy of Fayette County, PA 492
Lafourche Parish Library 242
Lafourche Parish Public Library-Cut Off Galliano Branch 237
Lafourche Parish Public Library-Martha Sowell Utley Memorial 242
Lagerstedt Family 474
Lagesse Family 524
LaGrange County Historical Society & Archives 188
LaGrange County Historical Society Newsletter 188
LaGrange County Library 188
LaGrange County Library Newsletter 188
Laguna Beach Historical Society 49
Lahaina Jottings 142

Lahaina Restoration Foundation 142
Laidlaw Historical Center 279
Laingsburg Public Library 295
Lair Linkage: A Family Newsletter 88
Lair: Cunningham Family Newsletter 185
Laird Township Historical Society 300
Lakahahmen Indian Band 649
Lake Alfred Public Library 115
Lake Babine Nation 648
Lake Benton Historical Society 309
Lake Blackshear Regional Library 125
Lake Blackshear Regional Library-Cordele-Crisp Carnegie 129
Lake Champlain Maritime Museum Archives 580
Lake Charlotte Area Heritage Society 675
Lake Chelan Historical Society & Library 600
Lake Chelan History Notes 600
Lake City Historical Society 309
Lake Country Museum Archives 653
Lake County Civic Center Association & Archives 87
Lake County Genealogical Society 164, 522
Lake County Genealogical Society & Archives 49, 455
Lake County Genealogical Society Newsletter 49
Lake County Genealogical Society Quarterly 164
Lake County Heritage 453
Lake County Historical Museum 49, 87, 123, 316, 450, 453
Lake County Historical Quarterly 453
Lake County Historical Society 182, 476
Lake County Historical Society & Archives 49, 123, 316, 450, 453
Lake County Historical Society & Library 164
Lake County Historical Society & Museum 192
Lake County Historical Society Newsletter 316, 450
Lake County History Review 453
Lake County Illinois Genealogical Society Newsletter 164
Lake County Library 49, 476
Lake County Library System 123
Lake County Library System-Cooper Memorial Library 110
Lake County Museum 177
Lake County Public Library 87, 189
Lake Court House Foundation 182
Lake Creek Historical Society 475
Lake Creek Pioneer Family Picnic 475
Lake Crystal Historical Society 309
Lake Elsinore Genealogical Society 49
Lake Elsinore Genealogical Society Newsletter 49
Lake Elsinore Historical Society 49
Lake Erie Islands Historical Society 456
Lake Erie Ledger 455
Lake Eufaula Area Genealogical Society 465
Lake Family 85
Lake Forest Public Library 164
Lake Forest-Lake Bluff Historical Society 164
Lake Geneva Public Library 624
Lake George Historical Association & Archives 402
Lake Guernsey Museum Archives 636
Lake Havasu Genealogical Society 17
Lake Havasu Genealogical Society & Library 17
Lake Havasu Genealogical Society Newsletter 17
Lake Havasu Historical Society 17
Lake Hopatcong Historical Museum 372
Lake Hopatcong Historical Society 372
Lake Hopatcong Historical Society Newsletter 372
Lake in the Hills Historical Society 164
Lake Jackson Historical Museum Archives 551
Lake Jackson Historical Museum Newsletter 551
Lake Lines 455
Lake McHenry County Historical Alliance 177
Lake Michigan Maritime Museum Archives 302
Lake Mills-Aztalan Historical Society & Archives 624
Lake Murray Historical Society 513
Lake Odessa Area Historical Society & Archives 295
Lake Odessa Historical Society 295
Lake of the Red Cedars Museum 181
Lake of the Red Cedars Museum Newsletter 181
Lake of the Woods Historical Museum 305
Lake of the Woods Historical Society & Archives 305
Lake of the Woods Museum Archives 684
Lake of the Woods Ojibway Cultural Centre 684
Lake Oroville State Historic Site Archives 58
Lake Oswego Public Library 476
Lake Park Area Historical Society 132, 309
Lake Park Public Library 115
Lake Perrid Regional Indian Museum Archives 59
Lake Placid Historical Society & Archives 115
Lake Placid Memorial Library 115
Lake Placid Public Library 402
Lake Placid Winter Olympic Museum Archives 402
Lake Placid-North Elba Historical Museum 402
Lake Placid-North Elba Historical Society & Archives 402
Lake Placid-North Elba Historical Society Newsletter 402
Lake Pleasant Town Historian 402
Lake Pontchartrain Basin Maritime Museum Archives 238
Lake Providence Historical Society 238
Lake Region Historical Society Association & Library 220
Lake Region Historical Society Association Newsletter 220
Lake Saint Louis Historical Museum 700
Lake Saint Louis Historical Society 700
Lake Shore Railway Historical Museum 496
Lake Shore Railway Historical Society & Archives 496
Lake Shore Timetable 496
Lake Station Historical Society 188
Lake Superior Maritime Museum Library 307
Lake Superior Railroad Museum Archives 307
Lake Superior Roots 297
Lake Tahoe Historical Museum 73
Lake Tahoe Historical Society & Archives 73
Lake Tahoe Historical Society Quarterly 73
Lake Tomahawk Historical Society & Archives 624
Lake View Historical Society 204
Lake View Public Library 204
Lake Villa Historical Society 164
Lake Villa Public Library District 164
Lake Waccamaw Depot Museum Archives 429
Lake Wales Museum and Cultural Center Archives 115
Lake Wales Museum and Cultural Center Quarterly 115
Lake Wales Public Library 115
Lake Winnipesaukee Historical Museum 362
Lake Winnipesaukee Historical Society & Archives 362
Lake Worth Public Library 115
Lakefield Public Library 684
Lakeland Area Genealogical Society 627

Lakeland Public Library 116
Lakeland Regional Library 708
Lake-Leake Newsletter 20
Lakes District Museum Archives 648
Lakes Region Historical Society 151
Lakeside Historical Society 49
Lakeside Museum Archives 705
Lakeside Reader 624
Lakeview Community Library 630
Lakeville Area Historical Society 309
Lakewood Heritage Center 87
Lakewood Historical Society & Archives 450
Lakewood Historical Society & Library 87
Lakewood Historical Society News 450
Lakewood Lore 450
Lakewood Memorial Library 402
Lakewood Public Library 450
Lam Family 500
Lamar Community College Library 87
Lamar County Genealogical and Historical Society 10
Lamar County Genealogical Society & Archives 555
Lamar County History and Genealogy 555
Lamar Public Library 87
Lamb County Library 552
Lamb Family 419, 605
Lambert Castle 376
Lambert Family 19, 121
Lambert Historical Society 345
Lambert-Lamberth Family Association Newsletter 74
Lamberton Area Historical Society 309
Lambertville Free Public Library 372
Lambertville Historical Society 372
Lambeth Family 544
Lambirth-Murphey-Hughes-Bowers-James-Briggs-Despain Museum 545
Lambton County Historical Society & Library 689
Lambton County Historical Society Bulletin 689
Lambton County Library 693
Lambton Heritage Museum Archives 683
Lamesa Area Genealogical Society & Archives 551
Lamesa Area Genealogical Society Bulletin 551
Lamie Family 303
Lamkin Family 63
Lamoni Public Library 204
Lamont Clan 433, 446
Lamont Memorial Free Library 404
Lamoure County Museum Archives 438
Lamplighter 63, 162
Lanark County Genealogical Society 688
Lanark Public Library 164
Lanawee County Library 285
Lancaster Community Library 589
Lancaster County Connections 489
Lancaster County Historical Commission & Library 516
Lancaster County Historical Society & Library 491
Lancaster County Historical Society Newsletter 491
Lancaster County Library 491, 516
Lancaster County Society for Historic Preservation 516
Lancaster County Society for Historic Preservation Newsletter 516
Lancaster Genealogical Society 551
Lancaster Historical Commission & Library 273
Lancaster Historical Museum 362
Lancaster Historical Society 402
Lancaster Historical Society & Archives 362
Lancaster Historical Society Newsletter 362
Lancaster Legend 402
Lancaster Mennonite Historical Society & Library 492
Lancaster Museum Archives 50
Lancaster Public Library 551
Lance Family 530
Lance-Lantz-Lentz-Lence People Newsletter 135
Lancer Centennial Museum Archives 707
Land O'Lakes Historical Society & Archives 624
Land of the Yankee Fork Historic Association 150
Land of the Yankee Fork Historic Museum 150
Lander Genealogical Society 636
Landis Valley Museum Archives 492
Landis-Keyes-Bogart-Ball Family 536
Landmark 37, 43, 508, 633
Landmark and Historical Society of Mount Vernon & Archives 405
Landmark Letter 7
Landmark Living Journal 151
Landmark Preservation Foundation Museum 409
Landmark Resource Center Archives 592
Landmark Society Historical Museum 414
Landmark Society of Western New York & Archives 414
Landmarker 134
Landmarkings 428
Landmarks Association of Saint Louis 339
Landmarks Bulletin 4
Landmarks Foundation-Old Alabama Town Archives 7
Landmarks of DeKalb County 4
Landmarks Quarterly 7
Landreth Family Historical Review 155
Landry Leader 549
Landsmannschaft der Bessarabiendeutschen 437
Landsmannschaft der Deutschen aus Russland 438
Landsmen 106
Lane Ancestors Newsletter 473
Lane County Historian 475
Lane County Historical Museum 213, 475
Lane County Historical Museum Library 475
Lane County Historical Society 475
Lane County Historical Society & Archives 213
Lane County Historical Society Newsletter 475
Lane Family Bulletin 68
Lane House Museum 479
Lane Library 137, 630
Lane Memorial Library 361
Lane Place Historic Home Museum 182
Lane Public Library 449
Lanesboro Historical Society 310
Laney Clan 116
Lang Pioneer Village Archives 683
Langan Family 404
Langdon Public Library 363
Langham and District Heritage Village Museum Archives 707
Langham Cultural Centre Archives 651
Langlade County Historical Society & Archives 617
Langlade County Historical Society Newsletter 617
Langley Air Force Base Library 589

Langley Centennial Museum Archives 649
Langley Mansion 532
Langsdale Library 256
Langsdale Library Link 256
Langston Family 25
Langworthy Public Library 507
Lanier County Historical Society 132
Lanier Mansion State Historic Site Archives 189
Lanigan and District Heritage Centre Archives 707
Lanpher Memorial Library 577
Lansdale Historical Society 492
Lansdale Public Library 492
Lansing Historical Museum 164
Lansing Historical Society & Archives 164
Lansing Historical Society & Library 217
Lansing Manor House Museum Archives 408
Lansing Newsletter 311
Lansing Veterans Memorial Museum Archives 164
Lansingburgh Historical Society & Library 402
Lanterman House Museum Archives 48
Lantern 104
Lantern Lite 294
Lantzville Historical Society 651
Lapeer County Genealogical Society & Archives 296
Lapeer County Genealogical Society Newsletter 296
Lapeer County Historical Society & Library 296
Lapeer County Library 296
Lapeer County Library-Goodland 294
Lapeer County Library-Marguerite de Angeli Branch 296
Lapeer County Library-Metamora Branch 297
Lapeer Legacy 296
Lapham Leader 291
Lapham-Patterson House Archives 138
LaPorte County Genealogical Society 188
LaPorte County Historical Museum 188
LaPorte County Historical Society & Archives 188
LaPorte County Public Library 188
Laramie County Community College Library 635
Laramie County Library 635
Laramie Peekers Genealogy Society of Platte County 638
Laramie Plains Museum Association Library 636
Larchmont Historical Museum 404
Larchmont Historical Society & Archives 404
Larchmont Public Library 402
Laredo Public Library 551
Largent Family Bulletin 62
Largo Library 116
Larimer County Genealogical Society 85
Larimer County Genealogical Society Newsletter 85
Larimer County Historic Alliance 85
Larkin Family 596
Lars Noak Blacksmith Shop Archives 248
Lars Noak Blacksmith Shop Newsletter 248
Larsson Log Home 248
Larue County Public Library 229
LaRues-Satterwhite-Jackson-Collins Family 504
Larussa Family 389
Larz Anderson Auto Museum Archives 268
Las Animas-Bent County Public Library 87
Las Calaveras 64
Las Casas Foundation 559
Las Cruces Historical Museum Archives 383
Las Cruces Historical Museum Newsletter 383
Las Vegas City Historical Society 383
Las Vegas Genealogical Society 383
Las Virgenes Historical Society & Library 35
LaSalle County Historical Museum 176
LaSalle County Historical Society & Archives 176
LaSalle County Historical Society and Genealogy Guild 169
LaSalle Genealogy Guild & Library 169
LaSalle Parish Library 237
LaSalle Public Library 164
Lashburn Centennial Museum Archives 707
Lasley Family 608
Lasqueti Island Historical Society 651
Lassen Community College Library 74
Lassen County Historical Society & Archives 74
Lassen Historical Museum Archives 74
Lassen Ledger 74
Last Indian Raid Museum 219
Last Word 154
Latah County Genealogical Society & Library 148
Latah County Genealogical Society Newsletter 148
Latah County Genealogical Society Quarterly 148
Latah County Historical Society & Library 148
Latchua News 113
Latchua Notes 113
Lathrop House Museum 62
Lathrop House Museum Archives 62
Latimer County Genealogical and Historical Society 471
Latimer County Public Library 471
Latimer Quest 100
Latrobe Area Historical Society & Library 492
Latt Maxcy Memorial Library 113
Latta Family 456
Latta Journal 428
Lattimore Family 474
Latty Family 325
Latvian History Museum Archives 691
Latvian Jewish Genealogy Special Interest Group 46
Latvian Jewish Genealogy Special Interest Group Newsletter 46
Latvian Museum 262
Laubach Family 495
Lauder Museum 387
Lauderdale County Library 532
Laudon Family 311, 315
Lauer Family 43
Lauer-Bohr Family 448
Laugenour Family 78
Laughlin Memorial Library 481
Laura Ingalls Wilder Historic Home and Museum Archives 334
Laura Ingalls Wilder Historical Museum 629
Laura Ingalls Wilder Lore 521
Laura Ingalls Wilder Memorial Society 521
Laura Ingalls Wilder Memorial Society & Archives 629
Laura Ingalls Wilder Museum 521
Laura Ingalls Wilder Museum Archives 198, 316
Laura Ingalls Wilder Museum Newsletter 316
Laura Riding Jackson Home Preservation Foundation 123
Laura Secord Homestead Museum Archives 686

Laurel County Historical Society & Library 230
Laurel County Public Library 230
Laurel Heritage Association 260
Laurel Historical Society & Library 103
Laurel Light 260
Laurel Messinger 502
Laurel Museum Archives 260
Laurel Public Library 103
Laurel-Jones County Library 321
Laurels 162, 406
Lauren Rogers Memorial Library and Museum Archives 321
Laurence C Jones Museum Archives 322
Laurens County Historical Commission 516
Laurens County Historical Society 516
Laurens County Historical Society & Archives 130
Laurens County Historical Society Newsletter 130
Laurens County Landmarks Foundation & Archives 516
Laurens County Library 516
Laurens District Genealogical Society 516
Laurens Genies-Pocahontas County Chapter, IGS 204
Laurier House Archives 687
Lauterbach Family 353
Lava Beds National Monument Archives 75
Lavender Line 112
Lavender Lines 1
Lavilla Museum Archives 114
Law Enforcement Memorial Association Archives 172
Lawco Lore 450
Lawn Heritage Museum Archives 667
Lawnside Historical Society 372
Lawrence Countian 450
Lawrence County Archives 7
Lawrence County Genealogical Society 153
Lawrence County Genealogical Society 529
Lawrence County Genealogical Society Newsletter 153
Lawrence County Genealogy Society & Library 450
Lawrence County Historical and Genealogical Society & Archives 179
Lawrence County Historical Commission & Library 7
Lawrence County Historical Museum 179
Lawrence County Historical Quarterly 32, 33
Lawrence County Historical Society 33, 164, 335, 529
Lawrence County Historical Society & Archives 450
Lawrence County Historical Society & Library 32, 495
Lawrence County Historical Society Bulletin 335
Lawrence County Historical Society, Jim Guthrie Chapter 179
Lawrence County Library 33
Lawrence County Public Library 230, 529
Lawrence Family 346
Lawrence Heritage State Park Archives 273
Lawrence History Center 273
Lawrence History News 273
Lawrence House Museum Archives 675
Lawrence L Lee Scouting Museum Archives 362
Lawrence Lee Pelletier Library 493
Lawrence Memorial Public Library 288, 435
Lawrence Public Library 217, 246, 273
Lawrence Town Historian 408
Lawrence Township Historical Society 368
Lawrenceburg Public Library 188
Lawrenceville Historical Society 499
Lawrenceville Public Library 164
Lawrence-Williams-Bradford-Brookshire Family 467
Laws Railroad Museum & Historical Site Library 37
Laws Railroad Museum & Historical Site Quarterly Bulletin 37
Lawshe Museum 315
Lawson Family 391
Lawson Letters 61
Lawson Memorial Research Center 316
Lawson State Community College Library 2
Lawton Family 31
Lawton Memorial Library 624
Lawton Public Library 466
Lawton Rangers Historical Society 466
Lax-Kw'alaams Indian Band 653
Laxqalts'ap Indian Band Council 650
Lay Family 339
Layland Museum Library 540
Layman-Duncan-Evans Family 303
Layman-Haun-Palm Family 116
Layton Family 260
LBJ Country 550
LC Bates Museum Archives 247
LCMM News 580
LDS Family History Center 109
Le Baton Rouge 235
Le Canado-Americain 362
Le Centre d'Etudes Madawaska 663
Le Circle Historique, Pointe Coupee Parish 240
Le Club Calumet, Genealogical Section & Library 243
Le Comite des Archives de la Louisiane & Library 235
Le Communique 236
Le Crescent Area Historical Society 310
Le Fevre Family 406
Le Musee Acadien 663
Le Noir Forge 673
Le Porche 238
Le Reconteur 235
Le Reveil Acadien: The Acadian Awakening 271
Lea County Genealogical Society & Library 384
Lea County Historical Society 384
Lea County Museum Archives 384
Lea County Western Heritage Center Archives 383
Lea County Western Heritage Center Newsletter 383
Leach Family 184
Leach Library 362
Leach Library News 362
Leach Public Library 439
Leaders' Letter 627
Leading Edge 159
Leadville Heritage Association 87
Leadville National Mining Museum Archives 87
Leaf of the Branch 659
Leaf Rpaids National Exhibition Centre 660
Leafy Branches 352
League City Genealogical Society 551
League for Yiddish 407
League of Americans of Ukranian Descent 156
Leaming's Run Colonial Farm Museum Archives 378
Leamington And Mersea Historical Society 685
Leamington Public Library 684

Learning Resource Center 4, 93, 649
Leasburg Missouri Historical Society 333
Lease Family 146
Leask Family 78
Leather Bucket 549
Leavenworth County Genealogical Society & Archives 217
Leavenworth County Historical Museum 217
Leavenworth County Historical Society & Archives 217
Leavenworth County Historical Society Gazette 217
Leavenworth Legacy 217
Leavenworth Public Library 217
Leaves and Saplings 43
Leaves from Our Family Tree 354
Leaves of Greene 460
Leaves of Lineage 219
Leaves of Thyme 194
Leaves to Taproots 218
Lebanon Area Library 245, 247
Lebanon Community Library 217, 492
Lebanon County Historical Society & Archives 492
Lebanon Genealogical Society & Archives 476
Lebanon Historical Museum 95
Lebanon Historical Society 164, 624
Lebanon Historical Society & Archives 95
Lebanon Public Library 188, 362, 476
Lebanon Township Museum at New Hampton Archives 371
Lebanon-Laclede County Library 334
Leblanc Family 96
Lec Sainte-Anne and District Pioneer Museum Archives 645
Lechler Museum Archives 60
Lecompton Historical Society & Library 217
Ledbetter Family 52
Ledbetter Historical Society 229
Ledding Library 477
Ledford Family 550
Ledom Clearinghouse 166
Leduc and District Historical Society 644
Leduc Public Library 644
Ledyard Public Library 95
Lee Cemetery Association Organization 328
Lee Chapel Museum Archives 589
Lee College Library 537
Lee County Genealogical and Historical Society 432
Lee County Genealogical Society 110, 158, 551
Lee County Genealogical Society & Library 203
Lee County Genealogical Society Newsletter 158
Lee County Genealogical Society of Iowa Newsletter 203
Lee County Historical and Genealogical Society 225, 589
Lee County Historical Commission 546
Lee County Historical Museum 6
Lee County Historical Society 158, 511
Lee County Historical Society & Archives 204
Lee County Historical Society & Library 6, 133
Lee County Historical Society Historical Yearbook 158
Lee County Library 322, 432
Lee County Library System-Cape Coral-Lee County Public Library 110
Lee County Library System-East County Regional 116
Lee County Library System-Fort Myers-Lee County 112
Lee County Public Library 225
Lee Davis Library 556
Lee Family 590
Lee Family Researchers Newsletter 328
Lee Hall Mansion Museum Archives 591
Lee Historical Museum 247
Lee Historical Society & Archives 247
Lee Library Association 273
Lee M Friedman Library 281
Lee Public Library 546
Lee Trust for Historic Preservation 113
Lee's Summit Historical Society 334
Leech Lake Tribal College Library 306
Leechburg Area Historical Museum 492
Leechburg Area Historical Society & Archives 492
Leeds Historical Commision 249
Leeds Jane Culbreth Public Library 6
Lee-Fendall House Museum Archives 583
Lee-Fendall House Museum Newsletter 583
Leelanau Historical Museum 296
Leelanau Historical Society & Archives 296
Leelanau Township Public Library 299
Leemuse 296
Lees College Campus Library 229
Leesburg Public Library 116
Leet Family 282
Leete Family 229, 230, 285
Leetonia Community Public Library 451
Leetonia Historical Society & Archives 451
Leeward Community College Library 142
Lefferts Historic House Museum Archives 391
Lefferts Historic House Museum Newsletter 391
LeFlore County Heritage 469
Leftingwell House Museum 97
Leftwich Family 591
Legacies 542
Legacies and Legends of Winn Parish 242
Legacy 52, 163, 228, 259, 557
Legacy Newsletter 571
Legacy: Annals of Herkimer County 399
Legacy: the Journal of the Reno County Historical Society 216
Legend 314
Legends 437
Legends of New Mexico Museum Archives 381
Legion of Honor 67
Legion of Valor Veterans Museum Archives 45
Legion Ville Historical Society 501
Legler Barn Museum 217
Lehigh Acres Genealogical Society 116
Lehigh County Historical Society 484, 486
Lehigh County Historical Society & Library 481
Lehigh County Historical Society Proceedings 481
Lehigh Valley Railroad Historical Society 416
Lehmann Family 45
Lehmer-Leamer-Lamer Newsletter 419
Lehnher Family 602
Lehnherr of Swiss Origins and Their Collateral Ties 602
Leiby Family 44
Leica Historical Society 230
Leica Historical Society of America 168
Leicester Historical Society 273
Leigh Library 2

Leinweber-Gerlitz Family 600
Leisure World Genealogical Workshop & Archives 72
Leisure World Historical Society 72
Leisure World Historical Society of Laguna Hills & Library 49
Leisure World Historical Society of Laguna Hills Newsletter 49
Leitch Collieries 642
LeJeune-Young Family 241
Leland Speed Library 319
Leland Stanford Mansion State Historic Park Archives 63
Leland Township Public Library 296
Lem(m)on(d)(s) Genealogical Society Descendants' Directory 50
LEMA News 172
LeMars Public Library 204
Lemaster-Brimberry-Stonbridge-Gunn-Hollyman (Holliman-Holleman-Hollomon-Hollyman) Family 71
Lemee House Museum Archives 239
Lemhi County Historical Museum 149
Lemhi County Historical Society & Archives 149
Lemhi County Historical Society Archives 149
Lemko (Slovakian) Society 421
Lemon Bay Historical and Genealogical Society 112
Lemon Family 569
Lemon Grove Historical Museum 50
Lemon Grove Historical Society & Archives 50
Lemon Hill Mansion Museum Archives 498
Lemont Area Historical Museum 164
Lemont Area Historical Society & Archives 164
LeMoyne House Museum 504
Lena Area Historical Society 164
Lena Armstrong Public Library-Belton City Branch 538
Lena Community District Library 164
Lenape Olam 481
Lenawee County Historical and Genealogical Society 285
Lenexa Historical Society & Archives 217
Lenni Lenape Historical Society & Archives 481
Lennox and Addington County Museum Library 686
Lennox and Addington County Public Library 686
Lennox Island Museum Archives 695
Lenox Library Association 273
Lenox Public Library 204
Lenox Township Library 298
Lent Van Lent Newsletter 394
Lentz Family 311
Leo Baeck Institute & Library 407
Leo Baeck Institute News 407
Leo Baeck Institute of Jews from Germany Yearbook 407
Leo Dehon Library 622
Leominster Historical Society & Library 273
Leominster Historical Society Newsletter 273
Leominster Public Library 273
Leon County Genealogical Society & Archives 540
Leon County Public Library System 122
Leon Hunters Dispatch 540
Leon Valley Public Library 551
Leonia Public Library 372
Leon-Saxeville Township Public Library 629
Leopold-Zurier-Shapiro-Maise Lap Family 160
Leora H McEachern Library of Local History 432
Lepper Library 451
Leroy and District Herigage Museum Archives 707
Leroy Community Library 296
Leroy Historical Society & Archives 402
Leroy Historical Society Newsletter 402
Leroy House Museum 402
Les Amis de la Genealogie du Quebec 698
Les Archives de la Ville de Quebec 701
Les Cahiers Nicholetains 700
Les Planteur de la Louisiane 238
Les Voyageurs 236
Leslie Clan 371, 488
Leslie County Historical Society & Archives 229
Leslie County Public Library 229
Leslie J Savage Library 86
Lesson Plans 29
Lest We Forget 112
Lester Family 470, 615
Lester Library 590
Lester Public Library 632
Lester-Garland Premesis Museum Archives 669
Lest-We-Forget: Wyoming County Pioneers 503
LeSueur County Historical Museum 307
LeSueur County Historical Society & Archives 307
LeSueur Historians & Library 310
LeSueur Museum Archives 310
Let's Connect We Wrote the Book on Libraries 73
Letcher County Historical and Genealogical Society 234
Letcher County Historical and Genealogical Society Newsletter 234
Letcher Public Library 522
Lethbridge Family Center Archives 644
Lethbridge Public Library 644
Lether E Frazar Memorial Library 238
Letzebuerger Sprooch, Luxembourg Society of Wisconsin 629
Leufroy-Lecoq-Ledoux-Richard-Robillard Family 52
Levere Memorial Temple Archives 159
Leverett Historical Museum 273
Leverett Historical Society & Archives 273
Levering Museum 442
Levi Coffin House 184
Levi E Coe Library 95
Levi Family 15
Levine Museum of the New South Archives 425
Leviston, Levingston, Levingstone, Livingston, Livingstone Family Exchange 454
Levitt Library 357
Levittown Historical Society 492
Levittown Public Library 402
Lewellen Public Library 353
Lewes Historical Society & Library 103
Lewes Public Library 103
Lewin-Paltiel Family 59
Lewis & Clark Boat House Museum Archives 338
Lewis & Clark Interpretive Center Archives 602
Lewis & Clark-Travel Planner & Guide 345
Lewis and Clark County Genealogical Society & Archives 345
Lewis and Clark Genealogical Society 161
Lewis and Clark Library 345
Lewis and Clark Museum Archives 524
Lewis Cooper Jr. Memorial Library 8
Lewis County Genealogical and Historical Society 615
Lewis County Genealogical Society 600

Lewis County Genealogical Society Newsletter 600
Lewis County Historian 403
Lewis County Historical Museum 403, 600
Lewis County Historical Society 147, 326, 403
Lewis County Historical Society & Archives 600
Lewis County Historical Society & Library 234, 403
Lewis County Log 600
Lewis County Public Library 234
Lewis Egerton Smoot Memorial Library 589
Lewis Family 536, 601
Lewis Library 329
Lewis Line 103
Lewis Listings 549
Lewis Town Historian 402
Lewis University Library 172
Lewis-Clark State College Library 148
Lewis-McClure-Sutton Family 607
Lewis-Smith Family 152
Lewiston Area Historical Society 296
Lewiston City Library 148
Lewiston Historical Commission 247
Lewiston Public Library 247
Lewiston Public Library 402
Lewiston-Auburn College Library 247
Lewistown Carnegie Public Library District 164
Lewistown Genealogy Society 345
Lewistown Public Library 345
Lewistown Society For Historical Preservation 164
Lewisville Public Library 551
Lexicon 294
Lexington Cemetery Archives 230
Lexington County Genealogical Association 516
Lexington County Historical Society 516
Lexington County Museum Archives 516
Lexington County Public Library 516
Lexington Genealogical and Historical Society 164
Lexington Genealogical Exchange 516
Lexington Genealogical Society & Archives 353
Lexington Historical Association 334
Lexington Historical Museum 273
Lexington Historical Society 412
Lexington Historical Society & Archives 273
Lexington Historical Society & Library 188
Lexington Historical Society Newsletter 188, 273
Lexington History Museum Archives 230
Lexington Public Library 230, 353
Ley Family 50
Leyden Historical Society 160
Lheit Lit'en Nation 654
Libby Family 250
Libby Heritage Center 345
Libby Museum Archives 365
Libby Newsletter 250
Liberal Area Genealogical Society & Archives 217
Liberal Memorial Library 217
Liberty Bell Memorial Museum Archives 117
Liberty County Historical Society 132, 343
Liberty County Library 343
Liberty County Museum Archives 343
Liberty Grove Historical Society 620
Liberty Hall Historic Center Archives 204
Liberty Hall Historic Center Quarterly 204
Liberty Hall Historic Site Archives 227
Liberty Hall Museum Archives 379
Liberty Hall Reflector 379
Liberty Historical Society 247
Liberty Memorial Association Museum Library 332
Liberty Memorial Museum of World War I 332
Liberty Municipal Library 552
Liberty Public Library 403
Libertyville-Mundelein Historical Society & Archives 164
Libertyville-Mundelein Historical Society Newsletter 164
LIBlines 240
Libra 585
LibRA: Library Society Newsletter 156
Libraries' Newsletter 340
Library Bookmarks 592
Library Company of Philadelphia 498
Library Company of Philadelphia Newsletter 498
Library Connection 304
Library Connections 446
Library Corner in Alpine Enterprise 53
Library Digest 175
Library Edition 222
Library Events 161
Library Focus Newsletter 320
Library Friends News 535
Library Herald 424
Library Journal 552
Library Lamplighter 563
Library Latest Byline 282
Library Leaves 151, 611
Library Letter 322, 369, 508, 597
Library Lexicon 291
Library Lines 63, 158, 169, 184, 268, 375, 431, 628
Library Lineup 372
Library Lingo 92
Library Link 170, 258, 274, 305, 338
Library Links 300
Library Lore 274
Library Matters 288, 401, 623
Library Messenger 474
Library Movers 204
Library News 181, 228, 256, 258, 282, 304, 320, 368, 391, 432, 467, 478, 495, 535, 537, 540, 552, 590, 635
Library News & Book Reviews 248
Library News Article 428
Library News Brief 505
Library Newsletter 404
Library Newsnotes 192
Library Notes 327, 373
Library of Congress 106
Library of Michigan 296
Library of the Presidents 555
Library of the Presidents Newsletter 555
Library of Virginia 593
Library of Virginia News 593
Library Pages 241
Library Paper 611
Library Pointes 293

Library Register 297
Library Scoop 441
Library Times Newsletter 225
Library Update 531
Libri Amicus 433
Licia & Mason Beekley Community Library 96
Licia & Mason Beekley Community Library Newsletter 96
Licking County Genealogical Society & Library 454
Licking County Historical Society & Archives 454
Licking County Historical Society Journal 454
Licking County Historical Society Quarterly 454
Licking Lantern 454
Liebeskind Family 99
Lieu Historique National de Coteau-du-Lac Archives 697
Lieu Historique National de Sir Wilfrid Laurier 704
Lieu Historique National des Forges du Saint-Maurice 703
Lieu Historique National du Canada de la Bataille-de-la-Ristigouche 700
Lieu Historique National du Commerce de la Fourrure 698
Lieu Historique National du Manoir-Papineau 699
Lieutenant General Ashton Armoury Museum 657
Life & Times of Ephraim McDowell 226
Life at Oneida Library 409
Life on the Ohio River History Museum Archives 195
Life Pacific College Alumni Library 66
Lifeline 418
Lifeliner 62
Lifelines 327, 411
Lifting the Veil 279
Ligda Lineage 76
Light Family 194
Light Family Newsletter 392
Lightbulb 170
Lightholder Family 161
Lighthouse Digest 252
Lighthouse Point Library 116
Lighthouse Preservation Society 360
Lightner Library 402
Lightner Museum Archives 121
Lightship 300
Ligonier Historical Museum 188
Ligonier Historical Society & Archives 188
Ligonier Public Library 188
Ligonier Valley Historical Society 492
Ligonier Valley Library Association 492
Likens-Adams Family Newsletter 350
Lillard Family 525
Lillian and Albert Small Jewish Museum 106
Lillian S Besore Memorial Library 488
Lillian Stevenson Nursing Archives Museum 668
Lillie M Evans Library District 171
Lillooet Indian Band 651
Lillooet Museum Archives 651
Lillooet Tribal Council 651
Lilly Historical and Genealogical Society 611
Lilly Letter 611
Lilly Library - Friends Collection 192
Lilly Pike Sullivan Municipal Library 426
Lima Historical Society 344
Lima Public Library 403, 451
Limbach Family 183
Limberlost State Historic Site Archives 184
Limberlost State Historic Site Newsletter 184
Lime Creek-Winnebago County Genealogical Society 202
Limerick Township Historical Society 501
Limestone County Archives 1
Limestone County Genealogical Society & Archives 1, 553
Limestone County Historical Society & Archives 1
Limestone Legacy 1
Limestone Ridge Historical Society 420
Limon Heritage Museum Archives 87
Limon Memorial Public Library 87
Linch-Lynch Family Association Newsletter 44
Linck-Ragatz Family 542
Lincoln Boyhood National Memorial Library 188
Lincoln Carnegie Library 217
Lincoln City Libraries 353
Lincoln County Chronicle 245, 252
Lincoln County Cultural and Historical Association & Library 252
Lincoln County Genealogical Society 252, 330, 612
Lincoln County Genealogical Society Newsletter 330
Lincoln County Genealogy and Historical Society 32
Lincoln County Heritage Trust 383
Lincoln County Historical Association 429
Lincoln County Historical Association & Archives 245
Lincoln County Historical Museum 217, 354, 600
Lincoln County Historical Society 86, 133, 382, 635, 636
Lincoln County Historical Society & Archives 217, 309, 354, 464, 477, 600
Lincoln County Historical Society Newsletter 217, 354, 464, 600
Lincoln County Historical Society Quarterly 477
Lincoln County Library 636
Lincoln County Museum Archives 86
Lincoln County Public Library 345, 429
Lincoln Fire & Rescue Department Museum Archives 353
Lincoln Herald 527
Lincoln Heritage Public Library 182
Lincoln Herndon Law Offices State Historic Site Archives 174
Lincoln Historical Society 273, 577
Lincoln Historical Society & Library 273
Lincoln Home National Historic Site Archives 174
Lincoln Homestead State Park Archives 233
Lincoln in Beloit 617
Lincoln Letters 527
Lincoln Library 174, 218
Lincoln Library Bulletin 174
Lincoln Lineage 612
Lincoln Log Cabin State Historic Site Archives 164
Lincoln Lore 183
Lincoln Memorial Shrine Archives 61
Lincoln Memorial Shrine Newsletter 61
Lincoln Museum Archives 183
Lincoln Parish Library 241
Lincoln Parish Museum and Historical Society & Library 241
Lincoln Parish Museum and Historical Society Newsletter 241
Lincoln Park Historical Museum 296
Lincoln Park Historical Society & Archives 296
Lincoln Park Historical Society News Letter 296
Lincoln Park Public Library 372
Lincoln Public Library 164, 273, 362, 508, 679
Lincoln Public Library Newsletter 508
Lincoln State Monument Museum Archives 383

INDEX

Lincoln Tomb State Historic Site Archives 174
Lincoln Township Public Library 303
Lincoln Train Museum Archives 488
Lincoln's New Salem State Historic Site Archives 170
Lincoln's New Salem State Historic Site Newsletter 170
Lincoln-Lancaster County Genealogical Society Newsletter 353
Lincoln-Lancaster County Genealogy Society 353
Lincoln-Lawrence-Franklin Regional Library 319
Lincoln-Tallman Museum Archives 623
Lincolnville Historical Society & Library 248
Lincolnville Historical Society Newsletter 248
Lincolnwood Library Acorn 164
Lincolnwood Public Library District 164
Lindberg Family 556
Linden Free Public Library 372
Linden Mills Historical Society 296
Linden Railroad Museum Archives 188
Lindenhurst Historical Society 403
Lindenhurst Historical Society & Library 403
Lindenhurst Memorial Library 403
Lindenhurst Memorial Library Newsletter 403
Linden-Madison Township Historical Society 188
Linderman Family 501
Lindmeyer Family 312
Lindsay Clan 135, 302
Lindsay Family 407, 425, 596,
Lindsay Letters 529
Lindsay Library 280
Lindsay Links and Legacy 183
Lindsay Recorder 135
Lindsborg Community Library 217
Lindstrom Historical Society 310
Line Spokesman 170
Line Upon Line 262
Lineage 395
Lineback Family 446
Linebaugh Public Library System of Rutherford County 531
Lines and By Lines 230
Lines and Pathways 433
Linesville Historical Society 492
Lingle Family 67
Link News 594
Links and Bridges 110
Links to Lamar 10
Linn County District Library 212
Linn County Heritage Hunters 198
Linn County Heritage Museum 198
Linn County Heritage Society & Archives 198
Linn County Historical and Genealogical Society & Archives 220
Linn County Historical Museum 474
Linn County Historical Museum Archives 474
Linn County Historical Society 480
Linn County Historical Society & Archives 474
Linn County Historical Society & Library 198
Linn County Historical Society Newsletter 220, 474
Linn County History Center 198
Linn County Library 217
Linn Genealogical Society 473, 480
Linn Genealogical Society & Archives 473
Linn-Benton Community College Library 473
Linnell Family 106
Linschoten Family 573
Linscott Family 251
Linton Public Library 438
Linus A Sims Memorial Library 237
Linwood Community Library 217
Linwood Historical Society 372
Linwood Historical Society Newsletter 372
Linwood Public Library 372
Lion and Thistle 232
Lion of White Hall 233
Lionberger Family 157
Lipscomb Family 458
Lisbon Falls Community Library 248
Lisbon Falls Community Library Newsletter 248
Lisbon Historical Museum 451
Lisbon Historical Society 248
Lisbon Historical Society & Archives 451
Lisbon Public Library 204, 362
Lisle Heritage Society 164
Lisle Heritage Society Newsletter 164
Lisle Library District 165
Lisle Library District Newsletter 165
Lisle Station Park Museum 164
Listuguj Mi'gmaq First Nation Government 699
Litchfield Carnegie Public Library 165
Litchfield Historical Museum 95
Litchfield Historical Society 362, 451
Litchfield Historical Society & Archives 95
Litchfield Public Library 310
Literacy Newsletter 494
Literally Lyons 165
Literally Speaking 93
Literary and Historical Society of Quebec & Library 701
Literary Lines 166
Lithuanian Alliance of America 407
Lithuanian American Genealogy Society & Archives 156
Lithuanian Historical Museum 156
Lithuanian Museum Review 155
Lithuanian Museum-Archives of Canada 686
Lithuanian Research and Studies Center 156
Lithuanian-American Bulletin 156
Lithuanian-American Council & Archives 156
Lititz Historical Foundation & Library 493
Littell's Living Age 122
Little Beaver Historical Society 486
Little Bit 435
Little Black Bear First Nation 706
Little Brick House Museum 176
Little Canada Historical Society 310
Little Chute Historical Society 624
Little Compton Historical Museum 508
Little Compton Historical Society & Archives 508
Little Cornwall on the Prarie 523
Little Country School Restoration Project 340
Little Cowboy Bar and Museum Archives 344
Little Current-Howland Centennial Museum Archives 690
Little Dixie News 463
Little Dixie Regional Libraries 335
Little Dixie Regional Libraries-Dulany Memorial 336

Little Falls Free Public Library 372
Little Falls Historical Museum 403
Little Falls Historical Society & Archives 403
Little Family 40, 185, 435
Little Giant 521
Little Landers Historical Society & Archives 75
Little Landers Historical Society Newsletter 75
Little Nine Partners Historical Society & Library 411
Little Norway Museum Archives 618
Little Pine First Nation 709
Little Prairie Heritage Museum Archives 648
Little Red School House Museum Archives 634
Little Red Schoolhouse Museum 417
Little Red Schoolhouse-Living Library 212
Little River Community Library 217
Little River Historical Society & Archives 25
Little Rock Public Library 29
Little Rock Township Public Library Genealogy Group 171
Little School Museum Archives 675
Little Shuswap Indian Band 648
Little Snake River Museum Archives 637
Little Traverse Historical Museum 300
Little Traverse Historical Society & Archives 300
Little White House Historic Site Archives 139
Little White School House Archives 630
Little White Schoolhouse Museum Archives 676
Littlefield Family 466
Littlefield Family Newsletter 249
Littleton Historical Museum 87
Littleton Historical Society 87
Littleton Historical Society & Library 273
Littleton Public Library 362
Litz Family 449
Live Oak 57
Live Oak County Library 546
Live Oak Public Libraries 137
Live Wire 255
Lively Family 136
Livermore Heritage Guild & Library 50
Livermore Public Library 50, 204
Livermore Roots Tracer 50
Livermore-Amador Genealogical Society & Archives 50
Liverpool Public Library 403
Lives and Times 137
Livesay Family 72, 481, 494, 481
Livezey Family 481
Living Bible Museum Archives 452
Living Historian 580
Living History 286
Living History Association 580
Living History Farms Archives 208
Living History Journal 580
Living Memorial to the Holocaust Archives 407
Living Memorial to the Holocaust Newsletter 407
Living Museum 174
Living Tree News 555
Living Word National Bible Museum Archives 535
Livingston County Genealogical Society 294
Livingston County Genealogical Society & Archives 327
Livingston County Genealogical Society Newsletter 327
Livingston County Historical and Genealogical Society 233
Livingston County Historical Society 294
Livingston County Historical Society & Archives 171, 398
Livingston Depot Center Archives 345
Livingston Library 136
Livingston Lord Library 311
Livingston Newsletter 6
Livingston Parish Library 238
Livingston-Steuben County Genealogical Society 395
Livonia Historical Society 296
Livonia Public Library 296, 403
Lizenbery Family 90
Llano County Public Library 552
Llano Estacado Genealogical Society 552
Llewellyn Family 355
Llewellyn Traces 89
Lloyd Family 536, 568
Lloyd Harbor Historical Society 400
Lloydminster Public Library 644, 707
LNN News 526
Lobdell Family 395, 410, 419
Local Historian 446
Local History or Genealogical Resource Booklet 493
Local Jewish History Society News 281
Local Sheaves 626
Locke Family 269
Locke Family 514
Locke Family News 532
Locke, Sickle and Sword: Newsletter of the Locke Family Association 269
Lockehaven Schoolhouse Museum Archives 360
Lockhart Clan 262
Lockhart Family 6, 549
Locklender 486
Lockport Public Library 403
Lockwood Family 416
Lockwood Public Library 334
Lockwood-Matthews Mansion Archives 97
Lockwood-Matthews Mansion Newsletter 97
Locust Creek Covered Bridge State Historic Site Archives 333
Locust Grove Historic Home Archives 230
Locust Grove Newsletter 230
Locust Grove-Samuel Morse Historic Site Archives 412
Locust Grove-Samuel Morse Historic Site Newsletter 412
Locust Lawn and Terwilliger House Museum Archives 398
Locust Valley Library 403
Lodgepole Historical Society 353
Lodi Historical Society 451
Lodi Memorial Library 372
Lodi Public Library 50
Lodi Valley Historical Society & Archives 624
Loeffler-Luther-Rodgers Family 62
Loertscher Family 188, 414
Log 247, 356
Log & Tally 28
Log Cabin Genealogical Society 297
Log Cabin Museum 624, 632
Log Cabin Museum Archives 695
Log Cabin News 302, 626
Log Cabin Sentinel 451
Log Cabin Society of Michigan 302

INDEX

Log Cabin Village Archives 545
Log Chain 185
Log Farm Museum Archives 686
Log House Gazette 336
Log House Museum 336
Log House Museum 606
Log Line 557
Log Mark 293
LOG: Ledger of Genealogy 612
Logan County Ancestree 613
Logan County Archives 233
Logan County District Library 442
Logan County Genealogical and Historical Society 164
Logan County Genealogical Society 90, 442, 613
Logan County Genealogical Society & Library 233, 465
Logan County Genealogical Society Quarterly 465
Logan County Historical Museum 442
Logan County Historical Society 357
Logan County Historical Society & Archives 442
Logan County Historical Society & Library 30
Logan County Historical Society Newsletter 30, 442
Logan County Museum Archives 31
Logan County Public Library 233
Logan Newsletter 173
Logan Public Library 217
Logan Public Library 567
Logan Roots and Branches 164
Logan-Helm Woodford County Public Library 234
Logan-Hocking County District Library 451
Logansport Public Library 188
Logberg-Heimskringla 662
Lois E Woods Museum Archives 592
Lois Wagner Memorial Library 300
Lois Wagner Memorial Library Newsletter 300
Lokrig Family 545
Lola Montez Home Museum Archives 46
Lombard Historical Museum 165
Lombard Historical Society & Archives 165
Lombard Historical Society Newsletter 165
Lombardy Hall Foundation & Library 104
Lomira Public Library 624
Lomita Historical Society 50
Lomita Railroad Museum Archives 50
Lompoc Legacy 50
Lompoc Museum Archives 50
Lompoc Public Library 50
Lompoc Valley Genealogical Society 50
Lompoc Valley Historical Museum 50
Lompoc Valley Historical Society & Archives 50
Londerry Mines Museum Archives 675
London and Middlesex Historical Museum 685
London and Middlesex Historical Society & Archives 685
London Leaf 685
London Public Libraries 685
London Town News 258
London Town Publik House and Gardens Library 258
Londonderry Historical Society 579
Londonderry Historical Society & Library 362
Lone Sailor 107
Lone Star Flight Museum Archives 546
Lone Star Flight Museum Newsletter 546
Lonesome Pine Regional Library 597
Long Beach Heritage Coalition 51
Long Beach Historical and Preservation Society 403
Long Beach Public Library 51, 403
Long Branch Free Public Library 372
Long Branch Historical Museum Archives 372
Long Family 549
Long Grove Historical Society 164
Long Grove Historical Society & Library 165
Long Hill Township Free Public Library 378
Long Hill Township Free Public Library Newsletter 378
Long Island Community Library 218
Long Island Forum 417
Long Island Historical Journal 417
Long Island History Museum Archives 394
Long Island Maritime Museum Archives 420
Long Island Museum of History Archives 417
Long Island Museum of History Newsletter 417
Long Lake (Kehewin) Cree Nation 641
Long Lake Town Historian 403
Long Pine Heritage Society 353
Long Point Genealogist 690
Long Trail News 580
Long-a-Coming Historical Society 367
Longfellow Evangeline State Historic Site Archives 241
Longfellow National Historic Site Library 268
Longfellow's Wayside Inn Archives 280
Longhorn Musem Archives 556
Longhunter 225
Longleaf 426
Longley Family 633
Longmeadow Historical Society & Archives 273
Longmire Family 608
Longmont Genealogical Society 87
Longmont Heritage 87
Longmont Heritage Association 87
Longmont Museum Archives 87
Longmont Museum Quarterly 87
Longmont Public Library 88
Longport Historical Society 372
Longstreet Farm Museum Archives 371
Longue Vue House Archives 240
Longue Vue House Quarterly 240
Longview Farm National Historic District 334
Longview Public Library 552, 603
Longwell Museum Archives 335
Longwood Public Library 404
Longwood Society For Historic Preservation, Genealogy Group 403
Longyear Historical Museum 268
Longyear Historical Society & Archives 268
Longyear Museum Library 269
Longyear Museum Quarterly News 268
Lonoke County Historical Society 30
Lonoke County Historical Society Newsletter 30
Lonoke Prairie County Regional Library 30
Lonoke Prairie County Regional Library-Des Arc 26
Lonoke Prairie County Regional Library-Devalls Bluff Public 26
Lonoke Prairie County Regional Library-Hazen Public 28
Loo Family 142

Lookin' for Lockes 480
Looking Backwards 620
Looking for Leads 229
Looking for Yesterday 633
Looking Glass 338
Looking: a Look Family Newsletter 59
Lookout Avenue 49
Looman-Prewit Museum 464
Loomings 97
Loomis Family 42
Loon Lake Historical Society 603
Looney Roots Researchers 341
Loop-Lupp-Leupp Family 359
Lopez Adobe Museum Archives 66
Lopez Island Historical Museum 603
Lopez Island Historical Society & Archives 603
Lopez Island Historical Society Newsletter 603
Lopez Island Library 603
Lorado Taft Museum 159
Lorain County Genealogical Society & Archives 448
Lorain County Historical Society & Archives 448
Lorain County Researcher 448
Lorain Public Library 451
Lord Family 250
Lord Selkirk Settlement Archives 695
Lord Strathcona's Horse Museum Archives 641
Lorenz Letters 314
Lorenzo Carriage House 393
Lorenzo State Historic Site Archives 393
Lorenzo State Historic Site Newsletter 393
Loring Parsonage 280
Lorne Philip Hudson Memorial Library 647
Lorne Scots Regimental Museum Archives 680
Lortscher-Loertscher-Lortsher Family 212
Los Alamitos Museum Association 51
Los Alamos County Historical Museum 383
Los Alamos County Historical Society & Archives 383
Los Alamos County Historical Society Newsletter 383
Los Alamos Family Historical Society Newsletter 383
Los Alamos Family History Society 383
Los Alamos Public Library System 384
Los Altos Hills Historical Society & Library 51
Los Altos Hills Historical Society Newsletter 51
Los Altos History Museum Archives 51
Los Altos History Museum Quarterly 51
Los Angeles City Historical Society & Library 52
Los Angeles City Historical Society Newsletter 52
Los Angeles Conservancy 52
Los Angeles Fire Department Historical Society 52
Los Angeles Fire Museum Archives 35
Los Angeles Harbor College Library 78
Los Angeles Maritime Museum Archives 69
Los Angeles Museum of the Holocaust Archives 52
Los Angeles Pierce College Library 78
Los Angeles Police Historical Museum 52
Los Angeles Police Historical Society & Archives 52
Los Angeles Public Library System 52
Los Angeles Public Library System-Vermont Square 52
Los Angeles Westside Genealogical Society 53
Los Angeles Westside Genealogical Society Newsletter 53
Los Banos Genealogical Society & Library 52
Los Bexarenos Genealogical Register 559
Los Bexarenos Genealogical Society 559
Los Californianos 67
Los Californianos, Hispanic Ancestors of Alta California 65
Los Fundadores-Santa Clara 68
Los Gatos Historic Preservation Commission 52
Los Gatos Museum Association 52
Los Gatos Public Library 52
Los Islenos de Galvez Heritage and Cultural Society 235
Los Nogales Museum 560
Los Tulares 76
Lost Creek Lineage 194
Lost Dutchman Museum 15
Lost in Canada? 308
Lost Lake-Randolph Historical Society 630
Lost Nation Public Library 204
Lost River State Park Archives 613
Lostant Community Library 165
Lot of Bunkum 423
Lothropp Family 266, 572
Lott Lineages 56
Loud Family 263
Louden-Thomas-Hamby Family 451
Loudonville Public Library 451
Loudoun Genealogy Society 589
Loudoun Heritage Farm Museum Archives 595
Loudoun Museum Archives 589
Loudoun: The 1757 Legacy 589
Loughmiller Family 561
Louis Bennett Public Library 615
Louis Bull Indian Band 644
Louis E May Museum 351
Louis R Comeau Bibliotheque 673
Louisa County Genealogical Society 209
Louisa County Historical Magazine 590
Louisa County Historical Museum 590
Louisa County Historical Society 209
Louisa County Historical Society & Archives 590
Louisa Gonser Community Library 491
Louise Steinman von Hess Foundation & Library 485
Louisiana Archives and Manuscripts Association & Library 240
Louisiana Archives and Manuscripts Association Newsletter 240
Louisiana Area Historical Museum Archives 334
Louisiana Cotton Museum Archives 238
Louisiana Czech Heritage Association 236
Louisiana Genealogical and Historical Society 235
Louisiana Genealogical Register 235
Louisiana Genealogical Seminar 240
Louisiana Historical Association 238
Louisiana Historical Association Quarterly Newsletter 238
Louisiana Historical Society 240
Louisiana History 238
Louisiana Life 240
Louisiana Marine Fisheries Museum Archives 238
Louisiana Naval War Memorial 235
Louisiana Naval War Memorial Quarterly 235
Louisiana Roots 239
Louisiana State Archives and Records 235
Louisiana State Exhibit Museum Archives 241

Louisiana State Library 235
Louisiana State Museum and Historic Center Library 240
Louisiana State Museum Patterson Archives 240
Louisiana Vital Records Registry 240
Louisiana's Old State Capitol Museum Archives 235
Louisville Free Public Library 230
Louisville Genealogical Society & Library 230
Louisville Historical Museum 88
Louisville Historical Society 88
Louisville Historical Society Quarterly 88
Louisville Public Library 451
Louisville Public Library 88
Louks-Loucks-Loukx Family Association 282
Loup City Public Library 353
Loup County Historical Society & Library 357
Louthan-Louthen Family 517
Loutit District Library 292
Louttit Library 509
Love County Historical Society & Library 466
Love County Historical Society Newsletter 466
Love Family 603
Love Letters 19, 49
Love Library 353
Lovejoy Imprints 158
Loveland Museum Archives 88
Loveland Public Library 88
Lovell Family 379
Lovell Historical Society 248
Lovell Lineage 352
Lovely Lane Museum Archives 256
Lovett Memorial Library 555
Lovettsville Historical Museum 590
Lovettsville Historical Society & Archives 590
Lovington Public Library 384
Low Country Courier 512
LOW County Newsletter 305
Lowe Family 302
Lowe News is Good News 302
Lowell Area Historical Museum Archives 296
Lowell Area Historical Museum Newsletter 296
Lowell Damon House Museum Archives 633
Lowell Family 604
Lowell Historical Society & Archives 273
Lowell Museum and Historical Society 30
Lowell National Historical Park Library 273
Lowell Public Library 188
Lowell's Boat Shop Museum Archives 265
Lowe-Low-Lau-Louew-Lough Family 294
Lower Altamaha Historical Society & Library 129
Lower Altamaha Historical Society Newsletter 129
Lower Arkansas Valley Regional Library 87
Lower Cape Fear Historical Museum 434
Lower Cape Fear Historical Society 434
Lower Cape Fear Historical Society Newsletter 434
Lower Columbia Genealogical Society & Archives 603
Lower Columbia Genealogical Society Newsletter 603
Lower Del-Mar-Va Genealogical Society & Library 262
Lower East Side Tenement Museum Archives 407
Lower Fort Garry Museum Archives 661
Lower Hudson Conference: Historical Agencies and Museums & Library 397
Lower Hudson Conference: Historical Agencies and Museums Newsletter 397
Lower Kootenay Indian Band 649
Lower Lakes Marine Historical Society 391
Lower MacUngie Township Historical Society 505
Lower Makefield Historical Society 506
Lower Merion Historical Society 482, 501
Lower Merion Library System 481
Lower Muskingum Historical Society & Archives 459
Lower Muskogee Creek Tribe Tama Creek Tribal Town Archives 139
Lower Nicola Indian Band 652
Lower Paxton Historical Society 489
Lower Shore Genealogical Society 261
Lower Similkameen Indian Band 651
Lower White River Museum Archives 26
Lower Wisconsin River Genealogical and Historical Society 633
Lowery Newsletter 262
Lowndes County Historical and Genealogical Society 5, 6
Lowndes County Historical Museum 139
Lowndes County Historical Society 4
Lowndes County Historical Society & Archives 139
Lowndes County Historical Society Newsletter 139
Lowndes County Historical Society Publications 4
Lowrance Family 340
Lowrey Family 337
Lowrey Ledger 95
Lowry Family 40
Lowry-Ledbetter Family 214
Lowville Free Library 403
Lowville Town Historian 403
Loxahatchee Currents 114
Loxahatchee River Historical Museum 114
Loxahatchee River Historical Society & Archives 114
Loyal Edmonton Regiment Military Museum Archives 643
Loyal Legion Historical Journal 497, 498
Loyalist Cultural Centre 679
Loyalist Gazette 692
Loyalist House Museum Library 665
Loyalist Record 432
LRC Newsletter 174
Lubbock Heritage Society 552
Lubbock Public Library 552
Lubcker Family 122
Lubec Memorial Library 248
Lubicon Lake Indian Nation 645
Lucan Historical Society 310
Lucas County Chapter, OGS & Archives 458
Lucas County Genealogical Society 458
Lucas County Genealogical Society & Archives 198
Lucas County Notes and Shakin the Family Tree 198
Lucas Family 383
Lucas Ledger 383
Lucas Quarterly 66
Lucasville Area Historical Society & Library 451
Luce County Historical Museum 299
Luce County Historical Society & Archives 299
Luce-Mackinac Genealogical Society 290
Luce-Mackinac Genealogical Society Newsletter 290
Lucerne Valley Library 53
Lucius Beebe Memorial Library 281
Luck Public Library 624

Luckens-Luken(s)-Lukin(s) Newsletter 63
Luckhard Museum Archives 302
Lucky Man First Nation 710
Lucretia Vaile Museum 88
Lucus County Historical Society 198
Lucy A Phillips Library 566
Lucy Carson Memorial Library 344
Lucy Craft Laney Museum of Black History Archives 127
Lucy Craft Laney Museum of Black History Newsletter 127
Lucy Hayes Heritage Center Archives 444
Lucy Hill Patterson Memorial Library 557
Lucy Maud Montgomery Birthplace Museum Archives 695
Lucy Robbins Welles Library 97
Ludden Memorial Library 245
Ludlam-Ludlow Newsletter 311
Ludlow Lines 65
Ludwig Family 68
Ludwig Welk Farmstead Archives 439
Lufkin Genealogical and Historical Society 552
Lugo Family 55
Luke Air Force Base Library 17
Luken Family History 571
Lum and Abner Museum Archives 31
Lumber Shover 418
Lumberton Public Library 552
Lummis Historic Home 52
Lumpkin County Historical Society 129
Lumsden Heritage Museum Archives 707
Lumsden Historical Museum 707
Lumsden Historical Society & Archives 707
Luna County Historical Society & Archives 382
Luna House Historical Society 148
Luna House Museum 148
Lundar Museum Archives 660
Lundy Newsletter 242
Lundy's Lane Historical Museum Library 686
Lunenburg County Historical Society 675
Lunenburg Historical Society 273
Lunnen Family 572
Lunney Museum 518
Lupton Family 423
Luptonian 423
Lura Woodside Watkins Museum 275
Luray Historical Society & Library 218
Lurleen B Wallace State Junior College Library 1
Luseland and Districts Museum Archives 707
Lussier Family Heritage Center 625
Luther Bean Museum Archives 81
Luther Burbank Home Museum Archives 71
Luther Family Newsletter 116
Luther L Gobbel Library 528
Luther Museum and Archives 405
Luther Valley Historical Society & Archives 621
Lutheran Church-Missouri Synod Rocky Mountain District Library 81
Lutheran Historical Society Gettysburg & Library 488
Lutheran Historical Society Gettysburg Newsletter 488
Lutheran Historical Society of Eastern Pennsylvania 498
Lutje Family 146
Lutt-Lutts-Luts Seekers 222
Lutz Family 491
Lutz Mountain Meeting House Archives 664
Luzerne County Historical Museum 505
Luzerne County Historical Society & Archives 505
Lybarger Family 447
Lyceum-Alexandria's History Museum Archives 583
Lycoming County Genealogical Society & Archives 505
Lycoming County Genealogical Society Newsletter 505
Lycoming County Historical Museum 505
Lycoming County Historical Society & Archives 505
Lycoming County Historical Society News 505
Lycoming Lineage 505
Lydia Bruun Woods Memorial Library 351
Lyle Family 499
Lyle-Lile Family 335
Lyles Station Historic Preservation Society 186
Lyman County Historical Museum Archives 355
Lyman Estate Museum Archives 281
Lyman Family 95
Lyman House Memorial Museum Library 141
Lyman Newsletter 328
Lyman Public Library 353
Lyman-Brule Genealogical Society 521
Lyme Heritage Center 393
Lyme Historical Society & Archives 97
Lyme Ledger 97
Lyme Lines 442
Lyme Public Library 95
Lyme Village Historical Museum 442
Lynchburg Museum Archives 590
Lynchburg Public Library 590
Lynden Pioneer Museum Archives 603
Lyndhurst Free Public Library 372
Lyndhurst House Museum Archives 418
Lyndon B Johnson National Historical Park Library 550
Lyndon Baines Johnson Library and Museum 536
Lyndon Carnegie Library 218
Lyndon Historical Society 165, 577
Lyndon Legacy 577
Lynn Historical Society & Archives 273
Lynn Lake Mining Town Museum Archives 660
Lynn Museum 273
Lynn Public Library 274
Lynn Township Historical Society 495
Lynnfield Historical Society & Library 274
Lynnfield Public Library 274
Lynnhaven House Museum Archives 596
Lynn-Linn Lineage Quarterly 166
Lyon County Historical Museum 213, 310
Lyon County Historical Society & Archives 213, 227, 310
Lyon County Historical Society Happenings 213
Lyon County Library District 211
Lyon County Lines 213
Lyon County Museum 227
Lyon County Public Library 227
Lyon Tale 310
Lyon Township Genealogical Society & Archives 298
Lyon Township Public Library 298
Lyon(s) Family 4, 325
Lyons Depot Library 88
Lyons Falls Village Historian 403

Lyons Historical Commission 165
Lyons Historical Society & Archives 88
Lyons Memorial Library 337
Lyons Public Library 165, 218
Lyons Redstone Museum 88
Lyons School District Public Library 403
Lyonsdale Town Historian 412
Lyster House Archives 620
Lytton Indian Band 651
Lytton Museum Archives 651

M

M D Anderson Library 549
M L Harris Library 29
M P Baker Library 540
M'Njikaning First Nation 689
Ma Hush Kah Historical Society 223
Mabee Farm Historic Site Archives 414
Mabee Library 219
Mabel Hartzell Historical Home Museum Archives 441
Mabel Zoe Wilson Library 599
Mabou Gaelic and Historical Society & Library 675
Mabry-Hazen House Archives 529
Mac's Antique Car Museum Archives 470
MacAlasdair Clan 5
MacAlister Clan 46
MacArthur Clan 431
MacArthur Museum of Arkansas Military History Archives 29
Macartney House Museum Archives 249
Macartney House Museum Newsletter 249
Macaulay Clan 518
Macaulay Museum of Dental History Archives 512
MacBean Clan 83
MacBeth Clan 508
MacBride Museum Archives 713
MacBride Museum Society & Archives 713
MacCallum More Museum Archives 585
MacCallum-Malcolm Clan 424
MacCartney Clan 458
MacCord Clan 53, 382
MacCubbin Clan Lines 120
Macculloch Hall Historical Museum Archives 374
Macculloch Hall Newsletter 374
Macdonald DeWitt Library 417
MacDonald Family 81
MacDougall Clan 46, 227, 274
MacDuff Clan 542, 545
MacDuff Family 54
MacDuffee Clan 131
MacDuffee Clan of America Journal 131
MacDuffee-Macfie Clan 229
MacDuff-McDuff Family 568
MacEacain Family 338, 550
Macedon Historical Museum 404
Macedon Historical Society & Archives 404
MacEwan Newsletter 59
MacFaddien Family 517
MacFarlane Clan 9, 255, 303
MacFarlanes Lantern 255
Macfie Clan 515, 530
MacGill Family 225, 434
Macgillivray Clan 478
MacGregor Family 83
MacGunnigle Family 507
Machan House Museum 188
MAChappenings 603
Machen Family Courier 239
Machiasport Historical Museum 248
Machiasport Historical Society & Archives 248
MacInnes Clan 584
MacIntosh Clan 183, 262
MacIntyre Clan 263, 430, 599
Mackay Banner 134
MacKay Clan 134, 140, 682
MacKay Family 492
Mackenzie and District Museum Archives 652
MacKenzie Clan 3, 124
MacKenzie Heritage Museum Archives 688
Mackenzie House Museum Archives 691
Mackenzie King Estate Archives 687
MacKenzie Memorial Public Library 451
Mackey Family 555
Mackey Family Newsletter 567
Mackey-Mackie Family 257
Mackie Family 435
Mackinac Island Public Library 296
Mackinac Island State Park Library 296
Mackinaw Area Public Library 296
Mackinaw Historical Society 165
MacKinnon Clan 114
Mackintosh Clan 595
Mackley and Hume Historic Site Archives 298
Mackley and Hume Historic Site Newsletter 298
Macklin and District Museum Archives 707
Macktown Living History Center Archives 172
Macktown Living History Center Newsletter 172
MacLachlan Clan 43, 535, 595
MacLaine Clan 594, 600
MacLamroc Clan 432
MacLaren Standard 83
MacLean Clan 429, 606
MacLellan Clan 43, 233, 447, 544
MacLennan Clan 511
MacLeod Clan 548
MACline 603
Maclure Library 578
MacMillan Clan 323, 623
MacNab Clan 78
Macnachton Clan 61
Macnamara Clan 377
MacNeil Clan 8, 12, 53, 59, 112, 116, 141, 211, 228, 230, 240, 247, 261, 424, 434, 446, 478, 545, 635
MacNicol Clan 266, 281
Macomb City Public Library 165
Macomb County Genealogy Group & Archives 298
Macomb County Historical Society & Archives 298
Macomb County Historical Society Newsletter 298
Macomb Town Historian 399
Macon County Genealogical Society 9
Macon County Historical Museum 158

Macon County Historical Society 134, 334
Macon County Historical Society & Archives 158, 529
Macon County Historical Society Quarterly 529
Macon County Public Library 427, 529
Macon County Tennessee Historical Society Newsletter 529
Macon Heritage Foundation 133
Macon Public Library 334
Macoupin County Genealogical Society 174
Macoupin County Historical Society 153
Macoupin County Searcher 174
MacPhail Clan 565
MacPherson Clan 99, 136, 238
MacPherson's Mill and Farm Homestead 675
MacRae Clan 137, 311
MacRae Library 676
Macrorie Museum Archives 707
MacTavish Clan 64
MacTavish-Thompson Clan 122
MacThomas Clan 245
MacUngie Historical Society 493
Madam Brett Homestead Museum Archives 389
Madama Family 378
Madawaska Historical Society & Archives 248
Madawaska Historical Society Newsletter 248
Madawaska Public Library 248
Madden Family 447
Madden Library Update & Friendscript 45
Maddox Family 441
Madeleine Clark Wallace Library 276
Madeleine Clark Wallace Library Newsletter 276
Madeline Island Historical Museum Archives 624
Madera County Historian 53
Madera County Historical Museum 53
Madera County Historical Society & Library 53
Madera County Library 53
Madera Heritage Quarterly 53
Madill Genealogical and Historical Society 466
Madison African-American Alliance Group 6
Madison County Florida Genealogical Society 116
Madison County Genealogical and Historical Society 29
Madison County Genealogical Society 354, 451, 552
Madison County Genealogical Society & Library 158
Madison County Genealogical Society Newsletter 158, 354, 451
Madison County Genealogical Society Stalker 158
Madison County Genealogy Society & Library 209
Madison County Heritage 409
Madison County Heritage Foundation 129
Madison County Historical Museum 158, 209
Madison County Historical Society 319, 329, 590
Madison County Historical Society & Archives 158, 209, 409
Madison County Historical Society & Library 179, 233, 354, 451
Madison County Historical Society Gazette 179
Madison County Historical Society Museum Newsletter 158
Madison County Historical Society Newsletter 209
Madison County Library 590
Madison County Musings 29
Madison County Public Library 233
Madison County-Canton Public Library 319
Madison Family Newsletter 467
Madison Heights Public Library 296
Madison Historical Museum 451
Madison Historical Society & Archives 95, 451
Madison Lake Area Historical Society 310
Madison Library District 149
Madison Now & Then 95
Madison Parish Historical Society 242
Madison Parish Library 242
Madison Public Library 218, 372, 522
Madison Public Library Newsletter 372
Madison Station Historical Preservation Society 6
Madison Township Historical Society & Archives 373, 375
Madisonian 451
Madison-Jefferson County Public Library 189
Madison-Morgan Cultural Center Archives 133
Madison-Morgan Cultural Center Newsletter 133
Madisonville Heritage Center 238
Madisonville Public Library 529
Madonna House Pioneer Museum Archives 681
Madras Genealogical Society 476
Mad-River Courant 459
Maes Family 82
Maffett Memorial Library 547
Magale Library 30
Magar Zsido 445
Magazine of Albemarle County History 585
Magazine of History and Biography 612
Magazine of the Chinese Culture Association 51
Magazine of the Milwaukee County Historical Society 626
Magazine of Virginia Genealogy 594
Mageveny House Museum Archives 530
Maggie I Walker National Historic Site Archives 593
Magic Mirror 45
Magic Valley Chapter, Idaho Genealogical Society 147
Magin Family 113
Magnan Family 133
Magness Memorial Library 530
Magnetawan First Nation Public Library 680
Magnetawan Historical Museum Archives 685
Magnolia Grove-Historic House Museum Archives 5
Magnolia House Archives 539
Magnolia Manor 153
Magnolia Plantation Museum Archives 512
Magny Families Association Newsletter 101
Magny Family 408
Magoffin County Genealogical Society & Library 233
Magoffin County Historical Society & Library 233
Magoffin Home State Historic Site Archives 544
Magpie 218
Mahaffie Stagecoach Stop Museum Archives 219
Mahaffie Stagecoach Stop Museum Newsletter 219
Mahan Surname Booklet 147
Mahaney-Newlin Family 165
Mahanoy and Mahantongo Historical and Preservation Society 485
Mahanoy Area Historical Society 493
Mahasha County Historical Society & Library 206
Mahasha County Historical Society Newsletter 206
Maher-Gallen-Casey Family 339
Maher-Gauge-Thynne Family 565
Mahler Museum and History Center 442
Mahnomen County Historical Society & Library 310

Mahnomen County Historical Society Newsletter 310
Mahone Bay Founders Society & Archives 675
Mahoney Library 374
Mahoning County Chapter, OGS 442, 443, 461
Mahoning Meanderings 442, 443, 461
Mahoning Valley Historical Society & Archives 461
Mahopac Library 404
Mahwah Historical Society 372
Maidu Genealogical Society 63
Maidu Genealogical Society Newsletter 63
Maidu Interpretative Center Archives 63
Maier-Avril-Herrold-Zeltner-Vogel-Schwoder Family 594
Mail Call Journal: a Newsletter for American Civil War Enthusiasts 378
Mail Stop 378
Mailcall! 51
Maimy Etta Global Black Fine Arts Museum And Historical Society & Archives 426
Maimy Etta Historical Museum 426
Main Centre Heritage Museum Archives 707
Main Street Graham 547
Maine Aviation Historical Society 243
Maine Civil War Reinactment Society 246
Maine Department of Human Services Office of Vital Statistics 243
Maine Franco-American Genealogical Society 247
Maine Genealogical Society 246
Maine Genealogical Society Newsletter 246
Maine Genealogical Society, Pejepscot Chapter 248
Maine Genealogist 246
Maine Historical Museum 250
Maine Historical Society & Archives 250
Maine History 250
Maine Lighthouse Museum Archives 250
Maine Lighthouse Museum Newsletter 250
Maine Maritime Museum Library 243
Maine Maritime Museum Quarterly 243
Maine Military Historical Museum 243
Maine Military Historical Society & Archives 243
Maine Narrow Gauge Railroad Museum Archives 250
Maine Seine 246
Maine State Archives 243
Maine State Library 243
Maine State Museum Archives 243
Maine State Museum Quarterly 243
Maine West Historical Society 158
Maine's Franco-American Heritage 244
Maine's Swedish Colony Archives 248
Main-Mayne-Maine Gazette 19
Mains'l Haul 65
Maiorca-Maiorka Family 557
Maison Andre-Benjamin-Papineau 699
Maison d'Youville 690
Maison des Chapais 702
Maison du Citoyen 698
Maison Dumulon Museum Archives 701
Maison Hamel-Bruneau 702
Maison J A Vachon 702
Maison Lamontagne Museum Archives 701
Maison Louis-Hippolyte Lafontaine 697
Maison Medard-Bourgault 702
Maison Vittie 698
Maitland Clan 279
Maitland Historical Museum 116
Maitland Historical Museum Quarterly 116
Maitland Historical Society 116
Maitland Matters 279
Maize Maze 219
Major County Genealogical Research Library 465
Major County Genealogical Society 465, 467
Major General Frederick Funston Museum Archives 216
Major John Bradford House 273
Major John Bradford House Quarterly 273
Major(s) Family 608
Maki Library 293
Makiki Christian Church Archives 141
Making History 499
Making History Together 479
Makoti Threshers' Museum Archives 438
Makwa Sahgaiehcan First Nation 707
Malabar Farm State Park Archives 451
Malagash and Area Heritage Association 677
Malahat Indian Band 652
Malaspina University College Library 652
Malby Family 346
Malcolm Blue Historical Society & Library 423
Malden Historical Museum Archives 334
Malden Historical Society & Archives 274
Malden Historical Society Newsletter 274
Malden Public Library 274
Male Academy Museum 135
Malheur County Library 477
Malheur Historical Project 480
Malibu Lagoon Museum Archives 53
Malibu Lagoon Museum Newsletter 53
Malki Museum Archives 36
Mallet Library/Bibliotheque Mallet 510
Mallory Memorabilia 549
Mallory-Neely House Museum Archives 530
Malluege Family 563
Malory Family 334
Maloy Family 20
Malvern Public Library 204
Malverne Historical and Preservation Society 404
Mamaleleqala Qwe'Qwa'Sot'Enox Indian Band 648
Mamaroneck Historical Society 404
Mamaroneck Historical Society Newsletter 404
Mamaroneck Public Library District 404
Mamie Doud Eisenhower Birthplace Museum and Library 198
Mamie Doud Eisenhower Birthplace Museum Newsletter 198
Mamie Doud Eisenhower Public Library 82
Mamit Innuat Nation 703
Mammoth Happenings 232
Mammoth Spring State Park Depot Museum Archives 30
Man from Mainz and His Descendants 154
Managee Village Historical Park Archives 109
Manasota Genealogical Society & Library 109
Manassas Museum Archives 590
Manassas National Battlefield Park Archives 590
Manatee County Historical Society 109
Manatee County Public Library System 109
Mancelona Area Genealogy Society 296

Mancelona Area Historical Society 296
Manchester City Library 362
Manchester Community College Library 95
Manchester District Library 297
Manchester Historic Association & Library 362
Manchester Historical Museum 274
Manchester Historical Society 274, 452, 577
Manchester Historical Society & Archives 95
Manchester Historical Society & Library 274
Manchester Historical Society Newsletter 274
Manchester Public Library 95, 204
Mancil-Taft Family 135
Mandan Historical Society 438
Mandan Public Library 438
Mandarin Historical Museum 114
Mandarin Historical Society & Archives 114
Maner Memorial Library 540
Maner Messenger 540
Mangum Genealogical Society 466
Manhasset Public Library 404
Manhasset Public Library Quarterly Newsletter 404
Manhattan Beach Historical Museum 53
Manhattan Beach Historical Society & Archives 53
Manhattan Public Library 218
Manhattan Public Library District 165
Manhattan Township Historical Society 165
Manheim Heritage Center 493
Manheim Historical Society 493
Manifest 402
Manior Leboutillier 697
Manistee County Historical Museum Archives 297
Manistee County Library 297
Manistee Genealogical Society & Archives 297
Manistee Museum Log 297
Manito Historical Society 165
Manitoba Agricultural Hall of Fame Archives 659
Manitoba Agricultural Museum Archives 659
Manitoba Automobile Museum Archives 659
Manitoba Genealogical Society & Library 662
Manitoba Genealogical Society, Dauphin Branch 659
Manitoba Genealogical Society, East European Branch 662
Manitoba Genealogical Society, Prior Relations Branch 660
Manitoba Genealogical Society, Southwest Branch 659
Manitoba Genealogical Society, Swan Valley Branch 661
Manitoba Heritage Federation 659
Manitoba Historical Museum Archives 662
Manitoba Historical Society 662
Manitoba Historical Society Newsletter 662
Manitoba History 662
Manitoba Mennonite Historical Society 662
Manitou Pioneer Museum Archives 708
Manitou Springs Historical Society & Library 88
Manitou Springs Public Library 88
Manitowoc County Genealogical Society 625
Manitowoc County Historical Society & Library 625
Manitowoc County Historical Society Monographs 625
Manitowoc County Historical Society Pinecrest Spirit 625
Manitowoc Public Library 625
Manitowoc Public Library Newsletter 625
Manley Family 390
Manley Family Newsletter 390
Manlius Historical Museum 404
Manlius Historical Society & Archives 404
Mann Family 565
Manning Family 95
Mannix Family 2
Manoa Gardens Community Center 142
Manon Historical Society 189
Manor Museum 708
Mansardian 385
Mansberger Family 119
Manscen Academic Library 329
Mansell House & Gardens 125
Mansfield Area Historical Museum 334
Mansfield Area Historical Society & Archives 334
Mansfield Free Public Library 493
Mansfield Historical Museum 99, 552
Mansfield Historical Society 274, 552
Mansfield Historical Society & Archives 99, 552
Mansfield Historical Society Newsletter 274
Mansfield Public Library 274, 365
Mansfield State Historic Site Museum Archives 239
Mansfield Township Historical Museum 369
Mansfield Township Historical Society & Archives 369
Mansfield-Richland County Public Library 452
Manship House Museum Archives 320
Mansion 481
Mansion Museum 615
Mansion News 625
Mansion Notes 502
Manteca Historical Museum 53
Manteca Historical Society & Archives 53
Manteno Historical Society 165
Manti Public Library 567
Manton Area Historical Society 297
Mantor Library 246
Mantorville Restoration Association & Library 310
Manuscript Collection News 327
Mapes Family 380, 396
Maple Grove Historical Preservation Society 310
Maple Rapids Public Library 297
Maple Ridge Museum Archives 652
Maple Sugar Museum and Pioneer Home 690
Maple Syrup Museum Archives 689
Maple Valley Bugle 603
Maple Valley Historical Museum 603
Maple Valley Historical Society & Archives 603
Maplewood Area Historical Society 310
Maplewood Library News 372
Maplewood Memorial Library 372
Maplewood Public Library 334
Maquoketa Public Library 204
Marais des Cygnes Memorial Historic Site Archives 220
Maramec Museum Archives 338
Marathon County Genealogical Society 633
Marathon County Historical Society & Archives 633
Marathon County Public Library 633
Marble Chips 88
Marble Columns 91
Marble Historical Museum 88

INDEX

Marble Historical Society & Archives 88
Marble Mountain Community Museum 677
Marble Springs, Gov John Sevier Farm Home Archives 529
Marble Valley Historical Society 132
Marblehead Historical Museum 274
Marblehead Historical Society & Archives 274
Marblehead Historical Society Newsletter 274
Marblehead Light House Historical Society 450
Marcellus Free Library 404
Marcellus Historical Museum 404
Marcellus Historical Society & Archives 404
Marcellus Historical Society Newsletter 404
March Field Air Museum Archives 53
Marchant Family 565
Marcus Public Library 204
Mardi Gras Museum Archives 237, 319
Mardigian Library 289
Mare Island Historic Park Foundation 76
Marengo County Genealogical Society 3
Marengo County Historical Society & Library 3
Marengo Public Library 204
Marfa and Presidio County Museum Archives 552
Marfa Public Library 552
Margaret and Herman Brown Library 535
Margaret E Heggan Free Public Library 371
Margaret I King Library 230
Margaret Laurence Home Museum Archives 660
Margaret Mitchell House and Museum Archives 126
Margaret R Grundy Memorial Library 483
Margaret Reaney Memorial Library 415
Margaret Woolfolk Library 30
Marguerite d'Youville Museum 700
Mari Sandoz Heritage Society 350
Mari Sandoz Heritage Society Newsletter 350
Marian J Mohr Memorial Library 508
Marianist Province of the Pacific Archives 141
Marianna Black Library 424
Marianna Lee County Historical Society 30
Marianna-Lee County Museum Archives 30
Marianopolis College Library 700
Marias Museum of History Archives 346
Maricopa County Historical Society 22
Maricopa County Library District 19
Maricopa County Library District-George L Campbell Branch Library 19
Maries Countian 341
Marietta House Museum 259
Marietta Museum of History Archives 134
Marilla Historical Museum 404
Marilla Historical Society 396
Marilla Historical Society & Archives 404
Marin County Free Library 69
Marin County Genealogical Society & Archives 57
Marin County Historical Museum 69
Marin County Historical Society & Archives 69
Marin County Historical Society Bulletin 69
Marin County Historical Society Magazine 69
Marin County Historical Society Newsletter 69
Marin Heritage 69
Marin Museum of the American Indian Library 57
Marine Corps Historical Center Library 106
Marine Corps Recruit Depot Command Museum Archives 65
Marine Historical Museum 310
Marine Historical Society & Archives 310
Marine Historical Society of Detroit 294, 456
Marine History Lines 458
Marine Museum at Fall River Archives 270
Marine Museum at Fall River Quarterly 270
Marine Museum of Manitoba Archives 661
Marine Museum of the Great Lakes 684
Marine Museum of Upper Canada Archives 691
Marine Preservation Commission 310
Mariner 401
Mariners' Museum Archives 591
Mariners' Museum Newsletter 591
Mariners' Park Museum Archives 685
Marinette County Consolidated Public Library Services 625
Marinette County Historian 625
Marinette County Historical Museum 625
Marinette County Historical Society & Archives 625
Maring-Moehring Family 478
Marion and Ed Hughes Public Library 554
Marion Area Chapter, OGS 452
Marion Area Historical Society & Archives 625
Marion Carnegie Library 165
Marion City Library 218
Marion County Alabama Tracks 10
Marion County Genealogical and Historical Group 533
Marion County Genealogical and Historical Society 173
Marion County Genealogical Club & Archives 612
Marion County Genealogical Society 10, 186, 204, 218, 550
Marion County Genealogical Society & Library 204
Marion County Genealogical Society Quarterly 550
Marion County Historical and Genealogical Society 33
Marion County Historical Commission 27
Marion County Historical Museum 452, 479
Marion County Historical Society 186, 229, 319, 516
Marion County Historical Society & Archives 452, 479
Marion County Historical Society Newsletter 516
Marion County History 479
Marion County Library 33, 516, 612
Marion County Museum Archives 516
Marion County Newsletter 204
Marion County Public Library 229
Marion County-Indianapolis Historical Society 186
Marion County-Indianapolis Historical Society Circular 186
Marion Heritage Center Archives 205
Marion Historical Museum Library 218
Marion Memories 452
Marion Public Library & Museum 189
Marion Public Library System 118
Marion-Adams Historical and Genealogical Society 193
Marion-Perry County Library 6
Mariposa County Historical Museum 53
Mariposa County Historical Society 53
Mariposa County Library 53
Marissa Historical and Genealogical Society 165
Maritime and Yachting Museum Newsletter 122
Maritime and Yachting Museum of the Treasure Coast Archives 122
Maritime Command Museum Archives 674
Maritime Currents 70

Maritime Industry Museum at Fort Schuyler 390
Maritime Museum 609
Maritime Museum Library 423
Maritime Museum of British Columbia 657
Maritime Museum of Monterey Library 55
Maritime Museum of San Diego Archives 65
Maritime Museum of the Atlantic Archives 674
Marjorie Kinnan Rawlings Historic State Park Archives 111
Mark and Emily Turner Memorial Library 250
Mark and Helen Osterlin Library 303
Mark O Hatfield Library 479
Mark Twain Birthplace State Historic Site Archives 329
Mark Twain Birthplace State Historic Site Library 341
Mark Twain Home Museum Archives 330
Mark Twain House and Museum Archives 94
Mark Twain House and Museum Quarterly 94
Mark Twain Library 98
Marked Tree Historical Society 30
Marker Family 71
Markesan Historical Society & Archives 625
Markham Family 569
Markham Museum and Historic Village Archives 685
Markham Public Libraries 685
Markle Area Historical Society 186
Markle Family 194
Markley Family 441
Markofski Family 618
Marks-Merck Family 276
Marks-Quitman County Library 321
Marktown Preservation Society 182
Markwell Family 607
Markwell Newsletter 607
Marland's Grand Home Museum Archives 469
Marlboro County Library 511
Marlboro Free Library 404
Marlboro Historical Museum 577
Marlboro Historical Society & Archives 577
Marlboro Historical Society Newsletter 577
Marlboro Library Grapevine 404
Marlborough County Historical Preservation Commission & Library 511
Marlborough Historical Museum 511
Marlborough Historical Society 95
Marlborough Historical Society & Archives 511
Marlborough Historical Society & Library 274
Marlborough Historical Society Newsletter 274, 511
Marlborough Public Library 274
Marlette District Library 297
Marley Family Newsletter 218
Marmarth Historical Society 346
Marney Monitor Newsletter 529
Marois Family 596
Marostica Surname Organization 89
Marple Newtown Historical Society 483
Marple Newtown Historical Society Newsletter 483
Marple Public Library 483
Marpole Museum and Historical Society 656
Marquardt Family 184
Marquee 47
Marquette County Genealogical Society & Archives 297
Marquette County Historical Museum Archives 297
Marquette County Historical Society & Library 634
Marquette Heights Public Library 165
Marquette Historical Society 218
Marrett House Archives 251
Marringhurst Pioneer Park Museum Archives 660
Marriott Library 571
Mars Bluff Society 514
Marseilles Public Library 165
Marshall Area Historical Society 625
Marshall Center School Museum Archives 198
Marshall Community Library 625
Marshall County Genealogical and Historical Society & Archives 225
Marshall County Genealogical and Historical Society Newsletter 225
Marshall County Genealogical Society 180, 192
Marshall County Historical Center 192
Marshall County Historical Museum 192, 316, 320
Marshall County Historical Quarterly 529
Marshall County Historical Society 320, 439, 529
Marshall County Historical Society & Archives 192, 316, 320
Marshall County Historical Society & Library 164, 218
Marshall County Historical Society News 320
Marshall County Historical Society Newsletter 164
Marshall County Historical Society Quarterly 192
Marshall County Memorial Library 529
Marshall County Public Library 225
Marshall County Roots and Branches 192
Marshall Family 528, 571
Marshall Gold Discovery State Historic Park Archives 41
Marshall Historical Society & Archives 297
Marshall N Dana Memorial Library 477
Marshall Point Lighthouse Museum Archives 250
Marshall Public Library 149, 335, 553
Marshall Street Historical Society 267
Marshall W Butt Library 592
Marshall W Hamilton Library 116
Marshalltown Public Library 205
Marshfield Area Genealogy Group & Library 625
Marshfield Historical Society 270
Marshfield Public Library 625
Marshland to Heartland 456
Marston Family 116, 309
Marston House Archives 65
Marston House Museum 66
Marston Memorial Historical Center 187
Marstons Mills Public Library 274
Martello Magazine 115
Marten River Logging Museum Archives 685
Martha A Parsons House Museum Archives 93
Martha Canfield Memorial Free Library 575
Martha's Vineyard Historical Society & Archives 270
Martha's Vineyard Historical Society Messenger 270
Martiau Family 77, 424, 477
Martin and Osa Johnson Safari Museum Archives 212
Martin County Community College Library 434
Martin County Genealogical Society 122, 193, 434
Martin County Genealogical Society & Archives 308
Martin County Genealogical Society Newsletter 122
Martin County Historical Museum Archives 560
Martin County Historical Museum Newsletter 560
Martin County Historical Society 193

INDEX

Martin County Historical Society & Archives 308, 434
Martin County Historical Society Newsletter 308
Martin County Library 308
Martin County Library System 122
Martin County Museum Archives 193
Martin County Public Library 229
Martin Family 32, 260, 296, 514, 542, 591
Martin Family News 205
Martin Historian 554
Martin Luther King Jr Center for Nonviolent Social Change 126
Martin Luther King Jr National Historic Site Archives 126
Martin Luther King Memorial Library 106
Martin Mysteries 292
Martin Township Public Library 157
Martin Van Buren National Historic Site Archives 402
Martinez Historical Society 53
Martins Ferry Public Library 452
Martinsburg Community Library 493
Martinsburg Town Historian 403
Martinsburg-Berkeley County Public Library 613
Martinsville-Henry County Historical Society 590
Martius Museum 452
Martyrs' Shrine Archives 685
Marum Family 19
Marvin Newton House Museum 575
Marvin Samson Center for Pharmacy History Archives 498
Mary and Jeff Bell Library 541
Mary and John Gray Library 537
Mary B Blount Library 586
Mary Ball Washington Museum and Library 589
Mary Ball Washington Museum Newsletter 589
Mary Barnett Memorial Library 202
Mary Cotton Public Library 221
Mary Couts Burnett Library 545
Mary D Edwards Public Library 101
Mary E Seymour Memorial Free Library 417
Mary Evelyn Blagg-Huey Library 543
Mary F Shipper Library 613
Mary Fuller Frazier School Community Library 496
Mary Gage Rice Museum 249
Mary H Weir Public Library 615
Mary Illick Memorial Library 486
Mary L Cook Public Library 459
Mary Lou Johnson-Hardin County District Library 450
Mary M Arron Memorial Museum Archives 53
Mary March Regional Museum and Logging Exhibition 667
Mary McLeod Bethune Museum Archives 106
Mary Miller Smiser Heritage Library 342
Mary Norton Clapp Library 52
Mary Riley Styles Public Library 587
Mary S Biesecker Public Library 502
Mary Todd Lincoln House Archives 230
Mary Washington House Museum Archives 588
Mary Wood Weldon Memorial Library 228
Maryfield Museum Archives 708
Maryland Genealogical Society & Library 256
Maryland Genealogical Society Bulletin 256
Maryland Genealogical Society Newsletter 256
Maryland Heights Historical Society 339
Maryland Historian 258
Maryland Historical Magazine 256
Maryland Historical Society & Library 256
Maryland Historical Society Museum 256
Maryland Historical Society, News and Notes 256
Maryland Historical Trust 258
Maryland Historical Trust & Library 258
Maryland Magazine of Genealogy 256
Maryland Manual 255
Maryland State Archives 255
Maryland State Library 255
Maryland Steam Historical Society 263
Maryland TMG Users Group 260
Marymoor Museum Archives 605
Marystown Museum Archives 667
Marysville Public Library 218, 452
Maryville Public Library 335
Mascoutah Historical Society 166
Mascoutah Historical Society Newsletter 166
Mascroft-Mascraft Family 276
Mashantucket Pequot Museum & Research Center Archives 95
Masillon Museum Archives 452
Maskwachees Cultural College 644
Mason City Public Library 205
Mason County District Library 296
Mason County Genealogical and Historical Society 162
Mason County Genealogical and Historical Society 612
Mason County Genealogical Society 205, 296, 602, 607
Mason County Genealogical Society & Library 231
Mason County Genealogical Society Newsletter 231
Mason County Historical Museum 231, 553
Mason County Historical Society 231
Mason County Historical Society & Archives 296, 553, 607
Mason County Historical Society Newsletter 607
Mason County LDS Genealogical Project 162
Mason County LDS Genealogical Project Newsletter 162
Mason County Library Board 614
Mason County Museum 231
Mason County Public Library 231
Mason Depot Museum 625
Mason Dixon Historical Society 264
Mason Family 487, 585
Mason Historical Society 297
Mason Historical Society & Archives 452
Mason Library 271
Mason Memorial Public Library 153
Mason Memories 296
Mason Public Library 452
Masoner Family 464
Masonic Grand Lodge & Library 438, 562, 662
Masonic Library & Museum of Pennsylvania Archives 498
Masonic Library and Museum of Indiana 184
Masonic Public Library of Hawaii 141
Masonic Resources 292
Masontown Historical Society 493
Masontown Public Library 493
Mason-Wood Family 572
Massac County Genealogical Society 166
Massac County Historical Society 166
Massachusetts Genealogical Council 269
Massachusetts Genealogical Council Newsletter 269

Massachusetts Historical Commission 267
Massachusetts Historical Museum 267
Massachusetts Historical Review 267
Massachusetts Historical Society & Archives 267
Massachusetts Historical Society Miscellany 267
Massachusetts Historical Society Proceedings 267
Massachusetts Society of Genealogists 265, 283
Massachusetts Society of Mayflower Descendants & Library 267
Massachusetts State Archives and Library 267
Massachusetts State Library 267
Massacre Rocks State Park Archives 145
Massanutten Regional Library 589
Massapequa Historical Society 404
Massasoit Historical Association 509
Massena Historical Association & Archives 404
Massena Historical Museum 404
Massey Area Museum Archives 685
Massey Family 331, 423
Massey-Heath-Cunningham Family 498
Massillon Public Library 452
MASSOG: A Genealogical Magazine for the Commonwealth of Massachusetts 283
Mass-Pocha 276
Masterson Family Newsletter and Historical Journal 114
Mastics-Moriches-Shirley Community Library 416
Mastics-Moriches-Shirley Community Library Newsletter 416
Mastroianni-Mastone Family 96
Matagorda County Genealogical Society & Library 537
Matagorda County Museum Archives 537
Matagorda County Musings 537
Matawan Historical Society 373
Matawan Historical Society Newsletter 373
Matchaponix Journal 369, 378
Matchbox Road Museum Archives 374
Matchless Mine Museum Archives 87
Mather Homestead Museum Archives 420
MATHER Matters 445
Matheson Clan 339, 548
Matheson Historical Center Library 113
Mathews County Historical Society 590
Mathews Maritime Foundation 591
Mathias Ham House 201
Mathias Ham House Historic Site Archives 201
Mathias Ham House Newsletter 201
Matilda J Gibson Memorial Library 199
Matney Family 545
Matson Family 336, 353
Matson Public Library 171
Matsqui Indian Band 652
Matsqui-Sumas Abbotsford Museum Society & Library 647
Matt's Museum Archives 238
Mattaliano-Lumpkin-Heiderer-Shoe Family 599
Mattapoisett Historical Society & Archives 274
Mattatuck Historical Museum 100
Mattatuck Historical Society & Archives 100
Mattawa and District Museum Archives 685
Mattawa District Historical Society 685
Matteson Bell 166
Matteson Historical Society 166
Matthew Edel Blacksmith Shop Archives 203
Matthews Covered Bridge Historical Society 189
Matthews Family 167, 267
Matthews Family Newsletter 76
Matthews Historical Society 189
Matthews Museum of Maine Heritage Archives 252
Mattie Logsdon Memorial Library 463
Mattituck Historical Society 404
Mattole Valley Historical Society 60
Mattoon Public Library 166
Mattye Reed African Heritage Center Archives 427
Maturango Museum 62
Maturango Museum of Indian Wells Valley Archives 40
Mauch Chunk Historical Society 490
Maud Preston Palenske Memorial Library 302
Maud Shunk Public Library 626
Mauger-Roseborough-McIntosh Family 343
Maui Community College Library 142
Maui Genealogical Society 142
Maui Historical Society & Archives 143
Mauldin Family News 470
Maumee Valley Antique Steam and Gas Engines Associates 190
Maumee Valley Historical Society & Archives 452
Mauney Memorial Library 429
Maupin Family 216, 529
Maurath Family 153
Maureen and Mike Mansfield Library 346
Maurer-Brill-Geissinger-Mower Family 635
Mauricetown Historical Society 373
Maury County Historical Society & Library 526
Maury County Historical Society Newsletter 526
Maury County Public Library 526
Maury County Public Library-Mount Pleasant Branch 530
Mausolf Family 285
Max Milam Library 31
Maxfield Family 567
Maxton Historical Society 430
Maxwell Clan 528
Maxwell Community Historical Museum Archives 205
Maxwell Family 572
Maxwell News 149
Maxwell Public Library 205
May Family 426, 565, 566
May H Baker Memorial Library 504
May Museum Archives 426
Maybee Family 601
Maybee-Simpson Library 25
Mayberry-Gadberry Family 55
Mayberry-Maberry-Mabry Family 594
Mayer Notebook 292
Mayes County Genealogical Society 464
Mayes County Genealogical Society Newsletter 464
Mayes County Historical Society 464
Mayfield Township Historical Society & Library 452
Mayfield Township Historical Society Newsletter 452
Mayflower Descendant: A Magazine of Pilgrim Genealogy and History 267
Mayflower Descendants Historical Museum 277
Mayflower Descendants Society of California & Library 57
Mayflower Society of Florida 120
Mayflower Society Quarterly 277
Mayland Community College Library 433

Maymont Museum Archives 594
Maymont Newsletter 594
Maynard Family 12
Maynard Public Library 274
Maynardville Public Library 530
Mayne Island Museum Archives 652
Mayo Historical Society 713
Mayrand Family News 67
Mays-Mace-Mase Family 492
Maysville and Mason County Historical and Scientific Society 231
Maysville Community College Library 231
Maytown Historical Society 493
Mayville Area Museum of History and Genealogical Library 297
Mayville Area Museum of History and Genealogy Newsletter 297
Mayville Historical Museum 625
Mayville Historical Society 297
Mayville Historical Society & Archives 625
Mayville Historical Society Newsletter 625
Mayville Limestone School Museum Archives 625
Maywood Historical Society 166
Maywood Public Library 166
Mazomanie Free Library 625
Mazomanie Historical Museum 626
Mazomanie Historical Society & Archives 626
Mazomanie Historical Society Newsletter 626
Mazuran-Burkinshaw Family 567
McAdams Historical Society 72
McAdams Historical Society Newsletter 72
McAfee Library 336
McAlester Public Library 466
McAlister Clan 5
McAlister Newsletter 262
McAlister-McAllister Family 135
McAllen Genealogical Society & Archives 553
McAllen Memorial Library 553
McAllister House Museum Archives 82
McAllister-Carson-Harvey-Lindsay Family 549
McAlpin Clan 432
McAninch Family History Newsletter 47
McArdle Family 39
McArthur Public Library 244
McArtor Family Historical Review 155
McAtee Family 588
McBride Family 567
McBurney Family News 541
McBurney Newsletter 50
McBurney-Patterson Family 441
McCabe Library 503
McCain Library 320, 514
McCain-Whitehead Family 206
McCall City Library 148
McCall Family 502
McCallum Museum 207
McCallum's Museum Archives 659
McCallus Family 482
McCann Family 345, 571
McCanna Family 159
McCarroll-Longbotham-Bower Family 559
McCarthy Family 420
McCartney Family 290
McCarty Mills Gazette 151
McCauley Family 385
McChord Air Museum Archives 608
McClain County Historical Museum 469
McClain County Oklahoma Historical and Genealogical Society Quarterly 469
McClanahan Family 533
McCleave-Miller-Bond-Bates-Mouser Family 195
McClellan Aviation Museum Archives 53
McClendon House Archives 561
McClendon, McLendon Family Association Newsletter 62
McClintock Family 70
McClintock-Ensminger Library 10
McClung Family Association Journal 181
McClung Family Newsletter 341
McCollum-Chidester House Museum 26
McComack Family 170
McComb Public Library 452
McConaghy House Archives 47
McCone County Museum Archive 344
McConnaughey Bulletin 187
McConnell Area Historical Society 166
McConnell Family 21
McConnell Mansion 148
McConnell Mansion Archives 148
McCook Army Air Base Historical Society 354
McCook County Historical Museum 523
McCook County Historical Society & Archives 523
McCook House Civil War Museum 443
McCord and District Museum Archives 708
McCord Family 16
McCord Family Association Newsletter 16
McCord Memorial Library 496
McCormick Clan 429
McCormick County Historical Commission 516
McCormick County Historical Society 516
McCormick-Reid-Casebolt-Wooldridge-Haymore-Cook-McConnell-Douglas-Bottoms Family 571
McCosh Clan 211
McCoy Family 18
McCoy House Museum 492
McCoy House Museum Archives 492
McCoy Memorial Library 166
McCracken County Genealogical Society 232
McCracken County Public Library 232
McCracken Public Library 218
McCrary-Eslinger-Wallace Family 604
McCraw Family 7, 119, 342, 490, 559
McCrea Network Newsletter 117
McCreary County Public Library District 234
MCCS Base Library 142
McCubbin, Cubbin-McKibbon Clan Newsletter 77
McCuistion-Turk Family 532
McCullah-Wasson Family 325
McCullen Family 297
McCulley Family 539
McCullough-McCulloch Newsletter 85
McCune Family 487
McCurdy Family 83
McCurdy Family Association Newsletter 282
McCurtain County Genealogy Society & Library 466

McCutchen Newsletter 595
McCutchen Overland Inn Archives 453
McCutchen Overland Inn Newsletter 453
McDade Historical Museum 553
McDade Historical Society & Archives 553
McDaniel Family 19, 38, 62
McDavitt Family 337
McDermott Library 90
McDole-Joyce-Tyre Family 137
McDonald County Library 337
McDonald Family 565, 592
McDonald's #1 Store Museum Archives 158
McDonough County Genealogical Society 165
McDonough County Genealogical Society News Quarterly 165
McDonough County Historical Society 165
McDougal Family 354
McDougall Mill Museum Archives 689
McDowell County Public Library 430
McDowell House Museum Archives 226
McDowell Public Library 615
McDuffie County Historical Society 138
McElroy Family 618
McEntegart Hall Library 391
McEuen Family 399
McEver Family 469
McEwen-Samuels-Marr House 181
McFaddin-Ward House Archives 537
McFaddin-Ward House Newsletter 537
McFarland Curatorial Center 346, 347
McFarland Family 535
McFarland Historical Museum 626
McFarland Historical Society & Archives 626
McFarland Historical Society Newsletter 626
McFarland Historical State Park Archives 16
McFarland House Museum Archives 686
McFarlane Family 543
McFarlin Library 470
McFatridge Family 529
McFatridge Family Newsletter 529
McGahen-McGhan-McGhen-McGahn-McGahan Family 493
McGalliard Family 431
McGarry Family 447
McGaw Library 232
McGee Family 47
McGee Newsletter 60
McGill Family News 532
McGill University Libraries 700
McGillis Pioneer Home Archives 710
McGowan Family 603
McGowan House 621
McGrady Family 450
McGrady News 84
McGrath Community Library 13
McGrath Family 371
McGraw Family 594
McGraw-Page Library 584
McGray Family 278
McGray Family Newsletter 278
McGregor Family 20, 168
McGregor Public Library 205
McGuire Air Force Base Library 373
McHenry County College Library 157
McHenry County Genealogical Society 157
McHenry County Historical Museum 176
McHenry County Historical Society & Archives 176
McHenry County Illinois Connection 166
McHenry County Illinois Connection Newsletter 157
McHenry County Illinois Connection Quarterly 157
McHenry County Illinois Genealogical Society 166
McHenry Library 70, 166
McHenry Museum and Historical Society & Archives 54
McHenry Museum Quarterly 54
McIlhaney Family 470
McIntire-Mendenhall Family 258
McIntosh County Historical Museum 437
McIntosh County Historical Society & Archives 437
McIntosh County Lake Eufaula Area Genealogical Society 465
McIntosh County Lake Eufaula Area Genealogical Society Newsletter 465
McIver's Grant Public Library 527
McKay Clan 106
McKay Family 143
McKay Library 149, 286
McKay-MacKay Family 265
McKays Museum Archives 659
McKean County Genealogical Society 486
McKean County Historical Society & Library 502
McKee Family 300
McKee Library 526
McKeesport Carnegie Free Library 493
McKeesport Heritage Center Archives 493
McKeever Family Association Newsletter 189
McKeldin Library 258
McKelvey Family 58
McKenney Family 89
McKenzie County Historical Society & Archives 440
McKenzie Family 572
McKenzie Memorial Library 530
McKenzie-Doering Family 215
McKenzie-McKenzie Family 550
McKillop Library 508
McKinley Birthplace Home Museum Archives 454
McKinley Memorial Library 454
McKinley Presidential Library & Museum 443
McKinley Presidential Library Newsletter 443
McKinney Memorial Public Library 553
McKinney-Corley Family 550
McKinnon-MacKinnon Family 116
McKune-Comfort Family 370
McKusick Family 279
McLain Family 304
McLaren Clan 542
McLarty Treasure Museum Archives 123
McLean County Genealogical Society & Archives 152
McLean County Genealogical Society & Library 168, 438
McLean County Genealogical Society Newsletter 168
McLean County Historical Museum 439
McLean County Historical Society & Archives 152, 439
McLean Historical Society & Archives 553
McLean Mill Museum Archives 653
McLean-Alanreed Area Museum 553

McLean-Mercer Regional Library 439
McLemore Family 8
McLendon Library 322
McLeod County Historical Society & Library 309
McLeod County Historical Society Newsletter 309
McLeod Family 134
McLeod Lake Indian Band 652
McLouth-Pratt Family 541
McMahan Family 529
McMakin Family 466
McMillan Memorial Library 634
McMinn County Living Heritage Museum Archives 525
McMinn Historical Society 525
McMinnville Public Library 476
McNair Family 148
McNair Memories 549
McNamara House Museum Archives 562
McNatt Ancestry 554
McNaughton-Hearon Family 516
McNees Family 604
McNeil Family 237
McNew-Carroll-Hockett Family 540
McPherson County Historical Society 218, 357
McPherson County Old Mill Museum Archives 217
McPherson Genealogy Club 218
McPherson Museum Archives 218
McPherson Museum Newsletter 218
McPherson Public Library 218
McPherson-Capps Family 427
McQuade-Cooper-McGinn-Irons-Cilley-Bastable Family 542
McRae Family 128
McSpedon Family Newsletter 92
McSween-MacSwene-John Edwards-Guillot-Guillo(w) Family 265
McVay, McVeigh, McVey Family 322
McWethy-Detamore Family 169
McWh*rter Genealogy Newsletter 92
McWherter Library 530
McWilliams Family 636
MD and PA Railroad Preservation and Historical Society 256
Mead Public Library 631
Meade County Historian 218
Meade County Historical Museum 218
Meade County Historical Society & Archives 218
Meade County Public Library 226
Meader Family Association Newsletter 389
Meadow Brook Hall Museum Archives 301
Meadow Garden Historic House Museum Archives 127
Meadow Lake Museum Archives 708
Meadow Lake Tribal Council 708
Meadowlands Museum Archives 377
Meadowlands Museum Newsletter 377
Meadows Family 562
Meadows Heritage Newsletter 190
Meadows Library 4
Meaford Museum Archives 685
Meagher County City Library 347
Meagher County Historical Association & Archives 347
Meagher County Historical Museum 347
Meaney Family 445
Meanskinisht Museum Archives 651
Mears Library 523
Measures Family 531
Meates Family 529
Mechanicsburg Area Public Library 493
Mechanicsburg Museum Archives 493
Mechanicsburg Museum Association Newsletter 493
Mechanicville District Public Library 404
Mechling-Mechlin-Macklin Family 584
Mecklenburg Historical Association 425
Mecklenburg Messenger 425
Mecosta County Genealogical Society 286
Mecosta County Historical Museum 286
Mecosta County Historical Society 286
Medaille College Library 391
Medal of Honor Historical Society 333
Medallion 537
Medfield Historical Society & Library 274
Medford Historical Society 274, 373
Medford Library 516
Medford Public Library 274
Mediaevalia 295, 389
Medicine Hat Municipal Library 645
Medicine Hat Museum Archives 645
Medicine Lodge Historical Society 218
Medieval & Renaissance Texts & Studies 21
Medieval Academy of America 268
Medieval Association of the Pacific 40
Medieval Encounters 266
Medieval History Journal 74
Medina Community Library 553
Medina County District Library 453
Medina County Genealogical Society 453
Medina County Historical Society & Archives 453
Medina County Historical Society Newsletter 453
Medina County Story 453
Medina Railroad Museum Archives 404
Medina Railroad Museum Newsletter 404
Medora Centennial Commission 439
Medora Doll House Museum Archives 439
Medway Historical Society 274
Medway Public Library 274
Mee Family 544
Meeker County Historical and Genealogical Society & Archives 310
Meeker County Historical Museum 310
Meeker County Historical Society Newsletter 310
Meeker Family 146, 463
Meeker Mansion 605
Meeker Newsletter 178, 458
Meese-Meece Family 380
Meeteetse Museum Archives 637
Meeteetse Museum Newsletter 637
Meeting Notice Letter 276
Meetinghouse Galleries Archives 103
Meetinghouse Museum 252
Mefford Memories 202
Megaphone 455
Meherrin Regional Library 589
Meigs County Genealogical Society & Library 455
Meigs County Historical Museum 455
Meigs County Pioneer and Historical Society & Archives 455

Meigs Historian 455
Meints Family 337
Meiser, Miser, Mizar, Mizer, Myser, Myzer, Meisser Museum 454
Mel Fisher Maritime Heritage Museum 115
Mel Fisher Maritime Heritage Society & Archives 115
Mel Harrison Memorial Library 111
Melanson Family 41
Melbourne Campus Library 117
Melbourne Public Library 117
Melfort and District Museum Archives 708
Melick Library 159
Mellen Area Historical Museum 626
Mellen Area Historical Society & Archives 626
Mellette County Historical Society 351
Mellette House Museum Archives 524
Melrose Area Historical Society 310
Melrose Family 151, 606
Melrose Park Historical Society & Library 166
Melrose Plantation Home Archives 239
Melrose Public Library 274
Melting Pot 153
Melting Pot Genealogical Society 28, 29
Melting Pot Genealogical Society Newsletter 28
Melting Pot: A Genealogy Newsletter for Mohr Moore and Maurer Names 73
Melvil Dewey Library 420
Melville Heritage Museum Archives 708
Melville Railway Museum Archives 708
Melville-Qulin Historical Society 337
Melvin Gelman Library 106
Member Matters 479
Membership Roster and Directory 499
Memorial Day Museum Archives 420
Memorial Foundation of the Germanna Colonies 586
Memorial Hall Library 265
Memorial Hall Museum 269
Memorial Library 223, 269, 310
Memorial Library of Little Valley 403
Memorial Library of Nazareth 495
Memorial Library of Radnor Township 504
Memorial Library Quarterly Newsletter 310
Memorial Museum Archives 305
Memorial Presbyterian Church Greenhoe Library 297
Memorial Public Library of the Borough of Alexandria 481
Memorial University 668
Memorial University of Newfoundland 668
Memorial War Museum Archives 663
Memories 61
Memory Lane 169
Memory Lane Gazette 298
Memoryville USA 338
Memos From Mary 53
Memphis Belle B17 Flying Fortress Museum Archives 530
Memphis Pink Palace Museum Library 530
Memphis Theological Seminary Library 530
Memphis-Shelby County Public Library Center 530
Memphremagog Historical Society 578
Menahga Area Historical Museum 311
Menahga Area Historical Society & Archives 311
Menard Genealogical Society 553
Menasha Historical Society 626
Menasha Historical Society Resource Center 626
Menaul Historical Library of the Southwest 381
Menczer Museum of Medicine and Dentistry Archives 94
Mendenhall Family 21, 553
Mendham Borough Library 373
Mendham Township Library 373
Mendham Township Library Newsletter 373
Mendham Township Public Library 368
Mendocino Coast Genealogical Society & Library 45
Mendocino County Historical Society & Archives 75
Mendocino County Historical Society Newsletter 75
Mendocino County Library 76
Mendocino County Library-Willits Branch 78
Mendocino County Museum Archives 78
Mendocino Historical Research & Archives 53
Mendocino Historical Review 53
Mendon Township Library 297
Mendota Historical Museum 166
Mendota Historical Society & Archives 166
Mendota-West Saint Paul Historical Society 311
Menges Family 441
Menifee County Public Library 228
Menifee County Roots 228
Menige Family 99
Menlo Park Historical Association 53
Menlo Park Public Library 54
Menlo Public Library 205
Menning Family 202
Mennisenk 412
Menno Simons Historical Library and Archives 589
Mennonite Family History 494
Mennonite Family History Library 486
Mennonite Heritage 166
Mennonite Heritage Center 489
Mennonite Heritage Centre 662
Mennonite Heritage Museum 214
Mennonite Heritage Museum Archives 214, 710
Mennonite Heritage Village Archives 661
Mennonite Historian 662
Mennonite Historians of Eastern Pennsylvania & Library 489
Mennonite Historians of Eastern Pennsylvania Newsletter 489
Mennonite Historians of Eastern Pennsylvania Quarterly 489
Mennonite Historical and Genealogical Society of Oregon 479
Mennonite Historical Bulletin 184
Mennonite Historical Library 442
Mennonite Historical Library & Archives 219
Mennonite Historical Society 184
Mennonite Historical Society of Alberta 641
Mennonite Historical Society of Saskatchewan 710
Mennonite Immigrant Historical Foundation & Archives 214
Mennonite Life 219
Mennonite Quarterly Review 184
Mennonite Quilting Center Museum Archives 62
Mennonite Weekly Review 502
Menominee County Historical Museum 297
Menominee County Historical Society & Archives 297
Menominee County Historical Society Newsletter 297
Menomonee Falls Historical Society & Archives 626
Menomonee Falls Historical Society Newsletter 626
Menotomy 265

INDEX

Mentor Public Library 453
Menzies Clan 424
Mequon Historical Society 626, 632
Meramec Station Historical Society 341
Meramec Valley Genealogical and Historical Society 336
Merced County Genealogical Society & Library 54
Merced County Historical Society & Library 54
Merced County Library 54
Merced Old County Courthouse Museum 54
Mercedes Memorial Library 553
Mercer Area Historical Museum 626
Mercer Area Historical Society & Archives 626
Mercer Carnegie Library 151
Mercer Castle Museum 486
Mercer County Genealogical and Historical Society 611
Mercer County Genealogical and Historical Society & Archives 151, 337
Mercer County Genealogical and Historical Society & Library 614
Mercer County Genealogical and Historical Society Quarterly 151
Mercer County Genealogical Society 443
Mercer County Genealogical Society & Library 501
Mercer County Genealogical Society Newsletter 501
Mercer County Heritage 494
Mercer County Historical Museum 494
Mercer County Historical Society & Archives 443, 494
Mercer County Historical Society & Library 437
Mercer County Historical Society Newsletter 443
Mercer County Historical Society, Genealogical Division & Archives 151
Mercer County Library 337, 372
Mercer County Monitor 443
Mercer County Public Library 228
Mercer Dateline 614
Mercer Family 45, 114, 532
Mercer Family Historian Newsletter 549
Mercer Mosiac 486
Mercer University Library 133
Merchant's House Museum Newsletter 408
Merchantville School and Public Library 373
Mercury 255
Meredith Historical Society 362
Meredith House Museum 257
Meredith Public Library 362
Meredosia Area Historical and Genealogical Society 166
Mergy Family 459
Meriam Library 40
Mericle Family 39
Meriden Historical Museum 95
Meriden Historical Society 95
Meriden Historical Society Quarterly 95
Meriden Library 362
Meriden Public Library 95
Meridian District Library 148
Meridian-Lauderdale County Public Library 321
Merier-Gourley-Roark Family 127
Merito 83, 89
Meriwether Connections 65, 121
Meriwether Historical Society 131
Meriwether Lewis Dredge Museum Archives 350
Meriwether Lewis National Monument Archives 528
Meriwether Society 229
Merlet Family 258
Merner-Pfeiffer Library 525
Merrehope Archives 321
Merrell Family 52
Merriam-Gilbert Public Library 282
Merrick County Historical Society 350
Merrick Family 67
Merrick Library 404
Merrick Public Library 268
Merrile Family 123
Merrill District Library 297
Merrill Family 271
Merrill Historical Society & Archives 626
Merrill Library 248, 567
Merrill Memorial Library 253
Merrill Memorial Library Newsletter 253
Merrill Museum Archives 319
Merrill Roots and Branches 235
Merrill-Holcomb-Mason-Mills-Buck-Lewis Family 555
Merrillville-Ross Township Historical Society 189
Merrimac Public Library 274
Merrimack Historical Society 362
Merrimack Society Of Genealogists 360
Merrimack Society of Genealogists & Library 360
Merritt Family 20, 606
Merry Brook School Museum 210
Mershon Family 332
Mershon Newsletter 123, 223
Mervyn H Sterne Library 2
Merwin Family 483
Merwin House-Tranquility-Museum Archives 280
Mesa County Genealogical Society & Library 85
Mesa County Historical Society 85
Mesa County Historical Society Bulletin 85
Mesa County Public Library 85
Mesa Dwellers 85
Mesa Genealogical Society 17
Mesa Historical Museum 17
Mesa Historical Society 17
Mesa Historical Society Newsletter 17
Mesa Regional Family History Center 17
Mesa Southwest Museum Archives 17
Mesa Verde National Park Museum Archives 88
Mescalero Apache Cultural Center Archives 384
Mesenbring-Bratthaver Family 349
Meserve Family 283
Mesquite Historical and Genealogical Society 553
Mesquite Historical and Genealogical Society Newsletter 553
Mesquite Public Library 553
Mesquite Tree 553
Message from the Chairman 367
Messecar Surname Organization 92
Messenger 161, 177, 385, 406, 585
Messier Library 377
Messner Family 15, 21
Metamora Courthouse Historic Site Archives 166
Metcalf Family 364
Metcalfe County Historical Society 227, 233
Metcalfe County Public Library 227
Metchosin School Museum Archives 657
Metherell Family 560

Methodist Archives 329
Methodist Commission on Archives and History & Archives 103
Methodist Historical Center 497
Methodist History 353, 372
Methuen Historical Society 274
Metis Aboriginal Association 689
Metis Association of the Northwest Territories 671
Metlakatla Indian Band 654
Metropolis Public Library 166
Metropolitan Historic Structures Association 407
Metropolitan Historic Structures Association Newsletter 407
Metropolitan Library System 468
Metropolitan Library System-Downtown Library 468
Metropolitan Memorial United Methodist Church Library 106
Metropolitan Toronto Police Museum Archives 691
MetroScene 446
Mettlin Family 6
Metuchen Public Library 373
Metuchen-Edison Genealogy Club 369
Metuchen-Edison Historical Society 373
Metuchen-Edison Regional Historical Society 373
Metzgar-Putterbaugh Family 454
Meux Home Gazette 45
Meux Home Museum Archives 45
Mexican War Journal 557
Mexican-American Historical Society 356
Mexico Free Public Library 248
Mexico Historical Museum 404
Mexico Historical Society 248
Mexico Historical Society & Archives 404
Mexico Town Historian 404
Mexico-Audrain County Library District 335
Meyer Family 142, 570
Meyercord Library 542
Meyers Family 222
Meyersdale Area Historical Society 494
Meyersdale Public Library 494
MHA News 362
MHE Heritage Library 17
MHR Review 53
Miami County Genealogical Society 191
Miami County Genealogical Society & Library 220
Miami County Historical and Genealogical Society 458
Miami County Historical Society & Archives 191, 220
Miami County Museum 191
Miami County Trakker 191
Miami Meanderings 458
Miami Public Library 467
Miami Springs Historical Society 117
Miami Station Museum Archives 660
Miami Valley County Genealogical Society 447
Miami Valley County Genealogical Society Bulletin 447
Miami-Dade Public Library 117
Miami-Dade Public Library System-Homestead Branch 114
Miamisburg Historical Society 453
Micanopy Historical Museum 117
Micanopy Historical Society & Archives 117
Mich Family 633
Michael Family 447
Michel Brouillet House & Museum Archives 195
Michener-Worthington Family 405
Michiana Jewish Historical Society 193
Michiana Searcher 183
Michie Family 529
Michigan City Historical Society & Archives 189
Michigan City Public Library 189
Michigan Genealogical Council 296
Michigan Hammontree Questors 287
Michigan Historical Center 296
Michigan Historical Commission 296
Michigan Historical Review 285, 290, 298
Michigan History 296
Michigan History Magazine 296
Michigan History's The Mitten 296
Michigan Iron Industry Museum Archives 298
Michigan Jewish History 302
Michigan Masonic Museum & Library 292
Michigan Newsletter 288
Michigan State Archives-Historical Center 296
Michigan State University Archives 290
Michigan State University Museum Archives 290
Michigan Street Preservation Corporation 391
Michigan Transit Museum Archives 298
Michigan Transit Museum Gazette 298
Michigan's Habitant Heritage 295
Michigana 292
Mickelsen Community Library 545
Mickey Reily Public Library 541
Micmac Association of Cultural Studies 676
MicMac Historical Cultural Arts Society 643
Micmacs of Maria Band 699
MICOGESOQU 220
Mid-America Air Museum Archives 217
Mid-America Air Museum News 217
Mid-America All Indian Center Museum Archives 223
Mid-America Folklore 31
Mid-America Folklore Society 31
Mid-America Genealogical Society 200
Mid-Atlantic Air Museum Archives 500
Mid-Atlantic Association for Living Historical Farms 372
Mid-Atlantic Center for the Arts/Cape May Lighthouse Archives 368
Mid-Atlantic Germanic Society 260, 263, 379
Mid-Atlantic Regional Archives Conference 398
Mid-Cities Genealogical Society 537
Mid-Cities Genealogical Society Newsletter 537
Mid-Columbia Library 609
Mid-Columbia Library District 602
Mid-Columbia Library District-Kennewick Branch 602
Mid-Continent Public Library 331
Mid-Continent Public Library-North Independence Branch 331
Mid-Continent Railway Gazette 628
Mid-Continent Railway Historical Society 628
Mid-Continent Railway Museum Archives 628
Middaugh-Meddaugh-Maddaugh Family 301
Middle Border Museum Archives 523
Middle Country Public Library 393
Middle Georgia Archives 133
Middle Georgia College Library 128
Middle Georgia Historical Society & Library 133
Middle Georgia Historical Society Newsletter 133

Middle Georgia Railroad Association 139
Middle Haddam Public Library 95
Middle Lake Museum Archives 708
Middle Tennessee Genealogical Society 531
Middle Tennessee Journal of Genealogy and History 531
Middleborough Antiquarian 275
Middleborough Historical Association & Archives 275
Middleborough Historical Museum 275
Middleburg Library Association 404
Middlebury Historical Museum 421
Middlebury Historical Society 95
Middlebury Historical Society & Archives 421
Middlefield Historical Society 95, 453
Middleport Free Library 405
Middlesboro-Bell County Public Library 231
Middlesex Canal Association & Archives 273
Middlesex County Cultural & Heritage Commission Library 374
Middlesex County Historical Museum 96
Middlesex County Historical Society & Archives 96
Middlesex County Museum Archives 376
Middlesex County Public Library 596
Middlesex Genealogical Society 92
Middlesex Genealogical Society Newsletter 92
Middlesex Historical Society 577
Middleton Area Historical Museum 626
Middleton Area Historical Society & Archives 626
Middleton Area Historical Society Newsletter 626
Middleton Historical Society & Archives 275
Middleton Library 235
Middleton Place Foundation 512
Middleton Place Notebook 512
Middleton Public Library 626
Middletown First Settlers Descendants [1650-1700] Society 48
Middletown Historical Museum 405
Middletown Historical Society 103, 508
Middletown Historical Society & Archives 508
Middletown Historical Society & Library 453
Middletown Historical Society Newsletter 453
Middletown Historical Society Newsletter 508
Middletown Public Library 189, 453, 494, 508
Middletown Springs Historical Society & Library 577
Middletown Springs Historical Society Newsletter 577
Middletown Township Historical Society 372
Middletown Township Public Library 373
Middletown Valley Historical Museum 261
Middletown Valley Historical Society & Archives 261
Middletown-Fall Creek Township Historical Society 189
Middletown-Thrall Library 405
Middleville Museum Archives 684
Midfield Public Library 6
Mid-Hudson Library System 412
Mid-Island Tribal Council 649
Midkiff Family 599
Midland County Historical Archives 297
Midland County Historical Museum 554
Midland County Historical Society & Archives 297, 554
Midland County Public Library 554
Midland Genealogical Society & Archives 297, 554
Midland Genealogical Society Magazine 554
Midland Genealogical Society Newsletter 554
Midland Log 297
Midland Park Memorial Library 373
Midlothian Historical Society 166
Mid-Michigan Genealogical Society & Library 296
Mid-Michigan Genealogical Society Newsletter 296
Mid-Mississippi Regional Library System 321
Mid-Missouri Civil War Round Table 327
Mid-Missouri Genealogical Society & Archives 331
Mid-Missouri Railfans Club 327
Mid-Peninsula Library Cooperative 294, 295
Midvale District Library 148
Midway Heritage Association & Archives 134
Midway Museum 134
Midway Village & Museum Archives 172
Midway Village Museum 172
Midwest Archives Conference 159
Midwest Historical and Genealogical Register 223
Midwest Historical and Genealogical Society & Library 223
Midwest Old Settlers and Threshers Association & Archives 205
Midwest Old Settlers and Threshers Museum 205
Mid-West Tennessee Genealogical Society 528
Mifflin County Historical News 492
Mifflin County Historical Society & Archives 492
Mifflin County Historical Society & Library 492
Mifflin County Library 492
Mifflin County Mennonite Historical Society 482
Mifflinburg Buggy Museum Archives 494
Mighty 8th Air Force Museum Archives 135
Mighty 8th Air Force Museum News 135
Miklaszewsky-Piotrowski Family 297
Milaca Museum Archives 311
Milam County Genealogical Society & Archives 557
Milam County Historical Museum Archives 539
Milam News and Events 20
Milam Roots 20
Milan Historical Association & Archives 218
Milan Historical Museum 453
Milan Historical Museum Archives 453
Milan Historical Society 297
Milan Historical Society & Archives 453
Milan Public Library 297, 363, 453
Milbridge Historical Museum 248
Milbridge Historical Society & Archives 248
Milburn Family 17, 287
Milden Community Museum Archives 708
Mildred Stevens Williams Memorial Library 243
Milepost 502
Milepost 613 130
Miler Family 388
Miles City Genealogical Society & Archives 346
Miles City Historic Preservation Office 346
Miles City Public Library 346
Miles College Library 2
Miles Family 95
Miles-Raley Family 222
Milestones 374, 482
Milford Area Historical Society & Library 453
Milford Area Historical Society Newsletter 453
Milford Free Library 405
Milford Historical Museum 297

Milford Historical Society 103, 363
Milford Historical Society & Archives 96, 297
Milford Historical Society Newsletter 103
Milford Historical Society Newsletter 363
Milford Memorial Library 205
Milford Museum Archives 103
Milford Public Library 96, 103, 189
Milford Town Library 275
Milford Township Library 297
Milford Twp Historical Preservation Society 500
Military Chronicle 593
Military Communications and Electronics Museum Archives 684
Military Glider Pilots Association Museum Archives 561
Military Heritage Museum Archives 387
Military Historians Headquarters Museum Archives 101
Military History 589
Military History of the West 543
Military Medal Museum and Research Center Archives 68
Military Museum of Southern New England Archives 92
Military Order of the Loyal Legion of the US & Library 498
Military Order of the Loyal Legion of the US, Ohio Commandery 452
Military Police Corps History 329
Military Queries and Reviews 603
Military Veterans Museum Archives 627, 628
Milk River Genealogical Society 343
Mill Cart 72
Mill City Museum 314
Mill Hill Historic Museum 97
Mill Race Historical Village 299
Mill Race Quarterly 299
Mill Valley Historical Review 54
Mill Valley Historical Society 54
Mill Valley Public Library 54
Mill Wheel 369
Millan Family 570
Millard Family 557
Millard Fillmore House Museum Archives 396
Millbrae Historical Society & Archives 54
Millbrae Museum 54
Millbrook and Cavan Historical Society 685
Millbrook Public Library 6
Millbrook Society & Archives 489
Millburn-Short Hills Historical Society 378
Mille Lacs County Historical Society 313
Mille Lacs Indian Museum and Trading Post Archives 312
Mille Lacs Lake Historical Society 309
Milleman Family 46
Miller County Historical Society 27
Miller Family 6, 111, 587, 595
Miller House 204
Miller House Archives 259
Miller House Museum 259
Miller Library 218, 491, 575
Miller Monitor 62
Miller Newsletter 530
Miller Nichols Library 332
Miller-Cory House Museum Archives 380
Miller-Ely Family 42
Miller-Kimble Family 601
Millerton Courthouse Museum Archives 45
Millet and District Museum Archives 645
Millet Family 17
Millicent Library 270
Millicent Rogers Museum Library 385
Milligan Memories 355
Millinocket Memorial Library 248
Millis Public Library 275
Mills County Genealogical Society & Archives 202
Mills County Genealogical Society Newsletter 202
Mills County Historical Museum 202
Mills County Historical Society & Archives 202
Mills Family 265, 570, 577
Mills Musings 476
Millsboro Public Library 103
Milltown Public Library 373
Millville Army Air Field Museum Archives 373
Millville Army Air Field Museum Journal 373
Millville Historical Association 313
Millville Historical Society 373
Millville Public Library 373
Milne Family 570
Milner House Museum 681
Milo Free Public Library 248
Milo Public Library 205
Milpitas Cultural Resources Preservation Board 54
Milpitas Historical Society 54
Miltenberger Family 542
Milton Blacksmith Shop Museum Archives 675
Milton Chronicles 286
Milton Historical Museum 578
Milton Historical Society 494, 685
Milton Historical Society & Archives 275, 578
Milton Historical Society & Library 104, 626
Milton Historical Society Newsletter 578
Milton House 626
Milton Public Library 275, 494, 578
Milton S Eisenhower Library 256
Milton-Freewater Genealogical Club 477
Milton-Freewater Public Library 477
Milton-Union Public Library 460
Milwaukee County Genealogical Society 626
Milwaukee County Genealogical Society Reporter 626
Milwaukee County Historical Society & Library 626
Milwaukee History 626
Milwaukee Public Library 626
Milwaukee Public Museum Archives 626
Milwaukee Schools Historical Society 626
Minatare Public Library 354
Mind Matters 200
Mine Au Breton Historical Society & Library 337
Miner 342
Miner Family 569, 572
Miner's Journal 160
Mineral County Historical Landmark Commission 611
Mineral County Historical Museum 346
Mineral County Historical Society 611
Mineral County Historical Society & Archives 346
Mineral County Pioneer 346
Mineral County Public Library 346
Mineral Point Historical Society & Library 627

Mineral Point Public Library 627
Mineral-Gold Public Library District 166
Miners Foundry Cultural Center Archives 56
Minerva Public Library 453
Minerva Town Historian 405
Minetto Town Historian 405
Mingei International Museum of World Folk Art Archives 49
Mingling Family 441
Mingo County Genealogical Society 615
Mingo Heritage 615
Minidoka County Historical Museum 149
Minidoka County Historical Society & Archives 149
Mining Your History Foundation 611
Mininger Mysteries 219
Miniota Municipal Museum Archives 660
Minisink Valley Historical Museum 412
Minisink Valley Historical Society & Archives 412
Ministry of Aboriginal Affairs 657
Mink Family 159
Minker-Wasserman Family 506
Minneapolis Public Library 311
Minneapolis Public Library-Sumner 311
Minnedosa and District Museum Archives 660
Minnegazette 314
Minnesota Air National Guard Historical Foundation Museum Archives 314
Minnesota Genealogical Journal 313
Minnesota Genealogical Society & Library 308
Minnesota Genealogical Society Newsletter 308
Minnesota Genealogist 308
Minnesota Historical Society & Archives 314
Minnesota History 314
Minnesota History News 314
Minnesota Lake Area Historical Society & Archives 311
Minnesota Pioneer Park Library 305
Minnesota Pioneer Park Newsletter 305
Minnesota State Capitol Historic Site Archives 314
Minnesota Transportation Museum Archives 314
Minnesota Veterinary Historical Museum Archives 314
Minnetonka Historical Society & Library 311
Minnetonka Mill Wheel Newsletter 311
Minnetrista Cultural Center Archives 190
Minnilusa Historical Association & Archives 523
Minnilusa Historical Association Newsletter 523
Minnis Family 114
Minnis: Newsletter of Minnis Families of America 114
MinnKota Genealogical Society 307
Minnkota Genealogical Society 438
Minocqua Museum Archives 627
Minor Family 570
Minor Memorial Library 98
Minot Air Force Base Library 439
Minot Public Library 439
Mint Hill Historical Society 430
Mint Roots 187
Minter Field Air Museum Archives 72
Minto Museum Archives 664
Minute Man National Historic Park Library 269
Mira Loma Genealogy Library 54
Mirabeau B Lamar Library 536
Miracle of America Museum Archives 346
Miracle of America Museum Newsletter 346
Miracle Valley Regional Library System 613
Miracle Valley Regional Library System Newsletter 613
Miracosta College Library 57
Miramichi Historical Museum 664
Miramichi Historical Society & Archives 663, 664
Miramont Castle 88
Mirrilees Family Association News 177
Mirror 62, 338, 492
Mirror and District Museum Archives 645
Mischler Newsletter 445
Mishawaka-Penn Public Library 189
Mishpacha 256
Mishpochology 121
Miss DAR Magazine 321
Missaukee District Library 295
Mission Bell Historical Museum 464
Mission Bell Historical Society & Archives 464
Mission Community Archives 652
Mission Dolores Archives 67
Mission House Museum Archives 280
Mission Inn Museum Archives 62
Mission Mill Museum Association & Archives 479
Mission Museum Archives 652
Mission News 57
Mission Nuestra Senora de la Soledad Museum Archives 72
Mission Oaks Genealogy Club & Library 39
Mission Oaks Genealogy Club Newsletter 39
Mission Of Nombre De Dios and La Leche Shrine Archives 121
Mission Saint-Francois Xavier 698
Mission San Carlos Borromeo del Rio Carmelo Archives 39
Mission San Diego Historical Society & Library 65
Mission San Fernando Historical Museum & Archival Center 54
Mission San Juan Bautista Museum Archives 68
Mission San Juan Capistrano Museum Archives 68
Mission San Luis de Apalachee Archives 122
Mission San Luis Rey Museum Archives 57
Mission San Miguel Museum Archives 69
Mission San Rafael Arcangel Archives 69
Mission Santa Clara de Asis Museum Archives 70
Mission Santa Cruz Archives 70
Mission Viejo Library 54
Missisquoi Historical Society Reports 703
Missisquoi Valley Historical Museum 578
Missisquoi Valley Historical Society & Archives 578
Mississagi Strait Lighthouse Museum Archives 685
Mississauga Library System 686
Mississaugas of the New Credit Indian Reserve 683
Mississinewa Battlefield Society 189
Mississippi Agriculture, Forestry & Aviation Museum Archives 320
Mississippi Armed Forces Museum Archives 319
Mississippi Armed Forces Museum Newsletter 319
Mississippi Band of Choctaw Indians 322
Mississippi Baptist Historical Commission 319
Mississippi Bible and Cemetery Records 320
Mississippi Coast Genealogical and Historical Society 319
Mississippi Coast Historical and Genealogical Society Tri-Annual 319
Mississippi County Genealogical Society & Library 327
Mississippi County Historical and Genealogical Society 31
Mississippi County Historical Center 31

Mississippi County Historical Museum 327
Mississippi County Historical Society & Archives 327
Mississippi County Library 327
Mississippi County Library System-Osceola Branch 31
Mississippi Department of Archives and History 320
Mississippi Genealogical Society 320
Mississippi Governor's Mansion Museum Archives 321
Mississippi Headwaters Region: Scenes from the Past 305
Mississippi Historical Society 321
Mississippi History Newsletter 321
Mississippi Library Commission 321
Mississippi Memories Society 241
Mississippi River Museum Archives 201
Mississippi River Museum at Mud Island Archives 530
Mississippi River Museum Newsletter 201
Mississippi River Routes 323
Mississippi State Historical Museum Archives 321
Mississippi University Archives and Museum 319
Mississquoi Historical Society & Archives 703
Mississquoi Museum 703
Missoula Public Library 346
Missouri Alliance for Historic Preservation 327
Missouri Baptist Historical Society & Archives 334
Missouri Civil War Museum Archives 342
Missouri Federal Information Center 339
Missouri Folklore Society 327
Missouri Forest Heritage Center 331
Missouri Historical Museum 339
Missouri Historical Review 328
Missouri Historical Society & Archives 339
Missouri Historical Society Newsletter 339
Missouri Lewis and Clark Bicentennial Commission 331
Missouri Mansion Preservation 331
Missouri Messenger 325
Missouri Mines Museum Society 336
Missouri Mormon Frontier Foundation 331
Missouri Pacific Historical Society 340
Missouri Postal History Society 335
Missouri River Frontier Museum Archives 336
Missouri River Regional Library 331
Missouri Society for Military History 331
Missouri Sources, Queries and Reviews 603
Missouri State Archives 331
Missouri State Genealogical Association 328
Missouri State Genealogical Association Journal 328
Missouri State Library 331
Missouri State Museum Archives 331
Missouri State Museum Quarterly 331
Missouri Territorial Pioneers 331
Missouri Western State College Library 338
Mistawasis First Nations 707
Mistletoe Leaves 464, 468
Mists of Moigh 595
Mitchell Area Genealogical Society & Library 523
Mitchell Community Public Library 189
Mitchell Community Public Library Newsletter 189
Mitchell Company Historical Society 423
Mitchell County Historical Museum 206, 212
Mitchell County Historical Society & Archives 206, 212
Mitchell County Public Library 540
Mitchell Family 547
Mitchell Gallery of Flight Archives 626
Mitchell Indian Museum Archives 159
Mitchell Indian Museum Newsletter 159
Mitchell Memorial Library 321
Mitchell Museum at Cedarhurst Archives 167
Mitchell Public Library 293, 523
Mitchell-Rountree Stone Cottage Archives 629
Mittelungsblat 437
Mix Family 442
Mixon Family 41
Mizel Museum Archives 84
M-news letter 494
Moales-Cleveland Family 111
Moannanu Family 330
MO-ARK Regional Railroad Museum Archives 337
Mobile Genealogical Society 7
Mobile Public Library 7
Mochelbost Family 567
Mock Family 89, 605
Mock Family Historian Newsletter 42
Mockbee Family 336
Mockbeggar Plantation Museum Archives 667
Moclips by The Sea Historical Society & Archives 603
Moclips Historical Museum 603
Modern Western Museum Archives 554
Modoc County Historical Museum 35
Modoc County Historical Society & Archives 35
Modoc County Historical Society Journal 35
Modoc County Library 35
Moeller Family 468
Moffat Clan 443, 603
Moffat County Libraries 83
Moffatt Clan 532
Moffatt-Ladd House Museum Archives 364
Mogingo-Monzingo-Montzingo Family 539
Mohave County Historical and Genealogical Society & Archives 17
Mohave County Historical Museum 17
Mohave County Historical Museum Newsletter 17
Mohave County Library District 17
Mohave Historical Society 76
Mohave Valley Genealogical Society 18
Mohawk 413
Mohawk Historical Society 458
Mohegan & Thames Valley Learning Resource Centers 97
Mohican Historical Museum 451
Mohican Historical Society & Archives 451
Mohler Family 487
Mohn Family 482
Moira Historical Association 405
Moise Memorial Library 385
Mojave Desert Genealogical Society 37
Mojave Desert Heritage and Cultural Association 44
Mojave River Valley Museum Association & Archives 37
Mojave River Valley Museum Association Newsletter 37
Mokelumne Hill Historical Society 54
Mokomis and District Museum 708
Mokotoff-Mokotow Family 375
Moland House Museum Archives 504
Molen Family 56

Molenaar Family 565
Molina-Gamboa-Gardea Family 573
Moline Public Library 166
Molly Brown House Museum Archives 84
Molly Brown House Museum Newsletter 84
Molson Historical Society 604
Molstead Library 146
Molyneux Family 599, 603
Monacan Indian Tribe 583
Monahan Library 90
Moncrief Family 65
Moncrieffe Clan 510
Moncton Museum Archives 664
Moncur Family 149
MonDak Heritage Center 346
MonDak Heritage Center Newsletter 346
MonDak Historical and Arts Society & Archives 346
Monessen Public Library 494
Mongan Family 16
Mongol Tolbo 374
Mongol-American Cultural Association 374
Monhegan Cultural and Historical Association & Archives 248
Monhegan Historical Museum 248
Moniteau County Historical Society 326
Moniteau County Historical Society Newsletter 326
Monmouth Beach Library 373
Monmouth Connection 370
Monmouth County Genealogical Club & Library 370
Monmouth County Genealogy Society 372
Monmouth County Historical Association & Archives 370
Monmouth County Historical Museum 370
Monmouth County Library 372
Monmouth County Library-Holmdel Branch 371
Monmouth County Library-Howell Branch 371
Monmouth County Library-Marlboro Branch 373
Monmouth County Library-Township of Ocean 375
Monmouth County Library-Wall 379
Monmouth Historical Museum 248
Monmouth Historical Society & Archives 248
Monmouth Museum Archives 372
Monmouth Museum Newsletter 372
Monmouth Public Library 477
Mono County Free Library System-Northern Region 38
Monocacy National Battlefield Library 259
Monona County Genealogical Society 206
Monona Historical Society 205
Monona Public Library 627
Monongahela Area Historical Society 494
Monongahela Area Library 494
Monongalia Historical Society & Library 312
Monroe County Genealogical Society 109
Monroe County Genealogical Society 157, 158
Monroe County Genealogical Society 460
Monroe County Genealogical Society & Archives 197
Monroe County Genealogical Society Newsletter 197
Monroe County Heritage 460
Monroe County Heritage Museum 7
Monroe County Heritage Society & Archives 7
Monroe County Historian 180
Monroe County Historian's Department Library 414
Monroe County Historical and Cemetery Association 26
Monroe County Historical and Genealogical Society & Archives 180
Monroe County Historical Association & Archives 502
Monroe County Historical Commission & Archives 298
Monroe County Historical Museum 180, 197, 298, 502
Monroe County Historical Society 176, 336, 615
Monroe County Historical Society & Archives 197, 631
Monroe County Historical Society & Library 131, 460
Monroe County Historical Society Newsletter 180, 615, 631
Monroe County Library 26, 298
Monroe County Library System-Bedford Branch 303
Monroe County Local History Room & Library 631
Monroe County Public Library 7, 115, 180
Monroe Family 236
Monroe Free Library 405
Monroe Free Library Newsletter 405
Monroe Genealogy Society 239
Monroe Historical Museum 96
Monroe Historical Society 96
Monroe Historical Society & Archives 96
Monroe Historical Society Quarterly 96
Monroe Public Library 96, 205, 627
Monroe Township Historical Society & Library 380
Monroe Township Public Library 371
Monroe, Juneau, and Jackson Counties Genealogy Workshop & Library 618
Monroe, Juneau, and Jackson Counties Genealogy Workshop Newsletter 618
Monroe, Juneau, Jackson County Wisconsin Genealogy Workshop 632
Monroe, Juneau, Jackson County Wisconsin Genealogy Workshop Newsletter 632
Monroeville Historical Society 494
Monroeville Public Library 494
Monroeville Public Library Newsletter 494
Monrovia Historical Society 54
Monrovia Old House Preservation Group 54
Monrovia Public Library 54
Monson Free Library 275
Monson Historical Society & Library 275
Montage 62, 183
Montague Association for the Restoration of Community History 373
Montague County Genealogical Society 538
Montague County Historical Society 554
Montague Family 1
Montague Museum and Historical Association & Library 298
Montague Public Libraries 280
Montague Public Libraries-Millers Falls Branch 275
Montague Public Libraries-Montague Center Branch 275
Montana Heritage Commission At Virginia City 346
Montana Historical Museum 345
Montana Historical Society & Archives 345
Montana Indian Band 644
Montana Masonic Museum Archives 345
Montana State Genealogical Society 343
Montana State Library 345
Montana State University-Billings Library 343
Montana: The Magazine of Western History; Montana Post 345
Montauk Library 405
Montauk Museum 199
Montauk Pioneer 390
Montauk Point Lighthouse Museum Archives 405
Montclair Free Public Library 373

Montclair Historical Museum 373
Montclair Historical Society & Archives 373
Monte Rio Area Historical Society 55
Monte Vista Genies 17
Monte Vista Historical Association 559
Monte Vista Historical Society 88
Montecito History Committee & Library 55
Monteith Family 473
Montello Historic Preservation Society 627
Monterey Bay Family History Center 64
Monterey County Agricultural and Rural Life Museum Archives 48
Monterey County Genealogical Society 64
Monterey County Genealogical Society Newsletter 64
Monterey County Genealogical Society Quarterly 64
Monterey County Historical Society & Library 64
Monterey County Historical Society Newsletter 64
Monterey County Library 64
Monterey History and Art Association & Library 55
Monterey Library 275
Monterey Public Library & Local History Room 55
Monterey State Historic Park Archives 55
Monterey-Tippecanoe Township Public Library 189
Montezuma Public Library 205
Montgomery Area Public Library 494
Montgomery City Historical Museum 335
Montgomery City Historical Society & Archives 335
Montgomery City-County Library 7
Montgomery Clan 170, 371
Montgomery County Archives 7
Montgomery County Chapter, OGS & Library 447
Montgomery County Department of History and Archives 397
Montgomery County Genealogial Society 207
Montgomery County Genealogical and Historical Society 541
Montgomery County Genealogical Club & Library 496
Montgomery County Genealogical Club Newsletter 496
Montgomery County Genealogical Society 335
Montgomery County Genealogical Society & Archives 165, 212, 262
Montgomery County Genealogical Society Newsletter 335
Montgomery County Genealogical Society Quarterly 165
Montgomery County Historical Journal 526
Montgomery County Historical Museum 447
Montgomery County Historical Society 182, 216, 397, 526
Montgomery County Historical Society & Archives 7, 447, 526
Montgomery County Historical Society & Library 30, 207, 262, 496
Montgomery County Historical Society Herald 7
Montgomery County Historical Society News 496
Montgomery County Historical Society, Genealogy Section 182
Montgomery County Library 31, 541
Montgomery County Public Libraries 262
Montgomery County Public Library 433
Montgomery County Story 262
Montgomery County: Our Heritage 30
Montgomery County-Norristown Public Library 496
Montgomery Genealogical Society 7
Montgomery Genealogical Society Quarterly 7
Montgomery Historical Society 554
Montgomery Historical Society & Library 578
Montgomery House-Warrior Run Area Public Library 493
Montgomery Library 226
Montgomery Memorial Library 203
Montgomery Museum Archives 586
Montgomery Museum Newsletter 586
Montgomery's Inn Museum Archives 682
Montgomery-Floyd Regional Library 586
Monthly Note Book 76
Monticello Area Historical Society 627
Monticello Association 339
Monticello Association Annual Report 339
Monticello Historical Committee 311
Monticello Plantation 585
Monticello Railway Museum Archives 167
Monticello-Union Township Public Library 189
Montour County Genealogical Society 485
Montour County Historical Society 485
Montpelier Historical Society 190
Montpelier Mansion 260
Montpelier Mansion Archives 260
Montpelier Public Library 190
Montreal Lake Cree Nation 708
Montreal Quebec Cornish Association 703
Montrose County Historical Society 88
Montrose County Historical Society Quarterly 88
Montrose Historical Association & Archives 298
Montrose Library District 88
Montrose Public Library 205
Montville Historical Museum 373
Montville Historical Society & Archives 373
Monument 453
Monument Lefebvre 664
Monumental News 449
Moody Air Force Base Library 134
Moody Bible Institute Library 156
Moody County Genealogical Society 521
Moody County Historical Museum 522
Moody County Historical Society & Archives 522
Moody County Historical Society Newsletter 522
Moody County Library 522
Moody Family 618
Moody Mansion Museum Archives 546
Moody Mansion Museum Newsletter 546
Moody Memorial Library 549
Moody-Bradley House Museum Archives 544
Moody-Joyner -McCune Family 571
Mooers Town Historian 405
Moomaw Newsletter 449
Moon Tribune 549
Mooney Family 75
Moorcroft Historical Society 637
Moore County Genealogical Society 431
Moore County Genealogical Society Newsletter 431
Moore County Historical Association & Library 433
Moore County Historical Museum Archives 543
Moore County Library 424
Moore Family 169, 426, 470, 473, 565, 572
Moore Family News 532
Moore Family Newsletter 376
Moore Free Library 578
Moore Home Archives 164
Moore Memorial Library 399, 561
Moore Museum 419

INDEX

Moore Museum Archives 686
Moore-Lewis Family 463
Moore-Moor Family 50
Moores Creek Battlefield Archives 425
Moores Memorial Library 484
Mooresville Public Library 190
Moore-Youse Home Museum 190
Moorland-Spingarn Research Center 106
Moorpark Historical Society 55
Moose Factory Centennial Museum Archives 684
Moose Jaw Museum and Exhibition Centre Archives 708
Moose Lake Historical Society 312
Moose River Historical Museum Archives 247
Moosehead Historical Society 246
Moosehead Marine Museum Archives 246
Moosehorn Museum Archives 660
Moosilauke Public Library 363
Moosomin First Nation 705
Moquah Heritage Society 617
Moraga Historical Society & Library 55
Moraga Historical Society Newsletter 55
Moraine Valley Oral History Association & Archives 168
Moran Family 167
Morasha (Heritage) 168
Morava Krasna 76
Moravia Public Library 205
Moravian Heritage Society 76
Moravian Historian 495
Moravian Historical Society & Archives 495
Moravian Historical Society Transactions 495
Moravian Museum Archives 482
Mordecai Square Historical Museum 431
Mordecai Square Historical Society & Archives 431
Morden and District Museum Archives 660
Morden Quarterly Newsletter 297
More and More Detamores 169
More Family 496
More from the Shore 262
Morefield Family 475
Morehouse Parish Library 235
Morehouse Town Historian 400
Moreland Community Historical Society 134
Moreland Muster 37
Morenci Community Library 18
Moreton's Harbour Museum 667
Morey Maximum Reader 549
Morey-Mowry Family 483
Morgan Area Genealogical Society 163
Morgan City Public Library 239
Morgan Company Historical Society 234
Morgan County African-American Historical Museum 133
Morgan County African-American Historical Society 133
Morgan County Archives 3
Morgan County Genealogical and Historical Society 533
Morgan County Genealogical Society 3
Morgan County Genealogical Society & Library 453
Morgan County Historic Preservation Society 189
Morgan County Historical and Genealogical Society 611
Morgan County Historical and Genealogical Society Newsletter 611
Morgan County Historical Museum 341
Morgan County Historical Society 3, 163
Morgan County Historical Society & Archives 341
Morgan County Historical Society & Library 133
Morgan County History and Genealogy Association 189
Morgan County History and Genealogy Association News 189
Morgan County Library 341, 568
Morgan County Messenger 533
Morgan County Public Library 189, 611
Morgan County Records Archives 133
Morgan Family 591
Morgan Family News 532
Morgan Hill Architectural Cultural Resources Board 55
Morgan Hill Historical Society & Library 55
Morgan Hill Museum Archives 55
Morgan House 628
Morgan Library of Ohio Imprints Archives 460
Morgan Link 453
Morgan Row Museum 228
Morgantown Public Library 613
Morgrage-Morgridge-Boadway-Boardway-Boudway-Budway Family 250
Moriarty Clan Newsletter 160
Moriarty Historical Museum 384
Moriarty Historical Society & Archives 384
Moricetown Indian Band Council 652
Morikami Museum of Japanese Culture Library 111
Morley Library 455
Mormon History Association 567
Mormon Visitors Center Museum Archives 331
Morongo Basin Historical Society 79
Morrill Historical Society 243, 354
Morrill Memorial Library 276
Morrill Public Library 354
Morris and District Centennial Museum Archives 660
Morris Area Genealogy Society 369
Morris Area Genealogy Society Newsletter 369
Morris Area New Jersey Jewish Genealogical Society 374
Morris Area Public Library District 167
Morris County Free Library 380
Morris County Genealogical Society & Library 223
Morris County Historical Society & Archives 374
Morris County Historical Society & Library 213
Morris Family 493, 560, 567
Morris Gazette 374
Morris Historical Society & Library 96
Morris Historical Society Newsletter 96
Morris Journal 291
Morris Library 104, 425
Morris Members 292
Morris Museum Archives 374
Morris Museum Newsletter 374
Morris Public Library 312
Morris-Butler House Museum Archives 187
Morris-Earnest-Mills-Cunningham-Gatlin-Beatty-Stiger-Murray-Hodapp-Holte Family 535
Morris-Jumel Mansion Museum Archives 407
Morris-Jumel Mansion Museum Newsletter 407
Morrison Clan 48, 334, 536
Morrison County Historical Museum 310
Morrison County Historical Society & Archives 310
Morrison County Historical Society Newsletter 310

Morrison Family 478, 554, 567
Morrison Heritage Museum 167
Morrison Heritage Museum Archives 88
Morrison Historical Society & Archives 167
Morrison Memories 149
Morrison Museum of the Country School Archives 644
Morrison-Reeves Library 192
Morrison-Talbott Library 176
Morrisonville Historical Society 167
Morrisonville Times 167
Morristown Centennial Library 578
Morristown Historical Society 312
Morristown Historical Society & Archives 578
Morristown National Historic Park Library 374
Morristown Two Times 578
Morristown-Hamblen Public Library 530
Morrow County Genealogical Society 453
Morrow Family 389, 448
Morrow Memorial Church Library 372
Morse (Moss) Family 567
Morse Department of Special Collections 218
Morse Family 363, 545
Morse Institute Library 275
Morse Museum Archives 708
Mortensen Family 573
Mortensen-James Family 572
Morton B Weiss Museum of Judaica Archives 156
Morton County Historical Museum 213
Morton County Historical Society & Archives 213
Morton County Library 438
Morton Family 605
Morton Grove Historical Society & Archives 167
Morton Grove Public Library 167
Morton Homestead Museum Archives 500
Morton House Museum Archives 286
Morton House Museum Newsletter 286
Mortvedt Library 608
Morven House Museum Archives 376
Morven Park Museum Archives 589
Moscow-Latah County Library System 148
Moseley Family 540
Moser Family 553, 567
Moses Greeley Parker Memorial Library 270
Moses Lake Museum Archives 603
Moses Myers House Museum Archives 592
Mosher Family 337
Mosquito Bytes 556
Mosquito Grizzly Bear Head First Nation 705
Moss Family 235, 377
Moss Mansion 343
Moss Memorial Library 240
Mossbank and District Museum Archives 708
Mother Colony Household & Museum 35
Mother Whiteside Memorial Library 383
Motherwell Homestead Museum Archives 705
Motion Unlimited Museum Archives 523
Motley County Genealogical and Historical Society 553
Motley County Library 553
Motley Family 504
Motoring Museum News 241
Motown Historical Museum Archives 289
Mott Family 567
Motter-Marter-Matter-Schwartz-Swartz Family 172
Motts Military Museum Archives 449
Moulin Fleming Museum Archives 698
Moulin Legare 702
Moultonboro Public Library 363
Moultrie County Heritage 175
Moultrie County Historical and Genealogical Society 175
Moultrie County Historical and Genealogical Society & Library 175
Moultrie County Historical and Genealogical Society Newsletter 175
Moultrie Family 609
Moultrie-Colquitt County Regional Library 135
Mound City Public Library 167
Moundridge Historical Association 219
Moundville Public Library 7
Mount Ayr Public Library 205
Mount Caesar Union Library 364
Mount Carmel Lutheran Church Library 626
Mount Carmel Public Library 167, 494
Mount Carroll Township Public Library 167
Mount Clare Museum House Archives 256
Mount Clemens Public Library 298
Mount Currie Indian Band 652
Mount Desert Island Historical Museum 248
Mount Desert Island Historical Society 248, 251
Mount Desert Island Historical Society Journal 248
Mount Desert Island Historical Society Newsletter 248
Mount Diablo Genealogical Society & Library 77
Mount Diablo Genealogical Society Newsletter 77
Mount Diablo Surveyors Historical Society 68
Mount Greenwood Historical Society 156
Mount Healthy Historical Society 453
Mount Holly Historical Museum 575
Mount Holly Historical Society 374
Mount Holly Historical Society & Archives 575
Mount Holly Library 575
Mount Holly Public Library 374
Mount Hood Genealogical Forum & Library 477
Mount Hope Historical Society 410
Mount Horeb Area Historical Society & Library 627
Mount Horeb Area Museum Archives 627
Mount Horeb Public Library 627
Mount Horeb Reader 627
Mount Independence Historic Site Archives 578
Mount Joy Area Historical Society 495
Mount Juliet Public Library 530
Mount Juliet-West Wilson County Historical Society & Library 530
Mount Juliet-West Wilson Historical Society Chronicle 530
Mount Kisco Public Library 405
Mount Lassen Historical Society 72
Mount Lebanon Historical Society 237, 239
Mount Lebanon Public Library 499
Mount Lowe Preservation Society 67
Mount Mary College Historic Costume Collection 626
Mount Massaemet Shadows 279
Mount McGregor Cottage 421
Mount Morris Public Library 167
Mount Olive Public Library 167, 368
Mount Pleasant Area Historical Society 495

Mount Pleasant Free Public Library 495
Mount Pleasant Historical Society 419
Mount Pleasant Historical Society & Archives 453
Mount Pleasant Public Library 205, 411, 554
Mount Prospect Historical Museum 167
Mount Prospect Historical Society & Archives 167
Mount Prospect Public Library 167
Mount Pulaski Courthouse State Historic Site Archives 167
Mount Pulaski Public Library 167
Mount Pulaski Township Historical Society 167
Mount Pulaski Township Historical Society Newsletter 167
Mount Rushmore National Memorial Archives 522
Mount Sterling Montgomery County Library 231
Mount Tamalpais State Park Archives 54
Mount Union Historical Society 495
Mount Vernon and Knox County Public Library 453
Mount Vernon City Library 603
Mount Vernon Genealogical Society & Archives 167
Mount Vernon Genealogical Society & Library 583
Mount Vernon Genealogical Society Newsletter 167, 583
Mount Vernon Hotel Museum Archives 407
Mount Vernon Ladies' Association of the Union & Library 591
Mount Vernon Public Library 405
Mount Washington Museum and Observatory Archives 363
Mountain Diggings 87
Mountain Empire Historical Society & Archives 39
Mountain Farm Museum Archives 425
Mountain Gateway Museum Archives 431
Mountain Genealogists 88
Mountain Genealogists Society 84
Mountain Heritage 225
Mountain Heritage Center Archives 425
Mountain Historical Society 627
Mountain Home Air Force Base Library 148
Mountain Home Public Library 148
Mountain Iron Public Library 312
Mountain Lake Public Library 312
Mountain Life Museum Archives 230
Mountain Light 145
Mountain Mills Museum Archives 689
Mountain News 611
Mountain Regional Library 140
Mountain Signal 30
Mountain Top Historical Society 392
Mountain View Doukhobor Museum Archives 650
Mountain View Historical Newsletter 55
Mountain View Museum Archives 645
Mountain View Pioneer and Historical Association 55
Mountain View Public Library 55, 335
Mountainside Historical Society 374
Mountjoy Family 551
Mountrail County Historical Society 439
Mouse River Loop Genealogical Society & Library 439
Movement Newsletter 530
Movie Museum Archives 299
Movie Museum Newsletter 299
Mowachaht-Muchalaht Indian Band 650
Mowat Family International Newsletter 113
Moweaqua Area Historical Society 167
Moweaqua Public Library 167
Mower County Genealogical Society & Library 305
Mower County Genealogical Society News 305
Mower County Historical Society & Library 305
Mower Family 149
Mowreader-Robinson-Cox-McCoughey Family 599
Mowry Family 507
Moye Library 430
Moyer Family 496, 569
mperial-Saint Landry Genealogy and Historical Society Newsletter 240
Muchmore Family 453
Muchmore Family Newsletter 380
Muchmore-Muchemore-Mutchmore Family 445
Muckenthaler Cultural Center Archives 46
Muddy Creek Historical Society 354
Muddy Roots 327
Mueller Family 209, 454
Mugar Memorial Library 267
Mugford Family 78
Muhlenberg Community Library 492
Muhlenberg County Genealogical Society 226
Muhlenberg County Genealogical Society & Archives 228
Muhlenberg County Heritage 226
Muhlenberg County Libraries-Central City Branch 226
Muhlenberg County Library 228
Muir-Golding Family 569
Mukilteo Historical Society 603
Mukwonago Community Library 627
Mukwonago Historical Society 627
Mulberry Public Library 31
Muldrow Genealogical Society 467
Muldrow Genealogical Society Newsletter 467
Muldrow Public Library 467
Muleshoe Area Public Library 554
Mulford House and Farm Museum Archives 396
Mulfords in America and Their Kin 154
Mulkey Family Journal 219
Mulkey Family Newsletter 219
Mulkeytown Area Historical Society 167
Mullan Chronicles 346
Mullanix-Snider Family 612
Mullenuex Family 611
Muller House Museum Archives 69
Mulliken District Library 298
Mullins Library 27
Multicultural Heritage Centre Archives 646
Multicutural Genealogical Society 240
Multnomah County Public Library 478
Mulvane Historical Society & Library 219
Mulvane Historical Society News 219
Mumma-Mumaw Family 505
Mummers Museum News 498
Mumpower Family Newsletter 190
Muncie Center Township Public Library 190
Muncie-Center Township Public Library 190
Muncy Historic School House Museum 495
Muncy Historical Museum 495
Muncy Historical Society & Archives 495
Muncy Public Library 495
Munday-Monday-Mundy-Mondy Family 347
Mundelein College Archives-Chicago 156

Munger Family 148
Municipal Reference and Records Center Archives 142
Munro Clan 434
Munson Family 419
Munster Historical Society 190
Muntzell Family 542
Murbach Family 404
Murdo Genealogical Society 523
Murdock Historical Society 354
Murdock Library 477
Murer Family 350
Murfreesboro Historical Association & Archives 430
Murfreesboro Historical Museum 430
Murphey Family 557
Murphy House Museum 39
Murphy Library 624
Murphy Mates 292
Murphy Memorial Library 205, 552, 485
Murphy Public Library 430
Murphy-Fitzmeyer-Butler Family 114
Murray Clan 506
Murray County Historical Society 315
Murray Family 566
Murray Library 488
Murray Public Library 568
Murray State College Library 470
Murray's Mill Historic Site Archives 424
Murray's Museum of History 660
Murray-Holley Historical Society 400
Murray-Lindsay Mansion Museum Archives 466
Murrell Home Museum Archives 468
Murrell Memorial Library 130
Murrey Tower Museum Archives 684
Murrysville Community Library 495
Muscatine County Genealogical Society 206
Muscatine History Museum Archives 206
Muscoda Public Library 627
Muscogee Genealogical Society 129
Muscogiana: Journal of Muscogee Genealogical Society 129
Muscowpetung First Nation 706
Muse 49, 71
Muse Family 255
Muse News 194, 511, 594
Musee Acadien 695
Musee Acadien Archives 664, 673
Musee Acadien du Pubnico Ouest 677
Musee Acadien du Quebec 697
Musee Arouane 692
Musee Automobile 665
Musee Bealne Archives 697
Musee Bon-Pasteur 701
Musee Canadien des Civilisations 698
Musee D'Histoire de Saint-Roch Archives 703
Musee d'Histoire et de Traditions Populaires 697
Musee David M Stewart Archives 700
Musee de Baie Comeau 697
Musee de Charlevois 701
Musee de Haut-Richelieu 702
Musee de Kamouraska 698
Musee de l'Abeille 697
Musee de l'Eglise Notre-Dame 700
Musee de l'Oratoire Saint-Joseph 700
Musee de la Mer 698
Musee de la Mer Rimouski 701
Musee de Lachine 698
Musee de Saint Boniface Archives 661
Musee de Sainte-Anne 702
Musee de Saint-Pierre-Jolys 661
Musee de Seminaire de Saint-Hyacinthe 702
Musee des Anciens Canadiens 702
Musee des Augustines de l'Hopital General de Quebec 701
Musee des Papes 664
Musee des Pioneers 701
Musee des Soeurs de Sainte-Anne 698
Musee des Soeurs Grises de Montreal 700
Musee des Ursulines 701, 703
Musee du College de Levis 699
Musee du Fjord 698
Musee du Fort Saint-Jean Archives 702
Musee du Frere Andre 700
Musee du Manoir du Presbytere de Batiscan Archives 697
Musee du Saguenay-Lac-Saint-Jean Archives 697
Musee du Vieu-Phare 700
Musee et Centre de Transmission de la Culture 698
Musee François-Pilote Archives 698
Musee Gilles Villeneuve Archives 697
Musee Girouxville Archives 644
Musee Heritage Museum Archives 645
Musee Historique Charles le Moyne 699
Musee J Armand Bombardier 703
Musee Jean-Hotte 702
Musee Kateri Tekakwitha 698
Musee Kio-Warini 699
Musee Laure Conan Archives 701
Musee Laurier 704
Musee Le Chataud 700
Musee le Pionnier 661
Musee Les Retrouvailles 702
Musee Maison Saint-Gabriel 700
Musee Marc-Aurele Fortin 700
Musee Marguerite Bourgeoys 700
Musee Marie-Rose Durocher 699
Musee Maritime du Quebec 699
Musee Marius Barbeau 702
Musee Marsil 702
Musee Militaire du 12e Regiment Blinde du Canada 703
Musee Namesokanjik 698
Musee Pointe des Chenes 661
Musee Regimentaire les Fusiliers de Sherbrooke 703
Musee Regional d'Argenteuil 701
Musee Regional de la Cote-Nord 703
Musee Regional de Rimouski 701
Musee Regional de Vaudreuil-Soulanges 704
Musee Regional des Mines 699
Musee Royal 22e Regiment Archives 701
Musee Saint-Brieux 710
Musee Sainte-Marie 673
Musee Saint-Joachim 660
Musee Saint-Joseph 661
Musee Stewart au Fort de Ile Sainte-Helene 700

INDEX

Musee Territoire 702
MuseLetter 155, 355
Museline 536
MuseNews 552
Museo de las Americas 84
Museo de las Americas Newsletter 84
Museo ItaloAmericano 67
Museum and Archives of Georgia Education 134
Museum and Archives of the Big Bend Archives 535
Museum and Genealogy Library 196
Museum Association of the Fur Trade Archives 350
Museum Association of the Fur Trade Quarterly 350
Museum at Mountain Home 528
Museum at Mountain Home Archives 531
Museum at the Shore 367
Museum at Warm Springs Archives 480
Museum Briefs 313
Museum Carstairs Historical Society 642
Museum Center Archives 231
Museum Center Quarterly 231
Museum Chronicle 156, 524
Museum Dom Benoit 660
Museum Gazette 103
Museum Highlights 443
Museum Hi-Lites 187
Museum in the Community Archives 613
Museum in the Community Newsletter 613
Museum Light 601
Museum Memo 473
Museum Monitor 434
Museum Muse 349, 498, 511, 578, 631
Museum Musette 610
Museum Musings 189, 420, 427, 451, 543, 595, 603
Museum News 94, 552, 556
Museum Notes 40, 51, 235, 258, 415, 480, 607, 632
Museum of Afro-American History Archives 267
Museum of Amateur Radio Archives 97
Museum of Amateur Radio Magazine 97
Museum of American Frontier Culture Archives 595
Museum of American Heritage Archives 59
Museum of American Political Life 100
Museum of American Presidents Archives 595
Museum of American Treasures 55, 56
Museum of Apopkans 109
Museum of Appalachia Archives 526, 531
Museum of Art & History Archives 101
Museum of Art and History Archives 70
Museum of Art and History Newsletter 70
Museum of Automobiles Archives 30
Museum of Aviation at Robins AFB Archives 139
Museum of Boston Harbor Heritage Archives 272
Museum of Bronx History 390
Museum of Bus Transportation Archives 489
Museum of Cape Breton Heritage 675
Museum of Carousel Art & History Archives 457
Museum of Chicot County Arkansas Archives 29
Museum of Chinese in the Americas Archives 407
Museum of Church History Archives 571
Museum of Connecticut History 94
Museum of Connecticut History Archives 94
Museum of Discovery Archives 29
Museum of Early Trades & Crafts Archives 372
Museum of Early Trades & Crafts Newsletter 372
Museum of East Alabama Archives 8
Museum of East Texas Archives 552
Museum of East Texas Newsletter 552
Museum of Fife and Drum Archives 95
Museum of Flight Archives 606
Museum of Florida History 122
Museum of Florida History & Florida State Archives 122
Museum of Flying Archives 71
Museum of Funeral Customs Archives 174
Museum of Health Care Archives 684
Museum of History 122
Museum of History and Art Archives 57
Museum of History Archives 606
Museum of Idaho Archives 147
Museum of Indian Culture 481
Museum of Industry Archives 676
Museum of Jewish Heritage 407
Museum of Los Gatos Archives 52
Museum of Man in the Sea Archives 119
Museum of Migrating People Archives 390
Museum of Miniature Houses 181
Museum of Mobile Archives 7
Museum of Mobile Newsletter 7
Museum of Native American Cultures Library 607
Museum of New Mexico Archives 385
Museum of Newport History Archives 508
Museum of Newport Irish History Archives 508
Museum of North Idaho Archives 146
Museum of North Idaho Newsletter 146
Museum of Northern Arizona 16
Museum of Northern British Columbia Archives 654
Museum of Northern History Archives 684
Museum of Northwest Colorado Archives 83
Museum of Nursing History Archives 498
Museum of Orient and East Marion History 410
Museum of Pioneer History 464
Museum of Radio and Technology Archives 612
Museum of Rural Life Archives 258
Museum of Russian Culture Archives 67
Museum of San Diego History and Research Archives 65
Museum of San Rafael Archives 565
Museum of Science & History of Jacksonville 114
Museum of Science & History of Jacksonville Newsletter 114
Museum of Seminole County History 121
Museum of South East Alberta Archives 643
Museum of South Texas History Archives 543
Museum of South Texas History Newsletter 543
Museum of Southern History Archives 114, 560
Museum of Southern History Newsletter 560
Museum of Surveying Archives 296
Museum of Surveying Newsletter 296
Museum of Texas Tech University Archives 552
Museum of the Albemarle Archives 426
Museum of the Albemarle Newsletter 426
Museum of the American Philosophical Society Archives 498
Museum of the American Quilter's Society Archives 232
Museum of the American West Archives 52

Museum of the Arkansas Grand Prairie 33
Museum of the Arkansas Grand Prairie Newsletter 33
Museum of the Berkeley Springs Archives 611
Museum of the Berkeley Springs Newsletter 611
Museum of the Borough of Brooklyn Archives 391
Museum of the Cape Fear Historical Complex Archives 426
Museum of the Cariboo Chilcotin Archives 657
Museum of the Cherokee Indian Archives 425
Museum of the Cherokee Strip Archives 465
Museum of the Cherokee Strip Newsletter 465
Museum of the City of Lake Worth Archives 115
Museum of the City of New York Archives 407
Museum of the City of New York Newsletter 407
Museum of the City of San Francisco Archives 67
Museum of the Confederacy Archives 594
Museum of the Confederacy Journal 594
Museum of the Confederacy Newsletter 594
Museum of the Forest Archives 18
Museum of the Great Plains Library 466
Museum of the Gulf Coast 556
Museum of the Highwood Archives 644
Museum of the Islands Archives 120
Museum of the llano Estacado Archives 556
Museum of the Middle Appalachians Archives 595
Museum of the Middle Appalachians Newsletter 595
Museum of the New South Archives 425
Museum of the North American Indian Travelling College 681
Museum of the Northern Great Plains Archives 344
Museum of the Occidental Archives 635
Museum of the Plains Archives 556
Museum of the Red River Archives 466
Museum of the Regiments Archives 641
Museum of the Rockies Archives 343
Museum of the Royal Regment of Canada 691
Museum of the Soldier 192
Museum of the Southern Jewish Experience Archives 321
Museum of the Southwest Archives 554
Museum of the Southwest Newsletter 554
Museum of the Waxhaws and Andrew Jackson Memorial Archives 434
Museum of the Western Prairie 463
Museum of the Yellowstone Archives 347
Museum of Tolerance Archives 52
Museum of Transportation Archives 339
Museum of Vision Museum Archives 67
Museum of West Louisiana Archives 238
Museum of Western Colorado Library 86
Museum of Work and Culture Archives 510
Museum of Yarmouth History 253
Museum of York County Archives 517
Museum of York County Newsletter 517
Museum Railroad Baggage Car Annex 215
Museum Record 286
Museum Report 584
Museum Review 500
Museum Sparks 430
Museum Times 86
Museum Update 427
Museum Village Archives 405
Museum Village Newsletter 405
Museum Visitor 301
Museums Alaska Archives 11
Museums at Stony Brook Archives 417
Museums of the City of Mobile Archives 7
Museums Report 524
Musgamagw Tribal Council 647
Mushoka Lakes Museum Archives 688
Music Box Cassette 48
Musical Wonder House Museum Archives 252
Musig Family 569
Musings 30, 190, 235, 257, 511, 604
Muskeg Lake First Nation 708
Muskego Historical Society 627
Muskego Historical Society Newsletter 627
Muskegon County Genealogical Society & Archives 298
Muskegon County Library 298
Muskegon County Museum Archives 298
Muskegon County Museum Quarterly 298
Muskegon Railroad Historical Society 298
Muskingum County District Library System 461
Muskingum County Genealogical Library 461
Muskingum County Genealogical Society & Archives 461
Muskingum Journal 461
Muskoday First Nation 705
Muskogee County Genealogical Society & Archives 467
Muskogee County Genealogical Society Quarterly 467
Muskogee Public Library 467
Muskogee War Memorial Park and Military Museum Archives 467
Muskoka Pioneer Village and Museum Archives 683
Muskoka Steamship and Historical Society 683
Muskowekwan First Nation 707
Muskrat Tales 301
Musqueam Indian Band 656
Musquodoboit Harbour Heritage Society 675
Musquodoboit Railway Museum 675
Musselman Library 442, 488
Musselman-South Berkeley Community Library 613
Musselshell Valley Historical Museum Archives 346
Musser Public Library 206
Musson Family 543
Mutter Museum Archives 498
My Old Kentucky Home State Park Archives 225
Myakka City Historical Society 117
Myalusing Valley Museum Archives 506
Myers Library 220
Myers Memorial Library 398
Myers Mine 219
Myers-Meiers Family 344
Myers-Parkhurst Family 469
Myerstown Community Library 495
Mylorie Family 420
Mynderse Library 416
Myrin Library 485
Myrin Library News 485
Myrtle Lintner Spear Museum 629
Myrtleville House Museum Archives 680
Mystic and Noank Library 96
Mystic Nautical Heritage Society 94
Mystic River Historical Society & Library 96
Mystic River Historical Society Newsletter 96
Mystic Seaport Museum and Library 96

INDEX

N

N L Terteling Library 146
N.S.S. Almanac (N.S.S. Kalendar) 499
N'Oubliez Pas 240
Nachrichten der Donauschwaben in Chicago 158
Nacogdoches Genealogical Society & Library 554
Nadleh Whut'en Indian Band 649
NaeSmith Genealogical Society of the United States 114
NaeSmith Genealogical Society of the United States Annual Update 114
Nafzger Family 623
Nahant Historical Society 275
Nahant Public Library 275
Naicam Museum Archives 708
Nak'azdli Indian Band 649
Nakodabi: the Assiniboine People 347
Namgis First Nation 647
Nampa Municipal Library 645
Nampa Public Library 148
NANA Museum of the Arctic Archives 13
Nanaimo and District Museum Society & Library 652
Nanaimo Family History Society 652
Nanaimo First Nations 652
Nanaimo Historical Society 652
Nance County Historical Society & Library 351
Nancy Carol Roberts Memorial Library 538
Nancy Fawcett Memorial Library 353
Nancy Island Historic Site Archives 692
Nancy Museum & Library of Antiquity Archives 334
Nancy Museum Newsletter 334
Nancy Thompson Library 379
Nanoose First Nation 651
Nantahala Regional Library 430
Nanticoke Historical Society 495
Nanticoke Indian Association & Archives 104
Nanticoke Indian Association Historical Museum 104
Nanticoke Public Library 683
Nanticoke Public Library, Selkirk Branch 689
Nanton Lancaster Air Museum Archives 645
Nantucket Atheneum Library 275
Nantucket Historical Association & Library 275
Nantucket Life-Saving Museum Archives 275
Nantucket Lightship Basket Museum Archives 275
Nantucket Lightship Basket Museum Newsletter 275
Napa City-County Library 55
Napa City-County Library-Calistoga Branch 38
Napa County Historical Society & Library 55
Napa County Landmarks Society 55
Napa Valley Genealogical and Biographical Society & Library 55
Napa Valley Model Railroad Historical Society 55
Napa Valley Museum Archives 78
Naper Settlement Museum 168
Naperville Heritage Society & Archives 168
Naperville Public Libraries 168
Napier Clan 8
Napier Family 221
Naples Historical Museum 248
Naples Historical Society & Archives 248
Naples Public Library 248
Napoleon Public Library 453
Napoleonic Society of America 110
Napoleonic Society of America Member's Bulletin 110
Naponee Historical Society 354
Nappanee Public Library 190
Naramata Museum Archives 652
Narcissa Prentiss House Museum Archives 412
NARFE Chapter 1320 Genealogy Group 559
Narodne Kalendar 484
Narragansett Historical Society & Library 280
Narragansett Historical Society Quarterly 280
Narragansett Indian Tribal Historic Preservation Office 510
Narrangansett Public Library 508
NASA Glenn Research Center Archives 445
Nase Ceske Dedictvi: Our Czech Heritage 198
Nase Rodina: Czechoslovak Genealogical Society Quarterly Newsletter 314
Nash County Historical Association & Archives 432
Nash Family 278, 478, 562
Nash Family Newsletter 54
Nash Library 464
Nash Notations 82
Nashotah House Library 627
Nashua Historical Society & Library 363
Nashua Historical Society Newsletter 363
Nashua Public Library 206, 363
Nashville Public Library 168, 531
Nashville Zoo and Historic Farm Archives 531
Nassau County Public Library System-Fernandina Beach Branch 112
Nassau Genealogist 112
Nassau Library System 418
Natchez Historical Society 321
Natchez Indians 321
Natchez Trace Genealogical Society 4
Natchez Trace Newsletter 4
Natchez Trace Traveler 4
Natchitoches Genealogical and Historical Association 239
Natchitoches Genealogist 239
Natchitoches Parish Library 239
Nathan Denison House Museum Archives 487
Nathan Hale Homestead Museum Archives 92
Nathan W Collier Library 117
Nathaniel W Faison Home Museum Archives 551
Natick Historical Museum 279
Natick Historical Society & Archives 279
Nation Family Newsletter 158
Nation Huronne-Wendat 704
National Aboriginal Forestry Association 687
National Afro-American Museum and Cultural Center Archives 460
National Afro-American Museum Newsletter 460
National Agricultural Center & Hall of Fame Archives 212
National Agricultural Center & Hall of Fame Archives Update 212
National Air and Space Museum Archives 106
National Air and Space Museum eNewsletter 106
National Apple Museum Archives 483
National Archives 258
National Archives - Alaska Branch 11
National Archives & Records Administration-Central Plains Region 332
National Archives & Records Administration-Great Lakes Region 156
National Archives & Records Administration-Mid Atlantic Region 498
National Archives & Records Administration-Northeast Region 277, 281
National Archives & Records Administration-Pacific Alaska Region 606
National Archives & Records Administration-Pacific Region 49, 64

National Archives & Records Administration-Rocky Mountain Region 84
National Archives & Records Administration-Southwest Region 545
National Archives and Records Administration 106
National Archives and Records Administration Library 267
National Archives Newsletter 687
National Archives of Canada 687
National Archives-Civilian Records Facility 339
National Archives-Military Personnel Records 339
National Archives-New York 407
National Archives-Southeast Region 130
National Association Civilian Conservation Corps Alumni, Chapter #55 65
National Association of Lively Families Quarterly Newsletter 136
National Atomic Museum Archives 381
National Baha'i Archives 160
National Border Patrol Museum Archives 544
National Buckeye Quarterly 256
National Buffalo Museum Archives 438
National Buildling Museum Archives 106
National Bydgelag Council & Library 306
National Capital Buckeye Chapter, Ohio Genealogical Society 256
National Capital Genealogy Club 687
National Capital Trolley Museum Archives 263
National Center for Constitutional Studies 148
National Christmas Center Museum Archives 496
National City Historical Society 55
National City Public Library-Hollingsworth Local History Room 56
National Civil Rights Museum Archives 530
National Civil War Association 70
National Civil War Museum Archives 489
National Colonial Dame of the 17th Century, Palo Verde Chapter 19
National Conference of State Historic Preservations Officers 106
National Council on Public History 21, 187
National Cowboy and Western Heritage Museum Archives 468
National Cowboy Hall of Fame 468
National Cryptologic Museum Archives 259
National Czech and Slovak Museum and Library 198
National D-Day Museum Archives 240
National Defense University Library 106
National Directory of Local Researchers 459
National Doukhobour Heritage Village 711
National Eaves Family Association Newsletter 131
National Episcopal Historians and Archivists 503
National Exhibition Centre 690
National Firearms Museum Archives 587
National First Ladies' Library 443
National First Ladies' Library Newsletter 443
National Flag Foundation 499
National Foundation for Jewish Culture 407
National Foundation for Jewish Culture Newsletter 407
National Frontier Trails Center Archives 331
National Genealogical Society & Library 584
National Genealogical Society Newsletter 584
National Genealogical Society Quarterly 584
National Genealogical Society, Computer Interest Group Digest 584
National Geographic Museum Archives 106
National Great Rivers Museum Archives 158
National Guard Memorial Library 106
National Hall of Fame for Famous American Indians Archives 463
National Headquarters, General Society of Mayflower Descendants & Archives 277
National Heritage Museum Archives 273
National Heritage Museum Quarterly 273
National Hibernian Digest 388
National Historic Oregon Trail Archives 473
National Historical Publications and Records Commission 106
National Historical Society 19, 489, 630
National Huguenot Society & Library 306
National Icarian Heritage Society 199, 544
National Icarian Heritage Society Newsletter 544
National Indian Arts and Crafts Corporation 687
National Infantry Museum Archives 131
National Institute on Genealogical Research 106
National Italian American Foundation 106
National Italian American Foundation News 106
National Japanese American Historical Society 67
National Kateri Shrine Museum Archives 397
National Kateri Shrine Museum Newsletter 397
National Liberty Ship Memorial 67
National Library of Canada 687
National Maritime Historical Society 411
National Medal of Honor Museum of Military History Archives 525
National Medal of Honor Museum of Military History Newsletter 525
National Military Heritage Museum Archives 338
National Military Heritage Society 338
National Museum of American History Library 106
National Museum of American Jewish History Archives 498
National Museum of American Jewish History Newsletter 498
National Museum of American Jewish Military History Archives 106
National Museum of American Jewish Military History Quarterly 106
National Museum of Catholic History Archives 407
National Museum of Catholic History Newsletter 407
National Museum of Civil War Medicine Archives 259
National Museum of Civil War Medicine Quarterly 259
National Museum of Communications Archives 557
National Museum of Funeral History Archives 549
National Museum of Health and Medicine Archives 106
National Museum of Industrial History Archives 483
National Museum of Naval Aviation Archives 120
National Museum of Patiotism Archives 126
National Museum of Polo Archives 115
National Museum of Polo Newsletter 115
National Museum of the American Indian Archives 407
National New York Central Railroad Museum Archives 183
National New York Central Railroad Museum Quarterly 183
National News (Narodyne Noviny) 499
National Odom Assembly News 43
National Odom Assembly Newsletter 110
National Odom Assembly Newsletter 33
National Oregon/California Trail Center 148
National Packard Museum Archives 459
National Park Community College Library 28
National Park Service-Midwest Regional Library 355
National POW Museum 125
National Preservation Institute 583
National Railroad Museum Archives 428, 622
National Railroad Museum Newsletter 622
National Railway Historical Society 260, 340, 478, 505, 585
National Railway Historical Society & Library 498
National Railway Historical Society, Chicago Chapter 169
National Railway Historical Society, Potomac Chapter 263

National Railway Historical Society, Roanoke Chapter 594
National Railway Historical Society, Rochester Chapter 414
National Records Center 263
National Rivers Hall of Fame Newsletter 201
National Route 66 Museum and Old Town Museum Archives 465
National Scouting Museum Archives 550
National Shaving and Barbershop Museum Archives 95
National Slovak Society News 484
National Slovak Society of the USA 484, 499
National Soaring Museum Archives 396
National Society of Andersonville 125
National Society of Colonial Dames of America in Georgia, Valdosta Town Committee 139
National Society of Descendants of Early Quakers 255
National Society of Hispanic Genealogy 84
National Society of New England Women 19
National Society of the British Empire in USA, Agin Court Chapter 17
National Society of the British Empire in USA, Plantagenet Chapter 20
National Society of the British Empire in USA, Stonehenge Chapter 20
National Society of the Colonial Dames of America & Library 106
National Society of the Colonial Dames of America in the State of Colorado & Archives 82
National Society of the Colonial Dames of America in the State of Georgia & Archives 137
National Society of the Colonial Dames of America in the State of New York & Library 407
National Society of the Colonial Dames of America in the State of Rhode Island & Archives 508
National Society of the Colonial Dames of America in the State of South Carolina & Library 512
National Society of the Colonial Dames of America, State of North Carolina & Library 434
National Society of the Daughters of the American Revolutions, New Mexico State 381
National Society, Children of the American Revolution 15
National Society, Children of the American Revolution & Archives 106
National Society, Colonial Dames of the 17th Century 19
National Society, Colonial Dames of the XVII Century & Library 106
National Society, Dames of the Court of Honor 19
National Society, Daughters of American Colonists 19
National Society, Daughters of American Colonists & Library 106
National Society, Daughters of Colonial Wars 20
National Society, Daughters of Founders-Patriots of America 16
National Society, Daughters of the American Revolution 17, 531
National Society, Daughters of the American Revolution & Library 106
National Society, Daughters of the American Revolution Museum 106
National Society, Daughters of the Revolution of 1776 413
National Society, Daughters of the Union 1861-1865 292
National Society, Daughters of Utah Pioneers & Library 571
National Society, Magna Carta Dames 20
National Society, Sons and Daughters of the Pilgrims 16, 311
National Society, Sons of the American Revolution & Library 230
National Society, Sons of Utah Pioneers & Library 571
National Society, United Daughters of 1812 16
National Society, Women Descendants of the Ancient and Honorable Artillery Company 19
National Steinbeck Center 64
National Steinbeck Center Newsletter 64
National Temple Hill Association & Archives 406
National Temple Hill Association Quarterly 406
National Temple Hill Historical Museum 406
National Toy Train Museum Archives 502
National Trail of Tears Association, Missouri Chapter 331
National Trust for Historic Preservation 106, 156
National Trust for Historic Preservation Museum 106
National Trust for Historic Preservation, South Region 512
National Trust for Historic Preservation, Western Regional Office 67
National Underground Railroad Freedom Center Archives 444
National Voting Rights Museum Archives 8
National Voting Rights Museum Newsletter 8
National Warplane Museum Archives 400
National Woman's Relief Corps, Auxiliary to the Grand Army of the Republic 174
National Yiddish Book Center Archives 265
Native Alliance of Quebec 698
Native American Heritage Commission 63
Native American Heritage Museum Archives 215
Native American Museum Archives 194
Native American Resource Center Archives 431
Native Council of Canada 687
Native Daughters of the Golden West Society & Library 67
Native Fishing Association 656
Native Mid-America All-Indian Center 223
Native Son 67
Native Sons of Greater Kansas City 332
Native Sons of the Golden West, Grand Parlor 67
Native Women's Association of Canada 687
Natrona County Genealogical Society 635
Natrona County Public Library 635
Natrona County Public Library Newsletter 635
Natural Bridge in the Kentucky Mountains 226
Natural Center for the American Revolution Archives 504
Natural News 414
Naugatuck Historical Museum 96
Naugatuck Historical Society & Archives 96
Naugatuck Historical Society News 96
Naumkeag Historic Home Museum Archives 280
Nautical Heritage Society 65
Nautical Museum 390
Nauticus Maritime Center Archives 592
Nauvoo Historical Museum 168
Nauvoo Historical Society & Archives 168
Nauvoo Historical Society Newsletter 168
Nauvoo Journal 567
Nauvoo Public Library 168
Navajo County Genealogical Society 22
Navajo Museum Archives 22
Navajo Nation Historic Preservation Department 16
Naval Air Station Library 120, 541, 545, 551
Naval Base Coronado Library 65
Naval Base Ventura County Library 60
Naval Historical Foundation & Library 106
Naval Historical Foundation Newsletter 106
Naval Institute History, Reference & Preservation Dept Library 255
Naval Museum of Alberta Archives 641
Naval Surface Warfare Center Library 260
Naval Training Center Library 161
Naval Undersea Museum Archives 602
Naval War College Museum Archives 508
Navarro County Genealogical Society & Archives 541
Navarro County Historical Society & Archives 541

Navarro Leaves and Branches 541
Navasota Public Library 554
Navigator 115, 460, 592
Nawash First Nation 692
Nazareth Archival Center 232
Nazko Indian Band 654
NCGS Bits & Bytes 22
NCTM Journal 263
ND Flickertale Newsletter 437
NEA Newsletter 267
Neal-Bateman Family 571
Nebeker Family 568
Nebraska Ancestree 353
Nebraska City Historical Society 354
Nebraska DAR & Library 349
Nebraska Historical Magazine 353
Nebraska Historical Society & Archives 350
Nebraska History 353
Nebraska History Network 356
Nebraska Jewish Historical Society & Library 355
Nebraska Jewish Historical Society Newsletter 355
Nebraska Library Commission 353
Nebraska Military Historical Society 352
Nebraska State Capitol Library & Museum 353
Nebraska State Genealogical Society 353
Nebraska State Genealogical Society & Archives 349
Nebraska State Historical Museum 353
Nebraska State Historical Society & Archives 351, 353
Nebraska State Historical Society Newsletter 353
Nebraskans of Irish and Scotch-Irish Ancestry 353
Nebraskans of Irish and Scotch-Irish Ancestry Newsletter 353
Ned Shed Museum Archives 685
Nederland Area Historical Society 88
Needham Free Public Library 275
Needham Historical Society & Library 275
Needles Regional Museum Archives 56
Neeley Family 609
Neelyville Historical Society 335
Neenah Historical Society & Archives 627
Neenah Public Library 627
Neenah Public Library Newsletter 627
Neerlandia School Public Library 645
Neese Family 256
Neese's Farm Museum Archives 516
Nee-Tahi-Buhn Indian Band 648
Neff Family 376
Neff News 376
Negaunee Historical Museum 298
Negaunee Historical Society & Archives 298
Negro Historical Association of Colorado Springs 82
Negro Leagues Baseball Museum Archives 332
NEHGS Educational Bulletin 267
NEHGS NEXUS 267
Neil Notes 63
Neill Museum Archives 545
Neill Public Library 605
Neill-Cochran House Museum Archives 536
Nekaneet First Nation 708
Neligh Mills Historical Society 354
Neligh Public Library 354
Nell Family 565
Nell Family Genealogical Society Newsletter 175
Nellis Family 420
Nelson City Historical Society 584
Nelson County Genealogical Roundtable 225
Nelson County Genealogist 225
Nelson County Public Library 225
Nelson Family 554
Nelson Municipal Library 652
Nelson Museum Association and Historical Society & Library 652
Nelson Notes 62
Nelson Pioneer Farm Museum Archives 206
Nelson Pioneer Farm Museum News Bulletin 206
Nelsonville Public Library 453
Nemaha County Genealogical Society 221
Nemaha County Genealogical Society Newsletter 221
Nemaha County Historical Society & Library 221
Nemaha Valley Genealogical Society 349
Nemaha Valley Genealogical Society Newsletter 349
Nemaha Valley Museum Library 349
Nemaiah Valley Indian Band 652
Nemours Foundation & Archives 104
Nenana Public Library 13
Neosho Historical Society & Archives 627
Neosho Museum Researcher 627
Neosho-Newton County Library 335
Nepean Central Library 686
Nepean Museum Archives 686
Neponset Public Library 168
Neponset Township Historical Museum 168
Neponset Township Historical Society & Archives 168
Neptune Public Library 374
Nesbitt Memorial Library 540
Nesbitt-Bryant-Mitchell-Guest Family 596
Nesbitt-Nisbet Family 506
Neshaminy-Warwick Presbyterian Church Library 504
Neshoba County Historical Society 322
Neshoba County Public Library 322
Neskonlith Indian Band 648
Nesmith Library 365
Nesmith Library News 365
Ness City Public Library 219
Ness County Historical Museum 219
Ness County Historical Society & Archives 219
Nessy 40
Nethercott-Marcum Family 150
Netherland Family 526
Netherland Inn House Museum Archives 528
Netherland Inn House Museum Newsletter 528
Nettle Creek Museum 185
Nettleton Family 585
Neuse Regional Library-Pollocksville Public Library 431
Nevada County Depot Museum Archives 32
Nevada County Depot Museum Association & Library 32
Nevada County Depot Museum Association Newsletter 32
Nevada County Genealogical Society 39
Nevada County Historical Society 32
Nevada County Historical Society & Library 56
Nevada County Historical Society Bulletin 56
Nevada County Historical Society Newsletter 56

INDEX

Nevada County Library 46, 56
Nevada County Library-Doris Foley Branch 56
Nevada Historical Society 206
Nevada Public Library 206, 336
Neversink Valley Area Museum Archives 395
Neversink Valley Area Museum Newsletter 395
Nevill Public Museum Newsletter 622
Nevill Public Museum of Brown County Library 622
New Albany-Floyd County Public Library 190
New Almaden Quicksilver County Park Association 56
New Almaden Quicksilver Mining Museum Archives 68
New At Your Library 276
New Baltimore Historical Society & Library 298
New Baltimore Historical Society Newsletter 298
New Bedford Fire Museum Archives 275
New Bedford Free Public Library 275
New Bedford Historical Society 275
New Bedford Whaling Museum 275
New Berlin Almanack 627
New Berlin Historical Museum 627
New Berlin Historical Society & Archives 627
New Berlin Library 405
New Berlin Public Library 628
New Bern-Craven County Public Library 430
New Bethlehem Area Free Public Library 495
New Book List 300
New Books at JCFL 272
New Books List 505
New Boston Genealogical Society 554
New Boston Historial Society 360
New Boston Historical Society & Library 168
New Boston Public Library 554
New Bostonian 554
New Braintree Historical Society 275
New Brass Key Newsletter 349, 353
New Braunfels Conservation Society & Archives 555
New Braunfels Conservation Society Newsletter 555
New Braunfels Historical Museum 555
New Braunfels Historical Railroad and Modelers Society 555
New Braunfels Public Library 555
New Bremen News 175
New Bremen Town Historian 393
New Brighton Area Historical Society & Library 312
New Britain Public Library 96
New Brunswick Free Public Library 374
New Brunswick Genealogical Society & Library 663
New Brunswick Genealogical Society, Carleton County Branch 664
New Brunswick Genealogical Society, Miramichi Branch 663
New Brunswick Genealogical Society, Restigouch Branch 663
New Brunswick Genealogical Society, Saint John Branch 665
New Brunswick Genealogical Society, Southeastern Branch 664
New Brunswick Healthcare Museum Archives 663
New Brunswick Mining Museum 664
New Brunswick Museum Archives 665
New Buffalo Township Public Library 298
New Canaan Historical Museum 96
New Canaan Historical Society & Archives 96
New Canaan Historical Society Annual 96
New Canaan Library 96
New Canaan Library News 96
New Carlisle and Olive Township Public Library 190
New Castle Historical Society & Archives 104
New Castle Historical Society & Library 393
New Castle Historical Society Newsletter 393
New Castle Public Library 104, 363, 495
New Castle-Henry County Public Library 190
New City Free Library 405
New Constellation 499
New Cumberland Public Library 495
New Denmark Historical Society 664
New Dimensions 497
New Directions 19
New Durham Public Library 363
New Echota State Historic Site Archives 127
New Egypt Historical Society 374
New England Air Museum 101
New England Archivists 267
New England Carousel Museum Archives 91
New England Civil War Museum Archives 98
New England Computer Genealogist 267
New England Fire and History Museum Archives 267
New England Historic Genealogical Society & Library 267
New England Historical and Genealogical Register 267
New England Historical Genealogical Society 271
New England Journal of History 281
New England Maple Museum Archives 578
New England Museum Association Archives 267
New England Pirate Museum Archives 278
New England Quarterly 267
New England Quilt Museum Archives 273
New England Wireless and Steam Museum Archives 507
New Fairfield Free Public Library 96
New Fairfield Historical Society & Library 96
New Glarus Historical Society 628
New Gleanings 387
New Gloucester Maine Historical Society & Library 248
New Greenville Mountaineer 515
New Growth 123
New Hampshire Antiquarian Museum 361
New Hampshire Antiquarian Society & Archives 361
New Hampshire Antiquarian Society Newsletter 361
New Hampshire Aviation Historical Society 362
New Hampshire Community Technical College Library 359
New Hampshire Farm Museum Archives 363
New Hampshire Farm Museum Newsletter 363
New Hampshire Genealogical Record 360
New Hampshire Genie 361
New Hampshire Historical Society & Library 360
New Hampshire Historical Society Newsletter 360
New Hampshire Records & Archives Library 360
New Hampshire Society of Genealogists 360
New Hampshire Society of Genealogists & Library 361
New Hampshire Society of Genealogists Newsletter 360
New Hampshire State Library 360
New Hampshire Technical Institute Library 360
New Hampshire-Maine Connection 362
New Hampton Historical Society 363
New Hampton Public Library 206
New Hanover County Public Library 434
New Hartford Historical & Archives 98

New Hartford Historical Museum 98, 405
New Hartford Historical Society 96
New Hartford Historical Society & Archives 405
New Haven Colony Historical Museum 96
New Haven Colony Historical Society & Archives 96
New Haven Colony Historical Society Journal 96
New Haven Community Library 578
New Haven Free Public Library 96
New Haven Town Historian 405
New Highland Sentinel 511
New Holstein Historical Society & Archives 628
New Holstein Historical Society Annual Newsletter 628
New Hope Historical Society 495
New Hope Historical Society Newsletter 495
New Hope Preservation Committee 312
New Hyde Park Public Library 405
New Jersey Genealogy Club of Passaic County 380
New Jersey Historical Commission 379
New Jersey Historical Commission Newsletter 379
New Jersey Historical Museum 374
New Jersey Historical Society & Archives 374
New Jersey Historical Society News 374
New Jersey History 374
New Jersey Messenger 374
New Jersey Museum of Agriculture Archives 375
New Jersey Museum of Agriculture Newsletter 375
New Jersey Naval Museum Archives 370
New Jersey Newsletter 375
New Jersey Office of Historic Sites 379
New Jersey State Archives 379
New Jersey State House Archives 379
New Jersey State Library 379
New Jersey State Museum Archives 379
New Jersey State Museum Newsletter 379
New Kent Historical Society 593
New Kirk Directory 329
New Kuban Historical Museum Archives 368
New Lebanon Library 405
New Lebanon Preservation Society 336
New Lenox Area Historical Society 168
New Lenox Public Library 168
New Light on Old Barratts 103
New London County Historical Museum 97
New London County Historical Society & Archives 97
New London County Historical Society Newsletter 97
New London Heritage Historical Society & Library 628
New London Historical Museum 363
New London Historical Society & Archives 363
New London Historical Society & Library 363
New London Historical Society Newsletter 363
New London Public Library 97, 454
New London Public Library and Museum 628
New Madison Public Library 454
New Madrid County Library 337
New Madrid Historical Museum Archives 336
New Market Battlefield Park Library 591
New Market Historical Society & Archives 363
New Martinsville Public Library 614
New Mexico Farm & Ranch Heritage Museum Archives 383
New Mexico Farm & Ranch Heritage Museum Newsletter 383
New Mexico Genealogical Society & Archives 381
New Mexico Genealogist 381
New Mexico Historical Review 381
New Mexico Jewish Historical Society 385
New Mexico Jewish Jewish Historical Society Newsletter 385
New Mexico Museum of Space History Archives 381
New Mexico Records Center and Archives 385
New Mexico Space Journal 381
New Mexico State Library 385
New Mexico State University Library 383
New Mexico State University Library Newsletter 383
New Mexico State University-Grants Branch Library 383
New Milan Ledger 453
New Milford Historical Museum 97
New Milford Historical Society & Archives 97
New Milford Public Library 97
New Milford Public Library Newsletter 97, 101
New Notes from Suggett House 395
New Ontario Chronicle 410
New Orleans Fire Department Museum Archives 240
New Orleans Genesis 240
New Orleans Pharmacy Museum Archives 240
New Orleans Public Library 240
New Palmer Vidette 97
New Paris Historical Society 190
New Port Richey Public Library 118
New Portico 400
New Prague Historical Society 312
New Providence Historical Society & Library 374
New Reader News 58
New Richmond Heritage Center 628
New Richmond Preservation Society 628
New River Historical Society 593
New River Historical Society & Archives 591
New River News 112
New Rochelle Public Library 406
New Rusyn Times 499
New Santa Fe Historical Society 332
New Series 700
New Sweden Farmstead Museum Archives 368
New Sweden Historical Society & Library 248
New Sweden Historical Society Newsletter 248
New Tecumseth Public Library 679
New Waterford and District Historical Society 675
New Westminster Indian Band 656
New Westminster Public Library 653
New Windsor Catonment State Historic Site Archives 419
New Windsor Public Library 168
New Year's Shooters and Mummers & Archives 498
New York Caledonian Club 407
New York City Fire Museum Archives 407
New York City Fire Museum Newsletter 407
New York City Municipal Reference and Research Center 407
New York City Police Museum Archives 407
New York City Police Museum Newsletter 407
New York Genealogical and Biographical Record 407
New York Genealogical and Biographical Society & Library 407
New York Genealogical and Biographical Society Newsletter 407
New York Historical Museum 407
New York Historical Society 367

INDEX

New York Historical Society & Archives 407
New York Historical Society Gazette 407
New York History 394
New York Irish History 407
New York Irish History Roundtable 407
New York Mills Finnish-American Historical Society 312
New York Museum of Transportation Archives 420
New York Newsletter 408
New York Pedigrees 145
New York Public Library 407, 408
New York State Bureau of Historic Sites Archives 419
New York State Council of Genealogical Organizations 418
New York State Historian 387
New York State Historical Association & Archives 394
New York State Library 387
New York State Military Museum Archives 415
New York State Museum Archives 387
New York State Office of Parks, Recration and Historic Preservation Library 387
New York State Queries 608
New York Transit Museum Archives 391
New York Wills: Richmond Co, Staten Island 607
Newark Historical Society & Library 104
Newark Historical Society Newsletter 104
Newark Landmark and Historic Preservation 374
Newark Museum Library 374
Newark Public Library 374, 408, 454
Newark Valley Depot Museum Archives 408
Newark Valley Depot Museum Newsletter 408
Newark Valley Historical Society & Library 408
Newark Valley Historical Society Newsletter 408
Newaygo County Museum 299
Newaygo County Society of History and Genealogy 292, 299, 304
Newaygo County Society of History and Genealogy Newsletter 304
Newaygo County Society of History and Genealogy Quarterly 299
Newberry County Historical Society 516
Newberry County Historical Society Bulletin 516
Newberry County Library 516
Newberry Library 156
Newberry Library's Friends of Genealogy 156
Newburgh Free Library 408
Newbury Park Library, Thousand Oaks Branch 56
Newburyport Maritime Society 265
Newburyport Maritime Society Archives 275
Newburyport Maritime Society Quarterly 275
Newburyport Public Library 275
Newcastle Historical Society 249
Newcomb Town Historian 408
Newcomb-Lampkin Family 290
Newcomen Society of the United States & Library 487
Newcomerstown Historical Society & Archives 454
Newell Museum Archives 523
Newetowne Chronicle 268
Newfane Historical Society 392
Newfields Public Library 363
Newfoundland Ancestor 668
Newfoundland and Labrador Genealogical Society 668
Newfoundland Historical Society & Library 668
Newfoundland Naval and Military Museum Archives 668
Newington Historical Society and Trust 97
Newington Neighbor 363
Newland House Museum 47
Newlin-Bush Family 89
Newman Family Society News 84
Newman Grove Public Library 354
Newman Library 584
Newmarket Public Library 363
Newmyer Family 325
Newnan-Coweta Historical Society & Archives 135
Newport Beach Historical Society 41
Newport Beach Public Library 56
Newport Gazette 508
Newport Harbor Nautical Museum Archives 56
Newport Historical Museum 363, 508
Newport Historical Society & Archives 363
Newport Historical Society & Library 508
Newport Historical Society Newsletter 508
Newport History 508
Newport News Library 591
Newport News Public Library System 591
Newport Public Library 508
Newport Restoration Foundation 508
Newport Township Historical Society 176
Newport-Vermillion County Library 191
Newrace Newsletter 346
News & Events at Brookings Public Library 521
News & Events Newsletter 376
News & Notes 259, 419, 493
News & Reviews 152
News & Views 222, 339
News and Notes 50, 197, 199, 261, 262, 277, 339, 414, 620
News and Notes of the Twenty-Nine Palms Historical Society 75
News and Notes Out of the Ordinary 272
News and Reviews 580
News and Views 104, 578
News and Views of the Underhill Society 410
News Etc Newsletter 432
News from Eldridge Street 406
News from Historic Hildene 577
News from Historic Speedwell 374
News from Home 628
News from Nickawackett 579
News from Northland 499
News from the Auburn Public Library 243
News from the Banks of the Elkhorn 335
News from the Board 444
News from the Congregational Christian Historical Society 266
News from the Customs House 260
News from the Evangelical and Reformed Historical Society 491
News from the Ford 292
News from the Frontier 595
News from the Northwest 167
News from the Northwoods 628
News from the Red Caboose 345
News in Tennessee History 531
News Letter of the Irish Family History Forum 414
News Notes 60, 312
News of Discovery 479
News of Note 93
News of the Family Circle 120

News of the Nehemiah Smith Clan 257
News of the North Central Illinois Genealogical Society 172
News of the Radio History Society 257
News of the Utah State Historical Society 572
News of the YIVO 408
News Packet 111
News Update 127
Newseum Archives 584
News-Journal Company Archives 104
Newsletter : A Word From The Weis 263
Newsletter for Friends of Special Collections 575
Newsletter from Scotland and the US Chapter 138
Newsletter Mission San Diego Historical Society Quarterly 65
Newsletter of 3rd Century Methodism 256
Newsletter of ACHM 583
Newsletter of Clan MacMillan Society of North America 323
Newsletter of Hartland Historical Society 577
Newsletter of South Suburban Genealogical and Historical Society 162
Newsletter of the Aiken-Barnwell Genealogical Society Chapter, SCGS 511
Newsletter of the Albemarle Genealogical Society 425
Newsletter of the Allegany County Historical Society 258
Newsletter of the Alton Area Historical Society 151
Newsletter of the Arizona Historical Society 22
Newsletter of the Arlington Genealogical Society 535
Newsletter of the Armstrong County Historical and Museum Society 491
Newsletter of the Bath County Historical Society 596
Newsletter of the Bluffton Historical Preservation Society 511
Newsletter of the Branch County Historical Society 288
Newsletter of the Brant County Branch, OGS 680
Newsletter of the Brattleboro Historical Society 575
Newsletter of the Brown County Historical Society 190
Newsletter of the Burnet County Genealogical Society; Shin Oaks Folks 539
Newsletter of the Butler County Historical Society 449
Newsletter of the Carbondale Historical Society and Museum 484
Newsletter of the Casa del Herrero 70
Newsletter of the Cass County Historical Society 330
Newsletter of the Cherryfield-Narraguagus Historical Society 245
Newsletter of the Clackamas County Family History Society 477
Newsletter of the Clark County Genealogical Society 609
Newsletter of the Clinton County Historical Society 493
Newsletter of the Cloverdale Historical Society 40
Newsletter of the Columbine Genealogical and Historical Society 86
Newsletter of the Coos County Historical Society 477
Newsletter of the Cumberland County Genealogical Society 426
Newsletter of the Cumberland County Historical Society 484
Newsletter of the Delaware County Historical Alliance 190
Newsletter of the Dorchester Historical Society 270
Newsletter of the Essex Society of Genealogists 274
Newsletter of the Farmington Genealogical Society 291
Newsletter of the Fayette County Genealogical Society 209
Newsletter of the Fayette County Historical Society 209
Newsletter of the Federation of Oklahoma Genealogical Societies 468
Newsletter of the Fort Gibson Genealogical and Historical Society 465
Newsletter of the Genealogical Society of New Jersey 374
Newsletter of the Genealogical Society of Santa Cruz County 70
Newsletter of the Genealogy Society of Pulaski County 328
Newsletter of the George Henton of Berks Co, PA Society 63
Newsletter of the Greenwood County Historical Society 213
Newsletter of the Gulf Coast Ancestry Researchers 562
Newsletter of the Gypsy Lore Society 257
Newsletter of the Hamilton County Historical Society 191
Newsletter of the Harrison Genealogical Society 293
Newsletter of the Henry Historical and Genealogical Society 162
Newsletter of the Historical and Genealogical Society of Indiana County 490
Newsletter of the Historical Society of Palm Beach County 119
Newsletter of the Historical Society of the Phoenixville Area 498
Newsletter of the Howard County Historical Society 259
Newsletter of the Hummelstown Area Historical Society 490
Newsletter of the Huntingdon County Historical Society 490
Newsletter of the Jewish Genealogical Society of North Jersey 376
Newsletter of the Kendall County Genealogical Society 169
Newsletter of the LaPorte County Genealogical Society 188
Newsletter of the Ligonier Valley Historical Society 492
Newsletter of the Livingston County Genealogical Society 294
Newsletter of the Macon County Historical Society 158
Newsletter of the Madison County Genealogy Society 209
Newsletter of the McKean County Historical Society 502
Newsletter of the Milwaukee County Historical Society 626
Newsletter of the Mississippi Memories Society 241
Newsletter of the Monmouth County Historical Association 370
Newsletter of the New England Historic Genealogical Society 267
Newsletter of the New York State Council of Genealogical Organizations 418
Newsletter of the Northeast Georgia Historical and Genealogical Society 131
Newsletter of the Northeast Pennsylvania Genealogical Society 501
Newsletter of the Okmulgee County Genealogical Society 468
Newsletter of the Ozarks Genealogical Society 341
Newsletter of the Pasadena Genealogy Society 59
Newsletter of the Perry County Genealogical and Historical Society 228
Newsletter of the Plains Genealogical Society 353
Newsletter of the Polk County Genealogical Society 474
Newsletter of the Pulaski County Historical Society 233
Newsletter of the Root Diggers Genealogical Society 344
Newsletter of the Saint Lawrence County Historical Association 392
Newsletter of the Saline County Genealogical Society 162
Newsletter of the Santa Barbara County Genealogical Society 70
Newsletter of the Schurch Family Association of North America 82
Newsletter of the Sheridan Genealogical Society 637
Newsletter of the Slovenian Genealogical Society 484
Newsletter of the Society Farsarotul 91, 100
Newsletter of the Society of Maine Archivists 247
Newsletter of the South Shore Genealogical Society 276
Newsletter of the South-Central Missouri Genealogical Society 342
Newsletter of the Southeastern New Mexico Genealogical Society 383
Newsletter of the Southwest Nebraska Genealogical Society 354
Newsletter of the Spencer County Historical Society 192
Newsletter of the Stanislaus County Genealogical Society 54
Newsletter of the Story County Genealogical Society 197
Newsletter of the Sullivan County Genealogical Society 194
Newsletter of the Upson Historical Society 138
Newsletter of the Verndale Historical Society 316
Newsletter of the West Augusta Historical and Genealogical Society 614
Newsletter of the Will County Historical Society 165
Newsletter of the Winnebago and Boone Counties Genealogical Society 172
Newsletter of the World Methodist Council 429
Newsletter of the Yadkin County Historical and Genealogical Society 435
Newsletter Scuttlebutt 261
Newsletter: The Gann Museum of Saline County 25
Newsline 529, 636
Newsome House Museum Archives 591
News-Rear View Notes 556

Newstead Historical Society & Library 387
Newstead Historical Society Newsletter 387
Newton County Historical and Genealogical Society 29
Newton County Historical Commission & Library 555
Newton County Historical Society 129, 187, 320
Newton County Historical Society and Genealogical Study Group & Archives 336
Newton County Historical Society Newsletter 29
Newton County Library 29
Newton County Library System 129
Newton County Museum Archives 29
Newton County Museum Library 336
Newton County Public Library-Roselawn Library 193
Newton County Roots 335
Newton County Saga 336
Newton Falls Public Library 454
Newton Family 449
Newton Family Newsletter 48
Newton Fire Department Museum Archives 375
Newton Free Library 276
Newton Free Library Newsletter 276
Newton Gresham Library 549
Newton Historical Society 276
Newton Public Library 219
Newton Public Library and Museum 168
Newton-Forsyth Family 352
Newtown Historic Association & Archives 495
Newtown Historical Museum 495
Newtown Historical Society 97
Newtown Library Company 495
Newville Historical Society & Library 496
Nez Perce County Historical Society & Archives 148
Nez Perce Historical Society 148
Nez Perce National Historical Park Library 150
Niagara Apothecary Archives 686
Niagara Area Historical Museum 628
Niagara Area Historical Society & Archives 628
Niagara County Community College Library 415
Niagara County Genealogical Society 388
Niagara County Genealogical Society & Archives 403
Niagara County Genealogical Society Newsletter 403
Niagara County Historical Society & Archives 403
Niagara County History Center 403
Niagara Falls Historical Society & Archives 408
Niagara Falls Public Library 408, 686
Niagara Falls Public Library Newsletter 408
Niagara Fire Museum Archives 686
Niagara Historical Museum 686
Niagara Historical Society & Archives 686
Niagara League News 487
Niagara-on-the-Lake Public Library 686
Nicholas County Historical and Genealogical Society 615
Nicholas County Public Library 226
Nicholas P Sims Library 562
Nichols Family 220
Nichols House Museum Archives 267
Nichols Memorial Library 362
Nichols Newsletter 104
Nichols Nostalgia 19
Nichols Professional Library 583
Nicholson Library 476
Nicholson Memorial Library 546
Nickels-Sortwell House Museum Archives 252
Nickerson Family 268, 276
Nicklas-Rogers Family 36
Nicodemus Family 482, 602
Nicodemus Historical Society & Library 212
Nicola Valley Historical Quarterly 652
Nicola Valley Museum Archives 652
Nicola Valley Museum Archives Association 652
Nicola Valley Tribal Council 652
Nicolas Denys Museum Library 676
Nicolaus Haugendobler-Hogendobler Family 176
Nicole Valley Historical Quarterly 652
Nicole Valley Museum Archives Association 652
Nicollet County Historical Museum 315
Nicollet County Historical Society & Archives 315
Nicomen Indian Band 651
Nielsen Library 81
Nienow Family 477
Niepodleglosc (Independence) 407
Niles Community Library 299
Niles Depot Museum Archives 45
Niles Historical Society 454
Niles Historical Society & Library 168
Niles Hotel and Saloon Museum Archives 35
Niles Trammel Learning Resources Center 117
Nilson-Smith Family 571
Nimitz Library 255
Nims Family 265, 269, 289, 398, 409, 596
Ninastako Cultural Centre 646
Nine Family 615
Nineteenth Century 498
Nineteenth-Century Studies 512
Ninety-Six National Historic Site Archives 517
Ninnau: North American Welsh Newspaper 367
Ninth Circuit Historical Society 59
Ninth Judicial Circuit Historical Society 478
Niobara County Historical Society & Archives 637
Niobrara Historical Society 354
Niobrara Public Library 354
Nipawin and District Historical Museum Archives 708
Nipigon Museum Archives 686
Nipigon Township Public Library 686
Nipissing Township Museum 686
Nisga'a Tribal Council 652
Nishna Heritage Museum 206
Nishnabotna Genealogical Society 203
Nisswa Area Historical Society 310
Nisswa Caboose Society 312
Niswaa Area Historical Society and Pioneer Park 309
Nita Stewart Haley Memorial Library 554
Nix-Nicks Family 470
Nixon Presidential Museum Archives 258
Nixon-Baccus Family 605
Nlaka'Pamux Nation Tribal Council 651
No Man's Land Historical Museum 465
No Man's Land Historical Society & Archives 465
Noah Webster Foundation and Historical Society of West Hartford & Library 101

Noank Historical Museum 94
Noank Historical Society & Archives 94, 97
Noank Historical Society Newsletter 94
Noank Historical Society Quarterly 97
Noble County Genealogical Society 469
Noble County Genealogical Society & Archives 179
Noble County Genealogical Society & Library 443
Noble County Historical Society 443
Noble County Historical Society & Archives 179
Noble County Library 179
Noble County Newsletter 443
Noble Family 339
Noble Maritime Collection Archives 417
Noble News 179
Nobleboro Historical Museum 249
Nobleboro Historical Society & Archives 249
Nobleboro Historical Society Newsletter 249
Nobles County Genealogical Society & Archives 317
Nobles County Genealogical Society Newsletter 317
Nobles County Historical Museum 317
Nobles County Historical Society & Archives 317
Nobles County Historical Society Newsletter 317
Nobles County Historical Society Pioneer Village Newsletter 317
Noblesville Public Library 191
Nodaway County Genealogical Society & Archives 335
Nodaway County Historical Museum 335
Nodaway County Historical Society & Archives 335
Noderer News 65
Noel Memorial Library 241
Nogales-Santa Cruz County Public Library 18
Nohl Family 57
Nokes Family 568
Nokomis Public Library 168
Nolan County Genealogical Association 561
Non Oblitus 122
Nooaitch Indian Band 652
Nor'Easter 307
Nor'Wester and Loyalist Museum Archives 679, 693
Nora E Larabee Memorial Library 221
Nora Springs Historical Society 206
Norborne Public Library 336
NorCal News 63
Norco Historical Society 56
Nordic Heritage Museum Library 606
Nordic News 606
Nordica Homestead 246
Nordica Memorial Association & Library 246
Nordland Heritage Foundation 523
Norelius Community Library 200
Norfolk County Historical Society of Chesapeake, VA & Archives 585
Norfolk Courier 592
Norfolk Genealogical Society 592
Norfolk Historical Museum 97, 592
Norfolk Historical Museum Archives 408
Norfolk Historical Society 97
Norfolk Historical Society & Archives 592, 690
Norfolk Public Library 354, 688, 692
Norfolklore 690
Norlin Library 81
Norman & Helen Asher Library 156
Norman and Cleveland County Historical Museum Archives 467
Norman County Historical Society & Library 305
Norman F Bourke Memorial Library 388
Norman Family 51
Norman Wells Historical Centre 671
Norman Williams Public Library 581
Normandy Area Historical Association 336
Norridgewock Historical Society 249
Norris City Memorial Public Library 168
Norris Family 48, 602
Norris L Brookens Library 174
Norris Public Library 432
Norseman 311
Norsemen Federation 311
North & South: The Official Magazine of the Civil War Society 75
North Adams Historical Society 276
North Alabama Genealogical Society 3
North Alabama Railroad Museum Archives 6
North Alabama Valley Leaves 6
North American Baptist Heritage Commission & Library 523
North American Baptists Archives 523
North American Black Historical Museum 679
North American Fiddlers Hall of Fame & Museum Archives 410
North American Indian Annex Archives 36
North American Indian Travelling College 681
North American Society for Sports History 492
North American Society for Sports History Proceedings 492
North American Swiss Alliance 443
North American Vexillological Association 379
North American Vexillological Association News 379
North Andover Historical Museum 276
North Andover Historical Society & Archives 276
North Anna Nuclear Information Center Archives 591
North Arkansas College Library 28
North Arkansas Regional Library 28, 33
North Arkansas Regional Library-Searcy County 30
North Arlington Free Public Library 375
North Atlantic Aviation Museum Archives 667
North Attleboro Historical Society 276
North Attleborough Historical Commission 276
North Aurora Public Library 81
North Babylon Public Library 408
North Baltimore Area Historical Society 454
North Baltimore Public Library 454
North Bay and Area Museum Archives 686
North Bay Public Library 686
North Beach Genealogical Society 604
North Beach Museum Archives 67
North Bend Public Library 477
North Bergen Free Public Library 375
North Berrien Historical Society 288
North Bingham County District Library 149
North Brevard Historical Museum 123
North Brevard Historical Society & Archives 123
North Brevard Public Library 123
North Carolina Division of Archives and History 431
North Carolina Friends Historical Society 427
North Carolina Genealogical Society 431
North Carolina Genealogical Society Journal 431
North Carolina Genealogical Society Newsletter; Ancestor Exchange 431

North Carolina Historical Review 431, 432
North Carolina Museum of Forestry Archives 434
North Carolina Museum of History Archives 431
North Carolina Office of Archives & History 432
North Carolina Preservation 431
North Carolina Society of County and Local Historians 427
North Carolina State Library 432
North Carolina Transportation Museum Archives 433
North Castle Historical Museum 388
North Castle Historical Society & Archives 388
North Castle Historical Society Newsletter 388
North Castle History 388
North Central Alabama Genealogical Society 3
North Central Illinois Genealogical Society & Library 172
North Central Indiana Genealogical Society 187
North Central Iowa Genealogical Society & Library 205
North Central Kansas Genealogical Society & Library 212
North Central Nebraska Genealogical Society 355
North Central North Dakota Genealogical Record 439
North Central Pennsylvania Historical Association 494
North Central Regional Library 609
North Central Regional Library-Ephrata Public Library 601
North Central Regional Library-Omak Community 604
North Central South Dakota Genealogical Society 522
North Chatham Free Library 408
North Chicago Public Library 168
North Coast Tribal Council 654
North Collins Historical Society 408
North Collins Town Library 408
North Country Community College Library 415
North County Chapter, NHSOG 362
North County Notes 411
North Cumberland Historical Society 676
North Dakota Heritage Center Archives 437
North Dakota History 437
North Dakota History: Journal of the Northern Plains 437
North Dakota Institute for Regional Studies Library 438
North Dakota State Genealogical Society 437
North Dakota State Library 437
North Dakota State University Library 438
North Eastern Illinois Historical Council 168
North Elba Town House 415
North English Public Library 206
North Fort Worth Historical Society & Library 545
North Georgia Genealogical Newsletter 134
North Georgia Journal 131
North Georgia Methodist Historical Society 126
North Hampton Public Library 363
North Hastings Heritage Museum Archives 679
North Haven Historical Society & Library 97
North Haven Historical Society Newsletter 97
North Hempstead Historical Museum 404
North Hennepin Historical Society 307
North Hero Public Library 578
North Highland Community Museum Archives 674
North Hills Genealogists 490, 499
North Hills Genealogists Newsletter 499
North Hills Museum Archives 674
North House Museum Archives 613
North Hudson Town Historian 408
North Indian River County Library 122
North Iowa Historical Society & Archives 205
North Jersey Highlands Historical Society 379
North Kingstown Free Library 508
North Lake Tahoe Historical Society & Archives 74
North Lake Tahoe Historical Society Newsletter 74
North Lanark Regional Museum Archives 679
North Lee County Historical Museum 202
North Lee County Historical Society & Archives 202
North Lee County Historical Society Newsletter 202
North Lee County Quarterly 202
North Lincoln County Historical Museum Archives 476
North Louisiana Genealogical Society & Archives 241
North Louisiana Genealogical Society Journal 241
North Louisiana Historical Association & Library 241
North Louisiana History 241
North Loup Public Library 354
North Madison County Public Library System 183
North Manchester Historical Society 191
North Manchester Historical Society Newsletter 191
North Manchester Public Library 191
North Merrick Public Library 409
North Miami Beach Public Library 118
North Miami Public Library 118
North Oakland Genealogical Society & Archives 295
North Olumpic Library System 604
North Pacific Cannery Village Museum Archives 653
North Palm Beach Public Library 118
North Palm Beach Public Library Newsletter 118
North Plainfield Exempt Fireman's Association Museum Archives 375
North Platte Genealogical Society 354
North Platte Public Library 354
North Platte Valley Historical Association & Archives 352
North Platte Valley Historical Association Newsletter 352
North Platte Valley Historical Museum 352
North Point Lighthouse Friends 626
North Port Public Library 118
North Providence Union Free Library 508
North Queens Heritage Society 673
North Reading Historical and Antiquarian Society & Library 276
North Reading Historical and Antiquarian Society Newsletter 276
North Richland Hills Public Library 555
North Saint Paul Historical Museum 312
North Saint Paul Historical Society & Archives 312
North Salem Historical Society 409
North San Diego County Genealogical Society & Archives 39
North Santiam Historical Society 477
North Scituate Public Library 508
North Shore Historical Society 653
North Shuswap Historical Society 648
North Smithfield Heritage Association 508
North Star Museum News 312
North Star Museum of Boy Scouting and Girl Scouting Archives 312
North Stonington Historical Society & Library 97
North Stonington Historical Society Newsletter 97
North Suburban Genealogical Society & Archives 178
North Suburban Genealogical Society Newsletter 178
North Suburban Library-Loves Park 165
North Sydney Historical Society 675
North Texas Cornish Society 536

North Texas Genealogical and Historical Association 563
North Texas Trail Tracers 563
North Thompson Indian Band 647
North Thompson Museum Archives 647
North Tonawanda History Museum Archives 409
North Tonawanda History Museum Newsletter 409
North Tonawanda Public Library 409
North Valley Public Library-Stevensville Library 346
North Vancouver City Library 653
North Vancouver Museum Archives 653
North West Company Fur Post Archives 313
North Wood County Historical Society & Archives 625
North York Public Library 691
Northampton Area Public Library 496
Northampton County Historical and Genealogical Society 486
Northampton Historical Museum 276
Northampton Historical Society & Archives 276
Northampton Notes 486
Northborough Free Library 276
Northborough Historical Museum 276
Northborough Historical Society & Archives 276
Northbrook Historical Society 168
Northeast Alabama Genealogical Society & Library 5
Northeast Alabama Settlers 5
Northeast Classic Car Museum Archives 409
Northeast Document Conservation Center 265
Northeast Georgia Historical and Genealogical Society 131
Northeast Georgia History Center Archives 131
Northeast Georgia History Center Archives Newsletter 131
Northeast Harbor Library 249
Northeast Iowa Genealogical Society & Archives 209
Northeast Kittias County Genealogical Society 607
Northeast Louisiana Delta African American Heritage Museum Archives 239
Northeast Louisiana Genealogical Society 239
Northeast Michigan Genealogical Society & Archives 285
Northeast Minnesota Historical Center 307
Northeast Mississippi Historical and Genealogical Quarterly 322
Northeast Mississippi Historical and Genealogical Society 322
Northeast Mississippi Historical and Genealogical Society Newsletter 322
Northeast Mississippi Museum Archives 319
Northeast Mississippi Museum News 319
Northeast Missouri Genealogical Society 326, 330
Northeast Missouri Genealogical Society Newsletter 326
Northeast Missouri Library Service 332
Northeast Missouri Library Service-H E Sever Memorial 332
Northeast Oakland Historical Museum 299
Northeast Oakland Historical Society & Archives 299
Northeast Oklahoma Genealogical Society 470
Northeast Ottawa District Library 288
Northeast Pennsylvania Genealogical Society 501
Northeast Regional Library 320
Northeast Scottish Society & Archives 356
Northeast Sumner Historical Society 533
Northeast Texas Genealogy and History 555
Northeast Texas Rural Heritage Museum Archives 556
Northeast Washington Genealogical Society & Archives 600
Northeastern Illinois Historical Council 161
Northeastern Montana Threshers Museum Archives 344
Northeastern Nebraska Genealogical Society 354
Northeastern Nebraska Genealogical Society Notes 354
Northeastern New York Genealogical Society 412, 415, 417
Northeastern Technical College Library 513
Northern Antelope County Genealogical Society 355
Northern Arizona Genealogical Society & Library 19
Northern Arizona Genealogical Society Bulletin 19
Northern California Chapter, Ohio Genealogical Society 63
Northern Cherokee Nation of the Old Louisiana Territory 328
Northern Gateway Museum Archives 706
Northern Gila County Genealogical Society & Library 18
Northern Gila County Historical Society & Archives 18
Northern Gila County Historical Society Newsletter 18
Northern Illinois Conference of the United Methodist Church 160
Northern Illinois Historical Society 167
Northern Illinois Record 167
Northern Indiana Historical Society & Archives 193
Northern Kentucky Heritage 226
Northern Kittitas County Genealogical Society 600
Northern Life Museum and National Exhibition Centre 671
Northern Lights College Library 649
Northern Lights Military Museum Archives 667
Northern Mariposa County History Center Archives 41
Northern Nebraska Genealogical Society 355
Northern Neck Historical Society & Library 591
Northern Neck of Virginia Historical Magazine 591
Northern New Mexico Community College Library 382
Northern New York American Canadian Genealogical Society 402
Northern New York American-Canadian Genealogical Society & Library 411
Northern NY Agricultural Historical Society 402
Northern Onondaga Public Library-Brewerton Branch 390
Northern Pacific Railway Museum Archives 609
Northern Pacific Railway Museum Newsletter 609
Northern Plains Public Library 81
Northern Virginia Genealogy 590
Northern Waters Museum 624
Northern Will County Genealogical Society 153
Northern Wisconsin Heritage 617
Northfield Historical Museum 312
Northfield Historical Society 578
Northfield Historical Society & Archives 312
Northfield Mass Historical Society 276
Northfield Public Library 312
Northhampton Township Historical Society 500
Northland Bulletin 306
Northland Genealogical Society 336
Northland Public Library 499
Northperth Public Library 685
Northport Historical Museum 409
Northport Historical Society & Archives 409
Northport Historical Society Newsletter 409
Northport Public Library 409
Northrup Family 478
Northumberland County Historical Society 589
Northumberland County Historical Society & Library 503
Northumberland County Public Library 681
Northumberland Fisheries Museum Archives 676
Northumberland Historical Society 361
Northup Library 477
Northville District Library 299
Northville Genealogical Society 299
Northville Genealogy Society Newsletter 299

Northville Historical Society & Library 299
Northwest Arkansas Genealogical Society & Archives 25
Northwest Arkansas Genealogical Society & Library 32
Northwest Carriage Museum Archives 605
Northwest Chronicle 449
Northwest Community College Library 656
Northwest Franklin County Historical Society & Library 449
Northwest Genealogical Society 350
Northwest Georgia Historical and Genealogical Society 136
Northwest Georgia Historical and Genealogical Society Quarterly 136
Northwest Georgia Regional Library System 129
Northwest Historian 453
Northwest Indiana Genealogical Society 185, 194
Northwest Iowa Genealogical Society & Archives 204
Northwest Iowa Root Diggers 204
Northwest Kansas Genealogical and Historical Society 219
Northwest Kansas Heritage Center 212
Northwest Kansas Library System 219
Northwest Missouri Genealogical Society & Library 338
Northwest Missouri Genealogical Society Journal 338
Northwest Missouri Genealogical Society Newsletter 338
Northwest Montana Historical Society 345
Northwest Museum 607
Northwest Nebraska Genealogical Society 349
Northwest Nebraska Genealogical Society Quarterly 349
Northwest Oakland County Historical Society & Library 294
Northwest Ohio Quarterly 452
Northwest Oklahoma Genealogical Society 471
Northwest Railway Museum Archives 607
Northwest Regional Library 10
Northwest Regional Library System-Bay County Public Library 119
Northwest Regional Library-Russellville Branch 8
Northwest Suburban Council of Genealogists & Library 167
Northwest Territories Genealogical Society 671
Northwest Territories Public Library Services 671
Northwest Territory French and Canadian Heritage Institute & Library 308
Northwest Territory Genealogical Society 195
Northwest Trail Tracer 195
Northwest Winds 471
Northwestern Michigan College Genealogy Group & Archives 303
Northwestern Ohio Genealogical Society 458
Northwestern Ohio Genealogical Society Newsletter 458
Northwestern Pacific Railroad Historical Society 71
Northwestern Railroad Depot Museum 625
Northwestern University Library, Special Collections 160
Northwood Historical Society 363
Northwoods Genealogical Society 630
Northwoods Historian 626
Norton County Genealogical Society & Archives 219
Norton County Historical Society 219
Norton County Tracers 219
Norton Historical Society & Library 276
Norton Notes 292
Norton Public Library 219, 276
Norum Family 604
Norvell Family 44
Norwalk Historical Society & Archives 97
Norwalk Museum Archives 99
Norwalk Museum Historical Reference Library 97
Norwalk Public Library 454
Norway Historical Museum 249
Norway Historical Society 634
Norway Historical Society & Archives 249
Norway House Band 660
Norway Memorial Library 249
Norwegian American Bygdelagenes Fellesraad do 306
Norwegian- American Historical Association Topical Studies 312
Norwegian American Museum Association & Archives 200
Norwegian Genealogy Group & Library 77
Norwegian Museum 200
Norwegian Tracks 625
Norwegian-American American Studies 312
Norwegian-American Historical Association & Archives 312
Norwegian-American Historical Association Newsletter 312
Norwegian-American Historical Association Travel and Description 312
Norwell Historical Society 273, 276
Norwell Historical Society Newsletter 276
Norwell Public Library 276
Norwich and District Historical Society Archives & Library 687
Norwich and District Museum Archives 687
Norwich Historical Museum 578
Norwich Historical Society 97
Norwich Historical Society & Archives 578
Norwich Historical Society Newsletter 578
Norwich Public Library 578
Norwin Public Library Association 490
Norwood Cole Library 603
Norwood Historical Association & Archives 409
Norwood Historical Museum 409
Norwood Historical Society & Library 276
Norwood Park Historical Society & Library 156
Norwood Village Historian 409
Nos Amis de la Genealogie 702
Nose Creek Valley Museum Archives 641
Nostalgia News 184
Nostalgic News 555
Notah Dineh Museum Archives 83
Notebook 263
Notes & Quotes; The Pocket Edition 188
Notes from Monument Square 492
Notes from the Old Jail 518
Notes n' Quotes of the Laney Clan USA 116
Notes, News and Nostalgia 373
Noticias 70, 381
Noticias del Puerto de Monterey 55
Noticias para Los Californianos 65
Notre Dame de Namur Library 37
Nott House 247
Nottawa Stone School Museum Archives 288
Nottoway County Historical Association 586
Nottoway County Library 592
Nottoway County Public Libraries 586
Nouvelles Nouvelles 446
Nova Scotia Archives and Records Management 674
Nova Scotia Genealogist 674
Nova Scotia Genealogy Network Association 676
Nova Scotia Historical Society 674
Nova Scotia Museum Library 674
Nova Scotia Provincial Library 674
Novato Historian 57

Novato History Museum Archives 57
Novel Events 446
Novel Ideas Newsletter 217
Novel News 163, 192
Novi Historical Society 299
Novi Public Library 299
Now and Then 169, 495
Nowata County Historical Museum 467
Nowata County Historical Society & Archives 467
Nowata County Historical Society Newsletter 467
Nowlin Newsletter 468
Noxon Family 549
Noxon Talk 87
Noxubee County Historical Society & Library 321
Noxubee County Historical Society Bulletin 321
Noxubee County Library System 321
Noyes House Museum 578
NSM Journal 396
NSM News 396
NSPL Newsletter 508
Nuantta Sunakkutaangit Museum Archives 671
Nuchatlaht Tribes 657
Nuckolls County Genealogical Society 357
Nuckolls County Historical Society 357
Nuckolls Kindred Worldwide Newsletter 138
Nuestra Herencia 407
Nuestras Raices 71, 83
Nugget 57, 66
Nuggets 617
Nuggets from Paradise 59
Nuggets of History 172
Nuggets of the Siskiyou County Historical Society 78
Nulton Family 259
Nunavut Arctic College Library 671
Nusee du Nativageur Rottant 702
Nute Library 363
Nutimik Lake Museum Archives 661
Nutley Free Public Library 375
Nutley Historical Society & Library 375
Nuts & Bolts 255
Nutter D Marvel Museum Archives 103
Nutter Family 591
Nutting Memorial Library 245
Nuu-chan-nulth Tribal Council 653
Nuxalk Indian Band 647
Nuzum Family 54
Nyack Public Library 409
Nyando Roots Genealogical Society & Library 404
Nye Family 270
Nygaard Family 313
Nylander Museum Archives 245

O

O Henry Museum Archives 536
O Mahony Family 264
O Meredith Wilson Library 311
O Progresso 64
O Winston Link Photography Museum Archives 594
O.H.I.O. Gazette 455
O'Brien-Diedrich Family Newsletter 78
O'Chiese Indian Band 645
O'Dell Inn Museum Archives 673
O'Dell Reunion Newsletter 19
O'Dochartaigh Family 328
O'Fallon Historical Society 169, 336
O'Fallon Public Library 169
O'Hara Family 274
O'Haras of County Down, Ireland 46
O'Lochlainns Irish Family Journal 332
O'Mahoney Family 117
O'Neill Museum 68
O'Nell-Nell-O'Neill-Cothren-Cochrane Family 60
O'Shaughnessy-Frey Library 314
Oak Brook Historical Society & Library 168
Oak Creek Historical Society & Archives 628
Oak Forest Historical Society 168
Oak Glen School House Museum Archives 79
Oak Hill and the Martha Berry Museum Archives 135
Oak Lawn Acorns 169
Oak Lawn Historical Society & Library 169
Oak Lawn Public Library 169
Oak Leaves 138, 367, 537
Oak Park Public Library 169
Oak Ridge Public Library 532
Oakdale Museum Archives 57
Oakdale Public Library 354
Oakdale-Lake Elmo Historical Society 309
Oakes Family 601
Oakey Family 146
Oakfield Historical Museum Archives 249
Oakfield Historical Society 249
Oakfield Pioneer Heritage Society 301
Oakfield Railroad Museum Archives 249
Oakland City-Columbia Township Public Library 191
Oakland County Genealogical Society 287
Oakland County Genealogical Society Surname Directory 287
Oakland County Historical Museum 300
Oakland County Pioneer and Historical Society & Archives 300
Oakland County Research Library 300
Oakland Gazette 300
Oakland Herald 126
Oakland Historical Foundation 169
Oakland Historical Society 206
Oakland Historical Society & Library 375
Oakland Museum of California 57
Oakland Museum of California Quarterly 57
Oakland Park City Library 118
Oakland Plantation Archives 133
Oakland Public Library 57, 249, 321
Oaklands Historic House Museum Archives 531
Oakleaf 339
Oakleigh House Museum Archives 7
Oakley 241
Oakley Library District 148
Oakley Park Museum Archives 514
Oakley Pioneer Museum Archives 148
Oakley Public Library 219
Oaklyn Memorial Library 375
Oakmont Carnegie Library 496
Oakridge Heritage Center 477

Oaks House Museum Archives 321
Oakville Historical Society & Archives 687
Oakville Public Library 687
Oakwood Historical Society & Library 447
Oakwood Public Library District 169
Oaly House Museum Archives 659
Oatlands Plantation Museum Archives 589
Oatlands Plantation Museum Newsletter 589
Obadiah Taylor Historical Association 188
Oberlin City Library 219
Oberlin College Library 455
Oberlin Historical and Improvement Organization & Archives 455
Oberlin Historical Museum 455
Oberlin Public Library 455
Obion County Genealogical Society & Library 533
Obion Origins 533
Oblinger-Oplinger-Uplinger Family 505
Observer 401
Occidental College History Society 52
Occurences 608
Ocean City Free Public Library 375
Ocean City Historical Museum Library 375
Ocean City Museum Society & Library 261
Ocean County Genealogical Society 372
Ocean County Genealogical Society Newsletter 372
Ocean County Historical Society & Library 379
Ocean County Library 379
Ocean Gate Historical Society 375
Ocean Grove Historical Museum 375
Ocean Man First Nation 711
Ocean Shores Public Library 604
Ocean Springs Genealogy Society 321
Ocean Springs Genealogy Society Newsletter 321
Ocean Star Offshore Drilling Rig and Museum Archives 546
Ocean Township Historical Museum Library 375
Oceana County Historical and Genealogical Society 293
Oceana County Historical and Genealogical Society Newsletter 293
Oceanside Historical Society 57
Oceanside Library 409
Oceanside Public Library 57
Ocenee County Genealogical Society 514
Ochapowace First Nation 711
Ocmulgee Regional Library System 130
Oconee County Library 518
Oconee County Museum Association & Archives 518
Oconee Heritage Center 518
Oconee Regional Library 130
Oconee Station Historic Site Archives 518
Oconomowoc Genealogical Club of Waukesha County & Library 628
Oconomowoc Historical Museum 628
Oconomowoc Historical Society & Archives 628
Oconto County Genealogical Society 632
Oconto County Historical Society & Archives 628
Octagon House 623, 633
Octagon House Museum 627
Octagon House Museum Archives 67
Octave Chanute Aerospace Museum Foundation Archives 171
Octave Chanute Aerospace Museum Newsletter 171
Octavia Fellin Public Library 383
Oddyssey-Heritage Tales 64
Odell Prairie Trails Historical and Genealogical Society 169
Odell Public Library 167
Odom Family 43, 110, 542
Odom Observer 129
Odon Winkelpleck Memorial Library 191
Odum Library 139
Odyssey Maritime Discovery Center Archives 606
Oelwein Area Genealogical Society Chapter, IGS & Archives 206
Oelwein Area Genealogical Society Chapter, IGS Newsletter 206
Oelwein Area Historical Society 206
Oelwein Public Library 206
Oesterle Library 168
Off The Shelf 177, 275, 364, 507, 542, 555, 620
Off the Shelves 159, 633
Off the Top Shelf 169
Office of Historic Alexandria 583
Office of Historic Preservation, Planning Services 63
Office of the City Historian 414
Ogden Family 563
Ogden Farmers' Library 417
Ogden Historical Museum 417
Ogden Historical Society & Archives 417
Ogden Union Station Museum Archives 568
Ogdensburg Public Library 409
Ogemaw District Library 301
Ogemaw Genealogical and Historical Society 304
Ogilvie Kith and Kin 25
Oglala Lakota College Library 522
Ogle County Genealogical Society & Library 169
Ogle County Historical Society 169
Ogle County Historical Society Gazette 169
Ogle County Links Newsletter 169
Ogle Family Association Newsletter 111
Ogle Genealogist 111, 114
Oglebay Institute & Archives 615
Ogle-Ogles Family 542
Oglethorpe University Library 126
Ogling for Ogles 114
Ogniwo Polish Museum Archives 662
Oh, Park Forest 170
Ohamil Indian Band 650
Ohef Sholom Temple Archives 592
Ohio Archivist 446
Ohio Association of Historical Societies and Museums 446
Ohio Cemetery Preservation Society 451
Ohio Civil War Genealogy Journal 452
Ohio Clues 452
Ohio County Historical Society 192
Ohio County Historical Society & Library 228
Ohio County Historical Society Newsletter 192
Ohio County Public Library 192, 228, 615
Ohio Genealogical Society & Library 452
Ohio Genealogical Society Newsletter 452
Ohio Genealogical Society Report 452
Ohio Historical Museum 446
Ohio Historical Society 455, 458
Ohio Historical Society & Archives 446, 452
Ohio History 446, 452
Ohio Palatine Heritage 446
Ohio Preservation Alliance 452

Ohio Railway Museum Archives 460
Ohio Records 285
Ohio Records and Pioneer Families 452
Ohio River Museum Archives 452
Ohio Society War of 1812 455
Ohio State Library 446
Ohio Statehouse Archives 446
Ohio Township Public Library System 190
Ohio Underground Railroad Society 460
Ohio Valley History 230, 444
Ohio, the Cross Road of Our Nation: Records and Pioneer Families 452
Ohio's Last Frontier 443
Ohioana Library 446
Ohnmeiss Family 502
Ohoopee Regional Library 139
Oil City Heritage Society 496
Oil City Historical Museum 240
Oil City Historical Society & Archives 240
Oil City Library 496
Oil Museum of Canada Archives 687
Oil Sands Discovery Centre 643
OIW Communique 29
Ojai Valley Historical Museum 57
Ojai Valley Historical Society & Archives 57
Ojai Valley Historical Society Newsletter 57
Ojibway and Cree Cultural Centre 691
Ojibway and Cree Cultural Centre Archives 691
Ojibway and Cree Nations 691
Ojibway Nation 684
Ojibwe Cultural Foundation 685
Okaloosa and Walton Counties Historical Museum 123
Okaloosa County Genealogical Society & Library 113
Okaloosa-Walton Community College Library 118
Okanagan Historical Society 656
Okanagan History 656
Okanagan Indian Band 656
Okanagan Tribal Council 653
Okanese First Nation 705
Okanogan County Genealogical Society & Library 604
Okanogan County Historical and Genealogical Research Center 604
Okeechobee County Historical Society 118
Okeechobee County Public Library 118
Okeechobee Historical Society 113
Okefenokee Heritage Center Archives 139
Okefenokee Historical and Genealogical Society 139
Okefenokee Regional Library 139
Okfuskee County Genealogical Society 467
Okfuskee County Historical Society 467
Oklahoma City National Memorial Archives 468
Oklahoma Department of Libraries 468
Oklahoma Firefighters Museum Archives 468
Oklahoma Genealogical Society 468
Oklahoma Genealogical Society Quarterly 468
Oklahoma Heritage Association & Library 468
Oklahoma Heritage News 468
Oklahoma Historical Society & Archives 463
Oklahoma Historical Society & Library 468
Oklahoma Museum of History 468
Oklahoma Museums Association 468
Oklahoma Pontotoc County Quarterly 463
Oklahoma Route 66 Museum Archives 464
Oklahoma State University Library 469
Oklahoma Territorial Museum Archives 465
Okmulgee County Genealogical Society 468
Okmulgee Public Library 468
Oktibbeha County Heritage Museum Archives 322
Oktibbeha County Historical Museum 322
Ol' Timer 75
Olana State Historic Site Archives 400
Olathe Historical Society & Library 219
Olathe Public Library 219
Old Abbeville District Historical Commission 516
Old Abington Historical Society 265
Old Academy Museum 271
Old Alna Meeting House 243
Old and New 280
Old Anderson House Museum 631
Old Bank Building Historical Museum 617
Old Bank of New Brunswick Museum Archives 664
Old Barracks Museum Archives 379
Old Berwick Historical Society & Library 251
Old Bethlehem Historical Society 91
Old Bethpage Village Restoration Archives 409
Old Bohemia Historical Society 263
Old Bridge Public Library 375
Old Bridgewater Historical Society & Library 282
Old Bridgewater Historical Society Newsletter 282
Old Brutus Historical Museum 420
Old Brutus Historical Society & Archives 420
Old Buncombe County Genealogical Society & Library 423
Old Campbell County Historical Society & Archives 130
Old Canada Road Historical Society 244
Old Capital Historical Society 134
Old Capitol Library 203
Old Capitol Museum of Mississippi History Archives 321
Old Carnegie Library 518
Old Carratunk Historical Society 244
Old Castle Museum Library 211
Old Catawba County Courthouse Museum 430
Old Cathedral Library 195
Old Cathedral Museum Archives 339
Old Charles Town Library 611
Old Christ Church (Episcopal) League & Library 103
Old Church Society 478
Old Clinton Historical Society 131
Old Colony Historical Museum 280
Old Colony Historical Society & Archives 280
Old Colony Historical Society Newsletter 280
Old Colorado City Historical Society 82
Old Constitution House Museum Archives 581
Old Conway Homestead 244
Old Courthouse Museum 70, 152, 177, 323, 524, 553
Old Courthouse Museum Society & Archives 70
Old Courthouse News 193
Old Cowtown Museum Archives 223
Old Crofton School Museum Archives 649
Old Crow Historical Society 713
Old Darlington District Chapter, SCGS 515
Old Darlington Flag Quarterly 515
Old Dartmouth Historical Society & Archives 275

Old Depot Museum 220
Old Depot Museum Archives 8, 220
Old Depot Railroad Museum Archives 307
Old Dobbs Trails 427
Old Dominion Railway Museum Archives 594
Old Dorchester State Historic Site Archives 518
Old Dutch Mill Museum Complex 223
Old Dutch Parsonage Museum Archives 378
Old Economy Village 481
Old Edgebrook Historical Society 156
Old Edgefield District Archives 514
Old Edgefield District Chapter, SCGS & Library 514
Old Exchange and Provost Dungeon Archives 512
Old Falls Village Museum 626
Old Firehouse Museum Archives 320
Old Florida Museum Archives 121
Old Force Library 409
Old Fort Bissell 220
Old Fort Boise Historical Society & Library 149
Old Fort Erie Museum Archives 686
Old Fort Genealogical Society & Library 202, 214
Old Fort Genealogical Society Quarterly 202
Old Fort Harrod State Park Mansion Archives 228
Old Fort House Museum 397
Old Fort Jackson Museum Archives 137
Old Fort Jackson Museum Newsletter 137
Old Fort Log 214
Old Fort Meade Museum Archives 522
Old Fort Museum Archives 243
Old Fort Museum Newsletter 243
Old Fort News 183
Old Fort Niagara Archives 422
Old Fort Niagara Association & Library 422
Old Fort Number 4 Archives 359
Old Fort William Historical Park Archives 691
Old Gaol Gazette 517
Old George's Authentic Collectibles Museum 711
Old Government House Archives 663
Old Governor's Mansion Archives 134
Old Governor's Mansion Museum Archives 227
Old Greer County Museum Archives 466
Old Guard Museum Archives 587
Old Guardhouse Museum 538
Old Hastings Mill Store Museum Archives 656
Old Hidalgo Pumphouse Archives 548
Old Hoxie House Museum Archives 278
Old Independence Regional Museum Archives 25
Old Iron County Courthouse Museum Archives 623
Old Jail Museum 179, 194, 285
Old Jail Museum Archives 182
Old Jail Museum Quarterly 182
Old Jefferson Town 220
Old Kent 257
Old Letter 188
Old Lighthouse Museum 189
Old Lighthouse Museum Archives 99
Old Lighthouse Museum News 189
Old Lincoln County Courthouse Museum Archives 383
Old Log Chain 185
Old Log Jail and Chapel Museums 185
Old Mackinac Point Lighthouse Museum Archives 296
Old Manchester Museum 95
Old Manse Museum Archives 269
Old Market House State Historic Site Archives 160
Old Massett Village Council 652
Old McLean County Courthouse Museum 152
Old Meeting House Museum Archives 673
Old Merchants House of New York Archives 408
Old Mill Hill Society 379
Old Mill Museum 382
Old Mill Museum Archives 69
Old Mill News 189, 295
Old Mill Wheel 369
Old Mines Area Historical Society & Library 336
Old Mission San Antonio de Padua Archives 48
Old Mission San Jose Museum Archives 45
Old Mission San Luis Obispo de Tolosa Archives 68
Old Mission Santa Ines Archives 72
Old Monterey Jail Museum Archives 55
Old Monterey Preservation Society 55
Old N' Newsletter 335
Old New Gate Prison and Copper Mine Museum Archives 93
Old New Hanover County Genealogical Society 434
Old Newberry District Chapter, SCGS 513
Old News 492, 606
Old Ninety Six District, SCGS & Library 515
Old North Yarmouth Townhouse 245
Old Onanquaga Historical Society & Archives 399
Old Orchard Beach Historical Museum 249
Old Orchard Beach Historical Society & Archives 249
Old Ordinary 272
Old Oroville Depot Historical Society 604
Old Pendleton District Chapter Newsletter 514
Old Pendleton District Chapter, SCGS 514, 518
Old Pike Post 260
Old Portage Trail Review 441
Old Prison Museum Archives 344
Old Randolph Historical Museum 377
Old Red Church 251
Old Red Review 540
Old Redmond Schoolhouse 605
Old Sacramento Schoolhouse Museum Archives 63
Old Sacramento State Historic Park Archives 63
Old Saint Bartholomew Chapter, SCGS 518
Old Saint Edward's Anglican Church Archives 673
Old Saint Paul's Cemetery 256
Old Salem Library 435
Old Salem Village Museum Archives 435
Old Santa Rosa Chapel Archives 39
Old Santee Canal Park Archives 516
Old Saybrook Historical Society & Archives 98
Old Schwamb Mill Museum Archives 265
Old Schwamb Mill Newsletter 265
Old Shawnee Town 221
Old Six Mile Historical Society & Library 161
Old Slater Mill Historic Site Library 508
Old Sod Post Office Museum Archives 438
Old South Meeting House Archives 267
Old South Meeting House Newsletter 267
Old Spanish Fort Museum 322

Old St Hilary's Landmark Archives 37
Old Stagecoach Stop Foundation 342
Old State Arsenal 227
Old State Bank Museum Archives 195
Old State House 266
Old State House Museum Archives 29, 94
Old State House Museum Newsletter 94
Old Stone Fort Museum 416
Old Stone House Museum 575, 578
Old Stone House Museum Archives 421
Old Stone House Museum Bulletin 578
Old Stone Jail Musuem 592
Old Stone Railroad Station 368
Old Store Museum 364
Old Store Museum Society of South Sutton & Archives 364
Old Sturbridge Village Library 280
Old Sturbridge Visitor 280
Old Sussex Almanac 375
Old Swedes Church and Hendrickson House Museum 104
Old Swedes' Church 104
Old Swedes' Foundation & Archives 104
Old Swedes' Foundation Newsletter 104
Old Sydney Society & Archives 675
Old Tavern Museum Archives 9
Old Timers Building 390
Old Timers Museum Archives 57
Old Town Brunswick Preservation Association 127
Old Town Hall Museum Archives 629
Old Town Museum Archives 249
Old Town Public Library 249
Old Town San Diego State Historic Park Archives 65
Old Towne Preservation Association 57
Old Trail Museum Archives 343
Old Trail Museum Newsletter 343
Old Trails Historical Society & Library 334
Old Trails Historical Society Newsletter 334
Old Village Hall Museum 403, 627
Old Village Union Historical Association 397
Old Wall Historical Society 367
Old Wall Historical Society & Library 379
Old Warren County Courthouse 402
Old Washington Historic State Park Archives 33
Old Wasilla Townsite Park 13
Old West 15
Old West Museum Archives 561
Old Westbury Gardens 409
Old Westbury Historic Home and Gardens 409
Old Westmoreland: The History and Genealogy of Westmoreland County, PA 492
Old Woodbury Historical Society 102
Old World Wisconsin Archives 620
Old Yarmouth Historical Museum 283
Old York Historical Museum 253
Old York Historical Society & Archives 253
Old York Historical Society Quarterly 253
Old York Road Genealogical Society 481
Old York Road Genealogical Society & Library 481
Old York Road Genealogical Society Quarterly 481
Old York Road Historical Museum 490
Old York Road Historical Society & Archives 490
Old York Road Historical Society Bulletin 490
Old-Brule Heritage Society 625
Olde Colonial Courthouse Museum Archives 266
Olde Mecklenburg Genealogical Society 425
Olde Mecklenburg Genealogical Society Quarterly 425
Olde Towne Ledger 228
Olde Towne Preservation Association of North Augusta 517
Oldest House Museum 121
Oldest House Museum Archives 115
Oldest Stone House Museum 450
Oldest Store Museum Archives 121
Oldham County Historical Society 229
Oldham County History Center 229
Oldham County Public Library 229
Oldman River Cultural Centre Archives 641
Olds Historical Society & Museum 645
Oldtimer 475
Ole Crawford 172
Olean Historical and Preservation Society 409
Olin C Bailey Library 26
Olin Family 420
Olin Library 124
Olin Memorial Library 96
Oliphant Clan 377
Olivas Adobe Archives 76
Olive G Pettis Library 361
Olive Warner Memorial Library 466
Oliver Cromwell Black History Society 368
Oliver Cromwell Carmichael Library 7
Oliver Family 478
Oliver House Museum 331
Oliver House News 411
Oliver Kelley Farm Museum Archives 307
Oliver Orator 549
Oliver Springs Historical Society 532
Oliver Springs Public Library 532
Oliver Tucker Museum 459
Oliver Tucker Museum Archives 442
Oliver Wolcott Library 95
Oliver Wolcott Library Newsletter 95
Olivia Public Library 312
Olivia Rodham Memorial Library 363
Ollie L Brown Afro-American Heritage Collection 7
Olmste(a)d Family 314
Olmstead County History Center Library 313
Olmstead Family 208
Olmstead Funeral & Historical Museum 28
Olmstead Historical Society 28
Olmstead Place State Park Archives 601
Olmstead-Olmsted Family 401
Olmsted County Genealogical Society & Library 313
Olmsted County Historical Society & Library 313
Olmsted Genealogical Society Newsletter 313
Olmsted Historian 313
Olmsted Historical Society 169, 454
Olne Community Library 555
Olney Community Library & Arts Center 555
Olney Public Library 169
Olompali State Historical Park Archives 57
Olschwanger Family 256

INDEX

Olustree Battlefield Historic State Park Archives 118
Olvera Family Association Newsletter 42
Olympia Genealogical Society 604
Olympia Genealogical Society Quarterly 604
Olympic Flight Museum Archives 604
Omaha Public Library-Charles B Washington Branch 355
OMII Genealogical Project 460
Omohundro Institute of Early American History and Culture & Library 597
Omro Area Historical Museum 628
Omro Area Historical Society & Archives 628
On Board 105
On Common Ground 481
On Eternal Patrol 142
On Huguenot Street 406
On the Big Horn 345
On the Garrard County Line 229
On the Level 373
On the Ramage Trail 22
On the Square 51, 52
On the Trail 223, 449
Onaga Historical Society 219
Onalaska Area Historical Museum 628
Onalaska Area Historical Society & Archives 628
Onawa Public Library 206
Onaway Library 299
Once Upon a Time 491
One Arrow First Nation 710
One Room Schoolhouse Museum 621
Oneida Community Journal 409
Oneida Community Library 628
Oneida Community Mansion Museum Archives 409
Oneida County Free Library 148
Oneida County Genealogical Club 419
Oneida County Genealogical Society 630
Oneida County Historical Museum 419
Oneida County Historical Society 419
Oneida County Pioneer Museum Archives 148
Oneida Library 409
Oneida Nation Museum Archives 620
Oneida National Museum Archives 628
Oneonta Public Library 8
Oney Family 496
Ong Family 589
Onion Lake First Nation 708
Onionskin 174
Oniota 419
Onondaga County Public Library 418
Onondaga Free Library 418
Onondaga Historical Association & Archives 418
Onondaga Historical Association Annual Report 418
Onondaga Historical Museum 418
Onslow County Genealogical Society 428
Onslow County Genealogical Society Newsletter 428
Onslow County Museum Archives 432
Onslow County Public Library 428
Onsted Community Historical Society 299
Ontario Agricultural Museum Archives 685
Ontario Black History Society 691
Ontario City Library 57
Ontario County Genealogical Society & Library 392
Ontario County Historical Museum 392
Ontario County Historical Society & Archives 392
Ontario County Historical Society Chronicles 392
Ontario Genealogical Society & Library 686, 691
Ontario Genealogical Society Membership 691
Ontario Genealogical Society Newsletter 691
Ontario Genealogical Society, Brant County Branch 680
Ontario Genealogical Society, Bruce and Grey Branch 687
Ontario Genealogical Society, Elgin County Branch 689
Ontario Genealogical Society, Guerin Dit la Fontaine Chapter 680
Ontario Genealogical Society, Haldimand County Branch 681
Ontario Genealogical Society, Halton-Peel Branch 687
Ontario Genealogical Society, Hamilton Branch 683
Ontario Genealogical Society, Huron County Branch 682
Ontario Genealogical Society, Kawartha Branch & Library 688
Ontario Genealogical Society, Kent County Branch 681
Ontario Genealogical Society, Kingston Branch 684
Ontario Genealogical Society, Kingston Branch Newsletter 684
Ontario Genealogical Society, Lambton County Branch 689
Ontario Genealogical Society, Leeds and Grenville Branch 680
Ontario Genealogical Society, London and Middlesex Branch 685
Ontario Genealogical Society, Niagara Peninsula Branch 689
Ontario Genealogical Society, Nipissing District Branch 686
Ontario Genealogical Society, Norfolk County Branch 681
Ontario Genealogical Society, Ottawa Branch 687
Ontario Genealogical Society, Oxford County Branch 693
Ontario Genealogical Society, Perth County Branch & Library 690
Ontario Genealogical Society, Quinte Branch 679
Ontario Genealogical Society, Saint Lawrence United Empire Loyalist Branch 686
Ontario Genealogical Society, Sault Sainte Marie and District Branch 689
Ontario Genealogical Society, Simcoe County Branch 679, 692
Ontario Genealogical Society, Sudbury District Branch 690
Ontario Genealogical Society, Thunder Bay District Branch 691
Ontario Genealogical Society, Toronto Branch 691
Ontario Genealogical Society, Waterloo-Wellington Branch 684
Ontario Genealogical Society, Whitby-Oshawa Branch 692
Ontario Genealogical Society, Windsor Branch 693
Ontario Heritage 57
Ontario Heritage Center 691
Ontario Heritage Square Museum 409
Ontario Historical Society 686, 693
Ontario Historical Society & Archives 409
Ontario Historical Society Bulletin 693
Ontario Historical Society Newsletter 409
Ontario History 693
Ontario Library Service 684
Ontario Museum of History Newsletter 57
Ontonagon County Genealogical Society 299
Ontonagon County Historical Lighthouse Archives 299
Ontonagon County Historical Museum 299
Ontonagon County Historical Society & Archives 299
Ontonagon Township Library 299
Oologah Historical Society 468
Oothoudt, Oathout, Oothout, Oathoudt, Othoudt Family 305
Op Dyck Genealogy 184
Opelousas Museum Archives 240
Opelousas-Eunice Public Library 240
Open Book 164, 179, 470
Open Door 149

Opetchesaht First Nation 653
Opp Historical Society 8
Opus 40 and the Quarryman's Museum Archives 415
Oracle 489
Oracle Historian 18
Oracle Historical Society & Archives 18
Oradell Free Public Library 375
Oral History Association 484
Oral History Association Newsletter 484
Oral History Center 145
Oral History Review 37
Oran's Black Americana Historical Society 355
Orange Beach Indian and Sea Museum Archives 8
Orange Beach Public Library 8
Orange City Public Library 206
Orange Community Historical Society 57
Orange County California Genealogical Society Journal 58
Orange County California Genealogical Society Newsletter 58
Orange County Genealocial Society 58
Orange County Genealogical Society 48, 191
Orange County Genealogical Society & Library 398
Orange County Historical Commission 70
Orange County Historical Museum Archives 428
Orange County Historical Society & Archives 191
Orange County Historical Society & Library 70, 119, 388, 592
Orange County Historical Society Newsletter 592
Orange County Historical Society Quarterly 119
Orange County Library System 119
Orange County Library-Wilderness 590
Orange County Pioneer Council 70
Orange County Public Library 70, 428, 592
Orange County Public Library-El Toro Branch 49
Orange County Public Library-Garden Grove Regional Library 46
Orange County Public Library-San Juan Capistrano Regional Library 68
Orange County Railway Historical Society 56
Orange Empire Railway Museum Archives 59
Orange Empire Railway Museum Gazette 59
Orange Genealogical Society Quarterly 398
Orange Historical Society & Library 98, 277
Orange Historical Society Newsletter 98, 277
Orange Johnson House Archives 446
Orange Peelings 191
Orange Public Library 58, 98, 375, 555
Orangeburg County Historical Society 517
Orangeburg County Historical Society Newsletter 517
Orangeburg County Library 517
Orangeburg German-Swiss Genealogical Society 512
Orangeburg Historical and Genealogical Record 517
Orangeburg Historical and Genealogical Society 517
Orangeburg Public Library 409
Orangeburgh German-Swiss Genealogical Society & Library 517
Orangeburgh German-Swiss Newsletter 517
Orangedale Railway Museum Archives 676
Orangetown Historical Museum Archives 411
Orangeville Public Library 687
Orator 427
Orbisonia-Rockhill Furnace Historical Society 496
Orcas Island Historical Museum 601
Orcas Island Historical Museum Archives 604
Orcas Island Historical Society & Archives 601
Orcas Islander 604
Orchard Historical Society 355
Orchard House Museum Archives 269
Orchard Park Historical Museum 409
Orchard Park Historical Society & Archives 409
Orchard Public Library 355
Orcutt Ranch Museum Archives 39
Ord Township Library 355
Order Board 531
Order of AHEPA 106
Order of Founders and Patriots of America 19, 20
Order of Saint Benedict 607
Order of the First World War 113
Order of the Founders and Patriots of America, Michigan Society 287
Order of the Indian Wars 29
Order of the Second World War 113
Order of the Sons of Italy in America 106
Order of the Sons of Italy in America News; Italian America 106
Order of the Three Crusades 20
Ordway Family Journal 418
Orebaugh Family 47
Oreck Family News 19
Oregon Air & Space Museum Archives 475
Oregon Archives Division 479
Oregon Area Historical Museum 628
Oregon Area Historical Society & Archives 628
Oregon Aviation Historical Society 474
Oregon City Public Library 477
Oregon Coast History Center Archives 477
Oregon County Genealogical Society & Library 325
Oregon County Genealogical Society Newsletter 325
Oregon Electric Railway Historical Museum 479
Oregon Electric Railway Historical Society & Archives 479
Oregon Genealogical Society & Library 475
Oregon Genealogical Society Bulletin 475
Oregon Genealogical Society Quarterly 475
Oregon Historic Cemeteries Association 473
Oregon Historic Cemeteries Association Ledger 473
Oregon Historic District Society 455
Oregon Historical Family 478
Oregon Historical Quarterly 478
Oregon Historical Society & Archives 478
Oregon Historical Society Newsletter 478
Oregon History Center Archives 478
Oregon History Magazine 478
Oregon Jack Creek Indian Band 647
Oregon Jerusalem Historical Museum 455
Oregon Jerusalem Historical Society & Archives 455
Oregon Jerusalem Historical Society Newsletter 455
Oregon Lewis and Clark Heritage Foundation 480
Oregon Military Museum Archives 474
Oregon Public Library District 169
Oregon State Library 479
Oregon State University Archives 474
Oregon Trail Library 473
Oregon Trail Museum 352
Oregon Trail Regional Museum Archives 473
Oregon Trail Sources, Queries and Reviews 603
Oregon-California Trails Association 331
Orem Public Library 569

Orestes Historical Society 191
Orford Free Library 363
Organ Historical Society 594
Organization of American Historians 180
Organization of American Historians Newsletter 180
Original Narratives of Early American History 408
Origins 292
Orillia Museum of Art and History 687
Orillia Public Library 687
Orinda Historical Society & Library 58
Orion Township Public Library 295
Orion Township Public Library Quarterly Newsletter 295
Oriskany Battlefield State Historic Site Archives 410
Orland Free Library 58
Orland Historical and Cultural Society 58
Orland Historical Highlights 249
Orland Historical Museum 249
Orland Historical Society 169
Orland Historical Society & Library 249
Orleans County Historical Society & Archives 575, 578
Orleans County Historical Society Bulletin 575
Orleans Historical Society & Library 277
Orleans Public Library 402
Orleans Town & Township Public Library 191
Orm Mikkelson Family 208
Ormond Beach Public Library 119
Oromocto Nation 664
Orono Maine Folklife Center Archives 249
Orono Public Library 249
Oroville Chinese Temple Museum Archives 58
Orphan Train Heritage Society of America 213
Orphan Train Heritage Society of America & Library 32
Orphan Voyage Library 314
Orphans Cemetery Association 130
Orrell Family 257
Ortega Adobe Museum Archives 76
Orthodox Church in America 417
Ortstadt-Ottstadt-Otstot(t) Family 584
Orval Berry Museum Archives 682
Orwell Garner Historic Village Museum 695
Orwell Town Historian 410
Osage County Genealogical Society 218
Osage County Genealogical Society Quarterly 218
Osage County Historical Museum 218, 468
Osage County Historical Society 334
Osage County Historical Society & Archives 218, 468
Osage County Historical Society Newsletter 334
Osage Mission-Neosho County Historical Society 221
Osage Nation Tribal Museum Archives 468
Osage Public Library 206
Osage Village State Historic Site Archives 333
Osakis Heritage Center 312
Osawatomie and Its People 219
Osawatomie Historical Society & Library 219
Osawatomie Public Library 219
Osborn-Cambron-Moser-Israelovitch-Auster-White-Lambert-Reeves-Mulinax-Primak-Robinson-Black-Gibson Family Association 263
Osborne County Genealogical and Historical Society 219
Osborne County Genealogical Society Quarterly 219
Osborne Family 442
Osborne Homestead Museum Archives 92
Osborne Public Library 219
Osborn-Jackson House Museum 396
Osbourne-Haywood Family 57
Osburn Public Library 149
Oscar Anderson House Archives 11
Osceola County Department of Genealogical Research 121
Osceola County Genealogical Society & Library 300
Osceola County Genealogical Society Reader 300
Osceola County Historical Museum 115
Osceola County Historical Society & Archives 115, 207
Osceola Depot Archives 628
Osceola Historical Society 191
Osceola Historical Society & Archives 628
Osceola Library 365
Osceola Public Library 206
Osceola Town Historian 392
Oscoda County Library 298
Osgood Public Library 191
Osgoode Township Historical Society & Archives 692
Osgoode Township Museum Archives 692
Oshawa Historical Society Archives & Library 687
Oshawa Public Library 687
Oshawa Sydenham Museum Archives 687
Oshkosh Public Library 355, 628
Oshkosh Public Museum Archives 628
Oshkosh Public Museum Newsletter 628
Oskaloosa Public Library 206, 220
Osler Historical Museum Archives 708
Osoyoos Indian Band 653
Osoyoos Museum Archives 653
Osseo Historical Society 628
Ossining Historical Museum 410
Ossining Historical Society & Archives 410
Ossipee Historical Society & Library 363
Ossipee Public Library 359
Osterhout Free Library Newsletter 505
Osterhout Free Public Library 505
Ostertag-Easterday Newsletter 170
Osterville Free Library 277
Osterville Historical Museum 277
Osterville Historical Society & Archives 277
Osterville Historical Society Museum Newsletter 277
Ostfriesian Heritage Society 202
Ostfriesland Society of Iowa 197
Ostrander Family 398
Ostrander Reunion 310
Ostrem-Reierson Family 623
Oswayo Valley Historical Society 502
Oswego City Historian 410
Oswego County Archives 410
Oswego County Historical Society & Archives 410
Oswego County Historical Society Newsletter 410
Oswego County Records Center 410
Oswego Historical Museum 220
Oswego Historical Society & Archives 220
Oswego Public Library District 169
Oswego School District Public Library 410
Oswego Town Historian 410
Otero Museum Archives 86

Otis Chidester Scout Museum of Southern Arizona Archives 22
Otis Community Library 220
Otis Library 97
Otisfield Historical Society 249
Otisville Historical Society 299
Otoe County Historical Society 354, 357
Otsego County Library 292
Otsego District Public Library 299
Ottawa Branch News 687
Ottawa Church Historical Society 310
Ottawa County Chapter, OGS 456
Ottawa County Genealogical Society & Library 467
Ottawa County Historical Museum Archives 219
Ottawa County Historical Society 467
Ottawa Public Library 220, 687
Ottawa Scouting Museum Archives 169
Ottenheimer Library 29
Otter Tail County Genealogical Society & Library 308
Otter Tail County Genealogical Society Newsletter 308
Otter Tail County Historical Museum 308
Otter Tail County Historical Society & Archives 308
Otter Tail County Historical Society Newsletter 308
Otter Tail Record 308
Otterbein Public Library 191
Otto Bruyns Public Library of Northfield 375
Otto F Linn Library 478
Otto Family 118, 429
Otto G Richter Library 111
Ottumwa Public Library 206
Ouachita County Historical Society & Archives 26
Ouachita County Historical Society Quarterly 26
Ouachita Genealogical Society 242
Ouachita Parish Public Library 239
Ouachita-Calhoun Genealogical Society 26
Ouderkerk Family Newsletter 134
Ouilmette Heritage 177
Our Birthright and Heritage 137
Our Clay Heritage 334
Our Harrison Heritage 443
Our Heritage 148, 168, 226, 460, 461, 469, 539, 559
Our House State Memorial Archives 448
Our Lady of Mercy Museum Archives 668
Our Lady of the Rock Library 607
Our Memories Museum Archives 146
Our Missing Links 195
Our Name's the Game 506
Our Polish Ancestors 445
Our Proud Heritage 591
Our Roots 83
Our Savior's Lutheran Church Library 172
Ouray County Historical Society 88
Ousley Newsletter 542
Out of the Mist 408
Out of the Past 122
Out on a Limb 633
Outagamie County Historical Society 623
Outagamie County Historical Society & Archives 617
Outer Banks History Center Archives 429
Outlook 630
Outlook and District Heritage Museum Archives 708
Over the Fence Post 316
Over the Years 315
Overall Family 525
Overfield Tavern Museum Archives 458
Overhiser Family 297, 302
Overhiser Highlights 297
Overholser Family 504
Overholser Mansion Museum Archives 468
Overland and Underground 636
Overland Historical Society & Archives 336
Overland Journal 331
Overland Park Historical Society 220
Overland Trail Museum Archives 90
Overstreet-Kerr Historical Farm Archives 466
Overton County Public Library 529
Overton Observer 529
Overview 211
Overview 231
Oviatt Family 579
Ovid Historical Society 299
Owascoag Notes 251
Owatonna Public Library 312
Oweekeno Nation 653
Oweekeno-Kitasoo-Nuxalk Tribal Council 647
Owen County Historical and Genealogical Society 193
Owen County History and Genealogy 193
Owen County Public Library 193, 232
Owen D Young Library, Special Collections 392
Owen Family 505, 584
Owen Sound Marine and Rail Museum Archives 688
Owen Sound Museum Archives 688
Owen Sound Public Library 688
Owenby-Ownby Family 529
Owen-Owens Newsletter 553
Owens Family 285
Owensboro Area Museum of History Archives 232
Owens-Stuart-Skipper Family 3
Owens-Thomas House Museum Library 137
Owensville Carnegie Library 191
Owls Head Transportation Museum Archives 249
Ownbey-Ownby Family 32
Owsley Company Historical Society 225
Owsley County Public Library 225
Owsley Family Historical Society Newsletter 73
Owyhee County Historical Museum 148
Owyhee County Historical Society & Archives 148
Owyhee Outpost 148
Oxford County Library 683
Oxford Family 28
Oxford Free Library & Museum 277
Oxford Historical Museum 261
Oxford Historical Society 98, 249, 261, 410
Oxford Municipal Library 355
Oxford Public Library 98, 191, 220, 496
Oxford Tracer 693
Oxnard Public Library 58
Oxon Cove Park Archives 261
Oyer Family 414
Oyster and Maritime Museum of Chincoteague Archives 586
Oyster Bay Historical Museum 410

INDEX

Oyster Bay Historical Society & Archives 410
Oyster Bay-East Norwich Public Library 410
Oyster Bay-East Norwich Public Library Newsletter 410
Oysterponds Historical Society & Archives 410
Oysterponds Historical Society Museum News 410
Ozar'kin: The People Who Settled the Missouri Ozarks 341
Ozark County Genealogical and Historical Society 329
Ozark Folk Center Archives 31
Ozark Happenings 330
Ozark Heritage Museum Archives 29
Ozark Regional Library-Ironton Branch 331
Ozark-Dale County Public Library 8
Ozarks Genealogical Society & Library 341
Ozarks Watch Magazine 340
Ozaukee County Historical Society & Library 619
Ozaukee County Historical Society Newsletter 619
Ozaukee County Pioneer Village Archives 630

P

P K Yonge Library of Florida History 113
P T Boat Museum Archives 527
P T Boats Museum & Library 530
Pa/e/urdue Family 444
Paarlberg Farmstead Homestead Archives 174
Pabineau Indian Band 663
Pace Family 550
Pace Family 597
Pacem in Terris House Museum Archives 419
Pacer-Hunt County Genealogical Society 557
Pacheenaht Indian Band 653
Pacific Asia Museum Archives 59
Pacific Beach Historical Society 65, 71
Pacific Coast Air Museum Archives 71
Pacific Coast Historical Association & Archives 605
Pacific Coast Historical Museum 605
Pacific County Genealogical Society & Library 604
Pacific County Historical Museum 607
Pacific County Historical Society & Archives 607
Pacific Great Eastern Station Archives 653
Pacific Grove Heritage Society & Library 58
Pacific Heritage Museum Archives 67
Pacific Historical Review 37, 51
Pacific Northwest Conference Depository, United Methodist Church 608
Pacific Northwest Cornish Association 606
Pacific Northwest Quarterly 606, 608
Pacific Northwest Truck Museum Archives 473
Pacific Northwest Truck Museum Newsletter 473
Pacific Palisades Historical Society & Library 58
Pacific Palisades Historical Society Newsletter 58
Pacific Railroad Society 69
Pacific Tsunami Museum Archives 141
Pacific University Museum Archives 475
Packard Family 400
Packer Family 567
Packet 292
Pack-Peck-Peek Pioneers 314
Packwood House Museum Archives 492
Paddlewheel Press 438
PAF-Finders Club 432
PAFinder Newsletter 68
PAFology 569
Page County Genealogical Society 207
Page Family 146, 601
Page Family Newsletter 478
Page One Newsletter 201
Page Public Library 18
PAGES 52
Pages From the Past 198, 294
Pahkisimon Nuye Ah Library 707
Pahquidque Packet 92
Paine Memorial Free Library 421
Painted Forest Folk Art Museum 634
Paipoonga Historical Museum Archives 691
Paisley Family Journal 206
Pajaro Valley Genealogical Society 45
Pajaro Valley Historical Association & Archives 77
Pajaro Valley Historical Association Newsletter 77
Pakn Treger 265
Palace of the Governors Library 385
Pal-Am Mountaineer 613
Palama Settlement Archives 142
Palatine Germans of the Mohawk Valley 415
Palatine Historical Society & Archives 169
Palatine Immigrant 446
Palatine Palaver 169
Palatine Patter 446
Palatines to America, Colorado Chapter 81, 87
Palatines to America, Illinois Chapter 170
Palatines to America, Illinois Chapter Newsletter 170
Palatines to America, Indiana Chapter 187
Palatines to America, Indiana Chapter Newsletter 187
Palatines to America, Michigan Chapter 292
Palatines to America, National Chapter & Library 446
Palatines to America, New York Chapter 392, 404, 416
Palatines to America, Ohio Chapter 446
Palatines to America, Pennsylvania Chapter 502
Palatines to America, Virginia Chapter 583, 587
Palatines to America, West Virginia Chapter 613
Palatka Railroad Preservation Society 119
PALCO Logging Museum Archives 72
Palermo Town Historian 411
Palestine Public Library 555
Palestine Public Library District 169
Paley Library 498
Palimpsest 203
Palisades Free Library 410
Palliser Regional Library 708
Palliser Regional Library-Moose Jaw Branch 708
Palm Bay Campus Library 119
Palm Beach County Genealogical Society & Library 124
Palm Beach County Public Library System 124
Palm Breezes Newsletter 553
Palm Harbor Historical Museum 119
Palm Harbor Historical Society & Archives 119
Palm Harbor Library 119
Palm Springs Air Museum Archives 58
Palm Springs Desert Museum Archives 58
Palm Springs Genealogical Society 58
Palm Springs Historical Society & Library 58
Palm Springs Public Library 58

Palmdale City Library 58
Palmer Historical Society & Archives 13
Palmer House Museum 454
Palmer Lake Historical Society & Archives 88
Palmer Museum Archives 216
Palmer Newsletter 418
Palmer Public Library 13, 277
Palmer-Gullickson Octagon House Archives 634
Palmer-Gullickson Octagon House Newsletter 634
Palmers of NY, Ontario, Canada, and Williams County, OH 77
Palmerton Library Association 496
Palmer-Weaver Family 21
Palmetto Trust for Historic Preservation 513
Palmyra Area Genealogical Society 496
Palmyra Bicentennial Public Library 336
Palmyra Historical Museum 191, 410
Palmyra Historical Society & Archives 191, 628
Palmyra Historical Society Newsletter 628
Palmyra King's Daughters' Free Library 410
Palo Alto City Library 59
Palo Alto County Genealogical Society 201
Palo Alto County Genealogical Society & Archives 201
Palo Alto Historic Resources Board 59
Palo Alto Historical Association & Library 59
Palo Verde Historical Museum 37
Palo Verde Historical Society & Archives 37
Palo Verde Valley District Library 37
Palomar College Library 69
Palos Heights Historical Society 169
Palos Heights Public Library 170
Palos Historical Society & Archives 170
Palos Park Public Library 170
Palos Verdes Library District 63
Palos Verdes Library District-Malaga Cove Plaza 59
Palumbo-Passero Families: the Cousins 103
Pamlico County Library 423
Pampa Genealogical and Historical Society 555
Pamplin Park Civil War Site Archives 592
Pamunkey Indian Museum Archives 589
Pamunkey Regional Library 588
Pangburn Letter 51
Panhandle Plains Historical Museum 539
Panhandle Plains Historical Review 539
Panhandle Plains Historical Society & Archives 539
Pankaskie Family 602
Panlener Papers 314
Pannebakker Family 624
Panning for Nuggets of Old 25
Panola County Historical and Genealogical Association 540
Panorama 549
Paoli Public Library 191
Papago Park Museum 21
Paper Airplane Museum Archives 142
Paperclips: Haywood County Public Library & Friends Newsletter 434
Papillion Area Historical Society 355
Paradis Family 246
Paradise Fact and Folklore 59
Paradise Family Newsletter 247
Paradise Genealogical Society & Library 59
Paradise Genealogical Society Newsletter 59
Paradise Schoolhouse 508
Paramus Historical and Preservation Society 377
Paramus Public Library 375
Parc de l'Artillerie 701
Parc Historique National du Fort Chambly Archives 697
Parchment Community Library 299
Parco-Sinclair Historical Society 637
Pardee Home Museum 57
Pardee Home Museum Newsletter 57
Pardue Family 587
Pardue Times & Historical Gazette 587
Paris Area Genealogical Society 532
Paris Cape Historical Museum 251
Paris Cape Historical Society & Archives 251
Paris Hill-Hamlin Memorial Library 249
Paris Historical Museum 688
Paris Historical Society & Archives 688
Paris Public Library 251, 555
Parish Public Library 410
Parish Town Historian 410
Paris-Henry County Heritage Center Archives 532
Parish-Parrish Family 46
Parishville Historical Association & Archives 410
Parishville Historical Museum 410
Parishville Museum Newsletter 410
Park City Historical Museum 569
Park City Historical Society & Archives 569
Park City Historical Society Quarterly 569
Park City Library 569
Park College Historical Society & Archives 336
Park County Genealogy Society 345, 635
Park County Historical Society & Archives 345
Park County Historical Society & Library 635
Park County Library 635
Park County Public Library 81, 345
Park Falls Public Library 629
Park Forest Historical Society & Archives 170
Park Forest Public Library 170
Park Hills Public Library 336
Park House Museum 218
Park Ridge Historical Society 170
Park Ridge Public Library 170, 375
Park University Library 336
Parkdale-Maplewood Community Museum Archives 673, 675
Parke County Historical Society 192
Parke Family 296, 626
Parke Society 477
Parker Community Historical Society 220
Parker County Genealogical Society & Archives 563
Parker Family 161, 607
Parker John Historical Society 456
Parker Public Library 18, 523
Parker Tavern Museum 278
Parker Williams Library 549
Parker-Lumpkin Family 513
Parker-O'Malley Air Museum Archives 398
Parkersburg-Wood County Public Library 614
Parkesburg Free Library 496
Parkinson Family 572
Parkland Community Library 481

Parkland Regional Library 644
Parkland Regional Library-Govan Branch 706
Park-McCullough House Archives 578
Parks Family 338
Parks Library 197
Parkside Library 624
Parks-Reese Family 339
Parksville and District Historical Society 653
Parlett Moore Library 256
Parlin Ingersoll Public Library 153
Parlour Talk 51
Parma Area Historical Society & Library 455
Parma Cuyahoga Chapter, OGS 455
Parma Public Library 400
Parma-Cuyahoga Newsletter 455
Parma-Hilton Historical Society 400
Parmenter Family 88, 208
Parmly Billings Library 343
Parnell Memorial Library 7
Parowan Public Library 569
Parris Island Heritage Library 515
Parris Island Historical Society 515, 517
Parris Island Museum Archives 517
Parris Island Museum Quarterly 517
Parrish Family 605
Parrott Family 560
Parrott-Perrotte Family 381
Parrsboro Shore Historical Society 676
Parry Mansion Museum 495
Parsley Family 187
Parson Fisher House Archives 244
Parsonfield-Porter Historical Society 250
Parsons Family 272, 460
Parsons Family Newsletter 22, 567
Parsons Historical Commission Museum Archives 220
Parsons Historical Society 220
Parsons Public Library 220
Parsonsfield Public Library 249
Parsonsfield-Porter Historical Society & Library 247
Partee-Purtee Family 622
Parten Family 71
Partin Family Archives 554
Partridge Public Library 220
Pasadena City College Library 59
Pasadena Genealogy Society 59
Pasadena Heritage 59
Pasadena Historical Society & Archives 59
Pasadena Historical Society Newsletter 59
Pasadena Public Library 59, 556
Pasadena Public Library-La Pintoresca 59
Pascack Historical Museum 375
Pascack Historical Society & Library 375
Paschill Family 532
Pasco County Genealogical Society 111
Pasco County Library System 114
Pasco County Line 111
Pas-Ka-Poo Historical Park 645
Paso Robles Public Library 59
Pasqua First Nation 79 706
Pasquerilla Library 493
Passages 170
Passaic County Community College Library 376
Passaic County Historical Society & Library 376
Passaic County, New Jersey Genealogy Club 376
Passenger Pigeon 300
Passey Family 603
Passiac Public Library 376
Password 544
Past & Present 223, 424
Past Heritage 59
Past Times 155, 430, 501
Past Times of Amador 48
Past to Present 96
Past, Present & Future 624
PastFinder 47, 113, 169, 286, 302, 441, 452
Pastfinders of South Lake County 110
PasTimes 314
Past-Present Prints 287
Pat Hathaway Collection of Historical Photos 55
Patagonia Public Library 18
Patch Gleanings 100
Patchen-Beverly Family 481
Patch-Latimer-Wright Family 100
Patchogue-Medford Central Library 410
Patchwork History of Tiverton 509
Pate Museum of Transportation Archives 541
Patee House Museum 338
Patents 412, 417
Paterson Free Public Library-Danforth Memorial Library 376
Paterson Historic Preservation Commission 376
Paterson Museum Archives 376
Pathfinders 295
Paths to the Past 39
Pathways 86, 416, 453
Pathways and Passages 96
Pathways: History and Genealogical Journal 530
Patnode-Patenade-Patenotre Family 299
Patricia Romanko Public Library 149
Patrick Air Force Base Library 119
Patrick County Genealogical Society 596
Patrick County Historical Museum 596
Patrick County Historical Society & Archives 596
Patrick Henry National Memorial Archives 585
Patrick Henry Sullivan Foundation & Archives 196
Patrick Henry Sullivan Museum and Genealogy Library 196
Patrick Power Library 674
Patriot Report 370
Patriots Point Naval and Maritime Museum Archives 516
Patrol Squadron Colorado Archives 81
Patrol Squadron Colorado Newsletter 81
Patron 165
Patrons' Pages 154
Patt Family 277
Pattee & Paterno Library 503
Patten Free Library 243
Patten Lumbermen's Museum Archives 249
Patterson Genies 59
Patterson Homestead Archives 447
Patterson Inn Museum 394
Patterson Library 421

Patterson Memorial Library 634
Patterson People 292
Patterson Points 262
Patterson Township Historical Society 59
Patterson-Tiner-Lemaster Family 381
Patton Exchange Letter 127
Patton Museum of Cavalry and Armor Library 227
Patuxent Rural Life Museum Archives 263
Paul and Matilda Wegner Grotto Archives 619
Paul Bunyan Logging Camp Museum Archives 620
Paul Bunyon Historical Society & Library 305
Paul Dresser Memorial Birthplace 194
Paul Family 27, 247
Paul G Blazer Library 227
Paul Horgan Library 384
Paul Indian Band 642
Paul Laurence Dunbar Library 447
Paul M Adams Memorial Library 343
Paul Meek Library 529
Paul Revere House 267
Paul Revere Memorial Association & Archives 267
Paul Revere Memorial Association Newsletter 267
Paulding County Carnegie Public Library 455
Paulding County Chapter, OGS & Archives 455
Paulding County Historical Museum 129
Paulding County Historical Society & Archives 129
Paulding History House Archives 69
Paulding House Archives 36
Paulding Pathways 455
Pauline E Glidden Toy Museum Archives 359
Pauline E Glidden Toy Museum Newsletter 359
Paulson House Museum Archives 286
Pauquachin Indian Band 647
Pautard Families Newsletter 124
Pavek Museum of Broadcasting Archives 314
Pavilion Indian Band 648
Paw Paw District Library 299
Paw Paw Public Library District 170
Paw Prints 54
Pawhuska Genealogical Society 468
Pawhuska Public Library 468
Pawlet Public Library 578
Pawlett Historical Society 578
Pawnee Bill Ranch Museum Archives 468
Pawnee City Historical Museum 356
Pawnee City Historical Society & Archives 356
Pawnee City Historical Society Newsletter 356
Pawnee County Historical Museum 469
Pawnee County Historical Society & Archives 469
Pawnee Genealogy Scouters 349
Pawnee Indian Village State Historic Park Archives 221
Pawnee Natural Historic Site Archives 86
Pawnee Public Library 170
Pawtucket Public Library 509
Pawtuxet Valley Preservation and Historical Society 510
Paxton Public Library 356
Payette County Historical Society 149
Payette Public Library 149
Payeur Family 273
Payne County Genealogical Society & Archives 469
Payne County Genealogical Society Quarterly 469
Payne County Historical Society & Library 469
Payne County Historical Society Review 469
Paynes Creek Historic State Park Archives 109
Paynesville Historical Society 312
Payson City Library 569
Payson Library 53
Payson Public Library 18
Pea Ridge Military Park Library 31
Pea Ridge National Military Park Archives 27
Pea River Historical and Genealogical Society 4
Pea River Historical and Genealogical Society & Archives 4
Pea River Historical Museum 4
Pea River Historical Society 4
Pea River Trails 4
Peabody Essex Museum 278
Peabody Historical Society & Library 220, 277
Peabody Historical Society Newsletter 220
Peabody Institute Library 269
Peabody Museum of Salem Library 278
Peabody Public Library 181
Peace Church Museum Archives 484
Peace River Centennial Museum Archives 645
Peach Public Library 131
Peachland Museum Archives 653
Peacock Family 537
Peacock Paths 537
Peak, Peake Family 42
Pearce Collections Museum Archives 541
Pearce Organization Bulletin 118
Pearcy/Pierce Family Association Newsletter 468
Pearcy-Piercy Family 468
Pearisburg Public Library 592
Pearl A Wanamaker Library 608
Pearl Button Newsletter 206
Pearl River Community College Library 322
Pearl River County Library System 322
Pearl River Historical Society 322
Pearl S Buck Birthplace Museum Archives 612
Pearl S Buck House Museum Archives 496
Pearsall Library 432
Pearson Air Museum Archives 609
Pearson Family 3
Pearson Museum Archives 174
Pearson's Places and Things 175
Pearsons Places and Things 3
Peary-MacMillan Arctic Museum Archives 244
Pease Public Library 364
Peavey Memorial Library 246
Peavler Newsletter 84
Pebble Hill Plantation Archives 138
Pecan Valley Genealogical Society 539
Pecatonica Historical Society 170
Pecos National Historical Park Archives 384
Pecos Trails 382
Peddy Family 175, 527
Peddycoart Family 1
Pedigree Pointers 631
Pedigree Searchers 58
Pee Dee Chapter, SCGS 516

INDEX

Pee Dee Chapter, SCGS & Library 516
Pee Dee Queue 516
Pee Wee Press 56
Peekskill Museum Archives 411
Peekskill Museum Newsletter 411
Peel Heritage Complex Archives 680
Peel House Museum 25
Peel Mansion Carriage House 32
Peel Mansion Museum 25
Peepeekisis First Nation 705
Peg a Parten Line 71
Peguis Cultural Centre 660
Peguis Nation 660
Pejepscot Historical Museum 244
Pejepscot Historical Society 251
Pejepscot Historical Society & Archives 244
Pekin Historical Society 190, 191
Pekin Public Library 170
Pekin Public Library Newsletter 170
Pelham Historical Museum 265
Pelham Historical Society 277
Pelham Historical Society 363
Pelham Historical Society & Archives 265
Pelham Historical Society Newsletter 265
Pelham Masonic Historical Society of City Island 390
Pelham Public Library 277
Pelican Lake First Nation 707
Pell City Library 8
Pella Historical Society & Archives 207
Pella Historical Village 207
Pella Public Library 207
Pelletier Family 252, 703
Pellien-Jaeger-Loretan-Steiner-Ross Family 627
Pellissippi Genealogical and Historical Society 526
Pellissippian 526
Pelly Crossing Historical Society 713
Pemaquid Historical Association 245
Pemaquid Historical Association & Library 249
Pember Library and Museum 399
Pemberton Museum Archives 653
Pemberville Public Library 455
Pemberville-Freedom Area Historical Society 455
Pembina City Library 439
Pembina Lobstick Historical Museum Archives 643
Pembina State Museum Archives 439
Pembina Threshermen's Museum Archives 662
Pembroke Historical Museum 277
Pembroke Historical Society & Archives 277
Pembroke Historical Society Quarterly 277
Pembroke Public Library 688
Pemiscot County Historical Society & Library 327
Pemiscot County Missouri Quarterly 327
Pemtcoe Tracings 434
Pena-Peck House Museum Archives 121
Pend Oreille County Historical Society & Library 603
Pend Oreille County Library District 603
Pendarvis State Historic Site Archives 627
Pender County Historical Society 424
Pender County Public Library 424
Pender County Public Library-Hampstead Branch 428
Pendle Hill Library 504
Pendleton Community Library 191
Pendleton County Historical and Genealogical Society 227
Pendleton County Historical and Genealogical Society Newsletter 227
Pendleton County Historical Society 612
Pendleton County Public Library 227
Pendleton District Agricultural Museum Archives 517
Pendleton District Historical, Recreational and Tourism Commission & Library 517
Pendleton Family 529
Pendleton Family Newsletter 211
Pendleton Foundation for Black History and Culture 517
Pendleton Historic Foundation 517
Pendleton Historic Foundation Newsletter 517
Pendleton Public Library 477
Penelakut Indian Band 648
Penetanguishene Centennial Museum Archives 688
Penfield Homestead Foundation 395
Penfield Library 410
Penfield Public Library 411
Peninsula 62
Peninsula and Saint Edmunds Township Museum Archives 691
Peninsula Historical Society & Library 455
Peninsula Historical Society Newsletter 455
Penland Historical Society 604
Penland Historical Society Quarterly 604
Penn Area Library 489
Penn Family 138
Penn Hills Library 499
Penn Hills Library-Lincoln Park Satellite 499
Penn in Hand 497
Penn Pal 502
Penn Yan Public Library 411
Pennesseewassee Sketches 249
Pennington County Historical Society 316
Pennington Family 59, 541
Pennington Public Library 376
Penns Valley Area Historical Museum Archives 481
Pennsauken Historical Society 376
Pennsbury Manor Library 494
Pennsilfaanisch Agitsch Barichta 491
Pennsville Public Library 376
Pennsville Township Historical Society 376
Pennsylvania 1800-1850 492
Pennsylvania Anthracite Heritage Museum Archives 501
Pennsylvania Deutch Society 183
Pennsylvania Dutch Folk Culture Society & Library 491
Pennsylvania Dutch News and Views 491
Pennsylvania Federation of Museums and Historical Organizations & Library 489
Pennsylvania Folklife 485
Pennsylvania Folklife Society & Library 485
Pennsylvania Freemason 498
Pennsylvania Genealogical Magazine 497
Pennsylvania Genealogical Research 529
Pennsylvania Genealogist and Historian 492
Pennsylvania German Heritage Library 491
Pennsylvania German Research Society 502
Pennsylvania German Society 491
Pennsylvania Heritage 489

Pennsylvania Heritage Society 489
Pennsylvania Historical and Museum Commission & Library 481, 489
Pennsylvania Historical and Museum Commission Archives 503
Pennsylvania Historical Association 502
Pennsylvania History 502
Pennsylvania in the Civil War 492
Pennsylvania in the Revolution 492
Pennsylvania Legacies 497
Pennsylvania Lumber Museum Archives 488
Pennsylvania Magazine of History and Biography 497
Pennsylvania Mennonite Heritage 492
Pennsylvania Military Museum and 28th Division Shrine Archives 483
Pennsylvania Trolley Museum Archives 504
Pennsylvanian Cornish Society 481
Pennville Township Public Library 191
Penny Lots 486
Penny Sketches 404
Pennypacker Mills Archives 501
Pennypacker Mills Newsletter 501
Pennyroyal Area Museum Archives 229
Penobscot Marine Museum Library 251
Penobscot Nation Historical Museum 249
Penobscot Nation Historical Society 249
Penrose Library 84
Penrose Memorial Library 609
Pensacola Historical Museum 120
Pensacola Historical Society & Archives 120
Pensacola History Illustrated 120
Pentagon Library 584
Penticton Indian Band 653
Penticton Public Library 653
Pentwater Township Library 300
Peoples Library 495
Peoria Arizona Historical Society 18
Peoria Genealogical Society & Library 170
Peoria Genealogical Society Newsletter 170
Peoria Heights Public Library 170
Peoria Historical Museum 170
Peoria Historical Society & Archives 170
Peoria Historical Society Newsletter 170
Peoria Public Library 18, 170
Peotone Public Library District 170
Pepin County Historical Society 620
Pequannock Township Public Library 376
Pequot Lakes Historical Society 313
Pequot Library 99
Peralta Adobe & Fallon House Archives 68
PerArdua 430
Perez Family 535
Perigo-Perrigo Newsletter 311
Periman Pathways Newsletter 174
Perinton Historical Museum 397
Perinton Historical Society & Archives 397
Perinton Historigram 397
Perkins Bull Collection Archives 688
Perkins County Genealogical Society 352
Perkins County Historical Society & Library 352
Perkins Family 493, 607
Perkins Family Newsletter 54
Perkins History Museum Archives 281
Perkins Library 351, 352
Permian Basin Genealogical Society & Archives 555
Permian Basin Genealogical Society Newsletter 555
Permian Historical Annual 555
Permian Historical Society & Archives 555
Perpetual Flame 161
Perquimans County Library 428
Perrault's Museum Archives 711
Perrigo-Perego-Peregy Family 109, 297
Perrin Family 292
Perrot Memorial Library 97
Perry and Long Genealogy 118
Perry Area Historical Society 135
Perry Carnegie Library 469
Perry County Public Library 529
Perry County Chapter, OGS & Library 450
Perry County District Library 454
Perry County Genealogical and Historical Society 228
Perry County Genealogical Society 10
Perry County Heirlines 450
Perry County Historical and Genealogical Society 29, 31
Perry County Historical and Preservation Society 6
Perry County Historical Society 158, 192, 194, 337, 457, 529
Perry County Historical Society & Archives 171
Perry County Historical Society Quarterly 529
Perry County Jail Museum 171
Perry County Lutheran Historical Museum 325
Perry County Lutheran Historical Society & Archives 325
Perry County Public Library 228
Perry Family 495
Perry Historical Museum 455
Perry Historical Society 120
Perry Historical Society of Lake County & Archives 455
Perry Library 592
Perry Memorial Library 556
Perry Public Library 411, 455
Perry Township-Southport Historical Society 193
Perry United Methodist Church Library 135
Perry's Victory and International Peace Memorial Archives 456
Perryopolis Area Heritage Society 497
Perryville Battlefield Museum Archives 232
Perryville Heritage Center 232
Persimmon Hill 468
Person County Historical Society 432
Person County Public Library 432
Perspectives 105
Perth Amboy Free Public Library 376
Perth County Profiles 690
Perth Museum Archives 688
Perth Regiment Museum Archives 690
Peru Historical Foundation News 356
Peru Historical Society & Library 356
Peru Public Library 170, 191
Peru State College Library 356
Peru Town Historian 411
Peshtigo Fire Museum 629
Peshtigo Fire Museum Newsletter 629
Peshtigo Historical Society & Archives 629
Pessner Family 567
Petaluma Adobe State Historic Park Archives 60

Petaluma Museum Association & Historical Library 60
Petaluma Regional Library 60
Peter Ballantyne Cree Nation 709
Peter Conser House Archives 466
Peter M Khan Memorial Library 52
Peter Rice Homestead 274
Peter Watne Memorial Library 314
Peter Wentz Farmstead Library 506
Peter White Public Library 297
Peter Whitmer Sr Home Museum Archives 420
Peter Willcocks Society 219
Peter Yegen Yellowstone County Museum Archives 343
Peterborough Centennial Museum Archives 688
Peterborough Historical Museum 363
Peterborough Historical Society 688
Peterborough Historical Society & Archives 363
Peterborough Historical Society Bulletin 688
Peterborough Historical Society Newsletter 363
Peterborough Public Library 688
Peterborough Town Library 363
Peters Colony Historical Society of Dallas County 540
Peters Family 460
Peters Indian Band 650
Peters Township Public Library 493
Petersburg National Battlefield Library 592
Petersburg Public Library 13, 170, 592
Petersen Automotive Museum Archives 52
Petersen Quarterly 52
Petersham Historical Museum 277
Petersham Historical Society & Archives 277
Petersham Memorial Library 277
Peterson Air & Space Museum Archives 89
Peterson Family 568
Peterstown Heritage Society 176
Petit Musee 663
Petite Angelicane Museum Archives 697
Petosky Public Library 300
Petroleum County Community Library 347
Petroleum Museum Archives 554
Petrolia Discovery Museum 688
Pettaquamscutt Historical Museum 508
Pettaquamscutt Historical Society & Archives 508
Pettaquamscutt Reporter 508
Pettee Memorial Library 580
Pettigrew Home Museum Archives 523
Pettigrew Regional Library 431
Pettingell Newsletter 39
Pettis County Historical Museum 340
Pettis County Historical Society & Archives 340
Pettis County Historical Society Newsletter 340
Petty Family 538
Pewaukee Area Historical Museum 629
Pewaukee Area Historical Society & Archives 629
Peyton Family 256, 593
Pfluger Family Digest 425
Pflugerville Community Library 556
Pharr Memorial Library 556
Pheasant Rump Nakota First Nation 707
Phelps Community Memorial Library 411
Phelps Connections 173
Phelps County Genealogical Society & Library 338
Phelps County Genealogical Society Quarterly 338
Phelps County Historical Museum 352
Phelps County Historical Society 338
Phelps County Historical Society & Archives 352
Phelps County Historical Society Newsletter 338
Phelps Family 512
Phelps Helps 352
Phelps Historical Society 411
Phelps House 327
Phelps House Museum Archives 198
Phelps House Museum Newsletter 198
Phelps-Bailey Family 566
Phelps-Swingley Family 606
Pheps Store Museum Archives 410
Phi Kappa Psi Fraternity Heritage Hall Archives 187
Philadelphia Archdiocesan Historical Research Center 506
Philadelphia City Archives 498
Philadelphia Historical Commission & Library 498
Philadelphia Society for the Preservation of Landmarks & Museum 498
Philadelphia Society for the Preservation of Landmarks Newsletter 498
Philadelphia Yearly Meeting Library 498
Philbrick and Philbrook Family Association Newsletter 58
Philbrick Family 49
Philip Read Memorial Library 364
Philip Read Memorial Library Newsletter 364
Philip Schaff Library 492
Philippi Public Library 614
Philipse Manor Hall State Historic Site Archives 421
Phillip G Hamm Library 3
Phillip Hamman Echo 1
Phillip-Chandler Family 529
Phillips County Genealogical Society 346
Phillips County Genealogical Society & Archives 220
Phillips County Historical Museum 86
Phillips County Historical Review 28
Phillips County Historical Society 86, 346
Phillips County Historical Society & Archives 28
Phillips County Historical Society & Library 220
Phillips County Library 28
Phillips County Museum Archives 28
Phillips Family 173, 215
Phillips Family Finder 19
Phillips Historical Museum 249
Phillips Historical Society & Archives 249
Phillips Memorial Library 509
Phillips News Letter 215
Phillips Public Library 250
Phillipsburg Area Historical Society & Library 376
Phillipsburg Area Historical Society Newsletter 376
Phillipsburg City Library 220
Phillipsburg Free Public Library 376
Phillips-Hollandsworth Family 586
Phillips-Lee-Monroe Regional Library-Lee County Library 30
Phillips-Lee-Monroe Regional Library-West Helena Library 33
Phillips-Quesenberry Family 586
Philmont Museum Archives 382
Philmont Scout Ranch 382
Philomathean Library 389
Phineas Upham House Society 274

Phipps Family 487
Phipps Quarterly 78
Phippsburg Historical Society 250
Phoebe Apperson Hearst Historical Society & Library 338
Phoebe Apperson Hearst Library 522
Phoebe Griffin Noyes Library 97
Phoebe News 97
Phoenix 159
Phoenix Genealogical Society 19
Phoenix Genealogical Society Newsletter 19
Phoenix Historical Society 474
Phoenix Museum of History Archives 19
Phoenix Museum of History Newsletter 19
Phoenix Police Museum Archives 19
Phoenix Police Museum Newsletter 19
Phoenix Public Library 19, 411
Phoenixville Public Library 498
Photographic Archives 230
Photographic Resource Center Archives 267
Photography Quarterly 421
Piapot First Nation 712
Piatt County Historical and Genealogical Society & Archives 167
Piatt County Historical and Genealogical Society Newsletter 167
Piatt County Historical and Genealogical Society Quarterly 167
Piatt County Museum Archives 167
Piatt County Museum Newsletter 167
Piatt Family 446
Piccadilly Museum of Transportation Archives 343
Pickaway County Genealogical Society & Library 445
Pickaway County Historical Society 445
Pickaway Quarterly 445
Pickens County Chapter, SCGS 511
Pickens County Genealogical Society 535
Pickens County Genealogical Society & Archives 5
Pickens County Historical Museum Newsletter 517
Pickens County Historical Society 517
Pickens County Library 514
Pickens County Museum Archives 517
Pickering Museum Village Archives 688
Pickering Public Library 688
Pickering-Beach Historical Museum 414
Pickering-Beach Historical Society & Archives 414
Pickett Library 614
Pickford Historical Society 300
Pickle Family 60
Pickler Mansion Museum 521
Pickler Memorial Library 333
Pico Rivera Historical and Heritage Society 60
Picton Public Library 688
Pictoral History of Lewes 103
Pictou County Genealogy and Heritage Society 676
Pictou County Historical Museum Archives 675
Pictou County Historical Society 675
Piece of History 311
Pied Cow 249
Piedmont Aviation Historical Society 435
Piedmont Historical and Genealogical Society 9
Piedmont Historical Society 518
Piedmont Lineages 586
Piedmont Regional Genealogical Society 126
Piedmont Regional Genealogy Society 140
Piedmont Regional Library 140
Pieper News 159
Pierce County Genealogical Society 601
Pierce County Heritage Center 629
Pierce County Historical and Genealogical Society 127
Pierce County Historical Association 629
Pierce County Historical Association & Archives 620
Pierce County Historical Society 356
Pierce County Library System 608
Pierce County's Heritage 620
Pierce District Library 149
Pierce Family 219, 579
Pierce House Museum 575
Pierce Manse-New Hampshire Political Library 360
Pierceton & Washington Township Library 192
Piermont Public Library 411
Pierpont Morgan Library 408
Pierre Menard Home State Historic Site Archives 159
Pierre-Fort Pierre Genealogical Society & Library 523
Pierre-Fort Pierre Genealogical Society Newsletter 523
Pierrepont Museum Archives 392
Pierson Family 282
Pierson Library 579
Pieter Claesen Wyckoff House Museum Archives 391
Pieter Claesen Wyckoff House Museum Bulletin 391
Pietrusiewicz Family 156
Pigeon District Library 300
Pigg Family 46
Pigg Family Newsletter 231
Pike and Calhoun Counties Genealogical Society 171
Pike County Archives and History Society & Library 31
Pike County Genealogical Society 326, 459
Pike County Genealogical Society Quarterly 326
Pike County Historical and Genealogical Society 5, 9
Pike County Historical and Genealogical Society Papers 5
Pike County Historical Museum 171
Pike County Historical Review 232
Pike County Historical Society 191, 334, 405
Pike County Historical Society & Archives 171
Pike County Historical Society & Library 494
Pike County Historical Society Newsletter 171
Pike County Public Library 191, 232
Pike County Society for Historical and Genealogical Research 232
Pike Pioneer Museum Archives 9
Pike Speaks 459
Pike Township Historical Society 187
Pike-Amite-Walthall Library System 321
Pikes Peak Genealogical Society 82
Pikes Peak Genealogical Society Newsletter 82
Pikes Peak Historical Society 85
Pikes Peak Library District 82
Pile-Pyle Family 262
Pilesgrove-Woodstown Historical Society 380
Pilgrim 388
Pilgrim Congregational Church Library 307
Pilgrim Edward Doty Society 277
Pilgrim Edward Doty Society Newsletter 277
Pilgrim Hall Museum 277
Pilgrim John Howland Society 253

INDEX

Pilgrim Journal 277
Pilgrim Newsletter 311
Pilgrim Society & Archives 277
Pilgrim Society News 277
Pilgrim Society Notes 277
Pilgrim's Progress 42
Pillars 620
Pillsbury Free Library 365
Pilot Mound Centennial Museum Archives 660
Pilot Point Community Library 556
Pima Air and Space Museum Archives 22
Pima County Public Library 22
Pima Public Library-Graham County 19
Pimeria Alta Historical Museum 18
Pimeria Alta Historical Society & Archives 18
Pimeria Alta Historical Society Newsletter 18
Pinal County Arizona Genealogy Society 15
Pinal County Historical Museum 15, 16
Pinal County Historical Society & Archives 15, 16
Pinckney Community Public Library 300
Pinckney District Chapter Quarterly 518
Pinckney District Chapter, SCGS 518
Pine Aire News 305
Pine Barrens 135, 138
Pine Bluff and Jefferson Counties Public Library 31
Pine Bluff-Jefferson County Historical Museum Archives 31
Pine Bluff-Jefferson County Historical Museum Newsletter 31
Pine County Historial Museum 305
Pine County Historial Society & Archives 305
Pine County Historical Society 315
Pine Creek Grist Mill Archives 206
Pine Forest Regional Library 322
Pine Grove Historical Museum Library 300
Pine Grove Historical Society 499
Pine Grove Public Library 614
Pine Log Historical Society 136
Pine Mountain Regional Library 133
Pine River Public Library 81
Pine Torch 322
Pine, the Plow and the Pioneer 632
Pinecrest Historical Village 625
Pinellas Genealogy Society 116
Pinellas Park Historical Society 120
Pinellas Park Public Library 120
Pinellas Park Public Library Newsletter 120
Pinery 631
Pinery Logging Museum 626
Pinery Pedigree 633
Pinetop-Lakeside Historical Society 17
Pineville-Bell County Public Library 232
Piney Woods Pioneer Genealogical Society 551
Pinion Whispers 89
Pinkerton Family 256, 328
Pinkstaff Family 74
Pintlala Historical Association 5
Pio Pico State Historic Park Archives 77
Pioneer 67, 217, 319, 482
Pioneer and Historical Society of Muskingum County & Library 461
Pioneer Arizona Living History Museum Archives 19
Pioneer Arizona Living History Museum Newsletter 19
Pioneer Association-Pioneer Women 85
Pioneer Auto Museum Archives 523
Pioneer Auto Trails Historical Museum 22
Pioneer Auto Trails Historical Society & Archives 22
Pioneer Beloit 617
Pioneer Branches 600
Pioneer Club of Western South Dakota & Archives 522
Pioneer Corner Museum 628
Pioneer Crier 311
Pioneer Echoes 179
Pioneer Families of Hopkins County 560
Pioneer Farm Museum and Ohop Indian Village 601
Pioneer Florida Museum Archives 111
Pioneer Genealogical Society 469
Pioneer Genealogical Society Newsletter 469
Pioneer Heritage Center Archives 241, 437
Pioneer Heritage Library 204
Pioneer Heritage Museum 204
Pioneer Historical Connors Museum Archives 663
Pioneer Historical Museum of South Dakota 522
Pioneer Historical Society of Bedford County 482
Pioneer Historical Society of Riverside 62
Pioneer History 189
Pioneer Journey Museum 523
Pioneer Library 482
Pioneer Library System 467
Pioneer Log Cabin Museum 218, 623
Pioneer Log Cabin Museum Newsletter 218
Pioneer Magazine 571
Pioneer Memorial Association Newsletter 291
Pioneer Memorial Association of Fenton-Mundy Townships & Library 291
Pioneer Memorial Museum Archives 344
Pioneer Messenger 600
Pioneer Mothers Memorial Cabin Museum Archives 479
Pioneer Museum 16, 298, 308, 309, 343, 344, 440, 475, 480, 679
Pioneer Museum and Vereins Kirche 546
Pioneer Museum Archives 12, 561, 634
Pioneer Museum Newsletter 546
Pioneer Pathfinder 524
Pioneer People and Places 688
Pioneer Press 221
Pioneer Record 297
Pioneer School Museum 316
Pioneer Settlement Museum Archives 109
Pioneer Sons and Daughters Chapter, IGS 200
Pioneer Times 220, 331
Pioneer Town Archives 563
Pioneer Traces 337
Pioneer Trail 351
Pioneer Trails 2, 331, 477
Pioneer Tunnel Coal Mine & Steam Train Museum Archives 481
Pioneer Village 382, 439
Pioneer Village & Virgil Girssom Memorial Archives 189
Pioneer Village and Museum of Saskatchewan 708
Pioneer Village Archives 32, 566
Pioneer Village Gazette 619
Pioneer Village Museum 437, 541, 619, 628
Pioneer Village Museum Archives 659
Pioneer Wagon 331
Pioneer Woman Museum Archives 469

Pioneer's Cemetery Association & Library 19
Pioneering Parmenters of America Newsletter 208
Pioneer-Krier Museum 211
Pioneers of Hart County 126
Pioneers of Macedon 404
Pioneers, Trail Drivers and Former Texas Rangers Association Archives 559
PipeLine 240
Pipeline 326
Pipelines 71
Piper 388
Piper Aviation Museum Archives 493
Piper City Community Historical Society 171
Piper City Public Library District 171
Pipers 85
Pipestem 313
Pipestone County Genealogical Society & Archives 313
Pipestone County Historical Museum 313
Pipestone County Historical Society & Archives 313
Pipestone County Historical Society News 313
Pipestone National Monument Library & Archives 313
Pipkin Family Association Newsletter 22, 217
Pipost 630
Piqua Historical Society & Archives 455
Pirate House Museum 370
Pirate Soul Museum Archives 115
Piscataqua Pioneers & Archives 360
Piscataway Township Free Public Library 376
Piseco Lake Historical Society 411
Pisgah Pathfinder 596
Pithole Museum Archives 499
Pitkin County Library 81
Pitman-Pittman Family 537
Pitot House Museum Archives 240
Pitt County Family Researchers 427
Pitt Meadows Museum Archives 653
Pittenger Family 84
Pittman Family 81, 123, 134
Pittock Mansion Museum Archives 478
Pittock Mansion Museum Newsletter 478
Pitts Family 330, 341
Pitts Library 129
Pitts Theology Library 126
Pittsburg County Genealogical and Historical Society 466
Pittsburg Historical Museum 60
Pittsburg Historical Society & Archives 60
Pittsburg Public Library 220
Pittsburg Public Library News 220
Pittsburg-Camp County Library 556
Pittsburgh History and Landmarks Foundation & Library 499
Pittsburgh History: A Magazine of the City and Its Region 499
Pittser-Greenfield Family 74
Pittsfield Historical Society 578
Pittsfield Historical Society & Archives 250
Pittsfield Public Library 171, 250
Pittsford Historical Museum 411
Pittsford Historical Society 579
Pittsford Historical Society & Archives 578
Pittsford Historical Society Newsletter 578
Pittstown Historical Society 419
Pittsylvania Historical Society 585
Pittsylvania Historical Society & Library 585
Pittsylvania Packet 585
Piulimatsivik-Nain Museum Archives 667
Pixley Family 123
Place Family 209
Placentia Area Museum Archives 668
Placentia Founders Society & Archives 60
Placentia Historical Committee 60
Placentia Library District 60
Placer County Genealogical Society & Library 36
Placer County Museum Archives 36
Placer Trails 36
Plain City Public Library 455
Plainfield Free Public Library 376
Plainfield Historical Society 171
Plainfield Public Library 192, 629
Plainfield Public Library District 171
Plains Genealogical Society 353
Plains Genealogical Society Country 353
Plains Historical Society 353
Plains Indians and Pioneer Museum Archives 471
Plains Public Library District 346
Plains Talk 437
Plains Talk: Quarterly Newsletter of the State Historical Society of North Dakota 437
Plainsboro Free Public Library 376
Plainsboro Historical Society & Library 376
Plainsman Museum 349
Plainsman News 349
Plainview Historical Society 356
Plainview History Association 313
Plainview Public Library 313
Plainview-Old Bethage Public Library 411
Plainville Historical Society & Library 98
Plainville Public Library 277
Plaistow Historical Society 364
Plamondon and District Museum Archives 645
Plamondon Municipal Library 645
Plane Talk 222
Planes of Fame Museum Archives 40
Plank 158
Plano Community Library District 171
Plano Public Library 556
Plano Public Library-Gladys Harrington Library 556
Plantagenet Connection 81
Plantation Agriculture Museum Archives 32
Plantation Historical Museum Archives 120
Plantation Historical Museum Quarterly 120
Plantation News 143
Plantation Quarterly 596
Plantation Society in the Americas 240
Plaquemines Parish Genealogical Society 242
Plaquemines Parish Library 236
Plaster Rock Museum Archives 664
Platt Newsletter 96
Platt R Spencer Memorial Archives 449
Platte County Historical and Genealogical Bulletin 337
Platte County Historical and Genealogical Society 337
Platte County Historical Museum 350
Platte County Historical Society & Archives 350

Platte County Public Library 638
Platte Heritage Club 523
Platte Valley Kinseekers & Library 350
Platte Valley Kinseekers Quarterly 350
Plattekill Historical Society 394
Platteville Mining Museum Archives 629
Platteville Public Library 89, 629
Plattsburgh City Historian 411
Plattsburgh Public Library 411
Plattsburgh Town Historian 411
Plattsmouth Public Library 356
Pleasant Grove Public Library 569
Pleasant Hill Historical Society 337
Pleasant Mount Historical Society 499
Pleasant Reading 554
Pleasanton Public Library 60, 556
Pleasanton-Lincoln Library 220
Plimoth Plantation & Archives 277
Plimoth Plantation Historical Museum 277
Plimoth Plantation Newsletter 277
Plough Library 530
Plough Shares 168
Plover Public Library 207
Plow 42, 477
Plum City Public Library 629
Plum Coulee and District Museum Archives 660
Plum Creek Almanac 552
Plum Grove Historic Home Archives 203
Plum Lake Public Library 630
Plumas County Historical Museum 61
Plumas County Historical Society & Archives 61
Plumas County Library 61
Plumas County Museum Association & Library 61
Plumas County Museum Association Newsletter 61
Plumas Memories 61
Plumas-Eureka State Park Archives 37
Plumb Family 219
Plumb Farm Learning Center Archives 86
Plumb Farm Learning Center Newsletter 86
Plumb Memorial Library 99
Plutko Family Newsletter 40
Plymouth Antiquarian Society & Library 277
Plymouth Antiquarian Society Newsletter 277
Plymouth Area Historical Society 455, 460
Plymouth Center Museum 629
Plymouth Colony Genealogists 268
Plymouth District Library 300
Plymouth Genealogical Society 629
Plymouth Historical Family 300
Plymouth Historical Society 311, 313, 364, 500
Plymouth Historical Society & Archives 300, 629
Plymouth Historical Society & Library 98
Plymouth Historical Society Newsletter 500
Plymouth Library Association 98
Plymouth Meeting Historical Society 500
Plymouth Notch News 578
Plymouth Notch Newsletter 578
Plymouth Public Library 192, 277, 500, 629
Plymouth Rock Foundation 277
Plympton Historical Society 277
Poage Papers 313
Pobst-Richardson Family 597
Pocahontas County Genealogical Society 207
Pocahontas County Historical Museum 613
Pocahontas County Historical Society & Archives 613
Pocahontas County Iowa Historical Museum 204
Pocahontas County Iowa Historical Society & Archives 204
Pocahontas County Iowa Historical Society Quarterly 204
Pocahontas County Newsletter 613
Pocahontas Foundation 584
Pocahontas Library 207
Pocahontas Trails Genealogical Society 466
Pocahontas Trails Genealogical Society 49, 54
Pocahontas Trails Newsletter 49
Pocahontas Trails Quarterly 49
Pocatello Branch Genealogical Society 149
Pocock Family 17
Pocono Mountains Chapter National Railway Historical Society 503
Pocumtuck Valley Memorial Association & Archives 269
Poe Messenger 593
Poe Pages 146
Poe-Hamilton and Allied Families 187
Poestenkill Historical Society 411
Pohick Episcopal Church Archives 590
Poindexter-Poingdestra Family 470
Poinsett County Historical Society 28
POINT (Pursuing Our Italian Names Together) 59
Point Amour Lighthouse Museum Archives 668
Point Arena Lighthouse Museum Archives 60
Point Ellice House Museum Archives 657
Point Fermin Lighthouse Museum Archives 69
Point of Honor Archives 590
Pointe Coupee Historical Society 240
Pointe Coupee Museum Archives 240
Pointe Coupee Parish Library 240
Pointe de l'Eglise Historical and Genealogical Society 236
Pointe-Noire-Parc Marin du Saguencay 697
POINTers 59
POINTers in Person, San Diego County Area Chapter No. 16 77
Points Northeast Historical Society 608
Poland Township Historical Society 451
Polar Prioritites 499
Polar Trails 494
Pole Line 246
Police and Pioneer Museum Archives 661
Polish American Cultural Center Archives 498
Polish American Historic Site Association 289
Polish American Historical Association 299
Polish American Historical Association & Archives 156
Polish American Historical Association Bulletin 156
Polish American Historical Association Newsletter 299
Polish American Museum Archives 412
Polish American Museum Journal 412
Polish American Museum Newsletter 412
Polish American Studies 156, 299
Polish Eaglet 289
Polish Footprints 554
Polish Genalogical Interest Group of Arizona 21
Polish Genealogical Society of America 170
Polish Genealogical Society of America & Archives 156

Polish Genealogical Society of America Bulletin 156
Polish Genealogical Society of California 54
Polish Genealogical Society of California Bulletin 54
Polish Genealogical Society of Connecticut & Library 96
Polish Genealogical Society of Greater Cleveland 445
Polish Genealogical Society of Massachusetts 276
Polish Genealogical Society of Texas 554
Polish Genealogical Society of Western New York & Library 391
Polish Genealogical Society of Wisconsin 627, 630
Polish Genealogical Society of Wisconsin Newsletter 630
Polish Heritage 120
Polish Heritage Society 292
Polish Heritage Society Bulletin 292
Polish Library 700
Polish Museum of America 156
Polish Museum of America Newsletter 156
Polish Nobility Association & Library 256
Polish-American Archives 96
Polish-American Cultural Society of Saint Louis 339
Polk County Genealogical Society 28, 325, 433
Polk County Genealogical Society & Library 474
Polk County Genealogical Society Newsletter 28
Polk County Genealogical Society Quarterly 28
Polk County Genealogical Society, Polk County Pioneers 30
Polk County Heritage Museum 200
Polk County Heritage Society 552
Polk County Historama 325
Polk County Historical and Genealogical Association & Archives 109
Polk County Historical and Genealogical Library 109
Polk County Historical and Genealogical Society 128, 525
Polk County Historical and Genealogical Society Quarterly 525
Polk County Historical Association 433
Polk County Historical Association Newsletter 109
Polk County Historical Commission & Archives 552
Polk County Historical Museum 200, 307, 355, 479, 552, 617
Polk County Historical Quarterly 109
Polk County Historical Society 128, 325
Polk County Historical Society & Archives 200, 307, 355, 617
Polk County Historical Society Archives 200
Polk County Historical Society Newsletter 200, 307
Polk County Historical Society, Saint Croix Falls Chapter 630
Polk County Museum Archives 617
Polk County Public Library 425
Polk County-Tree Shakers Genealogical Society 209
Polk Cultural Center 531
Polk Family 526, 538
Polk Library News 628
Polk Public Library 356
Polk-Abell Family 559
Poll-Aalderink-Nugteren-Ryerkerk Family 232
Pollag 231
Pollard Memorial Library 273
Pollock Clan 109, 231
Pollock Family 165, 591
Pollocksville Public Library 431
Polo Historical Society 171
Polson Flathead Historical Society 346
Polson Museum News 602
Polson Park and Museum Historical Society & Archives 602
Polson Park Historical Museum 602
Polynesian Cultural Center Archives 142
Polynesian Voyaging Society 142
Pomeroy Living History Museum Archives 610
Pomfret Free Public Library 98
Pomfret Historical Society 98
Pommerscher Verein Freistadt & Library 622
Pommerscher Verein Freistadt Rundschreiben 622
Pomo Bulletin 49
Pomona Public Library 60
Pomona Valley Genealogical Society 60
Pomona Valley Genealogical Society Newsletter 60
Pomona Valley Historical Society 60
Pompano Beach Historical Society 120
Ponca City Library 469
Ponca Historical Society & Library 356
Ponca Public Library 356
Ponce de Leon Inlet Lighthouse Preservation Association 120
Ponce de Leon Inlet Lighthouse Preservation Association Quarterly 120
Pond Papers 313
Pond Spring - General Joe Wheeler Home Archives 5
Ponte Vedra Historical Society 120
Pontiac Area Historical and Genealogical Society 300
Pontiac Public Library 171, 300
Pontifical Institute of Medieval Studies 691
Pontius Family 147, 408, 446
Pontius Family Association Newsletter 408
Ponto Historic Society 39
Pontotoc County Historical and Genealogical Society 463
Pony Express 73
Pony Express Mail 338
Pony Express Museum Archives 338
Pony Express Station Archives 352
Pony Trails 338
Ponytales 457
Pool Family 133, 138
Pope Air Force Base Library 431
Pope County Historical Association 32
Pope County Historical Museum 308
Pope County Historical Society 161
Pope County Historical Society & Archives 308
Pope County Historical Society Newsletter 308
Pope County Library 32
Pope County Library System-Atkins Centennial Library 25
Pope County Library System-Dover Public Library 26
Pope Family 314, 563
Pope Memorial Library 576
Pope's Tavern Museum Archives 4
Pope-Leighey House Museum Archives 583
Popham-Patton Family 203
Popkum Indian Band 648
Poplar Creek Genealogical Society 175
Poplar Creek Public Library 175
Poplar Forest Newsletter 587
Poplar Grove Plantation Archives 434
Poplar Grove Plantation Newsletter 434
Poplar Row 450
Popplewell Family 339
Porciones Genealogical Society 543
Porciones Genealogical Society Journal 543
Porcupine Plain and District Museum Archives 709

Porritt Family 570
Port Arthur Historical Society & Archives 556
Port Arthur Public Library 556
Port Austin Township Library 300
Port Carling Pioneer Museum Archives 688
Port Chester Public Library 411
Port City Ram 129
Port Clements Historical Society 653
Port Clements Museum Archives 653
Port Clinton Area Heritage Foundation & Archives 456
Port Clinton Historical Museum 456
Port Colborne Historical and Marine Museum Archives 688
Port Columbus National Civil War Naval Museum Archives 129
Port Deposit Heritage Center 261
Port Dover Harbour Museum Archives 688
Port Ewen Library 411
Port Gamble Historic Museum Archives 604
Port Hardy Museum Archives 653
Port Hastings Historical Museum and Archives 676
Port Hastings Historical Society 676
Port Hope Public Library 688
Port Huron Museum Archives 300
Port Jefferson Museum 412
Port Jervis Free Library 412
Port Leyden Community Library 412
Port Moody Station Museum 653
Port Orford District Library 478
Port Orford Genealogical Society 478
Port Orford Heritage Society 478
Port Orford Lifeboat Station Museum Archives 478
Port Penn Area Historical Society & Library 104
Port Royal National Historic Park Archives 673
Port Royal State Historic Area Archives 525
Port Townsend Public Library 605
Port Union Museum Archives 668
Port Washington Historical Society 629
Port Washington Historical Society Research Center 629
Port Washington Public Library 412
Port Wing Historical Society 629
Portage Community Historical Society 192
Portage County District Library 448
Portage County Genealogical Society & Library 456
Portage County Historical Museum 456, 631
Portage County Historical Society & Archives 456, 631
Portage County Historical Society Newsletter 456, 631
Portage County Public Library 631
Portage District Library 300
Portage Historical Museum 629
Portage Historical Society & Archives 629
Portage La Prairie City Library 660
Portage Path to Genealogy 456
Portage Public Library 629
Portal of the Folded Wings Shrine to Aviation Museum 56
Portales Public Library 384
Port-au-Port-Bay St George Heritage Association & Library 668
Port-aux-Basques Railway Heritage Centre 668
Porter County Historical Society & Archives 194
Porter County Public Library 194
Porter County Public Library Genealogical Group 194
Porter County Public Library System-Hebron Branch 185
Porter County Public Library System-Portage Branch 192
Porter Henderson Library 558
Porter Historical Museum 422
Porter Meeting House History 250
Porter Memorial Library 248, 266
Porter Settlements 19
Porter-Anderson-Robinson-Capers Family 595
Porter-Phelps-Huntington Foundation & Archives 271
Porter-Phelps-Huntington Historical Museum 271
Porterville Historical Museum Archives 61
Porterville Historical Museum Quarterly 61
Porterville Public Library 61
Portholes 453
Portholes into the Past Museum Archives 453
Portico 95
Port-la-Joye-Fort Amherst Museum Archives 695
Portland Area Historical Society 300
Portland District Library 300
Portland Harbor Beacon 251
Portland Harbor Museum Archives 251
Portland Historical Society 98
Portland Museum Archives 230
Portland Poynts 367
Portland Public Library 250, 532
Portland Public Library 98
Portola Railroad Museum Archives 61
Portsmouth Athenaeum 364
Portsmouth Athenaeum Newsletter 364
Portsmouth Free Public Library 509
Portsmouth Genealogical Society & Archives 592
Portsmouth Genealogical Society Newsletter 592
Portsmouth Genealogy Society 456
Portsmouth Historical Association & Archives 592
Portsmouth Historical Museum 509, 592
Portsmouth Historical Society & Archives 509
Portsmouth Historical Society & Library 364
Portsmouth Historical Society Newsletter 509
Portsmouth Museum Archives 592
Portsmouth Museum of Military History Archives 592
Portsmouth Public Library 364, 456, 593
Portuguese Genealogical Society of Hawaii 142
Portuguese Heritage Journal 111
Portuguese Historical and Cultural Society & Library 64
Portuguese Historical Museum Archives 68
Portuguese Library 72
Portville Free Library 412
Posey 190
Posey County Historical Society 190
Posey Family 569
Poseyville Carnegie Public Library 192
Possum Trotter 332
Post Falls Public Library 149
Post Public Library 556
Post Scripts 267
Postboy 413
Poste de Traite Chauvin 703
Postville Courthouse State Historic Site Archives 164
Poteau Valley Genealogical Society & Archives 469
Poteau Valley Genealogical Society Newsletter 469
Poteet Public Library 556

Potpourri 412
Potpourri, Strangers and Pilgrims 267
Potsdam Museum Newsletter 412
Potsdam Public Library 412
Potsdam Public Museum Archives 412
Potsdam Town Historian 412
Potsgrove Manor Museum Archives 500
Pottawatomie County Genealogical Society & Library 469
Pottawatomie County Genealogical Society Newsletter 469
Pottawatomie-Wabaunsee Regional Library 221
Pottawattamie County Genealogical Society 199
Potter County Historical Museum 485
Potter County Historical Society & Archives 485
Potter County Historical Society Quarterly 485
Potter Family 145
Potter Historical Society 356
Potter-Oswald-Gilbert Family 607
Potthast Newsletter 262
Potton House 538
Potts Inn Museum Archives 32
Pottstown Historical Society 500
Pottstown Public Library 500
Pottsville Free Public Library 500
Pouce Coupe Museum Archives 654
Pouch Cove Museum Archives 668
Poughkeepsie Public Library-Adriance Memorial 412
Poulson Family 567
Poultney Historical Society 579
Poultney Public Library 579
Pound Ridge Historical Museum 412
Pound Ridge Historical Society & Archives 412
Pounders-Cain Family 557
Poundmaker First Nation 709
Powder Magazine 339
Powder Magazine Museum Archives 512
Powder River Genealogical Society 343
Powder River Historical Society 343
Powderhouse Quarterly 272
Powell County Genealogical Society 344
Powell County Museum Archives 344
Powell Family 568
Powell Memorial Library 341
Powell Memorial Society 478
Powell People 153
Powell River District Library 654
Powell River Historical Museum Archives 654
Powell Times and Lines 28
Powell Valley Genealogical Club 637
Powell-Liberty Historical Society 456
Powers Memorial Library 628
Powers Museum Library 327
Powers Museum Newsletter 327
Poweshiek County Historical and Genealogical Society 205
Poweshiek County Historical and Genealogical Society Newsletter 205
Poweshiek County Searcher 205
Powhatan County Historical Society 593
Poynette Area Historical Museum 629
Poynette Area Historical Society & Archives 629
PPHM News 539
Prairie Ave News 155
Prairie Community Library 146
Prairie County Historical Society 26, 28
Prairie Creek Public Library District 158
Prairie du Chien Historical Society & Archives 629
Prairie du Chien Memorial Library 629
Prairie du Sac Public Library 629
Prairie Gleaner 342
Prairie Grove Battlefield State Park Archives 32
Prairie Homestead Museum Archives 523
Prairie Life Historical Foundation 342
Prairie Museum of History 212
Prairie Panorama Museum Archives 642
Prairie Pioneer 166
Prairie Pioneer Genealogical Society 352
Prairie Pioneer Genealogical Society Newsletter 352
Prairie Pioneer Museum Archives 705
Prairie River Museum Archives 709
Prairie Roots 170
Prairie Trails 169
Prairie Trails Museum 199
Prairie Trails Public Library District 153
Prairie Trails Public Library District Newsletter 153
Prairie Treaty Nations Alliance 643
Prairie Village Archives 522
Prairie West Historical Museum 706
Prairie West Historical Society & Archives 706
Prairie Winds 212
Prairieland Genealogical Society & Archives 310
Prairieland Pioneer 310
Prairieland Register 310
Prairie-River Library District 147
Prairie-River Library District-Kamiah Community 147
Prall Newsletter 381
Prater's Mill Foundation 129, 139
Praters in my Pocket 549
Praters Mill Historic Site Museum Archives 139
Prather Bulletin 327
Pratt Building Museum Archives 269
Pratt County Historical Museum 221
Pratt County Historical Society & Archives 221
Pratt County Historical Society Newsletter 221
Pratt Family 446, 550
Pratt Museum Archives 12
Pratt Museum Newsletter 12
Pratt Public Library 221
Pratuch Family 591
Pray Family 245
PRC Newsletter 267
Preator-Ault Family 337
Preble County Chapter, OGS & Library 448
Preble County District Library 448
Preble County Historical Society 451
Preble County Historical Society & Library 448
Preble's Pride 448
Precis 97
Predmore-Pridmore-Pridemore-Pregmore Association Journal 147
Preface 166, 451
Preface Newsletter 187
Premm Newsletter 46
Prentis Memorial Library 287

INDEX

Prentiss County Genealogical And Historical Society 319
Presby Mansion 602
Presbyterian Church Archives 594
Presbyterian Church of Canada Archives 691
Presbyterian Heritage 430
Presbyterian Historical Museum 498
Presbyterian Historical Society & Archives 498
Prescott City Public Library 221
Prescott Family 423
Prescott Historical Society & Archives 19
Prescott House Museum Archives 676
Prescott Memorial Library 241
Prescott Public Library 19, 629
Preservation 106, 240, 491
Preservation Action Council of San Jose 68
Preservation Bulletin 383
Preservation Dallas 542
Preservation Delaware & Library 104
Preservation Forum 106
Preservation Gazette 133
Preservation Greensboro 427
Preservation League of New York State 387
Preservation Matters 431
Preservation Network News 387
Preservation New Jersey & Library 379
Preservation New York 387
Preservation News 229
Preservation North Carolina 429
Preservation Notes 394
Preservation Notes 588
Preservation On-Line 83
Preservation Perspective 379
Preservation Progress 512
Preservation Resource Center 240
Preservation Society of Charleston 512
Preservation Society of Newport County & Library 508
Preservation Society of Newport County Annual Report 508
Preservation Texas 536
Preservation Trust of Spartanburg 518
Preservation Virginia Journal 593
Preservation Worcester 283
Preservationist 9, 456
Preserve Our Past Society 328
President Andrew Johnson Museum and Library 527
President Chester A Arthur Historic Site Archives 576
President's Cottage Archives 615
Presidential Families of America 293
Presidential Museum 555
Presidential Museum Archives 555
Presidential Museum Newsletter 555
Presidential Pet Museum Archives 260
Presidents' Journal 179
Presidio Army Museum Archives 67
Presidio La Bahia Archives 547
Presidio of Monterey Museum Archives 55
Presidio State Historic Park Archives 70
Presley-Preslar-Presly Family 381
Presley-Pressley Family 587
Presqu'ile Provincial Park Museum Archives 680
Presque Isle County Genealogical Society 299
Presque Isle County Historical Museum Archives 301
Presque Isle County Historical Museum Newsletter 301
Presque Isle District Library 301
Presque Isle Heritage Society 629
Presque Isle Historical Society & Archives 250
Pressley Family 424
Preston County Historical Society 615
Preston Historical Society 313
Preston Public Library 98
Preston Scoop 512, 518
Preston Town-County Library of Hot Springs 345
Prestwould Foundation Museum Archives 586
Preus Library 200
Preview 167
Prevostal 199
Prevost-Provost Family 199
Prewitt-Pruitt Newsletter 200
Prezell R Robinson Library 432
Price City Library 569
Price County Historical Society & Archives 621
Price County Historical Society Newsletter 621
Price Gilbert Memorial Library 126
Price-Bryson Family 114
Pricketts Fort Archives 612
Priddy Family 227
Priddy Press 529
Pride Family 183
Priest Lake Public Library 149
Priest Quarterly Newsletter 297
Priestley-Forsyth Memorial Library 496
Primary Source 413
Prince Albert Grand Council 709
Prince Albert Historical Museum 709
Prince Albert Historical Society & Archives 709
Prince Edward County Museum Library 688
Prince Edward Island Genealogical Society & Library 695
Prince Edward Island Museum and Heritage Foundation & Library 695
Prince Edward Island Old and News 695
Prince Edward Island Potato Museum Archives 695
Prince Edward Island Provincial Library Service 695
Prince Edward Island Regiment Museum Archives 695
Prince George Genealogy Society 654
Prince George Public Library 654
Prince George's County Genealogical Society 257
Prince George's County Genealogical Society Bulletin 257
Prince George's County Historical Society 259, 260
Prince George's County Historical Society & Archives 262
Prince George's County Memorial Library System 260
Prince George's County Memorial Library System-Hyattsville Branch 260
Prince George's County Memorial Library System-Oxon Hill Branch 261
Prince George's County Memorial Library System-Public Documents Reference 263
Prince Georges County Historic Historical and Cultural Trust 260
Prince Memorial Library 245
Prince of Wales Armouries Heritage Centre 642
Prince of Wales Fort Archives 659
Prince of Wales Martello Tower Museum Archives 674
Prince of Wales Northern Heritage Centre 671
Prince Rupert Fire Museum Archives 654
Prince Rupert Library 654

Prince William County Genealogical Society 590
Prince William Public Library System 593
Prince William Public Library System-Bull Run Regional 590
Princess Anne County Historical Society 596
Princess Anne County Historical Society Newsletter 596
Princess Patricia's Canadian Light Infantry Regimental Museum Archives 641
Princeton and District Museum Archives 654
Princeton Battlefield State Park Archives 376
Princeton Historical Society & Library 630
Princeton History 376
Princeton History Project & Archives 376
Princeton Public Library 192, 376, 614
Princeton Recollector 376
Prison Chronicle 23
Pritchett(ard) Family 17
Pro Rodeo Hall of Fame Museum Archives 82
Pro Rodeo Hall of Fame Museum Newsletter 82
Proceedings of the American Antiquarian Society 283
Proceedings of the Bostonian Society 266
Proceedings of the Cambridge Historical Society 268
Proceedings of the Northumberland County Historical Society 503
Proceedings of the Pennsylvania German Society 491
Proceedings of the Unitarian Universalist Historical Society 267
Proctor Free Library 579
Proctor House Museum Archives 680
Proctor Library 575
Proctor-Wright Family 390
Professional Genealogists of Arkansas 26
Professional Genealogists of Arkansas Newsletter 26
Program 105
Prologue 170, 207
Promont House Museum 453
Promotion and Preservation of Iberville Parish 241
Prophet River Band 649
Prophetstown Area Historical Society 171
Prophetstown Dispatch 179
Proprietary House Newsletter 376
Proprietary House-Royal Governor's Mansion Archives 376
Prospect 387
Prospect Historical Society 98
Prospector 145
Prospector Quarterly 50
Prospectors, Diggers and Doers 214
Prosser Public Library 91
Prosser Public Library Newsletter 91
Prosveta: Enlightenment 490
Proudfoot Family 544
Prouty Register Newsletter 47
Prouty-Chew House Museum 398
Providence Athaneum 509
Providence Historical Society & Library 123
Providence Preservation Society & Archives 509
Providence Preservation Society News 509
Providence Public Library 509
Providence Public Library Newsletter 509
Providence Public Library-Knight Memorial 509
Province House Museum Archives 695
Provincetown Heritage Museum Archives 278
Provincetown Monument and Museum 277
Provincetown Public Library 278
Provincial Archives of Alberta 643
Provincial Archives of British Columbia 657
Provincial Archives of Manitoba 662
Provincial Archives of New Brunswick 663
Provincial Archives of Newfoundland and Labrador 668
Provincial Information and Library Resources Board 668
Provincial Museum of Alberta Archives 643
Provincial Museum of Newfoundland and Labrador Archives 668
Provincial Public Library Services 668
Provincial Resource Library 668
Provo City Public Library 570
Prowers County Genealogical Society & Archives 87
Prowers County Genealogical Society Newsletter 87
Prowers County Historical Society & Archives 87
Prowers County History 87
Prudence Crandall Museum Library 91
Pruitt-Black Family 545
Pryor Family Courier 239
Pryor Public Library 469
Public Archives of Nova Scotia 674
Public Archives of Prince Edward Island 695
Public Historian 37, 187
Public History News 187
Public Libraries of Saginaw 301
Public Library of Anniston and Calhoun County 1
Public Library of Cincinnati and Hamilton County 444
Public Library of Des Moines 200
Public Library of Enid and Garfield County 465
Public Library of Johnston County and Smithfield 433
Public Library of Steubenville and Jefferson County 457
Public Library of Youngstown and Mahoning County 461
Public Works Historical Society 160
Public Works History 160
Publick Post 93
Puddingstone Press 423
Pueblo County Historical Society 89
Pueblo de Cochiti Community Library 382
Pueblo Grande Museum Research Library 19
Pueblo History Museum Archives 89
Pueblo Horizons 381
Pueblo Lore 89
Pueblo Regional Library 89
Pueblo Weisbrod Aircraft Museum Archives 89
Pueblo Weisbrod Aircraft Museum Newsletter 89
Puerto Rican Cultural Heritage House 407
Puerto Rican-Hispanic Genealogical Society 389
Puget Sound Coast Artillery Museum Archives 605
Puget Sound Genealogical Society 605
Pulaski Area Historical Society 630
Pulaski County Genealogical Society 196
Pulaski County Heritage Seekers 31
Pulaski County Historical Society 30
Pulaski County Historical Society & Archives 233
Pulaski County Historical Society & Library 196
Pulaski County Indiana Genealogical Society Newsletter 196
Pulaski County Library 593
Pulaski County Public Library 196. 233
Pulaski Historical Society 412
Pulaski Public Library 412
Pulaski Village Historian 412

Pulliam Point 549
Pullman Historical Museum 155
Pullman, Washington Branch Genealogical Library 148
Pultneyville Historical Society 421
Pump House Steam Museum Archives 684
Pumphrey Family 256
Punahou School Archives 141, 142
Pun-Intended 536
Punxsutawney Area Historical and Genealogical Society 500
Purcell Family 447
Purcell-Cotter Family 115
Purchase Free Library 412
Purinton Family 577
Purviance Family 610
Purysburg Preservation Foundation 515
Pushmataha County Historical Society & Library 463
Puskarich Public Library 443
Putman Family 287
Putnam Cottage Archives 94
Putnam County Chapter, OGS & Library 455
Putnam County District Library 455
Putnam County Genealogical Club 179
Putnam County Genealogical Quarterly Journal 119
Putnam County Genealogical Society 119
Putnam County Genealogical Society Newsletter 119, 450
Putnam County Heritage 450
Putnam County Historical Museum 450
Putnam County Historical Society 171, 341
Putnam County Historical Society & Archives 184, 394, 450
Putnam County Historical Society & Library 162
Putnam County Historical Society Newsletter 394
Putnam County Library 526, 613
Putnam County Library Newsletter 613
Putnam County Library System 119
Putnam County Museum Archives 119, 184
Putnam County Public Library 184, 341
Putnam District Library 298
Putnam Museum of History Archives 200
Putnam Past Times 162
Putnam Past, Present and Future 184
Putnam Pastfinder 455
Putnam Public Library 98
Putnam Valley Historical Society & Library 412
Putney Historical Museum 579
Putney Historical Society & Archives 579
Putney Historical Society Newsletter 579
Putterbaugh/Butterbaugh Newsletter 192
Puukohola Heiau National Historic Site Archives 142
Puyallup Public Library 605
Puyallup Valley Heritage 605
Pyle House Museum Archives 522
Pyne Family 255

Q

Quaboag Historical Society 282
Quaco Historical and Library Society & Archives 665
Quaco Museum 665
Quaich 456
Quaker History 489
Quaker Yeoman 473
Quakertown Historical Society 500
Quakertown Train Station Historical Society 500
Qualicum Beach Historical Museum 654
Qualicum Beach Historical Society & Archives 654
Qualicum Indian Band 654
Qualla Boundary Public Library 425
Quapaw Quarter Association & Library 30
Quapaw Tribe of Oklahoma 469
Quarles Queries 529
Quarry News 359
Quarter Notes Quickie 66
Quarterdeck 473
Quarterly Connections 181
Quarterly Express 349
Quarterly Journal of Military History; Columbiad: a Journal for Amateur Historians Interested in the Civil War 589
Quarterly Newsletter of the Fred Hart Williams Genealogical Society 289
Quarterly of the Benzie Area Historical Society 286
Quarterly of the Cumberland and Coles County Genealogical Society 175
Quarterly of the Huntington Historical Society and Genealogical Workshop 400
Quarterly of the Middleborough Historical Association 275
Quarterly of the Upper Cumberland Genealogical Association 526
Quarterly Review of the Eastern North Carolina Genealogical Society 430
Quarterly Wisconsin Genealogical Council Newsletter 630
Quartzsite Historical Society 19
Quartzsite Public Library 19
Quasdorf Blacksmith and Wagon Museum Archives 201
Quatsino Indian Band 648
Quebec Diocesan Archives 699
Quebec Family History Society 700
Quebec Family History Society & Library 701
Queen Anne's County Free Library 257
Queen Anne's County Historical Society & Archives 257
Queen Charlotte Islands Museum Society & Library 655
Queen City Heritage 444
Queen Elizabeth II Library 668
Queen Emma Summer Palace Archives 142
Queen Emma's Summer Palace 141
Queen Mary Foundation 35
Queen Mary Museum Archives 51
Queen Village Historical Society & Archives 392
Queen's Own Cameron Highlanders Museum Archives 662
Queen's Own Rifles of Canada Regimental Museum Archives 691
Queen's York Rangers Regimental Museum 691
Queens Borough Public Library 401
Queens County Farm Museum Archives 397
Queens County Historical Museum 675
Queens County Historical Society & Archives 675
Queens County Museum Library 675
Queens County Tilley House Museum Archives 663
Queens Genealogy Workshop & Archives 413
Queens Genealogy Workshop Newsletter 413
Queens Historical Society & Library 397
Queens Historical Society Newsletter 397
Queensbury Historical Association & Archives 398
Quente West Public Library 692
Quesnel and District Museum Archives 654
Quesnel Library 654
Quest 120, 626

Questing Heirs Genealogical Society 51
Questing Heirs Genealogical Society Newsletter 51
Quetico Provincial Park Museum Library 679
Quick Family 351
Quid Nuc 558
Quidi Vidi Battery Museum Archives 668
Quiet Valley Living Historical Farm Archives 502
Quiet Valley Living Historical Farm Newsletter 502
Quigley Museum 441
Quigley Quest 441
Quill 514
Quill Pen 585
Quilter's Hall of Fame 189
Quincy and Adams County Historical Museum 171
Quincy Historical Society & Library 278
Quincy History 278
Quincy Museum Archives 171
Quincy Museum Quarterly 171
Quincy Public Library 171
Quinta Educational Museum Archives 680
Quintilla Geer Bruton Archives Center 120
Quintilla Geer Bruton Memorial Library 120
Quiram Family 307
Quirams Unlimited 341
Quirke-McIlraith-Grace Family 85
Quitman Public Library 557
Quittner Family 565
Quivey Memorial Library 354
R
R E Olds Transportation Museum Archives 296
R E Olds Transportation Museum Newsletter 296
R F Sink Memorial Library 227
R H Johnson Library 21
R P Strathearn Historical Park Archives 72
R T Elethorp Historical Museum 399
R T Elethorp Historical Society & Archives 399
R W Norton Art Gallery Library 241
R's Relatives: Robison, Robinson, Robson, Robertson, Roberson, Roberts, Robbins 37
Rabb Family 82
Rabbit Tracks Quarterly 74
Rabun County Historical Society 128
Racine County Heritage Museum 630
Racine County Historical Society & Archives 630
Racine Public Library 630
Rackett-Bradway-Broadway Family 408
Rader Ramblings 61
Radford City Historical Society 591
Radio & Television Museum Archives 257
Radio Museum News 612
Radnor Historical Society & Library 504
Radnor Historical Society Bulletin 504
Rae and Joseph Gann Library 276
Rag Sheet 562
Ragersville Historical Society 458
Ragged Edge Library 484
Ragsdale Register 529
Ragsdales of America 71
Rahway Historical Society 376
Rahway Public Library 377
Rail and Wire 176
Rail Fax 460
Rail Newsletter 257
Railroad and Heritage Museum Archives 561
Railroad Historical Society 64
Railroad House Historical Society 432
Railroad House Historical Society Newsletter 432
Railroad House Museum 432
Railroad Museum 233
Railroad Museum of Long Island Archives 413
Railroad Museum of Niwot 439
Railroad Museum of Pennsylvania 502
Railroad Ties 354
Railroaders Memorial Museum Archives 481
Rails and Trails Museum Archives 148
Railsback Family 557
Railsback Lines 557
Railtown 1897 State Historic Park Archives 48
Railway and Forestry Museum Archives 654
Railway Exposition Company Archives 226
Railway Heritage News 188
Railway Historical Society of Northern NY 389
Railway Locomotive Historical Museum 60
Railway Locomotive Historical Society 60
Railway Locomotive Historical Society Newsletter 60
Railway Museum of San Angelo Archives 558
Railway Reporter 402
Railway Station Museum Archives 648
Railway to Yesterday Library 481
Railway, Agricultural, Industrial Lineage Society 209
Railways to Yesterday Museum Archives 500
Rainey Family 560
Rainier City Library 479
Rainier Family 119
Rainier Valley Historical Society 606
Rainwater Researcher 36
Rainwater-Christensen-Moore-Pettijohn Family 148
Rainy Hills Historical Museum 644
Rainy Hills Historical Society 644
Rainy River District Women's Institute Museum Archives 682
Rainy River Public Library 689
Rainy River Valley Genealogical Society 309
Raleigh City Museum 431
Raleigh City Museum Archives 432
Raleigh County Public Library 611
Raleigh Historic Districts Commission 432
Raley Family 311
Ralls County Historical Museum 337
Ralls County Historical Society 327
Ralls County Historical Society & Archives 337
Ralls Historical Museum Archives 557
Ralph Allen Memorial Museum Archives 708
Ralph Ellison Library 468
Ralph Foster Museum Archives 337
Ralph J & Virginia A Fulton Library 484
Ralph L Milliken Museum Archives 52
Ralph Mark Gilbert Civil Rights Museum Archives 137
Ralph Pickard Bell Library 664
Ralph Shepard Family Organization Information Newsletter 126
Ralph W Steen Library 554

INDEX

Ralph Waldo Emerson House Museum Archives 269
Ralston Genealogical Society 356
Rama and Area Native Women's Association 679
Ramah Historical Society 384
Ramaker Library 206
Ramapogue Historical Society & Library 282
Ramapogue Historical Society Newsletter 282
Rambler 133, 424
Ramey Ramblings 74
Ramona Museum of California History Archives 52
Ramona Pioneer Historical Society & Archives 61
Rampant Lion 481
Rampart Regional Library District 90
Ramsay Clan 596
Ramsay House Museum Archives 583
Ramsey County Historical Society & Library 314
Ramsey County History 314
Ramsey County Public Library 315
Ramsey Family 114
Ramsey Free Public Library 377
Ramsey House Museum Plantation Archives 529
Ramsey House Museum Plantation Newsletter 529
Ramsey Reader 377
Ramsey Report 112
Ramsey-Ramsay Family 599
Ranchester Historical Society 637
Rancho Bernardo Genealogy Group 65
Rancho Buena Vista Adobe Archives 77
Rancho Camulos Museum Archives 60
Rancho Cucamonga Public Library 61
Rancho de Quadalupe Historical Society 47
Rancho Los Alamitos Historic Site Archives 51
Rancho Review 51
Rancho Santa Fe Historical Society 61
Ranck-Rank Family 491
Ranconteur 444
Rand Family 478
Randall Family Newsletter 339
Randall House Museum 677
Randall House Museum Archives 677
Randall Library & Museum 280
Randleman-Rendleman-Rentleman Newsletter 474
Randolf Historical Society 579
Randolph Air Force Base Library 557
Randolph Area Genealogical Society & Library 562
Randolph C Watson Library 551
Randolph County Genealogical Journal 423
Randolph County Genealogical Society 196
Randolph County Genealogical Society & Archives 423
Randolph County Genealogical Society & Library 154
Randolph County Historical and Genealogical Society 32
Randolph County Historical and Genealogical Society & Archives 196
Randolph County Historical Museum 196, 612
Randolph County Historical Quarterly 32
Randolph County Historical Society 174
Randolph County Historical Society & Archives 612
Randolph County Historical Society & Library 335
Randolph County Historical Society Report 335
Randolph County Library 32
Randolph County Museum 611
Randolph County Public Library 423
Randolph Free Library 412
Randolph Historical Museum 579
Randolph Historical Society 129, 579
Randolph Historical Society & Archives 579
Randolph Public Library 207
Randolph Township Historical Society 445
Range Genealogical Society & Library 306
Range Genealogical Society Newsletter 306
Range History 308
Range Reminiscing 308
Rangeley Historical Society 250
Rangeley Lakes Region Historical Society & Library 250
Rangeley Lakes Region Logging Museum Archives 250
Rangely Outdoor Museum Archives 89
Ranger Historical Preservation Society 557
Rankin County Historical Society & Library 319
Rankin House 456
Rankin House Museum Archives 664
Rankin Museum Archives 426, 557
Ranney Family 405
Ransom County Historical Society 438
Ransom County Historical Society & Library 438
Ransom Family 50, 473
Ransom Note 393
Rapid City Museum Archives 660
Rapid City Public Library 523
Rapid City Society for Genealogical Research & Library 523
Rapides Parish Library 235
Rappahannock Community College Library 597
Rappahannock Historical Society 597
Raquette Lake Free Library 412
Raquette Lake Town Historian 412
Raritan Library News 377
Raritan Public Library 377
Rashid Memorial Library 202
Rasmuson Family 263
Ratcliff Family 554
Rathbone Family 225
Rathbun Family Historian 225
Rathbun-Rathbone-Rathburn Family 587
Rathburn Free Library 93
Raton Historical Society 384
Raton Museum Newsletter 384
Ratzlaff Family 159
Ratzlaff Report Quarterly 159
Rauchholz Memorial Library 293
Raugust Library 438
Ravalli County Historical Society 345
Ravalli County Museum 344
Ravalli County Museum Library 345
Raven: a Journal of Vexillology 379
Ravenna Genealogical Society 356
Ravenswood-Lake View Historical Association & Archives 156
Ravenswood-Lake View Historical Association Newsletter 156
Rawhide Press 609
Rawlins County Chronicle 211
Rawlins County Genealogical Society & Library 211
Rawlins County Historical Museum 211
Rawlins County Historical Society & Archives 211

Rawlins Family Association Newsletter 39
Rawlins Municipal Library 523
Rawson Family 271
Ray County Genealogical Association & Library 338
Ray County Historical Society & Library 338
Ray County Historical Society News Letter 338
Ray County Mirror 338
Ray County Reflections 338
Ray Researchers: Rae, Rea, Rhea, Wray 354
Ray-Fouts Family 553
Raymer (Ramer) Roots 225
Raymer-Roemer Family Newsletter 262
Raymond A Sapp Memorial Library 178
Raymond and District Historical Society 645
Raymond Gustafson Archives 287
Raymond Public Library 605
Raymond Village Library 250
Raymond-Casco Historical Society 245, 250
Raymont H Fogler Library 249
Raymore Historical Society 337
Raymore Pioneer Museum Archives 709
Rayne Historical Association 241
Raynham Hall Museum Library 410
Raynham Hall Museum Newsletter 410
Raynham Historical Commission 278
Raynham Historical Society 278
Raynor Memorial Library 627
Raytown Historical Museum 337
Raytown Historical Society & Archives 337
RCMP Centennial Celebration Museum Archives 643
RCS Community Library 412
RCS Community Library Newsletter 412
Reach 482
Read Out 151
Readers News 360
Readers Review 297
Readfield Historical Society 250
Readfield Historical Society Newsletter 250
Reading Antiquarian Society & Archives 278
Reading Company Historical Society 492
Reading Historical Museum 456, 579
Reading Historical Society & Archives 456, 579
Reading in Indianapolis 186
Reading Public Library 278, 500
Reading Public Museum Library 500
Reading Railroad Heritage Museum Archives 500
Readings in Bulloch County History 137
Readington Township Library 380
Readsboro Historical Museum 579
Readsboro Historical Society & Archives 579
Reap-Reep Family 429
Reardan Memorial Library 605
Reasoner Family Bulletin 172
Rebe Newsletter 262
Rebecca M Arthurs Memorial Library 483
Rebecca Nurse Homestead Archives 269
Rebecca Nurse Homestead Quarterly 269
Rebecca Winters Genealogical Society 356
Rebee Family 320, 469
Rebel State Historic Site Archives 239
Rebele Family 263
Reber-Grasser-Croft-Waldron-Willie Family 572
Recent Titles 538
Reckart Family 258
Recollections 128
Record 28, 84, 106, 159, 229
Recorder 444, 469
Rector Public Library 32
Red Bank Indian Band 664
Red Bank Public Library 377
Red Banks Revue 228
Red Banner 61
Red Barn Museum Archives 405
Red Bay Historic Site Archives 668
Red Bird Missionary Conference, United Methodist Church 233
Red Bluff Indian Band 654
Red Bud Public Library 171
Red Clay Creek Presbyterian Church Archives 104
Red Clay State Historic Park Archives 526
Red Creek Free Library 412
Red Deer and District Museum and Archives 645
Red Deer Public Library 645
Red Dragon 51
Red Earth First Nation 709
Red Earth Museum Archives 468
Red Hill Quarterly 585
Red House Interpretive Center Archives 326
Red Lake County Historical Society 313
Red Lake Museum Archives 689
Red Lion Area Historical Society 500
Red Lion Area Historical Society Newsletter 500
Red Mill Museum Library 369
Red Oak Public Library 207
Red Pheasant First Nation 705
Red Pheasant Healing Lodge 705
Red River County Genealogical Society & Archives 540
Red River County Public Library 540
Red River County Texas Genealogical Society Newsletter 540
Red River Heritage Association 236
Red River Historical Museum 226
Red River Historical Museum Archives 560
Red River Historical Society & Archives 226
Red River Regional Studies Center 241
Red River Review 241
Red River Valley Genealogical Society Newsletter 438
Red River Valley Genealogy Society & Library 438
Red River Valley Museum Archives 562
Red Rock Historical Society 383, 396
Red Rock Public Library 689
Red Tower 118
Red Waller Community Library 552
Red Willow Historical Society 353
Red Wing Public Library 313
Redcliff Museum and Historical Society 645
Redd Family 568
Reddick Library 169
Reddick Roster 59
Redding Historical Society 98
Redding Museum of Art & History Archives 61
Redfield Town Historian 413

Redford Family Newsletter 560
Redford Township Genealogical Society 300
Redington Museum 252
Redington Museum Archives 252
Redlands Area Historical Society 61
Redlands Area Historical Society Newsletter 61
Redmen Nanticoke Tribe 103
Redmond Family 597
Redmond Historical Society & Archives 605
Redmond Historical Society Newsletter 605
Redondo Beach Historical Society 62
Redpath Museum Archives 700
Redwater and District Museum Archives 645
Redwood City Heritage Association & Archives 62
Redwood City Public Library 62
Redwood County Historical Museum 313
Redwood County Historical Society & Library 313
Redwood Falls Public Library 313
Redwood Family; Dorland Family Redwood 84
Redwood Genealogical Society & Library 45
Redwood Library and Athenaeum 508
Redwood National Park Archives 41
Reece's Pieces 549
Reed City Public Library 300
Reed Family 289, 301, 561
Reed Gold Mine Museum Archives 433
Reed Gold Mine State Historic Site Archives 430
Reed Institute Library 117
Reed Memorial Library 392, 456
Reed Review 549
Reeder Family 568
Reedley Historical Museum 62
Reedley Historical Society & Archives 62
Reed-Read-Reid Family 603
Reed-Reid Family 117
Reedsburg Area Historical Society & Library 630
Reedsburg Area Historical Society Newsletter 630
Reedsburg Log Village 630
Reedville Fishermen's Museum Archives 593
Reep Family 256
Reese Library 127
Reeves County Library 556
Reeves Memorial Library 488
Reeves-Reaves Family 322
Reflections 66, 221, 362, 368, 376, 446, 464, 533, 541
Reflections .... Then and Now 451
Reflections Along the Muskingum 459
Reflections/Reflecciones 544
Reflector 535
Reformed Presbyterian Theological Seminary Library 499
Reformed Theological Seminary Library 119, 321
Refugio County Historical Society & Archives 557
Refugio County Historical Society Newsletter 557
Refugio County Museum 557
Regensburg Library 155
Regi Magparorszag: Old Hungary 63
Regina Firefighters Museum Archives 709
Regina Plains Museum Archives 709
Regina Public Library 709
Reginald E Lewis Museum of Maryland African American History Archives 256
Reginald J P Dawson Library 699
Region 1 Archives, Evangelical Lutheran Church in America 608
Regional Archivist 339
Regional History Center 119
Regional History Center Archives 157
Regional History Collection & Archives 295
Regional Museum News 214
Regional Museum of Cultural History Library 673
Register 123
Registered Nurses Historical Museum 642
Registry of American Black Ancestry 571
Rehoboth Beach Historical Society & Archives 104
Rehoboth Beach Public Library 104
Reich Family 512
Reid Family 513
Reid Memorial Library 161
Reidville Historical Society 517
Reimer Family 419
Reimschussel Family 570
Reitz Home Museum Archives 183
Relatively Searching the Griffith Family 215
Relatively Seeking 213
Relatively Speaking 305, 642
Relics 375
Remains to be Found 355
Remember When Toy Museum and Historic Village of Cedar Falls Archives 326
Remick Country Doctor Museum and Farm Archives 364
Remick Review 364
Remington Carriage Museum Archives 642
Remington Firearms Museum Archives 401
Remington-Carpenter Township Public Library 192
Remsen-Steuben Historical Society 413
Rena Herald Newsletter 424
Renaissance Quarterly 408
Renaissance Society of America 408
Renaissance Studies 424
Rench Family 637
Rend Lake College Library 163
Renegade Root Diggers 47
Renfrew Museum Archives 504
Renfrew Museum Newsletter 504
Renfrew Public Library 689
Renfro Library 430
Renn Memorial Library 211
Rennison Ramblings 339
Rennollet Family 451
Reno County Genealogical Society & Library 216
Reno County Historical Museum 216
Reno County Historical Society & Archives 216
Rensselaer County Historical Museum 418
Rensselaer County Historical Society & Archives 418
Rensselaer County Historical Society Newsletter 418
Rensselaer Falls Library 413
Rensselaer Falls Village Historian 413
Rensselaer Russell House Museum Archives 209
Renton Historical Museum 605
Renton Historical Quarterly 605
Renton Historical Society & Archives 605

Renton Historical Society and Museum Newsletter 605
Renton Public Library 605
Rentsch-Herold Family 325
Renville County Genealogical Society & Library 313
Renville County Historical Museum 312, 439
Renville County Historical Society & Archives 312, 439
Renville Historical Museum 313
Reorganized Church of Jesus Christ of Latter Day Saints Archives 331
Repass Family Newsletter 597
Report: A Journal of German American History 256
Republic County Genealogical Society & Archives 212
Republic County Genealogical Society Quarterly 212
Republic County Historical Museum 212
Republic County Historical Society & Archives 212
Republic Historical Society 337
Research News 572
Researcher 430, 608
Researchin' Ouachita-Calhoun Counties AR 26
Reserve Indienne d'Odanak 700
Reshaw Exhibit Archives 636
Resource 176
Resources for Jewish Genealogy in the Boston Area 276
Restigouche Regional Museum Archives 663
Reston and District Historical Museum Archives 661
Restoration Chronicle 289
Restoration House Museum Archives 310
Restoration Trail Forum 331, 450
Restoration Trail Foundation 331
Restoration Witness 330
Resurrection Bay Historical Society & Library 13
Resurrection Bay Historical Society Newsletter 13
Reta E King Library 350
Reu Memorial Library 201
Reuben Hoar Library 273
Reuben's Notes 273
Reuel B Pritchett Museum Archives 585
Rev Dan Foster House 578, 580
Rev Dan Foster House Museum 580
Reveille 78, 396
Revelstoke Court House Museum Archives 654
Revelstoke Museum Archives 654
Revelstoke Railway Museum Archives 654
Revere Public Library 278
Revere Society for Cultural and Historic Preservation 278
Review 73, 122, 165, 294
Review of the Society for the History of Czechoslovak Jews 400
Revista 570
REVIVA 515
Revolutionary War Genealogy 529
Revue D'Histoire de L'Amerique Francaise 700
Revue d'Histoire de la Societe Historique Nicolas-Denys 665
Revue: Au Pays de Matane 699
Rex Allen Museum Archives 22
Reynold Rapp Museum Archives 710
Reynolds County Genealogy and Historical Society 328
Reynolds Family 209, 410, 583, 591
Reynolds Homestead Museum Archives 586
Reynolds Museum Archives 646
Reynolds Records 292
Reynolds Township Library 294
Rhamy Family 469
Rhea County Historical and Genealogical Society 526
Rhinebeck Aerodrome Museum Archives 413
Rhinehart Family 59
Rhinelander District Library 630
Rhinelander Historical Museum 630
Rhinelander Historical Society & Archives 630
Rhinelander Logging Museum Archives 630
Rhines Family 629
Rhines-Kepple Family 491
Rhoads Family 255, 539
Rhoads Quarterly: Descendants of Henry Rhoads of Bedford County, PA 6
Rhode Island Black Heritage Museum 509
Rhode Island Black Heritage Society & Archives 509
Rhode Island Black Heritage Society Bulletin 509
Rhode Island Families Association 277, 584
Rhode Island Genealogical Register 277, 584
Rhode Island Genealogical Society 507
Rhode Island Historical Museum 509
Rhode Island Historical Preservation and Heritage 509
Rhode Island Historical Society & Archives 509
Rhode Island History 509
Rhode Island Jewish Historical Association & Library 509
Rhode Island Jewish Historical Association Newsletter 509
Rhode Island Jewish Historical Notes 509
Rhode Island Labor History Society & Archives 508
Rhode Island Mayflower Descendants 509
Rhode Island Roots 507
Rhode Island State Historical Society & Library 509
Rhode Island State Library & Archives 509
Rhodes Crossroads Newsletter 3
Rhodes Family 350
Rhodes Family Quarterly 3
Rhodes Family Trails Quarterly 64
Rhpl Reader 301
RHS Newsletter 62
Rialto Historical Society 62
Ribble Family 550
Ricardian Register 289
Rice County Genealogical Society 312
Rice County Historian 308
Rice County Historical Museum 308
Rice County Historical Society & Archives 218, 308
Rice Family 147, 268
Rice Gleanings 312
Rice Lake Public Library 630
Rice Museum 236
Rice Museum Archives 515
Rice Planter 518
Rice Public Library 247
Rice-Smith Newsletter 328
Rice-Wiese-Hamblin Family 145
Rich Family 281, 565
Richard B Russell Library 125
Richard Bland College Library 592
Richard I Bong WWII Heritage Center Archives 632
Richard III Society 289
Richard J Daley Library 156
Richard R Russell Library 125
Richard Salter Storrs House 273

Richard Salter Storrs Library 273
Richard Sparrow House Archives 277
Richard Sudgen Library 279
Richard W Norton Memorial Library 240
Richards Free Library 363
Richards Library 419
Richards-Dar House Museum Archives 7
Richardson County Historical Society 351
Richardson Family 350
Richardson Family Researcher and Historical News 350
Richardson Historical and Genealogical Society 557
Richardson Library 535
Richardson Maritime Museum Archives 257
Richardson Maritime Museum Newsletter 257
Richardson Public Library 557
Richardson-Bates House Museum 410
Richardson-Sloan Genealogical Society & Library 200
Richelieu-Vix Family 252
Richey Historical Museum 346
Richey Historical Society & Archives 346
Richfield County Illinois Genealogical and Historical Society 169
Richfield Historical Park Archives 630
Richfield Historical Society 313, 456, 630
Richfield Historical Society Newsletter 313
Richfield Springs Public Library 413
Richford Historical Society 579
Richibucto River Museum Archives 664
Richland County Genealogical and Historical Society 169
Richland County Genealogical Society 452
Richland County Genealogical Society Newsletter 169
Richland County Historical Museum 439
Richland County Historical Society 452
Richland County Historical Society & Archives 439
Richland County Museum Archives 451
Richland County Public Library 513
Richland Hills Public Library 557
Richland Historical Society 500
Richland Parish Library 241, 605
Richland Town Historian 412
Richland-Shelby Chapter, OGS 457
Richmond Area Historical and Genealogical Society 300
Richmond Community College Library 428
Richmond County Historical Museum 699
Richmond County Historical Society 432
Richmond County Historical Society & Archives 127, 699
Richmond County History 127
Richmond County Public Library 597
Richmond County Record 432
Richmond Hill Historical Museum 135
Richmond Hill Historical Society & Archives 135
Richmond Hill Public Library 689
Richmond Historical Museum Archives 62
Richmond Historical Society 250, 509
Richmond Memorial Library 389
Richmond Museum Archives 654
Richmond National Battlefield Park Library 594
Richmond Public Library 62
Richmond Township Historical Society 299
Richmond Township Public Library 299
Richmondtown Restoration 417
Richville Free Library 413
Richville Historical Association 413
Richwood North Union Public Library 456
Rickel-Ruckel Family 195
Rickey-Smithson Family 479
Ricks Family 530
Riddick's Folly Archives 596
Riddick's Folly Newsletter 596
Rideau District Museum Archives 692
Rideau Lakes Union Library 682
Ridge Genealogical Society 109
Ridge Heritage Association 516
Ridge Historical Society & Library 156
Ridge Historical Society Newsletter 156
Ridge House Museum Archives 689
Ridge Route Communities Historical Museum 45
Ridge Route Communities Historical Society & Archives 45
Ridgecrest Historical Society 62
Ridgefield Historical Association & Library 98
Ridgefield Historical Society & Archives 98
Ridgefield Public Library 377
Ridgetop Historical Society 527
Ridgeville Public Library 192
Ridgewood Historical Society & Archives 377
Ridgewood Public Library 377
Ridgway Family 55
Riding Line 537
Riegel-Riggle Family 452
Riel House Museum Archives 662
Rifle Creek Museum Archives 89
Riggle-Edwards Family 188
Rikard's Mill Historical Park Museum 7
Riker-Ryker Newsletter 189
Riley County Genealogical Society & Library 218
Riley County Historical Society & Archives 218
Riley County Historical Society Newsletter 218
Riley Home Museum 443
Riley House Museum of African American History 122
Riley-Hickingbotham Library 25
Rim Country Museum 18
Rimbey Historical Society & Archives 645
Rimrock Historical Museum 88
Rimrock Historical Society Newsletter 88
Rimrock Historical Society of West Montrose County 88
Rimrocker Historical Museum Archives 88
Rincon County West RV Resort Genealogy Club 22
Rindge Historical Society 364
Riney Family 126
Ringgold County Genealogical Society 200, 205
Ringgold Roots 205
Ringo Family 71
Ringwood Manor House Museum Archives 377
Ringwood Public Library 377
Rinker Family 124
Rio Arriba County Historical Society 385
Rio Grande County Historical Society 83
Rio Grande Filipino American National Society 383
Rio Grande History 385
Rio Grande Researchers 544
Rio Grande Valley Museum Archives 547

Rio Rancho Public Library 384
Rio Vista Historical Museum Archives 62
Riordan Mansion State Historic Park Archives 16
Rios Caladonia Adobe 69
Rios-Caledonia Adobe Museum Archives 69
Rip Chord 608
Rip Van Winkle House Museum Archives 239
Rip Van Winkle House Museum Newsletter 239
Ripley County Heritage 328
Ripley County Historical and Genealogical Society & Archives 328
Ripley County Historical Museum 194
Ripley County Historical Society & Archives 194
Ripley County Historical Society Bulletin 194
Ripley Heritage Society & Archives 456
Ripley Museum Archives 456
Ripon Historical Museum 630
Ripon Historical Society & Archives 630
Ripon Public Library 630
Rippas-Gerber Family 597
Rising Sun Tavern Museum Archives 588
Risley Family 76, 393
Ritchie County Historical Society 614
Ritchie County Historical Society Newsletter 614
Ritchie County Public Library 612
Ritchie House and Freedom's Pathway Archives 222
Rittenhouse Family 339
Rittman Historical Museum 456
Rittman Historical Society & Archives 456
Ritzville Library District Two 605
River Bluffs History Center 617
River Bluffs Regional Library-Belt Branch 338
River City Library Times 183
River City Memoirs 634
River Falls Public Library 630
River Grove Public Library 171
River Heritage Museum Archives 232
River Museum 459
River Road Historical Society & Library 236
River Rouge Public Library 301
River Valley District Library 171
River Valley School Museum Archives 661
River Yarns 201
River's Bend 336
Riverdale Historical Society 171
Riverdale House Mansion 262
Riverdale Letter 262
Riverdale Library 171
Riverhead Free Library 413
Riverhead Free Library Newsletter 413
Riverside County Historical Commission & Library 62
Riverside Heritage House Museum Archives 62
Riverside Historical Commission 172
Riverside Historical Museum Archives 172
Riverside Metropolitan Museum Archives 62
Riverside Metropolitan Museum Newsletter 62
Riverside Museum Archives 624
Riverside Public Library 62, 172
Riverside Public Library Newsletter 172
Riverside Regional Library 331
Riverside Review 230
Riverside-Farnsley-Moremen Landing Museum Archives 230
Riverton Historical Society 637
Riverton Museum 637
Riverview House at Hobson Grove Archives 225
Riverview Observer 225
Riviera Beach Public Library 120
Roachdale-Franklin Township Public Library 192
Roane County Genealogical Society & Archives 528
Roane County Heritage Commission 528
Roane County Historical Society 614
Roane County Museum of History Archives 528
Roane County Public Library 614
Roane Ramblings 528
Roann Paw Paw Township Public Library 192
Roanoke City Public Library 594
Roanoke City Public Library System-Gainsboro 594
Roanoke County Public Library 594
Roanoke Public Library 192, 557
Roanoke Rapids Public Library 432
Roanoke Valley Historical Society 594
Roanoke Valley Historical Society Journal 594
Roanoke Valley Historical Society Newsletter 594
Roaring Twenties Antique Car Museum Archives 589
Robb Family 309, 502
Robbins Historical Society 172
Robbins Hunter Museum Archives 449
Robbins Hunter Museum Newsletter 449
Robbins Journal 602
Robbins Library 265
Robbinsdale Historical Society 313
Roberson Museum Archives 389
Robersonville Public Library 432
Robert A Bogan Fire Museum Archives 236
Robert A Frost Memorial Library 248
Robert A Nicholson Library 179
Robert E Kennedy Library 69
Robert E Lee Memorial Association & Library 595
Robert E Lee Memorial Association Archives 596
Robert E Lee Memorial Museum Archives 584
Robert F Kidd Library 612
Robert Frost Farm Museum Archives 360
Robert Fulton Birthplace Museum 500
Robert J Kleberg Public Library 551
Robert L Pierce Library 626
Robert Louis Stevenson House Museum Archives 55
Robert Louis Stevenson Memorial Cottage 415
Robert Louis Stevenson Silverado Museum Library 64
Robert Manning Strozier Library 122
Robert McKay Clan Newsletter 106
Robert Morris University Library 494
Robert R Jones Public Library 157
Robert R McCormick Museum at Cantigny 177
Robert Russell Rhodes House 445
Robert S Kerr Museum Archives 469
Robert Scott Small Library 512
Robert Toombs House Archives 139
Robert W Richardson Railroad Library 85
Robert W Woodruff Library 126
Roberts County Historical Commission & Archives 553
Roberts County Historical Society & Archives 524

Roberts County Museum 553
Roberts Family 481, 613
Roberts Family Journal 418
Roberts Memorial Library 128
Roberts Register 323
Robertsdale Public Library 8
Roberts-LaForge Library 319
Robertson County Public Library 231
Robertson Family 56, 607
Robertson Quarterly Roundup 227
Roberts-Smith Family 220
Robeson County Public Library 429
Robeson Family 6
Robey Memorial Library 209
Robey-Robie-Roby Family 261
Robinett Family Association Newsletter and Journal 17
Robinson Family 570, 596
Robinson Public Library District 172
Robinson Township Historical Society 493, 499
Robinson Visitors Center Museum Archives 515
Robinson-Gregson Family 567
Robinson-Robison Family 459
Robinson-Rolls Family 5
Robinson-Rose House Museum Archives 65
Roby Newsletter 262
Rocanville and District Museum Archives 709
Rocenka 314
Rocheport Historical Museum 338
Rochester Area Historical Society 633
Rochester Avon Historical Society 301
Rochester Community Library 645
Rochester Genealogical Society 414
Rochester Hills Museum Archives 301
Rochester Hills Public Library 301
Rochester Historical Museum 414
Rochester Historical Society 579
Rochester Historical Society & Archives 414
Rochester Historical Society & Library 364
Rochester Historical Society Newsletter 364
Rochester History 414
Rochester Museum & Science Center Archives 414
Rochester Public Library 313, 364, 414, 579
Rochester Public Library-Charlotte 414
Rock Castle Archives 527
Rock County Genealogical Society & Library 623
Rock County Genealogical Society Member's Newsletter 623
Rock County Historical Museum 623
Rock County Historical Society 309, 349
Rock County Historical Society & Archives 623
Rock County Recorder 623
Rock Creek Station State Historic Park Archives 351
Rock Creek Valley Historical Society & Library 223
Rock House Musuem 597
Rock Island Arsenal Historical Museum 172
Rock Island Arsenal Historical Society 172
Rock Island County Historical Society & Archives 166
Rock Island County Historical Society Newsletter 166
Rock Island Historical House 166
Rock Island Library Lines 172
Rock Island Public Library 172
Rock River Historical Society 637
Rock River Thresheree 620
Rock Springs Historical Museum Archives 637
Rock Springs Historical Society 637
Rock Springs Public Library 630
Rock Valley Public Library 207
Rockaway Borough Library Newsletter 377
Rockaway Free Public Library 377
Rockaway Township Free Public Library 377
Rockbridge Area Genealogical Society 595
Rockbridge Historical Museum 590
Rockbridge Historical Society & Archives 590
Rockbridge Historical Society Proceedings 590
Rockbridge Regional Library 590
Rockcastle County Historical Society & Library 231
Rockcastle County Library 231
Rockcastle Reminiscence 231
Rockdale County Historical Society & Library 129
Rockdale Genealogical Society 129
Rockefeller Archive Center 416
Rocket(t)-Rockette-Mowry-Whitlock-Garson-Challenor Family 69
Rockford Area Historical Society 301
Rockford Area Historical Society 313
Rockford Historical Society & Archives 172
Rockford Public Library 172
Rockingham County Historical Society 589
Rockingham County Historical Society & Library 434
Rockingham County Historical Society Newsletter 434
Rockingham County Public Library 426
Rockingham County Public Library-Madison Branch 429
Rockingham Free Public Library and Museum 575
Rockingham Heritage Society 674
Rockingham House Museum Archives 371
Rockingham Recorder 586
Rockingham Society of Genealogists & Library 361
Rockland County Historical Museum 405
Rockland Historical Society 250
Rockland Memorial Library 278
Rockland Public Library 250
Rockmore Family 498
Rockport Public Library 250, 278
Rockstad Family 316
Rockton Township Historical Society 172
Rockville Public Library 100
Rockwall County Genealogical Society 558
Rockwall County Genealogical Society Quarterly 558
Rockwall County Historical Foundation 558
Rockwall County Library 558
Rockwell City Public Library 207
Rockwell Family 623
Rockwell-Wilcox Family 304
Rockwood Area Historical and Genealogical Society 500
Rockwood Area Historical Society 301
Rockwood Museum Archives 104
Rockwood Public Library 532
Rocky Beach Dam Museum Archives 609
Rocky Comfort Museum Archives 27
Rocky Ford Historical Museum Archives 89
Rocky Hill Historical Society & Archives 98
Rocky Hill Historical Society Newsletter 98

Rocky Lane School Museum Archives 643
Rocky Mount Gazette 532
Rocky Mount Historical Association & Archives 532
Rocky Mount Museum 532
Rocky Mountain Buckeye 87
Rocky Mountain House National Historic Park Archives 645
Rocky Mountain Jewish Historical Notes 84
Rocky Mountain Jewish Historical Society & Archives 84
Rocky Mountain Medieval and Renaissance Association 16
Rocky Mountain Quilt Museum Archives 85
Rocky Mountain Quilt Museum Quarterly 85
Rocky Mountain Rangers Museum Archives 650
Rocky Ridge Review 334
Rocky River Public Library 456
Rockyford Municipal Library 645
Rod Library 198
Roddenbery Memorial Library 127
Rodeo Historical Society 468
Rodgers Tavern Museum Archives 261
Rodgers-Ferguson Family 149
Rodziny 156
Roe Family 624
Roebling Historical Society & Library 377
Roebling Record 377
Roebuck 535
Roebuck Springs Historic Preservation Society 2
Roedde House Museum Archives 656
Roesch House Report 116
Roger E Darling Memorial Library 441
Roger Mills County Genealogical Society 464
Roger Williams National Memorial Archive 509
Roger Williams University Library 507
Rogers County Genealogical and Historical Society 464
Rogers Family 17, 313, 603
Rogers Free Library 507
Rogers Historical Museum 32
Rogers Historical Museum Archives 32
Rogers Historical Society & Archives 32
Rogers Memorial Library 417
Rogers Park Historical Society 156
Rogers Park-West Ridge Historical Society 156
Rogers Roots 549
Rogers-Rodgers Family 614
Rogue Digger 477
Rogue Valley Genealogical Society 477
Rogue Valley Genealogical Society & Archives 477
Rohrbach Family 49
Rohrer Family 225
Rokeby Estate Museum Archives 576
Rokeby Messenger 576
Roland R Renne Library 343
Rolette County Historical Society 439
Rolfe Public Library 207
Roll of Arms 267
Rolla Free Public Library 338
Roller Family Association Newsletter 220
Rolling Meadows Public Library 172
Rolling River Band 659
Rolling River Cultural Centre 659
Rollo Jamison Museum Archives 629
Rolvaag Memorial Library 312
Roman L & Victoria E Hruska Memorial Public Library 351
Romanian American Heritage Center Archives 295
Romanian Bulletin 408
Romanian Folk Art Museum Archives 160
Romanian Library 408
Rombach Recorder 460
Rome Area Heritage Foundation 136
Rome Area History Museum Archives 136
Rome Historical Museum 414
Rome Historical Society & Archives 414
Rome Historical Society Newsletter 414
Rome-Delta Lake Historic Preservation 414
Romeo Historical Museum 301
Romeo Historical Society & Archives 301
Romeo Historical Society & Library 301
Romeoville Historical Society 172
Romeril Family 52
Romig-Romich Family 449
Romulus Historical Society & Library 301
Ron Morel Memorial Museum Archives 683
Ronald Reagan Boyhood Home Archives 158
Ronald Reagan Presidential Library 72
Ronald Reagan Presidential Library Newsletter 72
Ronald V Jensen Living Historical Farm Archives 573
Ronald Williams Library 156
Ronan City Library 346
Roniger Memorial Museum Archives 213
Rook Roots 529
Rooks County Historical Museum 222
Rooks County Historical Society & Archives 222
Rooneys of County Down, Ireland 46
Roop-Royer Family 258
Roopville Historical Society & Library 136
Roose-Ruoss National Family 611
Roosevelt Campobello International Park 665
Roosevelt Campobello International Park Commission & Archives 248
Roosevelt County Library 347
Roosevelt County Museum Archives 384
Roosevelt County Searchers 384
Roosevelt Warm Springs Institute & Library 139
Rooster's Crow 97
Root and Branch 581
Root Cellar Preserves 40
Root Digger 109, 208
Root Digger Newsletter 44
Root Digger Quarterly 44
Root Diggers 234, 335
Root Diggers Genealogical Society 344
Root Diggers, Lucerne Valley Genealogy Association & Archives 53
Root Family 381
Root House Museum 134
Root House Museum Archives 134
Root Seekers Genealogical Society 552
Rooting Around Leavenworth 217
Roots 314
Roots 'n' Branches 199
Roots and Branches 9, 111, 285, 395, 465
Roots and Branches Genealogical Society of West Volusia County & Library 111

Roots and Leaves 351
Roots and Shoots 450
Roots Branches and Twigs 681
Roots Family 536
ROOTS Users Group of Cape Cod 267
Roots-Key 72
Rootstalkers 285
Roper Family 571
Rosa Ponselle Museum Archives 95
Rosalie House Museum 321
Rosalie House Museum Archives 27
Rosalie Whyel Museum of Doll Art 599
Rosalie Whyel Museum of Doll Art Newsletter 599
Roscoe L West Library 370
Roscoe Village 446
Roscoe Village Foundation 446
Roscoe Village News 446
Roscommon County Genealogical Society 300
Rose Association Newsletter 68
Rose City Area Historical Society & Archives 301
Rose City Area Historical Society Newsletter 301
Rose Clan 434
Rose Family Bulletin 68
Rose Hill Mansion Museum Archives 398
Rose Hill Museum 442
Rose Hill Plantation Museum Archives 518
Rose House Museum Archives 688
Rose Lawn Museum Archives 128
Rose Memorial Library Association 417
Rose Mont Archives 527
Rose Valley and District Heritage Museum Archives 710
Rosebrooks Family 92
Rosebud Centennial Museum Archives 645
Rosebud County Library 344
Rosebud County Pioneer Museum Archives 344
Rosedale Historical Museum 425
Roseland Cottage Archives 102
Roseland Free Public Library 377
Roseland Historical Society 377
Roselle Free Public Library 377
Roselle Historical Foundation 172
Roselle Park Historical Society & Library 377
Roselle Park Public Library 377
Rosemead Library 63
Rosemont Plantation 323
Rosemount Area Historical Society 313
Rosemount Museum Archives 89
Rosemount Museum Quarterly 89
Rosenbach Museum Library 498
Rosenberg Library and Museum 546
Rosendale Historical Society 630
Rosetown Museum and Art Center 710
Rosette 595
Roseville Historical and Genealogical Society 301
Roseville Historical and Genealogical Society Newsletter 301
Roseville Historical Museum 63
Roseville Historical Society 313, 456
Roseville Historical Society & Archives 63
Roseville Public Library 63, 301
Rosier Family 464
Roslyn Historical Museum Society 605
Roslyn Landmark Society & Library 414
Roslyn Public Library 605
Ross Clan 591
Ross County Genealogical Society & Library 444
Ross County Genealogical Society Newsletter 444
Ross County Historical Museum 444
Ross County Historical Society & Archives 444
Ross Family 62, 172, 190
Ross Family Newsletter 48
Ross Farm Museum Archives 675
Ross House Museum Archives 662
Ross River Historical Society 713
Ross Thompson Museum Archives 674
Ross Thomson House 676
Rossburn Museum Archives 661
Rosseau County Historical Museum 313
Rosseau County Historical Society & Archives 313
Ross-Fish-Layman-Lehman Family 607
Rossie Town Historian 413
Rossland Historical Museum Association & Library 654
Ross-South Ross Ramblings 173
Rossville Historical Society & Library 173
Rostad Library 495
Roster of Persons Certified 105
Rostraver Public Library 501
Rostron-Townsden-Blackham-Smyth Family 567
Roswell Genealogical Society 384
Roswell Historic Preservation Commission 136
Roswell Historical Museum 384
Roswell Historical Society 384
Roswell Historical Society & Library 136
Roswell Historical Society Newsletter 136
Roswell Museum Bulletin 384
Roswell P Flower Memorial Library 420
Roswell Public Library 384
Roswell Research Library 136
Rotan Public Library 558
Rotary Museum of Police and Corrections Archives 709
Rotary Ramblings 413
Rotary Regional Library 695
Rotch-Jones-Duff House Museum Archives 275
Rotch-Jones-Duff House Museum Newsletter 275
Rothermel Family 492, 494
Rothko Chapel Museum Archives 549
Rothschild House State Park Archives 605
Rothschild Peterson Patent Model Museum Archives 393
Rotunda Museum Archives 585
Roudabush Family 589
Rough and Tumble Engineers' Historical Association 491
Rough and Tumble Engineers' Museum 491
Rouleau and District Museum Archives 710
Roulston Museum Archives 642
Round Lake Library 414
Round Rock Public Library 558
Round the Table 269
Round Top Family Library 558
Round Top Historical Society 544
Round Tower 467
Roundhouse Review 255

Roundtable 431
Roundy Family 16
Rouses Point Village Historian 414
Rouses Point-Champlain Historical Society 414
Rowan County Historical Society 231
Rowan County Public Library 231
Rowan County Register 432
Rowan Museum Archives 432
Rowan Museum Newsletter 432
Rowan Oak Home Museum Archives 321
Rowan Public Library 432
Rowayton Historical Society & Library 98
Rowden Family Newsletter 174
Rowe Family 290, 599
Rowe Historical Museum 278
Rowe Historical Society & Archives 278
Rowe Massachusetts Yearbook 278
Rowe Register 359
Rowe Town Library 278
Rowell Family 555
Rowlett Historical Society 558
Rowley Historical Museum 278
Rowley Historical Society & Archives 278
Rowley Historical Society Newsletter 278
Rowley Public Library 278
Rowley Researcher 40
Rowry-White Family 504
Roxbury Heritage News 278
Roxbury Historical Society 98
Roxbury Historical Society & Archives 278
Roxbury Library 414
Roxbury Township Public Library 378
Roy and Christine Sturgis Library of Cleveland Library 32
Roy Bailey African American History Center Archives 529
Roy O West Library 184
Roy R Estle Memorial Library 200
Roy Rogers and Dale Evans Museum Archives 76
Roy Whalen Regional Heritage Centre Archives 667
Royal Canadian Air Force Memorial Museum Archives 679
Royal Canadian Artillery Museum Archives 661
Royal Canadian Legion Branch 18 663
Royal Canadian Military Institute Museum Archives 691
Royal Canadian Mint Museum Archives 662
Royal Canadian Mounted Police Museum Archives 709
Royal Canadian Ordnance Corps Museum Archives 700
Royal Canadian Regiment Museum Archives 685
Royal Center-Boone Township Public Library 193
Royal Gorge Regional Museum & History Center 82
Royal Gorge Regional Museum Newsletter 82
Royal Hamilton Light Infantry Heritage Museum Archives 683
Royal Historical Society Transactions 406
Royal Military College of Canada Museum Archives 684
Royal Newfoundland Constabulary Museum Archives 668
Royal Nova Scotia Historical Society 674
Royal Oak Public Library 301
Royal Ontario Museum Library 691
Royal Saint John's Regatta Museum Archives 668
Royal Westminster Regiment Historical Society & Library 653
Royal Winnipeg Rifles Museum Archives 662
Royall House Association 274
Royall House Museum 274
Royalton Historical Society 314
Royalton Historical Society & Archives 579
Royce Quarterly 6
Royce-Rhoads Family 6
Royellou Museum Archives 117
RRHM Newsletter 561
Ruben Salazar Library 63
Ruby E Dare Library 162
Rudisill Family 196
Rudisill Family Association Newsletter 49
Rudisill North Regional Library 470
Rudyard Historical Society 346
Rue-Cox Family 353
Rufe Family 504
Rufus M Reed Public Library 231
Rugbeian 532
Rugeley Family 549
Rugg Family 449
Ruggles House Society 245
Rugh Family 185
Ruhlman(n) Family 603
Rumford Area Historical Society & Library 250
Rumford Historical Association & Archives 276
Rumford Historical Museum 276
Rumford Public Library 250
Runge Public Library 558
Runkle Family 377
Runyan Family 25
Rural Historical Society 633
Rural Retreat Historical Society 595
Rural Roots 308
Rush County Historical Society 216
Rush County Historical Society & Library 193
Rush Family 496, 602
Rush Rhees Library 414
Rushford Area Historical Organization 314
Rushford Public Library 314
Rushville Public Library 193, 356
Rusin (Slovakian) Association 311
Rusk County Genealogical Society 548
Rusk County Historical Association & Archives 548
Rusk County Historical Commission 548
Rusk County Historical Museum 624
Rusk County Historical Society & Archives 624
Rusk County Memorial Library 548
Rusk Family 602
Ruskin Public Library 356
Russell County Historical Commission 8
Russell County Historical Society 8, 229
Russell County Historical Society & Archives 221
Russell County Historical Society Newsletter 229
Russell County Public Library 229, 589
Russell Library 96
Russell Memorial Library 265
Russell Public Library 414
Russell Register 62
Russell Relatives and Balengee Trails 341
Russellville Heritage Preservation Society 8
Russian American Genealogical Archival Source 106

Russian American Genealogical Archival Source Resources 106
Russian Gulch State Park Archives 53
Russian River Recorder 47
Russian-Baltic Information Center 69
Rust Family Newsletter 529
Rusty Relics Museum Archives 705
Rutenschroer Reunion 179
Ruth A Haas Library 92
Ruth E Wheeler House 361
Ruth Enlow Library of Garrett County 261
Ruth L Lockwood Memorial Library 372
Ruth Riggs Library Association 12
Rutherford County Farm Museum Archives 427
Rutherford County Genealogical Society 5
Rutherford County Historical Society 531
Rutherford County Historical Society Newsletter 531
Rutherford County Historical Society Publications 531
Rutherford County Library 433
Rutherford House Archives 643
Ruthmere Historic Home Museum Archives 183
Ruthmere Historic Home Museum Quarterly 183
Rutland Free Library 579
Rutland Historical Society 278
Rutland Historical Society & Library 579
Rutland Historical Society Quarterly 579
Rutland Library 337
Rutter 96
RV/MH Heritage Foundation 183
RX News 240
Ryan Family 607
Rye Free Reading Room 414
Rye Historical Society 364
Rye Historical Society & Archives 414
Rye Public Library 364
Ryerss Museum & Library 498
Ryker Family 538
Ryker-Riker Family 595
Ryther Family 308

S

S S Meteor Maritime Museum Archives 617
S White Dickinson Memorial Library 282
Saanich Historical Artifacts Society 654
Saanich Historical Museum 654
Saanich Nation 647
Saanich Pioneer Log Cabin Museum Archives 654
Sabbath Recorder 623
Sabin Family 477
Sabine Parish Library 239
Sabin-Sabine-Sabean Genealogical Newsletter 141
Sac and Fox National Public Library 470
Sac City Public Library 207
Sac County Genealogical Society & Library 207
Sac County Genealogical Society News 207
Sacajawea Interpretive Center Archives 604
Sachem Historical Society & Library 389
Sachem Public Library 400
Sachem Public Library Newsletter 400
Sachs Harbour Museum Archives 671
Sackets Harbor Battlefield State Historic Site Archives 414
Sackets Harbor Historical Museum 420
Sackets Harbor Historical Society & Archives 420
Sackville and District Assistance Center 664
Sackville Heritage Society 676
Saco Museum Archives 250
Saco Museum Quarterly 250
Sacramento Archives and Museum Center 64
Sacramento County Historical Museum 64
Sacramento County Historical Society & Archives 64
Sacramento Genealogical Association 64
Sacramento Genealogical Society & Library 40
Sacramento German Genealogy Society & Library 64
Sacramento German Genealogy Society Newsletter 64
Sacramento Mountains Historical Museum 382
Sacramento Mountains Historical Society & Archives 382
Sacramento Museum and History Commission 64
Sacramento Old City Cemetery Archives 64
Sacramento Public Library 64
Sacramento Public Library-Carmichael Regional Library 39
Sacramento River Delta Historical Society 77
Sacramento Valley Museum Archives 77
Sacramento Valley Museum Association & Archives 78
Sacred Heart Area Historical Society 314
Sadawga Springs 580
Saddle Lake Indian Band 645
Saddleback Area Historical Society 43, 49
Saddlebag 48
SaddleBrooke Genealogy Club 22
Safe Haven Museum Archives 410
Safety Harbor Museum of Regional History Archives 121
Safety Harbor Museum of Regional History Newsletter 121
Safety Harbor Public Library 121
Safford City-Graham County Library 20
Safford Historic House Museum Archives 123
Safley-Saufley-Sofley Family 30
Sag Harbor Historical Society 414
Sag Harbor Whaling and Historical Museum Library 415
Sagacity: the Magazine of Early Wichita & Sedwick County History 223
Sagadahoc Preservation Archives 243
Sagadohoc Preservation 243
Sagamore Hill National Historic Site Archives 410
Sage Family 420
Saginaw County Historian 301
Saginaw Genealogical Society & Archives 301
Saginaw Public Library 558
Saginaw River Marine Historical Society 286
Saguache County Museum Archives 89
Saguache County Public Library 89
Saguenayensia 697
Sailor's Memorial Museum Archives 247
Saint Agatha Historical Society & Library 250
Saint Agatha Historical Society Newsletter 250
Saint Albans Free Library 579
Saint Albans Historical Museum 579
Saint Albans Historical Society & Archives 579
Saint Albans Historical Society Newsletter 579
Saint Albert Hall Library 55
Saint Albert Public Library 645
Saint Andrew's College Library 662, 710
Saint Andrews Blockhouse Archives 664

Saint Angela's Museum Archives 709
Saint Armand Town Historian 415
Saint Augustine Genealogical Society & Archives 121
Saint Augustine Historical Society 239
Saint Augustine Historical Society & Library 121
Saint Augustine Lighthouse Museum Archives 121
Saint Basil College Library 99
Saint Bernard Genealogical Society 236
Saint Bernard Parish Library 236
Saint Catharines Historical Museum 689
Saint Catharines Public Library 689
Saint Catherines Historical Museum Archives 689
Saint Charles City County Library District 340
Saint Charles City County Library District-Linnemann 338
Saint Charles County Genealogical Society & Archives 338
Saint Charles County Historical Museum 338
Saint Charles County Historical Society & Library 338
Saint Charles District Library 301
Saint Charles Heritage Center 173
Saint Charles Historical Society 301
Saint Charles Historical Society & Archives 173
Saint Charles Parish Library 238, 314
Saint Charles Public Library District 173
Saint Clair County Family History Group & Library 300
Saint Clair County Genealogical Society & Library 152
Saint Clair County Genealogical Society Newsletter 152
Saint Clair County Genealogical Society Quarterly 152
Saint Clair County Historical Museum 152
Saint Clair County Historical Society 8, 336
Saint Clair County Historical Society & Library 152
Saint Clair County Historical Society Journal 152
Saint Clair County Library 1, 300, 336
Saint Clair Historical Museum Archives 338
Saint Clair Historical Society 8
Saint Clair Historical Society & Archives 1
Saint Clair Shores Genealogy Group & Archives 301
Saint Clair Shores Historical Commission & Library 301
Saint Clair Shores Public Library 301
Saint Claude Museum Archives 661
Saint Clement's Island Heritage Group 258
Saint Clements Island-Potomac River Museum Archives 258
Saint Cloud Area Genealogists 314
Saint Croix County Historical Society & Library 623
Saint Croix County Historical Society Bulletin 623
Saint Croix Falls Public Library 630
Saint Croix Historical Society 244
Saint Croix Valley Farm Life Museum Archives 309
Saint Croix Valley Genealogical Society 630
Saint Elie Pioneer Church Museum Archives 660
Saint Ephrem Educational Center 461
Saint Frances County Museum Archives 27
Saint Francis County Historical Association 27
Saint Francis Historical and Genealogical Society 328
Saint Francis Historical Society 54, 314, 630
Saint Francis Hook and Ladder Society 67
Saint Francis Xavier University Archives 673
Saint Francois Historical Society 328
Saint Gemme-Beauvais Family Association Newsletter 208
Saint George Historical Society 661
Saint George's Society of New York 408
Saint George's Society of New York Newsletter 408
Saint George's United Methodist Church Museum Archives 498
Saint George's United Methodist Church Newsletter 498
Saint Helena Historical Society 235
Saint James Depot Museum Archives 314
Saint James Parish Library 238
Saint James Santee Parish Historical Society 518
Saint James' House Museum Archives 588
Saint John Historical Society 193
Saint John Jewish Historical Museum 665
Saint John Regional Library 665
Saint John the Baptist Parish Library 238
Saint John's Cathedral Library 84
Saint John's Church and Parish Museum Archives 588
Saint John's Episcopal Church Museum Archives 594
Saint John's Northwestern Military Academy Archives 620
Saint Johns County Public Library 121
Saint Johns Episcopal Church Library 357
Saint Johnsbury Athenaeum 579
Saint Joseph County Historical Society 288
Saint Joseph County Public Library 193
Saint Joseph Genealogical Society 304
Saint Joseph Historical Society 338
Saint Joseph Island Museum Village 689
Saint Joseph Museum Archives 338
Saint Joseph Preservation 338
Saint Joseph Public Library 338
Saint Joseph Valley Record 193
Saint Joseph's Mountain Site Museum Archives 683
Saint Lawrence Chronicler 392
Saint Lawrence County Historical Association & Archives 392
Saint Lawrence County Historical Association Quarterly 392
Saint Lawrence County Historical Museum 392
Saint Lawrence Memorial Miner's Museum 668
Saint Lawrence Valley Genealogical Society & Library 394
Saint Lawrence Valley Genealogical Society News 394
Saint Louis Christian College Library 329
Saint Louis County Historical Museum 307
Saint Louis County Historical Society 305
Saint Louis County Historical Society & Archives 307
Saint Louis County Historical Society Newsletter 307
Saint Louis County Library 339
Saint Louis County Library Newsletter Journal 339
Saint Louis County Library-Tesson Ferry 339
Saint Louis Genealogical Society 339
Saint Louis Genealogical Society & Library 339
Saint Louis Genealogical Society Quarterly 339
Saint Louis Historical Society 302
Saint Louis Park Historical Society 314
Saint Louis Public Library 340
Saint Lucie County Library System 113
Saint Lucie County Library System-Fort Pierce Branch 113
Saint Lucie Historical Commission & Archives 113
Saint Lucie Historical Museum 113
Saint Luke's Museum 399
Saint Marks Historic Landmark Fund 408
Saint Martin Parish Library 241
Saint Mary Genealogical and Historical Society 239
Saint Mary Parish Library 237
Saint Mary's College of Maryland Library 262

INDEX

Saint Mary's County Genealogical Society 260
Saint Mary's County Historical Society & Library 260
Saint Mary's Indian Band 649, 663
Saint Mary's Museum of Maxstone 705
Saint Mary's Pioneer Historical Society 331
Saint Mary's Public Library 689
Saint Mary's Submarine Museum Archives 136
Saint Mary's University Academic Library 559
Saint Mary-of-the-Woods College Library 193
Saint Marys and Benzinger Township Historical Museum 501
Saint Marys Genealogy Center 89
Saint Marys Historic Preservation Commission 136
Saint Marys Historical Society 221
Saint Marys Museum Archives 689
Saint Marys Public Library 501
Saint Michael's Historical Museum Archives 663
Saint Michael's Historical Society 357
Saint Nazianz Area Historical Society 630
Saint Nicholas Society of New York City 408
Saint Norbert Abbey 620
Saint Norbert Provincial Heritage Park Museum Archives 662
Saint Olaf Heritage Association 309
Saint Patrick's Church Museum Archives 676
Saint Patrick's Museum Archives 676
Saint Paul Historical Society 479
Saint Paul Museum Archives 432
Saint Paul Public Library 314
Saint Paul's Church Archives 127
Saint Paul's College Library 106
Saint Peter Lutheran Church Museum Archives 173
Saint Peter's Abbey & College Library 708
Saint Petersburg Museum of History Archives 121
Saint Petersburg Public Library 121
Saint Photios Greek Orthodox National Shrine Archives 121
Saint Piran Society of Minnesota 307
Saint Simons Lighthouse Museum Archives 136
Saint Simons Lighthouse Museum Quarterly 136
Saint Tammany Genealogical Society 238
Saint Tammany Genealogical Society & Archives 236
Saint Tammany Genealogical Society Information Bulletin 236
Saint Tammany Genealogical Society Newsletter 236
Saint Tammany Genealogical Society Quarterly 236
Saint Tammany Historical Society 238
Saint Tammany Historical Society & Archives 236
Saint Tammany Parish Library 236
Saint Thomas Public Library 689
Saint Thomas University Library 117
Saint Thomas' Old Garrison Church Museum 668
Saint Vincent College & Seminary Library 492
Saint Vladimir Institute Library & Library 692
Saint Volodymyr's Ukranian Orthodox Cultural Centre Library and Archives 641
Saint Vrain Historical Society & Library 88
Saint Walburg and District Historical Museum 710
Saint-Basile Chapel Museum Archives 665
Saint-Domingue Newsletter 240
Saint-Domingue Special Interest Group 240
Sainte Genevieve Historical and Genealogical Society & Archives 340
Sainte Marie Among the Iroquois Archives 403
Saints Herald 330
Sakimay First Nation 706
Salamanca Public Library 415
Salamanca Rail Museum Archives 415
Salem Area Historical Society 302
Salem County Historical Society & Library 377
Salem County Historical Society Quarterly Newsletter 377
Salem Free Public Library 377
Salem Historical Museum 456, 595
Salem Historical Society & Archives 456, 595
Salem Historical Society Newsletter 595
Salem Maritime National Historic Site Archives 278
Salem Public Library 193, 278, 340, 457, 479, 489
Salem Public Library Newsletter 479
Salem Witch Museum Archives 278
Salem-Ragatz Church Museum Archives 629
Salem-South Lyon District Library 302
Salida Museum Archives 89
Salida Regional Library 89
Salina Public Library 221
Salinas Pueblo Missions Research Library 384
Saline 26
Saline Area Historical Society 302
Saline County Genealogical Society 351
Saline County Genealogical Society & Library 162
Saline County Historical and Heritage Society 25
Saline County Historical Commission & Archives 25
Saline County Historical Museum 162, 351
Saline County Historical Society 335
Saline County Historical Society & Archives 162, 351
Saline County Historical Society & Library 221
Saline County Historical Society & Library 351
Saline County History and Heritage Society 25
Saline County History and Heritage Society & Library 26
Saline County Pastfinders & Library 351
Saline County Public Library 25
Saline District Library 302
Saling Family 148, 150
Salisbury Association & Archives 98
Salisbury Historical Museum 364
Salisbury Historical Newsletter 364
Salisbury Historical Society 415
Salisbury Historical Society & Archives 364
Salisbury House Foundation Archives 200
Salisbury Public Library 278
Salisbury Watchman 432
Salk Trails 288
Salkehatchie Regional Campus Library 511
Sally Stretch Keen Memorial Library 379
Salmo Museum Archives 654
Salmon Arm Museum Archives 655
Salmon Brook Historical Society 252
Salmon Brook Historical Society & Library 94
Salmon Family 432
Salmon Public Library 149
Salmon Ruins Museum 382
Salmon Ruins Museum Archives 382
Salt Lake City Public Library 571
Salt Lake County Library System 571
Salt Museum Archives 403
Salt Spring Island Historical Society 655

Salt Spring Island Museum Archives 650
Saltbox House Museum Archives 374
Salter Museum 211
Salubris 415
Saluda County Historical Society 517
Saluda County Historical Society Newsletter 517
Saluda County Library 517
Salvage Fisherman's Museum Archives 668
Salvation Army George Scott Railton Museum Archives 692
Salvation Army Southern Historical Center Archives 126
Salvation Army Western Territorial Museum Archives 61
Salvo 66
Salzmann Library 630
Sam Bell Maxey House State Historic Structure Library 555
Sam Brown Log House Museum 306
Sam Davis Home Memorial Association 532
Sam Houston Historical Schoolhouse Archives 530
Sam Houston Memorial Museum Archives 549
Sam Houston Regional Library 552
Sam Houston Regional Library and Research Center 552
Sam Houston Regional Library and Research Center News 551
Sam Rayburn Library & Museum Archives 538
Sam Rayburn Library Newsletter 538
Sam Waller Museum Archives 661
Samahquam Indian Band 652
Samford University Library 2
Samoa Cookhouse & Logging Museum Archives 44
Sampler 263, 444
Sampson County Historical Society 425
Sampson-Livermore Library 431
Samson Cree Indian Band 644
Samson V Maritime Museum Archives 653
Samuel Adams Society 584
Samuel Colgate Historical Library 413
Samuel Family 2
Samuel Freudenthal Memorial Library 90
Samuel H Wentworth Library 359
Samuel K Fox Museum Archives 12
Samuel K Fox Museum Newsletter 12
Samuel Moss House 484
Samuel Parsons House Museum 100
Samuel Searcher 11
Samuels Public Library 588
San Angelo Genealogical and Historical Society 558
San Angelo Genealogical and Historical Society Newsletter 558
San Anselmo Public Library 64
San Antonio Central Library 559
San Antonio College Library 559
San Antonio Conservation Newsletter 559
San Antonio de Pala Asistencia Museum Archives 58
San Antonio Genealogical and Historical Society 559
San Antonio Genealogical and Historical Society Newsletter 559
San Antonio Library, San Pedro Branch 559
San Antonio Missions National Historic Park Library 559
San Antonio Valley Historical Association 48
San Antonio Valley Historical Museum 50
San Antonio Valley Historical Society & Archives 50
San Augustine Public Library 559
San Benito County Free Library 47
San Benito County Genealogical Society 47
San Benito County Historical Society 47
San Bernardino County Archives 64
San Bernardino County Library & Historical Archives 64
San Bernardino County Library-Montclair Branch 54
San Bernardino County Museum Archives 61
San Bernardino County Museum Newsletter 61
San Bernardino Historical and Pioneer Society & Library 64
San Bernardino Public Library 64
San Bernardino Public Library-Inghram 64
San Bernardino Valley Genealogical Society & Library 64
San Bruno Public Library & Local History Room 64
San Buena Ventura Mission Museum Archives 76
San Buenaventura Heritage & Archives 76
San Buenaventura Historic Preservation Commission 76
San Carlos Historical Museum Archives 65
San Clemente Historical Society & Library 65
San Diego Aerospace Museum Archives 65
San Diego African-American Genealogy Research Group 65
San Diego Automotive Museum Archives 65
San Diego Civil War Roundtable 65
San Diego County Genealogical Association 61
San Diego County Historical Days Association 65
San Diego County Library 65
San Diego Electric Railway Association 66
San Diego Family History Center 66
San Diego Genealogical Society 66
San Diego Genealogical Society & Library 43
San Diego Historical Society & Library 66
San Diego Historical Society History Notes 66
San Diego Historical Society Times 66
San Diego History News 66
San Diego Maritime Museum Archives 66
San Diego Military Heritage Society 66
San Diego Public Library 66
San Diego State University Library 66
San Dieguito Heritage Museum Archives 43
San Dieguito Heritage Museum Quarterly Newsletter 43
San Dimas Historical Museum 66
San Dimas Historical Society & Archives 66
San Fernando Valley Genealogical Society 39
San Fernando Valley Genealogy Society 78
San Fernando Valley Historical Museum 54
San Fernando Valley Historical Society & Archives 54
San Francisco African-American Historical and Cultural Society & Library 67
San Francisco African-American Historical and Cultural Society Quarterly 67
San Francisco Bay Area Jewish Genealogical Society 39, 67
San Francisco Cable Car Museum Archives 67
San Francisco Fire Department Museum Archives 67
San Francisco Historical Society & Museum 67
San Francisco History Association 67
San Francisco Maritime National Historical Park Archives 67
San Francisco Public Library 67
San Francisco State University Library 67
San Francisco's Architectural Heritage 67
San Francisco's Gold Rush Trail Foundation 67
San Gabriel Historical Association & Library 67
San Gabriel Historical News 67
San Gabriel Mission Museum Archives 67
San Gorgonio Pass Genealogical Society 36
San Ildefonso Historical Society 385

INDEX

San Jacinto County Heritage Society and Historical Commission 540
San Jacinto Museum Archives 67
San Jacinto Museum of History Archives 551
San Jacinto Museum of History Newsletter 551
San Jacinto Valley Museum Association & Library 67
San Joaquin County Historical Museum 50
San Joaquin County Historical Society & Archives 50
San Joaquin Genealogical Newsletter 73
San Joaquin Genealogical Society & Library 73
San Joaquin Historian 50
San Joaquin Pioneer and Historical Society & Archives 73
San Jose Historical Landmarks Commission 68
San Jose Historical Museum Association & Library 68
San Jose Museum of Quilts and Textiles Archives 68
San Jose Public Library 68
San Juan Bautista Historical Society 68
San Juan Capistrano Historical Society & Archives 68
San Juan College Library 383
San Juan County Archaeological Research Center Archives 382
San Juan County Historical Museum 89
San Juan County Historical Society & Archives 89
San Juan Courier 89
San Juan Historical Society & Archives 601
San Juan Historical Society Newsletter 601
San Juan Island National Historic Site Archives 602
San Juan Island Public Library 602
San Juan State Historic Park Archives 68
San Leandro Historical Commission & Library 68
San Leandro Historical Railway Society 68
San Leandro Historical Society 68
San Lorenzo Valley Museum Archives 38
San Luis Obispo City-County Library 69
San Luis Obispo County Genealogical Society 69
San Luis Obispo County Genealogical Society & Library 36
San Luis Obispo County Genealogical Society Bulletin 36
San Luis Obispo County Genealogical Society Newsletter 36
San Luis Obispo County Historical Museum 69
San Luis Obispo County Historical Society 69
San Luis Valley Historian 81
San Luis Valley Historical Society 81
San Marcos de Apalache Historic State Park Archives 121
San Marcos Historical Society & Museum 69
San Marcos Public Library 559
San Marcos-Hays County Genealogical Society 559
San Marino Historical Society & Library 69
San Marino Public Library 69
San Mateo County Genealogical Society & Library 69
San Mateo County Genealogical Society Newsletter 69
San Mateo County Historical Association & Archives 69
San Mateo County Historical Association & Library 62
San Mateo Public Library 69
San Miguel Mission Church Museum Archives 385
San Pablo Historical and Museum Society & Library 69
San Pasqual Battlefield State Historic Park Archives 44
San Patricio County Library 560
San Pedro Bay Historical Society & Archives 69
San Rafael Public Library 69
San Ramon Valley Genealogical Society 42
San Ramon Valley Genealogical Society Newsletter 42
San Ramon Valley Historical Society & Library 42
San Ramon Valley Historical Society Record 42
San Ramon Valley Historical Society Roster 42
San Tan Historical Society 19
Sanborn Area Historical Museum 415
Sanborn Area Historical Society 415
Sanborn Family 265
Sanbornton Historical Society 365
Sanbornton Public Library 364
Sanchez Adobe Historic Site Archives 58
Sand Lake Historical Society & Library 420
Sand Lake Town Library 388
Sand Springs Cultural and Historical Museum Archives 469
Sand Springs Reflections 469
Sandefur-Taylor Family 600
Sanders Family 145
Sanders Family News 129
Sanders Newsletter 557
Sanders-Hurst Family 571
Sanderson-Saunderson Quarterly 557
Sandlin Family 135
Sandon Historical Museum 655
Sandon Historical Society & Archives 655
Sandon Museum Archives 652
Sandor Teszler Library 518
Sandoval County Historical Society & Library 382
Sandown Historical Society & Library 364
Sandpoint Lighthouse Archives 291
Sands of Time 19
Sands Sentinel 291
Sandstone History and Art Center 315
Sands-Willets House 412
Sandusky County Historical Society 448
Sandusky County Kin Hunter Society 448
Sandusky Library 457
Sandusky Public Library 302
Sandwich District Library 173
Sandwich Historical Museum 173
Sandwich Historical Society & Archives 173, 278
Sandwich Historical Society & Library 359
Sandwich Historical Society Annual Excursion Publication 359
Sandwich Islands Genealogical Society 142
Sandy Bay Historical Museum 278
Sandy Bay Historical Society & Archives 278
Sandy Creek Covered Bridge State Historic Site Archives 329
Sandy Creek Town Historian 415
Sandy Ground Historical Society 417
Sandy Historical Society 479
Sandy Spring Heritage Group 262
Sandy Spring Museum Archives 262
Sandy Spring Museum Legacy 262
Sanford Family 599
Sanford Historical Committee & Library 250
Sanford Historical Society & Library 302
Sanford Museum Archives 121
Sangamon County Genealogical Society 174
Sangamon County Historical Society & Library 174
Sanger Public Library 559
Sanibel Public Library 121
Sanilac County Historical Museum 300
Sanilac County Historical Society & Archives 300

Sanilac County Historical Society Newsletter 300
Sanilac District Library 300
Sanks Family 619
Sans Tache 8
Santa Ana Army Air Base CADET 41
Santa Ana Historical Preservation Society 70
Santa Ana Mountain Historical Society 72
Santa Ana Public Library 70
Santa Anna Library 559
Santa Barbara County Genealogical Society & Library 46, 70
Santa Barbara Courthouse Museum Archives 70
Santa Barbara Historical Museum 70
Santa Barbara Historical Museum Newsletter 70
Santa Barbara Historical Society & Archives 70
Santa Barbara Maritime Museum Archives 70
Santa Barbara Mission Museum Archives 70
Santa Barbara Old Mission 70
Santa Barbara Orchid Estate Archives 70
Santa Barbara Public Library 70
Santa Barbara Trust for Historic Preservation & Library 70
Santa Clara Arts and Historical Consortium 70
Santa Clara County Connections 70
Santa Clara County Historical and Genealogical Society 70
Santa Clara County Historical and Genealogical Society Newsletter 70
Santa Clara County Historical Heritage Commission & Library 68
Santa Clara County Historical Pharmacy Association 68
Santa Clara Historical Landmarks Commission 70
Santa Clara Public Library 70
Santa Clara River Valley Railroad Historical Society 44
Santa Clarita Valley Historical Society & Library 56
Santa Cruz City-County Library System 71
Santa Cruz County Railroad Historical Society 45
Santa Cruz Historical Society & Library 71
Santa Cruz Historical Society Newsletter 71
Santa Cruz Mission State Historic Park Archives 71
Santa Fe County Genealogical Society 384
Santa Fe County Historical Society 385
Santa Fe Depot Museum 211
Santa Fe Historical Society 385
Santa Fe Public Library 385
Santa Fe Springs City Library 71
Santa Fe Springs Historical Committee & Library 71
Santa Fe Trail Center 217
Santa Fe Trail Genealogical Society & Library 222
Santa Fe Trail Historical Society 211
Santa Fe Trail Museum Archives 90, 216
Santa Fe Trail Researchers Genealogical Society 329
Santa Fe Trail Rider 211
Santa Maria Museum of Flight Archives 71
Santa Maria Public Library 71
Santa Maria Valley Genealogical Society & Library 71
Santa Maria Valley Genealogical Society Quarterly 71
Santa Maria Valley Historical Museum 71
Santa Maria Valley Historical Society Archives 71
Santa Maria Valley Historical Society Quarterly 71
Santa Monica Historical Museum 71
Santa Monica Historical Society & Archives 71
Santa Monica Historical Society Newsletter 71
Santa Monica Mountains National Recreational Area Archives 75
Santa Monica Public Library 71
Santa Paula Historical Society 71
Santa Rosa Historical Society 117
Santa Ynez Valley Historical Society & Library 71
Santa Ysabel Asistencia Museum Archives 71
Santarella Museum Archives 281
Santuario de Nuestra Senora de Guadalupe Museum 384
Santuit and Cotuit Historical Museum 269
Sapit Journal 456
Sapp Family Association Newsletter 113
Sapp-Charlebois-Shalibo Family 113
Sappington Cemetery State Historic Site Archives 335
Sappington Family 300
Sappington House Foundation & Archives 328
Sappington House Museum 328
Sappington House Newsletter 328
Sapulpa Genealogical Association 469
Sapulpa Historical Museum 469
Sapulpa Historical Society & Archives 469
Sara Hightower Regional Library 136
Sarah A Mooney Housel Museum 50
Sarah Carpenter Memorial Library 577
Sarah Orne Jewett House Archives 251
Sarah Stewart Bovard Memorial Library 503
Sarah Vaughan Museum Archives 690
Saranac Lake Free Library 415
Saranac Lake Village Archives 415
Sarasota County Archives 121
Sarasota County Courthouse Archives 121
Saratoga Automobile Museum Archives 415
Saratoga Chips 415
Saratoga County Historical Society & Archives 389
Saratoga County Museum 389
Saratoga Heritage Preservation Commission 72
Saratoga Historical and Cultural Association & Archives 637
Saratoga Historical Foundation & Archives 72
Saratoga Historical Museum 637
Saratoga Historical Museum 72
Saratoga Springs Historical Museum 415
Saratoga Springs Library 389
Saratoga Springs Public Library 415
Saratoga Valley Quarterly 413
Saratogian Library 415
Sarcee People's Museum Archives 641
Sargent House Museum Archives 271
Sargent Newsletter 346
Sarguinetti House Museum 22
Sarine-Sirrine-Surine Family 288
Sarpy County Historical and Genealogical Society & Archives 349
Sarpy County Historical and Genealogical Society Newsletter 349
Sarpy County Historical Museum 349
Sartain Family Newsletter 150
Saskachewan Pharmacy Museum Archives 709
Saskatchewan Archives 709, 710
Saskatchewan Archives Board 709, 710
Saskatchewan Genealogical Society & Library 709
Saskatchewan Genealogical Society Bulletin 709
Saskatchewan Genealogical Society, Battlefords Branch 708
Saskatchewan Genealogical Society, Biggar Branch 705
Saskatchewan Genealogical Society, Border Branch 645
Saskatchewan Genealogical Society, Central Butte Branch 705

Saskatchewan Genealogical Society, Craik Branch 705
Saskatchewan Genealogical Society, Estevan Branch 711
Saskatchewan Genealogical Society, Grasslands Branch 707
Saskatchewan Genealogical Society, Kindersley Branch 707
Saskatchewan Genealogical Society, Moose Jaw Branch 705
Saskatchewan Genealogical Society, North-East Branch 708
Saskatchewan Genealogical Society, Pangman Branch 708
Saskatchewan Genealogical Society, Pipestone Branch 708
Saskatchewan Genealogical Society, Porcupine Plain Branch 710
Saskatchewan Genealogical Society, Prince Albert Branch 709
Saskatchewan Genealogical Society, Quill Plains Branch 710
Saskatchewan Genealogical Society, Regina Branch 709
Saskatchewan Genealogical Society, Saskatoon Branch 710
Saskatchewan Genealogical Society, Southeast Branch 705
Saskatchewan Genealogical Society, Swift Current Branch 711
Saskatchewan Genealogical Society, Turnor Lake Branch 711
Saskatchewan Genealogical Society, West Central Branch 706
Saskatchewan Genealogical Society, Weyburn Branch 711
Saskatchewan Genealogical Society, Yorkton Branch 711
Saskatchewan History 709
Saskatchewan History and Folklore Society 709
Saskatchewan Military Museum Archives 709
Saskatchewan Provincial Library 709
Saskatchewan Western Development Museum Archives 711
Saskatoon Heritage Society 710
Saskatoon Public Library 710
Saskatoon Tribal Council 710
Sassaman-Sossaman-Sossamon Family News 74
Satagoa National Historical Park Archives 417
Satellite Beach Public Library 121
Satilla Regional Library 130
Satterfield Quarterly 129
Satterlee Clark House Museum 623
Satwiwa Native American Indian Culture Center Archives 56
Sauermann Newsletter 262
Saugatuck-Douglas Historical Society 290, 302
Saugerties Historical Society & Archives 415
Saugerties Public Library 415
Saugus Historical Society 279
Saugus Iron Works National Historic Site Archives 279
Saugus Public Library 279
Sauk Centre Area Historical Society 315
Sauk City Public Library 630
Sauk County Historical Museum 617
Sauk County Historical Society & Archives 617
Sauk Prairie Area Historical Society & Archives 629
Sauk Trails 617
Sauk Valley Community College Library 158
Saukville Area Historical Society 630
Saul Silber Memorial Library 173
Sault de Sainte Marie Historical Sites Archives 302
Sault Sainte Marie Museum Archives 689
Sault Sainte Marie Public Library 689
Saulteaux First Nation 705
Saulteaux Indian Band 648
Saunders County Genealogical Seekers 357
Saunders County Genealogical Seekers Newsletter 357
Saunders County Historical Museum 357
Saunders County Historical Society & Archives 357
Saunders County Historical Society Newsletter 357
Saunders Family 27
Saunders Memorial Museum Archives 25
Saunders Newsletter 557
Sausalito Historical Society & Archives 72
Sausalito Historical Society Newsletter 72
Sautee-Nacoochee Center Archives 136
Sautee-Nacoochee Community Association 136
Savage Family 477
Savanna Public Library 173
Savannah Area Genealogical Association & Library 137
Savannah History Association 137
Savannah History Museum 137
Savannah Ogeechee Canal Society 137
Savannah River Valley Genealogical Society & Archives 132
Savannah River Valley Genealogical Society Newsletter 132
Save Historic Old Torrance 75
Save Our Heritage Organization & Library 66
Savery Library 9
Savitz Library 370
Savory Family 271
Sawin Museum 270
Sawin Society Newsletter 91
Sawtelle Research Center 243
Sawyer County Historical Museum 623
Sawyer County Historical Society & Archives 623
Sawyer Family 55
Sawyer Free Library 271
Sawyer Free Library Newsletter 271
Sawyer House 266
Sawyer's Sandhills Museum Archives 357
Saxon News Volksblatt 445
Saxonburg Area Library 501
Saxton B Little Free Library 92
Saxton Community Library 501
Saxtons River Historical Society & Library 579
Saybrook Colony Founders Association 98
Sayre Historical Society 501
Sayre Historical Society & Archives 469
Sayre Public Library 469, 501
Sayville Historical Museum 415
Sayville Historical Society & Archives 415
Sayville Public Library 415
Sayward-Wheeler House Museum Archives 253
Sborrik Museia Russkoy Kultury 67
SCAD Department of Architectural History 137
Scadaddles 54
Scadding Cabin Museum Archives 692
Scadlock Family 54
Scaggel Family 475
Scandia Museum Archives 221
Scandinavian American Genealogical Society 315
Scandinavian Genealogical Society of Oregon 479
Scandinavian Queries 25
Scandinavian Saga 308
Scandinavian-American Genealogical Society & Library 308
Scantic Academy Museum 93
Scappoose Public Library 479
Scarb(o)hough-Ha(y)worth Family 342
Scarborough Historical Museum 251
Scarborough Historical Museum Archives 689

Scarborough Historical Society & Archives 251
Scarborough Library 614
Scarborough Memorial Library 383
Scarce-Scearce Family 466
Scarsdale Historical Museum 415
Scarsdale Historical Society & Archives 415
Scarsdale Public Library 415
Scattered Seeds 111
SCCHS Archives Newsletter 338
Scenic Region Library 336
Scenic Regional Library 341
Scenic Regional Library-Hermann 330
Scenic Regional Library-Warrenton 342
SCGS Bulletin 518
Schaarschmidt Family 637
Schaffer Library 415
Schale (Westfallen) Newsletter 163
Schalick Museum 373
Schalm Memorial Library 643
Schartzer-Schertzer Connection 154
Schaub Family 522
Schauf-Hommell Family 584
Schaumburg Genealogical Society 173
Schaumburg Township District Library 173
Scheible Family 30
Schell-Shell Family 232
Schenectady County Historical Museum 415
Schenectady County Historical Society & Archives 415
Schenectady County Historical Society Newsletter 415
Schenectady County Public Library 415
Schenectady Museum Archives 415
Scherer Family 157
Schererville Historical Society 193
Schertz Public Library 559
Schewe Library 163
Schiele Museum of Southeastern Native American Studies Archives 427
Schifferstadt Architectural Museum Archives 259
Schifferstadt Architectural Museum Quarterly 259
Schiller Park Historical Society 173
Schimpfessel Newsletter 46
Schindel-Shindel-Shindle Family 264
Schindler House Archives 77
Schingoethe Center for Native American Cultures Archives 151
Schlegelmilch-McDaniel House Archives 620
Schleicher County Public Library 544
Schleswig Public Library 207
Schletzbaum Family 211
Schley County Historical Society 130
Schliem-Schlem Family 631
Schlow Memorial Library 502
Schmidt Quarterly 171
Schminck Museum 476
Schmucker-Smucker-Smoker Newsletter 184
Schnabel-Weare Family 325
Schnaible Family 68
Schneider Connections 154
Schneider Family 531
Schneider-Seeman Family 414
Schoenbaum Library 611
Schoenbrunn Village Archives 461
Schofield House Museum Archives 189
Schoharie Colonial Heritage Association & Archives 415
Schoharie County Historical Review 416
Schoharie County Historical Society & Library 416
Schoharie Crossing State Historic Site Archives 397
Scholderer-Sholder Family 443
Scholte House Museum Archives 207
Schomburg Center for Research in Black Culture 408
Schomburg Center Journal 408
Schoolcraft Historical Society 302
Schoolcraft Historical Society & Archives 297
Schoolcraft Historical Society Newsletter 297
Schoolhouse History Center Archives 344
Schoolhouse Museum 377
Schoolhouse Sentinel 93
Schoonmaker Family 406
Schrader Family 50
Schreiber Scriba 111
Schreiber Township Public Library 689
Schroeder Area Historical Society 315
Schroeppel Town Historian 411
Schroon-North Hudson Historical Society & Library 416
Schroon-North Hudson Historical Society Newsletter 416
Schuette Bierman Farmhouse Museum Archives 159
Schultheiss Family 625
Schultz Mansion Archives 461
Schulz-Marks Family 539
Schumacher Farm County Park 633
Schurch Family 82
Schutt Newsletter 262
Schutz Family 408
Schuyler County Historical Museum 405
Schuyler County Historical Society 333
Schuyler County Historical Society & Archives 405
Schuyler County Historical Society Journal 405
Schuyler Falls Town Historian 405
Schuyler Family 387
Schuyler Historical Society 356
Schuyler Jail Museum 173
Schuyler Mansion Museum 387
Schuyler-Brown Historical and Genealogical Society & Archives 173
Schuyler-Hamilton House Museum Archives 374
Schuylerite 173
Schuylerville Public Library 416
Schuylkill Haven Free Public Library 501
Schwartz Collection of Skiing Heritage Archives 75
Schwartz Heritage House Museum Archives 659
Schwarz Family 304
Schwenkfelder Historical Society & Archives 496
Schwenkfelder Library & Heritage Center 496
Schwenkfelder Museum Archives 496
Schweppe Family 633
Scio Free Library 416
Scio Historical Society 479
Scioto County Chapter Newsletter 456
Scioto County Genealogy Society & Library 456
Scioto County Historical Society 456
Scioto Historical Society 444
Sciple's Water Mill Archives 320
Scituate Historical Society & Archives 279

Scituate Historical Society Bulletin 279
Scituate Historical Society News 279
Scituate Maritime and Irish Mossing Museum Archives 279
Scituate Town Library 279
Scoby-Shobe Scribe 19
Scotch Plains Public Library 377
Scotch-Irish Society of the U.S.A. 498
Scotchtown Museum Archives 584
Scotia History Center Archives 416
Scotland County Genealogical Society 335, 429
Scotland County Historical Society & Archives 335
Scotland County Memorial Library 335, 429
Scotland Heritage Chapel and Museum Archives 523
Scotland Historical Society 99, 193
Scott Air Force Base Library 173
Scott Clan 536
Scott County Genealogical Society 188, 193, 228, 320
Scott County Genealogical Society & Archives 200
Scott County Genealogical Society Newsletter 188, 228
Scott County Historical and Genealogical Society 33, 325
Scott County Historical Society 178, 193, 315
Scott County Historical Society & Library 528
Scott County Historical Society Newsletter 528
Scott County Iowan 200
Scott County Journal 188
Scott County Library System 201, 315
Scott County Museum Archives 33
Scott County Public Library 193, 228
Scott Family 130, 241, 470, 538
Scott House 98
Scott One-Name Study 264
Scott Scanner 183
Scott Searcher 549
Scott-Fanton Museum 92
Scottish District Families Association 428
Scottish Genealogy Group of the Illinois Saint Andrew Society & Library 163
Scottish Genealogy Group of the Illinois Saint Andrew Society Quarterly 163
Scottish Heritage USA 431
Scottish Heritage USA Newsletter 431
Scottish Historic and Research Society of the Delaware Valley & Library 481
Scottish Queries 607
Scottish Rite Journal 106
Scottish Rite Masonic Library 66, 273
Scottish Rite Masonic Library Newsletter 66
Scottish Rite Supreme Council & Library 106
Scottish Society of Northern Colorado 85
Scottish Tartans Museum Archives 427
Scottish-American Military Society 111
Scotts Bluff National Monument Library 352
Scotts Valley Band of Pomo Indians 49
Scottsbluff Public Library 356
Scottsboro Public Library 8
Scottsboro-Jackson Heritage Center 8
Scottsboro-Jackson Heritage Center Library 8
Scottsdale Historical Society 20
Scottsdale Historical Society Newsletter 20
Scottsdale Public Library 20
Scott-Sebastian Regional Library 28
Scott-Sebastian Regional Library-Scott County 33
Scottsville Museum Archives 595
Scout 349
Scout Memorabilia 362
Scout's Dispatch 85
Scoville Family 98
Scoville Memorial Library 98
Scowlitz Indian Band 651
Scranton Historical Society 221
Scranton Public Library 501
Scratches in the Sand 48
Screven-Jenkins Regional Library 138
Scriba Town Historical Association 410
Scribe, Boyhood Memories and Family Ties 89
Scriven-Bowater-Jacobsen Family 567
Scriver Scribbler 312
Scrogg's House News 443
Scruggs Family 2
Scudder Family 378
Scudder Searches Newsletter 361
Scugog Shores Historical Museum Archives 688
Scurry County Genealogical Society 560
Scurry County Museum 560
Scurry County Museum Genealogical Group & Archives 560
Scurry County Museum Newsletter 560
SDSU Library Newsletter 66
Sea Breeze 121
Sea Cliff Village Museum Archives 416
Seabee Museum Archives 60
Seabhach Abu 73
Seabird Island Band 647
Seabrook Village Museum Archives 134
Seaford District Library 104
Seaford Historical Museum 416
Seaford Historical Quarterly 416
Seaford Historical Society 416
Seaford Historical Society & Library 104
Seaford Historical Society Quarterly 104
Seaforth Highlanders Regimental Museum Archives 656
Seagraves Family 423
Seagraves-Loop Museum Archives 559
Seal Cove Campus Library 668
Seal Island Light Museum Archives 673
Sealaska Heritage Foundation 12
Seaport Journal 399
Search 65
Search Notes 50
Search: International Quarterly for Researchers of Jewish Genealogy 168
Searcher 496
Searchers 282, 391
Searchers and Researchers 562
Searching for Searcy's 554
Searching for the Hidden Dale 19
Searchlight 480
Searchlight-The Light (and Variants) Family Newsletter 194
Searcy County Historical Museum 30
Searcy County Historical Society 30
Searcy Family 337
Searles Valley Historical Society & Library 75
Searls Historical Library 56
Sears Family 277
Sears Family Association Newsletter 277

Searsport Historical Society 251
Seashore Trolley Museum Archives 247
Seaside Community Library 72
Seaside Historical Museum 479
Seaside Historical Society & Archives 479
Seasons 196
Seasons Readings 426
Seaton Family 36
Seattle and King County Historical Museum 606
Seattle Genealogical Society 606
Seattle Genealogical Society & Library 606
Seattle Genealogical Society Bulletin 606
Seattle Genealogical Society Newsletter 606
Seaver Center for Western History Research 52
Seay House Museum 518
Sebastian Area Historical Museum 122
Sebastian Area Historical Society & Archives 122
Sebeka Finnish-American Historical Society, Chapter 38 315
Sebewaing Township Library 302
Sebring Historical Society 122
SEC Historical Society 106
Secaucus Free Public Library 377
Sechelt Indian Band 655
Second Section 167
Secoy Family 614
Security Public Library 89
Secwepemc Cultural Education Society 650
Secwepernc Museum and Heritage Park Archives 650
Sedalia Public Library 340
Sedgewick County Genealogical Society 86
Sedgewick Museum Archives 646
Sedgwick-Brooklin Historical Museum 251
Sedgwick-Brooklin Historical Society & Archives 251
Sedgwick-Brooklin Historical Society Newsletter 251
Sedona Genealogy Club 20
Sedona Genealogy Club Newsletter 20
Sedona Historical Society 20
Sedona Public Library 20
See Gull 57
Seeds Family 195
Seeds of History 492
Seefeld(t) Reunion Newsletter 111
Seefeldt Family 617
Seeker 220
Seeking and Searchin' Ancestors 338
Seeley Family 400
Seeley G Mudd Library 617
Seeley Genealogical Society 42, 99, 211
Seeley Genealogical Society Newsletter 42, 84, 99
Seeley Newsletter 217
Segler Family 607
Segrist Family 459
Seguin Conservation Society & Archives 560
Seguine-Burke Plantation Archives 417
Seguin-Guadalupe County Public Library 560
Segwun Heritage Centre Archives 683
Seideman Family 633
Selby Family 226
Selby Public Library 121
Selby Township Library District 157
Selby-England-Stamps Family 187
Self Family Newsletter 127
Selke-Holcomb Family 631
Selkirk College Archives and Local History Collection 648
Sellers Family 11, 523
Selma and Dallas County Public Library 8
Selma Museum Historical Society 72
Selma-Dallas County Friends Of The Trail 8
Selma-Dallas County Historic and Preservation Society 8
Selma-Sanders Family 585
Selover Public Library 444
Semiahmoo Indian Band 657
Seminaire De Chicoutimi Bibliotheque 697
Seminaire De Nicolet Library & Museum 700
Seminaire De Sherbrooke Bibliotheque 703
Seminaire Des Peres Maristes Bibliotheque 703
Seminold Canyon State Park and Historic Site Archives 541
Seminole County Genealogical Group 110
Seminole County Historical Society 121, 130
Seminole County Public Library System 121
Seminole Historical Society 469
Seminole Nation Museum 471
Seminole Nation Museum Newsletter 471
Seminole Nation of Oklahoma & Archives 471
Seminole National Historical Museum 471
Seminole National Historical Society & Archives 471
Seminole Public Library 469
Seminole Tribe of Florida Library 118
Senate House State Historic Site Library 402
Senator George Norris State Historic Site Archives 354
Senator John Heinz Regional History Center 499
Senator Wilson Home 521
Seneca County Genealogical Society & Library 458
Seneca County Historical Society & Archives 458
Seneca County Museum 458
Seneca Falls Historical Museum 416
Seneca Falls Historical Society & Archives 416
Seneca Falls Historical Society Newsletter 416
Seneca Free Library 221
Seneca Historical Committee 340
Seneca Nation Historical Society 401
Seneca Public Library District 173
Seneca Searches 458
Seneca-Iroquois National Museum Archives 415
Senior Newsletter 404
Senoia Area Historical Society 137
Sentinel 53, 688
Sentry 635
Sephardic Scholar 406
Septs 314
Sepulveda Historic House Museum Archives 52
Sequels 299
Sequim Museum Archives 607
Sequoia Genealogical Society & Archives 75
Sequoia Genealogical Society Newsletter 75
Sequoyah Cabin Museum Archives 469
Sequoyah Genealogical Society 469
Sequoyah Regional Library System-R T Jones Memorial 128
Sequoyan 214
Seraph 404

INDEX

Serb National Federation 499
Serbian Heritage Museum of Windsor 693
Serbian National Shield Society of Canada 693
Sergeant Rodney J Yano Main Library 143
Sergeants Major Academy Library 545
Service de la Bibliotheque de Ville de Laval 699
Sesquicentennial Museum Archives 692
Seton Centre Archives 659
Seton Lake Indian Band 655
Settler 503
Settlers' Museum and Cultural Centre 675
Settles Family 133
Settle-Suttle Family 187
Setzekorn Family 44
Seven Oaks House Museum Archives 662
Seven Springs Historical Society 135
Seven Valleys Historical Society 350
Seventeenth Century Review 106
Seventeenth-Century News 540
Seventh Day Baptist Historical Society & Library 623
Seventh Day Baptist Historical Society Annual Report 623
Seventh Town Historical Society 679
Sevier County Genealogical Society & Archives 26
Sevier County Genealogical Society Quarterly 26
Sevier County Historical Museum 26
Sevier County Historical Society & Archives 26
Sevier County Historical Society Newsletter 26
Sevier County Library, DeQueen Branch 26
Sevier County Public Library 532
Sevier Family 106, 430
Seville Historical Society 457
Seward Community Library 13
Seward County Genealogical Society & Library 356
Seward County Historical Museum 352, 356
Seward County Historical Society 217, 356
Seward County Historical Society & Archives 352, 356
Seward County Historical Society Newsletter 352
Seward House Museum 388
Seward Museum 13
Seward Public Library 356
Seward-Rose (Rowell) Family 635
Sewickley Public Library 501
Sewickley Public Library Newsletter 501
Sewickley Valley Historical Society & Library 501
Seymour Community Historical Museum 631
Seymour Community Historical Society & Archives 631
Seymour Community Museum Archives 631
Seymour Historical Society & Library 99
Seymour Public Library 388, 390
Seymour Public Library 99
Sgian Dubh 48
Sgorr A Bhreac 281
SGS Newsletter 98
Sgurr Uaran 137
Shackan Indian Band 652
Shackelford Quarterly 113
Shadek-Fackenthal Library 492
Shadelands News 77
Shadelands Ranch Historical Museum 77
Shades of the Past Archives 667
Shadow Family 71
Shadows Chronicle 71
Shadows-on-the-Teche Museum Archives 239
Shady Side Rural Heritage Society & Archives 262
Shady Side Rural Heritage Society Newsletter 262
Shafer Historical Museum Archives 610
Shafer-Kilts-Waltermire Family 393
Shafter Historical Society & Library 72
Shaftsbury Historical Museum 579
Shaftsbury Historical Society & Archives 579
Shaker Heights Public Library 457
Shaker Heritage Society & Library 387
Shaker Historical Museum 457
Shaker Historical Society & Archives 457
Shaker Historical Society Journal 457
Shaker Library at Sabbathday Lake 248
Shaker Museum Archives 225, 248, 409
Shaker Museum at South Union Archives 233
Shaker Quarterly 248
Shakers World 95
Shakertown at Pleasant Hill Museum Library 228
Shakertown at Pleasant Hill Museum Quarterly 228
Shakespeare Ghost Town Museum Archives 383
Shakespeare Quarterly 105, 383
Shakin' and Diggin' 234
Shaklee Family 465, 466, 468
Shakopee Heritage Society 315
Shakowi Cultural Center Archives 409
Shalshelet 478
Shambaugh Families Newsletter 200
Shamokin-Coal Township Public Library 501
Shamrock Museum Archives 710
Shand House Museum Archives 677
Shandy Hall House Museum Archives 449
Shank Bone 114
Shankland Family 295
Shanks Family 633
Shannon County Historical and Genealogical Society 342
Shannon Library 710
Shapleigh Community Library 251
Shapleigh Family 247
Shapley Family 557
Shappell Family 489
Sharing History 213, 216
Sharlot Hall Gazette 19
Sharlot Hall Journal 19
Sharlot Hall Museum 19
Sharon Historical Preservation Society 631
Sharon Historical Society 279
Sharon Historical Society & Archives 99
Sharon Historical Society Newsletter 99
Sharon Public Library 279
Sharon Springs Public Library 221
Sharon Temple Historic Site Archives 690
Sharon Township Heritage Society 457
Sharon Woods Village 457
Sharp County Historical Society 25
Sharp County Historical Society Newsletter 25
Sharp County Library 28
Sharp Family 174, 197, 490

Sharp Points 174
Sharpsteen Museum Archives 39
Sharpsteen Museum Newsletter 39
Sharpsville Historical Society 501
Sharptown Historical Society 260
Sharr Family 326
Shasta College Library 61
Shasta College Museum and Research Center Archives 61
Shasta College Museum Report 61
Shasta County Genealogical Society 61
Shasta County Library 61
Shasta Historical Society & Library 61
Shasta State Historic Park Archives 72
Shatook Museum Archives 469
Shattuck Public Library 469
Shaull, Shedenhelm, Slaymaker, Rosenberger, Rumple, Mouser Family 200
Shaver Family 421
Shaw Clan 16, 126, 259
Shaw Family 44, 261
Shaw Historical Library 476
Shaw Historical Society 476
Shaw Island Historical Museum 607
Shaw Island Library and Historical Society & Archives 607
Shawano City-County Library 631
Shawano County Historical Museum 631
Shawano County Historical Society & Archives 631
Shawnee 162
Shawnee County Historical Society & Library 222
Shawnee County Historical Society Newsletter 222
Shawnee Historical Association 188
Shawnee Historical Society & Library 221
Shawnee Library System 154
Shawneetown Historic Site Archives 173
Shawneetown Public Library 173
Shawnigan Lake Historical Museum Archives 655
Shearwater Aviation Museum Archives 676
Sheboygan County Genealogical Society & Library 631
Sheboygan County Genealogist 631
Sheboygan County Historical Museum Archives 631
Sheboygan County Historical Museum Newsletter 631
Sheboygan County Historical Research Center 631
Sheboygan County Historical Society & Archives 631
Sheboygan County Historical Society Quarterly 631
Sheboygan Falls Memorial Library 631
Sheboygan Historical Research Center 631
Sheel(e)y-Schilling-Fisher Family 347
Sheff Family 178
Sheffield Family 268
Sheffield Historical Museum 173
Sheffield Historical Society & Archives 173
Sheffield Historical Society & Library 279
Sheffield Public Library 9, 173
Shelbina Carnegie Public Library 340
Shelbina Genealogical Society & Archives 340
Shelburn(e) Family 608
Shelburne County Genealogical Society & Library 676
Shelburne County Museum Archives 676
Shelburne Historical Society 279
Shelburne Historical Society & Library 676
Shelburne Museum Archives 579
Shelburne Museum Newsletter 579
Shelburne Public Library 364
Shelby County Ancestors 173
Shelby County Genealogical Society 457
Shelby County Genealogical Society & Archives 193
Shelby County Historical and Genealogical Society 173
Shelby County Historical and Genealogical Society Newsletter 173
Shelby County Historical Commission 540
Shelby County Historical Museum 203
Shelby County Historical Quarterly 3
Shelby County Historical Society 457
Shelby County Historical Society & Archives 193, 203, 540
Shelby County Historical Society & Library 340
Shelby County Historical Society & Museum 3
Shelby County Library District 233
Shelby County Museum Archives 540
Shelby Exchange 160
Shelby Family 550
Shelby House Hotel Museum 442
Shelby Iron Works Park Archives 9
Shelby Spirits 457
Shelby Township Historical Association 195
Shelbyville Free Public Library 173
Shelbyville Public Library 193
Sheldon Family 442, 536
Sheldon Jackson Museum Archives 13
Sheldon Museum and Cultural Center Archives 12
Sheldon Peck Homestead Archives 165
Sheldon Public Library 207
Shelf Life 156, 315, 441
Shell Lake Museum Archives 710
Shell Lake Public Library 631
Shell Newsletter 262
Shelley Family 566
Shelter House Archives 487
Shelter House Society 487
Shelter Island Historical Museum 416
Shelter Island Historical Society 415
Shelter Island Historical Society & Archives 416
Shelter Island Historical Society Newsletter 416
Shelter Island Public Library 416
Shelton Historical Society 99
Shelton Historical Society News 99
Shem Tov 691, 693
Shenando News 586
Shenandoah County Historical Society & Archives 586
Shenandoah County Library 586
Shenandoah Valley Discovery Museum Archives 597
Shenango Valley Library 501
Shenendehowa Public Library 394
Shenendehowa Public Library Newsletter 394
Shepard Family 126
Shepard Pruden Memorial Library 426
Shepherd Area Genealogical Society 302
Shepherd Area Historical Society & Library 302
Shepherd Family 607
Shepherdstown Public Library 614
Sheppard Arthur Watson Library 460
Sheppard Family 135, 521
Sheppard Memorial Library 428

Sheppard's Pie 135
Sherbon-Cattermole Family 468
Sherbondy Beacon 220
Sherbrooks Village Museum Archives 676
Sherburn Historical Society 315
Sherburne County Historical Museum 305
Sherburne County Historical Society & Archives 305
Sherburne Memorial Library 577
Sheridan County Fulmer Public Library 637
Sheridan County Historical Museum 637
Sheridan County Historical Society & Archives 637
Sheridan County Historical Society & Library 215, 356
Sheridan County Historical Society Newsletter 215
Sheridan County Library 215, 346
Sheridan Daybreakers Genealogical Society 346
Sheridan Genealogical Society & Archives 637
Sheridan Historical Society 89, 193
Sheridan Memorial Library 560
Sherman County Historical and Genealogical Society 214
Sherman County Historical and Genealogical Society Quarterly 214
Sherman County Historical Society & Library 353, 477
Sherman County Public Library 560
Sherman County: For the Record 477
Sherman Free Library 412
Sherman Historical Society & Library 99
Sherman Historical Society Newsletter 99
Sherman House Museum Archives 451
Sherman Indian Museum Archives 62
Sherman Library and Gardens 41
Sherman Preservation League 560
Sherman Public Library 251, 560
Sherrod Library 528
Sherwin Miller Museum of Jewish History Archives 470
Sherwin Miller Museum of Jewish History Newsletter 470
Sherwood Forest Plantation Archives 585
Sherwood Historical Museum 480
Sherwood Historical Society 480
Sherwood Public Library 480
Sherwood-Davidson House Museum 454
Shiawassee County Genealogical Society & Library 299
Shiawassee County Historical Society & Library 299
Shiawassee District Library-Durand Memorial Branch 290
Shiawassee District Library-Owosso Branch 299
Shiawassee Gazette 299
Shiawassee Stepping Stones 299
Shield 187
Shields Library 42
Shikany Family 341
Shiloh Museum of Arkansas History Archives 32
Shiloh Museum of Arkansas History Newsletter 32
Shiloh National Military Park Library 532
Shiloh Regional Library 528
Shimmin Tveit Museum Archives 439
Shindafer Family 478
Shinebarger-Shoenberger-Shaumberger Family 291
Ship 'N Shore 391
Ship Ashore Resort Museum Archives 72
Ship's Bell 302
Ship's Lamp 302
Shipbuilding Museum 270
Shipley Family 263
Shipman Library 285
Shippensburg Historical Museum 502
Shippensburg Historical Society & Archives 502
Ships of the Sea Maritime Museum Archives 137
Shipshape 507
Shipshewana Area Historical Society 193
Shirley Association Newsletter 42
Shirley Centennial Historical Museum 193
Shirley Centennial Historical Society & Archives 193
Shirley Historical Society & Library 279
Shirley Plantation Archives 585
Shirley-Eustis House Museum Archives 267
Shirley-Eustis Newsletter 267
Shively Newsletter 156, 221
Shivers Newsletter 552
Shoal Creek Living History Museum Archives 332
Shoal Lake Cree Nation 708
Shoal Lake Historical Society & Archives 661
Shoals Public Library 193
Shockey Family 611
Shoemaker Signpost Family Newsletter 549
Shoen Library 476
Shoestring 419
Shomers Journey to America 112
Shop Talk 433
Shorashim 49
Shore Line Trolley Museum Archives 93
Shore Line Trolley Museum Newsletter 93
Shore Village Museum Library 250
Shore Village Museum Library Newsletter 250
Shoreham Historical Society 579
Shoreline Historical Museum Archives 606
Shoreline Memories 606
Shores Memorial Museum Archives 577
Shoreview Historical Society 315
Shorewood Historical Society 631
Shorewood-Troy Public Library District 173
Shorter Mansion Museum Archives 4
Shortgrass Country Museum 469
Shoshone Bannock Tribal Museum Archives 146
Shoshone County Genealogical Society 147
Shoshone County Genealogical Society Quarterly 147
Shoshone Public Library 150
Shoshone Tribal Cultural Center Archives 636
Shoshone-Bannock Library 146
Shoun-Shown-Shawn Family 470
Shove Family 414
Show Low Historical Museum 20
Show Low Historical Society & Archives 20
Show Low Public Library 20
Show Me State Genealogical News 328
Shreve Memorial Library 241
Shreve Memorial Library-Broadmoor 241
Shreveport Campus Library 241
Shrewsbury Historical Society 279
Shrewsbury Historical Society & Library 378
Shrewsbury Public Library 279
Shrewsbury Windle House Archives 189
Shrigley Family 87

Shrigliana 87
Shrine Foundation Historical Society 66
Shumate Newsletter 262
Shupe Family 567, 568
Shurtliff Signatures 549
Shuswap Indian Band 650
Shuswap Nation Tribal Council 651
Shutt Newsletter 262
Sibley County Historical Museum 309
Sibley County Historical Society & Archives 309
Sibley County Historical Society Newsletter 309
Sibley-Cone Memorial Library 134
Sicamous and District Historical Museum 655
Sicamous and District Historical Society & Archives 655
Sicamous and District Museum Archives 655
Sidell Community Historical Society 173
Sidney and North Saanich Historical Society 655
Sidney B Coulter Library 418
Sidney Historical Association & Archives 416
Sidney Historical Association Newsletter 416
Sidney Historical Museum 416
Sidney Historical Museum Archives 655
Sidney Historical Society 173
Sidney Lanier Cottage Museum 133
Sidney Marine Historical Museum Archives 655
Sidney Memorial Public Library 416
Sidney Memorial Public Library Newsletter 416
Sidney Public Library 207, 356
Sidwell-Hufstetler-Hufstutler-Gordy-Frazee Family 568
Siege Museum Archives 592
Siems-Damkroger Family 39
Sierra County Genealogical Society & Archives 385
Sierra County Historical Society & Archives 385
Sierra County Historical Society & Museum 72
Sierra Historic Sites Association & Library 57
Sierra Joint Community College Library 62
Sierra Madre Historical Society 72
Sierra Mono Indian Museum Archives 56
Sierra Museum Archives 66
Sierra Sacramento Valley Medical Society Museum Archives 64
Sierra Vista Genealogical Society 20
Sierra Vista Public Library 20
Sierran 72
Siggard-Grimshaw Family 565
Sigler Family 530
Sign Post 99
Signal Hill National Historic Site Museum Archives 668
Signal Hill Public Library 72
Signal Peak 538
Signal Tower 138
Signals 501, 592
Sikes Adobe Farmstead Archives 66
Sikes-Sykes Family 100, 223
Siksika Cultural Centre 646
Siksika Nation Museum Archives 646
Sila Lydia Bast Bell Museum Archives 622
Silas Bronson Library 100
Silence Family 341
Silent Wings Museum Archives 552
Silicon Valley PAF Users Group 68
Silliman Family 259
Siloam Springs Museum Archives 32
Siloam Springs Museum Newsletter 32
Silsby Free Public Library 359
Silt Historical Museum 89
Silt Historical Society & Archives 89
Silver Bay Public Library 315
Silver City Historical Museum 385
Silver City Historical Society & Archives 385
Silver City Public Library 385
Silver Cliff Museum Archives 89
Silver Falls Library District 480
Silver Ledge Hotel Museum Archives 647
Silver River Museum Archives 118
Silver Spring Historical Society 263
Silvercreek Museum Archives 160
Silverman Heritage Museum Archives 692
Silvers-Rogers Family 587
Silverstein and Hofman Family Ties Newsletter 70
Silverthorn(e) Family 70
Silverton Country Historical Society 480
Silverton Public Library 89
Silvery Slocan Historical Society 652
Silvery Slocan Museum Archives 652
Silz Family 133
Simcock-Simcox Family 40
Simcoe County Ancestors' News 679
Simcoe County Archives 686
Simcoe County Historical Association & Genealogy Branch 679
Simcoe County Museum Archives 679, 686
Simcoe Public Library 690
Simeon Perkins Museum Archives 675
Simi Valley Historical Museum 72
Simi Valley Historical Society & Archives 72
Simkins-Walker Family 570
Simmon Family 203
Simmons Family 463
Simmons Newsletter 50
Simon & Louise Henderson Library 550
Simon Fairfield Public Library 270
Simon Paneak Memorial Museum Archives 11
Simon Schwob Memorial Library 129
Simon Wiesenthal Center Library and Archives 52
Simonian Farms Museum Archives 45
Simonis Family 623
Simpson County Historical Museum 228
Simpson County Historical Society & Archives 228
Simpson Library 588
Simpson-Reed-Corum Family 605
Simpsons: A Gathering of the Clan 37
Simpsonville Historical Society 518
Sims Seeker 154
Simsbury Genealogical and Historical Research Library 99
Simsbury Historical Museum 99
Simsbury Historical Society & Archives 99
Simsbury Public Library 99
Sinclair Clan 362, 424
Sinclair Lewis Museum Archives 315
Sinclairville Free Library 416
Sindecuse Museum of Dentistry Archives 285

INDEX

Sinex Family 608
Singing Bird 437
Singletary Memorial Library 558
Sinking Spring Historical Society 500
Sinkler, Sinclair, St Clair Quarterly 538
Sinton Public Library 560
Sinyard Family 132
Sioux Center Public Library 208
Sioux City Public Library-Wilbur Aalfs Main Library 208
Sioux City Public Museum and Historical Association & Archives 208
Sioux County Historical Society 352
Sioux County Kith and Kin 208
Sioux Empire Medical Museum Archives 523
Sioux Lookout Museum Archives 690
Sioux Lookout Public Library 690
Sioux Rapids Memorial Library 208
Sioux Valley Genealogical Society & Archives 524
Siouxland Heritage Museums Library 524
Siouxland Libraries 524
Sipayik Museum Archives 249
Sippican Historical Society & Library 274
Sir Alexander Galt Museum Archives 644
Sirrine Family 17
Siska Indian Band 652
Siskihou County Museum 78
Siskiyou County Historical Society & Archives 78
Siskiyou County Museum Archives 78
Siskiyou County Public Library 78
Siskiyou Pioneer and Yearbook 78
Sisseton Memorial Library 524
Sisseton Wahpeton Community College Library 524
Sissing Family 304
Sisson Family 275
Sisson Memorial Library 88
Sisson Mirror 55
Sisson Museum Archives 55
Sisson Newsletter 50
Sister Bay Historical Society & Archives 631
Sisterhood B'nai Jacob Library 498
Sisters Of Saint Joseph Of Saint Hyacinthe Bibliotheque 701
Sisters of the Sacred Hearts Archives, Pacific Province 142
Site-Historique du Banc-de-Paspebiac 700
Sitka Historical Society & Archives 13
Sitka Historical Society Newsletter 13
Sitka National Historical Park Archives 13
Sitting Bull College Library 438
Siuslaw Genealogical Society & Archives 475
Siuslaw Public Library 475
Six Mile Regional Library 161
Six Nations Indian Museum Archives 409
Sixteenth Century Journal 333
Sixth Cavalry Museum Archives 131
Sixth Floor Museum at Dealey Plaza Archives 542
Sixth Floor Museum at Dealey Plaza Newsletter 542
Sixth Regiment United States Colored Troops 379
Skaggs Family 338
Skaggs-Miller Family 535
Skagit County Historical Museum 602
Skagit County Historical Museum Library 602
Skagit County Historical Society & Archives 602
Skagit County Historical Society Quarterly Newsletter 602
Skagit Valley Genealogical Society 600
Skagit Valley Genealogical Society Newsletter 600
Skagway Museum Archives 13
Skamokawa Library 607
Skaneateles Historical Society 416
Skaneateles Library Association 416
Skawahlook Indian Band 647
Skeen-Skeins-Skenes Newsletter 553
Skeer Family Organization Newsletter 62
Skeetchestn Indian Band 655
Skelton Family 515
Skene Clan 528
Sketches of Tyler County 563
Skidegate Indian Band 655
Skidompha Library 245
Skinner Kinsmen Update 61
Skinner Museum of Mount Holyoke College Archives 279
Skinner-Legutki-Geshewick Family 61
Skinner-McQueen Family 38
Skippack Historical Society 502
Skipwith Historical and Genealogical Society 321
Skirball Museum 444
Skokie Historical Society & Library 173
Skokie Public Library 173
Skokie Public Library Update 173
Skookumchuck Indian Band 653
Skowhegan History House Museum Archives 251
Skowkale Indian Band 655
Skubinna Family 106
Skunk Museum 446
Skuppah Indian Band 652
Skwah Indian Band 648
Skway Indian Band 648
Sky City Cultural Center 384
Sky Valley Genealogical Society 608
Slagle Family 602
Slagle World 602
Slate 441
Slate Family 44
Slate Run Living Historical Farm Archives 441
Slate Valley Museum Archives 399
Slate Valley Museum Newsletter 399
Slater Public Library 208, 340
Slaton-Slatton Family 5
Slaughter Ranch Museum Archives 16
Slavonic Benevolent Order of the State of Texas & Archives 561
Slavonic Benevolent Order of the State of Texas Archives 561
Slavonic Historical Museum 561
Sleeper Family 576
Sleepy Eye Historical Society 315
Sleepy Hollow and Tarrytown Historical Museum 418
Sliammon Cultural Center 654
Sliammon Nation 654
Slidell Cultural Center Archives 242
Slidell Museum Archives 242
Slifer House Museum Archives 492
Slippery Rock Heritage Association 502
Slippery Rock Heritage Association Newsletter 502
Sloan Family 568

Sloan Public Library 208
Sloane-Stanley Museum and Kent Furnace Archives 95
Sloatsburg Public Library 416
SLO-CO Gen-News 36
Sloss Furnaces National Historic Landmark Archives 2
Sloughhouse Area Genealogical Society 61
Slovak Genealogy Research Center 40
Slovak Heritage and Cultural Society of British Columbia 648
Slovak Heritage and Folklore Society International 414
Slovak Heritage and Folklore Society International Newsletter 414
Slovak Heritage Live 648
Slovak Institute & Library 445
Slovene National Benevolent Society 490
Slovenian Genealogical Society 484
Slovenian Genealogical Society, Canadian Chapter 649
Slovenian Genealogical Society, Colorado Chapter 86
Slovenian Genealogy Society 109
Slovo 198
Smackover Genealogical and Historical Society 32
Small Family 55, 533, 601
Smallwood Family 223
Smallwood State Park Archives 261
Smart Family 542
Smiley Memorial Library 329
Smith County Genealogical Society 322
Smith County Historical and Genealogical Society 525
Smith County Historical Society 216
Smith County Historical Society & Archives 562
Smith County Public Library 525
Smith Family 133, 257, 269, 320, 394, 432, 449, 474, 554, 573, 590, 602
Smith Family Journal 418
Smith Hedrick Newsletter 29
Smith Library 428
Smith Library of Regional History 455
Smith Memorial Library 393
Smith Museum 265
Smith Plantation Home Preservationists 136
Smith Robertson Museum Archives 321
Smith Robertson Museum News 321
Smith Township-Ennismore Historical Society 692
Smith's Castle 508
Smith's Cove Historical Museum Archives 676
Smith's Cove Historical Society 676
Smith's Fort Plantation Archives 596
Smithers Public Library 655
Smithfield Plantation Archives 584
Smithfield Review 584
Smith-Hannah-Terrell Family 119
Smith-Hedrick Family 29
Smith-Myers Family 530
Smiths Falls Public Library 690
Smiths Falls Railway Museum of Eastern Ontario 690
Smithsburg Historical Society 263
Smithsonian Institute Archives 106
Smith-Taylor Connections 442
Smithtown Historical Museum 416
Smithtown Historical Society & Archives 416
Smithtown Library 416
Smith-Trahern Mansion Archives 526
Smithville Community Historical Society 457
Smithville Historical Society 340
Smith-Zimmerman State Museum Archives 522
Smith-Zimmerman State Museum Newsletter 522
Smoke and Cinders 526
Smoke Signal 40
Smoke Signals 335, 345, 475
Smokey Bear Museum Archives 382
Smoki Museum of American Indian Culture Library 19
Smoky Hill Museum 221
Smoky Hill Museum Archives 221
Smoky Mountain Historical Society 532
Smoky Mountain Historical Society Newsletter 532
Smoky Mountain Trains Museum Archives 424
Smoky Mountain Trains Museum Newsletter 424
Smoky Valley Genealogical Society & Archives 221
Smoky Valley Genealogical Society and Library Newsletter 221
Smoky Valley Historical Association & Archives 217
Smurtwaite House Museum 19
Smyrna Heritage Association 104
Smyrna Heritage Association Museum 104
Smyrna Historical and Genealogical Society & Archives 137
Smyrna Museum 137
Smyrna Public Library 104, 137
Smyser Family 506
Smyth County Historical and Museum Society & Archives 590
Smyth County Historical Museum 590
Smyth Public Library 359
Smyth-Bland Regional Library 590
Snake River Genealogical Society of Southeastern Idaho 150
Snake River Heritage Center Archives 150
Snakeroot Extract 186
Snap Roll II 72
Snead Family 447
Sneary Family Association Newsletter 128
Snell-Timmerman-Zimmerman Newsletter 403
Snider Family 338
Snipes Family 384
Snodgrass Clan 596
Snohomish County Historical Association & Archives 601
Snohomish Historical Society & Archives 607
Snoqualmie Valley Historical Museum 603
Snoqualmie Valley Historical Society & Archives 603
Snoqualmie Valley Historical Society Quarterly 603
Snow Family 258, 569
Snow Library 277
Snowflake-Taylor Public Library 20
Snow-Isle Regional Library 603
Snug Harbor Cultural Center Archives 417
Snyder County Historical Society & Library 494
Snyder County Library 501
Snyder Family 115
Snyder Museum Archives 235
Snyder-Snider-Schneider Family 458
Soboba Band of Mission 67
Socie Scroll 379
Societe d'Histoire d'Amos & Bibliotheque 697
Societe d'Histoire de L'Epiphanie 699
Societe d'Histoire de Lanoraie D'Autray 699
Societe d'Histoire de Lavaltrie 699
Societe d'Histoire de MRC L'Assomption 699

INDEX

Societe d'Histoire de Saint-Calixte 701
Societe d'Histoire de Saint-Donat 702
Societe d'Histoire de Saint-Paul 702
Societe d'Histoire de Shefford & Bibliotheque 698
Societe d'Histoire de St-Jean-de-Matha 702
Societe d'histoire et d'archeologie des Monts 702
Societe d'histoire et d'Archeologie des Monts & Bibliotheque 702
Societe d'histoire et de genealogie de la Matapedia 698
Societe d'histoire et de genealogie de Maria Chapdeleine 697
Societe d'Histoire et de Genealogie de Matane 699
Societe d'histoire et de genealogie de Matane 699
Societe d'histoire et de genealogie de Riviere-du-Loup 701
Societe d'histoire et de genealogie de Saint-Prosper 702
Societe d'histoire et de genealogie de Salaberry 703
Societe d'histoire et de genealogie de Verdun 704
Societe d'histoire et de genealogie des Bois-Francs 704
Societe d'Histoire et Genealogie Sainte-Julienne 702
Societe d'Histoire et Souvenirs Saint-Roch 703
Societe d'Histoire Region Terrebonne 698
Societe d'Histoire Regionale de Nicolet & Bibliotheque 700
Societe de Developpement Culturel de Terrebonne 703
Societe de genealogie de Drummondville 697
Societe de Genealogie de l'Outaouais & Bibliotheque 698
Societe de genealogie de la Cote-Nord 703
Societe de Genealogie de Lanaudiere 698
Societe de Genealogie de Quebec & Bibliotheque 702
Societe de Genealogie des Cantons de l'Est & Bibliotheque 703
Societe de genealogie des Laurentides 702
Societe de genealogie Saint-Hubert 702
Societe de genealogie Salaberry de Valleyfield 703
Societe des Filles du roi et soldats du Carignan 394
Societe du patrimoine et de genealogie de Rouyn-Noranda 701
Societe du patrimoine et de genealogie du Canton Nedelec 700
Societe Franco-Ontarienne d'Histoire et de Genealogie, Region Saint-Laurent 681
Societe Genealogigue du Nord-Ouest 643
Societe Genealogique Canadienne-Francaise & Bibliotheque 700
Societe Genealogique Canadienne-Francaise Memoires 700
Societe genealogique d'Argenteuil 699
Societe Genealogique de l'Est du Quebec 701
Societe Genealogique de L'est du Quebec & Bibliotheque 701
Societe genealogique de la Presqu'ile 702
Societe genealogique de la region de l'Amiante 703
Societe genealogique de Montmagny 699
Societe genealogique du KRT 702
Societe Genealogique du Saguenay & Bibliotheque 697
Societe genealogique Les Patriotes 703
Societe Historique Acadienne 664
Societe Historique Acadienne de la Baie Sainte-Marie 673
Societe Historique de la Cote du Sud & Bibliotheque 698
Societe Historique de la Gaspesie & Bibliotheque 698
Societe historique de la Saskatchewan 709
Societe Historique de Madawaska 663
Societe Historique de Saint Boniface Bulletin 661
Societe Historique des Bernier d'Amerique & Bibliotheque 697
Societe Historique du Madawaska & Archives 663
Societe Historique du Madawaska Revue 663
Societe historique et genealogique de Sainte-Julienne 702
Societe Historique et Genealogique de Smoky River 642
Societe historique et genealogique de Trois-Pistoles 703
Societe Historique Nicolas-Denys & Archives 665
Societe Monteregienne de genealogie 697
Society for Creative Anachronism 54
Society for Georgia Archaeology 125
Society for German Genealogy in Eastern Europe 642
Society for Historical Archaeology 262
Society for Italian Historical Studies 269
Society for Italian Historical Studies Newsletter 269
Society for the Historic Preservation of Franklin County & Library 152
Society for the History of Czechoslovak Jews 400
Society for the History of Germans in Maryland 256
Society for the Preservation of Laurel Grove 137
Society for the Preservation of Long Island Antiquities & Archives 394
Society for the Preservation of Long Island Antiquities Museum 394
Society for the Preservation of Ohio One Room Schools 453
Society for the Preservation of Old Mills 295
Society for the Preservation of Old Mills & Library 189
Society for the Preservation of the Eastern Head, Digby Neck and Islands Genealogical Division 675
Society Happenings 315
Society of Acadian Descendants 66
Society of American Archivists 156
Society of Architectural Historians, Southern California Chapter 59
Society of Automotive Historians, Wisconsin Chapter 622
Society of California Archivists 37
Society of California Pioneers & Library 67
Society of California Pioneers Museum 67
Society of Civil War Families of Ohio 452
Society of Civil War Families of Ohio Report 452
Society of Colonial Wars 408
Society of Colonial Wars Bulletin 406, 408
Society of Colonial Wars in the State of Illinois 158
Society of Descendants of the Signers of the Constitution 498
Society of First Families of South Carolina 1670-1700 & Library 512
Society of Friends & Library 498
Society of Georgia Archivists 125
Society of Georgia Archivists Newsletter 125
Society of Hispanic Historical and Ancestral Research 54
Society of Historic Sharonville 457
Society of Indiana Pioneers 187
Society of Indiana Pioneers Year Book 187
Society of Loyalist Descendants of the American Revolution 432
Society of Maine Archivists 247
Society of Mayflower Descendants 516
Society of Mayflower Descendants & Library 408
Society of Mayflower Descendants in Connecticut 100
Society of Mayflower Descendants in Connecticut & Library 94
Society of Mayflower Descendants in the State of Arizona 15, 16, 22
Society of Middletown First Settlers Descendants 1650-1700 96
Society of Ohio Archivists & Library 446
Society of Pioneers of Montgomery & Library 7
Society of Richmond County, North Carolina Descendants 432
Society of Rocky Mountain Archivists 84, 635
Society of the Cincinnati 20
Society of the Cincinnati & Library 106
Society of the Danube Swabians in Chicago 158
Society of the Descendants of Washington's Army at Valley Forge, Alabama Brigade 6
Society of the Founders of Norwich Connecticut & Archives 97
Society of the History of the Early American Republic 195

Society of the Old Creek Cross 590
Society of The Sacred Heart Archives 340
Society of the War of 1812 in the State of Georgia 126
Society of the War of 1812 in the State of Illinois 169
Society Page 46
Society Story 176
Society Times 627
Society's Page 176
Socorro County Historical Society & Library 385
Socorro Public Library 385
Sod Buster Museum Archives 346
Sod House Museum Archives 352, 463, 671
Sod Line Historical Museum Archives 711
Soda Creek Indian Band 657
Soda Springs Public Library 150
Sodbuster Archives Museum Archives 646
Sodus Bay Historical Museum 416
Sodus Bay Historical Society & Archives 416
Sodus Bay Historical Society Newsletter 416
Sodus Township Library 302
Soeurs Ursulines De Quebec Archives 701
Sokol South Omaha Czechoslovak Society 355
Solana Beach Civic Historical Society 72
Solano County Genealogical Society & Library 44
Solano County Historic Records Commission 44
Solano County Historical Society & Library 76
Solano County Library 44
Solano Historian 76
Soldiers & Sailors Memorial Bldg Museum Archives 400
Soldiers Memorial Library 247
Soldiers National Museum Archives 488
Soldiers' Memorial Military Museum Archives 340
Soldotna Historical Museum 13
Soldotna Historical Society 13
Solliday-Sallade Family 371
Solomon Family 133
Solomon Harkey House 162
Solomon R Baker Library 281
Solomon Steele Williams and Eliza Ann Miller Bulletin 17
Solon Springs Historical Society & Archives 631
Solvay Public Library 416
Sombra Township Museum Archives 690
Somers Historical Society & Archives 416
Somers Historical Society & Library 99
Somers Library Friends 416
Somers Mansion Museum Archives 378
Somers Public Library 99, 416
Somerset County Historial Center 502
Somerset County Historical Society 261
Somerset County Historical Society & Library 368
Somerset County Library 368
Somerset County Library System 261
Somerset Historical Society 279
Somerset Place State Historic Site Archives 425
Somerset Place State Historic Site Newsletter 425
Somerset Public Library 279, 631
Somersworth Public Library 364
Somervell County Historical Society & Archives 547
Somervell County Museum 547
Somerville Family 19
Somerville Historical Museum 279
Somerville Historical Museum Library 279
Somerville Historical Society & Archives 279
Somerville Public Library 279
Somerville Public Library 378
Somerville-Fayette County Library 532
Sommerfeld Family 357
Songhees Indian Band 657
Sonnenberg Gardens & Mansion Museum Archives 392
Sonnenschein 483
Sonoma County Genealogical Society 71
Sonoma County Historical Society 71
Sonoma County Library-Santa Rosa Local History and Genealogy Annex 71
Sonoma County Museum Archives 71
Sonoma League for Historic Preservation & Library 73
Sonoma Searcher 71
Sonoma State Historic Park Archives 73
Sonoma Valley Historical Society & Archives 73
Sonoma Valley Legacy 73
Sonoma Valley Notes 73
Sons and Daughters of the Blue and Gray Civil War Roundtable 335
Sons and Daughters of the Cherokee Strip Pioneers 465
Sons and Daughters of the Province and Republic of West Florida 236
Sons and Daughters of the Province and Republic of West Florida, 1763-1810 236
Sons of Confederate Veterans 20, 258
Sons of Confederate Veterans & Library 526
Sons of Confederate Veterens, McDaniel-Curtis Camp #165 128
Sons of Italy Times 498
Sons of Italy, Grand Lodge of Pennsylvania 498
Sons of Norway & Library 311
Sons of Norway Viking 311
Sons of Sherman's March to the Sea 21
Sons of the American Revolution & Library 46
Sons of the American Revolution Magazine 230
Sons of the American Revolution, Alabama Society 7
Sons of the American Revolution, Alaska Society 11
Sons of the American Revolution, Arizona Society 18, 19, 21, 22
Sons of the American Revolution, Arkansas Society 25
Sons of the American Revolution, Colorado Society 81
Sons of the American Revolution, Connecticut Society 93
Sons of the American Revolution, Delaware Society 104
Sons of the American Revolution, Empire State Society 404
Sons of the American Revolution, Florida Society 113
Sons of the American Revolution, Georgia Society 129
Sons of the American Revolution, Hawaii Society 142
Sons of the American Revolution, Illinois Society 156, 168
Sons of the American Revolution, Indiana Society 187
Sons of the American Revolution, Iowa Society 205
Sons of the American Revolution, Louisiana Society 236
Sons of the American Revolution, Maine Society 248
Sons of the American Revolution, Maryland Society 264
Sons of the American Revolution, Massachusetts Society 267
Sons of the American Revolution, Michigan Society 301
Sons of the American Revolution, Minnesota Society 311
Sons of the American Revolution, Mississippi Society 321
Sons of the American Revolution, Montana Society 343
Sons of the American Revolution, Nebraska Society 353
Sons of the American Revolution, New Jersey Society & Library 377
Sons of the American Revolution, New Mexico Society 381

Sons of the American Revolution, North Carolina Society 434
Sons of the American Revolution, Northeastern Ohio Chapter 450
Sons of the American Revolution, Ohio Department 457
Sons of the American Revolution, Ohio Society 447
Sons of the American Revolution, Oklahoma Society 470
Sons of the American Revolution, Oregon Society 473
Sons of the American Revolution, Pennsylvania Society 496
Sons of the American Revolution, Rhode Island Societ 507
Sons of the American Revolution, South Carolina Society 518
Sons of the American Revolution, Utah Society 573
Sons of the American Revolution, Vermont Society 578
Sons of the American Revolution, Virginia Society 586
Sons of the American Revolution, Virginia Society 594
Sons of the American Revolution, Washington Society 606
Sons of the American Revolution, West Virginia Chapter 613
Sons of the American Revolution, Wisconsin Society 627
Sons of the American Revolution, Wyoming Society 637
Sons Of The Revolution, Gen John Sevier Chapter 532
Sons of the Union Veterans of the Civil War, Ohio Department (and Auxilliary) 455
Sons of Union Veterans of the Civil War 489
Sons of Union Veterans of the Civil War, Illinois Department 168, 177
Sons of Union Veterans of the Civil War, Ohio Department 457
Sooke Region Museum Library 655
Soowahlie Indian Band 649
Sophienburg Musuem 555
Sorrells Family 375
Sosa-Carillo-Fremont House Museum Archives 22
Sotterley Plantation Museum Archives 260
Sou'wester 607
Soule Family 387
Sound Historian: Journal of the Texas Oral History Association 562
Sounder 607
Sounding Board 484
Soundings 627
Sounds Like 314
Source 178, 180
Sourisseau Academy for State & Local History Archives 68
South Arkansas Historical Foundation 27
South Arkansas Historical Society 27
South Bannock County Historical Museum 147
South Bannock County Historical Society & Archives 147
South Bay Cities Genealogical Society & Library 75
South Bay Genealogy Club 122
South Bay Historical Railroad Society 70
South Bay Historical Society 56
South Beloit Historical Society 174
South Bend Area Genealocial Society 189
South Bend Area Genealogical Society 193
South Bend Area Genealogical Society Quarterly 189
South Bethlehem Historical Society 483
South Boston-Halifax County Museum Newsletter 595
South Boston-Halifax County Museum of Fine Arts and History Archives 595
South Brevard Historical Society 114, 117
South Bristol Historical Society 251
South Brunswick Public Library 373
South Cariboo Historical Museum Archives 648
South Carolina Archives Department 513
South Carolina Confederate Relic Room and Museum Library 513
South Carolina Cotton Museum Archives 511
South Carolina Cotton Museum Newsletter 511
South Carolina Department of Archives and History 513
South Carolina Genealogical Research 529
South Carolina Genealogical Society 513
South Carolina Historical Magazine 512
South Carolina Historical Museum 512
South Carolina Historical Society & Archives 512
South Carolina Law Enforcement Officers Hall of Fame 513
South Carolina Magazine of Ancestral Research 513
South Carolina Military Museum Archives 513
South Carolina National Guard Museum Archives 518
South Carolina Railroad Museum Archives 519
South Carolina State Library 513
South Carolina State Museum Archives 513
South Caroliniana Society & Library 514
South Central Area Library 437
South Central Genealogical Society 308
South Central Kentucky Historical and Genealogical Society 228
South Central Kentucky Historical and Genealogical Society Quarterly 228
South Central Nebraska Genealogical Society 354
South Central Pennsylvania Genealogical Society 506
South Central Virginia Genealogical Society 592
South Central Wisconsin Genealogical Society 625
South Charleston Museum Archives 614
South Charleston Public Library 614
South China Library 251
South Cities Genealogical Society Newsletter 75
South Coast Railroad Museum at Goleta Depot Archives 46
South County Historical Society & Archives 36
South County Library 389
South County Library Newsletter 389
South County Museum Archives 508
South Custer County Historical Society 148
South Dakota Genealogical Society 523
South Dakota Genealogical Society Newsletter 523
South Dakota Genealogical Society Quarterly 523
South Dakota Hall of Fame Archives 521
South Dakota Hall of Fame Magazine 521
South Dakota History 523
South Dakota National Guard Museum Archives 523
South Dakota State Archives 523
South Dakota State Historical Society & Library 523
South Dakota State Library 523
South Dakota Tractor Museum Archives 522
South Delta Library Services 323
South Dumfries Historical Society & Archives 690
South East Missouri Record 333
South End Historical Society 267
South Florida History Magazine 117
South Florida Museum Archives 109
South Florida Museum Archives Newsletter 109
South Florida Railway Museum Archives 111
South Georgia Genealogical Society 135, 138
South Georgia Regional Library 139
South Georgia Regional Library System-Statenville Branch 137
South Grey Museum and Historical Library 682
South Hadley Library System 279
South Hampton Free Public Library 364
South Haven Memorial Library 302
South Hero Bicentennial Museum Archives 579

South Hillsborough Genealogists 119
South Holland Historical Society 174
South Howard County Historical Society 336
South Humboldt Historical and Genealogical Society 46
South King County Genealogical Society & Library 602
South King Newsletter 602
South Kingstown Public Library 509
South Londonderry Free Library 579
South Lyon Area Historical Society 302
South Milwaukee Historical Museum 631
South Milwaukee Historical Society 631
South Milwaukee Historical Society Quarterly 631
South Mississippi Genealogical Society & Library 320
South of the Mountains 405
South Okanagan Genealogical Society & Archives 653
South Orange County, California Genealogical Society 54
South Park City Museum 84
South Park Historical Foundation & Archives 84
South Pasadena Public Library 73
South Pass City State Historic Site Archives 637
South Peace Historical Society & Archives 649
South Peach Centennial Museum 641
South Piedmont Community College Library 431
South Pierce County Historical Society 601
South Plains Genealogical Society & Library 552
South Plains Genealogical Society Newsletter 552
South Platte Valley Historical Society 85
South Portland Public Library 251
South Portland-Cape Elizabeth Historical Society 251
South Rawdon Museum Archives 676
South River Historical and Preservation Society 378
South River Meeting House Archives 590
South River-Machar Union Public Library 690
South Ryegate Public Library 579
South Saint Paul Historical Society 315
South Saint Paul Public Library 315
South San Francisco Public Library 73
South San Francisco Public Library, Grand Avenue Branch 73
South Sebastian County Historical Society 28
South Shore Genealogical Society 675
South Shore Genealogical Society & Library 276
South Simcoe Pioneer Museum Archives 679
South Similkameen Museum Archives 651
South Sioux City Public Library 356
South Street Seaport Museum Archives 408
South Suburban College Library 174
South Suburban Genealogical and Historical Society 162, 174
South Suburban Genealogical and Historical Society Newsletter 174
South Suburban Heritage Association 175
South Texas Genealogical Society 538, 547
South Texas Genealogical Society Quarterly 538
South Texas Museum Archives 535
South Thurston County Historical Society & Archives 609
South Thurston County Historical Society Newsletter 609
South Umpqua Historical Museum 477
South Umpqua Historical Society 474
South Umpqua Historical Society & Archives 477
South Union Messenger 225
South Vernon Genealogical Society 340
South Western Public Libraries 449
South Whidbey Genealogical Group 601
South Whidbey Historical Society 603
South Whitley-Cleveland Township Public Library 193
South Windsor Historical Society 99
South Windsor Public Library 99
South Wood County Historical Corporation Newsletter 634
South Wood County Historical Society & Archives 634
Southampton Colonial Society & Archives 417
Southampton Colonial Society Museum 417
Southampton Colonial Society Newsletter 417
Southampton Historical Society & Library 379
Southard Family 435
Southard Genealogy Research Center 3
Southard House Museum Archives 250
Southborough Historical Society 279
Southbury Historical Society & Library 99
Southbury Historical Society Newsletter 99
South-Central Missouri Genealogical Society 342
Southdown Plantation 237
Southeast Alabama Genealogical and Historical Society & Library 3
Southeast Alabama Genealogical and Historical Society Quarterly 3
Southeast Arkansas Genealogical Society & Archives 30
Southeast Arkansas Historical Museum 30
Southeast Arkansas Regional Library 30
Southeast Arkansas Regional Library-Dermott Branch 26
Southeast Arkansas Regional Library-Dumas Branch 27
Southeast Arkansas Regional Library-McGehee Branch Library 30
Southeast Arkansas Regional Library-Star City Branch 33
Southeast Arkansas Regional Library-Warren Branch 33
Southeast Florida Regional Preservation Office 112
Southeast Kansas Genealogical Society & Archives 216
Southeast Louisiana Historical Association 237
Southeast Louisiana Historical Association Papers 237
Southeast Missouri Regional Museum Archives 326
Southeast Museum Association Archives 390
Southeast Nebraska Genealogical Society & Archives 349
Southeast Sentinel 390
Southeast Side Historical Museum Archives 153
Southeast Steuben County Library 394
Southeast Texas Genealogical and Historical Society 537
Southeast Treaty 4 Tribal Council 711
Southeastern Colorado Genealogical Society & Library 89
Southeastern Community College Library 434
Southeastern Lincoln County Historical Society 608
Southeastern New Mexico Genealogical Society & Archives 383
Southeastern North Carolina Genealogical Society 434
Southeastern Railway Museum Archives 130
SoutheastTexas Genealogical and Historical Society Newsletter 537
Souther Family 267
Southern Aroostook Historical Society & Archives 247
Southern Baptist Convention Archives Center 594
Southern Baptist Historical Library and Archives 531
Southern Baptist Periodical Index 325
Southern California Chapter, OGS 77
Southern California Chapter, Ohio Genealogical Society 51
Southern California Genealogical Society 46
Southern California Genealogical Society & Library 38
Southern California Historical Aviation Foundation & Archives 47
Southern California Jewish Historical Society 52
Southern California Quarterly 52

Southern Californian 52
Southern Dutchess News 395, 419
Southern Echoes 126
Southern Forest Heritage Museum Archives 238
Southern Friend: Journal of the North Carolina Friends Historical Society 427
Southern Genealogist's Exchange Society & Library 114
Southern Genealogists Exchange Quarterly 114
Southern Highland Handicraft Guild Museum and Library 423
Southern Historian 9, 230, 549
Southern Humboldt Roots and Trails 46
Southern Indiana Genealogical Society 188, 190
Southern Indiana Genealogical Society Newsletter 190
Southern Indiana Genealogical Society Quarterly 190
Southern Jewish Historical Society 424
Southern Kentucky Genealogical Society & Library 225
Southern Lancaster County Historical Society 500
Southern Lancaster County Historical Society Newsletter 500
Southern Lorain County Historical Society & Archives 459
Southern Lorain County Historical Society Newsletter 459
Southern Methodist University Central Library 542
Southern Michigan Genealogical Society 285, 296
Southern Michigan Genealogical Society Newsletter 285
Southern Mono Historical Society 53
Southern Museum of Flight Archives 2
Southern Museum of Flight Newsletter 2
Southern Museum of Flight Quarterly 2
Southern New Mexico Genealogical Society 383
Southern Newfoundland Seamen's Museum Archives 667
Southern Ohio Genealogical Society 450
Southern Ohio Museum and Cultural Center Archives 456
Southern Ohio Museum Newsletter 456
Southern Ontario Heritage Village Archives 684
Southern Oregon Heritage 477
Southern Oregon Historical Museum 477
Southern Oregon Historical Society & Archives 477
Southern Oregon University Library 473
Southern Peaks Public Library 81
Southern Pines Public Library 433
Southern Plains Indian Museum Archives 463
Southern Queries 426
Southern Roots and Shoots 136
Southern Society of Genealogists & Library 2
Southern Studies Institute 239
Southern Studies Journal 239
Southern Tier Genealogy Club of Broome County 419
Southern Tier Genealogy Club of Broome County Newsletter 419
Southern Tier Library System 410
Southern Tier Library System-Mabel D Blodgett Memorial 414
Southern Tuolumne County Historical Society 46
Southern Ute Indian Cultural Center 86
Southern Wasco County Library-Maupin Library 476
Southey and District Museum Archives 710
Southington Genealogical Society & Library 98
Southington Historical Museum 99
Southington Historical Society & Archives 99
Southington Public Library 99
Southold Free Library 417
Southold Historical Museum 417
Southold Historical Society & Archives 417
Southold Historical Society Newsletter 417
Southport Echo 623
Southport Historical Society & Library 433
Southport Newsletter 623
Southside Regional Library 584
Southside Virginian: A Journal of Genealogy and History 594
Southwest Arkanasas Regional Archives 33
Southwest Arkansas Genealogical Society 30
Southwest Arkansas Regional Historical Society 33
Southwest Arkansas Regional Library 28, 31
Southwest Arkansas Regional Library-Howard County 31
Southwest Arkansas Regional Library-Nevada County 32
Southwest Arkansas Regional Library-Polk County 30
Southwest Baptist University Library 325
Southwest Butler County Genealogical Society 449
Southwest Butler County Genealogical Society Newsletter 449
Southwest Chronicle 552
Southwest Collection Special Collections Library 552
Southwest Cuyahoga Chapter, OGS 455, 458
Southwest Cuyahoga Chapter, OGS Newsletter 458
Southwest Dairy Museum Archives 561
Southwest Florida Historical Society 113
Southwest Florida Museum of History Archives 113
Southwest Florida Museum of History Newsletter 113
Southwest Genealogical Society 559
Southwest Georgia Genealogical Society 125
Southwest Georgia Regional Library 127
Southwest Georgia Regional Library-Seminole County Public Library 130
Southwest Harbor Public Library 251
Southwest Historical Quarterly 537
Southwest Louisiana Genealogical Society 238
Southwest Louisiana Genealogy and History Library 238
Southwest Louisiana Historical Association 238
Southwest Minnesota Historical Center 310
Southwest Mississippi Community College Library 322
Southwest Missouri Genealogical Society 327
Southwest Museum 51
Southwest Museum Archives 52
Southwest Nebraska Genealogical Society & Archives 354
Southwest Oklahoma Genealogical Society & Library 466
Southwest Pennsylvania Genealogical Service 492
Southwest Railroad Historical Society & Archives 542
Southwest Seattle Historical Society & Library 606
Southwest Texas Genealogical Society & Library 562
Southwest Virginia Museum Historical State Park Archives 584
Southwest Wisconsin Cornish Society 627
Southwest Wisconsin Library System 621
Southwestern Bell Library 340
Southwestern Community College Library 433
Southwestern Historical Quarterly 537
Southwestern Indiana Historical Society 183
Southwestern Michigan College Museum Archives 290
Southwestern Michigan College Museum Newsletter 290
Southwestern North Carolina Genealogical Quarterly 430
Southwestern North Carolina Genealogical Society & Library 430
Southwestern North Dakota Genealogical Society 439
Southwestern Ontario Heritage Village Archives 693
Southwestern Oregon Community College Library 474
Southwestern Saskatchewan Oldtimer's Museum Archives 708
Southwestern Virginia Genealogical Society 594
Southworth Chronicle 150

Southworth Family 565
Southworth Hall Newsletter 38
Southworth Library 392
Southworth Library Association 395
Souza-de Souza Family 142
Space Center Houston Archives 549
Spadina Museum 692
Spalding Memorial Library 482
Spalding University Library 230
Spallumcheen Indian Band 649
Spanaway Historical Society 607
Spanish American Genealogical Association 541
Spanish Governor's Palace Archives 559
Spanish History Museum Archives 381
Spanish River Papers 109
Spanishtown Historical Society & Library 47
Spannuth-Kohlmeier Family 266
Sparta Public Library 174, 378
Sparta Township Library 302
Sparta-Hancock County Historical Society 137
Spartanburg County Historical Association & Library 518
Spartanburg County Public Library 518
Spartanburg County Regional Museum Archives 518
Spartanburg Historical Association 518
Spartanburg Historical Association & Archives 517
Sparwood Public Library 655
Spaulding Memorial Library 251
Speak! 105
Speaking Relatively 451
Speaking Trumpet 272
Speakman Family 566
Spear News 116
Special Edition 189
Speculum: A Journal of Medieval Studies 268
Speedreader 193
Speedway Public Library 193
Speedwell Historical Museum 374
Speer Memorial Library 554
Spence Newsletter 82
Spencer Brook Historical Society 313
Spencer County Historical and Genealogical Society 233
Spencer County Historical Society & Archives 192
Spencer County Public Library 192
Spencer Family 527
Spencer Family Historical and Genealogical Society 113
Spencer Historical Society 457
Spencer Library 48
Spencer Public Library 208
Spencer Research Library 217
Spencer-Pierce-Little Farm Museum Archives 275
Spertus Institute of Jewish Studies 156
Spertus Museum 155
Spialaseequtt Museum Archives 671
Spiceland Town-Township Public Library 194
Spiegel Grove 448
Spillman Library 628
Spindletop-Gladys City Boomtown Museum Archives 537
Spink County Historical Society 523
Spipweske Museum Archives 661
Spire Historic Building Archives 549
Spirit 58, 431
Spirit Creek Baptist Church Archives 127
Spirit Family 334
Spirit Lake Historical Society 150
Spirit Lake Public Library 208
Spirit of '76 Museum 459
Spirit River and District Historical Museum 646
Spirit River and District Historical Society & Archives 646
Spjst Museum 561
Spjst Vestnik 561
Split Rock Lighthouse Archives 316
Spokane County Historic Preservation Office 607
Spokane County Library District 607
Spokane House Interpretative Center Archives 603
Spokane Public Library 607
Spokane Tribe of Indians Tribal Council 609
Spoke Wheel Car Museum Archives 695
Spolight 182
Spoon River Public Library 157
Sporran 31
Spotswood Family 218
Spotswood Public Library 378
Spotsylvania Historical Association & Archives 595
Spotsylvania Historical Museum 595
Spradling-Baker Newsletter 180
Sprague Family 629
Sprague Historical Society 91
Sprague Museum 399
Sprayberry-Spraberry-Sprabary Family 551
Spreading Wings 151
Spring Creek County Historical Association & Archives 561
Spring Creek County Historical Association Newsletter 561
Spring Creek County Historical Museum 561
Spring Ford Area Historical Society 501
Spring Green Community Library 631
Spring Grove Area Historical Preservation Society 502
Spring Grove Hospital Museum Archives 257
Spring Hill Genealogy and Historical Society 533
Spring Hill Genealogy and Historical Society Newsletter 533
Spring Hill Historic Home Archives 452
Spring Lake Historical Society & Library 378
Spring Lake Historical Society Newsletter 378
Spring Street Historical Museum Archives 241
Spring Street Historical Museum Newsletter 241
Spring Valley Community Historical Society & Archives 315
Spring Valley Historical Museum 315
Spring Valley Historical Society 73, 315
Springboro Historical Museum 457
Springboro Historical Society & Archives 457
Springbrook Church Museum Archives 631
Springdale School Museum Archives 261
Springer-Pricket Family 447
Springfield Area Historical Society 315
Springfield Armory National Historic Site Library 280
Springfield City Library 280
Springfield Free Public Library 378
Springfield Free Public Library Newsletter 378
Springfield Historical Museum 378
Springfield Historical Society 502
Springfield Historical Society & Archives 378

INDEX

Springfield Historical Society & Library 580
Springfield Museum Archives 480
Springfield Museum of Old Domestic Life Archives 428
Springfield Public Library 315, 480
Springfield Town Library 580
Springfield Township Historical Society 289
Springfield Township Library 502
Springfield-Greene County Library 341
Springhill Miner's Museum Archives 676
Springs Historical Society of the Casselman Valley & Archives 502
Springville Museum 73
Springville Public Library 572
Spritsail 271
Spruce Grove Public Library 646
Spruce Pine Public Library 433
Spruce Row Museum Archives 692
Spur and Phoenix 203
Spurlock Family 525
Spurlock Family Quarterly 525
Spuzzum Indian Indian Band 657
Spy Hill Museum Historical Museum 710
Spy Hill Museum Historical Society & Archives 710
Spyglass 121
Squamish Nation 653
Squamish Public Library 655
Squamish Valley Museum Archives 650, 655
Squan Village Historical Society 372
Square Notes 431
Squiala Indian Band 648
Squires Family 425
SS Jeremiah O'Brien 67
SS Moyle National Historic Site Archives 651
SSGHS Research Series 174
Stabler-Leadbeater Apothecary Museum Archives 583
Stabler-Stabley Family 481
Stack Talk 66
Stackhouse Newsletter 262
Stacy Stories 153
Stacy's Tavern Museum 161
Stacyville Public Library 208
Stadel Family 288
Staff Reporter 238
Stafford Air and Space Museum Archives 471
Stafford County Historical and Genealogical Society 221
Stafford Historical Society & Library 99
Stafford Historical Society Newsletter 99
Stag and Thistle 536
Stage Lines 56
Stagecoach Inn Museum 56
Stagecoach Inn Museum Archives 56
Stagecoach Library for Genealogical Research 84
Stagecoach Museum 637
Stagecoach Stops 86
Stageline 635
Stairs to Stubbs 149
Staked Plains 554
Stalkin' Kin 558
Stamford Historical Museum 99
Stamford Historical Society & Archives 99
Stamford Historical Society Newsletter 99
Stamford Museum Archives 99
Stamford Museum Newsletter 99
Stamford Village Library 417
Stammbaum 124
Stan Hywet Hall and Gardens Magazine 441
Stan Hywet Hall Museum Archives 441
Stanback Family 427
Standard Bearer 499
Standing Buffalo Dakota Nation 706
Standing Rock Sioux Tribal Offices 521
Standish Historical Society & Library 251
Standridge Kith n' Kin 30
Standt-Stoudt-Stout Family 501
Stanfield Public Library 480
Stanford Historian 73
Stanford Historical Society 73
Stanford University Museum Archives 73
Stanislaus County Free Library 54
Stanislaus County Genealogical Society 54
Stanislaus Library 75
Stanislaus Researcher 54
Stanislaus Stepping Stones 54
Stanley County Genealogical Society 423
Stanley County Genealogical Society Journal 423
Stanley County Public Library 423
Stanley Family 457
Stanley Heritage Association 150
Stanley Historical Museum 631
Stanley Historical Society Newsletter 631
Stanley Hotel Museum Archives 84
Stanley Museum Archives 247
Stanley Museum Quarterly 247
Stanley Ranch Museum 46
Stanley Stepping Stones 190
Stanley Tubbs Memorial Library 469
Stanley Whitman House Library 93
Stanley Whitman House Library Newsletter 93
Stanley-Whitman House 93
Stannard Historical Society 576
Stansberry Family 45
Stansbury Home Preservation Association 40
Stanstead County Historical Society & Library 703
Stanstead Historical Society Journal 703
Stanton Community Library 208
Stanton County Historical Museum 356
Stanton County Historical Society & Library 216
Stanton Family 98, 109
Stanton House Museum Archives 92
Stanwood Area Historical Society 608
Stanzel Model Aircraft Museum Archives 559
Staples Historical Society 315
Stapleton Library 490
Star 546
Star and Scabbard 19
Star Blanket First Nation 705
Star City Heritage Museum Archives 711
Star Genealogical Journal 163
Star Mound School Museum Archives 661
Star of the Republic Museum Library 562
Star of the Republic Museum Newsletter 562

Star Valley Historical Society 635
Starbuck Depot Society 315
Stargazer 457
Stark County Chapter, OGS & Library 454
Stark County District Library 443
Stark County Genealogical Society 175
Stark County Genie Quarterly 175
Stark County Historical Museum 443
Stark County Historical Society 175
Stark County Historical Society & Archives 443
Stark Family 548
Starke County Genealogical Society 187
Starke County Historical Museum 187
Starke County Historical Society & Archives 187
Starks Historical Society 242
Starkville-Oktibbeha County Library System 322
Starr Family Home State Historic Site Archives 553
Starr Library 413
Starr News 285
Starry Banner 593
Stars and Stripes Museum Archives 325
Starsmore Center for Local History 82
Starved Rock State Park Archives 176
State Agricultural Heritage Museum Archives 521
State Archives of Iowa 200
State Board 167
State Capital Pulishing Museum Archives 465
State Capitol Historical Association 604
State Capitol Museum Archives 94
State Historic Site of Fort Loudoun Archives 484
State Historical Museum of Wisconsin Archives 625
State Historical Society Museum 200
State Historical Society of Iowa & Library 200, 203
State Historical Society of Missouri & Library 328
State Historical Society of North Dakota & Library 437
State Historical Society of Wisconsin & Library 625
State Library of Iowa 200
State Library of Pennsylvania 489
State Museum of Pennsylvania 489
State of Connecticut Department of Public Health Certifications Unit 94
State of New Hampshire Historic Preservation Office 360
State of Rhode Island and Providence Plantations Department of Health Division of Vital Records 509
State of Vermont Historic Preservation Office 578
State of Washington Archaeology and Historic Preservation 599
State Preservation Board 536
StatelyOaks Plantation 132
Staten Island Historian 417
Staten Island Historical Museum 417
Staten Island Historical Society & Archives 417
Staten Island Institute of Arts and Sciences Archives 417
Statesboro Regional Library 137
Statesman 186, 448
Station 15 Museum Archives 219
Station Lamp 232
Station Log 272
Statlers Museum Archives 595
Statler-Stetler-Stotler Newsletter 64
Stattsburgh State Historic Site Archives 417
Stauffer Library 684
Staunton Public Library 174, 595
Stayton Public Library 480
Steam & Steel 117
Steam Railroading Institute Archives 299
Steam Railroading Institute Magazine 299
Steam Whistle 197
Steamboat Arabia Museum Archives 332
Steamboat Bertrand Museum Archives 205
Steamboat Bill 256
Steamboat Dock Museum Newsletter 371
Steamboat Log 93
Steamship Historical Society 256, 509
Steamship Keewatin Museum Archives 290
Steamship William G Mather Museum Archives 445
Steamtown National Historic Site Archives 501
Stearns County Historical Museum 314
Stearns County Historical Society & Archives 314
Stebbins Ancestral Society 580
Steel Family 54
Steele County Historical Museum 438
Steele County Historical Society & Archives 438
Steele County Historical Society & Library 312
Steele Memorial Library 396
Steele Memorial Library Newsletter 396
Steele-Brooks Family 573
Steep Falls Public Library 251
Steere Family 509
Steffel Chronicle 112
Steffy Family Connection 170
Steger Family 261
Steigerwalt Newsletter 483
Steilacoom Historical Museum Association & Library 608
Steilacoom Historical Museum Quarterly 608
Steinauer Historical Society 357
Steiner's History of Guilford & Madison 94
Stella Hill Memorial Lbirary 535
Stella Historical Society 341
Stella'ten First Nation 650
Stengel-True Museum Archives 452
Stephanson House Museum Archives 643
Stephen A Douglas Tomb Archives 156
Stephen C Foster State Park Museum Archives 130
Stephen Foster Folk Center Archives 124
Stephen Girard Museum Archives 498
Stephen House Museum 613
Stephen Leacock Memorial Library Museum Archives 687
Stephen Phillips Memorial Trust House Archives 278
Stephens African American Museum Archives 241
Stephens African American Museum Newsletter 241
Stephens County Genealogical Society & Archives 538
Stephens County Genealogical Society & Library 464
Stephens County Historical Museum 464
Stephens County Historical Society 138
Stephens County Historical Society & Archives 464
Stephens Indian Mission Foundation 637
Stephens Museum 329
Stephenson County Genealogical Society 160
Stephenson County Historical Museum 160
Stephenson County Historical Society & Archives 160
Stephenson County Swoghen 160

Stephenson Memorial Library 361
Stephens-Stevens-Stephenson-Stevenson Bulletin 77
Stephentown Historical Society & Library 417
Stephenville Historical Museum Archives 560
Stephenville Public Library 560
Stepping Back in Time 433
Stepping Stones 504
Steppingstone Museum Archives 260
Steppingstones 260
Sterling C Evans Library 540
Sterling Heights Genealogical and Historical Society 303
Sterling Heights Public Library 303
Sterling Hill Mining Museum Archives 375
Sterling Hill Mining Museum Newsletter 375
Sterling Historical Society & Archives 417
Sterling Historical Society & Library 280
Sterling Historical Society Newsletter 280, 417
Sterling Library 96
Sterling Municipal Library 537
Sterling North Society & Archives 620
Sterling Public Library 90, 174
Sterling Surname Organization Newsletter 237
Sterling-Rock Falls Historical Museum 174
Sterling-Rock Falls Historical Society & Archives 174
Sterling-Rock Falls Historical Society Newsletter 174
Sterne-Hoya Library & Museum Archives 554
Stetson Family 268
Stetson House 272
Stettler Town and Country Museum Archives 646
Steuben County Genealogical Society 179
Steuben County Historical Society 179
Steuben County Historical Society & Library 389
Steuben Family 413
Steuben House Museum Archives 377
Steuben Memorial State Historic Site Archives 413
Steven & Dorothea Green Library 117
Stevens County Genealogical Society 215
Stevens County Genealogical Society & Archives 312
Stevens County Genealogical Society Newsletter 312
Stevens County Historical Museum 215, 312, 600
Stevens County Historical Society & Archives 312, 600
Stevens County Historical Society Quarterly 312
Stevens County Library 215
Stevens Family 490, 609
Stevens Memorial Library 276, 388
Stevens Museum 193
Stevens Point Area Genealogical Society & Archives 631
Stevens-Coolidge Place Museum Archives 276
Stevenson Society of America 415
Steves Homestead Archives 559
Steveston Historical Society 654
Stewart B Lang Memorial Library 393
Stewart Clan 528
Stewart County Historical Society 527
Stewart Family 262
Stewart Family Newsletter 514
Stewart Free Library 245
Stewart Historical Museum 655
Stewart Historical Society & Archives 655
Stewart Library 129, 202
Stewart M Lord Historical Society, Museum & Archives 244
Stewart M Lord Historical Society Newsletter 244
Stewart M Lord Memorial Historical Society & Library 247
Stewart Sentinel 490
Stewartstown Historical Society 502
Stewartville Area Historical Society 315
Stibbens Family 557
Stickley Museum at Craftsman Farms Archives 375
Stickley Museum at Craftsman Farms Newsletter 375
Sticks and Stones House Archives 667
Stieber Family 193
Stiens-Feipel Family 156
Stiles Family 115, 178, 411
Stiles Family and Affiliated Families Newsletter 99
Stillaguamish Star Newsletter 599
Stillaguamish Valley Genealogical Society & Library 599
Stillians Newsletter 82
Stillwater County Library 344
Stillwater Public Library 315, 470
Stilson-Stillson Family 478
Stinnett Family Newsletter 529
Stires Family 248
Stirling Historical Society 399, 646
Stirling Historical Society Newsletter 399
Stirpes 552, 559
STM Newsletter 535
Stockbridge Family 518
Stockbridge Library & Museum 280
Stockholm Historical Museum 251
Stockholm Historical Organization 421
Stockholm Historical Society & Archives 251
Stockholm Historical Society Newsletter 251
Stockman Family 385
Stockment Family 117
Stockton Family 152
Stockton Links 529
Stockton Public Library 222
Stockton Township Public Library 175
Stockton-San Joaquin County Public Library 73
Stockwell-Mudd Libraries 285
Stoddard County Genealogical Society 328
Stoddard Family 159
Stoffel Family 560
Stokely Family 551
Stokely Memorial Library 531
Stokes County Historical Society 434
Stokes Family Quarterly 235
Stone County Genealogical Society 31
Stone County Historical and Genealogical Society 329
Stone County Historical Museum 31
Stone County Historical Society & Archives 31
Stone County Historical Society Newsletter 31
Stone County Library 329
Stone Family 6, 135
Stone Fort Days 416
Stone Fort Museum Archives 554
Stone House Museum 266
Stone House Newsletter 480
Stone Indian Band 650
Stone Lagoon Red Schoolhouse Museum Archives 75

Stone Lake Area Historical Museum 631
Stone Lake Area Historical Society & Archives 631
Stone Mountain Park Archives 138
Stone Newsletter 563
Stone Park Historical Society & Library 175
Stone Ridge Library 417
Stone School Museum 363
Stone Shop Museum Archives 683
Stone Store Museum 39
Stone's Tavery Museum Archives 188
Stone's Trace Historical Society 188
Stoneboro Community Historical Society 501
Stonefield State Historic Site Archives 619
Stoneham Public Library 280
Stonehouse Museum 480
Stone-Otis House 98
Stones River National Battlefield Archives 531
Stonewall House Museum 432
Stonewall Jackson House Library 590
Stonewall Jackson Museum at Hupp's Hill 595
Stoney Creek Current 586
Stoney Creek Elders Cultural Society 656
Stoney Creek Indian Band 656
Stonington Free Library Association 99
Stonington Historical Society & Library 99
Stony Hill School Museum Archives 621
Stony Plain and District Pioneer Museum Archives 646
Stony Point Battlefield Historic Site Archives 417
Storm Lake Public Library 208
Stormont, Dundas and Glengarry Historical Society & Library 681
Storrowton Village Museum Library 282
Storrs Family 95, 97
Story County Genealogical Society 197
Story Source 110
Stoughton and District Museum Archives 711
Stoughton Historical Museum 631
Stoughton Historical Society & Archives 631
Stoughton Historical Society & Library 280
Stoughton Historical Society Newsletter 280
Stoughton Public Library 280
Stout Family 497, 606
Stovall Family 321, 545
Stovall Journal 453
Stow House Museum 46
Stow Munroe Falls Public Library 457
Stow West 1825 School Museum Archives 280
Stow(e) Family 571
Stowe Free Library 580
Stowe Historical Society 580
Stowell Family 145
Stowitts Museum & Library 58
Strafford County Society of Genealogists & Library 360
Strafford Historical Society 364
Strafford Historical Society & Library 580
Straight Scoop 71
Strain Family 129
Strait News 604
Stranahan House Museum Archives 112
Strange Branches and Twigs 187
Strasbourg and District Museum Archives 711
Strasburg Museum Archives 595
Strategic Air and Space Museum Archives 349
Strater Hotel Archives 84
Stratford Area Historical Museum 631
Stratford Area Historical Society & Archives 631
Stratford Armoury 690
Stratford Hall Plantation 595, 596
Stratford Historical Society 73
Stratford Historical Society & Archives 100
Stratford Historical Society Newsletter 100
Stratford Library Association 100
Stratford Oklahoma Roots 470
Stratford Public Library 208, 690
Stratford Roots Genealogical Society 470
Stratham Historical Society 364
Strathclair Museum Archives 661
Strathcona County Heritage Museum Archives 646
Strathcona County Library 646
Strathroy-Middlesex Museum Archives 690
Stratton Free Library 365
Stratton Library 13
Straus Historical Society 416
Strawberry Point Historical Society & Archives 208
Strawbery Banke Museum Archives 364
Strawbery Banke Museum Newsletter 364
Strawn Family 264
Strayer Family 446, 506
Stream of History 31
Streamwood Historical Museum 175
Streamwood Historical Society & Archives 175
Streator Public Library 175
Street Family 542
Streetcar and Electric Railway Museum Archives 685
Streeter Family 40
Stremba-Stramba Newsletter 500
Stretorland Historical Society & Library 175
Strock Family 455, 460
Stroehm Record Depository 149
Strom Thurmond Institute Archives 513
Strong Family 503
Strong Family Newsletter 339
Strong Historical Society & Archives 251
Strong House Museum 265
Strong Museum Archives 414
Strong Museum Newsletter 414
Strongstown Historical Society 502
Strongsville Historical Society 458
Strongsville Historical Society Newsletter 458
Strother Family 585
Stroud Public Library 470
Strut and Axle 249
Stuart Family 555
Stuart Heritage Museum Archives 122
Stuart House Museum Library 296
Stuart Public Library 208
Stubbs Schooner News 111
Studebaker Family 458
Studebaker National Museum Archives 193
Studebaker National Museum Quarterly 193
Studies in Medieval and Renaissance History 406

INDEX

Stuhr Museum of the Prairie Pioneer Archives 352
Stuhr Museum of the Prairie Pioneer Newsletter 352
Stull Family 442
Stump Family 153
Stump-Stumpf Shoots 153
Stumptown Historical Society 347
Sturdivant Hall Museum Archives 9
Sturgeon Lake First Nation 710
Sturgeon River House Museum Archives 690
Sturgeon Valley Historical Society 300
Sturgis Library 266
Sturgis Public Library 303
Sturgis Public Library 524
Sturgis Station House Museum Archives 711
Sturm Memorial Library 625
Stutsman County Memorial Museum Archives 438
Stutsman County Memorial Museum Newsletter 438
Stuttgart Public Library 33
Sublette County Genealogy Society 637
Sublette County Historical Museum 637
Sublette County Historical Society & Archives 637
Sublette County Library 637
Sudbury Ancestor Hunting 690
Sudbury Historical Society 280
Sudbury Public Library 690
Sueltenfuss Library 559
Suffern Free Library 417
Suffern Free Library Newsletter 417
Suffield Historical Society 100
Suffolk County Historical Society & Archives 413
Suffolk County Historical Society Register 413
Suffolk County Vanderbilt Museum Library 393
Suffolk Museum Archives 596
Suffolk Museum Quarterly 596
Suffolk Resolves House 275
Sugar Creek Historical Society 194
Sugar Grove Historical Society 175
Sugar Hill Historical Society 362
Sugarland Genealogical Society 560
Sullens-Sullins Family 6
Sullivan County Genealogical Society 194, 525, 585
Sullivan County Genealogy Club 525
Sullivan County Historical Museum 401
Sullivan County Historical Society 495
Sullivan County Historical Society & Archives 401, 491
Sullivan County Historical Society & Library 194, 335
Sullivan County Historical Society Newsletter 194
Sullivan County Library 486
Sullivan County Public Library 194, 335, 525
Sullivan Museum and History Center 578
Sullivan-Sorrento Historical Society & Library 252
Sumas Indian Band 647
Summer Events Schedule 244
Summerfield Public Library 222
Summerland Museum and Arts Society & Archives 655
Summers Family 152
Summersville Public Library 615
Summerville Neighborhood Association 127
Summerville Preservation Society 518
Summerville Public Library 502
Summit County Genealogical Society 441
Summit County Historical Museum 81, 441
Summit County Historical Society 81
Summit County Historical Society & Archives 441
Summit County Historical Society Newsletter 81
Summit County Public Library 85
Summit Historian 378
Summit Historical Museum 84
Summit Historical Society & Archives 84, 378
Summitville Van Buren Township Historical Society 194
Sumner County Archives 527
Sumner County Genealogical Society 223
Sumner County Historical Society 527
Sumner County Historical Society & Library 219
Sumner County Public Library 527
Sumner Family 531
Sumner Genealogical Group 608
Sumpter Black River Watchman 518
Sumter County Genealogical Society & Archives 518
Sumter County Historical and Preservation Society 5, 6, 9
Sumter County Historical Commission & Library 518
Sumter County Historical Museum 518
Sumter County Historical Society & Archives 518
Sumter County Library 518
Sumter County Museum Archives 518
Sumter County Museum Newsletter 518
Sumter Historic Trust 125
Sun Cities Area Historical Society & Library 20
Sun Cities Genealogical Society & Library 20
Sun Cities Genealogist Quarterly 20
Sun Cities Genealogy Society & Library 22
Sun City Library 20
Sun City Vistoso Genealogical Society 18
Sun Inn Historical Museum 483
Sun Inn Preservation Association 483
Sun Prairie Historical Library and Museum Archives 632
Sun Prairie Historical Museum 632
Sun Prairie Historical Society & Archives 632
Sun Prairie Historical Society Newsletter 632
Sun Prairie Public Library 632
Sunapee Historical Society 364
Sunbright Public Library 533
Sunbury West Historical Society 663
Sunchild First Nations 645
Suncoast Genealogy Society 119
Suncoast Genealogy Society Newsletter 119
Sundridge-Strong Union Public Library 690
Sunflower 216
Sunflower County Historical Society & Archives 320
Sunflower County Library System 320
Sunlit Road 119
Sunnyside Museum and Historical Association & Library 608
Sunnyslope Historical Society 19
Sunnyvale Heritage Preservation Commission 74
Sunnyvale Historical Museum 74
Sunnyvale Historical Society & Archives 74
Sunnyvale Historical Society and Museum Association Guild 74
Sunnyvale Historical Society and Museum Association Newsletter 74
Sunnyvale Public Library 74
Sunrise Museum Archives 611

Sunrise Research Institute 252
Sunrise Trail Museum Archives 676
Sunscripts 370
Sunshine Coast Museum Archives 650
Sunshine Township Library 354
SUNY Potsdam College Library 412
Suomi Conference of the Lutheran Church in America Archives 384
Superior Historical Society 21
Superior Public Library 632
Superior Signal 290
Superstition Mountain Historical Museum 15
Superstition Mountain Historical Society & Archives 15
Superstition Mountain Historical Society Newsletter 15
Superstition Mountain Journal 15
Supreme Court Historical Society 107
Supreme Court Historical Society 257
Supreme Court Judicial Records Center 509
Supreme Court of Missouri Historical Society 331
Supreme Judicial Court Historical Society 267
Suquamish Museum Archives 605
Suquamish Museum Newsletter 605
Suquamish Tribal Cultural Center Archives 608
Surette Family 265
Surf-Bal-Bay Library 122
Surname Searcher 38
Surratt Courier 257
Surratt House Museum Archives 257
Surrey Historical Society 655
Surrey Museum Archives 655
Surrey Public Library 655
Surrey Public Library, Guildford Branch 655
Surrey Public Library-Cloverdale 655
Surry Community College Library 425
Surry County Genealogical Association Quarterly 425
Surry County Genealogical Society & Archives 425
Surry County Historical Museum 596
Surry County Historical Society & Archives 596
Surveyor 444
Surveyor's Historical Society 43
Surveyors Historical Society & Library 188
Surveyors' Historical Society 64
Surveyors' Historical Society & Library 47
Susan B Anthony House Museum Archives 414
Susan B Anthony House Museum Newsletter 414
Susanville District Library 74
Susquehanna County Free Library 494
Susquehanna County Historical Society & Archives 494
Susquehanna County Historical Society Newsletter 494
Susquehanna Depot Historical Society 503
Susquehanna Museum of Havre de Grace Archives 260
Susquehanna Museum Quarterly 260
Susquehanna Times & Magazine 492
Susquehanna Trails Genealogy Club, Vallerchamp Council 503
Sussex County Department of Libraries 103
Sussex County Historical Museum 375
Sussex County Historical Society & Archives 375
Sussex County Historical Society Newsletter 375
Sussex County Library System 375
Sussex County Library System-Dennis Library 375
Sussex-Lisbon Area Historical Society 632
Sutherland Clan 172, 273, 597, 599
Sutherland Public Library 208
Sutherland Steam Mill Archives 674
Sutter County Free Library 79
Sutter County Historical Society 79
Sutter County Historical Society News Bulletin 79
Sutter's Fort State Historic Park Archives 64
Sutter-Ulrich-Plank Family 202, 624
Sutter-Yuba Genealogical Society & Library 79
Sutton County Historical Museum 560
Sutton County Historical Society 560
Sutton Family 597
Suwanee Historical Association 138
Suwannee River Regional Library 116
Suwannee Valley Genealogical Society 116
Svendsen-Christensen-Miller-Olsen Family 573
Svoboda, Ukrainian Weekly 375
Swab Family 506
Swadley Family 262
Swain County Genealogical and Historical Society 424
Swamp Angel II News 486
Swampscott Historical Society & Archives 280
Swampscott Historical Society Newsletter 280
Swampscott Public Library 280
Swan Historical Foundation 371
Swan Library 387
Swan River Museum 220
Swan River Valley Historical Museum 661
Swan River Valley Historical Society & Archives 661
Swaney Memorial Library 614
Swanger Family 562
Swann Family 76
Swansea Free Public Library 280
Swanton Family 252
Swanton Historical Society 580
Swanton Public Library 458, 580
Swanton-Nyberg Family 535
Swarthout Museum 624
Swasey-Swesey Family 148, 602
Swayzee Public Library 194
Swecker Family 613
Sweden and America 311
Sweden Historical Society 244, 251
Swedish American Historical Museum 156
Swedish American Historical Quarterly 156
Swedish American Historical Society & Library 156
Swedish American Museum Association & Library 156
Swedish American Museum Association News 156
Swedish Ancestry Research Association 283
Swedish Colonial Society 498, 505
Swedish Colonial Society Newsletter 498
Swedish Council of America 311
Swedish Finn Historical Society Newsletter 606
Swedish Genealogy Society of Minnesota 315
Swedish Heritage 172
Swedish Heritage Center 355
Swedish Historical Society of Rockford & Archives 172
Swedish Pioneer Historical Quarterly 156
Swedish Pioneer Historical Society & Library 156
Swedish Press 656

Swedish-Finn Historical Society & Library 606
Sweet Briar Museum Archives 596
Sweet Home Genealogical Society & Library 480
Sweet Home Public Library 480
Sweet Springs Historical Society 341
Sweetgrass First Nation 706
Sweeton Family 92
Sweet-Wallace-Wright-Zimmerman-Hitt-Galbraith-Cooksey-Lawson-Brisbin-Morrow-Horn-Kenton-Lansdowne-Barney-Bookout-McClurg-Henderson-Russell Family 585
Sweetwater County Historical Museum 636
Sweetwater County Historical Museum Archives 636
Sweetwater County Historical Society & Archives 636
Sweetwater County Library 636
Sweetwater County-City Library 561
Sweetwater Creek State Park Archives 133
Sweetwater Public Library 533
Swegle Family 74
Swenson Memorial Museum of Stephens County Archives 538
Swenson Swedish Immigration Research Center 172
Swift County Historical Museum 306
Swift County Historical Society & Archives 306
Swigart Museum Library 490
Swindler's Ridge Museum Archives 618
Swink Historical Preservation Association 470
Swinney Homestead Archives 184
Swisher County Archives and Museum Archives 561
Swisher County Library 561
Swiss American 443
Swiss American Historical Society 156
Swiss Connection, a Genealogical and Cultural Newsletter 627
Swiss Echoes 180
Swiss Heritage Society & Library 180
Swiss Historical Village 628
Swiss Mennonite Cultural and Historical Society 219
Swiss-American Historical Society Review 156
Swissvale Historical and Genealogical Society 503
Switzerland County Historical Museum 195
Switzerland County Historical Society & Archives 195
Switzerland County Public Library 195
Swope Family 571
Sycamore Historical Society 175
Sycamore Leaves 194
Sycamore Public Library 175
Sydney and Louisburg Railway Museum 675
Sylvia Plotkin Judaica Museum Archives 20
Syms-Sims-Symes Family 301
Syosset Public Library 418
Syracuse Turkey Creek Township Public Library 194
Szukala-Bratek-Sitek-Kucyba-Kilian-Kielijan-Brzeski-Bloniarz-Blumarz-Jesionowki Family 287

T

T B Ferguson Home Museum Archives 471
T B Scott Library 626
T C Steele State Historic Site Archives 190
T Cartter & Margaret Rawlings Lupton Library 526
T Cartter & Margaret Rawlings Lupton Library Newsletter 526
T J Elder Community Center Archives 136
T L L Temple Memorial Library 543
T T Wentworth Florida State Museum 120
T'Sou-ke Indian Nation 655
Taber and District Museum Archives 646
Taber Tree 28
Table Rock Historical Museum 357
Table Rock Historical Society & Archives 357
Table Talk 317
Tabor College Library 215
Tabor Family 385
Tabor Opera House Museum Library 87
Tabusintac Centennial Museum Archives 665
Tackett Family Journal 41
Tacoma Family History Center 608
Tacoma Historical Society 608
Tacoma Public Library 608
Tacoma Public Library-Fern Hill Branch 608
Tacoma Public Library-Kobetich Branch 608
Tacoma Public Library-Moore Branch 608
Tacoma Public Library-Mottet Branch 608
Tacoma Public Library-South Tacoma 608
Tacoma Public Library-Swasey Branch 608
Tacoma Public Library-Wheelock Branch 608
Tacoma-Pierce County Genealogical Society & Library 608
Taconic Valley Historical Society 389
TADL-Tales 303
Taft Family 283
Taft Genealogical Society 74
Taft Public Library 274, 561
Taggart Family Organization Newsletter 74
Tagish Historical Society 713
TAGS: The Alliance Genealogical Society Newsletter 441
Tague Family 227
Tailings 44
Takla Lake Indian Band 649
Takoma Park Campus Library 263
Takoma Park Library 263
Taku River Tlingit First Nation 647
Talbert-DeLaney-Perkins Family 550
Talbot County Free Library 258
Talbot County Free Library's Weathervane 258
Talbot County Historical Museum 258
Talbot County Historical Society 258
Talbot Family 76
Talbot Library and Museum 464
Talbot Library and Museum Archives 464
Talent Historical Society 477, 480
Tales & Trails 480
Tales and Trails 437
Tales of Air Warriors 589
Tales of the Paradise Ridge 59
Taliaferro County Historical Society & Library 129
Taliaferro County, Georgia, Records & Notes 129
Talisi Historical Preservation Society 9
Talisi Historical Society 9
Talkeetna Historical Museum 13
Talkeetna Historical Society & Archives 13
Talkeetna Historical Society Newsletter 13
Tall Pines Monthly 37
Tall Talk 239
Tall Tree 59
Talladega County Historical Association 9

Talladega County Historical Association Newsletter 9
Tallahassee Genealogical Society 122
Tallahassee Genealogical Society Bulletin 122
Tallahassee Genealogist 122
Tallahassee Museum of History Archives 122
Tallapoosa County Historical Society and Genealogical Committee 1
Talledega Public Library 9
Tallmadge Church Archives 458
Tallmadge Historical Society & Library 458
Tallmadge Historical Society Bulletin 458
Tallow Light 452
Tallyboard 87
Tam Kernewek 291, 374
Tama County Historical Museum 208
Tama County Historical Society & Archives 208
Tama County Museum News 208
Tama County Tracers Genealogical Society & Library 208
Tamaqua Historical Society 503
Tamarack District Library 295
Tamastsklikt Cultural Center Archives 477
Tampa Bay History Center 123
Tampa Bay History Center Archives 123
Tampa Bay Library Consortium 123
Tampa Campus Library 123
Tampa Historical Society 123
Tampa Public Library 123
Tampico Area Historical Society 175
Tamworth Historical Society 364
Tanakteuk Indian Band 647
Tanana-Yukon Historical Society & Archives 12
Tanana-Yukon Historical Society Newsletter 12
Taneyhills Community Library 326
Taneyhills Community Library Newsletter 326
Tangelo 123
Tangipahoa Parish Historical Society 238
Tangipahoa Parish Library 235
Tangled Roots 338
Tangled Roots Genealogical Society 344
Tannehill Historical State Park Archives 6
Tannehill Historical State Park Newsletter 6
Tannenbaum Historic Park Archives 427
Tanner Family 120, 343, 637
Tantaquidgeon Indian Museum Archives 100
Tante Blanche Museum 248
Taoist Temple and Museum Archives 47
Taos County Historical Society & Library 385
Tap Root 12, 561
Tapestry 489
Tappan Library 418
Tappan Library Newsletter 418
Tappantown Historical Museum 418
Tappantown Historical Society & Archives 418
Tappantown Historical Society Newsletter 418
Taproot Newsletter 76
Taproots 260
Tar River Connections Genealogical Society 432
Tarentum Genealogical Society & Archives 503
Tarentum Genealogical Society Newsletter 503
Tarkio College Alumni Historical Museum 341
Tarpon Springs Area Historical Society & Archives 123
Tarpon Springs Cultural Center Archives 123
Tarpon Springs Heritage Museum Archives 123
Tarpon Springs Public Library 123
Tarrant County Black Historical and Genealogical Society 545
Tarrant County Black Historical and Genealogical Society Newsletter 545
Tarrant Public Library 9
Tartan 227
Tarvin Family 377, 444
Tasset Tree Trunks 219
Tate County Genealogical and Historical Society 322
Tate County Genealogical Library 322
Tate House Gazette 250
Tate House Museum Archives 250
Tate Trails 322
Tatge Family 305
Tattnall County Historical Society 135
Taunton Public Library 280
Taunton Public Library Newsletter 280
Tavares Public Library 123
Tavern Tidings 282
Tawakoni Area Public Library 557
Taylor Butler House Archives 373
Taylor County Genealogical Society 197
Taylor County Genealogical Society & Library 202
Taylor County Genealogical Society Newsletter 202
Taylor County Historical and Genealogical Society 612
Taylor County Historical Society & Archives 626
Taylor County Historical Society & Library 226
Taylor County Historical-Genealogical Society 127
Taylor County in Profile 612
Taylor County Public Library 226, 612
Taylor Family 153, 485, 571, 585
Taylor Family Journal 418
Taylor Heritage Society & Library 561
Taylor House Museum 256
Taylor Memorial Library 370
Taylor Memorial Public Library 446
Taylor Surname Newsletter 18
Taylor Times 571
Taylor-Armstrong Family 543
Taylor-Grady House Archives 125
Taylor-Kellum-Kellam-Webb-Loving-Goodman-Hale Family 591
Taylors Falls Historical Society 315
Taylors Falls Public Library 316
Taylorville Breeze Courier 167
Taymouth Township Library 287
Tazewell County Genealogical and Historical Society & Library 170
Tazewell County Historical Society 596, 611
Tazewell County Historical Society Newsletter 596
Tazewell County Public Library 596
Tazewell Genealogical and Historical Monthly 170
TCHA News 188
Tea Chronicles 109
Tea Family 109
Teachout-Crull Family 559
Teagle Family 138
Teague Public Library 561
Teaneck Public Library 378
Teas Family 303
Teck Centennial Library 684

Tecumseh Area Historical Society 693
Tecumseh Public Library 303
Ted Smallwood's Store Museum Archives 110
Teeterville Pioneer Museum Archives 681, 690
Tefft Family Association Chronicles 50
Tehachapi Heritage League 74
Tehama County Library 61
Tehama County Museum Foundation & Library 74
Tehama Genealogical and Historical Society 61
Tehkummah Township Museum Archives 690
Teinert Memorial Public Library 537
Tejas Gazette 549
Tekeyan Armenian Cultural Association 701
Telegram 548
Telegraph 309
Telephone Historical Collection Museum Archives 674
Telephone Museum Archives 246
Telephone Pioneer Museum of New Mexico Archives 381
Telescope 289
Telfair Academy Historic House Museum Archives 137
Telkwa Museum Archives 656
Tell City Historical Society & Library 194
Tell City-Perry County Public Library 194
Telling-Drake-VanScoyk Family 36
Tell-Tales 448
Telluride Historical Museum Archives 90
Telluride Historical Society 90
Temecula Library 74
Temecula Valley Genealogical Society 74
Temecula Valley Genealogical Society Newsletter 74
Temecula Valley Museum Archives 74
Temecula Valley Museum Newsletter; High Country Magazine 74
Temiskaming Genealogy Group 686
Tempe Historical Highlights 21
Tempe Historical Museum 21
Tempe Historical Society 21
Tempe Public Library 21
Temperance Tavern Museum 454
Temple Area Genealogical Library 567
Temple Beth Israel Library 45
Temple Beth Sholom Library 117
Temple Branch Genealogical Library 260
Temple De Hirsch Sinai Library 606
Temple Emanuel Library 22
Temple Israel Library 267, 304
Temple Israel Library of Judaica 124
Temple Judea 111
Temple Judea Museum Archives 486
Temple Mickve Israel Museum Archives 137
Temple Public Library 561
Templeton Historical Museum Archives 74
Templin Family 478
Templin Family Newsletter 121
Ten Broeck Mansion 387
Ten Broeck Newsletter 387
Tenafly Public Library 378
Tenement Times 407
Tennant Family 538
Tennessee Ancestors 529
Tennessee Central Railway Museum Archives 531
Tennessee Civil War Museum Archives 526
Tennessee Conservationist 531
Tennessee Genealogical Magazine: Ansearchin' News 525, 530
Tennessee Genealogical Society 525, 530
Tennessee Genealogist & Family Historian 531
Tennessee Genealogy and History 532
Tennessee Historical Commission & Archives 531
Tennessee Historical Commission Museum 531
Tennessee Historical Quarterly 531
Tennessee Historical Society & Archives 531
Tennessee Museum of Aviation Archives 532
Tennessee State Library and Archives 531
Tennessee State Museum Archives 531
Tennessee State Museum Newsletter 531
Tennessee Valley Authority Archives 529, 531
Tennessee Valley Genealogical Society 6
Tennessee Valley Historical Society & Archives 4
Tennessee Valley Historical Society & Library 9
Tennessee Valley Historical Society Newsletter 9
Tennessee Valley Railroad Museum Archives 526
Tennessee Western History Library 531
Tennessee-Kentucky Queries 607
Tenney Memorial Library 578
Tenney Times 17
Tensas Parish Library 241
Tense Past Present Future 170
Tequesta 117
Terra Alta Public Library 615
Terrace Bay Public Library 690
Terrace Hill 200
Terrace Hill Historic Site and Governor's Mansion 200
Terrace Public Library 656
Terrebonne Genealogical Society & Library 237
Terrebonne Genealogical Society Newsletter 237
Terrebonne Historical and Cultural Society & Archives 237
Terrebonne Historical and Cultural Society Newsletter 237
Terrebonne Life Lines 237
Terrebonne Parish Library 237
Terrell County Historic Preservation Society 130
Terrell County Restoration Society 130
Terrell Family 49, 425
Terrell Public Library 561
Terrell Trails 127
Terril Community Library 208
Territorial Capital-Lane Museum Archives 217
Territorial Statehouse State Park Archives 566
Territory Town Archives 467
Terry Family 603
Terryville Public Library 100
Terwiliger Museum 420
Teslin Historical Society 713
Teslin Tlingit Council 713
Teton County Historical Museum 636
Teton County Historical Society & Archives 636
Teton County Historical Society Quarterly 636
Teton County Library 636
Teton County Library-Huff Memorial Library 636
Teulon and District Museum Archives 661
Teutopolis Monastery Museum Archives 175
Tevebaugh-Teverbaugh Family 292

Tewksberry Historical Society 372
Tewksbury Historical Society 280
Tex Ark Antique Auto Museum Archives 33
Tex Ark Antique Auto Museum Newsletter 33
Texana Museum and Library 544
Texarkana Genealogical Society 561
Texarkana Historical Museum 561
Texarkana Historical Society & Archives 561
Texarkana Museums System Archives 561
Texarkana Public Library 561
Texarkana Quarterly 561
Texarkana USA Genealogical Society Quarterly 561
Texarkana USA Genealogy Society 561
Texas African American Photography Archives 542
Texas Air Museum Archives 557
Texas Association of Museums & Library 536
Texas Athens Genealogical Organization Newsletter 536
Texas Baptist Historical Center Archives 538
Texas Catholic Historian 536
Texas Catholic Historical Society 536
Texas Catholic Historical Society Newsletter 536
Texas City Ancestry Searchers & Archives 561
Texas City Museum Archives 561
Texas Collection 562
Texas County Genealogical and Historical Society 330
Texas County Library 330
Texas County Missouri Newsletter 330
Texas Energy Museum Archives 537
Texas Forestry Museum Archives 552
Texas General Land Office-Archives & Records Division Library 537
Texas Governor's Museum Archives 537
Texas Historian 537
Texas Historical Commission & Library 537
Texas Historical Foundation & Library 537
Texas Kin 542
Texas Maritime Museum Archives 557
Texas Military Forces Museum Archives 537
Texas Military Forces Museum Newsletter 537
Texas Oral History Association 562
Texas Oral History Association Newsletter 562
Texas Pharmacy Museum Archives 535
Texas Prison Museum Archives 550
Texas Ranger Hall of Fame and Museum Archives 562
Texas Research Library 537
Texas Research Ramblers 539
Texas Research Ramblers Newsletter 539
Texas Seaport Museum Archives 546
Texas State Afro-American Genealogical Society 549
Texas State Genealogical Society 546, 552, 559
Texas State Historical Association 537
Texas State Library 537
Texas Supreme Court Historical Society 537
Texas Tech University Library 552
Texas Transportation Museum Archives 559
Texas Wendish Heritage Society & Library 546
Texian Heritage Society 537
Teysen's Woodland Indian Musuem Archives 296
Thames Valley Museum School Archives 680
Thames, Tims, Timms Family 122
Thayer County Genealogical Society & Library 349
Thayer County Historical Society & Archives 349
Thayer County Museum 349
Thayer Family 267
Thayer Memorial Library 273
Thayer Public Library 267
Thayer Quarterly: A Quest for Your Heritage 267
The New York Public Library-The Research Libraries 408
The Pas Public Library 661
The Reynolds Family Circle 556
The Valley Library 474
Thebes Historical Society 175
Thedes Newsletter 71
Thelma Miles Museum Archives 685
Then and Now 205
Theodore Austin Cutler Memorial Library 302
Theodore Roosevelt Association 418
Theodore Roosevelt Association Journal 418
Theodore Roosevelt Birthplace National Historic Site Archives 408
Theodore Roosevelt Historical Museum 439
Theodore Roosevelt Inaugural Historic Site Archives 391
Theodore Roosevelt Nature and History Association & Library 439
Theresa & Edward O'Toole Library 371
Theresa Free Library 418
Theresa Public Library 632
Thetford Historical Society & Library 580
Thetford Historical Society Newsletter 580
Thetford Town Library 580
Thienemann Family 590
Think On 43, 447, 544
Third Century Methodism 256
Third Street Echoes 106
This is the Place Heritage Park Archives 571
This Month at the Urbana Free Library 176
This Week in Cape May 368
Thistle 378
Thistle and the Bee 584
Thistle Hill House Museum Archives 546
Thistle: Griesemer Family Association Newsletter 50
Thomas B Norton Public Library 5
Thomas Branigan Memorial Library 383
Thomas Burne Memorial Library 7
Thomas Clarke House 376
Thomas College Library 138
Thomas Cooper Library 514
Thomas County Genealogical Society 357
Thomas County Genealogical Society & Archives 212
Thomas County Historical Society 357
Thomas County Historical Society & Archives 212
Thomas County Historical Society & Library 138
Thomas County Library 357
Thomas County Public Library System 138
Thomas Crane Public Library 278
Thomas D Russell Library 1
Thomas Darling House 101
Thomas Downs House Museum Archives 181
Thomas E McMillan Museum Archives 2
Thomas Edison Birthplace Museum Archives 453
Thomas Edison House Archives 231
Thomas Elwood Lindley House 191
Thomas Erskine Birch Family Newsletter 76

Thomas F Reed Library 295
Thomas Family 572
Thomas Foster Memorial Temple Museum 688
Thomas G Carpenter Library 114
Thomas Griswold House Museum 94
Thomas H Leath Memorial Library 432
Thomas Hackney Braswell Memorial Library 432
Thomas Hale Hamilton Library 142
Thomas Haney House Museum Archives 652
Thomas Hart Benton Home Museum Archives 332
Thomas J Boyd Museum Archives 597
Thomas Jefferson Library 340
Thomas Jefferson Memorial Foundation & Library 585
Thomas Jefferson's Poplar Forest Archives 587
Thomas L Kane Memorial Chapel Museum Archives 491
Thomas Lee House 93, 97
Thomas McCulloch House 676
Thomas Memorial Library 244
Thomas P Kennard House Museum Archives 353
Thomas R Brendle Memorial Library 501
Thomas Stanton Society Newsletter 109
Thomas Tredway Library 172
Thomas Warne Historical Museum 373, 375
Thomas Warne Historical Museum Archives 375
Thomas Whaley House Museum Archives 66
Thomas Wilhite Memorial Library 469
Thomas Winston Cole, Sr Library 553
Thomas Wolfe Memorial Museum Archives 423
Thomas Wolfe Memorial Museum Newsletter 423
Thomas-Foreman Home Archives 467
Thomason Newsletter 479
Thomasson Family 135
Thomasson Traces 1
Thomaston Historical Society 100
Thomaston Historical Society & Library 251
Thomaston Public Library 100, 251
Thomaston Public Library Gazette 100
Thomaston-Upson Archives 138
Thomasville Cultural Center Library 138
Thomasville Genealogical and Historical Library 138
Thomasville Genealogical History & Library 138
Thomasville Landmarks 138
Thompson Ames Historical Society of Gilford 361
Thompson Family 15, 179, 331, 593, 622
Thompson Free Library 245
Thompson Historical Society 100
Thompson Home Public Library 294
Thompson House Archives 470
Thompson Museum Archives 709
Thompson Public Library 97, 661
Thompson-Nicola Regional District Library 651
Thompson-Nicola Regional District Library System-Barriere Library 647
Thompson-Thomson-Tomson Family 325
Thomsens Genealogical Center 565
Thoreau Institute 273
Thoreson House 634
Thorn Family 613
Thornbury Historical Society 488
Thorn-Courtney-Hall-Glisson-McDonough Famil 571
Thorn-Dowman-Hall-Edge-Bates-Penman Family 570
Thorne Bay Community Library 13
Thornhill Foundation 7
Thornhill Newsletter 7
Thornton Family 35
Thornton Family Bulletin 567
Thornton Historical Museum 175
Thornton Historical Society & Archives 175
Thornton Newsletter 553
Thornton Township Historical Society & Library 162
Thornton W Burgess Museum Archives 278
Thorntown Public Library 194
Thorny Trail 554
Thorold Public Library 691
Thorp Area Historical Museum 632
Thorp Area Historical Society 632
Thorp Area Historical Society & Archives 632
Thorp Family 32
Thorp Mill Town Historical Preservation Society 609
Thousand Islands Museum Archives 394
Thousand Islands Museum Newsletter 394
Thousand Oaks Library 75
Thrailkill Genealogical Society 332
Thrasher Carriage Museum Archives 259
Threads of Life 551
Three Creeks Historical Association 189
Three Forks Genealogical Society & Library 470
Three Forks Genealogical Society Bulletin 470
Three Island Crossing State Park Archives 146
Three Lakes Historical Museum 632
Three Lakes Historical Society & Archives 632
Three Oaks Township Library 303
Three Rivers Chronicle 515, 516
Three Rivers Genealogy Club 303
Three Rivers Historical Society 75
Three Rivers Historical Society & Library 515
Three Rivers Museum Archives 467
Three Rivers Public Library 154, 303
Three Rivers Public Library District, Minooka Branch Library 166
Three Rivers Public Library Newsletter 154
Three Valley Museum Archives 464
Three Village Historian 396
Three Village Historic Society 416
Three Village Historic Society Newsletter 416
Three Village Historical Museum 416
Three Village Historical Society & Library 396
Threshers Chaff 205
Thronateeska Heritage Foundation & Archives 125
Thronateeska Heritage Foundation Museum 125
Thronateeska Heritage Foundation Newsletter 125
Through the Porthole 448
Through the Spyglass 561
Thunder Bay Historical Museum Society & Library 691
Thunder Bay Historical Museum Society Papers and Records 691
Thunder Bay Military Museum Archives 691
Thunder Bay Public Library 691
Thunderbird Museum Archives 626
Thunderbolt Museum Archives 137
Thunderchild First Nation 711
Thurber-Barnett Family 87
Thurgood Family 568

Thurgood Marshall Library 257
Thurlow Family 301
Thurman Family 29, 543
Thurmond Clarke Memorial Library 58
Thurmont Historical Society 263
Thurston County Heritage Society 356
TIARA 280
Ticasuk Library 13
Tichenor Cemetery Newsletter 327
Tichenor Family 335
Tickle Family 595
Ticonderoga Historical Society & Archives 418
Tid Bits 628
Tidbits 20
Tiddy Family 98
Tideline 66
Tidewater Afro-American Historical and Genealogical Society 596
Tidewater Genealogical Society 588, 591
Tidewater Virginia Families 597
Tidewater Virginia Families: a Magazine of History and Genealogy 597
Tidings 55, 369, 375
Tidningen 315
Tidwell-Ledford Family 527
Tiedgen Family 349
Tietsort Family Newsletter 285
Tiffin-Seneca Public Library 458
Tiger Tales 319
Tigerton Area Historical Society 632
Tignish Cultural Centre Museum Archives 695
Tiles 117
Tillamook County Historical Society 480
Tillamook County Library 480
Tillamook County Pioneer Museum and Research Library 480
Tillamook Genealogy Study Group 480
Tillamook Naval Air Station Museum Archives 480
Tillman County Historical and Educational Society & Library 465
Tillman County Historical and Educational Society Newsletter 465
Tillotson Family 62
Tillsonburg and District Historical Museum Archives 691
Tilson-Tillson Family 412
Tilton Historical Society 175, 365
Tilton Library 279
Timber Trails 477
Timber Village Museum Archives 680
Timber, Tides and Tales 601
Timberland Regional Library 604, 609
Timberland Regional Library-Aberdeen Branch 599
Timberland Regional Library-Olympia Branch 604
Timbertown Log 301
Time Flys 115
Time Line 452
Time Lines 21, 662
Time Machine 459
Time Piece 428
Timekeeper 544
Timeline 18, 170, 304, 446
Timelines 118, 204, 212, 630
Timen Stiddem Society 283
Timen Stiddem Society Newsletter 283
Timepiece 118, 375
Times 432, 451
Times of Bath 243
Timescape 633
Timetable 447
Timexpo Museum Archives 100
Timmers Family 631
Timmins Museum Archives 690
Timmons Family 311
Timms-Tims Researcher 58
Timpson Area Genealogical and Heritage Society 561
Timrod Library 518
Tiner Times 529
Tingen Family 22
Tingley Memorial Library 110
Tingleys United Association Newsletter 47
Tinicum Township Historical Society 500
Tinker Swiss Cottage Museum Archives 172
Tinker Topics 172
Tinkertown Museum Archives 384
Tinklepaugh Family Newsletter 104
Tinley Moraine Genealogical Society 175
Tinley Park Historical Museum 175
Tinley Park Historical Society & Archives 175
Tinmouth Historical and Genealogical Society 580
Tintic Mining Museum Archives 566
Tioga County Historical Museum 410
Tioga County Historical Society & Archives 410
Tioga County Historical Society & Library 505
Tioga County Historical Society Newsletter 410, 505
Tioga Point Museum Archives 482
Tioga Point Museum Newsletter 482
Tip O'Texas Genealogical Society & Archives 548
Tippah County Historical and Genealogical Society 322
Tippah County Historical and Genealogical Society News and Journal 322
Tippecanoe Battlefield Museum Archives 179
Tippecanoe Battlefield Museum Newsletter 179
Tippecanoe County Area Genealogical Society & Archives 188
Tippecanoe County Area Genealogical Society Newsletter 188
Tippecanoe County Historical Association & Archives 188
Tippecanoe County Historical Museum 188
Tippecanoe County Public Library 188
Tippecanoe Historical Society 458
Tipton County Heritage Center Archives 194
Tipton County Historical Society 179, 194
Tipton County Historical Society 526
Tipton County Museum Veterans Memorial Archives 526
Tipton County Public Library 194, 526
Tipton Public Library 208
Tipton-Haynes Historic Site Archives 528
Tishomingo County Historical and Genealogical Society 320
Tishomingo County Historical and Genealogical Society Newsletter 320
Tiskilwa Township Library 175
Titanic Historical Society 272
Title Pages 192
Titus Family 72
Titus Times 39
Titusville Campus Library 123
Titusville Historical Society 503
Tiverton Historical Society 509
Tiverton Library Services 509

INDEX

Tl'azt'en Nation 649
Tla-o-qui-aht First Nation 656
Tlatlasikwala Indian Band 647
Tlowitsis-Mumtagila Band & Whe-la-la-u Area Indian Council 647
To Absent Friends 390
To the Point 516
Tobacco Farm Life Museum Archives 429
Tobacco Farm Life Museum Newsletter 429
Tobacco Plains Band 650
Tobias Community Historical Museum 357
Tobias Community Historical Society & Archives 357
Tobique Indian Band 664
Tobucksey News 466
Toccoa Historical Group 138
Today Is Tomorrow's History 542
Todd County Historical Newsletter 310
Todd County Historical Society 310
Todd County Public Library 227
Todd Family 600
Todd Library 531
Todd Wehr Memorial Library 624, 633
Todmorden Mills Historic Site Archives 692
Toe Valley Genealogical Society 433
Tofield Historical Museum Archives 646
Tofte Historical Society 316
Together We Are Strong 503
Toledo Area Genealogical Society 458
Toledo Firefighters Museum Archives 458
Toledo Public Library 208, 480
Toledo-Lucas County Public Library 458
Toledoth: These Are the Generations 230
Toler Family 542
Tolland Genealogical Society & Library 100
Tolland Historical Society & Archives 100
Tolland Historical Society Newsletter 100
Tolleson Public Library 21
Toll-Gate Keeper 299
Tolman Family 565
Tolono Public Library 175
Tolson-Toalson Family 557
Tom & Ada Beam Library 468
Tom Bevill Public Library 5
Tom Burnett Memorial Library 550
Tom Green County Library 558
Tom Mix Museum Archives 464
Tom's River Seaport Society 379
Tomaguag Indian Memorial Museum Archives 507
Tomah Area Historical Museum 632
Tomah Area Historical Society & Archives 632
Tomahawk Historical Society & Archives 632
Tomales Regional Local History Center Library 75
Tomb with a View 451
Tombigbee Regional Library 323
Tombigbee Regional Library System-Evans Memorial 319
Tombstone 19
Tombstone City Library 21
Tombstone Courthouse State Historic Park Archives 21
Tombstone Epitaph 21
Tombstone Trails 305
Tome Parish Museum Archives 385
Tomlinson Library 86
Tommaney Library 217
Tompkins Family 406, 611
Tompkins Memorial Library 514
Tonasket Genealogical Society 609
Tonawanda Historical Museum 418
Tonawanda-Kenmore Historical Museum 418
Tonawanda-Kenmore Historical Society & Archives 418
Toney Family 588
Tonganoxie Community Historical Society & Library 222
Tonganoxie Genealogical Society & Library 222
Tonganoxie Public Library 222
Tongass Historical Museum Archives 12
Tonkawa Public Library 470
Tooele Public Library 572
Toole County Free Library 346
Toombs County Historical Society 139
Toomer Herald 384
Toone-Toon-Tune Family 592
Toosey Indian Band 654
Top of Oklahoma Historical Museum 463
Top of Oklahoma Historical Society & Archives 463
Topanga Historical Society 75
Topeka Area Historical Society 194
Topeka Genealogical Society & Library 222
Topeka Genealogical Society Newsletter 222
Topeka Genealogical Society Quarterly 222
Topeka High School Historical Society & Library 222
Topeka Public Library 222
Tophan Brown Gallery Archives 657
Toponas Public Library 90
To-Po-Ska 213
Toppenish Museum Archives 609
Toppenish Museum Newsletter 609
Topsfield Historical Museum 280
Topsfield Historical Society & Archives 280
Toquaht Indian Band 656
Torbay Museum Archives 669
Toronto Aerospace Museum Archives 692
Toronto Cornish Association 692
Toronto Family 571
Toronto Public Library 692
Toronto Scottish Regimental Museum Archives 692
Toronto's Waterfront Museum Archives 692
Torrance Historical Museum 75
Torrance Historical Society 75
Torrance Public Library 75
Torrey Family Newsletter 48
Torreya State Park Archives 110
Torreyson Library 26
Torrington Historical Museum 100
Torrington Historical Society & Library 100
Torrington Historical Society Newsletter 100
Tosco Bay Historical Society 290
Totah Tracer 382
Totah Tracers Genealogical Society & Archives 382
Totem Heritage Center 12
Totoket Historical Society & Library 97
Touchwood-File Hills-Qu' Appelle Tribal Council 707
Tougaloo College Museum Archives 322

Tournament House Museum Archives 59
Tournaments Illuminated Journal 54
Touro Synagogue Archives 508
Towanda District Public Library 176
Towanda Public Library 222, 503
Towe Auto Museum Archives 64
Towe Auto Museum Newsletter 64
Tower Soudan Historical Society 316
Tower: Hinckley Family Newsletter 141
Town Creek Indian Mound State Historic Site Archives 430
Town Crier 273, 281, 453, 481, 496
Town Hall Museum 580, 621
Town of Bernalillo Public Library 382
Town of Bethelehem Historical Association & Archives 416
Town of Bethelehem Historical Association Newsletter 416
Town of Carmel Historical Society 404
Town of Carmel Historical Society Newsletter 404
Town of Cobleskill Historical Society 394
Town of Dayton Historical Society 395
Town of Greensboro Historical Society 576
Town of Moriah Historical Society 412
Town of Ontario Historical and Landmark Preservation Society & Library 409
Town of Ontario Historical and Landmark Preservation Society Newsletter 409
Town of Porter Historical Society & Archives 422
Town of Signal Mountain Library 532
Town of Tonawanda Public Library 402
Town of Ulster Public Library 402
Town of Ulster Public Library Quarterly Newsletter 402
Town of Whitby Archives 692
Towne Family 363, 426
Towns County Historical and Genealogical Society 132
Townsend Family 382
Townsend Historical Society 280
Townsend Newsletter 410
Townsend Public Library 280
Townsend Quarterly Newsletter 398
Townsend Society of America 398, 410
Townshend Public Library 580
Township Lines 491
Township of Cramahe Public Library 681
Township of Hamilton Historical Society 373
Township of Neptune Historical Society & Archives 374
Township of Neptune Historical Society Newsletter 374
Towpath Post 373
Towpath Topics 273
Towry-Towery Family 475
Toy & Miniature Museum Newsletter 332
Toy & Miniature Museum of Kansas City 332
Toy Train Depot Museum Archives 381
Toyn Family 569
Tracer 176, 218, 444, 448
Traces 228
Traces of Indiana & Midwestern History 186
Tracht Family 151
Tracings 555
Track and Trace 450
Tracking in Crawford County, Ohio 448
Tracks 119
Tracks and Traces 27
Tracy Area Genealogical Society 75
Trading Path 424
Trading Post Historical Museum 220
Trading Post Historical Society & Archives 220
Trading Post Times 537
Traditions 122
Traffic Report 445
Trail and District Public Library 656
Trail Blazer 456
Trail Breakers 609
Trail Dust 587
Trail End Historic Center 637
Trail Family 28
Trail Guide 333
Trail Historical Society 656
Trail Mix 473
Trail Museum Archives 656
Trail of `98 City Museum Archives 13
Trail Ruts 217
Trail Seekers 356
Trail Tales 197, 206
Trail's End: Rediscovering the Old West 466
Trailblazer 67
Traill County Historical Society & Library 438
Trails 693
Trails and Tales of Boom Town USA 539
Trails in History 6
Trails Regional Library 342
Trails to the Past 215
Trails West 563
Trailside Museum Archives 171
Train Collectors Quarterly 502
Train of Artillery Armory Museum Archives 507
Trainsheet 226
Transactions and Studies of the College of Physicians of Philadelphia 498
Transactions of Huguenot Society of South Carolina 512
Transactions of the London and Middlesex Historical Society 685
Transcona Historical Museum Archives 662
Transcription 557
Trans-Swiya Museum Archives 655
Transylvania County Historical Society 423
Transylvania County Library 424
Transylvania Hungary & Beyond 112
Transylvania Saxon Genealogy and Heritage Society 461
Transylvania Saxon Tapestry 461
Transylvania University Library & Museum 230
Trant Memorial Library 216
Trappe Historical Museum 485
Trappe Historical Society & Archives 485
Trapper Creek Public Library 13
Trascinsici-Chodorowsky-Burright-Leasy-Klawa-Moorehouse Family 64
Trautman Family 556
Trautman-Troutman Family 482
Travel Town Museum Archives 52
Traveler's Rest State Historic Site Archives 138
Travellers Rest Plantation Museum Archives 531
Traverse Area District Library 303
Traverse Area Heritage Center 303
Traverse County Historical Museum 316
Traverse County Historical Society & Archives 316
Traverse de Sioux Library System 310

INDEX

Traverse des Sioux Genealogical Society 312
Traylor-Trouillar Family 383
Treackle Mansion 261
Tread of Pioneers Museum Archives 90
Treasure Chest News 118
Treasure Coast Genealogical Society 113
Treasure Coast Genealogical Society Newsletter 113
Treasure Island Museum Archives 67
Treasure State Lines 344
Treasure Valley Chapter, Idaho Genealogical Society 145
Treasures of the Sea Archives 103
Treaty 8 Tribal Association 650
Treaty Site History Center Archives 315
Tredyffrin Public Library 504
Tredyffrin Public Library-Paoli Branch 496
Tree 521
Tree Branches 81
Tree Builders 229
Tree Climber 221, 308, 454, 516
Tree Climbers 453
Tree Climbers Notes 333
Tree Shaker 225
Tree Shakers 52
Tree Stumpers 205
Tree Talk 550
Tree Talks 418
Tree Tips 46, 70
Tree Tracers 35, 466
Tree Tracker 220
Tree Trackers & Library 328
Treebark 216
Trees and Trails 345
Trees from the Grove 474
Treesearcher 213
Treeshaker 555
Trefethen-Trefren Family 477
Treffry-Trefry Family 605
Trego County Historical Museum 222
Trego County Historical Society & Archives 222
Treherne Museum Archives 661
Treleven Family 622
Trembowla Cross of Freedom Museum Archives 659
Tremont District Public Library 176
Tremont Historical Society & Library 176
Trempealeau Community Heritage Society 632
Trempealeau County Historical Society & Archives 621
Trenton City Museum Archives 379
Trenton City Museum Newsletter 379
Trenton Historical Museum Archives 303
Trenton Historical Society 379
Trenton Public Library 176, 379
Trepassey Area Museum Archives 669
Trescott Family 604
Treutlen County Historical Society & Archives 137
Treutlen County Museum of Local History 137
Tri State Railway Historical Society 374
Triannual Musings 255
Tribal Chief's Association 645
Triboulet Family 223
Tribune des Francophiles 239
Tri-Cities Historical Museum 292
Tri-Cities Historical Society & Archives 292
Tri-City Genealogical Society & Library 605
Tri-City Genealogical Society Bulletin 605
Tri-county Family History Association 31
Tri-County Genealogical Society 151, 179, 336
Tri-County Genealogical Society & Library 30, 551
Tri-County Genealogical Society Newsletter 179
Tri-County Heritage Society 151, 494
Tri-County Historical Museum 215, 333
Tri-County Historical Society & Archives 215
Tri-County Historical Society of King City & Archives 333
Tri-County Newsletter 215, 551
Tri-County Researcher 614
Tri-County Searcher 343
Trimble County Historical Society 232
Trimble County Public Library 225
Trimble Library 82
Trimont Area Historical Society 316
Trinidad Historical Society 90
Trinidad History Museum Archives 90
Trinity Cathedral Historical Society 355
Trinity College Library 94
Trinity County Historical Society & Archives 77
Trinity County Historical Society Yearbook 77
Trinity County Library 77
Trinity Historical Society 669
Trinity Interpretation Centre Archives 669
Trinity Museum and Archives 669
Trinity Museum Archives 408
Tripoli Public Library 208
Tripp County Historical Society 524
Tripp County Library 524
Tripp Family 480
Tripp Memorial Museum 629
Tripp-Rice-Royce-Buck(e)ridge-Tucker-Toocker-Dickinson Family 101
Tri-State Corners Genealogical Society & Archives 351
Tri-State Genealogical and Historical Society 614
Tri-State Genealogical Society 15, 18, 183, 303, 521
Tri-State Genealogical Society & Archives 447
Tri-State Genealogical Society Quarterly Newsletter 447
Tri-State Packet 183
Tri-States Genealogical Society 16
Triton Community History Organization & Library 171
Triton Museum Archives 70
Tri-Township Public Library 176
Tritt Family 449, 484
Triumph of the Past 446
Trocaire College Library 391
Trochu and District Museum Archives 646
Trochu Municipal Library 646
Trogdon Family 341
Trolley Fare 504
Trolley Gazette 620
Trolley Museum of New York Archives 402
Trolley Museum Retriever 500
Trona Mining Museum of Bridger Valley Archives 637
Tropic Lightning Museum 143
Troup County Historical Society & Library 132
Troup County Historical Society Newsletter 132

Troup-Harris-Coweta Regional Library 132
Trousdale Place Archives 527
Troutdale Historical Museum 480
Troutdale Historical Society & Archives 480
Troy Historical and Genealogical Society 458
Troy Historical Society 303
Troy Museum and Historic Village 303
Troy Public Library 9, 303, 418
Troy State University Library 9
Troy Times 458
Troy Village Press 303
Truckee-Donner Historical Society 75
Trudeau Institute 415
True West 15
Truett Memorial Library 542
Truett Memorial Library Newsletter 542
Truman Farm Home Museum Archives 329
Trumbull County Genealogical Society 459
Trumbull County Historical Society & Archives 459
Trumbull Historical Society & Library 100
Trump of Fame 459
Truro Historical Museum 280
Truro Historical Society & Archives 280
Truro Historical Society Newsletter 280
Trussville Public Library 9
Truth or Consequences Public Library 385
TRW Genealogical Society 62
Tryon Palace Restoration Complex Archives 430
Ts'ilhqot'in Tribal Council 657
Tsa Mo Ga Memorial Museum Archives 556
Tsaile Campus Library 21
Tsawataineuk Indian Band 651
Tsawout Indian Band 654
Tsawwassen First Nation 649
Tsay Keh Dene Indian Band 654
Tseshaht Indian Band 653
Tseycum Indian Band 655
Tsimshian Tribal Council 654
Tuba City Public Library 21
Tubac Historical Society & Library 21
Tubac Presidio State Historic Park Archives 21
Tubb-May Memorial Library 322
Tubman African-American Museum Archives 133
Tuck Museum 361
Tuckahoe Public Library 418
Tucker Family 4
Tucker Family 601
Tucker Free Library 361
Tuckerton Historical Society 379
Tuckerton Seaport Museum Archives 379
Tuckerton Seaport Museum Newsletter 379
Tucson Rodeo Parade Museum Archives 22
Tucumcari Historical Research Institute Archives 385
Tucumcari Public Library 385
Tudor Place Museum Archives 107
Tudor Place Museum Newsletter 107
Tu-Endie-Wei State Park Archives 614
Tuftonboro Free Library 359
Tufts Family 269
Tufts Library 282
Tulare City Historical Society 75
Tulare County Historical Museum 76
Tulare County Historical Society & Archives 76
Tulare County Library System 76
Tulare Public Library 75
Tularosa Basin Historical Museum 381
Tularosa Basin Historical Society & Archives 381
Tularosa Basin Historical Society Newsletter 381
Tule River Historical Society & Archives 73
Tule Tree Tracers 61
Tule Tree Tracers Newsletter 61
Tulip Grove Mansion Archives 527
Tully Area Historical Society & Library 418
Tully Area Historical Society Newsletter 418
Tully Free Library 418
Tulpehocken Settlement Historical Society & Library 505
Tulpehocken Settlement Historical Society Newsletter 505
Tulpehocken Tattler 505
Tulsa Annals 470
Tulsa Central Library 470
Tulsa Genealogical Society & Library 470
Tulsa Genealogical Society Newsletter 470
Tulsa Historical Society 470
Tumacacori National Historical Park Archives 22
Tunbridge Public Library 580
Tungate Family 444
Tunica-Biloxi Native American Museum Archives 239
Tuolumne County Free Library 73
Tuolumne County Genealogical Society & Library 73
Tuolumne County Historian 73
Tuolumne County Historical Society & Library 73
Tupelo Automobile Museum Archives 322
Tupperville School Museum Archives 673
Tuquoise Museum Archives 381
Turin Town Historian 418
Turk Family 543
Turkey Talk 22
Turkey Tracks 374
Turlock Historical Society 75
Turman Family 567, 586
Turnage Family 301
Turnage Family Newsletter 28, 470
Turnbull Clan 167
Turner Family 118, 129
Turner House Museum Archives 320
Turner Tracing 292
Turner-Helm Family Newsletter 53
Turney Historical Society 341
Turning Page 343
Turquoise Unearthed 381
Turtle Mountain Chippewa Historical Society 437
Tuscaloosa County Preservation Society 9
Tuscaloosa Genealogical Society 9
Tuscaloosa Genealogical Society, Morning Group & Library 9
Tuscaloosa Genealogical Society, Night Group 9
Tuscaloosa Public Library 9
Tuscarawas County Genealogy Society & Library 454
Tuscarawas County Public Library 454
Tuscarora Historical Society 294
Tuscarora Township Historical Society 491

Tuscawaras County Pioneer Footprints 454
Tuskegee Institute National Historic Site Archives 9
Tussey Newsletter 553
Tusten-Cochecton Library 405
Tustin Area Historical Society & Museum 75
Tuttle Family 44
Tuttleman Library 494
Tuxedo Historical Society 418
Tuxedo Park Historic Preservation 418
Tuxedo Park Library 418
Tuxedo Park Library Newsletter 418
Tuzzy Consortium Library 11
TVGS Tidings 6
Twamley Family 511
TWANAT 480
Tweed and Area Heritage Centre Archives 692
Tweed-Siedenburg Family 635
Twenty Mile Post Historical Society 644
Twenty Mule Team Museum Archives 38
Twenty-Nine Palms Historical Society & Library 75
Twigs 194
Twigs and Branches 172
Twillingate Museum Association & Library 669
Twin Bridges Public Library 346
Twin Falls County Museum Archives 146
Twin Falls Public Library 150
Twin Falls State Park Museum Archives 614
Twin Lakes Library System 134
Twin Mountain Public Library 359
Twin Oaks Genealogy 180
Twin Ports Genealogical Society 307
Twin Rivers District Public Library 157
Twin Rivers Genealogical Society 148
Twin Tiers Genealogical Society 396
Twinsburg Historical Museum 458
Twinsburg Historical Society & Archives 458
Twinsburg Historical Society Newsletter 458
Twinsburg Public Library 458
Two Hills and District Museum Archives 646
Two Mile House Museum 484
Two Rivers Bulletin 483
Two Rivers Historical Society & Archives 632
Two Rivers Historical Society & Library 632
Two Rivers Historical Society Newsletter 632
Two Rivers History Museum Archives 632
TX-OK Panhandle Genealogical Society & Archives 556
TX-OK Panhandler 556
Tybee Island Historical Society & Archives 138
Tye Preston Memorial Library 539
Tyler County Genealogical Society 563
Tyler County Heritage and Historical Society 613
Tyler County Heritage Society & Archives 563
Tyler Memorial Library 268
Tyler Public Library 562
Tyndall Air Force Base Library 123
Tyomies Society 632
Tyre-Tyree Family 191
Tyrone Area Historical Society & Library 503
Tyrone Area Historical Society Annual Report 503
Tyrone Area Historical Society Newsletter 503
Tyrone-Snyder Township Public Library 503
Tyrrell County Genealogical and Historical Society 425
Tyrrell County Public Library 425
Tyrrell Historical Library 537
Tyrrell Historical Library Association Newsletter 537
Tyson Library 194
Tyson-Theisen-Teissen (Doors-Dahrs) Newsletter 63
Tzeachten Indian Band 655

U

U Grant Miller Library 504
U'Mista Cultural Centre Archives 647
U'Mista Nation 647
Uchucklesant Indian Band 653
Ucluelet Indian Band 656
Udall Historical Society 222
UDT-Seal Museum Archives 113
uernsey County Historical Museum 443
Uinta County Historical Society 636
Uinta County Library 636
Uintah County Library 573
Ukiah Tree Tracers Genealogical Society 76
Ukraine Museum Archives 710
Ukrainian Catholic Women's League 643
Ukrainian Catholic Women's League Historical Museum 643
Ukrainian Cultural Heritage Museum 661
Ukrainian Cultural Heritage Village Archives 643
Ukrainian Cultural Institute 437
Ukrainian Cultural Institute Newspaper 437
Ukrainian Fraternal Association & Library 501
Ukrainian Genealogical and Historical Society of Canada 642
Ukrainian Museum Archives 408, 445
Ukrainian Museum of Canada - Alberta Branch 643
Ukrainian Museum of Canada Archives 656
Ukrainian Museum of Canada Library 662, 692
Ukrainian National Home Association Library 662
Ukrainian National Museum & Archives 156
Ukrainian Public Library of Ivan Franko 662
Ukrainian Research Institute Reference Library 268
Ukranian Canadian Archives and Museum 643
Ukranian Cultural and Education Centre Library 662
Ukranian Cultural Heritage Village 646
Ukranian Genealogical and Heraldic Society 117
Ukranian Genealogical and Historical Society of Canada 642
Ukranian Museum of Canada Library 710
Ukranian National Association 375
Ukranian-American Museum Archives 303
Ulen Historical Society 316
Ulkatcho Indian Band 647
Ulster County Gazette 402, 404
Ulster County Genealogical Society & Library 401
Ulster County Historical Museum 404
Ulster County Historical Society & Archives 404
Ulster County Historical Society & Library 402
Ulster Gazette 401
Ulster Genie 401
Ulysses Historical Society & Library 418
Ulysses S Grant Cottage Historic Site Archives 421
Umatilla County Historical Society & Archives 477
Umhauer Family 558

Umpqua Discovery Center Archives 479
Umpqua Trapper 479
Unabridged 446
Unalaska Public Library 13
Uncle Remus Museum Archives 130
Uncle Remus Regional Library System-Greene County Library 131
Uncle Remus Regional Library System-Hancock County Library 137
Uncle Remus Regional Library System-Jasper County Library 134
Uncle Remus Regional Library System-Monroe-Walton County Library 134
Uncle Remus Regional Library System-Morgan County Library 133
Uncle Remus Regional Library System-O'Kelly Memorial Library 133
Uncle Remus Regional Library System-Putnam County Library 130
Uncle Remus Regional Library System-W H Stanton Memorial Library 137
Uncle Tom's Cabin Historic Site Archives 681
Uncommon Sense 597
Under Construction 45
Under the Mulberry Tree 272
Underground Gold Miners Museum Archives 35
Underground Gold Miners Museum Archives Newsletter 35
Underhill Family 410
Undersea Quarterly 602
Underwood Family Organization Newsletter 41
Underwood Memorial Library 246
Unger Memorial Library 556
Unger Ululations 556
Uniacke Estata Museum Archives 675
Unicoi County Public Library 527
Union Bar Indian Band 650
Union Bay Historical Society 656
Union Cemetery Historical Society & Library 332
Union City Genealogical Society 303
Union City Historical Museum 503
Union City Historical Museum Archives 76
Union City Historical Society 303
Union City Historical Society & Archives 503
Union City Public Library 194, 503
Union College Library 353
Union County Carnegie Library 518
Union County Chapter, OGS & Library 452
Union County District Library 231
Union County Genealogical and Historical Research Committee 151
Union County Genealogical Society & Archives 27, 199
Union County Heritage 492
Union County Heritage Museum Archives 321
Union County Heritage Room 430
Union County Historical Complex Archives 199
Union County Historical Foundation & Archives 518
Union County Historical Foundation Newsletter 518
Union County Historical Museum 127, 231, 321, 452, 518
Union County Historical Society 188, 321, 369, 382, 480, 521, 530
Union County Historical Society & Archives 127, 231, 452, 492
Union County Historical Society & Library 199
Union County Museum Archives 480
Union County Public Library 115, 188, 430, 492
Union County Public Library Newsletter 492
Union County-Jennie Stephens Smith Library 321
Union Covered Bridge State Historic Site Archives 336
Union Echoes 452
Union for Reform Judaism Museum Archives 408
Union Historical Society 252
Union Historical Society & Library 100
Union League of Philadelphia Genealogy Affinity Club 500, 502
Union League of Philadelphia Library 498
Union Library County of Hatborough 489
Union Mills Homestead & Grist Mill Archives 264
Union Mills Homestead Quarterly 264
Union of British Columbia Indian Chiefs 656
Union of New Brunswick Indians 663
Union of Nova Scotia Indians 676
Union of Ontario Indians 692
Union Pacific Historical Society 635
Union Pacific Railroad Museum Archives 199
Union Roots 199
Union Springs Public Library 10
Union Station Kansas City Museum & Archives 333
Union Station Kansas City Museum Newsletter 333
Union Township Public Library 456
Uniontown Public Library 503
Unionville Dispatch 175
Unitarian Universalist Association of Congregations Archives 267
Unitarian Universalist Historical Society 267
United Baltic Appeal 390
United Brethren Archives 186
United Christian Church Archives 492
United Church of Canada Central Archives 692
United Counties Museum Archives 681
United Daughters of the Confederacy & Library 594
United Daughters of the Confederacy Magazine 594
United Daughters of the Confederacy, Hot Springs Chapter 28
United Daughters of the Confederacy, James Jackson Gillcoatt Chapter 25
United Daughters of the Confederacy, John R. Baylor Chapter 22
United Daughters of the Confederacy, Louisiana Chapter 241
United Daughters of the Confederacy, Thunderbird Chapter 22
United Empire Loyalist Museum Archives 679
United Empire Loyalist Museum Library 680
United Empire Loyalists' Association of Canada & Library 692
United Methodist Church Archives 360
United Methodist Church, Southern New England Conference 267
United Methodist Historical Society 185
United Methodist Historical Society & Library 256
United Methodist Publishing House Library 531
United Native Nations 656
United Society of Shakers & Library 248
United States Catholic Historical Society 408
United States Civil War Center 236
United States Historical Society 594
United States Internet Genealogical Society 38
United States Lighthouse Society 67
United Theological Seminary Library 447
Unity and District Heritage Museum Archives 711
Unity Free Public Library 359
Unity Historical Society 251
Unity Library 341
Univ of Arkansas-Monticello Library 30
Univ of South Florida Library 123
Universal Genealogical Society of Bellflower 37
Universite de Montreal Dept. d'Histoire 700
Universite du Quebec a Chicoutimi Bibliotheque 697
Universite Saint-Anne 675
University Archives and Records Center 231

University at Buffalo Library 391
University Baptist Church Library 236
University City Historical Society 498
University City Public Library 341
University College of Cape Breton Library 676
University Libraries of Notre Dame 191
University Library 7, 62, 355, 450, 526, 631
University Museum Archives 153, 159, 168, 490, 529
University of Alabama Library 9
University of Alaska Library 11
University of Alaska Museum Archives 12
University of Alberta Archives 643
University of Alberta Museum Archives 643
University of Arizona Library 22
University of Arkansas Libraries 27
University of Auburn-Montgomery Library 7
University of British Columbia 656
University of British Columbia Library 656
University of California Library 48
University of California-Santa Barbara Library 70
University of Central Florida Library 119
University of Chicago Library 156
University of Connecticut Library 100
University of Dubuque Library 201
University of Hawaii Center 142
University of Idaho Library 148
University of Illinois Library 176
University of Iowa Libraries 203
University of Iowa Medical Museum Archives 203
University of King's College Archives 674
University of Lethbridge Library 644
University of Louisiana at Monroe Library 239
University of Maine at Presque Isle Library 250
University of Mississippi Museum Archives 322
University of Mississippi Museum Newsletter 322
University of Missouri-Kansas City Library 333
University of Nebraska State Museum Archives 353
University of Nebraska-Lincoln Library 353
University of New Brunswick Library 663
University of New Mexico-Los Alamos Campus Library 384
University of North Texas Library 543
University of Northern Iowa Museum Archives 198
University of Northern Iowa Museum Newsletter 198
University of Oklahoma Library 467
University of Pennsylvania Museum Archives 498
University of Pittsburgh Library 499
University of Rhode Island Library 508
University of Richmond Museum Archives 594
University of Saskatchewan Library 710
University of South Carolina at Beaufort Library 511
University of South Carolina Historical Association 516
University of Southern Colorado Library 89
University of Texas at Arlington Library 536
University of Texas at El Paso Library 544
University of Texas-Pan American Library 544
University of Texas-San Antonio Library 559
University of Toronto Library 692
University of Winnipeg Library 662
University of Wisconsin-Madison Library 625
University of Wisconsin-Wausau Library 633
University of Wyoming Library 636
untington County Historical Museum 185
Up and Down the Valley 611
Up the Gatineau 700
Upchurch Family 333
Upchurch-Bright Family 6
Upchurch-Bright Family Newsletter 6
Update: Newsletter of the Kershaw County Historical Society 512
Upham Family 274
Upjohn Library 295
Upland Area Historical Society 194
Upland Public Library 76
Upper Blackfoot Historical Society 345
Upper Canada Village Archives 686
Upper Cumberland Genealogical Association 526
Upper Cumberland Genealogical Association Bulletin 526
Upper Cumberland Researcher 526
Upper Darby Free Public Library 504
Upper Darby Historical Society 504
Upper Merion Township Library 491
Upper Mooreland Free Public Library 505
Upper Moreland Historical Association 505
Upper Musselshell Historical Museum 345
Upper Musselshell Historical Society & Archives 345
Upper Musselshell Historical Society Newsletter 345
Upper Nicola Indian Band 652
Upper Ohio Valley Historical Review 615
Upper Ottawa Valley Genealogical Group 688
Upper Room Chapel Museum Archives 531
Upper Saddle River Historical Society 379
Upper San Juan Historical Museum 88
Upper San Juan Historical Society & Archives 88
Upper Sandusky Community Library 458
Upper Sandusky Historical Society 458
Upper Shore Genealogical Society Membership Surnames 258
Upper Shore Genealogical Society of Maryland 258
Upper Similkameen Indian Band 651
Upper Snake River Valley Historical Society & Library 149
Upper South Carolina Genealogy and History 518
Upper Township Historic Preservation Society 380
Uppertown Firefighters Museum Archives 473
Uppertown Firefighters Museum Newsletter 473
Upsala Area Historical Society 316
Upsala Area Historical Society Newsletter 316
UPSCOPE 298
Upshaw Family Journal 129
Upshur County Genealogical Society 611
Upshur County Historical Society 611
Upshur County Historical Society Newsletter 611
Upshur County Library 546
Upson Historical Society & Library 138
Upstairs & Downstairs 617
Upstate History Alliance 409
Upstate History Alliance Quarterly Museum 409
Up-to-Date 286
Upton County Genealogical Society 557
Upton County Public Library 553
Upton Historical Society 281
Upton Historical Society Newsletter 281
Urbain Baudreau Graveline Genealogical Association 277

Urbana Free Library 176
Urbandale Historical Society 208
Urbandale Public Library 208
Urhobo Historical Society 391
Urich Community Historical Society 341
Urquhart Clan 441
Ursuline Sisters Archives 231
US Air Force Academy Visitor Center 90
US Air Force Museum Archives 460
US Air Force-Historical Research Agency 6
US Army Air Defense Artillery Museum Archives 545
US Army Aviation Museum Archives 4
US Army Center for Army Analysis 587
US Army Center of Military History 107
US Army Center of Military History Archives 107
US Army Chaplain Museum Archives 514
US Army Chaplain Museum Newsletter 514
US Army Chemical Corps Museum Archives 4
US Army Consolidated Library 385
US Army Finance Corps Museum Archives 514
US Army Fort Myer Post Library 587
US Army Garrison 143
US Army Groninger Library 587
US Army Headquarters, US Army Fort Monroe Technical Library 587
US Army Heritage & Education Center 484
US Army Infantry School 131
US Army Medical Department Museum Archives 545
US Army Medical Department Museum Newsletter 545
US Army Military History Institute 484
US Army Military Police Corps Museum Archives 329
US Army Military Police Corps Regimental Museum Archives 4
US Army Museum of Hawaii 141
US Army Ordnance Center & Ordnance Museum Library 255
US Army Post Library 23
US Army Publications Center 256
US Army Quartermaster Museum Archives 587
US Army Signal Corps Museum Archives 131
US Army Transportation Museum Library 587
US Army War College Library 484
US Army Women's Museum Archives 587
US Army Women's Museum Newsletter 587
US Army-Institute of Heraldry Library 587
US Army-Transportation School Library 587
US Army-Transportation School LibraryQuarterly Newsletter 587
US Army-Van Noy Library 587
US Brig Niagara 487
US Capitol Historical Society & Archives 107
US Catholic Historian 112
US Catholic Historical Society 112
US Cavalry Association & Library 214
US Cavalry Memorial Research Library 214
US Coast Guard Academy Library 97
US Coast Guard Base Library-Otis 265
US Coast Guard Historian's Office 107
US Coast Guard Museum Archives 97
US Daughters of 1812 559
US District Court for the Northern District of California Historical Society 67
US Geological Survey Library 16, 54, 84, 593
US Grant's Home State Historic Site 160
US Holocaust Memorial Museum Archives 107
US Holocaust Memorial Museum Quarterly 107
US Marconi Museum Archives 359
US Marine Corps Air Station Library 511
US Marine Corps Air-Ground Museum Archives 593
US Marine Corps James Carson Breckinridge Library 593
US Marine Corps Quantico Family Library 593
US Maritime Administration Archives 107
US Merchant Marine Museum Archives 179
US Mint Philadelphia Museum Archives 498
US Mormon Battalion, California South Division 66
US Naval Academy Museum Archives 255
US Naval Shipbuilding Museum Archives 278
US Naval War College Library 508
US Navy Memorial Foundation 107
US Navy Museum 106
US Navy Resource Center 600
US Navy Supply Corps School Station Museum Archive 125
US Navy-Naval Amphibious Base Library
US Patent and Trademark Office Museum Archives 583
Usher Family 145
Ushers Ferry Historic Village 198
US-Japan Meritime Foundation 408
USMC Air Station Library 425
USMC MCAS Station Library 428
USS Alabama Battleship Memorial Park Archives 7
USS Arizona Memorial Library 142
USS Bowfin Submarine Museum & Park Library 142
USS Constellation Museum Archives 256
USS Constitution Museum Archives 267
USS Lexington Museum Archives 541
USS Lexington Museum Newsletter 541
USS Radford National Naval Museum Archives 454
USS Radford National Naval Museum Newsletter 454
Utah Cornish Association 566
Utah Genealogical Association & Library 571
Utah Genealogical Association News 571
Utah Genealogical Association, Morgan Valley Chapter 566
Utah Genealogical Association, Salt Lake Valley Chapter 571
Utah Genealogical Association, Snake River Chapter 149
Utah Genealogical Association, Tooele Chapter 566
Utah Genealogical Association, Utah Valley Chapter 570
Utah Historical Quarterly 572
Utah Preservation 567, 572
Utah Preservation Society 572
Utah State Archives 572
Utah State Historical Society 567
Utah State Historical Society & Library 572
Utah State Library 572
Utah Valley PAF Users Group 569
Ute Indian Museum Archives 88
Ute Indian Tribe Museum Archives 566
Ute Mountain Tribal Library 90
Ute Mountain Ute Tribal Research Archives Library Tribal Compound 90
Ute Pass Historical Society & Library 90
Utica Historical Society & Archives 345, 453
Utica Museum 345
Utica Public Library 303, 419
Utica Public Library District 176
Utley Family 528
UVAN Historical Museum Archives 662

INDEX

Uxbridge-Scott Historical Society & Archives 692

V

Vacaville Museum Archives 76
Vachel Lindsay Home State Historic Site Archives 174
Vahey Family 478
Vail Family 242
Vaile Mansion and Dewitt Museum Archives 331
Vaile Victorian Society Newsletter 331
Val A Browning Library 570
Val Verde County Genealogy Society 543
Val Verde County Library 543
Valdez Consortium Library 13
Valdez Historical Museum 13
Valdez Historical Society & Library 13
Valdez Museum & Historical Archives 11
Vale Lyman Estate 281
Valemount and Area Museum Archives 656
Valencia Community College Library 119
Valencia County Historical Society 382
Valens Log Cabin Museum Archives 679
Valentine Prentice Newsletter 46
Valentine Richmond History Center Archives 594
Valentine Richmond History Center Newsletter 594
Valentine-Varian House 390
Valentown Historical Museum 419
Valentown Historical Society 419
Valentown Historical Society Newsletter 419
Valentown Museum Archives 397
Valiant Air Command Warbird Air Museum Archives 123
Valiant Air Command Warbird Air Museum Newsletter 123
Valiant Defender 497
Vallejo Historical Museum 76
Vallejo Naval and Historical Museum Archives 76
Vallejo Naval and Historical Museum Newsletter 76
Vallerchamp Council #25 503
Valley 54
Valley Center Historical and Cultural Society 222
Valley City Historical Society 459
Valley City-Barnes County Public Library 439
Valley Community Library 381
Valley Cottage Free Library 419
Valley County 344
Valley County Genealogical Society & Archives 146
Valley County Genealogical Society & Library 355
Valley County Genealogical Society Newsletter 146
Valley County Heritage 146
Valley County Historical Society 146
Valley County Historical Society & Archives 344, 355
Valley East Public Library 683
Valley Falls Historical Society 222
Valley Forge Historical Society 498
Valley Forge Historical Society & Library 504
Valley Forge Journal 504
Valley Forge National Historical Park Archives 504
Valley Forge National Historical Park Library 491
Valley Gazette 492
Valley Genealogist 47
Valley Heritage 71
Valley Historical Museum 357
Valley Historical Society & Archives 357
Valley Museum Archives 652
Valley Park Community Library 341
Valley Quarterly 64
Valley Stream Historical Society 419
Valor 548
Valparaiso Community Library 123
VAM Membership Directory 594
VAM Quarterly Newsletter 594
Van Aersdalen Family 554
Van Aken-Van Auken Newsletter 92
Van Alstyne Public Library 562
Van Arsdale Newsletter: Van to Van 178
Van Blaricom Family 197
Van Buren County Genealogical Society Chapter, IGS & Library 204
Van Buren County Historical Journal 26, 533
Van Buren County Historical Museum 26, 204
Van Buren County Historical Society 293
Van Buren County Historical Society & Archives 26, 204
Van Buren County Historical Society & Library 533
Van Buren County Historical Society Newsletter 533
Van Buren County Library 289
Van Buren County Quill 204
Van Buren District Library 289
Van Buren Echoes 289
Van Buren Public Library 33
Van Buren Regional Genealogical Society & Archives 289
Van Buren-Henke-Mohme Family 176
Van Buskirk News 187
Van Cortlandt House Museum Archives 390
Van Der Veer Family 325
Van Hoosen Farm 301
Van Horn Public Library 313
Van Kouwenhoven-Conover Family 369, 375
Van Lear Historical Society & Archives 234
Van Meter State Park Archives 335
Van Nostrand-Starkins House Museum Archives 414
Van Nuys Notes 313
Van Pelt Library 498
Van Riper-Hopper House 380
Van Schaick Family 269
Van Steenwyk Family 198
Van Valkenburg Family 187
Van Valkenburg Family 454
Van Veghten House 368
Van Voorhees Family 369, 379
Van Wert and Surrounding Counties, Ohio-Early Records 459
Van Wert Connection 459
Van Wert County Genealogical Quarterly 459
Van Wert County Genealogical Society 459
Van Wert County Historical Society & Library 459
Van Wyck Dispatch 397
Van Wyck Homestead Museum Library 397
Van Wye Family History Research Newsletter 55
Van Wylen Library 294
Van Zandt County Library 539
Van Zandt Family 492, 500
VA-NC Piedmont Genealogical Society & Archives 586
Vance & Dorothy Hammond Museum 251
Vance County Historical Society 428

Vance Family 281, 599
Vance Township Library 160
Vanceboro Historical Society 252
Vancortlandtville Historical Society 395
Vancouver Cornish Association 653
Vancouver Historical Society 656
Vancouver Holocaust Education Centre 656
Vancouver Island Regional Library 652
Vancouver Maritime Museum Archives 656
Vancouver Museum Archives 656
Vancouver Museum Library 656
Vancouver Naval Museum Archives 657
Vancouver Police Centennial Museum Archives 656
Vancouver Public Library 656
Vandal Family 289
Vandalia Historical Society & Archives 176
Vandalia State House Archives 176
Vande Bogart Library 345
Vandenberg Air Force Base Library 76
Vandenberg Genealogical Society & Library 50
Vander Ende-Onderdonk House 413
Vanderbilt Mansion National Historic Site Archives 401
Vanderburgh County Historical Society 183
Vandergrift Historical Museum 504
Vandergrift Historical Society & Archives 504
Vanderhoof Community Museum Archives 656
Vanderpool Newsletter 62
Vanguard Centennial Museum Archives 711
Vann House State Historical Park Archives 128
Varnado Family 319
Varner Newsletter 120
Varner-Hogg Plantation State Historic Site Archives 563
Varnum Family 281
Varnum Memorial Armory and Military Museum Archives 507
Varnum Memorial Armory and Military Museum Newsletter 507
Vasa Luthern Church Museum Archives 306
Vashon Maury Island Heritage Association & Archives 609
Vashon Maury Island Heritage Association Newsletter 609
Vashon Maury Island Historical Museum 609
Vassalboro Historical Museum 245
Vassalboro Historical Society 252
Vassalboro Historical Society & Archives 245
Vassalboro Public Library 245
Vaugh'a'n Family 561
Vaughan Memorial Library 677
Vaughan-Vaughn Family Annals 554
Vaughan-Vaughn Family Research Bulletin 74
Vaughn Library 562
Vaughn Public Library 617
Vaught Family 531
Vawter-Vauter-Vaugher(s) Newsletter 193
Vcera a dnes 16
Veazey-Veasey Family 435
Vegreville Regional Museum Archives 646
Veitch-Veach-Veatch-Veech Family 444
Velline Family Organization Newsletter 75
Venable Family 528
Venango County Genealogical Club & Archives 496
Venango County Genealogical Club Newsletter 496
Venango County Historical Society & Library 487
Venango Intelligencer 487
Venice Archives and Area Historical Collection 123
Venice Archives and Historical Society 123
Venice Historical Society 76
Vent Haven Museum Archives 227
Ventress Memorial Library 274
Ventura County Genealogical Society & Archives 76
Ventura County Genealogical Society Quarterly 76
Ventura County Historical Museum 76
Ventura County Historical Society & Archives 76
Ventura County Historical Society Quarterly 76
Ventura County Library 76
Ventura County Library Services Agency 76
Ventura County Maritime Museum Archives 58
Ventura County Maritime Museum Newsletter 58
Vera Estey House 250
Verandah House Archives 320
Verde Valley Historical Society 15
Verdier House Museum 511
Verdigre Heritage Society 357
Vermazen-Vermason Family 204
Vermilion County Museum Society & Library 157
Vermilion County Museum Society Newsletter 157
Vermilion Heritage Museum Archives 646
Vermilion Parish Library-Cow Island 235
Vermilion Parish Library-Delcambre Branch 236
Vermilion Parish Library-Erath Branch 237
Vermilion Parish Library-Gueydan Branch 237
Vermilion Parish Library-Kaplan Branch 237
Vermilion Parish Library-Maurice Branch 239
Vermilion Parish Library-Vaugh-Copel Memorial Branch-Pecan Island 237
Vermilion Public Library 646
Vermillion Community College Library 307
Vermillion County Historical Society 191
Vermillion Genealogical Society 235
Vermillion Historic Foundation 238
Vermillion Historical Society 235
Vermillion Parish Library 235
Vermillion Public Library 524
Vermont Department of Libraries 578
Vermont Folklife Center Archives 577
Vermont French-Canadian Genealogical Society 575
Vermont Genealogy 579
Vermont Historical Museum 578
Vermont Historical Society & Archives 578
Vermont Historical Society & Library 575
Vermont History 578
Vermont History News 578
Vermont Life 578
Vermont Marble Museum Archives 579
Vermont State House Museum Archives 578
Vermontville Historical Society 303
Verndale Historical Society & Library 316
Vernon and District Family History Society 657
Vernon Area Public Library District 164
Vernon County Genealogical Society & Library 336
Vernon County Historical Museum 632
Vernon County Historical Museum Archives 632
Vernon County Historical Society & Archives 336
Vernon County Historical Society & Archives 632

Vernon Family 427
Vernon Historians 580
Vernon Historians Newsletter 580
Vernon Historical and Genealogical Society 235, 238
Vernon Historical Museum 100, 580
Vernon Historical Society 371
Vernon Historical Society & Archives 100
Vernon Parish Library 238
Vernon R Alden Library 441
Verona Public Library 632
Versailles Area Genealogical and Historical Newsletter 176
Versailles Area Genealogical and Historical Society 176
Verwood Community Museum Archives 711
Veselik Historical Society 590
Vespasian Warner Public Library 157
Vesper Public Library 632
Vesta Legion Pioneer Society 316
Vestal Historical Museum 419
Vestal Historical Society 419
Vestal Historical Society Newsletter 419
Vestal Public Library 419
Vesterheim Genealogical Society & Library 625
Vesterheim Norwegian-American Museum Archives 200
Vesterheim Norwegian-American Museum Newsletter 200
Vest-Lindsey House Archives 227
Vestnik 157
Veteran's Museum of Hardy Archives 28
Veterans Depot Museum Archives 177
Veterans Memorial Library 261, 298
Veterans' Memorial Military Museum Archives 695
VHPS News 139
Via Family 78
Vick Family 498
Vickers Family 138
Vicksburg and Warren County Historical Society & Archives 323
Vicksburg and Warren County Historical Society Newsletter 323
Vicksburg Battlefield Museum Archives 323
Vicksburg District Library 303
Vicksburg Genealogical Society 323
Vicksburg Genealogical Society Newsletter 323
Vicksburg Historical Society 303
Vicksburg National Military Park Archives 323
Victor Heritage Association 347
Victor Historical Museum 347
Victor Public Library 90
Victor Township Historical Society 295
Victor Valley Museum Archives 35
Victoria College Library 562
Victoria Cornish Association 657
Victoria County Genealogical Society 562
Victoria County Historical Museum 684
Victoria County Historical Society 684
Victoria County Library Museum and Archives 673
Victoria Genealogical Society 657
Victoria Heritage Foundation 657
Victoria Historical Society 657
Victoria Mansion Archives 250
Victoria Mansion Newsletter 250
Victoria Preservation 562
Victoria Public Library 562
Victoria School Museum and Archives 643
Victoria School Museum Archives 680
Victoria-Crossroads of South Texas 562
Victorian 498
Victorian Alliance 67
Victorian Carthage 327
Victorian Dress Museum Archives 439
Victorian Preservation Society of Santa Clara Valley 68
Victorian Review 643
Victorian Society Historical Museum 498
Victorian Society in America & Archives 498
Victorian Studies 180
Victorian Studies Association of Western Canada 643
Victorian Times 492
Victorville Public Library 76
Victory Garden 592
Vidette 230
Vidor Public Library 562
Viebrock Family 334
Vieille Maison des Jesuites 701
Vienna Historic Preservation Society 139
Vienna Public Library 615
Viers-Veirs Quarterly Newsletter 60
Viet Nam Generation 101
Vietnam Era Educational Center Archives 371
Vietnamese Association 692
View from Evergreen 255
View from Kimberly Crest 61
View from the Cupola 278
Viewpoints in Georgia History 133
Views a-Foot 491
Views from Clermont 394
Views from the Verandah 125
Vigilant Crane 116
Vigo County Historical Museum 194
Vigo County Historical Society & Archives 194
Vigo County Public Library 194
Viking Historical Museum Archives 646
Viking Historical Society 646
Vikingsholm Museum Archives 74
Vilas County Historical Society 630
Villa Bagatelle 703
Villa Louis Historic Site Archives 629
Villa Montezuma Museum Archives 66
Villa Park Historical Society 76
Villa Park Historical Society & Library 176
Villa Park Public Library 176
Village Crier 214
Village Dispatch 244
Village Genealogical Society Newsletter 29
Village Green Heritage Center 58
Village Guide 447
Village Hall Museum 308
Village Historical Museum 449
Village Historical Society & Archives 449
Village Historique Acadien 663
Village Inn Museum 369
Village Library of Morris 405
Village Minier de Bourlamaque 703
Village of Dannemora Historian 395

Village of East Davenport Association 200
Village of Elsah Museum 159
Village of Gouverneur Town Historian 398
Village of Thornton Historical Society 175
Village Ouebecois d'Antan 697
Village Progress 501
Village Square Mall 213
Village Star 367
Village Yesterdays 169
Villager 293
Villages Genealogical Society 115
Vilyeu-Workman Blood Lines Quarterly Newsletter 603
Vimy Barracks 684
Vinalhaven Historical Museum 252
Vinalhaven Historical Society & Archives 252
Vincennes Historical and Antiquarian Society 195
Vincennes State Historic Site Archives 195
Vincent Family 414, 605
Vincentian Studies Institute 337
Vineland Historical and Antiquarian Society & Library 379
Vineland Historical Magazine 379
Vineyard Haven Public Library 281
Vineyard Library 470
Vineyard Museum 270
Vining Library 613
Vinings Historic Preservation Society 126
Vinita Public Library 470
Vintage Flyer 69
Vintage Flying Museum Archives 546
Vinton County Heritage 449
Vinton County Historical Society and Chapter, OGS & Library 449
Vinton Historical Society 596
Viola Public Library 632
Violent Kin 117
Violette Family 274
Virden Pioneer Museum Archives 661
Virgie Speights Memorial Library & Museum Archives 548
Virgil B McCain Jr Learning Resource Center 2
Virginia Aeronautical Historical Society 594
Virginia Air and Space Center Museum Archives 588
Virginia Appalachian Notes 594
Virginia Area Heritage Center 316
Virginia Area Historical Society & Archives 316
Virginia Association of Museums 594
Virginia Aviation Museum Archives 594
Virginia Aviation Museum Newsletter 594
Virginia Baptist Historical Society & Archives 594
Virginia Baptist Register 594
Virginia Beach Central Library 596
Virginia Beach Department of Public Libraries 596
Virginia Beach Department of Public Libraries Update 596
Virginia Beach Maritime Museum Archives 596
Virginia City-J Spencer Watkins Historical Museum Archives 347
Virginia Department of Conservation and Preservation 594
Virginia Department of Historic Resources Archives-Research Library 594
Virginia Genealogical Research 529
Virginia Genealogical Society 594
Virginia Genealogical Society Newsletter 594
Virginia Historical Society & Library 594
Virginia Historical Society Documents 594
Virginia Historical Society History Notes 594
Virginia Historical Society Occasional Bulletin 594
Virginia Holocaust Museum Archives 594
Virginia Magazine of History and Biography 594
Virginia Masonic Herald 593
Virginia Memorial Public Library 176
Virginia Military Institute Museum Archives 590
Virginia Museum of Transportation Archives 594
Virginia Society for Black Historical and Genealogical Research 591
Virginia Society for Black Historical and Genealogical Research News 591
Virginia State Library and Archives 594
Virginia Technical University Library 584
Virginia Tidewater Genealogy 588
Virginia War Memorial Archives 594
Virginia War Musuem Archives 591
Virginia-West Virginia Queries 608
Vision 119, 626
Visit'N 577
Vista Ranchos Historical Museum 77
Vista Ranchos Historical Society 77
Vista Ranchos Historical Society Newsletter 77
Vista-View 69
Vizcaya Museum and Gardens Archives 117
Vogel Genealogical Research Library 162
Vogel Library 209
Voice 15
Voice of the Past 45
Voice of the White Eagle 256
Voices 99
Volendam Windmill Museum Archives 373
Volk auf dem Weg 438
Volney Town Historian 398
Volo Antique Auto Museum and Village Archives 176
Volpe Library 526
Volunteer Firemen's Mall Museum Archives 402
Volunteer News 379
Voluntown Historical Society 100
Voluntown Public Library 100
Volusia County Genealogical and Historical Society 111
Volusia County Library Center 111
Von Bargen Family 476
Von Bellor Family 469
Von Canon Library 585
Von Riesen Library 354
Voorheesville Public Library 419
Voss-Lohmeier-Reikofski Family 356
Voter Family 531
Vox Nemenis 465
Voyager 429
Voyages 606
Voyageur Heritage Centre Archives 685
Voyageur: Northeast Wisconsin's Historical Review 622
Vulcan and District Historical Society 646
Vuntut Gwitch'in First Nation 713

W

W A C Bennett Library 648
W A Rankin Memorial Library 219
W C Bradley Memorial Library 129
W C Handy Home Museum & Library 4

INDEX

W Dale Clark Library 355
W G Rhea Library 532
W H Over State Museum Archives 524
W H Over State Museum Newsletter 524
W H Passon Historical Society 537
W H Stark House Archives 555
W K Gordon Center for Industrial History of Texas Archives 554
W L Moody Jr Library 538
W M Logan Library 550
W T Bland Public Library 117
W Walworth Harrison Public Library 547
Waba Cottage Museum Archives 692
Wabash Carnegie Public Library 195
Wabash County Genealogical Society 195
Wabash County Historical Museum 195
Wabash County Historical Museum Archives 195
Wabash County Historical Society 167
Wabash County Historical Society & Archives 195
Wabash County Historical Society Newsletter 167, 195
Wabash Frisco and Pacific Railroad Museum 329
Wabash Valley Genealogical Society 194
Wabash Valley Magazine 194
Wabash Valley Trust for Historic Preservation 188
Wabasha County Historical Society & Archives 313
Wabasha County Historical Society & Library 309
Wabasha Public Library 316
Wabaunsee County Historical Museum 211
Wabaunsee County Historical Society & Archives 211
Wabaunsee County Historical Society Newsletter 211
Waboden Historical Museum Archives 661
Wach Family 40
Wachovia Historical Society 435
Waco Heritage and History 562
Waco-McLennan County Library 562
Waco-McLennan County Library System-East Waco 562
Waconda Roots and Branches 212
Waddington Historian & Archives 419
Wade Family 595, 607
Wade House Stagecoach Inn Museum Archives 622
Wadena and District Museum Archives 711
Wadena County Historical Society & Library 316
Wadena County Historical Society Quarterly Newsletter 316
Wadena Public Library 209
Wadleigh Memorial Library 363
Wadsworth Atheneum 94
Wadsworth Family 568
Wadsworth Library 276
Wagnalls Memorial Archives 451
Wagner Family 621
Wagon Road 583, 587
Wagon Tracks on Prairie Trails 203
Wagon Wheel Newsletter 601
Wagon Wheel Regional Museum Archives 641
Wagon Wheels 30
Wagon Yard Museum Archives 27
Wagoner Journal 349
Wahkaw 208
Wahkiakum County Historical Museum 600
Wahkiakum County Historical Society & Archives 600
Wahlert Memorial Library 201
Wahoo Genealogical Seekers 357
Wahpeton Dakota First Nation 709
Waidner-Spahr Library 484
Wailoa Center Museum Archives 141
Wainfleet Township Public Library 692
Wainwright Museum Archives 646
Waiste Newsletter 82
Waitsfield Historical Society 580
Waitsfield Historical Society Newsletter 580
Wakarusa Historical Society 195
Wakarusa-Olive & Harrison Township Public Library 195
Wakaw Heritage Museum Archives 711
Wake County Genealogical Society & Library 432
Wake County Genealogical Society Updates 432
Wake County Public Library 432
Wake County Public Library System-Cameron Village Regional 432
Wake County Public Library System-Olivia Raney Local History 432
Wake Forest College Birthplace Society & Archives 434
Wake Forest College Birthplace Society Newsletter 434
Wake Forest Historical Museum 434
Wake Treasures 432
WaKeeney Public Library 222
Wakefield Brookfield Historical Society 360
Wakefield Historical Society 303
Wakefield Historical Society & Library 281
Wakefield House Museum 306
Wakefield Museum Archives 223
Wakefield Museum Newsletter 223
Wakefield Public Library 223
Wakerobin Newsletter 420
Wakpa Sica Historical Society 349, 522
Wakulla County Historical Society 111
Wakulla County Public Library 111
Walden and Wallkill Valley Historical Museum 419
Walden Community Library 580
Walden Public Library 685
Waldensian Heritage Museum Archives 434
Waldoboro Historical Museum 252
Waldoboro Historical Society & Archives 252
Waldoboro Historical Society Newsletter 252
Waldo-Staten-Mack Family 109
Waldport Heritage Museum Archives 480
Waldwick Public Library 379
Walker Association Newsletter 151
Walker County Genealogical Society 550
Walker County Historical Society 132
Walker County Historical Society Netwsletter 132
Walker Family 162
Walker Memorial Library 252, 539
Walkerton Area Historical Society 195
Walkerton-Lincoln Township Historical Society 195
Walkerton-Lincoln Township Public Library 195
Walking Back in Time 6
Walla Walla Public Library 609
Walla Walla Valley Genealogical Society 609
Walla Walla Valley Pioneer and Historical Society & Library 609
Wallace Area Museum Archives 677
Wallace Clan 263
Wallace District Mining Museum Archives 150
Wallace E Mason Library 362

Wallace Family 289
Wallace House Museum Archives 378
Wallace Library 542, 559
Wallace Museum Foundation Archives 7
Wallace Name File 63
Wallace Public Library 150
Wallace Reunion Newsletter 59
Wallace-Wallis-Wallice Connections Newsletter 188
Wallenpaupack Historical Society 496
Waller County Historical Society 538
Waller County Library 548
Waller Wanderings 529
Wallingford Branches 355
Wallingford Historical Society & Archives 100, 580
Wallingford Public Library 100
Wallis Family 570
Wallis Museum Archives 471
Wallisville Heritage Society & Library 562
Wallowa County Library 475
Wallpack Historical Society 368, 372
Walney Visitor Center Archives 585
Walney Visitor Center Newsletter 585
Walnut Creek Historical Society & Archives 77
Walnut Grove Plantation Museum 517
Walnut Public Library 176
Walpole Historical Society 365
Walpole Historical Society Newsletter 365
Walpole Town Library 365
Walrath Family Association Newsletter 38
Walsh County Historical Society 439
Walsh Library 378
Walt Whitman Association Newsletter 368
Walt Whitman Birthplace Historic Site Archives 400
Walt Whitman Birthplace Historic Site Newsletter 400
Walt Whitman House Museum Library 368
Walter Cecil Rawls Library and Museum 586
Walter E Helmke Library 184
Walter Elwood Museum Library 388
Walter F George Law Office Museum Archives 139
Walter Harris Memorial Library 685
Walter M Pierce Library 476
Walter M Pierce Library Newsletter 476
Walter P Carter Library 256
Walter P Chrysler Boyhood Home and Museum Archives 213
Walter P Chrysler Museum Archives 286
Walter Palmer Society 97
Walter Reed Birthplace Museum Archives 588
Walter Royal Davis Library 424
Walter T A Hansen Memorial Library 248
Walter W Stiern Library 36
Walter Wright Pioneer Village Archives 649
Walters Public Library 471
Waltham Historical Museum 281
Waltham Historical Society & Archives 281
Waltham Historical Society Quarterly 281
Waltham Museum Library 281
Waltham Museum Newsletter 281
Walton Historical Society 419
Walton House Museum Archives 443
Walton-Tipton Township Public Library 195
Walworth County Genealogical Society 618, 620
Walworth County Genealogical Society Newsletter 620
Walworth County Historical Society & Library 620
Walz-Johnson Family 565
Wamego Historical Society & Archives 223
Wamego Historical Society Newsletter 223
Wamego Public Library 223
Wanamingo Historical Society & Library 316
Wanapum Dam Heritage Center Archives 599
Wanatah Historical Society 195
Wanatah Public Library 195
Wanigan 633
Wantagh Historical and Preservation Society & Archives 419
Wantagh Historical Museum 419
Wantagh Public Library 419
Wapello County Genealogical Society & Library 207
Wapello County Genealogical Society Newsletter 207
Wapello County Historical Museum 207
Wapello County Historical Society & Archives 207
Wapello County Historical Society Quarterly 207
Waponahki Resource Center 249
War Eagle Air Museum Archives 385
War Vet Museum Archive 443
Ward County Genealogical Society & Library 554
Ward County Heritage 554
Ward County Historical Museum 439
Ward County Historical Society & Archives 439
Ward County Historical Society Library 439
Ward Family 149, 310, 445, 538
Ward Hall Museum Archives 228
Ward Surname Newsletter 18
Ward W O'Hara Agricultural Museum Archives 388
Warden Memorial Library 532
Warden's House Museum 315
Warder Public Library 457
Wardner Family 579
Wareham Free Library 281
Warhawk Air Museum Archives 148
Waring Historical Medical Museum Archives 513
Warkentin House Archives 219
Warner Family 95
Warner Family Redwood 84
Warner Hall Graveyard Archives 588
Warner House Museum Archives 364
Warner House Museum Newsletter 364
Warner Library 418
Warner Library News 418
Warner Museum 417
Warner: Who, When and Where? 292
Warren County Chapter Newsletter 451
Warren County Genealogical Association & Archives 530
Warren County Genealogical Association Bulletin 530
Warren County Genealogical Society 139, 203, 342, 451, 496
Warren County Genealogical Society & Library 166
Warren County Historical and Genealogical Society & Library 367
Warren County Historical Museum 504
Warren County Historical Society 151
Warren County Historical Society 196, 203, 398
Warren County Historical Society & Archives 504
Warren County Historical Society & Library 173, 342, 451

INDEX

Warren County Historical Society Newsletter 342
Warren County Library 367
Warren County Public Library 166
Warren County Reflections 196
Warren County-Vicksburg Public Library 323
Warren County-Vicksburg Public Library Newsletter 323
Warren Heritage Museum Archives 638
Warren Historical Society 303
Warren Historical Society & Library 252
Warren Hunting Smith Library 398
Warren Memorial Library 252
Warren Public Library 195, 281, 303, 504
Warren Public Library-Walt Whitman Branch 303
Warren Rifles Confederate Museum Archives 588
Warren Township Historical Society 162
Warren Township Public Library 176
Warren-Newport Public Library District 162
Warrenton Historical Society 597
Warren-Trumbull County Public Library 459
Warrenville Historical Society 176
Warrenville Public Library District 176
Warrick County Historical Society 180
Warroad Area Historical Society 316
Warsaw Community Public Library 195
Warsaw Historical Society & Archives 419
Warsaw Historical Society & Library 176
Warsaw Public Library 176
Warther Museum Archives 447
Warwick Historical Museum 419
Warwick Historical Society & Library 509
Warwick Public Library 509
Warwick Roots 419
Wasco County Historial Museum Archives 480
Wasco County Historical Society 480
Wasco Historical Society & Museum 77
Waseca Area Genealogy Society & Library 316
Waseca Area Genealogy Society Rag 316
Waseca County Historical Society & Library 316
Waseca County Historical Society Newsletter 316
Waseca-Le Sueur Regional Library 316
Washakie County Historical Society 638
Washakie Museum 638
Washburn County Genealogical Society & Library 631
Washburn County Historical Museum 631
Washburn County Historical Society & Archives 631
Washburn Historial Society 633
Washburn Historical Museum Archives 633
Washburn Memorial Library 252
Washington 452
Washington Carnegie Public Library 195
Washington County Chapter, OGS & Archives 452
Washington County Courthouse Museum 633
Washington County Family History Society 476
Washington County Free Library 259
Washington County Genealogical Society 233, 244, 249, 260, 431
Washington County Genealogical Society & Archives 209, 350
Washington County Genealogical Society Journal 431
Washington County Genealogical Society Newsletter 209
Washington County Heritage Society 538
Washington County Historian 478
Washington County Historical and Genealogical Society 223
Washington County Historical Association & Archives 351
Washington County Historical Association News Bulletin 351
Washington County Historical Museum 351
Washington County Historical Society 3, 136, 168, 431, 452
Washington County Historical Society & Archives 193, 259, 260, 315, 478, 504, 633
Washington County Historical Society & Library 27, 223, 452
Washington County Historical Society Quarterly 193, 223
Washington County Library 317, 337, 431, 570
Washington County Library Newsletter 570
Washington County Library System-William Alexander Percy Memorial Library 320
Washington County Museum Archives 3, 81
Washington County Public Library 3, 233, 452, 583
Washington County Rural Heritage Museum Archives 257
Washington County-Jonesboro Public Library 528
Washington Crossing Historic Park Library 504
Washington Free Public Library 379
Washington Heritage Bulletin 604
Washington Historical Museum 342
Washington Historical Society 365
Washington Historical Society & Archives 176, 342
Washington History: The Magazine of the Historical Society of Washington D.C. 105
Washington Irving Trail Museum Archives 469
Washington Island Farm Museum Archives 633
Washington Museum Archives 242
Washington Parish Library System 237
Washington Parish Library System, Bogalusa Branch 236
Washington Public Library 209
Washington Public Library-Warrensburg Branch 342
Washington State Archives, Central Regional Branch 601
Washington State Capital Museum Archives 604
Washington State Division Archives & Records Management 604
Washington State Genealogical Society 604
Washington State Genealogical Society Newsletter 604
Washington State Historical Museum 608
Washington State Historical Society 604, 608
Washington State Historical Society & Archives 608
Washington State Jewish Historical Society 606
Washington State Library 604
Washington Township Historical Museum 139
Washington Township Historical Society 139
Washington Township Historical Society & Library 45, 372
Washington Township Public Library 189
Washington University Library 340
Washington's Headquarters Museum Archives 379
Washington's Headquarters Museum Newsletter 379
Washington's Headquarters State Historic Site Library 408
Washington's Lands Museum 614
Washingtons of Pontotoc County, Mississippi 530
Washington-Wilkes Historical Foundation 139
Washington-Wilkes Historical Museum 139
Washtenaw County Historical Society 285
Washtenaw Impressions 285
Wasilla Public Library 13
Wasilla-Knik-Willow-Creek Historical Society & Archives 13
Waskada Museum Archives 661
Wasyl Negrych Pioneer Homestead Archives 660

Watauga Ancestry 423
Watauga County Public Library 423
Watauga Regional Library Center 528
Water Cooler 156
Water Mill Museum Archives 419
Waterborough 245
Waterborough Historical Society 245
Waterbury Historical Society & Library 580
Waterbury Republican & American Library 100
Waterbury Village Public Library 580
Waterford Echoes 249
Waterford Historical Museum 252
Waterford Historical Museum Archives 419
Waterford Historical Society 100, 303
Waterford Historical Society & Archives 249, 252
Waterford Township Public Library 304
Waterfront Museum Archives 391
Waterhen Lake First Nation 711
Waterloo Area Farm Museum Archives 292
Waterloo Area Historical Museum 633
Waterloo Area Historical Society & Archives 633
Waterloo Area Historical Society & Library 303
Waterloo Area Historical Society Quarterly Newsletter 303
Waterloo Historical Society & Archives 420
Waterloo Historical Society & Library 684
Waterloo Historical Society Annual Volume 684
Waterloo Public Library 209, 692, 704
Watermen's Museum Archives 597
Waterous Family 149
Waters Family 367
Waterson-Watterson Family 47, 190
Watertown City Historian 420
Watertown Daily Times Newspaper Archives 420
Watertown Free Public Library 281
Watertown Genealogical Society & Library 524
Watertown Historical Museum 100
Watertown Historical Society 420
Watertown Historical Society & Archives 100
Watertown Historical Society & Library 633
Watertown Historical Society Newsletter 100
Watertown Public Library 633
Watertown Regional Library 524
Waterville Historical Society & Archives 252
Waterville Public Library 252
Waterville Public Library 420
Watervliet Arsenal Museum Archives 420
Watervliet District Library 304
Watervliet Public Library 420
Watervliet Shaker Journal 387
Waterways 477
Watkins Community Museum 217
Watkins Family 625
Watkins Mill Association & Library 333
Watkins Museum Archives 322
Watkins Woolen Mill State Historic Site 333
Watkinson Library 95
Watkins-Wood Family 525
Watonawan County Historical Center 310
Watonawan County Historical Society & Archives 310
Watonga Public Library 471
Watonwan County Library 314
Watson Cabin Museum Archives 74
Watson Crossley Community Museum Archives 660
Watson Family Surname Newsletter 18
Watson Farm Museum Archives 508
Watson Lake Historical Society 713
Watson Library 217
Watson Town Historian 403
Watson's Mill Museum Archives 685
Watson-Curtze Mansion Museum Archives 487
Watt's Crossing 215
Watters Smith Memorial State Park Archives 613
Watts Family 215
Wattsburg Area Historical Society & Library 504
Wattsburgh Occasional 504
Wauconda Township Historical Museum 177
Wauconda Township Historical Society & Archives 177
Wauconda Township Historical Society Newsletter 177
Waukegan Historical Society & Archives 177
Waukegan Public Library 177
Waukesha County Genealogical Society 633
Waukesha County Genealogical Society Newsletter 633
Waukesha County Historical Museum 633
Waukesha County Historical Society & Archives 633
Waukesha County Historical Society News 633
Waukesha Engine Historical Society 633
Waukesha Public Library 633
Waunakee Public Library 633
Waupaca Area Genealogical Society 624
Waupaca Area Public Library 633
Waupaca County Historical Society 628
Waupaca Historical Society & Genealogy Center 633
Waupaca Historical Society Newsletter 633
Waupun Historical Museum 633
Waupun Historical Society & Archives 633
Waupun Public Library 633
Waushara County Historical Museum 633
Waushara County Historical Society 633
Waushara County Historical Society Newsletter 633
Wauwatosa Historical Society 627
Wauwatosa Historical Society & Library 633
Wauwatosa Public Library 633
Waveland State Historic Site Archives 230
Waveland-Brown Township Public Library 195
Wavelength 373
Waverley Heritage Society 677
Waverly Free Library 420
Waverly Genealogical and Historical Newsletter 177
Waverly Genealogical and Historical Society 177
Waverly Public Library 209
Waverly Town Historian 415
Waves and Furrows 252
Wawina Area Historical Society 316
Wawota and District Museum Archives 711
Wayland Area Tree Tracers Genealogical Society & Library 304
Wayland Free Library 420
Wayland Free Public Library 281
Wayland Historical Society 234
Wayland Historical Society & Library 281
Wayland Historical Society Newsletter 281

Wayne City Public Library 177
Wayne Community College Library 427
Wayne County Genealogical And Historical Society 615
Wayne County Genealogical Society 357
Wayne County Genealogical Society & Archives 192
Wayne County Genealogical Society & Archives 199
Wayne County Genealogical Society & Archives 460
Wayne County Genealogy Organization 323
Wayne County Genie News 199
Wayne County Historian 533
Wayne County Historical and Genealogical Society 231
Wayne County Historical Association & Library 427
Wayne County Historical Association Reflections 427
Wayne County Historical Museum 192, 403, 460, 490
Wayne County Historical Society 132, 160, 199, 337, 357, 533
Wayne County Historical Society & Archives 192, 199, 403, 460, 490
Wayne County Historical Society Newsletter 199, 403, 490
Wayne County Historical Society Quarterly 192
Wayne County Historical Society Quarterly Newsletter 460
Wayne County Irish Society 304
Wayne County Public Library 231, 427, 460
Wayne Historical Museum Archives 304
Wayne Historical Society 304
Wayne Public Library 357, 380
Wayne Township Historical Commission & Library 380
Wayne Township Historical Society 187
Waynesboro Historical Society 504
Waynesboro Public Library 597
Waynesville Historical Society 459
Waynoka Historical Society & Library 471
Waynoka Public Library 471
Wayzata Historical Society 316
WCPL Newsletter 435
We're Making History 537
Wead Library 404
Weakley County Genealogical Society & Library 530
Weatenotes 188
Weatherbee Round-Up 158
Weathercock 408
Weatherford College Library 563
Weatherford Family 367
Weatherford Public Library 471, 563
Weathermon Family 22
Weathersfield Historical Society 580
Weathersfield Historical Society & Archives 578
Weathersfield Historical Society Newsletter 580
Weathers-Withers-Wethers Museum 417
Weathervane 503
Weathervane Newsletter 276
Weaver-Oates House 540
Weaverville Joss House State Historic Park Archives 72
Weaverville Joss House State Park Archives 77
Webb City Area Genealogical Society 342
Webb City Historical Society 342
Webb City Public Library 342
Webb County Heritage Foundation & Library 551
Webb House Museum Archives 454
Webb Newsletter 122
Webb Public Library 209
Webb Shadle Memorial Library 207
Webb Wanderings 292
Webb-Deane-Stevens Museum Library 101
Webb-Deane-Stevens Museum Newsletter 101
Webbers Falls Historical Museum 471
Webbers Falls Historical Society & Archives 471
Weber County Library 569
Webster County Genealogical Society 202
Webster County Historical and Genealogical Society & Archives 226
Webster County Historical Museum 356
Webster County Historical Society 335
Webster County Historical Society & Archives 356
Webster County Historical Society Journal 335
Webster County Public Library 227
Webster Groves Archives 342
Webster Groves Historical Society & Archives 342
Webster Groves Historical Society Newsletter 342
Webster Groves Public Library 342
Webster Home 189
Webster House 620
Webster House Museum Newsletter 620
Webster Parish Library 239
Webster Public Library 524
Webster's Wagon Wheel 226
Webster-Addison Public Library 615
Webster-McCracken Family 165
Wedell-Williams Memorial Aviation Museum Archives 240
Wedmore Clan 563
Wedsworth Memorial Library 343
Weedman Family 231
Weedsport Free Library 420
Weekly Arizonian 21
Weekly Newspaper 217
Weeks Family 33, 287, 361, 539
Weeks Public Library 361
Weeks-Townsend Memorial Library 225
Week-Weeks-Weekes Family 607
Weems-Botts Museum 586
Weeping Water Valley Historical Museum 357
Weeping Water Valley Historical Society & Archives 357
Weese Family 549
Wefel Family 474
Wehrman Family 341
Wehrung Family 301
Weimer Family 381
Weiner Judaic Museum 262
Weiner Library 378
Weir Farm National Historic Site Archives 101
Weir Farm News 101
Weirs and Woods 244
Weis Library 263
Weiser Family 495
Welborn-Wellbourne-Wilburn Family 470
Welch Family 150
Welch Library 531
Welcome Historical Society 316
Weld County Genealogical Society & Archives 86
Weld County Genealogical Society Quarterly 86
Weld County Library District-Centennial Park 86
Weld Historical Society & Library 252
Weld Historical Society Newsletter 252

Weld Library District 86
Weld Library District, Lincoln Park Branch 86
Weld Library District-Lincoln Park 86
Welker-Lund Family 149
Welland Historical Museum Archives 692
Wellauer-Winz-Wintz-Buel Family 627
Welles Family 99
Wellesley Free Library 281
Wellesley Historical Society & Library 281
Wellesley Historical Society Newsletter 281
Wellesprings 99
Welles-Turner Memorial Library 93
Wellfleet Historical Museum 281
Wellfleet Historical Society & Archives 281
Wellfleet Public Library 281
Wellington Community Historical Museum Archives 692
Wellington County Historical Society 682
Wellington County Museum and Archives 682
Wellington County Public Library 682
Wellington Genealogical Group 459
Wellington Genealogical Workshop 459
Wellington Public Library 90
Wells Auto Museum Archives 252
Wells County Historical Museum 180, 438
Wells County Historical Society & Archives 180, 438
Wells County History 438
Wells County Museum Archives 438
Wells County Public Library 180
Wells Family 169, 416, 602, 609
Wells Fargo History Museum 66
Wells Fargo History Museum Archives 19, 52, 64, 67, 311, 478
Wells Fargo Museum Archives 64
Wells Historical Society 580
Wells Memorial Library 419
Wells Museum Archives 657
Wells Researcher Newsletter 157
Wells Town Historian 420
Wellsburg Public Library 209
Wellsville Carnegie Public Library 459
Wellsville City Library 223
Wellsville Depot Museum Archives 342
Wellsville Historical Society & Archives 459
Welsh Society of Richville 413
Welsh-American Genealogical Society & Library 579
Welsh-American Genealogical Society Newsletter 579
Welsh-American Heritage Musuem Archives 455
Wenatchee Area Genealogical Society & Library 609
Wenatchee Valley Museum Archives 609
Wenatchee Valley Museum Newsletter 609
Wendell Gilley Museum Archives 251
Wendler-Guetzke Family 627
Wenger-Winger Family 481
Wenham Historical Association & Archives 281
Wenham Historical Association Newsletter 281
Wenham Public Library 281
Wenrich Family 591
Wentworth Gardner & Tobias Lear Houses Association 364
Wentworth Library 683
Wentworth-Coolidge Mansion Archives 364
Wentz Post 506
Wentzville Community Historical Society 342
Werner Family 264
Werner-Sass Family 426, 483
Wernersville Public Library 505
Wert Family 500
Wertz Newsletter 262
Wertz-Cell(e)-Sell(s) Family 81
Wescott Family 57
Weslaco Museum Archives 563
Weslaco Museum Newsletter 563
Weslaco Public Library 563
Wessels Library 517
Wessington Public Library 524
Wessington Springs Carnegie Library 524
West Allis Historical Museum 633
West Allis Historical Society & Archives 633
West Augusta Historical and Genealogical Society 614
West Baden Historical Society 195
West Bank Genealogy Society 237
West Bank Regional Library 239
West Baton Rouge Genealogical Society & Library 241
West Baton Rouge Genealogical Society Newsletter 241
West Baton Rouge Historical Association & Archives 241
West Baton Rouge Historical Museum 241
West Baton Rouge Parish Library 241
West Bell Genealogical Society 551
West Boylston Historical Society 282
West Branch Public Library 304
West Bridgewater Public Library 282
West Caldwell Public Library 380
West Carroll Parish Library 240
West Carrollton Historical Society 447
West Carter County Genealogy Society 341
West Central Georgia Genealogical Society 132
West Central Georgia Genealogical Society Newsletter 132
West Central Kentucky Family Research Association & Library 232
West Central Kentucky Family Research Association Bulletin 232
West Central Minnesota Historical Center 312
West Central Missouri Genealogical Society & Library 342
West Chester Public Library 505
West Chicago City Museum Archives 177
West Chicago Historical Society & Archives 177
West Chickasaw County Historical and Genealogical Society 320
West Coast Maritime Museum Archives 656
West Coast Museum of Flying Archives 655
West Concord Historical Society 309, 316
West Covina Museum 77
West Custer County Library District 90
West Des Moines Historical Society & Archives 209
West Elmore County Historical Society 6
West Family 55, 259
West Fargo Public Library 440
West Feliciana Historical Museum 241
West Feliciana Historical Society & Archives 241
West Feliciana Parish Public Library 241
West Florida Footprints 120
West Florida Genealogical Society 120
West Florida Railroad Museum Archives 117
West Florida Regional Library 120
West Franklin Historical District and Genealogical Society 157

West Georgia Genealogical Society & Archives 132
West Georgia Museum of Tallapoosa Archives 138
West Georgia Regional Library 128
West Gray Public Library 682
West Greenwich Historical Preservation Society 509
West Hanover Township Historical Society 489
West Hants Historical Society & Library 677
West Hartford Historical Society 101
West Hartford Library 580
West Hartford Public Library 101
West Haven Public Library 101
West Hawaii Center 142
West Hennepin County Pioneers Association & Archives 310
West Hennepin County Pioneers Association Newsletter 310
West Hennepin Historical Museum 310
West Hurley Public Library 420
West Indianapolis Historical Society 190, 196
West Islip Public Library 420
West Islip Public Library Quarterly Newsletter 420
West Jefferson County Historical Society 1
West Liberty Historical Society 209
West Lincoln Historical Society 690
West Long Branch Public Library 380
West Memphis Public Library 33
West Milford Museum Archives 380
West Milwaukee Historical Society & Library 634
West Moberly Lake Indian Band 652
West Monroe Historical Society 420
West Monroe Town Historian 420
West Nassau Historical Society 110
West New York Public Library 380
West Newton Public Library 505
West of the Pecos Museum Archives 556
West of the Pecos Museum Newsletter 556
West Overton Museums Archives 501
West Palm Beach Public Library 124
West Parry Sound District Museum Archives 688
West Pasco County Genealogical Society 120
West Pasco County Genealogical Society Quarterly 120
West Pasco Genealogical Society 118
West Pasco Historical Museum 118
West Pasco Historical Society & Archives 118
West Pasco Historical Society Newsletter 118
West Point Lighthouse Museum Archives 695
West Point Museum Archives 420
West Region Tribal Council 659
West River Museum Society & Archives 523
West Routt Library District-Hayden Public Library 86
West Roxbury Historical Society 282
West Sacramento Historical Museum 77
West Sacramento Historical Society 77
West Salem Historical Society & Archives 634
West Salem Historical Society Newsletter 634
West Seneca Historical Society & Library 421
West Side Historical Society 156
West Side Historical Society 315
West Tennessee Historical Society & Library 530
West Tennessee Historical Society Papers 530
West Texas Genealogical Society & Library 535
West Texas Genealogical Society Bulletin 535
West Texas Historical Association & Archives 535
West Texas Historical Association Year Book 535
West Toronto Junction Historical Society 692
West Turin Town Historian 394
West Valley Genealogical Society & Library 20
West Valley Museum Archives 78
West Vancouver Museum Archives 657
West Virginia & Regional History Collection 613
West Virginia and Regional History Association & Archives 613
West Virginia and Regional History Collection Newsletter 613
West Virginia Camp Washington Museum Archives 611
West Virginia Genealogy Society & Library 612
West Virginia Hillbilly 614
West Virginia Historical Museum 611
West Virginia Historical Society & Archives 611
West Virginia Historical Society Newsletter 611
West Virginia Independence Hall Archives 615
West Virginia Northern Community College Museum 615
West Virginia State Farm Museum Archives 614
West Volusia Historical Society 111
West Volusia Historical Society & Library 111
West Warwick Public Library 510
West Warwick Public Library Newsletter 510
West Wayne Genealogical Society 404
West Wilson County Historical Society 530
West Windsor Historical Society 575
West Woodstock Library 102
Westampton Historical Society 374
Westbank Indian Band 651
Westborough Historical Commission & Archives 282
Westborough Historical Society & Library 282
Westborough Historical Society Newsletter 282
Westborough Public Library 282
Westbrook Heritage Society 316
Westbrook Historical Society 101
Westbrook Maine Historical Society 252
Westbrook-Hood Family 470
Westby Area Historical Society & Archives 634
Westchester Connections 421
Westchester County Dept of Parks and Conservation 405
Westchester County Genealogical Society & Library 421
Westchester County Genealogical Society Newsletter 421
Westchester County Historical Museum 397
Westchester County Historical Society & Archives 397, 419
Westchester Historian 397
Westchester Historical Happenings 397
Westchester Historical Society 177
Westchester Public Library 181
Westcott Family 279, 453
Westcott Family Newsletter 98
Westerly Historical Society 510
Westerly Public Library 510
Western Bayfield County Historical Society 623
Western Canada Aviation Museum Archives 662
Western Counties Regional Library 677
Western Development Museum Archives 710
Western District Historic Preservation 398
Western District Library 169
Western Genesis 344
Western Heritage Bee 355

Western Heritage Society & Archives 355
Western Historical Manuscript Collection 338
Western Historical Quarterly 381, 567
Western History Association 381, 567
Western History Collection 467
Western Hotel Museum Archives 50
Western Illinois University Library 165
Western Kenosha County Historical Society & Archives 632
Western Kentucky Journal 190
Western Lake Erie Historical Society & Library 458
Western Manitoba Regional Library 659
Western Manitoba Regional Library-Glenboro Branch 660
Western Manitoulin Historical Society & Archives 682
Western Maryland Genealogy 261
Western Maryland Railway Historical Society 263
Western Massachusetts Genealogical Society & Library 280
Western Michigan Genealogical Society 292
Western Michigan Genealogical Society Newsletter 292
Western Monroe Historical Society 390
Western Monroe Historical Society Newsletter 390
Western Montana Genealogical Society & Library 346
Western Montana Genealogical Society Newsletter 346
Western Museum Archives 211
Western Museum of Flight 47
Western Museum of Mining & Industry Library 82
Western New Mexico University Museum Archives 385
Western New York Association of Historical Agencies & Library 389
Western New York Genealogical Society & Library 399
Western New York Genealogical Society Journal 399
Western New York Heritage Institute 392
Western North Carolina United Methodist Commission on Archives and History 425
Western Pennsylvania Genealogical Society & Library 499
Western Pennsylvania Genealogical Society Quarterly 499
Western Pennsylvania History 499
Western Places: a Chronicle of Western Settlement 476
Western Plains Heritage Series 212
Western Plains Plainsman 471
Western Plains-Weatherford Genealogical Society & Archives 471
Western Pocono Community Library 483
Western Railway Museum Archives 73
Western Reserve Historical Society & Archives 445
Western Reserve Historical Society News 445
Western Reserve Historical Society, Genealogy Club 445
Western Rhode Island Civic Historical Society & Archives 507
Western Rhode Island Historical Museum 507
Western Seminary Cline-Tunnell Library 478
Western Sonoma County Historical Society & Library 72
Western South Dakota Historical Museum 522
Western Springs Historical Society & Library 177
Western States Jewish History 78
Western States Jewish History Association 78
Western Texas College Library 560
Western Texas Genealogical Association 560
Western Trail Genealogical Society & Archives 463
Western Trail Newsletter 463
Western Trails Historical and Genealogical Society 463
Western Virginia Historical Museum 594
Western Wayne County Genealogical Society 296
Westerners International & Library 468
Westerners International, San Francisco Corral 38
Westerners, Kansas City Posse 333
Westerners, Stockton Corral 73
Westerville Historical Society & Library 460
Westerville Public Library 460
Westfield Athanaeum and Historical Museum Archives 282
Westfield Heritage Centre Archives 683
Westfield Heritage Village Archives 689
Westfield Historical Society 460
Westfield Historical Society & Library 380
Westfield Historical Society Newsletter 380
Westfield Memorial Library 380
Westfield Public Library 195, 634
Westfield-Washington Historical Society 196
Westford Library 580
Westhampton Beach Historical Society 421
Westhampton Free Library 421
Westhampton Free Library Newsletter 421
Westlake-Porter Public Library 460
Westminster Historical Museum 580
Westminster Historical Society 77, 81, 90
Westminster Historical Society & Archives 580
Westminster Historical Society & Library 282
Westminster Historical Society Newsletter 282
Westmont Historical Society & Library 177
Westmoreland Chronicle 488
Westmoreland County Historical Society & Library 488
Westmoreland History 488
Westmoreland Library Historical Society 421
Westmoreland-Fayette Historical Society & Archives 501
Westmorland Historical Society 665
Westmorland Historical Society Newsletter 665
Westmount Historical Association & Bibliotheque 704
Westmount Public Library 704
Weston County Genealogical Society 637
Weston County Historical Society & Archives 637
Weston County Public Library 637
Weston Historical Museum 282
Weston Historical Museum Archives 342
Weston Historical Society 101
Weston Historical Society & Archives 282, 580
Weston Historical Society Bulletin 282
Weston Historical Society Newsletter 580
Weston Public Library 282, 460
Westonka Historical Society 312
Westphalia Historical Society 342
Westphalian Heritage Society 342
Westport Historical Museum 101
Westport Historical Society & Archives 101
Westport Historical Society & Library 282, 333
Westport Historical Society News Notes 101
Westport Library Association 101
Westport Public Library Newsletter 101
Westport Town Historian 421
Westporter 333
Westport-South Beach Historical Society & Archives 609
Westside Center Museum Archives 630
Westside Public Library 209
Westville Historic Handicrafts 133
Westville Historic Handicrafts Museum Archives 133

INDEX

Westville Historical Organization 394
Westville Mirror 133
Westville Public Library District 177
Westville Town Historian 394
Westville-New Durham Township Public Library 196
Westward into Nebraska 355
Westwood Historical Society 282
Westwood Holmby Historical Society 52
Wetaskiwin and District Museum Archives 646
Wethersfield Historical Museum 101
Wethersfield Historical Society 95
Wethersfield Historical Society & Archives 101
Wethersfield Historical Society & Library 580
Wethersfield Newsletter 101
Wetzel County Genealogical Society & Library 614
Wetzel County Ggenealogical Society Newsletter 614
Wetzel Family 72
Wexford County Historical Museum 287
Wexford County Historical Society & Archives 287
Wexford County Historical Society Newsletter 287
Weyerbacher Family 494
Weymouth Historical Society 282, 676
WGTL Newsletter 364
Whaleback Log 632
Whalers Village Museum Archives 142
Whales Tale 394
Whaley Family Newsletter 529
Whaley Historical House 291
Whaling Account 394
Wharf Lane Newsletter 96
Wharton County Historical Museum Archives 563
Wharton County Historical Museum Newsletter 563
Wharton County Library 563
What's Happening 320, 415
Whatcom County Public Library 599
Whatcom Genealogical Society 599
Whatcom Moments & Memoirs 603
Whatcom Museum of History and Art Archives 599
Whealton Family 423
Wheat Ridge Historical Museum 90
Wheat Ridge Historical Society & Library 90
Wheatland Mansion Newsletter 491
Wheaton History Center Archives 177
Wheaton Public Library 177
Wheeler County Historical Society 356
Wheeler Cousins Newsletter 341
Wheeler Family 341, 530
Wheeler Historic Farm Archives 572
Wheeler Library 97
Wheeler Memorial Library 277
Wheeler Writings 292
Wheeling Area Genealogical Society 615
Wheeling Historical Museum 177
Wheeling Historical Society & Archives 177
Wheeling Historical Society Newsletter 177
Wheels O'Time Museum Archives 170
Wheels O'Time Museum Quarterly 170
Wheels of Time 332
Wheelwright Museum of the American Indian Archives 385
Whelden Memorial Library 281
Where the Trails Cross 174
Whetnall Family 599
Whidbey Island Genealogical Searchers 603
Whiffenpoof 329
Whippany Railway Museum Archives 380
Whipple Family 273, 479
Whipple House Museum 359
Whispering Palms 58
Whispering Pines Indian Band 651
Whispers Near the Inglenook 394
Whistle 491
Whistle Stop Newsletter 442
Whit(e)l(e)y Family 468
Whitaker Library 430
Whitbourne Museum Archives 669
Whitby Public Library 692
Whitchurch-Stouffville Museum Archives 682
Whitchurch-Stouffville Public Library 690
White 1 Foundation Military Museum Archives 115
White 1 Foundation Military Museum Newsletter 115
White Bear First Nation 705
White Bear Lake Area Historical Society 316
White Bear Lake Genealogical Society 316
White Bear Lake Genealogical Society Newsletter 316
White Buffalo Tales 560
White Cloud Community Library 304
White Cockade 43
White County Genealogical and Historical Society 532
White County Genealogy Society 189
White County Heritage 32
White County Historian 153
White County Historical Museum 128, 153, 189
White County Historical Museum Archives 32
White County Historical Society 32
White County Historical Society & Archives 128, 153, 189
White County Historical Society Newsletter 128
White County Public Library 32, 532
White Deer Land Museum Archives 555
White Family 41
White Fox Museum 711
White Hall State Historic Site Archives 233
White Hall Township Library 177
White House Historical Association 107
White House Historical Society 533
White House History Journal 107
White House Museum 107
White James Fort Association Archives 529
White Lake Area Historical Society 298
White Lake Community Library 304
White Lake Historical Society 304
White Mountain Apache Tribe 22
White Pillars Museum 620
White Pine Genealogical Society 625
White Pine Library 302
White Pine Public Library 533
White Pine Village Museum 296
White Plains Historical Society 420, 421
White Plains Public Library 421
White River Museum Archives 88
White River Regional Library 25

White River Trace Genealogical Society 88
White River Valley Historical Museum 599
White River Valley Historical Quarterly 337
White River Valley Historical Society 329, 337
White River Valley Historical Society & Archives 599
White River Valley Historical Society Newsletter 599
White Rock Museum Archives 657
Whitecap Dakota-Sioux First Nation 710
Whitefield House Museum 495
Whitefish Bay Public Library 634
Whitefish Bay Public Library Newsletter 634
Whitefish Lake Indian Band 128 644
Whitehall Historic House 119
Whitehall Historical Preservation Society 505
Whitehall Museum House 508
Whitehall Township Public Library 505
Whitehaven 232
Whitehaven Mansion Archives 232
Whitehead Family 382
Whitehead Memorial Museum Archives 543
Whitehorn Historic House Archives 683
Whitehorse Historical Society 713
Whitemouth Municipal Museum Archives 662
Whiteriver Public Library 22
Whitesboro Public Library 563
Whitesburg Campus Library 234
Whiteside County Genealogical News 175
Whiteside County Genealogists & Library 175
Whitestone Hill Battlefield State Historic Site Archives 438
Whitesville Public Library 421
Whitewater Canal State Historic Site Archives 189
Whitewater Historical Museum 634
Whitewater Historical Society & Archives 634
Whitewood Historical Museum Archives 711
Whitfield Family 43, 428
Whitfield-Hurst-Lane-Exum-Murphy-Kirkland Family 572
Whitfield-Murray Historical Quarterly 129
Whitfield-Murray Historical Society & Library 129
Whiting Family 571
Whiting Library 576
Whiting Public Library 196
Whiting-Fannin-Brimhall Family 572
Whitingham Historical Museum 577, 580
Whitingham Historical Society 580
Whitingham Historical Society & Archives 577
Whiting-Robertsdale Historical Society & Library 196
Whiting-Robertsdale Historical Society Newsletter 196
Whitinsville Social Library 282
Whitley County Historical and Genealogical Society 234
Whitley County Historical Bulletin 181
Whitley County Historical Museum 181
Whitley County Historical Society & Archives 181
Whitman County Genealogical Society & Library 605
Whitman County Genealogical Society Newsletter 605
Whitman County Historical Society & Archives 605
Whitman County Historical Society & Library 600
Whitman County Library 600
Whitman Mission National Historic Site Library 609
Whitman Public Library 282
Whitmeyer Genealogy Library 563
Whitney Family 497
Whitney Pier Historical Society 676
Whiton Family Newsletter 93
Whittier Area Genealogical Society 77
Whittier Area Genealogical Society Newsletter 77
Whittier Club of Haverhill 272
Whittier Historical Society & Library 77
Whittier Home Museum Archives 265
Whittier Newsletter 272
Whittier Public Library 77
Whittington W Clement Library 586
Whittlers' Bench 433
Whitworth Family 228
Whitworth Family 549
Who When Where 194
Who, When and Where of Lincoln County, West Virginia 612
Who's Who in Acadian-Cajun Genealogical Research 66
Who's Who in American Melroses 606
Who's Your Ancestor Genealogical Society 182
WHS Newsletter 421
Whycocomagh and District Historical Society 677
Whyte Museum of the Canadian Rockies & Archives 641
Wichita County Heritage Society & Archives 563
Wichita County Historical and Genealogy Society 217
Wichita County Historical Society 563
Wichita County Library 217
Wichita Falls Museum Library 563
Wichita Falls Public Library 563
Wichita Genealogical Society & Library 223
Wichita Public Library 223
Wichita-Sedgwick County Historical Museum Archives 223
Wichita-Sedgwick County Historical Museum Association & Archives 223
Wickenburg Public Library 22
Wickersham House Museum 12
Wickliffe Public Library 460
Wicomico County Free Library 262
Wicomico County Historical Society 262
Wicomico County Historical Trust Newsletter 262
Widdows Web 163
Wide Awake Club Library 397
Widrick-Wuthrich Family 395
Wiggin Memorial Library 364
Wiggins Cabin Museum 26
Wiggins Family 133
Wight Family Organization Newsletter 113
Wignall Museum Archives 61
Willkinsburg Historical Society & Archives 499
Wiingashk Kwek Women's Group 679
Wil(l)banks Trees 20
Wilbarger County Historical Society 562
Wilber Czech Museum Archives 357
Wilber Historical Society 357
Wilbraham Public Library 282
Wilbur Wright Birthplace Museum Archives 185
Wilbur Wright Birthplace Museum Newsletter 185
Wilcox County Library 2
Wilcox Historical Society 2
Wilcox Library 206
Wild Rose Historical Society & Archives 634
Wild Rose Pioneer Museum 634

Wild West 589
Wilder Library 198
Wilder Memorial Museum 208
Wilder Public Library District 150
Wildermuth Family 446
Wilderness Road 233
Wilderness Road Museum 591
Wildwood Center Archives 354
Wildwood Historical Society & Archives 380
Wildwood Historical Society Newsletter 380
Wile Carding Mill Museum Archives 673
Wiler Family 76
Wiley House Museum 161
Wiley-Woods-Wyatt-Austin Family 467
Wilhelm Where Are You? 219
Wiliam Henry Harrison Mansion - Grouseland Archives 195
Wiliam K Kohrs Memorial Library 344
Wilkes Community College Library 434
Wilkes County Genealogical Society Bulletin 431
Wilkes County Library 431
Wilkes Genealogical Society & Archives 431
Wilkie and District Museum Archives 711
Wilkin County Historical Museum 306
Wilkin County Historical Society & Archives 306
Wilkinsburg Historical Society 499
Wilkinsburg Public Library 499
Wilkinson County Historical Society 131, 323
Wilkinson County Museum Archives 323
Wilkinson County Museum News 323
Wilkinson Family 623
Will C Miller Memorial Library 562
Will County Historical Society & Archives 165
Will County Historical Society Quarterly 165
Will Grundy Counties Genealogical Society Newsletter 177
Will Grundy Counties Genealogical Society Quarterly 177
Will Mayfield Heritage Foundation 334
Will Reed Log Home Museum Archives 25
Will Rogers Library 464
Will Rogers Memorial Museum Archives 464
Will Rogers State Historic Park Archives 58
Willa Cather Memorial and Educational Foundation 356
Willa Cather Memorial and Educational Foundation Newsletter 356
Willamette Valley Genealogical Society & Archives 479
Willamette Valley Genealogical Society Newsletter 479
Willapa Harbor Genealogical Society 605
Willapa Seaport Museum Archives 605
Willard Family 273, 279
Willard Family Association of America Newsletter 279
Willard Historical Society 634
Willard House Museum Archives 271
Willard House Newsletter 271
Willard Library 183
Willard Library 286
Willard Memorial Library 460
Willard V Way Public Library 455
Willcox Family 138
Willett Memorial Library 133
Willey-Reinbold-Hopkin-Jubb-Cliff-Johnson-Lane-Fike-Richardson-Trachsel-Troxell-McKitrick Family 570
Will-Grundy Counties Genealogical Society & Library 177
William A Farnsworth Library 250
William Allen White Library 213
William and Evelyn Banks Library 132
William and Lucy Rand Memorial Library 578
William and Mary Quarterly: A Magazine of Early American History and Culture 597
William and Norma Harvey Library 588
William Anderson's National Historical General Store Archives 117
William B Ide Adobe Archives 61
William B Ogden Free Library 419
William Breman Jewish Heritage Museum Archives 126
William Brewster Nickerson Memorial Room 282
William C Jason Library-Learning Center 103
William Clapp House 270
William Clark Market House Museum Archives 232
William Clarke Quantrill Society 331
William Cullen Bryant Homestead Archives 269
William D Lawrence House Museum Archives 674
William D McIntyre Library 620
William D Weeks Memorial Library 362
William E Dermody Free Public Library 368
William E Dermody Free Public Library Newsletter 368
William E Morgan Library 85
William F Ekstrom Library 231
William F Laman Public Library 31
William F Maag Library 461
William Fogg Library 246
William G Braude Library 509
William H Bush Memorial Library 404
William H Pratt Museum 74
William H Sheppard Library 9
William H Volck Memorial Museum 77
William Hammond Mathers Museum Archives 180
William Heath Davis House Museum Archives 66
William Henry Steeves House Museum Archives 664
William Holmes McGuffey Museum Archives 455
William Holtzclaw Library 322
William Howard Taft National Historic Site Archives 444
William Howard Taft National Historic Site Newsletter 444
William J Clinton Presidential Library & Museum 30
William Jeanes Memorial Library 491
William K Sanford Town Library 403
William Knox Holt Library 73
William Pryor Letchworth Museum Archives 392
William Ray House Archives 674
William Rusell Pullen Library 126
William S Carlson Library 458
William S Hart Museum Archives 56
William Spangler Library 373
William Strother Society 205
William T Boyce Library 46
William T Jerome Library 442
William T Young Library 230
William Wesley Pool Family Organization Newsletter 138
William Whitely House State Historic Site Archives 233
Williams County Genealogical Society 440
Williams County Genealogical Society & Library 443
Williams County Historical Museum 453
Williams County Historical Society & Archives 453
Williams County Public Library 443

Williams Family 88, 195, 455, 581, 601
Williams Lake Indian Band 657
Williams Lake Library 657
Williams Lake Museum Archives 657
Williams Newsletter 110
Williams Public Library 22
Williams Writings 313
Williamsburg County Historical Museum 516
Williamsburg County Historical Society & Archives 516
Williamsburg County Library 516
Williamsburg Public Library 505
Williamsburg Regional Library 597
Williamson Campus Library 615
Williamson County Genealogical Society & Library 558
Williamson County Historical Museum 165
Williamson County Historical Society 527
Williamson County Historical Society & Archives 165
Williamson County Historical Society Journal 527
Williamson County Public Library 527
Williamsport and North Branch Railroad Historical Society 499
Williamsport-Washington Township Public Library 196
Williamston Area Historic Commission 518
Williamstown Historical Society 404
Williamstown Historical Society 580
Williamstown House of Local History 282
Williamstown House of Local History Newsletter 282
Williamstown Town Historian 421
Williamstown Township Historical Society 505
Williamsville Historical Society 421
Willingboro Public Library 380
Willington Historical Society & Library 101
Willis Family 571
Willison Library Bulletin 467
Willistead Manor House Museum 693
Williston Community Library 440
Williston Historical Society & Library 580
Williston Historical Society Bulletin 580
Willmore City Heritage Association 51
Willmore County Heritage Association 51
Willoughby Historical Museum Archives 686
Willoughby Historical Society 460
Willoughby-Baylor House Archives 592
Willoughby-Eastlake Public Library 460
Willow Bunch Museum Archives 711
Willow Creek Historical Society & Archives 78
Willow Creek-China Flat Museum Archives 78
Willow Public Library 13
Willowbrook 249
Willowbrook Museum Village Archives 249
Willows Museum Archives 78
Willows Public Library 78
Wilmette Historical Museum 177
Wilmette Historical Society & Archives 177
Wilmette Public Library District 177
Wilmington Area Historical Society 177
Wilmington Family History Center 104
Wilmington Historical Society 78
Wilmington Institute Free Library 104
Wilmington Monthly Meeting of Friends & Library 104
Wilmington Public Library 460
Wilmington Public Library District 177
Wilmington Railroad Museum Archives 434
Wilmington Town Historian 421
Wilna Town Historian 392
Wilscam Family 98
Wilson Castle Museum Archives 579
Wilson County Genealogical Society 435
Wilson County Historical Society and Genealogical Chapter & Archives 214
Wilson County Historical Society Newsletter 214
Wilson County Public Library 435, 544
Wilson Family 418, 499, 583, 584
Wilson Family Journal 418
Wilson Historical Museum 421
Wilson Historical Society & Archives 421
Wilson Library 49, 321, 424
Wilson MacDonald Memorial School Museum Library 689
Wilson Museum 245
Wilson Museum Bulletin 245
Wilson Public Library 350
Wilson Research 153
Wilson's Creek National Battlefield Foundation 341
Wilson's Creek National Battlefield Library 337
Wilson-Cobb History and Genealogy Research Library 384
Wilson-Sunderhaus-Trugstad Family 552
Wilsonville Public Library 480
Wilsonville-Boones Ferry Historical Society 480
Wilson-Wulff History and Genealogy Library 328
Wiltbank Family 20
Wilton Free Public Library 252
Wilton Heritage Museum 101
Wilton Historical Society 252
Wilton Historical Society & Archives 101
Wilton Historical Society Newsletter 101
Wilton House 593
Wilton House Museum Archives 594
Wilton Library Association 101
Wilton Manors Public Library 124
Wilton Public Library 209
Wiltondale Pioneer Village Archives 667
Wimberley Valley Genealogical Society 563
Wimberley Village Library 563
Wimberly Library 109
Wimmer Family 496
Winchendon Historical Museum 282
Winchendon Historical Society & Archives 282
Winchendon Historical Society Quarterly 282
Winchester Area Historical Society 624
Winchester Community Library 196
Winchester Historical Society & Library 101
Winchester Historical Society & Library 283
Winchester Public Library 178, 283
Winchester-Frederick County Genealogical Society 597
Winchester-Frederick County Historical Society & Library 597
Winchester-Frederick County Historical Society Journal 597
Winchester-Frederick County Historical Society Newsletter 597
Wind River Historical Center 636
Wind River Mountaineer 636, 637
Wind River Rendezvous 637
Wind Rose 96
Windale Historical Center Library 558

INDEX

Windber-Johnstown Genealogical Society 491
Windbreak 87
Windemuth Family 15
Windemuth Family Organization Newsletter 36
Windermere District Historical Museum Archives 650
Windermere Valley Museum Archives 650
Windham Free Library Association 101
Windham Historical Society 246, 252
Windham Historical Society & Archives 94
Windham Historical Society Newsletter 252
Windham Textile and History Museum Archives 101
Windmill 595
Windmill Island Municipal Park Archives 294
Wind-Mill: A Periodical of Frisian-Germanic Heritage 43
Window 203
Windows 545
Windsor Family 419
Windsor Historical Society 78, 342
Windsor Historical Society & Library 101
Windsor Historical Society News 101
Windsor Locks Historical Society 101
Windsor Locks Journal 101
Windsor Public Library 581, 693
Windsor Square-Hancock Park Historical Society 52
Windsor's Community Museum Archives 693
Windswept 363
Windward Community College Library 142
Windytimes 217
Wine Press Newsletter 55
Winegar Family Newsletter 558
Winfield Family 637
Winfield Historical Society 178
Winfield Public Library 178
Winfield Public Library 224
Wing Family 270
Wing-Basford-Hall Family 569
Wingfield Family Society Newsletter 109
Wingham District Heritage and History Society & Archives 693
Wingham District Historical Museum 693
Wingo Family 614
Wings 349
Wings of History Air Museum Archives 69
Wings of Oregon 475
Wings Over Miami Museum Archives 117
Wings Over Miami Museum Newsletter 117
Wings Over the Rockies Air & Space Museum Archives 84
Wings Over the Rockies Newsletter 84
Winkler County Library 550
Winn Parish Genealogical and Historical Society 242
Winn Parish Library 242
Winnebago and Boone Counties Genealogical Society 165, 172
Winnebago Area Historical Museum 317
Winnebago Area Historical Society 317
Winnebago Area Museum Archives 317
Winnebago County Historical and Archaeological Society & Archives 628
Winnebago Public Library 178
Winnebagoland Genealogical Society 628
Winnebagoland Roots 628
Winneconne Historical Museum and Kay Wilde Doll Cottage 634
Winneconne Historical Society & Archives 634
Winneconne Public Library 634
Winneshieck County Genealogical Society 200
Winneshieck County Historical Society & Archives 200
Winneshiek County Genealogical Society Quarterly 200
Winneshiek County History News 200
Winnetka Historical Museum 178
Winnetka Historical Society & Archives 178
Winnetka-Northfield Public Library 178
Winnetoon Historical Society 357
Winnfield Historical Society 242
Winnie Davis Museum of History Archives 514
Winnipeg Police Museum Archives 662
Winnipegosis Historical Museum 662
Winnipegosis Historical Society & Archives 662
Winn-Wynn-Wynne-Wynns Family 619
Winona Area Genealogy Roundtable & Archives 317
Winona County Genealogical Roundtable Newsletter 317
Winona County Genealogical Society 317
Winona County Historical Society & Archives 317
Winona County Historical Society Memo 317
Winona Lake Historical Society 196
Winona Public Library 317
Winooski Historical Society 581
Winslow Crocker House Museum Archives 283
Winslow Family 487
Winslow Farr Family Organization Newsletter 54
Winslow Historical Society 252
Winslow Public Library 22
Winstead National Reunion and Genealogy Newsletter 111
Winston Churchill Memorial Library 329
Winston County Genealogical Society 3
Winston County Historical and Genealogical Society 321
Winston Family 529
Winston Historical Society 342
Wint-Dewalt-Lessig-Cooper-Huffschmidt-Huffsmith-Blattenberger-Plattenberger-George-Kichline-Altemore-Laubach-Custard-Meckes-Albright-Albrecht Family 496
Winter Harbor Historical Society & Library 252
Winter Park Public Library 124
Winterbottom-Ridgeway-Welsh-Matthews-Misner-Creager-Church-Fortesque-George-Hollingshead-Hollinshead-Rollins-Rawlins Family 568
Winterport Historical Association & Library 252
Winters Public Library 563
Winterset Public Library 209
Winterthur Heritage Association 104
Winterthur Museum and Garden 104
Winthrop Historical Society 245
Winthrop Historical Society 317
Winthrop Public Library 283
Winthrop Society 39
Winthrop Society Quarterly 39
Winton Family 563
Wintonbury Historical Society & Library 91
Wiregrass Roots 3
Wiscasset Public Library 252
Wiscasset, Waterfille & Farmington Railway Museum Archives 243
Wisconsin Automotive Museum Archives 622
Wisconsin Black Historical Museum 627
Wisconsin Black Historical Society & Archives 627
Wisconsin Genealogical Council 617, 624, 630

Wisconsin Genealogical Council Newsletter 617
Wisconsin Historical Museum Archives 625
Wisconsin Jewish Genealogical Society 627
Wisconsin Labor History Society 627
Wisconsin Lineage Links 618
Wisconsin Magazine of History 625
Wisconsin Marine Historical Society 627
Wisconsin National Guard Memorial Archives 619
Wisconsin National Guard Memorial Newsletter 619
Wisconsin Postal Historical Society 623
Wisconsin Preservation: National Register of Historic Places Newsletter 625
Wisconsin Slovak 619
Wisconsin Slovak Historical Society & Library 619
Wisconsin State Genealogical Society 625, 627
Wisconsin State Genealogical Society Newsletter 625, 627
Wisconsin State Genealogical Society, Waupaca County Chapter 633
Wisconsin State Old Cemetery Society 626
Wisconsin Veterans Home 624
Wisconsin Veterans Museum Archives 624
Wisconsin Veterans Museum Research Center Archives 625
Wisdom Family 569
Wise Ancestry 557
Wise County Genealogical Society 557
Wise County Historical Commission and Society Newsletter 542
Wise County Historical Museum 542
Wise County Historical Society & Archives 542
Wise County Historical Society & Library 597
Wise County Historical Society Bulletin 597
Wise County News 597
Wise Family 68
Wise Library 613
WISE Search Group (Wales, Ireland, Scotland, England) 84
Wiseman Family 456
Wisner Heritage Society 357
Wissahickon Valley Historic Society 483
Wissahickon Valley Historical Society 481, 483
Wissel-Wessel Family Newsletter 532
Wistariahurst Museum Archives 272
Wistariahurst Museum Newsletter 272
Witch's Chatter 302
Witchekan Lake First Nation 710
Witcraft-Stapleton Family 477
With(e)y, Weth(e)y Family 285
Witham Family 363
Withee Public Library 634
Witherell-Sponenburg Family 71
Witherle Memorial Library 245
Witherspoon Family 547
Withrow Family Corners Newsletter 82
Witt Memorial Public Library 178
Witt-Daux Family 547
Witte Family 341
Witte Museum Library 559
Wittenberg Area Historical Museum 634
Wittenberg Area Historical Society & Archives 634
Wixarika Research Center 57
Wixom Historical Society 304
Woburn Public Library 283
Woenne-Wonne Family 57
Wofford, Lottie, Brinker Family 333
Wolcott Community Public Library 196
Wolcott Family 101
Wolcott Historical Society 421
Wolcott House Museum 452
Wolf House Museum Archives 218
Wolf Point Area Historical Museum 347
Wolf Point Area Historical Society & Archives 347
Wolfe County Library 226
Wolfeboro Historical Museum 365
Wolfeboro Historical Society & Archives 365
Wolfensberger Family 468
Wolfgram Memorial Library 484
Wolfinger Newsletter 488
Wolfs Wandering 292
Wolfville Historical Society & Archives 677
Wolpert-Fajfer-Karlentowsky-Fox-Graetz-Shafran-Dittman-Friedman-Holtz Family 134
Wolseley Community Museum Archives 711
Wolston-Brockway Family 199
Wolverton Family 328
Wolvertons Unlimited 341
Womack Family 119, 340, 609
Womack Family Courier 239
Womack Workers 153
Wombles-Womble Newsletter 174
Womelsdorf Family Newsletter 117
Women's Army Corps Museum Archives 4
Women's Club of Welaka Library 123
Women's History Museum Archives 615
Women's Relief Corps, Ohio Dept 452
Wonewoc Public Library 634
Wood County Chapter, OGS Newsletter 442
Wood County District Public Library 442
Wood County Genealogical Society & Library 442, 557
Wood County Genealogical Society Newsletter 557
Wood County Historical Museum 442
Wood County Historical Society & Archives 442
Wood Dale Historical Society 178
Wood Dale Public Library District 178
Wood Family 569
Wood Library-Museum of Anesthesiology Archives 170
Wood Memorial Library 99
Wood Mountain First Nation 711
Wood Mountain Post Archives 709
Wood Mountain Ranch and Rodeo Museum Archives 711
Wood Place Library 326
Wood River Historical Society 147
Woodard Family 536
Woodbattle Farm 293
Woodbine International Fire Museum Archives 140
Woodbridge Public Library 380
Woodburn Historic House Archives 517
Woodburn Historic House Newsletter 517
Woodbury County Genealogical Society 208
Woodbury County Library 205
Woodbury Heritage Society 317
Woodbury Historical Society 400
Woodbury Public Library 102
Woodbury Public Library 400
Woodchester Ville 680

Wooden Nickel Historical Museum Archives 559
Woodford County Historical Society & Library 159, 234
Woodford Heritage News 234
Woodford Mansion Archives 498
Woodford Newsletter 262
Woodgate Free Library 421
Woodham Family Journal 129
Woodin Family 442, 444
Woodland Public Library 243
Woodlands Native American Indian Museum Archives 170
Woodlands Pioneer Museum Archives 662
Woodlawn Museum Archives 246, 583
Woodlawn Plantation Archives 591
Woodlief-Woodliff Family 594
Woodridge Area Historical Society 178
Wood-Ridge History Committee 380
Wood-Ridge Memorial Library 380
Woodrow Wilson Birthplace Foundation & Library 595
Woodrow Wilson Birthplace Foundation Newsletter 595
Woodrow Wilson House Archives 127
Woodrow Wilson House Museum Archives 107
Woodrow Wilson House Newsletter 107
Woodruff County Historical Society 30
Woodruff Family 572
Woodruff Family History Exchange 35
Woodruff Historical Society & Archives 634
Woodruff Memorial Library 87
Woodruff Museum of Indian Artifacts 368
Woods County Genealogist Journal 463
Woods County Genealogists & Archives 463
Woods Family 555
Woods Hole Library 283
Woods Memorial Library 266
Woodside National Historic Site Archives 684
Woodside Store Historic Site Archives 78
Woodson County Genealogical Society 224
Woodson County Historical Museum 224
Woodson County Historical Society & Library 224
Woodson County Kansas Genealogy Society Newsletter 224
Woodson Family 263
Woodson Watcher 314
Woodstock Historical Museum 102, 244, 581
Woodstock Historical Society & Archives 102, 244
Woodstock Historical Society & Library 581
Woodstock Museum National Historic Site 693
Woodstock Museum of Shenandoah County Archives 597
Woodstock Public Library 178, 693
Woodstown-Pilesgrove Public Library 380
Woodsville Free Public Library 365
Woodville Civic Club Annual Report 323
Woodville Civic Club, Friends of the Museum & Library 323
Woodville Community Library 634
Woodville Museum Archives 479
Woodville Public Library 10
Woodward Public Library 471
Woodwards We Search 132
Woodward-Woodard Family 60
Wood-Woods Family 525
Woodworth Family 36, 608
Woodworth Journal 554
Woody Family Tree 59
Woolaroc Museum Archives 463
Wooldridge Family 529
Woolford Newsletter 262
Woolley Family 570
Woolley-Hampton-Foster-Olpin-Dunbar-Ashbridge-Samuel Rose Parkinson-Chandler Family 572
Woolverton Family 342
Woolwich Historical Society 253
Woolworth Community Library 383
Woonsocket Harris Public Library 510
Woonsocket Historical and Preservation Society 510
Wooten-Wooton Newsletter 584
Worcester County Historical Society 261
Worcester County Library 263
Worcester Family 243
Worcester Historical Museum Library 283
Worcester Historical Society & Library 421
Worcester Public Library 283
Worch Memorial Public Library 459
Word from the Junction 590
Worden Family 297
Worden Memorial Library 215
Words to the Wise 68
Workman and Temple Family Homestead Museum Archives 40
Workman Family 567, 603
Workmen's Circle 408
World Chamberlain Society 286, 300
World Figure Skating Museum Archives 82
World Jewish Genealogy Organization & Library 391
World Methodist Historical Society & Library 372
World Methodist Museum Archives 429
World Museum of Mining Archives 343
World Newsletter of the International Molyneux Family Association 603
World of Scouting Museum Archives 504
World of Wings Pigeon Center Archives 468
World War II 589
World's Largest Toy Museum Archives 326
World's Smallest Museum Archives 21
Wormsloe State Historic Site Archives 137
Wornstaff Memorial Public Library 441
Worsham Family 361
Worth County Historical Society 138
Worth County Historical Society 329
Worthington Family 259
Worthington Historical Museum 460
Worthington Historical Society 196, 342
Worthington Historical Society & Archives 460
Worthington Public Library 196, 460
Wounded Knee Museum Archives 524
Wragg Family 553
Wrangell Genealogical Society 14
Wrangell Museum Archives 14
Wrather West Kentucky Museum Archives 232
Wray Heritage Association 90
Wrecker's Museum 115
Wregie Memorial Library 207
Wren Family 544
Wren's Nest Historic Home Museum 126
WRHS News 453

Wright Angles 155, 169
Wright Brothers National Memorial Archives 429
Wright Centennial Museum Archives 638
Wright County Genealogical Searchers 199
Wright County Genealogical Society 306
Wright County Historical and Genealogical Society 330
Wright County Historical Museum 306
Wright County Historical Society & Archives 306
Wright County Historical Society Newsletter 306
Wright County Library 330
Wright Family 44, 355
Wright Family Newsletter 339
Wright Family Organization 100
Wright Family Workbook 314
Wright Historical Museum Archives 711
Wright Information Center 109
Wright Memorial Public Library 455
Wright Museum Archives 365
Wright Museum Newsletter 365
Wright Potts Library 514
Wright's Chance 257
Wright's Ferry Mansion Museum 485
Wrightsboro Quaker Community Foundation & Library 138
Write Stuff 115
Wulastock Museum Archives 663
WVNCC Newsletter 615
WW II History 589
WW&F Newsletter 243
Wyalusing Public Library 506
Wyandot County Historical Museum 458
Wyandot County Historical Society & Archives 458
Wyandot County Historical Society Newsletter 458
Wyandot Tracers 458
Wyandot Tracers Genealogical Society & Library 458
Wyandotte County Genealogical Society 216
Wyandotte County Historical Museum 212
Wyandotte County Historical Society & Archives 212
Wyandotte Historical Commission & Archives 304
Wyandotte Historical Commission Newsletter 304
Wyandotte Historical Society & Archives 304
Wyandotte Historical Society Newsletter 304
Wyandotte Museum 304
Wyanet Historical Society & Library 178
Wyanet Historical Society Newsletter 178
Wyatt Earp Birthplace Archives 166
Wyck Museum Archives 498
Wyckoff Public Library 380
Wykoff Area Historical Society 317
Wylie House Museum Archives 180
Wylie House Newsletter 180
Wyman Tavern Museum Archives 362
Wyman Tavern Museum Newsletter 362
WyMonDak Messenger 521
Wynnewood State Historical Site Archives 525
Wynyard and District Museum 711
Wyoming County Genealogical Society 614
Wyoming County Historical Society & Library 503
Wyoming County Library System 614
Wyoming Historical and Cultural Commission 304
Wyoming Historical Society 445
Wyoming History News 635
Wyoming Pioneer Historical Society 635
Wyoming Pioneer Home Library 638
Wyoming Pioneer Memorial Musuem Archives 635
Wyoming State Archives 635
Wyoming State Historical Society & Library 635
Wyoming State Library 635
Wyoming State Museum Archives 635
Wyoming Territorial Prison and Old West Park Archives 636
Wyoming Transportation Museum Archives 635
Wythe County Historical Review 597
Wythe County Historical Society & Archives 597
Wythe-Grayson Regional Library 589
Wythe-Grayson Regional Library-Wythe County Public 597
Wytheville Community College Library 597
Wytheville Historical Society 597

X

Xavier University of Louisiana Library 240
Xaxli'p Indian Nation 651

Y

Y Draig Goch 51
Yadkin County Historical and Genealogical Society 435
Yadkinville Public Library 435
Yakima National Museum Archives 609
Yakima Valley Genealogical Society & Library 610
Yakima Valley Genealogical Society Bulletin 610
Yakima Valley Historical Association & Archives 610
Yakima Valley Historical Museum 610
Yakima Valley Regional Library 610
Yakima Valley Regional Library-Harrah Library 602
Yakweakwioose Indian Band 655
Yale First Nation 650
Yale University Library Gazette 96
Yalobusha County Historical Society 319
Yalobusha County Historical Society Quarterly 319
Yamhill County Genealogical Society & Archives 477
Yampa Public Library 90
Yancey County Library 424
Yankee Air Force Museum Archives 304
Yankee Genealogical Society 315
Yankton Community Library 524
Yankton County Historical Society & Archives 524
Yankton Genealogical Society 523, 524
Yaphank Historical Society 421
Yaquina Genealogical Society & Archives 480
Yaquina Pacific Railroad Historical Society 480
Yardley Historical Association & Library 506
Yarmouth County Historical Museum 677
Yarmouth County Historical Society & Archives 677
Yarmouth Historical Society & Archives 253
Yarmouth Historical Society Newsletter 253
Yarmouth Library 283
Yarmouth Town Libraries 279
Yarnall-Yarnell Family 478
Yarnell Public Library 22
Yates Community Library 403
Yates County Genealogical and Historical Society & Archives 411
Yates County Genealogical and Historical Society Newsletter 411

INDEX

Yates of Yore 529
Yavapai College Library 19
Yawkey House Museum 633
Yazoo Historical Society & Archives 323
Ye Old Dutch Mill 606
Ye Olde Alleganian 389
Yeadon Public Library 506
Yearbook of the Florida Genealogical Society 122
Yearbook of the Historical Society of Fairfax County 587
Yearbook of the Historical Society of Middletown and the Wallkill Precinct 405
Yeary Library Tidings Newsletter 551
Yeater Cousins: For All Yeaters and Their Kin 198
Yell County Historical and Genealogical Association Bulletin 26
Yell County Historical and Genealogical Society 26, 32
Yell County Library 26
Yella Board 167
Yellow Medicine County Heritage 308
Yellow Medicine County Historical Museum 308
Yellow Medicine County Historical Society & Archives 308
Yellowed Pages 537
Yellowhead Tribal Council 646
Yellowjacket 171
Yellowknife Public Library 671
Yellowquill First Nation 711
Yellowstone Gateway Museum of Park County Archives 345
Yellowstone Genealogy Forum & Archives 343
Yelm Prairie Historical Society 610
Yeshiva University Archives 408
Yesterday 554
Yesterday and Today in Lawrence County 529
Yesterday in Hudson 450
Yesterday in the Merricks 409
Yesterday's Children Antique Doll & Toy Museum 323
Yesterdays 547
Yesterdays of Brome County 698
Yesterdays Tuckaways 231
Yester-Year Artifacts Museum Archives 645
Yesteryear House and Central Mine Museum Archives 288
Yesteryear Museum Library 380
Yesteryear Village Archives 124
Yesteryear's Trails 447
Yesteryears 219
Yester-Years Community Museum Archives 706
Yesteryears Museum Association & Library 278
Yesteryears Museum News 278
Yesteryears: A Quarterly for New York State Historical and Genealogical Research 388
Yichus 376
YIVO Annual 408
Yivo Institute for Jewish Research & Library 408
Ymir Museum Archives 657
Yoakum County Library 556
Yocum Family 347
Yoder Newsletter 184
Yolo County Historical Museum Archives 78
Yolo County Historical Society 78
Yolo County Historical Society Newsletter 78
Yolo County Library 78
Yonkers Historian 421
Yonkers Historical Society & Archives 421
Yonkers Historical Society Newsletter 421
Yonkers Public Library 421
Yorba Linda Genealogical Society & Library 78
Yorba Linda Genealogical Society Newsletter 78
Yorba Linda Historical Museum 78
Yorba Linda Historical Society & Archives 78
Yorba Linda Public Library 78
Yorba-Slaughter Adobe Museum Archives 40
Yore Lore 4
York County Culture and Heritage Commission 517
York County Genealogical and Historical Society 517
York County Genealogical Society 249
York County Genealogical Society Journal 249
York County Genealogical Society Newsletter 249
York County Heritage Trust 506
York County Historical Association 357
York County Historical Commission 519
York County Library 517
York County Library System 506
York County Library-Rock Hill Public 517
York County Public Library 598
York County, South Carolina Quarterly 517
York Family Newsletter 145
York Gazette and Public Advertiser 506
York Pioneer 692
York Pioneer and Historical Society 692
York Public Library 253
York Region Native Women's Association 679
York Regional Library 663
York Township Historical Society 453
York Township Public Library 175
York Township Public Library 182
York W Bailey Museum Archives 517
Yorker Palatine 404, 416
Yorkshire Air Museum, Canada Branch 702
York-Sunbury Historical Museum 663
York-Sunbury Historical Society & Archives 663
Yorkton Tribal Council 705
Yorktown Historical Museum 563
Yorktown Historical Society & Archives 563
Yorktown Museum Archives 421
Yorktown Museum Newsletter 421
Yorkville Historical Society 519
Yorkville Public Library 178
Yosemite Gateway Museum Archives 46
Yosemite National Park Research Library 78
Young Chippewayan First Nation 710
Young Clan 250
Young County Historical Society 547
Young Family 315, 423
Young Historians of Sumter County High School 125
Young Historical Library 217
Young Library 228
Young Men's Library 281
Young Public Library 22
Young Research Library 52
Young Times 250
Youngblood News Letter 541
Youngs Family Newsletter 252
Youngstown Historical Center of Industry and Labor Archives 461

Youngtown Public Library 22
Younkin Family News Bulletin 260
Your Library 283
Yours Aye 362
Ypsilanti District Library 304
Ypsilanti Gleanings-Past Scenes and Old Times 304
Ypsilanti Historical Museum 304
Ypsilanti Historical Society & Archives 304
YRMA Newsletter 562
Yturri-Edmunds Historic Site Archives 559
Yuba County Library 53
Yuba Feather Historical Association & Archives 38
Yuba Historical Society 53
Yuba-Feather Museum Archives 44
Yucaipa Adobe Museum Archives 79
Yucaipa Valley Family Finders Quarterly 79
Yucaipa Valley Genealogical Society 79
Yucca Valley Branch Library 79
Yucipa Valley Historical Museum 79
Yucipa Valley Historical Society 79
Yugtarvik Regional Museum Archives 11
Yukon Heritage Resources Board 713
Yukon Historical and Museums Association & Library 713
Yukon Historical and Museums Association Newsletter 713
Yukon Historical and Museums Association Occasional Papers 713
Yukon Indian Cultural Education Society 713
Yukon Territory Archives 713
Yukon Transportation Museum Archives 713
Yule-Yool-Yuille-Zuil Connection 251
Yuma Area Genealogical Society 90
Yuma County Library District 23
Yuma Crossing State Historical Park Archives 23
Yuma Territorial Prison State Historic Park 23
Yupiit Piciryarait Cultural Center and Museum Archives 11
Yutan Historical Society 358

Z

Z Smith Reynolds Library 435
Z Taylor Brown-Saray Dorsey House Museum Archives 554
Z'chor (Remember) 499
Zach S Henderson Library 137
Zachariah Ferriss Chronicles 291
Zale Library 542
Zalud House Museum Archives 61
Zane Grey Museum Archives 454, 491
Zanesville Campus Library 461
Zapata County Public Library 563
Zdroik-Zdojewski-Belongia-Champau Family 633
Zearing Public Library 210
Zebulon B Vance Birthplace State Historic Site Archives 434
Zeeland Historical Society 304
Zeeland Historical Society Year Book 304
Zeimantz Family 608
Zelienople Historical Museum 506
Zelienople Historical Society & Archives 506
Zelienople Historical Society Newsletter 506
Zellwood Historical Society Library & Archives 124
Zellwood Historical Society Museum 124
Zephyrhills Public Library 124
Zichron Note: San Francisco Bay Area Jewish Genealogical Society Newsletter 67
Ziegler Family 20
Ziegler Newsletter 421
Ziegler-Abrill Family 240
Ziehlke Newsletter 262
Ziev Family 306
Ziibiwing Center of Anishinabe Culture Archives 298
Zilliox-Marshall Family 549
Zimmerman Library 381
Zinser House 176
Zion Benton Public Library 178
Zion Genealogical Society & Archives 178
Zion Historical Museum 178
Zion Historical Society & Archives 178
Zion Mennonite Church and Public Library 502
Zionsville Historical Society 196
Zirchron Note 39
Zirkle Family 593
Zoar State Memorial Archives 461
Zoar Village Archives 461
Zula-Bryant-Wylie Library 540
Zulpo Family 159
Zumberge Library 285
Zumwalt Family 376
Zumwalt-Sumwalt Family 478
Zuni Heritage and Historic Preservation Society & Library 385
Zwigart Family 429